COUNTY COURTHOUSE BOOK

COUNTY COURTHOUSE BOOK

3rd Edition

Elizabeth Petty Bentley

Copyright © 2009
Genealogical Publishing Company
3600 Clipper Mill Rd., Suite 260
Baltimore, Maryland 21211-1953
All Rights Reserved.
Library of Congress Catalogue Card Number 2009923999
ISBN 978-0-8063-1797-7
Made in the United States of America

CONTENTS

INTRODUCTION

The data in this compilation is based largely upon information found on the Internet and received in response to questionnaires sent to each and every county across the country. In my questionnaire I requested verification of address, telephone number, and the jurisdiction's date of organization and provenance. Of the major record groups that are of significant interest to genealogists and other researchers, I selected four—land records, naturalization records, vital records, and probate records—and asked that for each category my correspondent identify the particular office researchers should contact. (Even if a clerk or other official is listed by name, addressing his or her office is usually sufficient.) I also requested information about the dates covered in each record group as well as fees for an index search and photocopying, whether there was a minimum charge, and whether there were restrictions on the records' use (such as proof of relationship for vital records).

Some correspondents supplied more information than was requested, and I've included this additional data wherever possible. For instance, these same offices may hold other genealogically significant records such as assessments, bonds, marks and brands, voter registrations, licenses, fictitious names, name changes, school records, divorces, guardianships, adoptions, and criminal and civil court proceedings.

For offices whose information is sketchy, the reader can refer to the summary of the state's judicial organization at the beginning of the state's listing and to other jurisdictions in the state to determine the pattern of record-keeping and the average fees for the area. Note especially whether neighboring counties reported having naturalization records. I made a special effort to elicit information on naturalizations from those jurisdictions that previously claimed to have none, and I was surprised at the number that reported finding some or else reported that the records had been transferred elsewhere. For some time naturalizations have been recorded only by the Immigration and Naturalization Service, so those that were recorded earlier in the general court dockets, often undifferentiated and unindexed, are rarely consulted now and mostly forgotten. Vital records are also somewhat under-reported, since some offices didn't realize that I meant to include marriages in that category. Many states have relegated the recording of twentieth-century births, deaths and marriages to a state office, while New England vital records continue to be kept by town clerks. Those addresses can be found in my book *The Genealogist's Address Book*. Also note the information regarding a county's creation (usually carved out of a larger geographical area, but sometimes pieced together from parts of several existing jurisdictions). Events that occurred in a locality before it assumed its present boundaries should also be sought in the town, county, territory, or state from which the younger jurisdiction was formed, because the governing body that retained the area's original name usually retained all the records created before the split. Note that territorial records are held by the federal government, and newly independent Virginia cities may have records dating from the founding of the city. On the other hand, several county governments have recently been consolidated with the governments of cities that have long existed within their borders.

This present directory is aimed primarily at facilitating research done by mail, not in person, so, for the most part, I've omitted office hours, per diem reading-room fees, or charges for second copies of the same document, or for unassisted photocopying (usually somewhat less than for photocopies prepared by the staff for mailing). Most agencies allow, and even encourage, individuals to come and view their records in person. However, they may require positive identification, and they usually restrict the availability of fragile originals and curtail browsing in files which contain confidential information, such as adoptions or illegitimate births. It's always advisable to phone ahead for an appointment before visiting. But if a personal visit is impossible, mailed requests should be kept very specific when addressed to understaffed and underfunded offices that are primarily tasked with creating *current* records. Answering historical and genealogical inquiries is not their function. When requesting copies, give as much identifying information as possible. Some agencies provide a search service, but it is usually limited to determining whether a specific record exists, not searching every Smith will and deed to see if a daughter who married a Jones is mentioned in one. If you have that kind of project, it's best to hire a professional genealogist or a title search company. Local genealogical or historical societies usually maintain lists of researchers and their fees.

For their efforts in my behalf I would like to thank Michael Tepper, Editor-in-Chief of the Genealogical Publishing Company, and the thousands of correspondents who took the time to research their holdings and answer my letter.

I hope future editions of this work will contain more information, based on an even greater response from the agencies themselves. I would welcome additions and corrections to the present text from any readers who may find omissions or errors.

Elizabeth Petty Bentley
PO Box 58
Woodsboro, MD 21798
301.845.7040
epbentley@hotmail.com

COUNTY COURTHOUSE BOOK

ALABAMA

Capital: Montgomery. Statehood: 14 December 1819 (southern part claimed in Louisiana Purchase of 1803, the rest included in the Territory of Mississippi in 1798, became a territory in 1817)

Alabama's Municipal Courts handle city ordinance violations and misdemeanors. District Courts hear some civil actions, misdemeanors, traffic and juvenile matters. Probate Courts are convened in each county. Appeals from these three courts go to the Circuit Courts, which sit in each county.

First Judicial Circuit: Choctaw, Clarke and Washington counties; Second Judicial Circuit: Butler, Crenshaw and Lowndes counties; Third Judicial Circuit: Barbour and Bullock counties; Fourth Judicial Circuit: Bibb, Dallas, Hale, Perry and Wilcox counties; Fifth Judicial Circuit: Chambers, Macon, Randolph and Tallapoosa counties; Sixth Judicial Circuit: Tuscaloosa County; Seventh Judicial Circuit: Calhoun and Cleburne counties; Eighth Judicial Circuit: Morgan County; Ninth Judicial Circuit: Cherokee and DeKalb counties; Tenth Judicial Circuit: Jefferson County; Eleventh Judicial Circuit: Lauderdale County; Twelfth Judicial Circuit: Coffee and Pike counties; Thirteenth Judicial Circuit: Mobile County; Fourteenth Judicial Circuit: Walker County; Fifteenth Judicial Circuit: Montgomery County; Sixteenth Judicial Circuit: Etowah County; Seventeenth Judicial Circuit: Greene, Marengo and Sumter counties; Eighteenth Judicial Circuit: Clay, Coosa and Shelby counties; Nineteenth Judicial Circuit: Autauga, Chilton and Elmore counties; Twentieth Judicial Circuit: Henry and Houston counties; Twenty-first Judicial Circuit: Escambia County; Twenty-second Judicial Circuit: Covington County; Twenty-third Judicial Circuit: Madison County; Twenty-fourth Judicial Circuit: Fayette, Lamar and Pickens counties; Twenty-fifth Judicial Circuit: Marion and Winston counties; Twenty-sixth Judicial Circuit: Russell County; Twenty-seventh Judicial Circuit: Marshall County; Twenty-eighth Judicial Circuit: Baldwin County; Twenty-ninth Judicial Circuit: Talladega County; Thirtieth Judicial Circuit: Blount and St. Clair counties; Thirty-first Judicial Circuit: Colbert County; Thirty-second Judicial Circuit: Cullman County; Thirty-third Judicial Circuit: Dale and Geneva counties; Thirty-fourth Judicial Circuit: Franklin County; Thirty-fifth Judicial Circuit: Conecuh and Monroe counties; Thirty-sixth Judicial Circuit: Lawrence County; Thirty-seventh Judicial Circuit: Lee County; Thirty-eighth Judicial Circuit: Jackson County; Thirty-ninth Judicial Circuit: Limestone County.

Appeals from the Circuit Courts go to either the Court of Criminal Appeals at Montgomery or the Court of Civil Appeals at Montgomery or other locations at the court's discretion. Some appeals from the Circuit Courts and all those from the Appeals Courts go to the Supreme Court, which sits at Montgomery or elsewhere.

Autauga County
organized 1 November 1818 from Montgomery County

Autauga County Probate Office
176 West Fifth Street
Prattville, AL 36067
(334) 361-3731 (Archives); (334) 361-3730 (Clerk)
autaugacc@aol.com
http://www.autaugaco.org
Kathy Evans, Chief Clerk
(marriages from 1829-1898; probate records from 1810)

Prattville Municipal Court
101 West Main Street
Prattville, AL 36067

(334) 361-3621 (334) 361-3696 FAX
terri.mathis@prattville.com
http://www.prattville.com
Terri G. Mathis, Court Clerk

Baine County
(see Etowah County)

Baldwin County
organized 1809 from Washington County

Baldwin County Circuit Clerk
(312 Courthouse Square, Suite 10, Bay Minette, AL 36507—location)
PO Box 1354 (mailing address)
Bay Minette, AL 36536
(251) 937-0261; (251) 937-0280
jody.campbell@mchsi.com
http://www.deltacomputersystems.com/al/al05/drlinkquerya.html (Land Records);
http://www.deltacomputersystems.com/al/al05/mllinkquerya.html (Marriages)
Jody Wise Campbell, Circuit Clerk

Baldwin County Probate Office
(220 Court House Square—location)
PO Box 459 (mailing address)
Bay Minette, AL 36507
(251) 937-0230; (251) 580-2563 FAX
pdouvier@co.baldwin.al.us (Recording)
http://www.co.baldwin.al.us/Pageview.asp?PageType=R&edit_id=3
(probate records from 1810, post-1986 in online searchable database)
no probate search service; copies of probate records: $1.00 per page, no minimum

Fairhope Satellite Courthouse
(1100 Fairhope Avenue, Fairhope, AL 36532—location)
PO Drawer 2063 (mailing address)
Fairhope, AL 36533
(251) 928-3002, ext. 2637; (251) 580-2590 FAX
http://www.baldwincountydistrictattorney.com/Fairhopesatellite.html

Foley Satellite Courthouse
(201 East Section Street, Foley, AL 36535—location)
PO Drawer 2085 (mailing address)
Foley, AL 36536
(251) 943-5061, ext. 2881
http://www.baldwincountydistrictattorney.com/Foleysatellite.html

Barbour County
organized 1832 from Pike County and Original Territory

Barbour County Circuit Clerk
(1 Court Square—location)
PO Box 219 (mailing address)
Clayton, AL 36016-0219
(205) 775-8366
David S. Nix

Barbour County Probate Office
(1800 Fifth Avenue, North—location)
PO Box 398 (mailing address)
Clayton, AL 36016
(334) 775-8371

Benton County
(see Calhoun County)

Bibb County
organized 1818 from Monroe and Montgomery counties

Bibb County Circuit Clerk
(County Courthouse—location)
PO Box 185 (mailing address)
Centreville, AL 35042
(205) 926-3103
http://www.archives.state.al.us/counties/bibb.html (Alabama Department of Archives and History)
John Harper Stacy

Bibb County Probate Office
455 Walnut Street, Room #100
Centreville, AL 35042
(205) 926-3103
http://www.bibbcountyalabama.com

Blount County
organized 1818 from Montgomery County

Blount County Circuit Clerk
220 Second Avenue East, Room 208
Oneonta, AL 35121-1747
(205) 625-4153
info@co.blount.al.us
http://www.co.blount.al.us
Michael E. Criswell

Blount County Probate Office
(220 Second Avenue East, Room 101—location)
PO Box 549 (mailing address)
Oneonta, AL 35121
(205) 625-4191
info@co.blount.al.us
http://www.co.blount.al.us

Bullock County
organized 1866 from Barbour, Macon, Montgomery and Pike counties

Bullock County Circuit Clerk
(217 North Prairie Street—location)
PO Box 230 (mailing address)
Union Springs, AL 36089-0230
(205) 738-2280
http://www.archives.state.al.us/counties/bullock.html (Alabama Department of Archives and History)
Wilbert M. Jernigan
(land records, divorces)

Bullock County Probate Office
(217 North Prairie—location)
PO Box 71 (mailing address)
Union Springs, AL 36089
(334) 738-2250
http://www.archives.state.al.us/counties/bullock.html (Alabama Department of Archives and History);
http://www.unionspringsalabama.com (City of Union Springs)
Barbara Lewis, Chief Clerk
(probate records from 1853, marriages)

Butler County
organized 1819 from Conecuh and Montgomery counties

Butler County Circuit Clerk
(700 Court Square—location)
PO Box 236 (mailing address)
Greenville, AL 36037
(334) 382-7166; (334) 382-3521
http://www.archives.state.al.us/counties/butler.html (Alabama Department of Archives and History)
Allen W. Stephenson
(land records from 1853; births and deaths from 1899 to 1919)
copies: $1.00 (includes search), no minimum

Butler County Probate Office
(700 Court Square—location)
PO Box 756 (mailing address)
Greenville, AL 36037
(334) 382-3512
http://www.archives.state.al.us/counties/butler.html (Alabama Department of Archives and History)

Calhoun County
organized 1832 from Creek Cession, name changed from Benton County 1858

Calhoun County Circuit Clerk
25 West 11th Street, Suite 500
Anniston, AL 36201-4584
(256) 231-1750; (256) 231-1740
http://wwwcalhouncounty.org
H. Ted Hooks

(deeds from 1865)

Calhoun County Probate Office
Calhoun County Administration Building
1702 Noble Street, Suite 102
Anniston, AL 36201
(256) 241-2825; (256) 231-1728 FAX
probate@calhouncounty.org
http://www.calhouncounty.org/probate/index.
html
Ms. Sherre Green, Chief Clerk of Probate
(marriages from 1834, probate records, probate
minutes from 1850s)
no probate search service; copies of probate
records: 50¢ per page

Chambers County
organized 1832 from Creek Cession

Chambers County Circuit Clerk
Chambers County Courthouse
2 Lafayette Street
Lanett, AL 36862
(334) 864-4348; (334) 864-8411
http://www.chamberscounty.com
Charles W. Story
(land records, naturalization records, vital
records)

Chambers County Probate Office
Chambers County Courthouse
2 Lafayette Street
Lafayette, AL 36862
(334) 864-4397
probatejudge@chamberscounty.com
http://www.chamberscounty.com/probate.html
Romona Barber, Chief Clerk

Cherokee County
organized 1836 from Cherokee Cession

Cherokee County Circuit Clerk
Cherokee County Courthouse
100 Main Street, Room 203
Centre, AL 35960-1510
(256) 927-3637
http://www.cherokeecounty-al.gov
Ms. Carolyn M. Smith
(deeds and mortgages 1882 to present, marriages
[but no births])

Cherokee County Probate Office
Cherokee County Courthouse
100 East Main Street
Centre, AL 35960
(256) 927-3363
MattSims@CherokeeCounty-AL.gov
http://www.cherokeecounty-al.gov
no probate search service; copies of probate
records: $1.00 per page

Chilton County
organized 1868 from Bibb, Perry, Autauga and
Shelby counties; name changed from Baker
County in 1874

Chilton County Circuit Clerk
(500 Second Avenue North—location)
PO Box 1946 (mailing address)
Clanton, AL 35046-1946
(205) 755-4275
http://www.chiltoncounty.org
Mike Smith

Chilton County Probate Office
PO Box 270
Clanton, AL 35045
(205) 755-1555
http://www.newchiltoncounty.org/probatejudg
e.htm

Choctaw County
organized 1847 from Sumter and Washington
counties

Choctaw County Circuit Clerk
(Choctaw County Courthouse, 117 South
Mulberry, Suite 10—location)
PO Box 428 (mailing address)
Butler, AL 36904-0428
(205) 459-2155

http://www.archives.state.al.us/counties/chocta
w.html (Alabama Department of Archives
and History)
Donald R. Gibson
(land records from 1873)

Choctaw County Probate Office
Choctaw County Courthouse
117 South Mulberry Street
Butler, AL 36904
(205) 459-2417
http://www.archives.state.al.us/counties/chocta
w.html (Alabama Department of Archives
and History)
(probate records from 1873)
no probate search service; copies of probate
records: 50¢ per page

Clarke County
organized 1812 from Washington County

Clarke County Circuit Clerk
(117 Court Street—location)
PO Box 921 (mailing address)
Grove Hill, AL 36451
(251) 275-3163
http://www.clarkecountyal.com
Alex W. Brunson

Clarke County Probate Office
(114 Court Street—location)
PO Box 10 (mailing address)
Grove Hill, AL 36451
(251) 275-3251
http://www.clarkecountyal.com
(no probate search service; copies of probate
records: $1.00 per page for each of the first
ten pages and 50¢ for each additional page)

Clay County
organized 1866 from Talladega and Randolph
counties

Clay County Circuit Clerk
(20 First Street North—location)
PO Box 816 (mailing address)
Ashland, AL 36251
(205) 354-7310 (Revenue Commission); (205)
354-7926 (Circuit Clerk)
http://www.archives.state.al.us/counties/clay.ht
ml (Alabama Department of Archives and
History)
(land records in Revenue Commission,
naturalization records in Circuit Court)

Clay County Probate Office
(Court Square—location)
PO Box 187 (mailing address)
Ashland, AL 36251
(256) 354-2198
http://www.archives.state.al.us/counties/clay.ht
ml (Alabama Department of Archives and
History)
no probate search service; copies of probate
records: 25¢ per page, no minimum

Cleburne County
organized 1866 from Calhoun and Randolph
counties

Cleburne County Circuit Clerk
120 Vickery Street, Suite 202
Heflin, AL 36264
(205) 463-2651
http://www.archives.state.al.us/counties/clebur
ne.html (Alabama Department of Archives
and History)
Jerry Paul Owen

Cleburne County Probate Office
406 Vickery Street, Room 101
Heflin, AL 36264
(205) 463-5655
http://www.archives.state.al.us/counties/clebur
ne.html (Alabama Department of Archives
and History)
Recording Clerk
no probate search service; copies of probate
records: $1.00 per page

Coffee County
organized 1841 from Dale County

Coffee County Circuit Clerk
(99 Edward Street—location)
PO Box 311284 (mailing address)
Enterprise, AL 36331
(334) 347-2519
http://www.archives.state.al.us/counties/coffee
.html (Alabama Department of Archives and
History)
James M. "Mickey" Counts
(some land records from 1823, marriages from
1877)

Coffee County Probate Office
(995 Edward Street—location)
PO Box 1256 (mailing address)
Enterprise, AL 36330
(334) 347-2688
http://www.archives.state.al.us/counties/coffee
.html (Alabama Department of Archives and
History)
(wills from early 1900s, probate minutes from
1861 with Judge William O. Gammill)
no probate search service; copies of probate
records: varies, usually about $1.00 per page,
no minimum

Colbert County
organized 1867 from Franklin County

Colbert County Circuit Clerk
201 North Main Street
Tuscumbia, AL 35674-2060
(256) 386-8512; (256) 386-8511
http://www.colbertcounty.org
Nancy Hearn
(land records from 1867)

Colbert County Probate Office
(201 North Main Street—location)
PO Box 47 (mailing address)
Tuscumbia, AL 35674
(256) 386-8546 (Records Department); (256)
386-8547
http://www.colbertprobatejudge.org
(probate records from 1861)
no probate search service; copies of probate
records: $1.00 per page, $3.00 for certified
copies, no minimum

Conecuh County
organized 1818 from Monroe County

Conecuh County Circuit Clerk
(409 Belleville Street, Suite 4—location)
PO Box 107 (mailing address)
Evergreen, AL 36401-0107
(251) 578-2066
http://www.conecuhcounty.us;
http://www.archives.state.al.us/counties/con
ecuh.html (Alabama Department of Archives
and History)
George E. Hendrix

Conecuh County Probate Office
(Jackson Street—location)
PO Box 149 (mailing address)
Evergreen, AL 36040
(251) 578-1221
http://www.conecuhcounty.us;
http://www.archives.state.al.us/counties/con
ecuh.html (Alabama Department of Archives
and History)

Coosa County
organized 1832 from Creek Cession

Coosa County Circuit Clerk
(Main Street—location)
PO Box 98 (mailing address)
Rockford, AL 35136-0098
(256) 377-4988
http://www.archives.state.al.us/counties/coosa.
html (Alabama Department of Archives and
History)
Jeffrey A. Wood
(land records from 1834, marriages from 1834
[published through 1865])

Alabama

Coosa County Probate Office
(Main Street—location)
PO Box 218 (mailing address)
Rockford, AL 35136
(256) 377-4919
http://www.archives.state.al.us/counties/coosa.html (Alabama Department of Archives and History)
(probate records from 1834)
no probate search service; copies of probate records: $1.00 per page by mail, 50¢ in person (if researcher makes copies)

Covington County
organized 1821 from Henry County

Covington County Circuit Clerk
1-K North Court Square
Andalusia, AL 36420-3995
(334) 428-2520
http://www.archives.state.al.us/counties/covingto.html (Alabama Department of Archives and History)
Roger A. Powell

Covington County Probate Office
(1 Court Square—location)
PO Box 188 (mailing address)
Andalusia, AL 36420
(334) 428-2510
http://www.archives.state.al.us/counties/covingto.html (Alabama Department of Archives and History)

Crenshaw County
organized 1866 from Covington, Butler, Coffee, Lowndes and Pike counties

Crenshaw County Circuit Clerk
(29 South Glenwood Avenue, Second Floor—location)
PO Box 167 (mailing address)
Luverne, AL 36049-0167
(334) 335-6575
http://www.archives.state.al.us/counties/crenshaw.html (Alabama Department of Archives and History)
Ann W. Tate
(land records from 1866)

Crenshaw County Probate Office
(Glenwood Avenue—location)
PO Box 328 (mailing address)
Luverne, AL 36049-0328
(334) 335-6568, ext. 101
http://www.archives.state.al.us/counties/crenshaw.html (Alabama Department of Archives and History)
probate search service: $5.00; copies of probate records: $1.00 each, $2.00 for certified copies, no minimum

Cullman County
organized 1877 from Blount, Morgan and Winston counties

Cullman County Circuit and District Courts Clerk
500 Second Avenue, S.W., Suite 303
Cullman, AL 35056-4137
(256) 775-4654; (256) 775-4770
http://www.co.cullman.al.us/recording_department.htm
Robert G. Bates
(naturalization records from 1883 to 1912)

Cullman County Probate Office
PO Box 970
Cullman, AL 35056
(256) 775-4803
http://www.co.cullman.al.us/serv03.htm
charges for probate search and copy services vary

Dale County
organized 1824 from Covington and Henry counties

Dale County Circuit Clerk
(Dale County Courthouse, Court Square—location)
PO Box 1350 (mailing address)
Ozark, AL 36360-1350
(334) 774-5003
http://www.dalecountyal.org
Mary M. Bludsworth
(land records from 1884 [earlier records destroyed in fire], divorce records)

Dale County Probate Office
(Court Square—location)
PO Box 580 (mailing address)
Ozark, AL 36361
(334) 774-2754
http://www.dalecountyal.org
Mary Bludsworth
(probate records from 1884, marriages)
no probate search service; copies of probate records: $1.00 per page, no minimum

Dallas County
organized 1818 from Montgomery County

Dallas County Circuit Clerk
(105 Lauderdale Street—location)
PO Box 1148 (mailing address)
Selma, AL 36702
(334) 874-2523
http://www.dallascounty-al.org
Cheryl Curtis-Strong

Dallas County Probate Office
(105 Lauderdale Street—location)
PO Box 997 (mailing address)
Selma, AL 36701
(334) 874-2516
http://www.dallascounty-al.org
copies: $1.50 per page for each of the first twenty pages and $1.00 for each additional page, $2.00 for certification

DeKalb County
organized 1836 from Cherokee Cession

DeKalb County Circuit Clerk
(300 Grand Avenue South—location)
PO Box 681149 (mailing address)
Fort Payne, AL 35968-1149
(256) 845-8535
http://www.archives.state.al.us/counties/dekalb.html (Alabama Department of Archives and History); http://www.tourdekalb.com (DeKalb County Tourist Association)
Danny R. Lamunyon

DeKalb County Probate Office
111 Grand Avenue, Suite 200
Fort Payne, AL 35967
(256) 845-8525
http://www.archives.state.al.us/counties/dekalb.html (Alabama Department of Archives and History)
Probate Clerk

Elmore County
organized 1866 from Montgomery, Coosa and Autauga counties, and from Tallapoosa County in 1867

Elmore County Circuit Clerk
(8935 U.S. Highway 231 North—location)
PO Box 310 (mailing address)
Wetumpka, AL 36092-0310
(334) 567-1123
http://www.elmoreco.org
Larry Dozier
(land records, marriages)
copies: 50¢ per page

Elmo County Probate Office
200 Commerce Street
Wetumpka, AL 36092
(334) 567-1143
http://www.elmoreco.org

Escambia County
organized 1868 from parts of Baldwin and Conecuh counties

Escambia County Circuit Clerk
(314 Belleville Avenue—location)
PO Box 856 (mailing address)
Brewton, AL 36427-0856
(251) 867-0225
http://www.co.escambia.al.us
James K. Taylor

Escambia County Probate Office
(315 Belleville Avenue—location)
PO Box 557 (mailing address)
Brewton, AL 36427
(251) 867-0301
http://www.co.escambia.al.us

Etowah County
organized 1867 from Blount, Calhoun, Cherokee, DeKalb, Marshall and St. Clair counties, formerly Baine County

Etowah County Circuit Clerk
Etowah County Judicial Building
801 Forrest Avenue, Suite 202
Gadsden, AL 35901
(205) 546-2181; (256) 549-2150
http://www.etowahcounty.org/circuit
Billy Yates, Clerk
(land records, naturalization records, marriages)

Etowah County Probate Office
Etowah County Courthouse
800 Forrest Avenue
Gadsden, AL 35901-3641
(256) 549-2159
http://www.etowahcounty.org/probate.html
Bobby M. Junkins, Judge of Probate

Fayette County
organized 1824 from Marion and Pickens counties

Fayette County Circuit Clerk
(113 North Temple Avenue—location)
PO Box 206 (mailing address)
Fayette, AL 35555-0206
(205) 932-4617
http://www.fayetteal.org (City of Fayette)
Juston Eddy Smith
(land records, naturalization records)

Fayette County Probate Office
(113 North Temple Avenue—location)
PO Box 509 (mailing address)
Fayette, AL 35555-0509
(205) 932-5916
http://www.fayetteal.org (City of Fayette)

Franklin County
organized 1818 from Cherokee Cession

Franklin County Circuit Clerk
(410 Jackson Street—location)
PO Box 160 (mailing address)
Russellville, AL 35653-0160
(256) 332-8861
http://www.franklinchamber.org; http://www.archives.state.al.us/counties/franklin.html (Alabama Department of Archives and History)
Joseph T. Newton
(land records)

Franklin County Probate Office
(410 Jackson Street—location)
PO Box 1438 (mailing address)
Russellville, AL 35653
(256) 332-1210
http://www.franklinchamber.org; http://www.archives.state.al.us/counties/franklin.html (Alabama Department of Archives and History)
probate search service: $4.00; copies of probate records: $1.00 per page for each of the first ten pages and 50¢ for each additional page if the staff looks them up

Geneva County
organized 1868 from Coffee, Dale and Henry counties

Geneva County Circuit Clerk
(200 North Commerce Street—location)
PO Box 86 (mailing address)

Geneva, AL 36340-0086
(334) 684-5620
http://www.genevacounty.net
Ms. Gale Laye
(land records from 1898, marriages from 1898)

Geneva County Probate Office
PO Box 430
Geneva, AL 36340-0340
(334) 684-5640
http://www.genevacounty.net
R. Milton, Recording Clerk
(probate records from 1898)
no probate search service; copies of probate
    records: $1.00 per page   •

Greene County
organized 1819 from Marengo and Tuscaloosa
    counties

Greene County Circuit Clerk
(440 Morrow Avenue—location)
PO Box 307 (mailing address)
Eutaw, AL 35462
(205) 372-3598
http://www.archives.state.al.us/counties/greene
    .html (Alabama Department of Archives and
    History)
Ms. Johnnie M. Knott
(deeds and mortgages from 1820)

Greene County Probate Office
(440 Morrow Avenue—location)
PO Box 790 (mailing address)
Eutaw, AL 35462
(205) 372-3340
http://www.archives.state.al.us/counties/greene
    .html (Alabama Department of Archives and
    History)
(probate records from 1820)
probate search service: $2.00; copies of probate
    records: 50¢ per page, $2.50 if certified,
    minimum $2.00 by correspondence

Hale County
organized 1867 from Greene, Marengo and
    Perry counties

Hale County Circuit Clerk
(Hale County Courthouse, Room 8AA—
    location)
PO Box 99 (mailing address)
Greensboro, AL 36744
(334) 684-4334
http://www.archives.state.al.us/counties/hale.ht
    ml (Alabama Department of Archives and
    History)
Ms. Gaynell Ficker

Hale County Probate Office
(1001 Main Street—location)
PO Box 396 (mailing address)
Greensboro, AL 36744-0396
(334) 624-8740; (334) 624-4257
http://www.archives.state.al.us/counties/hale.ht
    ml (Alabama Department of Archives and
    History)

Henry County
organized 1819 from Conecuh County

Henry County Circuit Clerk
101 Courtsquare, Suite J
Abbeville, AL 36310-2135
(205) 585-2753
http://www.archives.state.al.us/counties/henry.
    html (Alabama Department of Archives and
    History)
Ms. Connie J. Burdeshaw

Henry County Probate Office
PO Box 337
Abbeville, AL 36310-0337
(334) 585-3257
http://www.archives.state.al.us/counties/henry.
    html (Alabama Department of Archives and
    History)

Houston County
organized 1903 from Dale, Geneva, and Henry

counties

Houston County Circuit Clerk
(Houston County Courthouse, 114 North Oates
    Street—location)
PO Drawer 6406 (mailing address)
Dothan, AL 36302
(334) 677-4858
http://www.houstoncounty.org
Judy C. Byrd

Houston County Probate Office
Probate Filing and Recording Department
(462 North Oates Street—location)
PO Drawer 6406 (mailing address)
Dothan, AL 36303
(334) 677-4723; (334) 677-4724; (334) 677-4725;
    (334) 677-4726; (334) 677-4733 FAX
http://www.houstoncounty.org/Probate_Depar
    tment/Probate_Filing_And_Recording.htm
(deeds, mortgages, judgments)
copies: $1.00 each

Jackson County
organized 1819 from Cherokee Cession

Jackson County Circuit Clerk
(112 East Laurel—location)
PO Box 397 (mailing address)
Scottsboro, AL 35768-0397
(256) 574-9320; (256) 259-9981 FAX
kferrell@hijackson.net
http://www.jacksoncountyal.com/courthouse/c
    ircuit_clerk/circuitclerk%20index.htm
William K. "Kenn" Ferrell
(land records from 1830, including mortgages
    and miscellany, scattered unindexed births
    from 1920 to 1934, unindexed births and
    deaths from 1892 to 1896, marriages from
    1851)

Jackson County Probate Office
(102 East Laurel Street, Suite 11—location)
PO Box 128 (mailing address)
Scottsboro, AL 35768
(256) 574-9290; (800) 617-8408; (256) 574-9318
    FAX
http://www.jacksoncounty.al.com/courthouse/
    probate_office/probindex.htm
Cathy Bullock, Chief Clerk
(probate records from 1850)
no probate search service; copies of probate
    records: $1.00 per page, no minimum

Jefferson County
organized 1819 from Blount County

Jefferson County Circuit Clerk
Jefferson County Courthouse
716 Richard Arrington Jr. Boulevard North,
    Room 400
Birmingham, AL 35203-0001
(205) 325-5360
http://www.jeffcointouch.com/jeffcointouch/i
    eindex.asp
Annie Marie Adams
(deeds and mortgages from 1812)

Jefferson County Probate Office
Jefferson County Courthouse
Probate Court, Probate Records Room
716 Richard Arrington Jr. Boulevard North,
    Suite 130
Birmingham, AL 35263-0068
(205) 325-5411 (Recording Department); (205)
    325-5512 (Record Room)
http://www.jeffcointouch.com/jeffcointouch/i
    eindex.sp
Jackie Rhodes, Recording; Benny Dodd, Record
    Room
(probate records from 1818, marriages from
    1818)
no probate search service without date; copies
    of probate records: $1.00 per page plus SASE,
    $2.00 per document for certification, no
    minimum

Lamar County
organized 1867 from Marion, Pickens and
    Fayette counties

Lamar County Circuit Clerk
(330 First Street NE—location)
PO Box 434 (mailing address)
Vernon, AL 35592-0434
(205) 695-7193
http://www.archives.state.al.us/counties/lamar.
    html (Alabama Department of Archives and
    History)
Curtis L. Graham
(land records)

Lamar County Probate Office
(Courthouse Square, South Pond Street—
    location)
PO Box 338 (mailing address)
Vernon, AL 35592-0338
(205) 695-9119
http://www.archives.state.al.us/counties/lamar.
    html (Alabama Department of Archives and
    History)

Lauderdale County
organized 1818 from Cherokee Cession

Lauderdale County Circuit Clerk
(200 South Court Street—location)
PO Box 795 (mailing address)
Florence, AL 35631
(256) 760-5720 (4th Floor); (256) 760-4710 (5th
    Floor)
http://www.lauderdalecountyonline.com
Kenneth C. Austin
(land records, marriages)

Lauderdale County Probate Office
(200 South Court Street—location)
PO Box 1059 (mailing address)
Florence, AL 35631-1059
(256) 760-5800 (Probate Judge); (256) 766-5180
http://www.lauderdalecountyonline.com
no probate search service; copies of probate
    records: $1.00 per page, no minimum

Lawrence County
organized 1818 from Cherokee Cession

Lawrence County Circuit Clerk
(Lawrence County Courthouse, 14330 Court
    Street, Suite 101—location)
PO Box 249 (mailing address)
Moulton, AL 35650-0265
(256) 974-2432
http://www.lawrenceco-al.org;
    http://www.lawrencealabama.com (Chamber
    of Commerce)
Mr. Harce M. Hill

Lawrence County Probate Office
(Lawrence County Courthouse, 14330 Court
    Street, Suite 102—location)
PO Box 310 (mailing address)
Moulton, AL 35650
(256) 974-0663; (256) 974-2439 (Probate Judge's
    Office)
http://www.lawrenceco-al.org; http://www.
    lawrencealabama.com (Chamber of Commerce)
no probate search service (contact Lawrence
    County Archives and Historical Commission)

Lee County
organized 1866 from Chambers and Macon
    counties

Lee County Circuit Clerk
2311 Gateway Drive, Room 104
Opelika, AL 36801-6847
(334) 749-7141
cthurst@aol.com
http://www.leeco.us
Ms. Corrinne Tatum Hurst

Lee County Probate Office
(215 South Ninth Street, Opelika, AL 36802—
    location)
PO Box 2266 (mailing address)
Opelika, AL 36803-2266
(334) 745-9761
bfreeman@leeco.us
http://www.leeco.us/probate/index.html
BBecky Freeman, Chief Clerk

Limestone County

organized 1818 from Cherokee and Chickasaw cessions

Limestone County Circuit Clerk
200 Washington Street West
Athens, AL 35611
(256) 233-6406
http://co.limestone.al.us/index.html
Charles D. Page, Jr.

Limestone County Probate Office
Limestone County Courthouse
100 South Clinton Street
Athens, AL 35611
(256) 233-6427
lcpro@hiwaay.net
http://www.co.limestone.al.us/probate/pj_docs
/probate.htm
Edria Ann Norton, Chief Clerk

Lowndes County

organized 1830 from Butler and Dallas counties

Lowndes County Circuit Clerk
(1 Washington Street—location)
PO Box 876 (mailing address)
Hayneville, AL 36040-0876
(334) 548-2252
http://www.geocities.com/lowndes_county;
http://www.archives.state.al.us/counties/low
ndes.html (Alabama Department of Archives
and History)
Ruby Jones
(land records, marriages from the 1830s)
copies: $1.00 per page, plus $3.00 for
certification for marriages

Lowndes County Probate Office
(Washington Street—location)
PO Box 5 (mailing address)
Hayneville, AL 36040
(205) 584-2365; (205) 584-2331
http://www.geocities.com/lowndes_county;
http://www.archives.state.al.us/counties/low
ndes.html (Alabama Department of Archives
and History)

Macon County

organized 1832 from Creek Cession

Macon County Circuit Clerk
PO Box 830723
Tuskegee, AL 36083-0723
(334) 724-2614
http://www.archives.state.al.us/counties/maco
n.html (Alabama Department of Archives and
History)
Mr. Eddie Dean Mallard
(land records from 1832, marriages from 1832)

Macon County Probate Office
Macon County Courthouse
101 East Northside Street, Suite 101
Tuskegee, AL 36083-1750
(334) 724-2611
http://www.archives.state.al.us/counties/maco
n.html (Alabama Department of Archives and
History)
(probate records from 1832)
probate search service: $5.00; copies of probate
records: $1.00 per page

Madison County

organized 1808 from Cherokee Cession

Madison County Circuit Clerk
Madison County Courthouse
100 North Side Square
Huntsville, AL 35801-4820
(256) 532-3380; (256) 532-3768 FAX
jane.smith@alacourt.gov
http://www.madisoncountycircuitclerk.org
Jane Chandler Smith

Madison County Probate Office
Madison County Courthouse
100 North Side Square, Room 101
Huntsville, AL 35801
(256) 532-3330 (Chief Clerk); (256) 532-2347

(Genealogy Archives)
http://www.co.madison.al.us/probate/home.sh
tml
Patty Hanson, Chief Clerk; Rhonda Larkin,
Genealogy Archives

Marengo County

organized 1818 from Choctaw Cession

Marengo County Circuit Clerk
(101 East Coats Avenue, Linden, AL 36748-
1546—location)
PO Box 480566 (mailing address)
Linden, AL 36748-0566
(334) 295-2222
http://www.archives.state.al.us/counties/maren
go.html (Alabama Department of Archives
and History)
Robert Rusty Nichols
(deed and mortgage records from 1818)

Marengo County Probate Office
101 East Coats Avenue
Linden, AL 36748
(334) 295-2210
http://www.archives.state.al.us/counties/maren
go.html (Alabama Department of Archives
and History)
(wills, administrations, and guardianships)
probate search service: $5.00; copies of probate
records: $1.00 per page, no minimum

Marion County

organized 1818 from Indian Lands

Marion County Circuit Clerk
(132 Military Street South—location)
PO Box 1595 (mailing address)
Hamilton, AL 35570
(205) 921-7451
http://www.sonet.net/marioncounty;
http://www.archives.state.al.us/counties/mar
ion.html (Alabama Department of Archives
and History)
Betty McDonald
(land records, naturalization records, vital
records)

Marion County Probate Office
(132 Military Street South—location)
PO Box 1687 (mailing address)
Hamilton, AL 35570
(205) 921-2471
http://www.sonet.net/marioncounty;
http://www.archives.state.al.us/counties/mar
ion.html (Alabama Department of Archives
and History)
Annette Bozeman, Judge of Probate

Marshall County

organized 1836 from Blount County and
Cherokee Cession

Marshall County Circuit Clerk
(423 Gunter Avenue—location)
PO Box 248 (mailing address)
Guntersville, AL 35976
(205) 571-7768
http://www.marshallco.us/marshallco/index.php
Sherry Griep

Marshall County Probate Office
424 Gunter Avenue
Guntersville, AL 35976
(256) 571-7764
probate@marshallco.org
http://www.marshallco.us/marshallco/probate.
php

Mobile County

county created by proclamation 18 December
1812 by Governor Holmes of the Mississippi
Territory; on 13 April 1813 Major General
James Wilkinson took possession of Mobile
when the Spanish, who did not recognize the
Louisiana Purchase, surrendered at Fort
Charlotte

Mobile County Circuit Clerk
205 Government Street, Room C-936

Mobile, AL 36644-2936
(251) 574-8420
http://www.mobilecounty.org
Susan F. Wilson
(deeds from 25 May 1813 through 12 September
1958, real property records from 12
September 1958 to date [earliest land record is
a Spanish Land Grant circa 1715],
miscellaneous books from 12 Jan 1819
through 12 September 1958 [including early
records of slave sales as well as some
contracts for house and building plans])

Mobile County Probate Office
(Mobile County Courthouse, 304 Government
Street—location)
PO Box 7 (mailing address)
Mobile, AL 36601
(251) 574-8497 (Recording); (251) 574-8490
(Records); (251) 574-4939 FAX (Recording);
(251) 574-5580 FAX (Records)
probatecourt@mobile-county.net
http://www.mobile-county.net/probate
Grace Dixon, Recording Supervisor; Gerald
Stork, Records Division Chief
(will books from 22 September 1812 to date,
judicial records from 1819 [containing wills,
estate cases, any judicial occurrence], white
marriage licenses from 3 March 1813, colored
marriage licenses from 29 May 1865)
no probate search service; copies of probate
records: $1.00 per page for each of the first
ten pages and 50¢ per page thereafter per
instrument; pay by money order or cashier's
check only

Monroe County

organized 1815 from Creek Cession of 1814 and
Washington County

Monroe County Circuit Clerk
65 North Alabama Avenue
Monroeville, AL 36460
(251) 743-2283
http://www.monroecountyal.com
John M. Sawyer

Monroe County Probate Office
PO Box 8
Monroeville, AL 36461-0008
(334) 743-4107
http://www.monroecountyal.com
(wills, estates and inventories from about 1830)

Montgomery County

organized 1816 from Monroe County

Montgomery County Circuit Clerk
(251 South Lawrence Street, Montgomery, AL
36104—location)
PO Box 1667 (mailing address)
Montgomery, AL 36102-1667
(334) 832-1290
http://www.mc-ala.org/Home
Melissa A. Rittenour

Montgomery County Probate Office
(Administration Building [Annex], 100 South
Lawrence Street, Montgomery, AL 36104—
location)
PO Box 5625 (mailing address)
Montgomery, AL 36103
(334) 206-5418; (334) 832-1233 (Recorder)
probate@mc-ala.org
http://www.mc-ala.org/Home/
Elected%20Officials/Probate%20Judge

Morgan County

organized 1818 from Indian Lands; name
changed from Cotaco County in 1821

Morgan County Circuit Clerk
(302 Lee Street, NE—location)
PO Box 668 (mailing address)
Decatur, AL 35602-0668
(256) 351-9600
http://www.co.morgan.al.us
John Pat Orr
(deeds, mortgages, plats, original land survey
from 1819 to date, incomplete births and

County Courthouse Book

deaths from 1893 to 1912, marriages from 1821 to date, black marriages from 1865 to the 1920s)

Morgan County Probate Office
(302 Lee Street, NE—location)
PO Box 848 (mailing address)
Decatur, AL 35602
(256) 350-4678; (256) 351-4680 (Recording)
http://www.co.morgan.al.us;
http://www.morgancountyprobate.com
(wills from 1819 to date)
no probate search service; copies of probate records: $1.00 per page (records indexed in-house, but indices are not available in a published form, except through private compilations by the local genealogical society)

Perry County
organized 1819 from Tuscaloosa County

Perry County Circuit Clerk
(300 Washington Street—location)
PO Box 505 (mailing address)
Marion, AL 36756
(334) 683-6106
http://www.perrycountyalabama.org
Mary C. Moore
(land records, naturalization records)

Perry County Probate Office
PO Box 478
Marion, AL 36756-0478
(334) 683-2210; (334) 683-2211
http://www.perrycountyalabama.org

Pickens County
organized 1820 from Tuscaloosa County

Pickens County Circuit Clerk
(County Courthouse—location)
PO Box 418 (mailing address)
Carrollton, AL 35447-0418
(205) 367-2050
http://www.archives.state.al.us/counties/picken
s.html (Alabama Department of Archives and History)
Mr. Bobby Cowart
(land records from 1876, probate records from 1876)
no probate search service; copies of probate records: 50¢ per page, no minimum

Pickens County Probate Office
(Courthouse Square—location)
PO Box 370 (mailing address)
Carrollton, AL 35447
(205) 367-2010
http://www.archives.state.al.us/counties/picken
s.html (Alabama Department of Archives and History)

Pike County
organized 1821 from Henry and Montgomery counties

Pike County Circuit Clerk
(120 West Church Street—location)
PO Box 948 (mailing address)
Troy, AL 36081
(334) 566-4622
brenda.peacock@alacourt.gov
http://www.pikecountychamber.net (Chamber of Commerce)
Brenda Meadows Peacock
(land records from 1830)

Pike County Probate Office
(1 West Church Street—location)
PO Box 1008 (mailing address)
Troy, AL 36081
(334) 566-6374
http://www.pikecountychamber.net (Chamber of Commerce)
(some wills and estate records)
no probate search service; copies of probate records: 50¢ per page, no minimum

Randolph County
organized 1832 from Creek Cession

Randolph County Circuit Clerk
(1 Main Street—location)
PO Box 328 (mailing address)
Wedowee, AL 36278-0328
(205) 357-4551
http://www.ircusa.com/randolph/county.htm
(Chamber of Commerce);
http://www.archives.state.al.us/counties/ran
dolph.html (Alabama Department of Archives and History)
Ms. Kim S. Benefield
(land records from early 1900s)

Randolph County Probate Office
PO Box 328
Wedowee, AL 36278-0328
(256) 357-4933
http://www.ircusa.com/randolph/county.htm
(Chamber of Commerce);
http://www.archives.state.al.us/counties/ran
dolph.html (Alabama Department of Archives and History)
(probate records from early 1900s)

Russell County
organized 1832 from Creek Cession

Russell County Circuit Clerk
(501 14th Street—location)
PO Box 518 (mailing address)
Phenix City, AL 36868-0518
(334) 298-0516, ext. 224
http://www.russellcountyala.com
Kathy Coulter

Russell County Probate Office
(501 14th Street—location)
PO Box 518 (mailing address)
Phenix City, AL 36868-0518
(334) 298-7963; (334) 298-7979
http://www.russellcountyala.com
(wills, guardianships, veterans' discharges, bonds, miscellaneous, real estate deeds, mortgages, marriages)
no probate search service; copies of probate records: $1.00 per page, no minimum

St. Clair County
organized 1818 from Shelby County

St. Clair County Circuit Clerk
(St. Clair County Courthouse, Sixth Avenue and Court Street West—location)
PO Box 1569 (mailing address)
Ashville, AL 35953-1569
(205) 594-2184
http://www.stclairco.com
Jeff Wyatt
(land records from 1818)

St. Clair County Probate Office
(129 Fifth Avenue—location)
PO Box 220 (mailing address)
Ashville, AL 35953-0220
(205) 594-2120
probate@stclairco.com
http://www.stclairco.com
Johnnie H. Bagwell, Probate Clerk
(marriages from 1818 to date, estate records from 1818)

St. Clair County Probate Office
1815 Cogswell Avenue, Suite 212
Pell City, AL 35128
(205) 338-9449
http://www.stclairco.com
Probate Clerk

Shelby County
organized 1818 from Montgomery County

Shelby County Circuit Clerk
(Shelby County County Courthouse, Main Street, Columbiana, AL 35051-1627—location)
PO Box 1810 (mailing address)
Columbiana, AL 35051-1810
(205) 669-3760
maryharrisclerk@charter.net
http://www.maryharrisclerk.com

Mary H. Harris
(deeds and mortgages in Recording Office)

Shelby County Probate Office
(Shelby County Courthouse, Main Street, Columbiana, AL 35051-1627—location)
PO Box 825 (mailing address)
Columbiana, AL 35051
(205) 669-3720 (Recording); (205) 669-3884 FAX (Recording)
kimm@shelbycountyalabama.net
http://www.shelbycountyalabama.com/probate
/default.htm
Kimberly A. Melton, Chief Clerk

Sumter County
organized 1832 from Choctaw Cession

Sumter County Circuit Clerk
(126 Franklin Street—location)
PO Box 936 (mailing address)
Livingston, AL 35470-0936
(205) 652-2291
http://www.archives.state.al.us/counties/sumte
r.html (Alabama Department of Archives and History)
Odessa Mack

Sumter County Probate Office
PO Box 1040
Livingston, AL 35470
(205) 652-7281
http://www.archives.state.al.us/counties/sumte
r.html (Alabama Department of Archives and History)
Judge Willie Pearl Watkins Rice
(probate records)

Talladega County
organized 1832 from Creek Cession

Talladega County Circuit Clerk
(148 East Street North—location)
PO Box 432 (mailing address)
Talladega, AL 35160
(256) 761-2102
http://www.talladegacountyal.org
Clarence E. Haynes

Talladega County Probate Office
(Court Square—location)
PO Box 755 (mailing address)
Talladega, AL 35160-0755
(256) 362-4175
http://www.talladegacountyal.org

Tallapoosa County
organized 1832 from Chicksaw Cession

Tallapoosa County Circuit Clerk
Tallapoosa County Courthouse
125 North Broadnax Street, Room 132
Dadeville, AL 36853-1371
(256) 825-1098
http://www.tallaco.com/probate.asp
Frank Lucas

Tallapoosa County Probate Office
Tallapoosa County Courthouse
125 North Broadnax Street, Room 126
Dadeville, AL 36853
(256) 825-4268
http://www.tallaco.com/probate.asp

Tuscaloosa County
organized 1818 from Indian Lands

Tuscaloosa County Courthouse
714 Greensboro Avenue
Tuscaloosa, AL 35401
(205) 349-3870, ext. 259 (Circuit Clerk, Room 214); (205) 349-3870, ext. 201 (Probate Department, PO Box 20067, Tuscaloosa, AL 35402-0067); (205) 349-3870, ext. 208 (Records Room)
http://www.tuscco.com
Doris T. Turner
(land records from 1818, marriages from 1823, probate records from 1821 in Record Room)
no probate search service; copies of probate records: $1.00 per page, no minimum

Walker County

organized 26 December 1823 from Marion and Tuscaloosa counties

Walker County Circuit Clerk
(Walker County Courthouse, Third Avenue and 19th Street, Second Floor—location)
PO Box 749 (mailing address)
Jasper, AL 35501-0749
(205) 384-7268
http://www.walkercounty.com/constitutional/clerk/index.htm
Vinita B. Thompson
(land records from about 1877)
copies: $1.00 per page for land records

Walker County Probate Office
(1900 Third Avenue—location)
PO Box 502 (mailing address)
Jasper, AL 35502-0502
(205) 384-7281
http://www.walkercounty.com/constitutional/probatecourt/index.htm
(probate records from about 1877, marriages from about 1877)
copies: $1.50 per page for probate records, $2.50 each plus $1.00 for certification for marriages

Washington County

organized 1800, original county, formed from Mississippi; Territory

Washington County Circuit Clerk
(1 Court Street—location)
PO Box 548 (mailing address)
Chatom, AL 36518-0548
(251) 847-2239
http://www.archives.state.al.us/counties/washingt.html (Alabama Department of Archives and History)
Steven P. Grimes
(marriages from 1826)

Washington County Probate Office
(Courthouse Square—location)
PO Box 549 (mailing address)
Chatom, AL 36518
(251) 847-2208
http://www.archives.state.al.us/counties/washingt.html (Alabama Department of Archives and History)
probate search service: $5.00 per surname from Mrs. Barbara Waddell, PO Box 421, Chatom, AL 36518, (205) 847-3156; copies of probate records: $1.00 per page

Wilcox County

organized 1819 from Dallas and Monroe counties

Wilcox County Circuit Clerk
(12 Water Street—location)
PO Box 608 (mailing address)
Camden, AL 36726-0608
(334) 682-4126
contactus@wilcoxcountyalabama.com
http://wilcoxcountyalabama.com
Ralph W. Ervin

Wilcox County Probate Office
PO Box 656
Camden, AL 36726
(334) 682-4881
contactus@wilcoxcountyalabama.com
http://wilcoxcountyalabama.com

Winston County

organized 1858 from Walker County

Winston County Circuit Clerk
(Highway 195, Main Street—location)
PO Box 309 (mailing address)
Double Springs, AL 35553-0309
(205) 489-5533
john.snoddy@alacourt.gov;
  wakefield_snoddy@ala.nu
http://www.winstoncountycircuitclerk.org
John Snoddy

Winston County Probate Office

(Main Street—location)
PO Box 27 (mailing address)
Double Springs, AL 35553
(205) 489-5219
http://www.winstoncountyalabama.org

ALASKA

Capital: Juneau. Statehood: 3 January 1959 (ceded by Russia by treaty in 1867, organized in 1884, obtained territorial status in 1884)

Magistrate Courts formerly in many Alaskan cities, no longer handle small civil cases, small claims and misdemeanors. District Courts established in each judicial district in 1959 are trial courts hearing misdemeanors and violations of city and borough ordinances. They also record vital statistics in some areas and hear civil cases and small claims cases, plus some cases involving children and domestic violence.

Superior Courts have jurisdiction over civil and criminal matters, including cases involving juveniles, probate, guardianship, and domestic relations, and serves as an appellate court for appeals from civil and criminal cases tried in the district court.

A Court of Appeals in Anchorage and Fairbanks hears appeals from the Superior Courts, and a Supreme Court in Anchorage, Fairbanks, Juneau and occasionally in other locations is the court of last resort. For a map of Alaska's judicial district and court locations, see http://www.state.ak.us/courts/map.pdf

The following boroughs or reservations were organized after statehood in lieu of counties: Aleutian Islands, Anchorage, Angoon, Barrow, Bethel, Bristol Bay, Cordova-McCarthy, Fairbanks, Haines, Juneau, Kenai-Matanuska-Susitna, Nome, Outer Ketchikan, Prince of Wales, Seward, Sitka, Skagway-Yakutat, Southeast Fairbanks, Upper Yukon, Valdez-Chitina-Whittier, Wade-Hampton, Wrangell-Petersburg, and Yukon-Koyukuk.

First Judicial District
Court and Office Building
Juneau, AK 99811
(907) 465-3420
http://www.state.ak.us/courts/ctinfo.htm
(probate records)
probate search service: $3.00 by correspondence only; copies of probate records: 20¢ per page from paper originals, $1.25 per page from microfilm originals, no minimum

Fourth Judicial District
604 Barnette Street, Room 342
Fairbanks, AK 99701-4569
(907) 452-9317
http://www.state.ak.us/courts/ctinfo.htm
(land records with Fairbanks Recorder's Office, 210 Cushman, Fairbanks, AK 99701, naturalization records with U.S. District Court, 101 12th Avenue, Fairbanks, AK 99701, vital records with Courthouse, Coroner's Office, 604 Barnette Street, Fairbanks, AK 99701, probate records with Courthouse, Probate Office, 604 Barnette Street, Fairbanks, AK 99701)
probate search service: $3.00; copies of probate records: 20¢ per page, $3.00 for certified copies

Second Judicial District
Box 100
Nome, AK 99762-0100
(907) 443-5216
http://www.state.ak.us/courts/ctinfo.htm

Third Judicial District
303 K Street
Anchorage, AK 99501-2083
http://www.state.ak.us/courts/ctinfo.htm
(vital records with Sandra Weatherman, Supervisor; marriages and deaths are not open to the public for fifty years, births for 100 years; inquirer must prove relationship to the subject of inquiry prior to the fifty- or 100-year period, probate records with Kathleen Harrington, Probate Master)
probate search service: varies; copies of probate records: 20¢ per page, $5.00 for certified copies, $7.00 for authenticated copies, no

County Courthouse Book

minimum (requests must be in writing, including as much information as possible)

Aleutians East Borough

Akutan, Belkofski, Cold Bay, False Pass, King Cove, Nelson Lagoon, Pauloff Harbor, Sand Point, and Unga

Valdez District Court
(serves Sand Point, see Valdez-Cordova Census Area)

Aleutians West Census Area

Adak, Atka, Attu Station, Nikolski, St. George, St. Paul, Shemya Station (Eareckson Air Force Station), and Unalaska (including Dutch Harbor)

Unalaska Court
Box 245
Unalaska, AK 99685-0245
(907) 581-1379
http://www.state.ak.us/courts/ctinfo.htm
Karla Utter, Magistrate

Anchorage Superior Court
Anchorage District Court
Anchorage Trial Court
825 West Fourth Avenue
Anchorage, AK 99501-2004
(907) 264-0436 (Probate Division); (907) 264-0491 (Records)
http://www.state.ak.us/courts/ctinfo.htm

Bethel Census Area

Akiachak, Akiak, Aniak, Atmautluak, Bethel, Chefornak, Chuathbaluk, Crooked Creek, Eek, Goodnews Bay, Kasigluk, Kipnuk, Kongiganak, Kwethluk, Kwigillingok, Lime Village, Lower Kalskag, Mekoryuk, Napakiak, Napaskiak, Newtok, Nightmute, Nunapitchuk, Oscarville, Platinum, Quinhagak, Red Devil, Sleetmute, Stony River, Toksook Bay, Tuluksak, Tuntutuliak, Tununak, and Upper Kalskag

Aniak Court
Box 147
Aniak, AK 99557-0147
(907) 675-4325
http://www.state.ak.us/courts/ctinfo.htm
David H. Woodmancy, Magistrate
(also serves McGrath)

Bethel Court
Box 130
Bethel, AK 99559-0130
(907) 543-2298 (Bethel); (907) 543-1105 (Quinhagak)
http://www.state.ak.us/courts/ctinfo.htm
(also serves Quinhagak)

Bristol Bay Borough

King Salmon, Naknek, South Naknek

Naknek Court
Box 229
Naknek, AK 99633-0229
(907) 246-4240
http://www.state.ak.us/courts/ctinfo.htm
Julie Jedlicka, Magistrate

Denali Borough

Anderson, Cantwell, Ferry, Healy, Lignite, and McKinley Park

Healy Court
Box 298
Healy, AK 99743-0298
(907) 683-2213
http://www.state.ak.us/courts/ctinfo.htm
Paul Verhagen, Magistrate

Dillingham Census Area

Aleknagik, Clark's Point, Dillingham, Ekwok, Koliganek, Manokotak, New Stuyahok, Portage Creek, Togiak, and Twin Hills

Dillingham Court
Box 909
Dillingham, AK 99576-0909

(907) 842-5215
http://www.state.ak.us/courts/ctinfo.htm
Fred Torrisi, Superior Court Judge

Fairbanks North Star Borough

College, Eielson AFB, Ester, Fairbanks, Fox, Harding-Birch Lakes, Moose Creek, North Pole, Pleasant Valley, Salcha, and Two Rivers

Fairbanks Superior Court
Fairbanks District Court
101 Lacey Street
Fairbanks, AK 99701
(907) 452-9277 (Clerk's Office); (907) 452-9256 (Probate Department)
http://www.state.ak.us/courts/ctinfo.htm

Haines Borough

Covenant Life, Excursion Inlet, Haines, Lutak, Mosquito Lake, and Mud Bay

Haines Court
Box 169
Haines, AK 99827-0169
(907) 766-2801
http://www.state.ak.us/courts/ctinfo.htm
John Hutchins, Magistrate

Juneau City and Borough

Juneau Superior Court
Juneau District Court
PO Box 114100
Juneau, AK 99811-4100
(907) 463-4700 (Clerk of Court)
http://www.state.ak.us/courts/ctinfo.htm

Kenai Peninsula Borough

Anchor Point, Bear Creek, Beluga, Clam Gulch, Cohoe, Cooper Landing, Crown Point, Diamond Ridge, Fox River, Fritz Creek, Funny River, Halibut Cove, Happy Valley, Homer, Hope, Kachemak, Kalifornsky, Kasilof, Kenai, Lowell Point, Miller Landing, Moose Pass, Nanwalek, Nikiski, Nikolaevsk, Ninilchik, Port Graham, Primrose, Ridgeway, Salamatof, Seldovia, Seldovia Village, Seward, Soldotna, Sterling, Sunrise, and Tyonek

Homer District Court
3670 Lake Street, Suite 400
Homer, AK 99603-7686
(907) 235-8171
http://www.state.ak.us/courts/ctinfo.htm
Margaret L. Murphy, District Court Judge

Kenai Superior Court
Kenai District Court
125 Trading Bay Drive, Suite 100
Kenai, AK 99611-7717
(907) 283-3110 (Clerk of Court)
http://www.state.ak.us/courts/ctinfo.htm

Seward Court
Box 1929
Seward, AK 99664-1929
(907) 224-3075
http://www.state.ak.us/courts/ctinfo.htm
George Peck, Magistrate

Ketchikan Gateway Borough

Ketchikan and Saxman

Ketchikan Superior Court
Ketchikan District Court
415 Main Street, Room 400
Ketchikan, AK 99901-6399
(907) 225-3195 (Clerk of Court)
http://www.state.ak.us/courts/ctinfo.htm

Kodiak Island Borough

Afognak, Akhiok, Aleksashkina, Aleneva, Chiniak, Kanatak, Karluk, Kodiak, Kodiak Station, Larsen Bay, McCord, Old Harbor, Ouzinkie, Port Hobron, Port Lions, Port O'Brien, Port Wakefield, Port William, and Womens Bay

Kodiak Superior Court
204 Mission Road, Room 124
Kodiak, AK 99615-7312

(907) 486-1600 (Clerk of Court)
http://www.state.ak.us/courts/ctinfo.htm

Lake and Peninsula Borough

Chignik, Chignik Lagoon, Chignik Lake, Egegik, Fish Village, Hallersville, Igiugig, Iliamna, Ivanof Bay, Kaskanak, Kokhanok, Kvichak, Levelock, Meshik, Nakeen, Newhalen, Nondalton, Pedro Bay, Perryville, Pilot Point, Pope-Vannoy Landing, Port Alsworth, Port Heiden, Seversens, and Ugashik

Matanuska-Susitna Borough

Big Lake, Buffalo Soapstone, Butte, Chase, Chelatna Lodge, Chickaloon, Chulitna, Colorado, Cottonwood, Curry, Eska, Eureka Roadhouse, Farm Loop, Fishhook, Gateway, Glacier View, Houston, Jonesville, Knik River, Knik-Fairview, Lake Louise, Lakes, Lazy Mountain, Matanuska, Meadow Lakes, Montana, Palmer, Petersville, Point MacKenzie, Skwentna, Sunshine, Susitna, Sutton-Alpine, Talkeetna, Tanaina, Trapper Creek, Wasilla, Willow, Willow Lake, and Y

Palmer Superior Court
Palmer District Court
435 South Denali
Palmer, AK 99645-6437
(907) 746-8109 (Clerk of Court)
http://www.state.ak.us/courts/ctinfo.htm

Nome Census Area

Brevig Mission, Diomede, Elim, Gambell, Golovin, Koyuk, Nome, Port Clarence, Savoonga, Shaktoolik, Shishmaref, St. Michael, Stebbins, Teller, Unalakleet, Wales, and White Mountain

Nome Superior Court
(113 Front Street, Room 230—location)
Box 1110 (mailing address)
Nome, AK 99762-1110
(907) 443-5216
http://www.state.ak.us/courts/ctinfo.htm

Unalakleet Court
Box 250
Unalakleet, AK 99684-0250
(907) 624-3015
http://www.state.ak.us/courts/ctinfo.htm
Heidi Erickson, Magistrate

Barrow Court
Box 270
Barrow, AK 99723-0270
(907) 852-4800
http://www.state.ak.us/courts/ctinfo.htm

Kotzebue Superior Court
(serves Point Hope, see Northwest Arctic Borough)

Northwest Arctic Borough

Ambler, Buckland, Deering, Kiana, Kivalina, Kobuk, Kotzebue, Noatak, Noorvik, Red Dog Mine, Selawik, and Shungnak

Kotzebue Superior Court
Box 317
Kotzebue, AK 99752-0317
(907) 442-3208 (Clerk of Court)
http://www.state.ak.us/courts/ctinfo.htm
(also serves Ambler, Kiana, Kobuk, Noorvik, Point Hope, and Shungnak)

Selawik Court
PO Box 231
Selawik, AK 99770
http://www.state.ak.us/courts/ctinfo.htm
Joseph Ballott, Magistrate

Prince of Wales-Outer Ketchikan Census Area

Coffman Cove, Craig, Edna Bay, Hollis, Hydaburg, Hyder, Kasaan, Klawock, Metlakatla, Meyers Chuck, Naukati Bay, Point Baker, Port Protection, Thorne Bay, and Whale Pass

Craig Court
Box 646
Craig, AK 99921-0646
(907) 826-3316
http://www.state.ak.us/courts/ctinfo.htm
Kay Clark, Magistrate

Sitka City and Borough

Sitka Superior Court
304 Lake Street, Room 203
Sitka, AK 99835-7759
(907) 747-3291 (Clerk of Court)
http://www.state.ak.us/courts/ctinfo.htm

Skagway-Hoonah-Angoon Census Area

Angoon, Cube Cove, Elfin Cove, Game Creek, Gustavus, Hobart Bay, Hoonah, Klukwan, Pelican, Skagway, Tenakee Springs, and Whitestone Logging Camp

Angoon Court
Box 250
Angoon, AL 99820-0250
http://www.state.ak.us/courts/ctinfo.htm
Daniel Johnson, Jr., Magistrate

Hoonah Court
Box 430
Hoonah, AK 99829-0430
(907) 945-3668
http://www.state.ak.us/courts/ctinfo.htm
Maureen DesRosiers, Magistrate

Skagway Court
Box 495
Skagway, AK 99840-0495
(907) 983-2368
http://www.state.ak.us/courts/ctinfo.htm
Susan Reed, Magistrate

Southeast Fairbanks Census Area

Alcan Border, Big Delta, Chicken, Delta Junction, Deltana, Dot Lake Village, Dot Lake, Dry Creek, Eagle, Eagle Village, Fort Greely, Healy Lake, Northway, Northway Junction, Northway Village, Tanacross, Tetlin, and Tok

Delta Junction Court
Box 401
Delta Junction, AK 99737-0401
(907) 895-4211; (907) 895-4212
http://www.state.ak.us/courts/ctinfo.htm
Tracy L. Blais, Magistrate

Tok Court
Box 187
Tok, AK 99780-0187
(907) 883-5171; (907) 883-5172
http://www.state.ak.us/courts/ctinfo.htm
Evelyn Martiniuk, Magistrate

Valdez-Cordova Census Area

Chenega, Chisana, Chistochina, Chitina, Copper Center, Copperville, Cordova, Gakona, Glennallen, Gulkana, Kenny Lake, McCarthy, Mendeltna, Mentasta Lake, Nelchina, Paxson, Silver Springs, Slana, Tatitlek, Tazlina, Tolsona, Tonsina, Valdez, Whittier, and Willow Creek

Cordova Court
Box 898
Cordova, AK 99574-0898
(907) 424-7312
http://www.state.ak.us/courts/ctinfo.htm
Vincent DiNapoli, Magistrate

Glennallen Court
Box 86
Glennallen, AK 99588-0086
(907) 822-3405
http://www.state.ak.us/courts/ctinfo.htm
Jean Wilkinson, Magistrate

Valdez District Court
Box 127
Valdez, AK 99686-0127
(907) 835-2266

http://www.state.ak.us/courts/ctinfo.htm
(also serves Sand Point)

Whittier Court
(post vacant)
(907) 264-0456 (Rural Court Training Assistant)

Wade Hampton Census Area

Alakanuk, Chevak, Emmonak, Hooper Bay, Kotlik, Marshall, Mountain Village, Pilot Station, Pitkas Point, Russian Mission, St. Mary's, Scammon Bay, and Sheldon Point (Nunam Iqua)

Chevak Court
Box 238
Chevak, AK 99563-0238
(907) 858-7232
http://www.state.ak.us/courts/ctinfo.htm
Doris Atchak, Magistrate

Emmonak Court
Box 176
Emmonak, AK 99581-0176
(907) 949-1748
http://www.state.ak.us/courts/ctinfo.htm
Darlene Johnson, Magistrate

St. Mary's Court
Box 269
St. Mary's, AK 99658-0269
(907) 438-2912
http://www.state.ak.us/courts/ctinfo.htm
Renea Hootch, Magistrate

Wrangell-Petersburg Census Area

Kake, Kupreanof, Petersburg, Port Alexander, Thoms Place, and Wrangell

Kake Court
Box 100
Kake, AK 99830-0100
(907) 785-3651
http://www.state.ak.us/courts/ctinfo.htm
Mike Jackson, Magistrate

Petersburg Court
Box 1009
Petersburg, AK 99833-1009
(907) 772-3824
http://www.state.ak.us/courts/ctinfo.htm
Darlene A. Whitethorn, Magistrate

Wrangell Court
Box 869
Wrangell, AK 99929-0869
(907) 874-2311; (907) 874-2313
http://www.state.ak.us/courts/ctinfo.htm
Christine P. Ellis, Magistrate

Yakutat City and Borough

Yakutat Court
Box 426
Yakutat, AK 99689-0426
(907) 784-3274
http://www.state.ak.us/courts/ctinfo.htm
Bertrand Adams, Magistrate

Yukon-Koyukuk Census Area

Alatna, Allakaket, Anvik, Arctic Village, Beaver, Bettles, Birch Creek, Central, Chalkyitsik, Circle, Coldfoot, Evansville, Flat, Fort Yukon, Four Mile Road, Galena, Grayling, Holy Cross, Hughes, Huslia, Kaltag, Koyukuk, Lake Minchumina, Livengood, Manley Hot Springs, McGrath, Minto, Nenana, New Allakaket, Nikolai, Nulato, Rampart, Ruby, Shageluk, Stevens Village, Takotna, Tanana, Venetie, and Wiseman

Aniak Court
(serves McGrath, see Bethel Census Area)

Fort Yukon Court
Box 211
Fort Yukon, AK 99740-0211
(907) 662-2336
http://www.state.ak.us/courts/ctinfo.htm
Dacho Alexander, Magistrate

Galena Court
Box 167

Galena, AK 99741-0167
(907) 656-1322
http://www.state.ak.us/courts/ctinfo.htm
Brian D. Fisher, Magistrate
(also serves Tanana)

Nenana Court
Box 449
Nenana, AK 99760-0449
(907) 832-5430
http://www.state.ak.us/courts/ctinfo.htm
Paul Verhagen, Magistrate

County Courthouse Book

ARIZONA

Capital: Phoenix. Statehood: 14 February 1912 (annexed through the Treaty of Guadalupe-Hidalgo, 1848, and the Gadsden Purchase, 1853, organized as a territory in 1863)

Arizona's Municipal Courts and Justices of the Peace handle civil actions and misdemeanors. Superior Courts in each county have jurisdiction over probate and domestic relations. Appeals are made to one of two Courts of Appeal. Division One includes Apache, Coconino, La Paz, Maricopa, Mohave, Navajo, Yavapai and Yuma counties and sits at Phoenix and elsewhere as needed. Division Two includes Cochise, Gila, Graham, Greenlee, Pima, Pinal and Santa Cruz counties and sits in Tucson and elsewhere. The state's Supreme Court is the court of last resort and sits in Phoenix.

Apache County
organized 1879 from Mohave County

Apache County Recorder
(Apache County Annex Building, First Floor, 75 West Cleveland Street—location)
PO Box 425 (mailing address)
St. Johns, AZ 85936
(928) 337-7514; (928) 337-7676 FAX
ljohnson@co.apache.az.us
http://www.co.apache.az.us/recorder
LeNora Y. Johnson
(land records)
copies: $1.00 per page

Apache County Superior Court
(Apache Superior Court House, 70 West Third South—location)
PO Box 365 (mailing address)
St. Johns, AZ 85936
(602) 337-4364 (County Switchboard); (928) 337-7550 (Clerk); (928) 337-2771 FAX (Clerk)
clerkofcourt@co.apache.az.us
http://www.co.apache.az.us/clerk
Sue Hall, Clerk of the Court %

Cochise County
organized 1881 from Pima County

Cochise County Recorder
1415 Melody Lane Building B
Bisbee, AZ 85603
(520) 432-8350; (520) 432-8368 FAX
recorder@co.cochise.az.us
http://www.co.cochise.az.us/recorders
Christine Rhodes
(land records)

Cochise County Superior Court
PO Drawer CK
Bisbee, AZ 85603
(520) 432-8570; (520) 432-4850 FAX
dlundin@courts.sp.state.az.us
http://www.co.cochise.az.us/Court/ClerkOfCourt/Crtclerk.htm
Denise I. Lundin, Clerk
(naturalization records, vital records, probate records)
records search service: $11.00 per year or source; copies of records: 50¢ per page, $11.00 for certification, no minimum

Coconino County
organized 1891 from Yavapai County

Coconino County Recorder
110 east Cherry Avenue
Flagstaff, AZ 86001
(928) 779-6585; (800) 793-6181
recrdr@coconino.az.gov
http://www.coconino.az.gov/recorder.aspx
Candace D. Owens
(land records)
copies: $1.00 per page

Coconino County Superior Court

Court House
200 North San Francisco Street
Flagstaff, AZ 86001
(928) 779-6535
http://www.coconino.az.gov/courts.aspx?id=295
Deborah Young, Clerk
(probate records from 1891)
probate search service: $3.00 per year; copies of land records: $1.00 per page, $3.00 per document for certification; copies of probate records: 50¢ per page, $3.00 minimum

Gila County
organized 1881 from Maricopa and Pinal counties

Gila County Recorder
1400 East Ash Street
Globe, AZ 85501
(928) 425-3231; (800) 291-4452; (928) 425-9270 FAX
webmaster@co.gila.az.us
http://recorder.gilacountyaz.gov
Linda Haught Ortega
(land records)
copies: $1.00 per page

Gila County Superior Court
Globe Courthouse
1400 East Ash Street
Globe, AZ 85501-1414
(602) 425-3231
gilacosc@courts.sp.state.az.us
http://www.supreme.state.az.us/gilasc
Anita Escobedo, Clerk
(probate, marriages)
copies: 50¢ per page

Graham County
organized 1881 from Apache and Pima counties

Graham County Recorder
921 Thatcher Boulevard
Safford, AZ 85546
(928) 428-3560
wjohn@graham.az.gov
http://www.graham.az.gov/county_offices.asp?id=1394
Wendy John
(land records)

Graham County Superior Court
Graham County Courthouse
800 Main Street
Safford, AZ 85546-2828
(602) 428-3310 (Court); (602) 428-3100 (Clerk)
dmaylen@graham.az.gov
http://www.graham.az.gov/county_offices.asp?id=1391&section=Judicial
Darlee Maylen, Clerk
(probate records)
probate search service: $11.50 per year; copies of probate records: $1.25 per page, no minimum

Greenlee County
organized 1909 from Graham County

Greenlee County Recorder
(253 Fifth Street—location)
PO Box 1625 (mailing address)
Clifton, AZ 85533
(928) 865-2632; (928) 865-1717 FAX
bmanuz@co.greenlee.az.us
http://www.co.greenlee.az.us/Recorder/RecorderHomePage.aspx
Berta Manuz, Clerk
(land records)

Greenlee County Superior Court
(223 Fifth Street—location)
PO Box 1027 (mailing address)
Clifton, AZ 85533
(602) 865-4242; (928) 865-5358 FAX
http://www.co.greenlee.az.us/Courts/ClerkHomePage.aspx
Cheryl Bowen, Clerk
(probate records)
probate search service: $3.00 per year; copies of probate records: 50¢ per page, no minimum

La Paz County
organized 1983 from Yuma County

La Paz County Recorder
1112 Joshua Avenue, Suite 201
Parker, AZ 85344
(928) 669-6136; (888) 526-8685 (within the county)
recorder@co.la-paz.az.us
http://www.co.la-paz.az.us/recorder.htm
Shelly Baker
(land records)

La Paz County Superior Court
(1316 Kofa Avenue, Suite 607—location)
PO Box 729 (mailing address)
Parker, AZ 85344
(602) 669-6131 (Clerk)
snewman@courts.sp.state.az.us
http://www.co.la-paz.az.us/courts.htm
Sheri Newman, Clerk

Maricopa County
organized 1871 from Yavapai and Yuma counties

Maricopa County Recorder
111 South Third Avenue
Phoenix, AZ 85003
(602) 506-3535
http://www.recorder.maricopa.gov
Helen Purcell
(land records)
copies: 50¢ per page

Maricopa County Superior Court
Maricopa County Central Court Building
201 West Jefferson Street
Phoenix, AZ 85003
(602) 506-3763 (Probate)
coccustomerrelations@mail.maricopa.gov
http://clerkofcourt.maricopa.gov/default.asp
Michael K. Jeanes, Clerk

Mohave County
organized 1864, original county, and in 1871 annexed Pah-Ute County, which had been organized in 1865

Mohave County Recorder
(700 West Beale Street—location)
PO Box 70 (mailing address)
Kingman, AZ 86402-0070
(928) 753-0701; (928) 753-0727
joan.mccall@co.mohave.az.us
http://www.co.mohave.az.us/depts/recorder/recorder_default.asp
Joan McCall, Clerk
(land records)

Mohave County Superior Court
(County Courthouse, 401 East Spring Street, Kingman, AZ 86401—location)
PO Box 7000 (mailing address)
Kingman, AZ 86402
(928) 753-0713
clerkofcourt@mohavecourts.com
http://www.mohavecourts.com/clerk/homepage.htm
Virlynn Tinnell, Clerk
(marriages, divorces, and probate records)
probate search service: $3.00 per year; copies of probate records: 50¢ per page, no minimum

Navajo County
organized 1870, original county

Navajo County Recorder
(Navajo County Governmental Complex, 100 East Carter Drive, South Highway 77—location)
PO Box 668 (mailing address)
Holbrook, AZ 86025
(928) 524-4194; (928) 524-4308 FAX
laurie.justman@co.navajo.az.us
http://co.navajo.az.us/recorder
Laurette Justman
(land records)

Navajo County Superior Court

(Navajo County Governmental Complex, 100
East Carter Drive, South Highway 77—
location)
PO Box 668 (mailing address)
Holbrook, AZ 86025
(602) 524-4188 (Clerk); (800) 634-2392
http://www.co.navajo.az.us/JusticeCourts/Justi
ce_Courts_Start_Page.aspx

Pima County
organized 1870, original county

Pima County Recorder
(115 North Church Avenue—location)
PO Box 3145 (mailing address)
Tucson, AZ 85702-3145
(520) 740-4350; (520) 623-1785 FAX
webmaster@recorder.pima.gov
http://www.recorder.co.pima.az.us
F. Ann Rodriguez
(land records)

Pima County Superior Court
Pima County Superior Courts Building
110 West Congress Street
Tucson, AZ 85701-1317
(520) 740-3200; (520) 798-3531 FAX
clerkprobate@sc.co.pima.az.us
http://www.cosc.pima.gov
Patricia A. Noland
(land records Property ownership records from
1924 with The Assessor's Office,
grantor/grantee index from 1912 [statehood]
with The Pima County Recorder in the "old"
Courthouse, 115 North Church, Tucson, AZ
85701, marriage licenses with Clerk of the
Superior Court, Probate Division, Pima
County Superior Courts Building, 110 West
Congress, Tucson, AZ 85701-1317, births and
deaths with Pima County Health and Welfare,
150 West Congress, Tucson, AZ 85701,
probate records with Clerk of the Superior
Court)
probate search service: $11.50; certified copies
of marriage licenses: $11.50 plus $3.50
postage; copies of probate records: $1.15 per
page, rounded up to next quarter dollar, $1.25
minimum, plus $3.50 postage

Pinal County
organized 1875 from Pima County

Pinal County Recorder
(31 North Pinal Street, Building E—location)
PO Box 848 (mailing address)
Florence, AL 85232
(520) 866-6830; (520) 866-6831 FAX
Recorder@co.pinal.az.us
http://co.pinal.az.us/Recorder
(land records)

Pinal County Superior Court
(Pinal County Criminal Justice Complex, 971
Jason Lopez Circle, Building A/Highway
79—location)
PO Box 2730 (mailing address)
Florence, AZ 85232-0827
(520) 866-5300 (Main Line); (520) 866-5381
(Clerk); (520) 866-5320 FAX
STipping@courts.sp.state.az.us
http://co.pinal.az.us/Clerk/SC
Kristi Youstey-Ruiz, Clerk of the Superior Court
(probate records)
probate search service: $11.50 per source (each
docket book for records before 1985 or
computer index from 1985 to date); copies of
probate records: $1.15 per page (cashier's
check or money order only), no minimum

Santa Cruz County
organized 1899 from Pima County

Santa Cruz County Recorder
2150 North Congress Drive, Suite 101
Nogales, AZ 85621
(520) 375-7990
ssainz@co.santa-cruz.az.us
http://www.co.santa-
cruz.az.us/recorder/index.html
Suzanne Sainz
(land records)

Santa Cruz County Superior Court
(2150 North Congress Drive, Nogales, AZ
85621—location)
PO Box 1265 (mailing address)
Nogales, AZ 85628
(520) 375-7700; (520) 375-7703 FAX
dbauch@courts.sp.state.az.us
http://www.co.santa-
cruz.az.us/clerk/index.html
Delfina Bauch, Clerk
(naturalization records from 18 July 1899
through 25 May 1984, marriage licenses and
applications, probate records from 9 May
1899)
probate search service: $3.00 per year; copies of
land records: $1.15 per page, rounded up to
next quarter dollar, $1.25 minimum, plus
$3.50; certified copies of vital records: $11.50
each plus $3.50 postage; copies of probate
records: $1.15 per page, $1.25 minimum, plus
$3.50 postage

Yavapai County
organized 1860, original county

Yavapai County Recorder
Administrative Services Building
1015 Fair Street, #228
Prescott, AZ 86305
(928) 771-3244; (928) 771-3258 FAX
web.recorder@co.yavapai.az.us
http://www.co.yavapai.az.us/departments/rec/
rechome.asp
Ana Wayman-Trujillo
(land records)

Yavapai County Superior Court
Yavapai County Courthouse
120 South Cortez, Room 207
Prescott, AZ 86303
(928) 771-3312 (Clerk); (928) 777-3062 (Probate
Specialist); (928) 771-3312 (Marriage
Licenses); (928) 771-3111 FAX (Clerk)
web.coc.probate@co.yavapai.az.us (Probate
Specialist);
web.coc.marriage@co.yavapai.az.us (Marriage
Licenses)
http://www.co.yavapai.az.us/departments/Cls/
ClsHome.asp
Jeanne Hicks, Clerk

Yuma County
organized 1864, original county

Yuma County Recorder's Office
410 South Maiden Lane, Suite B
Yuma, AZ 85364-2311
(928) 373-6020; (928) 373-6021 (Document
Recording); (928) 373-6022 (Recorder); (928)
373-6024 FAX
diana.brumley@co.yuma.az.us
http://www.co.yuma.az.us/recorder/index.htm
Dianna Brumley, Chief Deputy, Document
Recording; Susan Marler, Recorder
(land records)
copies: $1.00 per page, $3.00 for certification

Yuma County Superior Court
250 West Second Street
Yuma, AZ 85364
(928) 817-4210 (Clerk); (928) 817-4237 (Clerk);
(928) 817-4223 (Clerk)
cindy.joslin@co.yuma.az.us
http://www.co.yuma.az.us
Beverly Frame, Clerk

ARKANSAS

*Capital: Little Rock. Statehood: 15 June 1836
(Arkansas Territory organized 1819 from parts of
Louisiana and Missouri territories)*

Arkansas has several courts of limited
jurisdiction: Police Courts, City Courts,
Municipal Courts, Courts of Common Pleas,
and County Courts. The last have jurisdiction in
county taxes, county expenditures and claims
against the county as well as bastardy
proceedings and juvenile cases.

Twenty-four Chancery and Probate Courts,
sitting in each county, have jurisdiction in land
disputes, domestic relations, probate matters and
adoptions. Twenty-four Circuit Courts also meet
in each county and have jurisdiction over civil
and criminal cases. First Judicial Circuit: Cross,
Lee, Monroe, Phillips, St. Francis and Woodruff
counties; Second Judicial Circuit: Clay,
Craighead, Crittenden, Greene, Mississippi and
Poinsett counties; Third Judicial Circuit:
Jackson, Lawrence, Randolph and Sharp
counties; Fourth Judicial Circuit: Madison and
Washington counties; Fifth Judicial Circuit:
Franklin, Johnson and Pope counties; Sixth
Judicial Circuit: Perry and Pulaski counties;
Seventh Judicial Circuit: Grant, Hot Spring and
Saline counties; Eighth Judicial Circuit:
Hempstead, Lafayette, Miller and Nevada
counties; Ninth Judicial Circuit-East: Clark and
Pike counties; Ninth Judicial Circuit-West:
Howard, Little River and Sevier counties; Tenth
Judicial Circuit: Ashley, Bradley, Chicot, Desha
and Drew counties; Eleventh Judicial Circuit-
East: Arkansas County; Eleventh Judicial
Circuit-West: Jefferson and Lincoln counties;
Twelfth Judicial Circuit: Crawford and Sebastian
counties; Thirteenth Judicial Circuit: Calhoun,
Cleveland, Columbia, Dallas, Ouachita and
Union counties; Fourteenth Judicial Circuit:
Baxter, Boone, Marion and Newton counties;
Fifteenth Judicial Circuit: Conway, Logan, Scott
and Yell counties; Sixteenth Judicial Circuit:
Cleburne, Fulton, Independence, Izard and
Stone counties; Seventeenth Judicial Circuit-
East: Prairie and White counties; Seventeenth
Judicial Circuit-West: Lonoke County;
Eighteenth Judicial Circuit-East: Garland
County; Eighteenth Judicial Circuit-West:
Montgomery and Polk counties; Nineteenth
Judicial Circuit: Benton and Carroll counties;
Twentieth Judicial Circuit: Faulkner, Searcy and
Van Buren counties.

Six District Courts of Appeal sit in any of
their respective county seats. District One: Clay,
Craighead, Crittenden, Cross, Greene, Lee,
Mississippi, Monroe, Phillips, Poinsett, St.
Francis and Woodruff counties; District Two:
Baxter, Boone, Cleburne, Faulkner, Fulton,
Independence, Izard, Jackson, Lawrence,
Lonoke, Marion, Newton, Prairie, Randolph,
Searcy, Sharp, Stone, Van Buren and White
counties; District Three: Benton, Carroll,
Crawford, Franklin, Johnson, Madison, Pope,
Sebastian and Washington counties; District
Four: Clark, Conway, Garland, Grant,
Hempstead, Hot Spring, Howard, Lafayette,
Little River, Logan, Miller, Montgomery,
Nevada, Pike, Polk, Saline, Scott, Sevier and Yell
counties; District Five: Arkansas, Ashley,
Bradley, Calhoun, Chicot, Cleveland, Columbia,
Dallas, Desha, Drew, Jefferson, Lincoln,
Ouachita and Union counties; District Six: Perry
and Pulaski counties. A Supreme Court meets in
Little Rock.

Arkansas County
organized 1813, original county

Arkansas County Circuit Clerk
(Arkansas County Courthouse, 101 Court
Square—location)
PO Box 719 (mailing address)
DeWitt, AR 72042
(870) 946-4219; (870) 946-1394 FAX

circuitclerksd@centurytel.net;
    circuitclerknd@centurytel.net
http://local.arkansas.gov/local.php?agency=Ark
    ansas%20County
Tommy Sue Keffer
(land records)

Arkansas County Clerk
(Arkansas County Courthouse, 101 Court
    Square—location)
PO Box 719 (mailing address)
DeWitt, AR 72042
(870) 946-4349 voice & FAX
ArkansasClerk@ArkansasClerks.com
http://local.arkansas.gov/local.php?agency=Ark
    ansas%20County
Aline Ellenburg
(naturalization records, vital records, probate
    records)

Ashley County
organized 1848 from Union and Drew counties

Ashley County Circuit Clerk
215 East Jefferson Street
Hamburg, AR 71646
(870) 853-2030; (870) 853-2034 FAX
http://local.arkansas.gov/local.php?agency=As
    hley%20County
Bob Rush
(land records from 1849)

Ashley County Clerk
215 East Jefferson Street
Hamburg, AR 71646
(870) 853-2020; (870) 853-2082 FAX
ashleyclerk@arcounties.com;
    ashleycoclerk@sbcglobal.net
http://local.arkansas.gov/local.php?agency=As
    hley%20County
Regina Kersten
(marriages from 1848 , probate records from
    1921 and index of some before that year)
no probate search service; copies of probate
    records: 50¢ per page; courthouse burned in
    1921

Baxter County
organized 1873 from Fulton County

**Baxter County Circuit Clerk and County
    Clerk**
1 East Seventh Street
Mountain Home, AR 72653-4065
(501) 425-3475; (870) 424-5105 FAX
baxterclerk@centurybel.net
http://www.baxtercounty.org
Rhonda J. Porter
(land records and probate records from 1895,
    marriages and deaths that were recorded)
no probate search service; copies of probate
    records: 25¢ per page, no minimum;
    adoptions and juvenile records are not public
    record; courthouse burned in the late 1800s

Benton County
organized 1836 from Washington County

Benton County Circuit Clerk and Recorder
215 East Central
Bentonville, AR 72712-0699
(479) 271-1015; (479) 271-5719 FAX
bdeshields@co.benton.ar.us
http://www.co.benton.ar.us
Brenda DeShields
(land records from 1837 to date)

Benton County Clerk
215 East Central
Bentonville, AR 72712-0699
(479) 271-1013 (County Clerk); (479) 271-5723
    (Archives); (479) 271-5727 (Probate); (479)
    271-1019 FAX (County Clerk)
mslinkard@co.benton.ar.us
http://www.co.benton.ar.us/BCClerk/index.html
Mary L. Slinkard, County and Probate Clerk
(naturalization records from 1907 to 1929,
    marriages from 1868 to date, probate records
    from 1859 to date, wills from 1837 to date)
records search service: $3.00; copies of records:

50¢ per page

Boone County
organized 1869 from Carroll and Marion
    counties

Boone County Circuit Clerk
100 North Main Street
Harrison, AR 72601
(870) 741-5560; (870) 741-4335 FAX
jeanniesteen@hotmail.com
http://local.arkansas.gov/local.php?agency=Bo
    one%20County
Jennie Steen

Boone County Clerk
(100 North Main Street, Harrison, AR 72601—
    location)
PO Box 846 (mailing address)
Harrison, AR 72602-0846
(501) 741-8428; (870) 741-9724 FAX
http://local.arkansas.gov/local.php?agency=Bo
    one%20County
Kristie Blevins

Bradley County
organized 1840 from Union County

Bradley County Circuit Clerk
100 East Cedar Street
Warren, AR 71671
(870) 226-2272; (870) 226-8404 FAX
http://local.arkansas.gov/local.php?agency=Bra
    dley%20County
Dona Smith

Bradley County Clerk
100 East Cedar Street
Warren, AR 71671
(870) 226-3464; (870) 226-8404 FAX
http://local.arkansas.gov/local.php?agency=Bra
    dley%20County
Janet Kimbrell

Calhoun County
organized 1850 from Dallas, Ouachita, and
    Union counties

**Calhoun County Circuit Clerk and County
    Clerk**
(Second and Main Streets—location)
PO Box 626 (mailing address)
Hampton, AR 71744-0626
(501) 798-2517; (870) 798-2428 FAX
CalhounClerk@ArkansasClerks.com
http://local.arkansas.gov/local.php?agency=Cal
    houn%20County
Alma Davis
(land records from 1851, probate records from
    1862)
no probate search service; copies of probate
    records: 25¢ per page (50¢ for 11" x 17"), no
    minimum

Carroll County
organized 1833 from Izard County

Carroll County Circuit Clerk
210 West Church Street
Berryville, AR 72616-4233
(870) 423-2422; (870) 423-4796 FAX
http://local.arkansas.gov/local.php?agency=Car
    roll%20County
Ramona Wilson
(land records from the late 1860s, divorces)

Carroll County Clerk
210 West Church Street
Berryville, AR 72616-4233
(870) 423-2022; (870) 423-7400 FAX
http://local.arkansas.gov/local.php?agency=Car
    roll%20County
Shirley Doss
(marriages, probate records)
no probate search service; copies of probate
    records: 25¢ each, $3.00 for certified copies,
    minimum $5.00 if typed

Chicot County
organized 1823 from Arkansas County

Chicot County Circuit Clerk
108 Main Street
Lake Village, AR 71653
(870) 265-8010; (870) 265-8012 FAX
chicotcirclk@cei.net
http://local.arkansas.gov/local.php?agency=Chi
    cot%20County
Floy P. Bostick

Chicot County Clerk
108 Main Street
Lake Village, AR 71653
(870) 265-8000; (870) 265-8006 FAX
chicotclerk@arkansasclerks.com
http://local.arkansas.gov/local.php?agency=Chi
    cot%20County
Pam Donaldson
(probate records)
no probate search service (must have a year);
    copies of probate records: $3.00 each, $5.00
    for certified copies, no minimum

Clark County
organized 1818 from Arkansas County

Clark County Circuit Clerk
401 Clay Street
Arkadelphia, AR 71923
(870) 246-4281; (870) 246-1419 FAX
penny@clarkcountyarkansas.com
http://www.clarkcountyarkansas.com/dept/clerk
Penny Ross

Clark County Clerk
401 Clay Street
Arkadelphia, AR 71923
(501) 246-4491; (870) 246-6505 FAX
rhonda@clarkcountyarkansas.com
http://www.clarkcountyarkansas.com
Rhonda Williams Cole
(probate records)
probate search service: no charge; copies of
    probate records: $1.00 per page, $3.00 per
    certified document, 32¢ postage

Clay County
organized 1873 from Randolph County and
    Greene counties

Clay County Circuit Clerk
151 South Second Avenue
Piggott, AR 72454
(870) 598-2524; (870) 598-1107 FAX
http://local.arkansas.gov/local.php?agency=Cla
    y%20County
Janet Luff
(land records)

Clay County and Probate Clerk
(151 South Second Avenue—location)
PO Box 306 (mailing address)
Piggott, AR 72454-0306
(870) 598-2813; (870) 598-2813 FAX
http://local.arkansas.gov/local.php?agency=Cla
    y%20County
Sharon Williams
(probate records)

Cleburne County
organized 1883 from White, Van Buren and
    Independence counties

Cleburne County Circuit Clerk
301 West Main Street
Heber Springs, AR 72543
(501) 362-8149; (501) 362-4650 FAX
http://local.arkansas.gov/local.php?agency=Cle
    burne%20County
Karen Giles
(land records)

Cleburne County Clerk
301 West Main Street
Heber Springs, AR 72543
(501) 362-4620; (501) 362-4622 FAX
cleburneclerk@arkansasclerks.com
http://local.arkansas.gov/local.php?agency=Cle
    burne%20County
Dana Guffey
(probate records)

Arkansas

probate search service: $3.00; copies of probate records: 25¢ per page, $3.00 minimum; enclose SASE

Cleveland County
organized 1873 as Dorsey County, renamed 5 March 1885 as Cleveland County, and by provision of the organic act, portions of the counties of Lincoln, Jefferson, Dallas, and Bradley were integrated in the new county

Cleveland County Circuit Clerk and County Clerk
(20 Magnolia Street—location)
PO Box 368 (mailing address)
Rison, AR 71665-0368
(870) 325-6521 (County Clerk); (870) 325-6902 (Circuit Clerk); (870) 325-6144 FAX (County Clerk)
clevelandclerk@arkansasclerks.com
http://local.arkansas.gov/local.php?agency=Cleveland%20County
Sharron K. Gray
(land records, marriages, and probate records)

Columbia County
organized 1852 from Lafayette County

Columbia County Circuit Clerk
(1 Court Square, Suite 3, Magnolia, AR 71753—location)
PO Box 327 (mailing address)
Magnolia, AR 71754
(870) 235-3700; (870) 235-3786 FAX
circuitclerk@countyofcolumbia.net
http://www.countyofcolumbia.net
Janet Linkous
(land records)

Columbia County Clerk
1 Court Square, Suite 1
Magnolia, AR 71753
(870) 235-3774; (870) 235-3773 FAX
countyclerk@countyofcolumbia.net
http://www.countyofcolumbia.net
Sherry L. Bell
(marriage licenses and probate records)
probate search service: $2.00; copies of probate records: 50¢ per page

Conway County
organized 1825 from Pulaski County

Conway County Circuit Clerk
117 South Moose Street
Morrilton, AR 72110-3427
(501) 354-9617; (501) 354-9612 FAX
circlrk@conwaycounty.org
http://local.arkansas.gov/local.php?agency=Conway%20County
Carolyn Gadberry

Conway County Clerk
117 South Moose Street
Morrilton, AR 72110-3427
(501) 354-9621; (501) 354-9610 FAX
dhartman@conwaycounty.org
http://local.arkansas.gov/local.php?agency=Conway%20County
Debbie Hartman

Craighead County
county formed 19 February 1859 from parts of Greene, Mississippi and Poinsett counties

Craighead County Circuit Clerk
511 South Main Street
Jonesboro, AR 72401-2849
(870) 933-4530; (870) 933-4534 FAX
ann@craigheadcounty.org
http://www.craigheadcounty.org

Craighead County Clerk
511 South Main Street
Jonesboro, AR 72401-2849
(870) 933-4520; (870) 933-4514 FAX
nancy@craigheadcounty.org
http://www.craigheadcounty.org
Nancy Helms
(land records, vital records, and probate records)
copies: 25¢ per page

Crawford County
organized 1820 from Pulaski County; courthouse burned in 1876

Crawford County Circuit Clerk
300 Main Street
Van Buren, AR 72956-5765
(479) 474-1821; (479) 471-0622 FAX
linda.howard@crawford-county.org
http://www.crawford-county.org
Linda Howard
(land records)

Crawford County Clerk
300 Main Street
Van Buren, AR 72956-5765
(479) 474-1312; (479) 471-3236 FAX
patti.hill@crawford-county.org
http://www.crawford-county.org
Patti Hill
(marriages and probate records)
no probate search service; copies of probate records: 50¢ per page, $5.00 for certified copies, no minimum; send SASE

Crittenden County
organized 1825 from Phillips County

Crittenden County Circuit Clerk
100 Court Square
Marion, AR 72364
(870) 739-3248; (870) 739-3287 FAX
http://www.crittendencountywebsite.com/Crittenden_County_Arkansas_local_government_officlas_representative_committee_board_election_AR.html
Donna Palmer
(land records)

Crittenden County Clerk
100 Court Square
Marion, AR 72364
(870) 739-4434; (870) 739-3072 FAX
http://www.crittendencountywebsite.com/Crittenden_County_Arkansas_local_government_officlas_representative_committee_board_election_AR.html
Ruth Trent
(marriage licenses and probate records)

Cross County
organized 15 November 1862 from Crittenden, Poinsett and St. Francis counties

Cross County Circuit Clerk
705 East Union Street
Wynne, AR 72396-3039
(870) 238-5720; (870) 238-5722 FAX
http://local.arkansas.gov/local.php?agency=Cross%20County
Vernon Horton
(deeds from 1863)

Cross County Clerk
705 East Union Street
Wynne, AR 72396-3039
(870) 238-5735; (870) 238-5739 FAX
crossclerk@arkansasclerks.com
http://local.arkansas.gov/local.php?agency=Cross%20County
Peggy T. Jones
(marriages from 1863, probate records from 1864)
no probate search service; copies of marriage license: no charge for verification, $5.00 for certified copy; copies of probate records: $1.00 per page

Dallas County
organized 1845 from Clark and Hot Spring counties

Dallas County Circuit Clerk and County Clerk
Third and Oak Streets
Fordyce, AR 71742
(870) 352-2307; (870) 352-7179 FAX
http://local.arkansas.gov/local.php?agency=Dallas%20County
Janic McDaniel

Desha County
organized 1838 from Arkansas County

Desha County Circuit Clerk
Robert Moore Street
Arkansas City, AR 71630
(870) 877-2411; (870) 877-3407 FAX
deshaco@seark.net
http://local.arkansas.gov/local.php?agency=Desha%20County
Skippy Leek

Desha County Clerk
(Robert Moore Street—location)
PO Box 188 (mailing address)
Arkansas City, AR 71630-0188
(870) 877-2323; (870) 877-3413 FAX
http://local.arkansas.gov/local.php?agency=Desha%20County
Brenda Smith Morgan

Dorsey County
(see Cleveland County)

Drew County
organized 1846 from Arkansas County

Drew County Circuit Clerk
210 South Main
Monticello, AR 71655-4731
(870) 460-6250; (870) 460-6246 FAX
http://local.arkansas.gov/local.php?agency=Drew%20County
Pat Scifres Savage

Drew County Clerk
210 South Main
Monticello, AR 71655-4731
(870) 460-6260; (870) 460-6246 FAX
drewclerk@arkansasclerks.com
http://local.arkansas.gov/local.php?agency=Drew%20County
Lyna Gulledge

Faulkner County
organized 1873 from Pulaski County

Faulkner County Circuit Clerk
(801 Locust Street, Conway, AR 72032—location)
PO Box 9, Conway (mailing address)
Conway, AR 72033
(501) 450-4911; (501) 450-4948 FAX
srimmer@faulknercc.org
http://local.arkansas.gov/local.php?agency=Faulkner%20County
Sharon Rimmer
(land records)

Faulkner County Clerk
801 Locust Street
Conway, AR 72032
(501) 450-4904; (501) 450-4938 FAX
msreynolds@conwaycorp.net
http://local.arkansas.gov/local.php?agency=Faulkner%20County
Melinda Reynolds
(probate records)
probate search service: $2.00 (long search); copies of probate records: 25¢ per page

Franklin County
organized 1837 from Crawford County

Franklin County Circuit Clerk
211 West Commercial
Ozark, AR 72949
(479) 667-3818; (479) 667-5174 FAX
http://local.arkansas.gov/local.php?agency=Franklin%20County
Wilma Brushwood
(land records from 1860, naturalization records)

Franklin County Clerk
211 West Commercial
Ozark, AR 72949
(479) 667-3607; (479) 667-4247 FAX
http://local.arkansas.gov/local.php?agency=Franklin%20County
Sharon Needham

(marriages from 1850, probate records from 1886, unindexed, Quorum Court Records, Ministerial Records, Articles of Incorporation, Record of Administrator's Settlements, Real Estate Tax Books, etc.)
no probate search service; copies of marriages and probate: $1.00 plus SASE copies: $1.00 plus SASE

Fulton County
organized 1842 from Izard County

Fulton County Circuit Clerk and County Clerk
(123 South Main—location)
PO Box 485 (mailing address)
Salem, AR 72576-0485
(870) 895-3310; (870) 895-3383 FAX
http://local.arkansas.gov/local.php?agency=Fulton%20County
Vickie Bishop
(land records from 1879 to date, probate records from 1870 to date [courthouse fire in 1890 destroyed records])
searches and copies not available in fragile, old records bound in unindexed books

Garland County
organized 1873 from Hot Spring County

Garland County and Probate Clerk
501 Ouachita Avenue, Room 103
Hot Springs, AR 71901-5154
(501) 622-3610; (501) 624-0665 FAX
marriage@garlandcounty.org
http://www.garlandcounty.org
Judy Hughes
(marriages, probates, adoptions [sealed] and guardianships)
probate search service: no charge; certified copies of marriages: $5.00 each (includes search); copies of probate records: $1.00 per page

Garland County Circuit Clerk
501 Ouachita Avenue, Room 207
Hot Springs, AR 71901-5154
(501) 622-3636; (501) 609-9043 FAX
vicki@garlandcounty.org
http://www.garlandcounty.org
Vicki Rima
(deeds and divorces)

Grant County
organized 4 Feb 1869 from territory taken from Hot Spring, Jefferson, and Saline counties

Grant County Circuit Clerk and County Clerk
(Main at Center Street—location)
PO Box 364 (mailing address)
Sheridan, AR 72150
(870) 942-2631; (870) 942-3564 FAX
gcclerk@seark.net
http://local.arkansas.gov/local.php?agency=Grant%20County
Carol Ewing

Greene County
organized 1833 from Lawrence County

Greene County Circuit Clerk
(320 West Court Street—location)
PO Box 364 (mailing address)
Paragould, AR 72451-0364
(870) 239-6330; (870) 239-3550 FAX
http://local.arkansas.gov/local.php?agency=Greene%20County
Ellen Johnson
(land records from 1876)

Greene County Clerk
(320 West Court Street—location)
PO Box 62 (mailing address)
Paragould, AR 72450
(870) 239-6345; (870) 239-3550 FAX
http://local.arkansas.gov/local.php?agency=Greene%20County
Linda Heritage
(marriages from 1876, probate records from

1876)
copies of probate records: $1.00 each, no minimum

Hempstead County
organized 1818 from Arkansas County

Hempstead County Circuit Clerk
400 South Washington Street
Hope, AR 71801
(870) 777-2384; (870) 777-7827 FAX
http://local.arkansas.gov/local.php?agency=Hempstead%20County
Carolyn Neel

Hempstead County Clerk
400 South Washington Street
Hope, AR 71801
(870) 777-2241; (870) 771-7829 FAX
http://local.arkansas.gov/local.php?agency=Hempstead%20County
Velora B. Haltom
(marriages and probate records)
probate search service: charges vary, depending on time spent; copies of probate records: 50¢ per page, no minimum

Hot Spring County
organized 1829 from Clark County

Hot Spring County Circuit Clerk
210 Locust Street
Malvern, AR 72104
(501) 332-2281; (501) 332-2221 FAX
http://local.arkansas.gov/local.php?agency=Hot%20Spring%20County
Sue Jones
(land records from 1829)

Hot Spring County Clerk
210 Locust Street
Malvern, AR 72104
(501) 332-2291; (501) 332-2221 FAX
http://local.arkansas.gov/local.php?agency=Hot%20Spring%20County
Mary Ann Walters
(probate records from 1829)
probate search service: charges vary

Howard County
organized 1873 from Pike County

Howard County Circuit Clerk
Howard County Courthouse
421 North Main Street
Nashville, AR 71852-2008
(870) 845-7506; (870) 845-7505 FAX
bobbie.jo.green@arkansas.gov
http://local.arkansas.gov/local.php?agency=Howard%20County
Bobbie Jo Green

Howard County Clerk
Howard County Courthouse
421 North Main Street
Nashville, AR 71852-2008
(870) 845-7502; (870) 845-7505 FAX
HowardClerk@ArkansasClerks.com
http://local.arkansas.gov/local.php?agency=Howard%20County
Janice Huffman

Independence County
organized 1820 from Arkansas County

Independence County Circuit Clerk
192 East Main Street
Batesville, AR 72501-3135
(870) 793-8833; (870) 793-8888 FAX
http://local.arkansas.gov/local.php?agency=Independence%20County
Claudia Nobles

Independence County Clerk
192 East Main Street
Batesville, AR 72501-3135
(870) 793-8828; (870) 793-8831 FAX
IndependenceClerk@ArkansasClerks.com
http://local.arkansas.gov/local.php?agency=Independence%20County
Margaret Boothby

Izard County
organized 1825 from Independence County

Izard County Circuit Clerk and County Clerk
Izard County Courthouse
Melbourne, AR 72556
(870) 368-4316; (870) 368-4748 FAX
http://local.arkansas.gov/local.php?agency=Izard%20County
Rhonda Halbrook

Jackson County
organized 1829 from Independence County

Jackson County Circuit Clerk
208 Main Street
Newport, AR 72112
(870) 523-7423; (870) 523-3682 FAX
cclerk@ipa.net
http://www.jacksoncountyar.org
Pam Graham

Jackson County Clerk
(208 Main Street—location)
PO Box 641 (mailing address)
Newport, AR 72112-0641
(501) 523-7420; (870) 523-7404 FAX
JacksonClerk@ArkansasClerks.com
http://www.jacksoncountyar.org
Dottie Calhoun
(naturalization records, vital records [restrictions on adoption records and juvenile records], probate records)

Jefferson County
organized 1829 from Arkansas and Pulaski counties

Jefferson County Circuit Clerk
101 East Barraque Street
Pine Bluff, AR 71601
(870) 541-5304; (870) 541-5324 FAX
http://www.jeffersoncountyark.com

Jefferson County Clerk
(101 East Barraque Street—location)
PO Box 6317 (mailing address)
Pine Bluff, AR 71601
(501) 541-5322; (870) 541-5324 FAX
hbradley@jcclerk@sbcglobal.net
http://www.jeffersoncountyark.com
Helen Bradley
(naturalization records, vital records, and probate records)
copies 25¢ per page

Johnson County
organized 1833 from Pope County

Johnson County Circuit Clerk
215 West Main Street
Clarksville, AR 72830
(479) 754-2977 (Circuit Clerk); (479) 754-7724 (Sheriff); (479) 754-3371 (Collector); (479) 754-3863 (Assessor); (479) 754-4235 FAX
jocotrea@cswnet.com (Collector)
http://local.arkansas.gov/local.php?agency=Johnson%20County
Jane Houston, Circuit Clerk; Wesley Kendrick, County Sheriff; Carol Williams, County Collector; Don R. Hurst, Jr., County Assessor
(copy of tax books, assessment books, plat maps with Assessor, deeds, mortgages, oil and gas leases with Circuit Clerk, current tax books with Sheriff and Collector, a few very old naturalization records with Circuit Clerk [District Courts for all others])

Johnson County Clerk
(215 West Main Street—location)
PO Box 57 (mailing address)
Clarksville, AR 72830
(479) 754-3967; (479) 754-2286 FAX
http://local.arkansas.gov/local.php?agency=Johnson%20County
Kathy B. Pitts
(tax books, marriages from 1855 with County Clerk, veteran discharge records, wills,

administrations, guardianships, voter registration, minister credentials, doctors' and nurses' credentials, articles of incorporation, county officials' commissions, and affidavit for collection of small estates by distributees) probate search service: $5.00; copies of probate records: 25¢ per page, $5.00 minimum

Lafayette County
organized 1827 from Hempstead County

Lafayette County Circuit Clerk
(Third and Spruce Streets—location)
PO Box 986 (mailing address)
Lewisville, AR 71845
(870) 921-4878; (870) 921-4879 FAX
lafcocirclerk@whti.net
http://local.arkansas.gov/local.php?agency=Lafayette%20County
Mary Joe Rogers
(deeds, civil and chancery records)
certified copies of land records: $3.00 plus 80¢ per page, survey plats $6.00 each

Lafayette County Clerk
(Third and Spruce Streets—location)
PO Box 945 (mailing address)
Lewisville, AR 71845
(870) 921-4633; (870) 921-4505 FAX
lafcoclerk@whti.net
http://local.arkansas.gov/local.php?agency=Lafayette%20County
Diane Fletcher
(marriage licenses, probate, small estate, assumed name, county court cases)
no probate search service; certified copies of marriage licenses: $5.00 each; copies of probate records: from 40¢ to $1.00 plus certification and postage

Lawrence County
organized 1815 from New Madrid County, Missouri

Lawrence County Circuit Clerk
(315 West Main—location)
PO Box 581 (mailing address)
Walnut Ridge, AR 72476
(870) 886-1112; (870) 886-1128 FAX
lawcocir@bscn.com
http://local.arkansas.gov/local.php?agency=Lawrence%20County
Kristi Murphy
(deeds)

Lawrence County Clerk
(315 West Main—location)
PO Box 526 (mailing address)
Walnut Ridge, AR 72476
(870) 886-1111; (870) 886-1122 FAX
LawrenceClerk@ArkansasClerks.com
http://local.arkansas.gov/local.php?agency=Lawrence%20County
Tina Stowers
(probate records)
copies: $1.00-$2.00

Lee County
organized 1873 from Phillips and Monroe counties

Lee County Circuit Clerk
15 East Chestnut Street
Marianna, AR 72360-2302
(870) 295-7710; (870) 295-7712 FAX
http://local.arkansas.gov/local.php?agency=Lee%20County
Mary Ann Wilkinson
(deeds)

Lee County Clerk
15 East Chestnut Street
Marianna, AR 72360-2302
(870) 295-7715; (870) 295-7783 FAX
pwilson@cablelynx.com
http://local.arkansas.gov/local.php?agency=Lee%20County
Pat Wilson
(tax books [only], marriages, probate records)
probate search service: no charge for index

search [staff limited, public invited to do searches]; copies of marriages: 25¢ each, $5.00 if certified; copies of probate records: $1.00 per page

Lincoln County
organized 1871 from Arkansas, Bradley, Desha, Drew and Jefferson counties

Lincoln County and Probate Clerk
300 South Drew Street
Star City, AR 71667
(870) 628-5114; (870) 628-5794 FAX
LincolnClerk@ARkansasClerks.com
http://local.arkansas.gov/local.php?agency=Lincoln%20County
Katherine Lawson Denmon
(probate records)
probate search service: $3.00; copies of probate records: 25¢ per page, $5.00 for certified copies

Lincoln County Circuit Clerk and Recorder
300 South Drew Street
Star City, AR 71667
(870) 628-3154; (870) 628-5546 FAX
lincocircuitclerk@centurytel.net
http://local.arkansas.gov/local.php?agency=Lincoln%20County
Vera Reynolds
(deeds, etc.)

Little River County
organized 1867 from Hempstead County

Little River County Circuit Clerk
351 North Second
Ashdown, AR 71822
(870) 898-7212; (870) 898-5783 FAX
http://local.arkansas.gov/local.php?agency=Little%20River%20County
Deanna M. Bishop
(land records)

Little River County Clerk
351 North Second
Ashdown, AR 71822
(870) 898-7208; (870) 898-7207 FAX
LittleRiverClerk@ArkansasClerks.com
http://local.arkansas.gov/local.php?agency=Little%River%20County
Linda Coleman
(probate records)
probate search service: $3.00; copies of probate records: 50¢ per page, no minimum

Logan County
organized 1871 from Franklin County; name changed from Sarber County in 1875

Logan County Circuit Clerk
Courthouse Square
Paris, AR 72855
(501) 963-2164; (479) 963-3304 FAX
http://local.arkansas.gov/local.php?agency=Logan%20County
Everly Kellar
(land records from 1877)

Logan County Clerk
Courthouse Square
Paris, AR 72855
(479) 963-2618; (479) 963-9017 FAX
LoganClerk@ArkansasClerks.com
http://local.arkansas.gov/local.php?agency=Logan%20County
Lynda Brooks
(probate records from 1877)
no probate search service; copies of probate records: 25¢ per page, no minimum, no photocopies available of records prior to 1940, transcriptions only

Lonoke County
organized 1873 from Pulaski and Jefferson counties

Lonoke County Circuit Clerk
(301 North Center Street—location)
PO Box 431 (mailing address)

Lonoke, AR 72086
(501) 676-2316; (501) 676-3014 FAX
http://local.arkansas.gov/local.php?agency=Lonoke%20County
Deborah Oglesby
(land records)

Lonoke County Clerk
(301 North Center Street—location)
PO Box 431 (mailing address)
Lonoke, AR 72086
(501) 676-2368; (501) 676-3038 FAX
http://local.arkansas.gov/local.php?agency=Lonoke%20County
Prudie Percefull
(probate records)
copies of probate records: $1.00 per page, $5.00 for certified copies

Madison County
organized 1836 from Washington County

Madison County Circuit Clerk
201 West Main Street
Huntsville, AR 72740
(479) 738-2215; (479) 738-1544 FAX
http://local.arkansas.gov/local.php?agency=Madison%20County
Phyllis Vilines
(deeds from 1848, mortgages from 1883, deaths from 1848-1972 [previously recorded in the Deed Books])

Madison County Clerk
(201 West Main Street—location)
PO Box 37 (mailing address)
Huntsville, AR 72740-0037
(479) 738-2747; (479) 738-2735 FAX
MadisonClerk@ArkansasClerks.com
http://local.arkansas.gov/local.php?agency=Madison%20County
Faron Ledbetter
(marriage licenses from 1901, probate records from 1860)
no probate search service; copies of probate records: 25¢ per page, $3.00 for certified copy, no minimum

Marion County
organized 1835 from Izard County

Marion County Circuit Clerk and County Clerk
Marion County Courthouse
Yellville, AR 72687
(870) 449-6226; (870) 449-4979 FAX
http://local.arkansas.gov/local.php?agency=Marion%20County
Dee Carleton
(land and probate records from late 1887 to date)
land and probate records search service: $6.00; copies of probate records: $50¢ per page

Miller County
organized 1862 from Lafayette County, abolished 1863, reestablished 1874

Miller County Circuit Clerk
400 Laurel Street
Texarkana, AR 71854
(870) 774-4501; (870) 772-5293 FAX
http://local.arkansas.gov/local.php?agency=Miller%20County
Wanda Davis
(land records)

Miller County Clerk
400 Laurel Street
Texarkana, AR 71854
(870) 774-1501; (870) 774-4090 FAX
http://local.arkansas.gov/local.php?agency=Miller%20County
Ann Nicholas
(probate records)
probate search service: no charge; copies of probate records: $1.00 per page, $5.00 for certified copies, no minimum, send SASE

Mississippi County
organized 1883 from Crittenden County

Mississippi County Circuit Clerk
200 West Walnut Street
Blytheville, AR 72315
(870) 762-2332; (870) 762-8148 FAX
ocse.Mississippi.clerk.2@ocse.state.ar.us
http://www.mcagov.com
Donna Bray

Mississippi County Clerk
200 West Walnut Street
Blytheville, AR 72315
(870) 762-2411; (870) 838-6674 FAX
mississippiclerkb@arkansasclerks.com
http://www.mcagov.com
Lib Shippen
(probate records)
probate search service: no charge; copies of
probate records: 25¢ per page, no minimum

Monroe County
organized 1839 from Phillips and Arkansas
counties

Monroe County Circuit Clerk
123 Madison Street
Clarendon, AR 72029-2742
(870) 747-3615; (870) 747-3710 FAX
http://local.arkansas.gov/local.php?agency=Mo
nroe%20County
Phyllis Stinson

Monroe County Clerk
123 Madison Street
Clarendon, AR 72029-2742
(870) 747-3632; (870) 747-5961 FAX
MonroeClerk@ArkansasClerks.com
http://local.arkansas.gov/local.php?agency=Mo
nroe%20County
Janet E. Tweedle

Montgomery County
organized 1842 from Clark County

**Montgomery County Circuit Clerk and
County Clerk**
(105 Highway 270 East—location)
PO Box 717 (mailing address)
Mt. Ida, AR 71957-0717
(870) 867-3521; (870) 867-2177 FAX
MontgomeryClerk@ArkansasClerks.com
http://local.arkansas.gov/local.php?agency=Mo
ntgomery%20County
Debbie Baxter

Nevada County
organized 1871 from Hempstead County

Nevada County Circuit Clerk
(Courthouse Square—location)
PO Box 552 (mailing address)
Prescott, AR 71857
(870) 887-2511; (870) 887-5795 FAX
http://circuitcourt.co.nevada.ar.us
Carolyn Steed
(land records from 1871, naturalization records
from 1871)

Nevada County Clerk
(Courthouse Square—location)
PO Box 618 (mailing address)
Prescott, AR 71857
(870) 887-2710; (870) 887-5795 FAX
NevadaClerk@ArkansasClerks.com
http://co.nevada.ar.us
Julie Stockton
(probate records from 1871)
no probate search service; copies of probate
records: $1.00 each, $5.00 for certified copies

Newton County
organized 1842 from Carroll County

**Newton County Circuit Clerk and County
Clerk**
(Court Street—location)
PO Box 410 (mailing address)
Jasper, AR 72641
(870) 446-5125; (870) 446-5755 FAX
http://local.arkansas.gov/local.php?agency=Ne
wton%20County
Donnie Davis
(unindexed land records from 1870s, probate
records from 1870s)

Ouachita County
organized 1842 from Clark County

Ouachita County Circuit Clerk
(Town Square—location)
PO Box 644 (mailing address)
Camden, AR 71701
(870) 837-2230; (870) 837-2252 FAX
http://local.arkansas.gov/local.php?agency=Ou
achita%20County
Betty Lemons

Ouachita County Clerk
(Town Square—location)
PO Box 644 (mailing address)
Camden, AR 71701
(870) 837-2220; (870) 837-2217 FAX
http://local.arkansas.gov/local.php?agency=Ou
achita%20County
Britt Williford
(probate records)
probate search service: 50¢ per page; copies of
probate records: 50¢ per page; enclose fees
with request

Perry County
organized 1840 from Pulaski County

**Perry County Circuit Clerk and County
Clerk**
(310 West Main Street—location)
PO Box 358 (mailing address)
Perryville, AR 72126-0358
(501) 889-5126; (501) 889-5759 FAX
PerryClerk@ArkansasClerks.com
http://www.perrycountyarkansas.com
Barbara L. Lovell

Phillips County
organized 1820 from Arkansas County

Phillips County Circuit Clerk
620 Cherry Street
Helena, AR 72342
(870) 338-5515; (870) 338-5513 FAX
http://local.arkansas.gov/local.php?agency=Phi
llips%20County
Wanda W. McIntosh
(land records from 1873)

Phillips County Clerk
620 Cherry Street, Suite 202
Helena, AR 72342-3399
(870) 338-5505; (870) 338-5509 FAX
ocse.phillips.clerk@ocse.state.ar.us
http://local.arkansas.gov/local.php?agency=Phi
llips%20County
Linda White
(marriages from 1831, probate records from
1821)
records search service: copies: 25¢ each, $5.00
for certified copies

Pike County
organized 1833 from Carroll and Clark counties

Pike County Circuit Clerk
Courthouse Square
Murfreesboro, AR 71958
(870) 285-2231; (870) 285-3281 FAX
pikedwhite@alltel.net
http://local.arkansas.gov/local.php?agency=Pik
e%20County
Donna White

Pike County Clerk
Courthouse Square
Murfreesboro, AR 71958
(870) 285-2743; (870) 285-3900 FAX
http://local.arkansas.gov/local.php?agency=Pik
e%20County
Sandy Campbell

Poinsett County
organized 1838 from Greene County

Poinsett County Circuit Clerk
401 Market Street
Harrisburg, AR 72432
(870) 578-4420; (870) 578-4427 FAX
admin@poinsettcounty.us
http://www.poinsettcounty.us//officials.htm
Claudia Mathews

Poinsett County Clerk
401 Market Street
Harrisburg, AR 72432
(870) 578-4412; (870) 578-2441 FAX
PoinsettClerk@ArkansasClerks.com
http://www.poinsettcounty.us//officials.htm
Fonda Condra

Polk County
organized 1844 from Montgomery County

Polk County Circuit Clerk
507 Church Street
Mena, AR 71953-3257
(479) 394-8100; (479) 394-8135 FAX
polk.clerk@ocse.state.ar.us
http://www.visionmena.com/polk_count_arka
nsas_government/polk_county_arkansas_gov
ernment.htm
Sharon Simmons

Polk County Clerk
507 Church Street
Mena, AR 71953-3257
(479) 394-8123; (479) 394-8115 FAX
polkcountyclerk@yahoo.com
http://www.visionmena.com/polk_count_arka
nsas_government/polk_county_arkansas_gov
ernment.htm
Terri Harrison
(marriages from 1893, probate records from
1920)
no probate search service; copies of probate
records: 25¢ per page, no minimum

Pope County
organized 1829 from Pulaski County

Pope County Circuit Clerk
100 West Main Street
Russellville, AR 72801
(479) 968-7499; (479) 880-8463 FAX
fernpopecounty@centurytel.net
http://local.arkansas.gov/local.php?agency=Po
pe%20County
Fern Tucker

Pope County Clerk
100 West Main Street
Russellville, AR 72801
(479) 968-6064; (479) 967-2291 FAX
http://local.arkansas.gov/local.php?agency=Po
pe%20County
Don Johnson

Prairie County
organized 1846 from Monroe County

**Prairie County Circuit Clerk and County
Clerk**
(Courthouse Square—location)
PO Box 278 (mailing address)
Des Arc, AR 72040-0278
(870) 256-4434 voice & FAX
PrairieClerk@ArkansasClerks.com
http://local.arkansas.gov/local.php?agency=Pra
irie%20County
Karan Skarda

Pulaski County
organized 1818 from Arkansas County

**Pulaski County Circuit Clerk and County
Clerk**
(401 West Markham Street, Suite 100—location)
PO Box 2659 (mailing address)
Little Rock, AR 72201-2659
(501) 340-8500; (501) 340-8340 FAX
circuit@co.pulaski.ar.us

Arkansas

http://www.pulaskiclerk.com
Mr. Pat O'Brien
(land records from 1819 with Circuit Clerk,
marriage licenses and probate records with
County Clerk)
probate search service: $3.00 per name; copies
of probate records: 75¢ for the first page and
38¢ for each additional page; need date (year)
case was opened

Randolph County
organized 1835 from Lawrence County

Randolph County Circuit Clerk
107 West Broadway
Pocahontas, AR 72455
(870) 892-5522; (870) 892-8794 FAX
http://local.arkansas.gov/local.php?agency=Ra
ndolph%20County;
http://www.randolphchamber.com
Debbie Wise
(land records from 1836)

Randolph County Clerk
107 West Broadway
Pocahontas, AR 72455
(870) 892-5822; (870) 892-5829 FAX
rcoclerk@tcac.net
http://local.arkansas.gov/local.php?agency=Ra
ndolph%20County;
http://www.randolphchamber.com
Janis Mock
(probate records from 1836)
copies of probate records: 25¢ per page, 15¢ to
20¢ for copies of papers in files (since paper is
smaller), no minimum

St. Francis County
organized 1827 from Phillips

St. Francis County Circuit Clerk
313 South Izard Street
Forrest City, AR 72335-3856
(870) 261-1715; (870) 261-1723 FAX
http://local.arkansas.gov/local.php?agency=Sai
nt%20Francis%20County
Bette Green

St. Francis County Clerk
313 South Izard Street
Forrest City, AR 72335-3856
(870) 261-1725; (870) 630-1210 FAX
http://local.arkansas.gov/local.php?agency=Sai
nt%20Francis%20County
Elizabeth Smith
(land records, naturalization records, vital
records, probate records from 1900s)
probate search and copy fees vary

Saline County
organized 1835 from Pulaski County

Saline County Circuit Clerk
200 North Main Street
Benton, AR 72015
(501) 303-5615; (501) 303-5675 FAX
dkidd@salinecounty.org
http://www.salinecounty.org
Doug Kidd
(deeds from 1836)

Saline County Clerk
200 North Main Street
Benton, AR 72015
(501) 776-5630; (501) 303-5684 FAX
SalineClerk@ArkansasClerk.com
http://www.salinecounty.org
Freddy Burton
(probate records from 1836, tax records from
1890)
no probate search service; copies of probate
records: 50¢ per page, no minimum

Sarber County
(see Logan County)

Scott County
organized 1833 from Crawford and Pope
counties

Scott County Circuit Clerk and County Clerk
(Courthouse Square—location)
PO Box 1578 (mailing address)
Waldron, AR 72958-1578
(479) 637-2642; (479) 637-0124 FAX
http://local.arkansas.gov/local.php?agency=Sco
tt%20County
Lenny McDaniel
(land records, naturalization records, vital
records, probate records)

Searcy County
organized 1838 from Marion County

Searcy County Circuit Clerk and County Clerk
Courthouse Square
Marshall, AR 72650
(870) 448-3807; (870) 448-5005 FAX
SearcyClerk@ArkansasClerks.com
http://local.arkansas.gov/local.php?agency=Sea
rcy%20County
Wesley Smith
(deeds from 1878, births from 1919 to 1920,
deaths from 1919 to 1921, marriages from
1881, probate records from 1879)
no land, probate, or vital records search service;
copies of probate records: 10¢ per page, no
minimum

Sebastian County
organized 1851 from Crawford County

Sebastian County Circuit Clerk
35 South Sixth Street
Fort Smith, AR 72901
(479) 782-1046; (479) 784-1580 FAX
nbrewer@co.sebastian.ar.us
http://www.sebastiancountyonline.com
Nancy Brewer

Sebastian County Clerk
35 South Sixth Street
Fort Smith, AR 72901
(479) 782-5065; (479) 784-1567 FAX
dtate@co.sebatian.ar.us
http://www.sebastiancountyonline.com
Doris Tate

Sevier County
organized 1828 from Hempstead County

Sevier County Circuit Clerk
115 North Third Street
De Queen, AR 71832
(870) 584-3055; (870) 642-3119 FAX
sccirclk@alltel.net
http://www.seviercounty-ar.com
Laurie Green
(land records)

Sevier County Clerk
115 North Third Street
De Queen, AR 71832
(870) 642-2852; (870) 642-3896 FAX
SevierClerk@ArkansasClerks.com
http://www.seviercounty-ar.com
Sandra Dunn
(probate records)
probate search service: no charge; copies of
probate records: $1.00 per page if request
includes book and page numbers, no
minimum

Sharp County
organized 1868 from Izard County

Sharp County Circuit Clerk and County Clerk
718 Ash Flat Drive
Ash Flat, AR 72513
(870) 994-7361; (870) 994-7712 FAX
sharpclerk@centurytel.net
htt://www.sharpcounty.org
Tommy Estes

Stone County
organized 1873 from Independence and Izard
counties

Stone County Circuit Clerk and County Clerk
(107 West Main—location)
PO Drawer 120 (mailing address)
Mountain View, AR 72560
(870) 269-3271 (Circuit Clerk); (870) 269-5550
(County Clerk); (870) 269-2303 FAX (Circuit
Clerk); (870) 269-9058 FAX (County Clerk)
djwilson@mvtel.net
http://local.arkansas.gov/local.php?agency=Sto
ne%20County
Donna Wilson
(land records, marriages and probate records
from 1873)
probate search service: $2.00 ("will do as we
have time"); copies of probate records: 50¢
each, $2.00 minimum

Union County
organized 1829 from Hempstead and Clark
counties

Union County Circuit Clerk
101 North Washington Street
El Dorado, AR 71730
(870) 864-1940; (870) 864-1994 FAX
UnionClerk@ArkansasClerks.com
http://www.co.union.ar.us
Cheryl Cochran-Wilson
(land records)

Union County Clerk
101 North Washington Street
El Dorado, AR 71730
(870) 864-1910; (870) 864-1927 FAX
UnionClerk@ArkansasClerks.com
http://www.co.union.ar.us
Connie Chandler
(probate records)
probate search service: $1.00 per name; copies
of probate records: $1.00 per page plus SASE

Van Buren County
organized 1833 from Independence County

Van Buren County Circuit Clerk and County Clerk
(451 Main Street—location)
PO Box 80 (mailing address)
Clinton, AR 72031-0080
(501) 745-4140; (501) 745-7400 FAX
http://local.arkansas.gov/local.php?agency=Va
n%20Buren%20County
Ester Bass
(deeds, mortgages, etc., from late 1860s,
marriage licenses, probate records from 1903)
certified copies of marriages: $5.00; copies of
probate records: 25¢ each from paper original,
50¢ each from microfilm original, plus SASE

Washington County
organized 1828 from Crawford County and a
tract known as Lovely's Purchase

Washington County Circuit Clerk
280 North College Avenue
Fayetteville, AR 72701
(479) 444-1538; (479) 444-1537 FAX
bstamps@co.washington.ar.us
http://www.co.washington.ar.us
Bette Stamps

Washington County Clerk
280 North College Avenue
Fayetteville, AR 72701
(479) 444-1711; (479) 444-1894 FAX
kpritchard@co.washington.ar.us
http://www.co.washington.ar.us
Karen Pritchard

White County
organized 1835 from Pulaski, Jackson, and
Independence counties

White County Circuit Clerk
300 North Spruce Street
Searcy, AR 72143-7720
(501) 279-6203; (501) 279-6218 FAX
http://www.whitcountyar.org
(divorces, deeds, mortgages, etc.)

White County Clerk
300 North Spruce Street
Searcy, AR 72143-7720
(501) 279-6204; (501) 279-6260 FAX
whitecountyclerk@cablelynx.com
http://www.whitecountyar.org
Tanya Burleson
(marriages, probate records)
probate search service: no charge; copies of
	marriages: $1.00 each, $5.00 for certified
	copies; copies of probate records: $1.00 per
	page, $3.00 for certified copies, no minimum;
	copies are typed due to the condition of the
	records

Woodruff County
organized 1862 from White County

Woodruff County Circuit Clerk
500 North Third Street
Augusta, AR 72006-2056
(870) 347-2391; (870) 347-8703 FAX
http://local.arkansas.gov/local.php?agency=Wo
	odruff%20County
Jean Carter Root
(land records from 1862)

Woodruff County Clerk
500 North Third Street
Augusta, AR 72006-2056
(870) 347-2871; (870) 347-2608 FAX
http://local.arkansas.gov/local.php?agency=Wo
	odruff%20County
Becky Hicks
(probate records from 1868)
copies of probate records: $1.00 per page, no
	minimum

Yell County
organized 1840 from Pope County; courthouse
	burned in 1865

Yell County Circuit Clerk and County Clerk
(Fifth and Main Streets—location)
PO Box 219 (mailing address)
Danville, AR 72833
(479) 495-4850; (479) 495-4875 FAX
YellClerk@ArkansasClerks.com
http://local.arkansas.gov/local.php?agency=Yel
	l%20County
Carolyn Morris
(land records from circa 1868, vital records from
	circa 1868, probate records from circa 1868)
vital records search service ("as time permits");
	no probate search service; copies of probate
	records: 25¢ per page, certified copies $3.00

Capital: Sacramento. Statehood: 9 September 1850
(annexed after the Treaty of Guadalupe-Hidalgo, 1848)

California's Municipal Courts and Justice
Courts handle civil disputes, small claims,
misdemeanors and infractions. Superior Courts
have jurisdiction over all felonies as well as civil
and criminal cases, juvenile, probate and family
law, etc., and sit at the county seats.
	Courts of Appeal are divided into six districts.
First District at San Francisco: Alameda, Contra
Costa, Del Norte, Humboldt, Lake, Marin,
Mendocino, Napa, San Francisco, San Mateo,
Solano and Sonoma counties; Second District at
Los Angeles and Ventura: Los Angeles, Santa
Barbara and Ventura counties; Third District at
Sacramento: Alpine, Amador, Butte, Calaveras,
Colusa, El Dorado, Glenn, Lassen, Modoc,
Mono, Nevada, Placer, Plumas, Sacramento, San
Joaquin, Shasta, Sierra, Siskiyou, Sutter, Tehama,
Trinity, Yolo and Yuba counties; Fourth District
at San Diego, San Bernardino and Santa Ana:
Imperial, Inyo, Orange, Riverside, San
Bernardino and San Diego counties; Fifth
District at Fresno: Fresno, Kern, Kings, Madera,
Mariposa, Merced, San Luis Obispo, Stanislaus,
Tulare and Tuolumne counties; Sixth District at
San José: Monterey, San Benito, Santa Clara and
Santa Cruz counties. The Supreme Court sits in
San Francisco, Los Angeles and Sacramento,
with special sessions elsewhere.

Alameda County
organized 1853 from Contra Costa and Santa
	Clara counties

Alameda County Clerk-Recorder
1106 Madison Street, Room 136
Oakland, CA 94607
(510) 272-6362; (888) 280-7708
http://www.acgov.org/auditor/clerk/index.htm
(land records from 1853, vital records from
	1905)

Alameda County Superior Court
René C. Davidson Alameda County Courthouse
1225 Fallon Street, Room 105
Oakland, CA 94612-4216
(510) 272-6763 (File Room - Records)
courtfeedback@alameda.courts.ca.gov
http://www.alameda.courts.ca.gov/courts/inde
	x.shtml
(naturalization records from 11 April 1853,
	probate records from 1853)
probate search service: $1.75 per year; copies of
	probate records: 50¢ per page plus $1.75 for
	certification

Alpine County
organized 1864 from Calaveras, Amador, El
	Dorado, Mono and Tuolumne counties

Alpine County Clerk
(County Administration Building, 99 Water
	Street—location)
PO Box 158 (mailing address)
Markleeville, CA 96120
(530) 694-2281; (530) 694-2491 FAX
coclerk@alpinecountyca.com
http://www.alpinecountyca.gov
Barbara Howard

Alpine County Superior Court
(14777 State Route 89—location)
POBox 518 (mailing address)
Markleeville, CA 96120-0518
(530) 694-2113; (530) 694-2119 FAX
http://www.alpine.courts.ca.gov

Amador County
organized 1854 from Calaveras County

Amador County Recorder-Clerk
500 Argonaut Lane
Jackson, CA 95642

---

(209) 223-6468
http://www.co.amador.ca.us/depts/recorder/in
	dex.htm
Sheldon Johnson
(land records, births from 1873, deaths from
	1872, and marriages)
copies of vital records: $13.00 each for births
	and marriages, $9.00 each for deaths

Amador County Superior Court
Amador County Courthouse
108 Court Street
Jackson, CA 95642-2308
(209) 223-6463
http://www.amadorcourt.org
(naturalization records, probate records with
	Court Clerk)
copies of land records: $2.00 for the first page
	and 50¢ for each additional page, $1.00 for
	certification

Butte County
organized 1850, original county

Butte County Clerk-Recorder
County Administration Building
25 County Center Drive, Lower Level
Oroville CA 95965
(530) 538-7691; (530) 538-7690; (530) 538-7975
	FAX
clerk@buttecounty.net;
	cgrubbs@buttecounty.net
http://clerk-recorder.buttecounty.net
Candace J. Grubbs

Butte County Superior Court
1 Court Street
Oroville, CA 95965-3303
(916) 532-7002
http://www.buttecourt.ca.gov

Calaveras County
organized 1850, original county

Calaveras County Clerk-Recorder
Calaveras County Government Center
891 Mountain Ranch Road
San Andreas, CA 95249
(209) 754-6372
http://www.co.calaveras.ca.us/departments/rec
	order.asp
Karen Varni
(land records, vital records)

Calaveras County Superior Court
Calaveras County Government Center
891 Mountain Ranch Road
San Andreas, CA 95249
(209) 754-6311; (209) 754-6310 (Clerk)
courtinfo@calaveras.courts.ca.gov
http://www.calaveras.courts.ca.gov
(naturalization records, probate records)

Colusa County
organized 1850, original county (records
	included in Butte County for the first few
	years)

Colusa County Clerk and Recorder
546 Jay Street
Colusa, CA 95932
(530) 458-0500
info@colusacountyclerk.com;
	ccclerk@colusanet.com
http://www.colusacountyclerk.com
Kathleen Moran
(land records, vital records, naturalization
	records)

Colusa County Superior Court
(547 Market Street—location)
532 Oak Street (mailing address)
Colusa, CA 95932
(530) 458-5149; (530) 458-2230
kathy.torres@colusa.courts.ca.gov
http://www.colusa.courts.ca.gov
Clerk
(probate records)
probate search service: $1.75 per year of search;
	copies of probate records: 50¢ per page, no

minimum

Colusi County
(see Colusa, Glenn, and Tehama counties)

Contra Costa County
organized 1850, original county

Contra Costa County Clerk Recorder
(730 Las Juntas Street—Recorder's Office
location; 822 Main Street—Clerk's Office
location)
PO Box 350 (mailing address)
Martinez, CA 94553
(925) 646-2360
http://www.co.contra-
costa.ca.us/dept/elect/clerk/index.html

Contra Costa County Superior Court
(725 Court Street, Room 103—probate location)
PO Box 911 (mailing address)
Martinez, CA 94553
(925) 646-2950 (Probate)
ctweb@contracosta.courts.ca.gov
http://cc-courts.org;
http://www.criis.com/contracosta/official.htm
(Recorded Document Search Menu)
Clerk

Del Norte County
organized 1857 from Klamath County

Del Norte County Clerk Recorder
981 H Street, Suite 160
Crescent City, CA 95531
(707) 464-7216; (707) 465-0321 FAX
clerkrecorder@co.del-norte.ca.us
http://www.co.del-norte.ca/us
Vicki Frazier

Del Norte County Superior Court
450 H Street, Room 209
Crescent City, CA 95531
(707) 464-8115; (707) 465-4005
http://www.delnorte.courts.ca.gov/probate.htm
copies of land and probate: 50¢ per page, $1.75
for certification; certified copies of marriages:
$12.00 each

El Dorado County
organized 1850, original county

El Dorado County Clerk Recorder
360 Fair Lane
Placerville, CA 95667
(530) 621-5719 (County Assessor's Office);
(530) 621-5490; (530) 621-2147 FAX
recorderclerk@co.el-dorado.ca.us
http://www.co.el-dorado.ca.us/countyclerk
William E. Schultz
(land records with Recorder's Office or
Assessor's Office, births and deaths with
Recorder's Office)

El Dorado County Superior Court
495 Main Street
Placerville, CA 95667-5628
(530) 621-6426
http://eldocourtweb.eldoradocourt.org
(naturalization records, probate records)
no probate search service; copies of probate
records: 50¢ per page, no minimum

Fresno County
organized 1856 from Mariposa and Merced
counties

Fresno County Assessor-Recorder
Hall of Records
2281 Tulare Street, Room 302
Fresno, CA 93721
(209) 488-1830; (559) 488-3476 (Vital Records)
http://www.co.fresno.ca.us/0420/recorders_we
b/index.htm
Robert C. Werner
(land records, vital records)
land and vital records search service: $5.00

Fresno County Superior Court
1100 Van Ness, Room 402
Fresno, CA 93721-0002

(559) 488-3618; (559) 488-3334 FAx
infodexk@fresno.courts.ca.gov
http://www.fresnosuperiorcourt.org/probate
Clerk
(naturalization records, probate records)

Glenn County
organized 1891 from Colusa County

Glenn County Clerk Recorder
526 West Sycamore Street
Willows, CA 95988
(530) 934-6412; (530) 934-6305 FAX
http://www.countyofglenn.net/Recorder/home
_page.asp
Vince Minto
(land records from 1891; births, deaths and
marriages from 1905, plus a few delayed birth
registrations going back to 1887)
no land records search service; copies of land
records: $1.00 for the first page and 50¢ for
each additional page per document; certified
copies of vital records: $13.00 each for births
and marriages, $9.00 each for deaths

Glenn County Superior Court
(526 West Sycamore Street—location)
PO Box 391 (mailing address)
Willows, CA 95988-0391
(530) 934-6446; (530) 934-6449 FAX
http://www.glenncourt.ca.gov/index.html
Clerk
(naturalization records before 1931, probate
records)
naturalization records search service: $5.00 per
file or name; copies of naturalization records:
50¢ per page

Humboldt County
organized 1853 from Trinity County, and in
1874 annexed part of Klamath County, which
was formed in 1851

Humboldt County Assessor
825 Fifth Street, Room 300
Eureka, CA 95501
(707) 445-7663; (866) 240-0485
http://www.co.humboldt.ca.us/assessor
Linda Hill
(land records)

Humboldt County Recorder
825 Fifth Street, Fifth Floor
Eureka, CA 95501-1172
(707) 445-7593; (707) 445-7382 (Vital Records
Division)
http://www.co.humboldt.ca.us/recorder
Carolyn Crinch
(vital records)

Humboldt County Superior Court
(421 I Street—entrance location)
825 Fifth Street (mailing address)
Eureka, CA 95501-1153
(707) 445-7256
http://www.courtinfo.ca.gov/courts/trial/hum
boldt
Civil, Criminal, Traffic, and Small Claims
Matters (includes Probate)
(naturalization records, probate records)
probate search service: $1.75 per name per year;
copies of probate records: 50¢ per page, no
minimum; certification: $1.75 (enclose SASE)

Imperial County
organized 1907 from San Diego County

Imperial County Clerk Recorder
County Administration Center
940 Main Street, Room 202
El Centro, CA 93343
9760) 482-4272
http://www.co.imperial.ca.us

Imperial County Superior Court
939 Main Street
El Centro, CA 92243
(760) 482-4374; (612) 339-4256
http://www.imperial.courts.ca.gov
copies: 50¢ per page, $15.00 for certification

Inyo County
organized 1866 from Tulare County

Inyo County Clerk Recorder
(168 North Edwards Street—location)PO Box F
(mailing address)
Independence, CA 93526
(760) 878-0222 (Recorder); (760) 867-0223
(Clerk)
http://www.countyofinyo.org
Beverly J. Harry
(land records from 1866, naturalization records
from 1866 to 1971, births and deaths from
1905)
copies of birth certificate: $14.00 each; copies of
death certificates: $12.00

Inyo County Superior Court
(168 North Edwards Street—location)
PO Drawer U (mailing address)
Independence, CA 93526
(760) 878-2411; (760) 878-0218 (Clerk, Dept. 1);
(760) 878-0218 (Clerk, Dept. 2); (760) 878-
0319 (Clerk, Dept. 3)
http://www.inyocourt.ca.gov
(probate records from 1866, marriages from
1875)
probate search service: 50¢ per name per year;
copies of probate records: 50¢ for the first
page and 25¢ for each additional page;
certification: $15.00, no minimum

Kern County
organized 1866 from Los Angeles and Tulare
counties

Kern County Probate Office
Justice Building
1415 Truxtun Avenue, Room 100
Bakersfield, CA 93301
(661) 868-5393
http://www.kern.courts.ca.gov/probate.asp
Gale S. Enstad, County Clerk's Office
(naturalization records, probate records)
probate search service: $1.75 per name per year;
copies of probate records: 50¢ per page, $1.75
for certification, 50¢ minimum

Kern County Recorder
Hall of Records
1655 Chester Avenue
Bakersfield, CA 93301
(661) 868-6400
response@co.kern.ca.us
http://recorder.co.kern.ca.us
Jim Fitch, Assessor-Recorder
(land records, vital records)

Kings County
organized 1893 from Tulare County

Kings County Superior Court
1426 South Drive
Hanford, CA 93230
(559) 582-1010
http://www.kings.courts.ca.gov
Todd H. Barton, Executive Officer, Clerk of
Court & Jury CommissionerMon–Fri 8:00–
5:00
(land records from 1894, naturalization records
from 1894 to 1957, vital records from 1904,
probate records from 1894)
no probate search service; copies of probate
records: 50¢ per page, $1.75 minimum if file is
in warehouse

Kings County Clerk Recorder
Kings County Government Center
1400 West Lacey Boulevard
Hanford, CA 93230
(559) 582-3211, ext. 2470; (559) 582-6639 FAX
http://www.countyofkings.com/acr/clerk/inde
x.htm

Lake County
organized 1861 from Tuolumne County

Lake County Clerk and Recorder
255 North Forbes Street
Lakeport, CA 95453

(707) 263-2293; (707) 263-2311 (Clerk); (707)
  263-2302 (Recorder)
Recorder@co.lake.ca.us
http://www.co.lake.ca.us
Pam Cochrane, County Clerk/Auditor-
  Controller; Douglas W. Wacker,
  Assessor/Recorder

Lake County Superior Court
Lakeport Division (Departments One [Probate],
  Two, Three, Commissioner, and Court
  Executive Officer)
255 North Forbes Street, Fourth Floor
Lakeport, CA 95453-4731
(707) 263-2374; (707) 262-1327 FAX
http://www.courtinfo.ca.gov/courts/trial/lake
Mary E. Smith, Court Executive Officer

Lassen County
organized 1864 from Plumas and Shasta
  counties

Lassen County Clerk Recorder
220 South Lassen Street, Suite 5
Susanville, CA 96130
(530) 251-8217 (Clerk); (530) 251-8234
  (Recorder); (530) 257-3480 FAX
lcclerk@co.lassen.ca.us
http://clerk.lassencounty.org/clerk.htm;
http://clerk.lassencounty.org/recorder.htm
Theresa Nagel
(land records from 1857, births and deaths from
  1864)

Lassen County Superior Court
220 South Lassen Street
Susanville, CA 96130
http://www.lassencourt.ca.gov
(naturalization records from about 1867 to 1974,
  marriages from 1864 [incomplete], probate
  records from 1864)
probate search service: $5.00 per case; copies of
  probate records: $1.50 for the first page and
  50¢ for each additional page, no minimum;
  please send SASE

Los Angeles County
organized 1850, original county

**Los Angeles County Registrar-
  Recorder/County Clerk**
12400 Imperial Highway
Norwalk, CA 90650
(562) 462-2137 (Birth, Death and Marriage
  Records); (562-462133 (Real Estate Records)
recorder@rrcc.co.la.ca.us
http://www.lavote.net
Conny McCormack

Los Angeles County Superior Court
Probate Department (Central District)
111 North Hill Street, Room 258
Los Angeles, CA 90012
(213) 974-5471
http://www.lasuperiorcourt.org/probate
Ron Cyger, Probate Manager

Madera County
organized 1893 from Fresno County

Madera County Clerk Recorder
209 West Yosemite Avenue
Madera, CA 93637
(559) 675-7703 (General Information)
info@madera-county.com (General
  Information)
http://www.madera-
  county.com/countyclerk/recorder
Rebecca Martinez
copies: $14.00 for births, $12.00 for deaths

Madera County Superior Court
Probate Department, Civil Division
209 West Yosemite Avenue
Madera, CA 93637
info@maderacourt.org
http://madera.courts.ca.gov

Marin County
organized 1850, original county

Marin County Recorder
3501 Civic Center Druive, Suite 232
San Rafael, CA 94903
(415) 499-7215
mpioli@co.marin.ca.us
http://199.88.77.35/depts/AR/main/index.cfm
Joan C. Thayer, Assessor-Recorder

Marin County Superior Court
Civic Center, Hall of Justice, Room 113
San Rafael, CA 94903
(415) 499-6407
probate@marincourt.org
http://www.co.marin.ca.us/depts/MC/main/pr
  obate.cfm

Mariposa County
organized 1850, original county

Mariposa County Clerk Recorder
(4982 Tenth Street—location)
PO Box 247 (mailing address)
Mariposa, CA 95338
(209) 966-2007
coclerk@mariposacounty.org
http://www.maripsoacounty.org

Mariposa County Superior Court
(5088 Bullion Street—location)
PO Box 28 (mailing address)
Mariposa, CA 95338-0247
(209) 966-2005
grycelb@mariposacourts.org
http://www.mariposacourts.org/Dept_Probate.
  htm

Mendocino County
organized 1850, original county

Mendocino County Clerk Recorder
501 Low Gap Road, Room 1020
Ukiah, CA 95482
(7078) 463-4370 (Clerk); (707) 463-4376
  (Recorder); (707) 463-4257 FAX
acr@co.mendocino.ca.us
http://www.co.mendocino.ca.us/acr/clerk.htm
Marsha A. Young
(land records, vital records)

Mendocino County Superior Court
100 North State Street, Room 108
Ukiah, CA 95482-4416
(707) 463-4481; (707) 463-6850 FAX
webmaster@mendocino.courts.ca.gov
http://www.mendocino.courts.ca.gov/probate.
  html
Mon–Fri 8:00–2:30
(naturalization records, vital records)

Merced County
organized 1855 from Mariposa County

Merced County Recorder
2222 M Street, Main Floor
Merced, CA 95340-3729
(209) 385-7627; (209) 385-7626 FAX
http://www.co.merced.ca.us/recorder
M. Stephen Jones
(land records, vital records)

Merced County Superior Court
Merced County Courts Building
627 West 21st Street
Merced, CA 95340
(209) 725-4100
http://www.mercedcourt.org
(naturalization records, probate records)
probate search service: $5.00; copies of probate
  records: 50¢ per page, $1.75 for certification,
  no minimum; include SASE

Modoc County
organized 1874 from Siskiyou County

Modoc County Auditor-Recorder
204 Court Street
Alturas, CA 96101
(530) 233-6204
http://www.modoccounty.us
(land records, vital records)

Modoc County Superior Court
Probate Court
Robert A. Barclay Justice Center
205 South East Street
Alturas, CA 96101
(530) 233-6515
http://www.frontiernet.net/~ldier
(naturalization records, probate)
probate search service: no charge; copies of
  probate records: 50¢ per page, no minimum

Mono County
organized 1861 from Calaveras and Fresno
  counties

Mono County Recorder
(Annex I, 74 School Street, Library Building,
  First Floor—location)
PO Box 237 (mailing address)
Bridgeport, CA 93517
(760) 932-5530
commdev@mono.ca.gov
http://www.monocounty.ca.gov
(land records, vital records)
search request: $2.00 per name per year; copies:
  25¢ per page; certified copies of vital records:
  $9.00

Mono County Superior Court
(State Highway 395 North, Main Street—
  location)
PO Box 537 (mailing address)
Bridgeport, CA 93517-0537
(760) 932-5239; (760) 932-7520 FAX
http://www.monosuperiorcourt.ca.gov
(naturalization records, probate records)
probate search service: $2.00 per year; copies of
  probate records: $1.00 per page, minimum
  $2.00

Monterey County
organized 1850, original county

Monterey County Clerk-Recorder
(Monterey County Government Center
  Administration Building, 168 West Alisal
  Street, First Floor—location)
PO Box 29 (mailing address)
Salinas, CA 93902
(831) 755-5041; (831) 755-5064 FAX
vandegriftb@co.monterey.ca.us
http://www.co.monterey.ca.us/recorder
Stephen L. Vagnini, Assessor-County Clerk-
  Recorder
(vital records)

Monterey County Superior Court
Monterey County Courthouse
240 Church Street, Suite 318
Salinas, CA 93901
(831) 647-5800 (Salinas); (831) 647-5800
  (Monterey)
http://www.monterey.courts.ca.gov
Lenor Noll, Civil, Family Law, Probate, Small
  Claims
(naturalization records with Clerk of the
  Superior Court [Salinas office only], probate
  records with Clerk of the Superior Court in
  Salinas or at the Branch Courthouse on the
  Monterey Peninsula [Courthouse, 1200
  Aguajito Road, Monterey, CA 93940],
  depending on the residence of the decedent)
probate search service: $5.00 per year; copies of
  probate records: 75¢ per page, no minimum

Napa County
organized 1850, original county

Napa Napa County Recorder-County Clerk
(900 Coombs, Room 116—location)
PO Box 298 (mailing address)
Napa, CA 94559-0298
(707) 253-4246
recorder-clerk@co.napa.ca.us
http://co.napa.ca.us/Gov/Departments/Dept
  Default.asp?DID=28000
John Tuteur, Director

Napa County Superior Court
Historic Courthouse

825 Brown Street, First Floor
Napa, CA 94559
(707) 299-1140 (Civil - Research/Records)
http://www.napa.courts.ca.gov/Civil/civil_prob
ate.htm

Nevada County
organized 1851 from Yuba County

Nevada County Clerk-Recorder
(Eric W. Rood Administrative Center, 950
Maidu Avenue—location)
Box 6100 (mailing address)
Nevada City, CA 95959
(530) 265-1221; (530) 265-9842 FAX
jacqueline.pollard@co.nevada.ca.us
http://new.mynevadacounty.com/recorder
Kathleen Smith
(land records from 1851 to date, vital records
from 1851 to date)

Nevada County Superior Court
Courthouse Annex
201 Church Street
Nevada City, CA 95959
(916) 265-1293 (Family Law Court)
info@nevadacountycourts.com
http://court.co.nevada.ca.us/services/civil_pro
bate/probate.htm
(probate records from 1851 to date)
probate search service: $5.00; copies of probate
records: 50¢ per page

Orange County
organized 1889 from Los Angeles County

Orange County Clerk Recorder
(The Hall of Finance and Records, 12 Civic
Center Plaza, Rooms 101 and 106, Santa Ana,
CA 92701—location)
PO Box 238 (mailing address)
Santa Ana, CA 92702
(714) 834-2500
CR_Webmaster@rec.ocgov.com
http://www.oc.ca.gov/recorder
Tom Daly
(land records, vital records)

Orange County Superior Court
Lamoreaux Justic Center
341 The City Drive
Orange, CA 92868
(714) 834-2225 (Clerk)
feedback@occourts.org
http://www.occourts.org/probate
(probate records)
probate search service: $1.75 per year; copies of
probate records: 50¢ per page, $1.75 for
certified copies, no minimum, include SASE
("if you do not know the correct amount
needed, leave it blank and write 'not to exceed
$_____' on the check. We will fill in the
amount necessary")

Placer County
organized 1851 from Yuba and Sutter counties

Placer County Clerk Recorder
2954 Richardson Drive
Auburn, CA 95603
(530) 886-5600; (530) 886-5687 FAX
clerk@placer.ca.gov
http://www.placer.ca.gov/clerk
Jim McCauley
(land records, marriages)

Placer County Superior Court
(101 Maple Street—location)
PO Box 5228 (mailing address)
Auburn, CA 95604-5228
(916) 823-4471 (County Clerk); (916) 823-4621
(Recorder)
http://www.placercourts.org
(naturalization records naturalization papers
from 1852 to 1893 and from 1903 to 1906,
declarations of intention from 1893 to 1906
and from 1913 to 1939, certificates of
citizenship [District Court from 1874 to 1879,
County Court from 1876 to 1897, and
Superior Court from 1897 to 1903], petitions

and records from 1906 to 1942, and petitions
for naturalization 1943 to 1960, probate
records from late 1800s)
probate search service ("Supply all info possible
when requesting a search of our records"):
$1.75 (from 1974 to present), additional $1.75
per year per name (prior to 1974); copies of
marriages: $5.00 each; copies of probate
records: 50¢ for the first page, 25¢ for each
additional page of the same document, 10¢
per page for each additional copy of same
document, no minimum

Plumas County
organized 1854 from Butte County

Plumas County Clerk/Recorder
520 Main Street, Room 102
Quincy, CA 95971
(530) 283-6218; (916) 283-6380 (Assessor); (530)
283-6155 FAX
kathywilliams@countyofplumas.com
http://www.countyofplumas.com/clerkrecorder
/index.htm
Kathleen Williams
(land records with Assessor, PO Box 11016,
vital records with Clerk-Recorder)
copies: 50¢ per page, $1.00 per page if copy
entails research, $1.75 for certification;
certified copies of vital records: $13.00 each
for births and marriages, $9.00 each for
deaths

Plumas County Superior Court
520 Main Street, Room 104
Quincy, CA 95971
(530) 283-6305 (Civil Matters)
Information@plumascourt.org
http://www.pluascourt.ca.gov
(probate records)
records search service: $1.75 per year; copies:
50¢ per page, $1.00 per page if copy entails
research

Riverside County
organized 1893 from San Bernardino and San
Diego counties

**Riverside County Assessor-County Clerk-
Recorder**
(County Administrative Center, 4080 Lemon
Street, First Floor—location)
PO Box 12004 (mailing address)
Riverside, CA 92502-2204
(951) 486-7000 (Clerk-Recorder); (951) 955-6200
(Assessor)
accrmail@co.riverside.ca.us
http://riverside.asrclkrec.com
(land records, vital records)

Riverside County Superior Court
Riverside Probate Court
4050 Main Street
Riverside, CA 92501
(951) 275-1970 (Probate Section)
http://www.courts.co.riverside.ca.us/probate.htm
(probate records)

Sacramento County
organized 1850, original county

Sacramento County Clerk/Recorder
(600 Eighth Street, Sacramento, CA 95814—
location)
PO Box 839 (mailing address)
Sacramento, CA 95812-0839
(916) 874-6334
http://www.ccr.saccounty.net
Craig A. Kramer
(land records, vital records)

Sacramento County Superior Court
William R. Ridgeway Family Relations
Courthouse
3341 Power Inn Road
Sacramento, CA 95826
(916) 875-3400
court-info@saccourt.com
http://www.saccourt.com/index/probate.asp
(probate records)

probate search service: $1.75 per name; copies
of probate records: 50¢ per page, $1.75 per
document for certification ("fees change
periodically; if unsure of the amount needed
you may write a check payable to the
'Sacramento County Clerk' leaving the dollar
amount blank and writing 'Not to exceed
$5.00' on the check; do not send cash")

San Benito County
organized 1874 from Monterey County

San Benito County Clerk-Auditor-Recorder
440 Fifth Street, Room 206
Hollister, CA 95023-3843
(831) 636-4029; (831) 636-2939 FAX
jhodges@elections.co.san-benito.ca.us
http://www.san-benito.ca.us
John R. Hodges
(land records from 1850s [transcribed from
Monterey County until 1870s], vital records
from 1874, but not mandatory until 1905)
search service ("Specific questions should be
made either to the Clerk's Office or
Recorder's Office"): $1.75 per year searched;
50¢ per page (Clerk's office), $2.00 for the
first page and $1.00 for each additional page
(Recorder's Office), no minimum

San Benito County Superior Court
440 Fifth Street, Room 205
Hollister, CA 95023-3833
(831) 636-4057; (831) 636-2046 FAX
http://www.sanbenito.courts.ca.gov;
http://www.superior-court.co.san-
benito.ca.us
Honorable Harry J. Tobias, Presiding Judge;
Honorable Steven R. Sanders
(some naturalization records from 1874 and
some not available to the public, probate
records from 1874)

San Bernardino County
organized 1853 from Los Angeles County

**San Bernardino County Auditor/Controller-
Recorder**
Hall of Records
222 West Hospitality Lane
San Bernardino, CA 92415-0022
(909) 387-8322; (909) 387-8314 (Birth, Marriage
and Death Certificates)
http://www.co.san-
bernardino.ca.us/ACR/default.asp
Larry Walker
(land records from 1854, vital records from
1880)

San Bernardino County Superior Court
351 North Arrowhead Avenue
San Bernardino, CA 92415-0240
(909) 387-3922 (Civil/Family Law Clerk's
Office); (909) 888-4260 (Civil/Small Claims
Information)
http://www.sbcounty.gov/courts
(probate records from 1856)
probate search service: $1.75 per source; 50¢ per
page, no minimum

San Diego County
organized 1850, original county

San Diego County Recorder/Clerk
County Administration Center
1600 Pacific Highway, Room 260
San Diego, CA 92101
(619) 237-0502 (Birth/Marriage/Death); (619)
238-8158 (Real Property)
http://www.sdcounty.ca.gov/arcc/arcc_home.h
tml

San Diego County Superior Court
Madge Bradley Building
1409 Fourth Avenue, Third Floor
San Diego, CA 92101
(619) 687-2000
http://www.sdcourt.ca.gov/portal/page?_pagei
d=53,130146&_dad=portal&_schema=POR
TAL
Jeri Porch, Court Clerk

San Francisco County
organized 1850, original county

San Francisco County Assessor-Recorder
1 Dr. Carlton B. Goodlett Place, City Hall, Room 190
San Francisco, CA 94102-4698
(415) 554-5516; (415) 554-7915 FAX
assessor@sfgov.org
http://www.sfgov.org/site/assessor_index.asp
Phil Ting

San Francisco County Superior Court
Civic Center Courthouse
400 McAllister Street, Room 202
San Francisco, CA 94102-4514
(415) 551-3650 (Probate); (415) 551-3804 (Archives)
http://sfgov.org/site/courts_index.sp
Linda Gorham, Court Manager

San Joaquin County
organized 1850, original county

San Joaquin County Recorder/County Clerk
(Pacific State Bank Building, 6 South El Dorado Street, Second Floor, Stockton, CA 95202—location)
PO Box 1968 (mailing address)
Stockton, CA 95201
(209) 468-3939; (209) 468-8040 FAX
recorder@co.san-joaquin.ca.us
http://www.co.san-joaquin.ca.us/Recorder
Gary W. Freeman

San Joaquin County Superior Court
Stockton Courthouse
222 East Weber Avenue, Room 303
Stockton, CA 95202-2702
(209) 468-2843 (Probate Clerk); (209) 468-2355 (Information, Records Unit)
http://www.stocktoncourt.org/courts/probate.htm
(naturalization records, probate records)
copies of naturalization records and probate records: 50¢ per page, payable in advance

San Luis Obispo County
organized 1850, original county

San Luis Obispo County Clerk-Recorder
County Government Center
1055 Monterey Street, Room 102
San Luis Obispo, CA 93408
(805) 781-5088
http://www.slocounty.ca.gov/Page113.aspx
Julie Rodewald
(land records, vital records)

San Luis Obispo County Superior Court
1035 Palm Street, Room 385
San Luis Obispo, CA 93408
(805) 781-5706 (Court Clerk's Division)
slocourt@slo.courts.ca.gov
http://www.slocourts.ca.gov
(naturalization records, probate records)

San Mateo County
organized 1856 from San Francisco County

San Mateo County Assessor- County Clerk-Recorder
555 County Center, First Floor
Redwood City, CA 94063-1665
(650) 363-4500; (650) 363-1903 FAX
countyclerk@smcare.org; recorder@smcare.org
http://www.smcare.org
Warren Slocum
(vital records, land records, naturalization records)

San Mateo County Hall of Justice and Records
400 County Center
Redwood City, CA 94063
(415) 363-4711 (Clerk's Office/Probate)
http://www.sanmateocourt.org
(probate records)
probate search service: $1.75; copies of probate records: 50¢ per page

Santa Barbara County
organized 1850, original county

Santa Barbara County Clerk-Recorder-Assessor
Hall of Records
1100 Anacapa Street
Santa Barbara, CA 93101-0159
(805) 568-2250; (805) 568-2266 FAX
Mbryson@co.santa-barbara.ca.us (Clerk's Office); morales@co.stantabarbara.ca.us (Recorder's Office)
http://www.sb-democracy.com/carehome.aspx
Joseph E. Holland
(land records, vital records)

Santa Barbara County Superior Court
(1100 Anacapa Street—location)
PO Box 21107 (mailing address)
Santa Barbara, CA 93121-1107
(805) 568-2220; (805) 568-2219 FAX
http://www.sbcourts.org/index.asp
(naturalization records [mark request "Attn: Certification"] probate records)
probate search service: $1.75 per name per year; copies of probate records: 50¢ per page, no minimum; inquiries should be sent by correspondence

Santa Clara County
organized 1850, original county

Santa Clara County Clerk Recorder
70 West Hedding Street, East Wing, First Floor
San José, CA 95110
(408) 299-2481
ClerkRecorder@rec.sccgov.org
http://www.sccgov.org/portal/site/rec
(land records, vital records)

Santa Clara County Superior Court
191 North First Street
San José, CA 95113
(408) 882-2100
ssprobinfo@scscourt.org
http://sccsuperiorcourt.org/probate
Stephen V. Love, Clerk
(naturalization records from 1850 to 1970, probate records from 1800)
probate search service: $4.00 per year; copies of probate records: 50¢ per page, no minimum

Santa Cruz County
county incorporated 18 February 1850, original county

Santa Cruz County Clerk Recorder
701 Ocean Street
Santa Cruz, CA 95060
(831) 454-2800
rcd.web@co.santa-cruz.ca.us
http://www.co.santa-cruz.ca.us/rcd
Gary E. Hazelton

Santa Cruz County Superior Court
Santa Cruz Main Courthouse
701 Ocean Street, Room 110
Santa Cruz, CA 95060-4027
(408) 425-2175 (Special Services); (831) 454-2012 (Clerk)
court@santacruzcourt.org
http://www.santacruzcourt.org
Alex Calvo, Executive Officer and Clerk
(naturalization records with Special Services, Room 210D, probate records with Clerk)
probate search service: $1.75 per year; copies of probate records: 50¢ per page, no minimum (enclose SASE)

Shasta County
organized 1850, original county

Shasta County Clerk Recorder
(1643 Market Street, Redding, CA 96001—location)
PO Box 990880 (mailing address)
Redding, CA 96099-0880
(530) 225-5730; (530) 225-5454 FAX
countyclerk@co.shasta.ca.us
http://www.co.shasta.ca.us/departments/

CountyClerkRegistrarOfVoters/index.shtml
Cathy Darling
(land records, vital records)

Shasta County Superior Court
(Courthouse, 1500 Court Street, Redding, CA 96001—location)
PO Box 880 (mailing address)
Redding, CA 96009
(530) 245-6789
genmail@shastacourts.com
http://www.shastacourts.com
Ann Reed, Clerk
(naturalization records, probate records)
probate search service: $1.75 per year searched; copies of probate records: 50¢ per page, no minimum

Sierra County
organized 1852 from Yuba County

Sierra County Clerk-Recorder
(100 Courthouse Square, Suite 11—location)
PO Drawer D (mailing address)
Downieville, CA 95936-0398
(530) 289-3295; (530) 289-2830 FAX
clerk-recorder@sierracounty.ws
http://www.sierracounty.ws
Mary J. Jungi
(land records from 1852 to date, births from 1857 to date, deaths from 1864 to date, marriages from 1852 to date)
certified copies of vital records: $13.00 each for births and marriages, $9.00 each for deaths (includes search)

Sierra County Superior Court
(100 Courthouse Square, Second Floor—location)
PO Box 476 (mailing address)
Downieville, CA 95936
(530) 289-3698; (530) 289-0205 FAX
hamilton@sierracourt.org
http://www.sierracourt.org/probate.html
Ms. Jan Hamilton, Court Executive Officer, Court Administration
(naturalization records from 1852 to date with Court Administrator, PO Box 95, Downieville, CA 95936, probate records from 1852 to date with Court Administrator)

Siskiyou County
organized 1852 from Klamath and Shasta counties, and in 1874 annexed part of Klamath County, which was formed in 1851

Siskiyou County Clerk
(510 North Main Street—location)
PO Box 338 (mailing address)
Yreka, CA 96097-9910
(916) 842-8084; (530) 842-8093 FAX
cbaker@co.siskiyou.ca
http://www.co.siskiyou.ca.us/clerk/index.htm
Colleen Baker

Siskiyou County Recorder
(311 Fourth Street, Room 101—location)
PO Box 8 (mailing address)
Yreka, CA 96097
(530) 842-8065; (530) 842-8036 (Assessor); (530) 842-8077 FAX
http://www.co.siskiyou.ca.us/recorder/index.htm
(land records with Assessor, Room 108, vital records with Recorder)

Siskiyou County Superior Court
(311 Fourth Street—location)
PO Box 1026 (mailing address)
Yreka, CA 96097
(530) 842-8239; (530) 842-0164 FAX
personnel@siskiyou.ca.gov
http://www.siskiyou.courts.ca.gov
(naturalization records, probate records)
probate search service: $1.75 per year ("if files are stored, it may take some time to retrieve them"); copies of probate records: 50¢ per page, no minimum

Solano County
organized 1850, original county

Solano County Assessor/Recorder
675 Texas Street, Suite 2700
Fairfield, CA 94533
(707) 784-6200
http://www.co.solono.ca.us/Department/Depa
rtment.asp?NavID=65
Marc C. Tonnesen, Acting Assessor/Recorder
(land records)

Solano County Superior Court
Hall of Justice
600 Union Avenue
Fairfield, CA 94533
(707) 207-7340 (Family Law/Probate)
courtoutreach@solanocounty.com
http://www.solanocourts.com
(probate records)
probate search service: $1.75 per name per year;
copies of probate records: 50¢ per page, no
minimum

Sonoma County
organized 1850, original county

Sonoma County Clerk-Recorder-Assessor
(585 Fiscal Drive, Suite 103-F, Santa Rosa, CA
95403—location)
PO Box 1709 (mailing address)
Santa Rosa, CA 95402
(707) 565-2651
Recorder@sonoma-county.org
http://www.sonoma-
county.org/recorder/aboutus.asp
Eeve Lewis
(land records, vital records)

**Sonoma County Superior and Municipal
Court**
(Sonoma County Hall of Justice, 600
Administration Drive, Room 107, Santa Rosa,
CA 95403—location)
PO Box 11187 (mailing address)
Santa Rosa, CA 95406-5000
(707) 527-1100 (Mon–Fri 8:00–noon)
info@sonomacourt.org
http://www.sonomasuperiorcourt.com/index.php
(only limited naturalization records, probate
records)
probate search service: $15.00 per hour, $5.00
minimum

Stanislaus County
organized 1854 from Tuolumne County

Stanislaus County Clerk-Recorder
(1029 I Street—location)
PO Box 1670 (mailing address)
Modesto, CA 95353-1670
(209) 525-5250; (209) 525-5265 (Vital Records)
webmaster@mail.co.stanislaus.ca.us
http://www.stanvote.com
Lee Lundrigan
(land records, naturalization records, births,
deaths, and marriages)
certified copies of vital records: $13.00 each for
births and marriages, $9.00 each for deaths

Stanislaus County Superior Court
800 11th Street, Room 222
Modesto, CA 95354
(209) 558-6000
http://www.stanct.org/courts/probate/index.html
(probate records)
no probate search service; copies of probate
records: 50¢ for the first page, 30¢ for each
additional page, $1.75 per page for
certification, plus SASE

Sutter County
organized 1850, original county

Sutter County Clerk Recorder
433 Second Street
Yuba City, CA 95991
(530) 822-7134
http://www.co.sutter.ca.us/doc/government/d
epts/cr/crhome
Joan Bechtel
(land records from 1849, vital records from

1873)

Sutter County Superior Court
Courthouse, 446 Second Street, Room 211
Yuba City, CA 95991-5524
(530) 822-7352 (Press 8 to reach a clerk)
etodd@suttercourts.com
http://www.suttercourts.com

Tehama County
organized 1856 from Butte, Colusa and Shasta
counties

Tehama County Clerk-Recorder
(444 Oak Street, Room C—location)
PO Box 250 (mailing address)
Red Bluff, CA 96080
(530) 527-8190; (530) 527-1140 FAX
http://www.smartvoter.org/ca/th
Mary Alice George
(land records from 1856, births and deaths from
1889, marriages from 1856)

Tehama County Superior Court
Department 1
(633 Washington Street—location)
PO Box 310 (mailing address)
Red Bluff, CA 96080-0250
(916) 527-3350
http://www.courtinfo.ca.gov/courts/trial/tehama
(probate records)
no probate search service

Trinity County
organized 1850, original county

Trinity County Clerk/Recorder
(11 Court Street—location)
PO Box 1215 (mailing address)
Weaverville, CA 96093
(530) 623-1215; (530) 623-8398 FAX
http://www.trinitycounty.org/departments/asse
ssor-clerk-elect/clerkrecorder.htm
Dero Forslund
(land records, vital records)

Trinity County Superior Court
(101 Court Street—location)
PO Box 1258 (mailing address)
Weaverville, CA 96093
(530) 623-1369; (530) 623-1208; (530) 623-3762
FAX
dregnani@trinitycounty.org
http://www.courtinfo.ca.gov/courts/trial/trinity
Donna Regnani, Court Executive Officer
(naturalization records, probate records)
no probate search service; copies of probate
records: 50¢ per page, no minimum; case
number preferred but not required

Tulare County
organized 1852 from Mariposa County

Tulare County Clerk Recorder
County Civic Center
221 South Mooney Boulevard
Visalia, CA 93291
(559) 733-6418 (Clerk, Courthouse, Room 105);
(559) 733-6377 (Recorder, Courthouse, Room
103); (559) 740-4329 FAX
TCWebmaster@co.tulare.ca.us
http://www.co.tulare.ca.us/government/clerk_r
ecorder/default.asp
Gregory B. Hardcastle
(land records from 1854, births, deaths and
marriages)
land records search service: $10.00 per name;
copies of land records: $1.00 for the first page
and 50¢ for each additional page of the same
document, $1.00 for certification; certified
copies of vital records: $16.00 each for births,
$9.00 each for deaths, $13.00 each for
marriages

Tulare County Superior Court
County Civic Center, 221 South Mooney
Boulevard, Room 201
Visalia, CA 93291-4593
(559) 733-6374
http://www.tularesuperiorcourt.ca.gov

(naturalization records, probate records from
1854)
probate search service: $5.00 per name; copies
of probate records: 50¢ per page, $1.75 for
certified copies, no minimum

Tuolumne County
organized 1850, original county

Tuolumne County Assessor-Recorder
Administration Center
2 South Green Street
Sonora, CA 95370
(209) 533-5570 (Clerk/Auditor/Controller);
(209) 533-5535 (Assessor); (205) 533-5510
FAX (Clerk)
http://www.smartvoter.org/2000/11/07/ca/tl
m#electoff;
http://proagency.tripod.com/ca-
tuolumnecounty.html
Tim R. Johnson

Tuolumne County Superior Court
Historic Courthouse
41 West Yaney Street
Sonora, CA 95370
(209) 533-5555
supcrt1@tuolumne.courts.ca.gov
http://www.tuolumne.courts.ca.gov/probate.htm
Jennifer Russ, Division Manager

Ventura County
organized 1 January 1873 from Santa Barbara
County

Ventura County Recorder's Office
Hall of Administration, Main Plaza
800 South Victoria Avenue
Ventura, CA 93009-1260
(805) 654-2290
http://recorder.countyofventura.org/venclrk.htm
Philip J. Schmit
(land records, vital records)

Ventura County Superior Court
Ventura Hall of Justice, Government Center
800 South Victoria Avenue
Ventura, CA 93009-5317
(805) 654-2269 (Naturalization Records); (805)
654-2264 (Probate Records)
sarah.waters@ventura.courts.ca.gov
http://www.ventura.courts.ca.gov
Sarah Waters, Probate, Court Program Manager
(naturalization records from 1873 to 1987,
probate records)
probate search service: $1.75 per year; copies of
probate records: 50¢ for the first page, 30¢ for
each additional copy at the same time from
same original ("need to have fee before
service can be rendered")

Yolo County
organized 1850, original county

Yolo County Clerk Recorder
(625 Court Street, Room B01, Woodland, CA
95695—location)
PO Box 1130 (mailing address)
Woodland, CA 95776
(530) 666-8130; (530) 666-8109 FAX
freddie.oakley@yolocounty.org
http://www.yolocounty.org/org/Recorder
Freddie Oakley
(current land records and vital records)
no records search service; certified copies
available

Yolo County Superior Court
Main Court House
725 Court Street
Woodland, CA 95695
(530) 406-6700 (Main Number); (530) 406-6831
(Administration); (530) 406-6835 FAX
(Administration)
webmaster@yolocourts.com
http://www.yolocourts.com
(current probate records)
no records search service; certified copies
available

Yuba County
organized 1850, original county

Yuba County Clerk/Recorder Division
915 Eighth Street, Suite 107
Marysville, CA 95901
(530) 749-7850; (530) 749-7854 FAX
http://www.co.yuba.ca.us/content/departments
/clerk
Terry A. Hansen, Clerk
(land records, naturalization records, vital
    records)

Yuba County Superior Court
215 Fifth Street, Suite 200
Marysville, CA 95901-5737
(530) 741-6341 (Clerk); (530) 749-7351 FAX
    (Civil Division)
http://ww.yubacourts.org
(probate records)
probate search service: $5.00 per case; copies of
    probate records: 50¢ per page

COLORADO

*Capital: Denver. Statehood: 1 August 1876 (annexed
as a result of the Louisiana Purchase, 1803, and the
Treaty of Guadalupe-Hidalgo, 1848, became a territory
in 1861)*

Colorado's Municipal Courts handle
ordinance violations and traffic matters. The
County Courts hear civil cases, misdemeanors,
felony preliminaries and small claims. Seven
Water Courts, in Greeley, Pueblo, Alamosa,
Montrose, Glenwood Springs, Steamboat
Springs, and Durango, determine water rights.

Twenty-two District Courts sit in each of the
counties and handle domestic relations, civil and
criminal cases, and (except in Denver) probate
and juvenile matters. First Judicial District:
Gilpin and Jefferson counties; Second Judicial
District: City and County of Denver; Third
Judicial District: Huerfano and Las Animas
counties; Fourth Judicial District: El Paso and
Teller counties; Fifth Judicial District: Clear
Creek, Eagle, Lake, and Summit counties; Sixth
Judicial District: Archuleta, La Plata, and San
Juan counties; Seventh Judicial District: Delta,
Gunnison, Hinsdale, Montrose, Ouray, and San
Miguel counties; Eighth Judicial District:
Jackson and Larimer counties; Ninth Judicial
District: Garfield, Pitkin, and Rio Blanco
counties; Tenth Judicial District: Pueblo County;
Eleventh Judicial District: Chaffee, Custer,
Fremont, and Park counties; Twelfth Judicial
District: Alamosa, Conejos, Costilla, Mineral,
Rio Grande, and Saguache counties; Thirteenth
Judicial District: Kit Carson, Logan, Morgan,
Phillips, Sedgwick, Washington, and Yuma
counties; Fourteenth Judicial District: Grand,
Moffat, and Routt counties; Fifteenth Judicial
District: Baca, Cheyenne, Kiowa, and Prowers
counties; Sixteenth Judicial District: Bent,
Crowley, and Otero counties; Seventeenth
Judicial District: Adams and Broomfield
counties; Eighteenth Judicial District: Arapahoe,
Douglas, Elbert, and Lincoln counties;
Nineteenth Judicial District: Weld County;
Twentieth Judicial District: Boulder County;
Twenty-first Judicial District: Mesa County;
Twenty-second Judicial District: Dolores and
Montezuma counties.

The Denver Probate Court and the Denver
Juvenile Court serve that city. A Court of
Appeals sits in Denver and occasionally at
Colorado Springs and Grand Junction. The
Supreme Court sits at Denver.

Adams County
organized 1901 from Arapahoe County, and
annexed part of Denver County in 1909

Adams County Clerk and Recorder
Adams County Courthouse
450 South Fourth Street
Brighton, CO 80601
(303) 654-6026; (303) 654-6009 FAX
http://www.co.adams.co.us/index.cfm?d=stand
    ard&b=1&c=9&s=84&p=180
(land records)
no probate search service; copies of probate
    records: 75¢ per page

Clerk of Court
Adams County Justice Center
1100 Judicial Center Drive
Brighton, CO 80601
(303) 659-1161; (303) 654-3216 FAX
http://www.courts.state.co.us/district/17th/17c
    lerks.htm
Eloise Cohen
(probate records)

Alamosa County
organized 1913 from Costilla County

Alamosa County Clerk and Recorder
(402 Edison Avenue—location)
PO Box 630 (mailing address)

Alamosa, CO 81101
(719) 589-6681; (719) 589-6118 FAX
clerkrecorder@alamosacounty.org;
    vitalstatistics@alamosacounty.org
http://www.alamosacounty.org/depts/Clerk_R
    ecorder/index.html
Holly Z. Lowder
(land records, naturalization records, vital
    records)

Clerk of Court
Alamosa Combined Court
Alamosa County Courthouse
Fourth and San Juan
Alamosa, CO 81101
(719) 589-4996 (District Court); (719) 589-6213
    (County Court); (719) 589-4998 FAX
shirley.skinner@judicial.state.co.us
http://www.courts.state.co.us/district/12th/12c
    lerks.htm
Shirley Skinner
(probate records)

Arapahoe County
organized 1861, original county

Arapahoe County Clerk and Recorder
Administration Building
5334 South Prince Street
Littleton, CO 80166-001
(303) 795-4200; (303) 794-4625 FAX
Clerk@co.arapahoe.co.us
http://www.co.arapahoe.co.us/Departments/C
    R/index.asp
Nancy Doty
(land records)

Clerk of Court
Arapahoe District Court
Arapahoe County Justice Center
7325 South Potomac Street
Centennial, CO 80112
(303) 649-6355; (303) 792-2401 FAX
http://www.courts.state.co.us/district/18th/18c
    lerks.htm
Tammy L. Herivel
(naturalization records, probate records)

Archuleta County
organized 1885 from Conejos County

Archuleta Clerk and Recorder
Archuleta County Courthouse
449 San Juan Street
Pagosa Springs, CO 81147
(970) 264-8350; (970) 264-5656 (Land Records);
    (970) 264-8357 FAX
jmadrid@archuletacounty.org
http://www.archuletacounty.org/Clerk/clerk.htm
June Madrid

Clerk of Court
Archulata Combined Court
(449 San Juan Street—location)
PO Box 148 (mailing address)
Pagosa Springs, CO 81147
(970) 264-5932; (970) 247-2304 (Naturalization
    Records); (970) 264-2407 FAX
Pamela.Thompson@judicial.state.co.us
http://www.courts.state.co.us/district/06th/6di
    stclerks.htm
Pamela S. Thompson
(probate records)

Baca County
organized 1889 from Las Animas County

Baca County Clerk and Recorder
(741 Main Street—location)
PO Box 116 (mailing address)
Springfield, CO 81073-0116
(719) 523-6532; (719) 523-4555 (vital records)
bacacr@ria.net
http://www.springfieldcolorado.com/bacacount
    ygov.html
Sheila Emick
(land records from 1889; some vital records
    from 1917, more consistently starting in the
    1920s with Betty Nutt, 732 College,
    Springfield, CO 81073)

Clerk of Court
Baca Combined Court
741 Main Street
Springfield, CO 81073
(719) 523-4555; (719) 523-4552 FAX
http://www.courts.state.co.us/district/15th/15c
lerks.htm
Linda Gibson
(probate records from 1911)
probate search service: no fee; copies of probate
records: 75¢ per page, no minimum

Bent County

organized 1870 from Greenwood County, which
was organized in 1874 and abolished in 1878
by being divided between Bent and Elbert
counties

Bent County Clerk and Recorder
(725 Bent Avenue—location)
PO Box 350 (mailing address)
Las Animas, CO 81054-0350
(719) 456-2009; (719) 456-2223 FAX
bentc&r@stateco.org
http://www.bentcounty.org/abc/countyfacts.ht
m (Bent County Development Foundation)
Patty Nickell
(land records from 1888 to date, marriage
licenses from 1888 to date)
no land records search service; copies of land
records: $1.25 per page, $1.00 additional for
certification; copies of vital records: $12.00
for the first copy of births or deaths and $6.00
for each additional copy of the same record
purchased on the same day (restricted to
immediate relatives), $2.00 each for marriage
licenses, $1.00 for certification

Clerk of Court
Bent Combined Court
725 Bent
Las Animas, CO 81054
(719) 456-1353; (719) 456-0040 FAX
http://www.courts.state.co.us/district/16th/16c
lerks.htm
Vicki Morlan
(probate records from 1888)
probate search service: $8.00 per name

Boulder County

organized 1861, original county

Boulder County Clerk and Recorder
1750 33rd Street, Suite 201
Boulder, CO 80301-2549
(303) 413-770 (Recording Division)
cjhcr@co.boulder.co.us
http://www.co.boulder.co.us/clerk/index.htm
Linda Salas
(land records, marriages)

Clerk of Court
Boulder County Justice Center
(1777 Sixth Street—location)
PO Box 4249 (mailing address)
Boulder, CO 80306-4249
(303) 441-3766 (Clerk); (303) 441-3750 (Main);
(303) 441-4750 FAX
http://www.courts.state.co.us/district/20th/20c
lerks.htm
Debra Crosser
(probate records)

Broomfield County

organized 1998 from parts of Adams, Boulder,
Jefferson, and Weld counties

Broomfield County Clerk and Recorder
1 DesCombes Drive
Bromfield, CO 80020
(303) 438-6332
info@Broomfield.org
http://www.ci.broomfield.co.us
(land records)

Clerk of Court
Broomfield County Court
17 DesCombes Drive
Broomfield, CO 80020
(720) 887-2100

http://www.courts.state.co.us/district/17th/17c
lerks.htm
Melinda Taylor
(probate records)

Chaffee County

organized 1861 from Lake County

Chaffee County Clerk and Recorder
(104 Crestone—location)
PO Box 699 (mailing address)
Salida, CO 81201-0699
(719) 539-4016 (County Assessor); (719) 539-
6913 (County Clerk and Recorder); (719) 539-
8558 FAX
jreno@chaffeecounty.org
http://www.chaffeecounty.org/GigPage.aspx?P
ageID=251
Joyce M. Reno
(land records with County Assessor,
naturalization records with County Clerk and
Recorder)

Clerk of Court
Chaffee Combined Court
(142 Crestone—location)
PO Box 279 (mailing address)
Salida, CO 81201
(719) 539-2561; (719) 539-6281 FAX
ida.hansen@judicial.state.co.us
http://www.courts.state.co.us/district/11th/11c
lerks.htm
Ida Hansen
(probate records)
no search service; copies of probate records: 50¢
to $2.00 depending on size

Cheyenne County

organized 1889 from Bent and Elbert counties

Cheyenne County Clerk and Recorder
PO Box 567
Cheyenne Wells, CO 80810
(719) 767-5685; (719) 767-5540 FAX
cheyclrk@rebeltec.com
http://www.co.cheyenne.co.us
Kay Feyh

Clerk of Court
Cheyenne Combined Court
(51 South First Street—location)
PO Box 696 (mailing address)
Cheyenne Wells, CO 80810-0696
(719) 767-5649; (719) 767-5671 FAX
http://www.courts.state.co.us/district/15th/15c
lerks.htm
Vicki Allen
(naturalization records, probate records)
no probate search service; copies of probate
records: 75¢ per page

Clear Creek County

organized 1861, original county

Clear Creek County Clerk and Recorder
(Courthouse, 405 Argentine—location)
PO Box 2000 (mailing address)
Georgetown, CO 80444-2000
(303) 679-2338; (303) 679-2357 (Archives); (303)
679-2441 FAX
clerk@co.clear-creek.co.us
http://www.co.clear-
creek.co/us/Depts/clerk.htm
Pam Phipps
(land records and marriages; marriages from
1882–1905 with Archives in Courthouse
basement)

Clerk of Court
Clear Creek Combined Court
(Fifth and Argentine—location)
PO Box 367 (mailing address)
Georgetown, CO 80444
(303) 569-3274; (303) 569-3274 FAX
kim.hill@judicial.state.co.us
http://www.courts.state.co.us/district/05th/05c
lerks.htm
Kimberlee A. Hill
(probate records)

Conejos County

organized 1861, original county

Clerk of Court
Conejos Combined Court
(Conejos County Courthouse, Main Street—
location)
PO Box 128 (mailing address)
Conejos, CO 81129
(719) 376-5465
shelly.quintana@judicial.state.co.us
http://www.courts.state.co.us/district/12th/12c
lerks.htm
Shelly Quintana
(naturalization records, vital records, probate
records)

Conejos County Clerk and Recorder
(6683 County Road 13—location)
PO Box 127 (mailing address)
Conejos, CO 81129
(719) 376-5422; (719) 376-5997 FAX
http://www.rockymountainbride.com/mtntown
resources/mountaintownresources/clerkandr
ecorders/tabid/88/Default.aspx
Lawrence Gallegos
(land records from 1900)

Costilla County

organized 1861, original county

Clerk of Court
Costilla Combined Court
(Costilla County Court Complex, 401 Church
Place—location)
PO Box 301 (mailing address)
San Luis, CO 81152
(719) 672-3681; (719) 672-4493 FAX
bernadette.lucero@judicial.state.co.us
http://www.courts.state.co.us/district/12th/12c
lerks.htm
Bernadette M. Lucero
(probate records)

Costilla County Clerk and Recorder
(Main Street—location)
PO Box 308 (mailing address)
San Luis, CO 811512
(719) 672-3301
http://www.costilla-county.com/clerk.html
Dolores Burns

Crowley County

organized 1911 from Bent County

Clerk of Court
Crowley Combined Court
110 East Sixth
Ordway, CO 81063
(719) 267-4468
http://www.courts.state.co.us/district/16th/16c
lerks.htm
Dawn Stallsworth
(probate records)

Crowley County Clerk and Recorder
631 Main Street
Ordway, CO 81063
(719) 267-5555, ext. 3; (719) 267-3114 FAX
lnichols@crowleycounty.net
http://www.crowleycounty.net/clerk.htm
Lucile Nichols
(land records and marriages)

Custer County

organized 1877 from Fremont County

Clerk of Court
Custer Combined Court
(County Courthouse Building, 205 South Sixth
Street—location)
PO Box 60 (mailing address)
Westcliffe, CO 81252
(719) 783-2274; (719) 783-2995 FAX
linda.urwiller@judicial.state.co.us
http://www.courts.state.co.us/district/11th/11c
lerks.htm
Linda Urwiller
(probate records)

Custer County Clerk and Recorder
(County Courthouse Building, 205 South Sixth
    Street—location)
PO Box 150 (mailing address)
Westcliffe, CO 81252
(719) 783-2441; (719) 783-0441; (719) 783-2885
    FAX
ccclerk@centurytel.net
http://www.custercountygov.com
Debbie Livengood

Delta County
organized 1883 from Gunnison County

Clerk of Court
Delta Combined Court
501 Palmer, Suite 338
Delta, CO 81416
(970) 874-6280; (970) 874-4306 FAX
MandyA@judicial.state.co.us
http://www.courts.state.co.us/district/07th/07c
    lerks.htm
Mandy Allen
(probate records)
no probate search service; copies of probate
    records: 75¢ per page

Delta County Clerk and Recorder
Delta County Courthouse
501 Palmer Street, Suite 211
Delta, CO 81416-1764
(970) 874-2150; (970) 874-2161 FAX
http://www.deltacounty.com/index.asp?ID=59
Ann B. Eddins
(land records; births, deaths, and marriages)

Denver County
organized 1901 from Adams County

Denver County Clerk and Recorder
Wellington E. Webb Municipal Office Building
201 West Colfax Avenue, Dept. 101
Denver, CO 80202
(720) 865-8400
Wayne.Vaden@ci.denver.co.us
http://www.denvergov.ofg/Clerk_and_Recorde
    r/default.asp
Wayne E. Vaden
(land records, marriages)

**Second Judicial District Administrator and
    Clerk of Court**
Denver County City-County Building
1437 Bannock Street
Denver, CO 80202
(720) 865-8301 (General Information)
http://www.courts.state.co.us/district/02nd/02
    admin.htm
Miles Flesche, District Administrator; Sabra A.
    Millett, Clerk of the District Court
(land records from 1800, probate)

Dolores County
organized 1881 from Ouray County

Clerk of Court
Dolores Combined Court
(409 North Main—location)
PO Box 511 (mailing address)
Dove Creek, CO 81324
(970) 677-2258; (970) 677-4156 FAX
Linda.Cressler@judicial.state.co.us
http://www.courts.state.co.us/district/22nd/22
    distclerks.htm
Linda L. Cressler
(probate records)

Dolores County Clerk and Recorder
(409 North Main Street—location)
PO Box 58 (mailing address)
Dove Creek, CO 81324-0058
(970) 677-2381; (970) 677-2815 FAX
dolocnty@fone.net
http://www.dolorescounty.org
Earlene White

Douglas County
organized 1861, original county

Clerk of Court
Douglas Combined Court
Douglas County Justice Center
4000 Justice Way, #2009
Castle Rock, CO 80109
(303) 663-7200; (303) 688-1962 FAX
http://www.courts.state.co.us/district/18th/18c
    lerks.htm
Cheryl Layne
(probate records)

Douglas County Clerk and Recorder
301 South Wilcox Street
Castle Rock, CO 80104-2440
(303) 660-7469; (303) 814-2750 FAX
cmurray@douglas.co.us
http://www.douglas.co.us/clerk/index.html
Carole Murray
(real estate records from 1864, marriages)
no records search service; copies of records:
    $1.25 per page

Eagle County
organized 1883 from Summit County

Clerk of Court
Eagle Combined Court
(885 Chambers Avenue—location)
PO Box 597 (mailing address)
Eagle, CO 81631
(970) 328-6373; (970) 328-6328 FAX
jackie.cooper@judicial.state.co.us
http://www.courts.state.co.us/district/05th/05c
    lerks.htm
Jackie Cooper
(probate records)

Eagle County Clerk and Recorder
(500 Broadway, Suite 101—location)
PO Box 537 (mailing address)
Eagle, CO 81631
(970) 328-8723 (Recording); (970) 328-8716
    FAX

teak.simonton@eaglecounty.us
http://www.eaglecounty.us/clerk
Teak Simonton

El Paso County
organized 1861, original county

Clerk of Court
El Paso Combined Court
El Paso County Judicial Building, 270 South
    Tejon Street—location)
PO Box 2980 (mailing address)
Colorado Springs, CO 80903
(719) 448-7700 (Information); (719) 448-7599,
    ext. 8 (Clerk)
http://www.courts.state.co.us/district/04th/04c
    lerks.htm
Mary V. Perry
(probate records)
probate search service: $8.00 per name; copies
    of probate records: 75¢ per page; no phone
    calls, correspondence only

El Paso County Clerk and Recorder
200 South Cascade Avenue
Colorado Springs, CO 80903
(719) 520-6216; (719) 520-6212 FAX
clerk_recorder@co.el.paso.co.us
http://car.elpasoco.com
Robert C. "Bob" Balink
(land records, marriages)

Elbert County
organized 1874 from Douglas and Greenwood
    counties, the latter of which was organized in
    1874 and abolished in 1878 by being divided
    between Bent and Elbert counties

Clerk of Court
Elbert Combined Court
(751 Ute Street—location)
PO Box 232 (mailing address)
Kiowa, CO 80117
(303) 621-2131; (303) 621-2722 FAX
http://www.courts.state.co.us/district/18th/18c
    lerks.htm
Diana Richards

(probate records)

Elbert County Clerk and Recorder
215 Comanche Street
Kiowa, CO 80117
(303) 621-3128
http://www.elbertcounty-co.gov/dept_clerk.asp
(marriage licenses, real estate transactions)

Fremont County
organized 1861, original county

Clerk of Court
Fremont Combined Court
136 Justice Center Road, Room 103
Canon City, CO 81212
(719) 269-0100; (719) 269-0134 FAX
debora.sather-stringari@judicial.state.co.us
http://www.courts.state.co.us/district/11th/11c
    lerks.htm
Deborah Sather-Stringari
(probate records)

Fremont County Clerk and Recorder
615 Macon Avenue, Room 100
Cañon City, CO 81212
(719) 276-7330 (General Information); (719)
    276-7333 (Clerk); (719) 276-7336, Recording
    Department, Room 102)
normahat@fremontco.com
http://www.fremontco.com/clerkandrecorder/i
    ndex.shtml
Norma Hatfield
(real property, marriages)
copies of land records: $1.25 per page; copies of
    marriages: $2.00; certification: $1.00

Garfield County
organized 1883 from Summit County

Clerk of Court
Garfield Combined Court
109 Eighth Street, Suite 104
Glenwood Springs, CO 81601
(970) 945-5075; (970) 945-8756 FAX
james.bradford@judicial.state.co.us
http://www.courts.state.co.us/district/09th/09c
    lerks.htm
James C. Bradford
(probate records)

Garfield County Clerk and Recorder
109 Eighth Street, Suite 200
Glenwood Springs, CO 81601-3362
(303) 945-2377, ext. 1760; (970) 947-1078 FAX
malsdorf@garfield-county.com
http://www.garfield-
    county.com/home/index.asp?page=562
Mildred Alsdorf
(land records from 1883, births, deaths and
    marriage licenses from 1884 to date, births
    and deaths)
no land records search service; certified copies
    of births and deaths: $12.00 each (includes
    search, some early birth and death records are
    very hard to find, and you have to be a
    member of the family and have permission to
    get a copy); copies of marriage licenses: $3.50
    each (includes search); copies of birth and
    death certificates: $15.00

Gilpin County
organized 1861, original county

Clerk of Court
Gilpin Combined Court
2960 Dory Hill Road, Suite 200
Golden, CO 80403-8780
(303) 582-5522 (Main); (303) 582-3112 FAX
http://www.courts.state.co.us/district/01st/01c
    lerks.htm
Deborah George
(probate records)

Gilpin County Clerk and Recorder
(203 Eureka Street, First Floor—location)
PO Box 3429 (mailing address)
Central City, CO 80427
(303) 582-5521; (303) 565-1797 FAX
gcclerk@co.gilpin.co.us

http://www.co.gilpin.co.us/ClerkRecorder/default.htm
Jessica Lovingier
(land records with Gilpin County Assessor's Office)

Grand County
organized 1874 from Summit County

Clerk of Court
Grand Combined Court
(Grand County Courthouse, 308 Byers Street—location)
Box 192 (mailing address)
Hot Sulphur Springs, CO 80451
(970) 725-3357
heather.harms@judicial.state.co.us
http://www.courts.state.co.us/district/14th/14clerks.htm
Heather J. Harms
(probate records)

Grand County Clerk and Recorder
(Grand County Courthouse, 308 Byers Avenue—location)
PO Box 120 (mailing address)
Hot Sulphur Springs, CO 80451-0120
(970) 725-3347; (970) 725-0100 FAX
grandclerk@co.grand.co.us;
srosene@co.grand.co.us
http://co.grand.co.us/Clerk/clerkand.htm
Sara L. Rosene
(land records, vital records)

Gunnison County
organized 1877 from Lake County

Clerk of Court
Gunnison Combined Court
200 East Virginia Avenue
Gunnison, CO 81230
(970) 641-3500; (970) 641-6876 FAX
http://www.courts.state.co.us/district/07th/07clerks.htm
Betsy Nesbitt
(naturalization records from 1890 to 1942, probate records from 1900)
probate search service: no charge; copies of probate records: 75¢ per page, no minimum

Gunnison County Clerk and Recorder
221 North Wisconsin, Suite C
Gunnison, CO 81230
(970) 641-1516 (Clerk); (970) 641-2038 (Recording); (970) 641-7956 FAX
http://www.gunnisoncounty.org/dept/clerk
Stella Dominguez
(land records from 20 April 1877, marriages from 1 December 1877)
copies of land records (must have book and page number or reception number or exact date with grantor and grantee names): $1.25 per page

Hinsdale County
organized 1874 from Conejos County

Clerk of Court
Hinsdale Combined Court
(317 Henson—location)
PO Box 245 (mailing address)
Lake City, CO 81235
(970) 944-2227; (970) 944-2289 FAX
Joan.Anastasion@judicial.state.co.us
http://www.courts.state.co.us/district/07th/07clerks.htm
Joan Anastasion
(probate records)
no probate search service; copies of probate records: 75¢ each, no minimum

Hinsdale County Clerk and Recorder
Hinsdale County Courthouse
Henson Street
Lake City, CO 81235
(970) 944-2228
hinsdaleclerk@yahoo.com
http://www.hinsdalecountycolorado.us/HCclerk.html
Linda Pavich Ragle

(land records, marriages, and deaths)

Huerfano County
organized 1861, original county

Clerk of Court
Huerfano Combined Court
Huerfano County Courthouse
401 Main Street, Room 304
Walsenburg, CO 81089
(719) 738-1040
http://www.courts.state.co.us/district/03rd/03clerks.htm
Lorraine Castro
(probate records)

Huerfano County Clerk and Recorder
Huerfano County Courthouse
401 Main Street, Suite 204
Walsenberg, CO 81089
(719) 738-2380; (719) 738-3996 FAX
judy@huerfano.us
http://www.huerfano.us
Judy Benine
(land records, marriages)

Jackson County
organized 1909 from Grand County

Clerk of Court
Jackson County Combined Court
(396 Lafever Street—location)
PO Box 308 (mailing address)
Walden, CO 80480
(970) 723-4363
http://www.courts.state.co.us/district/08th/08clerks.htm
Jennifer Weddle
(probate records)

Jackson County Clerk and Recorder
PO Box 337
Walden, CO 80480-0337
(303) 723-4334; (970) 723-3214 FAX
http://www.rockymountainbride.com/mtntownresources/mountaintownresources/clerkandrecorders/tabid/88/Default.aspx
Charlene Geer
(land records, vital records)

Jefferson County
organized 1861, original county

Clerk of Court
Jefferson Combined Court
100 Jefferson County Parkway
Golden, CO 80401-6002
(303) 271-6215 (Main); (303) 271-6135 (Probate)
http://www.courts.state.co.us/district/01st/01clerks.htm
Shirley Williams
(probate records)
probate search service: $5.00 per name; copies of probate records: 75¢ per page, $1.00 for certification, no minimum

Jefferson County Hall of Justice
100 Jefferson County Parkway
Golden, CO 80419
(303) 271-8168; (303) 271-8197 FAX
fgriffin@co.jefferson.co.us
http://jeffco.us/cr/index.htm
Faye Griffin
(land records, marriages)

Kiowa County
organized 1889 from Cheyenne and Bent counties

Clerk of Court
Kowa Combined Court
(200 East 13th Street—location)
PO Box 353 (mailing address)
Eads, CO 81036
(719) 438-5558; (719) 438-5300 FAX
http://www.courts.state.co.us/district/15th/15clerks.htm
Diane Crow
(probate records)

Kiowa County Clerk and Recorder

(County Courthouse, 1305 Goff—location)
PO Box 37 (mailing address)
Eads, CO 81036-0037
(719) 438-5421; (719) 438-5327 FAX
http://www.kiowacountycolo.com/countyclerk.htm
Betty V. Crow

Kit Carson County
organized 1889 from Elbert County

Clerk of Court
Kit Carson Combined Court
(251 16th Street, Suite 301—location)
PO Box 547 (mailing address)
Burlington, CO 80807-0547
(719) 346-5524; (719) 346-7805 FAX
http://www.courts.state.co.us/district/13th/13clerks.htm
Sharlene K. Mills
(probate records)

Kit Carson County Clerk and Recorder
(251 16th Street—location)
PO Box 249 (mailing address)
Burlington, CO 80807-0249
(719) 346-8638; (719) 346-7242
clerkandrecorder@kitcarsoncounty.org
http://www.kitcarsoncounty.org/Countyclerk.htm
Della Calhoon
(land records, marriage licenses)

La Plata County
organized 1874 from Conejos and Lake counties

Clerk of Court
La Plata Combined Court
1060 East Second Avenue, Room #106
Durango, CO 81301
(970) 247-2004; (970) 247-4348 FAX
leslie.davis@judicial.state.co.us
http://www.courts.state.co.us/district/06th/6distclerks.htm
Leslie Davis
(probate records)

La Plata County Clerk and Recorder
Court House, 1060 Second Avenue, Room #134
Durango, CO 81301-5157
(970) 382-6280; (970) 382-6281; (970) 382-6285 FAX
Recording@co.laplata.co.us
http://www.co.laplata.co.us/clerk/clerk.htm
Linda Daley
(deeds, plats, surveys, marriage licenses, and other historic documents dating back to the 1800s)
certified copies of marriage licenses: $3.00

Lake County
organized 1861, original county; name changed from Carbonate in 1879

Clerk of Court
Lake Combined Court
(Fifth and Harrison Avenue—location)
PO Box 55 (mailing address)
Leadville, CO 80461
(719) 486-0535; (719) 486-5006 FAX
brenda.bond@judicial.state.co.us
http://www.courts.state.co.us/district/05th/05clerks.htm
Brenda Bond
(probate records from 1860)
no probate search service; copies of probate records: 75¢ per page, no minimum

Lake County Clerk and Recorder
(505 Harrison Avenue—location)
PO Box 917 (mailing address)
Leadville, CO 80461
(719) 486-1410; (719) 486-3972 FAX
http://www.lakecountyco.com/clerkandrecorder
Patricia A. Berger
(land records from 1876, marriage records from 1876, some burials from 1885–1903)

Larimer County
organized 1861, original county

Clerk of Court
Larimer County Justice Center
201 La Porte Avenue, Suite 100
Fort Collins, CO 80521-2761
(970) 498-6100; (970) 498-6110 FAX
http://www.courts.state.co.us/district/08th/08c
lerks.htm
Sherlyn K. Sampson
(probate records from 1878)
copies of probate records: 75¢ per page

Larimer County Clerk and Recorder
200 West Oak Street, First Floor
Fort Collins, CO 80521
(970) 498-7860 (Recording Department); (970)
498-7830 FAX (Recording)
sdoyle@larimer.org
http://www.co.larimer.co.us/clerk
Scott Doyle
copies of land records: 75¢ per page

Las Animas County
organized 1866 from Huerfano County

Clerk of Court
Las Animas Combined Court
Las Animas County Courthouse
200 East First Street, Room 304
Tirinidad, CO 81082
(719) 846-3316
http://www.courts.state.co.us/district/03rd/03
clerks.htm
Bob Kreiman
(probate records)

Las Animas County Clerk and Recorder
(County Courthouse, 200 East First Street,
Room 207—location)
PO Box 115 (mailing address)
Trinidad, CO 81082
(719) 846-3314; (719) 846-0333 (Property
records); (719) 845-2573
FAXhttp://www.tlac.net (Trinidad Las
Animas County Economic Development)
bernard.gonzales@dorexch.state.co.us
http://www.rockymountainbride.com/mtntown
resources/mountaintownresources/clerkandr
ecorders/tabid/88/Default.aspx
Bernard J. Gonzales
(land records, marriages)

Lincoln County
organized 1889 from Elbert County

Clerk of Court
Lincoln County Court
(103 Third Avenue—location)
PO Box 128 (mailing address)
Hugo, CO 80821
(719) 743-2455; (719) 743-2636 FAX
http://www.courts.state.co.us/district/18th/18c
lerks.htm
Janet Bandy
(naturalization records, probate records)
no probate search service; copies of probate
records: 75¢ per page, no minimum

Lincoln County Clerk and Recorder
(103 Third Avenue—location)
PO Box 67 (mailing address)
Hugo, CO 80821
(719) 743-2444; (719) 743-2524 FAX
http://www.lincolncountyco.us/county_clerk.htm
Corinne M. Lengel
(land records, births, deaths, and marriages [for
Lincoln County only])

Logan County
organized 1887 from Weld County

Clerk of Court
Logan District Court
(110 North Riverview Road, Room 205—
location)
PO Box 71 (mailing address)
Sterling, CO 80751
(970) 522-6565; (970) 522-6566 FAX
http://www.courts.state.co.us/district/13th/13c
lerks.htm
Diana J. Kaufman

(naturalization records, probate records)
probate search service: no charge; copies of
probate records: 75¢ per page for filed
documents

Logan County Clerk and Recorder
Logan County Courthouse
315 Main Street, Suite 3
Sterling, CO 80751-4357
(970) 522-1544 (Recording/Election); (970) 522-
2063 FAX
loganclk@kci.net
http://www.loganco.gov/clerk/temp_index.htm
Roberta J. Perry
(land records, marriages)

Mesa County
organized 1883 from Gunnison County

Clerk of the District Court
Mesa County and District Court
Mesa County Justice Center
(544 Rood Avenue—location)
PO Box 20,000 (mailing address)
Grand Junction, CO 81502-5030
(970) 257-3660
sandra.casselberry@judicial.state.co.us
http://www.courts.co.us/district/21st/21clerks.
htm
Sandra Casselberry
(naturalization records, probate records)

Mesa County Clerk and Recorder
Recording Division
(544 Rood Avenue—location)
PO Box 20,000 (mailing address)
Grand Junction, CO 81502-5006
(970) 244-1607; (970) 244-1703
Janice.Ward@mesacounty.us
http://recorder.mesacounty.us
Janice Ward
(land records from 1883 to date, marriages from
1883 to date)
no land records search service; copies of land
records: $1.25 per page plus $1.00 per
document for certification; copies of
marriages: $2.00 each plus $1.00 for
certification

Mineral County
organized 1893 from Hinsdale County

Clerk of Court
Mineral Combined Court
(Mineral County Courthouse, North First
Street—location)
PO Box 337 (mailing address)
Creede, CO 81130
(719) 658-2575; (719) 658-0507 FAX
hollie.wheelwright@judicial.state.co.us
http://www.courts.state.co.us/district/12th/12c
lerks.htm
Hollie Wheelwright
(naturalization records, vital records, probate
records)

Mineral County Clerk and Recorder
(North First Street—location)
PO Box 70 (mailing address)
Creede, CO 81130-0070
(719) 658-2440
Mineralctr@stateco.org
http://www.creede.com/city_cty.htm
Virginia Wyley
(land records with Clerk, Assessor and
Treasurer,)

Moffat County
organized 1911 from Routt County

Clerk of Court
Moffat Combined Court
221 West Victory Way, Suite 300
Craig, CO 81625
(970) 824-8254
dianal.meyer@judicial.state.co.us
http://www.courts.state.co.us/district/14th/14c
lerks.htm
Diana L. Meyer
(probate records)

no probate search service; copies of probate
records: 75¢ per page, no minimum

Moffat County Clerk and Recorder
221 West Victory Way, Suite 200
Craig, CO 81625
(970) 824-9104; (970) 826-3413 FAX
esullivan@moffatcounty.net
http://www.co.moffat.co.us/ClerkandRecorder
/default.htm
Elaine Sullivan, Clerk and Recorder; Debbie
Winder, Recording Supervisor
(land records, limited marriages; no birt/death
certificates)
no land records search service; copies of land
records: $1.25 per page, certification: $1.00
per document

Montezuma County
organized 1889 from La Plata County

Clerk of Court
Montezuma District Court
Montezuma County Courthouse
109 West Main Street, Room 210
Cortez, CO 81321
(970) 565-1111; (970) 565-8516
desiree.lipe@judicial.state.co.us
http://www.courts.state.co.us/district/22nd/22
distclerks.htm
Desiree Lipe
(probate records)

Montezuma County Clerk and Recorder
Montezuma County Courthouse
109 West Main Street, Room 108
Cortez, CO 81321-3154
(970) 565-3728; (970) 564-0215 FAX
ctullis@co.montezuma.co.us
http://www.co.motezuma.co.us/newsite/clerkh
ome.html
Carol Tullis
(land records from 1889, vital records from
1879)

Montrose County
organized 1883 from Gunnison County

Clerk of Court
Montrose Combined Court
1200 North Grand Avenue, Bin A
Montrose, CO 81401
(970) 252-4300; (970) 252-4309 FAX
hendrika.wiley@judicial.state.co.us
http://www.courts.state.co.us/district/07th/07c
lerks.htm
Hendrika (Henny) Wiley
(naturalization records, probate records)

Montrose County Clerk and Recorder
(320 South First Street, Room 101—location)
PO Box 1289 (mailing address)
Montrose, CO 81402-1289
(970) 249-3362, ext. 2 (Recording and Vitals)
ckruse@co.montrose.co.us
http://www.co.montrose.co.us/clerks.htm
Carol Kruse
(land records, birth, death, and marriage records)
copies of land records: $1.25 per page, $5.00 per
sheet for plats or documents larger than of
8½" x 14"; certified copies vital records:
$15.00 for the first copy of births or deaths
and $6.00 for each additional copy ordered at
the same time, $2.00 for marriage licenses

Morgan County
organized 1889 from Weld County

Clerk of Court
Morgan Combined Court
(400 Warner Street—location)
PO Box 130 (mailing adress)
Fort Morgan, CO 80701
(970) 542-3435; (970) 542-3436 FAX
http://www.courts.state.co.us/district/13th/13c
lerks.htm
Cathlene J. Marshall
(probate records)
probate search service: no charge; copies of
probate records: 75¢ per page, certification

75¢ per page, no minimum

Morgan County Clerk and Recorder
(231 Ensign Street—location)
PO Box 1399 (mailing address)
Fort Morgan, CO 80701
(970) 542-3521; (970) 542-3525 FAX
mcclerk@co.morgan.co.us
http://www.co.morgan.co.us/CountyClerk.html
Connie Ingmire
(land records, marriages from 1889 to date)

Otero County

organized 1889 from Bent County

Clerk of Court
Otero Combined Court
13 West Third Street
La Junta, CO 81050
(719) 384-4951
http://www.courts.state.co.us/district/16th/16c
lerks.htm
Caren L. Stanley
(naturalization records, probate records)

Otero County Clerk and Recorder
(13 West Third Street—location)
PO Box 511 (mailing address)
La Junta, CO 81050-0511
(719) 383-3020 (Clerk); (719) 384-8701 (Deputy
Clerk and Recorder); (719) 384-7080 (Land
Use Administrator's Office); (719) 383-4225
FAX
oteroc&r@stateco.org; ssisnroy@oterogov.org
http://www.rockymountainbride.com/mtntown
resources/mountaintownresources/clerkandr
ecorders/tabid/88/Default.aspx
Sharon Sisnroy
(deeds, original subdivision plats, etc., marriages,
and probate records with Deputy Clerk and
Recorder, Room 210, maps with Kathy
Ehrlich, Land Use Administrator's Office,
Room 208)

Ouray County

organized 1877 from Hinsdale County

Clerk of Court
Ouray Combined Court
(541 South Fourth Street—location)
PO Box 643 (mailing address)
Ouray, CO 81427
(970) 325-4405; (970) 325-7364 FAX
jane.holmes@judicial.state.co.us
http://www.courts.state.co.us/district/07th/07c
lerks.htm
Jane Holmes
(naturalization records, probate records)

Ouray County Clerk and Recorder
(541 Fourth—location)
PO Box C (mailing address)
Ouray, CO 81427-0615
(303) 325-4961
ourayclerk@mail.co.ouray.co.us
http://ouraycountyco.gov/clerk.html
Michelle Nauer
(name changed from Uncompahgre County in
1883; land ownerships, marriages)

Park County

organized 1861, original county

Clerk of Court
Park Combined Court
(300 Fourth Street—location)
PO Box 190 (mailing address)
Fairplay, CO 80440
(719) 836-2940; (719) 836-2892 FAX
debra.mclimans@judicial.state.co.us
http://www.courts.state.co.us/district/11th/11c
lerks.htm
Debra McLimans
(probate records)

Park County Clerk and Recorder
(501 Main Street—location)
PO Box 220 (mailing address)
Fairplay, CO 80440-0220
(719) 836-2433; (719) 836-4348 FAX

pcclerk@parkco.us
http://www.parkco.us/county_offices.htm
Debra Green

Phillips County

organized 1889 from Logan County

Clerk of Court
Phillips Combined Court
221 South Interocean
Holyoke, CO 80734
(970) 854-3279; (970) 854-3179 FAX
http://www.courts.state.co.us/district/13th/13c
lerks.htm
Joy Strack
(probate records)

Phillips County Clerk and Recorder
221 South Interocean Avenue
Holyoke, CO 80734-1534
(970) 854-3131; (970) 854-4745 FAX
phillipsclerk@pctelcom.coop
http://www.phillipscountyco.org (Economic
Development Corporation)
Beth Cumming
(land records, vital records)

Pitkin County

organized 1881 from Gunnison County

Clerk of Court
Pitkin Combined Court
506 East Main, Suite E
Aspen, CO 81611
(970) 925-7635; (970) 925-6349 FAX
hans.jessup@judicial.state.co.us
http://www.courts.state.co.us/district/09th/09c
lerks.htm
Hans Jessup
(probate records)

Pitkin County Clerk and Recorder
Courthouse Plaza
506 Main Street, First Floor
Aspen, CO 81611-2923
(303) 920-5180; (970) 920-5196 FAX
county_info@co.pitkin.co.us
http://www.aspenpitkin.com/depts/5
Janice Vos Caudill
(land records, vital records [births and deaths
prior to 1907 with Grantee-Grantor Records])
copies of land records: $1.25 per page, $5.00 for
plats

Prowers County

organized 1889 from Bent County

Clerk of Court
Prowers Combined Court
301 South Main Street, Suite 300
Lamar, CO 81052
(719) 336-7416
http://www.courts.state.co.us/district/15th/15c
lerks.htm
Rose Ann Yates
(naturalization records, probate records)

Prowers County Clerk and Recorder
(301 South Main Street, Suite 210—location)
PO Box 1046 (mailing address)
Lamar, CO 81052-1046
(719) 336-8011 (Clerk); (719) 336-2209 (County
Assessor's Office); (719) 336-5306 FAX
cntyclrk@prowerscounty.net; cntyclerk@ria.net
http://www.prowerscounty.net
Dorothy J. McCaslin
(land records with County Assessor's Office)

Pueblo County

organized 1861, original county

Clerk of Court
Pueblo Combined Court
Pueblo County Judicial Building
320 West Tenth Street
Pueblo, CO 81003
(719) 583-7000 (Main); (719) 583-7017 (Clerk);
(719) 583-7184 FAX
munoz1@co.pueblo.co.us
http://www.courts.state.co.us/district/10th/10c

lerks.htm
Laura Lasater
(probate records)

Pueblo County Clerk and Recorder
Pueblo County Judicial Building
215 West Tenth Street
Pueblo, CO 81003
(719) 583-6507
munoz1@co.pueblo.co.us
http://www.co.pueblo.co.us/clerk
Chris Munoz, Department Head
(land records, marriages)

Rio Blanco County

organized 1889 from Garfield County

Rio Blanco Combined Courts
(555 Main Street—location)
PO Box 1150 (mailing address)
Meeker, CO 81641
(970) 878-5622; (970) 878-4295 FAX
solveig.olson@judicial.state.co.us
http://www.courts.state.co.us/district/09th/09c
lerks.htm
Solveig Olson
(probate records from 1891)
probate search service: no charge (but depends
on available time); copies of probate records:
75¢ per page from paper originals, $1.00 per
page from microfilm originals, plus postage;
no minimum; send written request with
payment and SASE

Rio Blanco County Clerk and Recorder
(555 Main Street—location)
PO Box 1067 (mailing address)
Meeker, CO 81641
(970) 878-9460; (970) 878-3587 FAX
clerk@co.rio-blanco.co.us
http://www.co.rio-blanco.co.us/clerkadrecorder
Nancy R. Amick
(land records, births, deaths, and marriage
licenses)
no land or vital records search service; copies of
land records: $1.25 per page, copies of births
and deaths: $12.00; copies of marriage
licenses: $2.00

Rio Grande County

organized 1874 from Conejos County

Clerk of Court
Rio Grande Combined Court
(Rio Grande County Courthouse, 925 Sixth
Street, Room 204—location)
PO Box W (mailing address)
Del Norte, CO 81132
(719) 657-3394; (719) 657-2636 FAX
jennifer.martinez@judicial.state.co.us
http://www.courts.state.co.us/district/12th/12c
lerks.htm
Jennifer Martinez
(naturalization records, probate records)
probate search service: $5.00; copies of probate
records: 75¢ per page, $5.00 for certification,
no minimum

Rio Grande County Clerk and Recorder
(Rio Grande County Courthouse, 965 Sixth
Street—location)
PO Box 160 (mailing address)
Del Norte, CO 81132
(719) 657-3334; (719) 657-2621 FAX
riograndecounty@yahoo.com
http://www.riograndecounty.org/page6.html
Sandy Jackson
(land records, vital records)
certified birth or death certificates: $17.00,
certified copies of marriage licenses: $3.00;
copies of land records: $1.25 per page;
certification: $1.00 per document

Routt County

organized 1877 from Grand County

Clerk of Court
Routt Combined Court
(522 Lincoln Avenue—location)
PO Box 773117 (mailing address)

Steamboat Springs, CO 80477
(970) 879-5020
tracey.epley@judicial.state.co.us
http://www.courts.state.co.us/district/14th/14c
  lerks.htm
Tracey L. Epley
(probate records)

Routt County Clerk and Recorder
(522 Lincoln Avenue—location)
Box 773598 (mailing address)
Steamboat Springs, CO 80477-3598
(970) 870-5556; (970) 870-1329 FAX
clerk@co.routt.co.us
http://www.co.routt.co.us/sections.php?op=vie
  warticle&artid=81296
Kay Weinland
(land records, marriage licenses)

Saguache County
organized 1866 from Costilla County

County Clerk and Recorder
(501 Fourth Street—location)
PO Box 176 (mailing address)
Saguache, CO 81149-0176
(719) 655-2512; (719) 665-2635 FAX
mmyers@saguachecounty-co.gov
http://www.saguachecounty.net/depts/clerk
(land records, marriages)

Saguache County Combined Courts
Saguache Combined Court
(Saguache County Courthouse, Fourth and
  Christy—location)
PO Box 197 (mailing address)
Saguache, CO 81149
(719) 655-2522; (719) 655-0109 FAX
lynn.thompson@judicial.state.co.us
http://www.courts.state.co.us/district/12th/12c
  lerks.htm
Lynne Thompson
(probate records)

San Juan County
organized 1876 from La Plata County

Clerk of Court
San Juan Combined Court
(1447 Greene Street—location)
PO Box 441 (mailing address)
Silverton, CO 81433
(970) 387-5790; (970) 387-0295 FAX
chris.tookey@judicial.state.co.us
http://www.courts.state.co.us/district/06th/6di
  stclerks.htm
Chris Tookey
(probate records)

San Juan County Clerk and Recorder
PO Box 466
Silverton, CO 81433
(303) 387-5671 voice & FAX
http://www.sanjuancountycolorado.us
Dorothy A. Zanoni
(land records, marriages)

San Miguel County
organized 1861 from Ouray County

Clerk of Court
(305 West Colorado—location)
PO Box 919 (mailing address)
Telluride, CO 81435
(970) 728-3891; (970) 728-6216 FAX
susan.wilson@judicial.state.co.us
http://www.courts.state.co.us/district/07th/07c
  lerks.htm
Susan Wilson
(probate records)

San Miguel County Clerk and Recorder
(305 West Colorado Avenue—location)
PO Box 548 (mailing address)
Telluride, CO 81435
(970) 728-3954; (970) 728-4808 FAX
http://www.sanmiguelcounty.org/clerk.htm
Doris Ruffe
(land records and marriages)

Sedgwick County
organized 1889 from Logan County

Clerk of Court
Sedgwick Combined Court
Third and Pine
Julesburg, CO 80737
(970) 474-3627; (970) 474-2026 FAX
http://www.courts.state.co.us/district/13th/13c
  lerks.htm
Susan S. Kinnison
(probate records)

Sedgwick County Clerk and Recorder
(315 Cedar Street—location)
PO Box 50 (mailing address)
Julesburg, CO 80737
(303) 474-3346; (303) 474-0954 FAX
pcarter@pctelcom.coop;
  sedgwickcogov@kci.net
http://www.sedgwickcountygov.net
Patrice Carter
(land records)

Summit County
organized 1861, original county

Clerk of Court
Summit Combined Court
(501 North Park Avenue—location)
PO Box 185 (mailing address)
Breckenridge, CO 80424
(970) 453-2241; (970) 453-1134 FAX
jan.reed@judicial.state.co.us
http://www.courts.state.co.us/district/05th/05c
  lerks.htm
Jan Reed
(probate records)

Summit County Clerk and Recorder
(208 East Lincoln Avenue—location)
PO Box 1538 (mailing address)
Breckenridge, CO 80424
(970) 453-3470; (970) 453-3540 FAX
clerkandrecorder@co.summit.co.us
http://www.co.summit.co.us/Clerk/index.htm
Cheri Brunvand
(land records, births, deaths, and marriage
  licenses)
copies of birth and death certificates: $15.00;
  copies of marriage licenses with certification:
  $3.00; copies of land records: $1.25 per page,
  $5.00 per page for plats; certification: $1.00
  per document

Teller County
organized 1899 from Fremont County

Clerk of Court
Teller Combined Court
(County Courthouse, 101 West Bennett
  Avenue—location)
PO Box 997 (mailing address)
Cripple Creek, CO 80813
(719) 689-2574

http://www.courts.state.co.us/district/04th/
  04clerks.htm
Sheri Porter
(probate records)

Teller County Clerk and Recorder
(County Courthouse, 101 West Bennett
  Avenue—location)
PO Box 1010 (mailing address)
Cripple Creek, CO 80813
(719) 689-2951; (719) 686-8030 FAX
crowsonp@co.teller.co.us
http://www.co.teller.co.us/Clerk%20and%20Re
  corder/clerk.htm
Patricia Crowson
(land records, marriages, births from 1876,
  deaths from 1902)
copies of birth or death certificates: $15.00

Washington County
organized 1887 from Weld and Arapahoe
  counties

Clerk of Court

Washington Combined Court
(26861 Highway 34—location)
PO Box 455 (mailing address)
Akron, CO 80720
(970) 345-2756; (970) 345-2829 FAX
http://www.courts.state.co.us/district/13th/13c
  lerks.htm
Gloria K. Hillier
(probate records)
probate search service: no charge; copies of
  probate records: 75¢ per page, $1.00 for
  certified copies, 75¢ minimum

Washington County Clerk and Recorder
(150 Ash—location)
PO Box L (mailing address)
Akron, CO 80720-0380
(970) 345-6565; (970) 345-6607 FAX
clerk@wcgov.com
http://www.wcgov.com
Garland Wahl
(land records, marriage licenses; vital records
  with Emma Howard, Registrar of Vital
  Statistics, 251 Hickory, Akron, CO 80720)

Weld County
organized 1861, original county

Clerk of Court
Weld County Combined Court
(901 Ninth Avenue—location)
PO Box 2038 (mailing address)
Greeley, CO 80632
(970) 351-7300; (970) 351-7300, ext. 5400
  (Probate, Room 418); (970) 356-4356 FAX
http://www.courts.state.co.us/district/19th/19c
  lerks.htm
Lauris Laue and Bridgette Owens, Probate
(probate records)

Weld County Clerk and Recorder
(1402 North 17th Avenue—location)
PO Box 459 (mailing address)
Greeley, CO 80631
(970) 304-6530, ext. 3065 (Recording
  Department); (970) 353-1964 FAX
smoreno@co.weld.co.us
http://www.co.weld.co.us/departments/clerkre
  corder.html
Steve Moreno

Yuma County
organized 1889 from Washington County

Clerk of Court
Yuma Combined Court
(200 East Third—location)
PO Box 347 (mailing address)
Wray, CO 80758-0347
(970) 332-4118; (970) 332-4119 FAX
yumac&r@stateco.org
http://www.courts.state.co.us/district/13th/13c
  lerks.htm
Betty J. Wilson
(probate records)

Yuma County Clerk and Recorder
310 Ash, Suite F
Wray, CO 80758
(970) 332-5809; (970) 332-5919 FAX
yumac&r@stateco.org
http://www.yumacounty.net/clerkrecorder.php
Beverly Wenger

Capital: Hartford. Statehood: 9 January 1788 (chartered 1662, relinquished western lands in 1786 and Western Reserve in 1800)

Connecticut is divided into 133 probate districts (up from 12 in 1978), consisting of one or more of the state's 169 towns and cities. In researching early probate matters, it's important to know which former probate district governed the area at any particular time. The State Library's enormously helpful "Research Guide to Connecticut Probate Districts" is available online at http://www.cslib.org/probate/districtsa.htm.

Probate Courts within each district have original jurisdiction over estate matters, trusts, guardianships, adoptions, name changes, etc. Appeals are taken to the Superior Court in the same Judicial District, which also handles all other civil and criminal cases. An Appellate Court and a Supreme Court sit in Hartford.

Birth records are restricted in Connecticut; a copy of a certificate can be obtained only by the person whose name appears on the certificate if eighteen years of age or older, a minor's parent or guardian, or a member of a legally incorporated genealogical society. If the last, a copy of a current, signed membership card must accompany all requests for certificates. However, microfilm copies of births, deaths, and marriages prior to 1900 are on deposit at the Connecticut State Library, 231 Capitol Avenue, Hartford, CT 06106.

Naturalization records from some of Connecticut's Municipal Courts were transferred to the U.S. District Courts for Connecticut and were subsequently transferred to the National Archives along with naturalization records from the Federal Courts for Connecticut (Record Group 21 and Record Group 200). The State Library retains records of pre-1790 naturalizations and photocopies of some records from Middlesex and New London Superior Courts as well as microfilm copies of some of the Municipal, County Court, and Court of Common Pleas records.

The State Library has most of the original estate papers prior to 1900 and some of later date, mostly on microfilm.

Fairfield County

organized 1666, original county; includes Bethel, Bridgeport, Brookfield, Danbury, Darien, Easton, Fairfield, Greenwich, Monroe, New Canaan, New Fairfield, Newtown, Norwalk, Redding, Ridgefield, Shelton, Sherman, Stamford, Stratford, Trumbull, Weston, Westport, and Wilton

Bethel Probate District (009)
(1 School Street—location)
PO Box 144 (mailing address)
Bethel, CT 06801
(203) 794-8508; (203) 794-8564 FAX (Finance Department)
Brenda M. Craig, Clerk

Bridgeport Probate District (015)
202 State Street
Bridgeport, CT 06604
(203) 576-3945; (203) 576-7898 FAX
Jeannette Sargent, Clerk
(contains the records of Stratford from May session 1782 to 4 June 1840, and the records of Easton, which include the records of Weston, Easton being a district of its own from 22 July 1875 until 4 March 1878)

Brookfield Probate District (018)
(Brookfield Municipal Center, 100 Pocono Road, Room 211—location)
PO Box 5192 (mailing address)
Brookfield, CT 06804
(203) 775-3700; 203) 775-5316
probate@brookfield.org

http://www.brookfield.org/Office/probate.htm
Meegan C. Buckley, Clerk

Danbury Probate District (034)
City Hall, 155 Deer Hill Avenue
Danbury, CT 06810
(203) 797-4521; (203) 796-1526 FAX (Finance Department)
http://www.ci.danbury.ct.us/content/45/468/default.aspx
Marjorie L. Cerveniski, Clerk

Darien Probate District (035)
Town Hall, 2 Renshaw Road, Room 204
Darien, CT 06820
(203) 656-7342
http://www.ci.darien.ct.us/officials/probate_judge.htm
Janet Ianniello, Clerk

Easton Probate Court
(see Trumbull Probate District)

Fairfield Probate District (051)
Independence Hall, 725 Old Post Road
Fairfield, CT 06824
(203) 256-3041; (203) 256-3080 FAX
Sybil Ann Mackenzie, Clerk

Greenwich Probate District (057)
(Town Hall, 101 Field Point Road, First Floor—location)
PO Box 2540 (mailing address)
Greenwich, CT 06836-2540
(203) 622-7879; (203) 622-3766; (203) 622-6451 FAX
http://www.greenwichct.org/probate/Probate.asp
Barbara Carbino, Clerk

Monroe Probate Court
(see Trumbull Probate District)

New Canaan Probate District (090)
Town Hall, 77 Main Street, First Floor (rear of building)
New Canaan, CT 06840
(203) 594-3050; (203) 594-3128 FAX
karen.smith@newcanaan.info
http://www.newcanaan.info
Karen P. Smith, Clerk

New Fairfield Probate District (091)
New Fairfield-Sherman Probate Court
New Fairfield Town Hall, 4 Brush Hill Road
New Fairfield, CT 06812
(203) 312-5627; (203) 312-5612 FAX
http://www.townofshermanct.org
Anna Lucchesi, Clerk
(probate records from 1846 to date)

Newtown Probate District (097)
Edmond Town Hall, 45 Main Street
Newtown, CT 06470
(203) 270-4280; (203) 270-4283 FAX
http://www.newtown-ct.gov/Public_Documents/NewtownCT_Judge/index
Margaret L. Gross, Clerk

Norwalk Probate District (103)
(City Hall, 125 East Avenue, Room 102—location)
PO Box 2009 (mailing address)
Norwalk, CT 06852-2009
(203) 854-7737; (203) 854-7825 FAX
Debra Lasprogato, Clerk
(includes Wilton)

Redding Probate District (117)
(Town Hall, 100 Hill Road—location)
PO Box 1125 (mailing address)
Redding, CT 06875
(203) 938-2326; (203) 938-8816 FAX
http://www.townofreddingct.org/Public_Documents/ReddingCT_Court/index
Michele R. Grande, Clerk

Ridgefield Probate District (118)
Town Hall, 400 Main Street
Ridgefield CT 06877
(203) 431-2776; (203) 431-2722 FAX
http://www.ridgefieldct.org/content/48/98/default.aspx
Jacqueline Buckle, Clerk

(probate district constituted 10 June 1841 from Danbury)

Shelton Probate District (126)
(60 Perry Hill Road—location)
PO Box 127 (mailing address)
Shelton, CT 06484
(203) 924-8462; (203) 924-8943 FAX
http://www.cityofshelton.org/gengov/probatecourt.htm
Loreen S. Michalak, Clerk

Sherman Probate Court
(see New Fairfield-Sherman Probate Court)

Stamford Probate District (135)
(Stamford Government Center, 888 Washington Boulevard, Eighth Floor—location)
PO Box 10152 (mailing address)
Stamford, CT 06904-2152
(203) 323-2149; (203) 964-1830 FAX
http://www.ci.stamford.ct.us/ProbateCourt/default.htm
Roselyn B. Ramist, Clerk

Stratford Probate District (138)
Birdseye Municipal Complex
468 Birdseye Street, Second Floor
Stratford, CT 06615
(203) 385-4023; (203) 375-6253 FAX
http://www.townofstratford.com/depts/probate.htm
Deirdre L. Bassett, Clerk

Trumbull Probate District (144)
Town Hall, 5866 Main Street, Mezzanine Level
Trumbull, CT 06611-5416
(203) 452-5068; (203) 452-5092 FAX
http://www.trumbullct.com/probate.htm
Judge John P. Chiota
(includes Easton and Monroe; naturalization records and probate records)

Weston Probate Court
(see Westport Probate District)

Westport Probate District (158)
Town Hall, 110 Myrtle Avenue, Room 100
Westport, CT 06880
(203) 341-1100; (203) 341-1153 FAX
http://www.westportct.gov/government/boards/pc.htm
ShirleyA. DeLuca, Clerk
(includes Weston)

Wilton Probate Court
(see Norwalk Probate District)

Hartford County

organized 1666, original county; includes Avon, Berlin, Bloomfield, Bristol, Burlington, Canton, East Granby, East Hartford, East Windsor, Enfield, Farmington, Glastonbury, Granby, Hartford, Hartland, Manchester, Marlborough, New Britain, Newington, Plainville, Rocky Hill, Simsbury, South Windsor, Southington, Suffield, West Hartford, Wethersfield, Windsor, and Windsor Locks

Avon Probate District (004)
Town Hall, 60 West Main Street
Avon, CT 06001
(860) 409-4348; (860) 409-4368 FAX
http://www.town.avon.ct.us/Public_Documents/AvonCT_Probate/probate
Maria L. Clarke, Assistant Clerk

Berlin Probate District (007)
(1 Liberty Square—location)
PO Box 400 (mailing address)
New Britian, CT 06050-0400
(860) 826-2696; (860) 826-2695 FAX
http://www.town.berlin.ct.us/content/1828/default.aspx
Ceil Hann, Clerk
(includes New Britain; naturalization records and probate records)

Bloomfield Probate District (011)
Town Hall, 800 Bloomfield Avenue
Bloomfield, CT 00602

(860) 769-3548; (860) 242-1167 FAX
probate@bloomfieldct.org
http://www.bloomfieldct.org/Pages/Bloomfiel dCT_Probate/index
Patricia Robillard, Clerk

Bristol Probate District (017)
City Hall Building
111 North Main Street, Third Floor
Bristol, CT 06010
(860) 584-6230; (860) 584-3818 FAX
http://www.ci.bristol.ct.content/3478/3655/de fault.aspx
Anne C. Holihan, Esq., Clerk

Burlington Probate District (020)
Town Hall, Route 4, 200 Spielman Highway
Burlington, CT 06013
(860) 673-2108; (860) 673-1527 FAX (First Selectman's Office)
Kay Matarese, Clerk

Canton Probate District (023)
(Town Hall, 4 Market Street—location)
PO Box 175 (mailing address)
Collinsville, CT 06022-0175
(860) 693-7851; (860) 693-7889 FAX
Rose Stepnick, Clerk

East Granby Probate District (040)
(Town Hall, 9 Center Street—location)
PO Box 542 (mailing address)
East Granby, CT 06026
(860) 653-3434; (860) 653-7085 FAX
info@egtownhall.org
http://www.eastgranby.net
Linda Y. Ridgeway, Clerk

East Hartford Probate District (043)
Town Hall, 740 Main Street
East Hartford, CT 06108
(860) 291-7278; (860) 291-7211 FAX (Town Hall)
Sally A. Madin, Clerk

East Windsor Probate District (047)
Town Hall, 1540 Sullivan Avenue
South Windsor, CT 06074
(860) 644-2511, ext. 271; (860) 648-5047 FAX
Annette Tarascio, Clerk
(includes South Windsor)

Enfield Probate District (049)
820 Enfield Street
Enfield, CT 06082
(860) 253-6305; (860) 253-6388 FAX
http://enfield-ct.gov/content/91/1008/default.aspx
Linda Chrzanowski, Clerk

Farmington Probate District (052)
Town Hall, 1 Monteith Drive
Farmington, CT 06034-0948
(860) 675-2360; (860) 673-8262 FAX
Francesca Lefante, Clerk

Glastonbury Probate District (054)
(Town Hall, 2155 Main Street—location)
PO Box 6523 (mailing address)
Glastonbury, CT 06033-6523
(860) 652-7629; (860) 368-2520 FAX
http://www.glasct.org/public_documents/glast onburyct_probate/index
Esther Buffington, Clerk

Granby Probate District (056)
(Town Hall, 15 North Granby Road—location)
PO Box 240 (mailing address)
Granby, CT 06035-0240
(860) 844-5314; (860) 653-8944; (860) 653-4769 FAX (Town Manager's Office)
http://www.granby-ct.gov/Public_Documents/ GranbyCT_Court/index
Judith Henry, Clerk

Hartford Probate District (064)
250 Constitution Plaza, Third Floor
Hartford, CT 06103-2814
(860) 757-9150; (860) 724-1503 FAX
Sondra J. Waterman, Clerk

Hartland Probate Court
(see New Hartford Probate District)

Manchester Probate District (077)
66 Center Street
Manchester, CT 06040
(860) 647-3227; (860) 647-3236 FAX
Sandra Haun, Clerk

Marlborough Probate District (079)
(26 North Main Street—location)
PO Box 29 (mailing address)
Marlborough, CT 06447
(860) 295-6239; (860) 295-6122 FAX (Town Hall)
Paula J. Verrier, Clerk

New Britain Probate Court
(see Berlin Probate District)

Newington Probate District (094)
66 Cedar Street, Rear
Newington, CT 06111
(860) 665-1285; (860) 665-1331 FAX
Rose Anne Adamowich, Clerk
(includes Rocky Hill and Wethersfield)

Plainville Probate District (110)
Municipal Center
1 Central Square, Room 201
Plainville, CT 06062
(860) 793-0221, ext. 250; (860) 793-2424 FAX
famiglietti@plainville-ct.gov
http://www.plainvillect.com/detpages/munigov 37.html
Carol A. LePage, Clerk
copies of probate records: $5.00 per document, up to five pages, certified copies $5.00 for the first two pages and $1.00 for each additional page

Rocky Hill Probate Court
(see Newington Probate District)

Simsbury Probate District (128)
(Belden Town Office Building, 933 Hopmeadow Street—location)
PO Box 495 (mailing address)
Simsbury, CT 06070-0495
(860) 658-3277; (860) 658-3204 FAX
http://www.simsburyct.virtualtownhall.net/Pub lic_Documents/Departments/SimsburyCT_P robate/index
Juliet Lavissiere, Clerk

South Windsor Probate Court
(see East Windsor Probate District)

Southington Probate District (131)
(Town Office Building, 75 Main Street—location)
PO Box 165 (mailing address)
Southington, CT 06489-0165
(860) 276-6253; (860) 276-6255 FAX
http://www.southington.org/departments/prob ate.shtml
Cynthia A. Houle, Clerk

Suffield Probate District (139)
(Town Hall Building, 83 Mountain Road, Lower Level—location)
PO Box 234 (mailing address)
Suffield, CT 06078-0234
(860) 688-3835; (860) 668-3029 FAX
http://www.suffieldtownhall.com/content/79/ 123/default.aspx
Judith A. Remington, Clerk

West Hartford Probate District (155)
Town Hall, 50 South Main Street, Room 318
West Hartford, CT 06107
(860) 561-7940; (860) 561-7941 FAX
whprobatecourt@westhartford.org
http://www.west-hartford.com/TownServices/ProbateCourt/P robateHomePage.htm
Janice D. Reynolds, Clerk
(probate records from 1983)

Wethersfield Probate Court
(see Newington Probate District)

Windsor Probate District (164)
(Town Hall, 275 Broad Street—location)
PO Box 342 (mailing address)
Windsor, CT 06095

(860) 285-1976; (860) 285-1909 FAX (Town Clerk's Office)
Katie Chiodo, Clerk

Windsor Locks Probate District (165)
Town Office Building, 50 Church Street
Windsor Locks, CT 06096-0412
(860) 627-1450; (860) 627-1451 FAX
Laurie Roberts, Clerk

Litchfield County

organized 1751 from Hartford and Fairfield counties; includes Barkhamsted, Bethlehem, Bridgewater, Canaan, Colebrook, Cornwall, Goshen, Harwinton, Kent, Litchfield, Morris, New Hartford, New Milford, Norfolk, North Canaan, Plymouth, Roxbury, Salisbury, Sharon, Thomaston, Torrington, Warren, Washington, Watertown, Winchester, and Woodbury

Barkhamsted Probate Court
(see New Hartford Probate District)

Bethlehem Probate Court
(see Woodbury Probate District)

Bridgewater Probate Court
(see New Milford Probate District)

Canaan Probate District (021)
(Town Hall, 107 Main Street, Falls Village, CT 06031—location)
PO Box 905 (mailing address)
Canaan, CT 06018-0905
(860) 824-7114; (860) 824-3139 FAX (First Selectman's Office)
Beth L. McGuire, Clerk
(includes North Canaan)

Colebrook Probate Court
(see Winchester Probate District)

Cornwall Probate District (031)
(Town Office Building, 26 Pine Street—location)
PO Box 157 (mailing address)
Cornwall, CT 06753-0157
(860) 672-2677; (860) 672-4069 FAX
Jill E. Gibbons, Clerk

Goshen Probate Court
(see Torrington Probate District)

Harwinton Probate District (066)
Town Offices, 100 Bentley Drive
Harwinton, CT 06791
(860) 485-1403; (860) 484-2716 FAX
Kay Matarese, Clerk
copies of probate records: $5.00 for from one to five pages and $1.00 for each additional page

Kent Probate District (068)
(Town Hall, 41 Kent Green Boulevard—location)
PO Box 678 (mailing address)
Kent, CT 06757
(860) 927-3729; (860) 927-1313 FAX (First Selectman's Office)
Carol L. Jarvis, Clerk
copies of probate records: 25¢ per page, $1.00 per page for certified copies

Litchfield Probate District (074)
(Town Office Building, 74 West Street—location)
PO Box 505 (mailing address)
Litchfield, CT 06759
(860) 567-8065; (860) 567-2538 FAX
Stephanie P. Brennan, Clerk
(includes Morris and Warren; naturalization records and probate records)

Morris Probate Court
(see Litchfield Probate District)

New Hartford Probate District (092)
(Town Hall, 530 Main Street—location)
PO Box 308 (mailing address)
New Hartford, CT 06057-0308
(860) 379-3254; (860) 379-8560 FAX (Judge's Law Office)
Suzanne Pombar, Clerk

(naturalizations and probate records; includes Barkhamsted and Hartland)

New Milford Probate District (096)
Town Hall, 10 Main Street
New Milford, CT 06776
(860) 355-6029; (860) 355-6024 FAX (Mayor's Office)
Marianne Arancio Stilson, Clerk
(includes Bridgewater)

Norfolk Probate District (098)
(Town Hall, 19 Maple Avenue—location)
PO Box 648 (mailing address)
Norfolk, CT 06058-0648
(860) 542-5134; (860) 542-5876 FAX (First Selectman's Office)
Barbara G. Gomez, Clerk

North Canaan Probate Court
(see Canaan Probate District)

Plymouth Probate District (111)
Town Hall, 80 Main Street
Terryville, CT 06786
(860) 585-4014; (860) 585-4099 FAX
http://www.plymouthct.us/government.htm#probate
Nancy B. Meyer, Clerk

Roxbury Probate District (120)
(Town Hall, 29 North Street—location)
PO Box 203 (mailing address)
Roxbury, CT 06783-0203
(860) 354-1184; (860) 355-3091 FAX
Marsh Dorin, Clerk

Salisbury Probate District (122)
(Town Hall, 27 Main Street—location)
PO Box 525 (mailing address)
Salisbury, CT 06068
(860) 435-5183; (860) 435-5172 FAX (Town Hall); (860) 435-6125 FAX (Judge's Law Office)
Maureen S. Erickson, Clerk

Sharon Probate District (125)
(Town Hall, 63 Main Street—location)
PO Box 1177 (mailing address)
Sharon, CT 06069-1177
(860) 364-5514; (860) 364-5789 FAX
Kathleen Visconti, Clerk

Thomaston Probate District (140)
(Town Hall Building, 158 Main Street—location)
PO Box 136 (mailing address)
Thomaston, CT 06787
(860) 283-4874; (860) 283-1013 FAX (Police Department)
Traci A. Fairchild, Clerk

Torrington Probate District (143)
City Hall, 140 Main Street, Second Floor
Torrington, CT 06790
(860) 489-2216; (860) 489-2215; (860) 496-5910 FAX
http://www.torringtonct.org/Public_Documents/TorringtonCT_Probate/index
Gale Pellegren, Clerk
(includes Goshen)

Warren Probate Court
(see Litchfield Probate District)

Washington Probate District (150)
(Bryan Memorial Town Hall, 2 Bryan Plaza, Main Level—location)
PO Box 295 (mailing address)
Wshington Depot, CT 06794-0295
(860) 868-7974; (860) 868-0512 FAX
probate@washingtonct.org
http://www.washingtonct.org/probate.html
Pamela L. Osborne, Clerk
copies of probate records: $1.00 per page

Watertown Probate Court
(see Woodbury Probate District)

Winchester Probate District (162)
(Town Hall, 338 Main Street, Second Floor—location)
PO Box 625 (mailing address)

Winsted, CT 06098-0625
(860) 379-5576; (860) 738-7053 FAX (Town Hall)
http://www.townofwinchester.org/town_departments_page.asp?SubCategoryID=probatecourt
Patricia Fradette, Clerk
(includes Colebrook)

Woodbury Probate District (168)
(Shove Building, 281 Main Street South—location)
PO Box 369 (mailing address)
Woodbury, CT 06798-0369
(203) 263-2417; (203) 263-2748 FAX
http://www.woodburyct.org
Gail D. Cesarello, Clerk
(includes Bethlehem and Watertown)
no records search service; copies: $1.00 per page

Middlesex County
organized 1785 from Hartford, New London and New Haven counties

Chester Probate Court
(see Saybrook Probate District)

Saybrook Probate District (026)
(203 Middlesex Avenue, Route 154—location)
PO Box 628 (mailing address)
Chester, CT 06412
(860) 526-0013, ext. 221; (860) 526-0004 FAX (First Selectman's Office)
Janet M. Gauger, Clerk
(includes Chester; naturalization records and probate records)

Clinton Probate District (027)
(Eliott House, 50 East Main Street—location)
PO Box 130 (mailing address)
Clinton, CT 06413-0130
(203) 669-6447 voice & FAX
Margaret A. Schroeder, Clerk

Cromwell Probate Court
(see Middletown Probate District)

Deep River Probate District (036)
(Town Hall, 174 Main Street—location)
PO Box 391 (mailing address)
Deep River, CT 06417
(860) 526-6026; (860) 526-6094 FAX
Marge Calltharp, Clerk

Durham Probate Court
(see Middletown Probate District)

East Haddam Probate District (041)
(Goodspeed Plaza—location)
PO Box 217 (mailing address)
East Haddam, CT 06423
(860) 873-5028; (860) 873-5025 FAX (First Selectman's Office)
probate@easthadam.org
http://www.easthadam.org
Marge B. Calltharp, Clerk

East Hampton Probate District (042)
Town Hall, 20 East High Street, Annex
East Hampton, CT 06424
(860) 267-9262; (860) 267-6453 FAX
probatejudge@easthamptonct.org
http://www.easthamptonct.org
Janice Visinski, Clerk
(probate records from 1915)

Essex Probate District (050)
Town Hall, 29 West Avenue
Essex, CT 06426
(860) 767-4347, ext. 125; (860) 767-8509 FAX (First Selectman's Office)
Valerie N. Shickel, Clerk
(Old Saybrook probate records from 4 July 1853 to 4 July 1859])

Haddam Probate District (061)
Town Office Building, Route 154, 30 Field Park Drive
Haddam, CT 06438
(860) 345-8531; (860) 345-3730 (First Selectman's Office)
Charles F. Riordan, Clerk

Killingworth Probate District (070)

Town Office Building, 323 Route 81
Killingworth, CT 06417
(860) 663-2304; (860) 663-3305 FAX (First Selectman's Office)
http://www.killingworthtoday.com/selectmen/townservices.html
Helene Yates, Clerk

Middlefield Probate Court
(see Middletown Probate District)

Middletown Probate District (083)
94 Court Street
Middletown, CT 06457
(860) 347-7424; (860) 346-1520 FAX
http://www.townofdurhamct.org/content/16445/default.aspx
Mary C. Woods, Clerk
(includes Cromwell, Durham, and Middlefield; naturalization records and probate records)

Old Saybrook Probate District (106)
251 Main Street
Old Saybrook, CT 06475
(860) 395-3128; (860) 395-3125 FAX
http://www.oldsaybrookct.org/Pages/OldSaybrookCT_Probate/index
Kathleen M. Delaney, Clerk

Portland Probate District (113)
(Town Hall, 33 East Main Street—location)
PO Box 71 (mailing address)
Portland, CT 06480-0071
(860) 342-6739; (860) 342-0001 FAX (Town Clerk's Office)
http://www.portlandct.org/Portland/departments/probate.htm
Judge Richard J. Guliani

Westbrook Probate District (154)
Town Hall, 866 Boston Post Road
Westbrook, CT 06498
(860) 399-5661; (860) 399-3092 FAX
Nancy Vadnais, Clerk

New Haven County
organized 1666, original county; Ansonia, Beacon Falls, Bethany, Branford, Cheshire, Derby, East Haven, Guilford, Hamden, Madison, Meriden, Middlebury, Milford, Naugatuck, New Haven, North Branford, North Haven, Orange, Oxford, Prospect, Seymour, Southbury, Wallingford, Waterbury, Wolcott, West Haven, and Woodbridge

Ansonia Probate Court
(see Derby Probate District)

Beacon Falls Probate Court
(see Naugatuck Probate District)

Bethany Probate District (008)
Town Hall, 40 Peck Road
Bethany, CT 06524-3338
(203) 393-2100, ext. 111; (203) 393-0821 FAX (Town Clerk's Office)
Judith Yale, Clerk

Branford Probate District (014)
(1019 Main Street—location)
PO Box 638 (mailing address)
Branford, CT 06405-0638
(203) 488-0318; (203) 315-4715 FAX
Leslie S. George, Clerk

Cheshire Probate District (025)
Town Hall, 84 South Main Street
Cheshire, CT 06410
(203) 271-6608; (203) 271-6628 FAX
http://www.cheshirect.org/probate/default.html
Margherita Bergstrand, Clerk
(includes Prospect)

Derby Probate District (037)
City Hall, 253 Main Street, Second Floor
Ansonia, CT 06401
(203) 734-1277; (203) 734-0922 FAX
Joan M. Lawlor, Clerk
(includes Ansonia and Seymour)

East Haven Probate District (044)
Town Hall, 250 Main Street
East Haven, CT 06512

(203) 468-3895; (203) 468-5155 FAX
http://www.townofeasthaven.com
Beverly J. Stanton, Clerk

Guilford Probate District (060)
Town Hall, 31 Park Street
Guilford, CT 06437
(203) 453-8006; (203) 453-8017 FAX (Tax Office)
Cynthia S. Dwyer, Clerk
copies of land and probate records: $1.00 per page

Hamden Probate District (062)
Hamden Government Center
2750 Dixwell Avenue
Hamden, CT 06518
(203) 287-7082; (203) 287-7087 FAX
http://www.hamden.com/content/43/85/140/1239/default.aspx
Christine L. Theriault, Clerk
(probate district constituted 8 January 1945 from New Haven)

Madison Probate District (076)
Madison Town Campus
8 Campus Drive
Madison, CT 06443
(203) 245-5661; (203) 245-5653 FAX
Mary J. DiMeola, Clerk

Meriden Probate District (080)
City Hall, 142 East Main Street, Room 113
Meriden, CT 06450
(203) 630-4150; (203) 630-4043 FAX
Janet Firulli, Clerk

Meriden Wallingford Regional Children's Probate Court
Probate District (202)
City Hall, 142 East Main Street, Room 113
Meriden, CT 06450
(203) 630-4620; (203) 238-8050 FAX
Emily E. Webster, Clerk

Middlebury Probate Court
(see Waterbury Probate District)

Milford Probate District (084)
(Parsons Complex, City Hall, 70 West River Street—location)
PO Box 414 (mailing address)
Milford, CT 06460
(203) 783-3205; (203) 783-3364 FAX
Karen Liskiewicz, Clerk

Naugatuck Probate District (088)
Town Hall, 229 Church Street
Naugatuck, CT 06770
(203) 720-7046; (203) 720-5476 FAX (Judge's Law Office)
Patricia Alegi, Clerk
(includes Beacon Falls)

New Haven Probate District (093)
(Kennedy Mitchell Hall of Records, 200 Orange Street, First Floor, New Haven, CT 06510—location)
PO Box 905 (mailing address)
New Haven, CT 06504-0905
(203) 946-4880; (203) 946-5962 FAX
Patricia Parkinson, Clerk

New Haven Regional Children's Probate Court
Probate District (200)
873 State Street
New Haven, CT 06511-3923
(203) 773-9556; (203) 773-9685 FAX
Amy Benjamin, Clerk

North Branford Probate District (099)
Town Hall, 909 Foxon Road
North Branford, CT 06471
(203) 484-6007; (203) 484-6017 FAX (Town Hall)
Diane B. Whalen, Clerk

North Haven Probate District (101)
(Town Hall, 18 Church Street—location)
PO Box 175 (mailing address)
North Haven, CT 06473-0175
(203)239-5321, ext. 775; (203) 239-1874 FAX

haven.ct.us/departments/community_serv_rec.s
html#probatecourt
Valerie A. Dondi, Clerk

Orange Probate District (107)
525 Orange Center Road
Orange, CT 06477
(203) 891-2160; (203) 891-2161 FAX
Marilyn Fusco, Clerk

Oxford Probate District (108)
Town Hall, 486 Oxford Road
Oxford, CT 06483
(203) 888-2543, ext. 3014; (203) 888-2136 FAX (Town Hall)
http://www.oxford-ct.gov/government/probate
Eugenia Purcella, Clerk

Prospect Probate Court
(see Cheshire Probate District)

Seymour Probate Court
(see Derby Probate District)

Southbury Probate District (130)
(421 Main Street, South—location)
PO Box 674 (mailing address)
Southbury, CT 06488-0674
(203) 262-0641; (203) 264-9310 FAX
Linda Leigh, Clerk

Wallingford Probate District (148)
Municipal Building
45 South Main Street, Room #108
Wallingford, CT 06492
(203) 294-2100; (203) 294-2109 FAX
http://www.town.wallingford.ct.us/Page.cfm?name=PROBATE%20COURT
Lucy Brann, Clerk

Wallingford Regional Children's Probate Court
(see Meriden Wallingford Regional Children's Probate Court)

Waterbury Probate District (151)
236 Grand Street
Waterbury, CT 06702
(203) 755-1127; (203) 597-0824 FAX
Cynthia Gilbode, Clerk
(includes Middlebury and Wolcott)

West Haven Probate District (156)
(City Hall, 355 Main Street, Second Floor—location)
PO Box 127 (mailing address)
West Haven, CT 06516
(203) 937-3552; (203) 937-3556 FAX
http://www.cityofwesthaven.com/contentpage.asp?page=Probate&nfolder=3
Maureen B. O'Connor, Clerk

Wolcott Probate Court
(see Waterbury Probate District)

Woodbridge Probate District (167)
Town Hall, 11 Meetinghouse Lane
Woodbridge, CT 06525
(203) 389-3410; (203) 389-3480 FAX
Jo-Marie Tamburrino, Clerk
(naturalization records and probate records)

New London County
organized 1666, original county; Bozrah, Colchester, East Lyme, Franklin, Griswold, Groton, Lebanon, Ledyard, Lisbon, Lyme, New London, Montville, North Stonington, Norwich, Old Lyme, Preston, Salem, Sprague, Stonington, Voluntown, and Waterford

Bozrah Probate District (013)
Town Hall, 1 River Road
Bozrah, CT 06334
(860) 889-2958; (860) 887-7571 FAX
Jessie Friedrich, Clerk

Colchester Probate District (028)
Town Hall, 40 Norwich Avenue
Colchester, CT 06415
(860) 537-7290; (860) 537-7298 FAX
probate@colchesterct.org
http://www.colchesterct.net/probate.html

Linda A. Neal, Clerk
(includes Lebanon; naturalization records and probate records)
no probate search service; copies of probate records: $1.00 per page

East Lyme Probate District (045)
(Town Hall, 108 Pennsylvania Avenue—location)
PO Box 519 (mailing address)
Niantic, CT 06357
(860) 739-6931; (860) 739-6930 FAX
Patricia A. Stratos, Clerk
copies of probate records: $1.00 per page

Franklin Probate Court
(see Norwich Probate District)

Griswold Probate District (058)
Town Hall, 28 Main Street, Second Floor
Jewett City, CT 06351
(860) 376-7060, ext. 213; (860) 376-6628 FAX
http://www.griswold-ct.org/judgeofprobate.html
Suzanne Devine, Clerk

Groton Probate District (059)
Town Hall, 45 Fort Hill Road
Groton, CT 06340
(860) 441-6655; (860) 441-6657 FAX
Helen M. Falvey, Clerk
(probate records from 1839 to date)
copies of probate records: $1.00 per page, certified copies: $5.00 for the first two pages and $2.00 for each additional page

Lebanon Probate Court
(see Colchester Probate District)

Ledyard Probate District (072)
Town Hall, 741 Colonel Ledyard Highway (Route 117)
Ledyard, CT 06339
(860) 464-3219; (860) 464-8531 FAX
Eleanora Marshall Quin, Clerk
(the records of Ledyard from May 1666 to October 1766 are in New London; from October 1766 to 6 June 1837 in Stonington)

Lisbon Probate Court
(see Norwich Probate District)

Lyme Probate District (075)
Town Hall, 480 Hamburg Road
Lyme, CT 06371
(860) 434-7733; (860) 434-2989 FAX (Town Hall)
Janet M. Gauger, Clerk
(probate records concerning Lyme, from 1 May 1666 to 4 June 1830, are in New London; from 4 June 1830 to 4 July 1869, are in Old Lyme; from 4 July 1869 to date, are in Lyme)

Montville Probate District (086)
Town Hall, 310 Norwich-New London Turnpike, First Floor
Uncasville, CT 06382
(860) 848-3030, ext. 319; (860) 848-2116 FAX
http://www.townofmontville.org/CMS/default.asp?CMS_AreaID=139
Linda Wisniewski, Clerk

New London Probate District (095)
(City Hall, 181 State Street, Second Floor—location)
PO Box 148 (mailing address)
New London, CT 06320
(860) 443-7121; (860) 437-8155 FAX
http://ci.new-london.ct.us/content/27/59/default.aspx
Doris Sanders, Clerk
(includes Waterford)

New London Regional Children's Probate Court
Probate District (204)
470 Bank Street
New London, CT 06320
(860) 437-6253; (860) 437-6259 FAX
Doris Sanders, Clerk

North Stonington Probate District (102)
(391 Norwich Westerly Road #2—location)

PO Box 204 (mailing address)
North Stonington, CT 06359-0204
(860) 535-8441 voice & FAX
Susan Cardinal, Clerk

Norwich Probate District (104)
(City Hall, 100 Broadway—location)
PO Box 38 (mailing address)
Norwich, CT 06360-0038
(860) 887-2160; (860) 887-2401 FAX
http://norwichct.org/content/155/495/default.
 aspx
Eileen M. Robbins, Clerk
(includes Franklin, Lisbon, Preston, and
 Sprague; naturalization records and probate
 records)

Old Lyme Probate District (105)
Old Lyme Memorial Town Hall, 52 Lyme Street
Old Lyme, CT 06371
(860) 434-1605, ext. 222 (Clerk); (860) 434-1605,
 ext. 223; (860) 434-9283 FAX (Town Clerk's
 Office)
http://www.oldlyme-
 ct.gov/Pages/OldlymeCT_Probate/index
Marilyn Campbell, Clerk

Preston Probate Court
(see Norwich Probate District)

Salem Probate District (121)
Town Office Building
270 Hartford Road, Route 85
Salem, CT 06415
(860) 859-3873; (860) 537-1433 FAX
Judge John W. Butts

Sprague Probate Court
(see Norwich Probate District)

Stonington Probate District (137)
(Town Hall Building, 152 Elm Street—location)
PO Box 312 (mailing address)
Stonington, CT 06378-0312
(860) 535-5090; (860) 535-0520 FAX
Carolyn Bessett, Clerk

Voluntown Probate Court
(see Ellington Probate District)

Waterford Probate Court
(see New London Probate District)

Tolland County

organized 1785 from Windham County;
 Andover, Bolton, Columbia, Coventry,
 Ellington, Hebron, Mansfield, Somers,
 Stafford, Tolland, Union, Vernon, and
 Willington

Andover Probate District (001)
(Notch Road Municipal Center, 104 Notch
 Road—location)
222 Bolton Center Road (mailing address)
Bolton, CT 06043
(860) 647-7979; (860) 649-8674 FAX
Patricia A. McPherson, Clerk
(includes Bolton and Columbia)
copies of probate records: $5.00 for the first five
 pages and $1.00 for each additional page

Bolton Probate Court
(see Andover Probate District)

Columbia Probate Court
(see Andover Probate District)

Coventry Probate Court
(see Mansfield Probate District)

Ellington Probate District (048)
(Memorial Building, 14 Park Place, Rockville,
 CT 06066—location)
PO Box 268 (mailing address)
Vernon, CT 06066-0268
(860) 872-0519; (860) 870-5140 FAX
http://www.jud.state.ct.us/probate/faq.html;
 http://www.ellington-
 ct.gov/town_services_page.asp?subCategoryI
 D=probate_court
Geraldine C. Miller, Clerk
(includes Vernon and Voluntown)

Hebron Probate District (067)

Town Office Building, 15 Gilead Street
Hebron, CT 06248
(860) 228-5971; (860) 228-4859 FAX (Mail
 Room)
Paula J. Verrier, Clerk

Mansfield Probate District (078)
Mansfield Town Hall
Audrey P. Beck Municipal Building
4 South Eagleville Road
Storrs, CT 06268
(860) 429-3313; (860) 429-4088 FAX
http://www.coventryct.org
Patricia H. Maines, Clerk
(includes Coventry)

Somers Probate Court
(see Stafford Probate District)

Stafford Probate District (134)
(Warren Memorial Town Hall, 1 Main Street—
 location)
PO Box 63 (mailing address)
Stafford Springs, CT 06076-0063
(860) 684-1783; (860) 684-1797 FAX
Brenda Wilde, Clerk
(includes Somers and Union)

Tolland Probate District (142)
Hicks Memorial Municipal Center
21 Tolland Green
Tolland, CT 06084
(860) 871-3640; (860) 871-3641 FAX
Diane D. DuBaldo, Clerk
(ncludes Willington)

Union Probate Court
(see Stafford Probate District)

Vernon Probate Court
(see Ellington Probate District)

Willington Probate Court
(see Tolland Probate District)

Windham County

organized 1726 from Hartford and New
 London counties; includes Ashford,
 Brooklyn, Canterbury, Chaplin, Eastford,
 Hampton, Killingly, Plainfield, Pomfret,
 Putnam, Scotland, Sterling, Thompson,
 Windham, and Woodstock

Ashford Probate District (003)
Ashford Town Office Building, 5 Town Hall
 Road
Ashford, CT 06278
(860) 487-4408; (860) 487-4436 FAX
Cheryl Bowen, Clerk
(includes Chaplin; probate records before 1832)

Brooklyn Probate District (019)
(Town Hall, 4 Wolf Den Road—location)
PO Box 356 (mailing address)
Brooklyn, CT 06234-0356
(860) 774-5973; (860) 779-3744 FAX
Khamleuang V. Kelley, Clerk

Canterbury Probate Court
(see Plainfield Probate District)

Chaplin Probate Court
(see Ashford Probate District)

Eastford Probate District (039)
(16 Westford Road—location)
PO Box 98 (mailing address)
Eastford, CT 06242
(860) 974-3024; (860) 974-0624 FAX
Probate@TownofEastford.com
http://www.munic.state.ct.us/eastford/judge.ht
 ml
Mary Ellen Ellsworth, Clerk

Hampton Probate District (063)
(Town Office Building, 164 Main Street—
 location)
PO Box 143 (mailing address)
Hampton, CT 06247
(860) 455-9132, ext. 8; (860) 455-0517 FAX
 (Town Clerk's Office)
probate@hamptonct.org
http://www.hamptonct.org/probate.htm

Lenore B. Case, Clerk

Killingly Probate District (069)
Town Hall, 127 Main Street
Killingly, CT 06239
(860) 779-5319; (860) 779-5394 FAX
 (Receptionist's Office)
Dorothy A. Roy, Clerk

Plainfield Probate District (109)
Town Hall, 8 Community Avenue
Plainfield, CT 06374
(860) 230-3031; (860) 230-3033 FAX (First
 Selectman's Office)
Michelle R. Gunn, Clerk
(includes Canterbury and Sterling)

Pomfret Probate District (112)
5 Haven Road, Route 44
Pomfret Center, CT 06259
(860) 974-0186; (860) 974-3950 FAX (First
 Selectman's Office)
http://www.pomfretct.com/pomfret.html
Judge Leah Schad

Putnam Probate District (116)
Town Hall, 126 Church Street
Putnam, CT 06260
(860) 963-6868; (860) 963-6817 FAX
Jennie Coffey, Clerk

Scotland Probate Court
(see Windham Probate District)

Sterling Probate Court
(see Plainfield Probate District)

Thompson Probate District (141)
(Town Office Building, 815 Riverside Drive, Rt.
 12—location)
PO Box 74 (mailing address)
North Grosvenor Dale, CT 06255
(860) 923-2203; (860) 923-7426 FAX
http://s113439721.onlinehome.us/25901.html
Theresa E. Muraco, Clerk

Windham Probate District (163)
(Town Building, 979 Main Street—location)
PO Box 34 (mailing address)
Willimantic, CT 06226
(860) 465-3049; (860) 465-3012 FAX
Pamela Shorey, Clerk
(includes Scotland)
copies of probate records: $1.00 each, $5.00
 minimum

Woodstock Probate District (169)
415 Route 169
Woodstock, CT 06281
(860) 928-2223; (860) 963-7557 FAX (Mail
 Room)
Roger W. Gale, Clerk

DELAWARE

Capital: Dover. Statehood: 7 December 1787 (separated from Pennsylvania in 1776)

Delaware's Alderman's Courts, by town or city charter, have jurisdiction over minor civil cases, minor misdemeanors, municipal and traffic matters. The Municipal Court of Wilmington has jurisdiction over misdemeanors, municipal violations, preliminary hearings for felonies and drug-related misdemeanors, plus traffic violations. Nineteen Justice of the Peace Courts throughout the state handle civil actions, some misdemeanors, motor vehicle cases (except felonies), and landlord-tenant cases. Family Courts in each county seat handle, among other matters, divorce, annulment, separate maintenance, property settlement, custody, adoptions, and termination of parental rights. Courts of Common Pleas in each county seat handle some civil actions and misdemeanors. The Delaware Court of Chancery, which sits at each county seat, handles equity cases, guardianships, trusts and estates. The Superior Court has general jurisdiction and sits at each county seat. The Supreme Court sits at Dover and receives appeals.

Kent County
organized 1680 from Horre Kill District, which was organized in 1664; name changed from St. Jones County in 1682

Kent County Recorder of Deeds
O'Brien Building
414 Federal Street, Room 218
Dover, DC 19901-3615
(302) 744-2314; (302) 736-2035 FAX
http://www.co.kent.de.us/Departments/RowOffices/Recorder
Betty Lou McKenna
copies: $1.00 per page mailed, $5.00 per page for certification

Kent County Register of Wills
O'Brien Building
414 Federal Street
Dover, DE 19901-3615
(302) 736-2230
carol.dill@co.kent.de.us
http://www.co.kent.de.us/Departments/RowOffices/Wills/index.htm
Carol A. Dill, Chief Deputy
(wills and estates)

New Castle County
organized 1673, original county

New Castle County Recorder of Deeds
Louis L. Redding City/County Building
800 French Street
Wilmington, DE 19899
(302) 395-7730
SupportPerson@NewCastle.co.de.org
http://www.ncc-deeds.com/recclkshr/default.asp
Anthony Camponelli, Support

New Castle County Register of Wills
(Louis L. Redding City/County Building, 800 French Street, Second Floor, Wilmington, DC 19899—location)
87 Reads Way (mailing address)
New Castle, DE 19720
(302) 395-7800; (302) 395-7801 FAX
Wills@nccde.org
http://www.co.new-castle.de.us/wills/home/webpage1.asp
Diane Clarke Streett, Esq.
no probate search service; copies of probate records: $1.00 per page

Sussex County
organized 1680 from Horre Kill District, which was organized in 1664, name changed from Deale County in 1682

Sussex County Recorder of Deeds
(2 The Circle—location)
PO Box 827 (mailing address)
Georgetown, DE 19947
(302) 855-7785; (302) 855-7787 FAX
http://www.sussexcountyde.gov
John Brady

Sussex County Register of Wills
(Court of Chancery Building, 34 The Circle—location)
PO Box 743 (mailing address)
Georgetown, DE 19947-0505
(302) 855-7875; (302) 853-5871 FAX
http://www.sussexcountyde.gov/departments/index.cfm?id=18
Howard Clendaniel

Deseret
(see Utah)

DISTRICT OF COLUMBIA

Authorized as a federal district in 1790 from Prince George's and Montgomery counties, Maryland, and from Fairfax County, Virginia; Alexandria retroceded to Virginia in 1846

The Superior Court of the District of Columbia has five divisions: Civil, Criminal, Family, Probate and Tax. The Family Division has jurisdiction over juveniles, divorce, custody and support, paternity, adoption, commitment of the mentally ill, etc. The District of Columbia Court of Appeals has some primary jurisdiction and hears appeals from the Superior Court.

District of Columbia Courthouse
Moultrie Courthouse, 500 Indiana Avenue, N.W.
Washington, DC 20001-2131
(202) 879-1010
http://www.dccourts.gov/dccourts/index.jsp

DC Superior Court
Moultrie Courthouse
500 Indiana Avenue, NW, Room 4485
Washington, DC 20001
(202) 879-1400 (Clerk); (202) 879-4800 (Register of Wills); (202) 879-4840 (Marriage Information); (202) 879-1261 (Divorce Information)
http://www.dccourts.gov/dccourts/superior
Duane B. Delaney, Clerk of the Court;
Constance G. Starks, Register of Wills
marriages: $10.00

FLORIDA

Capital: Tallahassee. Statehood: 3 March 1845 (annexed as part of the Louisiana Purchase, 1803, and the Adams-Onis Treaty, 1819, became a territory in 1822)

Florida's County Courts handle some civil actions, small claims, misdemeanors, ordinance violations, felony preliminaries and traffic. Circuit Courts meet in each county and have jurisdiction over felonies and actions over $5,000, plus juvenile cases, domestic relations, probate, guardianship, mental health and equity. First Judicial Circuit: Escambia, Okaloosa, Santa Rosa and Walton counties; Second Judicial District: Franklin, Gadsden, Jefferson, Leon, Liberty and Wakulla counties; Third Judicial District: Columbia, Dixie, Hamilton, Lafayette, Madison, Suwannee and Taylor counties; Fourth Judicial District: Clay, Duval and Nassau counties; Fifth Judicial District: Citrus, Hernando, Lake, Marion and Sumter counties; Sixth Judicial District: Pasco and Pinellas counties; Seventh Judicial District: Flagler, Putnam, St. Johns and Volusia counties; Eighth Judicial District: Alachua, Baker, Bradford, Gilchrist, Levy and Union counties; Ninth Judicial District: Orange and Osceola counties; Tenth Judicial District: Hardee, Highlands and Polk counties; Eleventh Judicial District: Dade County; Twelfth Judicial District: DeSoto, Manatee and Sarasota counties; Thirteenth Judicial District: Hillsborough County; Fourteenth Judicial District: Bay, Calhoun, Gulf, Holmes, Jackson and Washington counties; Fifteenth Judicial District: Palm Beach County; Sixteenth Judicial District: Monroe County; Seventeenth Judicial District: Broward County; Eighteenth Judicial District: Brevard and Seminole counties; Nineteenth Judicial District: Indian River, Martin, Okeechobee and St. Lucie counties; Twentieth Judicial District: Charlotte, Collier, Glades, Hendry and Lee counties.

Five District Courts of Appeal have appellate jurisdiction. First District at Tallahassee: First, Second, Third, Fourth, Eighth and Fourteenth Judicial Circuits; Second District at Lakeland: Sixth, Tenth, Twelfth, Thirteenth and Twentieth Judicial Circuits; Third District at Miami: Eleventh and Sixteenth Judicial Circuits; Fourth District at West Palm Beach: Fifteenth, Seventeenth and Nineteenth Judicial circuits; Fifth District at Daytona Beach: Fifth, Seventh, Ninth and Eighteenth Judicial Circuits. The Supreme Court, which sits at Tallahassee, is the court of last resort.

Alachua County

organized 1824 from Duval and St. Johns counties; land records from 1826; marriages from 1837

Alachua County Clerk of the Circuit Court
(Alachua County Courthouse, 201 East University Avenue—location)
PO Box 600 (mailing address)
Gainesville, FL 32602-0600
(352) 374-3636; (352) 338-3201 FAX
jpowelljr@gru.net
http://www.clerk-alachua-fl.org/Clerk/index.cfm; http://www.clerk-alachua-fl.org/archive/default.cfm (Ancient Records)
Jim Powell, Jr., Ancient Records Coordinator
(probate records from early 1800s)
probate search service: $1.00 per year per name, $4.00 minimum; copies of probate records: $1.00 per page, $2.00 for certified copies, $1.00 minimum

Baker County

organized 1861 from New River County

Baker County Clerk of the Circuit Court
339 East Macclenny Avenue

Macclenny, FL 32063
(904) 259-8113; (904) 259-4176 FAX
clerk@bakercountyfl.org
http://bakercountyfl.org/clerk
Al Fraser
(land records, naturalization records, vital records from 1877, probate records)

Bay County

organized 1913 from Calhoun and Washington counties; name changed from New River County in 1861

Bay County Clerk of the Circuit Court
300 East Fourth Street
Panama City, FL 32401
(850) 763-9061; (850) 747-5188 FAX
baycoclerk@baycoclerk.com
http://www.baycoclerk.com
Harold Bazzel
(land records, marriages and deaths, probate records)

Bradford County

organized 1858 from New River County

Bradford County Clerk of the 8th Circuit Court
(945 North Temple Avenue—location)
PO Drawer B (mailing address)
Starke, FL 32091
(904) 966-6280; (904) 966-4456 FAX
Ray_Norman@bradford-co-fla.org
http://www2.myfloridacounty.com/wps/wcm/connect/bradfordclerk
Ray Norman
(land records, marriages probate records from March 1875)
probate search service: $1.00 per year; copies of probate records: $1.00 per page, $2.00 for certified copies, no minimum

Brevard County

St. Lucie County organized 1844 from Mosquito County, name changed to Brevard County in 1855 (present-day St. Lucie County organized from Brevard County in 1905)

Brevard County Clerk of the Circuit Court
(Historic Titusville Court House, 506 South Palm Avenue, and Administration/Human Resources/Full-service counter, 400 South street, Second Floor, and Recording Department, Parkway Complex, 700 South Park Avenue, Building B—location)
PO Box 2767 (mailing address)
Titusville, FL 32781-2767
(321) 637-5413 (Main); (321) 637-2004 (Land Records); (321) 637-5413 (Probate); (321) 264-5246 FAX (Land Records)
scott.ellis@brevardclerk.us
http://199.241.8.125
Scott Ellis, Clerk of Courts
(land records, marriage license applications from 1938, probate records)
probate search service: $1.00 per year of search; copies of probate records: $1.00 per page, no minimum

Broward County

organized 1915 from Dade and Palm Beach counties

Broward County Clerk of the Circuit Court
Broward County Courthouse
201 S.E. Sixth Street, Room 230
Fort Lauderdale, FL 33301
(954) 831-7154 (Probate, Room 252); (954) 712-7899, ext. 7802 (Archived Records, 515 S.W. Second Avenue, Ft. Lauderdale, FL 33301)
http://www.browardclerk.org
Howard C. Forman
(probate records)
probate search service: $1.00 per year per name; copies of probate records: $1.00 per page, $1.00 for certification, no minimum; include period of time to be searched

Broward County Records Division
Broward County Government Center

115 South Andrews Avenue, Room 114
Fort Lauderdale, FL 33301-1801
(954) 831-1267; (407) 357-7286 (Search Department)
records@broward.org;
http://www.broward.org/records/cri02800.htm
Mon–Fri 7:30–5:00
(documents recorded only from 1978)

Calhoun County

organized 1838 from Jackson County

Calhoun County Clerk of the Circuit Court
20859 S.E. Central Avenue E, Room 130
Blountstown, FL 32424
(850) 674-4545; (850) 674-5553 FAX
http://www2.myfloridacounty.com/wps/wcm/connect/calhounclerk
Ruth Attaway

Charlotte County

organized 1921 from DeSoto County

Charlotte County Clerk of the Circuit Court
(Charlotte County Justice Center, 350 East Marion Avenue, Room 141—location)
PO Box 511687 (mailing address)
Punta Gorda, FL 33951-1687
(941) 637-2199
CasWeb@co.charlotte.fl.us
http://www.co.charlotte.fl.us/clrkinfo/clerk_default.htm
Barbara T. Scott, Clerk of the Circuit Court
(land records from 1921, marriages from 1921, probate records from 4 July 1921)
probate search service: $1.00 per year; copies of probate records: 25¢ each for unrecorded records, $1.00 each for recorded records, no minimum

Citrus County

organized 1887 from Hernando County

Citrus County Clerk of the Circuit Court
Inverness Courthouse, 110 North Apopka Avenue, Room 101
Inverness, FL 34450-4299
(352) 341-6400; (352) 341-6491 FAX
ClerkofCourts@clerk.citrus.fl.us
http://www.clerk.citrus.fl.us/home.jsp
Betty Strifler
(land records from 1887, marriages from 1887, probate records)

Clay County

organized 1858 from Duval County

Clay County Clerk of the Circuit Court
(Courthouse, 825 North Orange Avenue—location)
PO Box 698 (mailing address)
Green Cove Springs, FL 32043-0698
(904) 284-6317; (904) 284-6390 FAX
http://clerk.co.clay.fl.us
James B. Jett
(land records from 1835 [except from 1858 to 1872], some naturalization records in Circuit Court minutes, 1858 to date, probate records from 1858)
no probate search service; copies of probate records: $1.00 per page, no minimum; some old records are not indexed

Collier County

organized 1923 from Lee and Monroe counties

Collier County Clerk of the Circuit Court
3301 Tamiami Trail, Building L, Fifth Floor
Naples, FL 34112
(239) 732-2646; (239) 775-2755 FAX
collierclerk@clerk.collier.fl.us
http://www.clerk.collier.fl.us
Dwight E. Brock

Columbia County

organized 1832 from Alachua County

Columbia County Clerk of the Circuit Court
(173 NE Hernando Avenue—location)
PO Drawer 2069 (mailing address)

Lake City, FL 32056-2069
(386) 758-1342; (386) 719-7457 FAX
http://www2.myfloridacounty.com/wps/wcm/
connect/columbiaclerk
P. DeWitt Cason, Clerk of Courts
(deeds from 1 January 1875, plats from 1886,
mortgages from 7 December 1872, marriages
from 1876, delayed births from 1943, estate
files from 1895, dockets from 1871,
guardianships from 1868)
probate search service: $1.00 per year; copies of
probate records: $1.00 per page (to 8½" x
14"), $5.00 per page (over 8½" x 14"), $1.00
for certification, no minimum; visitors
welcome

Dade County
organized 1836 from Monroe County

**Miami-Dade County Clerk of the Circuit
Court**
Miami-Dade County Courthouse
73 West Flagler, Suite 242
Miami, FL 33130
(305) 275-1155
recording@miamidade.gov
http://www.miami-dadeclerk.com/dadecoc
Harvey Ruvin, Clerk

DeSoto County
organized 1887 from Manatee County

DeSoto County Clerk of the Circuit Court
(115 East Oak Street, Room 101—location)
PO Box 591 (mailing address)
Arcadia, FL 33821
(863) 993-4876; (863) 993-4669 FAX
Mitzie.McGavic@desotoclerk.com
http://www.desotoclerk.com
Mitzie W. McGavic
(deeds, marriage licenses, probate records)
probate search service: $1.00 per year; copies of
probate records: $1.00 per page, no minimum

Dixie County
organized 1921 from Lafayette County

Dixie County Clerk of the Circuit Court
PO Box 1206
Cross City, FL 32628
(352) 498-1200; (352) 498-1201 FAX
jallen@inetw.net
http://www2.myfloridacounty.com/wps/wcm/
connect/dixieclerk
Joe Hubert Allen

Duval County
organized 1822 from St. Johns County

Duval County Clerk of the Circuit Court
Downtown Courthouse, 330 East Bay Street,
Room 103
Jacksonville, FL 32202-2909
(904) 630-2028; (904) 630-2979 FAX
http://www.duvalclerk.com/ccWebsite
Jim Fuller
(land records, probate records)
land and probate records search service: $1.00
per year of index

Escambia County
organized 1822, original county

Escambia County Clerk of the Circuit Court
M. C. Blanchard Judicial Building
190 Governmental Center
Pensacola, FL 32501
(850) 595-4310; (850) 595-3930 (Official
Records Division, 223 South Palafox Place,
Pensacola, FL 32501-5845); (850) 595-4316
FAX; (850) 595-4827 FAX (Official Records
Division)
publicrecords@clerk.co.escambia.fl.us
http://www.clerk.co.escambia.fl.us
Ernie Lee Magaha

Flagler County
organized 1917 from St. Johns and Volusia
counties

Flagler County Clerk of the Circuit Court
(Flagler County Courthouse, 201 East Moody
Boulevard—location)
PO Box 787 (mailing address)
Bunnell, FL 32010-0787
(386) 437-7410; (386) 437-7406 FAX
clerk@clerk.co.flagler.fl.us
http://clerk.co.flagler.fl.us
Gail Wadsworth

Franklin County
organized 1832 from Jackson County

Franklin County Clerk of the Circuit Court
(33 Market Street, Suite 203—location)
PO Box 340 (mailing address)
Apalachicola, FL 32320-0340
(850) 653-8861, ext. 102; (850) 653-2261 FAX
http://www2.myfloridacounty.com/wps/wcm/
connect/franklinclerk
Marcia M. Johnson

Gadsden County
organized 1823 from Jackson County

Gadsden County Clerk of the Circuit Court
(Gadsden County Courthouse, 10 East Jefferson
Street—location)
PO Box 1649 (mailing address)
Quincy, FL 32353-1649
(850) 875-8601; (850) 875-8612 FAX
clerkofcourt@clerk.co.gadsden.fl.us
http://www.clerk.co.gadsden.fl.us
Nicholas Thomas

Gilchrist County
organized 1925 from Alachua County

Gilchrist County Clerk of the Circuit Court
(112 South Main Street—location)
PO Box 37 (mailing address)
Trenton, FL 32693-0037
(352) 463-3170; (800) 267-3182; (352) 463-3166
FAX
joeg@mail.co.gilchrist.fl.us
http://www2.myfloridacounty.com/wps/wcm/
connect/gilchristclerk
Joseph (Joe) W. Gilliam
land, vital records, or probate search service:
$1.00 per name per year for requests in
writing

Glades County
organized 1921 from DeSoto County

Glades County Clerk of the Circuit Court
(500 Avenue J—location)
PO Box 10 (mailing address)
Moore Haven, FL 33471-0010
(863) 946-6010; (863) 946-0560 FAX
gladesclerk@gladesclerk.com
http://www2.myfloridacounty.com/wps/wcm/
connect/gladesclerk
Joe Flint
(land records from 1921, probate records)
probate search service: $1.00 per year; copies of
probate records: $1.00 per page, no minimum

Gulf County
organized 1925 from Calhoun County

Gulf County Clerk of the Circuit Court
1000 Cecil G. Costin, Sr., Boulevard, Room 148
Port St. Joe, FL 32456
(850) 229-6112; (850) 639-5068; (850) 229-6174
FAX
http://www2.myfloridacounty.com/wps/wcm/
connect/gulfclerk
Rebecca L. Norris
(land records, probate records)
probate search service: $1.00 per year; copies:
$1.00 per page, no minimum (requests must
be in writing and include payment)

Hamilton County
organized 1827 from Duval County

Hamilton County Clerk of the Circuit Court
207 First Street NE, Room 106
Jasper, FL 32052-6669

(386) 792-1288; (386) 792-3524 FAX
Hamiltonclerk@flcjn.net
http://www.hamiltoncountyflorida.com/ced_cl
erk.html
Greg Godwin

Hardee County
organized 1921 from DeSoto County

Hardee County Clerk of the Circuit Court
(417 West Main Street—location)
PO Box 1749 (mailing address)
Wauchula, FL 33873-1749
(863) 773-4174; (863) 773-4422 FAX
http://www2.myfloridacounty.com/wps/wcm/
connect/hardeeclerk
B. Hugh Bradley
(land records, probate records)
probate search service: $1.00 per year; copies of
probate records: $1.00 per page, no minimum

Hendry County
organized 1923 from Calhoun County

Hendry County Clerk of the Circuit Court
(Clewiston Town Center, 931 West Sugarland
Highway, Clewiston and Courthouse
Complex, 25 East Hickpoochee Avenue, SR
80 corner SR 29, LaBelle—location)
PO Box 1760 (mailing address)
LaBelle, FL 33935-1760
(863) 675-5217; (863) 983-1586
clerk@hendryclerk.org
http://www.hendryclerk.org
Barbara S. Butler

Hernando County
organized 1843 from Benton County, which no
longer exists but was organized 1843 from
Alachua County

Hernando County Clerk of the Circuit Court
20 North Main Street, Room 130
Brooksville, FL 34601-2800
(352) 754-4201; (352) 754-4247 FAX
karenn@co.hernando.fl.us
http://www.clerk.co.hernando.fl.us
Karen Nicolai
(land records, probate records)
land and probate search service: $1.00 per year;
copies of land and probate records: $1.00 per
page, $1.00 minimum

Highlands County
organized 1921 from DeSoto County

Highlands County Clerk of the Circuit Court
590 South Commerce Avenue
Sebring, FL 33870-3867
(863) 386-6564; (863) 402-6768 FAX
clerk@hcclerk.org
http://www.clerk.co.highlands.fl.us/index_new.
html
L. E. "Luke" Brooker
(land records from 1921 in Recording Division,
probate records from 1921 in Probate
Division)
probate search service: $1.00 per year; copies of
probate records: $1.00 per page, no minimum

Hillsborough County
organized 1834 from Alachua and Monroe
counties

**Hillsborough County Clerk of the Circuit
Court**
(George E. Edgecomb Courthouse, 800 Twiggs
Street, Second Floor-Probate, Tampa, FL
33602, and 501 East Kennedy Boulevard,
Sixth Floor-Recording, Tampa, FL, 33602—
location)
PO Box 1110 (mailing address)
Tampa, FL 33601-1110
(813) 276-8100 (automated voice system for
property records information—touch 4, Clerk
of Circuit Court); (813) 272-6518 FAX
clekadmin@hillsclerk.com;
probated@hillsclerk.com
http://www.hillsclerk.com

Pat Frank
(land records [current records from Mr. Alton "Bud" Parker, Property Appraiser], probate records)
probate search service: $1.00 per person per year; copies of probate records: $1.00 per page, $3.00 minimum (three years or more)

Holmes County
organized 1848 from Walton and Calhoun counties

Holmes County Clerk of the Circuit Court
(201 North Oklahoma Street—location)
PO Box 397 (mailing address)
Bonifay, FL 32425-2243
(850) 547-1100; (850) 547-6630 FAX
wcta_99@yahoo.com
http://www2.myfloridacounty.com/wps/wcm/connect/holmesclerk
Cody Taylor
(land records from 1901, probate records, some patent deed records from late 1800s)
land records: copies $1.00 each; probate search service: $1.00 per year; copies of probate records: 15¢ per page, $1.00 for certified copies, no minimum

Indian River County
organized 1925 from St. Lucie County

Indian River County Clerk of the Circuit Court
(2000 16th Avenue, Vero Beach, FL 32960—location)
PO Box 1028 (mailing address)
Vero Beach, FL 32961-1028
(772) 770-5185; (772) 770-5008 FAX
clerk@clerk.Indian-River.org
http://www.clerk.indian-river.org
Jeffrey K. Barton, Clerk of Circuit Court, Recording Division
(land records in Recording Division, marriage licenses and probate records in Civil Division)
land and probate records search service: $1.00 per year

Jackson County
organized 1822 from Escambia County, and in 1834 annexed Fayette County, which was organized in 1832

Jackson County Clerk of the Circuit Court
PO Box 510
Marianna, FL 32446-0510
(850) 482-9552; (850) 482-7849 FAX
clerkjack@digitalexp.com
http://www2.myfloridacounty.com/wps/wcm/connect/jacksonclerk
Dale Rabon Guthrie

Jefferson County
organized 1827 from Leon County

Jefferson County Clerk of the Circuit Court
(10 Court House Circle—location)
PO Box 547 (mailing address)
Monticello, FL 32344
(850) 342-0218, ext. 32 (Clerk of Court); (850) 342-0218, ext. 25 (Marriage Clerk); (850) 342-0218, ext. 28 (Probate Clerk); (850) 342-0222 FAX
http://myjeffersoncounty.com;
http://www.co.jefferson.fl.us
Dale Boatwright
(property transactions from 1827, marriage licenses from 1827, probate records)
search service: $1.00 per year; copies: $1.00 per page

Lafayette County
organized 1856 from Madison County

Lafayette County Clerk of the Circuit Court
PO Box 88
Mayo, FL 32066-0088
(386) 294-1600; (386) 294-4231 FAX
rnlclerk@yahoo.com
http://www2.myfloridacounty.com/wps/wcm/connect/lafayetteclerk
Ricky Lyons

Lake County
organized 1887 from Orange and Sumter counties

Lake County Clerk of the Circuit Court
(Administration Building, 416 West Main Street—location)
PO Box 7800 (mailng address
Tavares, FL 32778-7800
(352) 742-4100 (General Information); (352) 742-4117 (Recording Division); (352) 742-4122 9Probate); (352) 742-4110 voice & FAX
webmaster@lakecountyclerk.org
http://www.lakecountyclerk.org/default1.asp
Jim Watkins
(deeds in Recording Division, marriages in Executive Division, probate records in Probate Division)
probate search service: $1.00 per year; copies of probate records: $1.00 per page

Lee County
organized 1887 from Monroe County

Lee County Justice Center
(2115 Second Street, Fort Myers, FL 33901—location)
PO Box 2469 (mailing address)
Fort Myers, FL 33902-2469
(813) 335-2283 (Probate Division)
LeeClerk_Info@leeclerk.org
http://www.leeclerk.org
Charlie Green
(land record; probate records from 1889)
probate search service: no charge; copies of probate records: $1.00 per page, no minimum

Leon County
organized 1824 from Gadsden County

Leon County Clerk of the Circuit Court
301 South Monroe Street
Tallahassee, FL 32302
(850) 577-4000 (Administration); (850) 577-4180 (Probate); (850) 577-4061 (Archives); (850) 577-4013 FAX
http://www.clerk.leon.fl.us
Bob Inzer
(land records from 1825, marriages from 1825, probate records from 1825)
probate search service: $1.00 per year; copies of probate records: $1.00 per page, no minimum

Levy County
organized 1845 from Alachua and Marion counties

Levy County Clerk of the Circuit Court
(Levy County Courthouse, 355 South Court Street—location)
PO Box 610 (mailing address)
Bronson, FL 32621-0610
(352) 486-5229; (352) 486-5166 FAX
LevyClerk@Circuit8.org
http://levyclerk.com
Danny J. Shipp
(land and probate records)
probate search service: $1.00 per name; copies of probate records: $1.00 per page

Liberty County
organized 1855 from Franklin and Gadsden counties

Liberty County Clerk of the Circuit Court
PO Box 399
Bristol, FL 32321-0399
(850) 643-2215; (850) 643-2866 FAX
liertycounty67@yahoo.com
http://www2.myfloridacounty.com/wps/wcm/connect/libertyclerk
Robert Hill

Madison County
organized 1827 from Jefferson County

Madison County Clerk of the Circuit Court

(125 S.W. Range Avenue—location)
PO Box 237 (mailing address)
Madison, FL 32341-0237
(850) 973-1500; (850) 973-2059 FAX
clerksoffice@digitalexp.com
http://www2.myfloridacounty.com/wps/wcm/connect/madisonclerk
Tim Sanders

Manatee County
organized 1855 from Hillsborough County

Clerk of Circuit Court and Comptroller
(1115 Manatee Avenue West—location)
PO Box 25400 (mailing address)
Bradenton, FL 34206
(941) 749-1800; (941) 741-4082 FAX
helpdesk@manateeclerk.com
http://www.clerkofcourts.com/index.htm
Chips Shore, Clerk

Marion County
organized 1844 from Alachua County

Marion County Clerk of the Circuit Court
(110 N.W. First Avenue—location)
PO Box 1030 (mailing address)
Ocala, FL 32670-1030
(352) 671-5604; (352) 671-5600 FAX
mcclerkinfo@yahoo.com
http://www.marioncountyclerk.org
David R. Ellspermann
(land records from 1845, probate records from 1845)
probate search service: $1.00 per year; copies of probate records: $1.00 per page, $2.00 for certified copies, no minimum

Martin County
organized 1925 from Palm Beach County

Martin County Clerk of the Circuit Court
100 East Ocean Boulevard, Suite 200
Stuart, FL 33495-9016
(772) 288-5576; (772) 288-5991 FAX
http://clerk-web.martin.fl.us/ClerkWeb
Marsha Ewing
(land records, marriage licenses)
land records and marriages search service: $1.00 per year; copies of land records: $1.00, plats $5.00

Monroe County
organized 1823 from St. Johns County

Monroe County Clerk of the Circuit Court
(500 Whitehead Street, Key West, FL 33040—location)
PO Box 1980 (mailing address)
Key West, FL 33041
(305) 292-3550
http://www.clerk-of-the-court.com
Danny L. Kalhage, Clerk
(land records, deaths, probate records)
probate search service: $1.00 per year, per name; copies of probate records: $1.00 per page, $2.00 for certified copies, no minimum

Nassau County
organized 1824 from Duval County

Nassau County Clerk of the Circuit Court
PO Box 456
Fernandina Beach, FL 32034-0456
(904) 548-4600; (904) 548-4508 FAX
clerk@nassauclerk.com
http://www.nassauclerk.org
J. M. Oxley, Jr., Clerk; Ms. Nancy Beasley, Deputy Clerk, Land; Margie Armstrong, Deputy Clerk, Marriages; Ms. June Stewart, Deputy Clerk, Probate
(land records from 1840, marriages from 1887, probate records from 1872)
probate search service: $1.00 per year; copies of probate records: $1.00 per page

Okaloosa County
organized 1915 from Santa Rosa and Walton counties

Okaloosa County Clerk of the Circuit Court
Okaloosa County Courthouse
101 East James Lee Boulevard
Crestview, FL 32536
(850) 689-5000
http://www.clerkofcourts.cc
Don W. Howard
(land records: Deeds, mortgages, judgments, plats, etc., marriages, probate records from 1915)
probate search service: $1.00 per year; copies of probate records: $1.00 per page, $1.00 extra for certification

Okeechobee County

organized 1917 from Osceola and Palm Beach counties

Okeechobee County Clerk of the Circuit Court
312 N.W. Third Street
Okeechobee, FL 34972
(863) 763-2131; (863) 763-1557 FAX
webmaster@clerk.co.okeechobee.fl.us
http://www.clerk.co.okeechobee.fl.us
Sharon Robertson

Orange County

organized 1824 from Indian lands; name changed from Mosquito County in 1845

Orange County Clerk of the Circuit Court
(425 North Orange Avenue—location)
PO Box 4994 (mailing address)
Orlando, FL 32801
(407) 836-5115 (Land Records); (407) 836-2025 (Vital Records/Civil); (407) 836-2058 (Probate); (407) 836-2060 (Administration); (407) 836-2269 FAX (Administration)
ContactAdminDiv@orange-clerk.org; ContactProbateDiv@orange-clerk.org; ContactCoCivDiv@orange-clerk.org
http://orangeclerk.orangecountyfl.net
Lydia Gardner
(land records [100 East Pine Street, Orlando, FL 32801], vital records [832 West Central Boulevard, Orlando, FL 32805], probate records from 1873 to date)
probate search service: $1.00 per year; copies of probate records: $1.00 per page, $1.00 additional per document for certification, no minimum

Osceola County

organized 1887 from Brevard and Orange counties

Osceola County Clerk of the Circuit Court
2 Courthouse Square, Suite 2000
Kissimee, FL 34741
(407) 343-3500 (Main Switchboard); (407) 343-3699 FAX
kmik@osceolaclerk.org (Recording Division)
http://www.osceolaclerk.com
Larry Whaley
(deeds, mortgages, satisfactions, etc., marriages, naturalizations, wills, probate of estates, guardianships, trusts)
copies: $1.00 per page (up to 8½" x 14"), $1.00 for certification

Palm Beach County

organized 1909 from Dade County

Palm Beach County Clerk of the Circuit Court
Central Courthouse
205 North Dixie Highway
West Palm Beach, FL 33401
(561) 355-2996; (561) 355-4638 (Records Services)
clerkweb@co.palm-beach.fl.us (subject: Terri Marlen, Records Services)
http://www.pbcountyclerk.com
Sharon R. Bock

Pasco County

organized 1887 from Hernando County

Pasco County Clerk of the Circuit Court
Pasco County Courthouse
38053 East Live Oak Avenue
Dade City, FL 33523-3894
(800) 368-4274
http://www.pascoclerk.com
Jed Pittman
(land records, naturalizations, vital records, probate records)

Pinellas County

organized 1911 from Hillsborough County

Pinellas County Clerk of the Circuit Court
Clearwater Courthouse
315 Court Street
Clearwater, FL 34616-5192
(727) 464-3267; (727) 464-4876 (Official Records Department); (727) 464-4162 FAX
http://www.pinellasclerk.org/aspInclude2/ASPInclude.asp?pageName=index.htm
Ken Burke
(land records from 1912 and old Hillsborough records that pertain to property that is now in Pinellas County, marriages from 1912 and death certificates which have been recorded in connection with the sale of real estate, probate records from 1912)
probate search service: $1.00 per year; copies of probate records: $1.00 per page, $2.00 for certified copies, no minimum

Polk County

organized 1861 from Brevard and Hillsborough counties

Polk County Clerk of the Circuit Court
(255 North Broadway Avenue—location)
PO Box 988 (mailing address)
Bartow, FL 33830
(863) 534-4540; (863); 534-4584 FAX
http://www.polkcountyclerk.net
Richard Weiss

Putnam County

organized 13 January 1849 from Alachua, Duval, Marion, Mosquito [now Orange] and St. Johns counties

Putnam County Clerk of the Circuit Court
(410 St. Johns Avenue, Palatka, FL 32177—location)
PO Box 758 (mailing address)
Palatka, FL 32078-0758
(386) 329-0361; (386) 329-0330 (Archivist); (386) 329-0258 (Recording); (386) 329-0350 (Marriage Department); (386) 329-0888 FAX
timsmith@putnam-fl.com
http://www1.putnam-fl.com/live/clkmain.asp
Mon–Fri 8:30–5:00
(land records from 1849 in Recording, 518 St. Johns Avenue, Palatka, FL 32078, naturalization records 1849–1910, from Janice S. Mahaffey, Archivist, Archives Office, PO Box 1976, Palatka, FL 32078-1976 [after 1915 contact the Bureau of Vital Statistics in Jacksonville], marriage records from 1849 in Marriage Department, probate records in Archives Department or Law Department)
probate search service from Law Department: $1.00 per year; probate search service from Archives Department: $5.00; copies from Law Department: $1.00 per page; copies from Archives Department: 25¢ per page

St. Johns County

organized 1822, original county

St. Johns County Clerk of the Circuit Court
4010 Lewis Speedway
St. Augustine, FL 32084
(904) 819-3600; (904) 819-3641 (Records Center); (904) 819-3661 FAX
reccoc2@sjccoc.us (Records Center)
http://www.clk.co.st-johns.fl.us/index.htm
Cheryl Strickland
(land records from 1820, marriages from 1840 [some years in 1800s missing], probate records from 1845 [some years in 1800s]

destroyed by fire])
search service: $1.00 per year; copies: $1.00 per page, $1.00 per document for certification

St. Lucie County

organized 1844 from Mosquito County; name changed to Brevard County in 1855; present-day St. Lucie County organized from Brevard County in 1905

St. Lucie County Clerk of the Circuit Court
(Research/Microfilm Department, Orange Blossom Business Center, 4132 Okeechobee Road, Fort Pierce, FL 34947—location)
PO Box 700 (mailing address)
Fort Pierce, FL 34954
(772) 462-6900; (772) 462-6960 (Microfilm); (772) 462-6930 (Research); (772) 462-1614 FAX
frye@stlucieco.gov
http://www.slcclerkofcourt.com/research/research.htm
Honorable Edwin M. Fry, Jr.

Santa Rosa County

organized 1845 from Escambia County

Santa Rosa County Clerk of the Circuit Court
PO Box 472
Milton, FL 32572
(801 Caroline S.E.—location)
PO Box 148 (mailing address)
Milton, FL 32570-4978
(850) 983-1987; (850) 981-5533 (Archives); (850) 626-9994 FAX
mary.johnson@co.orange.fl.us
http://www2.myfloridacounty.com/wps/wcm/connect/santarosaclerk
Mary M. Johnson
(land records from July 1869 to date [all earlier records destroyed by fire], marriages from 1869 to date, marriage applications from 1922 to date, probate records from 1869 to date)

Sarasota County

organized 1921 from Manatee County

Sarasota County Clerk of the Circuit Court
2000 Main Street
Sarasota, FL 34237
(941) 861-7400
cklinfo@scgov.net
http://www.sarasotaclerk.com
Karen E. Rushing
(deeds, mortgages, marriages, probate records)

Seminole County

organized 1913 from Orange County

Seminole County Clerk of the Circuit Court
(Downtown Courthouse, 301 North Park Avenue, Sanford, FL 32771, and Criminal Justice Center, 101 Bush Boulevard, Sanford, FL 32773—location)
PO Box 8099 (mailing address)
Sanford, FL 32772-8099
(407) 665-4330; (407) 323-4330, ext. 4407 (Land Records, PO Drawer C, Sanford, FL 32772-0659); (407) 323-4330, ext. 4376 (Probate Division); (407) 330-7193 FAX
clerk@seminoleclerk.org
http://www.seminoleclerk.org
Maryanne Morse
(land records, marriage licenses and a few death certificates having to do specifically with land recordings, probate records)
probate search service: $1.00 per year; copies of probate records: $1.00 per page, no minimum (money order or cashier's checks acceptable) plus SASE

Sumter County

organized 1853 from Marion and Orange counties

Sumter County Clerk of the Circuit Court
209 North Florida Street
Bushnell, FL 33513-9308

Georgia

41

(352) 793-0215 (Records Division); (352) 793-0233 FAX (Records Division)
http://www.sumterclerk.com/public
Gloria R. Hayward

Suwannee County
organized 1858 from Columbia County

Suwannee County Clerk of the Circuit Court
Suwannee County Courthouse
200 South Ohio/MLK Jr. Avenue
Live Oak, FL 32064
(386) 362-0500; (386) 362-0567 FAX
http://www.suwclerk.org
Kenneth Dasher
(land records from 1859, delayed birth certificates and death certificates, probate records from 1859)
probate search service: $1.00 per year, per name; copies of probate records: $1.00 per recorded instrument, 15¢ per unrecorded instrument, no minimum

Taylor County
organized 1856 from Madison County

Taylor County Clerk of the Circuit Court
Taylor County Courthouse
PO Box 620
Perry, FL 32347-0620
(850) 838-3506; (850) 838-3549 FAX
cindym@perry.qulfnet.com
http://www2.myfloridacounty.com/wps/wcm/connect/taylorclerk
Annie Mae Murphy
(land and probate records)

Union County
organized 1921 from Bradford County

Union County Clerk of the Circuit Court
Union County Courthouse
55 Main Street, West, Room 103
Lake Butler, FL 32054-1637
(386) 496-3711; (386) 496-1718 FAX
rhp@circuit8.org
http://www2.myfloridacounty.com/wps/wcm/connect/unionclerk
Regina H. Parrish
(land records; probate records)
probate search service: $1.00 per year; copies of probate records: $1.00 per page, no minimum

Volusia County
organized 1854 from St. Lucie County

Volusia County Clerk of the Circuit Court
(Volusia County Courthouse, 101 North Alabama, De Land, FL 32724—location)
PO Box 6043 (mailing address)
De Land, FL 32720-6043
(386) 736-5915; (386) 822-5711 FAX
http://www.clerk.org/index.jsp
Diane M. Matousek
(land records in Recording Department, naturalization records limited to name and date only, marriages and divorces, probate records)
probate search service: $1.00 per year, per name; copies of probate records: $1.00 per page, no minimum

Wakulla County
organized 1843 from Leon County

Wakulla County Clerk of the Circuit Court
(3056 Crawfordville Highway—location)
PO Box 337 (mailing address)
Crawfordville, FL 32326-0337
(850) 926-0300; (850) 926-0938 FAX
drichardson@wakullaclerk.com (Official Records)
http://www2.myfloridacounty.com/wps/wcm/connect/wakullaclerk
Brent X. Thurmond

Walton County
organized 1824 from Jackson County

Walton County Clerk of the Circuit Court

(571 U.S. Highway 90 East, De Funiak Springs, FL 32435—location)
PO Box 1260 (mailing address)
De Funiak Springs, FL 32434-1260
(850) 892-8115; (850) 892-8130 FAX
http://clerkofcourts.co.walton.fl.us
Martha Ingle

Washington County
organized 1825 from Jackson and Walton counties

Washington County Clerk of the Circuit Court
(203 West Cypress, Chipley, FL 32428-1821—location)
PO Box 647 (mailing address)
Chipley, FL 32428-0647
(850) 638-6285; (850) 638-6297 FAX
http://www2.myfloridacounty.com/wps/wcm/connect/washingtonclerk
Linda Hayes Cook
(land records, marriages, probate records)
probate search service: $1.00 per year, per name; copies of probate records: $1.00 per page, no minimum

Franklin
(The lost state of Franklin, see North Carolina and Tennessee)

GEORGIA

Capital: Atlanta. Statehood: 2 January 1788 (chartered by England in 1732, ceded western lands to Alabama and Mississippi in 1802, southern boundary settled in 1866)

Georgia has 361 Municipal Courts with local jurisdiction. The Municipal Court of Columbus has countywide jurisdiction in civil and some landlord-tenant cases as well as misdemeanor guilty pleas and preliminary hearings. The City Court of Atlanta deals with traffic violations. The Civil Courts of Bibb and Richmond counties exist in lieu of the original City Courts there and sit at the county seats. The County Recorder's Courts in Chatham, DeKalb, Gwinnett and Muscogee counties are courts of limited jurisdiction. There is a Magistrate Court in each of the counties to deal with criminal and civil matters, as well as a Juvenile and a Probate Court. The State Courts sit in each county seat and deal with some civil actions and misdemeanors.

The Superior Courts are the courts of general trial jurisdiction and sit at each county seat. The Court of Appeals and the Supreme Court of Georgia sit in Atlanta.

Appling County
organized 1818 from Creek Cession

Appling County Clerk of Superior Court
38 South Main Street, Suite B
Baxley, GA 31513
(912) 367-8126; (912) 367-8180 FAX
http://www.baxley.org/site/page5515.html
F. Floyd Hunter

Appling County Probate Court
38 South Main Street, Suite A
Baxley, GA 31513
(912) 367-8114; (912) 367-8166 FAX
dianehallman@hotmail.com
http://www.baxley.org/site/page5515.html
Judge Diane Hallman Brock

Atkinson County
organized 1917 from Coffee and Clinch counties

Atkinson County Clerk of Superior Court
PO Box 855
Pearson, GA 31642
(912) 422-3552
http://www.atkinson-ga.org
Wilson Paulk
(land records and naturalization records)

Atkinson County Probate Court
PO Box 855
Pearson, GA 31642
(912) 422-3552; (912) 422-7842 FAX
http://atkinsoncounty.georgia.gov
Judge Jeffery Paulk McGowan
(vital records; probate records from 1919)
probate search service: $3.00; copies of probate records: 25¢ each, $3.00 for certified copies, no minimum

Bacon County
organized 1914 from Appling, Pierce and Ware counties

Bacon County Clerk of Superior Court
(12 and Dixon Street—location)
PO Box 376 (mailing address)
Alma, GA 31510-0376
(912) 632-7661; (912) 632-4915
http://www.gsccca.org/clerks
Sherry Tillman
(land records)

Bacon County Probate Court
PO Box 146
Alma, GA 31510
(912) 632-7661; (912) 632-7662 FAX
probae@baconcounty.org
http://baconcounty.georgia.gov

Judge Joe Boatright
(vital records and probate records)
probate search service: $3.00; copies of probate
    records: $3.00, $3.00 minimum

Baker County
organized 1825 from Early County

Baker County Clerk of Superior Court
(Hoke Smith Drive, Room 2—location)
PO Box 10
Newton, GA 31770-0010
(229) 734-3004; (229) 734-7770 FAX
http://www.gsccca.org/clerks
Betty Bush

Baker County Probate Court
(Hoke Smith Drive, Room 1—location)
PO Box 548 (mailing address)
Newton, GA 31770-0548
(229) 734-3007; (229) 734-8822 FAX
http://bakercounty.georgia.gov
Judge Angela Hendricks

Baldwin County
organized 1803 from Creek Indian Lands and
    Hancock, Washington and Wilkinson
    counties

Baldwin County Clerk of Superior Court
121 North Wilkinson Street, Suite 209
Milledgeville, GA 31061
(478) 445-6324; (478) 445-6039 FAX
http://www.baldwincountyga.com/clerk.htm
Rosemary Fordham Phillips
(land records)

Baldwin County Probate Court
121 North Wilkinson Street, Suite 109
Milledgeville, GA 31061
(478) 445-4807; (478) 445-5178 FAX
baldwinprobate@yahoo.com
http://www.baldwincountyga.com/probate.htm
Judge Todd Blackwell
(births and deaths from 1917, marriages from
    1806, wills and estates from 1806)
probate search service: no charge; copies of
    probate records: 25¢ per page, $4.00 for
    certified copies, no minimum

Banks County
organized 1858 from Franklin and Habersham
    counties

Banks County Clerk of Superior Court
144 Yonah-Homer Road
Homer, GA 30547
(706) 677-6243
http://www.bankscountyga.org/gov.htm
Tim Harper

Banks County Probate Court
144 Yonah-Homer Road
Homer, GA 30547
(706) 677-6250
http://www.bankscountyga.org
Judge Betty Thomas
(births, deaths and marriages, wills and estates)
probate search service: $3.00; copies of probate
    records: 25¢ per page, $3.00 for certified
    copies

Barrow County
organized 1914 from Gwinnett, Jackson and
    Walton counties

Barrow County Clerk of Superior Court
233 East Broad Street
Winder, GA 30680
(770) 307-3035; (770) 867-4800 FAX
gloria.wall@gsccca.org
http://www.barrowga.org
Gloria Moon Wall
(deeds)

Barrow County Probate Court
233 East Broad Street
Winder, GA 30680
(770) 307-3045
http://www.barrowga.org
Janet T. Cape

(vital records and probate records)

Bartow County
organized 1832 from Indian Lands; name
    changed from Cass County in 1861

Bartow County Clerk of Superior Court
135 West Cherokee Avenue
Cartersville, GA 30120
(770) 387-5025; (770) 387-5611 FAX
http://www.bartowga.org/bccsc/index.html
Gary Bell
(land records Books A & B missing, C to P
    many gaps, P to present intact, a few scattered
    naturalization records in Superior Court
    Minutes)
no land records search service (contact Bartow
    County Genealogical Society)

Bartow County Probate Court
135 West Cherokee Avenue, Suite 243A
Cartersville, GA 30120
(770) 387-5075; (770) 387-5074 FAX
scogginsm@bartowga.org; clarkr@bartowga.org
http://www.bartowga.org/probate/index.html
Judge Mitchell Scoggins; Rhonda N. Clark, Chief
    Clerk
(marriages from 1832, births and deaths from
    1919 with Judge, Probate Court, wills from
    1836, probate from 1853 with Judge, Probate
    Court)
probate search service: no charge; copies of
    probate records: $1.00 per page, no minimum

Ben Hill County
organized 1906 from Irwin and Wilcox counties

Ben Hill County Clerk of Superior Court
(115 South Sheridan Street—location)
PO Box 1104 (mailing address)
Fitzgerald, GA 31750
(229) 426-5135; (229) 426-5487 FAX
Laverne.Wheeler@gsccca.org
http://www.benhillcounty.com/superiorcourt.htm
Laverne D. Wheeler

Ben Hill County Probate Court
111 South Sheridan Street
Fitzgerald, GA 31750
(229) 426-5137; (229) 426-5486 FAX
probate@benhillcounty.com
http://www.benhillcounty.com/probate.htm
Judge Tommy W. Ash; Virginia Luke, Chief
    Clerk

Berrien County
organized 1856 from Coffee, Irwin and
    Lowndes counties

Berrien County Clerk of Superior Court
PO Box 446
Nashville, GA 31639-0446
(229) 686-5421
http://www.gsccca.org/clerks
Carol Ross

Berrien County Probate Court
(205 North Jefferson Street—location)
PO Box 446 (mailing address)
Nashville, GA 31639-0446
(229) 686-5213; (229) 686-9495 FAX
bprobate@alltel.net
http://gaprobate.org/court_detail.asp?county=1
    0; http://berriencounty.georgia.gov
Judge Susan W. Griner

Bibb County
organized 1822 from Houston, Jones, Monroe
    and Twiggs counties

Bibb County Clerk of Superior Court
(601 Mulberry Street, Room 216, Macon, GA
    31201—location)
PO Box 4708 (mailing address)
Macon, GA 31298
(912) 749-6527; (478) 621-5823 FAX
dbrannen@co.bibb.ga.us
http://www.co.bibb.ga.us/superiorcourtclerk.asp
Dianne Brannen
(land records with Aline Byrd, Clerk of Court,

275 Second Street, Macon, GA 31201, births
    and deaths with Theresa Aultman, County
    Health Department, 175 Emery Highway,
    Macon, GA 31201, probate records with
    William J. Self, II, Probate Judge)

Bibb County Probate Court
(601 Mulberry Street, Macon, GA 31201—
    location)
PO Box 6518 (mailing address)
Macon, GA 31208
(478) 749-6494
wself@co.bibb.ga.us
http://www.co.bibb.ga.us/ProbateCourt/Proba
    teCourt.asp
Judge William J. Self, II

Bleckley County
organized 1912 from Pulaski County

Bleckley County Clerk of Superior Court
306 S.E. Second Street
Cochran, GA 31014-1622
(478) 934-3200; (478) 934-7942; (478) 934-4516
http://www.bleckley.org;
    http://www.gsccca.org/clerks
Diane Brown
(land records)

Bleckley County Probate Court
306 S.E. Second Street
Cochran, GA 31014
(478) 934-3204; (478) 934-3205 FAX
tfoskey@yahoo.com
http://www.bleckley.org;
    http://bleckleycounty.georgia.gov
Judge Kenneth Powell

Brantley County
organized 1920 from Charlton, Pierce and
    Wayne counties

Brantley County Clerk of Superior Court
117 Brantley Street
Nahunta, GA 31553
(912) 462-5256
http://www.brantleycounty.org/govt/govt.htm
M. Anthony Ham

Brantley County Probate Court
117 Brantley Street
Nahunta, GA 31553
(912) 462-5192
http://www.brantleycounty.org/govt/govt.htm
Judge Johnnie E. Crews
(vital records, probate records)
probate search service: $3.00

Brooks County
organized 1858 from Lowndes and Thomas
    counties

Brooks County Clerk of Superior Court
PO Box 630
Quitman, GA 31643
(229) 263-4747
http://quitmangeorgia.org/2005/govt/index.
    php (Chamber of Commerce)
Elizabeth D. Baker
(land records)

Brooks County Probate Court
PO Box 665
Quitman, GA 31643-0665
(229) 263-5567; (229) 263-5058 FAX
http://quitmangeorgia.org/2005/govt/index.
    php (Chamber of Commerce)
Judge Jo Ann K. Collins
no probate search service; copies of probate
    records: $3.00, no minimum

Bryan County
organized 1793 from Chatham, Effingham and
    Liberty counties

Bryan County Clerk of Superior Court
(151 South College Street—location)
PO Drawer 670 (mailing address)
Pembroke, GA 31321
(912) 653-3872; (912) 653-3870 FAX
Becky.Crowe@gsccca.org

http://wwwbryancountyga.org
Rebecca G. Crowe
(land records)

Bryan County Probate Court
(151) South College Street—location)
PO Box 418 (mailing address)
Pembroke, GA 31321
(912) 653-3856; (912) 653-4691 FAX; (912) 653-3845 FAX
samdavis@bryan-county.org
http://wwwbryancountyga.org
Sam C. Davis, Jr., Probate Judge; Carole H. Groover, Clerk
(vital records and probate records)
probate search service: $3.00; copies of probate records: 50¢ per page, $3.00 for certified copies

Bulloch County
organized 8 Feb 1796 from Bryan and Screven counties

Bulloch County Clerk of Superior Court
20 Siebald Street
Statesboro, GA 30458
(912) 765-9009; (912) 764-5953 FAX
info@bullochcounty.net
http://www.bullochcounty.net;
Sherri A. Akins, Superior Court Clerk
(court records from 1806, land records from 1796)

Bulloch County Probate Court
(Bulloch County Courthouse, 2 North Main Street, Room 103—location)
PO Box 1005 (mailing address)
Statesboro, GA 30459
(912) 489-8749; (912) 764-8740 FAX
probatecourt@bulloch.net
http://www.bullochcounty.net/departments/probate.htm
Judge Lee H. DeLoach; Patricia A. Lanier, Chief Clerk
(marriages, estates and guardianships)
probate search service: no charge; copies of probate records: 25¢ per page, no minimum; SASE helpful

Burke County
organized 1777 from St. George Parish

Burke County Clerk of Superior Court
(602 Liberty Street—location)
PO Box 803 (mailing address)
Waynesboro, GA 30830-0062
(706) 554-2279
sherri.cochran@gscca.org
http://www.burkechamber.org/burke-county/department-profile.php?Department_ID=2
Sherri J. Cochran
(no records before 24 January 1856, when courthouse burned; deeds and land records)

Burke County Probate Court
(602 Liberty Street—location)
PO Box 322 (mailing address)
Waynesboro, GA 30830
(706) 554-3000
http://www.burkechamber.org/burke-county/department-profile.php?Department_ID=7
Judge Preston B. Lewis, III; Denise S. Quick
(vital records and probate records)
probate search service: no charge; copies of probate records: 25¢ per page, no minimum

Butts County
organized 1825 from Henry and Monroe counties

Butts County Clerk of Superior Court
(County Administration Complex, 625 West Third Street—location)
PO Box 320 (mailing address)
Jackson, GA 30233
(770) 775-8215; (770) 504-1359 FAX
rhonda.waits@gscca.org
http://www.buttscounty.org/courts

Rhonda T. Waits-Smith
(land records)

Butts County Probate Court
(County Administration Complex, 625 West Third Street—location)
PO Box 91 (mailing address)
Jackson, GA 30233
(770) 775-8204; (770) 775-8004 FAX
buttsprobate@bellsouth.net
http://www.buttscounty.org/courts
Judge Vicki W. Johnston
(vital records, probate records)
probate search service: no charge; copies of probate records: 25¢ per page, $1.00 minimum; enclose SASE

Calhoun County
organized 1854 from Baker and Early counties

Calhoun County Clerk of Superior Court
(111 School Street—location)
PO Box 69 (mailing address)
Morgan, GA 31766-0069
(229) 849-2715; (229) 849-0072 FAX
clerk_calhoun@mail.gsccca.org
http://www.gsccca.org/clerks
James C. Shippey
(land records)

Calhoun County Probate Court
(31 Court Street, Suite C—location)
PO Box 87 (mailing address)
Morgan GA 31766-0087
(229) 849-2115; (229) 849-2117 FAX
projudgeholder@alltel.net
http://calhouncounty.georgia.gov
Judge Annie Doris Holder
(vital records and probate records)
probate search service: $3.00 (includes cost of copies)

Camden County
organized 1777 from St. Mary, St. Thomas parishes

Camden County Clerk of Superior Court
(109 Courthouse Square—location)
PO Box 550 (mailing address)
Woodbine, GA 31569-0578
(912) 576-5622; (912) 576-5648 FAX
http://www.co.camden.ga.us/departments/departments.htm
Susan Waldron

Camden County Probate Court
(109 Courthouse Square—location)
PO Box 818 (mailing address)
Woodbine, GA 31569-0818
(912) 576-3785; (912) 576-4484 FAX
http://www.co.camden.ga.us/departments/departments.htm
Shirley Wise

Campbell County
(see Fulton County)

Candler County
organized 1914 from Bulloch, Emanuel, and Tattnall counties

Candler County Clerk of Superior Court
705 North Lewis Street
Metter, GA 30439-3333
(912) 685-2835
http://www.gsccca.org/clerks
Linda Sewell

Candler County Probate Court
Courthouse Square
Metter, GA 30439
(912) 685-2357; (912) 685-5130 FAX
http://candlercounty.georgia.gov; http://www.metter-candler.com (Chamber of Commerce)
Judge Charles E. Beasley

Carroll County
organized 1826 from Indian Lands and Paulding County

Carroll County Clerk of Superior Court

PO Box 338
Carrollton, GA 30112-0006
(404) 830-5830
info@carrollcountyga.com
http://carrollcountyga.com
Kenneth Skinner
(deeds from 1828)

Carroll County Probate Court
(Carroll County Courthouse, 311 Newnan Street—location)
PO Box 338 (mailing address)
Carrollton, GA 30112
(770) 830-5840; (770) 830-5995 FAX
bcason@carrollcountyga.com
http://carrollcountyga.com
Judge Bette B. Cason; Carole C. Walker, Chief Clerk
no probate search service (contact private researcher)

Cass County
(see Bartow and Gordon counties)

Catoosa County
organized 1853 from Walker and Whitfield counties

Catoosa County Clerk of Superior Court
7694 Nashville Street
Ringgold, GA 30736
(404) 935-4231
http://www.catoosa.com/judicial.htm#Clerk%20of%20Superior
Norman Stone

Catoosa County Probate Court
875 Lafayette Street
Ringgold, GA 30736
(706) 935-3511; (706) 935-3519 FAX
genelowery@catt.com
http://www.catoosa.com/depts/probate%20court/probate-index.htm
Judge Gene Lowery; Sandra Cobos, Probate Clerk

Charlton County
organized 1854 from Camden and Ware counties

Charlton County Clerk of Superior Court
100 Third Street
Folkston, GA 31537-3706
(912) 496-2549
charltoncomm@planttel.net
http://www.gsccca.org/clerks
Mildred Carter

Charlton County Probate Court
100 Third Street
Folkston, GA 31537-3706
(912) 496-2230; (912) 496-1167 FAX
http://charltoncounty.georgia.gov
Judge Robert F. Phillips

Chatham County
organized 1777 from St. Phillips and Christ Church parishes

Chatham County Clerk of Superior Court
133 Montgomery Street
Savannah, GA 31401-3230
(912) 652-7197; (912) 652-7380 FAX
http://www.chathamcounty.org/supctclk.html
Dan W. Massey

Chatham County Probate Court
133 Montgomery Street, Room 509
Savannah, GA 31401-3242
(912) 652-7265; (912) 652-7262 FAX
JT_Missroon@chathamcounty.org
http://www.chathamcounty.org/probatecourt.html
Judge Harris Lewis; Kim H. Birge, Chief Clerk/Administrator

Chattahoochee County
organized 1854 from Marion and Muscogee counties; consolidted with the City of Cussetta in 2003

Chattahoochee County Clerk of Superior Court
(Courthouse, Broad Street—location)
PO Box 120 (mailing address)
Cusseta, GA 31805
(706) 989-3602
Marilyn.Hauck@gsccca.org
http://www.ugocc.us
Marilyn Hauck
(land records)

Chattahoochee County Probate Court
(Courthouse, Broad Street—location)
PO Box 119 (mailing address)
Cusseta, GA 31805
(706) 989-3603; (706) 898-2015 FAX
KenVanhorn@yahoo.com
http://www.ugocc.us
Judge Kenneth Van Horn
probate search service: $3.00; copies of probate
records: 25¢ per page, $3.00 minimum

Chattooga County
organized 1838 from Floyd and Walker counties

Chattooga County Clerk of Superior Court
PO Box 211
Summerville, GA 30747-0211
(706) 857-0706; (706) 857-0686 FAX
http://www.gsccca.org/clerks
Sam Cordle

Chattooga County Probate Court
PO Box 467
Sumerville, GA 30747-0467
(706) 857-0709 voice & FAX
jonm1966p@yahoo.com
http://chattoogacounty.georgia.gov
Judge Jon M. Payne

Cherokee County
organized 1832 from Cherokee Lands and
Carroll, DeKalb, Habersham, Hall and
Swinnett counties

Cherokee County Clerk of Courts
Cherokee County Justice Center
90 North Street
Canton, GA 30114-2725
(678-493-6511; (770) 479-0467 FAX
pbaker@cherokeega.com
http://www.cherokeega.com/ccweb/departmen
ts/clerkofcourts
Patty Baker
(land records from 1832)

Cherokee County Probate Court
Cherokee County Justice Center
90 North Street, Suite 340
Canton, GA 30114
(678) 493-6160
klmrss@aol.com
http://www.cherokeega.com/ccweb/departmen
ts/judicial/probate/index.cfm
Judge Kipling L. "Kip" McVay
(deaths from 1928, marriages from 1841, estates
from 1832)

Clarke County
organized 1801 from Greene and Jackson
counties; consolidated with the City of Athens
in 1990

**Athens-Clarke County Clerk, Superior and
State Courts**
325 East Washington Street, Room 450
Athens, GA 30601
(706) 613-3190; (706) 613-3189 FAX
http://athensclarke.allclerks.us
Beverly Logan
(land records)
no records search service; copies of land
records: $1.00 each (assisted)

Clarke County Probate Court
Athens-Clarke County Courthouse
325 East Washington Street
Athens, GA 30601
(706) 613-3320; (706) 613-3323 FAX
susantate@co.clarke.ga.us

http://www.athensclarkecounty.com/probateco
urt
Judge Susan P. Tate; Sherry Moore, Chief Clerk
(marriages from 1803, probate records from
1802)
no records search service; copies of probate
records: 25¢ per page

Clay County
organized 1854 from Early and Randolph
counties

Clay County Clerk of Superior Court
105 North Washington Street
Fort Gaines, GA 31751
(229) 768-3238
superiorcourtclerk@claycountyga.org;
deanna_bertrand@clay.gsccca.org
http://www.claycountyga.org/superior-court-
clerk.pp
Deanna Bertrand

Clay County Probate Court
Box 448
Fort Gaines, GA 31751
(229) 768-2445; (229) 768-2710 FAX
http://www.claycountyga.org/probate-
judge.php
Judge Melessa Shivers

Clayton County
organized 1858 from Fayette and Henry
counties

Clayton County Clerk of Superior Court
H. R. Banke Justice Center
9151 Tara Boulevard
Jonesboro, GA 30236-4912
(770) 477-3395 (Clerk of Superior Court)
linda.miller@co.clayton.ga.us
http://www.co.clayton.ga.us/superior_court/cle
rk_of_courts/index.htm
Linda T. Miller
(land records)

Clayton County Probate Court
Clayton County Administration, Annex 3
121 South McDonough Street
Jonesboro, GA 30236
(770) 477-3299; (770) 477-3301 (Vital Records);
(770) 477-3306 FAX
probate.court@co.clayton.ga.us
http://www.co.clayton.ga.us/probate_court/ind
ex.htm
Judge Pam Ferguson; Cathy M. Roark, Probate
Director/Chief Clerk
(vital records from 1919, probate records from
1859)
probate search service: no charge (estates);
copies of vital records: $10.00 for the first
page and $5.00 each additional page; copies of
probate records: 25¢ per page, no minimum

Clinch County
organized 1850 from Lowndes and Ware
counties

Clinch County Clerk of Superior Court
(100 Court Square—location)
PO Box 433 (mailing address)
Homerville, GA 31634
(912) 487-5854; (912) 487-3083
http://www.gsccca.org/clerks
Daniel V. Leceese

Clinch County Probate Court
100 Courth Square
Homerville, GA 31634-1415
(912) 487-5523; (912) 487-3083 FAX
http://clinchcounty.georgia.gov
Judge Karleen S. O'Berry

Cobb County
organized 1832 from Cherokee County

Cobb County Clerk of Superior Court
Real Estate Division
10 East Park Square, First and Second Floors
Marietta, GA 30090
(770) 528-1300; (770) 528-1382 FAX

supcourtclk@cobbcounty.org
http://www.cobbgasupctclk.com
Jay C. Stephenson
(land records)

Cobb County Probate Court
32 Waddell Street
Marietta, GA 30090
(770) 528-1900; (770) 528-1996 FAX
probatecourt@cobbcounty.org;
ddodd@cobbcounty.org
http://www.cobbcounty.org/judicial/index.htm
#pro
David Dodd, Chief Judge
(vital records and probate records)

Coffee County
organized 9 February 1854 from Clinch, Irwin,
Telfair and Ware counties

Coffee County Clerk of Superior Court
(101 South Peterson Avenue, Douglas, GA
31533—location)
PO Box 10 (mailing address)
Douglas, GA 31534
(912) 384-2865; (912) 393-3252 FAX
http://www.gsccca.org/clerks
Angela Spell
(land records)
no title work, but will furnish a copy of a deed if
sufficient information is given

Coffee County Probate Court
101 South Peterson Avenue
Douglas, GA 31533
(912) 384-5213; (912) 383-8116 FAX
coffeeprobate@yahoo.com
http://coffeecounty.georgia.gov
Judge Sylvia Stone

Colquitt County
organized 1856 from Lowndes and Thomas
counties

Colquitt County Clerk of Superior Court
(9 Main Street, Room 214, Moultrie, GA
31768—location)
PO Box 886 (mailing address)
Moultrie, GA 31776
(229) 616-7420; (229) 616-7029 FAX
http://www.ccboc.com/courts.htm
Carolyn M. Brazel

Colquitt County Probate Court
PO Box 264
Moulrie, GA 31776
(912) 891-7415; (229) 616-7489 FAX
http://www.ccboc.com/courts.htm
Judge Wesley J. Lewis

Columbia County
organized 1790 from Richmond County

Columbia County Clerk of Superior Court
(Justice Center, 640 Ronald Reagan Drive—
location)
PO Box 2930 (mailing address)
Appling, GA 30809
(706) 312-7139
cindy.mason@gsccca.org
http://www.columbiacountga.gov/home/index.
asp?page=2416
Cindy Mason

Columbia County Probate Court
(Justice Center, 640 Ronald Reagan Drive—
location)
PO Box 1520 (mailing address)
Appling, GA 30809
(706) 312-7254; (706) 541-4001 FAX
phardaway@columbiacountyga.gov
http://www.columbiacountyga.gov
Judge Pat Hardaway
(births and deaths from 1927, marriages from
1790, probate records from 1790)
records search service: $5.00 minimum in
advance

Cook County
organized 1918 from Berrien County

Cook County Clerk of Superior Court
212 North Hutchinson
Adel, GA 31620
(912) 896-7717; (229) 896-7589 FAX
http://www.gsccca.org/clerks
Chlois Lollis

Cook County Probate Court
212 North Hutchinson Avenue
Adel, GA 31620-2413
(912) 896-3941; (229) 896-6083 FAX
http://cookcounty.georgia.gov;
   http://www.cookcountyga.com
Judge Louise Cowart

Coweta County
organized 1826 from Indian Lands and DeKalb
   and Meriwether counties

Coweta County Clerk of Superior Court
72 Greenville Street, Newnan, GA 30263—
   location)
PO Box 943 (mailing address)
Newnan, GA 30264
(770) 254-2690; (770) 254-3700 FAX
http://www.coweta.ga.us/Resources/superiorcl
   erk1.html
Cindy G. Brown

Coweta County Probate Court
Coweta County Administration Building
22 East Broad Street
Newnan, GA 30263
(770) 254-2640; (770) 254-2648 FAX
mcranford@cowetaga.us
http://www.coweta.ga.us/Resources/probate.html
Judge Mary T. Cranford

Crawford County
organized 1822 from Houston, Macon, Marion
   and Talbot counties

Crawford County Clerk of Superior Court
(100 Georgia Highway 42 South, Knoxville, GA
   31050—location)
PO Box 1037 (mailing address
Roberta, GA 31078
(478) 836-3328; (478) 836-9170 FAX
http://www.gsccca.org/clerks
John D. Castleberry

Crawford County Probate Court
PO Box 1028
Roberta, GA 31078
(912) 836-3313; (478) 836-4111 FAX
pbusbee@pstel.net
http://crawfordcounty.georgia.gov
Judge Pamela L. Busbee

Crisp County
organized 1905 from Dooly County

Crisp County Clerk of Superior Court
(Crisp County Courthouse, 210 Seventh Street
   South, Rooms 206 & 208, Cordele, GA
   31015—location)
PO Box 747 (mailing address)
Cordele, GA 31010
(229) 276-2616; (229) 273-5750 FAX
http://www.crispcounty.com/departments/inde
   x.html
Jean H. Rogers

Crisp County Probate Court
PO Box 26
Cordele, GA 31010-0026
(229) 276-2621; (229) 273-9184 FAX
bgriffin@crispcounty.com
http://www.crispcounty.com/departments/inde
   x.html
Judge Belinda F. Griffin

Dade County
organized 1837 from Walker County

Dade County Clerk of Superior Court
(12371 Main Street—location)
PO Box 417 (mailing address)
Trenton, GA 30752-0417
(706) 657-4778; (706) 657-8284 FAX
dade@mail.gsccca.org

http://www.gsccca.org/clerks
Kathy D. Page

Dade County Probate Court
PO Box 605
Trengon, GA 30752
(706) 657-4414; (706) 657-4305 FAX
http://dadecounty.georgia.gov
Judge Jan Ellison

Dawson County
organized 1857 from Gilmer and Lumpkin
   counties

Dawson County Clerk of Superior Court
25 Tucker Avenue, Suite 106
Dawsonville, GA 30534
(706) 344-3510; (706) 344-3511 FAX
http://www.dawsoncounty.org/page.php?id=18
   0
Becky V. McCord

Dawson County Probate Court
(25 Tucker Avenue, Suite 102—location)
PO Box 252 (mailing address)
Dawsonville, GA 30534
(706) 344-3580; (706) 265-6155 FAX
jeffiferb-probate@syclone.net; julieh-
   probate@syclone.net;
   jenniferburt@cyclone.net
http://www.dawsoncounty.org/PROBATEJU
   DGEFILES/probatejudgepage1.htm
Judge Jennifer Evans Burt; Julia Honea, Clerk

Decatur County
organized 1823 from Gilmer and Lumpkin
   counties

Decatur County Clerk of Superior Court
(Decatur County Courthouse, 112 West Water
   Street—location)
PO Box 336 (mailing address)
Bainbridge, GA 31718
(229) 248-3026; (229) 248-3029 FAX
http://www.gsccca.org/clerks
Rebecca McCook
(land records)

Decatur County Probate Court
PO Box 234
Bainbridge, GA 31717
(229) 248-3016; (229) 248-3858 FAX
ejp@bellsouth.net
http://decaturcounty.georgia.gov
Judge Edwin J. Perry, III
(marriages, wills and estates)
probate search service: $1.50 per name; certified
   copies: $4.50

DeKalb County
organized 1822 from Fayette, Gwinnett, Henry
   and Newton counties

DeKalb County Clerk of Superior Court
556 North McDonough Street, Second Floor
Decatur, GA 30030-3356
(404) 371-2836
clerksup@co.dekalb.ga.us;
   Lacarter@co.dekalb.ga.us
http://dklbweb.dekalbga.org/courts/clerk/inde
   x.htmLinda Carter
(land and vital records)

DeKalb County Probate Court
DeKalb County Courthouse Annex, Room 1100
556 North McDonough Street
Decatur, GA 30030
(404) 371-2718; (404) 371-7055 FAX
jrrosh@co.dekalb.ga.us;
   amragas@co.dekalb.ga.us
http://dklbweb.dekalbga.org/courts/probate/in
   dex.htm
Judge Jeryl Debra Rosh; Arnold Ragas,
   Associate Judge/Chief Clerk

Dodge County
organized 1870 from Montgomery, Pulaski and
   Telfair counties

Dodge County Clerk of Superior Court
(5401 Anson Avenue—location)

PO Box 4276 (mailing address)
Eastman, GA 30123
(478) 374-2871; (478) 374-3035 FAX
http://www.gsccca.org/clerks
Rhett Walker

Dodge County Probate Court
PO Box 4276
Eastman, GA 31023
(912) 374-3775; (478) 374-9197 FAX
judgekelly_717@hotmail.com
http://dodgecounty.georgia.gov; http://www.
   eastman-georgia.com (Chamber of Commerce)
Judge John Kelley

Dooly County
organized 1821 from Indian Lands

Dooly County Clerk of Superior Court
(104 Second Street—location)
PO Box 326 (mailing address)
Vienna, GA 31092
(229) 268-4234; (229) 268-1427 FAX
betty.colter@gsccca.org
http://www.gsccca.org/clerks
Betty Colter

Dooly County Probate Court
(104 Second Street South, Room 11—location)
PO Box 304 (mailing address)
Vienna, GA 31092-0304
(229) 268-4217; (229) 268-6142 FAX
pbct@cowega.net
http://doolycounty.georgia.gov
Judge Dwayne D. Forehand

Dougherty County
organized 1853 from Baker County

Dougherty County Clerk of Superior Court
Dougherty Judicial Building
225 Pine Avenue, Room 126
Albany, GA 31701
(912) 431-2198
http://www.dougherty.ga.us/court_system/sup
   erior_court.htm
Evonne Mull
no land records search service; copies of land
   records: $1.00 per page, $2.00 for oversize
   copies, $2.50 for the first certified page and
   50¢ for each additional certified page

Dougherty County Probate Court
(Dougherty Judicial Building, 225 Pine Avenue,
   Suite 124—location)
PO Box 1827 (mailing address)
Albany, GA 31702
(229) 431-2102; (229) 434-2694 FAX
gnewberry@dougherty.ga.us
http://www.dougherty.ga.us/court_system/pro
   bate_court.htm
Gloria W. Newberry, Chief Clerk

Douglas County
organized 1870 from Campbell and Carroll
   counties

Douglas County Clerk of Superior Court
Douglas County Courthouse
8700 Hospital Drive, Main Floor
Douglasville, GA 30134
(770) 920-7252
clerksuperiorcourt@co.douglas.ga.us
http://www.celebratedouglascounty.com/cgi-
   bin/MySQLdb?VIEW=/departments/view_
   dept.txt&cdept=33&department=Clerk%20o
   f%20Superior%20Court
Cindy Chaffin
(land records)

Douglas County Probate Court
Douglas County Courthouse
8700 Hospital Drive, Third Floor, Judicial Side
Douglasville, GA 30134
(770) 920-7249; (770) 920-7381 FAX
probate@co.douglas.ga.us
http://www.celebratedouglascounty.com/cgi-
   bin/MySQLdb?VIEW=/departments/view_
   dept.txt&cdept=146&department=Probate%
   20Court

Judge Hal E. Hamrick
(vital records and probate records)
probate search service; copies of probate
records: no charge for one or two copies,
$4.00 plus 25¢ per page for certified copies,
no minimum

Early County
organized 1818 from Creek Indian Lands

Early County Clerk of Superior Court
(Courthouse Square, First Floor—location)
PO Box 849 (mailing address)
Blakey, GA 31723-0849
(229) 723-3033; (229) 723-4411 FAX
india.thompson@gscca.org
http://www.gsccca.org/clerks
India E. Thompson

Early County Probate Court
Early County Courthouse, Room 8
Blakey, GA 31723-0525
(229) 723-3454; (229) 723-5246 FAX
tonyaholley@alltel.net
http://earlycounty.georgia.gov;
http://www.blakelyearlychamber.com
Judge Tonya Holley
probate search service: $3.00; copies of probate
records: $3.00 for certification plus 25¢ per
page

Echols County
organized 1858 from Clinch and Lowndes
counties

Echols County Clerk of Superior Court
(Courthouse, 110 Highway 94 E—location)
PO Box 213 (mailing address)
Statenville, GA 31648
(229) 559-5642; (229) 559-5792 FAX
http://www.echolscountygeorgia.com/superior
Court.htm
Paula Goss

Echols County Probate Court
(Courthouse, 110 Highway 94 East—location)
PO Box 118 (mailing address)
Statenville, GA 31648-0118
(229) 559-7526; (229) 559-8128 FAX
judgerodgers@plnttel.net
http://www.echolscountygeorgia.com/courts.htm
Judge Carlos L. Rodgers, Jr.

Effingham County
organized 1777 from St. Mathew and St. Phillips
parishes

Effingham County Clerk of Superior Court
(901 North Pine Street—location)
PO Box 387 (mailing address)
Springfield, GA 31329-0307
(912) 754-2118
http://www.effinghamcounty.org/Departments
/ClerkofCourts/tabid/1387/Default.aspx
Elizabeth Z. Hursey
(land records)

Effingham County Probate Court
(901 North Pine Street—location)
601 North Laurel Street (mailing address)
Springfield, GA 31329
(912) 754-2112; (912) 754-3894 FAX
fseckinger@effinghamcounty.org;
jsuhor@effinghamcounty.org
http://www.effinghamcounty.org
Judy Suhor, Chief Clerk
(vital records and probate records)
probate search service: $3.00; copies of probate
records: 25¢ per page, $3.00 minimum

Elbert County
organized 1790 from Madison and Wilkes
counties

Elbert County Clerk of Superior Court
(Elbert County Government Complex, 45
Forest Avenue—location)
PO Box 619 (mailing address)
Elberton, GA 30635
(706) 283-2005; (706) 213-7286 FAX

pat.anderson@gsccca.org
http://www.elbertco.net/Department%20Pages
/clerkof courts.htm
Ms. Pat V. Anderson

Elbert County Probate Court
Elbert County Courthouse
8 South Oliver Street
Elberton, GA 30635-1498
(706) 283-2016; (706) 213-7286 FAX
http://www.elbertco.net/Department%20Pages
/clerkof courts.htm
Judge Susan R. Sexton

Emanuel County
organized 1812 from Bulloch and Montgomery
counties

Emanuel County Clerk of Superior Court
(125 South Main Street—location)
PO Box 627 (mailing address)
Swainsboro, GA 30401-0627
(912) 237-7091; (912) 237-3881
http://www.gsccca.org/clerks
J. Carlton Lawson

Emanuel County Probate Court
(201 West Main Street—location)
PO Drawer 70 (mailing address)
Swainsboro, GA 30401-2078
(706) 283-2016; (706) 283-9668 FAX
judgewilkes@yahoo.com
http://emanuelcounty.georgia.gov
Judge Don E. Wilkes

Evans County
organized 1914 from Bulloch and Tattnall
counties

Evans County Clerk of Superior Court
(123 West Main Street—location)
PO Box 845 (mailing address)
Claxton, GA 30417
(912) 739-3868; (912) 739-2504 FAX
gail.mccooey@evans.gsccca.org
http://www.gsccca.org/clerks
Gail B. McCooey
(land records from 1915 to date)

Evans County Probate Court
(Courthouse Square—location)
PO Box 852 (mailing address)
Claxton, GA 30417
(912) 739-4080; (912) 739-4077 FAX
judgemccoy@hotmail.com
http://evanscounty.georgia.gov;
http://www.claxtonevanschamber.com
(Chamber of Commerce)
Judge Darin McCoy
(vital records and probate records from 1915 to
date)

Fannin County
organized 1854 from Gilmer and Union
counties

Fannin County Clerk of Superior Court
(420 West Main Street—location)
PO Box 1300 (mailing address)
Blue Ridge, GA 30513
(706) 632-2039; (706) 258-5250 FAX
http://www.fannincountyga.org/clerkofcourt.htm
Dana Chastain
(land records from 1854)

Fannin County Probate Court
420 West Main Street, Suite 2
Blue Ridge, GA 30513
(706) 632-3011; (706) 632-7167 FAX
http://www.fannincountyga.org/probate.htm
Judge Linda K. Davis; Vicky W. Hughes, Chief
Clerk
(deaths from 1927, births [some delayed
certificates] from 1861, probate records from
1868)
probate search service: $10.00 (unlimited
search); copies of probate records: 25¢ per
page, no minimum; searches are done as time
permits

Fayette County
organized 1821 from Indian Lands and Henry
County

Fayette County Clerk of Superior Court
(Fayette County Justice Center, 1 Center
Drive—location)
PO Box 130 (mailing address)
Fayetteville, GA 30214
(770) 461-4703
srstuddard@aol.com
http://www.admin.co.fayette.ga.us/courts/clerk
court.asp
Sheila Studdard

Fayette County Probate Court
Fayette County Justice Center
1 Center Drive
Fayetteville, GA 30214
(770) 716-4220; (770) 461-9555, ext. 2136; (770)
716-4854 FAX; (770) 460-8685 FAX
probate@admin.co.fayette.ga.us
http://www.admin.co.fayette.ga.us/courts/prob
court/infoprobcourt.asp
Judge Martha Stephenson; Betty A. Johnson,
Chief Clerk
(vital records and probate records from 1890 to
date)
probate search service: $3.00; no copying
service, contact the Archives for copies

Floyd County
organized 1832 from Chattooga, Cherokee and
Paulding counties

Floyd County Clerk of Superior Court
Floyd County Judicial Building
3 Government Plaza, Suite 101
Rome, GA 30161
(706) 291-5190; (706) 235-0035 FAX
johnstonj@floydcountyga.org
http://www.floydcountyga.org/Courts/superior
.htm
Joe E. Johnston
(land records, naturalization records)

Floyd County Probate Court
3 Government Plaza, Suite 201
Rome, GA 30161
(706) 291-5136; (706) 291-5189 FAX
burkhals@floydcountyga.org
http://www.floydcountyga.org/Courts/Probate
_home.htm
Lisa Horton
(probate records)

Forsyth County
organized 1832 from Cherokee and Lumpkin
counties

Forsyth County Clerk of the Superior Court
100 Courthouse Square, Suite 010
Cumming, GA 30040
(770) 781-2120; (770) 886-2858 FAX
DESorrells@forsythco.com
http://www.forsythco.com/department.asp?De
ptID=2
Douglas Sorrells

Forsyth County Probate Court
112 West Maple Street, Suite 101
Cumming, GA 30040
(770) 781-2140; (770) 889-2839 FAX
ldjordan@forsythco.com
http://www.forsythco.com/department.asp?De
ptID=16
Judge Lynwood D. (Woody) Jordan, Jr.

Franklin County
organized 1784 from Cherokee Lands

Franklin County Clerk of Superior Court
(9592 Lavonia Road—location)
PO Box 70 (mailing address)
Carnesville, GA 30521
(706) 384-2483
info@franklincountyga.com
http://www.gsccca.org/clerks
Melissa Blakey Holbrook

Franklin County Probate Court
(9592 Lavonia Road—location)
PO Box 207 (mailing address)
Carnesville, GA 30521
(706) 384-2403; (706) 384-2636 FAX
sbanks@franklincountyga.com
http://franklincounty.georgia.gov;
    http://www.franklin-county.com/home
    (Chamber of Commerce)
Judge Eddy Fowler

Fulton County
organized 1853 from Campbell and DeKalb
    counties, on 1 January 1932 annexed
    Campbell County (organized 1828 from
    Carroll, Cherokee, Coweta, DeKalb and
    Fayette counties) and Milton County
    (organized 1857 from Cherokee, Cobb and
    Forsyth counties)

Fulton County Clerk of Superior Court
136 Pryor Street, S.W.
Atlanta, GA 30303-3519
(404) 730-5300; (404) 730-5313
clerk@fcclk.org
http://www.fcclk.org
Juanita Hicks

Fulton County Probate Court
141 Pryor Street
Atlanta, GA 30303
(404) 730-4640 (General Information); (404)
    730-4693 (Records)
pinkie.toomer@co.fulton.ga.us
http://www.co.fulton.ga.us/departments/proba
    te_court.html
Judge Pinkie T. Toomer

Gilmer County
organized 1832 from Cherokee and Union
    counties

Gilmer County Clerk of Superior Court
1 West Side Square
Elijay, GA 30540
(706) 635-4462 voice & FAX
http://www.gilmercounty-ga.gov
Glenda Sue Johnson
(land records)

Gilmer County Probate Court
51 Sand Street
Elijay, GA 30540
(706) 635-4763; (706) 635-4761 FAX
ahmprobate@hotmail.com
http://www.gilmercounty-ga.gov/probate.htm
Judge Anita Mullins; Amy Arnold, Probate
    Questions
(vital records from 1927, probate records from
    1837)
no probate search service; copies of probate
    records: 25¢ each, $3.00 for certified copies,
    25¢ minimum

Glascock County
organized 1857 from Warren County

Glascock County Clerk of Superior Court
(62 East Main Street—location)
PO Box 231 (mailing address)
Gibson, GA 30810-0231
(706) 598-2084; (706) 598-2577 FAX
http://www.glascockcountyga.com/LocalGov.h
    tml
Carla Stevens

Glascock County Probate Court
(62 East Main Street—location)
PO Box 277 (mailing address)
Gibson, GA 30810
(706) 598-3241; (706) 598-2471 FAX
http://www.glascockcountyga.com/LocalGov.h
    tml
Judge Denise Dallas

Glynn County
organized 1777 from St. David and St. Patrick
    parishes

Glynn County Clerk of the Superior Court
(701 H Street, Courthouse Square—location)
PO Box 1355 (mailing address)
Brunswick, GA 31520
(912) 554-7272; (912) 267-5625 FAX
http://www.gsccca.org/clerks
Lola B. Jamsky

Glynn County Probate Court
New Courthouse, 701 H Street, Third Floor
Brunswick, GA 31520
(912) 554-7231; (912) 466-8001 FAX
probatecourt@glynncounty-ga.gov
http://www.glynncounty.org/index.asp?nid=138
Judge Debra G. Howes; Linnie M. Torkildsen,
    Senior Deputy Clerk
(marriage licenses from the late 1800s, wills,
    estates, administrators' returns, inventories
    from the late 1800s)
vital records and probate records search service:
    no charge; copies 25¢ per page, $4.00 for
    certification of the first page and 25¢ for each
    additional page, no minimum

Gordon County
organized 1850 from Cass, Floyd and Murray
    counties

Gordon County Clerk of Superior Court
(100 South Wall Street, First Floor, Calhoun,
    GA 30703—location)
PO Box 580 (mailing address)
Calhoun, GA 30701
(706) 629-9533; (706) 629-2139 FAX
bbrannon@gordoncounty.org
http://www.gordoncounty.org/clerkofcourt.asp
Brian Brannon

Gordon County Probate Court
(100 South Wall Street—location)
PO Box 669 (mailing address)
Calhoun, GA 30703-0669
(706) 629-7314; (706) 629-4698 FAX
probatecourt@gordoncounty.org
http://www.gordoncounty.org/probate.asp
Judge Johnny R. Parker

Grady County
organized 1906 from Decatur and Thomas
    counties

Grady County Clerk of Superior Court
(250 North Broad Street, Cairo, GA 31728-
    4101—location)
Box 8 (mailing address)
Cairo, GA 31738
(229) 377-1512; (229) 377-7078 FAX
http://www.gsccca.org/clerks
Annette H. Alred
(land records)

Grady County Probate Court
(250 North Braod Street, First Floor—location)
Box 1 (mailing address)
Cairo, GA 39828
(229) 377-4621; (229) 378-8052 FAX
gradypc@alltel.net; swvoyles@alltel.net
http://gradycounty.georgia.gov
Judge Sadie W. Voyles; Lizzie S. Garrette, Clerk
probate search service available, send SASE;
    copies of probate records: $3.00 per page

Greene County
organized 1786 from Oglethorpe, Washington
    and Wilkes counties

Greene County Clerk of Superior Court
113 North Main Street, Suite 109
Greensboro, GA 30642-1107
(706) 453-3340; (706) 453-9179 FAX
deborah.jackson@gsccca.org
http://www.gsccca.org/clerks
Deborah D. Jackson
(land records, naturalization records)

Greene County Probate Court
113 North Main Street, Suite 113
Greensboro, GA 30642-1107
(706) 453-3346; (706) 453-7649 FAX
http://www.greenecountyga.gov
Tricia B. Kroeger, Chief Clerk

(vital records, and probate records)

Gwinnett County
organized 1818 from Cherokee Lands and Hall
    and Jackson counties

Gwinnett County Clerk of Superior Court
(75 Langley Drive, Lawrenceville, GA 30245-
    6900—location)
PO Box 880 (mailing address)
Lawrenceville, GA 30046
(770) 822-8100
http://www.gwinnettcourts.com/staff/cocs001.
    htm
Tom Lawler

Gwinnett County Probate Court
Gwinnett Justice and Administration center
75 Langley Drive
Lawrenceville, GA 30045
(770) 822-8250
Marlene.Duwell@gwinnettcounty.com
http://www.gwinnettcourts.com/courts/Proco
    urt.htm
Marlene Duwell, Chief Clerk

Habersham County
organized 1818 from Cherokee Lands and
    Franklin County

Habersham County Clerk of Superior Court
(Courthouse, 555 Monroe Street, First Floor—
    location)
PO Box 2320 (mailing address)
Clarkesville, GA 30523-0227
(706) 754-2924; (706) 754-8779 FAX
http://www.co.habersham.ga.us/habco/courts/
    clerk
David C. Wall

Habersham County Probate Court
(Courthouse, 555 Monroe Street—location)
PO Box 625 (mailing address)
Clarkesville, GA 30523-0625
(706) 754-2013; (706) 754-5093 FAX
http://www.co.habersham.ga.us/habco/courts/
    probate
Judge Ann Frye Adams-Jarrell

Hall County
organized 1819 from Cherokee Lands and
    Franklin and Jackson counties

Hall County Clerk of Superior Court
(County Courthouse Annex, 116 Spring Street,
    S.E., Bottom Floor, East Wing, Gainesville,
    GA 30501—location)
PO Box 1275 (mailing address)
Gainesville, GA 30503-1275
(770) 532-7058 (Real Estate Division); (770)
    536-0702 FAX
dwight.wood@gsccca.org
http://www.hallcounty.org/judicial/jud_superio
    rcourt.asp
Dwight Wood

Hall County Probate Court
(Hall County Courthouse, First Flooor, 225
    Green Street, S.E., 123, Gainesville, GA
    30501—location)
PO Box 826 (mailing address)
Gainesville, GA 30503-0826
(770) 531-6921; (770) 531-4946 FAX
pcornett@hallcounty.org
http://www.hallcounty.org/judicial/jud_probco
    urt.asp
Judge Patti P. Cornett
(marriage licenses and probate records)
probate search service: $2.00; certified copies of
    marriage licenses: $4.00; copies of probate
    records: 25¢ per page; send SASE

Hancock County
organized 1793 from Greene and Washington
    counties

Hancock County Clerk of Superior Court
(Courthouse Square—location)
PO Box 451 (mailing address)
Sparta, GA 31087-0451

(706) 444-6644; (706) 444-6221 FAX
http://www.gsccca.org/clerks
Leroy S. Wiley
(land records)

Hancock County Probate Court
Courthouse Square
Sparta, GA 31087-1114
(706) 444-5343; (706) 444-8024 FAX
ejiprobate@bellsouth.net
http://hancockcounty.georgia.gov
Judge Marva Rice
(births and deaths from 1927 [very few births before 1927], probate records from 1793)
probate search service: $3.00 (to verify availability), $8.00 for research before 1900; copies of probate records: 25¢ per page

Haralson County
organized 1856 from Carroll and Polk counties

Haralson County Clerk of Superior Court
(Courthouse, 4485 Georgia Highway 120—location)
PO Drawer 849 (mailing address)
Buchanan, GA 30113-0373
(770) 646-2005; (770) 646-8827 FAX
http://haralsoncounty.georgia.gov;
http://www.gsccca.org/clerks
Dorothy Parker

Haralson County Probate Court
(Courthouse, 4485 Georgia Highway 120—location)
PO Box 620 (mailing address)
Buchanan, GA 30113-0620
(770) 646-2008; (770) 646-3419 FAX
hcprob@randomc.com; ehulsey@bellsouth.net
http://haralsoncounty.georgia.gov
Judge J. Edward Hulsey, Jr.

Harris County
organized 1827 from Muscogee and Troup counties

Harris County Clerk of Superior Court
(102 North College Street—location)
PO Box 528 (mailing address)
Hamilton, GA 31811-0528
(706) 628-4944; (706) 628-7039 FAX
http://www.harriscountga.gov/departments/court-superior-juvenile.php
Stacy K. Haralson

Harris County Probate Court
(Harris County Courthouse, Room 116—location)
PO Box 569 (mailing address)
Hamilton, GA 31811
(706) 628-5038; (706) 628-7322 FAX
http://www.harriscountga.gov/departments/court-probate.php
Judge Martha M. Hartley
no probate search service ("County offices do not search *any records* with a professional genealogist or visit the Archives in Atlanta to see records on microfilm")

Hart County
organized 1853 from Elbert and Franklin counties

Hart County Clerk of Superior Court
(185 West Franklin Street—location)
PO Box 386 (mailing address)
Hartwell, GA 30643-0386
(706) 376-7189; (706) 376-1277 FAX
http://www.hartcountyga.org/ClerkCourt.htm
William E. (Bill) Holland, III
(land records)

Hart County Probate Court
(185 West Franklin Street—location)
PO Box 1159 (mailing address)
Hartwell, GA 30643-1159
(706) 376-2565; (706) 376-9032 FAX
probatecourt@hartcom.net
http://www.hartcountyga.org/probate.htm
Judge Bob Smith
(vital records [restricted to persons and parents],

probate records)
probate search service: $3.00; copies of probate records: 25¢ per page, $3.00 minimum

Heard County
organized 1830 from Carroll, Coweta, and Troup counties

Heard County Clerk of Superior Court
(215 East Court Square—location)
PO Box 249 (mailing address)
Franklin, GA 30217-0249
(706) 675-3301; (706) 675-0819 FAX
http://www.heardcountyga.com/clerkofcourt.htm
Bryan S. Owensby
(land records from 1894)

Heard County Probate Court
(215 East Court Square—location)
PO Box 478 (mailing address)
Franklin, GA 30217-0478
(706) 675-3353; (706) 675-0819 FAX
hcpcga@hotmail.com
http://www.heardcountyga.com/probae.htm
Judge Joseph Bledsoe
(marriages, deaths, and probate records from 1894)
certified copies of vital records: $10.00 each for births and deaths, $4.00 each for marriages; copies of probate records: 25¢ per page, $3.00 minimum

Henry County
organized 1821 from lands acquired from the Creek Nation

Henry County Probate Court
99 Sims Street
McDonough, GA 30253
(770) 954-2303; (770) 954-2308 FAX
dbuttrill@co.henry.ga.us
http://www.co.henry.ga.us/Probate/ProbateCourt.htm
Judge Kelley S. Powell
(vital records, probate records)

Henry County Superior Court Clerk
1 Courthouse Square
McDonough, GA 30253
(404) 954-2121
http://www.co.henry.ga.us/Superior%20Court/SuperiorCtMain.htm
Judith A. "Judy" Lewis
(land records)

Houston County
organized 1821 from Indian Lands

Houston County Clerk of Superior Court
201 Perry Parkway
Perry, GA 31069
(478) 218-4720
carolyn.sullivan@gsccca.org
http://www.houstoncountyga.com/SuperiorCt.htm
Carolyn V. Sullivan
copies: 25¢, certified copy: $2.50

Houston County Probate Court
(201 North Perry Parkway—location)
PO Box 1801 (mailing address)
Perry, GA 31069
(478) 218-4710; (478) 218-4715 FAX
jspires@houstoncountyga.org;
ychapman@houstoncountyga.org
http://www.houstoncountyga.com/Probate/probate_court.htm
Judge Janice Davidson Spires; Yvonne V. Chapman

Irwin County
organized December 1818 from Indian Lands (ceded from the Creek Nation in treaties of 1814 and 1818)

Irwin County Clerk of Superior Court
301 South Irwin Avenue, Suite 103
Ocilla, GA 31774
(229) 469-5356; (229) 468-9753 FAX
http;//www.irwincounty.net/Clerkofcourt.html

Sharon H. Martin
(land records and naturalization records)

Irwin County Probate Court
202 South Irwin Avenue
Ocilla, GA 31774
(229) 831-7520
icprobate@alltel.net
http://www.irwincounty.net/Probatecourt.html
Judge Allen Gay
(births and deaths from 1919, and probate records)
probate search service: $3.00; copies of land records: $3.00 minimum; certified copies of vital records: $10.00 each (birth records restricted for family only); copies of probate records: 25¢ per page, $3.25 minimum

Jackson County
organized 1796 from Franklin County

Jackson County Clerk of Superior Court
County Courthouse, 500 Jackson Parkway
Jefferson, GA 30549
(706) 387-6360; (706) 387-2468 FAX
cthomas@jacksoncountygov.com
http://jacksoncountygov.com/ClerkofCourtsload.asp
Connie W. Thomas
(deeds from 1796)
no land records search service; no copies available by mail

Jackson County Probate Court
County Courthouse, 5000 Jackson Parkway
Jefferson, GA 30549
(706) 387-6277; (706) 367-7211 FAX
probate@county.jackson.ga.us
http://jacksoncountygov.com/ProbateCourtload.asp
Judge Margaret Deadwyler; Susan Garmon, Chief Deputy Clerk
(vital records from 1919, marriages from 1806 to date, probate records)

Jasper County
organized 1807 from Baldwin, Newton and Walton counties; name changed from Randolph County in 1812 (present-day Randolph County was organized in 1828)

Jasper County Clerk of Superior Court
126 West Green Street, Room 200
Monticello, GA 31064
(706) 468-4901; (706) 468-4946 FAX
dan.jordan@gsccca.org
http://www.jaspercourt.com
Dan Jordan

Jasper County Probate Court
126 West Green Street, Suite 111
Monticello, GA 31064
(706) 468-4903; (706) 468-4926 FAX
jasperprobate@bellsouth.net
http://jaspercounty.georgia.gov
Judge Linda M. Mock

Jeff Davis County
organized 1905 from Appling and Coffee counties

Jeff Davis County Clerk of Superior Court
(14 Jeff Davis Street, Room 105—location)
PO Box 429 (mailing address)
Hazlehurst, GA 31539-0429
(912) 375-6615; (912) 375-6637 FAX
http://www.gsccca.org/clerks
Myra Murphy
(land records and naturalization records)

Jeff Davis County Probate Court
(14 Jeff Davis Street, Room 210—location)
PO Box 446 (mailing address)
Hazlehurst, GA 31539-0013
(912) 375-6626; (912) 375-0502 FAX
judgebuford@yahoo.com
http://jeffdaviscounty.georgia.gov;
http://www.hazlehurst-jeffdavis.com (Board of Tourism)
Judge Arthur F. Buford

Georgia

49

(vital records and probate records)

Jefferson County
organized 1796 from Burke and Warren counties

Jefferson County Clerk of Superior Court
(Courthouse, 202 East Broad Street—location)
PO Box 151 (mailing address)
Louisville, GA 30434–0151
(478) 625-7922; (478) 625-9589 FAX
http://www.jeffersoncounty.org
Michael (Mickey) R. Jones

Jefferson County Probate Court
(Courthouse, 202 East Broad Street—location)
PO Box 307 (mailing address)
Louisville, GA 30434-0307
(478) 625-3258; (478) 625-0245 FAX
jcpcbryan@bellsouth.net
http://www.jeffersoncounty.org/county_gover
nment.shtml
Judge Quillian L. Bryant, Jr.

Jenkins County
organized 1905 from Bulloch, Burke, Emanuel and Screven counties

Jenkins County Clerk of Superior Court
(Courthouse Square, 611 East Winthrop Avenue—location)
PO Box 659 (mailing address)
Millen, GA 30442
(478) 982-4683; (478) 982-1274 FAX
http://www.jenkinscountyga.com/govt_superio
r_court.html
Elizabeth T. Landing

Jenkins County Probate Court
(Courthouse Square, 611 East Winthrop Avenue—location)
PO Box 904 (mailing address)
Millen, GA 30442
(478) 982-5581; (478) 982-2829 FAX
jenkinscounty945@bellsouth.net
http://www.jenkinscountyga.com
Judge Wanda P. Burke

Johnson County
organized 1858 from Emanuel, Laurens and Washington counties

Johnson County Clerk of Superior Court
(Courthouse, East Elm Street, First Floor—location)
PO Box 321 (mailing address)
Wrightsville, GA 31096-0321
(912) 864-3484; (912) 864-1343 FAX
http://www.gsccca.org/clerks
Patricia T. Glover

Johnson County Probate Court
(Courthouse Square—location)
PO Box 264 (mailing address)
Wrightsville, GA 31096-0264
(478) 864-3316; (478) 864-0528 FAX
maryjobuxton@hotmail.com
http://johnsoncounty.georgia.gov
Judge Mary Jo Buxton

Jones County
organized 1807 from Baldwin, Bibb and Putnam counties

Jones County Clerk of Superior Court
(110 South Jefferson Street—location)
PO Box 39 (mailing address)
Gray, GA 31032
(478) 986-6671; (478) 986-2030 FAX
http://www.jonescountyga.org/depts_court.php
Bart W. Jackson
(land records from 1807)

Jones County Probate Court
(110 South Jefferson Street—location)
PO Box 1359 (mailing address)
Gray, GA 31032
(478) 986-6668; (478) 986-1715 FAX
http://www.jonescountyga.org/depts_court.ph
p; http://www.jonescounty.org (Chamber of
Commerce)

Judge J. Mike Greene
(births from 1871 [indexed], deaths from 1917 and marriages from 1811, wills from 1809, Court Dockets from 1829, Minutes from 1808)
probate search service: no charge; certified copies of vital records: $10.00 each for births and deaths (restricted to relatives, indexes not open for searches), $4.00 each for marriages; copies of probate records: 25¢ per page

Kinchafoonee County
(see Webster County)

Lamar County
organized 1920 from Monroe and Pike counties

Lamar County Clerk of Superior Court
(326 Thomaston Street—location)
Box 7 (mailing address)
Barnesville, GA 30204-1669
(404) 358-5145; (770) 358-5149 FAX
http://www.gsccca.org/clerks
Robert (Frank) Abbott
(land records and naturalization records)

Lamar County Probate Court
326 Thomaston Street
Barnesville, GA 30204-1669
(770) 358-5155; (770) 358-5348 FAX
kmartin358@aol.com
http://lamarcounty.georgia.gov
Judge Kathryn B. Martin
no probate search service; copies of probate records: $3.00, no minimum (must have genuine reason for interest)

Lanier County
organized 1920 from Berrien, Clinch and Lowndes counties

Lanier County Clerk of Superior Court
Lanier County Courthouse, 100 Main Street
Lakeland, GA 31635-1187
(229) 482-3594; (229) 482-8333 FAX
http://www.gsccca.org/clerks
Martha B. Neugent
(land records and naturalization records)

Lanier County Probate Court
Lanier County Courthouse, 100 Main Street
Lakeland, GA 31635-1186
(229) 482-3668; (229) 482-8333 FAX
lcpcjam@yahoo.com
http://laniercounty.georgia.gov
Judge Judy B. Mullis
(births, deaths and marriage licenses, probate records)
vital records search service: $10.00; copies of vital records: births and deaths $10.00 (confidential and limited to family members), marriage licenses $4.00

Laurens County
organized 1807 from Montgomery, Washington and Wilkinson counties

Laurens County Clerk of Superior Court
(Laurens County Courthouse, 101 North Jefferson Street, Room 106, Dublin, GA 31021—location)
PO Box 2028 (mailing address)
Dublin, GA 31040-2028
(478) 272-3210; (478) 277-2933 FAX
Allen.Thomas@gsccca.org
http://www.laurenscoga.org
Allen Thomas

Laurens County Probate Court
(Laurens County Courthouse, 101 North Jefferson Street, Dublin, GA 31021—location)
PO Box 2098 (mailing address)
Dublin, GA 31040-2098
(229) 272-2566; (229) 482-8333 FAX
HarperH@dlcga.com
http://www.laurenscoga.org
Judge Helen W. Harper
(marriage records, probate records from 1809)
probate search service: $10.00; copies of probate

records: 25¢ per page, no minimum

Lee County
organized 1826 from Indian Lands and Dooly County

Lee County Clerk of Superior Court
(County Courthouse, 100 Leslie Highway—location)
PO Box 597 (mailing address)
Leesburg, GA 31763-0597
(229) 759-6018; (229) 759-6019; (229) 759-6050 FAX
anix@lee.ga.us
http://www.lee.ga.us/departments/e_clerk.html
Ann E. Nix

Lee County Probate Court
(County Courthouse, 100 Leslie Highway—location)
PO Box 592 (mailing address)
Leesburg, GA 31763-0592
(229) 759-6005; (229) 759-6006; (229) 759-6050 FAX
jwheaton@lee.ga.us; leecounty@lee.ga.us
http://www.lee.ga.us/departments/3_probate.h
tml
Judge John Wheaton

Liberty County
organized 1777 from St. Johns Parish

Liberty County Clerk of Superior Court
(112 North Main Street—location)
PO Box 50 (mailing address)
Hinesville, GA 31310-0050
(912) 876-3625; (912) 369-5463 FAX
clerkofcourts@libertyco.com
http://www.libertycoga.com
F. Barry Wilkes, Clerk and Court Administrator
(land records from 1756)

Liberty County Probate Court
(112 North Main Street, Room 100—location)
PO Box 28 (mailing address)
Hinesville, GA 31310-0223
(912) 876-3635; (912) 876-3589 FAX
nancy.aspinwall@libertycountyga.com
http://www.libertycoga.com
Judge Nancy K. Aspinwall
(vital records and probate records)

Lincoln County
organized 1796 from Wilkes County

Lincoln County Clerk of Superior Court
(182 Huphrey Street—location)
PO Box 340 (mailing address)
Lincolnton, GA 30817-0340
(706) 359-5505; (706) 359-5027 FAX
bbeggs@lincolncountyga.com
http://lincolncountyga.com/SuperiorCourts.asp
Bruce C. Beggs

Lincoln County Probate Court
(182 Humphrey Street—location)
PO Box 205 (mailing address)
Lincolnton, GA 30817-0340
(706) 359-5528; (706) 359-5520 FAX
lmoss@lincolncountyga.com
http://lincolncountyga.com/Probate&Magistrat
eCourts.asp
Judge Lee D. Moss, Chief Judge; Melaina Murphy, Probate Clerk

Long County
organized 1920 from Liberty County

Long County Clerk of Superior Court
(49 East McDonald Street—location)
PO Box 458 (mailing address)
Ludowici, GA 31316-0458
(912) 545-2123; (912) 545-2020 FAX
http://www.gsccca.org/clerks
Frank S. Middleton
(land records)
copies of vital records: $10.00; proof of relationship required

Long County Probate Court
(49 East McDonald Street—location)

PO Box 426 (mailing address)
Ludowici, GA 31316-0426
(912) 545-2315; (912) 545-2131; (912) 545-2150
FAX
http://longcounty.georgia.gov
Judge Marie H. Middleton
(vital records, probate records)

Lowndes County
organized 1825 from Irwin County

Lowndes County Clerk of Superior Court
(108 East Central Avenue, Valdosta, GA
31601—location)
PO Box 1349 (mailing address)
Valdosta, GA 31603-1349
(229) 333-5127; (229) 333-7637 FAX
scrow@lowndescounty.com
http://www.lowndescounty.com/courts.asp
Sara Crow
(land records)

Lowndes County Probate Court
(Lowndes County Courthouse, 100 East Central
Avenue, Room 105—location)
PO Box 72 (mailing address)
Valdosta, GA 31603-0072
(229) 333-5103; (229) 671-2650; (229) 333-7646
FAX
rsirmans@lowndescounty.com
http://www.lowndescounty.com/courts.asp?id
=33
Judge Ruby K. Sirmans; Terri Adams, Chief
Clerk
no probate search service; copies of probate
records: depends on type of records, 25¢
minimum

Lumpkin County
organized 1832 from Cherokee, Habersham and
Hall counties

Lumpkin County Clerk of Superior Court
99 Courthouse Hill, Suite D
Dahlonega, GA 30533
(404) 864-3736; (706) 864-5298 FAX
edward.tucker@gsccca.org
http://www.lumpkincounty.gov
Edward E. Tucker
(deeds, surveys)

Lumpkin County Probate Court
99 Courthouse Hill, Suite C
Dahlonega, GA 30533
(706) 864-3847; (706) 864-9271 FAX
judgechastain@lumpkincounty.gov
http://www.lumpkincounty.gov
Judge Michael Chastain
(births from 1921, deaths from 1928, marriage
licenses from the 1830s, probate records)
vital records search service: births and deaths are
closed to the public, but with correct name
and date, the office will look them up at no
charge, open to relatives; copies of land
records: $1.00 per page for 8½" x 11", $2.00
per page for 8½" x 11", plus $1.00 postage;
copies of vital records: 25¢ per page, certified
copies $10.00 each for births and deaths,
$3.00 each for marriage licenses

Macon County
organized 1837 from Houston and Marion
counties

Macon County Clerk of Superior Court
(Macon County Courthouse, 121 South Sumter
Street—location)
PO Box 337 (mailing address)
Oglethorpe, GA 31068-0337
(478) 472-7661; (478) 472-4775 FAX
http://www.gsccca.org/clerks
Juanita M. Laidler

Macon County Probate Court
(Macon County Courthouse, 121 South Sumter
Street—location)
PO Box 216 (mailing address)
Oglethorpe, GA 31068-0216
(478) 472-7685; (478) 472-5643 FAX
http://www.montezuma-

ga.org/government.htm (unofficial site);
http://www.maconcountyga.org (Chamber of
Commerce); http://maconcounty.georgia.gov
Judge Mack S. McCarty
(vital records, probate records)

Madison County
organized 1811 from Clarke, Elbert, Franklin,
Jackson and Oglethorpe counties

Madison County Clerk of Superior Court
(91 Albany Avenue—location)
PO Box 247 (mailing address)
Danielsville, GA 30633
(706) 795-6310; (706) 795-2209 FAX
http://www.madisonco.us
Michelle H. Strickland
(land records with Tax Commissioners and Tax
Assessor's Office)

Madison County Probate Court
(91 Albany Avenue—location)
PO Box 207 (mailing address)
Danielsville, GA 30633
(706) 795-6365; (706) 795-5933 FAX
cchambers@madisonco.us
Judge Donald H. (Hoppy) Royston
(vital records and probate records)
no probate search service (due to understaffing)

Marion County
organized 1827 from Lee, Muscogee and Stewart
counties

Marion County Clerk of Superior Court
(Courthouse Building, 100 Broad Street—
location)
PO Box 41 (mailing address)
Buena Vista, GA 31803-0041
(229) 649-7321; (229) 649-7931 FAX
http://www.gsccca.org/clerks
Joy Smith

Marion County Probate Court
(Courthouse Building, 1 Broad Street—location)
PO Box 207 (mailing address)
Buena Vista, GA 31803-0207
(229) 649-5542; (229) 649-2059 FAX
bumpwelch@sowega.net
http://marioncounty.georgia.gov
Judge James R. Welch

McDuffie County
organized 17 October 1870 from Columbia and
Warren counties

McDuffie County Clerk of Superior Court
(337 Main Street, Room 104—location)
PO Box 158 (mailing address)
Thomson, GA 30824-0158
(706) 595-2134; (706) 595-9150 FAX
connie.cheatham@mcduffie.gsccca.org
http://www.thomson-mcduffie.com/
artman/publish/mc-clerk.shtml
Constance H. Cheatham
(land records)

McDuffie County Probate Court
(337 Main Street, Room 108—location)
PO Box 2028 (mailing address)
Thomson, GA 30824-2028
(706) 595-2124; (706) 595-4710 FAX
vburley@thomson-mcduffie.net
http://www.thomson-
mcduffie.com/artman/publish/mc-
probate.shtml
Judge Albert E. (Gene) Wells; Valerie Burley
(vital records and probate records)

McIntosh County
organized 1793 from Liberty County

McIntosh County Clerk of Superior Court
(Courthouse, 310 North Way—location)
PO Box 1661 (mailing address)
Darien, GA 31305-1661
(912) 437-6641; (912) 437-6673 FAX
http://www.mcintoshclerkofcourts.com
Ann W. Poppell

McIntosh County Probate Court

(Courthouse, 310 North Way—location)
PO Box 453 (mailing address)
Darien, GA 31305-0453
(912) 437-6636; (912) 437-6635 FAX
http://mcintoshcounty.georgia.gov
Judge Gordon S. Shurman

Meriwether County
organized 1827 from Troup County

Meriwether County Clerk of Superior Court
(Courthouse, 100 Court Square—location)
PO Box 160 (mailing address)
Greenville, GA 30222-0160
(706) 672-4416; (706) 672-9465 FAX
http://www.gsccca.org/clerks
Louise T. Garrett
(land records)

Meriwether County Probate Court
(Courthouse, 100 Court Square—location)
PO Box 608 (mailing address)
Greenville, GA 30222-0608
(706) 672-1817; (706) 672-6660 FAX
probatejudge@yahoo.com
http://www.meriwether.ga.us
Judge Stiles Estes; Laurie B. Harrison, Probate
Clerk
(probate records from 1828 to date and
marriages)

Miller County
organized 1856 from Baker and Early counties

Miller County Clerk of Superior Court
(155 South First Street, Room 103—location)
PO Box 66 (mailing address)
Colquitt, GA 31737
(229) 758-4102; (229) 758-6585 FAX
annie.middleton.miller@gsccca.org
http://www.gsccca.org/clerks
Annie Laura Middleton

Miller County Probate Court
155 South First Street, Suite 110
Colquitt, GA 31737
(229) 758-4111; (229) 758-4110; (229) 758-8133
FAX
mcprobatecourt@bellsouth.net;
mcll@surfsouth.com
http://www.colquitt-
georgia.com/site/page5973.html (Chamber of
Commerce)
Judge Brenda G. McNease

Milton County
(see Fulton County)

Mitchell County
organized 1857 from Baker County

Mitchell County Clerk of Superior Court
Mitchell County Courthouse
11 Broad Street
Camilla, GA 31730
(229) 336-2022; (229) 336-9866 FAX
adaynabroome@gsccca.com
http://www.mitchellcountyga.net/html/govern
ment.html
Adayna Broome

Mitchell County Probate Court
Mitchell County Courthouse
11 Broad Street, Room 102
Camilla, GA 31730
(229) 336-2015; (229) 336-2016; (229) 336-2004
FAX; (229) 336-2354 FAX
http://www.mitchellcountyga.net/html/govern
ment.html
Judge Susan D. Taylor

Monroe County
organized 1821 from Indian Lands

Monroe County Clerk of Superior Court
(1 Courthouse Square—location)
PO Box 450 (mailing address)
Forsyth, GA 31029-0450
(478) 994-7022; (478) 994-7053 FAX
http://www.monroecountygeorgia.com

Lynn W. Ham
(deeds and naturalization records)

Monroe County Probate Court
(1 Courthouse Square—location)
PO Box 817 (mailing address)
Forsyth, GA 31029-0817
(478) 994-7036; (478) 994-7054 FAX
kpitman@monroecountygeorgia.com
http://www.monroecountygeorgia.com
Judge Karen H. Pitman
(marriages and probate records)
probate search service: $3.00; copies of deeds: $2.25; copies of marriages: $2.00; copies: $3.50, no minimum

Montgomery County
organized 1793 from Washington County

Montgomery County Clerk of Superior Court
(400 South Railroad Avenue
PO Box 311 (mailing address)
Mt. Vernon, GA 30445-0311
(912) 583-4401; (912) 583-4343 FAX
http://www.montgomerycountyga.com
Keith Hamilton
(land records and naturalization records)

Montgomery County Probate Court
(400 South Railroad Avenue—location)
PO Box 444 (mailing address)
Mt. Vernon, GA 30445-0444
(912) 583-2681; (912) 583-4343 FAX
rmoxsand@hotmail.com
http://www.montgomerycountyga.com
Judge Rubie Nell Sanders
(vital records and probate records)

Morgan County
organized 1807 from Baldwin and Jasper counties

Morgan County Clerk of Superior Court
(149 East Jefferson Street, Room 101A—location)
PO Box 130 (mailing address)
Madison, GA 30650-0168
(706) 342-3605; (706) 342-5083 FAX
EMealor@morganga.org
http://www.morganga.org
Elaine M. Mealor
(land records)

Morgan County Probate Court
(149 East Jefferson Street, Room 108—location)
PO Box 857 (mailing address)
Madison, GA 30650-1370
(706) 342-1373; (706) 342-5085 FAX
MBracewell@morganga.org
Judge Michael F. Bracewell

Murray County
organized 1832 from Cherokee County

Murray County Clerk of Superior Court
(121 North Third Avenue—location)
PO Box 1000 (mailing address)
Chatsworth, GA 30705-1000
(706) 695-2932; (706) 517-9672 FAX
http://www.murraycoga.com
Loreine P. Matthews

Murray County Probate Court
115 Fort Street
Chatsworth, GA 30705
(706) 695-3812; (706) 517-1340 FAX
mcprobate@alltel.net
http://www.murraycoga.com
Judge Dale Adams

Muscogee County
organized 1826 from Creek Lands and Harris, Lee and Marion counties; consolidated with the City of Columbus in 1970

Muscogee County Clerk of Superior Court
(1000 Tenth Street, Columbus, GA 31901-2376—location)
PO Box 2145 (mailing address)
Columbus, GA 31902-1340
(706) 653-4351; (706) 653-4352; (706) 653-4353

lpierce@columbusga.org
http://www.columbusga.org/depts
Linda Pierce

Muscogee County Probate Court
(100 Tenth Street, Columbus, GA 31901-2376—location)
PO Box 1340 (mailing address)
Columbus, GA 31902-1340
(706) 653-4333; (706) 653-4023 FAX
JLumpkin@ColumbusGa.org
http://www.columbusga.org/depts
Judge Julia W. Lumpkin

Newton County
organized 1821 from Henry, Jasper, Morgan and Walton counties

Newton County Clerk of Superior Court
1132 Usher Street, Room 338
Covington, GA 30014
(770) 784-2035; (770) 385-8930 FAX
lhays@co.newton.ga.us
http://co.newton.ga.us/content/view/13/31
Linda D. Hays
(land records from 1822)

Newton County Probate Court
1132 Usher Street, Room 148
Covington, GA 30014
(770) 784-2047; (770) 784-2045; (770) 784-2145 FAX
hbaker@co.newton.ga.us
http://co.newton.ga.us/content/view/13/31
Judge Henry A. Baker
(births and deaths from 1927, marriages from 1822, and probate records from 1822)
probate search service: no charge; copies of vital records: $10.00 each; copies of probate records: $4.00, no minimum; request should be in writing

Oconee County
organized 1875 from Clarke County

Oconee County Clerk of Superior Court
(Oconee County Courthouse, 23 North Main Street, Room 208—location)
PO Box 1099 (mailing address)
Watkinsville, GA 30677
(706) 769-3940; (706) 769-3948 FAX
awatson@oconee.ga.us
http://www.oconeecounty.com/Government/Judiciary/index.htm
Angela Elder Watson

Oconee County Probate Court
(Oconee County Courthouse, 23 North Main Street, Room 304—location)
PO Box 54 (mailing address)
Watkinsville, GA 30677
(706) 769-3936
danglin@oconee.ga.us
http://www.oconeecounty.com/Government/Judiciary/index.htm#probate
Judge David Anglin; Virginia King, Senior Probate Clerk
(records from 1875)
birth and death records: $10.00 for the first copy and $5.00 for each copy thereafter

Oglethorpe County
organized 1793 from Clarke, Greene and Wilkes counties

Oglethorpe County Clerk of Superior Court
(111 West Main Street—location)
PO Box 68 (mailing address)
Lexington, GA 30648-0068
(706) 743-5731; (706) 743-5335 FAX
kellips@windstream.net
http://onlineoglethorpe.com
Kelli Smith
(land records from 1794)

Oglethorpe County Probate Court
(111 West Main Street—location)
PO Box 70 (mailing address)
Lexington, GA 30648-0070
(706) 743-5350; (706) 743-3514 FAX

nation56@alltel.net
http://onlineoglethorpe.com/departmnts/probate/default.aspx
Judge Beverly W. Nation
(births from 1919, deaths from 1927, marriages from 1794, and wills and estates from 1794)
probate search service: $3.00; copies of probate records: 25¢ per page, $3.00 for certified copies, $3.25 minimum

Paulding County
organized 1832 from Cherokee Lands and Carroll and Cobb counties

Paulding County Clerk of Superior Court
11 Courthouse Square, G2
Dallas, GA 30132-1401
(770) 443-7527; (770) 443-7528 9Real Estate Division); (770) 505-3863 FAX
tshelton@paulding.gov
http://www.paulding.gov/gov/clerksofcourt.asp
Treva W. Shelton

Paulding County Probate Court
25 Courthouse Square, Room 102
Dallas, GA 30132
(770) 443-7541; (770) 443-7631 FAX
deborah.andersen@paulding.gov
http://www.paulding.gov
Judge Deborah Andersen

Peach County
organized 1924 from Houston and Macon counties

Peach County Clerk of Superior Court
(205 West Church Street—location)
PO Box 389 (mailing address)
Fort Valley, GA 31030-0389
(478) 825-5331; (478) 825-7319; (478) 825-8662 FAX
joe.wilder@gsccca.org
http://www.peachcounty.net/government/clerkofcourt.cfm
Joe Wilder

Peach County Probate Court
(205 West Church Street, Suite 117—location)
PO Box 327 (mailing address)
Fort Valley, GA 31030-0327
(478) 825-2313; (478) 825-2678 FAX
debbie-hunnicutt@peachcounty.net
http://www.peachcounty.net/probate.cfm
Judge Deborah W. Hunnicutt

Pickens County
organized 1853 from Cherokee and Gilmer counties

Pickens County Clerk of Superior Court
(52 North Main Street, Suite 102—location)
PO Box 130 (mailing address)
Jasper, GA 30143
(706) 253-8763; (706) 253-8825 FAX
http://www.pickenscountyga.gov
Gail Brown

Pickens County Probate Court
50 North Main Street, Suite 203
Jasper, GA 30143-1598
(706) 253-8757; (706) 253-8910 FAX
pickensprobatejudge@hotmail.com
http://www.pickenscountyga.gov
Judge D. Rodney Gibson
(vital records, probate records)
probate search service: $1.00; copies of probate records: $3.00, $3.00 minimum

Pierce County
organized 1857 from Appling and Ware counties

Pierce County Clerk of Superior Court
(312 Nichols Street, Suite 5—location)
PO Box 588 (mailing address)
Blackshear, GA 31516
(912) 449-2020; (912) 449-2106 FAX
thomas.sauls@gsccca.org
http://www.piercecountyga.org
Thomas W. Sauls

Pierce County Probate Court

(Pierce County Courthouse, 3550 Highway 84
    West—location)
PO Box 406 (mailing address)
Blackshear, GA 31516-0406
(912) 449-2029; (912) 449-1417 FAX
bjchoward@yahoo.com
http://www.piercecountyga.org
Judge Brenda Howard

Pike County
organized 1822 from Monroe and Upson
    counties

Pike County Clerk of Superior Court
(Courthouse, 100 Barnesville Street—location)
PO Box 10 (mailing address)
Zebulon, GA 30295-0010
(770) 567-2000; (770) 567-2017 FAX
http://pikecounty.georgia.gov/clerk
L. Carolyn Williams

Pike County Probate Court
(Courthouse, 100 Barnesville Street—location)
PO Box 324 (mailing address)
Zebulon, GA 30295-0324
(770) 567-8734; (770) 567-2019 FAX
pikeco1@bellsouth.net; stevefrypike@aol.com
    (Steve Fry (Chairman);
    jedhwfarm@mindspring.com (James
    Davidson, Commissioner);
    spalpw@mindspring.com (Onree Garner,
    Commissioner);
    pikecomm@accessunited.com (Benjamin
    Dunn, Commissioner)
http://pikecounty.georgia.gov/probate
Judge Lynn Brandenburg

Polk County
organized 1851 from Floyd and Paulding
    counties

Polk County Clerk of Superior Court
(Polk County Courthouse No. 1, 100 Prior
    Street, Room 106—location)
PO Box 948 (mailing address)
Cedartown, GA 30125-0948
(770) 749-2114; (770) 749-2148 FAX
http://www.polkcountygeorgia.us
Sheila A. Wells

Polk County Probate Court
Polk County Courthouse No. 1
100 Prior Street, Room 102
Cedartown, GA 30125
(770) 749-2128; (770) 749-2150 FAX
polkprobate@polkcountygeorgia.us
http://www.polkcountygeorgia.us
Judge Joyce B. Jones

Pulaski County
organized 1808 from Dodge, Dooly, Houston
    and Laurens counties

Pulaski County Clerk of Superior Court
(350 Commerce Street—location)
PO Box 60 (mailing address)
Hawkinsville, GA 31036-0060
(912) 783-1911; (912) 892-3308 FAX
peggy.fauscett@pulaskico.com
http://www.pulaskico.com/superior_court_cler
    k.htm
Peggy G. Fauscett
(land records)

Pulaski County Probate Court
(350 Commerce Street—location)
PO Box 156 (mailing address)
Hawkinsville, GA 31036-0156
(478) 783-2061; (478) 783-9219 FAX
Jeff.Jones@pulaskico.com;
    penny.dunagan@pulaskico.com
http://www.pulaskico.com/probate_main.htm
Judge Jeffrey Jones; Penny Dunagan
(vital records and probate records)
probate search service: $3.00; copies of probate
    records: $3.00

Putnam County
organized 1807 from Baldwin County

Putnam County Clerk of Superior Court
100 South Jefferson Avenue
Eatonton, GA 31024-1095
(706) 485-4501; (706) 485-2515 FAX
sheila.layson@gsccca.org
http://www.putnamcountyga.us
Sheila Layson

Putnam County Probate Court
100 South Jefferson Avenue
Eatonton, GA 31024
(706) 485-5476; (706) 485-2515 FAX
putnamprobate@surfsouth.com
http://www.putnamcountyga.us
Judge Patrice Howard

Quitman County
organized 1858 from Randolph and Stewart
    counties; consolidated with the City of
    Georgetown in 2006

Quitman County Clerk of Superior Court
(Courthouse, Main Street, Suite 2—location)
PO Box 307 (mailing address)
Georgetown, GA 31754-0307
(912) 334-2578; (912)334-3991 FAX
clerk_quitman@mail.gsccca.org
http://www.gsccca.org/clerks
Rebecca S. (Becky) Fendley

Quitman County Probate Court
(Courthouse, Main Street—location)
PO Box 7 (mailing address)
Georgetown, GA 31754-0007
(229) 334-2224; (229) 334-6826 FAX
abennett@eufaula.rr.com
http://quitmancounty.georgia.gov
Judge Andrew Bennett

Rabun County
organized 1819 from Cherokee Land and
    Habersham County

Rabun County Clerk of Superior Court
(25 Courthouse Square, Suite 105—location)
PO Box 893 (mailing address)
Clayton, GA 30525
(706) 782-3615; (706) 782-1391 FAX
http://www.rabuncountygov.com
Holly E. Henry-Perry
(land records)

Rabun County Probate Court
(25 Courthouse Square, Suite 215—location)
PO Box 346 (mailing address)
Clayton, GA 30525
(706) 672-3614; (706) 782-9278 FAX
lilliangarrett_tabunlaw@alltel.net
http://www.rabuncountygov.com
Judge Lillian W. Garrett
(births from 1869, deaths from 1930, and
    marriages and probate records from 1820)
probate search service: $10.00 (not refundable,
    must have name of person, name of record
    requested, and date of record); copies of vital
    records: $10.00 each for births and deaths,
    $4.00 each for marriages; must show death
    certificate of person in order to obtain birth
    certificate; copies of probate records: 25¢ per
    page when mailed

Randolph County
organized 1828 from Baker and Lee counties (an
    earlier county of the same name was renamed
    Jasper County in 1812)

Randolph County Clerk of Superior Court
(208 Court Street—location)
PO Box 98 (mailing address)
Cuthbert, GA 31740-0098
(229) 732-2216; (229) 732-5881 FAX
http://www.gsccca.org/clerks
Kay Arnold

Randolph County Probate Court
(208 Court Street—location)
PO Box 424 (mailing address)
Cuthbert, GA 31740-0424
(229) 732-2671; (229) 732-5881 FAX
http://randolphcounty.georgia.gov

Judge Linda E. Jackson

Richmond County
organized 1777 from St. Paul Parish;
    consolidated with the City of Augusta in 1995

Richmond County Clerk of Superior Court
(City-County Building, 530 Greene Street Room
    503—location)
PO Box 2046 (mailing address)
Augusta, GA 30911
(706) 821-1837; (706) 821-2448 FAX
ej1335@co.richmond.ga.us
http://www.augustaga.gov/departments/clerk_
    sup/home.asp
Elaine C. Johnson
(land records)

Richmond County Probate Court
City-County Municipal Building (11)
530 Greene Street, Room 401
Augusta, GA 30911
(706) 821-2434; (706) 821-2442 FAX
ij8771@augustaga.gov
http://www.augustaga.gov/departments/probat
    e_court/home.asp
Lelia R. Botnick
(marriage licenses, probate records)
probate search service: no charge; copies of
    probate records: 25¢ per page

Rockdale County
organized 1870 from Henry and Newton
    counties

Rockdale County Clerk of Courts
(922 Court Street—location)
PO Box 937 (mailing address)
Conyers, GA 30012
(770) 929-4021 (Main Number); (770) 929-4068
    (Real Estate Division)
maryclerk@aol.com
http://www.rockdalecounty.org/rock.cfm?pid=49
Joanne P. Caldwell

Rockdale County Probate Court
Rockdale County Courthouse
922 Court Street, Room 107
Conyers, GA 30012
(770) 929-4058; (770) 918-6463 FAX
donna.foust@rockdalecounty.org
http://www.rockdalecounty.org/rock.cfm?pid=38
Donna B. Foust
(births and deaths from 1920, estates from 1871)
vital records search service: $10.00 (births are
    covered under the privacy act, but deaths are
    public if relationship can be established);
    probate search service: $10.00; copies of
    probate records: 25¢ each

Schley County
organized 1857 from Marion and Sumter
    counties

Schley County Clerk of Superior Court
(200 South Broad Street, Courthouse Square—
    location)
PO Box 7 (mailing address)
Ellaville, GA 31806-0007
(229) 937-5581; (229) 937-5047 FAX
ginger.eubanks@gsccca.org
http://www.gsccca.org/clerks
Ginger G. Eubanks

Schley County Probate Court
(200 South Broad Street, Courthouse Square—
    location)
PO Box 385 (mailing address)
Ellaville, GA 31806-0385
(229) 937-2905; (229) 937-5588 FAX
mway@alltel.net
http://schleycounty.georgia.gov
Judge Mitzi E. Way

Screven County
organized 1793 from Burke and Effingham
    counties

Screven County Clerk of Superior Court
(216 Mims Road—location)

PO Box 156 (mailing address)
Sylvania, GA 30467-0156
(912) 564-2614; (912) 564-2622 FAX
janis.reddick@gsccca.org
http://www.gsccca.org/clerks
Janis B. Reddick

Screven County Probate Court
216 Mims Road, Suite 107
Sylvania, GA 30467-2026
(912) 564-2783; (912) 564-9139 FAX
screvenprobate@yahoo.com
http://screvencounty.georgia.gov; http://www.
screvencounty.com (Chamber of Commerce)
Judge Debbie B. Wells

Seminole County
organized 1920 from Decatur and Early counties

Seminole County Clerk of Superior Court
(Courthouse, 200 South Knox Avenue—
location)
PO Box 672 (mailing address)
Donalsonville, GA 31745
(912) 524-2525; (912) 524-8883 FAX
http://www.gsccca.org/clerks
Earlene Bramlett
(land records)

Seminole County Probate Court
(Courthouse, 200 South Knox Avenue—
location)
PO Box 63 (mailing address)
Donalsonville, GA 31745
(229) 524-5256; (229) 524-8644 FAX
scpc@alltel.net
http://seminolecounty.georgia.gov;
http://www.donalsonvillega.com/governmen
t.php (Chamber of Commerce)
Judge J. E. "Bo" Earnest
(vital records and probate records)
probate search service: depends on what is
requested; certified copies: $3.00 plus 50¢ per
page, $5.00 minimum

Spalding County
organized 1851 from Henry, Fayette and Pike
counties

Spalding County Clerk of Superior Court
(132 East Solomon Street, Griffin, GA 30223-
3312—location)
PO Box 163 (mailing address)
Griffin, GA 30224-0163
(770) 467-4745
info@spaldingcounty.com
http://www.spaldingcounty.com
Marcia Norris

Spalding County Probate Court
132 East Solomon Street
Griffin, GA 30223-3342
(770) 467-4340; (770) 467-4243 FAX
dsimonton@spauldingcounty.com
http://www.spaldingcounty.com
Judge DeWitt Simonton, Jr.

Stephens County
organized 1905 from Franklin and Habersham
counties

Stephens County Clerk of Superior Court
Stephens County Government Building
205 North Alexander Street, Room 202
Toccoa, GA 30577
(706) 886-9496; (706) 886-5710 FAX
http://www.itoccoa.com
Mr. Aubre Grafton

Stephens County Probate Court
Stephens County Government Building
205 North Alexander Street, Room 108
Toccoa, GA 30577
(706) 886-2828; (706) 886-2631 FAX
gseprobate@alltel.net
http://www.itoccoa.com
Judge Glenda S. Ernest

Stewart County
organized 1830 from Randolph County

Stewart County Clerk of Superior Court
(Courthouse, Broad Street—location)
PO Box 910 (mailing address)
Lumpkin, GA 31815-0910
(912) 838-6220; (912) 838-4505 FAX
stcocomm@bellsouth.net
http://www.gsccca.org/clerks
Patti B. Smith

Stewart County Probate Court
(Courthouse, Broad Street—location)
PO Box 876 (mailing address)
Lumpkin, GA 31815-0876
(229) 838-4394; (229) 838-9084 FAX
jimmybrazier@cs.com
http://www.stewartcounty.net;
http://stewartcounty.georgia.gov
Judge Jimmy B. Brazier

Sumter County
organized 1831 from Lee County

Sumter County Clerk of Court
(Sumter County Courthouse, Lamar Street—
location)
PO Box 333 (mailing address)
Americus, GA 31709
(229) 928-4537; (229) 928-4539 FAX
http://www.sumter-
ga.com/courts/clerkofcourt.html
Nancy Smith

Sumter County Probate Court
(Sumter County Courthouse, Lamar Street—
location)
PO Box 246 (mailing address)
Americus, GA 31709
(229) 928-4551
judyr@sumter-ga.com
http://www.sumter-
ga.com/courts/probate.html
Judge Judy Reeves; Marianna Holloway, Clerk
(marriages and probate records)
copies of marriage records: 25¢ per page, $4.00
for certified copies, plus SASE; copies of
probate records: 25¢ per page

Swinnett County
(see Cherokee County)

Talbot County
organized 1827 from Crawford, Harris, Macon,
Marion and Muscogee counties

Talbot County Clerk of Superior Court
(1 Courthouse Square, 26 Washington Road—
location)
PO Box 325 (mailing address)
Talbotton, GA 31827-0325
(706) 665-3239; (706) 665-8637 FAX
http://www.gsccca.org/clerks
Linda Lucas

Talbot County Probate Court
(Courthouse Square, Washington Street—
location)
PO Box 157 (mailing address)
Talbotton, GA 31827-0157
(706) 665-8866; (706) 665-8240 FAX
talbotpro@yahoo.com
http://talbotcounty.georgia.gov
Judge Joe S. Johnson, Jr.

Taliaferro County
organized 1825 from Greene, Hancock,
Oglethorpe, Warren and Wilkes counties

Taliaferro County Clerk of Superior Court
(113 Monument Street—location)
PO Box 182 (mailing address)
Crawfordville, GA 30631-0182
(706) 456-2123; (706) 456-2749 FAX
http://www.gaclerks.org/Association/Clerks/D
efault.aspx?CountyID=131;
http://www.georgiacourts.org/courts/counti
es/taliaferro/index
Sandra S. Greene
(land records)

Taliaferro County Probate Court
(113 Monument Street—location)
PO Box 264 (mailing address)
Crawfordville, GA 30631
(706) 456-2253; (706) 456-3550 FAX
http://taliaferrocounty.georgia.gov
Judge Martha R. Mayo
(births and probate records)

Tattnall County
organized 1801 from Liberty and Montgomery
counties

Tattnall County Clerk of Superior Court
(108 Brazell Street—location)
PO Box 39 (mailing address)
Reidsville, GA 30453-0039
(912) 557-6716; (912) 557-4861 FAX
debbie.crews@gsccca.org
http://www.tattnall.com
Debbie Crews

Tattnall County Probate Court
(108 Brazell Street—location)
PO Box 699 (mailing address)
Reidsville, GA 30453-0039
(912) 557-6719; (912) 557-3976 FAX
glopurdub_98@hotmail.com;
tattnallprobatecourt@hotmail.com
http://home.alltel.net/tattnall/tattnall/Contact
Us.html
Judge Gloria Dubberly

Taylor County
organized 1852 from Macon, Marion and Talbot
counties

Taylor County Clerk of Superior Court
(1 Courthouse Square—location)
PO Box 248 (mailing address)
Butler, GA 31006-0248
(478) 862-5594; (478) 862-5334 FAX
http://www.taylorga.us/clerk.htm
Robert E. Taunton, Jr.
(land records from 1852 to date)

Taylor County Probate Court
(1 Courthouse Square—location)
PO Box 536 (mailing address)
Butler, GA 31006-0536
(478) 862-3357; (478) 862-9447 FAX
probate@pstel.net
http://www.taylorga.us/probate.htm
Judge Ronnie A. Parker
(vital records from 1927 to date [confidential,
restricted to family members], probate
records from 1852 to date)
copies of probate records: 20¢ per page

Telfair County
organized 1807 from Appling and Wilkinson
counties

Telfair County Clerk of Superior Court
Telfair Courthouse, 128 East Oak Street, Suite 2
McRae, GA 31055
(912) 868-6525; (912) 868-7956 FAX
http://www.gsccca.org/clerks
Gene Johnson
(deed records from 1807)

Telfair County Probate Court
128 East Oak Street, Suite 1
McRae, GA 31055-1670
(229) 868-6038; (229) 868-7620 FAX
judgedw@alltel.net
http://telfaircounty.georgia.gov
Judge Dianne M. Walker

Terrell County
organized 1856 from Lee and Randolph
counties

Terrell County Clerk of Superior Court
513 South Main Street
Dawson, GA 31742
(229) 995-2631; (229) 995-6453 FAX
Louise.Darley@gsccca.org
http://www.gsccca.org/clerks
Louise B. Darley
(land records, naturalization records)

Terrell County Probate Court
(Courthouse, 235 East Lee Street—location)
PO Box 67 (mailing address)
Dawson, GA 31742-0067
(229) 995-5515; (229) 995-5574 FAX
probatefryer@hotmail.com
http://terrellcounty.georgia.gov;
http://www.terrellcounty-
ga.com/government.htm (AdVenture
Publishing, Inc.)
Judge Nancy P. Fryer
(vital records and probate records)
probate search service: $3.00; copies of probate
records: 25¢ per page, $1.50 for certified
copies

Thomas County
organized 1825 from Baker, Decatur, Irwin and
Lowndes counties

Thomas County Clerk of Superior Court
(225 North Broad Street, Thomasville, GA
31792—location)
PO Box 1995 (mailing address)
Thomasville, GA 31799-1995
(229) 225-4108; (229) 225-4110 FAX
david.hutchings@gsccca.org
http://www.thomascoclerkofcourt.org
David Hutchings, Jr.
(land records)

Thomas County Probate Court
(225 North Broad Street—location)
PO Box 1582 (mailing address)
Thomasville, GA 31799
(229) 225-4116; (229) 227-1698 FAX
probbk@rose.net
http://www.georgiacourts.org/courts/probate/t
homas
Judge Vickie B. Burnette
probate search service: $3.00 in person only, not
by mail; copies of probate records: $1.00 per
page in person only, no minimum

Tift County
organized 1905 from Berrien, Irwin and Worth
counties

Tift County Clerk of Superior Court
(Courthouse, Second Street and Tift Avenue—
location)
PO Box 354 (mailing address)
Tifton, GA 31793-0354
(229) 386-7810; (229) 386-7815 FAX
gwen.pate@gsccca.org
http://www.tiftcounty.org/Departments/count
y_court/clerkofcourt.htm
Gwen C. Pate

Tift County Probate Court
(Administrative Building, Room 117—location)
PO Box 792 (mailing address)
Tifton, GA 31793-0792
(229) 386-7913; (229) 386-7926 FAX
sjohnson@tiftcounty.org
http://www.georgiacourts.org/courts/counties/
tift/index.html
Judge Suzanne C. Johnson

Toombs County
organized 1905 from Emanuel, Montgomery
and Tattnall counties

Toombs County Clerk of Superior Court
(Courthouse, 100 Courthouse Square—location)
PO Drawer 530 (mailing address)
Lyons, GA 30436-0530
(912) 526-3501; (912) 912-1004 FAX
http://www.gsccca.org/clerks
Chess Fountain

Toombs County Probate Court
(Courthouse, 100 Courthouse Square—location)
PO Box 1370 (mailing address)
Lyons, GA 30436-1370
(912) 526-8696; (912) 526-1008 FAX
driskell_tpc@accessvidalia.net
http://toombscounty.georgia.gov;
http://www.georgiacourts.org/courts/counti
es/toombs/index.html

Judge Jackie O. Driskell

Towns County
organized 1856 from Rabun and Union counties

Towns County Clerk of Superior Court
48 River Street, Suite E
Hiawassee, GA 30546
(706) 896-2130; (706) 896-1772 FAX
http://www.townscountyga.com/County_office
s.php
Cecil Ray Dye

Towns County Probate Court
48 River Street, Suite C
Hiawassee, GA 30546
(706) 896-3467; (706) 896-1772 FAX
tcjudge@alltel.net
http://www.townscountyga.com/County_office
s.php
Judge Wayne Garrett

Treutlen County
organized 1917 from Emanuel and Montgomery
counties

Treutlen County Clerk of Superior Court
203 Second Street South, Suite 301
Soperton, GA 30457
(912) 529-4215; (912) 529-6737 FAX
http://www.gsccca.org/clerks
Curtis (Buddy) J. Rogers, Jr.
(land records from 1919)

Treutlen County Probate Court
(Treutlen County Courthouse Annex, 114
Second Street South—location)
PO Box 88 (mailing address)
Soperton, GA 30457-0088
(912) 529-3842; (912) 529-6838 FAX
tj4treutlen@yahoo.com
http://treutlencounty.georgia.gov;
http://www.georgiacourts.org/courts/counti
es/treutlen/index.html
Judge Torri J. Hudson
(vital records and probate records from 1919)
probate search service: no charge; copies of
probate records: 25¢ per page, no minimum

Troup County
organized 1826 from Indian Lands and Carroll
County

Troup County Clerk of Superior Court
Troup County Government Services Center
100 Ridley Avenue, First Floor
La Grange, GA 30241
(706) 883-1740
jackie.taylor@gsccca.org
http://www.troupcountyga.org
Jackie Taylor

Troup County Probate Court
100 Ridley Avenue
La Grange, GA 30240
(706) 883-1690; (706) 812-7933 FAX
dboyd@troupco.org;
Troupprobate@mindspring.com
http://www.georgiacourts.org/courts/counties/
troup
Judge Donald W. Boyd; Debbie Wade, Chief
Clerk

Turner County
organized 1905 from Dooly, Irwin, Wilcox and
Worth counties

Turner County Clerk of Superior Court
(219 East College Avenue, Room #3—location)
PO Box 106 (mailing address)
Ashburn, GA 31714-0106
(229) 567-2011 (229) 567-0450 FAX
http://www.gsccca.org/clerks
Linda T. House
(land records)

Turner County Probate Court
PO Box 2506
Ashburn, GA 31714-2506
(229) 567-2151; (229) 567-0358 FAX
thomaspenny@gomail.doas.state.georgia.us

http://turnercounty.georgia.gov;
http://www.georgiacourts.org/courts/counti
es/turner/index.html
Judge Penny E. Thomas
(vital records and probate records)
vital records search service: $10.00 (index only
open to the public); probate search service:
$10.00; copies of vital records: first copy
included in search fee, $5.00 for each
additional copy (restricted to relatives); copies
of probate records: $1.00 per page

Twiggs County
organized 1809 from Wilkinson County

Twiggs County Clerk of Superior Court
(109 East Main Street—location)
PO Box 234 (mailing address)
Jeffersonville, GA 31044-0228
(478) 945-3350; (478) 945-6751 FAX
pgrimsley@twiggscounty.us
http://www.twiggscounty.us/Clerk%20of%20C
ourt.htm
Patti H. Grimsley

Twiggs County Probate Court
(109 East Main Street—location)
PO Box 307 (mailing address)
Jeffersonville, GA 31044-0307
(478) 945-3390; (478) 945-6070 FAX
http://www.twiggscounty.us; http://www.
georgiacourts.org/courts/counties/twiggs/in
dex.html
Judge Kenneth E. Fowler

Union County
organized 1832 from Cherokee Lands and
Lumpkin County

Union County Clerk of Superior Court
114 Courthouse Street, Suite 5
Blairsville, GA 30512
(706) 439-6022; (706) 439-6026 FAX
http://www.unioncountyga.gov/home.htm
Allen Conley
(land records from the 1860s)

Union County Probate Court
114 Courthouse Street, Suite 8
Blairsville, GA 30512
(706) 439-6006; (706) 439-6009 FAX
ucprobate@alltel.net
http://www.unioncountyga.gov/home.htm
Judge Dwain Brackett
(births and deaths from 1919, marriages from
1833, wills, administrations, etc. from 1835)
probate search service: $3.00; copies of probate
records: $1.00 per page, no minimum

Upson County
organized 1824 from Crawford and Pike
counties

Upson County Clerk of Superior Court
(116 West Main Street, Courthouse Annex
Building—location)
PO Box 469 (mailing address)
Thomaston, GA 30286-0468
(706) 647-5847; (706) 647-8999 FAX
http://www.gsccca.org/clerks
Nancy B. Adams
(land records with Tax Assessor's Office,
naturalization records with Clerk of Court)

Upson County Probate Court
(Thomaston-Upson County Government
Complex Building, 250 East Lee Street, Suite
210—location)
PO Box 906 (mailing address)
Thomaston, GA 30286-0012
(706) 647-7015; (706) 646-3341 FAX
garyhamby@msn.com
http://upsoncounty.georgia.gov; http://www.
georgiacourts.org/courts/counties/upson/in
dex.html
Judge Virgil Gary Hamby

Walker County
organized 1833 from Murray County

Walker County Clerk of Superior Court
(Walker County Courthouse, Duke Street—location)
PO Box 445 (mailing address)
Lafayette, GA 30728-0445
(706) 638-1742
clerkofcourt@co.walker.ga.us
http://www.co.walker.ga.us/Clerk_of_Court.htm
Bill McDaniel
(deeds with Clerk of Court, appraisal records with Property Records Office, marriage licenses with Walker County Health Department)
copies of marriage licenses: $3.00 each

Walker County Probate Court
(Walker County Courthouse, Duke Street—location)
PO Box 436 (mailing address)
LaFayette, GA 30728
(706) 638-2852; (706) 638-2869 FAX
probatecourt@co.walker.ga.us
http://www.co.walker.ga.us/Probate.htm
Judge Foye L. Johnson; Briggitt Garrett, Clerk
(probate records from 1882)
probate search service: $3.00; copies of probate records: 25¢ each, $3.00 for certified copies, no minimum

Walton County
organized 1803 from Cherokee Lands and Henry and Jackson counties

Walton County Clerk of Superior Court
(115 South Broad Street—location)
PO Box 745 (mailing address)
Monroe, GA 30655-0745
(770) 267-1305; (770) 267-1307; (770) 267-1365 FAX
ktrost@co.walton.ga
http://www.waltoncountyga.org
Kathy Keesee Trost
(land records, naturalization records)

Walton County Probate Court
(111 East Spring Street—location)
PO Box 629 (mailing address)
Monroe, GA 30655-0629
(770) 267-1345; (770) 267-1417 FAX
gadams@co.walton.ga.us
http://www.waltoncountyga.org/courts.html
Judge H. Greg Adams
(vital records, and probate records from 1819)
no probate search service; copies of probate records: 25¢

Ware County
organized 1824 from Appling County

Ware County Clerk of Superior Court
(800 Church Street, Room 124, Waycross, GA 31502—lcoation)
PO Box 776 (mailing address)
Waycross, GA 31501-0776
(912) 287-4340; (912) 287-2498 FAX
mfiveash@warecounty.com
http://warecounty.com
Melba H. Fiveash
(land records, naturalization records)

Ware County Probate Court
Ware County Courthouse
800 Church Street, Suite 123
Waycross, GA 31501
(912) 287-4315; (912) 287-4317 FAX
mclark@warecounty.com
http://warecounty.com
Judge Marcus Lee Sweat, Jr.; Mary Nell Clark, Clerk
(marriages from 1874, wills, administrations, guardianships from 1874)
probate search service: no charge; copies of probate records: 25¢ per page, no minimum

Warren County
organized 1793 from Columbia, Richmond and Wilkes counties

Warren County Clerk of Superior Court
(Courthouse, 100 East Main Street, Suite 201—location)
PO Box 227 (mailing address)
Warrenton, GA 30828-0227
(706) 465-2262; (706) 465-0232 FAX
http://www.gsccca.org/clerks
Shirley T. Cheeley

Warren County Probate Court
(Courthouse, 100 East Main Street—location)
PO Box 364 (mailing address)
Warrenton, GA 30828
(706) 465-2227; (706) 465-1300 FAX
http://warrencounty.georgia.gov; http://www.warrencountyga.com (Chamber of Commerce); http://www.georgiacourts.org/courts/counties/warren/index.html
Judge Janice Thigpen

Washington County
organized 1784 from Indian Lands

Washington County Clerk of Superior Court
(Washington County Courthouse, Courthouse Square Highway 15—location)
PO Box 231 (mailing address)
Sandersville, GA 31082-0231
(478) 552-3186; (478) 553-9969 FAX
http://www.washingtoncounty-ga.com/countygovernment.htm
Joy H. Conner
(deed records from 1865)

Washington County Probate Court
(Washington County Courthouse, Courthouse Square—location)
PO Box 669 (mailing address)
Sandersville, GA 31082-0669
(478) 552-3304; (478) 552-7424 FAX
rtl150washco@yahoo.com
http://www.washingtoncounty-ga.com/countygovernment.htm
Judge Rachel T. Lord
(probate records from 1828)
probate search service: no charge; copies of probate records: $1.00, no minimum

Wayne County
organized 1803 from Indian Lands and Appling, Camden and Glynn counties

Wayne County Clerk of Superior Court
(Courthouse, 174 North Brunswick Street—location)
PO Box 918 (mailing address)
Jesup, GA 31545
(912) 427-5930; (912) 427-5939 FAX
http://www.co.wayne.ga.us/home/departments/Courts
Stetson F. Bennett, Jr.

Wayne County Probate Court
Courthouse, 174 North Brunswick Street
Jesup, GA 31546
(912) 427-5940; (912) 427-5944 FAX
waynees@bellsouth.net
http://www.co.wayne.ga.us/home/departments/Courts
Judge Christine Burch

Webster County
organized 1853 from Stewart County; name changed from Kinchafoonee in 1856

Webster County Clerk of Superior Court
(Courthouse, U.S. Highway 28 East, 6330 Hamilton Street, Room 102—location)
PO Box 117 (mailing address)
Preston, GA 31824-0117
(912) 828-3525; (912) 828-6961 FAX
http://www.gsccca.org/clerks
Tina Blankenship

Webster County Probate Court
(Courthouse, Highway 28 West—location)
PO Box 135 (mailng address)
Preston, GA 31824-0135
(912) 828-3615; (912) 828-3616 FAX
magjudgetindol@hotmail.com
http://webstercounty.georgia.gov; http://www.georgiacourts.org/courts/counties/webster/

index.html
Judge Lorene W. Tindol

Wheeler County
organized 1912 from Montgomery County

Wheeler County Clerk of Superior Court
(Courthouse, 119 West Pearl Street—location)
PO Box 38 (mailing address)
Alamo, GA 30411-0038
(912) 568-7137; (912) 568-7543 FAX
wheelerco@alltel.net
http://www.gsccca.org/clerks
Michael A. (Sandy) Morrison
(land records, naturalization records)

Wheeler County Probate Court
(Courthouse, 119 West Pearl Street—location)
PO Box 477 (mailing address)
Alamo, GA 30411-0477
(912) 568-7133; (912) 568-1743 FAX
wprobate@alltel.net
http://wheelercounty.georgia.gov
Judge Roy O. Braswell, Jr.
(marriages, estate records)

White County
organized 1857 from Habersham County

White County Clerk of Superior Court
59 South Main Street, Suite B
Cleveland, GA 30528
(706) 865-2613; (706) 865-7749 FAX
dadams@whitecounty.net
http://www.whitecounty.net/clerk.htm
Dena M. Adams

White County Probate Court
59 South Main Street, Suite H
Cleveland, GA 30528
(706) 865-4141; (706) 865-1324 FAX
gbaker@whitecounty.net
http://www.whitecounty.net/probate.htm
Judge Garrison Baker

Whitfield County
organized 1851 from Murray and Walker counties

Whitfield County Clerk of Superior Court
205 North Selvidge Street
Dalton, GA 30720
(706) 275-7450; (706) 275-7456 FAX
http://www.whitfieldcountyga.com/Clerk%20of%20Court/clerk_of_court.htm; http://www.gaclerks.org/Association/Clerks/default.aspx
Melica Kendrick
(online record search)

Whitfield County Probate Court
(205 North Selvedge Street, Dalton, GA 30721—location)
301 West Crawford Street (mailing address)
Dalton, GA 30720-4290
(706) 275-7400; (706) 275-7486 FAX
rbroadrick@whitfieldcountyga.com
http://www.whitfieldcountyga.com/Probate%20Court/probate_court.htm
Judge Ray Broadrick
(vital records, probate records)
probate search service: no charge; vital records search service: $10.00; copies of marriages: 25¢ each, $5.00 if certified

Wilcox County
organized 1857 from Dooly, Irwin and Pulaski counties

Wilcox County Clerk of Superior Court
103 North Broad Street
Abbeville, GA 31001-1000
(229) 467-2442; (229) 467-2886 FAX
http://www.gsccca.org/clerks
Wanda F. Hawkins

Wilcox County Probate Court
103 North Broad Street
Abbeville, GA 31001-1000
(229) 467-2220; (229) 467-2000 FAX
http://wilcoxcounty.georgia.gov;
http://www.georgiacourts.org/courts/counti

es/wilcox/index.html
Judge Betty J. Anderson

Wilkes County
organized 1777 from original territory

Wilkes County Clerk of Superior Court
23 East Court Street, Room 205
Washington, GA 30673-1593
(706) 678-2523; (706) 678-2115 FAX
mildred.peeler@wilkes.gacourts.org
http://www.gsccca.org/clerks
Mildred Peeler
(real estate records from 1785)
land records search service: $3.00 plus SASE

Wilkes County Probate Court
23 East Court Street, Room 422
Washington, GA 30673-1595
(706) 678-2523; (706) 678-4854 FAX
j.c.burton@usa.net
http://wilkescounty.georgia.gov;
    http://www.washingtonwilkes.com (Chamber
    of Commerce); http://www.georgiacourts.
    org/courts/counties/wilkes/index.html
Judge James C. Burton
(land grants [not deeds], births and deaths from
    1927 [not public records], marriages from
    1800 and probate records from 1777)

Wilkinson County
organized 1803 from Creek Cession

Wilkinson County Clerk of Superior Court
(100 Bacon Street—location)
PO Box 250 (mailing address)
Irwinton, GA 31042-0250
(478) 946-2221; (467) 946-1497 FAX
http://www.wilkinsoncounty.net/wilco_sup_ct.
    htm
Cinda S. Bright
(courthouse burned five times, rebuilt in 1924)

Wilkinson County Probate Court
(100 Bacon Street—location)
PO Box 201 (mailing address)
Irwinton, GA 31042-0201
(478) 946-2222; (478) 946-3810 FAx
judgevivian@hotmail.com
http://www.wilkinsoncounty.net/Probate.htm
Judge Vivian L. Cummings
(births and deaths from 1919, marriages from
    1823 to 1828 and from 1865 to date and wills
    from 1820 to date)
copies: 25¢ per page

Worth County
organized 1853 from Dooly and Irwin counties

Worth County Clerk of Superior Court
201 North Main, Room 13
Sylvester, GA 31791-2100
(229) 776-8205; (229) 776-8205 FAX
joann.powell@gsccca.org
http://www.worthcountyboc.com/clerk-of-
    courts.html
Joann Ford Powell
(land records from 1892)

Worth County Probate Court
201 North Main Street, Room 12
Sylvester, GA 31791
(229) 776-8207; (229) 776-1540 FAX
virginiaandrews@hotmail.com
http://www.worthcountyboc.com/probate-
    court.html; http://www.worthcounty.com/
    communities; http://www.georgiacourts.org/
    courts/counties/worth/index.html
Judge Virginia Andrews
(births and deaths from 1919, marriages from
    1854, probate records from 1853, wills from
    1863)
probate search service: $3.00 per name; certified
    copies of vital records: $10.00 (cashier's check
    or money order only); copies of probate
    records: 25¢ per page, $4.00 for certified
    copies, $1.00 minimum plus postage (cashier's
    check or money order only)

HAWAII

*Capital: Honolulu. Statehood: 21 August 1959
(annexed in 1898, became a territory on 30 April
1900)*

Hawaii's Tax Appeal Court and Land Court
have statewide special jurisdiction and sit at
Honolulu. Four District Courts handle some
civil actions, small claims, landlord-tenant
disputes, misdemeanors, traffic violations and
felony preliminaries. Four Circuit Courts handle
civil matters, domestic relations, probate,
felonies, and juvenile matters. First Circuit:
Honolulu County, the Kalaupapa settlement in
Kalawao, Molokai and all other islands not
covered by other circuits; Second Circuit: Maui
County except the Kalaupapa settlement in
Kalawao, Molokai; Third Circuit: Hawaii
County; Fifth Circuit: Kauai County. An
Intermediate Court of Appeals and the state's
Supreme Court sit at Honolulu.

Land Court
Ka'ahumanu Hale
777 Punchbowl Street
Honolulu, HI 96813-5093
(808) 539-4777; (808) 539-4713 FAX
http://www.courts.state.hi.us/page_server/Gen
    Info/Contact/41D9CB209CB017DFE9A824
    8EB4.html

Hawaii County
organized 1905

Hawai'i Third Circuit
Circuit Court
(State Building, 75 Aupini Street—location)
PO Box 1007 (mailing address)
Hilo, HI 96720
(808) 961-7440 (Chief Court Administrator);
    (808) 961-7416 FAX
http://www.courts.state.hi.us/page_server/Gen
    Info/Contact/36331383F1BEADEAE9DB7
    361C7.html

Hawai'i Third Circuit
District Court
State Building, 75 Aupini Street
Hilo, HI 96720
(808) 961-7470 (Information)
http://www.courts.state.hi.us/page_server/Gen
    Info/Contact/36331383F1BEADEAE9DB7
    361C7.html

Honolulu County
organized 1905

O'ahu First Circuit
Circuit Court
Ka'ahumanu Hale
(777 Punchbowl Street—location)
PO Box 619 (mailing address)
Honolulu, HI 96813
(808) 539-4767
http://www.courts.state.hi.us/page_server/Gen
    Info/Contact/1315C15E545F2834E9A82B5
    A46.html

O'ahu First Circuit
District Court
1111 Alakea Street
Honolulu, HI 96813
(808) 538-5767
http://www.courts.state.hi.us/page_server/Gen
    Info/Contact/1315C15E545F2834E9A82B5
    A46.html

Kauai County
organized 1905

Kaua'i Fifth Circuit
Circuit Court
3970 Ka'ana Street
Lihu'e, HI 96766
(808) 482-2318 (Chief Court Administrator);
    (808) 482-2510 FAX
http://www.courts.state.hi.us/page_server/Gen
    Info/Contact/53BB4524E0939088E9DB73C

75E.html

Kaua'i Fifth Circuit
District Court
3970 Ka'ana Street
Lihu'e, HI 96766
(808) 482-2300 (Information)
http://www.courts.state.hi.us/page_server/Gen
    Info/Contact/53BB4524E0939088E9DB73C
    75E.html

Maui County
organized 1905

Maui - Second Circuit
Circuit Court
Hoapili Hale
2145 Main Street, Suite 106
Wailuku, HI 96793-1679
(808) 244-2929 (Court Administrator); (808)
    244-2932 FAX
http://www.courts.state.hi.us/page_server/Gen
    Info/Contact/7A050DD7D88D65C8E9DB7
    276C1.html
(vital records, probate records)

Maui - Second Circuit
District Court
Hoapili Hale
2145 Main Street
Wailuku, HI 96793
(808) 244-2800 (Information)
http://www.courts.state.hi.us/page_server/Gen
    Info/Contact/7A050DD7D88D65C8E9DB7
    276C1.html

IDAHO

Capital: Boise. Statehood: 3 July 1890 (became sole U.S. possession by treaty with Great Britain in 1846, was part of Oregon Territory in 1848, Washington Territory in 1853, and became a separate territory in 1863)

Idaho's District Courts sit at each county seat and have original jurisdiction over civil, personal injury, domestic relations, criminal, felony and other matters, including appeals from the Magistrate's Division of District Courts, which hear some civil actions and cases concerning property liens, probate, small claims, misdemeanors, traffic, juveniles, etc. First Judicial District: Benewah, Bonner, Boundary, Kootenai, and Shoshone counties; Second Judicial District: Clearwater, Idaho, Latah, Lewis, and Nez Perce counties; Third Judicial District: Adams, Canyon, Gem, Owyhee, Payette, and Washington counties; Fourth Judicial District: Ada, Boise, Elmore, and Valley counties; Fifth Judicial District: Blaine, Camas, Cassia, Gooding, Jerome, Lincoln, Minidoka, and Twin Falls counties; Sixth Judicial District: Bannock, Bear Lake, Caribou, Franklin, Oneida, and Power counties; Seventh Judicial District: Bingham, Bonneville, Butte, Clark, Custer, Fremont, Jefferson, Lemhi, Madison, and Teton counties. The Idaho Supreme Court sits at Boise and elsewhere.

Ada County
organized 1864 from Boise County

Ada County Clerk of the Fourth District Court/Auditor/Recorder
200 West Front Street, Room 1196
Boise, ID 83702-7300
(208) 287-6840; (208) 287-6849 FAX
daven@adaweb.net
http://www.adaweb.net/departments/ClerkAuditorRecorder
J. David Navarro
(land records from 1865)
copies: $1.00 per page

Magistrate Court Civil Clerk's Office
200 West Front Street, Fourth Floor
Boise, ID 83702
(208) 287-6900 (press 5)
http://www2.state.id.us/fourthjudicial/Ada%20County/Ada%20County.htm
(civil matters, unlawful detainers, adoptions, terminations, child protection proceedings, name changes, probates, guardianships, conservatorships, and registrations of trust)

Adams County
organized 1911 from Washington County

Adams County Clerk
(201 Industrial Avenue—location)
PO Box 48 (mailing address)
Council, ID 83612-0048
(208) 253-4561; (208) 263-4880 FAX
mfisk@co.adams.id.us
http://www.the3rdjudicialdistrict.com/adams.htm
Michael A. Fisk
(land records from about 1900, probate records from 1911)
probate search service (cost depends on what is requested); copies of probate records: $1.00 per page, no minimum

Alturas County
county abolished 1895 (see Blaine, Custer, Elmore, and Lincoln counties)

Bannock County
organized 1893 from Oneida and Bear Lake counties

Bannock County Clerk
624 East Center, Room 211

Pocatello, ID 83205
(208) 236-7352
http://www.co.bannock.id.us/clrk/index.htm
Mr. Dale Hatch
(probate records)
probate search service: no charge; copies of probate records: $1.00 per page, no minimum

Bannock County Clerk-Auditor-Recorder
(624 East Center, Room 211—location)
PO Box 6094 (mailing address)
Pocatello, ID 83205-6094
(208) 236-7334; (208) 236-7345 FAX
daleh@bannockcounty.us
http://www.co.bannock.id.us/clerkcrt.htm
Dale Hatch
(land records from 1893, naturalization records from 1903 to 1917, declarations of intention from 1893 to 1906)

District Court Clerk
624 East Center, Room 211
Pocatello, ID 83205
(208) 236-7352
http://www.co.bannock.id.us/6distct.htm
Dale Hatch
(probate records)
probate search service: no charge; copies of probate records: $1.00 per page, no minimum

Bear Lake County
organized 1875 from Oneida County

Bear Lake County Clerk
(7 East Center Street—location)
PO Box 190 (mailing address)
Paris, ID 83261-0190
(208) 945-2212, ext. 5; (208) 945-2236; (208) 945-2780 FAX
khaddock@dcdi.net
http://www.bearlakecounty.info/services.html#anchor68950
Kerry Haddock
(land transactions, birth and death records 1907–1911)

District Court Deputy Clerk
(7 East Center Street—location)
PO Box 190 (mailing address)
Paris, ID 83261-0190
(208) 945-2208, ext. 6; (208) 945-2209; (208) 945-2780 FAX
http://www.bearlakecounty.info/services.html#anchor30100
Rosemary Lloyd
(court documents and proceedings)

Benewah County
organized 1915 from Kootenai County

Benewah County Clerk
701 West College Avenue
St. Maries, ID 83861-1852
(208) 245-3212; (208) 245-3046 FAX
jreynolds@benewahcounty.org
http://www.state.id.us/aboutidaho/county/benewah.html
Michele Reynolds
(land records, naturalization records, vital records, probate records)
no probate search service; copies of probate records: $1.00 per page (all records have been microfilmed by the Family History Library in Salt Lake City)

Bingham County
organized 1885 from Oneida County

Bingham County Clerk
501 North Maple Street, #205
Blackfoot, ID 83221-1776
(208) 785-8040; (208) 785-4131 FAX
sstaub@co.bingham.id.us
http://www.co.bingham.id.us
Sara Staub
(land records from 1865, naturalization records from 1892 to about 1969, births and deaths from 1907 to 1911, marriages from 1865, probate records from 1894)
probate search service: no charge; copies of

probate records: $1.00 per page, $1.00 for certification, no minimum

Blaine County
organized 1895 from Alturas County, which was organized 1864 and abolished 1895, and whose records were deposited with Blaine County, along with those of Logan County, which was organized 1889 and abolished 1895

Blaine County Clerk
(206 First Avenue South #200—location)
PO Box 400 (mailing address)
Hailey, ID 83333-0400
(208) 788-5505; (208) 788-5501 FAX
mreimann@co.blaine.id.us
http://www.co.blaine.id.us
Marsha Reimann
(vital records from 1907 to 1913, probate records)
no probate search service; copies of probate records: $1.00 if recorded, 25¢ if not recorded, no minimum

Boise County
organized 1907, original county

Boise County Clerk, Auditor, Recorders Office
(420 Main Street—location)
PO Box 1300 (mailing address)
Idaho City, ID 83631-1300
(208) 392-4431; (208) 392-4473 FAX
cswearingen@co.boinse.id.us
http://www.co.boise.id.us
Constance Swearingen, Clerk, Ex Officio Auditor, Recorder
(some naturalization records from 1865 to 1916 and probate records from 1865)
probate search service: no charge; copies of probate records: $1.00 per page, $10.00 minimum

Bonner County
organized 1907 from Kootenai County

Bonner County Clerk
215 South First
Sandpoint, ID 83664-1392
(208) 265-1432; (208) 265-1447 FAX
mscott@co.bonner.id.us
http://www.co.bonner.id.us
Marie Scott
(land records from 1907, some naturalization records from 1890s to 1920s, births from 1907 to 1911, deaths from 1707 to 1911 and 1986 to present, marriages from 1907, probate records from 1907)
probate search service: no charge; copies of land, naturalization, vital, and probate records: $1.00 per page, $1.00 per document for certification, no minimum

Bonneville County
organized 1911 from Bingham County

Bonneville County Clerk and Clerk of Seventh Judicial District
605 North Capital Avenue
Idaho Falls, ID 83402-3582
(208) 529-1350, ext. 1355; (208) 529-1350, ext. 1350 (County Recorder); (208) 529-1350, ext. 1359 (Courts–Archivist); (208) 529-1350, ext. 1357 (Civil Courts); (208) 529-1188 FAX
rlongmore@co.bonneville.id.us
http://www.co.bonneville.id.us
Ron Longmore

Boundary County
organized 1915 from Bonner County

Boundary County Clerk
PO Box 419
Bonners Ferry, ID 83805-0419
(208) 267-2242; (208) 267-7814 FAX
gposton@boundarycounty.org
http://www.boundarycountyid.org
Glenda Poston
(land records, confidential naturalization

records, confidential vital records, probate records)

no probate search service; copies of probate records: 50¢ per page

Butte County
organized 1917 from Bingham, Blaine and Jefferson counties

Butte County Clerk-Recorder
PO Box 737
Arco, ID 83213-0737
(208) 527-3021; (208) 527-3916 FAX
butteclerk@atcnet.net
http://www.state.id.us/aboutidaho/county/butt e.html
Trilby McAffee
(land records, vital records, and probate records from 1917, naturalization records from 1909)
probate search service: $5.00; copies of probate records: $1.00

Camas County
organized 1917 from Blaine County

Camas County Clerk and Clerk of the District Court
PO Box 430
Fairfield, ID 83327-0430
(208) 764-2242 (County Clerk); (208) 764-2238 (Clerk of the District Court); (208) 764-2349 FAX
frb@northrim.net
http://www.co.twin-falls.id.us/5thDistrict2/Counties/Camas.htm
Rollie Bennett

Canyon County
organized 10 November 1892 from Owyhee and Ada counties

Canyon County Clerk
1102 East Chicago
Caldwell, ID 83605-3522
(208) 454-7562; (208) 454-6899 FAX
nhales@canyoncounty.org
http://www.canyoncounty.org
Noel Hales
(land records only by deeded owner's name, naturalization records Books 1 & 2, 1893 to 1906, births from May 1907 through June 1911, deaths from June 1907 through March 1912, marriages, probate records from 1892)
no probate search service: will search a five-year period or specific year; copies of probate records: $1.00 per page, $1.00 per instrument for certification (no certification available for naturalization records)

Caribou County
organized 1919 from Bannock and Oneida counties

Caribou County Clerk
(159 South Main Street, Soda Springs, ID 83276-1427—location)
PO Box 775 (mailing address)
Soda Springs, ID 83276-0775
(208) 547-4324; (208) 547-4759 FAX
ediei@caribouco.com
http://www.state.id.us/aboutidaho/county/cari bou.html
Edie Bush
(land records, marriages, probate records)
no probate search service; copies of probate records: $1.00 per page

Cassia County
organized 1879 from Oneida County

Cassia County Clerk and Clerk of the District Court
1459 Overland Avenue
Burley, ID 83318-1862
(208) 678-4367; (208) 878-1003 FAX
lmickelsen@cassiacounty.org
http://www.cassiacounty.org;
http://www.co.twin-falls.id.us/5thDistrict2/Counties/cassia.htm

Larry Mickelsen
(land records from 1878, naturalization records, births and deaths from 1907 through 1911 only, and marriages from 1879 to date with Recorder, estate files from January 1919 with Magistrate Division)
no probate search service; copies of probate records: $1.00 per page, no minimum

Clark County
organized 1919 from Fremont County

Clark County Clerk
PO Box 205
Dubois, ID 83423-0205
(208) 374-5304; (208) 374-5609 FAX
clarkclk@dcdi.net
http://www.state.id.us/aboutidaho/county/clar k.html
Lisa Black
(land records, naturalization records, vital records, probate records)

Clearwater County
organized 1911 from Nez Perce County

Clearwater County Clerk and Clerk of the District Court
(150 Michigan Avenue—location)
PO Box 586 (mailing address)
Orofino, ID 83544-0586
(208) 476-5615; (208) 476-9315 FAX
rchristensen@clearwatercounty.org
http://www.clearwatercounty.org; http://www2.state.id.us/2djudicial/contact.htm
Robin Christensen
(deeds, mortgages, leases, etc., marriages from 1911, probate records)
probate search service: $6.00; copies of probate records: $1.00 per page

Custer County
organized 1881 from Alturas County

Custer County Clerk and Clerk of the District Court
PO Box 385
Challis, ID 83226-0385
(208) 879-2360; (208) 879-5246 FAX
custerc@custertel.net
http://www.co.custer.id.us/Clerk.htm
Ethel Peck

Elmore County
organized 1889 from Alturas County

Elmore County Auditor/Recorder/Clerk
150 South Fourth East, Suite 5
Mountain Home, ID 83647-3000
(208) 587-2130, ext. 508; (208) 587-2130, ext. 507 (Assessor); (208) 587-2130, ext. 500 (Recorder); (208) 587-2159 FAX
mhilerr@elmorecounty.org; jgridley@elmore county.org; assessor@elmorecounty.org
http://www.elmorecounty.org
Merilee Hiler
(land records by legal description with Ms. Jo Gridley, Assessor, Suite 2, Drawer A, Mountain Home, ID 83647, land records by name with Merrilee Hiler, Recorder, naturalization records from 1889 to 1908 only, vital records from 1907 to 1911 only, probate records)
no probate search service; copies of probate records: $1.00 per page; searches must be made in person

Franklin County
organized 1913 from Oneida County

Franklin County Clerk and Clerk of the District Court
(39 West Oneida, Room 2, Preston, ID 83263-1232—location)
PO Box 231 (mailing address)
Preston, ID 83263-1234
(208) 852-1090; (208) 852-1094 FAX
velarsen@gemstate.net
http://www.co.bannock.id.us/6distct.htm/larse

n.htm; http://www.rootsweb.com/~idfrankl
V. Elliott Larsen
(probate records)
probate search service (cost depends on extent of search); copies of probate records: $1.00 per page

Fremont County
organized 1893 from Bingham and Lemhi counties

Fremont County Clerk of the District Court, Ex-officio Auditor, and Recorder
151 West First North, #12
St. Anthony, ID 83445-1548
(208) 624-7332; (208) 624-7335 FAX
amace@co.fremont.id.us
http://www.co.fremont.id.us
Abbie Mace
(land records from 1893, naturalization records, vital records from 1906 to 1917 [spotty], probate records from 1893)
probate search service: $17.00; copies of probate records: $1.00 per page, no minimum

Gem County
organized 1915 from Boise and Canyon counties

Gem County Clerk
415 East Main Street
Emmett, ID 83617-3096
(208) 365-4561; (208) 365-6172 FAX
clerk@co.gem.id.us
http://www.co.gem.id.us
Susan K. Howard
(land records from 1915 [some records recorded a little earlier, but possibly not available], marriages and divorces from 1915, no births, probate records from 1915)
probate search service: no charge; copies of probate records: $1.00 per page, $1.00 for certification, no minimum

Gooding County
organized 1913 from Lincoln County

Gooding County Clerk
PO Box 417
Gooding, ID 83330-0417
(208) 934-4841; (208) 934-5085 FAX
hedwards@co.gooding.id.us
http://www.state.id.us/aboutidaho/county/goo ding.html
Helen P. Edwards
(land records from 1913 to date, naturalization records from 1913 to 1941, marriages, and probate records to 1970 with Alberta Sites or Helen Piatt, Recorders Office, probate records after 1970 with court offices)
copies: $1.00 per page plus $1.00 if certified

Idaho County
organized 1864, original county

Idaho County Clerk and Clerk of the District Court
320 West Main Street, Room 5
Grangeville, ID 83530-1948
(208) 983-2751; (208) 983-1428 FAX
rgehring@idahocounty.org
http://www.idahocounty.org
Rose E. Gehring

Jefferson County
organized 12 January 1914 from Fremont County

Jefferson County Clerk
(134 North Clark—location)
PO Box 275 (mailing address)
Rigby, ID 83442-0275
(208) 745-7756; (208) 745-9215 (Land Records); (208) 745-7736 (Probate Records); (208) 745-6636 FAX
cboulter@co.jefferson.id.us
http://www.co.jefferson.id.us
Christine Boulter
(land records, naturalization records to 1940, probate records)

Jerome County

organized 1919 from Gooding and Lincoln counties

Jerome County Clerk
(300 North Lincoln, Room 301, Jerome, ID 83338-2344—location)
PO Box 407 (mailing address)
Jerome, ID 83338-0407
(208) 324-8811; (208) 324-2719 FAX
cwatts@co.jerome.id.us
http://www.jeromecounty.org
Cheryl Watts
(land records with Greg Heinrich, Assessor, probate records with Clerk)
no probate search service; copies of probate records: $1.00 per page

Kootenai County

formed 1864 from a portion of Nez Perce County, but was not organized or officered until 1881

Kootenai County Clerk
(451 Government Way, Coeur d'Alene, ID 83814—location)
PO Box 9000 (mailing address)
Coeur d'Alene, ID 83816-9000
(208) 446-1650; (208) 769-4428; (208) 765-1968 FAX
denglish@kcgov.us; kcclerk@kcgov.us
http://www.co.kootenai.id.us/departments/clerk
Dan English
(land records from 1881, declarations of intention and naturalizations from 1882 through 1939, births and deaths from 1907 to 1911, marriages from 1881)
no land records search service; copies of land records: $1.00 per page, $1.00 per certification

Kootenai County District Court
Civil Department
(324 West Garden Avenue, Coeur d'Alene, ID 83814—location)
PO Box 9000 (mailing address)
Coeur d'Alene, ID 83816-9000
(208) 446-1160
kccourt@kcgov.us
http://www.co.kootenai.id.us/departments/districtcourt
Diana Meyer, Court Services Director
(probate records)
no probate search service; copies of probate records: $1.00 per page, $1.00 for certification (make checks or money orders payable to the Clerk of the District Court)

Latah County

organized 1888 from Kootenai County

Latah County Clerk and Clerk of the District Court
(Latah County Courthouse, Fifth and VanBuren—location)
PO Box 8068 (mailing address)
Moscow, ID 83843-0568
(208) 882-8580; (208) 883-7203 FAX
spetersen@latah.id.us
http://www.latah.id.us; http://www2.state.id.us/2djudicial/contact.htm
Susan R. Petersen
(land records from 1888, births and deaths from 1907 to 1911, probate records)
probate search service: $4.00; copies of probate records: $1.00 per page, no minimum; include name and date of death

Lemhi County

organized 1869 from Idaho County

Lemhi County Clerk and Clerk of the District and Magistrate Courts
206 Courthouse Drive
Salmon, ID 83467-3900
(208) 756-2815; (208) 756-8424 FAX
lemhic@salmoninternet.com
http:www.lemhicountyidaho.org/clerkauditors.htm
Terri Morton
(land records, naturalization records, and marriages and divorces with County Clerk, probate records with Magistrate Court)
probate search service: no charge; copies of probate records: $1.00 per page, no minimum

Lewis County

organized 1911 from Nez Perce County

Lewis County Clerk and Clerk of the District Court
(510 Oak Street, Room 1, Nez Perce, ID 83543-5065—location)
PO Box 39 (mailing address)
Nez Perce, ID 83543
(208) 937-2661; (208) 937-9234 FAX
clarson@lewiscountyid.org
http://www.lewiscountyid.org; http://www2.state.id.us/2djudicial/contact.htm
Cathy Larson
(tract index with Assessor's Office, probate records with District Court)
no probate search service; copies of probate records: $1.00 per page, no minimum

Lincoln County

organized 1895 from Alturas County

Lincoln County Clerk
(111 West B Street, Suite C, Shoshone, ID 83352-5364—location)
PO Box A (mailing address)
Shoshone, ID 83352-0800
(208) 886-7641; (208) 886-2458 FAX
lkime@lincolncountyid.us
http://www.state.id.us/aboutidaho/county/lincoln.html
Elizabeth Kime
(land records from 1895, naturalization records from 1895 to 1930, births and deaths from 1907 to 1911, marriages from 1895, probate records from 1900)
probate search service: no charge; copies of probate records: $1.00 per page

Madison County

organized 1913 from Fremont and Teton counties

Madison County Clerk, Auditor, Recorder, Chief Elections Officer, and Clerk of the District Court
PO Box 389
Rexburg, ID 83440-0389
(208) 356-3662; (208) 356-8396 FAX
mrasmuss@co.madison.id.us
http://www.co.madison.id.us/modules/wfsection/index.php?category=2
Marilyn Rasmussen
(land records, some older naturalization records, probate records with Magistrate Court)
probate search service: $10.00; copies of probate records: $1.00 per page

Minidoka County

organized 1913 from Lincoln County

Minidoka County Clerk-Auditor-Recorder, Clerk of the Magistrate Court, and Clerk of the District Court
(Minidoka County Courthouse, 715 G Street and Sherman J. Bellwood Judicial Building, Eight and G Streets—location)
PO Box 368 (mailing address)
Rupert, ID 83350-0368
(208) 436-9511 (County Recorder); (208) 436-7186 (Clerk of the Magistrate Court); (208) 436-0737 FAX (County Recorder); (208) 436-5857 FAX (Clerk of the Magistrate Court)
duane.smith@co.minidoka.id.us
http://www.minidoka.id.us/clerk-auditor-recorder/default.htm
Duane D. Smith
(land records with County Recorder, marriages, probate records with Clerk of the Magistrate Court)
land records search service: no charge; copies of land records: $1.00 per page, $1.00 per unit for certification

Nez Perce County

organized 1864 from Shoshone County

Nez Perce County Clerk and Clerk of the District Court
(Nez Perce County Courthouse, 1230 Main Street—location)
PO Box 896 (mailing address)
Lewiston, ID 83501-0896
(208) 799-3020; (208) 799-3070 FAX
pattyweeks@co.nezperce.id.us
http://www.co.nezperce.id.us; http://www2.state.id.us/2djudicial/contact.htm
Patty O. Weeks
(land records with County Assessor, probate records from 1900)
probate search service: no charge; copies of probate records: $1.00 per page plus $1.00 for certification, no minimum

Oneida County

organized 1864, original county

Oneida County Clerk and Clerk of the District Court
10 Court Street
Malad City, ID 83252-1200
(208) 766-4116; (208) 766-2448 FAX
sblaisdell@co.oneida.id.us
http://www.co.oneida.id.us
Shirlee Blaisdell

Owyhee County

organized 1863, original county

Owyhee County Clerk
PO Box 128
Murphy, ID 83650-0128
(208) 495-2421; (208) 495-1173 FAX
csherburn@co.owyhee.id.us
http://owyheecounty.net/clerk/index.htm
Charlotte Sherburn
(land records from 1865, naturalization records from 1904, births and deaths from 1907 to 1911, marriages from 1886 to 1893, probate records from 1865)
probate search service: no charge; copies of probate records: $1.00 per page, $2.00 for certified copies, no minimum

Payette County

organized 1917 from Canyon County

Payette County Clerk
1130 Third Avenue North, Room 104
Payette, ID 83661-2473
(208) 642-6000; (208) 642-6011 FAX
bdressen@payettecounty.org
http://www.payettecounty.org
Betty Dressen
(land records, naturalization records, vital records, probate records)

Power County

organized 1913 from Bingham and Blaine counties

Power County Clerk-Auditor-Recorder
543 Bannock Street
American Falls, ID 83211-1200
(208) 226-7611; (208) 266-7612 FAX
csteinlicht@co.power.id.us
http://www.co.power.id.us/clerk-auditor-recorder/default.htm
Christine Steinlicht
(land records, naturalization records, marriages, probate records)
no probate search service; copies of probate records: $1.00 per page

Shoshone County

organized 1864, original county

Shoshone County Clerk
(700 Bank Street, #120, Wallace, ID 83873-2348—location)
PO Box 1049 (mailing address)
Wallace, ID 83873-1049
(208) 752-1264; (208) 753-2711 FAX

pwhite@co.shoshone.id.us
http://www.state.id.us/aboutidaho/county/sho
shone.html
Peggy Delange-White
(land records from 1871, naturalization records
from about 1906, vital records from 1907 to
1911, probate records from 1885)
probate search service: no charge; copies of
probate records: $1.00 per page, no minimum

Teton County
organized 1915 from Fremont County

Teton County Clerk
(89 North Main, #1, Driggs, ID 83422-5164—
location)
PO Box 756 (mailing address)
Driggs, ID 83422-0756
(208) 354-2905; (208) 354-8410 FAX
nboyle@co.teton.id.us
http://tetoncountyidaho.gov
Nolan G. Boyle
(land records, very early naturalization records,
marriage licenses, probate records)

Twin Falls County
organized 1907 from Cassia County

Twin Falls County Clerk
(425 Shoshone Street North, Second Floor—
location)
PO Box 126 (mailing address)
Twin Falls, ID 83303-0126
(208) 736-4004; (208) 736-4182 FAX
kglascoc@co.twin-falls.id.us
http://www.co.twin-falls.id.us/dir/clerk.htm;
http://twinfallscounty.org
Kristina Glascock
(land records, marriages, and probate records)
no probate search service; certified copies of
marriages: $2.00; copies of probate: $1.00 per
page

Valley County
organized 1917 from Boise County

**Valley County Clerk and Clerk of the
District Court**
PO Box 1350
Cascade, ID 83611-1350
(208) 382-7100; (208) 382-7107 FAX
lheinrich@co.valley.id.us
http://www.co.valley.id.us;
http://www2.state.id.us/fourthjudicial/Valley
%20County/Valley%20County.htm
Leland G. Heinrich
(land records from July 1917 with Valley County
Recorder, probate records from 1917 with
District Court Clerk)
no probate search service; copies of probate
records: $1.00 per page, no minimum

Washington County
organized 1879 from Boise County

Washington County Clerk
PO Box 670
Weiser, ID 83672-0670
(208) 549-2092; (208) 414-3925 FAX
wcclerk@ruralnetwork.net
http://www.co.washington.id.us
Sharon Widner
(land records from 1879, certificates of
naturalization from 27 September 1903 to 25
September 1906, intent from March 1885 to
12 December 1929, births from 13 May 1907
to 17 June 1911, deaths from 18 August 1907
to 19 June 1911, marriages from 19 June
1879, probate records from 1879)
no copying of certificates of naturalization
available, information must be written down
in person; no probate search service; copies
of probate records: $1.00 per page, $2.00 for
certified copies, no minimum

ILLINOIS

*Capital: Springfield. Statehood: 3 December 1818
(ceded by England in the Treaty of Paris, 1783, settled
claims with Virginia, Connecticut and Massachusetts in
1786, was part of the Northwest Territory in 1787,
Indiana Territory in 1800, and became a separate
territory in 3 February 1809)*

Illinois' Court of Claims sits in Chicago and
Springfield and is a quasi-judicial part of the
legislative branch, having jurisdiction on all
claims against the state. Twenty-two Circuit
Courts have general jurisdiction and sit at the
county seats and elsewhere, as needed. First
Judicial Circuit: Alexander, Jackson, Johnson,
Massac, Pope, Pulaski, Saline, Union and
Williamson counties; Second Judicial Circuit:
Crawford, Edwards, Franklin, Gallatin,
Hamilton, Hardin, Jefferson, Lawrence,
Richland, Wabash, Wayne and White counties;
Third Judicial Circuit: Bond and Madison
counties; Fourth Judicial Circuit: Christian, Clay,
Clinton, Effingham, Fayette, Jasper, Marion,
Montgomery and Shelby counties; Fifth Judicial
Circuit: Clark, Coles, Cumberland, Edgar and
Vermilion counties; Sixth Judicial Circuit:
Champaign, DeWitt, Douglas, Macon, Moultrie
and Piatt counties; Seventh Judicial Circuit:
Greene, Jersey, Macoupin, Morgan, Sangamon
and Scott counties; Eighth Judicial Circuit:
Adams, Brown, Calhoun, Cass, Mason, Menard,
Pike and Schuyler counties; Ninth Judicial
Circuit: Fulton, Hancock, Henderson, Knox,
McDonough and Warren counties; Tenth
Judicial Circuit: Marshall, Peoria, Putnam, Stark
and Tazewell counties; Eleventh Judicial Circuit:
Ford, Livingston, Logan, McLean and
Woodford counties; Twelfth Judicial Circuit:
Will County; Thirteenth Judicial Circuit: Bureau,
Grundy and LaSalle counties; Fourteenth
Judicial Circuit: Henry, Mercer, Rock Island and
Whiteside counties; Fifteenth Judicial Circuit:
Carroll, Jo Daviess, Lee, Ogle and Stephenson
counties; Sixteenth Judicial Circuit: DeKalb,
Kane and Kendall counties; Seventeenth Judicial
Circuit: Boone and Winnebago counties;
Eighteenth Judicial Circuit: DuPage County;
Nineteenth Judicial Circuit: Lake and McHenry
counties; Twentieth Judicial Circuit: Monroe,
Perry, Randolph, St. Clair and Washington
counties; Twenty-first Judicial Circuit: Iroquois
and Kankakee counties; and Circuit Court of
Cook County.
Five District Appellate Courts sit at Chicago,
Elgin, Ottawa, Springfield and Mount Vernon.
The Illinois Supreme Court sits at Springfield
and Chicago.

Adams County
organized 1825 from Pike County; Highland
County organized from Adams and Marquette
counties in 1847 and eliminated in 1848;
Marquette County organized 1843 from
Adams County and eliminated in 1847

Adams County Clerk and Recorder
507 Vermont Street
Quincy, IL 62301521
(217) 277-2150 (Clerk); (217) 277-2127
(Recorder); (217) 277-2155 FAX
countyclerk@co.adams.il.us;
recorder@co.adams.il.us
http://www.co.adams.il.us/county_clerk/index.
htm; http://www.co.adams.il.us/
recorder/index.htm
Georgia Volm
(land records from early 1800s with County
Recorder; births and deaths from 1878,
marriages from 1825 with County Clerk)

Adams County Clerk of the Circuit Court
521 Vermont Street
Quincy, IL 62301-2901
(217) 277-2100; (217) 277-2116 FAX
circuitclerk@co.adams.il.us;

---

rfrese@co.adams.il.us
http://www.co.adams.il.us
Randy Frese
(probate records from 1830)
probate search service: $4.00 per year; copies of
probate records: $1.00 for the first page, 50¢
for each of the next nineteen pages and 25¢
for each additional page, $1.00 for
certification

Alexander County
organized 1819 from Johnson County

Alexander County Clerk
2000 Washington Avenue
Cairo, IL 62914-1717
(618) 734-0509; (618) 734-3947
alexctyclk@sbcglobal.net
http://publicrecords.onlinesearches.com/Illinoi
s-Land-Records-and-Deeds.htm
Kent Thomas

Alexander County Clerk of the Circuit Court
2000 Washington Avenue
Cairo, IL 62914-1717
(618) 734-0107; (618) 734-7003 FAX
circuitclerk@lycos.com
http://www.state.il.us/court/CircuitCourt/Circ
uitCourtJudges/CCC_County.asp
Sharon McGinness

Bond County
organized 1817 from Madison County

Bond County Clerk of the Circuit Court
200 West College
Greenville, IL 62246-1057
(618) 664-3208; (618) 664-2257 FAX
clerk@johnkking.com
http://www.state.il.us/court/CircuitCourt/Circ
uitCourtJudges/CCC_County.asp
John K. King
(probate records from 1825)
no probate search service; copies of probate
records: 50¢ per page, $2.00 minimum

Bond County Clerk/Recorder
PO Box 407
Greenville, IL 62246-1088
(618) 664-0449
rcreitz@papadocs.com
http://publicrecords.onlinesearches.com/Illinoi
s-Land-Records-and-Deeds.htm
Randy Reitz
(land records from 1850, births and deaths from
1877, marriages from 1817)

Boone County
organized 1837 from Winnebago County

Boone County Clerk and Recorder
601 North Main Street, Suite 202
Belvidere, IL 61008-2708
(815) 544-3103; (815) 547-8701 FAX
countyclerk@boonecountyil.org;
pam@boonecountyil.org
http://www.boonecountyil.org/countyclerk.htm
Pamela D. McCullough
(land records with Recorder, vital records with
County Clerk)

Boone County Clerk of the Circuit Court
601 North Main Street, Suite 303
Belvidere, IL 61008-2644
(815) 544-0371; (815) 547-9213 FAX
circuitclerk@boonecountyil.org
http://www.boonecountyil.org/deptframeset.htm
Nora L. Ohlsen
(naturalization records, probate records)

Brown County
organized 1839 from Schuyler County

Brown County Clerk
(Courthouse Building, 200 Court Street, Room
4—location)
PO Box 142 (mailing address)
Mt. Sterling, IL 62353
(217) 773-3421
woodworthsieben@hotmail.com

http://publicrecords.onlinesearches.com/Illinoi
s-Land-Records-and-Deeds.htm
Judy J. Woodworth
(land records and vital records)

Brown County Clerk of the Circuit Court
#1 Court Street
Mt. Sterling, IL 62353-1233
(217) 773-2713; (217) 773-2433 FAX
dtodd@hotmail.com
http://www.state.il.us/court/CircuitCourt/Circ
uitCourtJudges/CCC_County.asp
Doris Todd
(naturalization records, probate records, divorce
records)
probate search service: $4.00 plus 35¢ per page
for copies

Bureau County
organized 1837 from Putnam County

Bureau County Clerk and Recorder
700 South Main Street, Room 104
Princeton, IL 61356
(815) 875-2014; (815) 879-4803 FAX
bureaucckami@yahoo.com
http://bureaucountyclerk.com;
http://bureaucounty.us/Government.php
Kamala S. "Kami" Hieronymus
(land records, births, deaths, and marriages
[access to birth records is restricted to the
person himself or his parents, unless the
person is proven deceased by presentation of
a death record; applicant must show proof of
relationship])

Bureau County Clerk of the Circuit Court
700 South Main Street
Princeton, IL 61356-2037
(815) 872-2001; (815) 872-0027 FAX
mmiroux@bccirclk.gov
http://www.state.il.us/court/CircuitCourt/Circ
uitCourtJudges/CCC_County.asp;
http://bureaucounty.us/Government.php
Michael Miroux
(naturalization records and probate records)

Calhoun County
organized 1825 from Pike County

Calhoun County Clerk of the Circuit Court
(Main and County Roads—location)
PO Box 486 (mailing address)
Hardin, IL 62047-0486
(618) 576-2451; (618) 576-9541 FAX
hilltop1@hotmail.com
http://www.state.il.us/court/CircuitCourt/Circ
uitCourtJudges/CCC_County.asp
Yvonne Macauley
(naturalization records from 1825, probate
records from 1825)
probate search service: $4.00; copies of probate
records: 10¢ short, 25¢ long, plus postage

Calhoun County Clerk/Recorder
(102 County Road—location)
PO Box 187 (mailing address)
Hardin, IL 62047-0187
(618) 576-2351
http://publicrecords.onlinesearches.com/Illinoi
s-Land-Records-and-Deeds.htm
Lucille "Susie" Kress
(land records from 1825 with County Recorder,
births and deaths from 1878, marriages from
1825 [indexed through 1979] with County
Clerk)

Carroll County
organized 1839 from Jo Daviess County

Carroll County Clerk and Recorder
(301 North Main—location)
PO Box 152 (mailing address)
Mt. Carroll, IL 61053-0152
(815) 244-0221; (815) 244-0223
cclerk1@carroll-county.net
http://www.gocarrollcounty.com/county_infor
mation.html
Judith A. Gray
(land records from 1839 with County Recorder,

vital records from 1877 with County Clerk)
copies of vital records: $5.00 each

Carroll County Clerk of the Circuit Court
301 North Main Street
Mt. Carroll, IL 61053
(815) 244-0230; (815) 244-3869 FAX
dowaditty50@hotmail.com
http://www.gocarrollcounty.com/county_infor
mation.html
Sherri A. Miller
naturalization and probate search service: $4.00
per year; copies of probate records: $1.00 for
the first page, 50¢ for each of the next
nineteen pages and 25¢ for each additional
page, $2.00 for certification, no minimum

Cass County
organized 1837 from Morgan County

Cass County Clerk
Virginia, IL 62691
(217) 452-7217
casscoclerk@casscomm.com
http://publicrecords.onlinesearches.com/Illinoi
s-Land-Records-and-Deeds.htm
Michael Kirchner
(births and marriages)
copies of vital records: $5.00 (includes search)

Cass County Clerk of the Circuit Court
PO Box 203
Virginia, IL 62691-0203
(217) 452-7225; (217) 452-7219 FAX
etrenterclk@casscomm.com
http://www.state.il.us/court/CircuitCourt/Circ
uitCourtJudges/CCC_County.asp
Evelyn K. Trenter
(naturalization records)

Champaign County
organized 1833 from Vermilion County

Champaign County Clerk of the Circuit Court
Courthouse, 101 East Main Street
Urbana, IL 61801-2736
(217) 384-3725; (217) 384-3879 FAX
lfrank@co.champaign.il.us
http://www.cccircuitclerk.com
Linda S. Frank

Champaign County Clerk's Office
Brookens Administrabive Center
1776 East Washington
Urbana, IL 61802
(217) 384-3720; (217) 384-1241 FAX
mvshelden@co.champaign.il.us;
mail@champaigncountyclerk.com
http://www.champaigncountyclerk.com
Mark Seldon
(births and deaths from 1878, marriages from
1833)

Champaign County Recorder of Deeds
Brookens Administrabive Center
1776 East Washington
Urbana, IL 61802
(217) 384-3774
RecorderOfDeeds@co.champaign.il.us
http://www.co.champaign.il.us/recorder.htm
Barbara Frasca

Christian County
organized 1839 from Sangamon, Montgomery
and Shelby counties

Christian County Clerk of the Circuit Court
(On the Square—location)
Box 617 (mailing address)
Taylorville, IL 62568-0617
(217) 824-4966; (217) 824-5030 FAX
christiancountycircuitclerk@hotmail.com
http://www.state.il.us/court/CircuitCourt/Circ
uitCourtJudges/CCC_County.asp
Donna Castelli
(naturalization records and probate records)

Christian County Clerk/Recorder
(101 South Main—location)
PO Box 647 (mailing address)

Taylorville, IL 62568-0647
(217) 824-4969
cclerk@ctitech.com
http://publicrecords.onlinesearches.com/Illinoi
s-Land-Records-and-Deeds.htm
Linda Curtin
(land records and vital records)

Clark County
organized 1819 from Crawford County

Clark County Clerk of the Circuit Court
(501 Archer Avenue—location)
Box 187 (mailing address)
Marshall, IL 62441-0187
(217) 826-2811; (217) 826-1391 FAX
treynoldscc@yahoo.com
http://www.clarkcountyil.org/circuit_clerk.htm
Terri Reynolds

Clark County Clerk/Recorder
County Courthouse
501 Archer Avenue
Marshall, IL 62441
(217) 826-8311
clerk@clarkcountyil.org;
coclerk@marshall.il.com
http://www.clarkcountyil.org/clerk.htm
William C. "Bill" Downey

Clay County
organized 1824 from Lawrence, Wayne and
Fayette counties

Clay County Clerk of the Circuit Court
(111 Chestnut—location)
PO Box 100 (mailing address)
Louisville, IL 62858-0100
(618) 665-3523; (618) 665-3543 FAX
circlk@wabash.net
http://www.claycountyillinois.org/index.aspx?p
age=14
Rita L. Porter

Clay County Clerk/Recorder
(111 East Chestnut, Room 106—location)
PO Box 160 (mailing address)
Louisville, IL 62858-0160
(618) 665-3626; (618) 665-3607 FAX
claycoclk@wabash.net
http://www.claycountyillinois.org/index.aspx?p
age=15
Brenda Britton

Clinton County
organized 1824 from Washington, Bond and
Fayette counties

Clinton County Clerk and Recorder
(850 Fairfax Street—location)
PO Box 308 (mailing address)
Carlyle, IL 62231
(618) 594-2464, ext. 0139; (618) 594-0195 FAX
ccclerk@clintonco.illinois.gov
http://www.clintonco.org/officials_county.htm
Thomas LaCaze
(land records and vital records)

Clinton County Clerk of the Circuit Court
(850 Fairfax Street—location)
PO Box 407 (mailing address)
Carlyle, IL 62231-0407
(618) 594-2464, ext. 620; (618) 594-0197 FAX
circlerk@clintonco.illinois.gov;
lubbersj@clintonco.illinois.gov;
luebbersj@yahoo.com
http://www.clintonco.org/officials_county.htm
Jeff Luebbers
(naturalization records and probate records)

Coles County
organized 1830 from Clark and Edgar counties

Coles County Clerk and Recorder of Deeds
(651 Jackson Avenue, Room 122—location)
PO Box 207 (mailing address)
Charleston, IL 61920
(217) 348-0501 (Charleston); (217) 258-0501
(Mattoon); (217) 348-7337 FAX (Charleston);
(217) 258-7337 FAX (Mattoon)

countyclerk@co.coles.il.us;
 bcoffrin@co.coles.il.us
http://www.co.coles.il.us/CoClerk/index.htm
Betty J. Coffrin
(land records from 1830, births from 1879 [but
 not required until 1916], deaths from 1879
 [but not required until 1916], marriages from
 1830)
land records search service: $5.00 per five-year
 search, per name, per document, $1.00 per
 additional year (supply full name, years to be
 searched, kind of document(s), and your
 relationship); vital records search service:
 $7.00 for a five-year search and $1.00 for each
 additional year; certified copies of vital
 records: $7.00, $2.00 for each additional copy
 requested at the same time (access to birth
 records after 1916 is restricted to the person
 himself or his parents, unless the person is
 proven deceased by presentation of a death
 record)

Coles County Clerk of the Circuit Court
(Sixth and Jackson—location)
Box 48 (mailing address)
Charleston, IL 61920-0048
(217) 348-0516; (217) 348-7324 FAX
vkirkpatrick@co.coles.il.us
http://www.judici.com/courts/index.jsp?court
 =IL015025J
Vicki Kirkpatrick
(probate records)
no probate search service; copies of probate
 records: 50¢ per page

Cook County
organized 1831 from Putnam County

Cook County Clerk
Vital Records Division
(Cook County Building, 118 North Clark Street
 [Randolph Street Entrance/lower concourse
 level], Chicago, IL 60602-1304—location)
PO Box 642570 (mailing address)
Chicago, IL 60664-2570
(312) 603-7790
dorr@cookcountygov.com
http://www.cookctyclerk.com;
 http://www.voterinfonet.com
David Orr

Cook County Clerk of the Circuit Court
50 West Washington, Room 1001
Chicago, IL 60602-1305
(312) 603-5030; (312) 629-6601 (Archives); (312)
 603-4557 FAX; (312) 443-5013 FAX
 (Archives)
courtclerk@cookcountycourt.com;
 dobrown@cookcountycourt.com
http://198.173.15.34
Dorothy A. Brown
(naturalization records from 1871 to 1903 from
 both County Court and Criminal Court and
 from 1871 to 1929 from both Circuit Court
 and Superior Court with Philip J. Costello,
 Archivist, Clerk of the Circuit Court of Cook
 County, Archives Department, Richard J.
 Daley Center, Room 1113, Chicago, IL
 60602, will index from 1850, Documented
 Record of Wills from 1851, Abstract of
 Probate Proceedings from 1861, all other
 probate records from 1871 with Aurelia
 Pucinski, Circuit Court Clerk, County Bureau,
 Probate Division, Richard J. Daley Center,
 Room 1202, Chicago, IL 60602, deceased
 estate indexes from 1871 to 1967, will indexes
 from 1871 to 1970, minors indexes from 1871
 to 1967, incompetents indexes from 1911 to
 1965 with Archives)
probate search service: $6.00 per year; copies of
 probate records: $2.00 for the first page, 50¢
 for each of the next nineteen pages and 25¢
 for each additional page or $2.00 for the first
 three certified and $1.00 for each additional
 certified page, plus postage

Cook County Recorder of Deeds
Cook County Building, 118 North Clark Street,
 Room 120
Chicago, IL 60602

(312) 603-5050; (312) 603-5063 FAX
countyclerk@co.coles.il.us
http://www.ccrd.info/CCRD/il031/index.jsp
Eugene "Gene" Moore
(land records from Chicago Fire of 1871 with
 County Recorder's Office; abstracts prior to
 1871 with Chicago Title Insurance Company;
 government land patents with Illinois State
 Archives)

Crawford County
organized 1816 from Edwards County

Crawford County Clerk of the Circuit Court
(Court Street—location)
PO Box 655 (mailing address)
Robinson, IL 62454-0655
(618) 544-3512; (618) 546-5628 FAX
circuitclerk@crawfordcountycentral.com
http://www.crawfordcountycentral.com/circuit
 clerk.htm
Denise Utterback
(probate records)

Crawford County Clerk/Recorder
(100 Douglas—location)
PO Box 602 (mailing address)
Robinson, IL 62454-0602
(618) 546-1212; (618) 544-2590; (618) 546-0140
 FAX
Coclerk@crawfordcountyclerk.com
http://www.crawfordcountycentral.com/cocler
 k
Patricia "Patty" Lycan
(land records from 1816, births and deaths from
 1877, and marriages from 1816)
vital records search service: $5.00 (extensive
 searches referred to Robinson Public Library
 District); copies of vital records: $2.00 each,
 $5.00 for the first certified copy, $2.00 for
 each additional certified copy of the same
 record

Cumberland County
organized 1843 from Coles County

Cumberland County Clerk and Recorder
(140 Courthouse Square—location)
PO Box 146 (mailing address)
Toledo, IL 62468-0146
(217) 849-2631; (217) 849-2968 FAX
jgentry@rrl.net
http://publicrecords.onlinesearches.com/Illinoi
 s-Land-Records-and-Deeds.htm
Julie Gentry
(deeds, marriage licenses)
land records search service: $10.00; certified
 copies of land records: $5.00 to $10.00 for the
 first copy, $2.00 for each additional copy

**Cumberland County Clerk of the Circuit
 Court**
(Courthouse Square—location)
Box 145 (mailing address)
Toledo, IL 62468-0145
(217) 849-3601; (217) 849-2655 FAX
courthouse@rr1.net
http://www.state.il.us/court/CircuitCourt/Circ
 uitCourtJudges/CCC_County.asp
Golda Dunn

DeKalb County
organized 1837 from Kane County

DeKalb County Clerk and Recorder
Administration Building, 110 East Sycamore
 Street
Sycamore, IL 60178-1448
(815) 895-7149 (Clerk's Office); (815) 895-7156
 (Recorder's Office); (815) 895-7148 FAX
sholmes@dekalbcounty.org
http://www.dekalbcounty.org/CoClerk/co_cler
 k.html
Sharon L. Holmes
(deeds, plat maps, land atlases, birth indexes
 from 1878 through 1915 [incomplete] and
 from 1916 to date [no personal access by
 visitors], death indexes from 1878 through
 1915 [incomplete] and from 1916 to date,
 marriage indexes from 1837 to date,

naturalization records from 1853 to 1906 and
 a small part of 1906 to 1908 [indexed], and a
 few additional early naturalization records)
vital records search service from DeKalb
 County Historical-Genealogical Society: $5.00
 per surname plus LSASE with two stamps
 (includes search of ten other indexed
 materials as well); copies of vital records:
 $8.00 for certified copies of records from
 1916 (access to births restricted to the person
 named, his parents or legal representative),
 $3.00 for uncertified copies of records before
 1916, marriages 1837-1877 from Sheila
 Larson, Society Genealogist; copies of
 naturalization records: $2.00

DeKalb County Clerk of the Circuit Court
DeKalb County Courthouse
133 West State Street
Sycamore, IL 60178-1416
(815) 895-7131; (815) 895-7140 FAX
mjosh@dekalbcounty.org
http://www.dekalbcounty.org/CirClrk/circuit_c
 lerk.html
Maureen A. Josh
(probate records)

DeWitt County
organized 1839 from McLean and Macon
 counties

DeWitt County Clerk and Recorder
(201 West Washington—location)
PO Box 439 (mailing address)
Clinton, IL 61727-0439
(217) 935-2119
Jusher@dewittcountyill.com
http://www.dewittcountyill.com/countyoffices.
 html
Jayne Usher
(land records from 1839, naturalization records
 from 1880, and vital records from 1916)
copies of vital records: $5.00 (births restricted
 after 1916; certified copies of probate records:
 $2.00 and $4.00, no minimum

DeWitt County Clerk of the Circuit Court
201 West Washington Street
Clinton, IL 61727-0439
(217) 935-2195; (217) 935-3310 FAX
Kweiss@dewittcountyill.com
http://www.dewittcountyill.com/CircuitClerk.html
Kathy A. Weiss
no probate search service

Douglas County
organized 1859 from Coles County

Douglas County Clerk and Recorder
(401 South Center—location)
PO Box 467 (mailing address)
Tuscola, IL 61953-0467
(217) 253-2411
clerk@douglascountyil.com;
 clerk&record@netcare-il.com
http://www.douglascountyil.com/clerkrecorder
 /contactlerkrecorder.html
James A. "Jim" Ingram

Douglas County Clerk of the Circuit Court
(401 South Center—location)
PO Box 50 (mailing address)
Tuscola, IL 61953-0050
(217) 253-2352; (217) 253-9006 FAX
douglasco2@yahoo.com
http://www.douglascountyil.com/circuitclerk.html;
 http://www.state.il.us/court/CircuitCourt/Ci
 rcuitCourtJudges/CCC_County.asp
Julie Mills

DuPage County
organized 1839 from Cook County

DuPage County Clerk
(Jack T. Knuepfer Administration Building, 421
 North County Farm Road, Wheaton, IL
 60187—location)
PO Box 1028 (mailing address)
Wheaton, IL 60189
(630) 407-5500

http://www.co.dupage.il.us/countyclerk/index.
cfm
Gary A. King
(vital records with County Clerk and Health
Department)

DuPage County Clerk of the Circuit Court
(505 North County Farm Road—location)
PO Box 707 (mailing address)
Wheaton, IL 60189-0707
(630) 407-8700; (630) 407-8575 FAX
Civil.CircuitClerk@dupageco.org;
ckachiroubas@dupageco.org
http://www.co.dupage.il.us/courtclerk
Chris Kachiroubas
(naturalization records to 1945 and probate
records)
naturalization records search service: no charge
for search by special deputy clerks
(Genealogical Section); probate search
service: $4.00 per name per year; copies of
naturalization records and probate records:
$2.00 for the first page, 50¢ for each of the
next nineteen pages and 25¢ for each
additional page; copies of probate records

DuPage County Recorder
(Jack T. Knuepfer Administration Building, 421
North County Farm Road, First Floor,
Wheaton, IL 60187—location)
PO Box 936 (mailing address)
Wheaton, IL 60189
(630) 407-5400; (630) 407-5401 (Research)
recorder@dupageco.org
http://www.co.dupage.il.us/recorder/index.cfm
Fred Bucholz
(land records)

Edgar County
organized 1823 from Clark County

Edgar County Clerk and Recorder of Deeds
115 West Court Street, Room "J"
Paris, IL 61944
(217) 466-7433; (217) 466-7430 FAX
coclk@edgarcounty-il.gov;
rrkcoclk@edgarcounty-il.gov
http://www.edgarcounty-il.gov/cntyclerk
Rebecca R. "Becky" Kraemer
(land records from 1827, births and deaths from
1877, marriages from 1823 [before 1878
marriages give only names of bride and
groom and date of marriage])
land records search service: $7.00 for search of
1827-1873 grantee/grantor index (includes
copy of index pages), other searches referred
to Edgar County Genealogy Library; copies of
deeds: $1.00 per page (to be billed), $7.00 for
certification; copies of vital records: $1.00 per
page, $7.00 for certification

Edgar County Clerk of the Circuit Court
115 West Court Street, Room "M"
Paris, IL 61944-1739
(217) 466-7447; (217) 466-7443 FAX
circlk@edgarcounty-il.gov
http://www.edgarcounty-
il.gov/circclerk/index.html
Karen Halloran
(naturalization records, probate records)

Edwards County
organized 1814 from Madison and Gallatin
counties

Edwards County Clerk
50 East Main
Albion, IL 62806
(618) 445-2115
edcc@fairfieldwireless.net
http://publicrecords.onlinesearches.com/Illinoi
s-Land-Records-and-Deeds.htm
Mary Beth (Saxe) Smith
(land records and vital records)

Edwards County Clerk of the Circuit Court
50 East Main Street
Albion, IL 62806-1262
(618) 445-2016; (618) 445-4943 FAX
ptayloredwcocirclk@hotmail.com

http://www.state.il.us/court/CircuitCourt/Circ
uitCourtJudges/CCC_County.asp
Patsy Taylor
(naturalization records and probate records)
probate search service: $4.00 per year; copies of
probate records: 30¢ per page; send SASE
and payment in advance

Effingham County
organized 1831 from Fayette and Crawford
counties

Effingham County Clerk of the Circuit Court
(100 East Jefferson, #101—location)
PO Box 586 (mailing address)
Effingham, IL 62401-0586
(217) 342-4065; (217) 342-6183 FAX
bjansen@co.effingham.il.us
http://www.co.effingham.il.us/circuitclerk.html
Becky Jansen
(naturalization records and probate records)
naturalization and probate search service
(requests in writing only): $4.00 per year;
copies of naturalization and probate records:
50¢ for each of the first nineteen pages and
25¢ for each additional page

Effingham County Clerk/Recorder
(Effingham County Office Building, 101 North
Fourth Street, Suite 201—location)
PO Box 628 (mailing address)
Effingham, IL 62401-0628
(217) 342-6535; (217) 342-3577 FAX
khirtzel@co.effingham.il.us;
countyclerk@co.effingham.il.us
http://www.co.effingham.il.us/clerkrecorder.html
Kerry Hirtzel
(land records from 1833 with Recorder, births
and deaths from 1878, marriages from 1833
[filing of births and deaths were not required
in the state until 1918] with Clerk)
copies of land records: $1.00; copies of vital
records: $7.00 per certified copy, $2.00 for
each additional copy of same record (access
to birth records is restricted to the person
himself or his parents, unless the person is
proven deceased by presentation of a death
record)

Fayette County
organized 1821 from Bond, Jefferson, Wayne
and Clark counties

Fayette County Clerk and Recorder
(221 South Seventh Street—location)
PO Box 401 (mailing address)
Vandalia, IL 62471
(618) 283-5000
fayettecoclk@swetlandcom.com
http://publicrecords.onlinesearches.com/Illinoi
s-Land-Records-and-Deeds.htm
Terri Braun
(land records from 1821, births and deaths from
1877 ["few and far between before 1916"],
marriages from 1821 [before 1878 the records
show only the bride's and groom's names,
date of marriage and who performed the
marriage])
land records search service: $5.00 for twenty-
year search (includes copy); certified copies of
vital records: $5.00 each (includes twenty-year
search)

Fayette County Clerk of the Circuit Court
221 South Seventh Street
Vandalia, IL 62471-2755
(618) 283-5009; (618) 283-4490 FAX
Fayettecircuitclk@yahoo.com
http://www.state.il.us/court/CircuitCourt/Circ
uitCourtJudges/CCC_County.asp
Marsha Wodtka
(wills and estate records from 1834)

Ford County
organized 1859 from Vermilion County

Ford County Clerk and Recorder
200 West State Street, Room 101
Paxton, IL 60957
(217) 379-2721

1keller@advancenet.net;
clerk@fordcountycourthouse.com
http://publicrecords.onlinesearches.com/Illinoi
s-Land-Records-and-Deeds.htm
Linda Kellerhals
(deeds, mortgages and releases, births, marriages
and deaths)

Ford County Clerk of the Circuit Court
(200 West State Street—location)
Box 80 (mailing address)
Paxton, IL 60957-0080
(217) 379-2641; (217) 379-3445 FAX
kamalenjohnson@yahoo.com
http://www.state.il.us/court/CircuitCourt/Circ
uitCourtJudges/CCC_County.asp
Kamalen K. Johnson
(naturalization records and probate records)

Franklin County
organized 1818 from White and Gallatin
counties

Franklin County Clerk and Recorder
(202 West Main—location)
PO Box 607 (mailing address)
Benton, IL 62812
(618) 438-3221
dobill@franklincountyil.org
http://wwwfranklincountyil.org
Dave Dobill
(deeds and mortgages, births, deaths and
marriages)
copies of land records: $1.00 for the first two
pages, 50¢ for each additional page; copies of
vital records: $2.00 each, $5.00 for certified
copies

Franklin County Clerk of the Circuit Court
(On the Square—location)
PO Box 485 (mailing address)
Benton, IL 62812-2264
(618) 439-2011; (618) 439-4119 FAX
donna7ski@hotmail.com
http://wwwfranklincountyil.org
Donna Sevenski
(naturalization records and probate records)

Fulton County
organized 1823 from Pike County

Fulton County Clerk and Recorder
(100 North Main Street, Lewistown, IL 61542-
1409—location)
PO Box 226 (mailing address)
Lewistown, IL 61542
(309) 547-3041, ext. 43 or 705
jnelson@fultonco.org
http://www.fultonco.org/countyclerk.html
James I. "Jim" Nelson
(grantee records from 1823, grantor records
from 1856, tract index from the 1820s, births
and deaths from 1878, marriages from 1824)
copies of land records: 50¢ per page, no
minimum; certified copies of vital records:
$7.00 for the first copy (includes search);
$2.00 for each additional copy

Fulton County Clerk of the Circuit Court
(100 North Main Street—location)
PO Box 152 (mailing address)
Lewistown, IL 61542-0152
(309) 547-3041; (309) 547-3674 FAX
mhampton@9thjudicial.org
http://www.state.il.us/court/CircuitCourt/Circ
uitCourtJudges/CCC_County.asp
Mary C. Hampton
(naturalization records with Circuit Clerk's
Office [records may be researched but not
photocopied], probate records from about
1850 with Circuit Clerk's Office)
probate search service: no charge; copies of
probate records: 50¢ per page, no minimum

Gallatin County
organized 1812 from Randolph County

Gallatin County Clerk
(484 North Lincoln Boulevard West—location)
PO Box 550 (mailing address)

Shawneetown, IL 62984-0550
(618) 269-3025
bawargel@shawneelink.net
http://publicrecords.onlinesearches.com/Illinoi
s-Land-Records-and-Deeds.htm
Elizabeth Wargel
(land records from 1813, births and deaths from
1878, marriages from 1830)
copies of land records: 25¢ per page, possible
search fee; certified copies of vital records:
$5.00 for the first copy, $2.00 for each
additional copy

Gallatin County Clerk of the Circuit Court
(Lincoln Boulevard—location)
PO Box 249 (mailing address)
Shawneetown, IL 62984-0249
(618) 269-3140; (618) 269-4324 FAX
mistyblue80@hotmail.com
http://www.state.il.us/court/CircuitCourt/Circ
uitCourtJudges/CCC_County.asp
Mona L. Moore
(probate records and wills)
probate search service: depends on how much
searching; copies of probate records: 25¢ per
page, $2.00 minimum

Greene County
organized 1821 from Madison County

Greene County Clerk and Recorder
519 North Main Street
Carrollton, IL 62016
(217) 942-5443
grctyclk@hotmail.com
http://publicrecords.onlinesearches.com/Illinoi
s-Land-Records-and-Deeds.htm
Deborah Banghart
(deeds from 1821, births and deaths from
December 1877, marriages from 1821
[indexed from 1845 to 1858 and from 5 May
1870 to 31 January 1901])
vital records search service: $8.00 (access to
birth records is restricted to the person
himself or his parents, unless the person is
proven deceased by presentation of a death
record, and members of Illinois genealogical
societies may look at indexes prior to 1916 if
they present a membership card)

Greene County Clerk of the Circuit Court
519 North Main Street
Carrollton, IL 62016-1093
(217) 942-3421; (217) 942-5431 FAX
tunie1@midwest.net
http://www.state.il.us/court/CircuitCourt/Circ
uitCourtJudges/CCC_County.asp
V. "Tunie" Brannan
(naturalization records, probate records)
probate search service: no charge; copies of
probate records: 25¢ per page, no minimum

Grundy County
organized 1841 from LaSalle County

Grundy County Clerk and Recorder
(111 East Washington Street, Morris, IL 60450-
2268—location)
PO Box 675 (mailing address)
Morris, IL 60450
(815) 941-3222
lphillips@mornet.org
http://www.grundyco.org/clerkrecorder/clerkre
corder.shtml
Lana J. Phillips
(land records from 1841 with County Recorder,
births and deaths from 1878, marriage records
from 1841 with County Clerk)

Grundy County Clerk of the Circuit Court
111 East Washington Street, Room 30
Morris, IL 60450-0707
(815) 941-3258; (815) 941-3265 FAX
kslattery@mornet.org; kslattery_circlk@yahoo.com
http://www.grundyco.org/circuitclerk/circuitcle
rk.shtml
Karen Slattery
(naturalization records from 1859 to 1906, wills
from 1836)
probate search service: $7.00; copies of probate

records: $1.00 per page, no minimum

Hamilton County
organized 1821 from White County

Hamilton County Clerk
100 South Jackson Street
McLeansboro, IL 62859
(618) 643-2721
coclerk@hamiltonco.us
http://publicrecords.onlinesearches.com/Illinoi
s-Land-Records-and-Deeds.htm
Lavella Cradlock
(land records from 1851 [possibly some from
1830], births and deaths from 1878, marriages
from 1821 [for births, need child's name, date
of birth, father's name, mother's maiden
name])

Hamilton County Clerk of the Circuit Court
100 South Jackson Street
McLeansboro, IL 62859-1490
(618) 643-3224; (618) 643-3455 FAX
bjoxford@hotmail.com
http://www.state.il.us/court/CircuitCourt/Circ
uitCourtJudges/CCC_County.asp
Bobbi Oxford
(naturalization records [no index], probate
records from 1830)
probate search service: $2.00; copies of probate
records: 75¢ per side when mailed

Hancock County
organized 1825 from Pike County and
unorganized territory

Hancock County Clerk
PO Box 39
Carthage, IL 62321
(217) 357-3911
kerryclerk@juno.com
http://www.hancockcountyil.com/Government
; http://www.outfitters.com/illinois/hancock
Mr. Kerry Asbridge
(land records, vital records)
copies of vital records: $7.00 (includes search)

Hancock County Clerk of the Circuit Court
(Courthouse Square—location)
Box 189 (mailing address)
Carthage, IL 62321-0189
(217) 357-2616; (217) 357-2231 FAX
jneally@9thjudicial.org
http://www.hancockcountyil.com/Government
John Neally
(naturalization records, probate records)

Hardin County
organized 1839 from Pope County

Hardin County Clerk
(Main and Market Streets—location)
PO Box 187 (mailing address)
Elizabethtown, IL 62931
(618) 287-2251
hcdenton@shawneelink.net
http://publicrecords.onlinesearches.com/Illinoi
s-Land-Records-and-Deeds.htm; http://
www.hardincountyil.org (Tourism Online)
Mary Ellen Denton
(land records and vital records from 1884)
land records search service: $10.00; copies of
land records: 25¢ per page; certified copies of
vital records: $5.00

Hardin County Clerk of the Circuit Court
(Main and Market—location)
PO Box 308 (mailing address)
Elizabethtown, IL 62931-0308
(618) 287-2735; (618) 287-2713 FAX
http://www.state.il.us/court/CircuitCourt/Circ
uitCourtJudges/CCC_County.asp
Diana Hubbard
(probate records from 1884)
probate search service: $5.00; copies of probate
records: 25¢ per page (certified copies higher)

Henderson County
organized 1841 from Warren County

Henderson County Clerk and Recorder
PO Box 308
Oquawka, IL 61469
(309) 867-2911
coclerk@accessus.net; coclerk@mchsi.com
http://publicrecords.onlinesearches.com/Illinoi
s-Land-Records-and-Deeds.htm;
http://www.outfitters.com/illinois/henderso
n; htp://www.hendersoncountyedc.com
(Economic Development Corporation)
Marcella L. Cisna
(land records from 1841, births and deaths from
1878, marriages from 1841)

**Henderson County Clerk of the Circuit
Court**
(Fourth and Warren—location)
Box 546 (mailing address)
Oquawka, IL 61469-0546
(309) 867-3121; (309) 867-3207 FAX
skeane@9thjudicial.org
http://www.state.il.us/court/CircuitCourt/Circ
uitCourtJudges/CCC_County.asp
Sandra D. Keane
(naturalization records from 1850 to 1920,
probate records from 1841)
probate search service: no charge; copies of
probate records: 25¢ per page, no minimum

Henry County
organized 1825 from Fulton County

Henry County Clerk of the Circuit Court
Henry County Courthouse
307 West Center Street
Cambridge, IL 61238
(309) 937-3572; (309) 937-3990 FAX
CircuitClerk@Henrycty.com;
ddoss@henrycty.com
http://www.henrycty.com/codepartments/Circ
uitClerk/index.html
Debra J. Doss
(naturalization records from the late 1800s to
1950, probate records from the late 1800s to
date)
naturalization records and probate records
search service: $4.00 per name; copies of
naturalization records and probate records:
$2.00 per case from automated system, 50¢
per page from non-automated system, $2.00
per document for certification

Henry County Clerk/Recorder
Henry County Courthouse
307 West Center Street
Cambridge, IL 61238
(309) 937-3575 (Clerk); (309) 937-3486
(Recorder)
CountyClerk@Henrycty.com;
blink@henrycty.com
http://www.henrycty.com/codepartments/cou
ntyclerk/index.html; http://www.henrycty.
com/codepartments/recorder
Barbara M. Link
(land records from the 1800s, births, deaths and
marriages from the late 1800s but not
required by law until after 1916)
no land records search service (must supply
document number); vital records search
service (access to births after 1916 restricted
to the person named or their legal guardian):
$5.00; copies of land records: $1.00 per page;
certified copies of vital records: $7.00 for the
first copy, $2.00 for each additional copy of
the same record

Iroquois County
organized 1833 from Vermilion County

Iroquois County Clerk and Recorder
1001 East Grant Street
Watseka, IL 60970
(815) 432-6960
iroquoiscountyclerk@iroquois-co.com
http://www.co.iroquois.il.us/?page_id=15#
Mark Hendricks
(land records from 1839, indexed by buyer or
seller and date of transaction, births and
deaths from 1878, indexed by name and date,

and marriages from 1868, indexed by bride or groom and date)
copies of land records: $2.00; copies of vital records: $3.00 each, $7.00 for certified copies; indexes closed to the public after 1916

Iroquois County Clerk of the Circuit Court
550 South Tenth Street
Watseka, IL 60970-1810
(815) 432-6950; (815) 432-0347 FAX
iroqcirclk@iroquois-co.com
http://www.co.iroquois.il.us; http://www.state.il.us/court/CircuitCourt/CircuitCourtJudges/CCC_County.asp
Arlene J. Hines
(probate records from about 1862, better indexes from about 1927)

Jackson County
organized 1816 from Randolph and Johnson counties

Jackson County Clerk and Recorder
Courthouse, 1001 Walnut Street, First Floor
Murphysboro, IL 62966
(618) 687-7360 (Vital Records); (618) 687-7363 (Recording)
lrein265@earthlink.net
http://www.co.jackson.il.us/elected/co_clerk.htm
Larry W. Reinhardt
(land records from 1873, births and deaths from 1874, marriages from 1843)
copies of vital records: $1.00 each for records before 1916, $7.00 each for records after 1916 (must be certified)

Jackson County Clerk of the Circuit Court
(Tenth and Walnut—location)
PO Box 730 (mailing address)
Murphysboro, IL 62966-0730
(618) 687-7300; (618) 684-6378 FAX
csvanda@neondsl.com
http://www.circuitclerk.co.jackson.il.us/CircuitClerk.htm
Cindy R. Svanda
(probate records from 1843)
no probate search service; copies of probate records: 50¢ per page

Jasper County
organized 1831 from Crawford and Clay counties

Jasper County Clerk
204 West Washington Street, Suite 2
Newton, IL 62448
(618) 783-3124
raydiel1@yahoo.com
http://www.jaspercountyillinois.org; http://publicrecords.onlinesearches.com/Illinois-Land-Records-and-Deeds.htm
Ray Diel
(land records, vital records)
copies of land and vital records: 50¢ per page, $2.00 to $5.00 for certification

Jasper County Clerk of the Circuit Court
100 West Jordan Street
Newton, IL 62448-1973
(618) 783-2524; (618) 783-8626 FAX
jaspercirclk@hotmail.com
http://www.jaspercountyillinois.org; http://www.state.il.us/court/CircuitCourt/CircuitCourtJudges/CCC_County.asp
Sheryl Frederick
(naturalization records, probate records)
copies of naturalization and probate records: 50¢ per page, $2.00 to $5.00 for certification

Jefferson County
organized 1819 from Edwards and White counties

Jefferson County Clerk and Recorder
Jefferson County Courthouse
100 South Tenth Street, Room 105
Mt. Vernon, IL 62864
(618) 244-8020
jeffcoclerk@jeffil.us
http://publicrecords.onlinesearches.com/Illinois-Land-Records-and-Deeds.htm
Donald K. Rector
(land records from 1819, births from 1878, deaths from 1877, marriages from 1830)

Jefferson County Clerk of the Circuit Court
(Tenth and Broadway—location)
Box 1266 (mailing address)
Mt. Vernon, IL 62864-1266
(618) 244-8007; (618) 244-8029 FAX
jeffcocircuitclerk@jeff.il.us
http://www.state.il.us/court/CircuitCourt/CircuitCourtJudges/CCC_County.asp
Gene Bolerjack
(a few naturalization records from 1880 through 1930, wills from 1866 to date, probate records from 1830 to date)

Jersey County
organized 1839 from Greene County

Jersey County Clerk
200 North LaFayette Street
Jerseyville, IL 62052
(618) 498-5571, ext. 113
countyclerk@jerseycounty-il.us
http://www.jcba.us
Linda J. Crotchett
(with Recorder's Office, naturalization records from 1839 to 1848 and from 1854 to 1903, births and deaths from 1 January 1875 [indexes to 1916 open to the public], marriages [females indexed 1839-1876] with County Clerk, Office of Vital Records, PO Box 216, Jerseyville, IL 62052)
vital records search service: $5.00 (includes first copy if found); additional copies of the same record: $2.00 each

Jersey County Clerk of the Circuit Court
201 West Pearl Street
Jerseyville, IL 62052-1852
(618) 498-5571; (618) 498-6128 FAX
circuitclerk@jerseycounty-il.us
http://www.jerseycounty-il.us
Charles E. Huebener

Jersey County Recorder
201 W. Pearl Street
Jerseyville, IL 62052-1675
(618) 498-5571
http://publicrecords.onlinesearches.com/Illinois-Land-Records-and-Deeds.htm
(original land grant records from 1830, field notes from 1856, Road Record A from 1839, grantor-grantee records [deeds, mortgages, etc.] from 1839, plats of towns and subdivisions from 1839)

Jo Daviess County
organized 1827 from Mercer, Henry and Putnam counties

Jo Daviess County Clerk of the Circuit Court
Jo Daviess County Courthouse
330 North Bench Street, Room 204
Galena, IL 61036-1828
(815) 777-0037; (815) 776-9146 FAX
swand@jodaviess.org
http://www.jodaviess.org
Sharon A. Wand
(probate records from 1850)
probate search service: $4.00 by mail; copies of vital records: $7.00 each; copies of probate records: 25¢ per page, 25¢ minimum

Jo Daviess County Clerk/Recorder
330 North Bench Street
Galena, IL 61036
(815) 777-0161 (Clerk); (815) 777-9694 (Recorder)
countyclerk@jodaviess.org; countyrecorder@jodaviess.org; jdimke@jodaviess.org
http://www.jodaviess.org
Jean Dimke
(land records from 1829 [tract index starts 1920s] with Recorder, naturalization records from 1800s with Recorder, births and deaths from 1877 [not public record after 1916], marriages from 1830 with County Clerk, First

Floor)

Johnson County
organized 1812 from Randolph County

Johnson County Clerk of the Circuit Court
(Courthouse Square—location)
PO Box 517 (mailing address)
Vienna, IL 62995-0517
(618) 658-4751; (618) 658-2908 FAX
newjccc@yahoo.com
http://www.state.il.us/court/CircuitCourt/CircuitCourtJudges/CCC_County.asp
Neal E. Watkins

Johnson County Clerk/Recorder
PO Box 96
Vienna, IL 62995
(618) 658-3611
macabud@hotmail.com
http://publicrecords.onlinesearches.com/Illinois-Land-Records-and-Deeds.htm
Robin Harper-Whitehead
(land records, vital records)
vital records search service: $5.00; copies of land records: $1.00 each; certified copies of vital records: $7.00 each (includes search)

Kane County
organized 1836 from LaSalle County

Kane County Clerk
(Kane County Government Center, 719 South Batavia Avenue, Building B—location)
PO Box 70 (mailing address)
Geneva, IL 60134
(630) 232-5990 (Vital Records)
cunninghamjohn@co.kane.il.us
http://www.co.kane.il.us/coc
John A. "Jack" Cunningham

Kane County Clerk of the Circuit Court
540 South Randall Road
St. Charles, IL 60174
(630) 232-3413; (630) 208-2172 FAX
seyllerdeb@co.kane.il.us
http://www.cic.co.kane.il.us
Deborah Seyller
(naturalization records from 1800 to 1943 [not complete due to fire], probate records from 1800)
probate search service: $4.00 per year; copies of probate records: $1.00 for the first page, 50¢ for each of the next ten pages, and 25¢ for each additional page, no minimum

Kane County Recorder
Kane County Government Center
719 South Batavia Avenue
Geneva, IL 60134
(630) 232-5935; (630) 232-5945 FAX
wegmansandy@kanecountyrecorder.net
http://www.kanecountyrecorder.net
Sandy Wegman

Kankakee County
organized 1853 from Iroquois and Will counties

Kankakee County Clerk
Kankakee County Administration Building
189 East Court Street
Kankakee, IL 60901
(815) 937-2990; (815) 939-8831 FAX
countyclerk@k3county.net
http://www.kankakeecountyclerk.com
Bruce Clark
(births from 1878 to date, deaths from 1877 to date, marriages from 1853 to date)
certified copies of vital records: $7.00 for the first copy and $2.00 for each additional copy of the same record (records after 1900 are restricted)

Kankakee County Clerk of the Circuit Court
Probate
450 East Court Street, Room 208
Kankakee, IL 60901-3917
(815) 937-2905; (815) 937-2908 (Probate); (815) 939-8830 FAX
circuitclerk@k3county.net;

kthomas@k3county.net
http://www.k3county.net/circuitclerk.htm
Kathryn Thomas

Kankakee County Recorder of Deeds
189 East Court Street, Rooms 203–207
Kankakee, IL 60901
(815) 937-2980; (815) 937-3657 FAX
recorder@k3county.net
http://www.k3county.net/recorder.htm
Dennis Coy

Kendall County
organized 1841 from LaSalle and Kane counties

Kendall County Clerk and Recorder
110 West Fox Street
Yorkville, IL 60560
(312) 553-4112 (County Clerk and Recorder);
    (312) 553-4104 (County Clerk)
panderson@co.kendall.il.us;
    andersonp@sisna.com
http://www.co.kendall.il.us
Paul P. Anderson
(land records and vital records with County
    Clerk and Recorder, 110 Fox Street, Yorkville,
    IL 60560)

Kendall County Clerk of the Circuit Court
(807 West John Street—location)
PO Box M (mailing address)
Yorkville, IL 60560-0259
(630) 553-4183; (630) 553-4964 FAX
rmorganegg@co.kendall.il.us
http://www.co.kendall.il.us
Becky Morganegg
(naturalization records and probate records)

Knox County
organized 1825 from Fulton County

Knox County Clerk
Knox County Courthouse
200 South Cherry Street
Galesburg, IL 61401-4992
(309) 345-3815; (309) 345-3801 FAX
info@knoxclerk.org; serickson@knoxclerk.org
http://www.knoxclerk.org
Scott G. Erickson
(vital records)

Knox County Clerk of the Circuit Court
Knox County Courthouse
200 South Cherry Street
Galesburg, IL 61401-4912
(309) 343-3121; (309) 343-0098 FAX
kcheesman@9thjudicial.org
http://www.knoxclerk.org/CountyDepartments
    .htm
Kelly A. Cheesman
(naturalization records and probate records)

Knox County Recorder of Deeds
Knox County Courthouse
200 South Cherry Street, First Floor
Galesburg, IL 61401
(309) 345-3818; (309) 345-3842 FAX
http://www.knoxclerk.org/CountyDepartments
    .htm
Nancy McCune
(land records)

Lake County
organized 1839 from McHenry County

Lake County Clerk
18 North County Street, Room 101
Waukegan, IL 60085-4339
(847) 377-2400
cntyclk@co.lake.il.us;
    CountyClerk@co.lake.il.us;
    whelander@co.lake.il.ushttp://www.lakecoun
tyil.gov/default.htm
http://www.co.lake.il.us/cntyclk
Ms. Willard R. Helander

Lake County Clerk of the Circuit Court
18 North County Street
Waukegan, IL 60085-4340
(847) 377-3380; (847) 360-6409 FAX
CircuitClerk@co.lake.il.us; scoffelt@co.lake.il.us

http://www.co.lake.il.us/circlk
Sally D. Coffelt

Lake County Recorder of Deeds
18 North County Street, Second Floor
Waukegan, IL 60085
(847) 377-2061; (847) 625-7038 FAX
MVanderventer@co.lake.il.us
http://www.co.lake.il.us/recorder
Mary Ellen Vanderventer

LaSalle County
organized 1831 from Putnam and Vermilion
    counties

LaSalle County Clerk
(707 East Etna Road—location)
PO Box 430 (mailing address)
Ottawa, IL 61350-0430
(815) 434-8202
countyclerk@lasallecounty.org
http://www.lasallecounty.org/ctyclerk/default.h
tm
Mary Jane Wilkinson
(births and deaths from 1877, marriages from
    1832)
copies of vital records: $7.00 each (includes
    search)

LaSalle County Clerk of the Circuit Court
Civil Division
(LaSalle County Courthouse, 119 West Madison
    Street, #201—location)
PO Box 617 (mailing address)
Ottawa, IL 61350-0617
(815) 434-8671; (815) 433-9198 FAX
joseph-carey@lasallecounty.com;
    postmaster@lasallecounty.com
http://www.lasallecounty.com
Joseph M. Carey
(naturalization records from the mid-1800s;
    probate records from 1830)
probate search service: $4.00 per year ; copies of
    probate records: 25¢ per page, $4.00
    minimum

LaSalle County Recorder
707 East Etna Road
Ottawa, IL 61350
(815) 434-8226; (815) 434-8260 FAX
recorder@lasallecounty.org
http://www.lasallecounty.org/recorder/index.ht
m
Thomas Lyons
(deeds from 1835)
copies of land records: $1.00 per page

Lawrence County
organized 1821 from Crawford and Edwards
    counties

Lawrence County Clerk and Recorder
County Courthouse
1100 State Street
Lawrenceville, IL 62439
(618) 943-2346 (Clerk); (618) 943-5126
    (Recorder)
nhokelawcoclk@yahoo.com
http://www.lawrencecountyillinois.com/govern
ment.html
Nancy J. Hoke
(land records, births from 1877, deaths from
    1878, marriages from 1821)
land records search service: $10.00; copies of
    vital records: $2.00 before 1916, $5.00 after
    1916 (must be certified), proof of relationship
    required

Lawrence County Clerk of the Circuit Court
1100 State Street
Lawrenceville, IL 62439-2390
(618) 943-2815; (618) 943-5205 FAX
c_clerk2000@hotmail.com
http://www.lawrencecountyillinois.com/govern
ment.html
Peggy Frederick
(naturalization records to 1957, probate records)
probate search service: $4.00 per year searched
    (include names, years and what you want);
    copies of probate records: $1.00 for the first

page, 50¢ for each of the next nineteen pages
and 25¢ for each additional page

Lee County
organized 1839 from Ogle County

Lee County Clerk and Recorder
(112 East Second—location)
PO Box 329 (mailing address)
Dixon, IL 61021
(815) 288-3309; (815) 288-6492 FAX
nnelson@countyoflee.org
http://www.countyoflee.org
Nancy Nelson
(land records, births from 1878 [with a few
    delayed births back to 1856], deaths from
    1877, marriages from 1839)
copies of land records: $1.00; certified copies of
    vital records: $7.00 for the first copy, $2.00
    for each additional copy

Lee County Clerk of the Circuit Court
(Lee County Courts Building, 309 South
    Galena—location)
Box 325 (mailing address)
Dixon, IL 61021-0325
(815) 284-5234; (815) 288-5615 FAX
dmccaffrey@countyoflee.org
http://www.countyoflee.org/circuit_clerk/circu
it_clerk_main.html
Denise A. McCaffrey
(naturalization records and probate records)

Livingston County
organized 1837 from LaSalle and McLean
    counties

Livingston County Clerk
112 West Madison Street
Pontiac, IL 61764
(815) 844-2006
coclerk@maxwire.net
http://publicrecords.onlinesearches.com/Illinoi
s-Land-Records-and-Deeds.htm;
    http://www.livingstoncounty-il.org
Kristy A. Masching
(land records from 1837, births from 1856,
    deaths from 1878, marriages from 1837)
copies of land records: $2.00 each, $5.00 for
    certified copies; certified copies of vital
    records: $5.00 each

Livingston County Clerk of the Circuit Court
112 West Madison Street
Pontiac, IL 61764-0320
(815) 844-2602; (815) 844-2322 FAX
jcremer@fcg.net
http://www.state.il.us/court/CircuitCourt/Circ
uitCourtJudges/CCC_County.asp
Judith K. Cremer
(naturalization records from 1837 through the
    early 1900s, probate records from 1837)
probate search service: $4.00 per year; copies of
    probate records: $1.00 for the first page, 50¢
    for each of the next nineteen pages and 25¢
    for each additional page, no minimum;
    request search in writing

Logan County
organized 1839 from Sangamon County

Logan County Clerk and Recorder
(Logan County Courthouse, 601 Broadway
    Street—location)
PO Box 278 (mailing address)
Lincoln, IL 62656
(217) 732-4148
slitterl@co.logan.il.us
http://www.co.logan.il.us/county_clerk
Sally J. Litterly

Logan County Clerk of the Circuit Court
Civil Division
(Logan County Courthouse, 601 Broadway,
    Room 21—location)
PO Box 158 (mailing address)
Lincoln, IL 62656-0158
(217) 732-1163; (217) 732-1164; (217) 732-1232
    FAX
cbender@co.logan.il.us

http://www.co.logan.il.us/circuit_clerk
Carla Bender

Macon County

organized 1829 from Shelby County

Macon County Clerk
141 South Main Street, Room 104
Decatur, IL 62523
(217) 424-1305; (217) 423-0922 FAX
sbean@co.macon.il.us
http://www.maconcounty-
il.gov/departments/countyclerk/index.htm;
http://www.maconcoclerk.org
Stephen M. Bean
(vital records)

Macon County Clerk of the Circuit Court
253 East Wood Street
Decatur, IL 62523-1489
(217) 424-1454; (217) 424-1350 FAX
khott@court.co.macon.il.us
http://www.maconcounty-
il.gov/departments/circuitcourt/index.htm
Kathy Hott
(naturalization records, probate records)
probate search service: $5.00; copies of probate
records: 30¢ first page, 10¢ each additional
page

Macon County Recorder of Deeds
141 South Main Street, Room 201
Decatur, IL 62523
(217) 424-1360
http://www.maconcounty-
il.gov/departments/recorder/index.htm
Mary Eaton
(land records)

Macoupin County

organized 1829 from Madison and Greene
counties

Macoupin County Clerk and Recorder
(201 East Main—location)
PO Box 107 (mailing address)
Carlinville, IL 62626
(217) 854-3214
michele.zippay@macoupincountyil.gov;
countyclerk@roe40.k12.il.us
http://www.macoupincountyil.gov/county_cler
k.htm
Michele Zippay

Macoupin County Clerk of the Circuit Court
201 East Main Street
Carlinville, IL 62626-1824
(217) 854-3211; (217) 854-7361 FAX
mikemathis@emailx.net; circuit@ctnet.net
http://www.macoupincountyil.gov/circuit_clerk
.htm
Michael Mathis

Madison County

organized 1812 from St. Clair County

Madison County Clerk
(Madison County Administration Building, 157
North Main Street, Room 109—location)
PO Box 218 (mailing address)
Edwardsville, IL 62025-0218
(618) 296-4482
mavonnida@co.madison.il.us
http://www.co.madison.il.us
Mark A. Von Nida
(births from late 1800s, deaths from 1878,
marriages from 1813)

Madison County Clerk of the Circuit Court
Madison County Courthouse, 155 North Main
Street, Suite 120
Edwardsville, IL 62025-1955
(618) 692-6240; (618) 692-6200, ext. 4521
(Probate Division); (618) 692-0676 FAX
mmelucci@co.madison.il.us
http://www.co.madison.il.us/CircuitClerk/Circ
uitClerk.htm
Matt Melucci
(naturalization records from 1900, probate
records from about 1815 with Probate

Division, Attn: Clerk)

Madison County Recorder
(Madison County Administration Building, 157
North Main Street, Suite 211—location)
PO Box 308 (mailing address)
Edwardsville, IL 62025-0308
(618) 296-4644; (618) 296-4475; (618) 296-4475
http://www.co.madison.il.us
Daniel Donohoo

Marion County

organized 1823 from Fayette and Jefferson
counties

Marion County Clerk
(100 East Main Street—location)
PO Box 637 (mailing address)
Salem, IL 62881-0637
(618) 548-3400
ilmarioncountyclerk@ussonet.net
http://publicrecords.onlinesearches.com/Illinoi
s-Land-Records-and-Deeds.htm
Steve Bailey

Marion County Clerk of the Circuit Court
(100 Main—location)
PO Box 130 (mailing address)
Salem, IL 62881-0130
(618) 548-3856; (618) 548-2358 FAX
http://www.state.il.us/court/CircuitCourt/Circ
uitCourtJudges/CCC_County.asp
Ronda Yates

Marshall County

organized 1839 from Putnam County

Marshall County Clerk and Recorder
(122 North Prairie—location)
PO Box 328 (mailing address)
Lacon, IL 61540
(309) 246-6325
mcoclerk@mtco.com
http://publicrecords.onlinesearches.com/Illinoi
s-Land-Records-and-Deeds.htm
Andrea J. Mahoney
(land records, vital records)
no land records search service; vital records
search service: $5.00 (includes one copy, but
no copies are available for records containing
a social security number); copies of land
records: 50¢ per page, $1.00 per page if mailed

Marshall County Clerk of the Circuit Court
(122 North Prairie—location)
PO Box 328 (mailing address)
Lacon, IL 61540-0328
(309) 246-6435; (309) 246-2173 FAX
ginanoe@marshallcountycourt.net
http://www.state.il.us/court/CircuitCourt/Circ
uitCourtJudges/CCC_County.asp
Gina M. Noe
naturalization records search service: $4.00;
probate search service: $4.00; copies of
probate records: 50¢ each

Mason County

organized 1841 from Tazewell County

Mason County Clerk and Recorder
(100 North Broadway—location)
PO Box 77 (mailing address)
Havana, IL 62644-0077
(309) 543-6661
cclerk@grics.net
http://www.masoncountyil.org
William R. Blessman
(land records from 1841, births and deaths from
1878, marriages from 1841 [records prior to
1916 are accessible to members of
genealogical societies, but after 1916 births
are available only to the person himself or his
parents, unless the person is proven deceased
by presentation of a death record])
vital records search service: $5.00 for five names;
certified copies of marriage and birth records:
$5.00 each; certified copies of death records:
$7.00 each; photocopies of vital records:
$3.00; copies of other records: 50¢ per page

Mason County Clerk of the Circuit Court
County Courthouse
125 North Plum
Havana, IL 62644-0377
(309) 543-6619; (309) 543-4214 FAX
masoncourt@grics.net
http://www.masoncountyil.org
Brenda Miller
(naturalization records, probate records)
probate search service: $4.00 per year; copies of
probate records: 50¢ for each of the first
nineteen pages and 25¢ for each additional
page, no minimum

Massac County

organized 1843 from Pope and Johnson
counties

Massac County Clerk
(1 Superman Squaare—location)
PO Box 429 (mailing address)
Metropolis, IL 62960-0429
(618) 524-5213
http://publicrecords.onlinesearches.com/Illinoi
s-Land-Records-and-Deeds.htm
John D. "Bubba" Taylor
(land records from 1843, births from 1864,
deaths from 1878, marriages from 1843)

Massac County Clerk of the Circuit Court
(Superman Square—location)
PO Box 152 (mailing address)
Metropolis, IL 62960-1882
(618) 524-5011; (618) 524-4850 FAX
lggrace53@yahoo.com
http://www.state.il.us/court/CircuitCourt/Circ
uitCourtJudges/CCC_County.asp
Larry Grace
(naturalization records and probate records)
no probate search service; certified copies: $5.00
each

McDonough County

organized 1826 from Schuyler County

McDonough County Clerk and Recorder
1 Courthouse Square
Macomb, IL 61455
(309) 833-2474
fmiller@mcdonoughcountyclerk.org
http://www.outfitters.com/illinois/mcdonough;
http://publicrecords.onlinesearches.com/Illin
ois-Land-Records-and-Deeds.htm
Florine Miller
(land records, births, deaths and marriages)
copies of vital records: $5.00 each (includes
search), $7.00 each after 1916 (must be
certified)

**McDonough County Clerk of the Circuit
Court**
(#1 Courthouse Square—location)
PO Box 348 (mailing address)
Macomb, IL 61455-0348
(309) 837-4889; (309) 833-4493 FAX
mccc@9thjudicial.org
http://www.outfitters.com/illinois/mcdonough;
http://www.state.il.us/court/CircuitCourt/Ci
rcuitCourtJudges/CCC_County.asp
Kimberly Wilson
(naturalization records, probate records)

McHenry County

organized 1836 from Cook County

McHenry County Clerk
Government Center, 2200 North Seminary
Avenue
Woodstock, IL 60098-2639
(815) 334-4242; (815) 334-8727 FAX
countyclerk@co.mchenry.il.us;
kcschult@co.mchenry.il.us
http://www.co.mchenry.il.us/CountyDpt/coun
tyclerk/default.asp
Katherine C. Schultz
(naturalization records from 11 September 1851
[for abstracted and published Declarations of
Intention contact McHenry County Illinois
Genealogical Society], births from 1877,
deaths from 1878 [both incomplete before

1916], marriages from 1837)
copies of land records: $2.00 for the first copy, 50¢ for each additional copy of the same document; certified copies of vital records: $7.00 for the first copy and $2.00 for each additional copy of the same record made at the same time

McHenry County Clerk of the Circuit Court
Government Center, 2200 North Seminary Avenue (Route 47)
Woodstock, IL 60098-2837
(815) 334-4310; (815) 338-8583 FAX
vwkays@co.mchenry.il.us;
circuitclerk@co.mchenry.il.us
http://www.co.mchenry.il.us/CountyDpt/circuit/default.asp
Vernon W. Kays, Jr.
(probate records from 1836)
no probate search service; copies of probate records: $2.00 for the first page, 50¢ for each of the next nineteen pages and 25¢ for each additional page

McHenry County Recorder
(Administration Building, 667 Ware Road, Room 109—location)
Government Center, 2200 North Seminary Avenue (mailing address)
Woodstock, IL 60098
(815) 334-4110; (815) 338-9612 FAX
recorder@co.mchenry.il.us
http://www.co.mchenry.il.us/CountyDpt/recorder/default.asp
Phyllis K. Walters
(deeds and mortgages)

McLean County
organized 1830 from Tazewell County

McLean County Clerk
(115 East Washington Street, Room 102—location)
PO Box 2400 (mailing address)
Bloomington, IL 61701-2400
(309) 888-5190; (309) 888-5932 FAX
countyclerk@mcleancountyil.gov;
peggyann.milton@mcleancountyil.gov
http://www.mcleancountyil.gov/countyclerk
Peggy Ann Milton
(births and deaths from 1878 [deaths indexed through 1964, but no family information on deaths until about 1912], marriages from 1831 [indexed through 1935, no family information until about 1878, filings not required until 1916])
vital records search service: $5.00 (none by phone); certified copies: $5.00

McLean County Clerk of the Circuit Court
Law and Justice Center
104 West Front Street, Room 404
Bloomington, IL 61702-2400
(309) 888-5301; (309) 888-5324; (309) 888-5281 FAX
circuitclerk@mcleancountyil.gov;
Sandra.parker@mcleancountyil.gov
http://www.mcleancountyil.gov/CircuitClerk
Sandra K. Parker
(naturalization records and probate records)

McLean County Recorder
(115 East Washington Street, Room M104—location)
PO Box 2400 (mailing address)
Bloomington, IL 61702-2400
(309) 888-5170; (309) 888-5927 FAX
recorder@mcleancountyil.gov
http://www.mcleancountyil.gov/recorder
Mr. Lee Newcom
(land records)

Menard County
organized 1839 from Sangamon County

Menard County Clerk
(102 South Seventh—location)
PO Box 465 (mailing address)
Petersburg, IL 62675
(217) 632-3201
gtreseler@co.menard.il.us
http://publicrecords.onlinesearches.com/Illinois-Land-Records-and-Deeds.htm;
http://www.visitmenardcounty.com
Gene Treseler
(land records from 1839 to date, births from 1877 to 1952, deaths from 1877 to date, and marriage licenses from 1839 to date)
land records search service: $10.00; copies of land records: $1.00 each; copies of vital records: $1.00 per document, $5.00 for certification

Menard County Clerk of the Circuit Court
PO Box 466
Petersburg, IL 62675-0466
(217) 632-2615; (217) 632-4124 FAX
phoke@co.menard.il.us
http://www.state.il.us/court/CircuitCourt/CircuitCourtJudges/CCC_County.asp
Penny Hoke
probate search service: $4.00 per year, payable in advance (personal check not accepted); copies of probate records: $1.00 for the first page, 50¢ for each of the next nineteen pages and 25¢ for each additional page plus estimated postage, $2.00 for certification, billed after search is completed

Mercer County
organized 1825 from Pike County

Mercer County Clerk
(100 Southeast Third Street—location)
PO Box 66 (mailing address)
Aledo, IL 61231
(309) 582-7021
countyclerk@mercercountycourthouse.com
http://publicrecords.onlinesearches.com/Illinois-Land-Records-and-Deeds.htm;
http://www.outfitters.com/illinois/mercer;
http://www.mercercountyil.org
Thomas L. Hanson

Mercer County Clerk of the Circuit Court
(100 Southeast Third Street—location)
PO Box 175 (mailing address)
Aledo, IL 61231-0175
(309) 582-7122; (309) 582-7121 FAX
jbenson@mercercounty.il.org
http://www.state.il.us/court/CircuitCourt/CircuitCourtJudges/CCC_County.asp
Jeff G. Benson

Monroe County
organized 1816 from Randolph and St. Clair counties

Monroe County Clerk
Monroe County Courthouse
100 South Main Street
Waterloo, IL 62298-1322
(618) 939-8681; (618) 939-8639 FAX
moclerk@htc.net
http://www.monroecountyil.org
Dennis M. Knobloch
(deeds and vital records)
copies of deeds: $1.00 per page; certified copies of vital records: $7.00 (includes search)

Monroe County Clerk of the Circuit Court
100 South Main Street, Room 115
Waterloo, IL 62298-1322
(618) 939-8681; (618) 939-1929 FAX
http://www.monroecountyil.org
Aaron Reitz
(naturalization records and probate records)
no probate search service; copies of probate records: 20¢ per page, no minimum

Montgomery County
organized 1821 from Bond and Madison counties

Montgomery County Clerk of the Circuit Court
(120 North Main Street—location)
Box C (mailing address)
Hillsboro, IL 62049-0210
(217) 532-9546 (Civil); (217) 532-9545 (Probate);
(217) 532-9614
FAXhttp://www.montgomeryco.com
Marywebb@consolidated.net
http://www.montgomeryco.com/circlerk.htm
Mary Webb
(naturalization records and probate records)

Montgomery County Clerk/Recorder
(1 Courthouse Square—location)
PO Box 595 (mailing address)
Hillsboro, IL 62049
(217) 532-9530
sandyleitheiser@hotmail.com
http://www.montgomeryco.com/coclerk.htm
Sandy Leitheiser
(land records, births and deaths from 1877, marriages from 1821)
certified copies of vital records: $5.00 if exact name and date are supplied

Morgan County
organized 1823 from Sangamon County

Morgan County Clerk and Recorder
(300 West State Street—location)
PO Box 1387 (mailing address)
Jacksonville, IL 62650
(217) 243-8581
bjgross@irtc.net
http://www.morgancounty-il.com/cty_clerk.htm;
http://www.morgancountyclerk.com
Barbara J. Gross
(land records from 1823, births and deaths from 1878 [parents' names were required as of 1911], birth and death index from 1878 to 1916, marriages from 1828 [parents' names were required as of 1911], marriage index from 1828 to 1916)
copies of land records: 50¢ each from paper originals, $1.00 each from microfilm originals; certified copies of vital records: $7.00 each, subject to restrictions

Morgan County Clerk of the Circuit Court
(300 West State Street—location)
Box 1120 (mailing address)
Jacksonville, IL 62650-1165
(217) 243-5419; (217) 243-2009 FAX
circlerk@morgancounty-il.com
http://www.morgancounty-il.com/cir_clerk.htm
Theresa Lonergan

Moultrie County
organized 1843 from Macon and Shelby counties

Moultrie County Clerk and Recorder
10 South Main, Suite 6
Sullivan, IL 61951
(217) 728-4389; (217) 728-8178 FAX
ctyclrk@moultrie.com
http://publicrecords.onlinesearches.com/Illinois-Land-Records-and-Deeds.htm
Georgia C. England
(land records, vital records)
no land records search service; copies of vital records: $5.00 for the first copy, $2.00 for each additional copy of the same record

Moultrie County Clerk of the Circuit Court
10 South Main Street, Suite 7
Sullivan, IL 61951-1969
(217) 728-4622; (217) 728-7833 FAX
dpreston@circuit-clerk.moultrie.il.us
http://www.state.il.us/court/CircuitCourt/CircuitCourtJudges/CCC_County.asp
Cynthia J. Braden
(naturalization records; probate records)

Ogle County
organized 1836 from Jo Daviess County

Ogle County Clerk and Recorder
Washington and South Fourth Streets—location)
PO Box 357 (mailing address)
Oregon, IL 61061
(815) 732-1110; (815) 732-6273 FAX
rebeccah@oglecounty.org

http://oglecountyclerk.org
Rebecca Huntley
(land records from 1836 with County Recorder's
Office, PO Box 357, Oregon, IL 61061,
births from 1860, deaths from 1878, and
marriages from 1836 with County Clerk's
Office)
land records search service: $5.00 per name (give
approximate year); vital records search
service: $5.00 per name (includes copy);
copies of vital records: $1.00 each

Ogle County Clerk of the Circuit Court
(106 South Fifth, Suite 300—location)
PO Box 337 (mailing address)
Oregon, IL 61061-0337
(815) 732-3201; (815) 732-1130 (Civil Division);
(815) 732-6273 FAX
circuitclerk@oglecounty.org
http://www.oglecounty.org/marty/circuitclerk.
html
Martin W. Typer
(naturalization records, probate records)
probate search service: $4.00 per year by statute;
copies of probate records: from 10¢ to $1.00
per page (depends on the size of the search)

Peoria County
organized 1825 from Fulton County

Peoria County Clerk
324 Main Street, Room 101
Peoria, IL 61602
(309) 672-6059; (309) 672-6063 FAX
jthomas@co.peoria.il.us;
jthomas@peoriacounty.org
http://www.peoriacounty.org/display.php?dept
=countyClerk&page=index
JoAnn Thomas
(grantee index only with Recorder of Deeds,
vital records with County Clerk)

Peoria County Clerk of the Circuit Court
Peoria County Courthouse, 324 Main Street,
Room G22
Peoria, IL 61602-1319
(309) 672-6989; (309) 672-6628 FAX
rspears@co.peoria.il.us
http://www.peoriacounty.org/display.php?dept
=circuitClerk&page=index
Robert Spears
(naturalization records, probate records)
no probate search service; copies of probate
records: 50¢ for each of the first twenty pages
and 25¢ for each additional page (policies may
change)

Peoria County Recorder
Peoria County Courthouse, 324 Main Street,
Room G-04
Peoria, IL 61602
(309) 672-6090; (309) 667-6202 FAX
http://www.peoriacounty.org/display.php?dept
=deedsRecorder&page=index
Brad Horton

Perry County
organized 1827 from Randolph and Jackson
counties

Perry County Clerk and Recorder
(Government Building, 3764 State Route
13/127–location)
PO Box 438 (mailing address)
Pinckneyville, IL 62274-0438
(618) 357-5116; (618) 357-3194 FAX
kkern@onecliq.net
http://www.perrycountyil.org/countyclerk
Kevin Kern
(land records and vital records)

Perry County Clerk of the Circuit Court
(County Courthouse, Courthouse Square, First
Floor—location)
Box 219 (mailing address)
Pinckneyville, IL 62274-0219
(618) 357-6726; (618) 357-8336 FAX
kkellermanpccc@onecliq.net
http://www.perrycountyil.org
Kim Kellerman

(naturalization records and probate records)

Piatt County
organized 1841 from De Witt and Macon
counties

Piatt County Clerk and Recorder
(101 West Washington Street, Monticello, IL
61856-1149—location)
PO Box 558 (mailing address)
Monticello, IL 61856-0558
(217) 762-9487
countyclerk@piattcounty.org
http://www.piattcounty.org
Patricia "Pat" Rhoades
(land records, births and deaths from late 1800s
[very few, most from 1916], marriages from
1841)

Piatt County Clerk of the Circuit Court
(101 West Washington Street—location)
PO Box 288 (mailing address)
Monticello, IL 61856-0288
(217) 762-4966; (217) 762-8394 FAX
piattcort@piattcounty.org
http://www.piattcounty.org
Charles A. Barre
(sketchy naturalization records from 1858
through 1928, guardianships sketchy from
mid 1800s, possibly written into old Court
Docket books)
probate search service: no charge; copies of
probate records: 20¢ per page (prior to 1964)
or $1.00 for the first page and 50¢ per each
additional page (after 1964), no minimum

Pike County
organized 1821 from Madison, Bond and Clark
counties

Pike County Clerk of the Circuit Court
100 East Washington
Pittsfield, IL 62363-1497
(217) 285-6612; (217) 285-4726 FAX
circlk@kcds.net
http://publicrecords.onlinesearches.com/Illinoi
s-Land-Records-and-Deeds.htm
Debbie Dugan
(naturalization records from 1859, probate
records from 1831)
probate search service: $5.00 per name; certified
copies: $5.00

Pike County Clerk/Recorder
100 East Washington
Pittsfield, IL 62363
(217) 285-6812
donnieapps@kcds.net
http://www.state.il.us/court/CircuitCourt/Circ
uitCourtJudges/CCC_County.asp;
http://www.pikeil.org (Chamber of
Commerce)
Donnie Apps
(land records from 1839, births and deaths from
1877, marriages from 1827)

Pope County
organized 1816 from Johnson and Gallatin
counties

Pope County Clerk
PO Box 216
Golconda, IL 62938
(618) 683-4466
http://www.popeco.net/government/governme
nt.html
Connie Gibbs
(land records from 1816, births from 1877 [few
delayed records from 1862], deaths from
1878, marriages from 1816, probate records
from 1816 to 1950)
probate search service: $5.00; copies of vital
records: $5.00 (includes search); copies of
probate records: 25¢ each, $5.00 for certified
copies, $5.00 minimum

Pope County Clerk of the Circuit Court
(Main Street—location)
PO Box 438 (mailing address)
Golconda, IL 62938-0502

(618) 683-3941; (618) 683-3018 FAX
pope_co_cc@yahoo.com
http://www.popeco.net/government/governme
nt.html
Penni R. Taber
(naturalization records from 1865 to 1896;
probate records from 1951)
probate search service: $5.00; copies of probate
records: 25¢ each, $5.00 for certified copies,
$5.00 minimum

Pulaski County
organized 1843 from Johnson County

Pulaski County Clerk
PO Box 118
Mound City, IL 62963-0118
(618) 748-9360
jsauerbrunn@yahoo.com
http://www.pulaskicountyil.net/departments.ph
p
Julie Sauerbrunn

Pulaski County Clerk of the Circuit Court
(500 Illinois Avenue—location)
PO Box 88 (mailing address)
Mound City, IL 62963-0088
(618) 748-9300; (618) 748-9329 FAX
ckennedy@pulaskicountyil.net
http://www.pulaskicountyil.net/departments.ph
p
Cindy Kennedy

Putnam County
organized 1825 from Fulton County

Putnam County Clerk and Recorder
(120 North Fourth Street—location)
PO Box 236 (mailing address)
Hennepin, IL 61327
(815) 925-7129
dankuhn@mchsi.com
http://www.outfitters.com/illinois/putnam;
http://publicrecords.onlinesearches.com/Illin
ois-Land-Records-and-Deeds.htm
Daniel Kuhn
(land records from 1831 with County Recorder,
births and deaths from 1877, marriages from
1831 with County Recorder)
land records search service: $10.00 per name
(includes copy); vital records search service
(through 1910): $5.00 (includes certified copy,
if found); vital records after 1910 subject to
restrictions

Putnam County Clerk of the Circuit Court
120 North Fourth Street
Hennepin, IL 61327-0207
(815) 925-7016; (815) 925-7492 FAX
coliveri@mchsi.com
http://www.state.il.us/court/CircuitCourt/Circ
uitCourtJudges/CCC_County.asp
Cathy J. Oliveri
(naturalization records, estates)

Randolph County
organized 1795 from St. Clair County

Randolph County Clerk and Recorder
1 Taylor Street, Room 202
Chester, IL 62233-0309
(618) 826-2510; (618) 826-3750 FAX
countyclerk@randolphco.org;
gwaley@email.com
http://www.randolphco.org/gov/elected/office
.cfm?officeid=22
Pat Laramore
(land records from 1724 to date [indexed from
1853 to date] with, County Clerk and
Recorder, some naturalization records, births
from 1857, deaths from 1878, marriages from
1805)
land and vital records search service: $5.00;
copies $1.00 each, $7.00 for certification

Randolph County Clerk of the Circuit Court
1 Taylor Street, Room 302
Chester, IL 62233-0329
(618) 826-3116; (618) 826-3761 FAX
circuitclerk@randolphco.org;

bbrowncc@yahoo.com
http://www.randolphco.org/gov/elected/office
  .cfm?officeid=12
Barbara Brown
(divorces, some naturalization records, and
  probate records)

Richland County
organized 1841 from Clay and Lawrence
  counties

Richland County Clerk
103 West Main Street
Olney, IL 62450-2170
(618) 392-3111
elections@richlandcogov.com
http://www.vitalrec.com/ilcounties14.html#Ric
  hland
Michael T. Buss
(general Entry Book from 1841, births and
  deaths from 1878, marriages from 1841)

Richland County Clerk of the Circuit Court
103 West Main Street, #21
Olney, IL 62450-2170
(618) 392-2151; (618) 392-5041 FAX
rccc080@hotmail.com
http://www.state.il.us/court/CircuitCourt/Circ
  uitCourtJudges/CCC_County.asp
Sandy Franklin
(naturalization index [General], probate records)

Rock Island County
organized 1831 from Jo Daviess County

Rock Island County Recorder of Deeds
Courthouse, 210 15th Street, Second Floor
Rock Island, IL 61201
(309) 558-3360
pveronda@co.rock-island.il.us
http://www.co.rock-island.il.us/Rec.asp?id=123
Patricia A. Veronda

Rock Island County Clerk
(1504 Third Avenue, First Floor—location)
PO Box 3577 (mailing address)
Rock Island, IL 61204
(309) 558-3569; (309) 786-7381 FAX
ricoclerk@revealed.net; rdl@revealed.net
http://www.co.rock-island.il.us/CoClk.asp
Richard "Dick" Liebovitz

**Rock Island County Clerk of the Circuit
Court**
(Courthouse, 210 15th Street, Third Floor—
  location)
Box 5230 (mailing address)
Rock Island, IL 61201-5230
(309) 786-4451; (309) 786-3029 FAX
lbierman@co.rock-island.il.us
http://www.co.rock-
  island.il.us/CirClk.asp?id=159
Lisa L. Bierman
(naturalization records from 1872 to 1962)
naturalization records search service: $4.00 per
  person

St. Clair County
organized 1790 from Northwest Territory

St. Clair County Clerk
10 Public Square, Second Floor
Belleville, IL 62220-1623
(618) 277-6600, ext. 2380
countyclerk@co.st-clair.il.us
http://www.stclaircountyclerk.com
Bob Delaney
(land records with Dick Weilmuenster, Mapping
  and Platting, naturalization records to 1900,
  vital records with County Clerk)
copies of vital records: $8.60 for births (includes
  search), $7.00 for deaths and marriages
  (includes search)

St. Clair County Clerk of the Circuit Court
10 Public Square
Belleville, IL 62220-1623
(618) 277-6832; (618) 277-1562 FAX
circuitclerk@co.st-clair.il.us
http://co.st-

clair.il.us/Departments/Circuit+Clerk+Depar
  tment/default.htm
C. Barney Metz

St. Clair County Recorder of Deeds
(10 Public Square—location)
PO Box 543 (mailing address)
Belleville, IL 62222
(618) 277-6600
http://co.st-
  clair.il.us/Departments/Record+of+Deeds+
  Office/default.htm
Michael Costello

Saline County
organized 1847 from Gallatin County

Saline County Clerk and Recorder
10 East Poplar
Harrisburg, IL 62946
(618) 253-8197
countyclerk@yourclearwave.com
http://publicrecords.onlinesearches.com/Illinoi
  s-Land-Records-and-Deeds.htm;
http://www.salinecountychamber.org
  (Chamber of Commerce)
William "Willie" McClusky
(land records, vital records)

Saline County Clerk of the Circuit Court
10 East Poplar
Harrisburg, IL 62946-1553
(618) 253-5096; (618) 253-3904 FAX
randynybergcc@yahoo.com
http://www.state.il.us/court/CircuitCourt/Circ
  uitCourtJudges/CCC_County.asp
Randy Nyberg
(limited naturalization records, probate records)
probate search service: $5.00 per year; copies of
  probate records: 25¢ per page, no minimum;
  all requests by mail

Sangamon County
organized 1821 from Bond and Madison
  counties

Sangamon County Clerk
County Complex, 200 South Ninth Street
Springfield, IL 62701
(217) 753-6700
joea@co.sangamon.il.us
http://www.co.sangamon.il.us/Offices/ctyclerk.
  htm
Joseph Aiello
(births and deaths from 1877, marriages from
  1988)
search fee: $17.00 for birth or marriage record
  (includes one certified copy), $19.00 for death
  record (includes one certified copy)

Sangamon County Clerk of the Circuit Court
200 South Ninth Street, Room 405
Springfield, IL 62701-1299
(217) 753-6674; (217) 753-6665 FAX
tonylibri@cs.com
http://www.sangamoncountycircuitclerk.org
Anthony P. Libri
probate search service: no charge; copies of
  probate records: $1.00 for the first page, 50¢
  for each of the next eighteen pages, and 25¢
  for each additional page, $4.00 minimum

Sangamon County Recorder
(200 South Ninth Street, Room 211—location)
PO Box 669 (mailing address)
Springfield, IL 62705-0669
(217) 535-3150; (217) 535-3159 FAX
http://www.co.sangamon.il.us/Offices/recorde
  r.htm
Mary Ann Lamm

Schuyler County
organized 1825 from Pike and Fulton counties

Schuyler County Clerk and Recorder
(102 South Congress—location)
PO Box 200 (mailing address)
Rushville, IL 62681
(217) 322-4734
clerk85@frontiernet.net

http://www.schuylercountyillinois.com/govern
  ment/county_clerk.html
Linda S. Ward
(land records from 1825, births and deaths from
  1877, marriages from 1825)

Schuyler County Clerk of the Circuit Court
(Lafayette and Congress—location)
PO Box 80 (mailing address)
Rushville, IL 62681-0189
(217) 322-4633; (217) 322-6164 FAX
circlerk85@frontiernet.net
http://www.schuylercountyillinois.com/govern
  ment;
  http://www.state.il.us/court/CircuitCourt/Ci
  rcuitCourtJudges/CCC_County.asp
Elaine Boyd
(naturalization records from 1859, probate
  records from 1827)
probate search service: $4.00 per year; copies of
  probate records: $1.00 for the first page, 50¢
  for each of the next nineteen pages and 25¢
  for each additional page, no minimum

Scott County
organized 1839 from Morgan County

Scott County Clerk
35 East Market
Winchester, IL 62694
(217) 742-3178
countyclerk@wincoinet.com
http://publicrecords.onlinesearches.com/Illinoi
  s-Land-Records-and-Deeds.htm
Barbara J. McDade
(land records, births from 1860, deaths from
  1877, marriages from 1839)
vital records search service: $5.00 per name with
  written request

Scott County Clerk of the Circuit Court
35 East Market Street
Winchester, IL 62694-1216
(217) 742-5217; (217) 742-5853 FAX
http://www.state.il.us/court/CircuitCourt/Circ
  uitCourtJudges/CCC_County.asp
Joni Garrett
(naturalization records, probate records)

Shelby County
organized 1827 from Fayette County

Shelby County Clerk
(301 East Main—location)
PO Box 230 (mailing address)
Shelbyville, IL 62565
(217) 774-4421
shelbycc@consolidated.net
http://www.shelbycounty-
  il.comcountyclerkandrecorder.htm
Kathy Lantz
(land records from 1833, births from 1848 to
  date, deaths from 1878 to date, marriages
  from 1827 to date)

Shelby County Clerk of the Circuit Court
PO Box 469
Shelbyville, IL 62565-0469
(217) 774-4212; (217) 774-4109 FAX
cherro@consolidated.net
http://www.shelbycounty-
  il.com/circuitclerk.htm
Cheryl Roley
(probate records)

Stark County
organized 1839 from Knox and Putnam
  counties

Stark County Clerk and Recorder
(130 West Main—location)
PO Box 97 (mailing address)
Toulon, IL 61483-0097
(309) 286-5911
starkcoclerk@webtv.net
http://strkco.illinois.gov/countyOffice.php?offi
  ceID=55;
  http://www.outfitters.com/illiois/stark
Linda K. Peyll
(land records from 1839, births from 1855,

deaths from 1878, marriages from 1839)
copies of vital records: $3.00

Stark County Clerk of the Circuit Court
(130 Main Street—location)
Box 426 (mailing address)
Toulon, IL 61483-0426
(309) 286-5941; (309) 286-4039 FAX
starkcourt@yahoo.com
http://strkco.illinois.gov/countyOffice.php?offi
ceID=54
Marian E. Purtscher
(very few naturalization records, probate
records)
no probate search service; copies of probate
records: $1.00 for the first page and 50¢ for
each additional page

Stephenson County
organized 1837 from Winnebago and Jo Daviess
counties

Stephenson County Clerk and Recorder
15 North Galena Avenue, Suite 1
Freeport, IL 61032-4348
(815) 235-8289
votte@co.stephenson.il.us
http://www.co.stephenson.i.us/clerk
Vici R. Otte
(land records from 1837, vital records from
1887)

**Stephenson County Clerk of the Circuit
Court**
15 North Galena Street, Second Floor
Freeport, IL 61032-0785
(815) 235-8266; (815) 233-1576 FAX
bkcurran@hotmail.com
http://www.co.stephenson.il.us/circuitclerk
Bonnie K. Curran
(naturalization records from 1850 to 1960,
probate records from 1850)
no probate search service; copies of probate
records: from $5.00 to $10.00

Tazewell County
organized 1827 from Fayette County

Tazewell County Clerk
McKenzie Building
11 South Fourth Street
Pekin, IL 61554
(309) 477-2264
cwebb@tazewell.com
http://www.tazewell.com
Christie A. Webb
(naturalization records from 1850s, births from
1854, deaths from 1878, marriages from 1869)
copies of vital records: $5.00 for the first copy,
$2.00 for each additional copy of the same
record

Tazewell County Clerk of the Circuit Court
(342 Court Street—location)
PO Box 69 (mailing address)
Pekin, IL 61554-0069
(309) 477-2214; (309) 353-7801 FAX
pgardner@tazewell.com
http://www.tazewell.com
Pamela J. Gardner
(probate records from 1830s)
no probate records search service (but Tazewell
County Genealogical Society will search for
$5.00 per surname plus SASE); copies of
probate records: $1.00 for the first page, 50¢
for each of the next nineteen pages and 25¢
for each additional page, $2.00 for
certification

Tazewell County Recorder of Deeds
Arcade Building
13 South Capital Street
Pekin, IL 61554
(309) 477-2210; (309) 477-2321 FAX
recodrer@ntslink.net
http://www.tazewell.com/Recorder/index.html
Robert A. Lutz
(land records somewhat incomplete from the
1830s [public domain records in Illinois State
Archives])

no land records search service (but Tazewell
County Genealogical Society will search for
$5.00 per surname plus SASE)

Union County
organized 1818 from Johnson County

Union County Clerk
(309 West Market—location)
PO Box H (mailing address)
Jonesboro, IL 62952
(618) 833-5711
btolerjr@hotmail.com
http://www.shawneeheartland.com/governmen
t.html (Chamber of Commerce)
Bobby Toler, Jr.

Union County Clerk of the Circuit Court
309 West Market Street, Room 101
Jonesboro, IL 62952-0360
(618) 833-5913; (618) 833-5223 FAX
lorrainemoreland@yahoo.com
http://www.shawneeheartland.com/governmen
t.html (Chamber of Commerce)
Lorraine Moreland

Vermilion County
organized 1826 from Edgar County

Vermilion County Clerk
Vermilion County Courthouse Annex
6 North Vermilion Street
Danville, IL 61832-5879
(217) 554-1900; (217) 554-1913 (Marilyn Lynn,
Records); (217) 554-1914 FAX
coclerk@vercounty.org;
ccrecords@vercounty.org
http://www.co.vermilion.il.us/ctyclk.htm
Lynn Foster
(land records from 1826, births from 1858,
deaths from 1877, marriages from 1926)
certified copies of vital records: $7.00 each
(access subject to restrictions)

Vermilion County Clerk of the Circuit Court
7 North Vermilion Street
Danville, IL 61832-5806
(217) 554-7730; (217) 554-7728 FAX
smiller@vercounty.org
http://www.co.vermilion.il.us/circlk.htm
Susan Miller
probate search service: no charge for a specific
year, $4.00 for each year searched (request
must be in writing)

Vermilion County Recorder
Courthouse Annex
6 North Vermilion Street, First Floor
Danville, IL 61832
(217) 554-6040; (217) 554-6047 FAX
recorder@vercounty.org
http://www.co.vermilion.il.us/recorder
Barbara H. Young

Wabash County
organized 1824 from Edwards County

Wabash County Clerk
(401 Market Street—location)
PO Box 277 (mailing address)
Mt. Carmel, IL 62863
(618) 262-4561
wccr1@shawneelink.net
http://publicrecords.onlinesearches.com/Illinoi
s-Land-Records-and-Deeds.htm
Marie L. Kolb
(land records from 1857, births and deaths from
1877)

Wabash County Clerk of the Circuit Court
(401 Market—location)
PO Drawer 997 (mailing address)
Mt. Carmel, IL 62863
(618) 262-5362; (618) 263-4441 FAX
akcrum@shawneelink.net
http://www.state.il.us/court/CircuitCourt/Circ
uitCourtJudges/CCC_County.asp
Angela K. Crum
(naturalization records from 1877, probate
records from 1857)

probate search service: no charge if found;
copies of probate records: 25¢ per page,
$10.00 minimum (with extra returned)

Warren County
organized 1825 from Pike County

Warren County Clerk of the Circuit Court
100 West Broadway
Monmouth, IL 61462-1795
(309) 734-5179; (309) 734-4151 FAX
dschreck@9thjudicial.org
http://www.warrencountyil.com/countyOffice.
php?officeID=13
Denise Schreck
(naturalization records, probate records from
1830)
probate search service: $5.00; copies of probate
records: 50¢ per page, $2.00 for certified
copies, no minimum

Warren County Clerk/Recorder
Warren County Courthouse
100 West Broadway
Monmouth, IL 61462
(309) 734-8592
tconard@warrencountyil.com;
countyclerk@maplecity.com;
warrencountyclerk@yahoo.com
http://www.warrencountyil.com/countyOffice.
php?officeID=7
Tina Conard
(land records from 1834, births and deaths from
about 1876, but are random until 1916)
copies of vital records: 50¢ per page before
1916, $7.00 for certified copies after 1916

Washington County
organized 1818 from St. Clair County

Washington County Clerk and Recorder
101 East St. Louis Street
Nashville, IL 62263
(618) 327-4800
wcclerk2@hotmail.com
http://publicrecords.onlinesearches.com/Illinoi
s-Land-Records-and-Deeds.htm
Thomas Ganz
(land records from 1821, births and deaths from
1877, marriages from 1832)
certified copies of vital records: $5.00 each

**Washington County Clerk of the Circuit
Court**
101 East St. Louis Street
Nashville, IL 62263-1100
(618) 327-4800; (618) 327-3583 FAX
wccirclk@hotmail.com
http://www.state.il.us/court/CircuitCourt/Circ
uitCourtJudges/CCC_County.asp
Carol Heggemeier
(naturalization records from 1865, probate
records from 1865)
probate search service: $4.00 per year

Wayne County
organized 26 March 1819 from Edwards
County, reduced to its present size by an Act
on 23 December 1895

Wayne County Clerk
(301 East Main—location)
PO Box 187 (mailing address)
Fairfield, IL 62837-0187
(618) 842-5182
donna@wabash.net;
donnae@fairfieldwireless.net
http://publicrecords.onlinesearches.com/Illinoi
s-Land-Records-and-Deeds.htm
Donna F. Endsley
(part of the courthouse burned on 17 November
1886, destroying many records of the
Recorder's Office; land records from 1887
with County Clerk, vital records from 1887
with County Clerk)
certified copies of vital records: $5.00 each
(includes search)

Wayne County Clerk of the Circuit Court
(301 East Main Street—location)

PO Box 96 (mailing address)
Fairfield, IL 62837-0096
(618) 842-7684; (618) 842-2556 FAX
circlerk@fairfieldwireless.net
http://www.state.il.us/court/CircuitCourt/Circ
uitCourtJudges/CCC_County.asp
Sharon L. Gualdoni
(naturalization records, probate records)

White County
organized 1815 from Gallatin County

White County Clerk of the Circuit Court
(301 East Main Street—location)
PO Box 310 (mailing address)
Carmi, IL 62821-0310
(618) 382-2321; (618) 382-2322 FAX
cclerk@whitecounty-il.gov
http://www.whitecounty-il.gov
Ellen I. Pettijohn
(probate records)

White County Clerk/Recorder
(301 East Main Street—location)
PO Box 339 (mailing address)
Carmi, IL 62821
(618) 382-7211, ext. 1; (618) 382-2322 FAX
pdee398@shawneelink.net
http://www.whitecounty-il.gov
Paula Dozier
(land records from 1816, births and deaths from
1878, marriages from 1816)

Whiteside County
organized 1836 from Jo Daviess and Henry
counties

Whiteside County Clerk
200 East Knox Street
Morrison, IL 61270
(815) 772-5189; (815) 772-7673 FAX
dnelson@whiteside.org; jhamstra@whiteside.org
(Vital Records)
http://www.whiteside.org/index.php?module=
pagesetter&func=viewpub&tid=13&pid=0
Dana Nelson
(birth and death records from 1878, marriage
records from 1839; genealogists may have
access to the indexes of vital records prior to
1916 and may obtain copies of birth records
older than 75 years and death records older
than 20 years)
noncertified copies: $8.00

Whiteside County Clerk of the Circuit Court
200 East Knox Street
Morrison, IL 61270-2819
(815) 772-5163 (Probate Division); (815) 772-
5187 FAX
sschipper@whiteside.org;
circuitclerk@whiteside.org
http://www.whiteside.org/index.php?module=
pagesetter&func=viewpub&tid=3&pid=0
Sheila Schipper

Whiteside County Recorder
200 East Knox Street
Morrison, IL 61270
(815) 772-5192; (815) 772-5241 FAX
dyoung@whiteside.org
http://www.whiteside.org/index.php?module=
pagesetter&tid=14&pid=0&func=viewpub
Dawn Young

Will County
organized 1836 from Cook and Iroquois
counties

Will County Clerk
302 North Chicago Street
Joliet, IL 60432
(815) 740-4615
coclrk@willcountyillinois.com;
nvoots@willcountyillinois.com
http://www.willclrk.com
Nancy Schultz Voots

Will County Clerk of the Circuit Court
14 West Jefferson Street, Suite 212
Joliet, IL 60432-4399

(815) 727-8585; (815) 727-8896 FAX
pmcguire@willcountyillinois.com;
circuit_clerk@willcountyillinois.com
http://willcountycircuitcourt.com
Pamela J. McGuire

Will County Recorder of Deeds
Executive Centre
58 East Clinton Street
Joliet, IL 60432-4143
(815) 740-4637; (815) 740-4638 FAX; (815) 740-
4697 FAX (Archive)
lweglarz@willcountyillinois.com
http://www.willcountyrecorder.com
Laurie McPhillips-Weglarz

Williamson County
organized 1839 from Franklin County

**Williamson County Clerk of the Circuit
Court**
200 West Jefferson Street
Marion, IL 62959-2494
(618) 997-1301; (618) 998-9401 FAX
http://www.williamsoncountycourthouse.com/
p/circuit_clerk.php
Stuart Hall
(naturalization records and probate records)
probate search service: $4.00 per year; copies of
naturalization records not permitted; copies
of probate records: $1.00 for the first page,
50¢ for each of the next nineteen pages and
25¢ for each additional page, no minimum

Williamson County Clerk/Recorder
(200 West Jefferson Street, Marion, IL 62959-
3061—location)
PO Box 1108 (mailing address)
Marion, IL 62959
(618) 997-1301
williamsoncountyclerk@yahoo.com
http://www.williamsoncountycourthouse.com/
p/county_clerk.php
Saundra K. Jent
(land records, vital records)

Winnebago County
organized 1836 from Jo Daviess County

Winnebago County Clerk
400 West State Street
Rockford, IL 61101-1212
(815) 987-3050 (Vital Records); (815) 969-0259
FAX
dfjohnson@co.winnebago.il.us
http://www.winnebagocountyclerk.com
David Johnson
(vital records)

**Winnebago County Clerk of the Circuit
Court**
400 West State Street
Rockford, IL 61101-1221
(815) 987-5464; (815) 987-3012 FAX
mgasparini@co.winnebago.il.us
http://www.cc.co.winnebago.il.us
Marc A. Gasparini
(probate records)
probate search service: $4.00 per year; copies of
probate records: $1.00 for the first page, 50¢
for each of the next nineteen pages and 25¢
for each additional page

Winnebago County Recorder
404 Elm State Street, Room 405
Rockford, IL 61101
(815) 987-3100
http://ww.co.winnebago.il.us/deptHome.asp?d
eptID=1074&pgID=54;
http://publicrecords.onlinesearches.com/Illin
ois-Land-Records-and-Deeds.htm
Kenneth Staaf
(land records)

Woodford County
organized 1841 from Tazewell and McLean
counties

Woodford County Clerk of the Circuit Court
(115 North Main Street—location)

PO Box 284 (mailing address)
Eureka, IL 61530-0284
(309) 467-3312; (309) 467-7377 FAX
wccclerk@mtco.com
http://www.woodford-
county.org/index.php?section=69
Carol J. Newtson
(naturalization records and probate records)

Woodford County Clerk/Recorder
115 North Main Street, Room 202
Eureka, IL 61530
(309) 467-2822
wococlerk@gmail.com
http://wwwwoodford-
county.org/index.php?section=73
Debbie Harms
(land records, births and deaths from 1877,
marriages from 1841)
land and vital records search service: $5.00 per
name with year; copies of land records: $1.00;
vital records search service: $5.00 per name
with year; copies of vital records: $1.00
(relationship required for births and deaths)

INDIANA

Capital: Indianapolis. Statehood: 11 December 1816 (annexed as a result of the Treaty of Paris, 1783, was part of the Northwest Territory in 1787, and became a separate territory 7 May 1800)

Indiana has seventy-eight city and town courts with local jurisdiction. The Small Claims Court of Marion County sits at Indianapolis, as does the Marion Municipal Court. A separate Probate Court for St. Joseph County sits in South Bend. County Courts exist in forty-nine of the ninety-two counties and meet at the county seats to hear contract and tort disputes, misdemeanors, traffic and local ordinance violations and some criminal matters. The Superior Courts are courts of general jurisdiction and sit in the county seats of forty-seven counties, where they deal with law, equity, domestic relations, felonies, misdemeanors, preliminary hearings, and sometimes juvenile matters. The Marion and Vanderburgh Courts have probate divisions. The Circuit Courts handle all civil and criminal matters except where exclusive jurisdiction is conferred on a lower court in a county. The Circuit Courts sit in each county seat, but two circuits contain two counties: Dearborn-Ohio and Jefferson-Switzerland. The Court of Appeals sits at Indianapolis and is divided into four districts. The Supreme Court at Indianapolis is the court of last resort.

Clerk of the Supreme Court, Court of Appeals, and Tax Court
200 West Washington Street
217 State House
Indianapolis, IN 46204
(317) 232-1930 (Clerk); (317) 232-7225 (Records Division, 401 West Washington, Room W062); (317) 232-8365 FAX (Clerk)
http://www.in.gov/judiciary/cofc

Adams County

organized 1835 from Adams New Purchase, which included portions of Allen, Delaware, and Randolph counties

Adams County Clerk of Court
(112 South Second—location)
PO Box 189 (mailing address)
Decatur, IN 46733-1618
(260) 724-5509; (260) 724-5313 FAX
clerk@co.adams.in.us;
  circuitcourt@co.adams.in.us
http://www.co.adams.in.us/clerk/Home.html
Nanette S. Nidlinger
(marriage records from 1836, divorces, naturalization records, and probate records; twelve civil townships: Blue Creek French, Hartford, Jefferson, Kirkland, Monroe, Preble, Root, St. Marys, Union, Wabash, and Washington)
probate search service: no charge; copies of probate records: $1.00 per page, no minimum

Adams County Recorder
313 West Jefferson Street, Suite 240
Decatur, IN 46733
(260) 724-5343
recorder@co.adams.in.us
http://www.co.adams.in.us/recorder.html
Constance J. Moser
(land records)

Allen County

organized 1823 from Indian lands

Allen County Clerk's Office
715 South Calhoun Street, #201
Fort Wayne, IN 46802-1804
(260) 449-7424; (260) 449-7658 FAX
therese.brown@co.allen.in.us
http://www.co.allen.in.us/index.php?option=com_content&task=category&sectionid=4&id=109&Itemid=402
Therese M. Brown
(requests for birth and death records are referred to the Fort Wayne-Allen County department of Health's Vital Records Division)

Allen County Recorder
City-County Building
1 East Main Street, Room 206
Fort Wayne, IN 46802
(260) 449-7165
johnb.mcgauley@co.allen.in.us
http://www.co.allen.in.us/index.php?option=com_content&task=category&sectionid=4&id=89&Itemid=426
John McGauley
(land records)

New Haven City Court
815 Lincoln Highway East
New Haven, IN 46774
(260) 748-7878; (260) 748-7979 FAX
ahageman@newhavenin.org
http://www.newhavenin.org/department/?fDD=5-0
Andrea Hageman, City Court Clerk

Bartholomew County

organized 1821 from Indian lands

Bartholomew County Clerk's Office
(234 Washington Street—location)
PO Box 924 (mailing address)
Columbus, IN 47201
(812) 379-1600; (812) 379-1503 (Archives Department); (812) 379-1675 FAX; (812) 379-1797 FAX (Archives Department)
ntrimpe@bartholomewco.com
http://www.bartholomewco.com/clerk/index.php
Norma Trimpe; Tina Jeffries, Archives Department
(original and early owners of land and Tract Book index, naturalization records, marriage licenses from March 1821 to date, marriage applications [called marriage records] from February 1882 to date, probate records from 1821; marriages, deeds, tax records, cemeteries, civil, etc. as far back as the 1800s with Archives Department)
probate search service: no charge; copies of probate records: $1.00 per page (billable), no minimum

Bartholomew County Recorder
County Government Building
(440 Third Street, Suite 203, Columbus, IN 47201—location)
PO Box 1121 (mailing address)
Columbus, IN 47202-1121
(812) 379-1520; (812) 375-5440 FAX
bjbeshear@bartholomewco.com
http://www.bartholomewco.com/recorder/index.php
Betty Jean Beshear
(land records)

Benton County

organized 1840 from Indian Lands

Benton County Courthouse
700 East Fifth Street
Fowler, IN 47944-1556
(884) 884-0930 (Clerk's Office); (765) 884-0322 FAX (Clerk's Office)
bcclerk@sbcglobal.net;
  bcrecorder@sbcglobal.net
http://www.in.gov/mylocal/benton_county.htm
Janet Hasser, Clerk of Courts; Tish Ringle, Recorder

Blackford County

organized 1838 from Jay County

Blackford County Courthouse
110 West Washington
Hartford City, IN 47348-2251
(765) 348-1130 voice & FAX
lcoons@blackfordcounty.com;
  dshady@blackfordcounty.com;
  ftobey@blackfordcounty.com
http://www.blackfordcounty.com/department/index.asp?DD=4-0
Laura Coons, Clerk of Courts; Derinda Shady, Recorder; Fred Tobey, Assessor
(land records with Assessor, naturalization records and probate records with Clerk)
no probate search service; copies of probate records: 25¢ per page plus postage, $1.00 for certification, no minimum; researchers welcome to search for themselves

Boone County

organized 1830 from Indian lands

Boone County Clerk's Office
212 Courthouse Square
Lebanon, IN 46052-2195
(765) 482-3510; (765) 485-0150 FAX
lgaroffolo@co.boone.in.us
http://www.bccn.boone.in.us/clerk/index.html
Lisa C. Garoffolo, Clerk Boone Circuit and Superior Courts

Boone County Recorder
212 Courthouse Square
Lebanon IN 46052
(765) 482-3070
sbaldwin@co.boone.in.us
http://boonecounty.in.gov/Default.aspx?tabid=151
Mary Alice "Sam" Baldwin
(assignments, contracts, deeds, liens, mortgages, plats, etc.)
copies: $1.00 per page

Brown County

organized 1836 from Monroe, Jackson and Bartholomew counties

Brown County Courthouse
(20 East Main Street—location)
PO Box 85 (mailing address)
Nashville, IN 47448
(812) 988-5512 (Clerk's Office); (812) 988-2788 (Auditor's Office); (812) 988-5562 FAX (Clerk's Office)
foxbf@bcingov.us
http://www.in.gov/judiciary/brown
Bonita Fox, Clerk of Courts; Glenda Stogsdill, Recorder
(grantor/grantee records from 1873 [earlier records destroyed by fire] with Recorder, no more than half a dozen naturalization entries from 1860 through 1890 with Clerk, probate records from 1836 to 1945 [abstracted and indexed by every name in 1992 publication by the Brown County Historical Society] with Clerk)
probate search service: no charge; copies of land records, naturalization records, and probate records: $2.00 per page plus postage, no minimum; all genealogical inquiries sent to the Clerk's Office or the Health Department are sent to Helen H. Reeve, Brown County Historical Society, 6431 South Christiansburg Road, Columbus, IN 47201

Carroll County

organized 1828 from Indian lands

Carroll County Clerk
Carroll County Courthouse
101 West Main Street
Delphi, IN 46923
(765) 564-4485; (765) 564-1835 FAX
cclerk@geetel.net;
  ccrecorder@carrollcountyin.gov
http://www.carrollcountin.gov
Laura Sterrett, Clerk of Courts
(naturalization records, marriages from 1828 to date, and probate records)
copies of naturalization records, marriages, and probate records: $1.00 per page

Carroll County Recorder
Carroll County Courthouse
101 est Main street
Delphi, IN 46923
(765) 564-2124
ccrecorder@carrollcountyin.gov
http://www.carrollcountyin.gov

Linda Parrett
(land records)

Cass County
organized 1828 from Indian lands

Cass County Clerk
Cass County Government Building
200 Court Park, #103
Logansport, IN 46947-3114
(219) 753-7740; (574) 722-1556 FAX
lindacrimmins@co.cass.in.us
http://www.cqc.com/%7Eccfsupc/index.html
Linda Crimmins, Clerk
(naturalization records and probate records with
    County Clerk)
marriage records: $2.00 each; wills/probates:
    $5.00 per record (money order only)

Cass County Recorder
Cass County Government Building
200 Court Park, #102
Logansport, IN 46947
(574) 753-7810
cassrecorder@cqc.com;
    recorder@casscountygov.org
http://www.in-map.net/counties/
    CASS/recorder
Kathy Adair
(deeds, mortgages, releases assignments, etc.)
search: $8.00 for the first name and $5.00 for
    each additional name

Clark County
organized 1801 from Knox County

Clark County Clerk
City-County Building
501 East Court Avenue
Jeffersonville, IN 47130-4063
(812) 285-6244; (812) 285-6372 FAX
kgroth@co.clark.in.us
http://www.co.clark.in.us
Keith Groth, Clerk of Courts

Clark County Recorder
City-County Building
501 East Court Avenue
Jeffersonville, IN 47130
(812) 285-6235
cindygl@msn.com
http://www.co.clark.in.us
Richard Jones, Sr.
(deeds)

Clay County
organized 1825 from Indian lands, sections of
    Owen and Vigo counties

Clay County Clerk
Clay County Courthouse
609 East National Avenue, #213
Brazil, IN 47834
(812) 448-9024; (812) 446-9602 FAX
mary@claycounty.org
http://www.claycountyin.gov/metadot/index.pl
    ?id=4168&isa=Category&op=show
Mary C. Brown, Clerk
(land records with Recorder's Office,
    naturalization records from 1850 and probate
    records from 1850 with Clerk's Office)
probate search service: $3.00 for ten years;
    copies of probate records: $1.00 per page, no
    minimum; make request in writing and
    include payment

Clay County Recorder
Clay County Courthouse
609 East National Avenue, Room 111
Brazil, IN 47834
(812) 448-9005
modesitta@claycountyin.gov
http://www.claycountyin.gov/metadot/index.pl
    ?id=4241&isa=Category&op=show
Angela Modesitt

Clinton County
organized 1830 from Indian lands

Clinton County Clerk

265 Courthouse Square
Frankfort, IN 46041-1993
(765) 659-6335; (775) 659-6347 FAX
lhuffer@clintonco.com
http://www.ccinchamber.org/Gov; http://
    www.in.gov/mylocal/clinton_county.htm
Laura Huffer, Clerk of Courts; Sue Marcum,
    Archivist
(naturalization records from 1882 to 1896,
    marriages from 1830 to date, some early
    marriage consents from 1850 to 1882,
    marriage applications from 1882 to date,
    probate records from 1830 to date with
    Archivist, c/o Clerk)
no probate search service; copies of
    naturalization records: 25¢ to $1.00 each plus
    SASE, $2.00 for certified copies; copies of
    marriages: 25¢ to $1.00 each plus SASE, $2.00
    for certified copies; copies of births and
    deaths: $1.00 each plus SASE, $2.00 for
    certified copies (proof required); copies of
    probate records: 25¢ to $1.00 each plus SASE,
    $2.00 for certified copies

Clinton County Recorder
50 North Jackson Street
Frankfort, IN 46041-1993
(317) 659-6320
vballard@clintonco.com
http://www.in.gov/mylocal/clinton_county.htm
Vicki Ballard
(land records from 1830)
copies of land records: $1.00 per page plus
    SASE

Crawford County
organized 1818 from Harrison County

Crawford County Clerk
(316 Court Street—location)
PO Box 375 (mailing address)
English, IN 47118-0375
(812) 338-2565; (812) 338-2507 FAX
clerk@crawfordcountyin.com
http://www.selectcrawfordcounty.com/goernm
    ent.html; http://www.crawfordcountyindiana.
    info; http://www.ccn.net
Terry L. Stroud, Clerk of Courts
(marriages from 1828, probate records)
no probate search service; copies of probate
    records: 25¢ per page plus postage, $2.00 for
    certified copies, $1.00 minimum

Crawford County Recorder
(Crawford County Courthouse, 316 South Court
    Street—location)
PO Box 214 (mailing address)
English, IN 47118-0214
(812) 338-2615
recorder@crawfordcountyin.com
http://www.selectcrawfordcounty.com
Charla Wright
(land records)

Daviess County
organized 1816 from Indian lands

Daviess County Clerk
(200 East Walnut Street—location)
PO Box 739 (mailing address)
Washington, IN 47501
(812) 254-8669; (812) 254-8698 FAX
clerk@daviess.org
http://www.in.gov/mylocal/daviess_county.htm
Rosemary Abel, Clerk of Courts

Daviess County Recorder
Daviess County Courthouse
PO Box 793
Washington, IN 47501
(812) 254-8675
recorder@daviess.org
http://www.in-
    map.net/counties/DAVIESS/recorder
Gail Doades
copies: 50¢ per page, $1.00 for certification

Dearborn County
organized 1803, original county

Dearborn County Clerk
Dearborn County Administration Building
215B West High Street
Lawrenceburg, IN 47025-1662
(812) 537-8867; (812) 532-2021 FAX
http://www.dearborncounty.org/govern2.html
Phil Weaver, Clerk of Courts
(land records with Recorder, naturalization
    records and probate records with Clerk)
probate search service: no charge if simply to see
    if will is on record, no service for further
    research; copies of probate records: $1.00 per
    page

Dearborn County Recorder
Dearborn County Administration Building
215B West High Street
Lawrenceburg, IN 47025
(812) 537-8837
http://www.dearborncounty.org/govern2.html
Barb Kaffenberer
(land records)

Decatur County
organized 1821 from Indian lands

Decatur County Clerk
Decatur County Courthouse
150 Courthouse Square, Suite 244
Greensburg, IN 47240-2091
(812) 663-8223; (812) 663-8642 FAX
clerk@decaturcounty.in.gov
http://www.decaturcounty.in.gov
Tami D. Wenning, Clerk of Courts
(no naturalization records [now with Indiana
    State Library], probate records with Clerk's
    Office)
probate search service: no charge if not
    extensive; copies of probate records: $1.00
    per page

Decatur County Recorder
Decatur County Courthouse
150 Courthouse Square
Greensburg, IN 47240
(812) 663-4681
recorder@decaturcounty.in.gov
http://www.decaturcounty.in.gov
Mary Vail
(deed recording from 1821 to date)

DeKalb County
organized 1835 from Allen County

DeKalb County Clerk of Courts
(DeKalb County Courthouse, 100 South Main
    Street, Second Floor—location)
PO Box 239 (mailing address)
Auburn, IN 46706
(260) 925-0912; (260) 925-5126 FAX
JRowan@co-dekalb-in.us
http://www.dekalbnet.org/County_Department
    s/Clerk%20of%20Courts.htm
Jacqueline Rowan
marriage records: $1.00 per page

DeKalb County Recorder
(DeKalb County Courthouse, 100 South Main
    Street, First Floor—location)
PO Box 810 (mailing address)
Auburn, IN 46706
(260) 925-2112
brynearso@co.dekalb.in.us
http://www.dekalbnet.org/County_Department
    s/recorder.htm
Burtie M. Rynearson
(land records)

Delaware County
organized 1827 from Indian Lands

Delaware County Clerk of the Circuit Court
(100 West Main Street, Room 211—location)
PO Box 1089 (mailing address)
Muncie, IN 47305
(765) 747-7726; (765) 747-7768 FAX
clerk@dcclerk.org
http://www.dcclerk.org
Karen D. Wenger, Clerk
(marriage records; records from 1827–1920 are

on microfilm)
copies: 10¢ per pcopy, certified copies: $1.00 per page

Delaware County Recorder
Delaware County Building
100 West Main Street, Room 312
Muncie, IN 47305
(765) 747-7804
jlasater@co.delaware.in.us
http://co.delaware.in.us/county
Jane Lasater
(land records)

Dubois County
organized 1817 from Orange and Perry counties

Dubois County Clerk
1 Courthouse Square
Jasper, IN 47546
(812) 481-7037; (812) 481-7044 FAX
clerk@duboiscountin.org
http://www.visitduboiscounty.com (Dubois County Visitors Center and Tourism Commission)
Kathleen M. Hopf, Clerk
(naturalization records from 1839, probate records from 1839 with Clerk's Office and Records Library)
no records search service; copies of naturalizations and vital records: $1.00 per page, no minimum

Dubois County Recorder
1 Courthouse Square
Jasper, IN 47546
(812) 481-7067
http://www.visitduboiscounty.com (Dubois County Visitors Center and Tourism Commission)
Brenda Schnarr
(land records with Auditor and Recorder)
copies of land records: $1.00 per page, $5.00 for copies from plat book

Elkhart County
organized 1830 from Indian lands

Elkhart County Clerk
101 North Main Street
Goshen, IN 46526
(219) 535-6433; (219) 535-6471 FAX
http://www.elkhartcountyindiana.com/clerk.html
Stephanie Burgess, Clerk
(marriages from the early 1830s with , probate records from the early 1830s with Clerk of Circuit Court; Superior Courts 3 & 4 in Goshen, Superior Courts 1, 2, 5, and 6, and Juvenile Court, 315 South Second Street, Elkhart, IN 46516)
probate search service: no charge; copies of probate records: $1.00 per page, $1.00 for certification

Elkhart County Recorder
(117 North Second Street, Room 205—location)
PO Box 837 (mailing address)
Goshen, IN 46527-0837
(219) 535-6474 (Recorder); (219) 535-6718 (Auditor)
http://www.elkhartcountyindiana.com/recorder.html
(land assessments with Auditor's Office, deeds, mortgages, assignments, releases, powers of attorney, real estate contracts, annexations, trustee elections, affidavits, final decrees, surveys, federal tax liens, mechanisc liens, military discharges, articles of incorporation, cemetery deeds, bonds, plats, condominiums, firms doing business under assumed names, ,delinquent sewer liens, and miscellaneous instruments with Recorder)
no deed search service, copies: $1.00 per page, certification: $5.00 per document

Fayette County
organized 1818 from Wayne County

Fayette County Clerk
(Fayette County Courthouse, 401 Central
Avenue—location)
PO Box 607 (mailing address)
Connersville, IN 47331-1903
(765) 825-1813; (765) 827-4902 FAX
clerk@co.fayette.in.us
http://www.co.fayette.in.us/clerk.htm
Melinda Sudhoff

Fayette County Recorder
Fayette County Courthouse, First Floor
401 Central Avenue
Connersville, IN 47331
(765) 825-3051
recorder@co.fayette.in.us
http://www.co.fayette.in.us/recorder.htm
Ann Frost
(land records)

Floyd County
organized 1819 from Harrison and Clark counties

Floyd County Clerk
311 Hauss Square, #235
New Albany, IN 47150
(812) 948-5415; (812) 948-4711 FAX
efreiberger@floydcounty.in.gov
http://www.floydcounty.in.gov/%20offices/clerk.asp
Eugenea (Jeannie) Freiberger, Clerk

Floyd County Recorder
311 West First Street, Room 115
New Albany, IN 47150
(812) 948-5430
lendris@floydcounty.in.gov
http://www.floydcounty.in.gov/county%20offices/Recorder.htm
Lois N. Endris
(land records)

Fountain County
organized 1825 from Montgomery County

Fountain County Clerk of Courts
(Fountain County Courthouse, 301 Fourth Street—location)
PO Box 183 (mailing address)
Covington, IN 47932
(765) 793-2192; (765) 793-5002 FAX
Clerk@K-inc.com
http://www.co.fountain.in.us/clerk
Mariann Martin
(naturalization records, probate records)
no probate search service; copies of probate records: $1.00 per page, $1.00 for certification, no minimum

Fountain County Recorder
Courthouse Square
PO Box 55
Covington, IN 47932
(765) 793-2431
http://www.co.fountain.in.us
(land records)

Franklin County
organized 1811 from Clark and Dearborn counties

Franklin County Clerk of Courts
459 Main Street
Brookville, IN 47012-1405
(765) 647-5111; (765) 647-3224 FAX
marlene@rbmsonline.com
http://www.franklincounty.in.gov/office/clerk;
http://www.in.gov/mylocal/franklin_county.htm
Marlene Flaspohler
(naturalization records from 1820 in miscellaneous order books [original naturalization records with Indiana State Library, index only from 1820 with Brookville Library, naturalization records from 1820 to date with Indiana State Library], marriages from 1811 to date [index to marriages from 1811 to 1920, index to marriage transcripts from 1882 to 1920 with Brookville Library], probate and wills from 1811 to date [indexed] [wills from 1813 to 1936 with Brookville
Library, wills from 1811 to date with Indiana State Library])
records search service: no charge for minimal search (contact local researchers for extended searches), copies: $1.00 per page

Franklin County Recorder
459 Main Street
Brookville, IN 47012
(317) 647-5131 (Recorder); (317) 647-4631 (Auditor)
recorder@franklincounty.in.gov
http://www.franklincounty.in.gov/office/recorder
Pamela K. Beneker
(deeds from 1811 to date [indexed], original tract books with Recorder, county maps with Auditor, earliest Tract Book, land entries from Cincinnati, Indianapolis and Jefferson districts with Brookville Library, land entries from 1803 to date with Indiana State Library)

Fulton County
organized 1835 from Indian lands

Fulton County Auditor
125 East Ninth Street, Suite 108
Rochester, IN 46975
(574) 223-2912; (574) 223-2211 FAX
http://www.co.fulton.in.us/auditor
Denise J. Bonnell, Auditor
(land records)

Fulton County Clerk
(Circuit Court, 815 Main Street, Rochester, IN 46975-1546—location)
PO Box 254 (mailing address)
Rochester, IN 46975
(574) 223-4824; (574) 223-8304 FAX
http://www.co.fulton.in.us
Karen Miller
(naturalization records with Clerk, probate records with Circuit Court)

Fulton County Recorder
125 East Ninth Street, Suite 120
Rochester, IN 46975
(574) 223-2914; (574) 223-4734 FAX
http://www.co.fulton.in.us/recorder
Cathy Ginther

Gibson County
organized 1813 from Knox County

Gibson County Clerk
(Gibson County Courthouse, Circuit Court, 101 North Main, Princeton, IN 47670-1562—location)
PO Box 630 (mailing address)
Princeton, IN 47670
(812) 385-2541; (812) 385-5025 FAX
http://www.gibsoncountyin.org;
http://www.princeton-indiana.com/pages/city-services/county/elected_county_officials.htm
Debbie S. Wethington
(some naturalization records, marriages from 1813 [no information on parents until 1882], probate records)
no probate search service; copies of vital records: $2.00 each; copies of probate records: $1.00 per page, $1.00 for certification, no minimum; need some dates to go by, no personal checks

Gibson County Recorder
Gibson County Courthouse
101 North Main
Princeton, IN 47670
(812) 386-8401
http://www.gibsoncountyin.org;
http://www.princeton-indiana.com/pages/city-services/county/elected_county_officials.htm
(land records)
copies: $1.00 per page, $5.00 for certification

Grant County
organized 1831 from Delaware County

Grant County Clerk
Grant County Courthouse
101 East Fourth Street
Marion, IN 46952
(765) 668-8121; (765) 668-6541 FAX
clerk@grantcounty.net
http://clerk.grant.in.uinquire.us
Carolyn J. Mowery
(a few naturalization records, probate records)
copies of naturalizations: $1.00 per page, $1.00
  for certification; copies of probate records:
  $1.00 per page, $1.00 for certification

Grant County Recorder
Grant County Complex
401 South Adams Street
Marion, IN 46953
(765) 668-6559
dconner@grantcounty.net
http://recorder.grant.in.uinquire.us
Dixi Fischer Conner
(land records)

Greene County
organized 1821 from Knox County

Greene County Clerk
PO Box 229
Bloomfield, IN 47424
(812) 384-8532; (800) 837-1601; (812) 384-8458
  FAX
clerk@co.greene.in.us
http://clerkgreenecounty.com
Thomas H. Franklin, Clerk

Greene County Recorder
Greene County Courthouse
PO Box 309
Bloomfield, IN 47424
(812) 384-3537; (812) 384-2020
recorder@co.greene.in.us
http://www.gcindiana.info/gov.shtml
(land records)

Hamilton County
organized 1823 from Hancock and Marion
  counties

Hamilton County Clerk
1 Hamilton County Suare, Suite 106
Noblesville, IN 46060
(317) 776-9629
http://www.co.hamilton.in.us/departments.asp?
  id=2100
Tammy Baitz, Clerk
(naturalizations, marriages, and probate records)
probate search service: no charge ("we accept
  written requests, however our work load is so
  heavy we find it difficult to get the searches
  done in speedy fashion"); copies of probate
  records: 50¢ each

Hamilton County Recorder
Hamilton County Historic Courthouse
33 North Ninth Street, Suite 309
Noblesville, IN 46060
(317) 776-9619; (317) 776-9619
http://www.co.hamilton.in.us/departments.asp?
  id=2320
Sharon K. Cherry
(land records)

Hancock County
organized 1827 from Madison County

Hancock County Clerk of Courts
Hancock County Courthouse
9 East Main Street, Room 201
Greenfield, IN 46140
(317) 462-1109; (317) 477-1163 FAX
lgrass@hancockcoingov.org
http://www.hancockcoingov.org/clerk_of_courts
Linda J. Grass
(naturalization records, marriages and divorces,
  probate records)
probate search service: no charge; copies of probate records: $1.00 per page, no mailing fee

Hancock County Recorder
111 American Legion Place, Suite 202

Greenfield, IN 46140
(317) 477-1142
http://www.hancockcoingov.org/recorder/defa
  ult.asp
Carolyn Grass
search: $10.00 for the first name, $5.00 for each
  additional name; copies: $1.00 per page, $2.00
  for copies larger than 8½" x 14"

Harrison County
organized 1808 from Northwest Territory

Harrison County Clerk
Harrison County Courthouse
300 North Capital Avenue
Corydon, IN 47112-1333
(812) 738-4289; (812) 738-1153 FAX
clerkharr@epowerc.net
http://harrisoncounty.in.gov/department/index
  .asp?fDD=5-0
Sherry Brown

Harrison County Recorder
Harrison County Courthouse
300 North Capitol Avenue, Room 204
Corydon, IN 47112
(812) 738-3788; (812) 738-1153 FAX
recorder@harrison.in.gov
http://0.43.125.21/department/index.asp?fDD
  =9-0
Barbara Mathes
(mortgages, deeds, contracts, powers of
  attorney, affidavits, etc.)

Hendricks County
organized 1823 from Indian lands

Hendricks County Clerk
(Courthouse, 1 Courthouse Square—location)
PO Box 599 (mailing address)
Danville, IN 46122
(317) 745-9231; (317) 745-9306 FAX
cspence@co.hendricks.in.us
http://www.co.hendricks.in.us/Courthouse/Cle
  rksOffice/tabid/70/Default.aspx
Cindy Spence, Clerk

Hendricks County Recorder
Government Center
355 South Washington Street
Danville, IN 46122
(317) 745-9224
tlynch@co.hendricks.in.us
http://www.co.hendricks.in.us/GovernmentCent
  er/RecordersOffice/tabid/182/Default.aspx
Theresa D. Lynch
(land records)
copies: $1.00 per page, $2.00 if larger than 8½ x
  11, $5.00 for certification

Henry County
organized 1821 from Delaware County

**Henry County Clerk of Henry Circuit and
  Superior Courts**
(1215 Race Street—location)
PO Box B (mailing address)
New Castle, IN 47362-4219
(317) 529-6401
clerk.henryco.net
http://clerk.henry.in.uinquire.us
Linda Ratcliff
(naturalizations, probate records from 1822)
no probate search service; copies of probate
  records: $1.00 per page, no minimum

Henry County Recorder
(101 South Main Street, Room 106—location)
PO Box K (mailing address)
New Castle, IN 47362
(765) 529-4304; (765) 521-7017 FAX
recorder.henryco.net
http://recorder.henry.in.uinquire.us
Terri L. Pope
(land records from 1823)

Howard County
organized 1844 from Indian lands

Howard County Clerk's Office

(Circuit Court, 701 South Berkley Road,
  Kokomo, IN 46901—location)
PO Box 9004 (mailing address)
Kokomo, IN 46904
(765) 456-2200; (765) 456-2204; (765) 456-2267
  FAX
mona.myers@co.howard.in.us;
  circourt@co.howard.in.us
http://co.howard.in.us/clerk1/index.htm;
  http://co.howard.in.us/circourt/index.htm
Mona Myers
(name changed from Richardville County in
  1846)

Howard County Recorder
(Administration Center, 220 North Main Street,
  Room 330, Kokomo, IN 46901—location)
PO Box 733 (mailing address)
Kokomo, IN 46903-0733
(765) 456-2210; (765) 456-2056 FAX
http://co.howard.in.us/Recorder/index.htm
Linda Koontz
(land records)

Huntington County
organized 1832 from Grant County

Huntington County Clerk
(201 North Jefferson Street, #201—location)
PO Box 228 (mailing address)
Huntington, IN 46750
(219) 358-4819; (260) 358-4880 FAX
county.clerk@huntington.in.us
http://www.huntington.in.us/county/clerk
Vickie E. Stoffel, Clerk
copies: $1.00, certification: $1.00

Huntington County Recorder
Courthouse, Room 101
201 North Jefferson Street
Huntington, IN 46750
(260) 358-4848; (260) 358-4849
angie.garner@huntington.in.us
http://www.huntington.in.us/county/recorder
(land records)

Jackson County
organized 1815 from Washington County

Jackson County Clerk
111 South Main Street
Brownstown, IN 47220-0122
(812) 358-6117; (812) 358-6187 FAX
http://www.in.gov/mylocal/jackson_county.htm
Sarah M. Benter, Clerk

Jackson County Recorder
PO Box 75
Brownstown, IN 47220
(812) 358-6113
http://www.in.gov/mylocal/jackson_county.htm

Jasper County
organized 1835 from Indian lands

Jasper County Clerk
115 West Washington Street
Rensselaer, IN 47978-2888
(219) 866-4926; (219) 866-4940 FAX
http://jaspercountyin.gov
Kara Fishburn, Clerk
(vital records from 1865, probate records from
  1853, [naturalization records with State
  Archives, where county records were
  deposited])
probate search service: no charge; copies of
  probate records: 25¢ per page

Jasper County Recorder
Jasper County Courthouse
Renselaer, IN 47978
(219) 866-4930 (Auditor); (219) 866-4681
  (Recorder)
recorder@co.jasper.in.us
http://jaspercountyin.gov
Phyllis L. Lanoue
(land records)

Jay County
organized 1835 from Randolph County

Jay County Clerk's Office
Jay County Courthouse
Portland, IN 47371
(260) 726-4951; (260) 6922 FAX
jarunyon@co.jay.in.us
http://www.co.jay.in.us/clerk
Jane Ann Runyon
(naturalization records, marriages from 1837,
probate records from the early 1840s)
probate search service: $1.00 for each surname,
plus postage; copies of marriages: $1.00 each;
copies of births and deaths: $3.00 each; copies
of probate records: $1.00 for the first page
and 35¢ for each additional page, plus postage

Jay County Recorder
Jay County Courthouse
Portland, IN 47371
(260) 726-4572
recorder@co.jay.in.us
http://www.co.jay.in.us/recorder.htm
Betty St. Myers
(deeds/land records from the 1830s)
copies: $1.00 per page, certified copies: $5.00;
search: $8.00 for the first name, $5.00 for
each additional name

Jefferson County
organized 1810 from Indian lands, chartered
1811

Jefferson County Clerk
300 East Main Street, #203
Madison, IN 47250
(812) 265-8922; (812) 265-8955 FAX
toksjcc@jeffersoncoin.org
http://madisonindiana.org/govern.html
Martha Jane Shimfessel
(naturalization records, marriages with, wills
from 1811)

Jefferson County Recorder
104 Courthouse
Madison, IN 47250
(812) 265-8900; (812) 265-8910 (Recorder);
(812) 265-8902 (Treasurer's Office)
http://madisonindiana.org/govern.html

Jennings County
organized 1816 from Indian lands

Jennings County Clerk
PO Box 385
Vernon, IN 47282
(812) 352-3070; (812) 352-3076 FAX
http://www.jenningscounty-in.gov; http://
www.in.gov/mylocal/jennings_county.htm;
http://www.jenningscountychamber.com/ph
p/index.php (Chamber of Commerce)
Janice L. Ramey, Clerk

Jennings County Recorder
Jennings County Courthouse
PO Box 394
Vernon, IN 47282
(812) 346-3152
http://www.jenningscounty-in.gov

Johnson County
organized 1822 from Indian Lands

Johnson County Clerk
Johnson County Courthouse, First Floor
5 West Jefferson
Franklin, IN 46131
(317) 736-3708; (317) 736-3749 FAX
http://www.co.johnson.in.us (click on
Administration)
Jill L. Jackson, Clerk
(recent documents only)

Johnson County Microfilm Department
Johnson County Courthouse, Basement
5 West Jefferson Street
Franklin, IN 46131
(317) 736-3720
http://www.co.johnson.in.us (click on
Administration)
Brenda Smith, Director
(naturalization records from 1867 to 1908,

marriage certificates, marriage applications
starting in 1882, estate files, guardianship files,
civil files, divorce files, criminal files, and
computer-printed inexes of the following:
marriages from 1823 throuth 1994 [indexed
by bride or groom's name], estates probated
from 1826 through 1994, civil files [including
divorce files] from 1935 throug 2001, divorce
files through 1994, criminal files from 1935
through 1997)
search service: no charge, but must have a
"range of years for a specific person"; copies:
$1.00 per page plus SASE

Johnson County Recorder
(Courthouse Annex Building, Second Floor, 86
West Court Street—location)
PO Box 489 (mailing address)
Franklin, IN 46131
(317) 736-3718
http://www.co.johnson.in.us (click on
Administration)
Susie Misiniec
(land records from 1823)
copies: $1.00 per page

Knox County
organized 1790 from Northwest Territory

Knox County Clerk
(111 North Seventh Street—location)
PO Box 906 (mailing address)
Vincennes, IN 47591-5338
(812) 885-2521; (812) 895-4929 FAX
http://www.knoxcountygov.com/modules.php?
name=Top
Brenda J. Hall, Clerk
(naturalization records, probate records)
probate search service: no charge; copies of
probate records: $1.00 per page, $1.00 for
certified copies, no minimum

Knox County Recorder
Knox County Courthouse
101 North Seventh Street
Vincennes, IN 47591
(812) 885-2508
http://www.knoxcountygov.com/modules.php?
name=Top
(land records)

Kosciusko County
organized 1835 from Indian lands

Kosciusko County Clerk
Kosciusko Circuit Court
121 North Lake Street
Warsaw, IN 46580
(574) 372-2334; (574) 372-2338 FAX (Clerk)
http://www.kcgov.com/o_index.asp?hdnSelect
edID=73
Sharon Christner
(naturalization records from 1855 to 1929,
marriages from 1882, probate records from
1836)
probate search service: no charge; copies of
probate records: $1.00 per page, no minimum

Kosciusko County Recorder
100 West Center Street, Room 203
Warsaw, IN 46580
(574) 372-2360
http://www.kcgov.com/o_index.asp?hdnSelect
edID=55
(land records from 1845)

LaGrange County
organized 1832 from unorganized territory in
Elkhart County

LaGrange County Clerk of Courts
105 North Detroit Street
LaGrange, IN 46761
(260) 499-6368; (260) 463-2187 FAX
belliott@lagrangecounty.org
http://www.lagrangecounty.org (click on
County Government)
Beverly Elliott
(naturalization records [microfilm copies with
State Archives, Public Records Commission,

402 West Washington Street, Room W472,
Indianapolis, IN 46204], marriages from 1832
to date, probate records from 1840 to date)
no probate search service; copies of
naturalization records, marriages, and probate
records (genealogy is done only when there is
time): $1.00 per page, $2.00 for certified
copies

LaGrange County Recorder
114 West Michigan Street
LaGrange, IN 46761
(260) 499-6320 (Recorder); (260) 499-6311
(Auditor)
smartin@lagrangecounty.org
http://www.lagrangecounty.org (click on
County Government)
Sharon Martin
(land records)

Lake County
organized 1836 from Porter and Newton
counties

Gary Clerk
15 West Fourth Avenue
Gary, IN 46402
(219) 881-6065; (219) 881-6068 FAX
http://lakecountyin/org/portal/media-
type/html/group/clerk/page/default.psml/js
_pane/P-fc5c491248-10002
Arlene Allen, Chief Deputy

Hammond Clerk
232 Russell Street
Hammond, IN 46320
(219) 933-2857; (219) 933-2805 FAX
http://lakecountyin/org/portal/media-
type/html/group/clerk/page/default.psml/js
_pane/P-fc5c48f7e0-10001
Cynthia Berdine, Chief Deputy

Lake County Clerk
Courts Building, First Floor
2293 North Main Street
Crown Point, IN 46307
(219) 755-3465; (219) 755-3520 FAX
http://www.lakecountyin.org/portal/media-
type/html/group/clerk
Thomas Philpot
(probate records, marriage and miscellaneous
licenses)

Lake County Recorder
Building 'A', Second Floor
2293 North Main Street
Crown Point, IN 46307
(219) 738-2030; (219) 755-3257 FAX
http://www.lakecountyin.org/portal/media-
type/html/group/recorder/page/default
(land records)

LaPorte County
organized 1832 from Indian lands

LaPorte County Clerk
LaPorte County Complex and Circuit
Courthouse
813 Lincolnway, Suite 105
LaPorte, IN 46350
(219) 326-6808 (Clerk, LaPorte); (219) 874-5611
(Clerk, Michigan City)
rbehler@laportecounty.org
http://www.laportecounty.org/judiciary/courts
/clerk.html
Robert J. Behler, Jr., County Clerk %

LaPorte County Recorder
813 Lincolnway, Suite 206
LaPorte, IN 46350
(219) 326-6808, ext. 280; (219) 326-0828 FAX
recorders@laportecounty.org
http://www.laportecounty.org/departments/rec
order/index.html
Barbara Dean
(land records)

Lawrence County
organized 1818 from Orange County

Lawrence County Clerk

916 15th Street, Room 31
Bedford, IN 47421
(812) 275-4145; (812) 277-2024 FAX
http://bedfordonline.com/content/view/21/40
Myron D. Rainey
(marriages from 1818, probate records from
    1818; naturalization records with Indiana
    Commission on Public Records, 402 West
    Washington Street, Indianapolis, IN 46204)
probate search service: no charge; copies of
    births and deaths: $1.00 each; copies of
    marriages: $1.00 each, $2.00 for certified
    copies; copies of probate records: $1.00 per
    page, send SASE

Lawrence County Recorder
Courthouse Room 21
Bedford, IN 47421
(812) 275-3245
http://bedfordonline.com/content/view/21/40
Jessica Allen
(land records from 1819)

Madison County
organized 1823 from Fayette County

Madison County Clerk of Courts
Madison County Government Center
16 East Ninth Street
Anderson, IN 46016-1538
(765) 641-9457; (765) 640-4203 FAX
http://madisoncty.com
Ludy Watkins
(land records, naturalization records, vital
    records, probate records)

Madison County Recorder
Madison County Government Center
16 East Ninth Street, Second House Box 19
Anderson, IN 46016
(317) 641-9443
http://madisoncty.com

Marion County
organized 1821 from Ohio County; consolidated
    with the City of Indianapolis in 1969

Marion County Clerk
City-County Building
200 East Washington Street, #W-122
Indianapolis, IN 46204-3307
(317) 327-4740; (317) 327-3893 FAX
http://www.indygov.org/eGov/County/Clerk/
home.htm
Doris Anne Sadler, Clerk of Courts
(land records with County Assessor, 1141 City-
    County Building, probate records with 17th
    Floor, City-County Building)
no probate search service; copies of probate
    records: $1.00 per page, no minimum

Marion County Recorder
721 City-County Building
200 East Washington Street
Indianapolis, IN 46204
(317) 327-4020
http://www.indygov.org/eGov/County/Recor
der/home.htm
Wanda J. Martin

Marshall County
organized 1836 from Indian lands

Marshall County Clerk
501 North Center Street
Plymouth, IN 46563-1707
(574) 936-8922; (574) 936-8893 FAX
clerk@co.marshall.in.us
http://www.co.marshall.in.us/Departments/Cle
rk/Clerk.htm
Janice Fisher
(naturalization records [until these records
    became part of the Federal Court system]
    with State Archives, marriages with Circuit
    Court Clerk, 211 West Madison Street,
    Plymouth, IN 46563, probate records with
    Circuit Court Clerk)
probate search service: $10.00 if done
    professionally; copies of births and deaths:
    $3.00 for the first copy of births and $1.00 for

each additional copy, $4.00 for the first copy
    of deaths and $2.00 for each additional copy
    (must show proof of relationship); copies of
    probate records: $1.00 per page, no minimum;
    searches will not be done without dates

Marshall County Recorder
Marshall County Building, Room 201
112 West Jefferson Street
Plymouth, IN 46563
(764) 935-8515; (574) 935-5009 FAX
http://www.co.marshall.in.us
Betty Engel
(land records)

Martin County
organized 1820 from Indian lands

Martin County Clerk
Martin County Courthouse
PO Box 120
Shoals, IN 47581
(812) 247-3651; (812) 247-2791 FAX
http://www.in.gov/mylocal/martin_county.htm
John Hunt
(probate records from 1820)
probate search service: no charge; copies of
    probate records: $1.00 per page, $2.00 for
    certified copies, no minimum

Martin County Recorder
PO Box 147
Shoals, IN 47581
(812) 247-2420
http://www.in.gov/mylocal/martin_county.htm
(land records)

Miami County
organized 1832 from Cass County

Miami County Clerk
(Miami County Courthouse, 25 South
    Broadway—location)
PO Box 184 (mailing address)
Peru, IN 46970
(765) 472-3901, ext. 256; (765) 472-1778 FAX
dwalker@miamicountyin.gov
http://www.miamicountyin.gov/Departments/
Clerks/Index.html
Debra Walker, Clerk of Courts

Miami County Recorder
PO Box 597
Peru, IN 46970
(765) 472-3901
http://www.miamicountyin.gov
Brenda Weaver

Monroe County
organized 1818 from Orange County

Monroe County Clerk
(Monroe County Justice Building, 301 North
    College Avenue, Room 201—location)
PO Box 547 (mailing address)
Bloomington, IN 47402-0547
(812) 333-3600; (812) 349-2610 FAX
http://www.co.monroe.in.us/clerk/index.htm
Jim Fielder, Clerk
(naturalization records from 1908 to 1918 with
    County Clerk's Office, Justice Building, wills
    and probates from 1818 to date with County
    Clerk)
naturalization and probate records search
    service: no charge for index search for a single
    name, $25.00 for a more complete search;
    copies of land and probate records: $1.00 per
    page; certified copies of vital records: $5.00
    for births, $6.00 for deaths (births restricted
    to the individual named, parent, guardian,
    grandparent, sibling, spouse or child, with
    photocopy of driver's license for
    identification)

Monroe County Recorder
Monroe County Courthouse
100 West Fifth Street, Room 122
Bloomington, IN 47404
(812) 349-2520
http://www.co.monroe.in.us/recorder/index.htm

(land records)

Montgomery County
organized 1823 from Indian lands

Montgomery County Clerk of Courts
100 East Main Street
Crawfordsville, IN 47933
(317) 364-6430; (765) 364-6355 FAX
jennifer.bentley@montgomeryco.net
http://www.montgomeryco.net/department/?f
DD=3-0
Jennifer Bentley
(naturalization records, marriages, probate
    records)
probate search service: no charge; copies of
    marriages: $1.00 per page, $2.00 for certified
    copies (specify photocopy or typed copy);
    copies of probate records: $1.00 per page, no
    minimum

Montgomery County Recorder
100 East Main Street
Crawfordsville, IN 47933
(317) 364-6415
recoder@montgomeryco.net
http://www.montgomeryco.net/department/?f
DD=12-0
Kathy Traugber
(land records)

Morgan County
organized 1821 from Delaware County

Morgan County Clerk
(Morgan County Courthouse, First Floor,
    Courthouse Square, 10 East Washington
    Street—location)
PO Box 1556 (mailing address)
Martinsville, IN 46151
(765) 342-1025; (765) 342-1111 FAX (Clerk)
http://scican3.scican.net/government/clerkmcc
.html
Vickie Kivett

Morgan County Recorder
(Morgan County Administration Building, 180
    South Main Street, Suite 125—location)
PO Box 1653 (mailing address)
Martinsville, IN 46151
(765) 342-1077
http://scican3.scican.net/government/recorder.
html
Karen Brummett
searches: $3.00 plus $5.00 per debtor name, plus
    SASE

Newton County
organized 1857 from Jasper County

Newton County Clerk
(Newton County Courthouse, 1 Courthouse
    Square, Main Level—location)
PO Box 49 (mailing address)
Kentland, IN 47951
(219) 474-6081; (219) 474-5749 FAX
administrative@newtoncountyin.com
http://www.newtoncountyin.com/gov_services.
htm
Janie M. Wilson

Newton County Recorder
1 Courthouse Square, Room 104
Kentland, IN 47951
(219) 474-6081
administrative@newtoncountyin.com
http://www.newtoncountyin.com/gov_services.
htm
John Hall

Noble County
organized 1835 from Elkhart County

Noble County Clerk of Courts
Noble County Courthouse
101 North Orange Street, Second Floor
Albion, IN 46701-1049
(219) 636-2736; (260) 636-4000 FAX (Clerk)
http://www.nobleco.org/Clerk/clerk_home.htm
Candace Myers, Clerk of Courts

(probate records)

Noble County Recorder
(Noble County Courthouse, 101 North Orange
Street, Room 210—location)
PO Box 75 (mailing address)
Albion, IN 46701
(219) 636-2672; (260) 636-3264 FAX
http://www.nobleco.org/Recorder/Recorder.htm
Judith K. Hass
(deeds, mortgages, assignments, releases, powers
of attorney, real estate contracts, annexations,
surveys, cemetery deeds, plats, bonds, etc.,
from 1834 to date)
copies: $1.00 per page, $5.00 for certification;
search: $10.00 for the first name and $7.00 for
each additional name

Ohio County
organized 1844 from Dearborn County

Ohio County Clerk of Courts
Ohio County Courthouse
North Main Street
Rising Sun, IN 47040
(812) 438-2610; (812) 438-1215 FAX
http://www.in.gov/mylocal/ohio_county.htm
Constance "Connie" Althoff
(naturalization and probate records from 1844)
no probate search service; copies 50¢ and $1.00
each, no minimum

Ohio County Recorder
Ohio County Courthouse
North Main Street
Rising Sun, IN 47040
(812) 438-3369 (Recorder); (812) 438-3264
(Assessor)
http://www.in.gov/mylocal/ohio_county.htm
(land records from 1844)

Orange County
organized 1815 from Crawford and Washington
counties

Orange County Clerk
1 Court Street
Paoli, IN 47454
(812) 723-2649; (812) 723-0239 FAX
http://www.co.orange.in.us/government/index.
html; http://www.orangecountyindiana.info
Beth Jones
(marriage, divorce, probate, civil court records)

Orange County Recorder
205 East Main Street
Paoli, IN 47454
(812) 723-3600
http://www.co.orange.in.us/government/index.
html
(land records from 1816)

Owen County
organized 1819 from Sullivan County, with
addition from Greene County in August 1821

Owen County Clerk
(Owen County Courthouse, 60 South Main
Street—location)
PO Box 146 (mailing address)
Spencer, IN 47460
(812) 829-5015; (812) 829-5147 FAX
http://www.owencounty.org/index.html; http://
bob.ivytech.edu/~bpigati/government.htm
Nick Robertson
(naturalization records from 1819, marriages
from 1819, probate records from 1819)
probate search service: no charge; copies of
probate records: $1.00 per page, no minimum

Owen County Recorder
Owen County Courthouse
60 South Main Street
Spencer, IN 47460
(812) 829-2260
http://www.owencounty.org
(land records from 1819)

Parke County
organized 1821 from Indian lands

Parke County Clerk of Courts
116 West High Street, Room 204
Rockville, IN 47872
(317) 569-5132; (765) 569-4222 FAX
http://www.in.gov/mylocal/parke_county.htm;
http://www.parkecountychamber.com;
Sue Ann Woody
(scattered naturalization records from 1832,
probate records from 1832)

Parke County Recorder
Court House Square
Rockville, IN 47872
(317) 569-3422
http://www.in.gov/mylocal/parke_county.htm
(land records from 1832)

Perry County
organized 1814 from Harrison and Warrick
counties

Perry County Clerk
2219 Payne Street
Tell City, IN 47586
(812) 547-3741; (812) 547-9782 FAX
http://www.perrycountyin.org/gov-
officials.html
Doris Davis
(naturalization records, probate records)
probate search service: $1.00 per page; copies of
probate records: $1.00 per page, $2.00 for
certified copies

Perry County Recorder
Perry County Courthouse
2219 Payne Street
Tell City, IN 47586
(812) 547-4261
http://www.perrycountyin.org/gov-
officials.html
Jane James
(land records)

Pike County
organized 1816 from Indian Lands

Pike County Clerk
(Pike County Courthouse, 801 Main Street—
location)
PO Box 125 (mailing address)
Petersburg, IN 47567
(812) 354-6025; (812) 354-6369 FAX
http://www.pikecountyin.org/chamber_of_co
mmerce_004.htm
Shirley Van Meter
(probate records)
probate search service: no charge ("be sure
records requested would be found in this
county; many randomly write all counties
when searching for such information");
copies of probate records: $1.00 per page, no
minimum

Pike County Recorder
Pike County Courthouse, Second Floor
Petersburg, IN 47567
(812) 354-8448
http://www.in.gov/mylocal/pike_county.htm
(land records)

Porter County
organized 1835 from Indian lands

Porter County Clerk
16 East Lincoln Way, Suite 211
Valparaiso, IN 46383
(219) 465-3450; (219) 465-3847 FAX
http://www.porterco.org/?0/1100/1/19
Dale Brewer

Porter County Recorder
155 Indiana Avenue, Suite 210
Valparaiso, IN 46383
(219) 465-3465
linda.recorder@porterco.org
http://www.porterco.org
Linda Trinkler,

Posey County
organized 1814 from Knox County

Posey County Clerk of Courts
(Posey County Courthouse, 300 West Main
Street—location)
PO Box 606 (mailing address)
Mt. Vernon, IN 47620
(812) 838-1306; (812) 838-1339 FAX
http://www.freewebs.com/lindagen/index.htm
David A. Angermeier
(some early naturalization records in Probate
Order Books [some naturalization records in
Civil Records Books in the Indiana State
Library, some naturalization docket books
and actual papers in the Indiana State
Archives], probate records)
copies of probate records: $1.00 per page

Posey County Recorder
Posey County Courthouse
PO Box 9
Mt. Vernon, IN 47620
(812) 838-1314
http://www.in.gov/mylocal/posey_county.htm
(land records)
copies of land records: $1.00 per page

Pulaski County
organized 1835 from Cass County

Pulaski County Clerk
112 East Main Street, #230
Winamac, IN 46996
(574) 946-3313; (219) 946-3653 FAX
http://www.pulaskionline.org/content/category
/6/21/50
Jennifer Shank-Maxwell

Pulaski County Recorder
Courthouse, Room 220
Winamac, IN 46996
(219) 946-3844
http://www.pulaskionline.org/content/view/40
/50
Lynette Wilder
(land records)

Putnam County
organized 1821 from Indian lands

Putnam County Clerk
1 Courthouse Square
Greencastle, IN 46135
(765) 653-2648; (765) 653-8405 FAX
Opal J. Sutherlin
(naturalization records, probate records from
1825)
probate search service: $2.00; copies of probate
records: $1.00 per page, $1.00 minimum

Putnam County Recorder
Courthouse Square, Room 25
Greencastle, IN 46135
(765) 653-5613
(land records from 1821)

Randolph County
organized 1818 from Wayne County

Randolph County Clerk of Courts
100 South Main Street, Third Floor
Winchester, IN 47394
(765) 584-4214; (765) 584-2958 FAX
http://www.winchesterareachamber.org/page/p
age/5970064.htm; http://www.randolph-
county.org (Community and economic
Development Foundation)
Claudia R. Thornburg
(some naturalization records in Civil Court
books [others removed to Indiana State
Library], marriages [some only partially
indexed] from 1819 to 1882 [no applications]
and from 1882 [with name and birthplaces of
parents, ages, and other information], wills,
probate books, guardianship records)
no probate search service (inquiries, other than
prepaid orders for copies, are forwarded to
Randolph County Historical/Genealogical
Society, Rt. 3, Box 61, Winchester, IN 47394);
copies of probate records: $1.00 per page,
$2.00 per certified copy

Randolph County Recorder
Randolph County Courthouse, Room 101
Winchester, IN 47394
(317) 584-7070
jgrove@randolphcounty.us
http://www.winchesterareachamber.org/page/p
age/5970064.htm
Jane Grove
(early land records, patent deeds, plat maps for
towns and cemeteries)
copies of land records: $1.00 per page

Ripley County
organized 1816 from Indian lands

Ripley County Clerk of Courts
(Ripley County Courthouse, 115 North Main
Street—location)
PO Box 177 (mailing address)
Versailles, IN 47042-0177
(812) 689-6115; (812) 689-6000 FAX
gbradford@ripleycounty.com
http://www.ripleycounty.com/clerk
Ginger J. Bradford
(naturalization records from 19th century,
marriages from 1818, wills and probate
records from 1818)
no probate search service; copies of probate
records: $1.00 per page, $2.00 for certified
copies, no minimum

Ripley County Recorder
(Ripley County Courthouse, 115 North Main
Street—location)
PO Box 404 (mailing address)
Versailles, IN 47042
(812) 689-5808
http://www.ripleycounty.com/recorder
Tammy Borgman
(land records from 1818)

Rush County
organized 1821 from Franklin County

Rush County Clerk of Courts
(101 East Second Street—location)
PO Box 429 (mailing address)
Rushville, IN 46173
(765) 932-2086; (765) 932-4165 FAX
clerk@rushcounty.in.gov
http://www.rushcounty.in.gov/Public/County
Offices/Clerk/index.cfm
Linda K. Sheehan
(very few naturalization records, probate records
from 1822)
probate search service for names given only;
copies of probate records: $1.00 per page, no
minimum ("no record sent before paid for;
furnish SASE")

Rush County Recorder
Courthouse, 100 East Second Street, Room 8
Rushville, IN 46173
(317) 932-2388
recorder@rushcounty.in.gov
http://www.rushcounty.in.gov/Public/County
Offices/Recorder/index.cfm
Sally Niedenthal
(land records from 1822)

St. Joseph County
organized 1830 from Indian lands

St. Joseph County Clerk's Office
101 South Main Street
South Bend, IN 46601
(574) 235-9635; (574) 235-9838 FAX (Clerk)
http://www.stjosephcountyindiana.com/index1.
htm
Rita Glenn, Clerk
(naturalization records from middle 1830s
through about 1955, marriages from 1832 and
divorces, probate records from 1830)
vital records search service from Health
Department: $5.00 for from one to six names;
probate search service: no charge; copies of
vital records: $1.00 each; copies of probate
records: $1.00 per page, no minimum

Saint Joseph County Recorder

227 West Jefferson Boulevard, Third Floor
South Bend, IN 46601
(574) 235-9525; (574) 235-5170 FAX
http://www.stjosephcountyindiana.com/index1.
htm
Terri J. Rethlake
(deeds, mortgages, liens, plat books, final estates
from 1830)

Scott County
organized 1820 from Clark and Jackson counties

Scott County Clerk
1 East McClain Avenue
Scottsburg, IN 47170
(812) 752-8420; (812) 752-5459 FAX
scottcountyclerk@scottsburg.com
http://greatscottindiana.org/Scott_County/Ele
cted%20Officials.htm
Fran Satterwhite, Clerk of the Circuit Court
(probate records)
no probate search service; copies of vital
records: $5.00; copies of probate records:
$1.00 per page in books

Scott County Recorder
75 North Seventh Street
Scottsburg, IN 47170
(812) 752-2571; (812) 752-8408 (County
Auditor)
teresavannarsdall@c3bb.com
http://greatscottindiana.org/Scott_County/Ele
cted%20Officials.htm
Teresa Vannarsdall, Auditor
(land records with County Auditor)

Shelby County
organized 1821 from Indian Lands

Shelby County Clerk of Courts
(407 South Harrison Street—location)
PO Box 198 (mailing address)
Shelbyville, IN 46176
(317) 392-6320; (317) 392-6339 FAX
http://www.co.shelby.in.us/subsubpage.asp?id_
parent=9&mainid=4&id=9
Carol Stohry
(naturalization records from 1821 [most of them
in Civil and Probate books], marriages from
1821, probate records from 1821)
no records search service from County Clerk's
Office (see online index 1822-1874:
www.rootsweb.com/~inshelby/courthouse/e
state_records/probate_index.htm); copies:
$1.00 per page (no personal checks, no copies
from large books)

Shelby County Recorder
407 South Harrison Street
Shelbyville, IN 46176
(317) 392-6370
http://www.co.shelby.in.us/subsubpage.asp?id_
parent=18&mainid=4&id=18
(deeds from 1821)

Spencer County
organized 1818 from Warrick County

Spencer County Clerk
(Spencer County Courthouse, 200 Main Street—
location)
PO Box 12 (mailing address)
Rockport, IN 47635-0012
(812) 649-6027; (812) 649-6030 FAX
Clerk@spencercounty.in.gov
http://spencercounty.in.gov/pages.cfm?Depart
mentid=396;
http://www.spencerco.org/business/busines
s_details.cfm?business_id=377spencercoclerk
@psci.net
GayAnn Harney
(naturalization records, probate records)
copies of naturalization records: $1.00 per page

Spencer County Recorder
Spencer County Courthouse
200 Main Street
Rockport, IN 47635
(812) 649-4376
recorder@spencercounty.in.gov

http://spencercounty.in.gov/pages.cfm?Depart
mentid=408
Sandra Coy

Starke County
organized 1835 from Marshall County

Starke County Clerk
(Starke County Courthouse, 53 East Washington
Street—location)
PO Box 395 (mailing address)
Knox, IN 46534
(574) 772-9128; (574) 772-9169 FAX
clerk75@co.starke.in.us
http://co.starke.in.us
Evelyn Skronski, Clerk of the Circuit Court
(naturalization records, vital records, probate
records)

Starke County Recorder
(53 East Mound Street—location)
PO Box 1 (mailing address)
Knox, IN 46534
(219) 772-9109
http://co.starke.in.us
Jackie A. Bridegroom
(land records)

Steuben County
organized 1835 from Indian lands

Steuben County Clerk of Courts
(Steuben County Courthouse, 55 South Public
Square—location)
PO Box 327 (mailing address
Angola, IN 46703
(260) 668-1000, ext. 2240; (260) 668-3702 FAX
http://www.co.steuben.in.us/departments/clerk
s/clerks.aspx
Diana Penick
(only a few naturalization records with County
Clerk, PO Box 327, Angola, IN 46703,
probate records with County Clerk)
no probate search service ("We need date");
copies of probate records: $1.00 per page,
$2.00 for certified copies, no minimum

Steuben County Recorder
317 South Wayne Street, Suite 2F
Angola, IN 46703
(260) 668-1000, ext. 1700; (260) 665-8483 FAX
http://www.co.steuben.in.us/departments/reco
rder/recorder.aspx
Pam Coleman
(land records)
copies: $1.00 per page ($2.00 if over 8½ x 14)

Sullivan County
organized 1816 from Knox County

Sullivan County Clerk of Courts
Sullivan County Courthouse
100 Courthouse Square
Sullivan, IN 47882
(812) 268-4657; (812) 268-4870 FAX
http://www.sullivancountyindiana.us
Shelly Hiatt Parris

Sullivan County Recorder
Sullivan County Courthouse
100 Courthouse Square
Sullivan, IN 47882
(812) 268-4844
http://www.sullivancountyindiana.us

Switzerland County
organized 1814 from Indian lands

Switzerland County Clerk of Courts
212 West Main Street
Vevay, IN 47043
(812) 427-3175; (812) 427-2017 FAX
circuitcourtclerk@switzerlandcountycourthouse.
org
http://switzerlandcountycourthouse.org
Ginger Peters
(marriages from 1814, wills from 1823, probates
1831)

Switzerland County Recorder
Switzerland County Courthouse

212 West Main Street
Vevay, IN 47043
(812) 427-2544
recorder@switzerlandcountycourthouse.org
http://switzerlandcountycourthouse.org
Nancy Barker
(deeds from 1816)

Tippecanoe County
organized 1826 from Montgomery County

Tippecanoe County Clerk
Tippecanoe County Courthouse
301 Main Street
Lafayette, IN 47901
(765) 423-9326; (765) 423-9194 FAX
clerk@tippecanoe.in.gov;
lphillips@tippecanoe.in.gov
http://www.tippecanoe.in.gov/courts
Linda Phillips
(Circuit Court and Superior Courts 1–6;
naturalization records, marriages, and probate
records with Clerk or with Tippecanoe
County Historical Association [TCHA] for
early originals, including marriages up to
1971)
probate search service: $10.00 per surname
(clerk will refer requests to Tippecanoe
County Area Genealogical Society (TIPCOA);
copies of probate records: 15¢ per page plus
SASE

Tippecanoe County Recorder
Tippecanoe County Office Building
20 North Third Street, Second Floor
Lafayette, IN 47901-1211
(765) 423-9343; (765) 423-9215; (765) 423-9311
(Recorder)
pberglund@tippecanoe.in.gov
http://www.tippecanoe.in.gov
Pam Berglund
(land records)

Tipton County
organized 1844 from Hamilton County

Tipton County Clerk of Courts
Tipton County Courthouse
101 East Jefferson Street, #3
Tipton, IN 46072
(765) 675-2795; (765) 675-4103 FAX
http://www.tiptonguide.com
Bonita G. Guffey
(probate records from 1800s)
probate search service: no charge ("extensive
research referred to a lady who does
research"); copies of probate records: $1.00
per page

Tipton County Recorder
Tipton County Courthouse
101 East Jefferson Street
Tipton, IN 46072
(765) 675-4614
http://www.tiptonguide.com

Union County
organized 1821 from Wayne County

Union County Clerk of Circuit Court
Union County Courthouse
26 West Union Street
Liberty, IN 47353-1350
(765) 458-6121; (765) 458-5263 FAX
ucclerk@msn.com
http://www.in.gov/mylocal/union_county.htm;
http://www.uniondeocrats.com/?q=node/2
Susan Ray
(naturalization records from 1821, marriages
from 1821, probate records from 1821)
probate search service: no charge; copies of
probate records: $1.00 per page, no minimum

Union County Recorder
(Union County Courthouse, 126 West Union
Street—location)
Box 106 (mailing address)
Liberty, IN 47353
(317) 458-5434
tlpersinger@peoplepc.com

http://www.in.gov/mylocal/union_county.htm;
http://www.uniondeocrats.com/?q=node/2
Loree Persinger@peoplepc.com
(land records from 1815)

Vanderburgh County
organized 1818 from Indian lands

Vanderburgh County Clerk
(Civic Center Courts Building, 825 Sycamore
Street, Room 216, Evansville, IN 47708-
1831—location)
PO Box 3356 (mailing address)
Evansville, IN 47732-3356
(812) 435-5160; (812) 435-5849 FAX
http://www.vanderburghgov.org/home/index.a
sp?page=66
Susan K. Kirk
(naturalization records, marriage records,
probate records [with Probate Department])
no probate search service; copies of probate
records: $1.00 per page, no minimum

Vanderburgh County Recorder
PO Box 1037
Evansville, IN 47706-1037
(812) 435-5215
http://www.vanderburghgov.org/home/index.a
sp?page=69
Betty Knight Smith
(land records)
photocopies: $1.00 (8.5 x 14), certification: $5.00
per document

Vermillion County
organized 1824 from Parke County

Vermillion County Clerk
(Vermillion County Courthouse, 255 South
Main—location)
PO Box 10 (mailing address)
Newport, IN 47966
(317) 492-3500; (765) 492-5001 FAX
mapvermclerk@hotmail.com
http://www.vermillionco.org
Martha A. Padish
(naturalization records, marriages, probate
records)
no probate search service; copies of
naturalizations, marriages, and probate
records: $1.00 per page

Vermillion County Recorder
(Vermillion County Courthouse, 255 South
Main—location)
PO Box 145 (mailing address)
Newport, IN 47966
(317) 492-3570
cheflorip@yahoo.com
http://www.vermillionco.org; http://www.in.
gov/mylocal/vermillion_county.htm
Lori Porter
(deeds)

Vigo County
organized 1818 from Indian lands

Vigo County Clerk
(County Court House Building, 33 South Third
Street, Room 22, Second Floor—location)
PO Box 8449 (mailing address)
Terre Haute, IN 47807-8449
(812) 238-8211
clerk@vigocounty.org
http://www.vigocounty.org/clerk
Patricia R. Mansard, Clerk of the Circuit,
Superior, and Juvenile Courts
(naturalization records, marriages from 1921 to
date, probate records)
copies of probate records: $1.00 per page

Vigo County Recorder
Vigo County Annex Building
199 Oak Street
Terre Haute, IN 47807
(812) 462-3301; (812) 232-2219 FAX
lamiller@vigocounty.org;
rlwatts@vigocounty.org
http://www.vigocounty.org/recorder
Lou Ann Miller, Chief Deputy; Ray Watts,

Recorder
(land records)

Wabash County
organized 1832 from Huntington County

Wabash County Clerk of Courts
69 West Hill Street
Wabash, IN 46992
(260) 563-0661; (260) 569-1352 FAX
http://clerk.wabashcounty85.us
Lori Draper
(naturalization records, probate records)
probate search service: no charge; copies of
probate records: $1.00 per page, no minimum

Wabash County Recorder
Wabash County Courthouse
49 West Hill Street
Wabash, IN 46992
(260) 563-0661
recorder@wabashcounty.in.gov
http://recorder.wabashcounty85.ushttp://www.
in.gov/mylocal/wabash_county.htm
Nancy Gribben

Warren County
organized 1827 from Indian lands

Warren County Clerk of Courts
125 North Monroe Street, Suite 11
Williamsport, IN 47993-1198
(317) 762-3510 (Clerk); (765) 762-7251 FAX
jbclerk@hotmail.com
http://warrenadvantage.com/Warren_Profile/
Government.htm
Jacki Brier
(naturalization records, marriages, probate
records)

Warren County Recorder
Warren County Courthouse
125 North Monroe Street
Williamsport, IN 47993
(317) 762-3510
http://warrenadvantage.com/Warren_Profile/
Government.htm; http://www.in.gov/
mylocal/warren_county.htm
Melissa Drake
(land records)

Warrick County
organized 1813 from Indian lands

Warrick County Clerk
Warrick County Judicial Center
1 County Square, Suite 200
Boonville, IN 47601
(812) 897-6160; (812) 897-6400 FAX
clerk@warrickcounty.gov
http://www.warrickcounty.gov/departments/cl
erk.htm
Shannon Weisheit, Clerk of the Circuit Court
(records begin in 1814)

Warrick County Recorder
Warrick County Judicial Center
(1 County Square—location)
PO Box 285 (mailing address)
Boonville, IN 47601
(812) 897-6165; (812) 897-6168 FAX
recorder@warrickcounty.gov
http://www.warrickcounty.gov/departments/re
corder
(land records)

Washington County
organized 1813 from Indian lands

Washington County Clerk of Courts
Washington County Courthouse
99 Public Square, Suite 102
Salem, IN 47167
(812) 883-5748; (812) 883-8108 FAX
rita.martin@washingtoncountyindiana.com
http://www.washingtoncountyindiana.com/cler
k.html
Rita Martin
(naturalization records, vital records, probate
records)

copies: $1.00 per page (no personal checks)

Washington County Recorder
Washington County Courthouse
99 Public Square, Suite 100
Salem, IN 47167
(812) 883-4001; (812) 883-4020
http://www.washingtoncountyindiana.com/rec
    order.html
Cynthia Zink
(land records from 1814, also land tract index
    for deeds earlier than 1814)

Wayne County
organized 1810 from Indian lands

Wayne County Clerk
(Wayne County Courthouse, 301 East Main
    Street, Second Floor—location)
PO Box 1172 (mailing address)
Richmond, IN 47375-1172
(765) 973-9200; (317) 973-9220 (Clerk's Office);
    (765) 973-9490 FAX
clerk@co.wayne.in.us
http://co.wayne.in.us/clerk
Sue Anne Lower, Clerk
(naturalization records, marriages [before 1882
    did not keep "parental info"], probate
    records)
marriage records: $1.00 each or $2.00 for a
    certified copy; no probate search service
    unless date range is supplied; copies of
    probate records: $1.00 per page, $2.00 for
    certified copies, no minimum

Wayne County Recorder
Wayne County Annex Building
401 East Main Street
Richmond, IN 47374
(765) 973-9235; (765) 973-9341 FAX
http://co.wayne.in.us/recorder;
    http://www.doxpop.com (Doxpop Recorded
    Documents)
Debby Resh
(land records)

Wells County
organized 1835 from Huntington and Allen
    counties

Wells County Clerk
Wayne County Courthouse
102 West Market Street, Suite 201
Bluffton, IN 46714
(260) 824-6482 (Circuit Court Clerk); (260) 824-
    6483 (Superior Court Clerk, Suite 302); (260)
    824-6559 FAX (Circuit Court Clerk); (260)
    824-6511 (Superior Court Clerk)
clerk@wellscounty.org
http://www.wellscounty.org/clerk.htm
Beth Davis

Wells County Recorder
Wells County Courthouse
Wayne County Courthouse
102 West Market Street, Suite 203
Bluffton, IN 46714
(260) 824-6507; (260) 824-1238 FAX
recorder@wellscounty.org
http://www.wellscounty.org/recorder.htm
Sandra K. Fair

White County
organized 1834 from Carroll County

White County Clerk
(110 North Main Street—location)
PO Box 350 (mailing address)
Monticello, IN 47960
(574) 583-1530; (574) 583-1532 FAX
http://www.in-map.net/counties/WHITE/
    government/clerk.htm
Kay P. Kiser
(probate records)
probate search service: no charge; copies of
    probate records: $1.00 per page, no minimum

White County Recorder
White County Building
PO Box 127

Monticello, IN 47960
(219) 583-5912; (574) 583-1521 FAX
http://www.in-map.net/counties/WHITE/
    government/recorder.htm
Donna J. Salomon
(land records with County Recorder and County
    Auditor)
copies: $1.00 per page ($2.00 if larger than 9 x
    14)

Whitley County
organized 1835 from Huntington County

Whitley County Clerk
Whitley County Courthouse
101 West Van Buren Street
Columbia City, IN 46725-2402
(260) 248-3102; (260) 248-3137 FAX (Clerk)
http://www.whitleybiz.com/main-agencies-
    county.htm
Cindy Greer
(naturalization records, vital records, and
    probate records from 1853)
no probate search service; copies of probate
    records: $1.00 per page, no minimum

Whitley County Recorder
Whitley County Courthouse
101 West Van Buren Street, Second Floor,
    Room 18
Columbia City, IN 46725
(219) 248-3106 (Recorder); (260) 248-31900
    (Auditor)
http://www.whitleybiz.com/main-agencies-
    county.htm
(land records from 1838)

IOWA

*Capital: Des Moines. Statehood: 28 December 1846
(annexed as a result of the Louisiana Purchase, 1803,
was part of the Missouri Territory from 1812 to 1821,
mostly unorganized from 1821 to 1834, part of the
Michigan Territory from 1834 to 1836, part of
Wisconsin Territory from 1836 to 1838, when it became
a separate territory)*

Iowa has eight District Courts of general
jurisdiction, which sit in each county seat. First
Judicial District: Allamakee, Black Hawk,
Buchanan, Chickasaw, Clayton, Delaware,
Dubuque, Fayette, Grundy, Howard and
Winneshiek counties; Second Judicial District:
Boone, Bremer, Butler, Calhoun, Carroll, Cerro
Gordo, Floyd, Franklin, Greene, Hamilton,
Hancock, Hardin, Humboldt, Marshall, Mitchell,
Pocahontas, Sac, Story, Webster, Winnebago,
Worth and Wright counties; Third Judicial
District: Buena Vista, Cherokee, Clay, Crawford,
Dickinson, Emmet, Ida, Kossuth, Lyon,
Monona, O'Brien, Osceola, Palo Alto,
Plymouth, Sioux and Woodbury counties;
Fourth Judicial District: Audubon, Cass,
Fremont, Harrison, Mills, Montgomery, Page,
Pottawattamie and Shelby counties; Fifth
Judicial District: Adair, Adams, Clarke, Dallas,
Decatur, Guthrie, Jasper, Lucas, Madison,
Marion, Polk, Ringgold, Taylor, Union, Warren
and Wayne counties; Sixth Judicial District:
Benton, Iowa, Johnson, Jones, Linn and Tama
counties; Seventh Judicial District: Cedar,
Clinton, Jackson, Muscatine and Scott counties;
Eighth Judicial District: Appanoose, Davis, Des
Moines, Henry, Jefferson, Keokuk, Lee, Louisa,
Mahaska, Monroe, Poweshiek, Van Buren,
Wapello and Washington counties. The Supreme
Court and Court of Appeals have appellate
jurisdiction.

Adair County
organized 1851 from Cass County

Adair County Clerk of Court
(Adair County Courthouse, 400 Public Square—
    location)
PO Box L (mailing address)
Greenfield, IA 50849-1290
(515) 743-2445
http://www.judicial.state.ia.us/Administration/
    Directories/Clerks_of_District_Court
(a few naturalization records, probate records)
probate search service: $1.00; copies of probate
    records: 25¢ each, $1.00 minimum

Adair County Recorder
Adair County Courthouse
400 Public Square
Greenfield, IA 50849
(515) 743-2411
adairrec@ll.net
http://www.iowacounties.org/News/Publicatio
    ns%20Information/2007CountyDirectory/A
    dairCounty.mht
Janelle Schneider
(land records, births from 1880 [few from 1921
    to 1941 when certificates were sent directly to
    the state office], deaths from 1880 [none from
    1921 to 1941], marriages from 1880)

Adams County
organized 1851 from Taylor County

Adams County Clerk of Court
Adams County Courthouse, 500 Ninth Street—
    location)
Box 484 (mailing address)
Corning, IA 50841
(641)322-4711; (641) 322-4523 FAX
Debbie.Loudon@jb.state.ia.us
http://www.adamscountyia.com/County%20&
    %20State%20Employees.htm
Deb Loudon
(naturalization records from 1880, probate

records from 1880)

Adams County Recorder
500 Ninth Street—location)
Box 28 (mailing address)
Corning, IA 50841
(641) 322-3744 voice & FAX
mmiller@mddc.com
http://www.adamscountyia.com/County%20T
%20State$20Employees.htm
Mary L. Miller
(land records from 1855, vital records from
1880)
certified copies of vital records: $10.00 each

Allamakee County
organized 1847 from Clayton County

Allamakee County Clerk of Court
Allamakee County Courthouse
(110 Allamakee Street—location)
PO Box 248 (mailing address)
Waukon, IA 52172
(319) 568-6351; (319) 568-6353 FAX
http://www.judicial.state.ia.us/Administration/
Directories/Clerks_of_District_Court
Carl R. Christianson
(naturalization records from 1850 to 1890,
probate records from 1852)
probate search service: $10.00 ("If search in
probate is lengthy, cost of search goes up");
copies of probate records: 50¢ each, no
minimum

Allamakee County Recorder
Allamakee County Courthouse
110 Allamakee Street
Waukon, IA 52172
(319) 568-2364; (319) 568-6419 FAX
dwinke@co.allamakee.ia.us
http://www.co.allamakee.ia.us/recorder.htm
Debbie Winke
(land records from 1851, births and deaths from
1880, marriages from 1849)

Appanoose County
organized 1843 from Davis County

Appanoose County Clerk of Court
(201 North 12th—location)
PO Box 400 (mailing address)
Centerville, IA 52544
(515) 856-6101
http://www.judicial.state.ia.us/Administration/
Directories/Clerks_of_District_Court
(naturalization records from 1884 to 1929,
probate records from 1847)
probate search service: no charge ("most of the
research that is uncertified is referred to our
local Genealogy Society"); copies of probate
records: 25¢ per page, no minimum

Appanoose County Recorder
201 North 12th
Centerville, IA 52544
(641) 856-6103; (641) 856-8023 FAX
twalker@appanoosecounty.net
http://www.appanoosecounty.net
Teddy Walker
(land records from 1850, births and deaths from
1880)

Audubon County
organized 1851 from Cass and Black Hawk
counties

Audubon County Clerk of Court
318 Leroy Street #6
Audubon, IA 50025
(712) 563-4275
http://www.judicial.state.ia.us/Administration/
Directories/Clerks_of_District_Court
Evelyn Wiges
(naturalization records, probate records)
probate search service: $6.00; copies of probate
records: 50¢ per page, no minimum

Audubon County Recorder
318 Leroy Street, #7
Audubon, IA 50025

(712) 563-2119; (712) 563-4677 FAX
acro@iowatelecom.net
http://www.iowacounties.org/News/Publicatio
ns%20Information/2007CountyDirectory/A
udubonCounty.mht
Mary Lou Johansen
(land records with County Recorder [by owner's
name] or County Auditor [by legal
description], vital records with County
Recorder)

Benton County
organized 1837 from Indian lands

Benton County Clerk of Court
Courthouse, 111 East Fourth Street
Vinton, IA 52349
(319) 472-2766; (319) 472-2747 FAX
http://www.cobentoniaus.com
(naturalization records from 1860, probate
records from 1860)
probate search service: $6.00; copies of probate
records: 25¢ per page, $1.00 minimum

Benton County Recorder
Courthouse, 111 East Fourth Street, First Floor
Vinton, IA 52349
(319) 472-3309
bcrecorder@co.benton.ia.us;
bjw@co.benton.ia.us
http://www.cobentoniaus.com
Betty Wright
(land records, vital records from 1880)

Black Hawk County
organized 1843 from Delaware County

Black Hawk County Clerk of Court
316 East Fifth Street, Third Floor
Waterloo, IA 50703-4712
(319) 291-2482
http://www.judicial.state.ia.us/Administration/
Directories/Clerks_of_District_Court
(naturalization records from 1869 to 1926,
probate records from 1880)
naturalization search service: $6.00; probate
search service: no charge ("Some records
show origination in Buchanan County");
copies of probate records: 50¢ per page, 50¢
minimum

Black Hawk County Recorder
316 East Fifth Street, Room 208
Waterloo, IA 50703-4774
(319) 833-3012; (319) 833-3170 FAX
recorder@co.black-hawk.ia.us;
patsass@co.black-hawk.ia.us
http://www.co.black-
hawk.ia.us/depts/recorder.htm
Patricia Sass
(land records from about 1860 with County
Auditor [plat room deed transfer books, atlas-
1937] or County Recorder [grantee/grantor
books, atlas-1896, records from 1854], births,
deaths and marriages from 1880 [except from
1936 to 1941 records in Des Moines] with
County Recorder)
vital records search service: $6.00; copies of land
records: 75¢ per page; copies of vital records:
$5.00 each

Boone County
organized 1846 from Polk County

Boone County Clerk of Court
Boone County Courthouse
201 State Street
Boone, IA 500364898
(515) 433-0561
http://www.co.boone.ia.us
(some naturalization records from 1867, probate
records from about 1850)
probate search service: no charge ("We do these
searches only when we have time"); copies of
probate records: 50¢ per page, $10.00 for
certification, no minimum

Boone County Recorder
Boone County Courthouse
201 State Street

Boone, IA 50036
(515) 433-0514
recorder@co.boone.ia.us
http://www.co.boone.ia.us
Sheryl Thul
(land records, births and deaths from 1880,
marriages from 1851)
certified copies of vital records: $10.00

Bremer County
organized 1851 from Winnebago Indian Reserve

Bremer County Clerk of Court
(Courthouse, 415 East Bremer Avenue—
location)
PO Box 328 (mailing address)
Waverly, IA 50677
(319) 352-5661; (319) 352-1054 FAX
http://www.co.bremer.ia.us/new/departments.
htm
(naturalization records, probate records)
probate search service: no charge; copies of
probate records: 50¢ per page, $5.00
minimum

Bremer County Recorder
Courthouse, 415 East Bremer venue
Waberly, IA 50677
(319) 352-0401; (319) 352-0518 FAX
dellison@co.bremer.ia.us
http://www.co.bremer.ia.us/new/recorder.htm
Donna Ellison
(land records, vital records)
certified copies of vital records: $10.00 each

Buchanan County
organized 1837 from Delaware County

Buchanan County Clerk of Court
(210 Fifth Avenue, NE—location)
PO Box 259 (mailing address)
Independence, IA 50644-1929
(319) 334-2196
http://www.independenceia.com/lorg.html
(naturalization records from about 1875 to 1923,
probate records from 1854)
probate search service: no charge (must have
SASE); copies of probate records: 50¢ per
page, $10.00 for certified copies, no minimum

Buchanan County Recorder
(210 Fifth Avenue, NE—location)
PO Box 298 (mailing address)
Independence, IA 50644
(319) 334-4259; (319) 334-7453 FAX
recorder@bcch.sbt.net
http://www.independenceia.com/lorg.html
Diane Curry
(land records, births and deaths from 1 July
1880, marriages from 1848)

Buena Vista County
organized 1851 from Sac and Clay counties

Buena Vista County Clerk of Court
(215 East Fifth Street—location)
PO Box 1186 (mailing address)
Storm Lake, IA 50588-1186
(712) 749-2546
http://www.judicial.state.ia.us/Administration/
Directories/Clerks_of_District_Court
(naturalization records, probate records from
1880)
copies of naturalization records and probate
records: 50¢ per page, $10.00 for certified
copies

Buena Vista County Recorder/Registrar
PO Box 454
Storm Lake, IA 50588
(712) 749-2539; (712) 749-2539 FAX
recorder@co.buena-vista.ia.us;
sobannon@co.buena-vista.ia.us
http://www.co.buena-vista.ia.us
Shari O'Bannon
(land records with Recorder and Auditor
Offices, vital records from 1880 with
Recorder)

Butler County

organized 1851 from Buchanan and Black Hawk counties

Butler County Clerk of Court
Butler County Courthouse, 428 Sixth Street
Allison, IA 50602
(319) 267-2487; (319) 267-2488 FAX
http://butlercoiowa.org/clerkofcourt.htm
Nancy Greenlee
(naturalization records, vital records, and probate records)
probate search service: no charge; copies of probate records: 50¢ per page, no minimum

Butler County Recorder
(Butler County Courthouse, 428 Sixth Street—location)
PO Box 346 (mailing address)
Allison, IA 50602
(319) 267-2735; (319) 267-2675 FAX
recorder@butlercoiowa.org
http://www.butlercoiowa.org/recordercontact.htm
Craig Franken
(land records, vital records)

Calhoun County

organized 1851 from Greene County; name changed from Fox County in 1853

Calhoun County Clerk of Court
(Calhoun County Courthouse, 416 Fourth Street—location)
PO Box 273 (mailing address)
Rockwell City, IA 50579
(712) 297-8122
http://www.calhouncountyiowa.com/service.htm
Shirley Redenius
(naturalization records, probate records)
probate search service: no charge; copies of probate records: 50¢ per page, no minimum

Calhoun County Recorder
Calhoun County Courthouse
416 Fourth Street, Suite 3
Rockwell City, IA 50579
(712) 297-8121
mminnick@calhouncountyiowa.com;
recorder@calhouncountyiowa.com
http://www.calhouncountyiowa.com/recorder.htm
Marty Minnick
(land records, vital records)
land records search service: no charge (extensive searches referred to Calhoun County Genies, c/o Mrs. Beverly Courter, 226 North Grant Street, Rockwell City, IA 50579); copies of land records: 25¢ each

Carroll County

organized 1851 from Guthrie County

Carroll County Clerk of Court
PO Box 867
Carroll, IA 51401-0867
(712) 792-4327
http://www.judicial.state.ia.us/Administration/Directories/Clerks_of_District_Court
(probate records)

Carroll County Recorder
(Carroll County Courthouse, 114 East Sixt Street, First Floor, Southeast Corner—location)
PO Box 782 (mailing address)
Carroll, IA 51401
(712) 792-3328
ccrecorder@co.carroll.ia.us
http://www.co.carroll.ia.us/Recorder/recorder.htm
Marilyn Dopheide
(land records, vital records)

Cass County

organized 1851 from Pottawatamie County

Cass County Clerk of Court
5West Seventh Street
Atlantic, IA 50022-1492
(712) 243-2105
http://www.judicial.state.ia.us/Administration/Directories/Clerks_of_District_Court
(only early naturalization records, probate records)
probate search service: no charge; copies of probate records: 25¢ per page, no minimum

Cass County Recorder
5 West Seventh Street
Atlantic, IA 50022
(712) 243-1692; (712) 243-6660 FAX
jjensen@casscoia.us
http://www.iowacounties.org/News/Publications%20Information/2007CountyDirectory/CassCounty.mht
Joyce Jensen
(land records, vital records from 1880)

Cedar County

organized 1837 from Wisconsin Territory

Cedar County Clerk of Court
(400 Cedar Street—location)
PO Box 111 (mailing address)
Tipton, IA 52772
(563) 886-2101; (563) 886-3594 FAX
http://www.cedarcounty.org/offices/clerkofcourt/index.htm
Julie C. Carlin
(some naturalization records but not well indexed, probate records from 1836)
probate search service: $10.00 per name; certified copies of vital records: $6.00 each; copies of probate records: 50¢ per page, $10.00 for certified copies

Cedar County Recorder/Registrar
400 Cedar Street
Tipton, IA 52772-1750
(563) 886-2230; (563) 886-2120
cthumm@cedarcounty.org
http://www.cedarcounty.org/offices/recorder/index.htm
Charline Thumm
(land records from 1839, births and deaths from 1880, marriages from 1839)

Cerro Gordo County

organized 1851 from Floyd County

Cerro Gordo County Clerk of Court
Cerro Gordo County Courthouse
220 North Washington Avenue
Mason City, IA 50401-3254
(641) 424-6431
http://www.judicial.state.ia.us/Administration/Directories/Clerks_of_District_Court
(naturalization records, probate records)

Cerro Gordo County Recorder
Cerro Gordo County Courthouse
220 North Washington Avenue
Mason City, IA 50401
(641) 421-3056; (641) 421-3154 FAX
cpearce@co.cerro-gordo.ia.us
http://www.co.cerro-gordo.ia.us/Recorder/Recorder.cfm
Colleen Pearce
(land records, vital records)

Cherokee County

organized 1851 from Crawford County

Cherokee County Clerk of Court
(520 West Main Street—location)
Drawer F (mailing address)
Cherokee, IA 51012
(712) 225-6744; (712) 225-6749
http://www.cherokeecountyiowa.com/offices/Clerk%20of%20Court/index.htm
Cheryl Kaskey
(naturalizations, probate records)
records search service: $10.00 (includes certified copy of vital records); copies of records: 50¢ per page, no minimum

Cherokee County Recorder
(520 West Main Street—location)
Drawer G (mailing address)
Cherokee, IA 51012
(712) 225-6735; (712) 225-6754 FAX

djcoombs@co.cherokee.ia.us
http://www.cherokeecountyiowa.com/offices/recorder/index.htm
Dawn Jones Coombs
(land records, vital records from 1880 to date)

Chickasaw County

organized 1851 from Fayette County

Chickasaw County Clerk of Court
PO Box 467
New Hampton, IA 50659-0467
(515) 394-2106
http://www.judicial.state.ia.us/Administration/Directories/Clerks_of_District_Court
(naturalization records from 1858 to 1906, probate records from 1880)
probate search service: $6.00 ("supply all information possible"); copies of probate records: 50¢ per page, no minimum

Chickasaw County Recorder
(Chickasaw County Courthouse, 8 East Prospect—location)
PO Box 14 (mailing address)
New Hampton, IA 50659
(641) 394-2336; (641) 394-5541 FAX
ccrecorder@hotmail.com
http://www.chickasawcoia.org/Recorder
Cindy Messersmith
(land records from 1866, births from 1880, deaths from 1880 to 1919 and from 1941, marriages from 1853)

Clarke County

organized 1846 from Lucas County

Clarke County Clerk of Court
Clarke County Courthouse
100 South Main Street
Osceola, IA 50213-1299
(641) 342-6096
http://www.judicial.state.ia.us/Administration/Directories/Clerks_of_District_Court
(very few naturalization records, probate records from late 1800s)
probate search service: $3.00 ("Cover letter must accompany request with all information needed"); copies of probate records: 25¢ per page, $3.00 minimum

Clarke County Recorder
Clarke County Courthouse
100 South Main Street, First Floor
Osceola, IA 50213
(641) 342-3313 voice & FAX
ccrecord@cecnet.net;
clarkerecorder1@iowatelecom.net
http://www.clarkecountyia.org/recorder/index.html
Pennie Gonseth
(land records from 1866, vital records from 1880)

Clay County

organized 1851 from Indian lands

Clay County Clerk of Court
(215 West Fourth Street—location)
PO Box 4104 (mailing address
Spencer, IA 51301-3818
(712) 262-4335
http://www.judicial.state.ia.us/Administration/Directories/Clerks_of_District_Court
(naturalization records from 1866, probate records from 1871)
no records search service; copies of probate records: 25¢ per page

Clay County Recorder
Clay County Administration Building
300 West Fourth Street, Suite 3
Spencer, IA 51301
(712) 262-1081; (712) 262-5793 FAX
sgoyette@co.clay.ia.us
http://www.co.clay.ia.us
Shirley Goyette
(land records, births and deaths from 1880, marriages from 1866)

Clayton County
organized 1837 from Dubuque County

Clayton County Clerk of Court
(Courthouse, 111 High Street NE—location)
PO Box 418 (mailing address)
Elkader, IA 52043
(563) 245-2204; (563) 245-2825
http://www.claytoncountyiowa.net/directory/offices&boards/court.htm
Susan K. Johnson
(naturalization records, probate records)
probate search service: $6.00; copies of probate records: 50¢ per page

Clayton County Recorder
(Courthouse, 111 High Street NE—location)
PO Box 278 (mailing address)
Elkader, IA 52043
(563) 245-2710; (563) 245-2353 FAX
smeyer@claytoncountyiowa.net
http://www.claytoncountyiowa.net/directory/offices&boards/recorder.htm
Sue Meyer
(land records, vital records)

Clinton County
organized 1837 from Dubuque County

Clinton County Clerk of Court
PO Box 157
Clinton, IA 52732-0157
(319) 243-6210; (563) 243-3655 FAX
http://www.clintoncountyiowa.com/directory.htm
(naturalization records from 1859, probate records from 1854)
probate search service: no charge; copies of probate records: 50¢ per page, no minimum

Clinton County Recorder/Registrar
(Clinton County Administration Building, 1900 North Third Street—location)
PO Box 2957 (mailing address)
Clinton, IA 52733-2957
(563) 244-0565; (563) 242-8412 FAX
recorder@clintoncountyiowa.com;
smangan@clintoncountyiowa.com
http://www.clintoncountyiowa.com/recorder/default.asp
Stephen Mangan
(land records from 1846, births and deaths from 1880, marriages from 1840)
certified copies of vital records: $6.00

Crawford County
organized 1851 from Shelby County

Crawford County Clerk of Court
(Crawford County Courthouse, 1202 Broadway—location)
PO Box 546 (mailing address)
Denison, IA 51442-0546
(712) 263-2242
http://www.judicial.state.ia.us/Administration/Directories/Clerks_of_District_Court
Karen Kahl
(naturalization records, probate records)
no probate search service: "Nothing done over telephone"

Crawford County Recorder
Crawford County Courthouse
1202 Broadway
Denison, IA 51442
(712) 263-3643; (712) 263-3413 FAX
dmeeves@crawfordcounty.org
http://www.iowacounties.org/News/Publications%20Information/2007CountyDirectory/CrawfordCounty.mht;
http://www.crawfordcounty.org
Denise Meeves
(land records, vital records)
certified copies of vital records: $6.00

Dallas County
organized 1846 from Polk County

Dallas County Clerk of Court
801 Court Street
Adel, IA 50003-1485
(515) 993-5816
http://www.co.dallas.ia.us
Gloria L. Ward
(probate records from 1860)
probate search service: no charge; copies of probate records: 50¢ per page, $1.00 minimum

Dallas County Recorder
(Dallas County Courthouse, 801 Court Street, Room 203—location)
PO Box 38 (mailing address)
Adel, IA 50003
(515) 993-5804; (515) 993-5970 FAX
chol@co.dallas.ia.us
http://www.co.dallas.ia.us/recorder/recorder.asp
Carol "Cindy" Hol
(land records, births and deaths from 1880 [except some omissions from 1921 through 1941], marriages from 1850)

Davis County
organized 1843 from Van Buren County

Davis County Clerk of Court
100 Courthouse Square
Bloomfield, IA 52537-1600
(641) 664-2011; (641) 664-2041 FAX
http://www.daviscountyiowa.org/clerk.htm
Jeannie Houser
(probate records from 1840)
probate search service: $6.00; certified copies: $6.00 ("Make check or money order payable to the Clerk District Court and enclose a SASE")

Davis County Recorder
100 Courthouse Square
Bloomfield IA 52537
(641) 664-2321; (641) 664-3082
daviscorec@netins.net;
davis_co_recorder@yahoo.com
http://www.daviscountyrecorder.org
Louise Frymoyer
(land records, births and deaths from 1880, marriages from 1840)

Decatur County
organized 1846 from Appanoose County

Decatur County Clerk of Court
Decatur County Courthouse
207 North Main
Leon, IA 50144-1647
(515) 446-4331
http://www.judicial.state.ia.us/Administration/Directories/Clerks_of_District_Court
(very few naturalization records from early 1900s, probate records from 1880)
probate search service: no charge; copies of probate records: $1.00 per page, $10.00 for certified copies, no minimum ("We do not run Xerox copies on our old books, as it breaks the backs down")

Decatur County Recorder
Decatur County Courthouse
207 North Main
Leon, IA 50144
(641) 446-4322; (641) 446-7159 FAX
http://www.iowacounties.org/News/Publications%20Information/2007CountyDirectory/DecaturCounty.mht
Gale Norman
(land records from 1874, births and deaths from 1880, marriages from 1874)

Delaware County
organized 1837 from Dubuque County

Delaware County Clerk of Court
(Delaware County Courthouse—location)
PO Box 527 (mailing address)
Manchester, IA 52057
(319) 927-4942
http://www.judicial.state.ia.us/Administration/Directories/Clerks_of_District_Court
(naturalization records, probate records)
probate search service: no charge; copies of probate records: 50¢ per page, no minimum

Delaware County Recorder
Delaware County Courthouse
301 East Main
Manchester, IA 52057
(563) 927-4665; (563) 927-3641 FAX
dpeyton@co.delaware.ia.us
http://www.delawarecountyia.com
Deborah Peyton
(land records, vital records)

Des Moines County
organized 1834 from Wisconsin Territory

Des Moines County Clerk of Court
(513 North Main Street—location)
PO Box 158 (mailing address)
Burlington, IA 52601-0158
(319) 753-8272
http://www.judicial.state.ia.us/Administration/Directories/Clerks_of_District_Court
(naturalization records from 1856 to 1906 and 1928 to 1955, probate records from 1835)
no probate search service (contact Mrs. Louise Strable, 719 South 12th, Burlington, IA 52601)

Des Moines County Recorder
(513 North Main Street—location)
PO Box 277 (mailing address)
Burlington, IA 52601
(319) 753-8221; (319) 753-8721 FAX
http://www.co.des-moines.ia.us/Recorder/RcrdrDefault.asp
Kathryn S. Waterhouse
(land records, births from 1880, deaths from 1880 to 1910 [no index] and from July 1941)

Dickinson County
organized 1851 from Kossuth County

Dickinson County Clerk of Court
(County Courthouse—location)
PO Drawer ON (mailing address)
Spirit Lake, IA 51360
(712) 336-1138
http://www.co.dicksinson.ia.us/Department/clerk.asp
(probate records)

Dickinson County Recorder
1802 Hill Avenue
Spirit Lake, IA 51360
(712) 336-1495
jbortscheller@co.dickinson.ia.us
http://www.co.dicksinson.ia.us/Department/recorder.asp
Janice Bortscheller
(land records, vital records)

Dubuque County
organized 1834 from Wisconsin Territory

Dubuque County Clerk of Court
Courthouse
720 Central Avenue
Dubuque, IA 52001-7053
(563) 589-4418
http://www.judicial.state.ia.us/Administration/Directories/Clerks_of_District_Court
(naturalization records, probate records)

Dubuque County Recorder
Courthouse
720 Central Avenue
Dubuque, IA 52001
(563) 589-4434
kathyrec@dbqco.org
http://www.dubuquecounty.org/offices/recorder/index.html
Kathy Flynn Thurlow
(land records, vital records)

Emmet County
organized 1851 from Kossuth and Dickinson counties

Emmet County Clerk of Court
Emmet County Courthouse
609 First Avenue North
Estherville, IA 51334-2254

(712) 362-3325
http://www.emmetcountyia.com/services.htm
(probate records)

Emmet County Recorder
Emmet County Courthouse
609 First Avenue North, Suite 7
Estherville, IA 51334-2255
(712) 362-4115; (712) 362-7454 FAX
record32@netins.net
http://www.emmetcountyia.com/recorder.htm
Sue Snyder
(land records, vital records)
copies of land records: 50¢ per page; certified
    copies of vital records: $15.00 each

Fayette County
organized 1837 from Clayton County

Fayette County Clerk of Court
(Fayette County Courthouse, 114 North Vine
    Street—location)
PO Box 458 (mailing address)
West Union, IA 52175-0458
(319) 422-5694
http://www.fayettecountyiowa.org/CLERKOF
    COURT.html
Elizabeth Nuss
(naturalization records, probate records)
probate search service: no charge; copies of
    land, naturlaization, vital, and probate
    records: 50¢ per page, no minimum

Fayette County Recorder
(Fayette County Courthouse, 114 North Vine
    Street—location)
PO Box 226 (mailing address)
West Union, IA 52175
(563) 422-3687; (563) 422-3739 FAX
kford@co.fayette.ia.us
http://www.fayettecountyiowa.org/RECORDE
    R.html
Karen Ford
(land records, vital records)

Floyd County
organized 1851 from Chickasaw County

Floyd County Clerk of Court
101 South Main Street, Second Floor
Charles City, IA 50616
(641) 228-777; (641) 228-7772 FAX
Barbara.Fuls@jb.state.ia.us
http://www.floydcoia.org/departments/clerkof
    court/index.asp
Barbara Fuls
(naturalization records from 1800s, probate
    records from 1854)
no probate search service

Floyd County Recorder
101 South Main Street
Charles City, IA 50616
(641) 257-6154; (641) 228-6458 FAX
droberts@floydcoia.org
http://www.floydcoia.org/departments/recorde
    r/index.asp
Deborah K. Roberts
(land records, births and deaths from 1880,
    marriages from 1854)
certified copies of vital records: $10.00

Fox County
(see Greene County)

Franklin County
organized 1851 from Chickasaw County

Franklin County Clerk of Court
(12 First Avenue, N.W., Hampton, IA 50441-
    0026—location)
PO Box 28 (mailing address)
Hampton, IA 50441
(515) 456-5626
http://www.judicial.state.ia.us/Administration/
    Directories/Clerks_of_District_Court
(probate records)

Franklin County Recorder
Box 26

Hampton, IA 50441
(641) 456-5675
recorder@co.franklin.ia.us
http://co.franklin.ia.us/pages/recorder
Toni Wilkinson
(land records, vital records)

Fremont County
organized 1847 from Pottawattamie County

Fremont County Clerk of Court
PO Box 549
Sidney, IA 51652-0549
(712) 374-2232
http://www.co.fremont.ia.us/County%20Offici
    als.htm
Marsha Smith
(probate records)

Fremont County Recorder
(506 Filmore Street—location)
PO Box 295 (mailing address)
Sidney, IA 51652-0295
(712) 374-2315
mhenkle@co.fremont.ia.us
http://www.co.fremont.ia.us/fremcorecd.htm
Margaret Henkle
(land records, vital records)
copies of certified copies of vital records:
    $15.00; copies of instruments of record: 50¢
    per page, $5.00 for certification

Greene County
organized 1851 from Dallas County

Greene County Clerk of Court
114 North Chestnut Street, Southeast Office on
    the Second Floor
Jefferson, IA 50129-2114
(515) 386-2516; (515) 386-2321 FAX
http://www.co.greene.ia.us/clerk/clerk.htm
(naturalization records, probate records)

Greene County Recorder
114 North Chestnut Street, Northeast Office on
    the Second Floor
Jefferson, IA 50129
(515) 386-5670; (515) 386-5274 FAX
recorder@co.greene.ia.us
http://www.co.greene.ia.us/recorder/recorder.htm
Marcia Tasler
(land records, vital records)

Grundy County
organized 1851 from Black Hawk County

Grundy County Clerk of Court
Grundy County Courthouse
706 G Avenue
Grundy Center, IA 50638
(319) 824-5229
http://www.grundycounty.org/clerkofcourt/ind
    ex.asp
(naturalization records from April 1870, probate
    records from August 1856, first complete
    probate November 1870)
probate search service: $10.00; copies of probate
    records: 50¢ per page; $10.00 minimum per
    index search

Grundy County Recorder
Grundy County Courthouse
706 G Avenue
Grundy Center, IA 50638
(319) 824-3234
ckruse@gccourthouse.org
http://www.grundycounty.org/recorder/index.asp
Charles E. Kruse
(land records from 1856, births from July 1877
    [incomplete through 1880 and from 1921 to
    1941], deaths from 1880 [incomplete to 1921,
    none from 1921 to 1941])

Guthrie County
organized 1851 from Jackson County

Guthrie County Clerk of Court
Guthrie County Courthouse
200 North Fifth Street
Guthrie Center, IA 50115

(515) 747-3415
http://www.guthriecounty.org/clrkcourt/index.
    html
Rebecca L. Carico
(probate records)

Guthrie County Recorder
Guthrie County Courthouse
200 North Fifth Street
Guthrie Center, IA 50115
(641) 747-3412; (641) 747-3081 FAX
guthrierecorder@netins.net
http://www.guthriecounty.org/recorder/index.
    html
Jackie Sloss
(land records, vital records)

Hamilton County
organized 1856 from Webster County

Hamilton County Clerk of Court
(2300 Superior Street [South Highway 17],
    Webster City, IA 50595-3158—location)
PO Box 845 (mailing address)
Webster City, IA 50595-0845
(515) 832-9600; (515) 832-9519 FAX
http://www.hamiltoncounty.org/page2.html
Darlene L. Dingman
(first and second naturalization papers [no
    applications] from 1880 to 1910, petition and
    records from May 1910 to September 1921,
    declarations of intention from October 1921
    to January 1930, probate records from about
    1857 to date)
records search service: $10.00 (includes cost of
    certified copy); copies of probate records: 50¢
    per page (if no search is needed)

Hamilton County Recorder
(2300 Superior Street [South Highway 17],
    Webster City, IA 50595-3158, Suite 6—
    location)
PO Box 126 (mailing address)
Webster City, IA 50595-0126
(515) 832-9535; (515) 832-8620 FAX
recorder@hamiltoncounty.org
http://www.hamiltoncounty.org/Hamilton%20
    County%20Recorder%20Homepage.html
Kim Anderson
(land records, births and deaths from 1880 to
    date, marriages from 1857 to date)
records search service: $10.00 (includes cost of
    certified copy); copies of land records: 50¢ per
    page (if no search is needed)

Hancock County
organized 1851 from Wright County

Hancock County Clerk of Court
(855 State Street, Garner, IA 50438-1645—
    location)
PO Box 70 (mailing address)
Garner, IA 50438
(515) 923-2532
http://www.hancockcountyia.org
(not very many naturalization records, probate
    records from 1880)
probate search service: $2.00; certified copies:
    $6.00

Hancock County Recorder
Hancock County Government Center
855 State Street
Garner, IA 50438
hanrecsb@hancockcountyia.org
http://www.hancockcountyia.org
Sandra Brunsen
(land records, vital records)

Hardin County
organized 1851 from Black Hawk County

Hardin County Clerk of Court
PO Box 495
Eldora, IA 50627
(515) 858-2328
diane.ryerson@iowacourts.gov
http://www.co.hardin.ia.us/pages/Clerk
Diane L. Ryerson
(limited naturalization records from 1860 to

1940, probate records from 1850s)
probate search service: $6.00 per name; copies
of probate records: 25¢ per page, $6.00 for
certified copies, $6.00 minimum

Hardin County Recorder
(Hardin County Courthouse, 1215 Edgington
Avenue, Suite 4—location)
PO Box 443 (mailing address)
Eldora, IA 50627
(641) 939-8178
bnuss@co.hardin.ia.us
http://www.co.hardin.ia.us/pages/Recorder
Barbara Nuss
(original land entries 1852, deeds from 1852 to
date, book of plats 1892, 1903, 1916 and
current, mortgage records from 1852 to date,
births from 1880 to 1932 and from 1942 to
date, deaths from 1880 to 1920 and from
1942 to date, marriages from 1854 to date)
copies of land records: 50¢ per page

Harrison County
organized 1851 from Pottawattamie County

Harrison County Clerk of Court
Harrison County Courthouse
111 North Second Avenue
Logan, IA 51546-1331
(712) 644-2665
http://www.judicial.state.ia.us/Administration/
Directories/Clerks_of_District_Court
(probate records)

**Harrison County Recorder and Registrar of
Vital Statistics**
Harrison County Courthouse
111 North Second Avenue
Logan, IA 51546
(712) 644-2545; (712) 644-3157 FAX
lthomp@harrisoncountyia.org
http://www.harrisoncountyia.org/recorder/ind
ex.html
Lorie Thompson
(land records, vital records)

Henry County
organized 1836 from Wisconsin Territory

Henry County Clerk of Court
(County Courthouse, 100 East Washington
Street, Suite 203—location)
PO Box 176 (mailing address)
Mt. Pleasant, IA 52641
(319) 385-3150; (319) 385-2632; (319) 385-4203
FAX (Criminal); (319) 385-4144 FAX (Civil)
christine.brakeville@jb.state.ia.us
http://www.henrycountyiowa.us/Clerk%20of%
20Court.html
Christine Brakeville
(probate records)

Henry County Recorder
(County Courthouse, 100 East Washington
Street—location)
PO Box 106 (mailing address)
Mt. Pleasant, IA 52641
(319) 385-0765; (319) 385-3601 FAX
bwallace@co.henry.ia.us
http://www.henrycountyiowa.us/Recorder.html
Bernise Wallace
(land records, vital records)

Howard County
organized 1851 from Chickasaw and Floyd
counties

Howard County Clerk of Court
137 North Elm Street
Cresco, IA 52136-1522
(319) 547-2661
http://www.judicial.state.ia.us/Administration/
Directories/Clerks_of_District_Court
(naturalization records and probate records from
1880)
probate search service: $10.00 per name
("Include dates [from? to?], names [also
maiden names when necessary], parents'
names, cities")

Howard County Recorder
137 North Elm Street
Cresco, IA 52136
(563) 547-3621; (563) 547-2629 FAX
ccaffrey@co.howard.ia.us
http://www.iowacounties.org/News/Publicatio
ns%20Information/2007CountyDirectory/H
owardCounty.mht; http://www.howard-
county.com (Economic Development);
http://www.crescochamber.com (Chamber
of Commerce)
Cherri L. Caffrey
(land records from 1867, vital records from
1880)

Humboldt County
organized 1851 from Webster County

Humboldt County Clerk of Court
(County Courthouse, 203 Main—location)
PO Box 100 (mailing address)
Dakota City, IA 50529
(515) 332-1806
http://www.judicial.state.ia.us/Administration/
Directories/Clerks_of_District_Court
(probate records from 1880)
no probate search service

Humboldt County Recorder
203 Main Street
Dakota City, IA 50529
(515) 332-3693(515) 332-3693; (515) 332-1738
FAX
lfort@humboldtcountyia.org
http://www.humboldtcountyia.org/content/vie
w/8/11
Linda Fort
(naturalization records from May 1871, deeds
from 1856, births and deaths from July 1880)

Ida County
organized 1851 from Cherokee County

Ida County Clerk of Court
401 Moorehead Street
Ida Grove, IA 51445-1429
(712) 364-2628
http://www.judicial.state.ia.us/Administration/
Directories/Clerks_of_District_Court
(naturalization records, probate records)
probate search service: $6.00; copies of probate
records: $6.00, certified $10.00, no minimum

Ida County Recorder
401 Moorehead
Ida Grove, IA 51445
(712) 364-2220; (712) 364-2746 FAX
idacoaud@pionet.net
http://www.iowacounties.org/News/Publicatio
ns%20Information/2007CountyDirectory/Id
aCounty.mht
Jim Clausen
(land records, vital records)

Iowa County
organized 1843 from Washington County

Iowa County Clerk of Court
PO Box 266
Marengo, IA 52301-0266
(319) 642-3914
http://www.co.iowa.ia.us/clerkofcourt.htm
(probate records)

Iowa County Recorder
(901 Court Avenue—location)
PO Box 185 (mailing address)
Marengo, IA 52301
(319) 642-3622; (319) 642-5562 FAX
recorder48@co.iowa.ia.us
http://www.co.iowa.ia.us/recorder.htm
Sue Peterson
(land records, vital records)

Jackson County
organized 1837 from Wisconsin Territory

Jackson County Clerk of Court
201 West Platt Street
Maquoketa, IA 52060-2243

(319) 652-4946
http://www.judicial.state.ia.us/Administration/
Directories/Clerks_of_District_Court
(probate records)

Jackson County Recorder
201 West Platt Street
Maquoketa, IA 52060
(563) 652-2504; (563) 652-6460
aschauf@co.jackson.ia.us
http://co.jackson.ia.us/deptdirectory.htm
Arlene Schauf
(land records, vital records)

Jasper County
organized 1846 from Mahaska County

Jasper County Clerk of Court
(Courthouse, 101 First Street North, Room
104—location)
PO Box 666 (mailing address)
Newton, IA 50208-0666
(515) 792-3255
http://www.co.jasper.ia.us/county_directory1.htm
(naturalization records from early 1900s, probate
records from 1850)
probate search service: no charge; copies of
probate records: 50¢ per page

Jasper County Recorder
Courthouse, 101 First Street North, Room 205
Newton, IA 50208
(641) 792-5442
recorder@co.jasper.ia.us
http://www.co.jasper.ia.us/recorder.htm
Nancy Potter-Parrott
(land records from 1870, births and deaths from
1880, marriage licenses from 1849)

Jefferson County
organized 1839 from Indian lands

Jefferson County Clerk of Court
PO Box 984
Fairfield, IA 52556-0984
(515) 472-3454
http://www.jeffersoncountyiowa.com/court.ht
m
Kay O'Mara
(incomplete naturalization records, probate
records)
probate search service: no charge; copies of
probate records: 25¢ per page, no minimum

Jefferson County Recorder
Jefferson County Courthouse
Court and Briggs
Fairfield, IA 52556
(641) 472-4331; (641) 472-2597 FAX
jeffcorecorder@iowatelecom.net
http://www.jeffersoncountyiowa.com/recorder
Charlotte Fleig
(land records from 1839 vital records from
1880)

Johnson County
organized 1837 from Des Moines County

Johnson County Clerk of Court
(County Courthouse, 417 South Clinton
Street—location)
PO Box 2510 (mailing address)
Iowa City, IA 52240
(319) 356-6060
http://www.johnson-
county.com/location.shtml
(naturalization records from 1880s to 1900s [no
searches or copies available by mail], probate
records from 1843)
vital records search service: $6.00 (includes free
certified copy); probate search service: $6.00,
includes copies

Johnson County Recorder
(Johnson County Administration Building, 913
South Dubuque Street, Iowa City, IA
52240—location)
PO Box 1350 (mailing address)
Iowa City, IA 52244
(319) 356-6093; (319) 339-6181 FAX

kpainter@co.johnson.ia.us
http://www.johnson-
county.com/recorder/index.shtml
Kim Painter
(land records , births and deaths from 1 July
1880, marriages from 1 July 1839)

Jones County
organized 1837 from Wisconsin Territory

Jones County Clerk of Court
(Courthouse, 500 West Main—location)
PO Box 19 (mailing address)
Anamosa, IA 52205-0019
(319) 462-4341
http://www.co.jones.ia.us/countyoffices.ws4d
Sharon Modracek
(probate records)

Jones County Recorder
Courthouse, 500 West Main Street, Room 116
Anamosa, IA 52205
(319) 462-2477; (319) 462-5802 FAX
recorder@co.jones.ia.us
http://www.co.jones.ia.us/recorder.html
Marie Krutzfield
(land records, vital records)

Keokuk County
organized 1844 from Washington County

Keokuk County Clerk of Court
Courthouse, 101 South Main
Sigourney, IA 52591
(515) 622-2210; (641) 622-2171 FAX
http://www.keokukcountyia.com/Clerk%20of
%20Court/Clerk%20of%20Court.com
Linda James, Deputy County Clerk
(naturalization records from 1851, probate
records from 1854)
probate search service: $6.00; copies of probate
records: $1.00 per page, $6.00 minimum;
"Give as much information as possible"

Keokuk County Recorder
Courthouse, 101 South Main Street
Sigourney, IA 52591
(641) 622-2540; (641) 622-3789 FAX
recorder@keokukcountyia.com
http://www.keokukcountyia.com
Nancy T. Snakenberg
(land records from 1845, birth and death records
from 1880, death transcripts 1906–1915,
marriage returns 1880–1906, marriage records
from 1844, record of wills 1851–1968, heir
and land records 1867–1917, cemetery
records, naturalization records 1840–1890,
index/court statements 1854–1867, index to
court records 1854–1864)

Kossuth County
organized 1851 from Webster County

Kossuth County Clerk of Court
114 West State Street
Algona, IA 50511-2613
(515) 295-3240
http://www.judicial.state.ia.us/Administration/
Directories/Clerks_of_District_Court
(probate records)

Kossuth County Recorder
114 West State Street
Algona, IA 50511
(515) 295-5660; (515) 295-3071 FAX
recorder@co.kossuth.ia.us
http://www.co.kossuth.ia.us/recorder/recorder.
htm
Karen Benschoter
(land records, vital records)

Lee County
organized 1836 from Des Moines County

Lee County Clerk of Court
(701 Avenue F—location)
PO Box 1443 (mailing address)
Ft. Madison, IA 52627
(319) 372-3523
http://www.judicial.state.ia.us/Administration/

Directories/Clerks_of_District_Court
(probate records)

Lee County Recorder/Registrar
933 Avenue H
Ft. Madison, IA 52627
(319) 372-4662; (319) 372-7033 FAX
lholtkamp@leecounty.org
http://www.leecounty.org/Services/RecorderSe
rvices.htm;
http://www.leecounty.org/Services/Recorder
/VitalsRequest.htm
Larry Holtkamp
(land records, vital records)

Linn County
organized 1837 from Wisconsin Territory

Linn County Clerk of Court
(Third Avenue Bridge, Cedar Rapids, IA
52401—location)
PO Box 1468 (mailing address)
Cedar Rapids, IA 52406-1468
(319) 398-3411
http://www.co.linn.ia.us/faq.asp?PM=details&
FAQ_Id=416&Content_Id=610
(probate records)
no probate search service ("we forward many
requests to Linn County Heritage Society");
copies of probate records: 25¢ per page, 25¢
minimum

Linn County Recorder
(931 First Street, SW, Cedar Rapids, IA 52404—
location; 930 First Street SW, Cedar Rapids,
IA 52404—temporary location)
PO Box 1406 (mailing address)
Cedar Rapids, IA 52406-1406
(319) 892-5420; (319) 892-5459 FAX
recorder@linncounty.org
http://www.linncountyrecorder.com
Joan McCalmant
(land records, vital records)
certified copies of vital records: $10.00 each
(available only to immediate family)

Louisa County
organized 1836 from Des Moines County

Louisa County Clerk of Court
(Louisa County Courthouse, 117 South Main
Street—location)
PO Box 268 (mailing address)
Wapello, IA 52653-0268
(319) 523-4541; (319) 523-4542 FAX
Melissa.Schoonover@jb.state.ia.us
http://www.louisacountyiowa.org/louisa/clerk/
clerk.html
Melissa Schoonover
(probate records)

Louisa County Recorder/Registrar
(Louisa County Courthouse, 117 South Main
Street—location)
PO Box 264 (mailing address)
Wapello, IA 52653-0264
(319) 523-5361; (319) 523-5364 FAX
recorder58@louisacomm.net
http://www.louisacountyiowa.org/louisa/recor
der/recorder.html
T. Jean Brauns
(land records, vital records)

Lucas County
organized 1846 from Monroe County

Lucas County Clerk of Court
Lucas County Courthouse
916 Braden Avenue
Chariton, IA 50049-1258
(515) 774-4421
http://www.judicial.state.ia.us/Administration/
Directories/Clerks_of_District_Court
(naturalization records [discontinued about
1929-30], probate records)
probate search service: $6.00; copies of probate
records: $1.00 per page

Lucas County Recorder
Lucas County Courthouse

916 Braden Avenue
Chariton, IA 50049
(641) 774-2413
whitet@lucasco.org
http://www.iowacounties.org/News/Publicatio
ns%20Information/2007CountyDirectory/Lu
casCounty.mht
(land records, vital records from 1880 [except
from 1935 to 1940])

Lyon County
organized 1851 from Woodbury County; name
changed from Buncombe County in 1862

Lyon County Clerk of Court
Lyon County Courthouse
206 South Second Avenue
Rock Rapids, IA 51246
(712) 472-2623
http://www.judicial.state.ia.us/Administration/
Directories/Clerks_of_District_Court
(naturalization records, probate records)
probate search service: no charge ("must have
names and dates as close as possible"); copies
of probate records: 25¢ per page, no
minimum

Lyon County Recorder
Lyon County Courthouse
206 South Second Avenue
Rock Rapids, IA 51246
(712) 472-2381; (712) 472-2829 FAX
ekruse@co.lyon.ia.us
http://www.lyoncountyiowa.com/recorder
Eldon Kruse
(land records, vital records)

Madison County
organized 1844 from Polk County

Madison County Clerk of Court
PO Box 152
Winterset, IA 50273-0152
(515) 462-4451
http://www.madisoncoia.us/deptdirectory.htm
(probate records from 1852)
probate search service: no charge; copies of
probate records: 25¢ per page plus postage,
no minimum

Madison County Recorder
112 North John Wayne Drive
Winterset, IA 50273
(515) 462-3771
lsmith@i-rule.net
http://www.madisoncoia.us/recorder/recorder.
html; http://65.240/48/155/rindex.html
(Recorder's Indexing Inquiry); http://www.
madisoncounty.com (Chamber of Commerce)
Lisa Smith
(land records from 1850, births and deaths from
1880, marriages from 1855)
certified copies of land records: $4.00 plus 50¢
per page; vital records search service: $15.00;
certified copies of vital records or
noncertified copies obtained by mail: $15.00;
noncertified copies of vital records obtained
in person: $5.00 copies of land records: $1.00
per page

Mahaska County
organized 1843 from Indian lands

Mahaska County Clerk of Court
(Mahaska County Courthouse, 106 South First
Street—location)
PO Box 1168 (mailing address)
Oskaloosa, IA 52577
(515) 643-7786
http://www.judicial.state.ia.us/Administration/
Directories/Clerks_of_District_Court
(naturalization records from about 1880, probate
records from 1845)
probate search service: $6.00; copies of probate
records: $1.00 per page from old records or
microfilm originals, 25¢ per page for current
records, $6.00 minimum

Mahaska County Recorder
Mahaska County Courthouse

106 South First Street, First Floor
Oskaloosa, IA 52577
(641) 673-8187
recorder@mahaskacounty.org
http://www.mahaskacounty.org/departments/r
ecorder/recorder.html
Diane Upton Crookham
(land records from 1845, vital records from
1880)

Marion County
organized 1845 from Washington County

Marion County Clerk of Court
PO Box 497
Knoxville, IA 50138-0497
(515) 828-2207
http://www.judicial.state.ia.us/Administration/
Directories/Clerks_of_District_Court
(naturalization records, probate records)
no probate search service; copies of probate
records: 20¢ per page in county, $1.00 per
instrument outside of county, no minimum
("If order is quite large and the postage is
going to be quite high, then we ask for
postage")

Marion County Recorder
Marion County Courthouse
214 East Main
Knoxville, IA 50138
(641) 828-2211; (641) 842-3593 FAX
kschwanebeck@co.marion.ia.us
http://co.marion.ia.us
Karen Schwanebeck
(land records from 1845, vital records)

Marshall County
organized 1846 from Jasper County

Marshall County Clerk of Court
17 East Main Street
Marshalltown, IA 50158
(515) 754-1603
http://www.judicial.state.ia.us/Administration/
Directories/Clerks_of_District_Court
(naturalization records, probate records)
no records search service; copies of probate
records: 50¢ per page, no minimum ("If there
is an exact date; no charge for search")

Marshall County Recorder
(1 East Main Street, Third Frloor—location)
PO Box 573 (mailing address)
Marshalltown, IA 50158
(641) 754-6355; (641) 754-6349 FAX
recorder@co.marshall.ia.us
http://www.co.marshall.ia.us/departments/reco
rder; http://www.marshallcountyrecorder.
com
Kathleen K. "Kathy" Baker
(land records, vital records)
certified copies of vital records: $10.00 each

Mills County
organized 1851 from Pottawattamie County

Mills County Clerk of Court
Mills County Courthouse
418 Sharp Street
Glenwood, IA 51534
(712) 527-4880
http://www.judicial.state.ia.us/Administration/
Directories/Clerks_of_District_Court
(probate records)
no probate search service; copies of probate
records: 50¢ each, no minimum

Mills County Recorder
Mills County Courthouse, Main Floor
418 Sharp Street
Glenwood, IA 51534
(712) 527-9315
vmcclintic@millscoia.us
http://www.millscoia.us/recorder/recorder.html
Vicki McClintic
(land records, naturalization records, vital
records)
copies of land records: 50¢ per page ("Our early
record books are bound books and we do not

make copies")

Mitchell County
organized 1851 from Chickasaw County

Mitchell County Clerk of Court
Mitchell County Courthouse
508 State Street
Osage, IA 50461
(515) 732-3726
http://www.mitchellcoia.us/index.php?option=co
m_content&view=article&id=48&Itemid=68
Carol Rossum
(naturalization records from 1857 to 1951,
probate records)
probate search service: no charge; copies of
probate records: 50¢ per page, no minimum

Mitchell County Recorder
Mitchell County Courthouse
508 State Street
Osage, IA 50461
(641) 732-5861; (641) 732-5218 FAX
pskuster@mitchellcoia.us
http://www.mitchellcoia.us/index.php?option=co
m_content&view=article&id=70&Itemid=71
Pat Skuster
(land records from 1854 to date, births from July
1880 to date, deaths from 1880 to date,
marriages from 1855 to date)

Monona County
organized 1851 from Harrison County

Monona County Clerk of Court
(Monona County Courthouse, 610 Iowa
Avenue—location)
PO Box 14 (mailing address)
Onawa, IA 51040-0014
(712) 423-2491
http://www.judicial.state.ia.us/Administration/
Directories/Clerks_of_District_Court
(naturalization records, probate records)
no probate search service; copies of probate
records: 25¢ per page from paper originals,
75¢ per page from microfilm originals, no
minimum

Monona County Recorder
(Monona County Courthouse, 610 Iowa
Avenue—location)
PO Box 53 (mailing address)
Onawa, IA 51040
(712) 433-2575; (712) 423-3034 FAX
mocotlh@longlines.com
http://www.iowacounties.org/News/Publicatio
ns%20Information/2007CountyDirectory/M
ononaCounty.mht
Tena Hinkel
(land records, vital records)

Monroe County
organized 1843 from Wapello County

Monroe County Clerk of Court
Monroe County Courthouse
10 Benton Avenue East
Albia, IA 52531
(515) 932-5212
http://www.judicial.state.ia.us/Administration/
Directories/Clerks_of_District_Court
(naturalization records, probate records)
probate search service: $6.00; copies of probate
records: 25¢ per page, no minimum

Monroe County Recorder
Monroe County Courthouse
10 Benton Avenue East
Abia, IA 52531
(641) 932-5164; (641) 932-5905 FAX
tcasady@monroecoia.us
http://www.iowacounties.org/News/Publicatio
ns%20Information/2007CountyDirectory/C
ounty.mht
Tracy Casady
(land records, vital records)
copies of vital records: $1.00

Montgomery County
organized 1851 from Polk County

Montgomery County Clerk of Court
PO Box 469
Red Oak, IA 51566-0469
(712) 623-4986
http://www.judicial.state.ia.us/Administration/
Directories/Clerks_of_District_Court
(probate records)
no probate search service (contact Fran
Woodworth, Red Oak Public Library)

Montgomery County Recorder
Montgomery County Courthouse
105 Coolbaugh Street
Red Oak, IA 51566
(712) 623-4363; (712) 623-2346 FAX
cbruning@montgomerycoia.us
http://www.iowacounties.org/News/Publicatio
ns%20Information/2007CountyDirectory/M
ontgomeryCounty.mht
Carleen Bruning
(land records, vital records)

Muscatine County
organized 1836 from Des Moines County

Muscatine County Clerk of Court
401 East Third Street
Muscatine, IA 52761
(319) 263-6511; (319) 264-3622 FAX
http://www.co.muscatine.ia.us/departments/cle
_cnt.shtml
Jeff Tollenaer
(sketchy early naturalization records, probate
records)
probate search service: no charge; copies of
probate records: 50¢ ("if we make them"), no
minimum

Muscatine County Recorder
401 East Third Street
Muscatine, IA 52761
(563) 263-7741; (563) 263-7248 FAX
recorder@co.muscatine.ia.us;
cgray@co.muscatine.ia.us
http://www.co.muscatine.ia.us/departments/re
c_cnt.shtml
Cindy Gray
(land records, vital records from 1890)

O'Brien County
organized 1851 from Cherokee County

O'Brien County Clerk of Court
(O'Brien County Courthouse, 155 South
Hayes—location)
Box 430 (mailing address)
Primghar, IA 51245
(712) 757-3255
http://www.judicial.state.ia.us/Administration/
Directories/Clerks_of_District_Court
(probate records)

O'Brien County Recorder
PO Box 340
Primghar, IA 51245
(712) 957-3045; (712) 957-3046 FAX
obrecord@tcacxpress.net
http://www.obriencounty.com/government/re
corder.htm
Kurt Brown
(land records, vital records)

Osceola County
organized 1851 from Woodbury County

Osceola County Clerk of Court
(Osceola County Courthouse, 300 Seventh
Street—location)
PO Box 156 (mailing address)
Sibley, IA 51249
(712) 754-3595; (712) 754-2480 FAX
http://www.osceolacountyia.com/info/courtho
use.php (Osceola County Economic
Development Commission)
Eileen Grave
(naturalization records, probate records from the
early 1880s)
no naturalization, vital, or probate records
search service; copies of naturalizations and
vital records: 25¢ per page, $10.00 for

certified copies, no minimum

Osceola County Recorder
Osceola County Courthouse
300 Seventh Street
Sibley, IA 51249
(712) 754-3345; (712) 754-3743 FAX
akuehl@osceolacoia.org
http://www.osceolacountyia.com/info/courtho
use.php (Osceola County Economic
Development Commission)
Arlene Kuehl
(deeds, mortgages and releases [earliest dated
1869], births, deaths, and marriages)
land records search service: no charge, as time
allows; copies of land records: $1.00 per page,
$2.00 per document for certification

Page County
organized 1847 from Pottawattamie County

Page County Clerk of Court
(Page County Courthouse, 112 East Main
Street—location)
PO Box 263 (mailing address)
Clarinda, IA 51632
(712) 542-3214
http://www.judicial.state.ia.us/Administration/
Directories/Clerks_of_District_Court
(naturalization records, probate records)
copies: 50¢ per document

Page County Recorder
Page County Courthouse
112 East Main Street
Clarinda, IA 51632
(712) 542-3130; (712) 542-5019 FAX
besaias@co.page.ia.us
http://www.co.page.ia.us/offices/recorder/inde
x.htm
Brenda Esaias
(recorded instruments and indexes of land
records, vital records)

Palo Alto County
organized 1851 from Kossuth County

Palo Alto County Clerk of Court
11th and Broadway—location)
PO Box 387 (mailing address)
Emmetsburg, IA 50536-0387
(712) 852-3603
http://www.judicial.state.ia.us/Administration/
Directories/Clerks_of_District_Court
(naturalization records from 1871, probate
records from 1864)

Palo Alto County Recorder
Palo Alto County Courthouse
1010 Broadway
Emmetsburg, IA 50536
(712) 852-3701; (712) 852-3704 FAX
bwhitney@co.palo-alto.ia.us
http://www.iowacounties.org/News/Publicatio
ns%20Information/2007CountyDirectory/Pa
loAltoCounty.mht
Bonnie Whitney
(land records from about 1860, vital records
from 1880)

Plymouth County
organized 1851 from Woodbury County

Plymouth County Clerk of Court
Plymouth County Courthouse
215 Fourth Avenue, S.E.
Le Mars, IA 51031
(712) 546-4215; (712) 546-8430 FAX
http://www.co.plymouth.ia.us/Departments/cl
erkofcourts.htm
Richard L. Kenyon
(naturalization records from 1871, probate
records from 1870)
no records search service (contact Northwest
Iowa Genealogical Society); copies of records:
50¢ each, no minimum

Plymouth County Recorder
Plymouth County Courthouse
215 Fourth Avenue, S.E.

LeMars, IA 51031
(712) 546-4020; (712) 546-7304 FAX
recorder@co.plymouth.ia.us;
jgoodchild@co.plymouth.ia.us
http://www.co.plymouth.ia.us/departments/rec
order.aspx
Jolynn Goodchild
(land records from 1856, births from 1871,
deaths from 1880, marriages from 1860)

Pocahontas County
county formed in part from the extensive limits
of Buchanan and in part from those of
Fayette, created in 1851 from Humboldt and
Greene counties, attached for governmental
purposes in succession to Polk, Boone and
Webster counties, surveyed during 1853-1855,
formally organized in March 1859

Pocahontas County Clerk of Court
County Courthouse, 99 Court Square
Pocahontas, IA 50574
(712) 335-4208
http://www.judicial.state.ia.us/Administration/
Directories/Clerks_of_District_Court
James D. Bartosh
(naturalization records from 1867 through about
1926 [many are incomplete], probate records)
probate search service: no charge for twenty-
year span ("We will look up a record for
genealogy purposes for a search fee of $6
when the request is reasonable and *if* the
information sought has specific dates and
names so that we don't have to spend a lot of
time, such as when the request is vaguely
submitted, i.e., 'I *think* it was *about*"; extensive
searches referred to Pocahontas
County/Laurens Genealogical Society); copies
of probate records: 25¢ or 50¢ per page,
depending on the size of paper, no minimum

Pocahontas County Recorder
County Courthouse, 99 Court Square
Pocahontas, IA 50574
(712) 335-4404
mbollard@pocahontascoia.us;
recorderboy@evertek.net
http://www.iowacounties.org/News/Publicatio
ns%20Information/2007CountyDirectory/Po
cahontasCounty.mhthttp://www.pocahontas-
county.com/communities/resource.htm
(Economic Development)
Michael Bollard
(deeds from mid-1856 , births, deaths, and
marriages [missing for 1905])
vital records search service: $6.00; certified
copies of vital records: $10.00 each; copies of
land records: 25¢ each

Polk County
organized 1846 from Indian lands

Polk County Clerk of Court
500 Mulberry Street, Room 115
Des Moines, IA 50309-4238
(515) 286-3772
http://www.judicial.state.ia.us/Administration/
Directories/Clerks_of_District_Court
William Albright, County Records Supervisor
(naturalization records through 1928, probate
records from 1907 to date [if a case is closed
and five years have passed, files will be on
microfilm])
copies of probate records: 20¢ per page for file
copies, 50¢ per page for microfilm copies,
$4.00 minimum for microfilm copies, plus
SASE, payable in advance

Polk County Recorder
Polk County Administration Building
111 Court Avenue, Suite 250
Des Moines, IA 50309-2251
(515) 286-3160
http://www.polkrecorder.com;
http://www.polkcountyiowa.gov/recorder
Julie Haggerty
(land records, births from 1880 to 1920 and
from 1941 to date, deaths from 1888 to 1907
and from 1941 to date, marriages from 1846
to date)

copies of vital records: $10.00 each, plus SASE,
payable in advance

Pottawattamie County
organized 1848 from Indian lands

Pottawattamie County Clerk of Court
(Pottawattamie County Courthouse, 227 South
Sixth Street—Council Bluffs, IA 51501-
4208—location)
PO Box 476 (mailing address)
Council Bluffs, IA 51502-0476
(712) 328-5604
http://www.pottcounty.com/html/Contact_Inf
o.asp
Ruth Godfrey
(naturalization records from 1890 to 1901,
probate records from the late 1800s to date)

Pottawattamie County Recorder
Pottawattamie County Courthouse
227 South Sixth Street
Council Bluffs, IA 51501
(712) 328-5725 (Information and Vital Records);
(712)-328-5612 (Office)
john.sciortino@pottcounty.com
http://www.pottcounty.com/html/Recorder_O
verview.asp
John Sciortino
(land records, births and deaths from 1880
through 1921 and from 1941 to date,
marriages from 1846 to date [births and
deaths from 1921 through 1941 with Iowa
Department of Public Health])
vital records search service: $10.00 (includes
certified copy)

Poweshiek County
organized 3 April 1843 from Keokuk, Iowa and
Mahaska counties

Poweshiek County Clerk of Court
PO Box 218
Montezuma, IA 50171-0218
(515) 623-5644
http://www.judicial.state.ia.us/Administration/
Directories/Clerks_of_District_Court
(naturalization records [discontinued in early
1990s], probate records from 1840s to date)
copies of naturalization records: $1.00 per page,
$10.00 for certified copies; copies of probate
records: 25¢ per page, $10.00 per document
for certified copies

Poweshiek County Recorder
(Poweshiek County Courthouse, 302 East Main
Street—location)
PO Box 156 (mailing address)
Montezuma, IA 50171
(641) 623-5434; (641) 623-2363 FAX
powcorec@netins.net
http://www.iowacounties.org/News/Publicatio
ns%20Information/2007CountyDirectory/Po
weshiekCounty.mht
Bev Malloy
(land records from 1850 , vital records from
1880 to date)
copies of land records: 25¢ per page; copies of
vital records: $1.00 per page, $10.00 for
certified copies (restricted to relatives or
attorneys)

Ringgold County
organized 1855 from Taylor County

Ringgold County Clerk of Court
Mt. Ayr, IA 50854
(515) 464-3234
cindy_johnson@jb.state.ia.us
http://www.ringgoldcountyiowa.com/crthse.ht
ml
Cindy Johnson
(very few naturalizations from the early 1900s,
probate records from 1915)
probate search service: no charge (as time
permits); copies of probate records: 50¢ per
page, $10.00 for certified copies

Ringgold County Recorder
109 West Madison, Suite 204

Mt. Ayr, IA 50854-1651
(641) 464-3231; (641) 464-2568 FAX
kschaef@iowatelecom.net
http://www.ringgoldcountyiowa.com/crthse.html
Karen Schaefer
(land records, births, deaths and marriages from
1880 ["All our vital records are on microfilm
at our County library"])

Sac County
organized 1851 from Greene County

Sac County Clerk of Court
PO Box 368
Sac City, IA 50583-0368
(712) 662-7791; (712) 662-7978 FAX
http://www.judicial.state.ia.us/Administration/
Directories/Clerks_of_District_Court
(very few naturalizations, probate records from
1888)
probate search service: $10.00 per search; copies
of probate records: 25¢ per page

Sac County Recorder
100 North West State Street
Sac City, IA 50583
(712) 662-7789; (712) 662-6298 FAX
nauen@saccounty.org
http://www.saccounty.org/recorder/index.asp
Nancy Auen
(land records, vital records from 1888)

Scott County
organized 1837 from Wisconsin Territory

Scott County Clerk of Court
Scott County Courthouse
400 West Fourth Street
Davenport, IA 52801-1104
(563) 326-8647; (563) 326-8298 FAX
julie.carlin@jb.state.ia.us
http://www.scottcountyiowa.com/courts/clerk.
php; http://www.scottcountyiowa.com/
courts/probate.php
Julie Carlin
(probate records)

Scott County Recorder
Administrative Center
600 West Fourth Street
Davenport, IA 52801-1003
(563) 326-8621; (563) 328-3225 FAX
recorder@scottcountyiowa.com
http://www.scottcountyiowa.com/recorder
Rita Vargas
(land records, births and deaths from 1880,
marriages from 1838)
certified copies of vital records: $10.00 each

Shelby County
organized 1851 from Cass County

Shelby County Clerk of Court
(Shelby County Recorder, 612 Court Street—
location)
PO Box 431
Harlan, IA 51537-0431
(712) 755-5543
http://www.shco.org/clerk_court.htm
Vicki Krohn
(naturalization records [not very complete],
probate records)
probate search service: no charge; certified
copies of vital records: $10.00 each; copies of
probate records: 50¢ per page, no minimum

Shelby County Recorder
(Shelby County Courthouse, 612 Court Street,
Room 201—location)
PO Box 67 (mailing address)
Harlan, IA 51537-0067
(712) 755-5640; (712) 755-7556 FAX
lfahn@shco.org
http://www.shco.org/recorder.htm
Linda Fahn
(land records , births and deaths from 1880,
marriages from 1853)

Sioux County
organized 1860 from Plymouth County

Sioux County Clerk of Court
PO Box 47
Orange City, IA 51041
(712) 737-2286
http://www.siouxcounty.org
(naturalization records, probate records)
no probate search service; copies of probate
records: 25¢ per page

Sioux County Recorder
(210 Central Avenue, S.W.—location)
PO Box 18 (mailing address)
Orange City, IA 51041
(712) 737-2229; (712) 737-2230 FAX
recorder@siouxcounty.org;
anitavb@siouxcounty.org
http://www.siouxcounty.org/recorder.htm
Anita Van Bruggen
(land records, vital records)

Story County
organized 1846 from Jasper, Polk and Boone
counties

Story County Clerk of Court
PO Box 408
Nevada, IA 50201
(515) 382-6581
http://www.storycounty.com/index.aspx?DN=
6,1,Documents
(probate records)

Story County Recorder
900 Sixth Street
Nevada, IA 50201
(515) 382-7230
recorder@storycounty.com;
svandekamp@storycounty.com
http://www.storycounty.com/index.aspx?DN=
22,6,1,Documents
Susan Vande Kamp
(land records, vital records)

Tama County
organized 1843 from Boone and Benton
counties

Tama County Clerk of Court
PO Box 306
Toledo, IA 52342-0306
(515) 484-3721
http://www.judicial.state.ia.us/Administration/
Directories/Clerks_of_District_Court
(probate records from 1890)
copies: 25¢ per page, no minimum

Tama County Recorder/Registrar
(Tama County Administration Building, 104
West State Street—location)
PO Box 82 (mailing address)
Toledo, IA 52342
(641) 484-3320; (641) 484-8246 FAX
dkupka@tamacounty.org
http://www.tamacounty.org/recorder.html
Deborah Kupka
(land records, births and deaths from 1880,
marriages from 1850 [proof of relationship
required for certified copies of births, deaths
and marriages])

Taylor County
organized 1847 from Page County

Taylor County Clerk of Court
Taylor County Courthouse
405 Jefferson Street
Bedford, IA 50833-1388
(712) 523-2095
http://www.bedford-
iowa.com/countyOffices.HTM
Lori Reed
(naturalization records from 1850, probate
records from 1858)
probate search service: $6.00; copies of probate
records: 50¢ each, no minimum

Taylor County Recorder
Taylor County Courthouse
405 Jefferson Street
Bedford, IA 50833

(712) 523-2275; (712) 523-2274 FAX
taylorrec@frontiernet.net
http://www.bedford-
iowa.com/countyOffices.HTM
Rick Sheley
(land records, vital records from 1880)

Union County
organized 1851 from Clarke County

Union County Clerk of Court
Union County Courthouse
300 North Pine Street, Suite 6
Creston, IA 50801
(515) 782-7315
http://www.unioncountyiowa.org/clerkcourt/in
dex.html
Marsha Parsons
(naturalization records, probate records)
probate search service: $6.00; copies of probate
records: 50¢ each, no minimum ("Payment
must accompany request")

Union County Recorder/Registrar
Union County Courthouse
300 North Pine Street, Suite 5
Crewston, IA 50801
(641) 782-1725; (641) 782-1709 FAX
uncorec@iowatelecom.net
http://www.unioncountyiowa.org/recorder/ind
ex.html
Paula White
(land records, vital records, marriages)
copies of land records: $1.00 per document,
payable in advance; plain paper copies: $5.00
per record

Van Buren County
organized 1836 from Des Moines County

Van Buren County Clerk of Court
(Fourth and Dodge—location)
PO Box 495 (mailing address)
Keosauqua, IA 52565-0495
(319) 293-3108
http://www.judicial.state.ia.us/Administration/
Directories/Clerks_of_District_Court
(wills from 1837 to date)

Van Buren County Recorder
(Va Buren County Courthouse, 406 Dodge
Street—location)
PO Box 455 (mailing address)
Keosauqua, IA 52565
(319) 293-3240; (319) 293-6327 FAX
ggraber@vbcoia.org
http://www.iowacounties.org/News/Publicatio
ns%20Information/2007CountyDirectory/Va
nBurenCounty.mht
Glenice Graber
(land records from 1837, births and deaths from
1880 to date, marriages from 1837 to date)
land records search service: no charge (as time
allows); copies of land records: 25¢ per page

Wapello County
organized 1843 from Indian lands

Wapello County Clerk of Court
101 West Fourth Street
Ottumwa, IA 52501-2518
(515) 683-0060
http://www.judicial.state.ia.us/Administration/
Directories/Clerks_of_District_Court
(probate records)

Wapello County Recorder
Wapello County Courthouse
101 West Fourth Street
Ottumwa, IA 52537
(641) 683-0046; (641) 683-0019 FAX
waprecorder@pcsia.net
http://www.wapellocounty.org;
http://www.iowacounties.org/News/Publica
tions%20Information/2007CountyDirectory/
WapelloCounty.mht
Joyce Hass
(land records, vital records)
vital records search service: $6.00 (must have a
"tangible reason" to obtain birth certificates)

Warren County

organized 1846 from Polk County

Warren County Clerk of Court
PO Box 379
Indianola, IA 50125-0379
(515) 961-1033
http://www.co.warren.ia.us/contacts.htm
Deb Lockwood
(naturalization records from 1862, probate
records from 1858)
probate search service: no charge ("Must request
in writing"); copies of probate records: 25¢
per page, $1.00 minimum

Warren County Recorder
301 North Buxton, Suite 109
Indianola, IA 50125
(515) 961-1089
pollyg@co.warren.ia.us
http://www.co.warren.ia.us/Recorder/recorder.
htm?Dept_Id=27&Page_Id=413
Polly Glascock
(land records, , births and deaths from 1880,
marriages from 1850)

Washington County

organized 1837 from Wisconsin Territory

Washington County Clerk of Court
PO Box 391
Washington, IA 52353-0391
(319) 653-7741
http://www.judicial.state.ia.us/Administration/
Directories/Clerks_of_District_Court
(some unindexed naturalization records, probate
records from 1856)
probate search service: no charge; copies of vital
records: $1.00 each, $6.00 for certified copies

Washington County Recorder
(Washington County Courthouse, 222 West
Main Street, First Floor—location)
PO Box 889 (mailing address)
Washington, IA 52353
(319) 653-7727; (319) 653-7788 FAX
recorder@co.washington.ia.us
http://co.washington.ia.us/electedofficials/reco
rder/index.html
Connie Pence
(land records from 1840, births and deaths from
1880, marriages from 1844)
land records search service: $5.00 for a search of
grantor-grantee indexes for a short period of
years; copies of land records: 25¢ per page

Wayne County

organized 1846 from Appanoose County

Wayne County Clerk of Court
PO Box 435
Corydon, IA 50060
(515) 872-2264
http://www.waynecountyiowa.com/countyInfo
rmation.asp
Traci Tharp
(some naturalization records, probate records
from the 1850s)
no naturalization records search service
(scattered among the records); no probate
search service

Wayne County Recorder
(Wayne County Courthouse, 100 North
Lafayette Street—location)
PO Box 435 (mailing address)
Corydon, IA 50060
(641) 872-1676
recwc@grm.net
http://www.waynecountyiowa.com/countyInfo
rmation.asp (Wayne County Development
Corporation)
Angela Horton
(land records from the 1850s, some naturaliza-
ion records, births and deaths from the 1880s,
marriages from 1851, a few birth certificates
for people born outside of Wayne County)
vital records search service: no charge if supplied
with an approximate date

Webster County

organized 1853 from Yell and Risley counties,
both of which were organized in 1851 and
abolished in 1853

Webster County Clerk of Court
Courthouse, 701 Central Avenue
Fort Dodge, IA 50501-3813
(515) 576-7115
http://www.judicial.state.ia.us/Administration/
Directories/Clerks_of_District_Court
(probate records)

**Webster County Recorder and Registrar of
Vital Statistics**
(Courthouse, 701 Central Avenue, Second
Floor, North Side—location)
PO Box 1253 (mailing address)
Ft. Dodge, IA 50501
(515) 576-2401; (515) 574-3723 FAX
recorder@webstercountyia.org
http://www.webstercountyia.org
Judy Cosgrove
(land records, vital records)

Winnebago County

organized 1847 from Kossuth County

Winnebago County Clerk of Court
PO Box 468
Forest City, IA 50436-0468
(515) 582-4520
http://www.judicial.state.ia.us/Administration/
Directories/Clerks_of_District_Court
(probate records)

Winnebago County Recorder
Winnebago County Courthouse
126 South Clark
Forest City, IA 50436
(641) 582-2094; (641) 585-2891 FAX
winnrec@wctatel.net
http://www.iowacounties.org/News/Publicatio
ns%20Information/2007CountyDirectory/W
innebagoCounty.mht
Kris Colby
(land records, vital records)

Winneshiek County

organized 1847 from Indian lands

Winneshiek County Clerk of Court
201 West Main
Decorah, IA 52101-1775
(319) 382-2469
http://www.judicial.state.ia.us/Administration/
Directories/Clerks_of_District_Court
(naturalization records, probate records)
no probate search service; copies of probate
records: 50¢ (except $1.00 from old books),
no minimum

Winneshiek County Recorder
Winneshiek County Courthouse
201 West Main
Decorah, IA 52101
(563) 382-3486; (563) 387-4083 FAX
lbjergum@co.winneshiek.ia.us
http://www.winneshiekcounty.org/recorder
LaVonne Bjergum
(land records, vital records)

Woodbury County

organized 1851 from Indian Lands

**Woodbury County Auditor and Recorder
and Commissioner of Elections**
Woodbury County Courthouse
620 Douglas Street, Room 103
Sioux City, IA 51101
(712) 279-6465; (712) 279-6629 FAX
pgill@sioux-city.org
http://www.woodburyiowa.com/departments/
Recorder
Patrick F. Gill
(land records from 1809, vital records from 1880
[excluding adoptions and single parent
births])

Woodbury County Clerk of Court

Woodbury County Courthouse
620 Douglas Street, Room 101
Sioux City, IA 51101-1248
(712) 279-6616
http://www.judicial.state.ia.us/Administration/
Directories/Clerks_of_Court
(naturalization records from 1870 to 1932,
probate records from 18 June 1868)
probate search service: no charge; copies of
probate records: 50¢ per page, no minimum

Worth County

organized 1851 from Mitchell County

Worth County Clerk of Court
PO Box 243
Northwood, IA 50459
(515) 324-2840
http://www.worthcounty.org/clerkofcourt.htm
(probate records)

Worth County Recorder
1000 Central Avenue
Northwood, IA 50459
(641) 324-2734; (641) 324-3682 FAX
recorder@worthcounty.org;
wocorec@mchsi.com
http://www.worthcounty.org/Recorder.htm
Liz Kenison
(land records, vital records)

Wright County

organized 1851 from Webster County (Polk
County, then Boone, then Webster), set up
1855

Wright County Clerk of Court
PO Box 306
Clarion, IA 50525-0306
(515) 532-3113
http://www.wrightcounty.org/county_offices.htm
Sue Harrison
(naturalization records from the 1860s to date,
probate records from 1880)
no records search service (contact Wright
County Genealogical Searchers); copies of
records: 25¢ per page (no copying service
with courthouse)

Wright County Recorder
(Courthouse, 115 North Main—location)
PO Box 187 (mailing address)
Clarion, IA 50525
(515) 532-3204; (515) 532-2669 FAX
recorder@co.wright.ia.us
http://www.wrightcounty.org/recorder.htm
Dwight Reiland
(land records from 1850 to date, vital records
from 1880)

KANSAS

Capital: Topeka. Statehood: 29 January 1861 (annexed as part of the Louisiana Purchase, 1803, territory created by the Kansas-Nebraska Act, 1854)

Kansas has about 384 Municipal Courts of limited jurisdiction. The thirty-one District Courts, sitting at each county seat, have general jurisdiction over civil and criminal matters, and probate. First Judicial District: Atchison and Leavenworth counties; Second Judicial District: Jackson, Jefferson, Pottawatomie and Wabaunsee counties; Third Judicial District: Shawnee County; Fourth Judicial District: Anderson, Coffey, Franklin and Osage counties; Fifth Judicial District: Chase and Lyon counties; Sixth Judicial District: Bourbon, Linn and Miami counties; Seventh Judicial District: Douglas County; Eighth Judicial District: Dickinson, Geary, Marion and Morris counties; Ninth Judicial District: Harvey and McPherson counties; Tenth Judicial District: Johnson County; Eleventh Judicial District: Cherokee, Crawford and Labette counties; Twelfth Judicial District: Cloud, Jewell, Lincoln, Mitchell, Republic and Washington counties; Thirteenth Judicial District: Butler, Elk and Greenwood counties; Fourteenth Judicial District: Chautauqua and Montgomery counties; Fifteenth Judicial District: Cheyenne, Logan, Rawlins, Sheridan, Sherman, Thomas and Wallace counties; Sixteenth Judicial District: Clark, Comanche, Ford, Gray, Kiowa and Meade counties; Seventeenth Judicial District: Decatur, Graham, Norton, Osborne, Phillips and Smith counties; Eighteenth Judicial District: Sedgwick County; Nineteenth Judicial District: Cowley County; Twentieth Judicial District: Barton, Ellsworth, Rice, Russell and Stafford counties; Twenty-first Judicial District: Clay and Riley counties; Twenty-second Judicial District: Brown, Doniphan, Marshall and Nemaha counties; Twenty-third Judicial District: Ellis, Gove, Rooks and Trego counties; Twenty-fourth Judicial District: Edwards, Hodgeman, Lane, Ness, Pawnee and Rush counties; Twenty-fifth Judicial District: Finney, Greeley, Hamilton, Kearny, Scott and Wichita counties; Twenty-sixth Judicial District: Grant, Haskell, Morton, Seward, Stanton and Stevens counties; Twenty-seventh Judicial District: Reno County; Twenty-eighth Judicial District: Ottawa and Saline counties; Twenty-ninth Judicial District: Wyandotte County; Thirtieth Judicial District: Barber, Harper, Kingman, Pratt and Sumner counties; Thirty-first Judicial District: Allen, Neosho, Wilson and Woodson counties. A Court of Appeals and the state's Supreme Court have appellate jurisdiction.

Allen County
organized 1855, original county

Allen County Clerk
1 North Washington
Iola, KS 66749
(620) 365-1407; (620) 365-1441 FAX
coclerk@allencounty.org
http://www.allencounty.org/clerk/index.htm
Sherrie L. Riebel
(vital records)

Allen County Clerk of District Court
(1 North Washington, Iola, KS 66749-2841—
location)
PO Box 630 (mailing address)
Iola, KS 66749-0630
(620) 365-1425; (620) 365-1429 FAX
jbarrow@aceks.com
http://www.allencounty.org/judicial/index.htm
Jennifer Barrow
(naturalization records, probate records)
no probate search service ("However, if you
have a date, we can check to see if there is an
estate filed."); copies of probate records: 25¢
per page plus postage, no minimum

Allen County Register of Deeds
1 North Washington
Iola, KS 66749-2835
(620) 365-1412; (620) 365-1414 FAX
regofdeeds@allencounty.org
http://www.allencounty.org/regdeeds/index.htm
Cara Barkdoll
(land records)

Anderson County
organized 1855, original county

Anderson County Clerk
County Courthouse
100 East Fourth Avenue
Garnett, KS 66032-1500
(785) 448-6841; (785) 448-5621 FAX
pgettler@hotmail.com;
 AN_County_Clerk@wan.kdor.state.ks.us
http://andersoncountyks.org/clerk.html
Phyllis Gettler
(vital records)

Anderson County Clerk of District Court
(100 East Fourth Avenue, Garnett, KS 66032-
1503—location)
PO Box 305 (mailing address)
Garnett, KS 66032-0305
(785) 448-6886; (785) 448-3230 FAX
kreynolds@aceks.com
http://www.kscourts.org/dstcts/4anco.htm
Kara Reynolds
(naturalization records and probate records)

Anderson County Register of Deeds
100 East Fourth
Garnett, KS 66032
(785) 448-3715; (785) 448-3275 FAX
ancoregofdeeds@terraworld.net
http://andersoncountyks.orgregister-of-
deeds.html
Sandra J. Baugher
(land records)

Atchison County
organized 1855, original county

Atchison County Clerk
423 North Fifth Street
Atchison, KS 66002
(785) 367-1653; (913) 367-0227 FAX
AT_County_Clerk@wan.kdor.state.ks.us
http://www.atchisoncountyks.org/index.asp?NI
D=3
Pauline M. Lee
(vital records)
certified copies of vital records: $6.00 each
(requests should be in writing)

Atchison County Clerk of District Court
(425 North Fifth Street—location)
PO Box 408 (mailing address)
Atchison, KS 66002-0408
(913) 367-7400; (913) 367-1171 FAX
http://www.atchisoncountyks.org/index.asp?NI
D=7
Donna M. Oswald
(naturalization records from 1858–1953, births
and deaths from 1891–1911 [sketchy,
formerly belonged to a doctor], marriage
records 1855 to date, probate records from
1855 to date)
research: $12.00 per hour; copies: 25¢ per page,
$1.00 for certification

Atchison County Register of Deeds
423 North Fifth Street
Atchison, KS 66002-1861
(913) 367-2568; (913) 367-8441 FAX
atcorod@sbcglobal.net
http://www.atchisoncountyks.org/index.asp?NI
D=4
Marlene Wagner
(land records from 1855)
land records search service: $8.00; copies of land
records: 25¢ each, $1.00 for certified copies

Barber County
organized 1873 from Harper County

Barber County Clerk
120 East Washington Street
Medicine Lodge, KS 67104-1421
(620) 886-3961
bacoclerk4@cyberlodg.com
http://www.kssos.org/forms/communication/c
ounty.pdf
Debbie Wesley
(vital records)

Barber County Clerk of District Court
118 East Washington Street
Medicine Lodge, KS 67104
(720) 886-5639; (620) 886-5854 FAX
http://www.kscourts.org/dstcts/30dstct.htm
Ann McNett

Barber County Register of Deeds
120 East Washington Street
Medicine Lodge, KS 67104
(620) 886-3981; (620) 886-5045 FAX
barod@cyberlodg.com
http://www.barbercounty.net (Barber County
Development)
Betty Jo Swayden
(land records)

Barton County
organized 1867 from Ellsworth County

Barton County Clerk
(1400 Main Street, Suite 202—location)
PO Box 1089 (mailing address)
Great Bend, KS 67530
(620) 793-1835; (620) 793-1990 FAX
clerk@bartoncounty.org;
 kevers@bartoncounty.org
http://www.bartoncounty.org/clerk/index.htm
Donna Zimmerman
(vital records)

Barton County Clerk of District Court
1400 Main Street, Room 306
Great Bend, KS 67530-4098
(620) 793-1856; (620) 793-1860 FAX
http://www.kscourts.org/districts/Courthouse-
info.asp?d=20&cid=65
Sandra Kennedy
(probate records)
probate search service: $9.00 per hour ("it is
very important for us to have correct spellings
and accurate dates"); copies of probate
records: 35¢ per page (Xerox), 50¢ per page
(microfilm), no minimum

Barton County Register of Deeds
1400 Main Street, Suite 205
Great Bend, KS 67530-4037
(620) 793-1849; (620) 793-1981 FAX
phyde@opiwireless.com;
 phyde@bartoncounty.org
http://www.bartoncounty.org/regdeeds/index.
htm
Pam Hyde
(land records)

Bourbon County
organized 1855, original county

Bourbon County Clerk
210 South National Street
Fort Scott, KS 66701-1328
(620) 223-3800
countyclerk@bourboncountyks.org
http://www.bourboncountyks.org
Joanne Long
(vital records)

Bourbon County Clerk of District Court
Sixth Judicial District
(210 South National Street—location)
PO Box 868 (mailing address)
Ft. Scott, KS 66701-0868
(620) 223-0780; (620) 223-5303 FAX
http://www.kscourts.org/dstcts/6bbco.htm
Karen Paddock
(marriages and divorces)

Bourbon County Register of Deeds
210 South National Street
Ft. Scott, KS 66701

(620) 223-3800; (620) 223-5241 FAX
selder@bourboncountyks.org;
bourbonrod@hotmail.com
http://www.bourboncountyks.org/register_of_
deeds.htm
Sharon Elder
(land records)

Brown County
organized 1855, original county

Brown County Clerk
Brown County Courthouse
601 Oregon Street
Hiawatha, KS 66434
(785) 742-2581; (785) 742-7705 FAX
dparker@brcoks.org
http://www.brown.kansasgov.com/MV2Base.as
p?VarCN=9
Debbie Parker
(vital records)

Brown County Clerk of District Court
(Brown County Courthouse, 601 Oregon Street,
Third Floor—location)
PO Box 417 (mailing address)
Hiawatha, KS 66434-0417
(785) 742-7481; (785) 742-3506 FAX
lsmith@brdistcrt.org
http://www.brown.kansasgov.com/MV2Contac
ts.asp?VarCN=8

Brown County Register of Deeds
Brown County Courthouse
601 Oregon Street
Hiawatha, KS 66434-2283
(785) 742-3741; (785) 742-7705 FAX
scarter@brcoks.org
http://www.brown.kansasgov.com/MV2Base.as
p?VarCN=2
Sandy Carter
(land records)

Butler County
organized 1855, original county

Butler County Clerk
Courthouse
205 West Central, Suite 205
El Dorado, KS 67042
(316) 322-4239; (800) 822-7119
rroberts@bucoks.com
http://www.bucoks.com/elected/clerk.htm
Ron Roberts
(vital records)

Butler County Clerk of District Court
201 West Pine, Suite 101
El Dorado, KS 67042-2947
(316) 322-4370; (800) 595-3651; (316) 321-9486
FAX
ca-neal@southwind.net
http://www.bucoks.com/butlerco.htm#jud

Butler County Register of Deeds
Courthouse
205 West Central, Suite 104
El Dorado, KS 67042
(316) 322-4113; (800) 822-6803; (316) 321-1011
FAX
regdeeds@bucoks.com; mmccoy@bucoks.com
http://www.bucoks.com/elected/register.htm
Marcia McCoy
(land records)

Chase County
organized 1859 from Butler County

Chase County Clerk
(300 Pearl—location)
Box 547 (mailing address)
Cottonwood Falls, KS 66845-0547
(620) 273-6423
http://www.kssos.org/forms/communication/c
ounty.pdf; http://www.chasecountychamber.
org (Chamber of Commerce); http://www.
chasecountyks.org (unofficial site)
(vital records)

Chase County Clerk of District Court
(300 Pearl—location)

PO Box 529 (mailing address)
Cottonwood Falls, KS 66845
(620) 273-6319; (620) 273-6890 FAX
http://www.lyoncounty.org/Dist_Crt_Director
y.htm
Barbara J. Davis

Chase County Register of Deeds
PO Box 529
Cottonwood Falls, KS 66845-0059
(620) 273-6398; (620) 273-6617 FAX
cscrod@yahoo.com
http://www.kssos.org/forms/communication/c
ounty.pdf
Kathy J. Swift
(land records)

Chautauqua County
organized 1875 from Howard County, which
was organized in 1855 (named Godfrey and
changed to Seward in 1867) and abolished at
the time of its division into Chautauqua and
Elk counties

Chautauqua County Clerk
215 North Chautauqua Street
Sedan, KS 67361-1326
(620) 725-3282
cqclerk@yahoo.com
http://www.kssos.org/forms/communication/c
ounty.pdf
Lori Martin
(vital records)

Chautauqua County Clerk of District Court
(215 North Chautauqua Street, Sedan, KS
67361-1326—location)
PO Box 306 (mailing address)
Sedan, KS 67361-0306
(620) 725-5870; (620) 725-3027 FAX
http://www.kscourts.org/districts/District-
Info.asp?d=14
(probate records)
no probate search service; copies of probate
records: 25¢ each

Chautauqua County Register of Deeds
215 North Chautauqua Street
Sedan, KS 67361
(620) 725-5830; (620) 725-3256 FAX
http://www.kssos.org/forms/communication/c
ounty.pdf
Laura Beeson
(land records)

Cherokee County
organized 1855 from unorganized territory;
name changed from McGee County between
1860 and 1870

Cherokee County Clerk
300 East Maple
Columbus, KS 66725-1806
(620) 429-2042
ck_county_clerk@wan.kdor.state.ks.us
http://www.kssos.org/forms/communication/c
ounty.pdf
Sandra Soper
(vital records)

Cherokee County Clerk of District Court
(Cherokee County Courthouse, 110 West
Maple—location)
PO Box 189 (mailing address)
Columbus, KS 66725-0189
(620) 429-3880; (620) 429-1130 FAX
http://www.kscourts.org/dstcts/11cherco.htm
research: $12.00 per hour; copies: 25¢ per page

Cherokee County Register of Deeds
PO Box 228
Columbus, KS 66725
(620) 429-3777; (620) 429-1362 FAX
christy.rod@cherokeecounty-ks.gov
http://www.kssos.org/forms/communication/c
ounty.pdf
Christy Grant
(land records)

Cheyenne County
organized 1886 from Rawlins County

Office of the Clerk of the District Court
(212 East Washington—location)
PO Box 646 (mailing address)
St. Francis, KS 67756-0646
(785) 332-8850; (785) 332-8851 FAX
cndist@stks.net
http://www.cheyennecounty.org/clerkofthecou
rt.htm
Sharon Elliott
(naturalization records, probate records)
no probate search service (contact Marilyn
Holzwarth, PO Box 671, St. Francis, KS
67756); copies of probate records: 25¢ per
page, 25¢ minimum

Office of the County Clerk
PO Box 985
St. Francis, KS 67756-0985
(785) 332-8800; (785) 332-8825 FAX
cn_county_clerk@wan.kdor.state.ks.us
http://www.cheyennecounty.org/clerk.htm
Terry Miller
(vital records)

Office of the Register of Deeds
PO Box 907
St. Francis, KS 67756
(785) 332-8820; (785) 332-8825 FAX
cn_county_rod@wan.kdor.state.ks.us
http://www.cheyennecounty.org/registerofdeed
s.html
Mary Morrow
(land records)

Clark County
organized 1873 from Ford County

Clark County Clerk
County Courthouse
PO Box 886
Ashland, KS 67831-0886
(620) 635-2813
cacoclrk@ucom.net
http://www.clarkcountyks.com/page.php?4
Rebecca Mishler
(vital records)

Clark County Clerk of District Court
(913 Highland—location)
PO Box 790 (mailing address)
Ashland, KS 67831
(620) 635-2753; (620) 635-2155 FAX
http://www.kscourts.org/dstcts/16courts.htm
Sherre Harrington
(naturalization records and probate records)

Clark County Register of Deeds
PO Box 222
Ashland, KS 67831
(620) 635-2812; (620) 635-2393 FAX
cacorod@ucom.net
http://www.clarkcountyks.com/page.php?8
Lynn Young
(land records)

Clay County
organized 1857, original county

Clay County Clerk
(Courthouse, 712 Fifth Street, First Floor—
location)
PO Box 98 (mailing address)
Clay Center, KS 67432-0098
(785) 632-2552; (785) 632-5856 FAX
cyclerk@sbcglobal.net
http://www.cckansas.org/county_clerk.php
Mary Brown
(vital records from 1885 to 1911)
vital records search service: $5.00 minimum

Clay County Clerk of District Court
(Courthouse, 712 Fifth Street—location)
PO Box 203 (mailing address)
Clay Center, KS 67432-0203
(785) 632-3443; (785) 632-2651 FAX
http://www.cckansas.org/county_officers.php
Kayla Ernsting

(naturalization records, probate records)
probate search service: $9.00 per hour; copies of
probate records: 25¢ per page

Clay County Register of Deeds
(Courthouse, 712 Fifth Street—location)
PO Box 63 (mailing address)
Clay Center, KS 67432-0063
(785) 632-3811; (785) 632-2736 FAX
claycorod@sbcglobal.net; cyrod@sbcglobal.net
http://www.cckansas.org/register_of_deeds.php
Virginia "Gayle" Link
(land records)

Cloud County
organized 1860 from unorganized territory;
   name changed from Shirley County in 1861

Cloud County Clerk
Courthouse
811 Washington Street
Concordia, KS 66901-3415
(785) 243-4319
clerk@cloudcountyks.org
http://www.cloudcountyks.org/MV2Base.asp?
   VarCN=39
Linda Bogart
(vital records to 1911)

Cloud County Clerk of District Court
(Courthouse, 811 Washington Street, Concordia,
   KS 66901-3415—location)
PO Box 314 (mailing address)
Concordia, KS 66901
(785) 243-8124; (785) 243-8188 FAX
leaw@12jd.org
http://www.kscourts.org/dstcts/12dstct.htm
Lea Welch
(naturalization records, probate records)
probate search service: $2.00 per search; copies
   of probate records: 25¢ per page, no
   minimum

Cloud County Register of Deeds
PO Box 96
Concordia, KS 66901-0096
(785) 243-8121; (785) 243-8123 FAX
tferguso@dustdevil.com;
   deeds@cloudcountyks.org
http://www.cloudcountyks.org/MV2Base.asp?
   VarCN=57
Terry Ferguson
(land records)

Coffey County
organized 1855 from Kiowa County

Coffey County Clerk
Courthouse
110 South Sixth
Burlington, KS 66839
(316) 364-2191
angiek@coffeycountyks.org
http://www.coffeycountyks.org/service5.html
Angie Kirchner
(births and deaths from 1892 to 1910)
certified copies of vital records: $1.15 each

Coffey County Clerk of District Court
(Courthouse, 110 South Sixth—location)
PO Box 330 (mailing address)
Burlington, KS 66839-0330
(620) 364-8628; (620) 364-8535 FAX
districtcourt@coffeycountyks.org
http://www.kscourts.org/dstcts/4coco.htm
Debbie Poire
(naturalization records, marriage licenses, and
   probate records)
probate search service: as time permits; copies
   of naturalization records: 15¢ per page; copies
   of probate records: from 15¢ to $1.00 per
   page, $1.00 minimum plus SASE

Coffey County Register of Deeds
Courthouse, 110 South Sixth, Room 205
Burlington, KS 66839-1791
(620) 364-2423; (620) 364-8975 FAX
GBirk@coffeycountyks.org
http://www.coffeycountyks.org/service13.html
Gwen R. Birk
(land records)

Comanche County
organized 1875 from Kiowa County

Comanche County Clerk
(Courthouse, 201 South New York—location)
PO Box 776 (mailing address)
Coldwater, KS 67029-0776
(316) 582-2361
cm.county.clerk@wan.kdor.state.ks.us
http://www.comanchecounty.com/contacts.htm
Alice Smith
(vital records from 1891 to 1912)

Comanche County Clerk of District Court
(201 South New York—location)
PO Box 722 (mailing address)
Coldwater, KS 67029-0722
(620) 582-2182; (620) 582-2603 FAX
http://www.kscourts.org/dstcts/16courts.htm
Patricia Hayse

Comanche County Register of Deeds
PO Box 576
Coldwater, KS 67029-0576
(620) 582-2152; (620) 582-2390 FAX
comcorod@giantcomm.net
http://www.kssos.org/forms/communication/c
   ounty.pdf
Guyneth Snyder
(land records from 1883)
copies of land records: $1.50 per page

Cowley County
organized 1867; name changed from Hunter
   County

Cowley County Clerk
Courthouse, 311 East Ninth Avenue
Winfield KS 67156
(620) 221-5400; (620) 441-4500 ; (620) 221-5498
   FAX
clclerk@cowleycounty.org
http://www.cowleycounty.org/clerk.htm
Karen Brooks
(vital records)

Cowley County Clerk of District Court
Arkansas City Office
(City Hall Building—location)
PO Box 1152 (mailing address)
Arkansas City, KS 67005
(620) 441-4520; (620) 442-7213 FAX
http://www.kscourts.org/districts/District-
   Info.asp?d=19
Marilyn Leith

Cowley County Clerk of District Court
Winfield Office
Courthouse, 311 East Ninth Avenue, #216
Winfield, KS 67156
(620) 221-5470; (620) 441-4530 FAX
http://www.kscourts.org/districts/District-
   Info.asp?d=19
Marilyn Leith

Cowley County Register of Deeds
(Courthouse, 311 East Ninth Avenue—location)
PO Box 741 (mailing address)
Winfield, KS 67156
(620) 221-5461; (620) 221-5463 FAX
registerofdeeds@cowleycounty.org
http://www.cowleycounty.org/register.htm
Nancy Horst
(land records)

Crawford County
organized 1867 from Bourbon and Cherokee
   counties

Crawford County Clerk
PO Box 249
Girard, KS 66743-0249
(620) 724-6115
countyclerk@ckt.net
http://www.crawfordcountykansas.org;
   http://www.crawfordcountykansas.com/cler
   k/index.html
R. J. Wilson
(births and deaths from 1886 to 1911)
certified copies of births and deaths: $3.00 each

Crawford County Clerk of District Court
Girard Division
(Crawford County Courthouse, 111 East Forest
   Street, Third Floor–location)
PO Box 69 (mailing address)
Girard, KS 66743-0069
(620) 724-6212; (620) 724-4987 FAX
http://www.kscourts.org/dstcts/11crawco2.htm
(naturalization records, marriage licenses,
   probate records)

Crawford County Clerk of District Court
Pittsburg Division
Crawford County Judicial Center
602 North Locust
Pittsburg, KS 66762-1348
(620) 231-0380; (620) 231-0316 FAX
http://www.kscourts.org/dstcts/11crawco2.htm

Crawford County Register of Deeds
PO Box 44
Girard, KS 66743
(620) 724-8218; (620) 724-8823 FAX
ncpote@ckt.net
http://www.kssos.org/forms/communication/c
   ounty.pdf
Jeanette Nepote
(land records)

Decatur County
organized 1873 from Norton County

Decatur County Clerk
120 East Hall Street
Oberlin, KS 67749
(785) 475-8102
mah_2000_67749@yahoo.com
http://www.kssos.org/forms/communication/c
   ounty.pdf
Marilyn Horn
(births from 10 November 1885 to 6 July 1911
   [with some gaps], deaths from 5 December
   1885 to 31 July 1911 [with some gaps])

Decatur County Clerk of District Court
(120 East Hall Street—location)
PO Box 89 (mailing address)
Oberlin, KS 67749-0089
(785) 475-8107; (785) 475-8170 FAX
http://www.kscourts.org/districts/District-
   Info.asp?d=17
Janet Meitl
(naturalization initial papers from 1881 to 1906,
   petitions and records from 1901 to 1929, first
   papers from 1880 to 1894, marriages from 21
   February 1880 [with some gaps], probate
   records from 2 March 1900)
no probate search service ("The Decatur County
   Historical Society will do research"); copies of
   probate records: 25¢ per page (8½" x 11"),
   30¢ (17" x 11") plus certification

Decatur County Register of Deeds
PO Box 167
Oberlin, KS 67749-0167
(785) 475-8105; (785) 475-8150 FAX
judydcrod@yahoo.com;
   dc.county.rod@wan.kdor.state.ks.us
http://www.kssos.org/forms/communication/c
   ounty.pdf
Judy B. Gaumer
(land records from 1885)

Dickinson County
organized 1855, original county

Dickinson County Clerk
(Courthouse, 109 East First—location)
PO Box 248 (mailing address)
Abilene, KS 67410-0248
(785) 263-3774
dk_county_clerk@wan.kdor.state.ks.us
http://www.dkcoks.com/clerk.htm
Sandra Emig
(births from 1895 to 1911, deaths from 1901 to
   1911)

Dickinson County Clerk of District Court
(Courthouse, 109 East First Street, Second
   Floor—location)
PO Box 127 (mailing address)

Abilene, KS 67410-0127
(785) 263-3142, ext. 300; (785) 263-4407 FAX
dkcdc@8thjd.com
http://www.8thjd.com;
http://www.dkcoks.com/Court.htm
Cindy J. MacDonald
(some naturalization records, marriages from the 1870s, probate records from the 1870s)
probate search service: usually no charge ("Have correct names and the dates as close as you can to the time that you are searching for"); copies of probate records: $1.00 per page, no charge

Dickinson County Register of Deeds
PO Box 517
Abilene, KS 67410
(785) 263-3073; (785) 263-0428 FAX
dkrod@dkcoks.com
http://www.dkcoks.com/directory.htm
Linda Jones
(land records from 1859 [deeds, mortgages, land patents, oil & gas leases and other miscellaneous documents])
land records search service: no charge; copies of land records: 25¢ per page from paper originals, $1.00 per page from microfilm

Doniphan County
organized 1855, original county

Doniphan County Clerk
Courthouse, 120 East Chestnut
Troy, KS 66087
(785) 985-3513
dp_county_clerk@wan.kdor.state.ks.us
http://www.dpcountyks.com
Peggy Franken
(vital records)

Doniphan County Clerk of District Court
(120 East Chestnut—location)
PO Box 295 (mailing address)
Troy, KS 66087
(785) 985-3582; (785) 985-2402 FAX
http://www.dpcountyks.com; http://www.
  kscourts.org/districts/District-Info.asp?d=22
Janice Kay Wanlass

Doniphan County Register of Deeds
PO Box 73
Troy, KS 66087
(785) 985-3932; (785) 985-3723 FAX
donrod@carsoncomm.com
http://www.dpcountyks.com
Susan J. Shuster
(land records)

Douglas County
organized 1855, original county

Douglas County Clerk
1100 Massachusetts Street
Lawrence, KS 66044
(785) 832-5267
jshew@douglas-county.com
http://www.douglas-county.com/clerk.asp
Jamie Shew
(vital records)

Douglas County Clerk of District Court
Judicial Center
111 East 11th Street
Lawrence, KS 66044-2966
(785) 832-5333; (785) 832-5256 (Court); (785) 832-5174 FAX; (785) 832-5258 FAX (Records Department)
courtrecords@douglas-county.com;
dhamilton@douglas-county.com
http://www.douglas-county.com/
  District_Court/dc.asp
Douglas A. Hamilton
(naturalization records from 1865 to 1920, probate records)
probate search service: $9.00 per hour; copies of probate records: 25¢ per page, no minimum ("Money must be estimated and paid in advance; request must be in writing or in person")

Douglas County Register of Deeds

(Courthouse, 1100 Massachusetts Street, Lawrence, KS 66044-3097—location)
PO Box 747 (mailing address)
Lawrence, KS 66044-0747
(785) 832-5282; (785) 330-2807 FAX
kpesnell@douglas-county.com
http://www.douglas-county.com/register_of_deeds/rd.asp
Kay Pesnell
(land records)

Edwards County
organized 1874 from Kiowa County

Edwards County Clerk
312 Massachusetts Avenue
Kinsley, KS 67547-1059
(620) 659-3121
edwardsclerk@edwards.kscoxmail.com
http://www.kssos.org/forms/communication/county.pdf; http://www.edwardscounty.org
Gina Schuette
(vital records)

Edwards County Clerk of District Court
(312 Massachusetts Avenue, Kinsley, KS 67547-1059—location)
PO Box 232 (mailing address)
Kinsley, KS 67547-0232
(620) 659-2442; (620) 659-2998 FAX
eddistct@edwards.kscoxmail.com
http://www.kscourts.org/dstcts/24direct.htm
Linda Atteberry
(naturalization records, probate records)

Edwards County Register of Deeds
PO Box 264
Kinsley, KS 67547
(620) 659-3131; (620) 659-2583 FAX
edwardsdeeds@edwards.kscoxmail.com
http://www.kssos.org/forms/communication/county.pdf
Emily Kay White
(land records)

Elk County
organized 1875 from Howard County, which was organized in 1855 (named Godfrey and changed to Seward in 1867) and abolished at the time of its division into Chautauqua and Elk counties

Elk County Clerk
Courthouse, 127 North Pine
Howard, KS 67349
(316) 374-2490; (877) 504-2490; (620) 374-2771 FAX
ekclerk@sktc.net
http://www.elk.kansasgov.com/MV2Base.asp?VarCN=6
Donna Kaminska
(vital records)
vital records search service: $5.00; copies of vital records: 25¢ plus postage

Elk County Clerk of District Court
(Courthouse, 127 North Pine—location)
PO Box 306 (mailing address)
Howard, KS 67349-0306
(620) 374-2370; (620) 374-3531 FAX
http://www.kscourts.org/districts/District-Info.asp?d=13
Sharle M. Watkins
(probate records)
probate search service: $3.00 plus extra time; copies of probate records: 25¢ (standard size), $1.00 (oversized), no minimum

Elk County Register of Deeds
(Courthouse, 127 North Pine—location)
PO Box 476 (mailing address)
Howard, KS 67349-0476
(620) 374-2472; (620) 374-2771 FAX
http://www.elk.kansasgov.com/MV2Base.asp?VarCN=7
Neva L. Walter
(land records)
land records search service: $5.00; copies of land records: 25¢ plus postage

Ellis County
organized 1867 from unorganized territory

Ellis County Clerk
(Courthouse, 1204 Fort Street—location)
PO Box 720 (mailing address)
Hays, KS 67601
(785) 628-9410; (785) 628-9413 FAX
ellisoclk@ellisco.net
http://www.ellisco.net/index.asp?DocumentID=222
Alberta Klaus
(vital records)

Ellis County Clerk of District Court
(Courthouse, 1204 Fort Street, Third Floor—location)
PO Box 8 (mailing address)
Hays, KS 67601-0008
(785) 628-9415; (785) 628-8415 FAX
http://www.23rdjudicial.org/ellis.htm
Phil Fielder
(naturalization records, probate records)

Ellis County Register of Deeds
(Courthouse, 1204 Fort Street—location)
PO Box 654 (mailing address)
Hays, KS 67601
(785) 628-9450; (785) 628-9451 FAX
bdeed@ellisco.net; rod@ellisco.net
http://www.ellisco.net/index.asp?DocumentID=228
Rebecca Herzog
(land records)

Ellsworth County
organized 1867 from Saline County

Ellsworth County Clerk
Courthouse, 210 North Kansas Avenue
Ellsworth, KS 67439
(785) 472-4161; (785) 472-3818 FAX
ewclerk@kans.com
http://www.ellsworthcounty.org/clerk.htm
Janet Andrews
(vital records)

Ellsworth County Clerk of District Court
Courthouse, 210 North Kansas Avenue
Ellsworth, KS 67439-3118
(785) 472-4052; (785) 472-5712 FAX
http://www.ellsworthcounty.org/Courts.html
Peggy Svaty
(naturalization records, probate records from 1881)
probate search service: no charge ("Written requests only"); copies of probate records: 35¢ per page, no minimum

Ellsworth County Register of Deeds
(Courthouse, 210 North Kansas Avenue—location)
PO Box 306 (mailing address)
Ellsworth, KS 67439
(785) 472-3022; (785) 472-4912 FAX
jsneath@ellsworth.net
http://www.ellsworthcounty.org/Register%20Deeds.html
Janice Sneath
(land records from 1872)
copies of land records: $1.00 per page

Finney County
organized 1883 from Arapahoe and Foote counties; Garfield County was annexed to Finney County in 1893

Finney County Clerk
(County Administrative Center, 311 North Ninth—location)
PO Box M (mailing address)
Garden City, KS 67846-0450
(620) 276-3051
clerk1@finneycounty.org
http://www.finneycounty.org/clerk.askp
Elsa Ulrich
(vital records)

Finney County Clerk of District Court
(425 North Eighth Street—location)

PO Box 798 (mailing address)
Garden City, KS 67846-0450
(620) 271-6120; (620) 271-6140 FAX
http://www.kscourts.org/districts/District-
Info.asp?d=25
Chrstine Blake

Finney County Register of Deeds
(County Administrative Center, 311 North
Ninth—location)
PO Box M (mailing address)
Garden City, KS 67846-0450
(620) 272-3628; (620) 272-3624 FAX
register@finneycounty.org
http://www.finneycounty.org/register
Rita Alsop
(land records)

Ford County
organized 1873 from unorganized territory

Ford County Clerk
Ford County County Center
100 Gunsmoke Street
Dodge City, KS 67801-4456
(620) 227-4550; (620) 227-4699 FAX
vwells@fordcounty.net
http://www.fordcounty.net/coclerk
Victoria Wells
(vital records)

Ford County Clerk of District Court
(Courthouse, 101 West Spruce—location)
PO Box 197 (mailing address)
Dodge City, KS 67801-0197
(620) 227-4609; (620) 227-6799 FAX
http://www.kscourts.org/dstcts/16courts.htm
Diane McElwain

Ford County Register of Deeds
PO Box 1352
Dodge City, KS 67801
(620) 227-4565; (620) 227-4566 FAX
bpogue@fordcounty.net
http://www.fordcounty.net/rod
Brenda Pogue
(land records)

Franklin County
organized 1855, original county

Franklin County Clerk
315 South Main
Ottawa, KS 66067
(785) 229-3410; (785) 229-3419 FAX
sperry@mail.franklincoks.org
http://www.franklincoks.org/clerk/clerk.html
Shari Perry
(vital records)

Franklin County Clerk of District Court
(301 South Main—location)
PO Box 637 (mailing address)
Ottawa, KS 66067-0637
(785) 242-6000; (785) 242-5970 FAX
vmills@mail.franklincoks.org
http://www.kscourts.org/dstcts/4frco.htm
Vicki Mills

Franklin County Register of Deeds
315 South Main, Room 103
Ottawa, KS 66067
(785) 229-3440; (785) 229-3441 FAX
smccay@mail.franklincoks.org
http://www.franklincoks.org
Sue A. McCay
(land records)

Geary County
organized 1876 from Riley County; name
changed from Davis County in 1889

Geary County Clerk
200 Easth Eighth
Junction City, KS 66441
(785) 238-3912; (785) 238-5419 FAX
rebecca.bossemeyer@gearycounty.org
http://www.geary.kansasgov.com/MV2Base.asp
?VarCN=3
Rebecca Bossemeyer
(vital records)

Geary County Clerk of District Court
(138 East Eighth Street—location)
PO Box 1147 (mailing address)
Junction City, KS 66441-1147
(785) 762-5221, ext. 1431; (785) 762-4420 FAX
gecdc@8thjd.com
http://www.8thjd.com
Alice Adams
(naturalization records and probate records)
probate search service: $9.00 per hour; copies of
probate records: $1.00 per page, no minimum

Geary County Register of Deeds
(Geary County Courthouse Annex, 200 East
Eighth Street—location)
PO Box 927 (mailing address)
Junction City, KS 66441
(785) 238-5531; (785) 762-2642 FAX
diane.briestensky@gearycounty.org;
briestensky@jcks.com
http://www.geary.kansasgov.com/MV2Base.asp
?VarCN=171
Diane Lynn Briestensky
(land records)

Gove County
organized 1880 from Rooks County

Gove County Clerk
PO Box 128
Gove, KS 67736-0128
(785) 938-2300
go_county_clerk@wan.kdor.state.ks.us
http://www.kssos.org/forms/communication/c
ounty.pdf
Julie Hawkey
(births and deaths to 1911)

Gove County Clerk of District Court
(420 Broad Street—location)
PO Box 97 (mailing address)
Gove, KS 67736-0097
(785) 938-2310; (785) 938-2726 FAX
http://www.23rdjudicial.org
Wanita Cook
(naturalization records and probate records)
no probate search service

Gove County Register of Deeds
PO Box 116
Gove, KS 67736
(785) 938-4465; (785) 938-4486
cristytuttle@hotmail.com; goregofd@ruraltel.net
http://www.kssos.org/forms/communication/c
ounty.pdf
Cristy Tuttle
(land records)

Graham County
organized 1881 from Rooks County

Graham County Clerk and Election Officer
410 North Pomeroi Avenue
Hill City, KS 67642-1645
(785) 421-3453; (785) 421-6374 FAX
grahcocl@ruraltel.net
http://www.grahamcountyks.com/page.php?2
Jana Irby
(vital records)

Graham County Clerk of District Court
Courthouse, 410 North Pomeroi Avenue
Hill City, KS 67642-1645
(785) 421-3458; (785) 421-5463 FAX
http://www.kscourts.org/districts/District-
Info.asp?d=17
Donna Elliott

Graham County Register of Deeds
Courthouse, 410 North Pomeroi Avenue
Hill City, KS 67642
(785) 421-2551; (785) 421-2784 FAX
ghdeeds@ruraltel.net
http://www.grahamcountyks.com/page.php?4
Juanita Toll
(land records)

Grant County
organized 1873 from Finney and Kearny
counties

Grant County Clerk
Courthouse, 108 South Glenn Street
Ulysses, KS 67880-2551
(620) 356-1335; (620) 356-3081 FAX
clerk@pld.com
http://www.grantcoks.org/index.asp?nid=55
Linda McHenry
(vital records)

Grant County Clerk of District Court
Courthouse, 108 South Glen Street
Ulysses, KS 67880-2551
(620) 356-1526; (620) 353-2131 FAX
http://www.grantcoks.org/Directory.asp?DID=7
Loyetta Skeen

Grant County Register of Deeds
Courthouse, 108 South Glenn Street
Ulysses, KS 67880
(620) 356-1538; (620) 356-5379 FAX
gtrod@pld.com
http://www.grantcoks.org/index.asp?nid=126
Mary K. Sullivan
(land records)

Gray County
organized 1887 from Finney and Ford counties

Gray County Clerk
(Courthouse—location)
PO Box 487 (mailing address)
Cimarron, KS 67835-0487
(620) 855-3618; (620) 855-3107 FAX
bswartz@grayco.org
http://www.kssos.org/forms/communication/c
ounty.pdf
Bonnie Swartz
(vital records)

Gray County Clerk of District Court
(300 South Main—location)
PO Box 487 (mailing address)
Cimarron, KS 67835-0487
(620) 855-3812; (620) 855-7037 FAX
http://www.kscourts.org/dstcts/16courts.htm
Sandy Salmans
(naturalization records, probate records)

Gray County Register of Deeds
PO Box 487
Cimarron, KS 67835-0487
(620) 855-3835; (620) 855-3107 FAX
mgriffin@grayco.org
http://www.kssos.org/forms/communication/c
ounty.pdf
Marla Griffin
(land records)

Greeley County
county attached to Hamilton County for judicial
purposes in March 1886, organized 6
November 1888

Greeley County Clerk
(208 Harper—location)
PO Box 277 (mailing address)
Tribune, KS 67879-0277
(620) 376-4256; (620) 376-2294 FAX
gl_county_clerk@wan.kdor.state.ks.us;
l_firner@hotmail.com
http://www.greeleycountygovernment.org/clerk
.html
Linda Firner
(vital records)

Greeley County Clerk of District Court
(616 Second Avenue—location)
PO Box 516 (mailing address)
Tribune, KS 67879-0516
(620) 376-4292; (620) 376-2351 FAX
http://www.kscourts.org/districts/District-
Info.asp?d=25
Debra Riley
(naturalization records, probate records)

Greeley County Register of Deeds
(616 Second Street—location)
PO Box 12 (mailing address)
Tribune, KS 67879
(620) 376-4275; (620) 376-2294 FAX
gcrods@sunflowertelco.com; gcrod@pld.com
http://www.greeleycountygovernment.org/regd

eed.html
Lisa K. Robertson
(land records)

Greenwood County
organized 1855, original county

Greenwood County Clerk
Courthouse, 311 North Main Street
Eureka, KS 67045
(620) 583-8121; (620) 583-8124 FAX
greenwoodcountyclerk@yahoo.com
http://www.greenwoodcounty.org
Debbie Wyckoff
(vital records from 1885 to 1911)

Greenwood County Clerk of District Court
Courthouse, 311 North Main Street
Eureka, KS 67045
(620) 583-8153; (620) 583-6818 FAX
http://www.kscourts.org/districts/District-Info.asp?d=13
Tami Evenson
(mostly complete naturalization records, probate records)
no probate search service; copies of probate records: 25¢; genealogical inquiries to the County Clerk are referred to the Greenwood County Historical Society (117 North Main, Eureka, KS 67045), which accepts donations for its volunteer services; (316) 583-8121; (316) 583-8124 FAX.

Greenwood County Register of Deeds
Courthouse, 311 North Main Street
Eureka, KS 67045
(620) 583-8162; (620) 583-8178 FAX
rodmarsharamsey@yahoo.com
http://www.greenwoodcounty.org
Marsha E. Ramsey
(patent and deed records from 1850s)

Hamilton County
organized 1873 from unorganized territory

Hamilton County Clerk
(Courthouse, 219 North Main—location)
PO Box 1167 (mailing address)
Syracuse, KS 67878
(620) 384-5629; (620) 384-5853 FAX
hm_county_clerk@wan.kdor.state.ks.us
http://www.hamiltoncountyks.com/departments/clerk.htm
Marcia Ashmore
(vital records)

Hamilton County Clerk of District Court
(Courthouse, 219 North Main—location)
PO Box 745 (mailing address)
Syracuse, KS 67878-0745
(620) 384-5159; (620) 384-7806 FAX
http://www.hamiltoncountyks.com/departments/court.htm
(probate records)
copies of probate records: $1.00 per page

Hamilton County Register of Deeds
PO Box 1167
Syracuse, KS 67878
(620) 384-6925; (620) 384-5853 FAX
hmcorod@wbsnet.org
http://www.hamiltoncountyks.com/departments/deeds.htm
Vicki Valentine
(land records)
copies of land records: $1.00 per page

Harper County
organized 1879 from Kingman County

Harper County Clerk
County Courthouse
201 North Jennings Street, Second Floor
Anthony, KS 67003-2799
(620) 842-5555; (877) 537-2110; (620) 842-3455 FAX
coclerk@midway.net; clerk@harpercountyks.gov
http://harpercountyks.gov/index.asp?NID=19
Cheryl Adelhardt
(vital records)

Harper County Clerk of District Court
(County Courthouse, 201 North Jennings Street—location)
PO Box 467 (mailing address)
Anthony, KS 67003
(620) 842-3721; (620) 842-6025 FAX
http://www.kscourts.org/dstcts/30dstct.htm
Tracy Aleshire
(probate records)
probate records search service: no charge; copies of probate records: 25¢ per page, $1.00 for certification, no minimum

Harper County Register of Deeds
County Courthouse
201 North Jennings Street
Anthony, KS 67003
(620) 842-5336; (877) 537-2110; (620) 842-3455 FAX
deeds@harpercountyks.gov
http://harpercountyks.gov/index.asp?NID=120
Rhonda Berry
(land records)
land records search service: no charge; copies of land records: $1.00 per page

Harvey County
organized 1872 from McPherson and Sedgwick counties

Harvey County Clerk
Courthouse, Eighth and Main
Newton, KS 67114-1807
(316) 284-6840; (316) 284-6856 FAX
jtruskett@harveycounty.com
http://www.harveycounty.com
Joyce Truskett
(vital records)

Harvey County Clerk of District Court
(Courthouse, Eighth and Main—location)
PO Box 665 (mailing address)
Newton, KS 67114-0665
(316) 284-6890; (316) 283-4601 FAX
http://www.harveycounty.com
Robin Becker
(naturalization records, probate records)

Harvey County Register of Deeds
PO Box 687
Newton, KS 67114-0687
(316) 284-6950; (316) 284-6951 FAX
mhermstein@harveycounty.com
http://www.harveycounty.com
Margaret Hermstein
(land records)

Haskell County
organized 1887 from Finney County

Haskell County Clerk
(Courthouse, 300 South Inman—location)
PO Box 518 (mailing address)
Sublette, KS 67877-0518
(620) 675-2263; (620) 675-2681 FAX
hscoclk@pld.com
http://www.haskellcounty.org/clerk.html
Sharon Hinkle
(vital records)

Haskell County Clerk of District Court
(300 South Inman—location)
PO Box 146 (mailing address)
Sublette, KS 67877
(620) 675-2671; (620) 675-8599 FAX
http://www.haskellcounty.org/clerkofcourt.html
Phyllis Merz

Haskell County Register of Deeds
(Courthouse, 300 South Inman—location)
PO Box 656 (mailing address)
Sublett, KS 67877-0656
(620) 675-8343; (620) 675-8142 FAX
hscoregofdeeds@hotmail.com
http://www.haskellcounty.org/register.html
Candy Huffine
(land records)

Hodgeman County
organized 1873 from Indian lands

Hodgeman County Clerk
(Courthouse, 500 Main—location)
PO Box 247 (mailing address)
Jetmore, KS 67854-0247
(620) 357-6421
hg_county_clerk@wan.kdor.state.ks.us
http://www.kssos.org/forms/communication/county.pdf
Barbara Smidt
(vital records)

Hodgeman County Clerk of District Court
(Courthouse, 500 Main—location)
PO Box 187 (mailing address)
Jetmore, KS 67854-0187
(620) 357-6522; (620) 357-6216 FAX
hgdistct@sunflowertelco.com
http://www.kscourts.org/dstcts/24direct.htm
Linda Burkhart

Hodgeman County Register of Deeds
PO Box 505
Jetmore, KS 67854-0505
(620) 357-8536; (620) 357-6161 FAX
paulajlonnberg@hotmail.com
http://www.kssos.org/forms/communication/county.pdf
Paula Lonnberg
(land records)

Jackson County
organized 1855 from Calhoun County

Jackson County Clerk
Courthouse, 400 New York Street
Holton, KS 66436-1787
(785) 364-2891; (785) 364-4204 FAX
jacountyclerk@yahoo.com;
 JA_County_Clerk@wan.kdor.state.ks.us
http://www.jackson.kansasgov.com/MV2Base.asp?VarCN=81
Kathy Mick
(vital records)

Jackson County Clerk of District Court
Courthouse, 400 New York Street, Room 311
Holton, KS 66436
(785) 364-2191; (785) 364-3804 FAX
creamer@holtonks.net
http://www.kscourts.org/dstcts/2jackco.htm
Mon–Fri 8:00–4:30
(naturalization records, marriages, and probate records from 1854)
probate search service: $9.00 per hour; copies of probate records: 25¢ per page, no minimum

Jackson County Register of Deeds
Courthouse, 400 New York Street, Room 203
Holton, KS 66436
(785) 364-3591; (785) 364-3420 FAX
jadeeds@hotmail.com
http://www.jackson.kansasgov.com/MV2Base.asp?VarCN=18
Tammy Moulden
(deeds, mortgages, etc. from 1959, school records from 1883 to 1966)

Jefferson County
organized 1855, original county

Jefferson County Clerk
PO Box 321
Oskaloosa, KS 66066-0321
(785) 863-2272; (877) 278-4118; (785) 863-3135 FAX
lbuttron@jfcountyks.com
http://county-clerk.jfcountyks.com
Linda Buttron
(vital records)

Jefferson County Clerk of District Court
(300 Jefferson Street—location)
PO Box 327 (mailing address)
Oskaloosa, KS 66066-0327
(785) 863-2461; (785) 863-2369 FAX
jfcodistct@ruralnet1.com
http://www.kscourts.org/dstcts/2jeffco.htm
Connie Milner

Jefferson County Register of Deeds
(Courthouse on the Square, Room 104—

location)
PO Box 352 (mailing address)
Oskaloosa, KS 66066-0352
(785) 863-2243; (785) 863-2602 FAX
dheston@jfcountyks.com
http://deeds.jfcountyks.com
Delia A. Heston
(land records)

Jewell County
organized 1867 from Mitchell County

Jewell County Clerk
307 North Commercial Street
Mankato, KS 66956
(913) 378-3121
JW_County_Clerk@wan.kdor.state.ks.us
http://www.nckcn.com/homepage/jewell_co/J
EWELL.HTM (Community Development
Association)
Carla Waugh
(vital records)

Jewell County Clerk of District Court
307 North Commercial Street
Mankato, KS 66956-2025
(785) 378-4030; (785) 378-4035 FAX
dixiea@12jd.org
http://www.kscourts.org/dstcts/12dstct.htm
Dixie Abram
(naturalization records from 1872 to 1937,
marriages from 1871 probate records from
1871)
probate records search service: no charge; copies
of probate records: 25¢ per page plus postage,
no minimum

Jewell County Register of Deeds
307 North Commercial
Mankato, KS 66956-2093
(785) 378-4070; (785) 378-4075 FAX
marypowell@hotmail.com
http://www.kssos.org/forms/communication/c
ounty.pdf
Mary L. Powell
(land ownership from when land patented,
assessment rolls from 1871, school records
from 1884, unofficial register of births,
marriages and deaths [only births are indexed]
from 1886 to 1894)
land and probate records search service: no
charge; copies of land records: $1.00 per page
plus postage

Johnson County
organized 1855, original county

Johnson County Clerk of District Court
Johnson County Courthouse
100 North Kansas Avenue
Olathe, KS 66061-3273
(913) 715-3300; (913) 715-3401 (Civil); (913)
715-3461 (Criminal); (913) 715-3371
(Probate); (913) 715-3317 FAX
court.admin@jocogov.org
http://courts.jocogov.org
(probate records)

**Johnson County Records and Tax
Administration**
Johnson County Administration Building
Johnson County Square
111 South Cherry Street, Suite 1200
Olathe, KS 66061
(913) 715-0775
john.bartolac@jocogov.org
http://www.jocogov.org
John Bartolac
(consolidation of the offices of County Clerk
and Register of Deeds)

Kearny County
organized 1873 from Finney County

Kearny County Clerk
(Courthouse, 304 North Main—location)
PO Box 86 (mailing address)
Lakin, KS 67860
(620) 355-6422
ke_county_clerk@wan.kdor.state.ks.us

http://www.kearnycountykansas.com/kearnyco
unty/countyofficials.html
Jana Jenkinson
(births, deaths and marriages from 1900 to 1910)

Kearny County Clerk of District Court
(Courthouse, 304 North Main—location)
PO Box 64 (mailing address)
Lakin, KS 67860-0064
(620) 355-6481; (620) 355-7462 FAX
(naturalization records, probate records)
probate search service: $9.00 per hour; copies of
probate records: 25¢ per page, no minimum

Kearny County Register of Deeds
PO Box 42
Lakin, KS 67860
(620) 355-6241; (620) 355-7382 FAX
keksrod@hotmail.com
http://www.kearnycountykansas.com/kearnyco
unty/countyofficials.html
Melissa (Missie) Gerritzen
(land records)

Kingman County
organized 1874 from unorganized territory

Kingman County Clerk
Courthouse, 130 North Spruce Street
Kingman, KS 67068
(620) 532-2521
km.county.clerk@wan.kdor.state.ks.us
http://skyways.lib.ks.us/towns/Kingman/govt.
html
Inge Luptsford
(vital records)

Kingman County Clerk of District Court
(Courthouse, 130 North Spruce Street—
location)
PO Box 495 (mailing address)
Kingman, KS 67068-0495
(620) 532-5151; (620) 532-2952 FAX
http://www.kscourts.org/dstcts/30dstct.htm
Staci Jackson
(naturalization records and probate records)
no land records search services; probate search
service: $9.00 per hour; copies of probate
records: 25¢ per page, $2.00 minimum

Kingman County Register of Deeds
Courthouse, 130 North Spruce Street, Fourth
Floor
Kingman, KS 67068
(620) 532-3211; (620) 532-5079 FAX
kmrod@sbcglobal.net
http://skyways.lib.ks.us/towns/Kingman/govt.
html
Susan Hubbell
(land records, deaths)

Kiowa County
organized 1886 from Comanche and Edwards
counties, abolished in 1875, and recreated in
1886 from Comanche and Edwards counties

Kiowa County Clerk of District Court
Courthouse, 211 East Florida Street, Second
Floor
Greensburg, KS 67054-0211
(620) 723-3317; (620) 723-2970 FAX
http://www.kowacounty.us/districtcourt.htm;
http://www.kscourts.org/dstcts/16courts.htm
Debra Schmidt
(probate records)
probate search service: $9.00 per hour; copies of
probate records: 25¢ per page plus SASE, no
minimum

Kiowa County Register of Deeds
Courthouse, 211 East Florida Street, First Floor
Greensburg, KS 67054
(620) 723-2441; (620) 723-3320 FAX
rod@kiowacounty.us
http://www.kowacounty.us/registerofdeeds.htm
Sharren Thatch
(land records)

Kiowa County Clerk
Courthouse, 211 East Florida Street, First Floor
Greensburg, KS 67054

(620) 723-3366; (620) 723-3234 FAX
clerk@kiowacounty.us;
kw_county_clerk@wan.kdor.state.ks.us
http://www.kowacounty.us/clerk.htm
Evelyn Grimm, Clerk
(vital records)

Labette County
organized 1867 from Neosho County

Labette County Clerk
PO Box 387
Oswego, KS 67356
(620) 795-2138; (620) 421-5255; (620) 795-2928
FAX
lschreppel@labettecounty.com
http://www.labettecounty.com/1_Directory/Di
rectory%20Clerk.htm
Linda Schreppel
(births from 1885 to 1896, deaths from 1885 to
1889)

Labette County Clerk of District Court
Oswego Division
Labette County Courthouse
417 Merchant Street, Third Floor
Oswego, KS 67356
(620) 795-4533, ext. 7; (620) 421-5255, ext. 7;
(620) 795-3056 FAX
dstrickland@labettecounty.com
http://www.kscourts.org/dstcts/11labeco2.htm
Donna Strickland
(probate records)
no probate search service; copies of probate
records: 25¢ per page

Labette County Clerk of District Court
Parsons Division
Labette County Judicial Center
201 South Central
Parsons, KS 67357
(620) 421-4120; (620) 421-3633 FAX
http://www.kscourts.org/dstcts/11labeco2.htm

Labette County Register of Deeds
501 Merchant
Oswego, KS 67356
(620) 795-4931; (620) 795-2138 FAX
dstrickland@labettecounty.com
http://www.labettecounty.com
Donna Strickland
(land records from 1869)

Lane County
organized 1873 from Finney County

Lane County Clerk
(Courthouse, 144 South Lane—location)
PO Box 788 (mailing address
Dighton, KS 67839-0788
(620) 397-5356; (620) 397-5419 FAX
c_torson@hotmail.com
http://www.kssos.org/forms/communication/c
ounty.pdf
Crysta Torson
(vital records from 1885 to 1915)

Lane County Clerk of District Court
(Courthouse, 144 South Lane—location)
PO Box 188 (mailing address)
Dighton, KS 67839-0188
(620) 397-2805; (620) 397-5526 FAX
ledistct@st-tel.net
http://www.kscourts.org/dstcts/24direct.htm
Pamela Davis
(naturalization records from 1885 to 1935,
marriage licenses from 1885, estates from
1885)
probate search service: $8.00 per hour; copies of
probate records: 25¢ per page plus postage

Lane County Register of Deeds
PO Box 805
Dighton, KS 67839
(620) 397-2803; (620) 397-5937 FAX
LECounty_RegisterofDeeds@wan.kdor.state.ks.us
http://www.kssos.org/forms/communication/c
ounty.pdf
Betty Terhune
(land records from 1885)

Leavenworth County

organized 1855, original county

Leavenworth County Clerk
Courthouse, 601 South Third Street
Leavenworth, KS 66048
(913) 684-0421
lscheer@leavenworthcounty.org
http://www.leavenworthcounty.org/clerk/defa
ult.htm
Linda Scheer
(vital records)

Leavenworth County Clerk of District Court
601 South Third Street, Suite 3051
Leavenworth, KS 66048-2868
(913) 684-0700; (913) 684-0492 FAX
http://www.leavenworthcounty.org/dc/default.
htm
Darla Farnsworth
(very few naturalization records available ["as
courthouse fire in 1911 destroyed a great
many of them"], marriages and probate
records)
probate search service: no charge at present;
copies of probate records: 25¢ per page, $1.00
for certified copies, no minimum ("If copies
are requested by mail, payment should be by
money order, not cash or personal check")

Leavenworth County Register of Deeds
300 Walnut
Leavenworth, KS 66048
(913) 684-0424; (913) 684-0406 FAX
sdriscoll@leavenworthcounty.org
http://www.leavenworthcounty.org/rod/defaul
t.htm
Stacy Driscoll
(land records)

Lincoln County

organized 1867 from Ellsworth County

Lincoln County Clerk
Courthouse, 216 East Lincoln Avenue
Lincoln, KS 67455
(785) 524-4757; (785) 524-5008 FAX
lcclerk@nckcn.com
http://www.lincolncoks.com/NV2Base.asp?Var
CN=6
Dawn Harlow
(vital records)

Lincoln County Clerk of District Court
Courthouse, 216 East Lincoln Avenue
Lincoln, KS 67455
(785) 524-4757; (785) 524-3204 FAX
joh@12jd.org
http://www.kscourts.org/dstcts/12dstct.htm
JoAnn Hachmeister
(naturalization records, marriages, probate
records)

Lincoln County Register of Deeds
Courthouse, 216 East Lincoln Avenue
Lincoln, KS 67455-2056
(785) 524-4657; (785) 524-5003 FAX
lcregdeeds@nckcn.com
http://www.lincolncoks.com/MV2Base.asp?Var
CN=4
Tami L. Kerth
(land records)
copies: 35¢ per page

Linn County

organized 1855, original county

Linn County Clerk
(Courthouse, 315 Main Street—location)
PO Box 350 (mailing address)
Mound City, KS 66056-0601
(913) 795-2668; (913) 795-2889 FAX
dlamb@linncountyks.com
http://www.linncountyks.com/html/clerk.html
David Lamb
(vital records)

Linn County Clerk of District Court
(Judicial Building, 318 Chestnut—location)
PO Box 350 (mailing address)

Mound City, KS 66056-0350
(913) 795-2660; (913) 795-2004 FAX
AWare@linncountyks.com;
clerksoffice@linncountyks.com
http://www.kscourts.org/dstcts/6linnco.htm
Ann Ware
(naturalization records [very limited information]
and probate records)
probate search service: $10.00 per hour by Linn
County Historical and Genealogical Society,
$5.00 for travel

Linn County Register of Deeds
(Courthouse, 315 Main Street—location)
PO Box 350 (mailing address)
Mound City, KS 66056
(913) 795-2226; (913) 795-2889 FAX
kschmitz@linncountyks.com
http://www.linncountyks.com/html/registerofd
eeds.html
Kristy S. Schmitz
(land records)
land search service: $10.00 per hour by Linn
County Historical and Genealogical Society,
$5.00 for trip to the courthouse; copies of
land records: 10¢ per page

Logan County

organized 1887 from the entirety of St. John
County, which was established 13 March 1881
out of what previously had been in the
eastern part of Wallace County

Logan County Clerk
Courthouse, 710 West Second Street
Oakley, KS 67748-1251
(785) 672-4244
lg_county_clerk@wan.kdor.state.ks.us
http://www.kssos.org/forms/communication/c
ounty.pdf
Pat Schippers
(vital records)

Logan County Clerk of District Court
Courthouse, 710 West Second Street
Oakley, KS 67748-1233
(785) 672-3654; (785) 672-3517 FAX
http://www.kscourts.org/districts/District-
Info.asp?d=15
Nancy Gladin
(probate records)
probate search service with Abstracters' Office;
copies of probate records: 25¢ per page, $1.00
minimum

Logan County Register of Deeds
Courthouse, 710 West Second Street
Oakley, KS 67748-1251
(785) 672-4224; (785) 672-3517 FAX
lgrod@ruraltel.net
http://www.kssos.org/forms/communication/c
ounty.pdf
Joyce Bosserman
(land records)

Lyon County

organized 1857 from Madison County (which
was abolished at the time it was divided
between Lyon and Greenwood counties);
name changed from Breckinridge County in
1862

Lyon County Clerk
402 Commercial Street
Emporia, KS 66801-4000
(620) 341-3243; (620) 341-3415 FAX
lyclerk@lyoncounty.org
http://www.lyoncounty.org/Clerk.htm
Karen Hartenbower
(vital records)

Lyon County Clerk of District Court
430 Commercial Street, Room 203
Emporia, KS 66801
(620) 341-3281; (620) 341-3497 FAX
http://www.lyoncounty.org/FifthJudicialDistric
t.htm
Jeanne S. Turner
(naturalization records and probate records)
probate search service: $6.60 per hour ("Most

things take one hour; send $6.60 in advance;
Lyon County Historical Society might help
you"); copies of probate records: 50¢ per
page, no minimum

Lyon County Register of Deeds
430 Commercial Street
Emporia, KS 66801
(620) 341-3241; (620) 341-3438 FAX
vlopez@lyoncounty.org
http://www.lyoncounty.org/Register%20of%20
Deeds.htm
Victoria Lopez
(land records)

Marion County

organized 1855 from Chase County

Marion County Clerk
(Courthouse, 200 South Third, Courthouse
Square—location)
PO Box 219 (mailing address)
Marion, KS 66861-0219
(620) 382-2185; (800) 305-8851; (620) 382-3420
FAX
cmaggard@marioncoks.net;
coclerk@marioncoks.net
http://www.marioncoks.net/MV2Base.asp?Var
CN=116
Carol Maggard
(vital records from 1885 to 1911)
vital records search service: $3.00

Marion County Clerk of District Court
(200 South Third Street—location)
PO Box 298 (mailing address)
Marion, KS 66861-0298
(620) 382-2104; (620) 382-2259 FAX
mncdc@8thjd.com
http://www.8thjd.com
Jan Helmer
(probate records)
no probate search service; copies of probate
records: 25¢ per page, 15¢ for ten or more

Marion County Register of Deeds
(Courthouse, 200 South Third, Courthouse
Square—location)
PO Box 158 (mailing address)
Marion, KS 66861
(620) 382-2151; (620) 382-3420 FAX
rod@marioncoks.net
http://www.marioncoks.net/MV2Base.asp?Var
CN=2
Faye Makovec
(land records)

Marshall County

organized 1855, original county

Marshall County Clerk
Courthouse, 1201 Broadway
Marysville, KS 66508-1844
(785) 562-5361; (785) 562-5262 FAX
msctyclk@bluevalley.net
http://www.marshall.kansasgov.com/MV2Base.
asp?VarCN=35
Sonya L. Stohs
(births from November 1885 to August 1911,
deaths from May 1889 to August 1911 [except
1890 and 1891])

Marshall County Clerk of District Court
(Courthouse, 1201 Broadway, Marysville, KS
66508-1844—location)
PO Box 149 (mailing address)
Marysville, KS 66508-0149
(785) 562-5301; (785) 562-2458 FAX
mcdc@bluevalley.net
http://www.marshall.kansasgov.com/MV2Base.
asp?VarCN=52
(naturalization records, probate records)
naturalization and probate records search
service: $9.00 per hour, $2.25 minimum;
copies of naturalization and probate records:
50¢ for the first page, 25¢ for each additional
page, $1.00 for certification

Marshall County Register of Deeds
(Courthouse, 1201 Broadway—location)
PO Box 391 (mailing address)

Marylsville, KS 66508-1844
(785) 562-3226; (785) 562-5685 FAX
mscrod@bluevalley.net
http://www.marshall.kansasgov.com/MV2Base.
asp?VarCN=63
Linda Fincham
(land records, school records, veterans'
discharges)

McPherson County
organized 1867 from unorganized territory

McPherson County Clerk
(Courthouse, 117 North Maple—location)
PO Box 425 (mailing address)
McPherson, KS 67460-0425
(620) 241-3656; (620) 241-1168 FAX
smeng@mcphersoncountyks.us
http://www.mcphersoncountyks.us/index.asp?
NID=151
Susan Meng
(vital records from 1888 to 1905)

McPherson County Clerk of District Court
(Courthouse, 117 North Maple—location)
PO Box 1106 (mailing address)
McPherson, KS 67460-1106
(620) 241-3422; (620) 241-1372 FAX
cindyt@kscourt.net
http://www.mcphersoncountyks.us/index.asp?
NID=9
Cindy Teter

McPherson County Register of Deeds
(Courthouse, 117 North Maple—location)
PO Box 86 (mailing address)
McPherson, KS 67460
(620) 241-5050; (620) 245-0749 FAX
lpaul@mcphersoncountyks.us
http://www.mcphersoncountyks.us/index.asp?
NID=155
Linda K. Paul
(land records)

Meade County
organized 1873 from unorganized territory;
proclamation November 1855

Meade County Clerk
PO Box 278
Meade, KS 67864-0278
(785) 294-3976
jhale@meadeco.org
http://www.meadeco.org/MV2Base.asp?VarC
N=3; http://www.meadechamber.com
Janet Hale
(vital records)

Meade County Clerk of District Court
(200 North Fowler—location)
PO Box 623 (mailing address)
Meade, KS 67864-0623
(620) 873-8750; (620) 873-8759 FAX
http://www.kscourts.org/dstcts/16courts.htm
Kristen Branson
(probate records)

Meade County Register of Deeds
PO Box 399
Meade, KS 67864
(620) 873-8705; (620) 873-8713 FAX
ldavis@meadeco.org
http://www.meadeco.org/MV2Base.asp?VarC
N=12
Loretta Davis
(land records)

Miami County
organized 1855; name changed from Lykins
County

Miami County Clerk
Miami County Administration Building
201 South Pearl Street, Suite 102
Paola, KS 66071-1756
(913) 294-3976; (913) 294-9544 FAX
kpeckman@miamicountyks.org
http://www.miamicountyks.org/clerk.html
Kathy Peckman
(vital records)

Miami County Clerk of District Court
(120 South Pearl Street—location)
PO Box 187 (mailing address)
Paola, KS 66071-0187
(913) 294-3326; (913) 294-2535 FAX
http://www.kscourts.org/dstcts/6miamico.htm
Janet England
(naturalization records, probate records)
no probate search service ("Please contact
Genealogy Society Research, PO Box 123,
Paola, KS 66071, Attn: Vera Dakin; we have
released our records to them through The
Church of Jesus Christ of Latter-day Saints,
and they also have additional resources")

Miami County Register of Deeds
Miami County Administration Building
201 South Pearl Street, Suite 101
Paola, KS 66071-1790
(913) 294-3716; (913) 294-9515 FAX
kforck@micoks.net
http://www.miamicountyks.org/register.html
Katie Forck
(land records)

Mitchell County
county formed 1870 from Kirwin Land District

Mitchell County Clerk
Courthouse, 111 South Hersey Avenue
Beloit, KS 67420
(785) 738-3652
mitchell_co@nckcn.com
http://www.mcks.org/Clerk%27s%20Office.htm
Chris Treaster
(vital records)

Mitchell County Clerk of District Court
115 South Hersey Avenue
Beloit, KS 67420
(785) 738-3753; (785) 738-4101 FAX
maryloub@12jd.org
http://www.kscourts.org/dstcts/12dstct.htm
Mary Lou Brummer
(naturalization records, marriage licenses, and
probate records from about 1876)

Mitchell County Register of Deeds
PO Box 6
Beloit, KS 67420
(785) 738-3854; (785) 738-5844 FAX
mcrod@nckcn.com
http://www.mcks.org/Register%20of%20Deed
s.htm; http://www.kssos.org/forms/
communication/county.pdf
Judy Pettijohn
(land records)
copies of land records: $1.00 each

Montgomery County
organized 1867 from Labette County

Montgomery County Clerk
(Courthouse, 217 East Myrtle—location)
PO Box 446 (mailing address)
Independence, KS 67301-3758
(620) 330-1200; (620) 330-1202
csschmidt@mgcountyks.org
http://www.mgcountyks.org/clerk
Charlotte A. Scott-Schmidt
(naturalization records; births and deaths from
1887 to 1911)
certified copies of vital records: $3.00 each

Montgomery County Clerk of District Court
Montgomery County Judicial Center
300 East Main Street, Suite 201
Independence, KS 67301
(620) 330-1070; (620) 331-6120 FAX
http://www.kscourts.org/districts/District-
Info.asp?d=14
Nancy Williams
(probate records)

Montgomery County Register of Deeds
PO Box 647
Independence, KS 67301
(620) 330-1140; (620) 330-1144 FAX
mcalhoun@mgcountyks.org
http://www.mgcountyks.org/reg_of_deeds.htm
Marilyn Calhoun

(land records)

Morris County
organized 1855 from Madison County

Morris County Clerk
Courthouse, 501 West Main
Council Grove, KS 66846
(620) 767-5518
morris@cgtelco.net
http://www.morriscountyks.org/MV2Base.asp?
VarCN=5
Michelle Garrett
(vital records)

Morris County Clerk of District Court
Courthouse, 501 West Main Street
Council Grove, KS 66846
(620) 767-6838; (620) 767-6488 FAX
mrcdc@8thjd.com
http://www.8thjd.com
Sondra Carlson

Morris County Register of Deeds
Courthouse, 501 West Main
Council Grove, KS 66846
(620) 767-5614; (620) 767-6712 FAX
morrisrod@cgtelco.net
http://www.morriscountyks.org/MV2Base.asp?
VarCN=20
Corrine L. Blosser
(land records)

Morton County
constructed out of the territory belonging to
Seward County in 1883, and comprising the
territory defined originally as Kansas County
(1873), except that it extends three miles
further east; it was organized 20 February
1886; prior to 1887, it was attached to
Hamilton County for judicial purposes

Morton County Clerk
(1025 Morton Street—location)
PO Box 1116 (mailing address)
Elkhart, KS 67950-1116
(620) 697-2157; (620) 697-2159 FAX
mgilmore@elkhart.com
http://www.mtcoks.com
Mary C. Gilmore
(vital records)

Morton County Clerk of District Court
(1025 Morton Street—location)
PO Box 825 (mailing address)
Elkhart, KS 67950-0825
(620) 697-2563; (620) 697-4289 FAX
mtcodist@elkhart.com
http://www.mtcoks.com/district_court/court.h
tml
Karensa Meek
(probate records)
probate search service: $9.00 per hour; copies of
probate records: 25¢ per page, no minimum

Morton County Register of Deeds
(1025 Morton Street—location)
PO Box 756 (mailing address)
Elkhart, KS 67950
(620) 697-2561; (620) 697-4838 FAX
sakers@elkhart.com
http://www.mtcoks.com
Sally Akers
(land records)

Nemaha County
organized 1855, original county

Nemaha County Clerk
Courthouse, 607 Nemaha, Upper Level
Seneca, KS 66538
nmclerk@carsoncomm.com
http://www.nemaha.kansasgov.com/NV2Base.
asp?VarCN=6
Leann Jones
(vital records 1885–1911, cemetery records
1800–1982, other county records 1885–1911)
certified copies of vital records: $2.00 each

Nemaha County Clerk of District Court
(Courthouse, 607 Nemaha, Ground Level—

location)
PO Box 213 (mailing address)
Seneca, KS 66538-213
(785) 336-2146; (785) 336-6450 FAX
http://www.kscourts.org/districts/District-Info.asp?d=22
Nancy Koch
(limited naturalization records from 1859 to 1946, marriage licenses from 1832 to date, probate records from 1857 to date)
probate search service: $9.00 per hour; certified copies of marriages: $1.25 each; copies of probate records: 25¢ each, $1.00 for certification

Nemaha County Register of Deeds
PO Box 186
Seneca, KS 66538
(785) 336-2120; (785) 336-3373 FAX
nmrod@carsoncomm.com;
nemaharod@carsoncomm.com
http://www.nemaha.kansasgov.com/MV2Base.asp?VarCN=8
Mary Ann Holsapple
(land records from 1858 to date)
copies of land records: 25¢ each for 8½" x 11" (35¢ two-sided), 35¢ each for 8½" x 14" (50¢ two-sided)

Neosho County
organized 1855 from Labette County

Neosho County Clerk
PO Box 237
Erie, KS 66733
(620) 244-3811; (620) 244-3810 FAX
randalneelyclerk@neoshocounty.kscoxmail.com
http://www.neoshocountyks.org/clerk.asp
Randal Neely
(very few births)

Neosho County Clerk of District Court
Chanute Division
(102 South Lincon—location)
PO Box 889 (mailing address)
Chanute, KS 66720
(620) 431-5700; (620) 431-5710 FAX
jfroehlich@cableone.net
http://www.31stjudicialdistrict.org/neosho.html
Judy Froehlich

Neosho County Clerk of District Court
Erie Division
(100 South Main—location)
PO Box 19 (mailing address)
Erie, KS 66733
(620) 244-3831; (620) 244-3830 FAX
jfroehlich@cableone.net
http://www.31stjudicialdistrict.org/neosho.html
Judy Froehlich
(naturalization records, marriages from 1867 to date, probate records from 1867)
copies of naturlization records, marriages, and probate records: 25¢ per page, $1.00 for certified copies

Neosho County Register of Deeds
PO Box 138
Erie, KS 66733
(620) 244-3858; (620) 244-3860 FAX
neoshorod@hotmail.com
http://www.neoshocountyks.org/regofdeeds.asp
Glenda Taylor
(land records from 1867)
copies of land records: $1.00 per page from large bound books, 25¢ per page from small books, $1.00 for certified copies

Ness County
organized June 1880

Ness County Clerk
202 West Sycamore Street
Ness City, KS 67560-1558
(785) 798-2401
NS.County.Clerk@wan.kdor.state.ks.us
http://www.nesscountyks.com/County_CLerk.html
Renee Kerr
(vital records)

Ness County Clerk of District Court
(100 South Kansas—location)
PO Box 445 (mailing address)
Ness City, KS 67560-0445
(785) 798-3693; (785) 798-3348 FAX
nsdistct@gbta.net
http://www.kscourts.org/dstcts/24direct.htm
Joby Henning
(naturalization records, marriages [may be received from the Clerk or the District Magistrate Judge], probate records from District Magistrate Judge [has affidavits of death in some earlier cases])
probate search service: no charge; copies of probate records: 25¢ per page, no minimum

Ness County Register of Deeds
PO Box 127
Ness City, KS 67560
(785) 798-3127; (785) 798-2166 FAX
nesscorod@gbta.net
http://www.nesscountyks.com/Register_of_Deeds.html
Mark Horchem
(land records)

Norton County
organized 1872 from unorganized territory

Norton County Clerk
(Courthouse, 101 South Kansas—location)
PO Box 70 (mailing address)
Norton, KS 67654-0070
(785) 877-5710
nt.county.clerk@wan.kdor.state.ks.us
http://www.kssos.org/forms/communication/county.pdf
Robert Wyatt
(vital records)

Norton County Clerk of District Court
(Courthouse, 101 South Kansas—location)
PO Box 70 (mailing address)
Norton, KS 67654-0070
(877) 877-5720; (785) 877-5722 FAX
http://www.kscourts.org/districts/District-Info.asp?d=17
Darla Engel
(naturalization records, vital records, and probate records)

Norton County Register of Deeds
PO Box 70
Norton, KS 67654-0070
(785) 877-5765; (785) 877-5703 FAX
ntrod@ruraltel.net
http://www.kssos.org/forms/communication/county.pdf
Wanda Vincent
(land records)

Osage County
organized 1855, original county; name changed from Weller County 11 February 1859

Osage County Clerk
(Courthouse, 717 Topeka Avenue—location)
PO Box 226 (mailing address)
Lyndon, KS 66451
(785) 828-4812; (785) 828-4749 FAX
os_county_clerk@wan.kdor.state.ks.us
http://www.osage.kansasgov.com/MV2Base.asp?VarCN=3
Rhonda Beets
(births, deaths and marriages from 1885 to 1912)

Osage County Clerk of District Court
(Courthouse, 717 Topeka Avenue—location)
PO Box 549 (mailing address)
Lyndon, KS 66451-0549
(785) 828-4514; (785) 828-4704 FAX
charnaos@earthlink.net
http://www.kscourts.org/dstcts/4osco.htm
Charna L. Williams
(naturalization records from 1906 to 1929, marriage licenses from 1960, probate records from 1875)
probate search service: $8.00 per hour; copies of probate records: 15¢ per page, $1.00 per page for certification, no minimum

Osage County Register of Deeds
(Courthouse, 717 Topeka Avenue—location)
PO Box 265 (mailing address)
Lyndon, KS 66451-0265
(785) 828-4523; (785) 828-3648 FAX
lmassey@osageco.org
http://www.osage.kansasgov.com/MV2Base.asp?VarCN=120
Linda L. Massey
(land records from 1859)

Osborne County
organized 1867 from Mitchell County

Osborne County Clerk
(Courthouse, 423 West Main Street—location)
PO Box 160 (mailing address)
Osborne, KS 67473-0160
(785) 346-2431
ob_county_clerk@wan.kdor.state.ks.us;
obcoclerk@ruraltel.net
http://www.osbornecounty.org/index.asp?DocumentID=199
Vienna Janis
(vital records)

Osborne County Clerk of District Court
(Courthouse, 423 West Main Street—location)
PO Box 160 (mailing address)
Osborne, KS 67473-0160
(785) 346-5911; (785) 346-5992 FAX
http://www.osbornecounty.org/index.asp?DocumentID=197
Sheryl Gorsuch
(naturalization records from 1876, marriages from 1872, and probate records from 1880)
probate search service: $9.00 per hour; copies of probate records: 25¢ per page, no minimum

Osborne County Register of Deeds
(Courthouse, 423 West Main Street, First Floor—location)
PO Box 160 (mailing address)
Osborne, KS 67473
(785) 346-2452; (785) 346-5252 FAX
obcorod@ruraltel.net
http://www.osbornecounty.org/index.asp?DocumentID=189
Bruce A. Berkley
(land records from 1870)
land records search service: $2.00 for searches under thirty minutes, otherwise $5.00 per hour; copies of land records: 25¢ per page

Ottawa County
organized 1866 from Saline County

Ottawa County Clerk
Courthouse, 307 North Concord Street, Suite 130
Minneapolis, KS 67467
(785) 392-2279; (785) 392-2011 FAX
occlerk@nckcn.com
http://www.ottawacounty.org/index.asp?DocumentID=284
Mary Arganbright
(vital records)

Ottawa County Clerk of District Court
Courthouse, 307 North Concord Street
Minneapolis, KS 67467
(785) 392-2917; (785) 392-3626 FAX
http://www.ottawacounty.org/index.asp?DocumentID=319
Cheryl Adams

Ottawa County Register of Deeds
Courthouse, 307 North Concord Street, Suite 220
Minneapolis, KS 67467-2140
(785) 392-2078; (785) 392-3605 FAX
ottawacorod@yahoo.com
http://www.ottawacounty.org/index.asp?DocumentID=291
Marilyn Heck
(land records)

Pawnee County
organized 1872 from Rush and Stafford counties

Pawnee County Clerk
Courthouse, 715 Broadway
Larned, KS 67550-3054
(620) 285-3721; (620) 285-2559 FAX
pn_county_clerk@wan.kdor.state.ks.us
http://www.pawneecountykansas.com/MV2Bas
e.asp?VarCN=19
Ruth M. Searight
(vital records)

Pawnee County Clerk of District Court
(Courthouse, 715 Broadway, Larned, KS 67550-
3054—location)
PO Box 270 (mailing address)
Larned, KS 67550-0270
(620) 285-6937; (620) 285-3665 FAX
pndistct@pawnee.kscoxmail.com
http://www.kscourts.org/dstcts/24direct.htm
Kay Schartz

Pawnee County Register of Deeds
Courthouse, 715 Broadway
Larned, KS 67550-3097
(620) 285-3276; (620) 285-2908 FAX
jsrod@pawnee.kscoxmail.com
http://www.pawneecountykansas.com/MV2Bas
e.asp?VarCN=5
Jacque Schulze
(land records)

Phillips County
organized 1872 from Kirwin Land District

Phillips County Clerk
Courthouse, 301 State Street
Phillipsburg, KS 67661
(785) 543-6825; (785) 543-6827 FAX
coclerk@ruraltel.net
http://www.phillipscounty.org//clerk.html
Linda McDowell
(vital records)

Phillips County Clerk of District Court
(Courthouse, 301 State Street—location)
PO Box 564 (mailing address)
Phillipsburg, KS 67661-0564
(785) 543-6830; (785) 543-6832 FAX
http://www.kscourts.org/districts/District-
Info.asp?d=17
Debra Grammon
(some naturalization records [some
naturalization records with Decatur County],
marriages and adoptions and probate records)

Phillips County Register of Deeds
Courthouse, 301 State Street
Phillipsburg, KS 67661
(785) 543-6875; (785) 543-6897 FAX
pcorods@yahoo.com
http://www.phillipscounty.org/registerdeeds.html
Robert Keesee
(land records)

Pottawatomie County
organized 1857 from Indian lands

Pottawatomie County Clerk
(Courthouse, 106 Main Street—location)
PO Box 187 (mailing address)
Westmoreland, KS 66549
(785) 457-3314: (785) 457-3507 FAX
sfigge@pottcounty.org
http://www.pottcounty.org/Clerk/Clerk.htm
Susan Figge
(births and deaths from 1857 to 1900)

Pottawatomie County Clerk of District Court
(Courthouse, 106 Main Street—location)
PO Box 129 (mailing address)
Westmoreland, KS 66549-0129
(785) 457-3392; (785) 457-2107 FAX
ptdistct@kscourts.net
http://www.kscourts.org/dstcts/2pottco.htm
Jane Shehi
(naturalization records, marriages, and probate
records)
probate search service: $2.00 per name (as time
permits); copies of probate records: 25¢ per
page, $2.00 for certified copies, $1.00
minimum

Pottawatomie County Register of Deeds
(Pottawatomie County Office Building, 207
North First—location)
PO Box 186 (mailing address)
Westmoreland, KS 66549
(785) 457-3471; (785) 457-3577 FAX
babitz@pottcounty.org
http://www.pottcounty.org/Office%20Links/
Deeds.htm
Betty Jo Abitz
(land records)

Pratt County
organized 1870 from Stafford County

Pratt County Clerk
(Courthouse, 300 South Ninnescah, Second
Floor—location)
PO Box 885 (mailing address)
Pratt, KS 67124
(620) 672-4110; (620) 672-9541 FAX
skruse@prattcounty.org; clerk@prattcounty.org
http://www.prattcounty.org/clerk.html
Sherry Kruse
(vital records)

Pratt County Clerk of District Court
(Courthouse, 300 South Ninnescah—location)
PO Box 984 (mailing address)
Pratt, KS 67124-0984
(620) 672-4100; (620) 672-2902 FAX
http://www.kscourts.org/dstcts/30dstct.htm
Johanna Roberts

Pratt County Register of Deeds
(Courthouse, 300 South Ninnescah, Second
Floor—location)
PO Box 873 (mailing address)
Pratt, KS 67124
(620) 672-4140; (620) 672-9541 FAX
swenrich@prattcounty.org;
registerofdeeds@prattcounty.org
http://www.prattcounty.org/register_deeds.html
Sherry L. Wenrich
(land records)

Rawlins County
organized 1873 from Kirwin Land District

Rawlins County Clerk
Courthouse, 607 Main Street
Atwood, KS 67730-1839
(785) 626-3351
http://www.kssos.org/forms/communication/c
ounty.pdf; http://www.rawlinsounty.info
Krystal Hutfles
(vital records)

Rawlins County Clerk of District Court
(Courthouse, 607 Main Street, #F, Atwood, KS
67730-1839—location)
PO Box 257 (mailing address)
Atwood, KS 67730-0257
(785) 626-3465; (785) 626-3394 (Delores A.
Luedke); (785) 626-3350 FAX
(naturalization records, probate records)
records search service: c/o Delores A. Luedke,
PO Box 42, Atwood, KS 67730: for donation
to The Rawlins County Genealogical Society
Reader Printer Fund

Rawlins County Register of Deeds
PO Box 201
Atwood, KS 67730
(785) 626-3726; (785) 626-3172; (785) 626-9481
FAX
camrod@ruraltel.net; marshalldc75@yahoo.com
http://www.kssos.org/forms/communication/c
ounty.pdf
Carolyn Marshall
(land records)

Reno County
organized 1872 from Sedgwick County

Reno County Clerk
Courthouse, 206 West First Avenue
Hutchinson, KS 67501-5245
(620) 694-2934
shari.gagnebin@renogov.com

http://www.renogov.com/clerk
Shari Gagnebin
(births and deaths from 1890 to 1910)
certified copies of vital records: $2.00 each

Reno County Clerk of District Court
Courthouse, 206 West First Avenue, Third
Floor
Hutchinson, KS 67501-5245
(620) 694-2956; (620) 694-2958 FAX (Div. 1 &
2); (620) 694-2948 FAX (Div. 3); (620) 694-
2960 FAX (Div. 4)
http://www.kscourts.org/districts/District-
Info.asp?d=27
Pam Moses
(naturalization records and probate records [to
be checked by local abstract company or the
persons themselves])
no probate search or copy service

Reno County Register of Deeds
Courthouse, 206 West First Avenue
Hutchinson, KS 67501
(620) 694-2945; (620) 694-2944 FAX
carol.sallee@renogov.com
http://www.renogov.com/deeds
Carol A. Sallee
(land records from 1872)
copies of land records: $1.00 per page

Republic County
organized 1868 from Washington and Cloud
counties

Republic County Clerk
(Courthouse, 1815 M Street—location)
PO Box 429 (mailing address)
Belleville, KS 66935-0429
(785) 527-7231
http://www.republiccounty.org/MV2Base.asp?
VarCN=15
Vickie Hall
(vital records)

Republic County Clerk of District Court
(Courthouse, 1815 M Street—location)
PO Box 8 (mailing address)
Belleville, KS 66935-0008
(785) 527-5691; (785) 527-5029 FAX
krisk@12jd.org
http://www.kscourts.org/dstcts/12dstct.htm
Kris Kling

Republic County Register of Deeds
Courthouse, 1815 M Street, Suite 3
Belleville, KS 66935-0429
(785) 527-7238; (785) 527-2659 FAX
rc9@nckcn.com
http://www.republiccounty.org/MV2Base.asp?
VarCN=16
Ruth Rahe
(land records)

Rice County
organized 1867 from Reno County

Rice County Clerk
Courthouse, 101 West Commercial Street
Lyons, KS 67554
(620) 257-2232; (620) 257-3039 FAX
ashow@ricecocthse.com
http://www.ricecounty.us/clerk.htm
Alicia Showalter
(vital records)

Rice County Clerk of District Court
Courthouse, 101 West Commercial Street, Third
Floor
Lyons, KS 67554-2797
(620) 257-2383; (620) 257-3826 FAX
http://www.ricecounty.us/districtcourt.htm
Jane E. Hrabik
(naturalization and probate records)

Rice County Register of Deeds
Courthouse, 101 West Commercial Street
Lyons, KS 67554
(620) 257-2931 voice & FAX
rhunt@ricecocthse.com;
rdeeds@ricecocthse.com
http://www.ricecounty.us/registerofdeeds.htm

Rhonda Hunt
(land records)

Riley County
organized 1855 from Wabaunsee County

Riley County Clerk
Riley County Office Building
110 Courthouse Plaza, First Floor, Room B118
Manhattan, KS 66502-6018
(785) 565-6200; (785) 537-6394 FAX
rl_county_clerk@wan.kdor.state.ks.us
http://www.rileycountyks.gov/index.asp?nid=16
Rich Vargo
(vital records)

Riley County Clerk of District Court
(Riley County Office Building, 110 Courthouse
    Plaza, Manhattan, KS 66502-6018—location)
PO Box 158 (mailing address)
Manhattan, KS 66505-0158
(785) 537-6364; (785) 537-6382 FAX
http://www.rileycountyks.gov/index.asp?NID=
    190
Lynda K. Wickstrum

Riley County Register of Deeds
Riley County Office Building
110 Courthouse Plaza
Manhattan, KS 66502-6018
(785) 537-6340; (785) 537-6343 FAX
cshawver@rileycountyks.gov
http://www.rileycountyks.gov/index.asp?nid=418
M. Charlotte Shawver
(land records)

Rooks County
organized 1872 from Kirwin Land District

Rooks County Clerk
Courthouse, 115 North Walnut Street, Second
    Floor
Stockton, KS 67669-1663
(785) 425-6391; (785) 425-6015 FAX
RO.County.Clerk@wan.kdor.state.ks.us
http://www.rookscounty.net/clerk.htm
Clara Strutt
(vital records)

Rooks County Clerk of District Court
(Courthouse, 115 North Walnut Street, Third
    Floor, Stockton, KS 67669-1663—location)
PO Box 532 (mailing address)
Stockton, KS 67669-0532
(785) 425-6718; (785) 425-6568 FAX
http://www.23rdjudicial.org
Geneva Mason
(births and deaths from 1888 to 1905 [not
    indexed], marriages from 1888, probate
    records from 1880)
probate search service: $9.00 per hour; copies of
    probate records: 25¢ per page

Rooks County Register of Deeds
Courthouse, 115 North Walnut Street, Second
    Floor
Stockton, KS 67669
(785) 425-6291; (785) 425-6497 FAX
http://www.rookscounty.net/register_of_deeds.
    htm
Rosalee Sprick
(land records)

Rush County
organized 1874 from unorganized territory

Rush County Clerk
(715 Elm—location)
PO Box 220 (mailing address)
LaCrosse, KS 67548-0220
(785) 222-2731; (785) 222-3559 FAX
rh.county.clerk@wan.kdor.state.ks.us
http://www.rushcounty.org/contact.html
Barbara Matal
(vital records)

Rush County Clerk of District Court
(715 Elm Street—location)
PO Box 387 (mailing address)
La Crosse, KS 67548-0387
(785) 222-2718; (785) 222-2748 FAX

rhdistct@gbta.net
http://www.kscourts.org/dstcts/24direct.htm
Virginia L. Keener
(naturalization records, marriage licenses, and
    probate records)
search service: $9.00 per hour if it is an extensive
    search ("on probates we need the name; on
    marriage licenses we need the name and
    approximate date"); copies of naturalization
    records and probate records: 25¢ each, no
    minimum

Rush County Register of Deeds
(715 Elm—location)
PO Box 117 (mailing address)
LaCrosse, KS 67548
(785) 222-3312; (785) 222-3559 FAX
rushdeeds@yahoo.com
http://www.rushcounty.org/contact.html
Gloria Anders
(land records)
copies of land records: $1.00 per instrument

Russell County
organized 1867 from Ellsworth County

Russell County Clerk
(Courthouse, 401 North Main Street—location)
PO Box 113 (mailing address)
Russell, KS 67665
(785) 483-4641
rs_county_clerk@wan.kdor.state.ks.us
http://www.russellcounty.org/index.asp?Docu
    mentID=285
Simone Ginther
(vital records)

Russell County Clerk of District Court
(Courthouse, 401 North Main Street—location)
PO Box 876 (mailing address)
Russell, KS 67665-0876
(785) 483-5641; (785) 483-2448 FAX
http://www.kscourts.org/districts/District-
    Info.asp?d=20
Peggy A. Beck

Russell County Register of Deeds
(Courthouse, 401 North Main Street, Second
    Floor—location)
PO Box 191 (mailing address)
Russell, KS 67665
(785) 483-4612; (785) 483-5725 FAX
russellcorod@ruraltel.net
http://www.russellcounty.org/index.asp?Docu
    mentID=287
Dee Ann Matheson
(land records)

St. John County
(see Logan County)

Saline County
organized 1860, original county

Saline County Clerk
(300 West Ash Street, Room 215—location)
PO Box 5040 (mailing address)
Salina, KS 67402-5040
(785) 309-5820; (785) 309-5826 FAX
don.merriman@saline.org
http://www.saline.org/MV2Base.asp?VarCN=70
Don Merriman
(vital records)

Saline County Clerk of District Court
(300 West Ash, Room 307, Salina, KS 67401-
    2396—location)
PO Box 1760 (mailing address)
Salina, KS 67402-1760
(785) 309-5831; (785) 309-5845 FAX
http://www.saline.org/MV2Base.asp?VarCN=99
Teresa Lueth
(probate records)

Saline County Register of Deeds
(300 West Ash, Room 212—location)
PO Box 5040 (mailing address)
Salina, KS 67401-5040
(785) 309-5855; (785) 309-5856 FAX
rebecca.seeman@saline.org

http://www.saline.org/MV2Base.asp?VarCN=8-
Rebecca Seeman
(land records from 1860 to date)

Scott County
organized 1873 from Finney County

Scott County Clerk
Courthouse, 303 Court Street
Scott City, KS 67871-1122
(620) 872-2420
SC_County_Clerk@wan.kdor.state.ks.us
http://www.scott.kansasgov.com/MV2Base.asp
    ?VarCN=6
Pamela J. Faurot
(vital records)

Scott County Clerk of District Court
Courthouse, 303 Court Street
Scott City, KS 67871-1122
(620) 872-7208; (620) 872-3683 FAX
http://www.kscourts.org/districts/District-
    Info.asp?d=25
Darlene Kohman
(probate records)
no probate search service; copies of probate
    records: 25¢ per page

Scott County Register of Deeds
Courthouse, 303 Court Street
Scott City, KS 67871
(620) 872-3155; (620) 872-7145 FAX
scregofdeeds@hotmail.com
http://www.scott.kansasgov.com/MV2Base.asp
    ?VarCN=29
Debbie Murphey
(land records)

Sedgwick County
organized 1867 from Butler County

Sedgwick County Clerk
Courthouse, 525 North Main, Suite 211
Wichita, KS 67203
(316) 660-9222; (316) 383-7961 FAX
dbrace@sedgwick.gov
http://www.sedgwickcounty.org/countyclerk
Donald C. Brace
(vital records)

Sedgwick County Clerk of District Court
Court Records
Courthouse, 525 North Main, Sixth Floor
Wichita, KS 67203-3773
(316) 383-7302; (316) 383-8071 (Criminal); (316)
    383-8072 (Domestic); (316) 383-8073
    (Probate); (316) 383-8070 FAX (Civil)
http://www.dc18.org
(probate records)
no probate search service; copies of probate
    records: 25¢ per page, $1.00 for certification,
    no minimum

Sedgwick County Register of Deeds
Courthouse, 525 North Main, Room 415
Wichita, KS 67201-3326
(316) 660-9400; (316) 383-8066 FAX
wmeek@sedgwick.gov
http://www.sedgwickcounty.org/deeds
William "Bill" Meek
(land records)

Seward County
county laid out, along with Kansas and Stevens
    counties, in 1873 from Indian lands; the
    legislature passed an act fixing the boundaries
    of the three counties on 7 March 1875; in
    1883 the three counties became one, with
    Seward county extending to the Colorado-
    Kansas line

Seward County Clerk
Courthouse, 415 North Washington Avenue,
    Suite 109
Liberal, KS 67901-3462
(620) 626-3201; (620) 626-3211 FAX
countyclerk@swko.net
http://www.seward.kansasgov.com/MV2Base.a
    sp?VarCN=3
Stacia Long

(vital records)

Seward County Clerk of District Court
Courthouse, 415 North Washington Avenue,
Suite 103
Liberal, KS 67901-3462
(620) 626-3375; (620) 626-3302 FAX
http://www.kscourts.org/districts/District-
Info.asp?d=26
Rhonda Truhlar
(probate records)
no probate search service ("You search your
own records or have an abstract company do
the searching")

Seward County Register of Deeds
Courthouse, 415 North Washington Avenue,
Suite 105
Liberal, KS 67901
(620) 626-3223; (620) 626-3362 FAX
rodeeds@swko.net
http://www.seward.kansasgov.com/MV2Base.a
sp?VarCN=4
Cynthia Sallaska
(land records)
land records search service: $3.00 per name
search on U.C.C. filings, otherwise $6.00 per
hour; copies of land records: 50¢ each

Shawnee County
organized 1855, original county

Shawnee County Clerk
Courthouse, 200 S.E. Seventh Street
Topeka, KS 66603-3933
(785) 233-8200, ext. 4155; (785) 291-4912 FAX
cyndi.beck@co.shawnee.ks.us
http://www.co.shawnee.ks.us/clerk
Cynthia "Cyndi" Beck
(vital records)

Shawnee County Clerk of District Court
Courthouse, 200 S.E. Seventh Street
Topeka, KS 66603-3922
(785) 233-8200, ext. 5156 (Probate); (785) 291-
4908 FAX (Probate, Criminal, and Traffic);
(785) 291-4911 FAX (Civil and Domestic)
http://www.shawneecourt.org
Joyce D. Reeves
(births and deaths from 1894 to 1911, marriages
from February 1856 through 10 June 1906
with Room 107, probate records with Room
209)
probate search service: $9.00 per hour; copies of
probate records: 50¢ per page, no minimum
("Release of Copy Request must be signed")

Shawnee County Register of Deeds
Courthouse, 200 S.E. Seventh Street, Suite 108
Topeka, KS 66603
(785) 233-8200, ext. 4020; (785) 291-4950 FAX
marilyn.nichols@co.shawnee.ks.us
http://www.co.shawnee.ks.us/rd
Marilyn Nichols
(land records)

Sheridan County
organized 1873 from unorganized territory

Sheridan County Clerk
PO Box 899
Hoxie, KS 67740-0899
(785) 675-3361
sdcoclk@ruraltel.net
http://www.accesskansas.org/sheridan
Paula Bielser
(vital records)

Sheridan County Clerk of District Court
(925 Ninth Street, 3rd Floor—location)
PO Box 753 (mailing address)
Hoxie, KS 67740-0753
(785) 675-3451; (785) 675-2256 FAX
dchoxie@ruraltel.net
http://www.accesskansas.org/sheridan

Sheridan County Register of Deeds
PO Box 899
Hoxie, KS 67740-0899
(785) 675-3741; (785) 675-3050 FAX
sdrd@ruraltel.net

http://www.accesskansas.org/sheridan
Kari Weis
(land records)

Sherman County
organized 1873 from Kirwin Land District

Sherman County Clerk
Courthouse, 813 Broadway, Room 102
Goodland, KS 67735
(785) 890-4800; (785) 890-4809 FAX
sh_county_clerk@wan.kdor.state.ks.us
http://www.sherman.kansasgov.com/MV2Base
.asp?VarCN=3
Janet Rumpel
(vital records)

Sherman County Clerk of District Court
Courthouse, 813 Broadway, Room 201
Goodland, KS 67735
(785) 899-4850; (785) 899-4858 FAX
http://www.kscourts.org/districts/District-
Info.asp?d=15
Linda Bowen
(probate records)

Sherman County Register of Deeds
Courthouse, 813 Broadway, Room 104
Goodland, KS 67735-3097
(785) 899-4845; (785) 899-4848 FAX
shcounty_registerofdeeds@wan.kdor.state.ks.us
http://www.sherman.kansasgov.com/MV2Base
.asp?VarCN=171
Carol S. Armstrong
(land records)

Smith County
organized 1872 from unorganized territory

Smith County Clerk
Courthous, 218 South Grant Street
Smith Center, KS 66967-2708
(785) 282-5110
sm_county_clerk@kdor.state.ks.us
http://www.kssos.org/forms/communication/c
ounty.pdf
Sharon Wolters
(vital records 1891–1897)

Smith County Clerk of District Court
(218 South Grant Street, Smith Center, KS
66967-2708—location)
PO Box 273 (mailing address)
Smith Center, KS 66967-0273
(785) 282-5140; (785) 282-5145 FAX
http://www.kscourts.org/districts/District-
Info.asp?d=17
Karen Blank
(naturalization records, probate records)
probate search service: no charge; copies of
probate records: 25¢ per page, no minimum

Smith County Register of Deeds
218 South Grant
Smith Center, KS 66967
(785) 282-5160; (785) 282-6257 FAX
SMCounty_RegisterofDeeds@wan.kdor.state.ks.us
Helen Baetz
http://www.kssos.org/forms/communication/c
ounty.pdf
(land records)

Stafford County
organized 1879 from unorganized territory

Stafford County Clerk
Courthouse, 209–215 North Broadway, Second
Floor
St. John, KS 67576
(620) 549-3509; (620) 549-3481 FAX
coclerk@stjohnks.net
http://www.staffordcounty.org/clerk.html
Nita Keenan
(vital records)

Stafford County Clerk of District Court
(Courthouse, 209–215 North Broadway, Third
Floor—location)
PO Box 365 (mailing address)
St. John, KS 67576-0366
(620) 549-3295 (Office); (620) 549-3296; (620)

549-3298 FAX
m_gatton@earthlink.net
http://www.staffordcounty.org/distct.html
Mary M. Gatton

Stafford County Register of Deeds
Courthouse, 209–215 North Broadway, Second
Floor
St. John, KS 67576
(620) 549-3505; (620) 549-3503 FAX
regofdeeds@stjohnks.net
http://www.staffordcounty.org/regofdeeds.html
Lu Ann Brister
(land records)

Stanton County
created in 1873, later abolished and made part of
Hamilton County; in 1887 Stanton County
was reorganized from Hamilton County

Stanton County Clerk
Courthouse, 201 North Main
Johnson, KS 67855
(620) 492-2140; (620) 492-2688 FAX
st_county_clerk@wan.kdor.state.ks.us
http://www.kssos.org/forms/communication/c
ounty.pdf
Sharon Dimitt
(some early vital records)

Stanton County Clerk of District Court
(Courthouse, 201 North Main—location)
PO Box 913 (mailing address)
Johnson, KS 67855-0913
(620) 492-2180; (620) 492-6410 FAX
http://www.kscourts.org/districts/District-
Info.asp?d=26
Bonnie Parks
(some naturalization records, probate records)
probate search service: $9.00 per hour; copies of
probate records: 25¢ per page, no minimum

Stanton County Register of Deeds
PO Box 716
Johnson, KS 67855
(620) 492-2190; (620) 492-2688 FAX
stcorod@pld.com
http://www.kssos.org/forms/communication/c
ounty.pdf
Susan L. Lucas
(land records)

Stevens County
county laid out, along with Kansas and Seward
counties, in 1873 from Indian lands; the
legislature passed an act fixing the boundaries
of the three counties on 7 March 1875; in
1883 the three counties became one, with
Seward county extending to the Colorado-
Kansas line; Stevens County was reorganized
by 1886

Stevens County Clerk
Courthouse, 200 East Sixth Street
Hugoton, KS 67951-2652
(620) 544-2541
sv_county_clerk@wan.kdor.state.ks.us
http://www.stevenscoks.org/clerk.htm
Pam Bensel
(vital records)

Stevens County Clerk of District Court
Courthouse, 200 East Sixth Street
Hugoton, KS 67951-2652
(620) 544-2484; (620) 544-2528 FAX
http://www.stevenscoks.org/distcourt.htm
Koleen Nosekabel
(probate records)
no probate search service ("Requests for copies
must be in writing"); copies of probate
records: 10¢ per page

Stevens County Register of Deeds
Courthouse, 200 East Sixth Street
Hugoton, KS 67951
(620) 544-2630; (620) 544-4081 FAX
ziprosel@hotmail.com
http://www.stevenscoks.org/regdeed.htm
Zilpha (Betty) Rosel
(land records)

Sumner County
organized 1867 from Cowley County

Sumner County Clerk
Courthouse, 501 North Washington
Wellington, KS 67152-4064
(620) 326-3395; (620) 326-2116 FAX
sucoclk@co.sumner.ks.us
http://www.co.sumner.ks.us/MV2Base.asp?Var CN=9
Shane J. Shields
(vital records)

Sumner County Clerk of District Court
(Courthouse, 501 North Washington Avenue, Wellington, KS 67152-4064—location)
PO Box 399 (mailing address)
Wellington, KS 67152-0399
(620) 326-5936 (Probate Department); (620) 326-5365 FAX
dcclerk@sutv.com
http://www.co.sumner.ks.us/MV2Base.asp?Var CN=58;
http://www.kscourts.org/dstcts/30dstct.htm
Carolyn A. Jones
(naturalization records, probate records)
probate search service: $6.60 per year; copies of probate records: 25¢ per page, no minimum

Sumner County Register of Deeds
(Courthouse, 501 North Washington, Room 103—location)
PO Box 469 (mailing address)
Wellington, KS 67152
(620) 326-2041; (620) 399-1087 FAX
jlowe@co.sumner.ks.us
http://www.co.sumner.ks.us/MV2Base.asp?Var CN=22
Joyce A. Lowe
(land records)

Thomas County
organized 1873 from Kirwin Land District; organized with elected officials in October 1885

Thomas County Clerk and Election Officer
Courthouse, 300 North Court Street
Colby, KS 67701-2439
(785) 462-2561
tcc01@st-tel.net
http://www.thomascountyks.com/page.php?4
Shelly Harms
(vital records from 1885 through June 1910)
vital records search service: $10.00 per hour; copies: 25¢ per page plus postage

Thomas County Clerk of District Court
(Courthouse, 300 North Court Street, Colby, KS 67701-2494—location)
PO Box 805 (mailing address)
Colby, KS 67701-0805
(785) 460-4540; (785) 460-2291 FAX
http://www.thomascounty.us
Kim Schwarz
(naturalization records through 1977, marriage licenses, probate records)
probate search service: $9.00 per hour if takes a lot of time; copies of probate records: 25¢ per page, $1.00 for certification, no minimum ("Not all things can be copied")

Thomas County Register of Deeds
Courthouse, 300 North Court Street
Colby, KS 67701
(785) 460-4535; (785) 460-4512 FAX
throd@st-tel.net
http://www.thomascountyks.com/page.php?9
Maybelle Moore
(land records from 1885)
land records search service: $10.00 per hour

Trego County
organized 1879 from Ellis County

Trego County Clerk
Courthouse, 216 North Main Street
WaKeeney, KS 67672-2102
(785) 743-5773; (785) 743-2461 FAX
clerk@ruraltel.net
http://www.tregocountyks.com/MV2Base.asp?VarCN=16
Lori Augustine
(vital records)

Trego County Clerk of District Court
Courthouse, 216 North Main Street
WaKeeney, KS 67672-2102
(785) 743-2148; (785) 743-2726 FAX
http://www.23rdjudicial.org
Tiffany Gillespie
(land records from homestead or patent, probate records)

Trego County Register of Deeds
Courthouse, 216 North Main Street
WaKeeney, KS 67672
(785) 743-6622; (785) 743-2461 FAX
tregord@ruraltel.net
http://www.tregocountyks.com/MV2Base.asp?VarCN=16
Evea M. Rumpel
(land records)

Wabaunsee County
organized 1855 from Riley and Morris counties

Wabaunsee County Clerk
(Courthouse, 215 Kansas Avenue, Alma, KS 66401-9797—location)
PO Box 278 (mailing address)
Alma, KS 66401
(785) 765-2421; (785) 765-3704 FAX
WB_County_Clerk@wan.kdor.state.ks.us
http://www.wabaunsee.kansasgov.com/MV2Base.asp?VarCN=3
Jennifer Savage
(vital records)

Wabaunsee County Clerk of District Court
(Courthouse, 215 Kansas Avenue, Alma, KS 66401-9797—location)
PO Box 278 (mailing address)
Alma, KS 66401
(785) 765-2406; (785) 765-2487 FAX
dctalma@earthlink.net
http://www.kscourts.org/dstcts/2wabco.htm
Krisena Silva
(very few naturalization records [not complete] and probate records)
no probate search service ("Contact the Wabaunsee County Abstract Office, Alma, KS 66401"); copies of probate records: 25¢ per page, no minimum

Wabaunsee County Register of Deeds
(Courthouse, 215 Kansas Avenue, Alma, KS 66401-9797—location)
PO Box 278 (mailing address)
Alma, KS 66401-0278
(785) 765-3822; (785) 765-3824 FAX
wabrod@wan.kdor.state.ks.us
http://www.wabaunsee.kansasgov.com/MV2Base.asp?VarCN=5
C. Suzanne Simon
(land records)

Wallace County
created in 1868 from Indian lands and was part of a territory that went to Wa Keeney, now the county seat of Trego County; Wallace was established with its present boundaries in 1881, but no form of county government was created until 1886

Wallace County Clerk
Courthouse, 313 Main
Sharon Springs, KS 67758
(785) 852-4282; (785) 852-4783 FAX
wa_county_clerk@wan.kdor.state.ks.us
http://www.wallacecounty.net/government/localgov.php (Economic Development Alliance); http://www.kssos.org/forms/communication/county.pdf
Melody Fulton
(births, deaths and marriages from 1895 to 1911)

Wallace County Clerk of District Court
(Courthouse, 313 Main—location)
PO Box 8 (mailing address)
Sharon Springs, KS 67758

(785) 852-4289; (785) 852-4271 FAX
http://www.kscourts.org/districts/District-Info.asp?d=15
Karlin Barton
(naturalization records, marriage licenses from 1887 to date, coroner's records from 1888 to date, and probate records from 1908 to date)

Wallace County Register of Deeds
PO Box 10
Sharon Springs, KS 67758
(785) 852-4283; (785) 852-4783 FAX
wallacerod@yahoo.com; wallace@pld.com
http://www.wallacecounty.net/government/localgov.php (Economic Development Alliance); http://www.kssos.org/forms/communication/county.pdf
Lillian F. Swartz
(deeds and mortgages from 1887)

Washington County
organized 1855, original county

Washington County Clerk
Courthouse, 214 C Street
Washington, KS 66967-1928
(785) 325-2974
wsclerk@bluevalley.net;
ws_county_clerk@wan.kdor.state.ks.us
http://www.washingtoncountyks.net/clerk.html
Louella Kern
(vital records from 1887 to 1911 only)

Washington County Clerk of District Court
Courthouse, 214 C Street
Washington, KS 66968-1928
(785) 325-2381; (785) 325-2557 FAX
shirleym@12jd.org
http://www.kscourts.org/dstcts/12dstct.htm
Shirley A. Marrs
(naturalization records and probate records)
no probate search service; copies of probate records: 10¢ to 50¢ each, no minimum

Washington County Register of Deeds
Courthouse, 214 C Street
Washington, KS 66968
(785) 325-2286; (913) 325-2830 FAX
washcoregdeed@washingtonks.net
http://www.washingtoncountyks.net/register.html
Marilyn K. Kolle
(land records)

Wichita County
organized 1873 from Indian lands

Wichita County Clerk
PO Drawer 968
Leoti, KS 67861
(620) 375-4454
coclerk@wbsnet.org
http://www.kssos.org/forms/communication/county.pdf
Karla Ridder
(vital records)

Wichita County Clerk of District Court
(Courthouse, 206 South Fourth—location)
PO Box 968 (mailing address)
Leoti, KS 67861-0968
(316) 375-2731; (620) 375-2999 FAX
http://www.kscourts.org/districts/District-Info.asp?d=25
Mary J. Downs

Wichita County Register of Deeds
PO Box 472
Leoti, KS 667861-0472
(620) 375-2733; (620) 375-4350 FAX
http://www.kssos.org/forms/communication/county.pdf
Connie Wilson
(land records)

Wilson County
organized 1855, original county

Wilson County Clerk
Courthouse, 615 Madison Street, Room 104
Fredonia, KS 66736-1340
(620) 378-2186; (620) 378-3841

Kentucky 107

wilsoncoclerk@twinmounds.com;
wilsonclerk1@twinmounds.com
http://www.wilson.kansasgov.com/MV2Base.as
p?VarCN=4
Rhonda Willard
(vital records)

Wilson County Clerk of District Court
(Courthouse, 615 Madison Street, Room 214—
location)
PO Box 246 (mailing address)
Fredonia, KS 66736
(620) 378-4533; (620) 378-4531 FAX
cdc@twinmounds.com
http://www.31stjudicialdistrict.org./wilson1.html
Janel Downey
(probate records)
no probate search service ("You may look for
yourself"); copies of probate records: 25¢ per
page, no minimum

Wilson County Register of Deeds
Courthouse, 615 Madison Street, Room 106
Fredonia, KS 66736-1396
(888) 394-9977; (620) 378-4762 FAX
wlcorod@twinmounds.com
http://www.wilson.kansasgov.com/MV2Base.as
p?VarCN=9
Teresa A. (Terri) Young
(land records)

Woodson County
organized 1855, original county

Woodson County Clerk
Courthouse, 105 West Rutledge Street
Yates Center, KS 66783
(620) 625-3162; (620) 625-8605; (620) 625-8606;
(620) 625-8670 FAX
coclerk@woodsoncounty.net
http://woodsoncounty.net/clerk/index.htm
Shelley Stuber
(births, deaths and marriages from 1885 to 1910)
copies of vital records: $1.00 for the first page
and 50¢ for each additional page

Woodson County Clerk of District Court
(Courthouse, 105 West Rutledge Street, Yates
Center, KS 66783-1497—location)
PO Box 228 (mailing address)
Yates Center, KS 66783-0228
(620) 625-8610; (620) 625-8674 FAX
kgrisier@woodsoncounty.net
http://www.31stjudicialdistrict.org
Kelley S. Grisier
(marriages from 1860 to date, probate records)
probate search service: $9.00 minimum; copies
of vital records, and probate records: 25¢ per
page (FAX: $1.00 per page to receive a FAX,
$5.00 to send a single page, $9.00 for two
pages, $12.00 for three pages, $14.00 for four
pages, $1.00 for each additional page)

Woodson County Register of Deeds
Courthouse, 105 West Rutledge Street
Yates Center, KS 66783-1499
(620) 625-8635; (620) 625-8670 FAX
regofdeeds@woodsoncounty.net
http://woodsoncounty.net/deeds/deeds.htm
Mardelle Pringle
(land records, deaths from 1940)
copies of land records and vital records: 25¢ per
page (FAX: $1.00 per page to receive a FAX,
$5.00 to send a single page, $9.00 for two
pages, $12.00 for three pages, $14.00 for four
pages, $1.00 for each additional page)

Wyandotte County
organized 1859, original county; consolidated
with the City of Kansas City in 1997

District Court
Unified Government of Wyandotte
County/Kansas City, Kansas
710 North Seventh Street, Mezzanine
Kansas City, KS 66101-3047
(913) 573-2901
http://www.wycokck.org/gen/wyco_generated
_pages/District_Court_m1830.html
(probate records)

probate search service: no charge; copies of
probate records: 25¢ per page if court file in
office, $2.00 per page from microfilm
originals, no minimum

Unified Government Register of Deeds
Unified Government of Wyandotte
County/Kansas City, Kansas
710 North Seventh Street
Kansas City, KS 66101-3084
(913) 573-2841; (913) 321-3075 FAX
bgolubski@wycokck.org
http://www.wycokck.org/gen/wyco_generated
_pages/Legal_Records_m1588.html
Barbara Golubski
(land records)

KENTUCKY

*Capital: Frankfort. Statehood: 1 June 1792 (organized
as a county of Virginia in 1776, separated 1783)*

Kentucky's fifty-nine District Courts, sitting
in each county seat, have jurisdiction over most
misdemeanors, civil cases under $4,000,
uncontested probate matters, and juvenile cases.
The fifty-six Circuit Courts, sitting in each
county seat, have general jurisdiction, including
all cases of real estate title questions, contested
probate matters, divorces, adoptions,
termination of parental rights, civil cases over
$4,000, capital offenses and felonies, and
appellate jurisdiction over the District Courts.
The Court of Appeals and the seven Districts of
the Supreme Court exercise appellate
jurisdiction.

Secretary of State Land Office
Room 80, Capitol Building
Frankfort, KY 40601
(502) 564-3490; (502) 564-6894 FAX
Kadkinson@mail.sos.state.ky.us
http://www.kysos.com
Kandie Adkinson, Administrative Supervisor
("Revolutionary War; land patents; digitized
records")
copies: $1.00 per warrant, $1.00 per survey,
$1.00 per grant, 50¢ for other pages

Adair County
organized 1802 from Green County

Adair County Circuit Clerk
Adair County Courthouse
500 Public Square, Suite 6
Columbia, KY 42728
(270) 384-2626
http://courts.ky.gov/Counties/Adair/default.htm
Dennis Loy
(probate records)
probate search service: $2.00; copies of probate
records: $1.00 per page, no minimum

Adair County Clerk
424 Public Square, Suite 2
Columbia, KY 42728-1493
(270) 384-2801; (270) 384-4805 FAX
adaircc2007@yahoo.com
http://www.adaircounty.ky.gov/cogov/departm
ents/coclerk.htm
Sheila Blair
(land records)

Allen County
organized 1815 from Barren and Warren
counties

Allen County Circuit Clerk
(Allen County Courthouse, 201 West Main
Street, Room 202—location)
PO Box 477 (mailing address)
Scottsville, KY 42164-0477
(270) 237-3561; (270) 237-4734
http://courts.ky.gov/Counties/Allen/default.htm
Todd B. Calvert
(probate records)

Allen County Clerk
(201 West Main Street, Room 6—location)
PO Box 336 (mailing address)
Scottsville, KY 42164-0036
(270) 237-3706; (270) 237-9206 FAX
alnclerk@nctc.com
http://www.allencountykentucky.com
Beverly Calvert
(land records)

Anderson County
organized 1827 from Franklin, Mercer and
Washington counties

Anderson County Circuit Clerk
Anderson County Courthouse
151 South Main Street
Lawrenceburg, KY 40342

(502) 839-3508
http://courts.ky.gov/Counties/Anderson/defau
lt.htm
Ms. Jan D. Rogers
(probate records)

Anderson County Clerk
151 South Main Street
Lawrenceburg, KY 40342-1192
(502) 839-3041; (502) 839-3043 FAX
http://www.andersoncounty.ky.gov/elected
Edith Hanks
(land records)

Ballard County
organized 1842 from Hickman and McCracken
counties

Ballard County Circuit Clerk
(Ballard County Courthouse, 134 North Fourth
Street—location)
PO Box 265 (mailing address)
Wickliffe, KY 42087
(270) 335-5123
http://courts.ky.gov/Counties/Ballard/default.
htm
Faye Oldham
(probate records)

Ballard County Clerk
PO Box 145
Wickliffe, KY 42087-0145
(270) 335-5168; (270) 335-3081 FAX
bcclerk@brtc.net
http://www.ballardconet.com
Lynn W. Lane
(land records)

Barren County
organized 1799 from Green and Warren
counties

Barren County Circuit Clerk
(Barren County Courthouse, 100 Courthouse
Square, Glasgow, KY 42141—location)
PO Box 1359 (mailing address)
Glasgow, KY 42142-1359
(270) 651-3763; (270) 651-2561; (270) 651-9830;
(270) 651-6203 FAX
http://courts.ky.gov/Counties/Barren/default.htm
Krissie Coe Fields
(probate records)

Barren County Clerk
117 North Public Square, Suite 1A
Glasgow, KY 42141
(270) 651-5200; (270) 651-1083 FAX
pshbrowning@hotmail.com
http://www.barrencounty.com
Pam Hodges Browning
(land records, naturalization records, vital
records)

Bath County
organized 1811 from Montgomery County

Bath County Circuit Clerk
(Bath County Courthouse Annex, 19 East Main
Street—location)
PO Box 558 (mailing address)
Owingsville, KY 40360
(606) 674-2186; (606) 674-6821; (606) 674-3996
FAX
http://courts.ky.gov/Counties/Bath/default.htm
Claudette Faudere
(probate records)

Bath County Clerk
PO Box 609
Owingsville, KY 40360-0609
(606) 674-2613; (606) 674-9526 FAX
annlykes2003@yahoo.com
http://www.bathcounty.ky.gov/elected
Carolyn Rogers
(land records from 1811, probate records from
1811)
probate search service: (depends on index);
copies of probate records: $3.00 per
document, $3.00 minimum

Bell County
organized 1867 from Harlan and Knox counties

Bell County Circuit Clerk
(Farmer Helton Judicial Center, 101 Park
Avenue—location)
PO Box 307 (mailing address)
Pineville, KY 40977
(606) 337-2942
http://courts.ky.gov/Counties/Bell/default.htm
Charles "Monk" Green
(probate records)

Bell County Clerk
PO Box 157
Pineville, KY 40977-0157
(606) 337-6143; (606) 337-5415 FAX
http://www.bellcounty.ky.gov/departments;
http://www.bellcountychamber.com
(Chamber of Commerce)
Becky Blevins
(land records, marriages)

Boone County
organized 1799 from Campbell County

Boone County Circuit Clerk
Boone County Justice Center
6025 Rogers Lane, Room 141
Burlington, KY 41005
(859) 334-2286
http://courts.ky.gov/Counties/Boone/default.h
tm
Ms. Pat Gutzeit
(wills, inventories, etc. from 1799)
probate search service: $10.00 per hour; copies
of probate records: 50¢ per page plus SASE,
no minimum

Boone County Clerk
PO Box 874
Burlington, KY 41005-0874
(859) 334-2130; (859) 334-3575 FAX
mrouse@boonecountyky.org
http://www.boonecountyclerk.com
Marilyn K. Rouse
(deeds, marriages, etc. from 1799, naturalization
records from about 1835 to 1900)
copies of marriages: $1.00 each, $5.00 for
certified copies

Bourbon County
organized 1786 from Fayette County

Bourbon County Circuit Clerk
Bourbon County Judicial Center
310 Main Street
Paris, KY 40361
(859) 987-2624
http://courts.ky.gov/Counties/Bourbon/defaul
t.htm
Sherry B. Rankin
(probate records)

Bourbon County Clerk
PO Box 312
Paris, KY 40361-0312
(859) 987-2142; (859) 987-5660 FAX
richard.eads@ky.gov;
bocojudgeexec@yahoo.com
http://bourboncountyclerk.ky.gov
Richard Stipp Eades
(land records)

Boyd County
organized 1860 from Carter, Greenup and
Lawrence counties

Boyd County Circuit Clerk
(Courthouse Annex—location)
PO Box 694 (mailing address)
Catlettsburg, KY 41129-0694
(606) 739-4131; (606) 739-4131; (606) 739-4133
http://courts.ky.gov/Counties/Boyd/default.htm
Linda Kay Baker
(probate records)

Boyd County Clerk
(2800 Louisa Street, Catlettsburg, KY 41129-
1116—location)

PO Box 523 (mailing address)
Catlettsburg, KY 41129-0523
(606) 739-5116; (606) 739-0430 FAX
debbiejones@zoominternet.net
http://www.boydcountyky.net
Debbie Jones
(land records)

Boyle County
organized 1842 from Lincoln and Mercer
counties (having the same county seat as the
now-abolished Kentucky County, Virginia,
which was organized in 1776 from Fincastle
County, Virginia)

Boyle County Circuit Clerk
Boyle County Courthouse
321 West Main Street
Danville, KY 40422
(859) 239-7442; (859) 239-7000 FAX
http://courts.ky.gov/Counties/Boyle/default.htm
Joni H. Terry
(probate records from 1978)

Boyle County Clerk
321 West Main Street Suite 123
Danville, KY 40422-1848
(859) 238-1110; (859) 238-1114 FAX
denise.curtsinger@ky.gov
http://boylecountyclerk.ky.gov
Denise B. Curtsinger
(deeds from 1842 and mortgages, wills 1842–
1978)
no records search service; copies: 50¢ per page,
no minimum

Bracken County
organized 1797 from Campbell and Mason
counties

Bracken County Circuit Clerk
(Bracken County Courthouse, 116 West Miami
Street—location)
PO Box 205 (mailing address)
Brooksville, KY 41004
(606) 735-3328; (606) 735-3900 FAX
http://courts.ky.gov/Counties/Bracken/default
.htm
Kathy B. Free
(probate records from 1797)
no probate search service (contact Miss
Margaret Whitehead, Wallin Avenue,
Brooksville, KY 41004); copies of probate
records: 50¢ each

Bracken County Clerk
PO Box 147
Brooksville, KY 41004-0147
(606) 735-2952; (606) 735-2687 FAX
bcclerk2006@yahoo.com
http://www.brackencounty.ky.gov/elected/co.htm
Rae Jean Poe
(land records from 1797 to date)
copies of land records: 50¢ each

Breathitt County
organized 1839 from Clay, Estill and Perry
counties

Breathitt County Circuit Clerk
Breathitt County Justice Center
1131 Main Street
Jackson, KY 41339
(606) 666-5768; (606) 666-4893 FAX
http://courts.ky.gov/Counties/Breathitt/defaul
t.htm
Patsy C. Williams
(probate records)

Breathitt County Clerk
1137 Main Street
Jackson, KY 41339-1194
(606) 666-3810; (606) 666-3807 FAX
tonywatts@kih.net
http://www.breathittcounty.ky.gov/elected/oth
er.htm
Tony G. Watts
(land records)

Breckinridge County
organized 1800 from Hardin County

Breckinridge County Circuit Clerk
(Breckinridge County Courthouse, 208 South
Main Street, Courthouse Square—location)
PO Box 111 (mailing address)
Hardinsburg, KY 40143-0111
(270) 756-2239; (270) 756-1129 FAX
http://courts.ky.gov/Counties/Breckinridge/de
fault.htm
Connie Whitworth
(probate records)

Breckinridge County Clerk
PO Box 538
Hardinsburg, KY 40143-0538
(270) 756-2246; (270) 756-6166; (270) 756-1569
FAX
http://www.breckinridgecounty.net/governmen
t.html#
Charles Allen Wilson
(land records)

Bullitt County
organized 1797 from Jefferson and Nelson
counties

Bullitt County Circuit Clerk
(505 Buffalo Run Road—location)
PO Box 746 (mailing address)
Shepherdsville, KY 40165
(502) 543-7104; (502) 955-7764
http://courts.ky.gov/Counties/Bullitt/default.htm
Doris A. Cornell
(probate records from 1978)

Bullitt County Clerk
PO Box 6
Shepherdsville, KY 40165-0006
(502) 543-2513; (502) 543-9121
bcelection@alltel.net
http://bullittcountyclerk.ky.gov
Nora McCawley
(probate records 1796–1977 and land records)
no probate search service; copies of probate
records: $3.50 per instrument

Butler County
organized 1810 from Logan and Ohio counties

Butler County Circuit Clerk
110 Main Street
Morgantown, KY 42261-0625
(270) 526-5631
http://courts.ky.gov/Counties/Butler/default.htm
Bonnie Howard
(probate records)

Butler County Clerk
PO Box 449
Morgantown, KY 42261-0049
(270) 526-5676; (270) 526-2658 FAX
shirley.givens@ky.gov
http://butlercoutny.ky.gov/elected/countyclerk.
htm
Shirley Givens
(land records and marriages)
no probate search service; copies of probate
records: 25¢ per page

Caldwell County
organized 1809 from Livingston County

Caldwell County Circuit Clerk
Caldwell County Courthouse Annex
105 West Court Square
Princeton, KY 42445
(270) 365-6884
http://courts.ky.gov/Counties/Caldwell/default
.htm
Jo Ann Newsom
(probate records)

Caldwell County Clerk
100 East Market Street, Room 23
Princeton, KY 42445-1696
(270) 365-6754; (270) 365-7447 FAX (Sheriff's
Office)
coclerk@caldwellcourthouse.com

http://www.caldwellcounty.ky.gov/elected/cocl
erk.htm
Toni Watson

Calloway County
organized 1821 from Hickman County

Calloway County Circuit Clerk
Calloway County Judicial Building
312 North Fourth Street
Murray, KY 42071
(270) 753-2773
http://courts.ky.gov/Counties/Calloway/defaul
t.htm
Vicki Wilson
(probate records)

Calloway County Clerk
101 South Fifth Street, Suite 5
Murray, KY 42071-2569
(270) 753-3923; (270) 759-9611 FAX
countyclerk@murray-ky.net;
callowayelections@murray-ky.net
http://elect.ky.gov/countyclerks.htm
Ray Coursey, Jr.
(land records)

Campbell County
organized 1794 from Harrison, Mason and Scott
counties

Campbell County Circuit Clerk
Campbell County Courthouse
330 York Street, Room #8
Newport, KY 41071
(859) 292-6314
http://courts.ky.gov/Counties/Campbell/defau
lt.htm
Thomas J. Calme
(probate records)

Campbell County Clerk
340 York Street
Newport, KY 41071-1682
(859) 292-3845; (859) 292-3887 FAX
jsnodgrass@campbellcountyky.org
http://www.campbellcountykyclerk.org;
http://www.campbellcounty.ky.gov
Jack Snodgrass
(land records, naturalization records, vital
records, and probate records)

Carlisle County
organized 1886 from Ballard County

Carlisle County Circuit Clerk
Carlisle County Courthouse
70 West Court Street
Bardwell, KY 42023
(270) 628-5425
http://courts.ky.gov/Counties/Carlisle/default.
htm
Kevin Hoskins
(probate records)

Carlisle County Clerk
PO Box 176
Bardwell, KY 42023-0176
(270) 628-3233; (270) 628-0191 FAX
http://www.carlislecounty.ky.gov/elected
Theresa Owens
(land records from 1886, marriages)

Carroll County
organized 1838 from Gallatin, Henry and
Trimble counties

Carroll County Circuit Clerk
Carroll County Hall of Justice
802 Clay Street
Carrollton, KY 41008
(502) 732-4305; (502) 732-4306; (502) 732-4307;
(502) 732-8138 FAX
ccfc@iglou.com
http://courts.ky.gov/Counties/Carroll/default.
htm
Laman L. Stark
(probate records)

Carroll County Clerk
440 Main Street

Carrollton, KY 41008-1064
(502) 732-7005; (502) 732-7007 FAX
http://www.carrollcountygov.us/officials.asp
Alice Marsh
(deeds from 1838, marriages from 1839, probate
records with Circuit Court Offices)
probate search service: $3.50 per name; copies
of probate records: 25¢ per page

Carter County
organized 1838 from Greenup and Lawrence
counties

Carter County Circuit Clerk
Carter County Justice Center
100 East Main Street
Grayson, KY 41143
(606) 474-5191
http://courts.ky.gov/Counties/Carter/default.htm
Larry D. Thompson
(probate records)

Carter County Clerk
300 West Main Street, Room 232
Grayson, KY 41143-1298
(606) 474-5188; (606) 474-6883 FAX
http://www.cartercounty.ky.gov/elected/count
y/coclerk.htm
Mike Johnston
(land records, marriages, probate records)
records search service: $5.00 for one to three
years, $10.00 for three to ten years; copies of
records: $1.00 per page, $5.00 for certified
copies

Casey County
organized 1807 from Lincoln County

Casey County Circuit Clerk
Casey County Judicial Center
231 Courthouse Square
Liberty, KY 42539
(606) 787-6510
http://courts.ky.gov/Counties/Casey/default.htm
Craig L. Overstreet
(probate records)

Casey County Clerk
PO Box 310
Liberty, KY 42539-0310
(606) 787-6471; (606) 787-9155 FAX
cccevamiller@yahoo.com
http://www.caseycounty.ky.gov/departments/c
oclerk.htm
Eva S. Miller

Christian County
organized 1797 from Logan County

Christian County Circuit Clerk
Christian County Justice Center
100 Justice Way
Hopkinsville, KY 42240
(270) 889-6539; (270) 889-6541; (270) 889-6542;
(270) 889-6592; (270) 889-6029 FAX
http://courts.ky.gov/Counties/Christian/defaul
t.htm
Gary J. Haddock
(probate records)

Christian County Clerk
511 South Main Street, Suite 15
Hopkinsville, KY 42240-2300
(270) 887-4105; (270) 887-4186 FAX
michael.kem@ky.gov
http://www.christiancounty.org/countyclerk
Michael A. Kem
(land records from 1797, probate records from
1797)
probate search service: $5.00; copies of probate
records: 25¢ per page, $1.00 minimum

Clark County
organized 1793 from Bourbon and Fayette
counties

Clark County Circuit Clerk
(Governor James Clark Judicial Center, 17
Cleveland Avenue, Winchester, KY 40391—
location)

PO Box 687 (mailing address)
Winchester, KY 40392-0687
(859) 737-7264; (859) 737-7005
http://courts.ky.gov/Counties/Clark/default.htm
David N. Hunt
(probate records)

Clark County Clerk
PO Box 4060
Winchester, KY 40392-4060
(859) 745-0280; (859) 745-4251 FAX
http://www.winchesterky.com/quick_ref.phtml;
   http://www.winchesterkychamber.com
Anita Shimfessel Jones
(land records from 1793 to date, probate
   records)
probate search service ("we do not have
   someone that does the genealogy research full
   time"): $3.00; copies of probate records: 50¢
   per page or $3.00 per document, no minimum

Clay County
organized 1807 from Floyd, Knox and Madison
   counties

Clay County Circuit Clerk
Clay County Justice Center
316 Main Street, Suite 108
Manchester, KY 40962-1377
(606) 598-3663; (606) 598-4047 FAX
http://courts.ky.gov/Counties/Clay/default.htm
James S. Phillips
(probate records from 1978)
no probate search service; copies of probate
   records: 15¢ per page

Clay County Clerk
102 Richmond Road, Suite 101
Manchester, KY 40962-1392
(606) 598-2544; (606) 599-0603 FAX
claycoclerk@alltel.net
http://www.claycounty.ky.gov/elected/county.
   htm
Freddy Wayne Thompson
(land records)

Clinton County
organized 1836 from Cumberland and Wayne
   counties

Clinton County Circuit Clerk
Clinton County Courthouse
100 South Cross Street
Albany KY 42602
(606) 387-6424; (606) 387-8181; (606) 387-8154
   FAX
http://courts.ky.gov/Counties/Clinton/default.
   htm
Jake Staton
(probate records)

Clinton County Clerk
Courthouse, 100 South Cross Street
Albany, KY 42602-1263
(606) 387-5234; (606) 387-5258 FAX
clintoncountyclerk@alltel.net
http://www.clintoncounty.ky.gov/elected
Jim Elmore
(land records)

Crittenden County
organized 1842 from Livingston County

Crittenden County Circuit Clerk
Crittenden County Courthouse
107 South Main Street
Marion, KY 42064
(270) 965-4200; (270) 965-4046
http://courts.ky.gov/Counties/Crittenden/defa
   ult.htm
Madeline Henderson
(probate records)
no probate search service; copies of probate
   records: 25¢ per page

Crittenden County Clerk
107 South Main Street, Suite 203
Marion, KY 42064-1507
(270) 965-3403; (270) 965-3447 FAX
cbyford@hotmail.com

http://www.the-press.com/county.html
Carolyn Byford
(land records with Crittenden County PVA or
   County Clerk Offices)

Cumberland County
organized 1799 from Green County

Cumberland County Circuit Clerk
(Cumberland County Justice Building, 112
   Public Square—location)
PO Box 395 (mailing address)
Burkesville, KY 42717-0395
(270) 864-2611
http://courts.ky.gov/Counties/Cumberland/de
   fault.htm
Hazel L. Jones
(probate records)

Cumberland County Clerk
PO Box 275
Burkesville, KY 42717-0275
(270) 864-3726; (270) 864-5884 FAX
kaking620@alltel.net
http://www.cumberlandcounty.ky.gov/elected
Kim King
(deeds from 1799, marriages from 1882 [older
   ones burned], wills and estate settlements
   from 1814)
probate search service: no charge; copies of
   probate records: $2.00 per instrument; $2.00
   minimum

Daviess County
organized 1815 from Ohio County

Daviess County Circuit Clerk
(Holbrook Judicial Center, 100 East Second
   Street—location)
Po Box 277 (mailing address)
Owensboro, KY 42302-0277
(270) 687-7327; (270) 687-7200
http://courts.ky.gov/Counties/Daviess/default.
   htm
Susan W. Tierney
(probate records)

Daviess County Clerk
PO Box 609
Owensboro, KY 42302-0609
(270) 685-8434; (270) 686-7111 FAX
rhouse@daviessky.org
http://daviessky.org
J. Michael Libs
(land records, marriages, older probate records
   and wills)
no probate search service; copies of probate
   records: $2.00 per instrument under three
   pages

Edmonson County
organized 1825 from Grayson, Hart and Warren
   counties

Edmonson County Circuit Clerk
Edmonson County Courthouse Annex
110 Main Cross Street
Brownsville, KY 42210-0739
(270) 597-2584; (270) 597-2884 FAX
http://courts.ky.gov/Counties/Edmonson/defa
   ult.htm
Sharon French
(probate records from early 1800s)
probate search service: $2.50 per person; copies
   of probate records: 50¢ per page (up to legal
   size), 75¢ (large size), no minimum

Edmonson County Clerk
PO Box 830
Brownsville, KY 42210-0830
(270) 597-2624; (270) 597-9714 FAX
http://www.edmonsoncounty.ky.gov/elected/c
   oclerk.htm
Larry "Butch" Carroll
(land records from early 1800s)

Elliott County
organized 1869 from Carter, Lawrence and
   Morgan counties

Elliott County Circuit Clerk
(Elliott County Courthouse Annex, 100 Court
   and Main Street—location)
PO Box 788 (mailing address)
Sandy Hook, KY 41171-0788
(606) 738-5232; (606) 738-5238; (606) 738-6962
   FAX
http://courts.ky.gov/Counties/Elliott/default.htm
Mr. Delmaine D. Dickerson
(probate records from 1978)

Elliott County Clerk
PO Box 225
Sandy Hook, KY 41171-0225
(606) 738-5421; (606) 738-4462 FAX
http://www.elliottcounty.ky.gov/elected.htm
Reeda S. Ison
(deeds from 1869, marriages from 1934, probate
   records 1957–1978 [courthouse burned 1957])
no probate search service; copies of probate
   records: $1.00 per page

Estill County
organized 1808 from Clark and Madison
   counties

Estill County Circuit Clerk
Estill County Courthouse
130 Main Street, Room 207
Irvine, KY 40336-1006
(606) 723-3970
http://courts.ky.gov/Counties/Estill/default.htm
Charlene I. Baker
(probate records)

Estill County Clerk
(130 Main Street—location)
PO Box 59 (mailing address)
Irvine, KY 40336-0059
(606) 723-5156; (606) 723-5158 (Record
   Inquiries); (606) 723-5108 FAX
http://www.estill.net/local_govt.htm
Sherry L. Fox
(land records, marriages, and probate records)
probate search service: $5.00 per name per
   category; copies of probate records: $1.00 per
   page, $5.00 for certified copies, no minimum
   ("we do not allow customers to make copies
   themselves")

Fayette County
organized 1780 from Kentucky County,
   Virginia; consolidated with the City of
   Lexington in 1972

Fayette County Circuit Clerk
Fayette County Courthouse
120 North Limestone, Room 103
Lexington, KY 40507-1152
(859) 246-2141
http://courts.ky.gov/Counties/Fayette/default.
   htm
Wilma Fields Lynch
(probate records from the 1960s and 1970s)
no probate search service ("We do not perform
   this type of research, we pass these requests
   on to a local genealogist"); copies of probate
   records: 50¢ per page

Fayette County Clerk
162 East Main Street, Room 131
Lexington, KY 40507-1318
(859) 253-3344; (859) 231-9619 FAX
info@FayetteCountyClerk.com
http://www.fayettecountyclerk.com
Donald W. Blevins

Fleming County
organized 1798 from Mason County

Fleming County Circuit Clerk
Fleming County Courthouse
100 Court Square
Flemingsburg, KY 41041
(606) 845-7011; (606) 849-2400 FAX
http://courts.ky.gov/Counties/Fleming/default
   .htm
Pam Lowe
(probate records)

Fleming County Clerk
(Court Square, Flemingsburg, KY 41041-1398—
location)
PO Box 324 (mailing address)
Flemingsburg, KY 41041-0324
(606) 845-8461; (606) 845-0212 FAX
countyclerk@flemingcountyky.org
http://www.flemingcountyky.org/page3.htm
Jarrod Fritz
(naturalization records from 1850s, deeds,
marriages, wills, settlements, inventories and
appraisements from 1798)

Floyd County
organized 1800 from Fleming, Mason and
Montgomery counties

Floyd County Circuit Clerk
Floyd County Courthouse
127 South Lake Drive
Prestonsburg, KY 41653
http://courts.ky.gov/Counties/Floyd/default.htm
Douglas Ray Hall
(probate records)

Floyd County Clerk
PO Box 1089
Prestonsburg, KY 41653-5089
(606) 886-3816; (606) 886-8089 FAX
http://elect.ky.gov/countyclerks.htm;
http://www.floydcountykentucky.com
(Chamber of Commerce)
Christopher Waugh

Franklin County
organized 1795 from Mercer, Shelby and
Woodford counties

Franklin County Circuit Clerk
(Franklin County Courthouse Annex, 218 St.
Clair Street, Frankfort, KY 40601—location)
PO Box 678 (mailing address)
Frankfort, KY 40602
(502) 564-7013; (502) 564-8380; (502) 564-8188
FAX
http://courts.ky.gov/Counties/Franklin/default
.htm
Sally Jump
(probate records)

Franklin County Clerk
(Courthouse Annex—location)
PO Box 338 (mailing address)
Frankfort, KY 40602-0338
(502) 875-8702; (502) 875-8718 FAX
guy.zeigler@ky.gov
http://www.franklincountyclerk.org
Guy Zeigler
(land records and marriages)

Fulton County
organized 1845 from Hickman County

Fulton County Circuit Clerk
(Fulton County Courthouse, 114 East
Wellington Street—location)
PO Box 198 (mailing address)
Hickman, KY 42050
(270) 236-3944; (270) 236-3729 FAX
http://courts.ky.gov/Counties/Fulton/default.htm
Sarah Bing Johnson
(probate records)

Fulton County Clerk
PO Box 126
Hickman, KY 42050-0126
(270) 236-2727; (270) 236-2522 FAX
betty.abernathy@ky.gov
http://www.fultoncounty.ky.gov/elected
Betty Abernathy
(land records)

Gallatin County
organized 1799 from Franklin and Shelby
counties

Gallatin County Circuit Clerk
Gallatin County Courthouse
100 Main Street
Warsaw, KY 41095

(859) 567-5241; (859) 567-2388
http://courts.ky.gov/Counties/Gallatin/default.
htm
Sue O'Connor
(probate records)

Gallatin County Clerk
PO Box 1309
Warsaw, KY 41095-0616
(606) 567-5411; (859) 567-5444 FAX
tracymiles@gallatincountyky.com
http://www.gallatincountyky.com;
http://elect.ky.gov/countyclerks.htm
Tracy Miles
(land records)

Garrard County
organized 1797 from Lincoln, Madison and
Mercer counties

Garrard County Circuit Clerk
Garrard County Courthouse Annex
7 Public Square
Lancaster, KY 40444
(859) 792-2961
http://courts.ky.gov/Counties/Garrard/default.
htm
Jennifer Grubbs
(probate records)

Garrard County Clerk
15 Public Square, Suite 5
Lancaster, KY 40444-1057
(859) 792-3071; (859) 792-6751 FAX
garrardcoclerk@yahoo.com
http://www.garrardcounty.ky.gov/elected/cocle
rk.htm
Stacy H. May
(land records, naturalization records, vital
records, probate records)
no probate search service; copies of probate
records: $2.50 per document

Grant County
organized 1820 from Pendleton County

Grant County Circuit Clerk
Grant County Courthouse
101 North Main Street
Williamstown, KY 41097
(859) 824-4467
http://courts.ky.gov/Counties/Grant/default.htm
Shirley C. Wilson
(probate records)

Grant County Clerk
107 North Main Street
Williamstown, KY 41097-1107
(859) 824-3321; (859) 824-3367 FAX
http://www.grantcounty.ky.gov/departments_a
gencies
Leatha Conrad
(land records)

Graves County
organized 1824 from Hickman County

Graves County Circuit Clerk
Graves County Courthouse
100 East Broadway
Mayfield, KY 42066
(270) 247-1733; (270) 247-7853
http://courts.ky.gov/Counties/Graves/default.
htm
Nedra Nall Shemwell
(probate records)

Graves County Clerk
101 East South Street, Suite 2
Mayfield, KY 42066-2324
(270) 247-1676; (270) 247-1274 FAX
barry.kennemore@gy.gov
http://www.gravescounty.ky.gov/elected
Barry Kennemore
(land records)

Grayson County
organized 1810 from Hardin and Ohio counties

Grayson County Circuit Clerk
Grayson County Judicial Building

125 East White Oak Street
Leitchfield, KY 42754
(270) 259-3040; (270) 259-9866 FAX
http://courts.ky.gov/Counties/Grayson/default
.htm
Ms. Elois Downs
(probate records)
no probate search service; copies of probate
records: 25¢ per page, $3.50 for certified
copies

Grayson County Clerk
10 Court Square
Leitchfield, KY 42754-1199
(270) 259-3201; (270) 259-9264 FAX
carlettafarris@ky.gov
http://www.graysoncounty.ky.gov/elected
Carletta Farris
(land records and marriages from 1896)

Green County
organized 1793 from Lincoln and Nelson
counties

Green County Circuit Clerk
Green County Courthouse
203 West Court Street
Greensburg, KY 42743
(270) 932-5631; (270) 932-4029
http://courts.ky.gov/Counties/Green/default.htm
John Frank
(probate records)

Green County Clerk
203 West Court Street
Greensburg, KY 42743-1522
(270) 932-5386; (270) 932-6241 FAX
cmscott@accesshsd.net
http://www.greencounty.ky.gov/elected
Carolyn M. Scott
(land records, marriages, and probate records
from 1793)
probate search service: $2.00; copies of
marriages and land and probate records: $1.50
each plus postage

Greenup County
organized 1804 from Mason County

Greenup County Circuit Clerk
Greenup County Courthouse Annex
101 Harrison Street
Greenup, KY 41144
(606) 473-9869; (606) 473-9860
http://courts.ky.gov/Counties/Greenup/defaul
t.htm
Allen K. Reed
(probate records)

Greenup County Clerk
PO Box 686
Greenup, KY 41144-0686
(606) 473-7394; (606) 473-5354 FAX (call first)
http://www.greenupcounty.ky.gov/elected
Patricia Hieneman
(land records)

Hancock County
organized 1829 from Breckinridge, Daviess and
Ohio counties

Hancock County Circuit Clerk
(Hancock County Courthouse, 200 Court
Square—location)
PO Box 250 (mailing address)
Hawesville, KY 42348-0250
(270) 927-8144; (270) 927-8355; (270) 927-8629
FAX
http://courts.ky.gov/Counties/Hancock/defaul
t.htm
Ms. Noel J. Quinn
(probate records from 1975)

Hancock County Clerk
(Hancock County Administration Building—
location)
PO Box 146 (mailing address)
Hawesville, KY 42348-0146
(502) 927-6117; (270) 927-8639 FAX
trtotb@aol.com; hcclerk@bellsouth.net

http://elect.ky.gov/countyclerks.htm
Trina Ogle
(land records from 1829, probate records 1829–1975)
probate search service: $4.00 per hour; copies of probate records: 50¢ per page, $3.50 for certified copies, $4.00 minimum

Hardin County
organized 1793 from Nelson County

Hardin County Circuit Clerk
Hardin County Justice Center
120 East Dixie Avenue
Elizabethtown, KY 42701-1469
(270) 766-5000; (270) 766-5036
http://courts.ky.gov/Counties/Hardin/default.htm
Ralph Baskett
(probate records)

Hardin County Clerk
R. R. Thomas Government Building, 14 Public Square, Elizabethtown, KY 42701—location)
PO Box 1030 (mailing address)
Elizabethtown, KY 42702-1030
(270) 765-2171; (270) 564-4212 (Birth and Death Records); (270) 766-5000 (Divorce Decrees and Name Changes); (270) 765-6193 FAX
ktabb.hcco@hcky.org
http://www.hccoky.org
Kenneth L. Tabb
(land records, vital records, and probate records)
no probate search service ("It is necessary to employ a private researcher for search of *any* Hardin County records; the county does not have any personnel to do this work")

Harlan County
organized 1819 from Knox County

Harlan County Circuit Clerk
Harlan County Justice Center
129 South First Street
Harlan, KY 40831
(606) 573-7114; (606) 573-5895
http://courts.ky.gov/Counties/Harlan/default.htm
Paul F. Williams
(probate records)

Harlan County Clerk
(205 Central Street—location)
PO Box 670 (mailing address)
Harlan, KY 40831-0670
(606) 573-3636; (606) 573-0064 FAX
http://elect.ky.gov/countyclerks.htm;
http://www.harlancounty.com
Wanda S. Clem

Harrison County
organized 1794 from Bourbon and Scott counties

Harrison County Circuit Clerk
Harrison County Justice Center
115 Court Street
Cynthiana, KY 41031-0010
(859) 234-1914
http://courts.ky.gov/Counties/Harrison/default.htm
Wanda C. Marsh
(probate records)

Harrison County Clerk
County Courthouse Annex
313 Oddville Avenue
Cynthiana, KY 41031-1242
(859) 234-7130; (859) 234-8049 FAX
harrcntyclrk@kih.net; harrclrk@setel.com
http://www.harrisoncounty.ky.gov/elected/county/fiscal.htm
Linda B. Furnish
(land records, vital records from 1794, probate records from 1794)
probate search service: variable ("research done by local citizen"); copies of probate records: 50¢ per page, 50¢ minimum

Hart County
organized 1819 from Barren and Hardin counties

Hart County Circuit Clerk
Hart County Courthouse
100 Main Street
Munfordville, KY 42765-0248
(270) 524-5181
http://courts.ky.gov/Counties/Hart/default.htm
Rita Doyle
(probate records)

Hart County Clerk
(200 Main Street—location)
PO Box 277 (mailing address)
Munfordville, KY 42765-0277
(270) 524-2751; (270) 524-0458 FAX
http://www.hartcounty.ky.gov/departments/clerk.htm
Lisa Hensley

Henderson County
organized 1799 from Christian County

Henderson County Circuit Clerk
Henderson County Judicial Center
5 North Main Street
Henderson, KY 42420
(270) 826-2405; (270) 826-1566
http://courts.ky.gov/Counties/Henderson/default.htm
Ruth London
(probate records)

Henderson County Clerk
PO Box 374
Henderson, KY 42420-0374
(502) 826-3906; (270) 826-9677 FAX
rmatthews@hendersonky.us
http://www.hendersonky.us/right-hendersonky.php?nav_ID=178
Renny Tapp Matthews

Henry County
organized 1799 from Shelby County

Henry County Circuit Clerk
(Henry County Courthouse, 30 North Main Street—location)
PO Box 359 (mailing address)
New Castle, KY 40050
(502) 845-2868
http://courts.ky.gov/Counties/Henry/default.htm
Mary Lou Roberts
(probate records)

Henry County Clerk
(30 North Main, Suite A—location)
PO Box 615 (mailing address)
New Castle, KY 40050-0615
(502) 845-5705; (502) 845-5708 FAX
hcjudgeexec@hotmail.com (John Brent, County Judge/Executive)
http://www.henrycountygov.com/directory.html
Juanita Lashley

Hickman County
organized 1822 from Caldwell and Livingston counties

Hickman County Circuit Clerk
Hickman County Annex
109 South Washington Street
Clinton, KY 42031-1439
(270) 653-3901; (270) 653-2026; (270) 653-3989 FAX
http://courts.ky.gov/Counties/Hickman/default.htm
Carolyn Kimbell
(probate records)

Hickman County Court Clerk
110 east Clay Street, Suite E
Clinton, KY 42031-1296
(270) 653-2131; (270) 653-4248 FAX
http://www.hickmancounty.ky.gov/elected/coclerk
James "Jimbo" Berry

(land records from 1822, five citizenship records from 1843, marriages from 1822, "1854–1906 very scattered in both birth and death records in a book [1850–1860 in a box]," probate records from 1822)
probate search service: "depends on how many people and the length of time it takes to go through the dates that are asked for"; copies of probate records: $2.00 per document if mailed, 25¢ per page if working in our office, no minimum

Hopkins County
organized 1807 from Henderson County

Hopkins County Circuit Clerk
Hopkins County Courthouse
30 South Main Street
Madisonville, KY 42431
(270) 824-7502
http://courts.ky.gov/Counties/Hopkins/default.htm
Carolyn A. Polley
(probate records)

Hopkins County Clerk
10 South Main Street, Room 12
Madisonville, KY 42431-2588
(270) 821-7361; (270) 821-3270 FAX
http://www.hopkinscounty.net/clerk/default.htm
Devra Steckler
(land records, marriages)

Jackson County
organized 1858 from Clay, Estill, Madison, Owsley, Laurel and Rockcastle counties

Jackson County Circuit Clerk
Jackson County Courthouse
105 Main Street
McKee, KY 40447
(606) 287-7783; (606) 287-3277 FAX
http://courts.ky.gov/Counties/Jackson/default.htm
Mr. Bobby G. Morris
(probate records)

Jackson County Clerk
(Courthouse, Main Street, Room 108—location)
PO Box 339 (mailing address)
McKee, KY 40447-0339
(606) 287-7800; (606) 287-7079 FAX
jcclerk@prtcnet.org
http://www.jacksoncounty.ky.gov/elected.htm;
http://www.eastky.net/jacksonco
Donald "Duck" Moore

Jefferson County
organized 1780 from Kentucky County, Virginia; consolidated with the City of Louisvillein 2000

Jefferson County Circuit Clerk
Louis D. Brandeis Hall of Justice
600 West Jefferson Street, Second Floor, Room 2008
Louisville, KY 40202
(502) 595-3055; (502) 595-4629 FAX
http://courts.ky.gov/Counties/Jefferson/default.htm
Michael Losavio

Jefferson County Circuit Court Civil Suit/File Room
700 West Jefferson Street
Louisville, KY 40202
(502) 595-3007; (502) (502) 595-4928 FAX
http://courts.ky.gov/Counties/Jefferson/default.htm
Michael Losavio

Jefferson County Clerk
527 West Jefferson Street, Suite 105
Louisville, KY 40202-2850
(502) 574-5700; (502) 574-5566 FAX
pmccraney@JeffersonCountyClerk.org
http://www.jeffersoncountyclerk.org;
http://www.louisvilleky.gov
Barbara Holsclaw

Jessamine County

organized 1799 from Fayette County

Jessamine County Circuit Clerk
Jessamine County Court Complex
107 North Main Street
Nicholasville, KY 40356
(859) 885-4531; (859) 887-1005; (859) 887-0425
FAX
http://courts.ky.gov/Counties/Jessamine/defau
lt.htm
Doug Fain
(probate records)

Jessamine County Clerk
101 North Main Street
Nicholasville, KY 40356-1270
(859) 885-4161; (859) 885-5837 FAX
cleva@windstream.net; coclk@alltel.net
http://www.jessamineco.com/services/servicct
ext1.htm#countyclerk
Eva L. McDaniel
(land records from 1799, probate records)

Johnson County

organized 1843 from Floyd, Lawrence and
Morgan counties

Johnson County Circuit Clerk
Johnson County Judicial Center
908 Third Street
Paintsville, KY 41240
(606) 297-9567; (606) 297-9573 FAX
http://courts.ky.gov/Counties/Johnson/default
.htm
Vickie Rice
(probate records)

Johnson County Clerk
230 Court Street, Suite 124
Paintsville, KY 41240-1607
(606) 789-2557; (606) 789-2559
johnsoncoclerk@charterinternet.com
http://elect.ky.gov/countyclerks.htm
Sallee Conley Holbrook
(land records and vital records)

Kenton County

organized 1840 from Campbell County

Kenton County Circuit Clerk
Kenton County Justice Center
230 Madison Avenue
Covington, KY 41011
(859) 292-6521
http://courts.ky.gov/Counties/Kenton/default.
htm
Karen Linn
(probate records)

Kenton County Clerk
PO Box 1109
Covington, KY 41012-1109
(859) 392-1652; (859) 392-1639 FAX
rodney.eldridge@kentoncounty.org
http://www.kentoncounty.org/county_officials
/county_clerk/index.html
Rodney Eldridge
(land records and probate records from 1860)

Kenton County Clerk
Independence Office
PO Box 38
Independence, KY 41051
(859) 392-1680
rodney.eldridge@kentoncounty.org
http://www.kentoncounty.org/county_officials
/county_clerk/index.html
Rodney Eldridge
(land records and probate records from 1840)

Knott County

organized 1884 from Breathitt, Floyd, Letcher
and Perry counties

Knott County Circuit Clerk
(Knott County Justice Center, 100 Justice
Drive—location)
PO Box 1317 (mailing address)
Hindman, KY 41822

(606) 785-5021; (606) 785-3994 FAX
http://courts.ky.gov/Counties/Knott/default.htm
Judy Watson-Conley
(probate records)

Knott County Clerk
PO Box 446
Hindman, KY 41822-0446
(606) 785-5651; (606) 785-0996 FAX
http://elect.ky.gov/countyclerks.htm
Kenneth R. Gayheart

Knox County

organized 1800 from Lincoln County

Knox County Circuit Clerk
(Knox County Courthouse Annex, 401 Court
Square—location)
PO Box 760 (mailing address)
Barbourville, KY 40906
(606) 546-3075
http://courts.ky.gov/Counties/Knox/default.htm
Greg Helton
(probate records)

Knox County Clerk
401 Court Square, Suite 102
Barbourville, KY 40906-1463
(606) 546-3568; (606) 546-3589 FAX
coclerk@barbourville.com
http://knoxcountyky.co/clerk.htm
Mike Corey
(deeds, wills)
probate search service: $2.00; copies of probate
records: $2.00 per instrument, no minimum

LaRue County

organized 1843 from Hardin County

LaRue County Circuit Clerk
(LaRue County Courthouse Annex, 209 West
High Street—location)
PO Box 191 (mailing address)
Hodgenville, KY 42748-0191
(270) 358-3421; (270) 358-3731
http://courts.ky.gov/Counties/Larue/default.ht
m
Larry C. Bell
(probate records)

LaRue County Clerk
209 West High Street
Hodgenville, KY 42748-1543
(270) 358-3544; (270) 358-4528 FAX
lcclerk@laruecounty.net
http://www.laruecounty.org/localofficials.shtml
Linda Carter
(deeds from 1843, marriage licenses from 1843,
wills [incomplete])
no probate search service; copies of land and
probate records and marriage licenses: $1.00

Laurel County

organized 1826 from Clay, Knox, Rockcastle
and Whitley counties

Laurel County Circuit Clerk
(Laurel County Courthouse Annex 2, 103 South
Broad Street, London, KY 40741—location)
PO Box 1798 (mailing address)
London, KY 40743
(606) 864-2863; (606) 864-7445
http://courts.ky.gov/Counties/Laurel/default.htm
Roger L. Schott
(probate records)

Laurel County Clerk
101 South Main Street, Room 203
London, KY 40741-2308
(606) 864-5158; (606) 864-7369 FAX
lcc10@windstream.net
http://elect.ky.gov/countyclerks.htm
Dean Johnson

Lawrence County

organized 1822 from Floyd and Greenup
counties

Lawrence County Circuit Clerk
Lawrence County Courthouse Annex
122 Main Cross Street

Louisa, KY 41230
(606) 638-4215
http://courts.ky.gov/Counties/Lawrence/defau
lt.htm
Martha S. Kiser
(probate records)

Lawrence County Clerk
122 South Main Cross Street
Louisa, KY 41230-1393
(606) 638-4108; (606) 638-0638 FAX
http://www.lawrencecounty.ky.gov/elected
Chris Jobe
(land records from early 1800s, marriages,
probate records)
probate search service: $5.00; copies of probate
records: 50¢ (letter size), 75¢ (legal size), $1.00
(ledger), 50¢ minimum

Lee County

organized 1870 from Breathitt, Estill, Owsley
and Wolfe counties

Lee County Circuit Clerk
(Lee County Courthouse, 256 Main Street,
Second Floor—location)
PO Box E (mailing address)
Beattyville, KY 41311-2005
(606) 464-8400
http://courts.ky.gov/Counties/Lee/default.htm
Emma C. Adams
(probate records)

Lee County Clerk
PO Box 551
Beattyville, KY 41311-0511
(606) 464-4115; (606) 464-4102 FAX
russells@sc-tel.com; leeclrk@mikrotec.com
http://www.leecounty.ky.gov/elected
Russell Stamper
(deeds and mortgages, marriages, and probate
records from 1870)
no probate search service; copies of probate
records: 25¢ per page, 25¢ minimum

Leslie County

organized 1878 from Clay, Harlan and Perry
counties

Leslie County Circuit Clerk
(Leslie County Courthouse, 22010 Main
Street—location)
PO Box 1750 (mailing address)
Hyden, KY 41749
(606) 672-2505; (606) 672-2503; (606) 672-5128
FAX
http://courts.ky.gov/Counties/Leslie/default.htm
Carmolitta Morgan-Pace
(probate records)

Leslie County Clerk
PO Box 916
Hyden, KY 41749-0916
(606) 672-2193; (606) 672-4264 FAX
leslieclerk@TDS.net
http://www.lesliecounty.ky.gov/elected
James Lewis

Letcher County

organized 1842 from Harlan and Perry counties

Letcher County Circuit Clerk
Letcher County Courthouse
156 Main Street, Suite 201
Whitesburg, KY 41858
(606) 633-7559; (606) 633-1048
http://courts.ky.gov/Counties/Letcher/default.
htm
Margaret S. Nichols
(probate records)

Letcher County Clerk
156 Main Street, Suite 102
Whitesburg, KY 41858-7286
(606) 633-2432; (606) 632-9282 FAX
letchercountyclerk@yahoo.com
http://www.letchercounty.ky.gov/government/
elected
Winston Meade
(land records, naturalization records, marriage

records, probate records before 1978)

Lewis County
organized 1807 from Mason County

Lewis County Circuit Clerk
Lewis County Courthouse
512 Second Street
Vanceburg, KY 41179
(606) 796-3053; (606) 796-6002
http://courts.ky.gov/Counties/Lewis/default.htm
Kathy Hardy
(probate records)

Lewis County Clerk
PO Box 129
Vanceburg, KY 41179-0129
(606) 796-3062; (606) 796-6511 FAX
lewiscoclerk@yahoo.com
http://lewiscounty.ky.gov/elected
Shirley A. Hinton
(land records and probate records from 30 April 1807)
probate search service: $3.50; copies of probate records: $1.50 per instrument, no minimum

Lincoln County
organized 1780 from Kentucky County, Virginia

Lincoln County Circuit Clerk
Lincoln County Judicial Building
101 East Main Street
Stanford, KY 40484
(606) 365-2535
http://courts.ky.gov/Counties/Lincoln/default.htm
Teresa Reed
(probate records)

Lincoln County Clerk
102 East Main Street, Suite 3
Stanford, KY 40484-1279
(606) 365-4570; (606) 365-4572 FAX
mtdora@bellsouth.net
http://www.lincolnky.com/government.htm
George Spoonamore, IV

Livingston County
organized 1798 from Christian County

Livingston County Circuit Clerk
(Livingston County Courthouse, 339 Courthouse Drive—location)
PO Box 160 (mailing address)
Smithland, KY 42081
(270) 928-2172
http://courts.ky.gov/Counties/Livingston/default.htm
Ms. Jackie Doom
(probate records)

Livingston County Clerk
(Court Street—location)
PO Box 400 (mailing address)
Smithland, KY 42081-0400
(270) 928-2162 voice & FAX
http://www.livingstonco.ky.gov/clerk
Carroll Walker
(deeds and mortgages from 1800, marriages from 1898, probate records from 1800 to 1978)
no probate search service; copies of probate records: vary in price, $2.00 minimum

Logan County
organized 1792 from Lincoln County

Logan County Circuit/District Clerk
(Logan County Courthouse, 200 West Fourth Street—location)
PO Box 420 (mailing address)
Russellville, KY 42276
(270) 726-2424; (270) 726-7893 FAX
http://courts.ky.gov/Counties/Logan/default.htm
Sherry Wilkins
(probate records)

Logan County Clerk
(Park Square—location)
PO Box 358 (mailing address)
Russellville, KY 42276-0358

(270) 726-6061; (270) 726-4355
loganclk@bellsouth.net
http://www.logancounty.ky.gov/elected
Scottie Harper
(deeds, probate records before 1977)
no probate search service; copies of probate records: 25¢ per page, no minimum

Lyon County
organized 1854 from Caldwell County

Lyon County Circuit Clerk
(Lyon County Judicial Center, 500A West Dale Avenue—location)
PO Box 565 (mailing address)
Eddyville, KY 42038
(270) 388-7231
http://courts.ky.gov/Counties/Lyon/default.htm
Rebecca "Becky" Howard
(probate records)

Lyon County Clerk
PO Box 310
Eddyville, KY 42038-0310
(270) 388-2331; (270) 388-0634 FAX
sdefew@bellsouth.com
http://www.lyoncounty.ky.gov/elected;
http://www.lyoncounty.com (Chamber of Commerce)
Sarah Defew
(land records from 1854 to date, probate records from 1854 to date)
no records search service

Madison County
organized 1786 from Lincoln County

Madison County Circuit Clerk
Madison County Courthouse
101 West Main Street
Richmond, KY 40475
(859) 624-4713
http://courts.ky.gov/Counties/Madison/default.htm
Linda Spurlock Cates
(probate records)

Madison County Clerk
101 West Main Street, Suite 7
Richmond, KY 40475-1415
(606) 624-4703; (859) 624-8474 FAX
madisoncoclerk@adelphia.net
http://www.madisoncountyky.us
Billy Gabbard
(land records and probate records)
no land records search service (contact Katherine Vockery, 128 Redwood Drive, Richmond, KY 40475, [606] 623-0862, or David Green, c/o Richmond Supply Company, 517 Leighway Drive, Richmond, KY 40475, [606] 623-1398); no probate search service

Magoffin County
organized 1860 from Floyd, Johnson and Morgan counties

Magoffin County Circuit Clerk
Magoffin County Justice Center
100 East Maple Street
Salyersville, KY 41465
(606) 349-2215; (606) 349-4050; (606) 349-2209 FAX
http://courts.ky.gov/Counties/Magoffin/default.htm
Roger Gullett
(probate records)

Magoffin County Clerk
PO Box 1535
Salyersville, KY 41465-0530
(606) 349-2216; (606) 349-2328 FAX
http://magoffincounty.ky.gov
Renee Arnett Shepherd

Marion County
organized 1834 from Washington County

Marion County Circuit Clerk
Marion County Courthouse

120 West Main Street, Suite 6
Lebanon, KY 40033
(270) 692-2681
http://courts.ky.gov/Counties/Marion/default.htm
Ms. Kim T. May
(probate records from 1978)

Marion County Clerk
223 North Spalding Avenue, Suite 102
Lebanon, KY 40033-1584
(270) 692-2651; (270) 692-9811 FAX
marioncountyclerk@alltel.net
http://www.lebanonky.org/county.html (City of Lebanon)
Karen Spalding
(land records and vital records from 1863 ["Our courthouse was burned in 1863, during the Civil War, and all records were lost"]; probate records from 1863 to 1978)
probate search service: no charge; copies of probate records: 25¢ per page

Marshall County
organized 1842 from Calloway County

Marshall County Circuit Clerk
Marshall County Judicial Building
80 Judicial Drive, Unit 101
Benton, KY 42025
(270) 527-3883
http://courts.ky.gov/Counties/Marshall/default.htm
Ms. L. Carol Fisk
(probate records)

Marshall County Clerk
1101 Main Street
Benton, KY 42025-1498
(270) 527-4740; (270) 527-4738 FAX
dan.duke@shrte.ky.us
http://www.marshallcounty.ky.gov;
http://www.marshalcounty.net (Chamber of Commerce)
Dan Duke

Martin County
organized 1870 from Floyd, Johnson, Lawrence and Pike counties

Martin County Circuit Clerk
Martin County Courthouse
430 Court Street
Inez, KY 41224
(606) 298-3508
http://courts.ky.gov/Counties/Martin/default.htm
Jack H. Horn
(probate records)

Martin County Clerk
PO Box 460
Inez, KY 41224-0460
(606) 298-2810; (606) 298-0143 FAX
martinclerk@hotmail.com
http://www.martincounty.ky.gov/elected
Carol Sue Mills
(deeds and mortgages, marriage licenses, and probate records)
no probate search service; certified copies of land records: $5.00 each; copies of probate records: $1.00 per page, $1.00 minimum plus SASE

Mason County
organized 1789 from Bourbon County

Mason County Circuit Clerk
Mason County Justice Center
100 West Third Street
Maysville, KY 41056
(606) 564-4340
http://courts.ky.gov/Counties/Mason/default.htm
Kirk Tolle
(probate records)

Mason County Clerk
(221 Stanley Reed Court Street—location)
PO Box 234 (mailing address)
Maysville, KY 41056-0234

(606) 564-3341; (606) 564-8979 FAX
http://www.masoncountykentucky.com/articles
/home.asp
Frances A. Cotterill
(land records from 1789 to 1988, naturalization
records, and probate records from 1789)
probate search service: $3.00; copies of probate
records: $2.00 each, no minimum

McCracken County
organized 1825 from Hickman County

McCracken County Circuit Clerk
(McCracken County Courthouse, 301 South
Sixth Street, Paducah, KY 42003—location)
PO Box 1455 (mailing address)
Paducah, KY 42002-1455
(270) 575-7280
http://courts.ky.gov/counties/McCracken
http://courts.ky.gov/Counties/McCracken/def
ault.htm
Mike Lawrence
(probate records)

McCracken County Clerk
(McCracken County Courthouse, 301 South
Sixth Street, Paducah, KY 42003—location)
PO Box 609 (mailing address)
Paducah, KY 42002-0609
(270) 444-4700; (270) 444-4704 FAX
mcckco@apex.net
http://paducahky.gov/county/elected_officials
/county_clerk.php
Jeff Jerrell

McCracken County District Court
(McCracken County Courthouse, 301 South
Sixth Street, Second Floor, Paducah, KY
42003—location)
PO Box 1436 (mailing address)
Paducah, KY 42002-1436
(270) 575-7270; (270) 575-7273 (Probate)
http://courts.ky.gov/McCracken
(probate records)

McCreary County
organized 1912 from Pulaski, Wayne and
Whitley counties

McCreary County Circuit Clerk
McCreary County Courthouse
Main Street, Courthouse Square
Whitley City, KY 42653
(606) 376-5041
http://courts.ky.gov/Counties/McCreary/defau
lt.htm
Mr. Othel King
(probate records)

McCreary County Clerk
PO Box 699
Whitley City, KY 42653-0699
(606) 376-2411; (606) 376-3898 FAX
http://www.mccrearycounty.com/government.
htm
Jo Kidd

McLean County
organized 1854 from Daviess, Muhlenberg and
Ohio counties

McLean County Circuit Clerk
McLean County Courthouse Annex
210 East Main Street
Calhoun, KY 42327
(270) 273-3966; (270) 273-5918 FAX
http://courts.ky.gov/Counties/McLean/default
.htm
Stephanie J. King
(probate records)

McLean County Clerk
PO Box 57
Calhoun, KY 42327-0057
(270) 273-3082; (270) 273-5084 FAX
lindar.johnson@ky.gov
http://www.mcleancounty.ky.gov
Linda Ray Johnson
(deeds from 1854, only a few naturalization
records found only in Court Order Books,

probate records from 1854)
no probate search service; copies of probate
records: 25¢ per page if book number and
page given, $3.50 for certified copies ("equity
files and civil suits found in Circuit Court
Clerk Office")

Meade County
organized 1824 from Breckinridge and Hardin
counties

Meade County Circuit Clerk
Meade County Courthouse
516 Fairway Drive
Brandenburg, KY 40108
(270) 422-4961; (270) 422-2147 FAX
http://courts.ky.gov/Counties/Meade/default.htm
Evelyn D. "Debbi" Medley
(probate records)

Meade County Clerk
PO Box 614
Brandenburg, KY 40108-0614
(270) 422-2152; (270) 422-2158 FAX
katrina.fitzgerald@ky.gov
meadecountyclerk.ky.gov
Katrina Fitzgerald
(marriages from 1976, wills from 1824; land
records from 1824 to date, births and deaths
from 1824 to 1911 with Kentucky State
Archives)
no probate search service; copies of marriages or
probate records: $2.00 each, $5.00 for
certified copies

Menifee County
organized 1869 from Bath, Montgomery,
Morgan, Powell and Wolfe counties

Menifee County Circuit Clerk
Menifee County Courthouse
12 Walnut Street
Frenchburg, KY 40322
(606) 768-2461; (606) 768-2462 FAX
http://courts.ky.gov/Counties/Menifee/default
.htm
Karen Wells-Sorrell
(probate records)
no probate search service (contact Barbara
Ingram, PO Box 114, Frenchburg, KY 40322)

Menifee County Clerk
PO Box 123
Frenchburg, KY 40322-0123
(606) 768-3512; (606) 768-6738 FAX
thegirls@mrtc.com
http://www.menifeecounty.ky.gov/elected
Jo Ann Spencer
(land records from 1869)

Mercer County
organized 1786 from Lincoln County

Mercer County Circuit Clerk
Mercer County Courthouse
224 South Main Street
Harrodsburg, KY 40330-1696
(859) 734-6306
http://courts.ky.gov/Counties/Mercer/default.
htm
Rose Bishop
(probate records)

Mercer County Clerk
(Main Street—location)
PO Box 426 (mailing address)
Harrodsburg, KY 40330-0426
(859) 734-6310; (859) 734-6309 FAX
http://www.merceronline.com/government.htm
Chris Horn
(land records and probate records)
land records search service: $5.00; copies 50¢
each

Metcalfe County
organized 1 May 1860 from Adair, Barren,
Cumberland, Green and Monroe counties

Metcalfe County Circuit Clerk
Metcalfe County Courthouse

201 East Stockton Street
Edmonton, KY 42129
(270) 432-3663
http://courts.ky.gov/Counties/Metcalfe/default
.htm
Mary M. Shive
(probate records)

Metcalfe County Clerk
PO Box 25
Edmonton, KY 42129-0025
(270) 432-4821; (270) 432-5176 FAX
Carol England

Monroe County
organized 1820 from Barren and Cumberland
counties

Monroe County Circuit Clerk
(Monroe County Courthouse, 200 North Main
Street, Suite B—location)
PO Box 245 (mailing address)
Tompkinsville, KY 42167
(270) 487-5480; (270) 487-0068 FAX
http://courts.ky.gov/Counties/Monroe/default.
htm
Joyce Emberton
(probate records)

Monroe County Clerk
200 North Main Street, Suite D
Tompkinsville, KY 42167-1548
(270) 487-5471; (270) 487-5976 FAX
monroecountyclerk@mchsi.com
http://www.monroecounty.ky.gov/elected
Teresa McMillin Sheffield

Montgomery County
organized 1797 from Clark County

Montgomery County Circuit Clerk
(Montgomery County Courthouse, 1 Court
Street—location)
PO Box 327 (mailing address)
Mt. Sterling, KY 40353
(859) 498-5966; (859) 498-5991
http://courts.ky.gov/Counties/Montgomery/de
fault.htm
Ms. Connie Martin Goodpaster
(probate records)

Montgomery County Clerk
PO Box 414
Mt. Sterling, KY 40353-0414
(859) 498-8700; (859) 498-8729 FAX
Judy.Witt@ky.gov
http://www.montgomerycounty.ky.gov/elected
Judy Long Witt
(deeds and mortgages from 1800, marriages
from 1864, wills from 1779; "All probate
packages in Frankfort" [see Meade County])
no probate search service; copies of probate
records: 50¢ per page plus postage, no
minimum

Morgan County
organized 1823 from Bath and Floyd counties

Morgan County Circuit Clerk
Morgan County Courthouse
518 Main Street
West Liberty, KY 41472
(606) 743-3763; (606) 743-2633 FAX
http://courts.ky.gov/Counties/Morgan/default.
htm
Dona L. Pelfrey
(probate records)

Morgan County Clerk
PO Box 26
West Liberty, KY 41472-0026
(606) 743-3949; (606) 743-2111 FAX
http://www.morgancounty.ky.gov/elected
Randy Williams
(land records, vital records, probate records)
probate search service: $4.00 for a period of
twenty years; copies of probate records: 50¢
per page plus postage, no minimum

Muhlenberg County
organized 1799 from Christian and Logan counties

Muhlenberg County Circuit Clerk
Muhlenberg County Judicial Building
136 South Main Street
Greenville, KY 42345
(270) 338-4850
http://courts.ky.gov/Counties/Muhlenberg/default.htm
Janet Hearld
(probate records)

Muhlenberg County Clerk
PO Box 525
Greenville, KY 42345-0525
(270) 338-1441; (270) 338-1774 FAX
muhlenbergcoclerk@yahoo.com
http://www.muhlenbergcounty.ky.gov
Gaylan L. Spurlin

Nelson County
organized 1785 from Jefferson County

Nelson County Circuit Clerk
Nelson County Justice Center
200 Nelson County Plaza
Bardstown, KY 40004
(502) 348-3648
http://courts.ky.gov/Counties/Nelson/default.htm
Diane Thompson
(probate records)

Nicholas County
organized 1800 from Bourbon and Mason counties

Nicholas County Circuit Clerk
Nicholas County Courthouse
125 Main Street
Carlisle, KY 40311
(859) 289-2336
http://courts.ky.gov/Counties/Nicholas/default.htm
Sandye Watkins
(probate records)

Nicholas County Clerk
PO Box 227
Carlisle, KY 40311-0227
(859) 289-3730; (859) 289-3709 FAX
judgeex@qx.net (Larry Tincher, County Judge/Executive)
http://www.nicholascounty.ky.gov/elected
Douglas Fryman
(deeds and mortgages from 1800, marriage records only from 1800, wills, settlements, inventories and appraisements from 1800)
land records search service: no charge for one record; probate search service: no charge if you have a name and an approximate date for one record; copies of land and probate records: SASE plus $5.00 per document up to three pages, and $1.50 for each additional page; copies of marriages: $2.00 each

Ohio County
organized 1799 from Hardin County

Ohio County Circuit Clerk
(Ohio County Courthouse, 130 East Washington Street—location)
PO Box 67 (mailing address)
Hartford, KY 42347-0067
(270) 298-3671; (270) 298-3238; (270) 298-9565 FAX
http://courts.ky.gov/Counties/Ohio/default.htm
Ms. Gaynell Allen
(probate records)

Ohio County Clerk
(301 South Main Street, Suite 201—location)
PO Box 85 (mailing address)
Hartford, KY 42347-0085
(270) 298-4422; (270) 298-4425 FAX
http://www.ohiocounty.ky.gov/elected
Bess Ralph
(probate records from 1826 to 1972)

probate search service: $3.50 per item; copies of probate records: 50¢ each, $2.00 minimum if mailed, plus record search fee

Oldham County
organized 1824 from Henry, Jefferson and Shelby counties

Oldham County Circuit Clerk
Oldham County Courthouse
100 West Main Street
LaGrange, KY 40031
(502) 222-9837; (502) 222-3047 FAX
http://courts.ky.gov/Counties/Oldham/default.htm
Linda G. Mason
(probate records)

Oldham County Clerk
100 West Jefferson Street
La Grange, KY 40031-1189
(502) 222-0047; (502) 222-3208 FAX
AnnBrownOldhamClerk@yahoo.com
http://oldhamcounty.state.ky.us
Ann B. Brown
(land records, marriages, wills)
probate search service; copies of probate records: 25¢ per page plus postage and handling; $2.00 minimum

Owen County
organized 1819 from Franklin, Gallatin, Pendleton and Scott counties

Owen County Circuit Clerk
Owen County Courthouse
100 North Madison Street
Owenton, KY 40359
(502) 484-2232; (502) 484-0625 FAX
http://courts.ky.gov/Counties/Owen/default.htm
Cindy Wright
(probate records)

Owen County Clerk
135 West Bryan Street
Owenton, KY 40359-1440
(502) 484-2213; (502) 484-1002 FAX
http://www.owenton.net
Mary Kay Duncan
(land records from 1819, probate records from 1819 to 1978)

Owsley County
organized 1843 from Breathitt, Clay and Estill counties

Owsley County Circuit Clerk
(Owsley County Courthouse, North Court Street—location)
PO Box 130 (mailing address)
Booneville, KY 41314
(606) 593-6226
mikemays@prtcnet.org
http://courts.ky.gov/Counties/Owsley/default.htm
Mike Mays
(probate records)

Owsley County Clerk
PO Box 500
Booneville, KY 41314-0500
(606) 593-5735; (606) 593-5737 FAX
http://www.owlseycountykentucky.org
Sid Gabbard

Pendleton County
organized 1799 from Bracken and Campbell counties

Pendleton County Circuit Clerk
(Pedleton County Courthouse, 233 Main Street—location)
PO Box 69 (mailing address)
Falmouth, KY 41040
(859) 654-3347
http://courts.ky.gov/Counties/Pendleton/default.htm
Michael D. Redden
(probate records, naturalization records)

Pendleton County Clerk

PO Box 112
Falmouth, KY 41040-0112
(859) 654-3380; (859) 654-5600 FAX
pendclerk1@fuse.net
http://www.pendletoncounty.ky.gov/elected/countyclourtclerk.htm
Rita Spencer
(land records and probate records from 1799
probate search service: cost varies; copies of probate records: $1.00 per page

Perry County
organized 1821 from Clay and Floyd counties

Perry County Circuit Clerk
(Perry County Hall of Justice, 545 Main Street—location)
PO Box 7433 (mailing address)
Hazard, KY 41702
(606) 435-6000
http://courts.ky.gov/Counties/Perry/default.htm
Roger D. Collins
(probate records)

Perry County Clerk
PO Box 150
Hazard, KY 41701-0150
(606) 436-4614; (606) 439-0557 FAX
perrycc@tgtel.com
http://www.perrycounty.ky.gov/elected
Haven King
(land records from 1821, marriages from 1821, some probate records to 1977)
no probate search service; copies of probate records: 50¢ per page, no minimum

Pike County
organized 1821 from Floyd County

Pike County Circuit Clerk
Pike County Hall of Justice
172 Division Street, Suite 336
Pikeville, KY 41502
(606) 433-7557
http://courts.ky.gov/Counties/Pike/default.htm
W. David Deskins
(probate records)

Pike County Clerk
(320 Main Street, Pikeville, KY 41501-1118—location)
PO Box 631 (mailing address)
Pikeville, KY 41502-0631
(606) 432-6211; (606) 432-6222 FAX
http://elect.ky.gov/countyclerks.htm
Lillian Pearl Elliott
(land records from 1821, birth and death index from 1911 to 1949, marriages from 1821 to date, probate records from 1821 to 1978)
no records search service (must supply book and page or name); copies of land and probate records: $5.00 for the first two pages and 50¢ for each additional page of the same instrument; copies of vital records: $5.00 each for marriages plus 50¢ postage (no copies of births)

Powell County
organized 1852 from Clark, Estill and Montgomery counties

Powell County Circuit Clerk
Powell County Courthouse
Court Street
Stanton, KY 40380
(606) 663-4141; (606) 663-4142
http://courts.ky.gov/Counties/Powell/default.htm
Patricia Darlene Drake
(probate records)

Powell County Clerk
(525 Washington Street, Room 109—location)
PO Box 548 (mailing address)
Stanton, KY 40380-0548
(606) 663-6444; (606) 663-6406 FAX
rhondaabarnett@yahoo.com
http://www.powellcounty.ky.gov/elected/coclerk.htm
Rhonda Allen Barnett

Pulaski County

organized 1799 from Green and Lincoln counties

Pulaski County Circuit Clerk
Pulaski County Courthouse
100 Main Street
Somerset, KY 42501
(606) 677-4029; (606) 677-4033
http://courts.ky.gov/Counties/Pulaski/default.htm
George Flynn
(probate records)

Pulaski County Clerk
PO Box 724
Somerset, KY 42502-0724
(606) 679-2042; (606) 678-0073 FAX
http://www.pulaskicountygovt.com/modules.php?name=Content&pa=showpage&pid=4
Trudy Denham
(land records, marriages, and wills from 1799)
no probate search service; copies of land and probate records: $3.50 per instrument, $5.00 for certified copies; copies of marriages: $2.00 each

Robertson County

organized 1867 from Bracken Harrison, Mason and Nicholas counties

Robertson County Circuit Clerk
(Robertson County Courthouse, 211 Court Street—location)
PO Box 63 (mailing address)
Mt. Olivet, KY 41064
(606) 724-5993
http://courts.ky.gov/Counties/Robertson/default.htm
Judy Walters
(probate records)

Robertson County Clerk
(Robertson County Courthouse, 26 Court Street—location)
PO Box 75 (mailing address)
Mt. Olivet, KY 41064-0075
(606) 724-5212; (606) 724-5022 FAX
http://www.robertsoncounty.ky.gov/elected
Stephanie A. Bogucki
(land records)
no probate search service; copies of probate records: 5¢

Rockcastle County

organized 1810 from Knox, Lincoln, Madison and Pulaski counties

Rockcastle County Circuit Clerk
Rockcastle County Courthouse Annex
205 East Main Street, Room 102
Mt. Vernon, KY 40456
(606) 256-2581; (606) 256-2433
http://courts.ky.gov/Counties/Rockcastle/default.htm
Teresa Vanzant
(probate records)

Rockcastle County Clerk
(205 East Main Street, #6, Mt. Vernon, KY 40456-2211—location)
PO Box 365 (mailing address)
Mt. Vernon, KY 40456-0365
(606) 256-2831; (606) 256-4302 FAX
http://www.rockcastlecountyky.com/page—Our-Government.html
Norma Lois Houk
(land records and vital records from 1873)

Rowan County

organized 1856 from Fleming and Morgan counties

Rowan County Circuit Clerk
Rowan County Courthouse
627 East Main Street, First Floor
Morehead, KY 40351-1398
(606) 784-4574; (606) 784-4210; (606) 784-1899 FAX
http://courts.ky.gov/Counties/Rowan/default.htm
Jim Barker
(probate records)

Rowan County Clerk
627 East Main Street
Morehead, KY 40351-1390
(606) 784-5212; (606) 784-2923 FAX
http://elect.ky.gov/countyclerks.htm
Jean W. Bailey

Russell County

organized 1826 from Adair, Cumberland and Wayne counties

Russell County Circuit Clerk
Russell County Courthouse
410 Monument Square, Suite 203
Jamestown, KY 42629
(270) 343-2185; (270) 343-2186; (270) 343-5808 FAX
http://courts.ky.gov/Counties/Russell/default.htm
Tony D. Kerr
(probate records)

Russell County Clerk
PO Box 579
Jamestown, KY 42629-0579
(270) 343-2125; (270) 343-4700 FAX
http://www.russellcounty.ky.gov/elected
Lisha Popplewell

Scott County

organized 1792 from Woodford County

Scott County Circuit Clerk
Scott County Justice Center
119 North Hamilton Street
Georgetown, KY 40324-0474
(502) 863-0474
http://courts.ky.gov/Counties/Scott/default.htm
Karen Boehm
(probate records)

Scott County Clerk
101 East Main street
Georgetown, KY 40324-1794
(502) 863-7875; (520) 863-7898 FAX
http://www.scottcountyclerk.com
Jackie R. Covington
(deeds from 1784 [very few that early], mixed naturalization records [hard to find], wills, administration bonds, settlements, appraisals, sale bills; "The courthouse burned in 1833 and 1837, destroying *all* marriages and lots of wills and deeds. What was left was recopied just as it was, with blank areas on lots of pages. All loose probate papers were destroyed or thrown away. The county court order books are mostly intact. They start 1792, indexed in back of book. Not all names were indexed, guardianship appointments are in there. Early deed index—up to 1837—is by last name only. It is cross-indexed, grantor-grantee")
probate search service: no charge; copies of probate records: $2.00 per page, $2.00 minimum

Shelby County

organized 1792 from Jefferson County

Shelby County Circuit Clerk
Shelby County Courthouse
501 Main Street
Shelbyville, KY 40065
(502) 633-1287
http://courts.ky.gov/Counties/Shelby/default.htm
Kathy H. Nichols
(probate records)

Shelby County Clerk
(501 Washington Street, Shelbyville, KY 40065-1119—location)
PO Box 819 (mailing address)
Shelbyville, KY 40066-0819
(502) 633-4410; (502) 633-7887 FAX
shelbyclerk@yahoo.com
http://www.shelbycountyclerk.com

Sue Carole Perry
(land records, naturalization records, vital records, probate records)
records search service: SASE for cost estimate

Simpson County

organized 1819 from Allen, Logan and Warren counties

Simpson County Circuit Clerk
Simpson County Justice Center
101 Court Street
Franklin, KY 42134
(270) 586-4241
http://courts.ky.gov/Counties/Simpson/default.htm
Ms. Jan J. Murphree
(probate records)

Simpson County Clerk
PO Box 268
Franklin, KY 42134-0268
(270) 586-8161; (270) 586-6464 FAX
simpsoncountyclerk@comcast.net
http://www.simpsoncountyclerk.ky.gov;
http://www.simpsoncounty.us
Bobby C. Phillips, Jr.
(current land, vital, and probate records)

Spencer County

organized 1824 from Bullitt, Nelson and Shelby counties

Spencer County Circuit Clerk
(Spencer County Courthouse Annex, 27 Est Main Street—location)
PO Box 282 (mailing address)
Taylorsville, KY 40071
(502) 477-3220; (502) 477-9368 FAX
http://courts.ky.gov/Counties/Spencer/default.htm
Phyllis H. Shafar
(probate records)

Spencer County Clerk
(321 Main Street—location)
PO Box 544 (mailing address)
Taylorsville, KY 40071-0544
(502) 477-3215; (502) 477-3216 FAX
judypucket@spencercountyky.gov
http://www.spencercountyky.gov
Judy Puckett
(land records, naturalization records, vital records, probate records)

Taylor County

organized 1848 from Green County

Taylor County Circuit Clerk
Taylor County Courthouse
203 North Court Street
Campbellsville, KY 42718
(270) 465-6686; (270) 789-4356 FAX
http://courts.ky.gov/Counties/Taylor/default.htm
Rodney Burress
(probate records)

Taylor County Clerk
203 North Court Street, Suite 5
Campbellsville, KY 42718-2298
(502) 465-6677; (270) 789-1144 FAX (call first)
tcclerk@alltel.net
http://www.taylor-county-clerk.com
Mark Carney

Todd County

organized 1820 from Christian and Logan counties

Todd County Circuit Clerk
Todd County Courthouse
200 Washington Street
Elkton, KY 42220
(270) 265-5631 voice & FAX
http://courts.ky.gov/Counties/Todd/default.htm
J. Mark Cowherd
(probate records)

Todd County Clerk
PO Box 307
Elkton, KY 42220-0307

(270) 265-2363; (270) 265-2588 FAX
illy.flowler@ky.gov
http://www.toddcounty.ky.gov/elected
Billy Fowler

Trigg County
organized 1820 from Caldwell and Christian
  counties

Trigg County Circuit Clerk
(12 Court Street—location)
PO Box 673 (mailing address)
Cadiz, KY 42211
(270) 522-6270; (270) 522-5828 FAX
http://courts.ky.gov/Counties/Trigg/default.htm
Pam W. Perry
(probate records)

Trigg County Clerk
PO Box 1310
Cadiz, KY 42211-1310
(270) 522-6661; (270) 522-6662 FAX
triggcoclerk@kih.net; wanda.thomas@ky.gov
http://www.triggcounty.ky.gov/elected
Wanda H. Thomas
(land records)
no probate search service; copies of probate
  records: 25¢ each

Trimble County
organized 1837 from Gallatin, Henry and
  Oldham counties

Trimble County Circuit Clerk
(Trimble County Courthouse, 30 Highway 42
  East—location)
PO Box 248 (mailing address)
Bedford, KY 40006
(502) 255-3213; (502) 255-3525
http://courts.ky.gov/Counties/Trimble/default.
  htm
June Ginn
(probate records)

Trimble County Clerk
PO Box 262
Bedford, KY 40006-0262
(502) 255-7174; (502) 255-7045 FAX
jpowell@iglou.com
http://www.trimblecounty.com/tcgov.htm
Jerry L. Powell
(deeds from 1837 [indexed], probate records;
  marriage records from 1862 with, marriages
  before 1863 with Kentucky Historical Society)
vital records search service: $7.50 per hour plus
  copying costs and postage; copies of deeds
  and probate records: 25¢ per page plus
  postage

Union County
organized 1811 from Henderson County

Union County Circuit Clerk
(Courthouse Annex Building, 121 South Morgan
  Street—location)
PO Box 59 (mailing address)
Morganfield, KY 42437-0059
(270) 389-2264; (270) 389-1811
http://courts.ky.gov/Counties/Union/default.htm
Sue W. Beaven
(probate records)

Union County Clerk
(100 West Main Street—location)
PO Box 119 (mailing address)
Morganfield, KY 42437-0119
(270) 389-1334; (270) 389-9135 FAX
http://unioncounty.ky.gov/cogov/clerk.htm
William Stephen Peak, Jr.

Warren County
organized 1797 from Logan County

Warren County Circuit Clerk
Warren County Justice Center
1001 Center Street, Suite 102
Bowling Green, KY 42101-2184
(270) 746-7400; (270) 746-7401; (270) 746-7402;
  (270) 746-7403; (270) 746-7501 FAX
http://courts.ky.gov/Counties/Warren/default.

htm
Ms. Pat Howel Goad
(probate records from 1978)

Warren County Clerk
(429 East Tenth Street, Bowling Green, KY
  42101-2250—location)
PO Box 478 (mailing address)
Bowling Green, KY 42101-0478
(270) 843-5306; (270) 843-5315 FAX
warrencountyclerk@yahoo.com
http://www.warrencounty.state.ky.us
Dot Owens
(land records from 1797, probate records from
  1797 to 1978)
probate search service: no charge; copies of
  probate records: 25¢ per page

Washington County
organized 1792 from Nelson County

Washington County Circuit Clerk
Washington County Courthouse
111 Cross Main Street
Springfield, KY 40069
(859) 336-3761; (859) 336-0734; (859) 336-9824
  FAX
http://courts.ky.gov/Counties/Washington/def
  ault.htm
George B. Graves
(probate records)

Washington County Clerk
PO Box 446
Springfield, KY 40069-0446
(859) 336-5425; (859) 336-5408 FAX
http://www.washingtoncountyky.com/clerk.html
Glenn Black

Wayne County
organized 1801 from Cumberland and Pulaski
  counties

Wayne County Circuit Clerk
Wayne County Justice Center
125 West Columbia Avenue
Monticello, KY 42633
(606) 348-5841; (606) 348-5983; (606) 348-4225
  FAX
http://courts.ky.gov/Counties/Wayne/default.
  htm
Richard R. Morrow
(probate records)

Wayne County Clerk
PO Box 565
Monticello, KY 42633-0565
(606) 348-5721; (606) 348-8303 FAX
countclerk8303@windstream.net
http://www.waynecounty.ky.gov/elected/clerk.
  htm
Melissa Turpin
(land records, marriages, probate records)

Webster County
organized 1860 from Henderson, Hopkins and
  Union counties

Webster County Circuit Clerk
(Webster County Judicial Center, 25 U.S.
  Highway 41A South—location)
PO Box 290 (mailing address)
Dixon, KY 42409
(270) 639-9160
http://courts.ky.gov/Counties/Webster/default
  .htm
Amy Villines
(probate records)

Webster County Clerk
PO Box 19
Dixon, KY 42409-0019
(270) 639-7006; (270) 639-7029
becky@kih.net; valerie.franklin@ky.gov
http://elect.ky.gov/countyclerks.htm
Valerie Franklin

Whitley County
organized 1818 from Knox County

Whitley County Circuit Clerk

(Williamsburg Courthouse, Courthouse Square,
  100 Main Street—location)
PO Box 329 (mailing address)
Williamsburg, KY 40769-0329
(606) 549-2973; (606) 549-5162; (606) 549-3393
  FAX
http://courts.ky.gov/Counties/Whitley/default.
  htm
Gary W. Barton
(probate records)

Whitley County Clerk
(Main Street—location)
PO Box 8 (mailing address)
Williamsburg, KY 40769-0008
(606) 549-6002; (606) 549-2790 FAX
wcclerk@tcnet.net
http://www.whitleycountyfiscalcourt.com/clerk
  .asp
Kay Schwartz
(land records)

Wolfe County
organized 1860 from Breathitt, Morgan, Owsley,
  and Powell counties

Wolfe County Circuit Clerk
(Wolfe County Courthouse, 10 Court Street—
  location)
PO Box 296 (mailing address)
Campton, KY 41301-0296
(606) 668-3092; (606) 668-3736
http://courts.ky.gov/Counties/Wolfe/default.htm
Debbie H. Sparks
(probate records)

Wolfe County Clerk
PO Box 400
Campton, KY 41301-0400
(606) 668-3515; (606) 668-3367 FAX
wolfeclerk@yahoo.com
http://elect.ky.gov/countyclerks.htm
Steve Oliver

Woodford County
organized 1789 from Fayette County

Woodford County Circuit Clerk
Woodford County Courthouse Annex
130 Court Street
Versailles, KY 40383
(859) 873-3711
http://courts.ky.gov/Counties/Woodford/defa
  ult.htm
Tricia Nave Kittinger
(probate records)

Woodford County Clerk
103 South Main Street, Suite 120
Versailles, KY 40383-1298
(859) 873-3421; (859) 873-6985 FAX
jwoolum@woodfordcountyky.org
http://woodfordcounty.ky.gov/gov/coclerk.htm
Corinne C. Woolums
(land records, naturalization records, vital
  records, probate records)

LOUISIANA

Capital: Baton Rouge. Statehood: 18 July 1812 (annexed as part of the Louisiana Purchase, 1803, organized as the Territory of Orleans in 1804)

Louisiana's parishes are roughly equivalent to other states' county designations. In 1804 the area was divided into two parts: the District of Louisiana and the Territory of New Orleans. In 1805 it was divided into twelve counties: Orleans, German Coast, Acadia, Lafourche, Iberville, Pointe Coupee, Attakapas, Opelousas, Natchitoches, Rapides, Ouachita (or Washita) and Concordia. In 1807 the Orleans Territory was divided into nineteen parishes, prior to being admitted to the Union in 1812. Today the Mayor's Court, Municipal Court of New Orleans, Traffic Court of New Orleans, City Courts, Justice of the Peace Courts, and Parish Courts are the state's courts of limited jurisdiction, handling municipal and city violations, some civil actions, and criminal offenses not punishable by hard labor. Three Juvenile Courts sit in Caddo, Jefferson and Orleans parishes, and there is an East Baton Rouge Family Court.

Forty-one District Courts, sitting in each parish seat, have general trial jurisdiction and have exclusive jurisdiction over real property and probate. Orleans District: Orleans Parish; First Judicial District: Caddo Parish; Second: Bienville, Claiborne and Jackson parishes; Third: Lincoln and Union parishes; Fourth: Morehouse and Ouachita parishes; Fifth: Franklin, Richland and West Carroll parishes; Sixth: East Carroll, Madison and Tensas parishes; Seventh: Catahoula and Concordia parishes; Eighth: Winn Parish; Ninth: Rapides Parish; Tenth: Natchitoches Parish; Eleventh: De Soto Parish; Twelfth: Avoyelles Parish; Thirteenth: Evangeline Parish; Fourteenth: Calcasieu Parish; Fifteenth: Acadia, Lafayette and Vermilion parishes; Sixteenth: Iberia, St. Martin and St. Mary parishes; Seventeenth: Lafourche Parish; Eighteenth: Iberville, Pointe Coupee and West Baton Rouge parishes; Nineteenth: East Baton Rouge Parish; Twentieth: East Feliciana and West Feliciana parishes; Twenty-first: Livingston, St. Helena and Tangipahoa parishes; Twenty-second: St. Tammany and Washington parishes; Twenty-third: Ascension, Assumption and St. James parishes; Twenty-fourth: Jefferson Parish; Twenty-fifth: Plaquemines Parish; Twenty-sixth: Bossier and Webster parishes; Twenty-seventh: St. Landry Parish; Twenty-eighth: La Salle Parish; Twenty-ninth: St. Charles Parish; Thirtieth: Vernon Parish; Thirty-first: Jefferson Davis Parish; Thirty-second: Terrebonne Parish; Thirty-third: Allen Parish; Thirty-fourth: St. Bernard Parish; Thirty-fifth: Grant Parish; Thirty-sixth: Beauregard Parish; Thirty-seventh: Caldwell Parish; Thirty-eighth: Cameron Parish; Thirty-ninth: Red River Parish; Fortieth: St. John the Baptist Parish. A Court of Appeals and a Supreme Court handle the appeals.

Fifth Circuit Court of Appeal
(200 Derbigny Street, Fourth Floor, Gretna, LA 70053—location)
PO Box 489 (mailing address)
Gretna, LA 70054
(504) 376-1400; (504) 376-1498 FAX
http://www.fifthcircuit.org/Default.htm
Peter J. Fitzgerald, Jr., Clerk

First Circuit Court of Appeal
(1600 North Third Boulevard—location)
PO Box 4408 (mailing address)
Baton Rouge, LA 70821
(225) 342-1500; (225) 342-1527 FAX
http://www.la-fcca.org/clerk.htm
Christine Lasseigne Crow, Clerk

Fourth Circuit Court of Appeal
400 Royal Street
New Orleans, LA 70130

(504) 412-6001; (504) 412-6019 FAX
http://4thcir-app.state.la.us/coc.aspx
Danielle A. Schott, Clerk

Second Circuit Court of Appeal
430 Fannin Street
Shreveport, LA 71101
(318) 227-3700; (318) 227-3735 FAX
clerkdpw@lasccoa.state.la.us
http://www.lacoa2.org/clerk's_office.htm
Diana Pratt Wyatt, Clerk

Supreme Court
400 Royals Street, Suite 4200
New Orleans, LA 70130-8102
(504) 568-5707; (504) 568-2846 FAX
www.lasc.org/clerk/default.asp
John Tarlton Olivier, Clerk

Third Circuit Court of Appeal
(1000 Main Street, Lake Charles, LA 70615—location)
PO Box 16577 (mailing address)
Lake Charles, LA 70616
(337) 433-9403; (337) 491-2590 FAX
http://www.la3circuit.org
Kelly McNeely, Clerk

Acadia Parish
organized 1886 from St. Landry Parish

Acadia Parish Clerk of Court and Ex-Officio Recorder
(Court Circle—location)
PO Box 922 (mailing address)
Crowley, LA 70527-0922
(337) 788-8881; (337) 788-1048 FAX
robby@acadiaparishclerk.com
http://www.acadiaparishclerk.com
Robert T. "Robby" Barousse

Allen Parish
organized 1910 from Calcasieu Parish

Allen Parish Clerk of Court
(400 West Sixth Avenue—location)
PO Box 248 (mailing address)
Oberlin, LA 70655-0248
(337) 639-4351; (337) 639-2030 FAX
http://www.lpgov.org/directory/parish_info.php?id=2
Gerald W. Harrington

Ascension Parish
organized 1807 from Acadia County

Ascension Parish Clerk of Court
(300 Houmas Street—location)
PO Box 192 (mailing address)
Donaldsonville, LA 70346
(225) 473-9866; (225) 473-8641 FAX
hartbourque@ascensioncourthouse.org;
cgipson@ascensioncourthouse.org
http://www.eatel.net/~apcc/Clerk_ofCourt/indexx.html
Kermit "Hart" Bourque; Cynthia Gipson, Supervisor, Recording Department
(land conveyances from 1833 and naturalization records from 1857 with Mr. James Regira or Ms. Margaret Martin, probate records from 1820 with Kermit Hart Bourque, Clerk of Court)
probate search service: $7.00 for each index search plus $2.00 for each entry found; copies of probate records: $1.00 for each of the first five copies, 75¢ for each of the next fifteen copies and 50¢ for each additional copy, no minimum

Assumption Parish
organized 1807 from Lafourche County

Assumption Parish Clerk of Court
(4809 LA Highway 1—location)
PO Box 249 (mailing address)
Napoleonville, LA 70390
(985) 369-6653; (985) 369-2032 FAX
diandry@assumptionclerk.com
http://www.assuptionla.com/ala/ClerkOfCourt.aspx

Darlene Landry

Avoyelles Parish
organized 1807, original parish

Avoyelles Parish Clerk of Court
(310 North Main Street—location)
PO Box 219 (mailing address)
Marksville, LA 71351
(318) 253-7523; (318) 253-4614 FAX
http://www.lpgov.org/directory/parish_info.php?id=5
Samuel G. "Sammy" Couvillion

Beauregard Parish
organized 1912 from Calcasieu Parish

Beauregard Parish Clerk of Court
(201 West First Street—location)
PO Box 100 (mailing address)
De Ridder, LA 70634
(337) 463-8595; (337) 462-3916 FAX
http://www.beauparish.org
Ronald L. "Ronny" Nichols
(land records, naturalization records, marriages, probate records)

Bienville Parish
organized 1848 from Claiborne Parish

Bienville Parish Clerk of Court
100 Courthouse Drive, Room 100
Arcadia, LA 71001
(318) 263-2123; (318) 263-7426 FAX
jimmartin@bienvilleparish.org
http://www.bielvilleparish.org/clerk
James W. "Jim" Martin
(land and probate records from 1848)
probate search service: $5.00; copies of probate records: 50¢ each, no minimum

Bossier Parish
organized 1843 from Claiborne Parish

Bossier Parish Clerk of Court
26th Judicial District
(Courthouse, 204 Burt Boulevard—location)
PO Box 430 (mailing address)
Benton, LA 71006
(318) 965-2336; (318) 965-2713 FAX
http://www.bossierclerk.com;
http://mybossier.com/index.asp
Joan L. Carraway
(land records, marriages, probate records)
records search service: call for estimate; copies of records: $1.00 per page

Caddo Parish
organized 1838 from Natchitoches Parish

Caddo Parish Clerk of Court
501 Texas Street, Room 103
Shreveport, LA 71101-5401
(318) 226-6780; (318) 227-9080
clerk@caddoclerk.com;
civil@criminal@caddoclerk.com;
records@caddoclerk.com;
civil@caddoclerk.com (Civil Suites);
minutes@caddoclerk.com (Civil Minutes)
http://www.caddoclerk.com
Gary Loftin

Calcasieu Parish
organized 1840 from St. Landry Parish

Calcasieu Parish Clerk of Court
(1000 Ryan Street—location)
PO Box 1030 (mailing address)
Lake Charles, LA 70602-1030
(337) 437-3550; (337) 437-3350 FAX
calclerkofcourt.com
http://www.calclerkofcourt.com
Mr. H. Lynn Jones
(land and probate records from 1910 [earlier records destroyed by fire], marriage index from 1910)
records search service: $10.00 per name; copies of records: $1.00 per page, plus $5.00 to certify each document

Caldwell Parish

organized 1838 from Catahoula and Ouachita parishes

Caldwell Parish Clerk of Court
(200 Main Street—location)
PO Box 1327 (mailing address)
Columbia, LA 71418
(318) 649-2272; (318) 649-2037 FAX
http://www.lpgov.org/directory/parish_info.ph
p?id=11
Eugene Dunn
(land records, naturalization records, vital records, probate records)

Cameron Parish

organized 1832 from Calcasieu and Vermilion parishes

Cameron Parish Clerk of Court
(119 Smith Circle, Room 21—location)
PO Box 549 (mailing address)
Cameron, LA 70631-0549
(337) 775-5316; (337) 775-7172 FAX
http://www.cameronparish.com
Carl E. Broussard
(land and probate records from 1874)
probate search service: no charge ("we need a letter of request for copies or to search the records; must file original or certified copy from another Louisiana Clerk of Court Office"); copies of probate records: $1.00 per page, no minimum

Catahoula Parish

organized 1808 from Rapides Parish

Catahoula Parish Clerk of Court
(Courthouse Square, Room 101—location)
PO Box 198 (mailing address)
Harrisonburg, LA 71340-0198
(318) 744-5497; (318) 744-5488 FAX
http://www.lpgov.org/directory/parish_info.ph
p?id=13
Janet T. Payne
(land records from 1808, probate records from 1846)
probate search service: $15.00; copies of probate records: $1.00 per page, $5.00 for certification

Claiborne Parish

organized 1828 from Natchitoches Parish

Claiborne Parish Clerk of Court
(512 East Main Street—location)
PO Box 330 (mailing address)
Homer, LA 71040
(318) 927-9601; (318) 927-2345 FAX
http://www.claiborneone.org/cppj/department
s1.html
James Patrick Gladney

Concordia Parish

organized 1807, original parish

Concordia Parish Clerk of Court
(4001 Carter Street, Suite 5—location)
PO Box 790 (mailing address)
Vidalia, LA 71373
(318) 336-4204; (318) 336-8777 FAX
http://www.concordiaclerk.org
Clyde R. Webber, Jr.

De Soto Parish

organized 1843 from Natchitoches Parish

De Soto Parish Clerk's Office
(Courthouse, 210 Texas Street, Second Floor—location)
PO Box 1206 (mailing address)
Mansfield, LA 71052
(318) 872-3110; (318) 872-4202 FAX
http://www.lpgov.org/directory/parish_info.ph
p?id=16
O.L. "Sonny" Stone, Jr.
(land records from 1843, marriage licenses, probate records)
probate search service: $10.00 per hour ("But we do not do these for lack of time"); copies of

probate records: $1.00 per page; "No one in Mansfield does research"

East Baton Rouge Parish

organized 1810 from Spanish West Florida

East Baton Rouge Parish Clerk of Court
(222 St. Louis Street, Baton Rouge, LA 70802-5817—location)
PO Box 1991 (mailing address)
Baton Rouge, LA 70821
(225) 389-3960; (225) 389-7837 (Genealogy Section); (225) 389-3988 (Archives); (225) 389-5594 FAX
http://www.ebrclerkofcourt.org
J. Douglas "Doug" Welborn; Brandon Abadie, Archives Supervisor
(land and probate records from 1782 [Spanish West Florida])
probate search service: $22.00 per name; copies of probate records: 50¢ per page, $2.20 per certification, plus $2.50 minimum mail-out charge

East Carroll Parish

organized 1877 from Carroll Parish

East Carroll Parish Clerk of Court
400 First Street
Lake Providence, LA 71254-2616
(318) 559-2399; (318) 559-1502 FAX
http://www.lpgov.org/directory/parish_info.ph
p?id=18
Edna Bishop Brock

East Feliciana Parish

organized 1824 from Feliciana Parish

East Feliciana Parish Clerk of Court
(Courthouse Square, 12220 St. Helena Street—location)
PO Box 599 (mailing address)
Clinton, LA 70722
(225) 683-5145; (318) 683-3556 FAX
http://www.lpgov.org/directory/parish_info.ph
p?id=19
Debbie D. Hudnall
(conveyances, donations, mortgages, suits from 1825, a few naturalization records, early 1800s, probate records from 1825)
no probate search service ("depending on the amount of research involved, there may not be a fee. If it is involved there is someone that will search the records for $8.00 per hour plus copy cost; direct inquiries to Amanda S. Thomas"); copies of probate records: $1.00 each, no minimum

Evangeline Parish

organized 1908 from St. Landry Parish

Evangeline Parish Clerk of Court
(Courthouse Building, 200 Court Street—location)
PO Drawer 347 (mailing address)
Ville Platte, LA 70586
(337) 363-5671; (337) 363-5780 FAX
http://www.lpgov.org/directory/parish_info.ph
p?id=20
Walter Lee

Franklin Parish

organized 1843 from Catahoula, Madison and Ouachita parishes

Franklin Parish Clerk of Court
(6500 Main Street—location)
PO Box 1564 (mailing address)
Winnsboro, LA 71295
(318) 435-5133; (318) 435-5134 FAX
http://www.lpgov.org/directory/parish_info.ph
p?id=21
Ann Johnson

Grant Parish

organized 1869 from Rapides and Winn parishes

Grant Parish Clerk of Court
(200 Main Street—location)
PO Box 263 (mailing address)

Colfax, LA 71417
(318) 627-3246; (318) 627-3201 FAX
http://www.lpgov.org/directory/parish_info.ph
p?id=22
J. Elray Lemoine

Iberia Parish

organized 1868 from St. Martin and St. Mary parishes

Iberia Parish Clerk of Court
(300 Iberia Street, New Iberia, LA 70560—location)
PO Drawer 12010 (mailing address)
New Iberia, LA 70562-2010
(337) 365-7282; (337) 365-7636 FAX
http://www.iberiaparishgovernment.com
Michael Thibodeaux
(conveyance records from 1868 to date, naturalization records from 1884, marriage licenses from 1868, probate records from 1868)
copies of land records: 50¢ per page, $5.50 per document for certification; certified copies of marriage licenses: $6.00 each

Iberville Parish

organized 1807 from Iberville County

Iberville Parish Clerk of Court
(58050 Meriam Street—location)
PO Box 423 (mailing address)
Plaquemine, LA 70765-0423
(225) 687-5160; (225) 687-5260 FAX
http://www.ibervilleparish.com
J. Gerald "Bubbie" Dupont, Jr.

Jackson Parish

organized 1845 from Claiborne, Ouachita and Union parishes

Jackson Parish Clerk of Court
(500 East Courthouse Avenue—location)
PO Drawer 730 (mailing address)
Jonesboro, LA 71251
(318) 259-2424; (318) 395-0386 FAX
http://www.jacksonparishpolicejury.org
Ann B. Walsworth
(land and probate records from 1880)
probate search service: $2.00 per name per ten years; copies of probate records: $1.10 for the first copy and 55¢ for each additional copy, $5.00 minimum by mail

Jefferson Parish

organized 1825 from Orleans Parish

Jefferson Parish Clerk of Court
(Second and Derbiney Street, Sixth Floor, Gretna, LA 70053—location)
PO Box 10 (mailing address)
Gretna, LA 70054
(504) 364-2900; (504) 362-6355 FAX
http://www.jpclerkofcourt.us
Jon A. Gegenheimer
(land and probate records)
no probate search service; copies of probate records: 75¢ per page, $1.50 minimum

Jefferson Davis Parish

organized 1912 from Calcasieu Parish

Jefferson Davis Parish Clerk of Court
(300 State Street—location)
PO Box 799 (mailing address)
Jennings, LA 70546
(337) 824-1160; (337) 824-1354 FAX
http://www.lpgov.org/directory/parish_info.ph
p?id=26
Carlton L. Duhon
(land and probate records from 1913, marriages from 1913)
probate search service: no charge; copies of probate records: $1.00 per page, no minimum; "All records are public except adoption and juvenile records."

Lafayette Parish

organized 1823 from Attakapas and St. Martin

parishes

Lafayette Parish Clerk of Court
(800 South Buchanan Street—location)
PO Box 2009 (mailing address)
Lafayette, LA 70502
(337) 291-6400; (337) 291-6392 FAX
clerkofcourt@lpclerk.com
http://www.lafayetteparishclerk.com
Louis J. Perret
(land and probate records from 1823)
no probate search service; copies of probate
records: 50¢ per page

Lafourche Parish
organized 1807 from Lafourche County

Lafourche Parish Clerk of Court
(Lafourche Parish Annex Building, 309 West
Third Street—location)
PO Box 818 (mailing address)
Thibodaux, LA 70301
(504) 447-4841; (504) 447-5800 FAX
http://www.lafourchegov.org/lafourchegov
Vernon H. Rodrigue
(land, vital, and probate records from 1808,
naturalization records)
probate search service: $5.50; copies of land
records: $1.10 per page from large books,
otherwise 50¢ per page, $2.20 per document
for certification; copies of vital records: $1.10
per page; copies of probate records: 55¢ per
page

La Salle Parish
organized 1910 from Catahoula Parish

La Salle Parish Clerk of Court
(Courthouse Square—location)
PO Box 1372 (mailing address)
Jena, LA 71342-1372
(318) 992-2158; (318) 992-2157 FAX
http://www.lpgov.org/directory/parish_info.ph
p?id=30
Steve H. Crooks
(land and probate records)
probate search service: $12.00 per name, $5.50
thereafter; copies of probate records: 50¢ per
page, no minimum ("please send a deposit
with request")

Lincoln Parish
organized 1873 from Bienville, Claiborne,
Jackson and Union parishes

Lincoln Parish Clerk of Court
Third Judicial District Court of Louisiana
(100 West Texas Avenue, Room 100—location)
PO Box 924 (mailing address)
Ruston, LA 71273-0924
(318) 251-5130; (318) 255-6004 FAX
http://www.clerk.lincolnparish.org;
http://www.lincolnparish.org
Linda Cook
(land records, marriage licenses, probate
records)
records search service: $10.00; copies of records:
$1.00 per page, $2.00 for certified copies

Livingston Parish
organized 1832 from St. Helena Parish

Livingston Parish Clerk of Court
(20180 Iowa Street—location)
PO Box 1150 (mailing address)
Livingston, LA 70754
(225) 686-2216; (225) 686-1867 FAX
tsullivan@livclerk.org
http://www.livclerk.org
Thomas "Tom" Sullivan, Jr.

Madison Parish
organized 1838 from Concordia Parish

Madison Parish Clerk of Court
(100 North Cedar Street, Tallulah, LA 71282—
location)
PO Box 1710 (mailing address)
Tallulah, LA 71284
(318) 574-0655; (318) 574-3961 FAX

http://www.lpgov.org/directory/parish_info.ph
p?id=33
Carolyn C. Caldwell

Morehouse Parish
organized 1844 from Ouachita Territory

Morehouse Parish Clerk of Court
(120 South Franklin, Bastrop, LA 71220—
location)
PO Box 1543 (mailing address)
Bastrop, LA 71221
(318) 281-3343; (318) 281-3775 FAX
http://www.lpgov.org/directory/parish_info.ph
p?id=34
Carol Jones
(deeds and mortgages from 1844, naturalization
records from 1871 to 1901, probate records
from 1870)
probate search service: $10.00; copies of probate
records: $1.00 per page plus SASE, $2.00 for
certification, no minimum

Natchitoches Parish
organized 1807 from Natchitoches County

Natchitoches Parish Clerk of Court
(New Courthouse, 200 Church Street, Room
104, Natchitoches, LA 71457—location)
PO Box 476 (mailing address)
Natchitoches, LA 71458-0476
(318) 352-8152; (318) 352-9321 FAX
http://nppj.org
Louie Bernard
(land records, naturalization records, vital
records, probate records)
records search service: $10.00 minimum

Orleans Parish
organized 1807 from Orleans County

Orleans Parish Civil District Court
Civil Courts Building
421 Loyola Avenue, Suite 402
New Orleans, LA 70112
(504) 592-9105; (504) 592-9128 FAX
daleatk@acadiacom.net
http://www.orleanscdc.com/clerk1.shtm
Dale N. Atkins, Clerk

Orleans Parish Criminal Clerk
2700 Tulane Avenue, Room 115
New Orleans, LA 70119
(504) 827-3520; (504) 827-3385 FAX
http//www.nocitycouncil.com
Kimberly Williamson Butler

Orleans Parish Recorder of Mortgages
Civil Courts Building
421 Loyola Avenue, Room B-1
New Orleans, LA 70112
(504) 592-9176; (504) 592-9192 FAX
dcharbonnet@orleanscdc.com
http://www.orleanscdc.com/recmort.shtm
Desiree Charbonnet, Recorder

Orleans Parish Register of Conveyances
Civil Courts Building
421 Loyola Avenue, Room B-3
New Orleans, LA 70112
(504) 592-9194; (504) 523-4320 FAX
schiro@orleanscdc.com
http://www.orleanscdc.com/regcon.shtm
Gasper J. Schiro, Registrar

Ouachita Parish
organized 1807 from Ouachita County

Ouachita Parish Clerk of Court
(300 St. John Street, Monroe, LA 71201-7326—
location)
PO Box 1862 (mailing address)
Monroe, LA 71210
(318) 327-1444; (318) 327-3087 FAX
http://www.oppj.org
W. J. "Bill" Hodge

Plaquemines Parish
organized 1807 from Orleans County

Plaquemines Parish Clerk of Court

25th Judicial District Court
(301 Main Street—location)
PO Box 40 (mailing address)
Belle Chasse, LA 70037
(504) 333-4377; (504) 333-9202 FAX
dlundin@clerk25th.com
http://www.plaqueminesparish.com/ClerkofCo
urt
Dorothy M. Lundin
(land records, marriages, probate records)
no probate search service; copies of probate
records: 50¢ per page, no minimum

Pointe Coupee Parish
organized 1807 from Pointe Coupee County

Pointe Coupee Parish Clerk of Court
(203 East Main Street—location)
PO Box 86 (mailing adress)
New Roads, LA 70760-0086
(225) 638-9596; (225) 638-9590 FAX
http://www.pcpolicejury.org
Lanell Swindler Landry

Rapides Parish
organized 1807 from Rapides County

Rapides Parish Clerk of Court
(701 Murray Street, Alexandria, LA 71301—
location)
PO Drawer 952 (mailing address)
Alexandria, LA 71309-0952
(318) 473-8153; (318) 473-4667 FAX
info@rapidesclerk.org
http://www.rapidesclerk.org
Carolyn C. Jones Ryland
(land records from 1864 [earlier records burned
during Civil War] with Clerk, Sheriff,
Assessor, naturalization records, marriages,
and probate records from 1864 with Clerk of
Court)
records search service: $11.00 per name per
index (as time permits, "offices do not do
research; contact local genealogists"); copies of
probate records: 50¢ per page, $2.00 for
certification

Red River Parish
organized 1871 from Bienville, Bossier, Caddo,
DeSoto and Natchitoches parishes

Red River Parish Clerk of Court
(615 East Carrol Street—location)
PO Box 485 (mailing address)
Coushatta, LA 71019-0485
(318) 932-6741; (318) 932-3126
http://www.lpgov.org/directory/parish_info.ph
p?id=41
Stuart Shaw
(land and probate records)
probate search service: $5.00; copies of probate
records: 50¢ per page, $1.00 minimum

Richland Parish
organized 1852 from Carroll, Franklin,
Morehouse and Ouachita parishes

Richland Parish Clerk of Court
(100 Julia Street, Suite 103—location)
PO Box 119 (mailing address)
Rayville, LA 71269
(318) 728-4171; (318) 728-7020 FAX
http://www.lpgov.org/directory/parish_info.ph
p?id=42
Ramona N. Haire

Sabine Parish
organized 1843 from Natchitoches Parish

Sabine Parish Clerk of Court
(South Capitol at Main Street—location)
PO Box 419 (mailing address)
Many, LA 71449
(318) 256-6223; (318) 256-9037 FAX
http://www.lpgov.org/directory/parish_info.ph
p?id=43
Dollie M. Knippers
(conveyance records from 1843, marriages from
1843, probate records from 1843)

vital records search service (give groom's and bride's names): $5.00; probate search service (give name and year of death): $5.00; copies of probate records: $5.00 each

St. Bernard Parish

organized 1807 from Orleans County

St. Bernard Parish Clerk of Court
(1100 West St. Bernard Highway, Chalmette, LA 70043—location)
PO Box 1746 (mailing address)
Chalmette, LA 70044
(504) 271-3434
http://www.sbpg.net
Lena R. Torres

St. Charles Parish

organized 1807 from German Coast County

St. Charles Parish Clerk of Court
(15045 River Road—location)
PO Box 424 (mailing address)
Hahnville, LA 70057
(985) 783-6632; (985) 783-2005 FAX
http://www.stcharlesgov.net/departments/clerk .htm
Charles J. Oubre, Jr.

St. Helena Parish

organized 1810 from Feliciana County

St. Helena Parish Clerk of Court
(Rt. 1, Box 87-AB, Greensburg, LA 70422—location)
PO Box 308 (mailing address)
Greensburg, LA 70441-0308
(225) 222-4514; (225) 222-3443 FAX
http://www.sthelenapj.org
Herman C. Newell
(land records, marriages, probate records)
no probate search service; copies of probate records: 50¢ each, no minimum

St. James Parish

organized 1807, original parish

St. James Parish Clerk of Court
(5800 LA Highway 44—location)
PO Box 63 (mailing address)
Convent, LA 70723
(225) 562-2270; (225) 562-2383 FAX
http://www.stjamesla.com
Edmond E. Kinler, Jr.
(land and probate records, vital records)
probate search service: $10.00; copies of probate records: 75¢ per page, no minimum

St. John the Baptist Parish

organized 1807 from German Coast County

St. John the Baptist Parish Clerk of Court
40th Judicial District Court
(2393 East Third Street, Highway 18—location)
PO Box 280 (mailing address)
Edgard, LA 70049
(985) 497-8836; (985) 497-3972 FAX
http://www.stjohnclerk.org;
http://www.sjbparish.com/clerkofcourt.asp
Eliana DeFrancesch

St. Landry Parish

organized 1807 from Opelousas County (1805-1807), encompassing most of Southwestern Louisiana prior to 1840; Imperial St. Landry Parish comprised the modern parishes of Acadia, Allen, Beauregard, Cameron, Calcasieu, Evangeline, Jefferson Davis, and present-day St. Landry

St. Landry Parish Clerk of Court
Twenty-Seventh Judicial District
(118 South Court Street, Suite 109, Opelousas, LA 70570-5166—location)
PO Box 750 (mailing address)
Opelousas, LA 70570-0750
(337) 942-5606; (337) 948-7265 FAX
stlancoc@bellsouth.net; info@blmedia.com
http://stlandry.org
Charles Jgneaux

(land records from 1805 to date [including Opelousas County], naturalization records from 1824 to 1912, marriages from 1808 to date, probate records from 1807 to date; Opelousas Colonial Post [1764-1805] with Clerk's Archives for microfilm copies [originals deposited at the Louisiana State Archives])

St. Martin Parish

organized 1815 from Attakapas County

St. Martin Parish Clerk of Court
(415 South Main Street—location)
PO Box 308 (mailing address)
St. Martinville, LA 70582-0009
(337) 394-2210; (337) 394-7772 FAX
Allen@StMartinParishClerkofCourt.com
http://www.stmartinparishclerkofcourt.com
Allen Blanchard, Sr.
(land records, naturalization records, marriages, probate records)

St. Mary Parish

organized 1811 from Attakapas County

St. Mary Parish Clerk of Court
(500 Main Street—location)
PO Box 1231 (mailing address)
Franklin, LA 70538
(337) 828-4100; (337) 828-2509 FAX
http://www.parish.st-mary.la.us
Cliff Dressel

St. Tammany Parish

organized 1810 from Feliciana County

St. Tammany Parish Clerk of Court
(701 North Columbia Street—location)
PO Box 1090 (mailing address)
Covington, LA 70434
(985) 809-8700
http://www.sttammanyclerk.org/main/index.asp; http://www.stpgov.org
Malise Prieto
(land records from 1810 [ask for vault records], probate records from 1810 [ask for civil records]; marriage licenses, civil suits, successions, criminal records, cemetery records, original records from the State Land Office, charters, partnerships, oaths, bonds, citizenship and naturalization, notaries' papers, Justice of the Peace court hearings by ward [ask for Archives Department])
search service: $15.00 per hour; copies of probate records: 25¢ per page, no minimum

Tangipahoa Parish

organized 1869 from Livingston, St. Helena, St. Tammany and Washington parishes

Tangipahoa Parish Clerk of Court
(Mulberry and Bay—location)
PO Box 667 (mailing address)
Amite, LA 70422
(985) 549-1610; (985) 748-6503 FAX
civil@tangiclerk.org; criminal@tangiclerk.org; recording@tangiclerk.org
http://www.tangiclerk.org
Julian E. Dufreche
(land records from 1820, naturalization records from 1911 to 1928, probate records from 1850)
probate search service: $10.00 per name; copies of probate records: $1.00 per page, no minimum

Tensas Parish

organized 1843 from Concordia Parish

Tensas Parish Clerk of Court
(Courthouse Square—location)
PO Box 78 (mailing address)
St. Joseph, LA 71366-0078
(318) 766-3921; (318) 766-3926 FAX
http://www.lpgov.org/directory/parish_info.ph p?id=54
Ernest L. Sikes

Terrebonne Parish

organized 1822 from Lafourche Parish

Terrebonne Parish Clerk of Court
Attn: Copy Request
(Old Courthouse, 400 East Main Street, First Floor—location)
PO Box 1569 (mailing address)
Houma, LA 70361-1569
(985) 868-5660; (985) 868-5143 FAX
http://www.tpcg.org
I. Robert "Bobby" Boudreaux
(land records from June 1806, naturalization records from December 1907 to December 1927, marriages from October 1814, probate records from September 1807)
probate search service: no charge ("give as much information as possible to aid search"); copies of probate records: 75¢ per page, $5.00 for certification

City Court of Houma
7887 Main Street
Houma, LA 70361
(985) 868-4232
http://www.tpcg.org/city_court/clerk-of-court.asp
Doug Holloway, Clerk/Court Administrator
(three divisions: Civil, Criminal/Traffic, and the Juvenile and Community Service division; Terrebonne Parish Consolidated Government)

Union Parish

organized 1839 from Ouachita Parish

Union Parish Clerk of Court
Courthouse Building, 100 East Bayou, Suite 105
Farmerville, LA 71241
(318) 368-3055; (318) 368-3861
http://www.lpgov.org/directory/parish_info.ph p?id=56
Sue Buckley
(land records, vital records, probate records)
probate search service: no charge; copies of probate records: 75¢ each, no minimum

Vermilion Parish

organized 1844 from Lafayette Parish

Vermilion Parish Clerk of Court
(100 North State Street, Abbeville, LA 70510-5199—location)
PO Box 790 (mailing address)
Abbeville, LA 70511-0790
(337) 898-1992; (337) 898-0404 FAX
http://www.lpgov.org/directory/parish_info.ph p?id=57
Dianne Meaux Broussard
(land records from 1884 with Public Service Department, probate records from 1884 with Civil Suit Library)
no probate search service ("must get abstracter or do searches in person unless it is very small"); copies of probate records: $1.00 each

Vernon Parish

organized 1871 from Natchitoches, Rapides and Sabine parishes

Vernon Parish Clerk of Court
(201 South Third Street, Leesville, LA 71446—location)
PO Box 40 (mailing address)
Leesville, LA 71496-0040
(337) 238-1384; (337) 238-9902 FAX
http://www.lpgov.org/directory/parish_info.ph p?id=58
Willie Deon, Jr.
(land and probate records from 1871)
probate search service: $15.00; copies of probate records: $1.00 each, no minimum

Washington Parish

organized 1819 from St. Tammany Parish

Washington Parish Clerk of Court and Ex-Officio Recorder
22nd Judicial District

(Courthouse Building, Washington and Main,
Bogalusa, LA—location)
PO Box 607 (mailing address)
Franklinton, LA 70438-0607
(985) 839-4663 (Franklinton); (985) 732-7189
(Bogalusa); (985) 839-3116 FAX
http://www.wpgov.org
Johnny D. Crain
(land records from 1897 [because of a fire in
March of that year, which destroyed all earlier
records], marriages, probate records)

Webster Parish
organized 1871 from Bienville, Bossier and
Claiborne parishes

Webster Parish Clerk of Court
(410 Main Street, Minden, LA 71055-3325—
location)
PO Box 370 (mailing address)
Minden, LA 71058
(318) 371-0366; (318) 371-0226 FAX
http://www.wppj.org
Cynthia Klimkiewicz

West Baton Rouge Parish
organized 1807 from Baton Rouge Parish

West Baton Rouge Parish Clerk of Court
(850 Eighth Street—location)
PO Box 107 (mailing address)
Port Allen, LA 70767
(225) 383-0378; (225) 383-3694 FAX
http://www.wbrparish.org/index.php
Mark J. Graffeo
(land records, marriages, probate records)
probate search service ("an index search of
probate records will be conducted when time
is available"): no charge; copies of probate
records: $1.00 per page, no minimum

West Carroll Parish
organized 1877 from Carroll Parish

West Carroll Parish Clerk of Court
(305 East Main Street, Room 101—location)
PO Box 1078 (mailing address)
Oak Grove, LA 71263-1078
(318) 428-2369; (318) 428-8889 FAX
http://www.lpgov.org/directory/parish_info.ph
p?id=62
Kay S. Bolding

West Feliciana Parish
organized 1824 from Feliciana Parish

West Feliciana Parish Clerk of Court
(4789 Prosperity Street, St. Francisville, LA
70767—location)
PO Box 1921 (mailing address)
St. Francisville, LA 70775
(225) 635-3794; (225) 635-3770 FAX
http://www.lpgov.org/directory/parish_info.ph
p?id=63
Felicia A. Daniel Hendl

Winn Parish
organized 1852 from Catahoula, Natchitoches
and Rapides parishes

Winn Parish Clerk of Court
(101 Main Street, Room 103—location)
PO Box 137 (mailing address)
Winnfield, LA 71483
(318) 628-3515
http://www.lpgov.org/directory/parish_info.ph
p?id=64
Donald E. "Don" Kelley
(land records from 1886 to date, marriage
licenses from 1886 to date, probate records
from 1886 to date)
probate search service: $10.00 per name for a
ten-year search; 50¢ per page, $3.00 minimum
for mailing copies

MAINE

*Capital: Augusta. Statehood: 15 March 1820 (was
part of Massachusetts from 1639 to 1820, established
boundary with Canada, 1842)*

Each of Maine's counties has a Probate Court
which sits at the county seat. The Maine
Administrative Court sits in the District Court
or Superior Court and handles cases involving
real estate licenses. Thirteen District Courts sit
in each county seat and elsewhere and hear
some civil actions and non-felony criminal cases.

The Superior Court sits at each county seat
and has original jurisdiction over all matters that
are not dealt with by the lower courts. The
Supreme Judicial Court hears appeals in
Portland and Bangor.

All cities, towns and plantations deposited
copies of their vital statistics, 1782-1922, with
the Maine State Archives.

Androscoggin County
organized 18 March 1854 from Cumberland,
Kennebec, Lincoln and Oxford counties;
includes fourteen cities and towns, plus East
Livermore, East Poland, Lisbon Falls, North
Turner, Poland Spring, West Minot, and West
Poland

Androscoggin County Courthouse
2 Turner Street
Auburn, ME 04210-5953
(207) 784-8390 (County Commissioners Office);
(207) 782-0191 (Register of Deeds); (207)
782-0281 (Register of Probate)
http://www.maine.gov/local/androscoggin
Tina Chouinard, Register of Deeds; John
Cleveland, Register of Probate
(land records, probate records)
probate search service: no charge; copies of land
and probate records: $1.00 for the first page
and 50¢ for each additional page, no
minimum

District Court
71 Lisbon Street
Lewiston, ME 04240
(207) 795-4801
http://www.courts.state.me.us/mainecourts/dis
trict/district_lewiston.html
Sue Bement, Clerk

Aroostook County
organized 16 March 1839 from Penobscot and
Washington counties; 21 March 1843 annexed
part of Penobscot County; 12 Mar 1844
annexed parts of Piscataquis and Somerset
counties; contains 2 cities, 54 towns, 11
plantations, and 108 unorganized townships

Aroostook County Probate Court
26 Court Street, Suite 103
Houlton, ME 04730
(207) 532-1502
joanne@aroostook.me.us
http://www.aroostook.me.us/probate.html
Joanne M. Carpenter, Regeister
(probate records)
copies of records: 25¢ per page (if done in
person), 50¢ per page (if done by registry
personnel), $1.00 per page (if mailed)

Caribou Courthouse
144 Sweden Street
Caribou, ME 04736
(207) 493-3318; (207) 493-3491 FAX
dougWaroostook.me.us
http://www.aroostook.me.us
Douglas F. Beaulieu, County Administrator
(County Commissioners' Office, County
Administrator's Office, Treasurer's Office,
Public Words Director's Office, Maine Law
Library, District Court and Superior Court
Offices, District Attorney's Office, Probation
and Parole Offices)

District Court
144 Sweden Street, Suite 104
Caribou, ME 04736
(207) 493-3144
http://www.courts.state.me.us/mainecourts/dis
trict/district_caribou.html
Vickie Harris, Clerk

District Court
139 Market Street, Suite 101
Fort Kent, ME 04743
(207) 834-5003
http://www.courts.state.me.us/mainecourts/dis
trict/district_fortkent.html
Linda Cyr, Clerk

District Court
(645 Main Street, Madawaska, ME 04756—
location)
c/o Maine District Court, PO Box 473 (mailing
address)
Fort Kent, ME 04743-0473
(207) 728-4700
http://www.courts.state.me.us/mainecourts/dis
trict/district_

District Court
25 School Street
Houlton, ME 04730
(207) 532-2147
http://www.courts.state.me.us/mainecourts/dis
trict/district_houlton.html
Mary-Ellen Knapp, Clerk
(naturalization records)

District Court
27 Riverside Drive
Presque Isle, ME 04769
(207) 764-2055
http://www.courts.state.me.us/mainecourts/dis
trict/district_presqueisle.html
Sandi Thomas, Clerk

Northern Register of Deeds
(22 Hall Street, Suite 201—location)
PO Box 47 (mailing address)
Fort Kent, ME 04743-0047
(207) 834-3925; (207) 834-3138 FAX
louise@aroostook.me.us
http://www.aroostook.me.us/deeds.html
Louise Caron
(land records north of Caribou from 1808;
"serves: Big Twenty Twp - Escourt, ME, T19
R12 WELS, T19 R11 WELS, T18 R13
WELS, T18 R12 WELS, T18 R10 WELS,
T18 R 6 & 7, Fort Kent, T18 R5 Frenchville
& St. Agatha, T18 R4 Madawaska, T18 R3
Grand Isle, T17 R14 WELS, T17 R13 WELS,
T17 R12 WELS, T17 R9 St. Francis, T17 R8
St. John Plantation, T17 R7 Wallagrass, T17
R6 New Canada Plantation, T17 R5 WELS
Cross Lake, T17 R4 WELS, Sinclair, T17 R3
WELS Long Lake, TM R2 Van Buren, TL R2
Cyr Plantation, TG R1 Hamlin, TK R2
Connor Township, TF R2 Caswell, T16 R14
WELS, T16 R13 WELS, T16 R12 WELS,
T16 R10 Allagash, T16 R9 WELS, T16 R8
WELS, T16 R7 Eagle Lake, T16 R6 WELS,
T16 R5 WELS Square Lake, T16 R4 WELS,
T16 R3 Stockholm, T15 R15 WELS, T15 R14
WELS, T15 R13 WELS, T15 R12 WELS,
T15 R11 WELS, T15 R10 WELS, T15 R9
WELS, T15 R8 WELS, T15 R7 Winterville
Plantation, T15 R6 WELS, T15 R5 WELS,
T15 R4 Westmanland, T14 R7 WELS, T14
R6 WELS, T14 R5 WELS")

Southern Register of Deeds
26 Court Street, Suite 102
Houlton, ME 04730
(207) 532-1500; (207) 532-7319 FAX
pat@aroostook.me.us
http://www.aroostook.me.us/deeds.html
Patricia Brown
("serves: T14 R16 WELS, T14 R15 WELS, T14
R14 WELS, T14 R13 WELS, T14 R12
WELS, T14 R11 WELS, T14 R10 WELS,
T14 R9 WELS, T14 R8 WELS, Perham, New
Sweden, Woodland, Caribou, Limestone, Fort
Fairfield, Presque Isle, Easton, Westfield,

Mars Hill, E Township, Blaine, Cox Patent, Bridgewater, Monticello, Hammond, Littleton, Ludlow, New Limerick, Houlton, Linneus, Hodgdon, Cary Plantation, Amity, Haynesville, Orient, Bancroft, Weston, TA R2 WELS, Forkstown Township, TD R2 WELS, Washburn, Mapleton, Chapman, Wade, Castle Hill, Ashland, Masardis, T13 R16 WELS, T13 R15 WELS, T13 R14 WELS, T13 R13 WELS, T13 R12 WELS, T13 R11 WELS, T13 R10 WELS, T13 R9 WELS, T13 R8 WELS, T13 R7 WELS, Portage Lake, T13 R5 WELS, T12 R17 WELS, T12 R16 WELS, T12 R15 WELS, T12 R14 WELS, T12 R13 WELS, T12 R12 WELS, T12 R11 WELS, T12 R10 WELS, T12 R9 WELS, T12 R8 WELS, T12 R7 WELS, Nashville Plantation, T11 R17 WELS, T11 R16 WELS, T11 R15 WELS, T11 R14 WELS, T11 R13 WELS, T11 R12 WELS, T11 R11 WELS, T11 R10 WELS, T11 R9 WELS, T11 R8 WELS, T11 R7 WELS, T11 R4 WELS, Garfield Plantation, T10 R8 WELS, T10 R7 WELS, T10 R6 WELS, Squapan Township, T10 R3 WELS, T9 R8 WELS, T9 R7 WELS, Oxbow Plantation, T9 R5 WELS, T9 R4 WELS, T9 R3 WELS, T8 R5 WELS, St. Croix Township, T8 R3 WELS, T7 R5 WELS, Webbertown Township, Dudley Township, Moro Plantation, Merrill, Smyrna, Hersey, Dyer Brook, Oakfield, Crystal, Island Falls, T4 R3 WELS, Sherman, T3 R4 WELS, T3 R3 WELS, Benedicta Township, Silver Ridge Township, T2 R4 WELS Glenwood Plantation, T1 R5 WELS, Upper Molunkus Township, North Yarmouth Academy Grant, Reed Plantation, Molunkus Township, Macwahoc Plantation")

Cumberland County

organized 19 June 1760 from York County; includes twenty-six cities and towns, plus Bailey Island, Birch Island, Bustins Island, Cape Cottage, Chebeague Island, Cliff Island, Cumberland Center, Cumberland Foreside, Cundys Harbor, Cushing Island, Diamond Cove, Diamond Island, East Baldwin, East Sebago, East Falmouth Foreside, Frye Island, Great Diamond Island, Little Diamond Island, NAS Brunswick, North Bridgton, Orrs Island, Peaks Island, Pine Point, Pond Cove, Sebago Lake, South Casco, South Freeport, South Harpswell, South Windham, Steep Falls, West Baldwin, and West Scarborough, etc. (see http://www.hometownlocator.com/DisplayCountyFeatures.cfm?FeatureType=populated%20place&SCFIPS=23005)

Cumberland County Courthouse
(142 Federal Street, Portland, ME 04101-4151
PO Box 7230 (mailing address)
Portland, ME 04112
(207) 871-8386 (Register of Deeds); (207) 871-8382 (Register of Probate)
probate@cumberlandcounty.org
http://www.cumberlandcounty.org
John B. O'Brien, Register of Deeds; Teri E. McRae, Register of Probate
(land records, probate records)

District Court
142 Federal Street
Portland, ME 04112
(207) 822-4200
http://www.courts.state.me.us/mainecourts/district/district_portland.html
Deborah L. Sullivan, Clerk

District Court
2 Chase Common
Bridgton, ME 04009
(207) 647-3535
http://www.courts.state.me.us/mainecourts/district/district_bridgton.html
Belinda Becher, Clerk

District Court
207 Penobscot Avenue
Millinocket, ME 04462

(207) 723-4786
http://www.courts.state.me.us/mainecourts/district/district_millinocket.html
Rebecca Hanscom, Clerk

Franklin County

organized 20 March 1838 from Cumberland, Kennebec, Oxford and Somerset counties; includes eighteen towns plus Coplin Plantation, Dallas Plantation, Dryden, East Central Franklin (unorganized area), East Dixfield, East Wilton, Farmington Falls, Freeman (disorganized), North Franklin (unorganized area), North Jay, Oquossoc, Perkins (disorganized), Rangeley Plantation, Salem (unorganized), Sandy River Plantation, South Franklin (unorganized area), Stratton, West Central Franklin (unorganized area), West Farmington, and Wyman (unorganized area)

District Court
129 Main Street
Farmington, ME 04938
(207) 778-8200
http://www.courts.state.me.us/mainecourts/district/district_farmington.html
Vicki Hardy, Clerk

Franklin County Courthouse
140 Main Street
Farmington, ME 04938
(207) 778-5889 (Register of Deeds); (207) 778-5888 (Register of Probate)
http://www.maine.gov/local/franklin
Susan A. Black, Register of Deeds; Joyce S. Morton, Register of Probate
(land records, records)
no probate search service; copies of probate records: $1.00 for the first page and 50¢ for each additional page, no minimum

Hancock County

organized 25 June 1789 from Lincoln County; includes City of Ellsworth and thirty-six towns, plus 7 SD BPP, 8 SD Township, Bass Harbor, Bernard, Birch Harbor, Central Hancock (unorganized area), Corea, East Blue Hill, East Hancock (unorganized area), East Orland, Harborside, Hulls Cove, Islesford, Little Deer Isle, Minturn, North Sullivan, Northeast Harbor, Otter Creek, Prospect Harbor, Salsbury Cove, Sargentville, Seal Cove, Seal Harbor, South Gouldsboro, Sunset, and West Tremont

District Court
50 State Street
Ellsworth, ME 04605
(207) 667-7141
http://www.courts.state.me.us/mainecourts/district/district_ellsworth.html
Cheryl Tims, Clerk

Hancock County Courthouse
60 State Street
Ellsworth, ME 04605-1926
(207) 667-9542; (207) 667-8353 (Register of Deeds); (207) 667-8434 (Register of Probate)
aott@co.hancock.me.us;
dsw.hancockprobate@co.hancock.me.us
http://www.co.hancock.me.us;
http://www.registryofdeeds.com
Alan Ott, Register of Deeds; Margaret Lunt, Register of Probate
(land records, probate records)
probate search service: no charge; copies of probate records: $1.00 for the first page and 50¢ for each additional page; "Send any info they are looking for; where person last resided and date of death"

Kennebec County

organized 20 February 1799 from Cumberland and Lincoln counties; includes twenty-nine cities and towns, plus China Village, East Vassalboro, East Winthrop, Kents Hill, North Monmouth, North Vassalboro, South China, South Gardiner, Togus, Unity (unorganized),

and Weeks Mills

District Court
18 Colby Street
Waterville, ME 04903
(207) 873-2103
http://www.courts.state.me.us/mainecourts/district/district_
Mon–Fri 8:00–4:00

District Court
145 State Street
Augusta, ME 04330
(207) 287-8075
http://www.courts.state.me.us/mainecourts/district/district_augusta.html
Judy Pellerin, Clerk

Kennebec County Courthouse
95 State Street
Augusta, ME 04330-5611
(207) 622-0971; (207) 622-0431 (Register of Deeds); (207) 622-7558 (Register of Probate); (207) 621-1639 FAX (Probate)
kicdeeds@msn.com; kenprob@gwi.net;
katayers@aol.com
http://www.kennebeccounty.org;
http://www.kennebec.me.us.landata.com;
http://www.datamaine.com/probate
Beverly Bustin-Hatheway, Register of Deeds; Kathleen Ayers, Register of Probate
(land records, probate records)
no probate search service; copies of probate records: $1.00 for the first page and 50¢ for each additional page, no minimum

Knox County

organized 5 March 1860 from Lincoln and Waldo counties; includes City of Rockland and sixteen towns, plus Glen Cove, Manticus Isle Plantation, Spruce Head, Stonington, Tenants Harbor, and West Rockport

District Court
62 Union Street
Rockland, ME 04841
(207) 596-2240
http://www.courts.state.me.us/mainecourts/district/district_rockland.html
Penny Reckards, Clerk
(naturalization records)

Knox County Courthouse
62 Union Street
Rockland, ME 04841
(207) 594-0422 (Register of Deeds); (207) 594-0427 (Probate); (207) 594-0444 (Probate); (207) 594-0863 FAX (Probate);
lsimmons@knoxcounty.midcoast.com;
ehallett@knoxcounty.midcoast.com
http://knoxcounty.midcoast.com/departments/deeds.html; http://knoxcounty.midcoast.com/departments/probate.html
Lisa Simmons, Register of Deeds; Elaine D. Hallett, Register of Probate
(land records from early 1700s, probate records and adoptions from 1860)
no probate search service; copies of probate records: $1.00 for the first page and 50¢ for each additional page, no minimum; "Inquiries should be made to the individual department"

Lincoln County

organized 19 June 1760 from York County; includes eighteen towns plus Capital Island, Chamberlain, Coopers Mills, Damariscove Island, East Boothbay, Head Tide, Hibberts Gore (unorganized township), Isle of Springs, Medomak, Monhegan Plantation, Monhegan Island, New Harbor, Newagen, Pemaquid, Round Pond, Smutty Nose Island, Southport Island, Squirrel Island, Trevett, Walpole, West Boothbay Harbor, and West Southport

District Court
32 High Street
Wiscasset, ME 04578
(207) 882-6363
http://www.courts.state.me.us/mainecourts/district/district_wiscasset.html

Sharon Simpson, Clerk

Lincoln County Courthouse
(High Street—location)
PO Box 249 (mailing address)
Wiscasset, ME 04578
(207) 882-6311; (207) 882-7341 (Register of
 Deeds); (207) 882-7515 (Register of Deeds);
 (207) 882-7392 (Register of Probate); (207)
 882-4061 FAX (Register of Deeds); (207)
 882-4324 FAX (Register of Probate)
silva@co.lincoln.me.us;
lincprob@co.lincoln.me.us
http://www.co.lincoln.me.us/dep.html
Marcia Silva, Register of Deeds; Chester Fossett,
 Register of Probate
(land records and naturalization records with
 Register of Deeds; probate records with
 Register of Probate)
no probate search service; copies of probate
 records: $1.00 per page

Oxford County

organized 4 March 1805 from Cumberland and
 York counties; includes thirty-four towns plus
 Albany Township, Batchelders Grant, Bryant
 Pond, Center Lovell, East Andover, East
 Stoneham, Franklin Plantation, Frye, Lincoln
 Plantation, Magalloway Plantation, Mason
 Township, Milton Township, North
 Fryeburg, North Oxford (unorganized area),
 North Waterford, Parish Hill, Rumford
 Center, Rumford Point, South Oxford
 (unorganized area), South Paris, South
 Waterford, Sweden, West Bethel, and West
 Peru

District Court
145 Congress Street
Rumford, ME 04276
(207) 364-7171
http://www.courts.state.me.us/mainecourts/dis
 trict/district_rumford.html
Trudy DeSalle, Clerk

District Court
26 Western Avenue
South Paris, ME 04281
(207) 743-8942
http://www.courts.state.me.us/mainecourts/dis
 trict/district_southparis.html
Mon–Fri 8:00–4:00

Oxford County Courthouse
(26 Western Avenue—location)
PO Box 179 (mailing address)
South Paris, ME 04281-1417
(207) 743-6359; (207) 743-6211 (East Register of
 Deeds); (207) 935-2565 (West Register of
 Deeds); (207) 743-6671 (Register of Probate)
oxprob@megalink.net
http://www.oxfordcounty.org
Jane Rich, Eastern District, Register of Deeds;
 Jean Watson, Western District, Register of
 Deeds; Tom Winsor, Register of Probate
(land records, probate records from 1795)
probate search service: no charge; copies of
 probate records: $1.00 for the first page and
 50¢ for each additional page of each
 document, no minimum; "We do not have
 time for extensive searches; we must have
 specific names"

Penobscot County

organized 16 February 1816 from Hancock
 County; includes fifty-five cities and towns,
 plus Argyle Township (unorganized area),
 Cardville, Carroll Plantation, Drew Plantation,
 East Corinth, East Holden, East Newport,
 Grand Falls Plantation, Greenfield Township
 (disorganized), Indian Island, Kingman
 Plantation, Lincoln Center, Mattamiscontis
 Township, North Penobscot (unorganized
 area), Olamon, Prentiss Plantation, Ripley,
 Seboeis Plantation, Sherman Station,
 Stillwater, Webster Plantation, West Enfield,
 and Whitney

District Court
73 Hammond Street

Bangor, ME 04401
(207) 941-3040
http://www.courts.state.me.us/mainecourts/dis
 trict/district_bangor.html
Susan Cure, Clerk

District Court
12 Water Street
Newport, ME 04953
(207) 368-5778
http://www.courts.state.me.us/mainecourts/dis
 trict/district_newport.html
Ronda Nelson, Clerk
(Town of Newport naturalization records)

District Court
52 Main Street
Lincoln, ME 04457
(207) 794-8512
http://www.courts.state.me.us/mainecourts/dis
 trict/district_lincoln.html
Sharon Webster, Clerk

Penobscot County Courthouse
(97 Hammond Street, Bangor, ME 04401-
 4996—location)
PO Box 2070 (mailing address)
Bangor, ME 04402-2070
(207) 942-8797 (Register of Deeds); (207) 942-
 8769 (Register of Probate)
http://www.maine.gov/local/penobscot
Susan F. Bulay, Register of Deeds; Susan M.
 Almy, Register of Probate
(land records, probate records)
no land records search service; probate search
 service: $10.00; copies of land records: $1.00
 per page; copies of probate records: $1.00 for
 the first page and 50¢ for each additional page

Piscataquis County

organized 23 March 1838 from Penobscot and
 Somerset counties; includes seventeen towns
 plus Barnard Plantation, Blanchard
 Plantation, Brownville Junction, Derby
 Elliotsville Plantation, Greenville Junction,
 Kingsbury Plantation, Lake View Plantation,
 Northeast Piscataquis (unorganized area),
 Northwest Piscataquis (unorganized area),
 Orneville Township, Sebec Lake, Shirley
 Mills, Southeast (unorganized), and
 Williamsburg Township

District Court
163 East Main Street
Dover-Foxcroft, ME 04426
(207) 564-2240
http://www.courts.state.me.us/mainecourts/dis
 trict/district_doverfoxcroft.html
Lisa Richardson, Clerk

Piscataquis County Courthouse
159 East Main Street
Dover-Foxcroft, ME 04426-1306
(207) 564-2161; (207) 564-2411 (Register of
 Deeds); (207) 564-2431 (Register of Probate);
 (207) 564-3022 FAX
pisccourt@foxcroft.pvt.k12.me.us
http://www.maine.gov/local/piscataquis
Linda Smith, Register of Deeds; Judith A.
 Raymond, Register of Probate
(land records, probate records)
no probate search service; copies of probate
 records: $1.00 for the first page and 50¢ for
 each additional page, no minimum

Sagadahoc County

organized 4 April 1854 from Lincoln County;
 includes the City of Bath, nine towns, plus
 Five Islands, MacMahan, Pejepscot, Sebasco
 Estates, and West Bowdoin

District Court
New Meadows Road
West Bath, ME 04530
(207) 442-0200
http://www.courts.state.me.us/mainecourts/dis
 trict/district_westbath.html
Anita Alexander, Clerk

Sagadahoc County Courthouse
(752 High Street—location)

PO Box 246 (mailing address)
Bath, ME 04530-0246
(207) 443-8200; (207) 443-8214 (Register of
 Deeds); (207) 443-9733 (Clerk of Courts);
 (207) 443-8218 (Register of Probate); (207)
 443-8213 FAX ; (207) 443-8216 FAX
 (Register of Deeds); (207) 443-8217 FAX
 (Register of Probate)
sabprob@gwi.net (Register of Probate)
http://www.sagcounty.com
Barbara J. Trott, Register of Deeds; Joan
 Atwood, Register of Probate
(land records from 1826 with Register of Deeds,
 some old naturalization records with Clerk of
 Courts, probate records from 1854 with
 Register of Probate)
probate search service: $10.00 per estate; copies
 of land records: $1.00 per page; copies of
 probate records: $1.00 for the first page and
 50¢ for each additional page, no minimum

Somerset County

organized 1 March 1809 from Kennebec
 County; includes twenty-seven towns plus six
 plantations (Brighton Plantation, Dennistown
 Plantation, The Forks Plantation, Highland
 Plantation, Pleasant Ridge Plantation, and
 West Forks Plantation), and eighty-two
 unorganized territories in four political
 subdivisions (Central Somerset [Lexington
 and Concord]), North East Somerset [Bald
 Mountain, Chase Stream WKR, East Moxie,
 Indian Stream EKR, Johnson Long Pond,
 Mountain, Mayfield, Misery, Misery Gore,
 Moxie Gore, Parlin Pond, Rockwood Strip
 (T1 R1), Rockwood Strip (T2 R2), Sandwich
 Academy Grant, Sapling, Square Town, and
 Taunton & Raynham], Northwest Somerset
 [Appleton, Attean, Bigelow, Bow Town,
 Bradstreet, Carrying Place, Carrying Place
 Town, Dead River, Flagstaff, Forsyth,
 Haynestown (T5 R6), Hobbstown, Holeb,
 King & Bartlett, Lower Enchanged, Pierce
 Pond, Rayton (T5 R7)Spring Lake (T3R5
 BKP WKR), T3R4 BKP WKR, and Upper
 Enchanted], Seboomook Lake [Alder Brook,
 Bald Mountain (T4R3), Big Six, Big Ten, Big
 W, Blake Gore, Brassua, Comestock, Dole
 Brook, Elm Stream, Hammond, Little W,
 Pittston Academy, Plymouth, Prentiss, Russell
 Pond, Saint John, Sandy Bay, Seboomook,
 Soldiertown, T4R5 NBKP, T4R17 WELS,
 T5R17 WELS, T5R18 WELS, T5R19 WELS,
 T5R20 WELS, T6R17 WELS, T6R18 WELS,
 T7R16 WELS, T7R17 WELS, T7R18 WELS,
 T7R19 WELS, T8R16 WELS, T8R17 WELS,
 T8R18 WELS, T8R19 WELS, T9R16 WELS,
 T9R17 WELS, T9R18 WELS, T10R16
 WELS, Thorndike, Tomhegan, and West
 Middlesex Canal Grant])

District Court
47 Court Street
Skowhegan, ME 04976
(207) 474-9518
http://www.courts.state.me.us/mainecourts/dis
 trict/district_skowhegan.html
Melanie Adams

Somerset County Courthouse
41 Court Street
Skowhegan, ME 04976-9801
(207) 474-9861; (207) 474-3421 (Register of
 Deeds); (207) 474-3322 (Register of Probate);
 (207) 474-7405 FAX
communications@somersetcounty-me.org;
 somerset@mainester.net
http://www.somersetcounty-me.org;
 http://somersetcountycommissioners.com/re
 gistry%20of%20deeds.htm
Diane Godin, Register of Deeds; Victoria Hatch,
 Register of Probate
(land transfers, probate records from 1809
 [microfiche])
no probate search service; copies of probate
 records: $1.00 for the first page and 50¢ for
 each additional page, no minimum; "Parties
 must do own search or hire genealogist"

Waldo County

organized 7 February 1827 from Hancock County (Waldo Patent was granted 13 March 1630 by the Plymouth Council and included all of Waldo County except the towns of Burnham and Troy); includes twenty-six cities and towns plus Lincolnville Center and Sandy Point

District Court
103 Church Street
Belfast, ME 04915
(207) 338-3107
http://www.courts.state.me.us/mainecourts/dis
trict/district_belfast.html
Terri Curtis, Clerk

Waldo County Register of Deeds
137 Church Street
Belfast, NE 04915
(207) 338-1710; (207) 338-6360 FAX
deeds@waldocountyme.gov
http://www.waldocountyme.gov
Deloris Page
(land records, probate records)
no land records search service; probate search
service: no charge; copies of land records:
$1.00 per page; copies of probate records:
$1.00 for the first page and 50¢ for each
additional page

Waldo County Register of Probate
39A Spring Street
Belfast, ME 04915
(207) 338-2780; (207) 338-2360 FAX
probate@waldocountyme.gov
http://www.waldocountyme.gov
Joanne Crowley

Washington County

organized 25 June 1789 from Lincoln County; includes forty-two cities and towns, plus Baring Plantation, Bucks Harbor, Codyville Plantation, East Central Washington (unorganized area), Forest City, Grand Lake Stream Plantation, Indian Township Reservation of Passamaquoddy, Lambert Lake, North Washington (unorganized area), Plantation Number 14, and Plantation Number 21

District Court
47 Courth Street
Machias, ME 04654
(207) 255-3044
http://www.courts.state.me.us/mainecourts/dis
trict/district_machias.html
Marilyn Braley, Clerk

District Court
382 South Street, Suite B
Calais, ME 04619
(207) 454-2055
http://www.courts.state.me.us/mainecourts/dis
trict/district_calais.html
Karen Moraisey, Clerk

Washington County Courthouse
(47 Court Street—location)
PO Box 297 (mailing address)
Machias, ME 04654-0297
(207) 255-3127; (207) 255-6512 (Register of
Deeds); (207) 255-6591 (Register of Probate);
(207) 255-3326 (Clerk of Superior Court);
(207) 255-3313 FAX
http://www.maine.gov/local/washington
Sharon Strout, Register of Deeds; Marilyn
Braley, Clerk of Superior Court; Carlene
Holmes, Register of Probate
(land records with Register of Deeds;
naturalization records with Clerk of Superior
Court, probate records with Register of
Probate)

York County

organized 20 November 1652, original county (originally called Yorkshire County, when Massachusetts assumed jurisdiction in 1658 to 1691); includes twenty-nine cities and towns, plus Bar Mills, Biddeford Pool, Cape

Neddick, Cape Porpoise, East Parsonfield, East Waterboro, Kezar Falls, Kittery Point, Maplewood, Moody, , Ocean Park, Springvale, West Buxton, West Kennebunk, West Newfield, York Beach, and York Harbor

District Court
25 Adams Street
Biddeford, ME 04005
(207) 283-1147
http://www.courts.state.me.us/mainecourts/dis
trict/district_biddeford.html
Kathy Jones, Clerk

District Court
447 Main Street
Springvale, ME 04083
(207) 459-1400
http://www.courts.state.me.us/mainecourts/dis
trict/district_springvale.html
Rita Howard, Clerk

District Court
11 Chases Pond Road
York, ME 03909
(207) 363-1230
http://www.courts.state.me.us/mainecourts/dis
trict/district_
Mon–Fri 8:00–4:00

York County Courthouse
(45 Kennebunk Road—location)
PO Box 339 (mailing address)
Alfred, ME 04002-0339
(207) 324-1571; (207) 324-1574 (Register of
Deeds); (207) 324-1577 (Register of Probate);
(207) 324-9494 FAX
commissioners@co.york.me.us
http://www.yorkcountyme.gov
Debra Anderson, Register of Deeds; Carol
Lovejoy Register of Probate
(land records from the early 1600s to date,
probate records)
probate search service: "We don't really have
time to do in-depth searches; we can look up
estates, but not a large quantity"; copies of
land records: $1.25 per page; copies of
probate records: $1.00 for the first page and
50¢ for each additional page of the same
document, no minimum

Capital: Annapolis. Statehood: 28 April 1788 (proprietary colony established 1632, Mason-Dixon Line settled 1763-1767)

Maryland has twenty-three counties, but Baltimore City, which is an independent city, is not contained within a county. The Maryland Tax Court has statewide jurisdiction. The Maryland Orphans' Courts deal with matters involving probate, guardianships, orphans, etc., and are established in Baltimore City and in each county except Montgomery and Harford, where the Circuit Court exercises the same authority.

The Maryland District Courts sit at each county seat and Baltimore City and handle some civil actions, felony thefts, misdemeanors, and ordinance violations. District One: Baltimore City; District Two: Dorchester, Somerset, Wicomico and Worcester counties; District Three: Caroline, Cecil, Kent, Queen Anne's and Talbot counties; District Four: Calvert, Charles and St. Mary's counties; District Five: Prince George's County; District Six: Montgomery County; District Seven: Anne Arundel County; District Eight: Baltimore County; District Nine: Harford County; District Ten: Carroll and Howard counties; District Eleven: Frederick and Washington counties; District Twelve: Allegany and Garrett counties.

The Circuit Court of Maryland has unlimited trial jurisdiction and sits in each county seat and Baltimore City. First Judicial Circuit: Dorchester, Somerset, Wicomico and Worcester counties; Second Judicial Circuit: Caroline, Cecil, Kent, Queen Anne's and Talbot counties; Third Judicial Circuit: Baltimore and Harford counties; Fourth Judicial Circuit: Allegany, Garrett and Washington counties; Fifth Judicial Circuit: Anne Arundel, Carroll and Howard counties; Sixth Judicial Circuit: Frederick and Montgomery counties; Seventh Judicial Circuit: Calvert, Charles, Prince George's and St. Mary's counties; Eighth Judicial Circuit: Baltimore City. The Court of Special Appeals of Maryland and the six circuits of the Court of Appeals of Maryland hear appeals. For infomration on Maryland Circuit Court Clerks, see http://www.courts.state.md.us/clerks/listing.ht ml

Many older county records are housed in the Maryland State Archives, including marriage records, see http://www.mdarchives.state.md.us/msa/refser v/html/comarria.html.

Records Management Division
Maryland Department of General Services
(7275 Waterloo Road, Routes 175 and U.S. 1—
location)
PO Box 275 (mailing address)
Jessup, MD 20794
(410) 799-1930
http://www.dgs.maryland.gov/overview/logisti
cs_dept.htm
William E. Taylor, State Records Administrator
("RMD doesn't provide information to the
general public.")

State of Maryland Register of Wills
http://www.registers.state.md.us
(links to local Registers)

Allegany County

organized 1789 from Washington County

Allegany County Circuit Court
30 Washington Street
Cumberland, MD 21502-3043
(301) 777-5923 (Clerk); (301) 777-5924 (Land);
(800) 988-9087; (301) 777-2100 FAX
dawne.lindsey@courts.state.md.us
http://www.courts.state.md.us/clerks/allegany/
index.html
Dawne D. Lindsey, Clerk
(deeds, mortgages and deeds of trust, leases,

releases of mortgages and deeds of trust, land contracts, plat records)

District Court
Allegany County Office Building
3 Pershing Street, Second Floor
Cumberland, MD 21502-3045
(301) 723-3100; (800) 946-3952
http://www.courts.state.md.us/district/directori es/courtmap.html
Kathleen M. Stafford, Administrative Clerk

Register of Wills
James S. Getty Annex, 59 Prospect Square, First Floor
Cumberland, MD 21502
(301) 724-3760; (888) 724-0148
http://gov.allconet.org; http://www.registers. state.md.us/county/al/html/allegany.html
Rebecca Drew

Anne Arundel County
organized 1650, original county

Anne Arundel County Circuit Court
(7 Church Circle–location)
PO Box 71 (mailing address)
Annapolis, MD 21404-0071
(410) 222-1397 (Clerk of Circuit Court); (410) 222-1425 (Land Records); (888) 246-0615
http://www.clerk-anne-arundel.net; http://www.co.anne-arundel.md.us/ CircuitCourt/index.cfm
Robert P. Duckworth
(deeds, mortgages and deeds of trust, leases, releases, plats)
copies of land records: 50¢ per page, $3.00 for certification

District Court
Robert F. Sweeney Building
251 Rowe Boulevrd
Annapolis, MD 21401
(410) 260-1370; (800) 944-2688
http://www.courts.state.md.us/district/directori es/courtmap.html
Rebecca A. Hoppa, Administrative Clerk

Register of Wills
(Circuit Court House, 7 Church Circle—location)
PO Box 2368 (mailing address)
Annapolis, MD 21404
(410) 222-1430; (800) 679-6665
http://www.registers.state.md.us/county/aa/ht ml/annearundel.html
George M. Nutwell, Jr.

Baltimore County
organized 1659, original county (Baltimore City made independent of the county in 1851)

Baltimore County Circuit Court
County Courts Building, 401 Bosley Avenue
Towson, MD 21204
(410) 887-2601 (Clerk); (800) 938-5802
circuitcourt@co.ba.md.us
http://www.co.ba.md.us/Agencies/circuit/inde x.html; http://www.courts.state.md.us/ baltcty.html
Suzanne Mensh, Clerk
(land records)

Baltimore County Department of Health
Drumcastle Government Center
6401 York Road, Third Floor
Baltimore, MD 21212-2130
(410) 887-3740; (410) 377-4751 FAX
pvigilance@co.ba.md.us
http://www.baltimorecountymd.gov/agencies/ health/index.html
(does not maintain birth or death records)

District Court
120 East Chesapeake Avenue
Towson, MD 21286-5307
(410) 512-2000; (800) 944-1826
http://www.courts.state.md.us/district/directori es/courtmap.html
Michael P. Vach, Administrative Clerk

Register of Wills
County Courts Building
401 Bosley Avenue, Room 500
Towson, MD 21204
(410) 887-6680; (410) 887-6681; (888) 642-5387 (within Maryland); (410) 583-2517 FAX
gconnolly@co.ba.md.us
http://www.registers.state.md.us/county/ba/ht ml/flash.html
Hon. Grace G. Connolly, Register

Baltimore City Circuit Court
Clarence M. Mitchell, Jr. Courthouse
100 North Calvert Street
Baltimore, MD 21202-3417
(410) 333-3750 (Criminal Division, Room 200); (410) 333-3722 (Civil Division, Room 462, Courthouse East); (410) 333-3738 (Paternity Division, Room 109, Courthouse East); (410) 333-3760 (Land Records Division, Room 610)
http://www.baltocts.state.md.us/clerks.htm; http://www.courts.state.md.us/baltcity.html
Frank M. Conaway, Clerk
(land records)

District Court
Bogerding District Court Building
5800 Wabash Avenue
Baltimore, MD 21215-3330
(40) 878-8000; (800) 939-4523
http://www.courts.state.md.us/district/directori es/courtmap.html
Lonnie P. Ferguson, Jr., Administrative Clerk

District Court, Civil Division
Fayette and Gay Streets
Baltimore, MD 21202
(410) 878-8900; (800) 939-4523
http://www.courts.state.md.us/district/directori es/courtmap.html

Register of Wills
111 North Calvert Street
Baltimore, MD 21202
(410) 752-5131; (888) 876-0035 (Maryland only)
http://www.registers.state.md.us/county/bc/ht ml/baltimorecity.html
Hon. Mary W. Conaway

Calvert County
organized 1650, original county

Calvert County Circuit Court
175 Main Street
Prince Frederick, MD 20678
(410) 535-1660 (Clerk); (410) 535-1600, ext. 2267 (Land Records); (888) 535-0113
kathy.smith@mdcourts.gov; kathy.smith@courts.state.md.us
http://www.courts.state.md.us/clerks/calvert/i ndex.html
Kathy P. Smith, Clerk
(land records from 1882)

District Court
Multi-Service Center
200 Duke Street
Prince Frederick, MD 20678-4136
(443-550-6700); (800) 941-3375
http://www.courts.state.md.us/district/directori es/courtmap.html
Richard A. Parker, Administrative Clerk

Register of Wills
Courthouse, 175 Main Street
Prince Frederick, MD 20678
(410) 535-0121; (888) 374-0015
http://www.registers.state.md.us/county/cv/ht ml/calvert.html
Margaret H. Phipps
(probate records from 1882)
no probate search service; copies of probate records: 50¢ each, no minimum

Caroline County
organized 1773 from Dorchester and Queen Anne's counties

Caroline County Circuit Court
(109 Market Stree, Room 104t–location)

PO Box 458 (mailing address)
Denton, MD 21629-458
(410) 479-1811 (Clerk); (410) 479-1142 FAX (Clerk)
dale.minner@courts.state.md.us
http://www.courts.state.md.us/caroline.html
F. Dale Minner, Clerk
(land records from 1773, naturalization records from 1773 to 1945, marriages from 1773)
no land search service; no naturalization search service (most records transferred to The Hall of Records in Annapolis; certified copies of land records, naturualization records, and vital records: $5.00 each

District Court
Multi-Service Center
207 South Third Street
Denton, MD 21629-1229
(410) 819-4600; (800) 940-4968
grace.achuff@courts.state.md.us
http://www.courts.state.md.us/district/directori es/courtmap.html
Grace D. Achuff, Administrative Clerk

Register of Wills
(Courthouse, 109 Market Street, Room 108— location)
PO Box 416 (mailing address)
Denton, MD 21629-0416
(410) 479-0717; (888) 786-0019
cdavisregister@dmv.com
http://www.registers.state.md.us/county/ca/ht ml/caroline.html
Charles O. Davis, Jr.
(wills from 1688, estate proceedings from 1852)
probate search service: no charge; copies of probate records: 50¢ per page, no minimum

Carroll County
organized 1836 from Baltimore and Frederick counties

Carroll County Circuit Court
55 North Court Street
Westminster, MD 21157
(410) 386-2026 (Clerk); (410) 386-2022 (Land Record Department); (888) 786-0039; (410) 876-0822 FAX
larry.shipley@courts.state.md.us
http://www.courts.state.md.us/carroll.html
Larry W. Shipley, Clerk
(land records)
no probate search service; copies of probate records: 50¢ each, no minimum

District Court
101 North Courth Street
Westminster, MD 21157
(410) 871-3500; (800) 943-9396
http://www.courts.state.md.us/district/directori ·es/courtmap.html
Nancy E. Mueller, Administrative Clerk

Register of Wills
55 North Court Streeet, Room 124
Westminster, MD 21157
(410) 848-2586; (888) 876-0034
http://www.registers.state.md.us/county/cr/ht ml/carroll.html
Paul G. Zimmermann

Cecil County
organized 1674 from Kent County

Cecil County Commissioners
Room 101, County Office Building
Elkton, MD 21921
(410) 996-5373 (General Information); (888) 287-0576; (410) 398-2097 TTY
http://www.courts.state.md.us/cecil.html

Clerk of Circuit Court
Room 108, County Office Building
Elkton, MD 21921
(410) 996-5370; (410) 392-6032 FAX
william.brueckman@courts.state.md.us
http://www.courts.state.md.us/clerks/cecil/ind ex.html
William C. Brueckman, Clerk
(land records)

District Court
170 East Main Street
Elkton, MD 21921-5943
(410) 996-2700; (800) 941-0408
grace.achuff@courts.state.md.us
http://www.courts.state.md.us/district/directori
es/courtmap.html
Grace D. Achuff, Administrative Clerk

Register of Wills
County Court House
(129 East Main Street, Suite 101—location)
PO Box 468 (mailing address)
Elkton, MD 21922-0468
(410) 996-5530; (888) 398-0301
lnickle@ccgov.org
http://www.registers.state.md.us/county/ce/ht
ml/cecil.html
Ms. Allyn Price Nickle
(probate records from 1674)
no probate search service; copies of probate
records: 25¢ per page (closed estates), 50¢ per
page (open estates), no minimum

Charles County
organized 1658, original county

Charles County Circuit Court
(200 Charles Street—location)
PO Box 970 (mailing address)
La Plata, MD 20646
(301) 932-3201; (301) 870-2659; (888) 932-2072
http://www.courts.state.md.us/clerks/charles/i
ndex.html
Sharon "Sherri" L. Hancock, Clerk
(land records on microfilm from 1655, marriages
from 1886)

Charles County Register of Wills
(200 East Charles Street—location)
PO Box 3080, Courthouse
La Plata, MD 20646-3080
(301) 932-3345; (888) 256-0054
http://www.registers.state.md.us/county/ch/ht
ml/charles.html
Susie C. Bowles
(probate records)
no probate search service ("we must have
reference number"); copies of probate
records: 50¢ per page, $1.00 minimum

District Court
(200 Charles Street—location)
PO Box 3070 (mailing address)
La Plata, MD 20646-3070
(301) 932-3300; (301) 932-3295 (Criminal); (301)
932-3290 (Civil); (800) 941-3463
http://www.courts.state.md.us/district/directori
es/courtmap.html
Richard A. Parker, Administrative Clerk

Dorchester County
organized 1668, original county

County Office Building
(501 Court Lane—location)
PO Box 26 (mailing address)
Cambridge MD 21613
(410) 228-1700; (410) 228-9641 FAX
info@docogonet.com
http://www.docogonet.com/index.html

District Court
(310 Gay Street—location)
PO Box 547 (mailing address)
Cambridge, MD 21613-1813
(410) 901-1420; (800) 939-2872
mary.kinnamon@courts.state.md.us
http://www.courts.state.md.us/district/directori
es/courtmap.html
Mary E. Kinnamon, Administrative Clerk

Dorchester County Circuit Court
(206 High Street—location)
PO Box 150 (mailing adress)
Cambridge, MD 21613
(410) 228-0481; (800) 340-9186
http://www.courts.state.md.us/dorchester.html
Michael L. Baker, Clerk
(land records)

Register of Wills
Courthouse, 206 High Street
Cambridge, MD 21613
(410) 228-4181; (888) 242-6257
http://www.registers.state.md.us/county/do/ht
ml/dorchester.html
Doris K. Lewis, Register

Frederick County
organized 1748 from Prince George's County

District Court
100 West Patrick Street
Frederick, MD 21701
(301) 694-2000; (800) 945-2119
http://www.courts.state.md.us/district/directori
es/courtmap.html
Dixie L. Scholtes, Administrative Clerk

Frederick County Circuit Court
100 West Patrick Street
Frederick, MD 21701
(301) 694-1976 (Clerk); (301) 694-1961 (Land
Record Department); (800) 341-8797
http://www.courts.state.md.us/frederick.html
Sandra K. Dalton, Clerk
(land records from 1748 , naturalization records
from 1801 to 1906, marriages from 1778,
index of names for whom licenses were
issued from 1778 to 1865)
copies of land records: 50¢ per page; certified
copies of marriages: $5.00 each

Frederick County Register of Wills
100 West Patrick Street
Frederick, MD 21701
(301) 663-3722; (888) 258-0526
http://www.registers.state.md.us/county/fr/ht
ml/frederick.html
Virginia P. Fifer, Register
(wills from 1744 and administration accounts
from 1750)

Garrett County
organized 1872 from Allegany County

District Court
205 South Third Street
Oakland, MD 21550-1526
(301) 334-8020; (800) 947-1029
http://www.courts.state.md.us/district/directori
es/courtmap.html
Kathleen M. Stafford, Administrative Clerk

Garrett County Circuit Court
(203 South Fourth Street, Room 109—location)
PO Box 447 (mailing address)
Oakland, MD 21550-1535
(301) 334-1937 (Clerk); (301) 334-1938 (Land
Record Department); (800) 989-9760; (301)
334-5027 TTY
david.martin@courts.state.md.us
http://www.co.garrett.md.us;
http://www.courts.state.md.us/garrett.html
David K. Martin, Clerk
(land records, naturalization records from 1872
to 1930)

Garrett County Register of Wills
Old Courthouse
313 East Adler Street, Room 103
Oakland, MD 21550
(301) 334-1999; (888) 334-2203
http://www.registers.state.md.us/county/ga/ht
ml/garrett.html
Joseph F. DiSimone
no probate search service; copies of probate
records: 50¢ each, no minimum

Harford County
organized 1773 from Baltimore County

District Court
2 South Bond Street
Bel Air, MD 21014-3737
(410) 836-4545; (800) 943-6344
http://www.courts.state.md.us/district/directori
es/courtmap.html
Arthur G. Ford, III, Administrative Clerk

Harford County Circuit Court
20 West Courtland Street
Bel Air, MD 21014-3833
(410) 638-3426; (410) 879-2000; (800) 989-8296
james.reilly@courts.state.md.us
http://www.courts.state.md.us/harford.html;
http://www.harfordcountymd.gov
James Reilly, Clerk
(land records from 1779)

Harford County Register of Wills
Courthouse, Room 304
20 West Courtland Street
Bel Air, MD 21014
(410) 638-3275; (888) 258-0525
http://www.registers.state.md.us/county/ha/ht
ml/harford.html
Harry L. W. Hopkins, Jr.
probate search service: no charge ("but due to
our small staff, we do not have the time to
search for records, only possibly during
summer months if we have summer help");
copies of probate records: 50¢ per page, no
minimum

Howard County
organized 1851 from Baltimore County

District Court
3451 Courthouse Drive
Ellicott City, MD 21043-4377
(410) 480-7700; (800) 944-8107
http://www.courts.state.md.us/district/directori
es/courtmap.html
Nancy E. Mueller, Administrative Clerk

Howard County Circuit Court
8360 Court Avenue
Ellicott City, MD 21043
(410) 313-2111 (Clerk)
http://www.courts.state.md.us/howard.html;
http://www.co.ho.md.us
Margaret D. Rappaport, Clerk
(land records)

Howard County Register of Wills
Courthouse, 8360 Court Avenue
Ellicott City, MD 21043
(410) 313-2133; (888) 848-0136
http://www.registers.state.md.us/county/ho/ht
ml/howard.html
Kay K. Hartleb

Kent County
organized 1642, original county

District Court
103 North Cross Street
Chestertown, MD 21620-1511
(410) 810-3360; (800) 941-3347
grace.achuff@courts.state.md.us
http://www.courts.state.md.us/district/directori
es/courtmap.html
Grace D. Achuff, Administrative Clerk

Kent County Circuit Court
103 North Cross Street
Chestertown, MD 21620
(410) 778-7460 (Clerk); (800) 989-2520
kentcc@counrts.state.md.us
http://www.courts.state.md.us/clerks/kent/ind
ex.html
Mark L. Mumford, Clerk
(land records from 1656)

Kent County Register of Wills
Courthouse, 103 North Cross Street
Chestertown, MD 21620
(410) 778-7466; (888) 778-0179
http://www.registers.state.md.us/county/mo/h
tml/kent.html
Nancy Lee Jewell
(probate records from 1669)
probate search service: no charge at present;
copies of probate records: 50¢ per page, no
minimum, $5.00 per certified copy ("wills
from 1669 to 1798 are on microfilm here and
cannot be copied; to obtain copies for that
period, write to Maryland State Archives")

Montgomery County
organized 1776 from Frederick County

District Court
27 Courth House Square
Rockville, MD 20850-2325
(301) 279-1500; (800) 944-1341
http://www.courts.state.md.us/district/directori
es/courtmap.html
Jeffrey L. Ward, Administrative Clerk

Montgomery County Circuit Court
The Montgomery County Judicial Center
50 Maryland Avenue, Room 122a
Rockville, MD 20850
(240) 777-9400; (240) 777-9466; (Clerk); (888)
287-0593
molly.ruhl@courts.state.md.us
http://www.montgomerycountymd.gov/mc/ju
dicial/circuit/mcccourt.html
Molly Q. Ruhl, Clerk
(land records)

Montgomery County Register of Wills
Judicial Center, Room 322
50 Maryland Avenue
Rockville, MD 20850
(240) 777-9600
http://www.registers.state.md.us/county/mo/h
tml/montgomery.html
Joseph M. Griffin

Prince George's County
organized 1695 from Calvert and Charles
   counties

District Court
14735 Main Street, Suite 173B
Upper Marlboro, MD 20772
(301) 952-4080; (800) 943-3853
mary.j.abrams@courts.state.md.us
http://www.courts.state.md.us/district/directori
es/courtmap.html
Mary Abrams, Administrative Clerk

Prince George's County Circuit Court
Marbury Wing, 14735 Main Street, Room
   #M1401
Upper Marlboro, MD 20772
(301) 952-3318 (Clerk); (301) 952-3352 (Land);
   (301) 952-3318 (Naturalization)
clhorty@co.pg.md.us; dacooke@co.pg.me.us
   (Land Records Division);
ckspiety@co.pg.md.us (Civil Division);
cjoneil@co.pg.md.us (Criminal Division)
http://www.goprincegeorgescounty.com/Gover
nment/JudicialBranch/clerk.asp?nivel=foldm
enu(2)
Rosalyn E. Pugh, Clerk of Circuit Court; Cheryl
   L. Horty, Chief Deputy Clerk
(land records, naturalization records)

Prince George's County Register of Wills
5303 Chrysler Way, Suite 300
Upper Marlboro, MD 20772
(301) 952-3250; (888) 464-4219 (Maryland only);
   (301) 952-4489 FAX
http://www.co.pg.md.us/Government/Judicial
   Branch/wills.asp
Lynn Loughlin Skerpon
no probate search service; copies of probate
   records: 50¢ per page, no minimum

Queen Anne's County
organized 1706 from Talbot County

District Court
120 Broadway
Centreville, MD 21617-1092
(410) 819-4000; (800) 941-3403
grace.achuff@courts.state.md.us
http://www.courts.state.md.us/district/directori
es/courtmap.html
Grace D. Achuff, Administrative Clerk

Queen Anne's County Register of Wills
(Liberty Building, 107 North Liberty Street,
   Suite 220—location)
PO Box 59 (mailing address)
Centreville, MD 21617

(410) 758-0585; (888) 758-0010
wacannon@friend.ly.net
http://www.registers.state.md.us/county/qa/ht
ml/queenannes.html
Winsie A. Cannon

St. Mary's County
organized 1637, original county

District Court
Joseph D. Carter State Office Building
23110 Leonard Hall Drive
Leonardtown, MD 20650
(410) 535-8876; (800) 943-0091
richard.parker@courts.state.md.us
http://www.courts.state.md.us/district/directori
es/courtmap.html
Richard A. Parker, Administrative Clerk

St. Mary's County Circuit Court
(41605 Courthouse Drive—location)
PO Box 676 (mailing address)
Leonardtown, MD 20650-0676
(301) 475-4567;(301) 475-4561 (Vital Records);
   (301) 475-4568 FAX
evelyn.arnold@courts.state.md.us
http://www.courts.state.md.us/stmarys.html
Evelyn W. Arnold, Clerk
(land records from 1827; marriages from 1794)

St. Mary's County Register of Wills
(41605 Court House Drive—location)
PO Box 602 (mailing address)
Leonardtown, MD 20650-0602
(301) 475-5566; (888) 475-4821; (301) 475-4968
   FAX
http://www.registers.state.md.us/county/sm/ht
ml/stmaarys.html
Dianne B. McWilliams
probate search service: no charge; copies of
   probate records: 50¢ per page

Somerset County
organized 1666, original county

District Court
12155 Elm Street, Suite C
Princess Anne, MD 21853-1358
(410) 845-4700; (800) 939-7306; (410) 845-4701
   FAX
mary.kinnamon@courts.state.md.us
http://www.courts.state.md.us/district/directori
es/courtmap.html
Mary E. Kinnamon, Administrative Clerk

Somerset County Circuit Court
(30512 Prince William Street—location)
PO Box 279 (mailing address)
Princess Anne, MD 21853-0279
(410) 651-1555
ted.phoebus@courts.state.md.us
http://www.courts.state.md.us/somerset.html
I. Theodore Phoebus, Clerk
(land records from 1665, marriages from 1797)
no records search service; copies of records: 50¢
   per page

Somerset County Register of Wills
Courthouse, 30512 Prince William Street
Princess Anne, MD 21853
(410) 651-1696; (888) 758-0039
http://www.registers.state.md.us/county/so/ht
ml/somerset.html
Gary W. Miller

Talbot County
organized 1662 from Kent County

District Court
108 West Dover Street
Easton, MD 21601-2620
(410) 819-5850; (800) 941-2195; (410) 819-5853
   FAX
grace.achuff@courts.state.md.us
http://www.courts.state.md.us/district/directori
es/courtmap.html
Grace D. Achuff, Administrative Clerk

Talbot County Circuit Court
(Courthouse, 11 North Washington Street—
   location)

PO Box 723 (mailing address)
Easton, MD 21601
(410) 822-2611; (410) 820-8168 FAX
http://www.courts.state.md.us/clerks/talbot/in
dex.html; http://talbotcountymd.gov
Mary Ann Shortall, Clerk
(land records)

Talbot County Register of Wills
Courthouse, 11 North Washington Street
Easton, MD 21601-0816
(410) 770-6700; (888) 822-0039
http://www.registers.state.md.us/county/ta/ht
ml/talbot.html
Alice W. Anderson
no probate search service ("do not provide
   index search other than reference number");
   copies of probate records: 50¢ each, no
   minimum

Washington County
organized 1776 from Frederick County

District Court
36 West Antietam Street
Hagerstown, MD 21740
(240) 420-4600; (240) 420-4664; (800) 945-1406
http://www.courts.state.md.us/district/directori
es/courtmap.html
Dixie L. Scholtes, Administrative Clerk

Washington County Circuit Court
Courthouse, 95 West Washington Street
Hagerstown, MD 21740-4831
(301) 79-3085
dennis.weaver@courts.state.md.us
http://www.courts.state.md.us/clerks/washingt
on/index.html
Dennis J. Weaver, Clerk
(land records from 1776, naturalization records
   from 1787 to 1979, index of marriages only
   from 1799 to 1886)

Washington County Register of Wills
Courthouse, 95 West Washington Street
Hagerstown, MD 21740
(301) 739-3612; (888) 739-0013
http://www.registers.state.md.us/county/wa/ht
ml/washington.html
John R. Bloyer II

Wicomico County
organized 1867 from Somerset and Worcester
   counties

District Court
201 Baptist Street
Salisbury, MD 21801
(410) 713-3500; (800) 940-3267
mary.kinnamon@courts.state.md.us
http://www.courts.state.md.us/district/directori
es/courtmap.html
Mary E. Kinnamon, Administrative Clerk

Wicomico County Circuit Court
(Courthouse, 101 North Division Street—
   location)
PO Box 198 (mailing address)
Salisbury, MD 21803-0198
(410) 543-6551, ext. 159 (Bowen); (410) 543-
   6551, ext. 171 (Justice); (800) 989-6592
robin.justice@courts.state.md.us
http://www.courts.state.md.us/wicomico.html
Mark S. Bowen, Clerk; Robin L. Justice, Lead
   Court Clerk
(land records from 1867, naturalization records
   from 1879 to 1975, marriage licenses only)

Wicomico County Register of Wills
101 North Division Street, Room 102
Salisbury, MD 21803-0787
(410) 543-6635; (888) 786-0018
http://www.registers.state.md.us/county/wi/ht
ml/wicomico.html
Karen A. Lemon

Worcester County
organized 1742 from Somerset County

District Court
301 Commerce Street

Snow Hill, MD 21863
(410) 219-7830; (800) 941-0282
mary.kinnamon@courts.state.md.us
http://www.courts.state.md.us/district/directori
es/courtmap.html
Mary E. Kinnamon, Administrative Clerk

Worcester County Circuit Court
Courthouse, 1 West Market Street, Room 104
Snow Hill, MD 21863
(410) 632-5500; (800) 340-0691
stephen.hales@courts.state.md.us
http://www.courts.state.md.us/worcester.html
Stephen V. Hales, Clerk
(land records, marriages)

Worcester County Register of Wills
1 West Market Street, Room 102
Snow Hill, MD 21863-1074
(410) 632-1529; (888) 256-0047
register@ezy.net
http://www.registers.state.md.us/county/wo/ht
ml/worcester.html
Charlotte K. Cathell

MASSACHUSETTS

Capital: Boston. Statehood: 6 February 1788 (settled 1620, became a charter colony in 1629)

The Trial Court of Massachusetts was organized in 1978 and consists of seven departments: Superior Court Department, District Court Department, Boston Municipal Court Department, Probate and Family Court Department, Land Court Department, Juvenile Court Department and Housing Court Department. The Superior Court Department sits in each county and has original jurisdiction over all criminal and civil matters except those under the original exclusive jurisdiction of other courts.

The District Court Department has general jurisdiction and is divided into five regions, consisting of thirteen or more divisions. Region One: parts of Barnstable, Bristol, Dukes, Nantucket, Norfolk and Plymouth counties; Region Two: parts of Essex, Norfolk and Suffolk counties; Region Three: parts of Essex and Middlesex counties; Region Four: parts of Middlesex, Norfolk and Worcester counties; Region Five: parts of Berkshire, Franklin, Hampden, Hampshire and Worcester counties.

The Probate and Family Court Department has a division in each county. The Land Court Department has jurisdiction throughout the state and sits primarily at Boston. The Massachusetts Appeals Court and the Massachusetts Supreme Judicial Court hear appeals.

Deeds, naturalizations and probates are kept on the county level, but vital statistics and property tax records are kept in each municipality.

Land Court
226 Causeway Street
Boston, MA 02114
(617) 788-7470; (617) 788-8951 FAX
http://www.mass.gov/courts/courtsandjudges/
courts/landcourt/index.html; http://www.
massgov/courts/courtsandjudges/courts/lcm
ain.html
Deborah J. Patterson, Recorder

Supreme Judicial Court
Division of Archives and Records Preservation
(Judicial Archives, Archives of the
Commonwealth, 220 Morrissey Boulevard,
Boston, MA 02125—location)
1300 New Court House (mailing address)
Boston, MA 02108
(617) 727-2816 (Judicial Archives); (617) 557-
1082 (Archivist); (617) 557-1088 FAX
http://www.mass.gov/courts/sjc/supreme-
judicial-court.html
Elizabeth C. Bouvier, Head of Archives
(locating and preserving inactive, historically
important judicial records)

Barnstable County
organized 1685 from Old Plymouth Colony

Barnstable County Register of Deeds
(3195 Main Street)
PO Box 368 (mailing address)
Barnstable, MA 02630
(508) 362-7733; (508) 362-5065 FAX
http://bcrd.co.barnstable.ma.us
John F. Meade

Barnstable County Register of Deeds
(Registry of Deeds Building, Railroad Avenue—
location)
PO Box 427 (mailing address)
Barnstable, MA 02630
(508) 362-7733
http://www.barnstablecounty.org/departments.
htm
John F. Meade
(land records)

Barnstable County Superior Court
(Superior Court House, 3195 Main Street,
Barnstable, MA 02630-1105—location)
PO Box 425 (mailing address)
Barnstable, MA 02630
(508) 375-6684
http://www.barnstablecounty.org
Scott Nickerson, Clerk of Courts
(card file with names of individuals who have
been naturalized [no original records])

Falmouth District Court
161 Jones Road
Falmouth, MA 02540
(508) 495-1500; (508) 495-0992 FAX
http://www.mass.gov/courts/courtsandjudges/
courts/famouthdistrictmain.html
Kenneth Halloran, Clerk
(jurisdiction over Bourne, Falmouth, and
Mashpee)

Orleans District Court
237 Rock Harbor Road
Orleans, MA 02653
(508) 255-4700; (508) 240-5024 FAX
http://www.mass.gov/courts/courtsandjudges/
courts/orleansdistrictmain.html
Stephen I. Ross, Clerk
(jurisdiction over Brewster, Chatham, Dennis,
Eastham, Orleans, Provincetown, Harwich,
Truro, and Wellfleet)

Probate and Family Court Department
(Main Street—location)
PO Box 346 (mailing address)
Barnstable, MA 02630-0346
(508) 362-2511, ext. 594
http://www.barnstablecounty.org
Frederic P. Clauseen, Register of Probate
(probate records from 1686)
attested copies: $1.50 per page, no minimum

Barnstable District Court
PO Box 427
Barnstable, MA 02630
(508) 375-6778 (Criminal Division); (508) 375-
6786 (Civil Department)
http://www.mass.gov/courts/courtsandjudges/
courts/barnstabledistrictmain.html
(jusrisdiction over Barnstable, Sandwich, and
Yarmouth)

Berkshire County
organized 1760 from Hampshire County

Berkshire Middle District Register of Deeds
44 Bank Row
Pittsfield, MA 01201
(413) 443-7438; (413) 448-6025 FAX
Mary.K.Obrien@sec.state.ma.us
http://www.berkshire.net/~mobdeeds
Mary K. O'Brien
(land records; jurisdiction over Becket, Dalton,
Hinsdale, Lee, Lenox, Otis, Peru, Pittsfield,
Richmond, Stockbridge, Tyringham, and
Washington)

**Berkshire Northern District Register of
Deeds**
65 Park Street
Adams, MA 01220
(413) 743-0035; (413) 743-1003 FAX
nbrd@sec.state.ma.us
http://www.berkshirenorthdeeds.com
Frances T. Brooks
(land records; jurisdiction over Adams, Cheshire,
Clarksburg, Florida, Hancock, Lanesboro,
New Ashford, North Adams, Savoy,
Williamstown, and Windsor)

Berkshire Probate and Family Court
44 Bank Row
Pittsfield, MA 01201
(413) 442-6941; (413) 443-3430 FAX
http://www.mass.gov/courts/courtsandjudges/
courts/berkprobmain.html
Francis B. Marinaro, Register
(probate records from 1760 [divorces from
1924, changes of name, and adoptions])
probate search service ("depends on
involvement"); copies of probate records: 50¢

per page, no minimum

Berkshire Southern District Register of Deeds
334 Main Street
Great Barrington, MA 01230
(413) 528-0146; (413) 528-6878 FAX
SBRD@sec.state.ma.us
http://www.berkshiresouthdeeds.com
Irene M. Skorput, Register of Deeds and
Assistant Recorder for Land Court
(land records; jurisdiction over Alford,
Egremont, Great Barrington, Monterey, Mt.
Washington, New Marlborough, Sandisfield,
Sheffield, and West Stockbridge)

Berkshire Superior Court
76 East Street
Pittsfield, MA 01201-5304
(413) 499-7487; (413) 442-9190 FAX
http://www.mass.gov/courts/courtsandjudges/
courts/berksupmain.html
Deborah S. Capeless, Clerk
(naturalization records)

Central Berkshire District Court
(Pittsfield District Court, 24 Wendell Avenue—
location)
PO Box 875 (mailing address)
Pittsfield, MA 01202-0875
(413) 442-5468; (413) 499-7327 FAX
http://www.mass.gov/courts/courtsandjudges/
courts/pittsfielddistrictmain.html
Leo F. Evans, Clerk
(jurisdiction over Becket, Dalton, Hancock,
Hinsdale, Lanesborough, Lenox, Peru,
Pittsfield, Richmond, Washington, and
Windsor [Northern Berkshire District Court
exercising concurrent jurisdiction over
Hancock and Windsor; Southern Berkshire
Division exercising concurrent jurisdiction
over Becket and Lenox])

Northern Berkshire District Court
111 Holden Street
North Adams, MA 01247
(413) 663-5339; (413) 664-7209 FAX
morey_5@jud.state.ma.us
http://www.mass.gov/courts/courtsandjudges/
courts/northadamsdistrictmain.html
Timothy J. Morey, Clerk
(jurisdiction over Adams, Cheshire, Clarksburg,
Florida, Hancock, New Ashford, North
Adams, Savoy, Williamstown, and Windsor
[Pittsfield Division exercising concurrent
jurisdiction over Hancock and Windsor])

Southern Berkshire District Court
9 Gilmore Avenue
Great Barrington, MA 01230
(413) 528-3520; (413) 528-0757 FAX
http://www.mass.gov/courts/courtsandjudges/
courts/southberkshiredistrictmain.html
Thomas F. Bartini, Acting Clerk
(jurisdiction over Alford, Becket, Egremont,
Great Barrington, Lee, Lenox, Monterey, Mt.
Washington, New Marlborough, Otis,
Sandisfield, Sheffield, Stockbridge,
Tyringham, and West Stockbridge [Pittsfield
Division exercising concurrent jurisdiction
over Becket and Lenox])

Bristol County
organized 1685 from Old Plymouth Colony

Attleboro District Court
88 North Main Street
Attleboro, MA 02703
(508) 222-5900
http://www.mass.gov/courts/courtsandjudges/
courts/attleborodistrictmain.html
(jurisdiction over Attleboro, Mansfield, North
Attleboro, and Norton)

Bristol County Register of Deeds (Fall River District)
441 North Main Street
Fall River, MA 02720
(508) 673-2910; (508) 673-1651; (508) 673-7633
FAX
frdeeds@verizon.net

http://fallriverdeeds.com/malr_ecom/MalrApp
/index.jsp
Bernard J. McDonald, III
(land records; jurisdiction over Fall River,
Freetown, Somerset, and Swansea)

Bristol County Register of Deeds (Northern District)
11 Court Street
Taunton, MA 02780
(508) 822-0502; (508) 880-4975 FAX
dmsimas@tauntondeeds.com
http://www.tauntondeeds.com
David M. Simas
(land records; jurisdiction over Attleboro,
Berkley, Dighton, Easton, Mansfield, North
Attleboro, Norton, Raynham, Rehoboth,
Seekonk, and Taunton)

Bristol County Register of Deeds (Southern District)
25 North Sixth Street
New Bedford, MA 02740
(508) 993-2603; (508) 997-4250 FAX
nbregistry@gis.net
http://newbedforddeeds.com/mason/main
J. Mark Treadup
(land records; jurisdiction over Acushnet,
Dartmouth, Fairhaven, New Bedford, and
Westport; also a research library for recorded
land transactions, some back to 1687)

Bristol Probate and Family Court
(11 Court Street—location)
PO Box 567 (mailing address)
Taunton, MA 02780
(508) 824-4004; (508) 822-9837 FAX
http://www.mass.gov/courts/courtsandjudges/
courts/bristolprobro.html
Robert E. Peck, Register
(probate records)

Bristol Superior Court
9 Court Street, Room 13
Taunton, MA 02780
(508) 823-6588
http://www.mass.gov/courts/courtsandjudges/
courts/bristolsupmain.html
Marc Santos, Clerk of Courts

Fall River District Court
45 Rock Street
Fall River, MA 02720
(508) 679-8161; (508) 675-5477 FAX
http://www.mass.gov/courts/courtsandjudges/
courts/fallriverdistrictmain.html
Ronald A. Valcourt, Clerk
(jurisdiction over Fall River, Freetown,
Somerset, Swansea, and Westport)

New Bedford District Court
75 North Sixth Street
New Bedford, MA 02740
(508) 999-9700
http://www.mass.gov/courts/courtsandjudges/
courts/newbedforddistrictmain.html
James B. Sheerin, First Assistant Clerk
(jurisdiction over Acushnet, Dartmouth,
Fairhave, Freetown, New Bedford, and
Westport)

Taunton District Court
120 Cohannet Street
Taunton, MA 02780
(508) 977-6105; (508) 824-2282 FAX
http://www.mass.gov/courts/courtsandjudges/
courts/tauntondistrictmain.html
Raymond S. Peck, Clerk
(jurisdiction over Berkley, Dighton, Easton,
Raynham, Rehoboth, Seekonk, and Taunton)

Dukes County
organized 1695 from Martha's Vineyard

Dukes County Register of Deeds
(81 Main Street—location)
PO Box 5231 (mailing address)
Edgartown, MA 02539
(508) 627-4025; (508) 627-7821 FAX
dpowers@dukescounty.org
http://www.dukescounty.org/Pages/DukesCou

ntyMA_Deeds/index
Dianne E. Powers
(land records)

Dukes Probate and Family Court
(81 Main Street—location)
PO Box 237 (mailing address)
Edgartown, MA 02539
(508) 627-4703; (508) 627-7664 FAX
http://www.mass.gov/courts/courtsandjudges/
courts/dukesprobmain.html
Elizabeth J. Herrmann, Register
(probate records from 1696)
probate search service: no charge; copies of
probate records: 50¢ per page, $1.50 if
attested, no minimum

Dukes Superior Court
(Courthouse, Main Street—location)
PO Box 1267 (mailing address)
Edgartown, MA 02539
(508) 627-4668; (508) 627-7571 FAX
http://www.mass.gov/courts/courtsandjudges/
courts/dukessupmain.html
Joseph E. Sollitto, Jr., Clerk
(naturalization records)

Edgartown District Court
(81 Main Street—location)
PO Box 1284 (mailing address)
Edgartown, MA 02539
(508) 627-4622; (508) 627-7070 FAX
info@dukescounty.org
http://www.mass.gov/courts/courtsandjudges/
courts/edgartowndistrictmain.html;
http://www.dukescounty.org/Pages/DukesC
ountyMA_WebDocmnts/contactus
Liza D. Williamson
(jurisdiction over all of Dukes County)

Essex County
organized 1643, original county

Essex County Register of Deeds (Northern District)
354 Merrimack Street, Suite #304 (Entry C)
Lawrence, MA 01843
(978) 683-2745; (978) 681-5409 FAX
Thomas.Burke@sec.state.ma.us
http://www.lawrencedeeds.com
Thomas J. Burke
(land records; jurisdiction over Andover,
Lawrence, Methuen, and North Andover)

Essex County Register of Deeds (Southern District)
36 Federal Street
Salem, MA 01970
(978) 741-0201, ext. 250; (978) 744-7679 FAX
jlodeeds1@salemdeeds.com
http://www.salemdeeds.com
John L. O'Brien
(land records; jurisdiction over Amesbury,
Beverly, Boxford, Danvers, Essex,
Georgetown, Gloucester, Groveland,
Hamilton, Haverhill, Ipswich, Lynn,
Lynnfield, Manchester, Marblehead,
Merrimac, Middleton, Nahant, Newbury,
Newburyport, Peabody, Rockport, Rowley,
Salem, Salisbury, Saugus, Swampscott,
Topsfield, Wenham, and West Newbury)

Essex Probate and Family Court Department
36 Federal Street
Salem, MA 01970
(978) 744-1020, ext. 321; (978) 741-2957 FAX
http://www.mass.gov/courts/courtsandjudges/
courts/essexprobmain.html
Pamela A. Casey O'Brien, Register of Probate
(probate records)
certified copies: $1.50 per page

Essex Superior Court
34 Federal Street
Salem, MA 01970
(978) 744-5500; (978) 741-0691 FAX
http://www.mass.gov/courts/courtsandjudges/
courts/essexsupmain.html
Thomas H. Driscoll, Jr.

Gloucester District Court
197 Main Street
Gloucester, MA 01915
(978) 283-2620; (978) 283-8784 FAX
http://www.mass.gov/courts/courtsandjudges/
    courts/gloucesterdistrictmain.html
Kevin P. Burke, Clerk
(jurisdiction over Essex, Gloucester, and
    Rockport)

Haverhill District Court
(J. P. Ginty Boulevard—location)
PO Box 1389 (mailing address)
Haverhill, MA 01831
(978) 373-4151, ext. 120; (978) 521-6886 FAX
http://www.mass.gov/courts/courtsandjudges/
    courts/haverhilldistrictmain.html
Brian Lawlor, Acting Clerk
(jurisdisction over Boxford, Bradford,
    Georgetown, Groveland, and Haverhill)

Ipswich District Court
Newburyport District Courthouse
188 State Road
Route 1 Traffic Circle
Newburyport, MA 01950-6637
(978) 462-2652
http://www.mass.gov/courts/courtsandjudges/
    courts/ipswichdistrictmain.html
Kathryn M. Early, Clerk

Lawrence District Court
Fenton Judicial Center
2 Appleton Street
Lawrence, MA 01840-1525
(978) 687-7184, ext. 2353; (978) 975-3171 FAX
http://www.mass.gov/courts/courtsandjudges/
    courts/lawrencedistrictmain.html
Keith E. McDonough, Clerk
(jurisdiction over Andover, Lawrence, Methuen,
    and North Andover)

Lynn District Court
580 Essex Street
Lynn, MA 01901
(781) 598-5200
http://www.mass.gov/courts/courtsandjudges/
    courts/lynndistrictmain.html
Jane Brady Stirgwolt, Clerk
(jurisdiction over Lynn, Marablehead, Nahant,
    Saugus, and Swampscott)

Newburyport District Court
188 State Road
Route 1 Traffic Circle
Newburyport, MA 01950-6637
(978) 462-2652
http://www.mass.gov/courts/courtsandjudges/
    courts/newburyportdistrictmain.html
Kathryn M. Early, Clerk
(jurisdiction over Amesbury, Merrimac,
    Newbury, Newburyport, Rowley, Salisbury,
    and West Newbury)

Peabody District Court
1 Lowell Street
Peabody, MA 01960
(978) 532-3100; (978) 531-8524 FAX
http://www.mass.gov/courts/courtsandjudges/
    courts/peabodydistrictmain.html
Kevin L. Finnegan, Clerk
(jurisdiction over Lynnfield and Peabody)

Salem District Court
65 Washington Street
Salem, MA 01970
(978) 744-1167, ext. 3019; (978) 744-3211 FAX
http://www.mass.gov/courts/courtsandjudges/
    courts/salemdistrictmain.html
Robert F. Arena, Clerk
(jurisdiction over Beverly, Danvers, Manchester
    by the Sea, Middleton, and Salem)

Franklin County
organized 1811 from Hampshire County

Franklin County Register of Deeds
(425 Main Street, Greenfield, MA 01301-3313—
    location)
PO Box 1495 (mailing address)
Greenfield, MA 013012-1495

(413) 772-0239; (413) 774-7150 FAX
peter.wood@sec.state.ma.us
http://www.franklindeeds.com
H. Peter Wood
(Hampshire abstract records 1663-1786 and
    Franklin County records to present)
copies: 75¢ per page for records, $1.00 per page
    for plans

Franklin Probate and Family Court
(425 Main Street—location)
PO Box 590 (mailing address)
Greenfield, MA 01302
(413) 774-7011, ext. 215; (413) 774-3829 FAX
http://www.mass.gov/courts/courtsandjudges/
    courts/frankprobmain.html
John F. Merrigan, Register of Probate
(probate records)
probate search service: no charge ("provide
    estate name and approximate year"); copies of
    probate records: 50¢ per page, no minimum

Franklin Superior Court
(Courthouse, 425 Main Street—location)
PO Box 1573 (mailing address)
Greenfield, MA 01302
(413) 774-5535, ext. 248; (413) 774-4770 FAX
http://www.mass.gov/courts/courtsandjudges/
    courts/franksupmain.html
Doris G. Doyle, Clerk
(naturalization records)

Greenfield District Court
425 Main Street
Greenfield, MA 01301
(413) 774-5533; (413) 774-5328 FAX
http://www.mass.gov/courts/courtsandjudges/
    courts/greenfielddistrictmain.html
Margaret E. Palmeri, Clerk
(jurisdiction over Ashfield, Bernardston,
    Buckland, Charlemont, Colrain, Conway,
    Deerfield, Gill, Greenfield, Hawley, Heath,
    Leyden, Monroe, Montague, Northfield,
    Rowe, Shelburne, Sunderland, and Whately)

Orange District Court
1 Court Square
Orange, MA 01364
(978) 544-8277; (978) 544-5204 FAX
http://www.mass.gov/courts/courtsandjudges/
    courts/orangedistrictmain.html
Laurie N. Dornig, Clerk
(jurisdiction over Athol, Erving, Leverett, New
    Salem, Orange, Shutesbury, Warwick, and
    Wendell)

Hampden County
organized 1812 from Hampshire County

Chicopee District Court
30 Church Street
Chicopee, MA 01020
(413) 598-0099, ext. 245; (413) 594-6187 FAX
http://www.mass.gov/courts/courtsandjudges/
    courts/chicopeedistrictmain.html
Paul M. Kozikowski, Clerk
(jurisdiction over Chicopee only)

Hampden County Probate and Family Court
Hall of Justice
50 State Street
Springfield, MA 01102
(413) 748-7760; (413) 781-5605 FAX
http://www.mass.gov/courts/courtsandjudges/
    courts/hampdenprobmain.html
Thomas P. Moriarty, Jr., Register of Probate
(land records with Registry of Deeds,
    naturalization records, probate records with
    Thomas P. Moriarty, Jr., Register of Probate)

Hampden County Register of Deeds
(Hall of Justice, 50 State Street—location)
PO Box 559 (mailing address)
Springfield, MA 01102-0559
(413) 755-1722; (413) 731-8190 FAX
hampden@sec.state.ma.us
http://www.hampdendeeds.com
Donald E. Ashe

Hampden Superior Court
(Hall of Justice, 50 State Street—location)

PO Box 559 (mailing address)
Springfield, MA 01102-0559
(413) 748-7631
http://www.mass.gov/courts/courtsandjudges/
    courts/hampdcnsupmain.html
Marie G. Mazza, Esq., Clerk

Holyoke District Court
20 Court Plaza
Holyoke, MA 01040
(413) 538-9710, ext. 225; (413) 533-7165 FAX
http://www.mass.gov/courts/courtsandjudges/
    courts/holyokedistrictmain.html
Manuel A. Moutinho, III
(jurisdiction over Holyoke only)

Palmer District Court
235 Sykes Street, Suite 3
Palmer, MA 01069-1190
(413) 283-8916; (413) 283-6775 FAX
http://www.mass.gov/courts/courtsandjudges/
    courts/palmerdistrictmain.html
Benjamin Barnes, Clerk
(jurisdiction over Brimfield, East Longmeadow,
    Hampden, Holland, Ludlow, Monson,
    Palmer, Wales, and Wilbraham)

Springfield District Court
(Hall of Justice, 50 State Street—location)
PO Box 2421 (mailing address)
Springfield, MA 01101-2421
(413) 748-8600; (413) 747-4841 FAX (Civil);
    (413) 747-4842 FAX (Criminal)
http://www.mass.gov/courts/courtsandjudges/
    courts/springfielddistrictmain.html
Stephen C. Poitrast, Clerk Magistrate *pro tempore*
(jurisdiction over Longmeadow, Springfield and
    West Springfield)

Westfield District Court
224 Elm Street
Westfield, MA 01085
(413) 568-8946; (413) 568-4863 FAX
http://www.mass.gov/courts/courtsandjudges/
    courts/westfielddistrictmain.html
Carol J. Kantany-Casartello
(jurisdiction over Agawam, Blandford, Chester,
    Granville, Montgomery, Russell, Southwick,
    Tolland, and Westfield)

Hampshire County
organized 7 May 1662 from Middlesex County

Eastern Hampshire District Court
(116 Russell Street, Route 9—location)
PO Box 778 (mailing address)
Hadley, MA 01035
(413) 587-3120, ext. 2249 (Criminal
    Department); (413) 587-3120, ext. 2245 (Civil
    Department); (413) 587-3709 FAX
http://www.mass.gov/courts/courtsandjudges/
    courts/easthampshiredistrictmain.html
William P. Nagle, Jr.
(jurisdiction over Amherst, Belchertown,
    Granby, Hadley, Pelham, South Hadley, and
    Ware)

Hampshire County Register of Deeds
Hall of Records, 33 King Street
Northampton, MA 01060
(413) 584-3637; (413) 584-4136 FAX
HampshireReg@sec.state.ma.us
http://www.hampshiredeeds.com
Marianne L. Donohue
(land records)

Hampshire Probate and Family Court
33 King Street, Suite 3
Northampton, MA 01060
(413) 586-8500, ext. 107; (413) 584-1132 FAX
http://www.mass.gov/courts/courtsandjudges/
    courts/hampprobmain.html
David E. Sullivan, Register of Probate

Hampshire Superior Court
(15 Gothic Street—location)
PO Box 1119 (mailing address)
Northampton, MA 01060
(413) 584-5810, ext. 293; (413) 586-8217 FAX
http://www.mass.gov/courts/courtsandjudges/
    courts/hampsupmain.html

Harry Jekanowski, Jr.
(naturalization records)

Northampton District Court
15 Gothic Street
Northampton, MA 01060
(413) 584-7400; (413) 586-1980 FAX
http://www.mass.gov/courts/courtsandjudges/
courts/northamptondistrictmain.html
Jacklyn Connly, Clerk
(jurisdiction over Chesterfield, Cummington,
Easthampton, Goshen, Hatfield, Huntington,
Middlefield, Northampton, Plainfield,
Southampton, Westhampton, Williamsburg,
and Worthington)

Middlesex County
organized 1643, original county

Ayer District Court
25 East May Street
Ayer, MA 01432
(978) 772-2100; (978) 772-5345 FAX (Clerk's
Office)
http://www.mass.gov/courts/courtsandjudges/
courts/ayerdistrictmain.html
(jurisdiction over Ashby, Ayer, Boxborough,
Dunstable, Groton, Littleton, Pepperell,
Shirley, Townsend, Westford, and Devens
Regional Enterprise Zone)

Combridge District Court
40 Thorndike Street
Cambridge, MA 02141
(617) 494-4300 (Criminal Department); (617)
494-4310 (Civil Department); (617) 494-9129
FAX
http://www.mass.gov/courts/courtsandjudges/
courts/cambridgedistrictmain.html
Robert Moscow, Clerk
(jurisdiction over Arlington, Belmont, and
Cambridge)

Concord District Court
305 Walden Street
Concord, MA 01742-3616
(978) 369-0500, ext. 638; (978) 371-2945 FAX
http://www.mass.gov/courts/courtsandjudges/
courts/concorddistrictmain.html
Ann T. Colicchio, Clerk
(jurisdiction over Acton, Bedford, Carlisle,
Concord, Lexington, Lincoln, Maynard, and
Stow)

Framingham District Court
(600 Concord Street—location)
PO Box 1969 (mailing address)
Framingham, MA 01701
(508) 875-7461; (508) 626-2503 FAX
http://www.mass.gov/courts/courtsandjudges/
courts/framinghamdistrictmain.html
Thomas J. Begley, Clerk
(jurisdiction over Ashland, Framingham,
Holliston, Hopkinton, Sudbury, and Wayland)

Lowell District Court
41 Hurd Street
Lowell, MA 01852
(978) 4101, ext. 229; (978) 937-2486 FAX
http://www.mass.gov/courts/courtsandjudges/
courts/lowelldistrictmain.html
William A. Lisano, Clerk
(jurisdiction over Billerica, Chelmsford, Dracut,
Lowell, Tewksbury, and Tyngsboro)

Malden District Court
89 Summer Street
Malden, MA 02148
(781) 322-7500, ext. 100; (781) 322-0169 FAX
http://www.mass.gov/courts/courtsandjudges/
courts/maldendistrictmain.html
Joseph E. Croken, Clerk
(jurisdiction over Everett, Malden, Melrose, and
Wakefield)

District Court
45 Williams Street
Marlborough, MA 01752
(508) 485-3700, ext. 219; (508) 485-1575 FAX
http://www.mass.gov/courts/courtsandjudges/
courts/marlboroughdistrictmain.html

Paul F. Malloy, Clerk
(jurisdiction over Hudson and Marlborough)

Newton District Court
1309 Washington Street
West Newton, MA 02465-2011
(617) 244-3600, ext. 207; (617) 243-7291 FAX
http://www.mass.gov/courts/courtsandjudges/
courts/newtondistrictmain.html
Henry H. Shultz, Clerk
(jurisdiction over Newton only)

**Middlesex County Register of Deeds
(Northern District)**
360 Gorham Street
Lowell, MA 01852
(978) 322-9000; (978) 322-9001 FAX
lowelldeeds@comcast.net
http://www.lowelldeeds.com
Richard P. Howe, Jr.
(jurisdiction over Billerica, Carlisle, Chelmsford,
Dracut, Dunstable, Lowell, Tewksbury,
Tyngsborough, Westford, and Wilmington)

**Middlesex County Register of Deeds
(Southern District)**
(208 Cambridge Street, Cambridge, MA 02141-
0005—location)
PO Box 68 (mailing address)
East Cambridge, MA 02141
(617) 679-6310; (617) 494-9083 FAX
middlesexsouth@sec.state.ma.us
http://www.cambridgedeeds.com
Eugene C. Brune
(land records; jurisdiction over Acton, Arlington,
Ashby, Ashland, Ayer, Bedford, Belmont,
Boxborough, Burlington, Cambridge,
Concord, Everett, Framingham, Groton,
Holliston, Hopkinton, Hudson, Lexington,
Lincoln, Littleton, Malden, Marlboro,
Maynard, Medford, Melrose, Natick, Newton,
North Reading, Pepperell, Reading, Sherborn,
Shirley, Somerville, Stoneham, Stow, Sudbury,
Townsend, Wakefield, Waltham, Watertown,
Wayland, Weston, Winchester, and Woburn)

Middlesex Probate and Family Court
Attn. Copy Department
(208 Cambridge Street, Cambridge, MA 02141-
0005—location)
PO Box 410480 (mailing address)
East Cambridge, MA 02141-0006
(617) 768-5808; (617) 225-0781 FAX
http://www.mass.gov/courts/courtsandjudges/
courts/middprobro.html
John R. Buonomo, Registrar of Probate
(probate records from 1872)
probate search service: no charge; copies of
probate records: 50¢ per page for unofficial
copies or $1.50 per attested page; no
minimum

Middlesex Superior Court
Edward J. Sullivan Courthouse
40 Torndike Street
Cambridge, MA 02141
(617) 494-4010
http://www.mass.gov/courts/courtsandjudges/
courts/middsupmain.html
Edward J. Sullivan, Clerk

Natick District Court
117 East Central Street
Natick, MA 01760
(508) 653-4332; (508) 655-8196 FAX
http://www.mass.gov/courts/courtsandjudges/
courts/natickdistrictmain.html
Brian J. Kearney, Clerk
(jurisdiction over Natick and Sherborn)

Somerville District Court
175 Fellsway
Somerville, MA 02145
(617) 666-8000, ext. 719
http://www.mass.gov/courts/courtsandjudges/
courts/somervilledistrictmain.html
Robert A. Tomasone, Clerk
(jurisdiction over Meford and Somerville)

Waltham District Court
38 Linden Street

Waltham, MA 02452
(781) 894-4500, ext. 235
http://www.mass.gov/courts/courtsandjudges/
courts/walthamdistrictmain.html
Michael J. Finucane, Clerk
(jurisdiction over Waltham, Watertown, and
Weston)

Woburn District Court
30 Pleasant Street
Woburn, MA 01801
(781) 935-4000, ext. 239; (781) 933-4404 FAX
http://www.mass.gov/courts/courtsandjudges/
courts/woburndistrictmain.html
Kathleen M. McKeon, Clerk
(jurisdiction over Burlington, North Reading,
Reading, Stoneham, Wilmington, Winchester,
and Woburn)

Nantucket County
organized 1695, original county; town organized
1687 (Sherburn, 1713; Tuckannock, 1795);
town comprises the whole of Nantucket
County

Nantucket District Court
(Town and County Building, 16 Broad Street,
Second Floor—location)
PO Box 1800 (mailing address)
Nantucket, MA 02554
(508) 228-0460; (508) 325-5759 FAX
http://www.mass.gov/courts/courtsandjudges/
courts/nantucketdistrictmain.html
Roxana E. Viera

Nantucket Register of Deeds
Town and County Building
16 Broad Street
Nantucket, MA 02554
(508) 228-7250; (508) 325-5331 FAX
joanne.kelley@sec.state.ma.us
http://www.masslandrecords.com/malr/control
ler
Joanne L. Kelley

Nantucket Superior Court
(Town and County Building, 16 Broad Street—
location)
PO Box 967 (mailing address)
Nantucket, MA 02554
(508) 228-2559; (508) 228-3725 FAX
http://www.mass.gov/courts/courtsandjudges/
courts/nansupmain.html
Patricia R. Church
(naturalization records)

Probate and Family Court Department
(Town and County Building, 16 Broad Street—
location)
PO Box 1116 (mailing address)
Nantucket, MA 02554
(508) 228-2669; (508) 228-3662 FAX
howard_s@jud.state.ma.us
http://www.mass.gov/courts/courtsandjudges/
courts/nanprobmain.html
Sylvia D. Howard, Register of Probate
(probate records)
copies of probate records: 50¢ per page, $1.50
per page if attested, no minimum

Norfolk County
organized 1793 from Suffolk County

Brookline District Court
360 Washington Street
Brookline, MA 02445
(617) 232-4660; (617) 739-0734 FAX
http://www.mass.gov/courts/courtsandjudges/
courts/brooklinedistrictmain.html
Rosemarie V. Connors
(jurisdiction over Brookline)

Dedham District Court
631 High Street
Dedham, MA 02026
(781) 329-4777, ext. 334; (781) 329-8640 FAX
http://www.mass.gov/courts/courtsandjudges/
courts/dedhamdistrictmain.html
Salvatore Paterna
(jurisdiction over Dedham, Dover, Medfield,
Needham, Norwood, Wellesley, and

Westwood)

Norfolk County Register of Deeds
(649 High Street—location)
PO Box 69 (mailing address)
Dedham, MA 02026-0069
(781) 461-6122; (781) 326-4742 FAX
registerodonnell@norfolkdeeds.org
http://www.norfolkdeeds.org
William O'Donnell
(land records)

Norfolk Probate and Family Court
Department
35 Shawmut Road
Canton, MA 02021
(781) 830-1271; (781) 830-4310 FAX
http://www.mass.gov/courts/courtsandjudges/
courts/norfolkprobmain.html
Patrick W. McDermott, Register of Probate
(probate records)

Norfolk Superior Court
650 High Street
Dedham, MA 02026
(781) 326-1600; (781) 326-3871 FAX (Civil);
(781) 320-9726 FAX (Criminal)
http://www.mass.gov/courts/courtsandjudges/
courts/norfsupmain.html

Quincy District Court
1 Dennis F. Ryan Parkway
Quincy, MA 02169
(617) 471-1650; (617) 472-1924 FAX
http://www.mass.gov/courts/courtsandjudges/
courts/quincydistrictmain.html
Arthur H. Tobin
(jurisdiction over Braintree, Cohasset, Holbrook,
Milton, Quincy, Randolph, and Weymouth)

Stoughton District Court
1288 Central Street
Stoughton, MA 02072
(781) 344-2131; (781) 341-8744 FAX
http://www.mass.gov/courts/courtsandjudges/
courts/stoughtondistrictmain.html
Donald M. Stapleton, Clerk
(jurisdiction over Avon, Canton, Sharon, and
Stoughton)

Wrentham District Court
60 East Street
Wrentham, MA 02093
(508) 384-3106, ext. 227; (508) 384-5052 FAX
http://www.mass.gov/courts/courtsandjudges/
courts/wrenthamdistrictmain.html
Edward J. Doherty, Clerk
(jurisdiction over Foxborough, Franklin,
Medway, Millis, Norfolk, Plainville, Walpole,
and Wrentham)

Milford District Court
(see Worcester County)

Plymouth County
organized 1685 from Old Plymouth Colony

Brockton District Court
(215 Main Street—location)
PO Box 7610 (mailing address)
Brockton, MA 02303-7610
(508) 897-2727; (508) 587-6791 FAX
http://www.mass.gov/courts/courtsandjudges/
courts/broctondistrictmain.html
Kevin P. Creedon
(jurisdiction over Abington, Bridgewater,
Brockton, East Bridgewater, West
Bridgewater, and Whitman)

Hingham District Court
28 George Washington Boulevard
Hingham, MA 02043
(781) 749-7000, ext. 226; (781) 740-8390 FAX
http://www.mass.gov/courts/courtsandjudges/
courts/hinghamdistrictmain.html
Joseph A. Ligotti, Clerk
(jurisdiction over Hanover, Hingham, Hull,
Norwell, Rockland, and Scituate)

Plymouth County Commissioners
11 South Russell Street
Plymouth, MA 02360

(617) 747-1350
http://www.seeplymouth.com (Plymouth
County Development council Convention &
Visitors Bureau)
(deeds from 1620 to 1692, probate records from
1620 to 1692)
copies of deeds and probate records: send SASE
with request for manuscript, transcript or
both if available, and you will be given a cost
quotation (50¢ per page, $2.00 minimum)

Plymouth District Court
South Russell Street
Plymouth, MA 02360
(508) 747-0500, ext. 300; (508) 830-9303 FAX
http://www.mass.gov/courts/courtsandjudges/
courts/plymouthdistrictmain.html
John A. Sullivan, Acting Clerk Magistrate
(jurisdiction over Duxbury, Halifax, Hanson,
Kingston, Marshfield, Pembroke, Plymouth,
and Plympton)

Plymouth Probate and Family Court
Division
PO Box 3640
Plymouth, MA 02361
(508) 583-8250; (508) 897-5440; (508) 584-4142
FAX
http://www.mass.gov/courts/courtsandjudges/
courts/plymouthprobmain.html
Robert E. McCarthy, Register of Probate
(probate records)

Plymouth County Superior Court
Court Street
Plymouth, MA 02360
(508) 747-6911; (508) 583-8250 (Brockton)
http://www.mass.gov/courts/courtsandjudges/
courts/plymouthsupmain.html
Francis R. Powers, Clerk of Courts
(naturalization records, births, deaths and
marriages from 1636 to 1686)

Plymouth County Register of Deeds
50 Obery Street
Plymouth, MA 02361
(508) 830-9200; (508) 830-9221 FAX
http://regdeeds.co.plymouth.ma.us
John Buckley, Jr.
(deeds after 1692)

Wareham District Court
2200 Cranberry Highway
West Wareham, MA 02576
(508) 295-8300, ext. 315; (508) 291-6376 FAX
http://www.mass.gov/courts/courtsandjudges/
courts/warehamdistrictmain.html
(jurisdiction over Carver, Lakeville, Marion,
Mattapoisett, Middleboro, Rochester, and
Wareham)

Suffolk County
organized 1643, original county

Chelsea District Court
120 Broadway
Chelsea, MA 02150
(617) 660-9200; (617) 660-9215 FAX
http://www.mass.gov/courts/courtsandjudges/
courts/chelseadistrictmain.html
Kevin G. Murphy
(jurisdiction over Chelsea and Revere)

Suffolk County Register of Deeds
(24 New Chardon Street—location)
PO Box 9660 (mailing address)
Boston, MA 02114-9660
(617) 725-8575; (617) 720-4163 FAX
contact@suffolkdeeds.com
http://www.suffolkdeeds.com
Francis "Mickey" Roache

Suffolk County Superior Court for Criminal
Business
Suffolk County Courthouse, 14th Floor
3 Pemberton Square
Boston, MA 02108
(6176) 788-8160 (Criminal); (617) 788-8175
(Civil); (617) 788-7798 FAX
http://www.mass.gov/courts/courtsandjudges/
courts/suffsupcrimmain.html

Joseph M. Rubino, Clerk for Criminal Business;
Michael Joseph Donovan, Clerk for Civil
Business

Suffolk Probate and Family Court
(Edward W. Brooke Courthouse, 24 New
Chardon Street, Third Floor—location)
PO Box 9667 (mailing address)
Boston, MA 02114
(617) 788-8304; (617) 788-8983 FAX
http://www.mass.gov/courts/courtsandjudges/
courts/suffprobmain.html
Richard Iannella, Register of Probate

Supreme Judicial Court for Suffolk County
Archives and Record Preservation Project
1300 New Court House, Room 1400
Boston, MA 02108
(617) 725-8044; (617) 725-8045
sjccountyclerk@sjc.state.ma.us
http://www.mass.gov/courts/sjc/suffolk_clerk.
html
Maura S. Doyle, Clerk
(probate records)

Boston Municipal Court, South Boston
Division
535 East Broadway
South Boston, MA 02127
(617) 268-9292; (617) 268-7321 FAX
http://www.mass.gov/courts/courtsandjudges/
courts/southbostondistrictmain.html
Margaret F. Albertson, Esq., Clerk

Boston Municipal Court, Brighton Division
52 Academy Hill Road
Brighton, MA 02135
(617) 782-6521; (617) 254-2127
http://www.mass.gov/courts/courtsandjudges/
courts/brightondistrictmain.html
James B. Roche, Clerk
(jurisdiction over Allston and Brighton)

Boston Municipal Court, Charlestown
Division
3 City Square
Charlestown, MA 02129
(617) 242-5400; (617) 242-1677 FAX
http://www.mass.gov/courts/courtsandjudges/
courts/charlestowndistrictmain.html
John Whalen, Clerk
(jurisdiction over Charlestown)

Boston Municipal Court Department
Edward W. Brooke Courthouse
24 New Chardon Street
Boston, MA 02114
(617) 788-8600 (Criminal Division); (617) 788-
8400 (Civil Division); (617) 788-8465 FAX
(Criminal); (617) 788-8675 FAX (Civil)
http://www.mass.gov/courts/courtsandjudges/
courts/bmcmain.html
Daniel J. Hogan, Esq., Clerk-Magistrate

Boston Municipal Court, Dorchester
Division
510 Washington Street
Dorchester, MA 02124
(617) 288-9500, ext. 201; (617) 436-8250 FAX
http://www.mass.gov/courts/courtsandjudges/
courts/dorchesterdistrictmain.html
Anthony S. Owens, Clerk
(jurisdiction over Charlestown)

Boston Municipal Court, East Boston
Division
37 Meridian Street
East Boston, MA 02128
(617) 569-7550, ext. 125; (617) 561-4988 FAX
http://www.mass.gov/courts/courtsandjudges/
courts/eastbostondistrictmain.html
Joseph R. Faretra, Clerk
(jurisdiction over East Boston and Winthrop)

Boston Municipal Court, Roxbury Division
85 Warren Street
Roxbury, MA 02119
(617) 427-7000, ext. 530; (617) 541-0286 FAX
http://www.mass.gov/courts/courtsandjudges/
courts/roxburydistrictmain.html
Michael W. Neighbors, Clerk

Boston Municipal Court, West Roxbury Division
445 Arborway
Jamaica Plain, MA 02130
(617) 971-1200; (617) 983-0243 FAX
http://www.mass.gov/courts/courtsandjudges/
courts/westroxburydistrictmain.html
Richard L. Walsh, Clerk
(jurisdiction over West Roxbury, Jamaica Plain, Hyde Park, Roslindale, parts of Mission Hill, and Mattapan sections of Boston)

Worcester County
county incorporated 2 April 1731 with the town of Brookfield from Hampshire County, the towns of Lancaster, Leicester, Lunenburg, Rutland, Shrewsbury, Southborough, Westborough, and Worcester from Middlesex County, and the towns of Mendon, Oxford, Sutton, Uxbridge, and Woodstock from Suffolk County

Clinton District Court
300 Boylston Street
Clinton, MA 01510
(978) 368-7811; (978) 368-7827 FAX
http://www.mass.gov/courts/courtsandjudges/
courts/clintondistrictmain.html
Leonard F. Tomaiolo, Clerk
(jurisdiction over Berlin, Bolton, Boylston, Clinton, Harvard, Lancaster, Sterling, and West Boylston)

Dudley District Court
(West Main Street—location)
PO Box 100 (mailing address)
Dudley, MA 01571
(508) 943-7123; (508) 949-0015 FAX
http://www.mass.gov/courts/courtsandjudges/
courts/dudleydistrictmain.html
Kenneth F. Candito
(jurisdiction over Charlton, Dudley, Oxford, Southbridge, Sturbridge, and Webster)

East Brookfield District Court
544 East Main Street
East Brookfield, MA 01515-1701
(508) 885-6305; (508) 885-7623 FAX
http://www.mass.gov/courts/courtsandjudges/
courts/eastbrookfielddistrictmain.html
Elizabeth M. Maunsell, Clerk
(jurisdiction over Barre, Brookfield, East Brookfield, Hardwick, Leicester, New Braintree, North Brookfield, Oakham, Paxton, Rutland, Spencer, Warren, and West Brookfield)

Fitchburg District Court
100 Elm Street
Fitchburg, MA 01420
(978) 345-2111; (978) 342-2461 FAX
http://www.mass.gov/courts/courtsandjudges/
courts/fitchburgdistrictmain.html
David W. Bishop, Acting Clerk Magistrate
(jurisdiction over Fitchburg and Lunenburg)

Gardner District Court
108 Matthews Street
Gardner, MA 01440-0040
(978) 632-2373; (978) 630-3902 FAX
http://www.mass.gov/courts/courtsandjudges/
courts/gardnerdistrictmain.html
Whitney J. Brown, Clerk
(jurisdiction over Gardner, Hubbardston, Petersham, and Westminster)

Leominster District Court
25 School Street
Leominster, MA 01453
(978) 537-3722; (978) 537-3970 FAX
http://www.mass.gov/courts/courtsandjudges/
courts/leominsterdistrictmain.html
Philip B. O'Toole, Clerk
(jurisdiction over Holden, Leominster, and Princeton)

Milford District Court
(161 West Street—location)
PO Box 370 (mailing address)
Milford, MA 01757

(508) 473-1260; (508) 634-8477 FAX
http://www.mass.gov/courts/courtsandjudges/
courts/milforddistrictmain.html
Thomas C. Carrigan, JD, Clerk
(jurisdiction over Hopedale, Mendon, Milford, Upton, Worcester County, and over Bellingham, Norfolk County)

Uxbridge District Court
261 South Main Street
Uxbridge, MA 01569-1690
(508) 278-2454; (508) 278-2929 FAX
http://www.mass.gov/courts/courtsandjudges/
courts/uxbridgedistrictmain.html
Peter D. Rigero, Clerk
(jurisdiction over Blackstone, Douglas, Millville, Northbridge, Sutton, and Uxbridge)

Westborough District Court
175 Milk Street
Westborough, MA 01581
(508) 366-8266; (508) 366-8268 FAX
http://www.mass.gov/courts/courtsandjudges/
courts/westboroughdistrictmain.html
Thomas X. Cotter
(jurisdiction over Grafton, Northborough, Shrewsbury, Southborough, and Westborough)

Winchendon District Court
80 Central Street
Winchendon, MA 01475
(978) 297-0156; (978) 297-0161 FAX
http://www.mass.gov/courts/courtsandjudges/
courts/winchendondistrictmain.html
Daniel F. Langelier
(jurisdiction over Ashburnham, Phillipston, Royalston, Templeton, and Winchendon)

Worcester County Register of Deeds
Courthouse, 2 Main Street
Worcester, MA 01608
(508) 798-7717; (508) 798-7746 FAX
linda.curran@sec.state.ma.us
http://www.worcesterdeeds.com
Anthony J. Vigliotti, Esq.

Worcester District Court
50 Harvard Street
Worcester, MA 01608
(508) 757-8350; (508) 797-0716 FAX
http://www.mass.gov/courts/courtsandjudges/
courts/worcesterdistrictmain.html
Thomas J. Noonan, Clerk
(jurisdiction over Auburn, Millbury, and Worcester)

Worcester Northern Register of Deeds
Putnam Place
166 Boulder Drive, Suite 202
Fitchburg, MA 01420
(978) 342-2637; (978) 345-2865 FAX
fitchreg@sec.state.ma.us
http://www.fitchburgdeeds.com
John B. McLaughlin

Worcester Probate and Family Court
2 Main Street
Worcester, MA 01608-1116
(508) 770-0825
http://www.mass.gov/courts/courtsandjudges/
courts/worcesterprobmain.html
Stephen G. Abraham, Register of Probate

Worcester Superior Court
2 Main Street
Worcester, MA 01608
(508) 770-1899
http://www.mass.gov/courts/courtsandjudges/
courts/worcsupmain.html
Francis A. Ford

MICHIGAN

Capital: Lansing. Statehood: 26 January 1877 (ceded to the U.S. in 1783, part of the Northwest Territory in 1787, part of Indiana Territory in 1800, became a separate territory 11 January 1805 with extensions in 1818 and 1834)

Michigan has Municipal Courts in East Detroit, Grosse Pointe, Grosse Pointe Farms, Grosse Pointe Park, Grosse Pointe Shores and Grosse Pointe Woods. Probate Courts sit at each county seat and at other locations. However, eight counties have joined to form four Probate Court districts: Alger-Schoolcraft, Clare-Gladwin, Emmet-Charlevoix and Mecosta-Osceola. Ninety-eight District Courts sit throughout the state and deal with some civil matters, misdemeanors, preliminary examinations, evictions, foreclosures, etc. The Court of Claims hears claims against the state. The Recorder's Court of Detroit handles criminal felonies.

Fifty-five Circuit Courts have general jurisdiction and sit in each county seat. The following Circuits include more than one county: Fifth Judicial Circuit: Barry and Eaton counties; Eighth Judicial Circuit: Ionia and Montcalm counties; Eleventh Judicial Circuit: Alger, Luce and Schoolcraft counties; Twelfth Judicial Circuit: Baraga, Houghton and Keweenaw counties; Thirteenth Judicial Circuit: Antrim, Grand Traverse and Leelanau counties; Nineteenth Judicial Circuit: Benzie and Manistee counties; Twenty-third Judicial Circuit: Iosco and Oscoda counties; Twenty-sixth Judicial Circuit: Alcona, Alpena, Montmorency and Presque Isle counties; Twenty-seventh Judicial Circuit: Newaygo and Oceana counties; Twenty-eighth Judicial Circuit: Missaukee and Wexford counties; Twenty-ninth Judicial Circuit: Clinton and Gratiot counties; Thirty-second Judicial Circuit: Gogebic and Ontonagon counties; Thirty-third Judicial Circuit: Charlevoix and Emmet counties; Thirty-fourth Judicial Circuit: Arenac, Ogemaw and Roscommon counties; Forty-first Judicial Circuit: Dickinson, Iron and Menominee counties; Forty-sixth Judicial Circuit: Crawford, Kalkaska and Otsego counties; Forty-ninth Judicial Circuit: Mecosta and Osceola counties; Fiftieth Judicial Circuit: Chippewa and Mackinac counties; Fifty-first Judicial Circuit: Lake and Mason counties; Fifty-fifth Judicial Circuit: Clare and Gladwin counties. The Court of Appeals and Supreme Court have appellate jurisdiction.

Alcona County
organized 1840 from Alpena County; officially organized 1869

Alcona County Clerk
(County Building, 106 Fifth Street, Harrisville, MI 48740-9789—location)
PO Box 308 (mailing address)
Harrisville, MI 48740-0308
(989) 724-5374
http://www.alconacountymi.com
Patricia Truman
(naturalization records from 1869 to the 1930s, births from 1869 to date [very few], deaths and marriages from 1869 to date)

Alcona County Probate Court
(County Building, 106 Fifth Street—location)
PO Box 328 (mailing address)
Harrisville, MI 48740
(517) 724-6880; (517) 724-6490 (Register)
http://courts.michigan.gov/scao/services/dirs/
county/Alcona%20County.html
Pamela Ashford, Register
probate search service: no charge; copies of land records: $1.00 per page; copies of vital records: $1.00 per document, $5.00 for certification (restrictions on viewing births); copies of probate records: $1.00 per

document, 25¢ per page for files, etc.

Alcona County Register of Deeds
PO Box 269
Harrisville, MI 48740
(517) 724-6802
http://www.alconacountymi.com/content/secti
on/12/58
Karen Healy

Alger County
organized 1885 from Schoolcraft County

Alger County Clerk/Register of Deeds
Alger County Courthouse Complex
101 Court Street
Munising, MI 49862-1103
(906) 387-2076; (906) 387-2156 FAX
alger_co@miquf.org
http://www.algercounty.com/govt.htm
Mary Ann Froberg
(land records from 1885, naturalization records
from about 1885, some births and deaths
from 1884, some marriages from 1885)
copies of land records: $1.00 per page; copies of
naturlization records: 25¢ per page; certified
copies of vital records: $5.00 for the first copy
and $2.00 for each additional copy of the
same record

Alger/Schoolcraft Probate District 5
Alger County Courthouse Complex
101 Court Street
Munising, MI 49862
(906) 387-2080
Ms. Stacey E. Masters, Register
(probate records from about 1885)
probate search service: no charge; copies of
probate: 25¢ per page, $3.00 for certified
copies

Allegan County
territory embracing Allegan County was first
claimed by the British who ceded it to France
in 1763; it was seized by George Rogers Clark
in the name of Virginia on 1 March 1784, and
was organized in 1805 from Wayne County; at
this time, Allegan County was considered part
of Indiana; on 21 August 1821, the Ottawa
Indians conveyed their interest to the federal
government by the Treaty of Chicago; the
county was a portion of the region which the
legislative council of the Territory of
Michigan declared in November 1826 to be
attached to and composed a part of Lenawee
County; in April 1827, an Act formed the
territory thus annexed to Lenawee County
into the Township of St. Joseph; on 4
November 1829, Ranges 11 and 12 were
made a part of St. Joseph County; Ranges 13
to 17 frl., inclusive, were made a part of Cass
County; on 2 March 1831, the present
confines of the county were set off into a
separate county by the name of Allegan; on
29 March 1833, a law was enacted, "that all
the district of country which has been set off
into a separate county by the name of
Allegan, shall be attached to the County of
Kalamazoo for all legal purposes
whatsoever"; in 1834 the county seat was
located at Allegan Village; an act which took
effect 1 September 1835 again separated
Allegan County from Kalamazoo County
when it was organized into four townships:
Newark Township, containing what is now
Laketown, Saugatuck, Ganges, Casco,
Fillmore, Manlius, Clyude and Lee; Allegan
Township, containing what is now Overisel,
Heath, Valley, Cheshire, Salem, Monterey,
Allegan and Trowbridge; Otsego Township,
containing what is now Dorr, Hopkins,
Watson and Otsego; and Plainfield Township,
containing what is now Leighton, Wayland,
Martin and GunPlain

Allegan County Clerk/Register of Deeds
113 Chestnut Street
Allegan, MI 49010-1332
(616) 673-0450; (269) 673-0298 FAX

jwatts@allegancounty.org
http://www.allegancounty.org
Joyce Watts
(land records; births from 24 Jan 1867, deaths
from 13 Feb 1867, and marriages from 17
Dec 1835)
vital records search service: $7.00 for the first
three years, $3.00 for each additional year per
person and event (includes a certified copy of
the record, if found)

Allegan County Probate Court
Juvenile Court Center
2243 33rd Street
Allegan, MI 49010
(269) 673-0250
http://www.allegancounty.org/Government/P
BC/Index.asp?pt=
Linda S. Hays
probate search service: no charge; copies of
probate records: 50¢ per page for "conformed
copies," no minimum

Alpena County
Anamickee County organized 1840 from
Mackinac and unorganized territory
(Saginaw); county organized 7 February 1857,
with the township containing Fremont,
renamed the City of Alpena on 2 February
1859, composing the entire county

Alpena County Clerk
720 West Chisholm Street, Suite #2
Alpena, MI 49707-2429
(989) 354-9520; (989) 354-9644 FAX
http://www.alpenacounty.org/alpena_county_cl
erk.htm
Bonnie Friedrichs
(naturalization records from 1871, births from
1869 to date, deaths and marriages from 1871
to date)
certified copies of vital records: $5.00 for the
first copy and $2.00 for each additional copy
of the same record (driver's license required
for ID)

Alpena County Probate Court
Alpena County Office Building
719 West Chisholm Street, Suite 4
Alpena, MI 49707-2452
(989) 354-9650; (989) 354-9782 FAX
http://www.alpenacounty.org/COURTS.HTM
Jane Ferris, Register

Alpena County Register of Deeds
Courthouse, 720 West Chisholm, Suite #4
Alpena, MI 49707
(989) 354-9547; (989) 354-9646 FAX
matashk@alpenacounty.org
http://www.alpenacounty.org/alpena_county_r
egister%20of%20deeds.htm
Kathy Matash

Antrim County
organized 1840 from Mackinac County; name
changed from Meegise County in 1843

Antrim County Clerk
(County Building, 203 East Cayuga Street—
location)
PO Box 520 (mailing address)
Bellaire, MI 49615
(231) 533-6353; (231) 533-6935 FAX
clerk@antrimcounty.org;
sextonl@antrimcounty.org
http://www.antrimcounty.org/clerk.asp
Laura Sexton
(naturalization records from 1873 to 1955 and
vital records from 1876)

Antrim County Probate Court
(County Building, 205 East Cayuga Street—
location)
PO Box 130 (mailing address)
Bellaire, MI 49615
(231) 533-6681; (231) 533-6600 FAX
probatecourt@antrimcounty.org
http://www.antrimcounty.org/probate.asp
Patricia A. Theobald, Register

Antrim County Register of Deeds

(County Building, 205 East Cayuga Street—
location)
PO Box 376 (mailing address)
Bellaire, MI 49615
(231) 533-6683
registerofdeeds@antrimcounty.org
http://www.antrimcounty.org/rod.asp
Patty Niepoth

Arenac County
organized 1883 from Bay County

Arenac County Clerk
(Courthouse, 120 North Grove—location)
PO Box 747 (mailing address)
Standish, MI 48658
(989) 846-4626
http://www.arenaccountygov.com
Rick Rockwell

Arenac County Probate Court
(Courthouse, 120 North Grove—location)
PO Box 666 (mailing address)
Standish, MI 48658
(989) 846-6941
http://courts.michigan.gov/scao/services/dirs/
county/Arenac%20County.html
June M. Baker, Register

Arenac County Register of Deeds
(Courthouse, 120 North Grove—location)
PO Box 747 (mailing address)
Standish, MI 48658
(989-846-6188; (989) 846-9177 FAX
http://www.arenaccountygov.com
Rose Smith

Baraga County
organized 1875 from Houghton County

Baraga County Clerk/Register of Deeds
Courthouse, 16 North Third Street
L'Anse, MI 49946-1085
(906) 524-6183 voice & FAX
http://www.baragacounty.org/CountyOfficials.
htm
Wendy Tollefson-Goodreau

Baraga County Probate Court
Courthouse, 16 North Third Street
L'Anse, MI 49946
(906) 524-6390
http://www.baragacounty.org
Ms. Evelyn Welch, Register
probate search service: "All records beginning
with 1875 under office
instruction/supervision"; $1.00 per page
("certified copies at the regular fee")

Barry County
organized 1829 from Eaton County

Barry County Clerk
220 West State Street
Hastings, MI 49058
(269) 945-1285 (Vital Records); (269) 945-0209
FAX
dsmith@barrycounty.org
http://www.barrycounty.org;
http://barryco.readyhosting.com/Departmen
ts/clerk.html
Debbie Smith
(births and deaths from 1867, marriages from
1839 [but few recorded before 1867])
copies of vital records: $10.00 for the first copy
and $3.00 for each additional copy of the
same record ("Births may not be researched;
with proof of relationship a staff member
[time permitting] will look up one or two")

Barry County Probate Court
Courts and Law Building
206 West Court Street, Suite 302
Hastings, MI 49058
(269) 945-1390; (269) 948-3322 FAX
http://barryco.readyhosting.com/Departments/
Probate.html
Pamela A. Jarvis, Register
(probate records from November 1863)
probate search service: no charge ("We do not

have any individual who does this on a regular basis, and consequently we cannot estimate when we will be able to provide information . ... We strongly recommend that if people wish to search our ledgers they call in to check the court schedule, as we have very limited space, and the attorneys' room is the only place we have for our microfilm reader"; copies of probate records: $1.00 per page "as long as the documents do not need to be microfilmed")

Barry County Register of Deeds
220 West State Street
Hastings, MI 49058
(269) 945-1289; (269) 945-1298 FAX
bcrod@barrycounty.org;
dburghdoff@barrycounty.org
http://barryco.readyhosting.com/Departments/
ROD.html
Darla Burghdoff
(land records from 1836)

Bay County
organized 1857 from Saginaw and Midland counties

Bay County Clerk
515 Center Avenue, Suite 101
Bay City, MI 48708-5122
(989) 895-4280; (989) 895-4284 FAX
http://www.co.bay.mi.us/bay/home.nsf/Public
/Bay_County_Clerk.htm
Cynthia Luczak
(deaths and marriages)
copies of vital records: 25¢ each, $8.50 for certified copies of old records that must be typed

Bay County Probate Court
1230 Washington Avenue, Suite 715
Bay City, MI 48708-5737
(989) 895-4205
http://www.co.bay.mi.us/bay/home.nsf/Public
/Probate_Court.htm
Cathy M. Odney, Register

Bay County Register of Deeds
515 Center Avenue, Suite 102
Bay City, MI 48708-5122
(989) 895-4228; (989) 895-4296 FAX
http://www.co.bay.mi.us/bay/home.nsf/Public
/Bay_County_Register_Of_Deeds.htm
Victoria Roupe

Benzie County
In 1859 the Township of Crystal Lake in Grand Traverse County included all of what is now Benzie County; county of Benzie formed 1863 and attached to Grand Traverse County for civic and municipal purposes; organized by an act of the legislature 30 March 1869

Benzie County Clerk
(Benzie County Government Center, 448 Court Place—location)
PO Box 398 (mailing address)
Beulah, MI 49617
(231) 882-9671; (231) 882-5941 FAX
http://www.benzieshoreslibrary.org/numbers.h
tml
Dawn Olney
(naturalization records, births from 6 March 1868, deaths from 27 April 1868, marriages from 25 May 1869)
no vital records search service ("Researcher should be able to describe the family research being done, some form of identification"); copies of vital records: $5.00 for the first copy and $2.00 for each additional copy of the same record made at the same time

Benzie County Probate Court
(Benzie County Government Center, 448 Court Place—location)
PO Box 377 (mailing address)
Beulah, MI 49617
(231) 882-9675
http://courts.michigan.gov/scao/services/dirs/
county/Benzie%20County.html

Kimberly Ireton, Register
no probate search service; copies of probate records: 35¢ per page, no minimum

Benzie County Register of Deeds
(Benzie County Government Center, 448 Court Place—location)
PO Box 398 (mailing address)
Beulah, MI 49617
(231) 882-9674 (County Planning Office); (231) 882-0016; (800) 315-3651
http://www.michigan.gov/treasury/0,1607,7-
121-1748_1904_1989-5791--,00.html;
http://www.benziecounty.org;
http://benzie.org (Chamber of Commerce)
Michelle Gray
(land records with County Planning Office [has records of historical homes, photos, locations, etc.])

Berrien County
organized 1829 from Indian lands

Berrien County Clerk
Courthouse, 811 Port Street
St. Joseph, MI 49085-1156
(269) 983-7111, ext. 8368; (269) 983-7111, ext. 8233 (Vital Records); (269) 982-8642 FAX
records@berriencounty.org
http://www.berriencounty.org/?dept=6
M. Louise Stine
(naturalization records from about 1842, births and deaths from 1867 to date [Death Liber B has limited access because of fragile condition], marriages from 1834)
copies of naturalization records: $3.00 per page; certified copies of vital records: $10.00 for the first copy or three-year search ("to view a birth since 1900, an heir must show proof of death such as death certificate or obituary notice")

Berrien County Probate Court
Family Division
Courthouse, 811 Port Street, Fourth Floor
St. Joseph, MI 49085-1192
(269) 982-8613; (269) 982-8644 FAX
http://www.berriencounty.org/?dept=8&pid=239
Cora Robinson, Register
(wills, deceased trusts, estates, guardianships, etc., from 1837 to date)
probate search service: no charge; copies of probate records: $1.00 per page plus SASE, $10.00 for the first page of a certified copy and $1.00 for each additional page, no minimum

Berrien County Register of Deeds
Berrien County Administration Center
701 Main Street
St. Joseph, MI 49085
(269) 983-7111, ext. 8562; (269) 982-8659 FAX
rod@berriencounty.org
http://www.berriencounty.org/?dept=24
Lori D. Jarvis
copies of land records: $1.00 per page, $3.00 for plats, $1.00 for certification

Branch County
organized 1829 from St. Joseph County (formerly attached for judicial purposes only)

Branch County Clerk
Courthouse, 31 Division Street
Coldwater, MI 49036-1904
(517) 279-4306; (517) 278-5627 FAX
http://www.co.branch.mi.us/dept.taf?dept_id=
102
Ms. Terry Kubasiak
(naturalization records, deaths from 1867 and marriages from 1833)
copies of vital records: $13.00 for the first copy and $4.00 for each additional copy of the same document made at the same time

Branch County Probate Court
Courthouse, 31 Division Street
Coldwater, MI 49036
(517) 279-4318; (517) 279-6444 FAX
http://www.countyofbranch.com/dept.taf?dept

_id=116
Sharon L. Lounds, Register
no probate search service; copies of probate records: $1.00 per page, no minimum

Branch County Register of Deeds
Courthouse Annex, 23 East Pearl Street
Coldwater, MI 49036
(517) 279-4320; (517) 279-6458 FAX
http://www.countyofbranch.com/dept.taf?dept
_id=118
Nancy Hutchins

Calhoun County
organized 1829 from Indian lands

Calhoun County Clerk and Register of Deeds
County Building, 315 West Green Street
Marshall, MI 49068-1518
(269) 781-0730; (269) 781-0720 FAX
gregory.moore@mail.house.gov (Gregory Moore, Commissioner, District 5);
katesegal@hotmail.com (Kate Segal, Commissioner, District 1)
http://co.calhoun.mi.us
Anne B. Norlander
(naturalization records from 1918 to 1970, deaths and marriages from 1867; land records from 1833)
copies: $10.00

Calhoun County Probate Court
Calhoun County Justice Center
161 East Michigan Avenue
Battle Creek, MI 49014-4066
(269) 969-6794; (269) 969-6762 (Register); (269) 969-6797 FAX
http://www.calhouncountymi.org/Departments
/ProbateCourt/OverviewProbateCourt.htm
Cindy K. Rude, Probate Register

Cass County
organized 1829 from Indian lands

Cass County Clerk/Register of Deeds
(Cass County Building, 120 North Broadway, Room 123—location)
PO Box 355 (mailing address)
Cassopolis, MI 49031
(269) 445-4464; (269) 445-4406 FAX
http://www.casscountymi.org
Barbara Wilson
(real estate records from 1829; naturalization records from 1929 to 1952; births and deaths from 1867; marriages from 1830)

Cass County Probate Court
Law and Courts Building
60296 M-62, Suite 10
Cassopolis, MI 49031
(269) 445-4454
http://courts.michigan.gov/scao/services/dirs/
county/Cass%20County.html
Donna M. Dodd, Register
(probate records from 1829)
probate search service: no charge at this time; copies of probate records: $1.00 per page

Charlevoix County
organized 1869 from Manitou and Otsego counties

Charlevoix County Clerk
Charlevoix County Building
203 Antrim Street
Charlevoix, MI 49720
(231) 547-7200; (800) 548-9157; (231) 547-7217 FAX
clerk@charlevoixcounty.org
http://www.charlevoixcounty.org/clerk.asp
Jane Brannon
(naturalization records from 1880, vital records from 1868)

Charlevoix County Register of Deeds
Charlevoix County Building
301 State Street
Charlevoix, MI 49720
(231) 547-7204; (231) 237-0106 FAX

http://www.charlevoixcounty.org/rod.asp
Charlene M. Novotny

Charlevoix/Emmet Probate District 7
Charlevoix County Building
301 State Street, Second Floor
Charlevoix, MI 49720
(231) 547-7214; (231) 547-7256 FAX
http://www.charlevoixcounty.org/govern0052.asp
Cyndie Lieberman, Register
no probate search service; certified copies: $3.00
    each, no minimum

Cheboygan County
organized 1840 from Antrim County

Cheboygan County Clerk/Register of Deeds
(Cheboygan County Building, 870 South Main
    Street—location)
PO Box 70 (mailing address)
Cheboygan, MI 49721
(616) 627-8808
clerk@cheboygancounty.net
http://www.cheboygancounty.net
Mary Ellen Tryhan
(land records from 1855, naturalization records
    from 1878, vital records from 1867)

Cheboygan County Probate Court
(Cheboygan County Building, 870 South Main
    Street—location)
PO Box 70 (mailing address)
Cheboygan, MI 49721
(231) 627-8875 (Register); (231)627-8823
    (Court)
http://www.cheboygancounty.net
Patricia A. Hansen, Register

Chippewa County
organized 1826 from Mackinac County; a census
    was taken by Sheriff John Hulbert in 1827 for
    the County of Chippewa; the Michigan
    Manual states that the county was organized
    in 1843

Chippewa County Clerk
Courthouse, 319 Court Street
Sault Ste. Marie, MI 49783-2183
(906) 635-6300; (906) 635-6325 FAX
dcork@chippewacountymi.gov
http://www.chippewacountymi.gov
Diane Cork
(births and deaths from 1869 to date, marriages
    from 1827 to date)
vital records search service: $5.00 for each
    twenty years; certified copies of vital records:
    $5.00 for the first copy and $3.00 for each
    additional copy

Chippewa County Probate Court
Courthouse, 319 Court Street
Sault Ste. Marie, MI 49783
(906) 635-6314
http://www.chippewacountymi.gov
Susan M. Wilds, Register

Chippewa County Register of Deeds
Courthouse, 319 Court Street
Sault Se. Marie, MI 49783
(906) 635-6312
skennedy@chippewacountymi.gov
http://www.chippewacountymi.gov
Sharon Kennedy

Clare County
set off 1840 from Isabella County; first named
    Kay-Ka-Knee; name changed to Clare in
    1843; courthouse burned 12 July 1877

Clare/Gladwin Probate District 17
(Courthouse, 225 West Main Street—location)
PO Box 96 (mailing address)
Harrison, MI 48625
(517) 539-7109
http://www.clareco.net
Margaret F. Douglas, Register
(probate records from 1876)
no probate search service; copies of probate
    records: $1.00 per page, $10.00 for certified
    copies, no minimum

Clinton County
organized 1831 from Shiawassee County

Clinton County Clerk/Clerk of the Court
Courthouse, 100 East State Street, Suite 2600
St. Johns, MI 48879-1571
(989) 224-5140; (989) 227-6421 FAX
clerk@clinton-county.org
http://www.clinton-county.org/clerk/clerk.htm
Diane Zuker
(naturalization records from 1870, births and
    deaths from 1867, marriages from about
    1839)
vital records search service: $10.00 per name for
    a three-year search (includes one certified
    copy); copies of vital records: $10.00 for the
    first certified copy and $3.00 for each
    additional certified copy made at the same
    time of any births or of deaths or marriages
    after 1933, $1.00 for uncertified copies of
    deaths or marriages before 1933 (births
    restricted to researchers who are heirs, have
    the full name and birth date and can prove
    that the registrant is deceased)

Clinton County Probate Court
Courthouse, 110 East State Street, Suite 4300
St. Johns, MI 48879
(989) 224-5190; (989) 224-5102 FAX
probatect@clinton-county.org
http://www.clinton-county.org/prob-
    juv/probate_court.htm
Ms. Jean Rayman, Register
(probate records from 1840)
probate search service: no charge ("Probate
    Court should be contacted prior to coming in
    to assure the availability of a researcher");
    copies of probate records: $1.00 per page, no
    minimum

Clinton County Register of Deeds
(Courthouse, 100 East State Street, Suite 2600—
    location)
PO Box 435 (mailing address)
St. Johns, MI 48879-0435
(989) 224-5270; (989) 224-5102 FAX
rod@clinton-county.org
http://www.clinton-
    county.org/rod/register_of_deeds.htm
Carol Wooley
(land records from 1837)

Crawford County
organized 1818, original county

46th Circuit Trial Court
200 West Michigan Avenue
Grayling, MI 49738-1745
(989) 348-2841
http://courts.michigan.gov/scao/services/dirs/
    county/Crawford%20County.html
Christina Ventline, Probate Register
no probate search service; copies of probate
    records: $1.00 per record copy, no minimum

Crawford County Clerk/Register of Deeds
200 West Michigan Avenue
Grayling, MI 49738-1741
(989) 348-2841; (989) 344-3223 FAX
smoore@crawfordco.org
http://www.crawfordco.org/clerk/clerk.htm;
    http://www.crawfordco.org/deeds/deeds.htm
Sandra Moore
(deaths and marriages [births are no longer
    public record])

Delta County
organized 9 March 1843 from Schoolcraft
    County

Delta County Clerk/Register of Deeds
Delta County Building, 310 Ludington Street,
    Suite 109
Escanaba, MI 49829-4057
(906) 789-5105; (906) 789-5196 FAX
dclerk@charterinternet.com
http://www.deltacountymi.org/clerk.php;
    http://www.deltacountymi.org/deeds.php
Nancy Kolich
(land records from 1863, naturalization records

from 1866, and vital records from 1867)

Delta County Probate Court
Delta County Building, 310 Ludington Street
Escanaba, MI 49829
(906) 789-5112
http://www.deltacountymi.org
Regina F. Howell, Register
probate search service: $10.00; copies of probate
    records: $1.50 per page, $3.00 for certified
    copies, $10.00 minimum

Dickinson County
organized 1891 from Marquette County

Dickinson County Clerk
(Courthouse, 705 South Stephenson Avenue—
    location)
PO Box 609 (mailing address)
Iron Mountain, MI 49801-0609
(906) 774-0988; (906) 774-4660 FAX
clerkdolly@dickinsoncountymi.org
http://www.dickinsoncountymi.gov/countyDep
    t/countyClerk.html
Dolly L. Cook
(naturalization records before June 1970, births
    from 1891, deaths and marriages from 1891 [a
    separate death index for the years 1934 and
    on is available; separate marriage index for
    years 1891 to present indexed under groom's
    name only])
certified copies of vital records and probate
    records: $5.00 each (no out-of-county
    personal checks accepted, includes ten-year
    search; "Births are no longer considered
    public record"; available to "the individual
    who is the subject of the birth record, a
    parent named in the birth record, an heir, a
    legal representative or legal guardian or a
    court of competent jurisdiction;" to view a
    birth record "they must show some proof the
    person is deceased and they are an heir" by
    being able to "describe or display the family
    research being done and the records sought;
    to prove heirship must show copy of death
    certificate, obituary or funeral card")

Dickinson County Probate Court
(Courthouse, 705 South Stephenson Avenue—
    location)
PO Box 609 (mailing address)
Iron Mountain, MI 49801
(906) 774-1555; (906) 774-1561 FAX
http://www.dickinsoncountymi.gov
Judy Dallaguarda, Register
no probate search service

Dickinson County Register of Deeds
(Courthouse, 705 South Stephenson Avenue—
    location)
PO Box 609 (mailing address)
Iron Mountain, MI 49801-0609
(906) 774-2573; (906) 774-3686 FAX
reqmary@dickinsoncountymi.org
http://www.dickinsoncountymi.org
Mary Linsmeyer
(land records from 1891 [by legal description
    only, not street addresses])

Eaton County
organized 1837 from Kalamazoo County

Eaton County Clerk/Register of Deeds
Courthouse, 1045 Independence Boulevard
Charlotte, MI 48813-1033
(517) 543-7500, ext. 2426 (County Clerk's
    Office); (517) 543-7500, ext. 4203 (Register of
    Deeds Office); (517) 541-0666 FAX (County
    Clerk's Office); (517) 543-7377 (Register of
    Deeds Office)
CountyClerk@eatoncounty.org;
    RegisterOfDeeds@eatoncounty.org
http://www.eatoncounty.org
Ms. M. Fran Fuller
(deaths from 1867 through 1970, marriages from
    1838 through 1970)
vital records search service with Joyce Leiken,
    Eaton County Genealogical Society; copies of
    vital records: $1.00 for the first page and 50¢
    for each additional page, $5.00 for the first

certified copy and $2.00 for each additional certified copy (very early birth records available for inspection with clerk's assistance in locating ancestors; "must sign form and show proper identification")

Eaton County Probate Court
Courthouse, 1045 Independence Boulevard
Charlotte, MI 48813
(517) 543-7500
http://207.74.121.25/juvenile%20division.html
Lori Barrett, Register

Emmet County
organized 1853 from Mackinac County

Emmet Charlevoix Probate District 7
Emmet County Building
200 Division Street
Petoskey, MI 49770
(231) 348-1764
http://www.co.emmet.mi.us/probate
Colleen Sarki, Register
(probate records from 1857)
no probate search service ("Requests to be in writing with SASE"); copies of probate records: 25¢ each, no minimum

Emmet County Clerk
Emmet County Building
200 Division Street
Petoskey, MI 49770
(231) 348-1744; (231) 348-0602 FAX
gmartin@co.emmet.mi.us;
     sburr@co.emmet.mi.us (Vital Records Clerk)
http://www.co.emmet.mi.us/clerk
Gail A. Martin
(naturalizations from 1867, immigration records early 1800s, deaths and marriages from 1867)
certified copies of vital records: $5.00 (births restricted, death record requested for proof of heirship)

Emmet County Register of Deeds
Emmet County Building
200 Division Street
Petoskey, MI 49770
(231) 348-1761
registerofdeeds@co.emmet.mi.us
http://www.co.emmet.mi.us/deeds
Michele Stine
(land records from 1852)

Genesee County
organized 1835 from Oakland County

Genesee County Clerk
Courthouse, 900 South Saginaw Street, Room 202
Flint, MI 48502
(810) 257-3228; (810) 257-3225; (810) 257-3464 FAX
http://www.co.genesee.mi.us/clerk
Michael J. Carr
(births, deaths and marriages from 1867 to date)
copies of vital records: $2.00 per page, $10.00 for the first certified copy and $5.00 for each additional certified copy (births restricted to records over 100 years old or if proof of death is presented)

Genesee County Probate Court
Courthouse, 900 South Saginaw Street, Room 502
Flint, MI 48502
(810) 424-4426; (810) 257-2713 FAX
http://www.co.genesee.mi.us/probate/index.html
James N. Bauer, Register

Genesee County Register of Deeds
1101 Beach Street
Flint, MI 48502
(810) 257-3060; (810) 768-7965 FAX
http://www.co.genesee.mi.us/registerdeeds
Melvin Phillip McCree

Gladwin County
organized 1855 from unorganized territory

Gladwin/Clare Probate District 17
Gladwin County Building

401 West Cedar Street
Gladwin, MI 48624
(989) 426-7451
http://www.gladwinco.com
Toni L. Seipke, Register

Gladwin County Clerk
Gladwin County Building
401 West Cedar Avenue
Gladwin, MI 48624-2088
(989) 426-7351; (989) 426-6917 FAX
clerk@gladwinco.com
http://www.gladwinco.com
Laura E. Flach
(births from 1875 to 1972, and deaths and marriages from 1875 to date)
vital records search service: $1.00 per name per five-year period; copies of vital records: 25¢ each, $7.00 for the first certified copy and $3.00 for each additional certified copy of the same record (requires driver's license number or social security number, death certificate for births, and relationship to person for births or deaths)

Gladwin County Register of Deeds
Gladwin County Building
401 West Cedar Street
Gladwin, MI 48624
(517) 426-7551; (989) 426-6902 FAX
http://www.gladwinco.com
Bonnie K. House

Gogebic County
organized 1887 from Ontonagon County

Gogebic County Clerk
Courthouse, 200 North Moore Street
Bessemer, MI 49911
(906) 663-4518; (906) 663-4660 FAX
gpelissero@gogebic.org
http://www.gogebic.org/clerk
Gerry Pelissero
(births ["1887—the staff will check the index for eligible people"], deaths and marriages)
certified copies of vital records: $7.00 for the first copy and $2.00 for each additional copy of the same record made at the same time (births restricted, proof of death required)

Gogebic County Probate Court
Courthouse, 200 North Moore Street
Bessemer, MI 49911
(906) 667-0421; (906) 667-4660 FAX
http://www.gogebic.org/probate.htm
Wendy Mesich, Register

Gogebic County Register of Deeds
Courthouse, 200 North Moore Street
Bessemer, MI 49911
(906) 667-0381; (906) 663-4090 FAX
rdeeds@gogebic.org
http://www.gogebic.org/deeds.htm
Gerry R. Pelissero
copies of land records: $1.00 per page

Grand Traverse County
organized by an act approved 7 April 1851, from a part of Mackinaw previously called Omena; enlarged 1856 to include Benzie and Leelanau counties

Grand Traverse County Clerk
Governmental Center
400 Boardman Avenue
Traverse City, MI 49684
(231) 922-4760; (231) 922-4658 FAX
gtclerk@co.grand-traverse.mi.us
http://www.co.grand-traverse.mi.us/departments/county_clerk.htm
Linda Coburn
(naturalization records and vital records)

Grand Traverse County Probate Court
Governmental Center
400 Boardman Avenue
Traverse City, MI 49684
(231) 922-6862
http://www.co.grand-trverse.mi.us
Shar Fay, Register

Grand Traverse County Register of Deeds
Governmental Center
400 Boardman Avenue
Traverse City, MI 49684
(231) 922-4753
phaines@co.grand-traverse.mi.us
http://www.grand-traverse.mi.us/departments/Register_of_Deeds.htm
Peggy Haines

Gratiot County
organized 1855 from Saginaw County

Gratiot County Clerk
Courthouse, 214 East Center Street
Ithaca, MI 48847
(989) 875-5215; (989) 875-5254 FAX
http://www.co.gratiot.mi.us
Carol A. Vernon
(births and deaths from 1867, marriages from 1855)
copies of vital records: $10.00 each

Gratiot County Probate Court
(Courthouse, 214 East Center Street—location)
PO Box 217 (mailing address)
Ithaca, MI 48847
(989) 875-5231; (989) 875-5331 FAX
probatecourt@co.gratiot.mi.us
http://www.co.gratiot.mi.us
Mary Kay Hunter, Register
(probate records from 1857)
probate search service: no charge; copies of probate records: $1.00 per page (microfilm), $3.00 per page certification

Gratiot County Register of Deeds
Courthouse, 214 East Center Street
Ithaca, MI 48847
(989) 875-5217
registerofdeeds@co.gratiot.mi.us
http://www.co.gratiot.mi.us
Janet Davis
(land records from 1847)
will assist with research but will not answer mail or telephone requests

Hillsdale County
organized 1835 from Lenawee County

Hillsdale County Clerk
Courthouse, 29 North Howell Street, Room 1
Hillsdale, MI 49242
(517) 437-3391
hillsdale-co@miqvf.org
http://www.co.hillsdale.mi.us
Thomas Mohr
(few naturalization records available, births and deaths from 1867, marriages from 1844)
copies of vital records: $3.00 for non-certified copies needing to be typed, $1.00 for photocopies, $10.00 for certified copies

Hillsdale County Probate Court
Courthouse, 29 North Howell Street, Room 4
Hillsdale, MI 49242
(517) 437-4643
http://www.co.hillsdale.mi.us
Darlene Stuchell, Register
no probate search service; copies of probate records: $1.00 per page

Hillsdale County Register of Deeds
Courthouse, 29 North Howell Street, Room 3
Hillsdale, MI 49242
(517) 437-2231
deeds@co.hillsdale.mi.us
http://www.co.hillsdale.mi.us
Bambi L. Somerlott

Houghton County
organized 19 March 1845 from parts of Marquette, Schoolcraft and Ontonagon counties

Houghton County Clerk/Register of Deeds
Courthouse, 401 East Houghton Avenue
Second Floor
Houghton, MI 49931-2016
(906) 482-1150 (Clerk); (906) 482-1311 (Register

of Deeds)
http://www.houghtoncounty.net/directory-hcclerk.shtml;
http://www.houghtoncounty.net/directory-hcdeeds.shtml
Mary Schoos
(land records from 1847 [indexed], naturalization records from 1848 [indexed], births and deaths from 1867, marriages from 1855)
copies of land records: $5.00 each (includes five-year search); uncertified copies of naturalization records: $5.00 each (includes five-year search); copies of vital records: $5.00 each (includes three-year search of unindexed records or five-year search of indexed records) (births available only to the subject named, parent, legal representative, guardian or heir)

Houghton County Probate Court
Courthouse, 401 East Houghton Avenue, Second Floor
Houghton, MI 49931
(906) 482-3120; (906) 487-5964 FAX
http://www.houghtoncounty.net/directory-probate.shtml
Sue A. Gassittie, Register
(estate records from 1872)
copies of probate records: $5.00 each (includes three-year search of unindexed records or five-year search of indexed records)

Huron County
organized 1840 from Sanilac and Tuscola counties

Huron County Clerk
County Building, 250 East Huron Avenue, Room 201
Bad Axe, MI 48413-1317
(989) 269-9942; (989) 269-6160 FAX
Peggy Koehler
(naturalization records from 1867 to 1953, deaths from 1867, marriages from 1850)
copies naturalization records: $1.00 per page; certified copies of vital records: $10.00 each

Huron County Probate Court
County Building, 250 East Huron Avenue, Room 206
Bad Axe, MI 48413
(989) 269-9944
http://www.co.huron.mi.us
Krisie S. Fritz
no probate search service; copies of probate records: 50¢ per page from paper originals, $1.00 per page from microfilm originals, $10.00 for certification plus $1.00 per page, no minimum

Huron County Register of Deeds
County Building, 250 East Huron Avenue
Bad Axe, MI 48413
http://www.co.huron.mi.us
Fran Holdwick
copies of land records: $1.00 per page

Ingham County
organized 1838 from unorganized territory

Ingham County Clerk
(Courthouse, 341 South Jefferson Street, First Floor—location)
PO Box 179 (mailing address)
Mason, MI 48854
(517) 676-7201; (517) 676-7254 FAX
mbryanton@ingham.org
http://www.ingham.org/cl/index.htm
Mike Bryanton
(deaths from 1867, marriages from 1837, deaths from 1907 with the city of East Lansing)
certified copies of vital records from the county: $5.00 for the first copy and $2.00 for each additional copy of the same document made at the same time

Ingham County Probate Court
Veterans Memorial Courthouse
313 West Kalamazoo Street
Lansing, MI 48933
(517) 483-6300; (517) 483-6150 FAX
GStrander@ingham.org
http://www.ingham.org/pr/default.htm
George Strander, Register

Ingham County Register of Deeds
(Courthouse, 341 South Jefferson Street, Room 201—location)
PO Box 195 (mailing address)
Mason, MI 48854
(517) 676-7216; (517) 676-7245; (517) 676-7287 FAX
pjohnson@ingham.org
http://www.ingham.org/rd/rodindex.htm
Paula Johnson

Ionia County
organized 1837 from unorganized territory

Ionia County Clerk
Courthouse, 100 Main Street
Ionia, MI 48846
(616) 527-5322
deeds@ioniacounty.org
http://www.ioniacounty.org/Clerk/Clerk_home.asp
Barbara Trieweiler
(births, deaths from 1867, marriages from 1837)
copies of vital records: $1.00 each, except for births, which are $10.00 for the first record or search and $3.00 for each additional copy or search included in the same request; "must state relationship; birth record access requires death certificate."

Ionia County Probate Court
Courthouse, 100 Main Street
Ionia, MI 48846
(616) 527-5326
http://www.ioniacounty.org/probate/probate_home.asp
Ms. Kim Courtnay, Register

Ionia County Register of Deeds
(Courthouse, 100 West Main Street—location)
PO Box 35 (mailing address)
Ionia, MI 48846
(616) 527-5320; (616) 527-8234 FAX
deeds@ioniacounty.org
http://www.ioniacounty.org/RoD/ROD_home.asp
Diane Adams

Iosco County
organized 1840 from unorganized territory

Iosco County Clerk
(County Building, 422 East Lake Street, Tawas City, MI 48763—location)
PO Box 838 (mailing address)
Tawas City, MI 48764-0838
(989) 362-3497; (989) 984-1012 FAX
mwelsch@ioscocounty.org
http://iosco.m33access.com/clerk.htm
Mike Welsch
(name changed from Kanotin County in 1843)

Iosco County Probate Court
(County Building, 422 East Lake Street, Tawas City, MI 48763—location)
PO Box 421 (mailing address)
Tawas City, MI 48764
(989) 362-3991
http://iosco.m33access.com/offices.htm
Mary Windsor, Register

Iosco County Register of Deeds
(422 East Lake Street—location)
PO Box 367 (mailing address)
Tawas City, MI 48764-0367
(989) 362-2021; (989) 984-1101 FAX
ROD@ioscocounty.org
http://iosco.m33access.com/register.htm
Bonita Coyle

Iron County
organized 1885 from Marquette County

Iron County Clerk
Courthouse, 2 South Sixth Street, Suite 9
Crystal Falls, MI 49920-1413
(906) 875-3221
jluhtanen@iron.org
http://www.iron.org; http://iron.org/edc/gov-clerk.php
Joan Luhtanen
(deaths and marriages from 1885)
copies of vital records: 25¢ per page plus $2.00 for each record researched

Iron County Probate Court
Courthouse, 2 South Sixth Street, Suite 10
Crystal Falls, MI 49920
(906) 875-0659
http://courts.michigan.gov/scao/services/dirs/county/Iron%20County.html
Karen Sue Strahan, Register
probate search service: $10.00 to $20.00; copies of probate records: 25¢ each, $3.00 for certified copies, $5.00 minimum

Iron County Register of Deeds
Courthouse, 2 South Sixth Street, Suite 11
Crystal Falls, MI 49920-1413
(906) 875-3321; (906) 875-0658 FAX
mselmo@iron.org
http://iron.org/edc/gov-register-of-deeds.php
Mark Selmo

Isabella County
organized 1831 from unorganized territory

Isabella County Clerk
200 North Main Street, Room 240
Mt. Pleasant, MI 48858-2321
(989) 772-0911, ext. 265; (989) 772-6347 FAX
clerk@isabellacounty.org
http://www.isabellacounty.org/clerk/index.html
Joyce Swan
(naturalization records from 21 March 1861 to 5 April 1965, deaths from 1867, marriages from 1860)

Isabella County Trial Court
Probate Division
County Building, 300 North Main Street
Mt. Pleasant, MI 48858
(989) 772-0911, ext. 276
http://www.isabellacounty.org/Dept/Courts/probate.html
Laura Plachta, Register
(probate records [closed to the public])

Isabella County Register of Deeds
200 North Main Street
Mt. Pleasant, MI 48858
(989) 772-0911, ext. 253; (989) 953-7219 FAX
sbrown@isabellacounty.org
http://www.isabellacounty.org/deeds
Sharon Brown
(land records from 24 November 1851)

Jackson County
organized 1832 from Washtenaw County

Jackson County Clerk
312 South Jackson Street
Jackson, MI 49201
(517) 788-4265 (Genealogy); (517) 788-4601 FAX; (517) 768-6768 FAX
scrowley@co.jackson.mi.us
http://www.co.jackson.mi.us/countyclerksoffice
Sandra Crowley
(naturalization records, births, deaths, and marriages from 1867)
copies of vital records ("access to original records is discouraged; office staff handle these or make copies"): 50¢ (from 1934 to date) or $1.00 (1867–1933), depending on size, $5.00 for the first certified copy and $2.00 for each additional certified copy

Jackson County Probate Court
Courthouse, 312 South Jackson Street, First Floor
Jackson, MI 49201
(517) 788-4290
http://www.co.jackson.mi.us/CNP.asp
Clifford Yard, Register

Jackson County Register of Deeds

Tower Building, 120 West Michigan Avenue,
11th Floor
Jackson, MI 49201
(517) 788-4350; (517) 788-4686 FAX
MReilly@co.jackson.mi.us
http://www.co.jackson.mi.us/rod
Mindy Reilly
(land records)

Kalamazoo County
organized 1829 from St. Joseph County

Kalamazoo County Clerk/Register of Deeds
County Administrative Building
201 West Kalamazoo Avenue
Kalamazoo, MI 49007-3734
(269) 383-8840 (Clerk Division); (269) 383-8970
(Register of Deeds Division); (269) 383-8837
(Circuit Court Division)
tasnow@kalcounty.com
http://www.kalcounty.com/clerk/index.htm
Timothy A. Snow
(vital records)

Kalamazoo County Probate Court
150 East Crosstown Parkway
Kalamazoo, MI 49001-2849
(269) 383-8666; (269) 383-8685 FAX
KalamazooProbate@Kalcounty.com
http://www.kalcounty.com/courts/probate/def
ault.asp
Steven E. Burnham, Register
(probate records from 1932 to date)
probate search service: no charge; copies of
probate records: $1.00 per page

Kalkaska County
organized 1870 from Crawford County

46th Circuit Trial Court
Family/Probate Division
(Kalkaska County Governmental Center, 605
North Birch Street—location)
PO Box 10 (mailing address)
Kalkaska, MI 49646
(231) 258-3330; (231) 258-9031
http://www.circuit46.org
Lori Garrock, Probate Register
(probate records from 1874)
probate search service: no charge; copies of
probate records: 30¢ each plus postage

Kalkaska County Clerk
(Kalkaska County Governmental Center, 605
North Birch Street—location)
PO Box 10 (mailing address)
Kalkaska, MI 49646
(231) 258-3300; (231) 358-3337 FAX
http://www.kalkaskacounty.net/clerk.asp
Patricia Rodgers
(vital records from 1871)

Kalkaska County Register of Deeds
Kalkaska County Governmental Center
605 North Birch Street
Kalkaska, MI 49646
(231) 258-3315; (231) 258-3345 FAX
http://www.kalkaskacounty.net/regdeeds.asp
Joan Hall
(deeds from 1856 [on microfilm])
copies of land records: $1.00 each ("We also
have an abstract office, the books can be used
for $45.00 per hour")

Kay-Ka-Knee County
(see Clare County)

Kent County
organized 1836 from unorganized territory

Kent County Clerk/Register of Deeds
County Administration Building
300 Monroe Avenue, N.W.
Grand Rapids, MI 49503-2208
(616) 632-7640 (Clerk); (616) 632-7610
(Register); (616) 632-7645 FAX (Clerk); (616)
632-7615 FAX (Register)
mary.hollinrake@kentcounty.org
http://www.accesskent.com/YourGovernment
/CountyClerk/default.htm
Mary Hollinrake
(births and deaths from 1867, marriages from
1845)

Kent County Probate Court
180 Ottawa Avenue, N.W., Suite 2500
Grand Rapids, MI 49503
(616) 632-5440; (616) 632-5430 FAX
http://www.accesskent.com/CourtsAndLawEn
forcement/ProbateCourt/probate_index.htm
John D. Flynn, Register

Keweenaw County
organized 11 March 1861 from Houghton
County

Keweenaw County Probate Court
Courthouse, 5095 Fourth Street
Eagle River, MI 49950
(906) 337-1927
http://www.lwvccmi.org/keweenaw.html
Kathy McEvers, Register
probate search service: no charge; copies of
probate records: $3.00 for the first page and
$1.00 for each additional page, no minimum

Lake County
organized 1870 from Osceola County

Lake County Clerk/Register of Deeds
(800 Tenth Street, Baldwin, MI 49304-7970—
location)
PO Box B (mailing address)
Baldwin, MI 49304-0902
(616) 745-4641; (231) 745-2241 FAX
Clerk@co.lake.mi.us
http://www.michigan.gov/hal/0,1607,7-160-
17449_18635_20736-56605--,00.html
Shelly Myers
(land records from 1870; deaths and marriages
from 1870)
copies of vital records: $1.00 per page, $5.00 for
certified copies

Lake County Trial Court
800 Tenth Street, Suite 300
Baldwin, MI 49304
(231) 745-4614
http://courts.michigan.gov/scao/services/dirs/
county/Lake%20County.html
Jeff Nadig, Probate Register
(probate records from 1871)
probate search service: no charge; copies of
probate records: $1.00 per page; $3.00 per
certified page, no minimum

Lapeer County
organized 1837 from Oakland and St. Clair
counties

Lapeer County Clerk
Lapeer County Complex, 255 Clay Street
Lapeer, MI 48446
(810) 667-0356
http://www.county.lapeer.org/Clerk/index.html
Marlene M. Bruns
(naturalization records from 1843, births and
deaths from 1867, marriages from 1833)
certified copies of naturalization records and
vital records: $7.00 each

Lapeer County Probate Court
Lapeer County Complex, 255 Clay Street
Lapeer, MI 48446
(810) 245-4841
http://www.county.lapeer.org/Courts/Probate/
index.html
Margaret Daly, Register
(probate records from 1837)
probate search service: no charge; copies of
probate records: 25¢ per page, no minimum

Lapeer County Register of Deeds
279 North Court
Lapeer, MI 48446
(810) 667-0211; (810) 667-0293 FAX
mdevaugh@lapeercounty.org
http://www.county.lapeer.org/Deeds/index.html
Melissa R. DeVaugh
(land records from 1835)

copies of land records: $1.00 per page

Leelanau County
organized 1863 from Grand Traverse County

Leelanau County Clerk
(Courthouse, 301 East Cedar Street—location)
PO Box 467 (mailing address)
Leland, MI 49654
(231) 256-9824; (231) 256-8295 FAX
http://www.leelanaucounty.com
Michelle Crocker
(naturalization records from 1883 to 1929 and
deaths and marriages from 1867)
vital records search service: $5.00; certified
copies of vital records: $5.00 for the first copy
and $2.00 for each additional copy of the
same document made at the same time (birth
requests require proof of death and proof of
heir, regardless of age)

Leelanau County Probate Court
(Courthouse, 301 East Cedar Street—location)
PO Box 595 (mailing address)
Leland, MI 49654
(616) 256-9803 (Deputy Register)
http://courts.michigan.gov/scao/services/dirs/
county/Leelanau%20County.html; http://
www.leelanaucounty.com/cocourts.asp
Julie Orr, Deputy Register
(probate records from 1874)
probate search service: no charge; copies of
probate records: 25¢ per page for
photocopies, $1.00 for the first page of a
certified copy and $1.00 for each additional
page, no minimum

Leelanau County Register of Deeds
Courthouse, 301 East Cedar Street
Leland, MI 49654
(616) 256-9682
http://www.leelanaucounty.com/coclerk.asp
Barbara Kirt
(land records from 1851)
copies of land records: $1.00 per page

Lenawee County
organized 1822 from Indian lands

Lenawee County Clerk
Rex B. Martin Judicial Building
425 North Main Street
Adrian, MI 49221
(231) 256-9824; (866) 256-9711, ext. 824; (231)
256-8295 FAX
mcrocker@co.leelanau.mi.us
http://www.leelanau.mi.us/coclerk.asp
Michelle L. Crocker
(naturalization records, births and deaths from
1867, marriages from 1852)
vital records search service: $5.00 for the first
five years and $1.00 for each additional year;
certified copies of vital records: $10.00 each

Lenawee County Probate Court
Rex B. Martin Judicial Building
425 North Main Street
Adrian, MI 49221
(517) 264-4622
http://www.leelanaucounty.com/probatecourt.asp
David Stanifer, Register
(deceased estates, guardianships, secret
marriages from 1827)
probate search service: no charge; copies of
probate records: $1.00 for the first page and
50¢ for each additional page, $10.00 for the
first page of certified copies and $3.00 for
each additional page, no minimum

Lenawee County Register of Deeds
(301 East Cedar Street—location)
PO Box 595 (mailing address)
Leland, MI 49654
(231) 256-9682; (231) 256-8149 FAX
bkirt@co.leelanau.mi.us
http://www.leelanaucounty.com/coROD.asp
Barbara J. Kirt

Livingston County
laid out 21 March 1833 from Shiawassee and

Washtenaw counties; organized 24 March 1836 composed of the townships of Green Oak (which included Brighton), Hamburg (which included Genoa), Putnam (which included Marion), Unadilla (which included Iosco), and Howell (which included the present Oceola, Deerfield, Cohactah, Conway, Handy and Tyrone)

Livingston County Clerk
Courthouse, 200 East Grand River
Howell, MI 48843-2399
(517) 546-0500; (517) 546-4354 FAX
countyclerk@co.livingston.mi.us
http://www.co.livingston.mi.us/CountyClerk
Margaret M. Dunleavy
(births and deaths from 1867, marriages from 1836)
certified copies of vital records: $5.00 for the first copy and $2.00 for each additional copy of the same record (in order to obtain births, genealogists must document direct lineage with birth certificates, death certificates or marriage licenses)

Livingston County Probate Court
Judicial Center Building
204 South Highlander Way, Suite 2
Howell, MI 48843
(517) 546-3750; (517) 552-2515; (517) 552-2510 FAX; (517) 552-2511 FAX
probatecourt@co.livingston.mi.us
http://www.co.livingston.mi.us/ProbateCourt
Kathy Jo Rosenbergh
(probate records from 1838)
probate search service: no charge; copies of probate records: $1.00 per page, no minimum

Livingston County Register of Deeds
(Courthouse, 200 East Grand River, Howell, MI 48843—location)
PO Box 197 (mailing address)
Howell, MI 48843
(517) 546-0270; (517) 546-5955 FAX
registerofdeeds@co.livingston.mi.us
http://www.co.livingston.mi.us/RegisterofDeeds
Sally Reynolds
(land records from 1837)
copies of land records: $1.00 per page ("have tract")

Luce County
organized 1887 from Chippewa County

Luce County Clerk/Register of Deeds
Courthouse, East Court Street
Newberry, MI 49868
(906) 293-5521; (906) 293-0050 FAX
lucecoclrk@sault.com
http://www.michigan.gov/hal/0,1607,7-160-17449_18635_20736-56613--,00.html
Kathy S. Mahar
(land records from 1885, births from 4 June 1886, deaths from 8 June 1886, marriages from 14 July 1887)
copies of vital records: $1.00 per page, $10.00 for the first certified copy and $3.00 for each additional certified copy of the same record

Luce Probate District 6
Luce County Government Building
407 West Harrie Street
Newberry, MI 49868
(906) 293-5601
http://courts.michigan.gov/scao/services/dirs/county/Luce%20County.html
Deborah J. Strohl, Register
(probate records from 1888)
probate search service: $15.00; copies of probate records: $1.00 per page, $10.00 for the first certified copy and $3.00 for each additional certified copy of the same record

Mackinac County
organized 1818, original county, formerly called Michilimackinac County

Mackinac County Clerk
Courthouse, 100 Marley Street
St. Ignace, MI 49781-1457

(906) 643-7300; (906) 643-7302 FAX
macclerk@lighthouse.net
http://www.mackinaccounty.net/govt_all4971747.asp
Mary Kay Tamlyn, Clerk's Office
(naturalization records, deaths from 1873, marriages from 1867)
certified copies of vital records: $5.00 for the first copy and $2.00 for each additional copy of same document

Mackinac County Register of Deeds
Courthouse, 100 South Marley Street
St. Ignace, MI 49781
(906) 643-7306; (906) 643-7302 FAX
http://www.mackinaccounty.net/govt_all4979457.asp
Diane Frankovich

Mackinac/Luce Probate District 6
Courthouse, 100 Marley Street
St. Ignace, MI 49781
(906) 643-7303; (906) 643-8861 FAX
http://www.mackinaccounty.net/govt_all4972438_2.asp
Judith L. Ryerse, Register
probate search service: no charge ("search only as time allows"); copies of probate records: 25¢ per page, $10.00 for the first page of certified copies and $1.00 for each additional page

Macomb County
organized 1818, original county

Macomb County Clerk
40 North Main Street, First Floor
Mt. Clemens, MI 48043
(586) 469-5120; (586) 783-8184 FAX
clerksoffice@macombcountymi.gov
http://www.macombcountymi.gov/clerksoffice/clerkindex.htm
Carmella Sabaugh
(births and deaths from 1867 [death index only from 1889], marriages from 1819 to date, deaths only from 1925 with Eastpointe [formerly known as East Detroit])
certified copies of vital records: $10.00 for the first copy and $3.00 for each additional copy of the same record ("Genealogists may inspect a particular certificate if heirship can be proved; heirship also necessary to purchase a certified copy of a deceased relative's birth registration")

Macomb County Probate Court
Wills and Estates Division
21850 Dunham Road
Mt. Clemens, MI 48043
(586) 469-5290; (586) 783-0971 FAX
http://www.macombcountymi.gov/probatecourt/index.htm
Donald Housey, Court Administrator
(probate records from 1830; cases from the 1970s in a searchable online database)
probate search service: no charge (need specific parameters); copies of probate records: 35¢ per page from paper originals, 50¢ per page from microfilm originals, no minimum

Macomb County Register of Deeds
10 North Main, Second Floor
Mt. Clemens, MI 48043
(586) 469-7953; (586) 469-5130 FAX
registerdeeds@macombcountymi.gov
http://www.macombcountymi.gov/clerksoffice/RegisterOfDeedsIndex.htm
Carmella Sabaugh

Manistee County
organized 1855 from Wexford County

Manistee County Clerk
Courthouse, 415 Third Street
Manistee, MI 49660-1606
(231) 723-3331; (231) 723-1492 FAX
clerk@manisteecounty.net
http://www.manisteecounty.net/Clerk/index.html
Marilyn I. Kliber
(naturalization and vital records from 1867)

Manistee County Probate Court
Courthouse, 415 Third Street
Manistee, MI 49660
(231) 723-3261; (231) 398-3558 FAX
probatecourt@manisteecounty.net
http://www.manisteecounty.net/Probate/index.html
Darlene Gardner, Register
(probate records from 1880)
probate search service: $5.00 (includes one certified copy if found); copies of probate records: $1.00 for the first copy and 25¢ for each additional copy, $1.00 minimum

Manistee County Register of Deeds
Courthouse, 415 Third Street
Manistee, MI 49660
(231) 723-2146; (231) 398-3544 FAX
deeds@manisteecounty.net
http://www.manisteecounty.net/Deeds/index.html
Penny A. Pepera
(land records from 1856)

Marquette County
organized 9 March 1843 from Schoolcraft County

Marquette County Clerk
Courthouse, 234 West Baraga Avenue
Marquette, MI 49855-4710
(906) 225-8330
countyclerk@mqtcty.org
http://www.co.marquette.mi.us
Connie Branam
(deaths from 1867, marriages from December 1850 [except from January 1882 to 1892])
vital records search service: $2.00 for each additional year searched beyond three years; certified copies only of vital records: $5.00 for the first copy (includes initial three-year search) and $2.00 for each additional copy made at the same time

Marquette County Probate Court
Courthouse, 234 West Baraga, Room #31
Marquette, MI 49855
(906) 225-8305
http://www.co.marquette.mi.us/probate
Marcia DeFant, Register
(probate records from 1856)

Marquette County Register of Deeds
Courthouse, 234 West Baraga Avenue
Marquette, MI 49855
(906) 225-8415; (906) 225-8420 FAX
pmanley@mqtcty.org
http://www.co.marquette.mi.us/register.htm
Patricia Manley
(land records from the early 1800s)

Mason County
organized 1855 from Ionia County

Mason County Clerk
Courthouse, 304 East Ludington Avenue
Ludington, MI 49431-2121
(231) 843-8202; (231) 843-1972 FAX
jriffle@masoncounty.net
http://www.masoncounty.net
Jim Riffle
(vital records)

Mason County Probate Court
Courthouse, 304 East Ludington Avenue
Ludington, MI 49431
(231) 843-8666
http://www.masoncounty.net/content.aspx?departmentid=8&page=home
Cathy Hudy, Register

Mason County Register of Deeds
Courthouse, 304 East Ludington Avenue
Ludington, MI 49431
(231) 843-4466; (231) 845-7977 FAX
dstark@masoncounty.net
http://www.masoncounty.net
Diane L. Stark

Mecosta County
organized 11 February 1859 from Newaygo and

Osceola counties

Mecosta County Clerk
County Building, 400 Elm Street, Room 131
Big Rapids, MI 49307-1849
(231) 592-0783; (231) 592-0193 FAX
MCClerk@co.mecosta.mi.us
http://www.co.mecosta.mi.us/clerk.asp
Marcee M. Purcell
(births and deaths from 1867, marriages from
1859)
copies of vital records: $7.00 for the first copy
and $3.00 for each additional copy of the
same record

Mecosta County Register of Deeds
County Building, 400 Elm Street, Room 136
Big Rapids, MI 49307
(231) 592-0148
reg-deed@co.mecosta.mi.us
http://www.co.mecosta.mi.us/deeds.asp
Joanne Brown

Mecosta/Osceola Probate District 18
County Building, 400 Elm Street, Room 109
Big Rapids, MI 49307
(231) 592-0136
FamilyCt@co.mecosta.mi.us
http://www.co.mecosta.mi.us/probate.asp
Deborah K. Youngs, Register
(probate records from 1859 [deceased estates,
guardianships, mentally ill persons, adoption
orders, poor persons, wills, juvenile records])
probate search service: no charge ("please
submit written requests"); copies of probate
records: $1.00 per page, $3.00 for certified
copies, no minimum

Menominee County
organized 1863 from Marquette County

**Menominee County Clerk/Register of
Deeds**
Courthouse, 839 Tenth Avenue
Menominee, MI 49858
(906) 863-9968 (Clerk); (906) 863-9969 (Clerk);
(906) 863-2822 (Register); (906) 863-5819
FAX (Clerk); (906) 863-8839 FAX (Register)
http://www.menomineecounty.com/courts/cle
rk/clrk.html; http://www.menomineecounty.
com/rod/rgstr1.html
Barbara Morrison
(land records and naturalization records from
1868, deaths and marriages from 1868)
copies of land records and naturalization
records: $1.00 each; copies of vital records:
$5.00 each

Menominee County Probate Court
Courthouse, 839 Tenth Avenue
Menominee, MI 49858
(906) 863-2634; (906) 863-8839 FAX
http://www.menomineecounty.com/courts/pro
bate/probate.html
Sharon A. Everson, Register
probate search service: ("they search the
indexes"); copies of probate records: $5.00
for the first page, $2.00 for each additional
page

Midland County
organized 1850 from Saginaw County

Midland County Clerk
Midland County Building
220 West Ellsworth Street
Midland, MI 48640-5194
(989) 832-6739; (989) 832-6680 FAX
kholcomb@co.midland.mi.us
http://www.co.midland.mi.us/departments/ho
me.php?id=7
Karen Holcomb
(naturalization records; deaths and marriages
from 1867)
copies of vital records: 50¢ for deaths and
marriages, $7.00 for the first certified copy
and $3.00 for each additional certified copy of
the same record made at the same time (birth
records available as a last resort and eligibility
must be proved to obtain a certified copy)

Midland County Probate Court
Courthouse, 301 West Main Street
Midland, MI 48640
(989) 832-6880; (989) 832-6607 FAX
http://www.co.midland.mi.us/departments/ho
me.php?id=23
Roberta Peless, Register
no probate search service; copies of probate
records: 25¢ each, $10.00 for the first page of
certified copies and $1.00 for each additional
page

Midland County Register of Deeds
Midland County Building
220 West Ellsworth Street
Midland, MI 48640
(989) 832-6820; (989) 832-6842 FAX
shaines@co.midland.mi.us
http://www.co.midland.mi.us/departments/ho
me.php?id=25
Scott Haines

Missaukee County
organized 1840 from unorganized territory

**Missaukee County Clerk and Register of
Deeds**
(Courthouse, 111 South Canal—location)
PO Box 800 (mailing address)
Lake City, MI 49651
(231) 839-4967; (231) 839-3684 FAX
clerk@missaukee.org
http://www.missaukee.org/clrkdept.htm;
http://www.missaukee.org/regdept.htm
Carolyn Flore
(land records from 1871, naturalizations from
1871, and deaths and marriages from 1871)
no vital records search service (requests must
include name and date); copies of vital
records: $1.00 per Xerox copy (no copies
allowed from old books) or $1.00 per page
from microfilm, $5.00 for the first certified
copy (typed) and $2.00 for each additional
certified copy ("if a mail request, it is required
the researchers list relationship and sign their
requests")

Missaukee County Probate Court
(Courthouse, 111 South Canal—location)
PO Box 800 (mailing address)
Lake City, MI 49651
(231) 839-2266; (231) 839-5856 FAX
probate@missaukee.org
http://www.missaukee.org/court.htm
Donna L. Beals, Register
(probate records from 1873)
probate search service: no charge; copies of
probate records: $1.00 per page/microfilm
copy

Monroe County
organized 1817, original county

Monroe County Clerk
Courthouse, 106 East First Street
Monroe, MI 48161-2143
(734) 240-7020; (734) 240-7045 FAX
http://www.co.monroe.mi.us/monroe/default.a
spx?PageId=370
Ms. Geri Allen
(deaths from 1867, marriages from 1818)
copies of vital records: $3.00 for the first copy
and $2.00 for each additional copy of same
record ("death record is requested for proof
of heirship if a birth record is requested, and
staff does searching of births")

Monroe County Probate Court
Courthouse, 106 East First Street
Monroe, MI 48161
(734) 240-7160 (Register); (734) 240-7346
(Court); (734) 240-7355; (734) 240-7354 FAX
http://www.co.monroe.mi.us/monroe/default.a
spx?PageId=382
Brenda Smith, Register
(probate records from 1817)
probate search service: no charge; copies of
probate records: $3.00 for the first page and
$1.00 for each additional page, no minimum

Monroe County Register of Deeds
51 South Macomb Street
Monroe, MI 48161
(734) 240-7390; (734) 240-7395 FAX
http://www.co.monroe.mi.us/monroe/default.a
spx?PageId=370
Ms. Geri Allen

Montcalm County
organized 1831 from Isabella County; set aside
as an independent political unit by the
Michigan Legislature 29 March 1850

Montcalm County Clerk
(Administrative Building, 211 West Main Street,
Second Floor—location)
PO Box 368 (mailing address)
Stanton, MI 48888-0368
(989) 831-7339; (989) 831-7375 FAX
http://www.montcalm.org/countyclerk.asp
Kristen Millard
(deaths and marriages from 1867 [with proper
ID, may look at a particular birth record if
subject is deceased])
certified copies of vital records: $5.00 for the
first copy and $2.00 for each additional copy
of the same record

Montcalm County Probate Court
(Court Complex, 625 North State Street—
location)
PO Box 309 (mailing address)
Stanton, MI 48888
(989) 831-5226 (Register); (989) 831-7316
(Court); (989) 831-7314 FAX
http://www.montcalm.org/probate.asp
Lisa Hoffman, Register

Montcalm County Register of Deeds
(Administrative Building, 211 West Main Street,
First Floor—location)
PO Box 368 (mailing address)
Stanton, MI 48888-0368
(989) 831-7337; (989) 831-7320 FAX
http://www.montcalm.org/registerofdeeds.asp
Lori Wilson

Montmorency County
organized 1881 from Alpena County

Montmorency County Clerk
PO Box 789
Atlanta, MI 49709
(989) 785-8022; (989) 785-8023 FAX
http://www.montmorencycountymichigan.us/C
OUNTYCLERK.html
Cheryl A. Neilsen
(deaths and marriages from 1881)
copies of vital records: $2.00 each, $5.00 for
certified copies (need proper ID with picture
or two other kinds without)

Montmorency County Probate Court
(Courthouse, 12265 M-32—location)
PO Box 789 (mailing address)
Atlanta, MI 49709
(989) 785-8064; (989) 785-8065 FAX
http://www.montmorencycountymichigan.us/P
ROBATE.html
Bonnie J. Turppa

Montmorency County Register of Deeds
PO Box 789
Atlanta, MI 49709
(989) 785-8079; (989) 785-8080 FAX
montrod@i2k.com
http://www.montmorencycountymichigan.us/R
egisterofDeeds.html
Teresa Walker

Muskegon County
organized 1859 from Newaygo County

Muskegon County Clerk
Michael E. Kobza Hall of Justice
990 Terrace Street, Second Floor
Muskegon, MI 49442-3301
(231) 724-6221; (231) 724-6262 FAX
clerk@co.muskegon.mi.us
http://www.co.muskegon.mi.us/clerk

Karen D. Buie
(naturalization records from 1941 [Hackley
Public Library has naturalization records from
1859 to 1906 on microfilm]; births [closed],
deaths from 1867, marriages from 1859
[Hackley Public Library has birth record index
1867-1949 and records to 1917, death record
index from 1867 to 1949 and records to 1918,
marriage record index from 1859 to 1949 and
records to 1912 on microfilm])
copies of vital records: $5.00 for the first copy
and $2.00 for each additional copy of same
record, $10.00 for birth records ("must
complete state-approved form upon request
to establish heirship; picture ID required;
Clerk's Office would prefer use of materials at
Hackley before using their offices")

Muskegon County Probate Court
Michael E. Kobza Hall of Justice
990 Terrace Street
Muskegon, MI 49442
(231) 724-6241
http://www.co.muskegon.mi.us
Nicholas J. Mason, Register
(probate records from 1859)
no probate search service; copies of probate
records: 25¢ per page

Muskegon County Register of Deeds
Michael E. Kobza Hall of Justice
990 Terrace Street, Second Floor
Muskegon, MI 49442
(231) 724-6271; (231) 724-6842 FAX
deeds@co.muskegon.mi.us
http://www.co.muskegon.mi.us/deeds
Mark F. Fairchild
(land records from 1859 [Hackley Public Library
has deeds and indexes to 1886 on microfilm])

Newaygo County
organized 1840 from unorganized territory

27th Circuit Court
(1092 Newell Street—location)
PO Box 885 (mailing address)
White Cloud, MI 49349
(231) 689-7252; (231) 689-7015 FAX
http://www.countyofnewaygo.com/Courts/Cir
cuit/CCHome.htm
(naturalization records)

Newaygo County Clerk
(Newaygo County Building, 1087 Newell
Street—location)
PO Box 885 (mailing address)
White Cloud, MI 49349
(231) 689-7235; (231) 689-7241 FAX
laurie@co.newaygo.mi.us
http://www.countyofnewaygo.com/Clerk/Cler
kHome.htm
Laurel J. Breuker
(deaths from 1867, marriages from 1851)
certified copies of vital records: $7.00 each
("form must be filled out [ID, etc.]; for births
since 1900, must show proof of death")

Newaygo County Probate Court
(1092 Newell Street—location)
PO Box 885 (mailing address)
White Cloud, MI 49349
(231) 689-7270; (231) 689-7276 FAX
kerrie@co.newaygo.mi.us
http://www.countyofnewaygo.com/Courts/Pro
bate/ProbateHome.htm
Lynette K. Daniels, Register

Newaygo County Register of Deeds
(Newaygo County Building, 1087 Newell
Street—location)
PO Box 885 (mailing address)
White Cloud, MI 49349
(231) 689-7246; (231) 689-7271 FAX
Linda@co.newaygo.mi.us
http://www.countyofnewaygo.com/ROD/RO
DHome.htm
Linda M. Landheer

Oakland County
organized 1819, original county

Oakland County Clerk/Register of Deeds
1200 North Telegraph Road
Pontiac, MI 48053-1008
(313) 858-0260; (313) 858-0560 (Register of
Deeds)
clerk@oakgov.com
http://www.oakgov.com/clerkrod
Ruth Johnson
(land records, naturalization records from 1867
to 1985, births [unavailable to the public],
deaths from 1867 [staff must do the search
after 1960], marriages from 1837 [staff must
do the search after 1960] with Clerk/Register;
deaths from 1955 with Madison Heights City,
deaths from 1985 with Rochester Hills City,
deaths from 1897 with Troy City)
copies of naturalization records and vital
records: $10.00 for the first copy and $5.00
for each additional copy

Oakland County Probate Court
Estates and Mental Health, First Floor, East
Wing
1200 North Telegraph Road, Department 457
Pontiac, MI 48341-0457
(248) 452-2016 (Estates Division); (248) 858-
0950 (Register)
http://www.oakgov.com/probate
Lisa Langton, Register

Oceana County
organized 1831 from Newaygo County

Oceana County Clerk
Courthouse, 100 State Street, Suite M-1
Hart, MI 49420
(231) 873-4328
readie@oceana.mi.us
http://www.oceana.mi.us/clerk/index.html
Rebecca J. Griffin
(naturalization records from 1856 [very sketchy],
births and deaths from 1867, marriages from
1856)
copies of vital records: $7.00 for the first copy
and $3.00 for the second copy ("must fill out
a form and have read Procedures Governing
the Inspection of Vital Records Documents,
and indicate which records are sought; if birth
records, must prove they are an heir and show
proof of death")

Oceana County Probate Court
(Oceana County Building, 100 South State
Street, Suite M-10—location)
PO Box 129 (mailing address)
Hart, MI 49420
(231) 873-3666
http://courts.michigan.gov/scao/services/dirs/
county/Oceana%20County.html
Georgia Dennison, Register
no probate search service; copies of probate
records: $1.00 per page

Oceana County Register of Deeds
(Courthouse, 100 State Street—location)
PO Box 111 (mailing address)
Hart, MI 49420
(231) 873-4158; (231) 873-9218 FAX
jfoster@oceana.mi.us
http://www.oceana.mi.us/regdeeds/index.html
Janice Foster
(land records from 15 January 1846)
copies of land records: $1.00 per page

Ogemaw County
organized 1875 from Iosco County

Ogemaw County Clerk
806 West Houghton Avenue
West Branch, MI 48661
(989) 345-0215; (989) 345-7223 FAX
ogemawcoclerk@m33access.com;
ogemawcoclerk@journey.com
http://www.infomi.com/county/ogemaw/gov.
php
Gary Klacking
(naturalization records from 1876, deaths from
1876, marriages from 1887)
copies of vital records: 50¢ each, $5.00 for the
first certified copy and $2.00 for each

additional certified copy (births restricted)

Ogemaw County Probate Court
Ogemaw County Building
806 West Houghton Avenue, Room 203
West Branch, MI 48661
(989) 345-0145
ogemawprobate@m33access.com
http://www.ogemawcountymi.gov/probate/ind
ex.php
Kristeen M. Howard

Ogemaw County Register of Deeds
806 West Houghton Avenue
West Branch, MI 48661
(989) 345-0728
ogemawcoregdeed@m33access.com
http://www.infomi.com/county/ogemaw/gov.
php
Wanda Muzik

Ontonagon County
organized 9 March 1843 from Michilimackinac
and Chippewa counties

Ontonagon County Clerk/Register of Deeds
Courthouse, 725 Greenland Road
Ontonagon, MI 49953-1423
(906) 884-4255; (906) 884-2916 FAX
ontclerk@jamadots.com
http://www.ontonagonmi.org/home.html
(Chamber of Commerce)
Judith Roehm
(land records from formation with Register of
Deeds, naturalization records from formation,
deaths from 12 June 1867, and marriages
from 9 February 1853 with County Clerk)
copies of land records: $1.00 per page; copies of
vital records: $5.00 for the first copy and
$2.00 for each additional copy made at the
same time (a written statement regarding
heirship is required for birth records)

Ontonagon County Probate Court
Courthouse, 725 Greenland Road
Ontonagon, MI 49953
(906) 884-4117
http://courts.michigan.gov/scao/services/dirs/
county/Ontonagon%20County.html
Lori Seigneurie, Register
(probate records from formation)
probate search service: no charge; copies of
probate records: 25¢ per page, $3.00 certified

Osceola County
organized 1869 from Missaukee County

Osceola County Clerk
Courthouse, 301 West Upton Avenue
Reed City, MI 49677-1149
(231) 832-3261
oscclerk1@charterinternet.com
http://www.osceola-county.org/
County%20Departments/Clerk.htm
Karen J. Bluhm
(births from 1869, deaths from 1870, marriages
from 1869)
copies of vital records: $1.00 each, $7.00 for the
first certified copy and $3.00 for each
additional certified copy

Osceola County Register of Deeds
Courthouse, 301 West Upton Avenue
Reed City, MI 49677
(231) 832-6113
oscregister@chartermi.net
http://www.osceola-county.org/County%20
Departments/Register_Deeds.htm
Nancy Crawford

Osceola/Mecosta Probate District 18
410 West Upton Avenue
Reed City, MI 49677
(231) 832-6125
http://courts.michigan.gov/scao/services/dirs/
county/Osceola%220County.html
Linda Backus, Register

Oscoda County
organized 1840 from unorganized territory

Oscoda County Clerk
(311 Morenci Street—location)
PO Box 399 (mailing address)
Mio, MI 48647
(989) 826-1110
jwinton@oscodacountymi.com
http://www.oscodacountymi.com/Oscoda%20
County%20Clerk.htm
Jeri Winton
(naturalization records; deaths from July 1880,
marriages from April 1881 [index books are
very fragile])
vital records search service: $3.00; copies of vital
records: $1.00 (photocopies not available on
some prior to 1934 or 1942; information may
be hand-copied for some of these records),
$10.00 for the first certified copy and $2.00
for each additional certified copy

Oscoda County Probate Court
(Courthouse Annex, Court Street—location)
PO Box 399 (mailing address)
Mio, MI 48647
(989) 826-1107; (989) 826-1158 FAX
office@oscodacountyprobatecourt.com
http://www.oscodacountyprobatecourt.com
Cynthia L. Masterson, Register
no probate search service; certified copies of
probate records: $3.00 for the first copy and
$1.00 for each additional copy, no minimum

Oscoda County Register of Deeds
(311 Morenci Street—location)
PO Box 399 (mailing address)
Mio, MI 48647
(989) 826-1116; (989) 826-1136 FAX
registerofdeeds@oscodacountymi.com
http://www.oscodacountymi.com/Register%20
of%20Deeds.htm
Jeri Winton

Otsego County
organized 1875 from Crawford County

46th Circuit Trial Court
Alpine Center
800 Livingston Boulevard, Suite 1C
Gaylord, MI 49735
(989) 731-0204
http://www.circuit46.org; http://www.
otsegocountymi.gov/courts/courts.htm
Julie Chudzinski, Probate Register

Otsego County Clerk and Register of Deeds
225 West Main Street, Room 203
Gaylord, MI 49735-1348
(989) 731-7500 (Office); (989) 731-7504 (Clerk);
(989) 731-7551 (Register); (989) 731-7519
FAX
sdefeyter@otsegocountymi.gov
http://www.otsegocountymi.gov/clerk/clerk.htm;
http://www.otsegocountymi.gov/rod/rod.htm
Susan I. DeFeyter
(land records; deaths and marriages from 1875)
copies of vital records: $5.00 for the first copy
and $2.00 for each additional copy ("if a birth
record is requested, a document proving
death is required, unless it is obvious the
person is deceased")

Ottawa County
organized 29 December 1837 from part of Kent
County

Ottawa County Clerk
414 Washington Avenue, Room 301
Grand Haven, MI 49417-1443
(616) 846-8310; (616) 846-8138 FAX
countyclerk@co.ottawa.mi.us
http://www.co.ottawa.mi.us/CoGov/Clerk
Daniel C. Krueger
(naturalization records from 1910 to 1962,
deaths from 1867, marriages from 1848)
vital records search service: no charge; certified
copies of vital records: $10.00 for the first
copy and $3.00 for each additional copy made
at the same time (births open before 1908,
restricted after 1908)

Ottawa County Probate Court

12120 Fillmore Street
West Olive, MI 494601
(616) 786-4110; (616) 738-4624 FAX
pdewitt@co.ottawa.mi.us
http://www.co.ottawa.mi.us/CourtsLE/Probate
Ms. Penni A. Payne

Ottawa County Register of Deeds
(414 Washington Avenue, Room 305—location)
PO Box 265 (mailing address)
Grand Haven, MI 49417
(616) 846-8131
register@co.ottawa.mi.us
http://www.co.ottawa.mi.us/CoGov/ROD
Gary Scholten

Presque Isle County
organized 1840 from unorganized territory

Presque Isle County Clerk
(Courthouse, 151 East Huron Street—location)
PO Box 110 (mailing address)
Rogers City, MI 49779-1316
(989) 734-3288; (800) 334-5690; (989) 734-7635
FAX
presqueisle-co@miqvf.org
http://www.michigangov/hal/0,1607,7-160-
17449_18635_20736-56647--,00.html
Susan Rhode
(naturalization records, deaths and marriages
from 1871)
copies of vital records: $1.00 each, $5.00 for
certified copies ("ID is requested and whether
the researcher is a relative; birth record
viewing requires that the record be of a
deceased relative")

Presque Isle County Probate Court
Courthouse, 151 East Huron Street
Rogers City, MI 49779
(989) 734-3268
http://courts.michigan.gov/scao/services/dirs/
county/Presque%20Isle%20County.html
Ann Madsen, Register

Presque Isle County Register of Deeds
151 East Huron Street
Rogers City, MI 49779
(989) 734-2676
http://www.presqueislecounty.org
Cathy Idalski

Roscommon County
organized 1875 from Crawford County

**Roscommon County Clerk/Register of
Deeds**
Courthouse, 500 Lake Street
Roscommon, MI 48653-7690
(989) 275-5923 (Clerk); (989) 275-5931
(Register); (989) 275-8640 FAX
http://www.roscommoncounty.net/clerk.htm
Ann Bonk
(naturalization records, births and deaths from
1874, marriages from 1875)
copies of vital records: 50¢ per page, $5.00 for
the first certified copy and $2.00 for each
additional certified copy of same record
("must be able to relate facts relative to their
family—discuss the research, etc.")

Roscommon County Probate Court
County Building
500 Lake Street, Room 132
Roscommon, MI 48653
(989) 275-7675 (Register); (989) 275-4620
(Court); (989) 275-5221 (Probate Division);
(989) 275-8537 FAX
probatecourt@roscommoncounty.net
http://www.roscommoncounty.net/Courts/ho
me.htm
Linda Terrian
no probate search service; copies of probate
records: $3.00 for the first page and $1.00 for
each additional page, no minimum

Saginaw County
organized 1835 from unorganized territory

Saginaw County Clerk

Saginaw County Government Center
111 South Michigan Avenue, Room 101
Saginaw, MI 48602-2019
(989) 790-5251; (989) 790-5254 FAX
skaltenbach@saginawcounty.com
http://www.saginawcounty.com/Clerk/index.html
Susan Kaltenbach
(vital records)

Saginaw County Probate Court
Saginaw County Government Center
111 South Michigan Avenue
Saginaw, MI 48602
(989) 790-5320; (989) 790-5510 FAX
tbeagle@saginawcounty.com
http://www.saginawcounty.com/Probate/index
.htm
Ms. Terry Kluck Beagle, Register
copies of probate records: $1.00 per page

Saginaw County Register of Deeds
Saginaw County Government Center
111 South Michigan Avenue
Saginaw, MI 48602
(989) 790-5270; (989) 790-5278 FAX
http://www.saginawcounty.com/ROD/index.h
tml
Mildred M. Dodak

St. Clair County
organized 28 March 1820, original county

St. Clair County Clerk
County Building, 201 McMorran Boulevard,
Room 1100
Port Huron, MI 48060-4006
(810) 985-2200; (810) 985-4796 FAX
mdunn@stclaircounty.org
http://www.stclaircounty.org/Offices/clerk
Marilyn Dunn
(naturalization records from 1864 to 1985,
deaths from 1880, marriages from 1833)
certified copies of vital records: $5.00 each,
$2.00 for each additional copy of the same
record (requires "driver's license or other
pictured ID; must also fill out and sign form
entitled Procedures Governing the Inspection
of Vital Records Documents")

St. Clair County Probate Court
County Building, 201 McMorran Boulevard,
Room 2700
Port Huron, MI 48060
(810) 985-2066; (810) 985-2179 FAX
gnixon@stclaircounty.org
http://www.stclaircounty.org/Offices/courts
Mrs. Kelly Strozeski
probate search service: no charge; copies of
probate records: $1.00 each, $3.00 for the first
certified copy and $1.00 for each additional
certified copy (include "who, what, where,
when, if possible")

St. Clair County Register of Deeds
County Building, 201 McMorran Boulevard,
Suite 103
Port Huron, MI 48060
(810) 989-6930; (810) 985-4795 FAX
mdunn@stclaircounty.org;
registerofdeeds@stclaircounty.org
http://www.stclaircounty.org/Offices/register_
of_deeds
Marilyn Dunn
(land records from 1822 to date)
no land records search service; copies of land
records: $1.00 each

St. Joseph County
organized 1829 from Indian lands

St. Joseph County Clerk's Office
(125 West Main Street, Second Floor—location)
PO Box 189 (mailing address)
Centreville, MI 49032-0189
(269) 467-5602 (General Division); (269) 467-
5628 FAX
countyclerk@stjosephcountymi.org
http://www.stjosephcountymi.org/clerk.htm
Pattie S. Bender
(naturalization records from 1850s to 1860s,

births and deaths from 1867, marriages from 1830)

vital records search service: $10.00 for a ten-year search (includes one copy); copies of naturalization records: $1.00 per page (cannot be certified); copies of vital records: $3.00 for each additional copy made at the same time (births are restricted to the registrant or to properly identified heirs of deceased registrants)

St. Joseph County Probate Court
(Courthouse, 125 Main—location)
PO Box 190 (mailing address)
Centreville, MI 49032
(269) 467-5500 (Register); (269) 467-5538 (Court); (269) 467-5560 FAX
http://www.stjosephcountymi.org/cprobate.htm
Eva R. Sylvester, Register

St. Joseph County Register of Deeds
(125 West Main Street, Second Floor—location)
PO Box 388 (mailing address)
Centreville, MI 49032
(269) 467-5552; (269) 467-5593 FAX
rod@stjosephcountymi.org
http://www.stjosephcountymi.org/deeds
Cynthia L. Jarratt

Sanilac County

executive proclamation of 28 March 1820 proclaimed the county's boundaries, then attached to Oakland County and later to St. Clair County and included part of Huron County

Sanilac County Clerk
Courthouse, 60 West Sanilac Avenue, Room 203
Sandusky, MI 48471-1094
(810) 648-3212; (810) 648-5466 FAX
lkozfkay@voyager.net
http://www.sanilaccounty.net/clerk
Linda I. Kozfkay
(births, deaths and marriages from 1867)
copies of vital records: $5.00 each, $10.00 for the first certified copy and $3.00 for each additional certified copy (with proper identification, births restricted to those over 100 years old)

Sanilac County Probate Court
Courthouse, 60 West Sanilac Avenue, Room 106
Sandusky, MI 48471
(810) 648-3221; (810) 648-2900 FAX
http://www.sanilaccounty.net/office.asp?id=probatecou
Sandra J. Schlaud

Sanilac County Register of Deeds
(Courthouse, 60 West Sanilac Avenue—location)
PO Box 168 (mailing address)
Sandusky, MI 48471
(810) 648-2313; (810) 648-5461 FAX
http://www.sanilaccounty.net/office.asp?id=registerof
Michele VanNorman

Schoolcraft County

organized 9 March 1843 from Michilimackinac and Chippewa counties

Schoolcraft/Alger Probate District 5
Courthouse, 300 Walnut Street, Room 129
Manistique, MI 49854
(906) 341-3641
http://www.manistique.org/government/countyofficials.html
Beth A. Edwards

Schoolcraft County Clerk/Register of Deeds
Courthouse, 300 Walnut Street, Room 164
Manistique, MI 49854-1414
(906) 341-3618; (906) 341-5680
http://www.manistique.org/government/countyofficials.html
Sigrid Doyle
(births and deaths from about 1867, marriages from 1849)
copies of vital records: $10.00 for the first copy and $3.00 for each additional copy (births

restricted to researchers who are able to document their relationship to a deceased registrant)

Shiawassee County

organized 1822 from Indian lands

Shiawassee County Clerk
Courthouse, 208 North Shiawassee Street
Corunna, MI 48817
(989) 743-2242; (989) 743-2241 FAX
clerk@shiawassee.net
http://www.shiawassee.net/Clerk1.htm
Lauri L. Braid
(naturalization records from 1867, vital records from 1867)
probate search service: no charge; copies of probate records: $1.00 per page

Shiawassee County Probate Court
Shiawassee County Courts Building
110 East Mack Street
Corunna, MI 48817
(989) 743-2211; (989) 743-2349 FAX
http://www.shiawassee.net/dirnoframe.htm
Claudia Howdyshell, Register
(probate records from 1836)

Shiawassee County Register of Deeds
Courthouse, 208 North Shiawassee Street
Corunna, MI 48817
(989) 743-2374; (989) 743-2459 FAX
rod@shiawassee.net
http://www.shiawassee.net/dirnoframe.htm
Lori Kimble
(land records from 1836)

Tuscola County

organized 1851 from Saginaw County

Tuscola County Clerk
Courthouse, 440 North State Street
Caro, MI 48723-1555
(989) 672-3780; (989) 672-4266 FAX
white-cormier@tuscolacounty.org
http://www.tuscolacounty.org/clerk
Margie A. White-Cormier
(naturalization records from 1852, births [not public] and deaths from 1867, marriages from 1852)
probate search service: no charge; copies of land records: $1.00 per page; no copies of naturalization records available; certified copies of vital records: $10.00 each, $3.00 for verification of records; copies of probate records: $1.00 per page

Tuscola County Probate Court
Courthouse, 440 North State Street
Caro, MI 48723
(989) 672-3850
http://www.tuscolacounty.org/probate%20court
Kerri Zelmer

Tuscola County Register of Deeds
Courthouse, 440 North State Street
Caro, MI 48723
(989) 672-3840
gmclaren@tuscolacounty.org
http://www.tuscolacounty.org/deeds
Virginia "Ginny" McLaren
(land records from 1852)

Van Buren County

organized 1829 from unorganized territory

Van Buren County Clerk
Courthouse Annex, 212 East Paw Paw Street
Paw Paw, MI 49079-1496
(269) 657-8218; (269) 657-7573 FAX; (269) 657-8298 FAX
http://www.vbco.org/government0102.asp
Christine Leary
(naturalization records from 1846 [very limited], births and deaths from 1867, marriages from 1836)
vital records search service: $1.00 per liber per name; probate search service: no charge; certified copies of vital records: $7.00 for the first copy and $3.00 for each additional copy

made at the same time (must present picture ID, births available only to the registrant, parents, guardian or legal representative or heir of deceased)

Van Buren County Probate Court
Courthouse Annex, Second Floor
212 East Paw Paw Street
Paw Paw, MI 49079
(269) 657-8225
http://www.vbco.org/government0112.asp
Barbara A. Dundon, Register
(probate records from 1839)
copies of probate records: $1.00 per page from microfilm, no minimum

Van Buren County Register of Deeds
Courthouse, 219 Paw Paw Street, Suite 102
Paw Paw, MI 49079
(269) 657-8242; (269) 657-0674 FAX
smithm@vbco.org
http://www.vbco.org/government0104.asp
Mark Smith
(land records from 1836)

Washtenaw County

organized 1826, original county

Washtenaw County Clerk/Register of Deeds
(200 North Main, Suite 110—location)
PO Box 8645 (mailing address)
Ann Arbor, MI 48107-8645
(734) 222-6700; (734) 222-6720 (Vital Records, Suite 100); (734) 222-6710 (Register); (734) 222-6528 FAX; (734) 222-6719 FAX
http://www.ewashtenaw.org/government/clerk_register/index_html
Lawrence Kestenbaum
(land records from 1824, deaths from 1867 to date, marriages from 1833 through 1969 for genealogy)
vital records search service: $3.00 minimum for five-years search (includes a single copy, if found); copies of vital records: $10.00 for the first copy and $3.00 for each additional copy made at the same time (all births and records from 1970 to date are confidential and require current ID, verification of legitimate interest and a certified copy of a death certificate in the case of requests for birth records)

Washtenaw County Probate Court
(Courthouse, 101 East Huron, Room 314—location)
PO Box 8645 (mailing address)
Ann Arbor, MI 48107-8645
(734) 222-3072 (Court); (734) 222-3039 (Register); (734) 222-3019 FAX
carabeck4@ewashtenaw.org
http://www.washtenawtrialcourt.org/probate/index_html
Robert Carbeck
(probate records from 1828)
probate search service: no charge; copies of probate records: $10.00 for the first page and $1.00 for each additional page

Wayne County

organized 15 August 1796, original county

Wayne County City-County Building
Coleman A. Young Municipal Center
2 Woodward Avenue
Detroit, MI 48226-3413
(313) 224-0286 (County Executive)

Wayne County Clerk
Coleman A. Young Municipal Center
2 Woodward Avenue, Room 201
Detroit, MI 48226
(313) 224-6262; (313) 224-5364 FAX
http://www.waynecounty.com/clerk
Cathy M. Garrett
(births, deaths from 1867 to 1820 and from 1920 to date for all areas of the county except Detroit; deaths from 1930 to 1983 on microfiche with Detroit City [anything before or after requires staff search])
vital records search service: $3.00; copies of vital records: $17.00 for the first certified copy and

Minnesota

147

$3.50 for each additional certified copy, $11.50 for uncertified marriages (births restricted to the person named, their parent or legal guardian)

Wayne County Probate Court
1305 Coleman A. Young Municipal Center
2 Woodward Avenue
Detroit, MI 48226
(313) 224-5706
jsoliman@wcpc.us
http://www.wcpc.us (click on Public Access)
Jeanne S. Takenaga, Register
probate records search service: $3.00; copies of probate records: $2.00 per page, no minimum

Wayne County Register of Deeds
International Center Building
400 Monroe Street, Seventh Floor
Detroit, MI 48226
(313) 224-5854; (313) 224-5884 FAX
http://www.waynecounty.com/register/default.htm
Bernard J. Youngblood

Wexford County
organized 1840 from unorganized territory

Wexford County Clerk
(Courthouse, 437 East Division Street—location)
PO Box 490 (mailing address)
Cadillac, MI 49601
(616) 779-9450; (231) 779-0447 FAX
clerk@wexfordcounty.org
http://wexfordcounty.org/services_clerk.php
Elaine L. Richardson
(some naturalization records from about 1850 [but they are hard to find], births, deaths and marriages)
vital records search service: $5.00 for a three-year search and $2.00 for each additional year; copies of vital records: $1.00 for deaths from 1934 or marriages from 1920, $10.00 for certified copies prior to those dates, births restricted to the individual named, parents, or heirs with proof

Wexford County Probate Court
Courthouse, 437 East Division Street
Cadillac, MI 49601
(231) 779-9510; (231) 779-9511; (231) 779-9485 FAX
http://www.wexfordcounty.org/courts_probate.php
Tammy Wenn
no probate search service; copies of probate records: $1.00 per page, $10.00 for certified copies, no minimum

Wexford County Register of Deeds
Courthouse, 437 East Division Street
Cadillac, MI 49601
(231) 779-9455; (231) 779-9458; (231) 779-0292 FAX
register@wexfordcounty.org
http://wexfordcounty.org/services_deeds.php
Lori L. Sorensen-Smith

MINNESOTA

Capital: St. Paul. Statehood: 11 May 1858 (part annexed in 1783 and part by the Louisiana Purchase, 1803, was in the Northwest Territory in 1787, Indiana Territory in 1800, and became a separate territory in 1849)

Minnesota's County and Municipal Courts were eliminated by 1987, having merged with the District Court, which has general jurisdiction and sits in each county seat. First Judicial District: Carver, Dakota, Goodhue, Le Sueur, McLeod, Scott and Sibley counties; Second Judicial District: Ramsey County; Third Judicial District: Dodge, Fillmore, Freeborn, Houston, Mower, Olmsted, Rice, Steele, Wabasha, Waseca and Winona counties; Fourth Judicial District: Hennepin County; Fifth Judicial District: Blue Earth, Brown, Cottonwood, Faribault, Jackson, Lincoln, Lyon, Martin, Murray, Nicollet, Nobles, Pipestone, Redwood, Rock and Watonwan counties; Sixth Judicial District: Carlton, Cook, Lake and St. Louis counties; Seventh Judicial District: Becker, Benton, Clay, Douglas, Mille Lacs, Morrison, Otter Tail, Stearns, Todd and Wadena counties; Eighth Judicial District: Big Stone, Chippewa, Grant, Kandiyohi, Lac qui Parle, Meeker, Pope, Renville, Stevens, Swift, Traverse, Wilkin and Yellow Medicine counties; Ninth Judicial District: Aitkin, Beltrami, Cass, Clearwater, Crow Wing, Hubbard, Itasca, Kittson, Koochiching, Lake of the Woods, Mahnomen, Marshall, Norman, Pennington, Polk, Red Lake and Roseau counties; Tenth Judicial District: Anoka, Chisago, Isanti, Kanabec, Pine, Sherburne, Washington and Wright counties. The Court of Appeals and Supreme Court hear appeals.

Aitkin County
organized 1857 from Cass and Itasca counties

Aitkin County Court Administrator
209 Second Street, N.W., Room 242
Aitkin, MN 56431-1257
(218) 927-7350
bonnie.lecocq@courts.state.mn.us
http://www.co.aitkin.mn.us
Bonnie LeCocq
(naturalization records, marriages, probate records)
probate search service: $8.00 per hour; copies of probate records: $5.00 per document, $10.00 per certified document

Aitkin County Recorder
209 Second Street, N.W., Room 205
Aitkin, MN 56431
(218) 927-7336; (218) 927-7324 FAX
dlafferty@co.aitkin.mn.us
http://www.co.aitkin.mn.us/departments/Recorder/recorder.htm
Diane Lafferty
(land records, births and deaths)

Anoka County
organized 1857 from Hennepin County, annexed Manomin County in 1869

Anoka County Court Administrator
Attention: File Room, First Floor, East Wing
Courthouse, 325 East Main Street
Anoka, MN 55303-2489
(763) 422-7350; (763) 422-6919 FAX
http://www.co.anoka.mn.us/departments/courts
Jane Morrow
(marriage records, probate records)
copies: $5.00 per document, $10.00 if certified

Anoka County Property Records and Taxation
Anoka County Government Center
2100 Third Avenue
Anoka, MN 55303-2281
(763) 323-5400; (763) 323-5415 (Recorder); (763) 323-5421 FAX

proptax@co.anoka.mn.us;
larry.dalien@co.anoka.mn.us
http://www.co.anoka.mn.us/v1_departments/div-property-rec-tax/index.asp
Maureen Devine, Division Manager; Larry Dalien, Recorder
(carries out the duties of the offices of the Auditor, Treasurer, Assessor, Registrar of Titles, and Recorder; land records, births and deaths)

Becker County
organized 1858 from Indian lands

Becker County Court Administrator
(Courthouse, 913 Lake Avenue, Third Floor—location)
PO Box 787 (mailing address)
Detroit Lakes, MN 56502
(218) 846-7305; (218) 847-7620 FAX
janice.cossette@courts.state.mn.us
http://www.co.becker.mn.us/court_administrator/d_court_administrator.html
Janice Cossette
(marriage records, probate records)
probate search service: no charge; copies of probate records: 25¢ per page (if court order), $3.50 for the first page and 25¢ for each additional page, $5.00 for the first certified page and 25¢ for each additional certified page, no minimum

Becker County Recorder
(Courthouse, 913 Lake Avenue, Second Floor—location)
PO Box 595 (mailing address)
Detroit Lakes, MN 56502
(218) 846-7304; (218) 846-7323 FAX
damanev@co.becker.mn.us
http://www.co.becker.mn.us/recorder/d_recorder.html
Darlene Maneval
(land records, births and deaths)

Beltrami County
organized 1866 from unorganized territory

Beltrami County Court Administrator
Courthouse Annex, 619 Beltrami Avenue, N.W., First Floor
Bemidji, MN 56601-3068
(218) 333-4120; (218) 333-8431
cindy.ebbighausen@courts.state.mn.us
http://www.co.beltrami.mn.us/Departments/court%20administration.html
Cindy Ebbighausen
(naturalization records and probate records)

Beltrami County Recorder
Administration Building, First Floor
701 Minnesota Avenue, N.W., Suite 120
Bemidji, MN 56601-3177
(218) 759-4170; (218) 333-8427; (218) 759-4171 FAX
ann.allen@co.beltrami.mn.us
http://www.co.beltrami.mn.us/departments/recorder
Ann F. Allen
(land records, births and deaths)

Benton County
organized 1849, original county

Benton County Court Administrator
(615 Highway 23—location)
PO Box 189 (mailing address)
Foley, MN 56329
(320) 968-5205; (320) 968-5353 FAX
http://www.co.benton.mn.us/departments/court_admin/courtadmin.htm
Timothy Roberts

Benton County Recorder
PO Box 129
Foley, MN 56329
(320) 968-5037; (320) 968-5329 FAX
mnovak@co.benton.mn.us
http://www.co.benton.mn.us/departments/recorder
Marilyn J. Novak

(land records, births and deaths)

Big Stone County

organized 1862 from Pierce County (which was abolished the same year)

Big Stone County Court Administrator
20 S.E. Second Street
Ortonville, MN 56278-1544
(320) 839-2536; (320) 839-2537 FAX
Roger.Strand@courts.state.mn.us
http://www.mncourts.gov/district/8/?page=205
Roger Strand
(marriages from 1881, probate records from 1881)
probate search service: $8.00 per hour; copies of probate records: $3.50 plus 25¢ per page, $8.00 minimum

Big Stone County Recorder
PO Box 218
Ortonville, MN 56278
(320) 839-2308 voice & FAX
gloria_a@co.big-stone.mn.us
http://www.bigstonecounty.org
Gloria Arndt
(land records, births and deaths from 1881)

Blue Earth County

organized 1853 from unorganized territory

Blue Earth County Court Administrator
(Courthouse, 204 South Fifth Street—location)
PO Box 0347 (mailing address)
Mankato, MN 56002-0347
(507) 304-4050: (507) 304-4437 FAX
http://www.co.blue-earth.mn.us/dept/courts.php
Judy Besemer

Blue Earth County Recorder
PO Box 8608
Mankato, MN 56002-8608
(507) 389-8802; (507) 389-8808 FAX
patty.oconnor@co.blue-earth.mn.us
http://www.co.blue-earth.mn.us/dept/recording.php3
Patty O'Connor
(land records, births and deaths)

Brown County

organized 1855 from Nicollet County

Brown County Court Administrator
(Courthouse, 14 South State Street—location)
PO Box 248 (mailing address)
New Ulm, MN 56073-0248
(507) 233-6670; (507) 359-9562 FAX
http://www.co.brown.mn.us/Departments/Crt house/CrtAdmn/crtadm.htmhttp://www.mn courts.gov/district/5/?page=1479
Carol Melick
(probate records)
probate search service: $10.00 per hour (supply dates to be searched); copies of probate records: $5.00 each, $10.00 for certified copies, $10.00 minimum

Brown County Recorder
(Courthouse, 14 South State Street—location)
PO Box 248 (mailing address)
New Ulm, MN 56073
(507) 233-6653 (Land Records); (507) 223-6657 (Vital Records); (507) 359-1430 FAX
tom.weilage@co.brown.mn.us; recorder@co.brown.mn.us
http://www.co.brown.mn.us/Departments/Crt house/Recordr/record.htm
Tom Weilage
(land records, births and deaths from 1870 [prior records destroyed by fire])

Carlton County

organized 1857 from Pine County

Carlton County Court Administrator
(Courthouse, 301 Walnut Street—location)
PO Box 190 (mailing address)
Carlton, MN 55718-0190
(218) 384-4281; (800) 862-3760; (218) 384-9182

FAX
http://www.mncourts.gov/district/6/?page=208
Bruce Ahlgren
(naturalization records, vital records, and probate records)

Carlton County Recorder
(Courthouse, 301 Walnut Street—location)
PO Box 70 (mailing address)
Carlton, MN 55718
(218) 384-9195; (218) 384-9157 FAX
kris.basilici@co.carlton.mn.us
http://www.co.carlton.mn.us/Recorder.htm
Kris Basilici
(land records, births and deaths)

Carver County

organized 1855 from Hennepin County

Carver County Court Administrator
Carver County Justice Center
604 East Fourth Street
Chaska, MN 55318
(952) 361-1420; (952) 361-1491 FAX
http://www.co.carver.mn.us/ElectedOfficials/ Courts/CourtAdmin/index
Carolyn M. Renn

Carver County Recorder
Government Center
Administration Building
600 East Fourth Street
Chaska, MN 55318-2158
(952) 361-1930; (952) 361-1934; (952) 361-1931 FAX
khanson@co.carver.mn.us
http://www.co.carver.mn.us/ElectedOfficials/ Recorder/index.html
Carl W. (Kelly) Hanson
(land records, births and deaths)

Cass County

organized 1851, original county

Cass County Court Administrator
(Courthouse, 300 Minnesota Avenue, Second Floor—location)
PO Box 3000 (mailing address)
Walker, MN 56484
(218) 547-7200
http://www.co.cass.mn.us/court_admin/court_ admin_home.html
Amy Turnquist
(naturalization filing cards; marriages from 1900 [only a few recorded before 1900]; probate records from 1896)
probate search service: a minimum of $5.00 per hour; copies of marriages: $8.00; copies of probate records: $3.50 for the first page and 25¢ for each additional page, $5.00 for the first certified page and 25¢ for each additional certified page

Cass County Recorder
(Courthouse, 300 Minnesota Avenue, Second Floor—location)
PO Box 3000 (mailing address)
Walker, MN 56484
(218) 547-7381; (218) 547-7292 FAX
cass.recorders@co.cass.mn.us
http://www.co.cass.mn.us
Kathryn Norby
(land records from 1887, births and deaths from 1900 [only a few recorded before 1900])
copies of land records: $1.00 per page, $1.00 per page for certified copies, $3.00 minimum; copies of vital records: $11.00 for births, $8.00 for deaths

Chippewa County

organized 1870 from Pierce County (which was abolished in 1862)

Chippewa County Court Administrator
629 North 11th Street
Montevideo, MN 56265
(320) 269-7774; (320) 269-7733 FAX
Cheryl.Eckhardt@courts.state.mn.us
http://www.mncourts.gov/district/8/?page=206
Cheryl Eckhardt

(probate records from 1870)
probate search service: $10.00 per hour ("if it's just a few names, there are no charges; please give us as much information on the parties as they have [father's name, mother's *maiden* name, etc.]")

Chippewa County Recorder
629 11th Street
Montevideo, MN 56265
(320) 269-9431; (320) 269-7168 FAX
jlenning@co.chippewa.mn.us
http://www.co.chippewa.mn.us/recorder.htm
Jan Lenning
(land records from 1870; births, deaths and marriages from 1870)
copies of vital records: $11.00 for births, $8.00 for deaths and marriages

Chisago County

organized 1851 from Washington County

Chisago County Court Administrator
(Chisago County Courthouse, 313 North Main Street—location)
PO Box 126 (mailing address)
Center City, MN 55012
(651) 213-8650
chisagocounty.districtcourt@courts.state.mn.us
http://www.mncourts.gov/district/10/?page=925
Kathleen Karnowski
(births and deaths from 1870, marriages from 1852 with County Court Administrator, Vital Statistics Division, probate records from 1864 with County Court Administrator, Genealogy Division)
probate search service: $10.00 per hour for genealogy; copies of vital records: $11.00 for births, $8.00 for deaths and marriages; copies of probate records: $3.50 for the first page and 25¢ for each additional page, $5.00 for the first certified page and 25¢ for each additional certified page ("Payment must be received with request")

Chisago County Recorder
Chisago County Courthouse
313 North Main Street
Center City, MN 55012
(651) 213-8580; (651) 213-8581 FAX
tgfisko@co.chisago.mn.us
http://www.co.chisago.mn.us
Thora G. Fisko
(land records)

Clay County

organized 9 March 1862; name changed from Breckenridge County in 1862

Clay County Court Administrator
807 11th Street North
Moorhead, MN 56560
(218) 299-5065; (218) 299-7307 FAX
janice.cossette@courts.state.mn.us
http://www.mncourts.gov/district/7/?page=471
Janice Cossette
(probate records)
probate search service: no charge if approximate year is given; copies of probate records: $5.00 per document, $10.00 per certified document

Clay County Recorder
PO Box 280
Moorhead, MN 56560
(218) 299-5031; (218) 299-7500 FAX
bonnie.rehder@co.day.mn.us
http://www.co.clay.mn.us/Depts/Recorder/Re corder.htm
J. Bonnie Rehder
(land records, vital records)
copies of vital records: $11.00 for births, $8.00 for deaths and marriages

Clearwater County

organized 1902 from Beltrami County

Clearwater County Court Administrator
Courthouse, Third Floor
213 Main Avenue N, Department 303
Bagley, MN 56621

(218) 694-6177; (218) 694-6213 FAX
http://www.co.clearwater.mn.us/Government/
deptlist/CourtAdminHome.aspx
Darlene Gerbracht

Clearwater County Recorder
Courthouse, Second Floor
213 Main Avenue North, Department 207
Bagley, MN 56621-8304
(218) 694-6129; (218) 694-6179 FAX
allen.paulson@co.clearwater.mn.us
http://www.co.clearwater.mn.us/Government/
deptlist/RecorderHome.aspx
Allen Paulson
(land records, births and deaths)

Cook County
organized 1874 from Lake County

Cook County Court Administrator
411 West Second Street
Grand Marais, MN 55604
(218) 387-3610; (218) 387-3007 FAX
larry.saur@courts.state.mn.us
http://www.co.cook.mn.us/courts/index.html
Larry J. Saur
(probate records from 1896)
and probate records search service: $10.00 per
hour; copies of probate records: $5.00 each,
$10.00 for certified copies

Cook County Recorder
411 West Secon Street
Grand Marais, MN 55604
(218) 387-3000; (218) 387-3043 FAX
dusty.nelms@co.cook.mn.us
http://www.co.cook.mn.us/recorder.html
Dusty Nelms
(land records, vital records from 1900)
vital records search service: $10.00 per hour;
copies of vital records: $11.00 for certified
births, $8.00 for certified deaths and
marriages and uncertified births

Cottonwood County
organized 1857 from Brown County

Cottonwood County Court Administrator
(900 Third Avenue, Windom, MN 56101-
1645—location)
PO Box 97 (mailing address)
Windom, MN 56101-0097
(507) 831-4551; (507) 831-1425 FAX
http://www.co.cottonwood.mn.us/countyadmi
nistrator.html
Cheryl Peters

Cottonwood County Recorder
(900 Third Avenue, Room 6—location)
PO Box 326 (mailing address)
Windom, MN 56101
(507) 831-1458; (507) 831-3675 FAX
http://www.rrcnet.org/~cotton/cotrec.html
Mary Ann Anderson
(land records, births and deaths)

Crow Wing County
organized 1857 from Cass and Aitkin counties

Crow Wing County Court Administrator
326 Laurel Street
Brainerd, MN 56401
(218) 824-1310; (218) 824-1311 FAX
http://www.mncourts.gov/district/9/?page=664
Darrell Paske
(probate records)
no probate search service; copies of probate
records: $5.00 per document, $10.00 per
certified document

Crow Wing County Recorder
PO Box 383
Brainerd, MN 56401
(218) 824-1280; (218) 824-1281 FAX
kathyl@co.crow-wing.mn.us
http://www.co.crow-
wing.mn.us/Recorder/recorder.htm
Kathy Ludenia
(land records, births and deaths)

Dakota County
organized 1849, original county, formerly called
Dakotah County

Dakota County Court Administrator
Dakota County Judicial Center
1560 Highway 55 West
Hastings, MN 55033-2343
(651) 438-8100
Dakota@courts.state.mn.us
http://www.mncourts.gov/district/1/?page=549
Van A. Brostrom
(probate records with District Court, Division 1)
no probate search service; copies of probate
records: $3.50 for the first page and 25¢ for
each additional page, $5.00 for the first
certified page and 25¢ for each additional
certified page, $3.50 minimum

Dakota County Recorder
1590 West Highway 55
Hastings, MN 55033
(612) 438-4319 (Vital Statistics Department);
(651) 438-4329; (651) 438-8176 FAX
joel.beckman@co.dakota.mn.us
http://www.co.dakota.mn.us/property_records
/index.htm
Joel Beckmann
(land records with Recorder; births, deaths and
marriages from 1870, with a very few
marriages before 1870 with Vital Statistics
Department)
vital records search service: $10.00 per hour;
copies of vital records: $11.00 for certified
copies of births, $8.00 for certified or
uncertified copies of deaths and marriages or
uncertified copies of births, or for verification
of information (make checks payable to
Dakota County Treasurer-Auditor)

Dodge County
organized 1855 from Olmstead County

Dodge County Court Administrator
22 East Sixth Street, Department 12
Mantorville, MN 55955-2220
(507) 635-6260; (507) 635-6271 FAX
dodge.admin@co.dodge.mn.us
http://www.co.dodge.mn.us/html/depts/court
_adm.html
Annette Hodge
(naturalization records, vital records, and
probate records)
probate search service: no charge unless lengthy;
copies of probate records: 25¢ per page for
the first ten pages and 10¢ for each additional
page, no minimum

Dodge County Recorder
PO ox 128
Mantorville, MN 55955
(507) 635-6250; (507) 635-6255 FAX
sue.alberts@co.dodge.mn.us
http://www.co.dodge.mn.us/html/depts/recor
der.html
Sue A. Alberts
(land records, births and deaths)

Doty County
(see Lake and St. Louis counties)

Douglas County
organized 1858 from Todd County

Douglas County Court Administrator
Courthouse, 305 Eighth Avenue West, First
Floor
Alexandria, MN 56308-1759
(320) 762-3033; (320) 762-3882; (320) 762-8863
FAX
http://www.co.douglas.mn.us/court_admin.htm
Rhonda Russell
(probate records)
probate search service: no charge; copies of
probate records: variable from 50¢ to $3.50,
50¢ minimum

Douglas County Recorder
Courthouse, 305 Eighth Avenue West
Alexandria, MN 56308

(320) 762-3839; (320) 762-2389 FAX
darlene.chermak@mail.co.douglass.mn.us
http://www.co.douglas.mn.us/recorder.htm
Darlene Chermak
(land records, births and deaths)

Faribault County
organized 1855 from Blue Earth County

Faribault County Court Administrator
(Courthouse, 415 North Main—location)
PO Box 130 (mailing address)
Blue Earth, MN 56013
(507) 526-6273; (507) 526-3054 FAX
http://www.mncourts.gov/district/5/?page=1481
Lori Goodrich
(naturalization records from 1880s to 1920s,
vital records and probate records)
probate search service: no charge; copies of
probate records: $3.50 plus 25¢ per page, no
minimum

Faribault County Recorder
(Courthouse, 415 North Main—location)
PO Box 130 (mailing address)
Blue Earth, MN 56013
(507) 526-6253; (507) 526-5272 FAX
nancy.huff@state.mn.us
http://faribaultcountyrecorder.com
Nancy Huff
(land records)

Fillmore County
organized 1853, original county

Fillmore County Court Administrator
(101 Fillmore Street—location)
PO Box 436 (mailing address)
Preston, MN 55965
(507) 765-3356; (507) 765-4571 FAX
http://www.mncourts.gov/district/3/?page=218
James Attwood
(probate records)
probate search service: no charge for index
search but a 50¢ charge for each register
needed

Fillmore County Recorder
PO Box 465
Preston, MN 55965
(507) 765-3852; (507) 765-4571 FAX
mensink@co.fillmore.mn.us
http://www.co.fillmore.mn.us/Departments.htm
Richard W. Mensink
(land records, births and deaths)

Freeborn County
organized 1855 from Blue Earth and Rice
counties

Freeborn County Court Administrator
(411 South Broadway—location)
PO Box 1147 (mailing address)
Albert Lea, MN 56007-1147
(507) 377-5153; (507) 377-5260 FAX
kristine.maiers@courts.state.mn.us
http://www.co.freeborn.mn.us/crtadmin.html
Kristine Maiers
(vital records from 1870 to date; probate
records)

Freeborn County Recorder
PO Box 1147
Albert Lea, MN 56007-1147
(507) 377-5130; (507) 377-5175 FAX
kelly.callahan@co.freeborn.mn.us
http://www.co.freeborn.mn.us/recorder.html
Kelly Callahan
(land records)

Goodhue County
organized with indefinite boundaries on 5 March
1853 from Wabasha County; after the
government survey of the greater part of the
county was completed, the boundaries were
defined in 1854; the Half Breed Tract,
however, had not been included in the survey,
and it was later found that the starting point
of the boundaries described in the act was in
Wisconsin, a few miles northeast of

Frontenac; in general, the boundary was as at present, except that Central Point Township was excluded, and the line between Welch Township in Goodhue County and Douglas Township in Dakota County was extended due north to the Mississippi River a few miles southeast of Hastings; the present boundaries were defined in 1855; a bill was introduced in the Legislature in 1858 to detach part of Goodhue, Olmsted and Wabasha counties and to form a new county to be called Zumbrota; a committee to which it was referred made an unfavorable report, and the bill was never brought to a vote; in 1861 the voters defeated a proposition to attach that part of Cannon Falls Township north of the Cannon River to Dakota County

Goodhue County Court Administrator
Goodhue County Justice Center
454 West Sixth Street
Red Wing, MN 55066
(651) 267-4800; (651) 267-4810 (Probate); (651) 267-4989 FAX
http://www.mncourts.gov/district/1/?page=610
Yvonne Black
(probate records; marriages)
no probate search service; copies of probate records: 25¢ per page, no minimum

Goodhue County Recorder
Goodhue County Government Center
509 West Fifth Street
Red Wing, MN 55066
(651) 385-3152 (Register of Deeds); (651) 385-3148 (Vitals); (651) 385-3022 FAX
http://www.co.goodhue.mn.us/recorder.html
Lisa M. Hanni
(land records, births and deaths)

Grant County
organized 1868 from Stearns County

Grant County Court Administrator
(Grant County Courthouse—location)
PO Box 1007 (mailing address)
Elbow Lake, MN 56531
(218) 685-4825; (218) 685-5349 FAX
http://www.mncourts.gov/district/8/?page=1052
Diane K. Fox
(vital records, probate records)
probate search service: $2.00 per name; copies of probate records: $5.00

Grant County Recorder
10 Second Street N.E.
Elbow Lake, MN 56531-4300
(218) 685-4133; (218) 685-4521 FAX
patti.nordby@co.grant.mn.us;
recorder@co.grant.mn.us
http://www.co.grant.mn.us/licensing.asp#recorder
Patti Nordby
(land records)

Hennepin County
organized 1852, original county

Hennepin County Court Records Center
Hennepin County Government Center
300 South Sixth Street, B-Level
Minneapolis, MN 55487-0999
(612) 348-3244 (Clerk of Probate Court, C-400); 9612) 348-3170 (Records Center)
http://www.mncourts.gov/district/4/?page=374 (Probate); http://www.mncourts.gov/district/6/?page=1748 (Records Center)
Mary Hawkinson, Clerk of Probate Court
(probate records [on microfiche] from 1859)
probate search service: no charge; copies of probate records: 50¢ per page, $7.00 for certified copies (includes nine pages), no minimum

Hennepin County Recorder
A-803 Government Center
Minneapolis, MN 55487-0060
(612) 348-3893; (612) 348-3051 (County Recorder); (612) 348-3070 (Registrar of Titles); (612) 348-2791 (Vital Records

Section); (612) 348-4948 FAX
michael.cunniff@co.hennepin.mn.us
http://www.co.hennepin.mn.us/vgn/portal/internet/hcdetailmaster/0,2300,1273_100015559_100373069,00.html;
http://www.co.hennepin.mn.us/taxsvcs/gstxmain.htm
Michael H. Cunniff
(land records with Property Tax and Public Records Department, County Recorder [Abstract], A-803 or Registrar of Titles [Torrens], A-803; births and deaths, marriage licenses, ministerial credentials and notary filings with Vital Records Section, Public Service Level)

Houston County
organized 1854 from Fillmore County

Houston County Court Administrator
304 South Marshall Street, Room 204
Caledonia, MN 55921-1324
(507) 724-5806; (507) 724-5550 FAX
Darlene.Kuhlers@courts.state.mn.us
http://www.houstoncounty.govoffice2.com
Darlene Kuhlers
(probate records)
probate search service: $10.00 per hour; certified copies of probate records: $5.00 per document (includes search), $10.00 per certified document (includes search)

Houston County Recorder
PO Box 29
Caledonia, MN 55921-0029
(507) 725-5813; (507) 725-2647 FAX
bev.bauer@co.houston.mn.us
http://www.houstoncounty.govoffice2.com
Beverly J. Bauer
(land records, births and deaths)
land records and vital records search service: $20.00 per hour; copies of land records: 50¢ per page, $1.00 per certified page, $5.00 minimum; copies of vital records: $11.00 for births, $8.00 for deaths

Hubbard County
organized 1883 from Cass County

Hubbard County Court Administrator
(Courthouse, 301 Court Avenue, Park Rapids, MN 56470-1483—location)
PO Box 72 (mailing address)
Park Rapids, MN 56470
(218) 732-5286; (218) 732-0137 FAX
http://www.mncourts.gov/district/9/?page=665
Darlene Gerbracht
(probate records)

Hubbard County Recorder
Courthouse, 301 Court Avenue
Park Rapids, MN 56470
(218) 732-3552; (218) 732-3645 FAX
nlueth@co.hubbard.mn.us
http://www.co.hubbard.mn.us/Recorder.htm
Nicole K. Lueth
(land records, vital records)

Isanti County
organized 1857 from Anoka County

Isanti County Court Administrator
555 18th Avenue S.W.
Cambridge, MN 55008
(763) 689-2292
http://www.mncourts.gov/district/10/?page=926
Sue LaBore
(probate records from 1873)
probate search service: $10.00 per hour; copies of probate records: depends on document length; $2.50 minimum for name search

Isanti County Recorder
503–555 18th Avenue, S.W.
Cambridge, MN 55008
(763) 689-1191; (763) 689-8226 FAX
karen.anderson@co.isanti.mn.us
http://www.co.isanti.mn.us/recorder.htm
Karen D. Anderson
(land records from 1860s, vital records from

1870s)
copies of vital records: $11.00 for births, $8.00 for deaths and marriages

Itasca County
organized 1850, original county

Itasca County Court Administrator
123 Fourth Street, N.E.
Grand Rapids, MN 55744
(218) 327-7454; (218) 327-2897 FAX
diane.gross@courts.state.mn.us
http://www.co.itasca.mn.us
Diane Gross
(probate records from late 1890s)
probate search service: no charge unless very large request; copies of probate records: $5.00 per document, $10.00 per certified document

Itasca County Recorder
123 Fourth Street, N.E.
Grand Rapids, MN 55744-2600
(218) 327-2856; (218) 327-0689 FAX
jean.winter@co.itasca.mn.us;
bonnie.drobnick@co.itasca.mn.us;
char.vercellino@co.itasca.mn.us
http://www.co.itasca.mn.us/Records/Gov_rec.htm
Jean Winter, Recorder/Registrar; Bonnie Drobnick (Vital Statistics Records Deputy; Char Vercellino, Real Estate Records Deputy
(land records from 1870s; births from 1891 [actual record 1941]; deaths from 1894 [actual record 1946]; marriages from 1891)

Jackson County
organized 1857 from unorganized lands

Jackson County Court Administrator
(Courthouse, 405 Fourth Street—location)
PO Box 177 (mailing address)
Jackson, MN 56143
(507) 847-4400; (507) 847-2566 (Probate); (507) 847-5433 FAX
http://www.mncourts.gov/district/5/?page=1482
Kelly Iverson
(births, deaths and marriages from 1870, probate records from 1867)
probate search service: no charge; copies of probate records: $5.00 per document, $10.00 for certified copies

Jackson County Recorder
(Courthouse, 405 Fourth Street, Second Floor)
PO Box 209 (mailing address)
Jackson, MN 56143
(507) 847-2580; (507) 847-4718 FAX
becky.mccann@co.jackson.mn.us
http://www.co.jackson.mn.us
Becky McCann
(land records from 1865)

Kanabec County
organized 1858 from Pine County

Kanabec County Court Administrator
Courthouse, 18 North Vine Street
Mora, MN 55051-1342
(320) 679-6400
http://www.mncourts.gov/district/10/?page=927
Rosemary Nelson
(marriages, probate records)
probate search service: $10.00 per hour; copies of probate records: variable, $10.00 minimum

Kanabec County Recorder
Courthouse, 18 North Vine Street, Suite 261B
Mora, MN 55051
(320) 679-6466; (30) 679-6431 FAX
rhonda.olson@co.kanabec.mn.us;
recorder@co.kanabec.mn.us
http://www.kanabeccounty.org
Rhonda Olson
(land records, births and deaths)

Kandiyohi County
organized 1858 from Meeker County, annexed Monongalia County in November 1870

Kandiyohi County Court Administrator
505 Becker Avenue SW
Willmar, MN 56201
(320) 231-6206; (320) 231-6276 FAX
Teresa.Fredrickson@courts.state.mn.us
http://www.mncourts.gov/district/8/?page=1068
Teresa Fredrickson
(probate records)

Kandiyohi County Recorder
(505 West Becker, Willmar, MN 56201—
location)
PO Box 736 (mailing address)
Willmar, MN 56201
(612) 231-6223 (County Recorder and Office of
Vital Statistics)
julie.kalkbrenner@co.kandiyohi.mn.us
http://www.co.kandiyohi.mn.us/depts/Vitalstat
s/default.htm
Julie Kalkbrenner
(land records from the mid 1850s; births and
deaths from the 1870s; marriages from the
1860s)
copies of land records: 50¢ each; copies of vital
records: $11.00 for births (except
"confidential" births under 100 years old,
which require the mother's permission), $8.00
for deaths and marriages

Kittson County
organized 8 April 1879 from unorganized lands;
name changed from Pembina County in 1878

Kittson County Court Administrator
(Courthouse, 410 South Fifth Street #204—
location)
PO Box 39 (mailing address)
Hallock, MN 56728
(218) 843-3632; (218) 843-3634 FAX
http://www.mncourts.gov/district/9/?page=667
Teresa McDonnell
(vital records, probate records)
probate search service: no charge; certified
copies of vital records: $11.00 for births,
$8.00 for deaths and marriages; copies of
probate record: $5.00 each, $10.00 per
certified copy

Kittson County Recorder
PO Box 639
Hallock, MN 56728
(218) 843-2842; (218) 843-2020 FAX
jak@co.kittson.mn.us
http://www.visitnwminnesota.com/Kittson.htm
Janice Klein
(land records)

Koochiching County
organized 1906 from Itasca County

Koochiching County Court Administrator
Courthouse, 715 Fourth Street
International Falls, MN 56649
(218) 283-1160; (218) 283-1162 FAX
http://www.mncourts.gov/district/9/?page=668
Carol Clauson
(naturalization records, probate records)
no probate search service; copies of probate
records: 25¢ each, $5.00 per certified copy, no
minimum

Koochiching County Recorder
Courthouse, 715 Fourth Street
International Falls, MN 56649
(218) 283-1193; (218) 283-1194 FAX
pam.rooney@co.koochiching.mn.us
http://www.co.koochiching.mn.us/dept/record
er/recordermain.htm
Pam Rooney
(land records, vital records)
birth certificates: $16.00 certified or $13.00
uncertified; death certificates: $13.00 certified
or uncertified; marriage certificates: $9.00

Lac qui Parle County
organized 1863 north of the Minnesota River,
disestablished in 1868, then recreated in 1871
south of the river

Lac qui Parle County Court Administrator

(600 Sixth Street, Madison, MN 56256-1233)
PO Box 36 (mailing address)
Madison, MN 56256
(612) 598-3536; (320) 598-3915 FAX
Becky.Knudson@courts.state.mn.us
http://www.mncourts.gov/district/8/?page=1069
Becky Knudson
(vital records, probate records)
probate search service: $10.00 per hour; copies
of vital records: $11.00 for births, $8.00 for
deaths and marriages ("Individuals may search
the marriage and death records, but do not
have access to births"); copies of probate
records: $3.50 for the first page and 25¢ for
each additional page, $5.00 for the first
certified page and 25¢ for each additional
page, $2.50 minimum "if our office searches
records")

Lac qui Parle County Recorder
PO Box 132
Madison, MN 56256-0132
(320) 598-3724; (320) 598-7555 FAX
jbornhorst@mail.co.lac-qui-parle.mn.us
http://www.ci.madison.mn.us
Janine Bornhorst
(land records)

Lake County
organized 1856; name changed from Doty
County

Lake County Court Administrator
Courthouse, 601 Third Avenue
Two Harbors, MN 55616
(218) 834-8330; (218) 834-8397 FAX
larry.saur@courts.state.mn.us
http://www.mncourts.gov/district/6/?page=210
Larry J. Saur
(births from 1888 to date, deaths and marriages
from 1891 to date, probate records)
probate search service: $10.00 per hour; copies
of vital records: $8.00 for uncertified copies
of births or certified copies of deaths and
marriages, $11.00 for certified copies of
births; copies of probate records: $5.00 per
document, $10.00 per certified document

Lake County Recorder
601 Third Avenue
Two Harbors, MN 55616
(218) 834-8311; (218) 834-8347; (218) 834-8358
FAX
ekoski@50hotmail.com
http://www.lakecnty.com/government/index.html
Erica Koski
(land records)

Lake of the Woods County
organized 1923 from Beltrami County

**Lake of the Woods County Court
Administrator**
(206 Eighth Avenue S.E., Suite 250—location)
PO Box 808 (mailing address)
Baudette, MN 56623-0808
(218) 634-1451 (Vital Records); (218) 634-1388
(Probate); (218) 634-9444 FAX
http://www.mncourts.gov/district/9/?page=669
Carol Clauson
(vital records; probate records from January
1923)
probate search service: $10.00 per 00; copies of
probate records: $5.00 for the first page and
25¢ for each additional page, no minimum

Lak of the Woods County Recorder
(206 Eighth Avenue S.E., Suite 280—location)
PO Box 808 (mailing address)
Baudette, MN 56623
(218) 634-1902; (218) 634-2509 FAX
susan_n@co.lake-of-the-woods.mn.us
http://www.co.lake-of-the-
woods.mn.us/recorder.htm
Susan Ney
(land records)

Le Sueur County
organized 1853 from unorganized lands

Le Sueur County Court Administrator
LeSueur County Courthouse
88 South Park Avenue
Le Center, MN 56057
(507) 357-2251; (507) 357-8259 (Probate); (507)
357-6433 FAX
http://www.mncourts.gov/district/1/?page=773
Joanne Kopet
(marriages and probate records)
probate search service: $8.00 per hour; copies of
probate records: $5.00 each, $10.00 for
certified copies; certified copies of marriage
records: $8.00

Le Sueur County Recorder
LeSueur County Courthouse
88 South Park Avenue
Le Center, MN 56057-1620
(612) 357-2251; (507) 357-6375 FAX
sexe@co.le-sueur.mn.us
http://www.co.le-sueur.mn.us/Recorder.html
David A. Sexe
(land records, births and deaths)
land records search service: $5.00 per ¼ hour;
copies of land records: 50¢ per page (from
microfiche originals), $1.00 per page (plats),
$1.00 per certified copy, plus $1.00 minimum
for postage; certified copies of vital records:
$11.00 for births, $8.00 for deaths

Lincoln County
organized 1873 from Lyon County

Lincoln County Court Administrator
(Lincoln County Government Center, 319
North Rebecca—location)
PO Box 15 (mailing address)
Ivanhoe, MN 56142-0015
(507) 694-1355; (507) 694-1717 FAX
Wendy.Rost@courts.state.mn.us
http://www.mncounties3.org/lincoln/Departm
ents/CourtAdmin.htm
Wendy Rost

Lincoln County Recorder
(Lincoln County Government Center, , 319
North Rebecca—location)
PO Box 119 (mailing address)
Ivanhoe, MN 56142
(507) 694-1360; (507) 694-1198 FAX
lundberg@co.lincoln.mn.us
http://www.co.lincoln.mn.us/Departments/Re
corder.htm
Loretta J. Lundberg
(land records, births and deaths)

Lyon County
organized 1871 from Yellow Medicine County

Lyon County Court Administrator
Lyon County Government Center
607 West Main
Marshall, MN 56258-3021
(507) 537-6734; (507) 537-6150 FAX
karen.bierman@courts.state.mn.us
http://www.lyonco.org/depts/court
Karen Bierman
(naturalization records, vital records, probate
records)
no probate search service; copies of probate
records: $3.50 for the first page and 25¢ for
each additional page, $5.00 for the first
certified page and 25¢ for each additional
certified page, no minimum ("records
destroyed by fire 1870-1874")

Lyon County Recorder
607 West Main Street
Marshall, MN 56258
(507) 537-6722; (507) 537-7988 FAX
barker@co.lyon.mn.us
http://www.co.lyon.mn.us/depts/recorder
Jeanine M. Barker
(land records, births and deaths)

Mahnomen County
organized 1906 from Norman County

Mahnomen County Court Administrator
(Courthouse, 311 North Main, Suite 311)

PO Box 459 (mailing address)
Mahnomen, MN 56557-0459
(218) 935-2251; (218) 935-2851 FAX
lori.wiebolt@courts.state.mn.us
http://www.mncourts.gov/district9/?page=670
Loretta Wiebolt
(probate records)

Mahnomen County Recorder
(Courthouse, 311 North Main—location)
PO Box 380 (mailing address)
Mahnomen, MN 56557-0379
(218) 935-5669; (218) 935-5528; (218) 935-5946
    FAX
susan.bendickson@co.mahnomen.mn.us
http://www.sosstate.mn.us/home/index.asp?pa
    ge=151
Susan Bendickson
(land records, births and deaths)

Marshall County
organized 1879 from Kittson County

Marshall County Court Administrator
Courthouse, 208 East Collin Avenue, Suite 18
Warren, MN 56762-1693
(218) 745-4816; (218) 745-4921; (218) 745-4343
    FAX
http://www.mncourts.gov/district/9/?page=671
Janice (Jan) Johnston
(naturalization records from 1883 to 1965,
    probate records from 1883)
probate search service: no charge; copies of
    probate records: $3.50 for the first page and
    25¢ for each additional page, $5.00 for the
    first certified page and 25¢ for each additional
    certified page ("Give name and year")

Marshall County Recorder
Courthouse, 208 East Collin Avenue, Suite 7
Warren, MN 56762
(218) 745-4801; (218) 745-5013 FAX
halvorson@co.marshall.mn.us
http://www.co.marshall.mn.us/marshallcounty/
    departments/recorder.htm
Marion C. Halvorson
(land records from 1879, vital records from
    1883)
birth certificates: $16.00 certified, $13.00
    uncertified; death certificate: $13.00, marriage
    certificate: $9.00

Martin County
organized 1857 from Faribault County

Martin County Court Administrator
Martin County Security Building
201 Lake Avenue
Fairmont, MN 56031
(507) 238-3205; (507) 238-1913 FAX
connie.belgard@courts.state.mn.us
http://www.co.martin.mn.us/Courts/Courts.htm
Connie Belgard

Martin County Recorder
PO Box 785
Fairmont, MN 56031
(507) 238-3213; (507) 235-8537 FAX
kay.wrucke@co.martin.mn.us
http://www.co.martin.mn.us/Recorder/RECO
    RDER.HTM
Kay Wrucke
(land records, births and deaths)

McLeod County
organized 1856 from Carver County

McLeod County Court Administrator
McLeod County Courthouse
830 11th Street East
Glencoe, MN 55336-2216
(320) 864-1281; (320) 864-5905 FAX
http://www.co.mcleod.mn.us/mcleodco.cfm?pa
    geID=14&sub=yes
Robert Schmidt
(probate records from 1865 with Probate Clerk)
probate search service: $10.00 per hour; copies
    of probate records: $5.00 per document,
    $10.00 per certified document

McLeod County Recorder
2389 Hennepin Avenue North
Glencoe, MN 55336
(320) 864-1327; (320) 864-1295 FAX
mcleod.recorder@co.mcleod.mn.us;
    lynnette.schrupp@co.mcleod.mn.us
http://www.co.mcleod.mn.us/mcleodco.cfm?pa
    geID=25&sub=yes
LynnEtte Schrupp
(land records from 1856, births and deaths from
    1870, marriages from 1865)

Meeker County
organized 1856 from Wright County

Meeker County Court Administrator
Courthouse, 325 North Sibley Avenue
Litchfield, MN 55355
(320) 693-5230; (320) 693-5254 FAX
Linda.Jagush@courts.state.mn.us
http://www.mncourts.gov/district/8/?page=1070
Linda Jagush Schmidt
(naturalization index with County Clerk, probate
    records with Court Administrator)
no probate search service; copies of probate
    records: $1.00 per page, $5.00 for the first
    certified page and 25¢ for each additional
    certified page

Meeker County Recorder
Courthouse, 325 North Sibley Avenue, Level 3
Litchfield, MN 55355
(320) 693-5440; (320) 693-5444 FAX
elainelenhard@co.meeker.mn.us
http://www.co.meeker.mn.us
Elaine Lenhard
(land records)

Mille Lacs County
organized 1857 from Kanabec County

Mille Lacs County Court Administrator
635 Second Street, S.E.
Milaca, MN 56353-1305
(320) 983-8313; (320) 983-8384 FAX
george.lock@courts.state.mn.us
http://www.co.mille-
    lacs.mn.us/Departments/Court%20Administ
    ration/Court%20Administration.html
George Lock
(marriages, probate records)
no probate search service; copies of probate
    records: $5.00 for the first page and 25¢ for
    each additional page, $5.00 minimum

Mille Lacs County Recorder
635 Second Street, S.E.
Milaca, MN 56353
(320) 983-8308; (320) 983-8388 FAX
jennifer.laduke@co.mille-lacs.mn.us
http://www.co.mille-lacs.mn.us/page17.html
Jennifer LaDuke
(land records, births and deaths)

Morrison County
organized 1856 from Benton and Stearns
    counties

Morrison County Court Administrator
Morrison County Administration Building-
    Government Center
213 S.E. First Avenue
Little Falls, MN 56345-3196
(320) 632-0327; (866) 401-111, ext. 327; (320)
    632-0340 FAX
Shari.Wicks@courts.state.mn.us
http://www.mncourts.gov/district/7/?page=474
Rhonda Russell, Court Administrator; Shari
    Wicks, Assistant Court Administrator
(probate records from 1857)
probate search service: $10.00 per hour; copies
    of probate records: 50¢ per page, no
    minimum

Morrison County Recorder
213 S.E. First Avenue
Little Falls, MN 56345
(612) 632-0145; (612) 632-0141 FAX
bunny@co.morrison.mn.us
http://www.co.morrison.mn.us/wsite/recorder

/recorder.htm
Elda Mae (Bunny) Johnston
(land records from 1860 [early years sketchy],
    births, deaths and marriages from 1870)
land and vital records search service: $20.00 per
    hour; copies of land records: $1.00 per page
    in person, $2.00 plus SASE if mailed out;
    certified copies of vital records: $10.00 for
    births, $8.00 for deaths and marriages

Mower County
organized 1855 from Fillmore County

Mower County Court Administrator
201 First Street, N.E.
Austin, MN 55912
(507) 437-9465; (507) 437-9474 (Probate
    Registrar); (507) 434-2702 FAX
http://www.mncourts.gov/district/3/?page=221
Patricia Ball
(probate records)
no probate search service; copies of probate
    records: $3.50 plus 25¢ per page, no minimum

Mower County Recorder
201 First Street, N.E.
Austin, MN 55912
(507) 437-9446; (507) 437-9471 FAX
sued@co.mower.mn.us
http://www.co.mower.mn.us/Recorder01.htm
Susan M. Davis
(land records, births and deaths)
copies of vital records: $11.00 for births, $8.00
    for deaths

Murray County
organized 1875 from Lyon County

Murray County Court Administrator
(2500 28th Street—location)
PO Box 57 (mailing address)
Slayton, MN 56172-0057
(507) 836-6163, ext. 135; (507) 836-6019 FAX
sharon.tellinghuisen@courts.state.mn.us
http://www.murray-countymn.com/directory.
    asp?building=All&office=Court+Administrat
    ion&position=All&secid=429
Steven Schulze, Court Administrator; Sharon
    Tellinghuisen, Deputy Court Administrator
(probate records with Clerk of Court's Office)

Murray County Recorder
(2500 28th Street—location)
PO Box 57 (mailing address)
Slayton, MN 56172-0057
(507) 836-6148, ext. 144; (507) 836-8904 FAX
jjohnson@co.murray.mn.us
http://www.murray-
    countymn.com/directory.asp?building=All&o
    ffice=Recorder&position=All&secid=429
Jim Johnson
(land records, births and deaths)

Nicollet County
organized 1853 from unorganized lands

Nicollet County Court Administrator
(Nicollet County Government Center, 510
    South Minnesota Avenue, St. Peter, MN
    56082-2508—location)
PO Box 496 (mailing address)
St. Peter, MN 56082
(507) 931-6800; (507) 931-9220 FAX
http://www.co.nicollet.mn.us/dept.php3?id=6
Shirley Eken
(vital records from 1870, probate records from
    1870)
probate search service: $10.00 per hour; copies
    of vital records: $11.00 for births, $8.00 for
    deaths and marriages; certified copies of
    probate records: $5.00 each

Nicollet County Recorder
(Nicollet County Government Center, 510
    South Minnesota Avenue, St. Peter, MN
    56082-2508—location)
PO Box 493 (mailing address)
St. Peter, MN 56082
(507) 931-6800; (507) 934-0320; (507) 934-4487
    FAX

kconlon@co.nicollet.mn.us;
recorder@co.nicollet.mn.us
http://www.co.nicollet.mn.us/dept.php3?id=16
Kathy Conlon, Recorder's Office
(naturalization records, land records)

Nobles County
organized 1857 from Jackson County

Nobles County Court Administrator
(Prairie Justice Center, 1530 Airport Road—
location)
PO Box 547 (mailing address)
Worthington, MN 56187
(507) 372-8263; (507) 372-4994 FAX
http://www.co.nobles.mn.us/court.htm
Nancy VanderKooi

Nobles County Recorder
(Nobles County Government Center, 315 Tenth
Street—location)
PO Box 757 (mailing address)
Worthington, MN 56187
(507) 372-8232; (507) 372-8236; (507) 372-8223
FAX
lwilson@co.nobles.mn.us
http://www.co.nobles.mn.us/recorder.htm
Lynn Wilson
(land records, births and deaths)

Norman County
organized 1881 from Polk County

Norman County Court Administrator
16 Third Avenue East
Ada, MN 56510-1362
(218) 784-5458; (218) 784-3110 FAX
lori.wiebolt@courts.state.mn.us
http://www.co.norman.mn.ushttp://www.mnc
ourts.gov/district/9/?page=672
Loretta Wiebolt

Norman County Recorder
(16 Third Avenue East—location)
PO Box 146 (mailing address)
Ada, MN 56510-0146
(218) 784-5481; (218) 784-2399 FAX
kari.aanenson@co.norman.mn.us
http://www.co.norman.mn.us
Kari Aanenson
(land records, births and deaths)
birth certificates: $16.00 certified or $13.00
uncertified; death certificates: $13.00 certified
or uncertified; marriage certificates: $9.00

Olmsted County
organized 1855 from unorganized lands

Olmsted County Court Administrator
Olmstead County Government Center
151 Fourth Street, S.E., Fifth Floor
Rochester, MN 55904-3710
(507) 285-8363 (General Information); (507)
285-8475 (Administrator); (507) 285-8484
(Probate Registrar); (507) 285-8996 FAX
http://www.mncourts.gov/district/3/?page=222
Chuck Kjos
(probate records from about 1900)
probate search service: $5.00 per name for
probate or judgment search, $4.00 per name
for probate claim search; copies of probate
records: $5.00 per document, $10.00 per
document for certified copies ("all fees must
be paid in advance; no searches done by
telephone")

Olmsted County License Bureau
Olmstead County Government Center
151 Fourth Street, S.E., First Floor
Rochester, MN 55904
(507) 285-8150
vitals@co.olmsted.mn.us
http://www.co.olmsted.mn.us/departments/rec
ords/index.asp
(births and deaths from 1870, marriages from
1855)

**Olmsted County Property Records and
Licensing**
Olmstead County Government Center

151 Fourth Street, S.E.
Rochester, MN 55904
(507) 285-8124
propertyweb@co.olmsted.mn.us
http://www.co.olmsted.mn.us/departments/lic
ensing/index.asp
(land records from 1855; formerly
Assessor/Recorder/Auditor/Treasurer/Licen
se Bureau)
land records search service: $50.00 minimum,
prepaid; copies of land records: $1.00 per
page

Otter Tail County
organized 1858 from Pembina and Cass counties

Otter Tail County Court Administrator
Courthouse, 121 Junius Avenue West, Suite 310
Fergus Falls, MN 56537
(218) 998-8420; (218) 998-8438 FAX
http://www.co.otter-
tail.mn.us/courtadmin/default.php
Kathy Ouren
(probate records)
no probate search service; copies of probate
records: $3.50 plus 25¢ per page per
document

Otter Tail County Recorder
(Government Services Center, 500 Fir Avenue
West—location)
PO Box 867 (mailing address)
Fergus Falls, MN 56538-0867
(218) 739-2271; (218) 739-3721 FAX
wmetcalf@co.ottertail.mn.us
http://www.co.otter-
tail.mn.us/recorder/default.php
Wendy L. Metcalf
(land records from 1870, vital records from
1870)
copies of land records: $2.00 each; copies of
vital records: $11.00 for births, $8.00 for
deaths and marriages

Pennington County
organized 1910 from Red Lake County

Pennington County Court Administrator
(Courthouse, 101 North Main—location)
PO Box 619 (mailing address)
Thief River Falls, MN 56701
(218) 683-7023; (218) 681-0907 FAX
http://www.mncourts.gov/district/9/?page=676
Janice Johnston
(naturalization records ["records are at the
Minnesota Historical Society, but I have
index"], vital records, probate records)
probate search service: no charge; copies of
probate records: $5.00 each, $10.00 for
certified copies

Pennington County Recorder
(Courthouse, 101 North Main—location)
PO Box 616 (mailing address)
Thief River Falls, MN 56701
(218) 683-7027; (218) 683-7026 FAX
kdschmalz@co.pennington.mn.us
http://www.visitnwminnesota.com/Pennington
.htm
Ken D. Schmalz
(land records, births and deaths)

Pierce County
abolished 1862 (see Big Stone, Chippewa,
Stevens, and Pope counties)

Pine County
organized 1856 from unorganized lands,
annexed Buchanan County in 1861

Pine County Court Administrator
Courthouse, 315 Main Street South
Pine City, MN 55063
(320) 629-5634; (320) 629-5636
http://www.mncourts.gov/district/10/?page=928
Lu Ann Blegen

Pine County Recorder
315 Sixth Street South, Suite 3
Pine City, MN 55063

(320) 629-5615; (320) 629-5604 FAX
tltricas@co.pine.mn.us
http://www.pinecounty.org/Officers
Tamara Tricas
(land records, births and deaths)

Pipestone County
organized 1857 from Murray County; name
changed from Rock County in 1862

Pipestone County Court Administrator
(416 South Hiawatha Avenue, Pipestone, MN
56164-1566—location)
PO Box 337 (mailing address)
Pipestone, MN 56164
(507) 825-6730; (507) 825-6733 FAX
steve.schulze@co.pipestone.mn.us
http://www.pipestone-county.com
Steven Schulze
(probate records from 1880)
probate search service: no charge; copies of
probate records: $3.50 for the first page and
25¢ for each additional page, $3.50 minimum

Pipestone County Recorder
416 South Hiawatha Avenue
Pipestone, MN 56164
(507) 825-6755; (507) 825-6767 FAX
maryann.degroot@co.pipestone.mn.us
http://www.mncounties.org/pipestone/depart
ments.htm
Mary Ann De Groot
(land records from 1885, vital records from
1877)

Polk County
organized 1858 from Indian lands

Polk County Court Administrator
Courthouse, 612 North Broadway, Suite 301
Crookston, MN 56716
(218) 281-2332, ext. 1312; (218) 281-2204 FAX
http://www.mncourts.gov/district/9/?page=69
0
Kathy Narlock

Polk County Recorder
(Courthouse, 612 North Broadway—location)
PO Box 397 (mailing address)
Crookston, MN 56716
(218) 281-3464; (218) 281-1636 FAX
marlene.hanson.co.polk.mn.us
http://www.co.polk.mn.us
Marlene Hanson
(land records, births and deaths)

Pope County
organized 1862 from Pierce County (which was
abolished the same year)

Pope County Court Administrator
Courthouse, 130 East Minnesota Avenue
Glenwood, MN 56334
(320) 634-5222; (320) 634-5527 FAX
http://www.mncourts.gov/district/8/?page=1071
Sandee Tollefson
(vital records from 1870, probate records from
1870)
probate search service: $10.00; copies of probate
records: $3.50 each, $5.00 per certified copy,
no minimum

Pope County Recorder
Courthouse, 130 East Minnesota Avenue
Glenwood, MN 56334
(320) 634-5723; (320) 634-5717 FAX
darby.bowen@co.pope.mn.us
http://www.mncounties.org/pope/recorders.htm
Darby Jergenson Bowen
(land records, births and deaths)

Ramsey County
organized 1849, original county

Ramsey County Court Administrator
15 West Kellogg Boulevard, Room 1700
St. Paul, MN 55102
(651) 266-8266; (651) 266-8145 (Probate); (651)
266-8149 FAX (Probate)
http://www.mncourts.gov/district/2/?page=524

Ramsey County Recorder
50 West Kellogg Boulevard
St. Paul, MN 55102
(651) 266-2052; (651) 266-2199 FAX
richard.j.wendt@co.ramsey.mn.us
http://www.co.ramsey.mn.us
Susan Roth
(land records, births and deaths)

Red Lake County
organized 1896 from Polk County

Red Lake County Court Administrator
(124 Langevin Avenue—location)
PO Box 339 (mailing address)
Red Lake Falls, MN 56750
(218) 253-4281; (218) 253-4287 FAX
http://www.mncourts.gov/district/9/?page=691
Kathy Narlock
(probate records)
copies of probate records: $5.00 per document,
$10.00 per certified document

Red Lake County Recorder
124 North Main
Red Lake Falls, MN 56750-0003
(218) 253-2997; (218) 253-4894 FAX
jepaquin@co.red-lake.mn.us
http://www.prairieagcomm.com/redlakecounty
/index.cfm
Joyce Paquin
(land records, vital records)

Redwood County
organized 1862 from Brown County

Redwood County Court Administrator
(Third and Jefferson—location)
PO Box 130 (mailing address)
Redwood Falls, MN 56283-0130
(507) 637-4020; (507) 637-4018; (507) 637-4021
FAX
patty.amberg@courts.state.mn.us
http://www.mncourts.gov/district/5/?page=1497
Patty Amberg

Redwood County Recorder
PO Box 130
Redwood Falls, MN 56283
(507) 637-4032; (507) 637-4064 FAX
joyce_a@co.redwood.mn.us
http://www.co.redwood.mn.us/departments.htm
Joyce Anderson
(land records, births and deaths)

Renville County
organized 1855 from unorganized lands

Renville County Court Administrator
500 East DePue Avenue
Olivia, MN 56277-1396
(320) 523-2080; (320) 523-3689 FAX
Susan.Stahl@courts.state.mn.us
http://www.mncourts.gov/district/8/?page=1072
Susan T. Stahl
(probate records)
probate search service: no charge; copies of
probate records: $5.00 each, $10.00 for
certified copies

Renville County Recorder
500 East DePue Avenue
Olivia, MN 56277
(320) 523-3669; (320) 523-3679 FAX
gail_m@co.renville.mn.us
http://www.co.renville.mn.us/recorder/index.h
tml
Gail M. Miller
(land records with Auditor's Office and
Registrar of Titles, naturalization records with
Ellen Smith, County Recorder's Office, vital
records with County Recorder's Office)

Rice County
organized 1853 from Nobles County

Rice County Court Administrator
Courthouse, 218 N.W. Third Street, Suite 300
Faribault, MN 55021-5146
(507) 332-6107

RCCourtAdmin@co.rice.mn.us
http://www.co.rice.mn.us/court/index.php
Robert (Bob) Langer
(probate records from 1870s)
probate search service: $10.00 per hour, $2.50
minimum; copies of probate records: $3.50
for the first page and 25¢ for each additional
page, $5.00 for the first certified page and 25¢
for each additional certified page

Rice County Recorder
320 N.W. Third Street, Suite 10
Faribault, MN 55021
(507) 332-6114; (507) 332-5999 FAX
mdegroot@co.rice.mn.us;
RCRecorder@co.rice.mn.us
http://www.co.rice.mn.us/Recorder/default.htm
Marsha DeGroot
(births and deaths from 1870, marriages from
1856)

Rock County
organized 1857 from Nobles County; name
changed from Pipestone County in 1862

Rock County Court Administrator
(204 East Brown Street—location)
PO Box 745 (mailing address)
Luverne, MN 56156-0745
(507) 283-5020; (507) 283-5017 FAX
http://www.mncourts.gov/district/5/?page=1498
Sandra Vrtacnik
(naturalization records, vital records, probate
records)
probate search service: $8.00 per hour; copies of
probate records: $5.00 each, $10.00 for
certified copies

Rock County Recorder
PO Box 509
Luverne, MN 56156-0509
(507) 283-5014; (507) 283-1343 FAX
jtom.houselog@co.rock.mn.us
http://www.co.rock.mn.us/page4.html
Tom Houselog
(land records)

Roseau County
organized 1894 from Kittson County

Roseau County Court Administrator
606 Fifth Avenue, S.W., Room 20
Roseau, MN 56751
(218) 463-2541; (218) 463-1889 FAX
http://www.mncourts.gov/district/9/?page=692
Teresa McDonnell

Roseau County Recorder
606 Fifth Avenue, S.W., Room 170
Roseau, MN 56751-1477
(218) 463-2061; (218) 463-4294 FAX
rick@co.roseau.mn.us
http://co.roseau.mn.us
Rick Kvien
(land records, births and deaths)

St. Louis County
organized 1855 from Lake County (then called
Doty County)

St. Louis County Court Administrator
100 North Fifth Avenue West
Duluth, MN 55802-1285
(218) 726-2460; (800) 450-9777, ext. 2460
http://www.mncourts.gov/district/6/?page=211
Cindy Stratioti
(vital records from 1870 with, Court
Administrator, Room 320, probate records
with Court Administrator, Room 301)
probate search service: $10.00 per hour; certified
copies of vital records: $11.00 for births,
$8.00 for deaths and marriages; copies of
probate records: $3.50 for the first page and
25¢ for each additional page, $5.00 for the
first certified page and 25¢ for each additional
page, no minimum

Saint Louis County Recorder
(100 North Fifth Avenue West, Room 101,
Duluth, MN 55802—location)

PO Box 157 (mailing address)
Duluth, MN 55801-0157
(218) 726-2677; (218) 725-5052 FAX
monacellim@co.st-louis.mn.us
http://www.co.st-
louis.mn.us/slcportal/SiteMap/HomePage/D
epartments/Recorder/tabid/91/Default.aspx
Mark A. Monacelli
(deeds and titles from 1850s with Register of
Deeds and Titles, Room 101)

Scott County
organized 1853 from Dakota County

Scott County Court Administrator
Scott County Justice Center
200 Fourth Avenue West
Government Center - JC115
Shakopee, MN 55379-1220
(952) 496-8200; (952) 496-8197 (Probate); (952)
496-8211 FAX
Greg.Ess@courts.state.mn.us
http://www.co.scott.mn.us
Greg Ess
(naturalization records, probate records)
probate search service: no charge; copies of
probate records: $5.00 per document, $10.00
per certified document

Scott County Recorder
200 Fourth Avenue West
Shakopee, MN 55379
(952) 496-8150; (952) 496-8142; (952) 496-8138
FAX
pboeckman@co.scott.mn.us
http://www.co.scott.mn.us
Ms. Pat Boeckman
(land records, births and deaths)

Sherburne County
organized 25 February 1856 from Benton
County

Sherburne County Court Administrator
(Sherburne County Government Center, 13880
Highway 10—location)
PO Box 318 (mailing address)
Elk River, MN 55330-1692
(612) 241-2800; (800) 433-5232; (763) 241-2816
FAX
courtadmin@co.sherburne.mn.us
http://www.co.sherburne.mn.us/courtadmin/d
efault.htm
Patricia Kuka
(probate records from 1893)
probate search service: $10.00 per hour; copies
of probate records: $5.00 per document,
$10.00 per certified document

Sherburne County Recorder
Sherburne County Government Center, 13880
Highway 10
Elk River, MN 55330-4601
(763) 241-2915; (800) 719-2826; (763) 241-2995
FAX
recorder@co.sherburne.mn.us;
2919ashe@co.sherburne.mn.us
http://www.co.sherburne.mn.us/recorder/defa
ult.htm
Michelle Ashe
(land ownership, etc., records from 1856; births
and deaths from 1870; marriage applications
from 1856)
copies of land records: $1.00 each, $5.00 for
certified copies

Sibley County
organized 1853 from unorganized lands

Sibley County Court Administrator
(400 Court Street—location)
PO Box 867 (mailing address)
Gaylord, MN 55334
(507) 237-4051; (507) 237-4062 FAX
http://www.mncourts.gov/district/1/?page=772
Karen Messner
(marriages and probate records)

Sibley County Recorder's Office
400 Court Avenue

Gaylord, MN 55334
(507) 237-4080; (507) 237-4079; (507) 237-4306
  FAX
kathyd@co.sibley.mn.us
http://www.co.sibley.mn.us/Dept_Frame.htm
Kathy Dietz, Department Head
(land records, births and deaths)
land records or vital records search service:
  $20.00 per hour

Stearns County
organized 20 February 1855 from unorganized
  lands

Stearns County Court Administrator
(815 Courthouse Square—Case Intake/Payment
  Center)
725 Courthouse Square—Service Center
  (mailing address)
St. Cloud, MN 56303
(612) 259-3620; (320) 656-3626 FAX
info@co.stearns.mn.us
http://www.co.stearns.mn.us/1223.htm
Timothy Roberts
(probate records)
probate search service: no charge ("need name
  and approximate year of death"); copies of
  land records: $1.00 per page, $5.00 minimum,
  $9.50 plus 50¢ for certification for plats;
  copies of probate records: $3.50 for the first
  page and 25¢ for each additional page, $5.00
  for the first certified page and 25¢ for each
  additional certified page, no minimum

Stearns County License Center
Administration Center Room 125–130
705 Courthouse Square
St. Cloud, MN 56302
(320) 259-3925; (320) 656-3932 FAX
vital.stats@co.stearns.mn.us
http://www.co.stearns.mn.us/682.htm
Randy Schreifels, Auditor/Treasurer
(vital records from 1870)

Stearns County Recorder
(Administration Center, 705 Courthouse Square,
  Room 131—location)
PO Box 186 (mailing address)
St. Cloud, MN 56302
(320) 259-3855; (320) 656-3982 FAX
diane.grundhoefer@co.stearns.mn.us
http://www.co.stearns.mn.us/1022.htm
Diane Grundhoefer
(land records from 1855)

Steele County
organized 1855 from unorganized territory

Steele County Court Administrator
(111 East Main Street—location)
PO Box 487 (mailing address)
Owatonna, MN 55060
(507) 444-7720; (507) 444-7728 FAX
infodest@co.steele.mn.us
http://www.co.steele.mn.us/COURTSVC/cour
  tsvc.html
Gordon Meiners
(vital records with County Court, probate
  records with Probate Court)
probate search service: no charge for initial
  search; copies of probate records: $3.50 for
  the first page and 25¢ for each additional
  page, $5.00 for the first certified page and 25¢
  for each additional certified page, no
  minimum

Steele County Recorder
PO Box 890
Owatonna, MN 55060
(507) 444-7450; (507) 444-7470 FAX
avis.lewison@co.steele.mn.us
http://www.co.steele.mn.us/recorder/recorder.
  html
Avis Lewison
(land records)
land records search service ("will not do phone
  searches; will do index searches but only
  when our regular work is caught up; it would
  be best to come to the office in person")

Stevens County
organized 1862 from Pierce County (which was
  abolished the same year)

Stevens County Court Administrator
(Courthouse, Fifth and Colorado—location)
PO Box 530 (mailing address)
Morris, MN 56267-0107
(320) 589-7287; (320) 589-7288 FAX
Sandee.Tollefson@courts.state.mn.us
http://www.mncourts.gov/district/8/?page=1073
Sandee Tollefson

Stevens County Recorder
PO Box 530
Morris, MN 56267
(320) 589-7414; (320) 589-7112 FAX
virginiamahoney@co.stevens.mn.us
http://www.co.stevens.mn.us/docs/department
  s/recorder/default.html
Virginia Mahoney
(land records, births and deaths)

Swift County
organized 1870 from Chippewa County

Swift County Court Administrator
(Courthouse, 301 14th Street, North—location)
PO Box 110 (mailing address)
Benson, MN 56215
(320) 843-2744; (320) 843-4124 FAX
Carol.Jensen@courts.state.mn.us
http://www.mncourts.gov/district/8/?page=1074
Carol Jensen
(probate records from 1870)
records search service: $10.00 per hour (no
  charge for minor assistance; "dates must be
  given at the time of the search"); copies of
  probate records: $3.50 for the first page and
  25¢ for each additional page, $5.00 for the
  first certified page and 25¢ for each additional
  certified page, no minimum

Swift County Recorder
(Courthouse, 301 14th Street, North—location)
PO Box 246 (mailing address)
Benson, MN 56215
(320) 843-3377; (320) 843-2275 FAX
donna.lilleberg@morris.state.mn.us
http://www.swiftcounty.com
Donna Lilleberg
(land records)

Todd County
organized 1855 from Stearns County

Todd County Court Administrator
215 First Avenue, South
Long Prairie, MN 56347-1351
(320) 732-7802; (320) 732-2506 FAX
tammie.chapin@courts.state.mn.us
http://www.co.todd.mn.us/Court/court.htm
Tammie Chapin
(probate records)
probate search service: $10.00 per hour; copies
  of probate records: $2.00 each, $2.00
  minimum ("if copies can be completed on
  copy machine, 25¢ per copy")

Todd County Recorder
221 First Avenue, South, Suite 300
Long Prairie, MN 56347
(320) 732-4428; (320) 732-4001 FAX
cheryl.perish@co.todd.mn.us
http://www.co.todd.mn.us/Recorder/recorder.
  htm
Cheryl Perish
(land records, births and deaths)

Toombs County
(see Traverse and Wilkin counties)

Traverse County
organized 1862 from Wilkin County (then called
  Toombs County)

Traverse County Court Administrator
(Courthouse, 702 Second Avenue North—
  location)
PO Box 867 (mailing address)

Wheaton, MN 56296-0867
(320) 563-4343; (320) 563-4311 FAX
Roger.Strand@courts.state.mn.us
http://www.mncourts.gov/district/8/?page=1075
Roger Strand

Traverse County Recorder
PO Box 487
Wheaton, MN 56296
(320) 563-4622; (320) 563-4424 FAX
leann.peyton@co.traverse.mn.us
http://www.sosstate.mn.us/home/index.asp?pa
  ge=151
LeAnn Peyton
(land records, births and deaths)

Wabasha County
organized 1849, original county, formerly called
  Wabashaw County

Wabasha County Court Administrator
625 Jefferson Avenue
Wabasha, MN 55981-1577
(651) 565-4070 (Vital Records); (651) 565-3524
  (Probate)
http://www.mncourts.gov/district/3/?page=225
Twila Holtan
(probate records from 1856 with Registrar)
probate search service: no charge; copies of
  probate records: $5.00 per document, $10.00
  per certified document

Wabasha County Recorder
625 Jefferson Avenue
Wabasha, MN 55981
(651) 565-3623; (651) 565-2774 FAX
jaitken@co.wabasha.mn.us
http://www.co.wabasha.mn.us/index.php?option
  =com_content&task=view&id=74&Itemid=68
Jeffery R. Aitken
(land records; births and deaths from 1870;
  marriages from 1865)

Wadena County
organized 1858 from Cass and Todd counties

**Wadena County Court Administrator (Clerk
of Court)**
Courthouse, 415 South Jefferson Street
Wadena, MN 56482-1596
(218) 631-7633; (218) 631-7635 FAX
Beverly.Paavola@courts.state.mn.us
http://www.co.wadena.mn.us/courtadministrat
  or.htm
Beverley Paavola
(probate records)
probate search service: no charge unless it takes
  more than ½ hour, then $5.00 per hour;
  copies of probate records: $5.00 each, $10.00
  for certified copies, no minimum

Wadena County Recorder
PO Box 415
Wadena, MN 56482
(218) 631-2362; (218) 631-5709 FAX
soledad.henriksen@co.wadena.mn.us
http://www.co.wadena.mn.us/recorder.htm
Soledad Henriksen
(land records from 1873, vital records from
  1880)

Waseca County
organized 1857 from Steele County ("most
  records in Steele County until 12 August
  1858, some even later, until the county seat
  was moved from Wilton to Waseca in 1870")

Waseca County Court Administrator
307 North State Street
Waseca, MN 56093
(507) 835-0540; (507) 835-0633 FAX
doug.prescher@co.waseca.mn.us
http://www.co.waseca.mn.us/depart.htm
Douglas Prescher
(vital records from 1870, marriages from 1858,
  probate records from 1871, will books from
  1858)
probate search service: $10.00 per hour; copies
  of probate records: $5.00 each, $10.00 for
  certified copies, no minimum ("items other

than documents in the file can be copied for
15¢ per page")

Waseca County Recorder
307 North State Street
Waseca, MN 56093
(507) 835-0670; (507) 835-0633 FAX
linda.karst@co.waseca.mn.us
http://www.co.waseca.mn.us/recorder.htm
Linda Karst
(land records from 1857)

Washington County
organized 1849, original county

Washington County Court Administrator
Washington County Government Center
(14949 62nd Street North—location)
PO Box 6 (mailing address)
Stillwater, MN 55082-0006
(651) 430-6263
http://www.co.washington.mn.us/info_for_resi
dents/courts_and_supporting_services/court
_administration
Christina M. Volkers, Court Administrator and
Clerk of District Court
probate search service: no charge; copies of
probate records: $3.50 for the first page and
25¢ for each additional page, $2.00 for the
first page of non-court documents and 25¢
for each additional page of non-court
documents, no minimum

Washington County Recorder
(14900 North 61st Street—location)
PO Box 6 (mailing address)
Stillwater, MN 55082-0006
(651) 430-6755 (Abstract Division); (651) 430-
6756 (Torrens Division)
http://www.co.washington.mn.us/info_for_resi
dents/recorder__registrar_of_titles
Kevin J. Corbid
(abstracts [Abstract Division] and titles [Torrens
Division])

Watonwan County
organized 1860 from Brown County

Watonwan County Court Administrator
(710 Second Avenue South—location)
PO Box 518 (mailing address)
St. James, MN 56081
(507) 375-1238; (507) 375-5010 FAX
http://www.mncourts.gov/district/5/?page=1500
Kelly Iverson
(vital records and probate records)
probate search service: no charge; copies of
probate records: $3.50 for the first page and
25¢ for each additional page, $5.00 for the
first certified page and 25¢ for each additional
certified page, no minimum

Watonwan County Recorder
PO Box 518
St. James, MN 56081
(507) 375-1216; (507) 375-8271 FAX
recorder@co.watonwan.mn.us
http://www3.extension.umn.edu/county/templ
ate/index.aspx?countyID=85
Joy Sing
(land records)

Wilkin County
organized 1858 from Cass County; name
changed from Toombs County to Andy
Johnson County in 1863; name changed from
Andy Johnson County to Wilkin County in
1868

Wilkin County Court Administrator
(Courthouse, 300 South Fifth Street—location)
PO Box 219 (mailing address)
Breckenridge, MN 56520
(218) 643-4972; (218) 643-7167 FAX
Diane.Fox@courts.state.mn.us
http://www.mncourts.gov/district/8/?page=1076
Diane K. Fox
(probate records from 1874)
no probate search service

**Wilkin County Recorder and Registrar of
Titles**
PO Box 29
Breckenridge, MN 56520
(218) 643-7164; (218) 643-7170 FAX
recorder@co.wilkin.mn.us
http://www.co.wilkin.mn.us/recorder.asp
Renae Niemi
(land records from 1872)

Winona County
organized 1854 from unorganized lands

Winona County Court Administrator
171 West Third Street, Second Floor
Winona, MN 55987-3102
(507) 457-6385 (Judgment Searches); (507) 457-
6386 (Probate); (507) 457-6392 FAX
http://www.co.winona.mn.us/se3bin/clientgeni
e.cgi
Sally Cumiskey
(probate records)
vital records search service: $20.00 per hour;
probate search service ("try to be as
reasonable as possible; cost will cover copies
and mailing expense"); copies of vital records:
$11.00 for certified copies of births, $8.00 for
certified copies of deaths and marriages and
non-certified copies of births

Winona County Recorder
171 West Third
Winona, MN 55987
(507) 457-6340; (507) 454-9371 FAX
bbambenek@nt1.co.winona.mn.us
http://www.mn.us/se3bin/clientgenie.cgi
Bob Bambenek
(land records)

Wright County
organized 1855 from Becker County

Wright County Court Administrator
Government Center
10 Second Street, N.W.
Buffalo, MN 55313-1187
(763) 682-7539; (763) 682-7300 FAX
http://www.co.wright.mn.us/department/court
admin
LaVonn Nordeen
(probate records from 1871 with Probate
Division)
probate search service: no charge; copies of
probate records: $1.00 per page, no minimum

Wright County Recorder
Government Center
10 Second Street, N.W., Room 210
Buffalo, MN 55313-1196
(763) 682-7357
larry.unger@co.wright.mn.us
http://www.co.wright.mn.us/department/recor
der;
http://www.co.wright.mn.us/department/rec
order/landtitle/index.htm
Larry A. Unger
(land records, births and deaths)
vital records search service: $20.00 per hour,
$2.50 minimum; copies of vital records: $8.00
for uncertified copies of births, $11.00 for
certified copies of births (includes search),
$8.00 for certified copies of deaths and
marriages (includes search, no uncertified
copies available)

Yellow Medicine County
organized 1871 from Redwood County

**Yellow Medicine County Court
Administrator**
415 Ninth Avenue, Suite 103
Granite Falls, MN 56241-1367
(320) 564-3325; (320) 564-4435 FAX
Cheryl.Eckhardt@courts.state.mn.us
http://www.mncourts.gov/district/8/?page=1077
Cheryl Eckhardt
(probate records)
probate search service: $10.00 per hour; copies
of probate records: $5.00 per page, $10.00 per
certified page

Yellow Medicine County Recorder
415 Ninth Avenue
Granite Falls, MN 56241
(320) 564-2529; (320) 564-3670 FAX
kay.zempel@co.yellow-medicine.mn.us
http://yellowmedicine.govoffice.com
Kay Zempel
(land records, vital records)

MISSISSIPPI

Capital: Jackson. Statehood: 10 December 1817 (annexed in 1783, became a separate territory in 1798 with extensions in 1804 and 1813)

Mississippi has about fifty Municipal Courts which handle municipal ordinance violations. Some 410 Justice Courts hear some civil actions, misdemeanors, and felony preliminaries. Seventeen County Courts handle some civil actions, misdemeanors, felony preliminaries and juvenile matters in Adams, Bolivar, Coahoma, DeSoto, Forrest, Harrison, Hinds (judicial elections stayed by injunction), Jackson, Jones, Lauderdale, Leflore, Madison, Pike, Rankin, Warren, Washington and Yazoo counties.

The Circuit Court is the state's trial court of general jurisdiction and sits at the county seats within each circuit. First Judicial District: Alcorn, Itawamba, Lee, Monroe, Pontotoc, Prentiss and Tishomingo counties; Second: Hancock, Harrison and Stone; Third: Benton, Calhoun, Chickasaw, Lafayette, Marshall, Tippah and Union; Fourth: Holmes, Humphreys, Leflore, Sunflower and Washington; Fifth: Attala, Carroll, Choctaw, Grenada, Montgomery, Webster and Winston; Sixth: Adams, Amite, Franklin, Jefferson and Wilkinson; Seventh: Hinds and Yazoo; Eighth: Leake, Neshoba, Newton and Scott; Ninth: Claiborne, Issaquena, Sharkey and Warren; Tenth: Clarke, Kemper, Lauderdale and Wayne; Eleventh: Bolivar, Coahoma, Quitman and Tunica; Twelfth: Forrest and Perry; Thirteenth: Covington, Jasper, Simpson and Smith; Fourteenth: Copiah, Lincoln, Pike and Walthall; Fifteenth: Jefferson Davis, Lamar, Lawrence, Marion and Pearl River; Sixteenth: Clay, Lowndes, Noxubee and Oktibbeha; Seventeenth: DeSoto, Panola, Tallahatchie, Tate and Yalobusha; Eighteenth: Jones County; Nineteenth: George, Greene and Jackson; Twentieth: Madison and Rankin.

Mississippi's Chancery Courts sit in each county seat and deal with matters of equity, alimony and divorce, probate, mental competency, real estate titles, etc. First District: Alcorn, Itawamba, Lee, Monroe, Pontotoc, Prentiss, Tishomingo and Union counties; Second: Jasper, Newton and Scott; Third: DeSoto, Grenada, Montgomery, Panola, Tate and Yalobusha; Fourth: Amite, Franklin, Pike and Walthall; Fifth: Hinds County; Sixth: Attala, Carroll, Choctaw, Kemper, Neshoba and Winston; Seventh: Bolivar, Coahoma, Leflore, Quitman, Tallahatchie and Tunica; Eighth: Hancock, Harrison and Stone; Ninth: Humphreys, Issaquena, Sharkey, Sunflower, Warren and Washington; Tenth: Forrest, Lamar, Marion, Pearl River and Perry; Eleventh: Holmes, Leake, Madison and Yazoo; Twelfth: Clarke and Lauderdale; Thirteenth: Covington, Jefferson Davis, Lawrence, Simpson and Smith; Fourteenth: Chickasaw, Clay, Lowndes, Noxubee, Oktibbeha and Webster; Fifteenth: Copiah and Lincoln; Sixteenth: George, Greene and Jackson; Seventeenth: Adams, Claiborne, Jefferson and Wilkinson; Eighteenth: Benton, Calhoun, Lafayette, Marshall and Tippah; Nineteenth: Jones and Wayne; Twentieth: Rankin County. The Mississippi Supreme Court handles appeals.

Adams County
organized 1799 from the Old Natchez District, one of two areas to which the British acquired title by treaty with the Indians in 1765

Adams County Chancery Clerk's Office
PO Box 1006
Natchez, MS 39120-1006
(601) 446-6684; (601) 445-7913
Chanceryclerk@adamscountyms.gov
http://www.adamscountyms.net/elected-officials/chancery-clerk

Thomas O'Beirne, Chancery Clerk
(land records and probate records from the 1800s)
no land records search service; no probate search service; copies of probate records: 50¢ per page, $1.00 for certification, 50¢ minimum

Adams County Circuit Clerk's Office
PO Box 1224
Natchez, MS 39121
(601) 446-6326; (601) 442-3329 FAX
http://www.deltacomputersystem.com/MS/MS01
Mr. M. L. "Binky" Vines, Circuit Clerk
(marriage records)

Alcorn County
organized 1870 from Tippah, Tishomingo and Wilkinson counties

Alcorn County Chancery Clerk's Office
(500 Waldron Street, Corinth, MS 38834—location)
PO Box 69 (mailing address
Corinth, MS 38835-0069
(601) 286-7700; (607) 286-7706 FAX
bmarolt@co.alcorn.ms.us
http://alcorncounty.org/chancery.aspx
Mr. Bobby Marlot, Chancery Clerk
(land and probate records)

Alcorn County Circuit Clerk's Office
po Box 430
Corinth, MS 33834
(601) 286-7740; (601) 286-5713 FAX
jcaldwell@co.alcorn.ms.us
http://alcorncounty.org/circuit.aspx
Joe Caldwell, Circuit Clerk
(marriage records)

Amite County
organized 1809 from Wilkinson County

Amite County Chancery Clerk's Office
PO Box 680
Liberty, MS 39645
(601) 657-8022; (601) 657-8288 FAX
hollism@telapex.com
http://www.mslawyer.com/chanceryclerks/amite.html
Mr. Ronnie Taylor, Chancery Clerk
(land records, naturalization records, probate records)

Amite County Circuit Clerk's Office
PO Box 312
Liberty, MS 39645
(601) 657-8932; (601) 657-8288 FAX
http://www.mississippi.gov/sub_sub_map.jsp?Category_ID=12&County_ID=114
Sharon Walsh, Circuit Clerk
(marriage records)

Attala County
organized 1833 from Choctaw Cession

Attala County Chancery Clerk's Office
230 West Washington Street
Kosciusko, MS 39090
(601) 289-2921; (601) 289-7662 FAX
http://www.mississippi.gov/sub_sub_map.jsp?Category_ID=12&County_ID=115
Ms. Gerry Taylor, Chancery Clerk
(land records and probate records)

Attala County Circuit Clerk's Office
118 West Washington Street
Kosciusko, MS 39090
(601) 289-1471; (610) 289-7666 FAX
http://www.mslawyer.com/mssc/cirlerk.html#attala
Sara Reese, Circuit Clerk
(marriages)
copies of marriages: $5.00 each

Benton County
organized 1870 from Marshall and Tippah counties

Benton County Chancery Clerk's Office
PO Box 218

Ashland, MS 38603-0218
(601) 224-6300; (601) 224-6303 FAX
http://www.mississippi.gov/sub_sub_map.jsp?Category_ID=12&County_ID=116
Mark M. Ormon, Chancery Clerk
(land records from 1870, probate records from 1890)
no probate search service; copies of probate records: 50¢ each, no minimum

Benton County Circuit Clerk's Office
PO Box 262
Ashland, MS 38603
(601) 224-6310; (601) 224-6301 FAX
Circlk@Bentoncountyms.gov
http://www.mslawyer.com/mssc/circlerk.html#benton
Martha G. Mitchell, Circuit Clerk
(marriage records)

Bolivar County
organized 1836 from Choctaw Cession

Bolivar County Chancery Clerk's Office
PO Box 789
Cleveland, MS 38732
(601) 843-2071; (601) 846-5880 FAX
jwalker@co.bolivar.ms.us
http://www.co.bolivar.ms.us/chanceryclerk.htm
Jeanne R. Walker, Chancery Clerk
(land and probate records)

Bolivar County Circuit Clerk's Office
po Box 670
Cleveland, MS 38732
(601) 843-2061; (601) 843-2943 FAX
http://www.co.bolivar.ms.us/circuitclerk.htm
Rosie S. Simmons, Circuit Clerk
(marriage records)

Calhoun County
organized 1852 from Chickasaw, Lafayette and Yalobusha counties

Calhoun County Chancery Clerk's Office
PO Box 8
Pittsboro, MS 38951-0008
(601) 983-3122; (601) 983-3128 FAX
http://www.mississippi.gov/sub_sub_map.jsp?Category_ID=12&County_ID=118
Martha Ann Martin, Chancery Clerk
(land records from 1923 ["County courthouse burned 22 December 1922, destroying *all* records *except* for five books of abstracts of land deed records (indexed by land sections, but *not* indexed by surname), the 1921-1922 tax roll, and a very few deeds re-recorded after the courthouse burned; the abstract books are in the process of being indexed, but at present the only way to check is by precise land location"], probate records from 1923)
probate search service: no charge, but will be done only as time permits; copies of probate records: 50¢ per page, plus $1.00 for each certification, no minimum

Calhoun County Circuit Clerk's Office
PO Box 25
Pittsboro, MS 38951
(601) 983-3101; (601) 983-3128 FAX
Ddunn@Calhouncoms.com
http://www.mslawyer.com/mssc/circlerk.html#calhoun
Deborah Dunn, Circuit Clerk
(marriages from 1923 [and several marriages prior to 1923, which were obtained elsewhere or re-recorded])

Carroll County
organized 1833 from Choctaw Cession

Carroll County Chancery Clerk's Office
PO Box 60
Carrollton, MS 38917-0060
(601) 237-9274
Suage@Duckwood.net
http://www.carrollcountyms.com/electedofficials.htm
Stanley Mullins, Chancery Clerk
(land and probate records)

Carroll County Circuit Clerk's Office
PO Box 6
Vaiden, MS 39176
(601) 464-5476; (601) 464-7745 FAX
http://www.carrollcountyms.com/electedofficia
  ls.htm
Durwood Stanton, Circuit Clerk
(marriage records)

Chickasaw County
organized 1836 from Chickasaw Cession 1832

Chickasaw County Chancery Clerk's Office
Courthouse Building
101 North Jefferson
Houston, MS 38851
(601) 456-2513; (601) 456-5295 FAX
http://www.chickasawcoms.com
W. David Thomas, Chancery Clerk
(land records from 1861 ["county records were
  destroyed by Yankee troops in 1863; one deed
  book and a few tax rolls and a very few other
  items of this nature survived"], probate
  records from 1861)
no probate search service; copies of probate
  records: 50¢ per page

Chickasaw County Circuit Clerk's Office
Courthouse
Houston, MS 38851
(601) 456-2331; (601) 456-5295 FAX
Swillis@Chicasawcoms.com
http://www.chickasawcoms.com
Sandra Nabors Willis, Circuit Clerk
(marriage records)

Choctaw County
organized 1833 from Chickasaw Cession 1832

Choctaw County Chancery Clerk's Office
PO Box 736
Ackerman, MS 39735-0736
(601) 285-6329; (601) 285-3444 FAX
http://www.mississippi.gov/sub_sub_map.jsp?
  Category_ID=12&CountyID=121;
  http://www.choctawcountyms.org
Don Threadgill, Chancery Clerk
(land and probate records)

Choctaw County Circuit Clerk's Office
PO Box 34
Ackerman, MS 39735
(601) 285-6245; (601) 285-3444 FAX
http://www.mississippi.gov/sub_sub_map.jsp?
  Category_ID=12&CountyID=121;
  http://www.choctawcountyms.org
Wanda H. Vowell, Circuit Clerk
(marriage records)

Claiborne County
organized 1802 from Jefferson County

Claiborne County Chancery Clerk's Office
(410 Main Street—location)
PO Box 449 (mailing address)
Port Gibson, MS 39150-0449
(601) 437-4992; (601) 437-4430 FAX
Chancery11@aol.com
http://www.ccmsgov.us;
  http://www.mississippi.gov/sub_sub_map.js
  p?Category_ID=12&County_ID=122
Gloria Kelly Dotson, Chancery Clerk
(land records, name changes and correcting birth
  certificates, probate records)
probate search service: $5.00; copies of probate
  records: 50¢ for each of the first twenty-five
  copies and 25¢ for each additional copy

Claiborne County Circuit Clerk's Office
PO Box 549
Port Gibson, MS 39150
(601) 437-5841
http://www.mslawyer.com/mssc/circlerk.html
  #claiborne
Ms. Sammie Good, Circuit Clerk
(marriage records)

Clarke County
organized 1812 from Choctaw Cession

Clarke County Chancery Clerk's Office
PO Box 689
Quitman, MS 39355-0689
(601) 776-2126; (601) 776-1013 FAX
Chancery@Clarkeco.net
http://www.visitclrkecounty.com
Angie Chisholm, Chancery Clerk
(land records, probate records)
no probate search service; copies of probate
  records: 50¢ per page, no minimum

Clarke County Circuit Clerk's Office
PO Box 216
Quitman, MS 39355
(601) 776-3111; (601) 776-1013 FAX
Circuit@Clarkeco.net
http://www.mslawyer.com/mssc/circlerk.html
  #clarke
Beth Doggett, Circuit Clerk
(marriage records)

Clay County
organized 1872 from Chickasaw, Oktibbeha and
  Lowndes counties; name changed from
  Colfax County in 1876

Clay County Chancery Clerk's Office
PO Box 815
West Point, MS 39773-0815
(601) 494-3124; (601) 495-2050 FAX
Chancery@claycounty.ms.gov
http://www.mississippi.gov/sub_sub_map.jsp?
  Category_ID=12&County_ID=124
Mr. H. A. "Robbie" Robinson, Chancery Clerk
(land records from about 1862, probate records
  from 1872)
probate search service: no charge; copies of
  probate records: 50¢ per page, $2.00
  minimum

Clay County Circuit Clerk's Office
PO Box 364
West Point, MS 39773
(601) 494-3384; (601) 495-2050 FAX
Rharrell@claycounty.ms.gov
http://www.mslawyer.com/mssc/circlerk.html
  #clay
Robert Harrell, Circuit Clerk
(marriage records)

Coahoma County
organized 1836 from Chickasaw Cession 1836

Coahoma County Chancery Clerk's Office
PO Box 98
Clarksdale, MS 38614-0098
(601) 624-3000; (601) 624-3029 FAX
Chanceryclerk@cableone.net
http://www.mississippi.gov/sub_sub_map.jsp?
  Category_ID=12&County_ID=125
Edward P. Peacock, III, Chancery Clerk
(land records, probate records)

Coahoma County Circuit Clerk's Office
PO Box 849
Clarksdale, MS 38614
(601) 624-3014; (601) 624-3075 FAX
Coahomacirclrk@yahoo.com
http://www.mslawyer.com/mssc/circlerk.html
  #coahoma
Charles Oakes, Circuit Clerk
(marriage records)

Copiah County
organized 1823 from Hinds County

Copiah County Chancery Clerk's Office
(121 South Lowe Street—location)
PO Box 507 (mailing address)
Hazlehurst, MS 39083-0507
(601) 894-3021; (601) 894-4081 FAX FAX
samos@copiahcountyms.gov
http://www.copiahcounty.org/chancery_clerk.htm
Steve Amos, Chancery Clerk
(land records from 1823 [first Deed Book A lost
  when county seat moved], naturalization
  records from 1823 to 1906 [indexed by
  W.P.A., found in minute books], probate
  records from 1823)
no probate search service ("will refer request to

a genealogist"); copies of probate records: 50¢
  each

Copiah County Circuit Clerk's Office
PO Box 467
Hazlehurst, MS 39083
(601) 894-1241; (601) 894-3026 FAX
estevens@copiahcountyms.gov
http://www.copiahcounty.org/Circuit%20Clerk
  .htm
Edna Edwards Stevens, Circuit Clerk
(marriage records)

Covington County
organized 1819 from Lawrence and Wayne
  counties

Covington County Chancery Clerk's Office
PO Box 1679
Collins, MS 39428-1679
(601) 765-6132; (601) 765-1052 FAX
http://www.mississippi.gov/sub_sub_map.jsp?
  Category_ID=12&County_ID=127
Ann Bullock, Chancery Clerk
(land and probate records)

Covington County Circuit Clerk's Office
PO Box 667
Collins, MS 39428
(601) 765-6506; (601) 765-1052 FAX
circuitclerk@covingtoncountyms.gov
http://www.mslawyer.com/mssc/circlerk.html
  #coving
Keith Earl Collins, Circuit Clerk
(marriage records)

DeSoto County
organized 1836 from Indian lands

DeSoto County Chancery Clerk's Office
Courthouse, 2535 Highway 51 South, Room 104
Hernando, MS 38632
(601) 429-1318; (601) 429-1311 FAX
http://www.desotoms.com/chancery.htm
William E. "Sluggo" Davis, Chancery Clerk
(land records from 1836, a few naturalization
  records in probate court records [but have no
  index], current probate records)
clerk copies: 50¢; certified copies: $1.00

DeSoto County Circuit Clerk's Office
Courthouse, 2535 Highway 51 South
Hernando, MS 38632
(601) 429-1325; (601) 429-1311 FAX
dalethompson@desotocountyms.org
http://www.desotoms.com
Dale Kelly Thompson, Circuit Clerk
(marriage records)

Forrest County
organized 1906 from Perry County

Forrest County Chancery Clerk's Office
(316 Forest Street—location)
PO Box 951 (mailing address)
Hattiesburg, MS 39403-0951
(601) 545-6014; (601) 545-6095 FAX
reidlance@hotmail.com
http://www.co.forrest.ms.us
Jimmy C. Havard, Chancery Clerk
(land and probate records)

Forrest County Circuit Clerk's Office
PO Drawer 992
Hattiesburg, MS 39403
(601) 582-3213; (601) 545-6093 FAX
ladams@co.forrest.ms.us
http://www.co.forrest.ms.us
Lou Ellen Adams, Circuit Clerk
(marriage records)

Franklin County
county incorporated 1809 from Adams County

Franklin County Chancery Clerk's Office
PO Box 297
Meadville, MS 39653
(601) 384-2330; (601) 384-5864 FAX
chance@telapex.com
http://www.franklincountyms.com/welcome.html
Jimmy W. Jones, Chancery Clerk

(deeds from 1806 [some books were destroyed in courthouse fire of 1876], mortgages and deeds of trust from 1806, land rolls from 1872, wills from 1877)
probate search service: no charge; copies of probate records: 50¢ per page, $1.00 for certification, no minimum

Franklin County Circuit Clerk's Office
PO Box 267
Meadville, MS 39653
(601) 384-2320; (601) 384-5864 FAX
fccircuit@telepak.net
http://www.franklincountyms.com/welcome.html
Millie Thornton, Circuit Clerk
(marriage records)

George County
organized 1811 from Greene and Jackson counties

George County Chancery Clerk's Office
Courthouse Square
355 Cox Street, Suite A
Lucedale, MS 39452
(601) 947-4801
http://www.mississippi.gov/sub_sub_map.jsp?Category_ID=12&CountyID=131; http://www.georgecounty.ms
Cammie Byrd, Chancery Clerk
(land and probate records)

George County Circuit Clerk's Office
355 Cox Street, Suite C
Lucedale, MS 39452
(601) 947-4881; (601) 947-8804 FAX
http://www.mississippi.gov/sub_sub_map.jsp?Category_ID=12&CountyID=131; http://www.georgecounty.ms
James C. Cochran, Circuit Clerk
(marriage records)

Greene County
organized 1811 from Amite, Franklin and Wayne counties

Greene County Chancery Clerk's Office
PO Box 610
Leakesville, MS 39451-0610
(601) 394-2377; (601) 394-2334
http://www.mississippi.gov/sub_sub_map.jsp?Category_ID=12&County_ID=132
Allen Wayne Pulliam, Chancery Clerk
(land and probate records)

Greene County Circuit Clerk's Office
PO Box 310
Leakesville, MS 39451
(601) 394-2347; (601) 394-5939 FAX
http://www.mslawyer.com/mssc/circlerk.html#greene
Scharlotte Fortinberry, Circuit Clerk
(marriage records)

Grenada County
organized 1870 from Carroll, Tallahatchie and Yalobusha counties at Coffeeville, Mississippi

Grenada County Chancery Clerk's Office
PO Box 1208
Grenada, MS 38901-1208
(601) 226-1821; (601) 226-0427 FAX
powellva@ayrix.com
http://www.mississippi.gov/sub_sub_map.jsp?Category_ID=12&County_ID=133
Powell Vance, Chancery Clerk
(land records, probate records)
no land records search service (contact Mrs. J. W. [Ruth] Martin or Henry Heggie, local historians)

Grenada County Circuit Clerk's Office
59 Greene Street #8
Grenada, MS 38901
(601) 226-1941; (601) 226-0427 FAX
lbcirclk@ayrix.net
http://www.mslawyer.com/mssc/circlerk.html#grenada
Linda Marter Barnette, Circuit Clerk
(marriage records)

Hancock County
organized 1812 from Mobile District

Hancock County Chancery Clerk's Office
150 Main Street
Bay St. Louis, MS 39520
(601) 467-5404; (601) 466-5994 FAX
http://www.hancockcountyms.gov
Timothy A. Kellar, Chancery Clerk
(land and probate records)

Hancock County Circuit Clerk's Office
PO Box 249
Bay St. Louis, MS 39520
(601) 467-5265; (601) 467-2779 FAX
http://www.hancockcountyms.gov
Pamela T. Metzler, Circuit Clerk
(marriage records)

Harrison County
organized 1841 from Hancock and Jackson counties

Harrison County Chancery Clerk's Office
(1801 23rd Avenue, Gulfport, MS 39501—location)
PO Drawer CC
Gulfport, MS 39502
(228) 865-4117; (228) 865-4118; (228) 868-1480 FAX
chanclerk@goldinc.com; chanceryclerk@co.harrison.ms.us
http://www.goldinc.com/~clerk; http://www.co.harrison.ms/departments/chanclerk/index.asp
John McAdams, Chancery Clerk
(land and probate records)

Harrison County Circuit Clerk's Office
(1801 23rd Avenue, Gulfport, MS 39501—location)
PO Box 998 (mailing address)
Gulfport, MS 39502
(601) 865-4167; (601) 865-4099 FAX
gkparker@aol.com
http://www.co.harrison.ms.us/departments/circlerk/index.asp
Ms. Gayle Parker, Circuit Clerk
(marriage records)

Hinds County
organized 1821 from Choctaw Cession

Hinds County Chancery Clerk's Office
(Chancery Court Building, 316 South President Street, Jackson, MS 39201—First Judicial District location)
PO Box 686 (First Judicial District mailing address)
Jackson, MS 39205-0686
(601) 968-6508 (First Judicial District, Land); (601) 968-6540 (First Judicial District, Court); (601) 857-8055 (Second Judicial District); (601) 973-5535 FAX
ecarr@co.hinds.ms.us
http://www.co.hinds.ms.us/pgs/elected/chanceryclerk.asp
Eddie Jean Carr, Chancery Clerk
("original Hinds County Courthouse is in Raymond, Mississippi [Main Street, Annex Building, Raymond, MS 39154—Second Judicial District location, PO Box 88 (mailing address), Raymond, MS 39154]; they have all the records for the entire county up to 1870; at that time, the county built another courthouse at Jackson, Mississippi; Raymond Courthouse continued to keep the records for the western ⏐ of the county, and Jackson started keeping the records for the eastern ⏐ of the county")
no probate search service; copies of probate records: 50¢ per page, no minimum

Hinds County Circuit Clerk's Office
PO Box 327 (First Judicial District)
Jackson, MS 39205
(601) 968-6628 (First Judicial District); (601) 857-8038 (Second Judicial District); (601) 973-5547 FAX
bdunn@co.hinds.ms.us

http://www.co.hinds.ms.us/pgs/elected/circuitclerk.asp
Barbara Dunn, Circuit Clerk
(marriage records [Second Judicial District, PO Box 999, Raymond, MS 39154])

Second Judicial District
121 West Main Street
Raymond, MS 39154
(601) 857-8038; (601) 857-0535 FAX
http://www.mississippidui.com/dui_court/list.html

Holmes County
organized 1833 from Yazoo County

Holmes County Chancery Clerk's Office
PO Box 239
Lexington, MS 39095-0239
(601) 834-2281
http://www.mslawyer.com/chanceryclerks/holmes.html
Jean Smith, Chancery Clerk
(land and probate records)

Holmes County Circuit Clerk's Office
PO Box 718
Lexington, MS 39095
(601) 834-2476
court2@dixie-net.com
http://www.mslawyer.com/circuitclerks/holmes.html
Earline Hart, Circuit Clerk
(marriage records)

Humphreys County
organized 1918 from Holmes, Washington, Yazoo and Sunflower counties

Humphreys County Chancery Clerk's Office
PO Box 547
Belzoni, MS 39038-0547
(601) 247-1740; (601) 247-3906 FAX
http://www.mississippi.gov/sub_sub_map.jsp?Category_ID=12&CountyID=138; http://www.catfishcapitalonline.com
Lawrence Browder, Chancery Clerk
(land records, probate records)
probate search service: $5.00; copies of probate records: 50¢ per page (25¢ per page if you do the copying), $1.00 for certified copies, $5.00 minimum plus SAE

Humphreys County Circuit Clerk's Office
PO Box 696
Belzoni, MS 39038
(601) 247-3065; (601) 247-3906 FAX
http://www.mississippi.gov/sub_sub_map.jsp?Category_ID=12&CountyID=138; http://www.catfishcapitalonline.com
Timaka Jones, Circuit Clerk
(marriage records)

Issaquena County
organized 1844 from Washington County

Issaquena County Chancery Clerk and Circuit Clerk
PO Box 27
Mayersville, MS 39113
(601) 873-2761; (601) 873-2061 FAX
http://www.mississippi.gov/sub_sub_map.jsp?Category_ID=12&County_ID=139
Erline Fortner, Chancery Clerk
(land and probate records, marriage records)

Itawamba County
organized 1836 from Indian lands

Itawamba County Chancery Clerk's Office
(201 West Main, Fulton, MS 38843-1153—location)
PO Box 776 (mailing address)
Fulton, MS 38843
(601) 862-3421; (601) 862-4006 FAX
jwitt@itwambacoms.com
http://www.mississippi.gov/sub_sub_map.jsp?Category_ID=12&County_ID=140
James E. Witt, Jr., Chancery Clerk
(land records, probate records from 1836)

no probate search service; copies of probate records: 50¢ each, no minimum

Itawamba County Circuit Clerk's Office
201 West Main Street
Fulton, MS 38843
(601) 862-3511; (601) 862-4006 FAX
cgates@itawambacoms.com
http://www.mslawyer.com/mssc/circlerk.html
#itawamba
Ms. Carol Gates, Circuit Clerk
(marriage records from 1836)

Jackson County
organized 1812 from Mobile District

Jackson County Chancery Clerk's Office
(Civic Center, Vaga Street—temporary location;
Jackson County Courts Building, 3104
Magnolia Street—permanent location)
PO Box 998 (mailing address)
Pascagoula, MS 39568-0998
(228) 769-3499; (228) 769-3414 FAX
Terry_Miller@co.jackson.ms.us
http://www.co.jackson.ms.us/DS/ChanceryClerk.html
Mr. Terry Miller, Chancery Clerk
(land records from 1875, although some records
which were destroyed by two courthouse fires
have been re-recorded back to the early
1800s, naturalization records from 1875
[temporarily misplaced], probate records from
1875 [some earlier records re-recorded])
no probate search service; copies of land
records: 50¢ per page, $3.00 and up for maps;
copies of probate records: 50¢ per page

Jackson County Circuit Clerk's Office
(2902 Shortcut Road [Fairground]—temporary
location; Jackson County Courts Building,
3104 Magnolia Street—permanent location)
PO Box 998 (mailing address)
Pascagoula, MS 39568-0998
(601) 769-3040; (601) 769-3180 FAX
http://www.co.jackson.ms.us/DS/CircuitClerk.html
Joe W. Martin, Jr., Circuit Clerk
(marriage records from 1875)

Jasper County
organized 1833 from Indian lands

Jasper County Chancery Clerk's Office
PO Box 1047
Bay Springs, MS 39422
(601) 764-3368; (601) 764-3026
http://www.co.jasper.ms.us
Barbara Ravenhorst, Chancery Clerk
(land and probate records)
no probate search service; copies of probate
records: 25¢ per page

Jasper County Circuit Clerk's Office
PO Box 447
Bay Springs, MS 39422
(601) 764-2245; (601) 764-3078 FAX
http://www.co.jasper.ms.us/county_officials.html
Billy G. Rayner, Circuit Clerk
(marriage records)

Jefferson County
organized 1799 from Pickering County

Jefferson County Chancery Clerk's Office
PO Box 145
Fayette, MS 39069-0145
(601) 786-3021; (601) 786-6000 FAX
http://www.mississippi.gov/sub_sub_map.jsp?
Category_ID=12&CountyID=143
Delorise Frye, Chancery Clerk
(land records, probate records)
probate search service: $5.00; copies of land
records: 50¢ per page (supply section,
township and range); copies of probate
records: 50¢ per page, no minimum

Jefferson County Circuit Clerk's Office
PO Box 305
Fayette, MS 39069
(601) 786-3422; (601) 786-6000 FAX

http://www.mississippi.gov/sub_sub_map.jsp?
Category_ID=12&CountyID=143
Burnell Harris, Circuit Clerk
(marriage records)

Jefferson Davis County
organized 1906 from Covington and Lawrence
counties

Jefferson Davis County Chancery Clerk's Office
PO Box 1137
Prentiss, MS 39474-1137
(601) 792-4204; (601) 792-2894 FAX
jacklbsr@yahoo.com
http://www.mslawyer.com/chanceryclerks/jeffdavi.html
Jack D. Berry, Chancery Clerk
(land and probate records)

Jefferson Davis County Circuit Clerk's Office
PO Box 1082
Prentiss, MS 39474
(601) 792-4231; (601) 792-2894 FAX
http://www.mississippi.gov/sub_sub_map.jsp?
Category_ID=12&County_ID=144
Cecil Anderson, Circuit Clerk
(marriage records)

Jones County
organized 1826 from Covington and Wayne
counties

Jones County Chancery Clerk's Office
PO Box 1468
Laurel, MS 39441-1468
(601) 428-0527; (601) 428-3602 FAX
http://www.edajones.com/Government/government.html (Economic Development
Authority)
Roy Hunt Boutwell, Chancery Clerk
(land and probate records)

Jones County Circuit Clerk's Office
PO Box 1336
Laurel, MS 39440
(601) 425-2556; (601) 428-3602 FAX
http://www.mslawyer.com/mssc/circlerk.html
#jones
Wayne Myrick, Circuit Clerk
(marriage records)

Kemper County
organized 1833 from Indian lands

Kemper County Chancery Clerk's Office
PO Box 188
De Kalb, MS 39328-0188
(601) 743-2460; (601) 743-2789 FAX
http://www.kempercounty.com
June Craig Aust, Chancery Clerk
(land and probate records)

Kemper County Circuit Clerk's Office
PO Box 130
DeKalb, MS 39328
(601) 743-2224; (601) 743-2789 FAX
RomaAllen@co.kemper.ms.us
http://www.kempercounty.com
Roma Allen, Circuit Clerk
(marriage records)

Lafayette County
organized 1836 from Chickasaw Cession 1832

Lafayette County Chancery Clerk's Office
(300 North Lamar Boulevard—location)
PO Box 1240 (mailing address)
Oxford, MS 38655-1240
(601) 234-2131; (601) 234-5402 FAX
swall@lafayettecoms.com
http://www.lafayettecoms.com
Bill Plunk, Chancery Clerk
(land and probate records)

Lafayette County Circuit Clerk's Office
1 Courthouse Squaare, Suite 101
Oxford, MS 38655
(601) 234-4951; (601) 234-5402 FAX
lafcirc@dixie-net.com;

mbusby@lafayettecoms.com
http://www.lafayettecoms.com
Mary Alice Busby, Circuit Clerk
(marriage records)

Lamar County
organized 1904 from Marion and Pearl River

Lamar County Chancery Clerk's Office
PO Box 247
Purvis, MS 39475-0247
(601) 544-4410; (601) 794-1049 FAx
http://www.lamarcounty.com
Wayne Smith, Chancery Clerk
(land records from 1880, probate records from
1905)
probate search service: no charge if you make
search; copies of probate records: 50¢ each
(25¢ each if you do the copying), no
minimum

Lamar County Circuit Clerk's Office
PO Box 369
Purvis, MS 39475
(601) 794-8504; (601) 794-1049 FAX
CircuitClerk@co.lamr.ms.us
http://www.lamarcounty.com
Mr. Leslie Wilson, Circuit Clerk
(marriage records)

Lauderdale County
organized 1833 from Choctaw Cession

Lauderdale County Chancery Clerk's Office
(500 Constitution Avenue, First Floor, Meridian,
MS 39301—location)
PO Box 1587 (mailing address)
Meridian, MS 39302
(601) 482-9701
chanceryclerk@lauderdalecounty.org
http://www.lauderdalecounty.org/chancery_clerk.htm
Ann Wilson Hayes, Chancery Clerk
(land and probate records)

Lauderdale County Circuit Clerk's Office
(500 Constitution Avenue, First Floor, Meridian,
MS 39301—location)
PO Box 1005 (mailing address)
Meridian, MS 39302
(601) 482-9731; (601) 484-3970 FAX
circuitclerk@lauderdalecounty.org
http://www.lauderdalecounty.org/circuit_clerk.htm
Donna Jill Johnson, Circuit Clerk
(marriage records)

Lawrence County
organized 1814 from Marion County

Lawrence County Chancery Clerk's Office
PO Box 40
Monticello, MS 39654-0040
(601) 587-7162; (601) 587-3003 FAX
krayborn@co.lawrence.ms.us
http://www.mississippi.gov/sub_sub_map.jsp?
Category_ID=12&County_ID=150
Kevin Rayborn, Chancery Clerk
(land and probate records)

Lawrence County Circuit Clerk's Office
PO Box 1249
Monticello, MS 39654
(601) 587-4791; (601) 587-3003 FAX
cstokes@co.lawrence.ms.us
http://www.mslawyer.com/mssc/circlerk.html
#lawrenc
Cindy Stokes, Circuit Clerk
(marriage records)

Leake County
organized 1833 from Choctaw Cession 1830

Leake County Chancery Clerk's Office
PO Box 72
Carthage, MS 39051-0072
(601) 267-7371; (601) 267-6132 FAX
http://www.mississippi.gov/sub_sub_map.jsp?
Category_ID=12&County_ID=151
Dot Merchant, Chancery Clerk
(land records, probate records)

probate search service: ("we don't wish to do searches because of insufficient time, however we will for $20.00 per hour"); copies of probate records: $1.00 per page if mailed (25¢ per page if you do the copying), $10.00 minimum

Leake County Circuit Clerk's Office
PO Box 67
Carthage, MS 39051
(601) 267-8357; (601) 267-8889 FAX
http://www.mslawyer.com/mssc/circlerk.html#leake
Rebecca Pearson, Circuit Clerk
(marriage records)

Lee County
organized 1866 from Itawamba and Pontotoc counties

Lee County Chancery Clerk's Office
PO Box 7127
Tupelo, MS 38802
(601) 841-9100; (601) 680-6091 FAX
http://www.mslawyer.com/chanceryclerks/lee.html; http://www.leecoms.com
Willima H. "Bill" Benson, Chancery Clerk
(land records and probate records from 1867)
no probate search service; copies of probate records: 50¢ per page, no minimum

Lee County Circuit Clerk's Office
PO Box 762
Tupelo, MS 38802
(662) 841-9024; (662) 680-6079 FAX
jloftin@leecoms.com
http://www.mslawyer.com/circuitclerks/lee.html
Joyce R. Loftin, Circuit Clerk
(marriage records)

Leflore County
organized 1871 from Carroll and Sunflower counties

Leflore County Chancery Clerk's Office
PO Box 250
Greenwood, MS 38935-0250
(601) 453-6203; (601) 455-7965 FAX
abraham@duckwood.net
http://www.mississippi.gov/sub_sub_map.jsp?Category_ID=12&County_ID=153
Sam Joseph Abraham, Chancery Clerk
(land and probate records)

Leflore County Circuit Clerk's Office
PO Box 1953
Greenwood, MS 38935
(601) 453-1435; (601) 453-7460 FAX
teclerk@netdoor.com
http://www.mslawyer.com/mssc/circlerk.html#leflore
Mr. Howard "Trey" Evans, III, Circuit Clerk
(marriage records)

Lincoln County
organized 1870 from Amite, Pike, Lawrence and Franklin counties

Lincoln County Chancery Clerk's Office
PO Box 555
Brookhaven, MS 39601-0555
(601) 833-3411; (835-3423 FAX
http://www.co.lincoln.ms.us
Tillman Bishop, Chancery Clerk
(land records and probate records from 1893)
no probate search service ("will refer to private person"); copies of probate records: 50¢ per page

Lincoln County Circuit Clerk's Office
PO Box 357
Brookhaven, MS 39601
(601) 835-3435; (601) 835-3482 FAX
http://www.co.lincoln.ms.us
Ms. Terry Watkins, Circuit Clerk
(marriage records)

Lowndes County
organized 1830 from Monroe County

Lowndes County Chancery Clerk's Office
PO Box 684
Columbus, MS 39703-0684
(601) 329-5805; (601) 329-5870 FAX
http://www.mslawyer.com/chanceryclerks/lowndes.html
Lisa Neese, Chancery Clerk
(land records and wills from 1832)
no land or probate records search service (contact Mrs. H. C. Johnson, Jr., Ridge Road, Columbus, MS 39701); copies of probate records: 50¢ per page in advance

Lowndes County Circuit Clerk's Office
PO Drawer 31
Columbus, MS 39703
(601) 329-5900; (601) 329-5870 FAX
lchsalazar@bellsouth.net
http://www.mslawyer.com/mssc/circlerk.html#lowndes
Mahala Nickles Salazar, Circuit Clerk
(marriage records)

Madison County
organized 1828 from Yazoo County

Madison County Chancery Clerk's Office
(146 West Center Street—location)
PO Box 404 (mailing address)
Canton, MS 39046-0404
(601) 859-1177; (800) 428-0584; (601) 859-0337 FAX
johnston@madison-co.com
http://www.madison-co.com/elected_offices/chancery_clerk/index.php
Arthur Johnston, Chancery Clerk
(land and probate records)

Madison County Circuit Clerk's Office
(128 West North Street—location)
PO Box 1626 (mailing address)
Canton, MS 39046
(601) 859-4365; (601) 352-2049; (601) 859-8555 FAX
http://www.madison-co.com/elected_offices/circuit_clerk/index.php
Ms. Lee Westbrook, Circuit Clerk
(marriage records)

Marion County
organized 1811 from Amite, Wayne and Franklin counties

Marion County Chancery Clerk's Office
250 Broad Street, Suite 2
Columbia, MS 39429
(601) 736-2691; (601) 736-1232 FAX
http://www.mississippi.gov/sub_sub_map.jsp?Category_ID=12&County_ID=157
Mr. Cass Barnes, Chancery Clerk
(land and probate records)

Marion County Circuit Clerk's Office
250 Broad Street, Suite 1
Columbia, MS 39429
(601) 736-8246
http://www.mslawyer.com/mssc/circlerk.html#marion
Jesse Loftin, Circuit Clerk
(marriage records)

Marshall County
organized 1836 from Indian lands

Marshall County Chancery Clerk's Office
PO Box 219
Holly Springs, MS 38635
(601) 252-4431; (601) 252-0004 FAX
http://www.mississippi.gov/sub_sub_map.jsp?Category_ID=12&County_ID=158
http://www.hollyspringsms.us/subdepartment.php?e=59&z=14
C. W. "Chuck" Thomas, Chancery Clerk
(land and probate records)

Marshall County Circuit Clerk's Office
PO Box 459
Holly Springs, MS 38635
(601) 252-3434; (601) 252-0004 FAX
http://www.hollyspringsms.us/subdepartment.php?e=60&z=13
Lucy Carpenter, Circuit Clerk
(marriage records)

Monroe County
organized 1821 from Chickasaw Cession 1821

Monroe County Chancery Clerk's Office
(614 Summit Street—location)
PO Box 578 (mailing address)
Aberdeen, MS 39730-0578
(601) 369-8143; (601) 369-7928 FAX
http://wwwmonroecountyms.org/chancery_clerk.htm;
http://www.mslawyer.com/chanceryclerks/monroe.html
Mr. Ronnie D. Boozer, Chancery Clerk
(land and probate records)

Monroe County Circuit Clerk's Office
PO Box 843
Aberdeen, MS 39730
(601) 369-8695; (601) 369-3684 FAX
http://wwwmonroecountyms.org/circuit_clerk.htm
Judy K. Butler, Circuit Clerk
(marriage records)

Montgomery County
organized 1871 from Carroll and Choctaw counties

Montgomery County Chancery Clerk's Office
PO Box 71
Winona, MS 38967
(601) 283-2333; (601) 283-2233 FAX
http://www.mississippi.gov/sub-sub_map.jsp?Category_ID=12&County_ID=160
Talmadge "Tee" E. Golding, Chancery Clerk
(land and probate records)

Montgomery County Chancery Clerk's Office
PO Box 71
Winona, MS 38967-0071
(601) 283-2333
http://www.mississippi.gov/sub_sub_map.jsp?Category_ID=12&County_ID=160

Montgomery County Circuit Clerk's Office
PO Box 765
Winona, MS 38967
(601) 283-4161; (601) 283-2233 FAX
http://www.mslawyer.com/mssc/circlerk.html#montgomery
Julie Halfacre, Circuit Clerk
(marriage records)

Neshoba County
organized 1833 from Choctaw Cession 1830

Neshoba County Chancery Clerk's Office
(401 East Beacon Street, Suite 107—location)
PO Box 67 (mailing address)
Philadelphia, MS 39350-0067
(601) 656-3581
http://www.neshoba.org
Larry McMillan, Chancery Clerk
(land and probate records)

Neshoba County Circuit Clerk's Office
401 East Beacon Street
Philadelphia, MS 39350
(601) 656-4781; (601) 650-3280 FAX
neshoba12@bellsouth.net
http://www.neshoba.org
Patti Duncan Lee, Circuit Clerk
(marriage records)

Newton County
organized 1836 from Neshoba County

Newton County Chancery Clerk's Office
PO Box 68
Decatur, MS 39327-0068
(601) 635-2367
http://www.mississippi.gov/sub_sub_map.jsp?Category_ID=12&County_ID=162
George T. Hayes, Jr., Chancery Clerk
(land and probate records from 1876)

probate search service: no charge; copies of
   probate records: 50¢ per page, no minimum

Newton County Circuit Clerk's Office
PO Box 447
Decatur, MS 39327
(601) 635-2368; (601) 635-3210 FAX
http://www.mslawyer.com/mssc/circlerk.html
   #newton
Rodney Bounds, Circuit Clerk
(marriage records)

Noxubee County
organized 1833 from Choctaw Cession 1830

Noxubee County Chancery Clerk's Office
PO Box 147
Macon, MS 39341-0147
(601) 726-4243; (601) 726-2938 FAX
http://www.mississippi.gov/sub_sub_map.jsp?
   Category_ID=12&County_ID=163
Mary R. Taylor Shelton, Chancery Clerk
(land and probate records from 1834)
no photocopies of older, bound records

Noxubee County Circuit Clerk's Office
505 South Jefferson
Macon, MS 39341
(601) 726-5737; (601) 726-2938 FAX
http://www.mississippi.gov/sub_sub_map.jsp?
   Category_ID=12&County_ID=163
Carl L. Mickens, Circuit Clerk
(marriage records)

Oktibbeha County
organized 1833 from Choctaw Cession 1830

Oktibbeha County Chancery Clerk's Office
101 East Main Street
Starkville, MS 39759
(601) 323-5834; (601) 338-1065 FAX
monicawbanks@hotmail.com
htp://www.gtpdd.com/counties/oktibbeh
Monica Banks, Chancery Clerk
(land and probate records)

Oktibbeha County Circuit Clerk's Office
Courthouse
Starkville, MS 39759
(601) 323-1356; (601) 338-1065 FAX
amcginnis@gtpdd.com
http://www.gtpdd.com/counties/oktibbeha/cir
   cuit_clerk
Angie McGinnis, Circuit Clerk
(marriage records)

Panola County
organized 1836 from Indian lands

Panola County Chancery Clerk's Office
151 Public Square
Batesville, MS 38606-2220
(601) 563-6205; (601) 563-8233 FAX
http://www.mississippi.gov/sub_sub_map.jsp?
   Category_ID=12&County_ID=165
Sally H. Fisher, Chancery Clerk
(land and probate records)

Panola County Circuit Clerk's Office
PO Box 346
Batesville, MS 38606
(601) 563-6210; (601) 563-8233 FAX
jocreid@panola.com
http://www.mslawyer.com/mssc/circlerk.html
   #panola
W. Joe Reid, Circuit Clerk
(marriage records)

Pearl River County
organized 1890 from Hancock and Marion
   counties

Pearl River County Chancery Clerk's Office
200 South Main Street
Poplarville, MS 39470
(601) 795-2300; (601) 749-7700; (601) 795-3024
   FAX
http://www.pearlrivercounty.net/chancery/inde
   x.htm
David Earl Johnson, Chancery Clerk
(land and probate records)

Pearl River County Circuit Clerk's Office
200 South Main Street
Poplarville, MS 39470
(601) 403-2300; (601) 749-7700; (601) 795-3017
   FAX
http://www.pearlrivercounty.net/circuit/index.
   htm
Vickie Hariel, Circuit Clerk
(marriage records)

Perry County
organized 1820 from Greene County

Perry County Chancery Clerk's Office
PO Box 198
New Augusta, MS 39462-0198
(601) 964-8398; (601) 964-8265 FAX
   http://www.perrycountyms.com
Vickie Walters, Chancery Clerk
(land records, probate records)
no probate search service; copies of probate
   records: 25¢ per page, no minimum

Perry County Circuit Clerk's Office
PO Box 198
New Augusta, MS 39462-0198
(601) 964-8663; (601) 964-8265 FAX
   http://www.perrycountyms.com
Martha Fillingane Clark, Circuit Clerk
(marriage records)

Pike County
organized 1815 from Marion County

Pike County Chancery Clerk's Office
PO Box 309
Magnolia, MS 39652-0309
(601) 783-3362; (601) 783-4101 FAX
dougt@co.pike.ms.us
http://www.co.pike.ms.us/chanceryclerk.html
Doug Touchstone, Chancery Clerk
(land records, naturalization records, and
   probate records from 1882)
probate search service: no charge; copies of
   probate records: 25¢ per page, $1.00 for
   certification, no minimum

Pike County Circuit Clerk's Office
(200 East Bay Street—location)
PO Drawer 31 (mailing address)
Magnolia, MS 39652
(601) 783-2581; (601) 783-6322 FAX
rogerg@co.pike.ms.us
http://www.co.pike.ms.us/circuitclerk.html
Roger A. Graves, Circuit Clerk
(marriage records from 1882)

Pontotoc County
organized 1836 from Chickasaw Cession

Pontotoc County Chancery Clerk's Office
PO Box 209
Pontotoc, MS 38863-0209
(601) 489-3900; (601) 489-3940 FAX
rcollums@pontotoccms.com
http://www.mississippi.gov/sub_sub_map.jsp?
   Category_ID=12&County_ID=169
Reggie M. Collums, Chancery Clerk
(land records, marriage licenses, probate
   records)
no probate search service; copies of probate
   records: 25¢ per page, no minimum

Pontotoc County Circuit Clerk's Office
PO Box 428
Pontotoc, MS 38863
(601) 489-3908; (601) 489-3940 FAX
http://www.mslawyer.com/mssc/circlerk.html
   #pontotoc
Ms. Tracy L. Robinson, Circuit Clerk
(marriage records)

Prentiss County
organized 1870 from Tishomingo County

Prentiss County Chancery Clerk's Office
(Historic Chancery Building, 101 North Main
   Street—location)
PO Box 477 (mailing address)
Booneville, MS 38829-0477

(601) 728-8151; (601) 728-2007 FAX
http://www.boonevillemississippi.com
Travis Childers, Chancery Clerk
(land records, probate records)

Prentiss County Circuit Clerk's Office
101-A North Main Street
Booneville, MS 38829
(601) 728-4611; (601) 728-2006 FAX
http://www.boonevillemississippi.com
J. F. "Budd" Green, Circuit Clerk
(marriage records)

Quitman County
organized 1877 from Coahoma, Panola
   Tallahatchie and Tunica counties

Quitman County Chancery Clerk's Office
230 Chestnut Street
Marks, MS 38646
(601) 326-2661; (601) 326-8004 FAX
quitman@gmi.net
http://www.mississippi.gov/sub_sub_map.jsp?
   Category_ID=12&County_ID=171
Mr. T. H. "Butch" Scipper, Chancery Clerk
(deeds, wills)
land records search service: $40.00 per hour;
   copies of land records: 50¢ per page, $1.00 for
   certification

Quitman County Circuit Clerk's Office
Courthouse
Marks, MS 38646
(601) 326-8003; (601) 326-8004 FAX
http://www.mslawyer.com/mssc/circlerk.html
   #quitman
Brenda A. Wiggs, Circuit Clerk
(marriage records)

Rankin County
organized 1828 from Hinds County

Rankin County Chancery Clerk's Office
(211 East Govermnent Street, Suite D—
   location)
PO Box 700 (mailing address)
Brandon, MS 39042
(601) 825-1469; (601) 824-7116 FAX
Madkins@Rankincounty.org
http://www.rankincounty.org/chl
Mr. Murphy Adkins, Chancery Clerk
(land and probate records)

Rankin County Circuit Clerk's Office
(215 East Government Street—location)
PO Box 1599 (mailing address)
Brandon, MS 39043
(601) 825-1466; (601) 825-1465 FAX
cswilley@Rankincounty.org
http://www.rankincounty.org/ci
Carol Swilley, Circuit Clerk
(marriage records)

Scott County
organized 1833 from Choctaw Cession 1832

Scott County Chancery Clerk's Office
PO Box 630
Forest, MS 39074-0630
(601) 469-1922; (601) 469-5180 FAX
balford@hotmail.com
http://scottcountms.gov
Billy Frank Alford, Chancery Clerk
(land records, probate records)
no probate search service; copies of probate
   records: 50¢ each (25¢ each if you do the
   copying), no minimum

Scott County Circuit Clerk's Office
PO Box 371
Forest, MS 39074
(601) 469-3601; (601) 469-3514 FAX
scottcircuitclerk@scottcountyms.gov
http://scottcountms.gov
Joe Rigby, Circuit Clerk
(marriage records)

Sharkey County
organized 1876 from Warren, Washington and
   Issaquena counties

Sharkey County Chancery Clerk and Circuit Clerk
PO Box 218
Rolling Fork, MS 39159-0218
(601) 873-2755 (Chancery); (601) 873-4317 (Circuit); (601) 873-6045 FAX
http://www.mississippi.gov/sub_sub_map.jsp?Category_ID=12&County_ID=174;
Murindia Williams
(land and probate records, marriage records)

Simpson County
organized 1824 from Copiah County

Simpson County Chancery Clerk's Office
PO Box 367
Mendenhall, MS 39114-0367
(601) 847-2626; (601) 847-7004 FAX
http://www.mississippi.gov/sub_sub_map.jsp?Category_ID=12&County_ID=175
Tommy Harvey, Chancery Clerk
(land records and probate records)
copies of land and probate records: 50¢ each, $1.00 for certified copies

Simpson County Circuit Clerk's Office
PO Box 307
Mendenhall, MS 39114
(601) 847-2474; (601) 847-4011 FAX
Simpsoncircuit@co.simpson.ms.us
http://www.mslawyer.com/mssc/circlerk.html
Cindy Jenson, Circuit Clerk
(marriage records)

Smith County
organized 1833 from Indian lands

Smith County Chancery Clerk's Office
PO Box 39
Raleigh, MS 39153
(601) 782-9811; (601) 782-4002 FAX
http://www.smithcounty.ms.gov
Beth Crumpton, Interim Chancery Clerk
(land records from 1892 [some deeds prior to 1892 re-recorded after 1892 fire], probate records from 1892)
no land records service ("we do not have sufficient office force to permit us to run land indexes"); probate search service: $5.00; copies of probate records: $5.00 per page, no minimum

Smith County Circuit Clerk's Office
PO Box 517
Raleigh, MS 39153
(601) 782-4751; (601) 782-9481 FAX
http://www.smithcounty.ms.gov/officials.html
Anthony, Grayson, Circuit Clerk
(marriage records from 1912)

Stone County
organized 1916 from Harrison County

Stone County Chancery Clerk's Office
(323 Cavers Avenue—location)
PO Drawer 7 (mailing address)
Wiggins, MS 39577
(601) 928-5266; (601) 928-5248 FAX
stonecty@datasync.com
http://www.stonecounty.com/stone_county_officials.htm
Gerald Bond, Chancery Clerk
(land records, probate records)
probate search service: no charge; copies of land records and probate records: 50¢ per page (25¢ per page if you do the copying), $1.00 for certified copies, no minimum

Stone County Circuit Clerk's Office
323 Cavers Avenue
Wiggins, MS 39577
(601) 928-5246; (601) 928-5248 FAX
khatten@stonecountyms.gov
http://www.stonecounty.com (Economic Development Partnership)
William Kenny Hatten, Circuit Clerk
(marriage records)

Sunflower County
organized 1844 from Bolivar County

Sunflower County Chancery Clerk's Office
PO Box 988
Indianola, MS 38751-0988
(601) 887-4703; (601) 887-7054 FAX
sykes1@capital2.com
http://www.mississippi.gov/sub_sub_map.jsp?Category_ID=12&County_ID=178
Paula Sykes, Chancery Clerk
(land and probate records)

Sunflower County Circuit Clerk's Office
PO Box 576
Indianola, MS 38751
(601) 887-1252; (601) 887-7054 FAX
scountycircuitclerk@yahoo.com
http://www.mslawyer.com/mssc/circlerk.html
Sharon McFadden, Circuit Clerk
(marriage records)

Tallahatchie County
organized 1833 from Indian lands

Tallahatchie County Chancery Clerk's Office
PO Box 350
Charleston, MS 38921-0350
(601) 647-5551; (601) 647-8490 FAX
http://www.mississippi.gov/sub_sub_map.jsp?Category_ID=12&County_ID=179
Anita Fountain, Chancery Clerk
(land and probate records)

Tallahatchie County Circuit Clerk's Office
PO Box 86
Charleston, MS 38921
(601) 647-8758; (601) 647-8490 FAX
ssims@co.tallahatchie.ms.us
http://www.mslawyer.com/mssc/circlerk.html
Stephanie Sims, Circuit Clerk
(marriage records)

Tate County
organized 1873 from DeSoto, Marshall and Tunica counties

Tate County Chancery Clerk's Office
201 Ward Street
Senatobia, MS 38668-2616
(601) 562-5661; (601) 562-7486 FAX
burkecomm@burke.net
http://www.mississippi.gov/sub_sub_map.jsp?Category_ID=12&County_ID=180
Wayne Crockett, Chancery Clerk
(land and probate records)

Tate County Circuit Clerk's Office
201 Ward Street
Senatobia, MS 38668
(601) 562-5211; (601) 562-7486 FAX
http://www.mslawyer.com/mssc/circlerk.html
Steve B. Lentz, Circuit Clerk
(marriage records)

Tippah County
organized 1836 from Chickasaw Cession

Tippah County Chancery Clerk's Office
PO Box 99
Ripley, MS 38663-0099
(601) 837-7374; (601) 837-1030 FAX
http://www.mississippi.gov/sub_sub_map.jsp?Category_ID=12&CountyID=181;
http://www.tippahcounty.ripley.ms (Tippah County Development Foundation)
Daniel T. Shackelford, Chancery Clerk
(land records from 1836, probate records from 1836 [partially destroyed 1864])
probate search service: $10.00; copies of probate records: 25¢ per page, $10.00 minimum, covers postage

Tippah County Circuit Clerk's Office
Ripley, MS 38663
(601) 837-7370; (601) 837-1030 FAX
http://www.mississippi.gov/sub_sub_map.jsp?Category_ID=12&CountyID=181;
http://www.tippahcounty.ripley.ms (Tippah County Development Foundation)
James E. Dees, Circuit Clerk
(marriage records from 1836 [partially destroyed 1864])

Tishomingo County
organized 1836 from Chickasaw Cession, divided 1870 into Alcorn, Prentiss and Tishomingo counties

Tishomingo County Chancery Clerk's Office
1008 Highway 25-S
Iuka, MS 38852-1020
(601) 423-7010; (601) 423-7005 FAX
http://www.tishomingo.org./index.htm (Tishomingo County Development Foundation)
Hayden Ables, Chancery Clerk
(land records from 1887 ["present Tishomingo County records burned in 1887], probate records from 1887 with Irene Barnes, Rt. 5, Box 210, Iuka, MS 38852)
probate search service: $5.00; copies of probate records: 25¢ per page, no minimum

Tishomingo County Circuit Clerk's Office
1008 Battleground
Iuka, MS 38852
(601) 423-7026; (601) 423-7005 FAX
tishcircuit@hotmail.com
http://www.mslawyer.com/mssc/circlerk.html
Donna H. Dill, Circuit Clerk
(marriage records)

Tunica County
organized 9 February 1836 by the Treaty of Pontotoc from Chickasaw Cession of 1832

Tunica County Chancery Clerk's Office
PO Box 217
Tunica, MS 38676-0217
(662) 363-2451; (662) 357-0378 FAX
susiewhite@tunicacounty.com
http://www.tunicacounty.com/departments/chancery_clerk/index.html
Susie White, Chancery Clerk
(deeds from 3 February 1837, probate records from 13 December 1837)
probate search service: $10.00; copies of probate records: 50¢ per page

Tunica County Circuit Clerk's Office
PO Box 184
Tunica, MS 38676
(662) 363-2842; (662) 363-2413 FAX
sharon.reynolds@tunicacounty.com
http://www.tunicacounty.com/departments/circuit_clerk/index.html
Sharon Granberry, Circuit Clerk
(marriage records)

Union County
organized 1870 from Pontotoc and Tippah counties

Union County Chancery Clerk's Office
PO Box 847
New Albany, MS 38652-0847
(601) 534-1900; (601) 534-1907 FAX
http://www.mississippi.gov/sub_sub_map.jsp?Category_ID=12&County_ID=184
Tom Cooper, Chancery Clerk
(land and probate records)

Union County Circuit Clerk's Office
PO Box 298
New Albany, MS 38652
(601) 534-1910; (601) 534-1961 FAX
pstanford@unioncoms.com
http://www.mslawyer.com/mssc/circlerk.html
Phyllis Stanford, Circuit Clerk
(marriage records)

Walthall County
organized 1910 from Marion and Pike counties

Walthall County Chancery Clerk's Office
PO Box 351
Tylertown, MS 39667-0351
(601) 876-3553; (601) 876-6688 FAX
http://www.mslawyer.com/chanceryclerks/walthall.html
Bob A. Bracey, Chancery Clerk

(land and probate records from 1914)
probate search service: $5.00; copies of probate records: 50¢ each, no minimum

Walthall County Circuit Clerk's Office
200 Ball Avenue
Tylertown, MS 39667
(601) 876-5677; (601) 876-6688 FAX
cindydillon@yahoo.com
http://www.mississippi.gov/sub_sub_map.jsp?
   Category_ID=12&County_ID=185http://w
   ww.genefinley.com
Pat Ginn Broussard, Circuit Clerk
(marriage records)

Warren County
organized 1809 from the Old Natchez District

Warren County Chancery Clerk's Office
(1009 Cherry Street—location)
PO Box 351 (mailing address)
Vicksburg, MS 39180-0351
(601) 636-4415; (601) 630-8185 FAX FAX
chanclk@co.warren.ms.us; dotm@
   co.warren.ms.us; dmcgee@co.warren.ms.us
http://www.co.warren.ms.us/ChanceryClerk/C
   hanceryClerk.htm
Dot McGee, Chancery Clerk
(land and probate records)

Warren County Circuit Clerk's Office
(1009 Cherry Street—location)
PO Box 351 (mailing address)
Vicksburg, MS 39181
(601) 636-3961; (601) 630-4100 FAX
circlk@co.warren.ms.us;
   spalmertree@co.warren.ms.us
http://www.co.warren.ms.us/CircuitClerk/circu
   it_clerk.htm
Shelly Ashley-Palmertree, Circuit Clerk
(marriage records)

Washington County
organized 1827 from Warren and Yazoo counties

Washington County Chancery Clerk's Office
PO Box 309
Greenville, MS 38702-0309
(601) 332-1595; (601) 334-2725 FAX
http://www.genefinley.com/officials.html
Marilyn Hansell, Chancery Clerk
(land records from 1827, naturalization records from 12 December 1890 until 1930s, probate records from 1827)
no probate search service; copies of probate records: 75¢ per page, no minimum

Washington County Circuit Clerk's Office
PO Box 1276
Greenville, MS 38702-1276
(601) 378-2747; (601) 334-2698 FAX
http://www.genefinley.com/officials.html
Barbara Esters-Parker, Circuit Clerk
(marriage records)

Wayne County
organized 1809 from Washington County

Wayne County Chancery Clerk's Office
Wayne County Courthouse
Waynesboro, MS 39367
(601) 735-2873; (601) 735-6248 FAX
chancery@netpathway.com
http://www.wayneco.com/html/body_wayne_c
   ounty.html
Marlon West, Chancery Clerk
(land and probate records from 1892)
probate search service: no charge; copies of probate records: 50¢ each, no minimum

Wayne County Circuit Clerk's Office
Wayne County Courthouse
Waynesboro, MS 39367
(601) 735-1171; (601) 735-6261 FAX
wctycc@netpathway.com
http://www.wayneco.com/html/body_wayne_c
   ounty.html
Rose Bingham, Circuit Clerk
(marriage records)

Webster County
organized 1874 from Sumner and Montgomery counties

Webster County Chancery Clerk's Office
PO Box 398
Walthall, MS 39771
(601) 258-4131; (601) 258-6657 FAX
http://www.mississippi.gov/sub_sub_map.jsp?
   Category_ID=12&County_ID=189
Lady H. Doolittle, Chancery Clerk
(land records, naturalization records, probate records)
probate search service: $5.00; copies of probate records: 50¢ per page, no minimum

Webster County Circuit Clerk's Office
PO Box 308
Walthall, MS 39771
(601) 258-6287; (601) 258-6657 FAX
http://www.mississippi.gov/sub_sub_map.jsp?
   Category_ID=12&County_ID=189
Deborah Hood Neal, Circuit Clerk
(marriage records)

Wilkinson County
organized 1802 from Adams County

Wilkinson County Chancery Clerk's Office
PO Box 516
Woodville, MS 39669-0516
(601) 888-4381; (601) 888-6776 FAX
http://www.mississippi.gov/sub_sub_map.jsp?
   Category_ID=12&County_ID=190;
   http://www.mslawyer.com/chanceryclerks/w
   ilkinso.html
Thomas C. Tolliver, Jr., Chancery Clerk
(land and probate records)

Wilkinson County Circuit Clerk's Office
PO Box 327
Woodville, MS 39669
(601) 888-6697; (601) 888-6984 FAX
http://www.mslawyer.com/mssc/circlerk.html
Mr. Mon Cree Allen, Circuit Clerk
(marriage records)

Winston County
organized 1833 from Indian lands

Winston County Chancery Clerk's Office
PO Drawer 69
Louisville, MS 39339
(601) 773-3631; (601) 773-3517; (601) 773-8831 FAX
pamr@winstoncounty.org
http://www.mississippi.gov/sub_sub_map.jsp?
   Category_ID=12&County_ID=191
Pam Reel, Chancery Clerk
(land and probate records)

Winston County Circuit Clerk's Office
PO Drawer 785
Louisville, MS 39339
(601) 773-3581; (601) 773-8831 FAX
kim@winstoncounty.org
http://www.mslawyer.com/mssc/circlerk.html
Kim Ming, Circuit Clerk
(marriage records)

Yalobusha County
organized 1833 from Choctaw Cession 1830

Yalobusha County Chancery Clerk's Office
PO Box 664
Water Valley, MS 38965-0664
(601) 473-2091; (601) 473-5020 FAX
http://www.mississippi.gov/sub_sub_map.jsp?
   Category_ID=12&County_ID=192
Amy Mcminn, Chancery Clerk
(land and probate records)
no probate search service; copies of probate records: 50¢ per page, $1.00 minimum

Yalobusha County Circuit Clerk's Office
PO Box 431
Water Valley, MS 38965
(601) 473-1341; (601) 473-5020 FAX
http://www.mslawyer.com/mssc/circlerk.html
Daryl Burney, Circuit Clerk

(marriage records)

Yazoo County
organized 1823 from Hinds County

Yazoo County Chancery Clerk's Office
PO Box 68
Yazoo City, MS 39194-0068
(601) 746-2661
http://www.mississippi.gov/sub_sub_map.jsp?
   Category_ID=12&County_ID=193
Noreene Girard, Chancery Clerk
(land and probate records)
no probate search service; copies of probate records: 50¢ per page (25¢ per page if you do the copying), no minimum

Yazoo County Circuit Clerk's Office
PO Box 108
Yazoo City, MS 39194
(601) 746-1872; (601) 746-3890 FAX
circlk@yazooco.ms.us
http://www.mslawyer.com/mssc/circlerk.html
Susie Bradshaw Outlaw, Circuit Clerk
(marriage records)

MISSOURI

Capital: Jefferson City. Statehood: 10 August 1821 (annexed as part of the Louisiana Purchase, 1803, became a separate territory in 1812)

Missouri has 114 counties and an independent city, St. Louis, which is not contained within any county. The state's Circuit Courts were reorganized as of January 1979, eliminating the former Magistrate Court, Probate Court, Municipal Court and Hannibal and Cape Girardeau Courts of Common Pleas. The courts now consist of five divisions: the Circuit Division, with jurisdiction over civil and criminal cases; the Juvenile Division; the Associate Division, with jurisdiction over some civil cases, small claims cases, felony preliminaries, misdemeanors, etc.; the Probate Division; and the Municipal Division.

First Judicial Circuit: Clark, Schuyler and Scotland counties; Second: Adair, Knox and Lewis; Third: Grundy, Harrison, Mercer and Putnam; Fourth: Atchison, Gentry, Holt, Nodaway and Worth; Fifth: Andrew and Buchanan; Sixth: Platte; Seventh: Clay; Eighth: Carroll and Ray; Ninth: Chariton, Linn and Sullivan; Tenth: Marion, Monroe and Ralls; Eleventh: St. Charles; Twelfth: Audrain, Montgomery and Warren; Thirteenth: Boone and Callaway; Fourteenth: Howard and Randolph; Fifteenth: Lafayette and Saline; Sixteenth: Jackson; Seventeenth: Cass and Johnson; Eighteenth: Cooper and Pettis; Nineteenth: Cole; Twentieth: Franklin, Gasconade and Osage; Twenty-first: St. Louis; Twenty-second: City of St. Louis; Twenty-third: Jefferson; Twenty-fourth: Madison, Perry, St. Francois, Sainte Genevieve and Washington; Twenty-fifth: Maries, Phelps, Pulaski and Texas; Twenty-sixth: Camden, Laclede, Miller, Moniteau and Morgan; Twenty-seventh: Bates, Henry and St. Clair; Twenty-eighth: Barton, Cedar, Dade and Vernon; Twenty-ninth: Jasper; Thirtieth: Benton, Dallas, Hickory, Polk and Webster; Thirty-first: Greene; Thirty-second: Bollinger and Cape Girardeau; Thirty-third: Mississippi and Scott; Thirty-fourth: New Madrid and Pemiscot; Thirty-fifth: Dunklin and Stoddard; Thirty-sixth: Butler and Ripley; Thirty-seventh: Carter, Howell, Oregon and Shannon; Thirty-eighth: Christian and Taney; Thirty-ninth: Barry, Lawrence and Stone; Fortieth: McDonald and Newton; Forty-first: Macon and Shelby; Forty-second: Crawford, Dent, Iron, Reynolds and Wayne; Forty-third: Caldwell, Clinton, Daviess, DeKalb and Livingston; Forty-fourth: Douglas, Ozark and Wright; Fourty-fifth: Lincon and Pike counties. The Court of Appeals and Supreme Court hear appeals from the lower courts.

Adair County
organized 1841 from Macon County

Adair County Courthouse
106 West Washington Street
Kirksville, MO 63501-2889
(660) 665-3350 (County Clerk); (660) 665-3890 (Recorder); (660) 665-2552 (Circuit Clerk); (660) 627-5950 FAX; (660) 785-3233 FAX (County Clerk); (660) 785-3212 FAX (Recorder); (660) 665-3420 FAX (Circuit Clerk)
cadaer@mail.sos.state.mo.us
http://www.morecorders.com/CountyData.asp?COUNTY=ADAIR; http://www.courts.mo.gov/circuits/index.nsf/County+/+Adair/$first?OpenDocument
Sandy Callop, County Clerk; Pat Shouse, Recorder of Deeds; Linda S. Decker, Circuit Clerk
no probate search service; copies of probate records: 25¢ per page

Andrew County
organized 1841 from Platte Purchase

Andrew County Circuit Clerk and Recorder of Deeds
(Courthouse, 410 Court Street—location)
PO Box 208 (mailing address)
Savannah, MO 64485
(816) 324-4221; (816) 324-5667 FAX
lanceyrl@andrewcounty.org;
  rosa.lancey@courts.mo.gov
http://www.andrewcounty.org/circuitclerk.htm; http://www.morecorders.com/CountyData.asp?COUNTY=ANDREW; http://www.courts.mo.gov/circuits/index.nsf/County+/+Andrew/$first?OpenDocument
Rosa Lea Lancey

Andrew County Clerk
(411 Court Street—location)
PO Box 206 (mailing address)
Savannah, MO 64485
(816) 324-3624; (816) 324-6154 FAX
clerk@andrewcounty.org;
  andrewcounty@hotmail.com
http://www.andrewcounty.org/clerk.htm
Dan Hegeman
(births and deaths from 1883 to 1893, probate)
no probate search service; copies of probate records: 50¢ each, no minimum

Atchison County
organized 1845 from Holt County

Atchison County Circuit Clerk-Recorder
(400 Washington Street—location)
PO Box 280 (mailing address)
Rock Port, MO 64482
(660) 744-2707; (660) 744-2700 (Probate Division); (660) 744-5705 FAX
lorie.hall@courts.mo.gov
http://www.courts.mo.gov/circuits/index.nsf/County+/+Atchison/$first?OpenDocument; http://www.morecorders.com/CountyData.asp?COUNTY=ATCHISON; http://www.atchisoncounty.org
Lorie K. Hall
(land records from 1845; naturalization records ["we have found these in various places"]; deaths only from 1883 through 1893, marriages from 1845 to date; probate records from 1845)
land records search service: $4.00; probate search service: $4.00; copies of land records: $1.00 per page; copies of vital records: $2.00 each, $9.00 for certification; copies of probate records: $1.00 per page plus $1.00 for certification, $1.00 minimum ("it helps if they would send a SASE")

Atchison County Clerk
400 Washington Street
Rock Port, MO 64482
(660) 744-6214; (660) 744-5499 FAX
acclerk@rpt.coop
http://www.atchisoncounty.org
Susette Taylor

Audrain County
organized 1836 from Pike, Callaway and Ralls counties

Audrain County Courthouse
101 North Jefferson
Mexico, MO 65265-2769
(573) 581-8211; (573) 473-5820 (County Clerk, Room 101); (573) 473-5830 (Recorder); (573) 473-5840 (Circuit Clerk); (573) 581-2380 FAX (County Clerk); (573) 581-8087 FAX (Recorder); (573) 581-3237 FAX (Circuit Clerk)
caudrain@sospublicmail.state.mo.us (County Clerk); V_Pehle@sbcglobal.net
http://www.morecorders.com/CountyData.asp?COUNTY=AUDRAIN; http://www.courts.mo.gov/circuits/index.nsf/County+/+Audrain/$first?OpenDocument
Shelley Harvey, County Clerk; Virginia Pehle, Recorder of Deeds; Penny J. Creed, Circuit Clerk
(land records with Collector's Office, vital records from 1883 to 1886 only with County

Barry County
organized 1835 from Greene County

Barry County Courthouse
700 Main Street
Cassville, MO 65625-1467
(417) 847-2613; (417) 847-2561 (County Clerk, Suite 2); (417) 847-4558 (Recorder, Suite 1); (417) 847-2361 (Circuit Clerk); (417) 847-5311 FAX (County Clerk); (417) 847-8740 FAX (Recorder); (417) 847-6298 FAX (Circuit Clerk)
cbarry@mail.sos.state.mo.us (County Clerk)
http://www.morecorders.com/CountyData.asp?COUNTY=BARRY; http://www.courts.mo.gov/circuits/index.nsf/County+/+Barry/$first?OpenDocument
Gary Youngblood, County Clerk; Craig Williams, Circuit Clerk-Recorder of Deeds

Barton County
organized 1855 from Jasper County

Barton County Courthouse
1004 Gulf Street
Lamar, MO 64759-1466
(417) 682-3529 (County Clerk, Room 102); (417) 682-2110 (Recorder, Room 107); (417) 682-2444 (Circuit Clerk); (417) 682-4100 FAX (County Clerk); (417) 682-4102 FAX (Recorder); (417) 682-2960 FAX (Circuit Clerk)
cbarton@sospublicmail.state.mo.us (County Clerk); bcrecorder@tiadon.com
http://www.courts.mo.gov/circuits/index.nsf/County+/+Barton/$first?OpenDocument; http://www.bartoncounty.com (Chamber of Commerce)
Kristina Crockett, County Clerk; Jean Keithly, Recorder of Deeds; Jerry A. Moyer, Circuit Clerk
(land records from 1857, naturalization records from about 1890 to 1940, births from 1833 to 1896, deaths from 1883 to 1899 [incomplete], marriages from 1866, probate records from 1866)
probate search service: "all charges vary by time involved in search; complete information provided decreases time involved"; copies of probate records: $1.00 per page, $2.00 for certified copies ("SASE *all* offices; no charge except postage for return if nothing found")

Bates County
organized 1841 from Cooper County

Bates County Courthouse
1 North Delaware Street
Butler, MO 64730
(660) 679-3371 (County Clerk's Office, First Floor, PO Box 288); (660) 679-3611 (Recorder of Deeds, PO Box 186); (660) 679-5171 (Circuit Clerk's Office, Second Floor); (660) 679-3311 (Associate Circuit Court and Probate Clerk); (660) 679-9922 FAX (County Clerk); (660) 679-4935 FAX (Recorder); (660) 679-4446 FAX (Circuit Clerk's Office)
cbates@sospublicmail.state.mo.us (County Clerk); bates@sos.mo.gov (County Clerk); Mundey@netection.net
http://www.batescounty.net/county_offices; http://www.morecorders.com/CountyData.asp?COUNTY=BATES; http://www.courts.mo.gov/circuits/index.nsf/County+/+Bates/$first?OpenDocument
Marlene Wainscott, County Clerk; Lucille Mundey, Recorder; Diana L. Rich, Circuit Clerk
(land records from 1840 to date with Recorder of Deeds; very few naturalization records from January 1867 to 1880 with Circuit Clerk's Office; births and deaths from 1883 to 1886 with County Clerk's Office; probate

records from 1850 to date with Associate Circuit Court)

Benton County
organized 1835 from Cooper County

Benton County Courthouse
(316 Van Buren—location)
PO Box 1238 (mailing address)
Warsaw, MO 65355-1238
(660) 438-7326 (County Clerk); (660) 438-7712 (Circuit Clerk, PO Box 37); (660) 438-3275 FAX (County Clerk); (660) 438-5755 FAX (Circuit Clerk)
cheryl.schultz@courts.mo.gov
http://www.morecorders.com/CountyData.asp?COUNTY=BENTON; http://www.positech.net/~dcourt/clerks.htm
Mary Lutman, County Clerk; Cheryl Schultz, Circuit Clerk-Recorder of Deeds
(land records from 1837; naturalization records; births and deaths from 1883 to 1888, marriages from 1839; probate records from 1854)
no probate search service ("mail is worked as time allows"); copies of probate records: $2.00 each, no minimum

Bollinger County
organized 1851 from Cape Girardeau, Madison, Stoddard and Wayne counties

Bollinger County Courthouse
204 High Street
Marble Hill, MO 63764
(573) 238-2126; (573) 238-1900, ext. 333 (County Clerk); (573) 238-1900, ext. 7 (Recorder); (573) 238-1900, ext. 6 (Circuit Clerk); (573) 238-4511 FAX (County Clerk); (573) 238-4511 FAX (Recorder); (573) 238-2773 FAX (Circuit Clerk)
jjboll@sospublicmail.state.mo.us (County Clerk)
http://www.morecorders.com/CountyData.asp?COUNTY=BOLLINGER; http://www.courts.mo.gov/circuits/index.nsf/County+/+Bollinger/$first?OpenDocument
Diane H. Holzum, County Clerk; Winonah Ossig, Recorder of Deeds; Sharon Lutes, Circuit Clerk

Boone County
organized 1820 from Howard County

Boone County Circuit Clerk
705 East Walnut
Columbia, MO 65201
(573) 886-4000 (General Information); (573) 886-4090 (Probate Division); (573) 886-4044 FAX
http://www.courts.mo.gov/hosted/circuit13
Cheryl Whitmarsh
(naturalization records with Circuit Court, probate records with Probate Division, Circuit Court)
probate search service ("try to give us as much information about the person as possible; if you know the middle name or initial it would help a lot, plus the date or year that the person died in"): no charge; copies of probate records: $1.00 per page, $1.00 for the first page and 25¢ for each additional page (after 1900), no minimum, certified check or money order only

Boone County Clerk and Recorder
801 East Walnut
Columbia, MO 65201-4470
(573) 886-4375 (County Clerk, Room 236); (573) 886-4345 (Recorder, Room 132); (573) 886-4300 FAX (County Clerk); (573) 886-4359 FAX (Recorder)
ckwendy@msn.com; bjohnson@boonecountymo.org
http://www.showmeboone.com; http://www.morecorders.com/CountyData.asp?COUNTY=BOONE
Wendy Noren, County Clerk; Bettie Johnson, Recorder
(land records with Recorder of Deeds)

Buchanan County
organized 1838 from Platte Purchase

Buchanan County Courthouse
411 Jules Street
St. Joseph, MO 64501
(816) 271-1412 (County Clerk, Room 121); (816) 271-1437 (Recorder of Deeds, Room 103); (816) 271-1462 (Circuit Clerk, Room 331); (816) 271-1477 (Probate Clerk, Circuit Court, Room 332); (816) 271-1535 FAX (County Clerk); (816) 271-1582 FAX (Recorder); (816) 271-1538 FAX (Circuit Clerk)
pconway@clerk.co.buchanan.mo.us; khigginb@co.buchanan.mo.us
http://www.co.buchanan.mo.us; http://www.morecorders.com/CountyData.asp?COUNTY=BUCHANAN; http://www.5thcircuit.net/circuit_clerk/buchanan.shtml
Mr. Pat Conway, County Clerk; Karen Higginbotham, Recorder of Deeds; Ireene Mooney, Circuit Clerk
(land records from 1839 with Recorder's Office, naturalization records with Circuit Clerk's Office, marriages from 1839 with Recorder's Office, probate records from 1839 with Probate Court)
no land or vital records search service (contact Northwest Missouri Genealogical Society), probate search service: $10.00; copies of probate records: $1.00 per page, $1.00 minimum

Butler County
organized 1849 from Wayne County

Butler County Courthouse
(105 Main Street—location)
PO Box 332 (mailing address)
Poplar Bluff, MO 63901-0332
(573) 686-8050 (County Clerk, Room 202); (573) 686-8086 (Recorder); (573) 686-8082 (Circuit Clerk); (573) 686-8066 FAX (County Clerk); (573) 778-8014 FAX (Recorder); (573) 686-8094 FAX (Circuit Clerk)
cbutler@sospublicmail.state.mo.us (County Clerk); dlundstrom@tcmax.net
http://www.morecorders.com/CountyData.asp?COUNTY=BUTLER; http://www.courts.mo.gov/circuits/index.nsf/County+/+Butler/$first?OpenDocument
Tonyi Deffendall, County Clerk; Debby Lundstorm, Recorder of Deeds; Betty L. Scott, Circuit Clerk

Caldwell County
organized 26 December 1836 from Ray County

Caldwell County Courthouse
(49 East Main—location)
PO Box 67 (mailing address)
Kingston, MO 64650-0067
(816) 586-2571 (County Clerk); (816) 586-3080 (Recorder); (816) 586-2581 (Circuit Clerk, PO Box 68; (816) 586-2771 (Circuit Clerk); (816) 586-3600 FAX (County Clerk); (816) 586-2705 FAX (Recorder); (816) 586-2333 FAX (Circuit Clerk
jjcald@sospublicmail.mo.us (County Clerk)
http://www.morecorders.com/CountyData.asp?COUNTY=CALDWELL; http://www.courts.mo.gov/circuits/index.nsf/County+/+Caldwell/$first?OpenDocument
Beverly Bryant, County Clerk; Charlene Ward, Recorder of Deeds; Carrie Miller, Circuit Clerk
(original land patents 1834, deeds from 1860 [plus records re-recorded after the courthouse fire of 1860], atlases [rural land owners] with Deputy Recorder, PO Box 86, Kingston, MO 64650, naturalization records from 1887 to about 1899 [only about ten in all] with Circuit Clerk, PO Box 86, Kingston, MO 64650, marriages only with Deputy Recorder, probate records with Sue Adkison, Probate Clerk, PO Box 5, Kingston, MO 64650)
land records search service: no charge (extensive searches referred to Mrs. Marilyn Williams,

Rt. 1, Box 38, Kingston, MO 64650); copies of land records: $2.00 for the first page and $1.00 for each additional page

Callaway County
organized 1820 from Howard, Boone and Montgomery counties

Callaway County Courthouse
10 East Fifth Street
Fulton, MO 65251
(573) 642-0730 (County Clerk); (573) 642-0787 (Recorder of Deeds); (573) 642-0780 (Circuit Clerk); (573) 642-7181 FAX (County Clerk); (573) 642-7929 FAX (Recorder); (573) 642-0700 FAX (Circuit Clerk)
ccallawa@sospublicmail.mo.us (County Clerk); lindal@callawaycounty.org; callrecord@callawaycounty.org;
http://callaway.county.missouri.org/Courthouse.html; http://www.morecorders.com/CountyData.asp?COUNTY=CALAWAY; http://www.callawaycounty.org; http://www.courts.mo.gov/hosted/circuit13
Linda Love, County Clerk; Kenneth Dillon, Recorder of Deeds; Curtis Quick, Circuit Clerk

Camden County
organized 1841 from Pulaski, Morgan and Benton counties

Camden County Courthouse
1 Court Circle NW
Camdenton, MO 65020
(573) 346-4440 (All Departments); (573) 317-3890 (County Clerk, Suite 2); (573) 346-4440, ext. 1220 (County Clerk); (573) 346-4440, ext. 1300 (Recorder of Deeds); (573) 346-4440, ext. 3130 (Circuit Clerk); (573) 346-8445 FAX (County Clerk); (573) 346-8367 FAX (Recorder); (573) 346-5422 FAX (Circuit Clerk)
Donnie_Snelling@camdenmo.org; Jo_McElwee@osca.state.mo.us
http://www.camdenmo.org; http://www.morecorders.com/CountyData.asp?COUNTY=CAMDEN; http://www.courts.mo.gov/circuits/index.nsf/County+/+Camden/$first?OpenDocument
Rowland A. Todd, County Clerk; Donnie Snelling, Recorder of Deeds; Ms. Jo McElwee, Circuit Clerk

Cape Girardeau County
organized 1812, original county

Cape Girardeau County Administration Building
1 Barton Square
Jackson, MO 63755
(573) 243-3547 (County Clerk, Third Floor); (573) 243-8123 (Recorder of Deeds, Second Floor); (573) 243-1755 (Circuit Clerk); (573) 334-6249 (Circuit Clerk, Division 4); (573) 204-2418 FAX (County Clerk); (573) 204-2477 FAX(573) 204-2405 FAX (Circuit Clerk)
kclark@capecounty.us; jfrobert@capecounty.us
http://www.showme.net/CapeCounty/departments; http://www.morecorders.com/CountyData.asp?COUNTY=CAPE%20GIRARDEAU; http://www.courts.mo.gov/circuits/index.nsf/County+/+Cape%20Girardeau/$first?OpenDocument
Kara Clark, County Clerk; Janet Fenimore-Robert, Recorder; Charles Hutson, Circuit Clerk
(land records with Recorder of Deeds, probate records with Division 4—Judicial)
no probate search service; copies of probate records: 15¢ each

Carroll County
organized 1833 from Ray County

Carroll County Courthouse
8 South Main
Carrollton, MO 64633
(660) 542-0615 (County Clerk, Suite 6); (660)

542-1466 (Circuit Clerk); (660) 542-0621 FAX (County Clerk); (660) 542-1444 FAX (Recorder); (660) 542-0621 FAX (Circuit Clerk)
ccarroll@sospublicmail.state.mo.us (County Clerk); cheryl.mansur@courts.mo.gov
http://www.morecorders.com/CountyData.asp ?COUNTY=CARROLL;
http://www.courts.mo.gov/circuits/index.nsf /County+/+Carroll/$first?OpenDocument
Peggy McGaugh, County Clerk; Cheryl A. Mansur, Circuit Clerk-Recorder
(land records from 1833, naturalization records from 1833, births from 1883 to 1894, deaths from 1883 to 1890, marriages from 1833)
copies of land records: $1.00 each, copies of naturalization records: 35¢ each; copies of vital records: $2.00 for marriages

Carter County
organized 1859 from Ripley, Reynolds, Shannon and Oregon counties

Carter County Courthouse
(105 Main Street—location)
PO Box 517 (mailing address)
Van Buren, MO 63965-0517
(573) 323-4527 (County Clerk); (573) 323-9656 (Recorder); (573) 323-4513 (Circuit Clerk); (573) 323-4182 FAX (County Clerk); (573) 323-4885 FAX (Recorder)
jjcart@sospublicmail.state.mo.us (County Clerk)
http://www.morecorders.com/CountyData.asp ?COUNTY=CARTER;
http://www.courts.mo.gov/circuits/index.nsf /County+/+Carter/$first?OpenDocument
Rebecca Simpson Gibbs, County Clerk; Pauline Peterman, Recorder of Deeds; Cathy Duncan Terry, Circuit Clerk

Cass County
organized 1835 from Jackson County; name changed from Van Buren County in 1849

Cass County Circuit Clerk
Justice Center
2501 West Wall
Harrisonville, MO 64701
(816) 380-8227; (816) 380-8225 FAX
court4@casscounty.com;
kelly.elliott@courts.mo.gov
http://www.casscounty.com (click on Justice Center)
Thomas Campbell, Circuit Court IV, Probate; Kelly Sue Elliott, Circuit Clerk
(probate records from 1836 to 1956 with Wade Archives, Cass County Historical Society; probate records from 1956 with Probate Office)
no probate search service; copies of probate records: 50¢ each, $2.00 for certified copies

Cass County Courthouse
102 East Wall Street
Harrisonville, MO 64701-2478
(816) 887-2393 (Wade Archives); (816) 380-8102 (County Clerk, First Floor); (816) 380-8123 (Recorder, First Floor); (816) 380-8101 FAX (County Clerk); (816) 380-8165 FAX (Recorder)
janetb@casscounty.com;
gregoryjesagreg@aol.com
http://www.casscounty.com; http://www.morecorders.com/CountyData.asp?COUNTY=CASS
Janet Burlingame, County Clerk; Sandra Gregory, Recorder of Deeds
(land records from December 1840 to September 1960 with Wade Archives, Cass County Historical Society; land records from 1960 with Recorder's Office; marriages from 1835 with Recorder's Office)

Cedar County
organized 1845 from Dade and St. Clair counties

Cedar County Courthouse
(113 South Street—location)
PO Box 126 (mailing address)

Stockton, MO 65785-0126
(417) 276-6700, ext. 221 (County Clerk); (417) 276-6700, ext. 246 (Recorder); (417) 276-6700, ext. 234 (Circuit Clerk); (417) 276-3461 FAX (County Clerk); (417) 276-5499 FAX (Recorder); (417) 276-5001 FAX (Circuit Clerk)
ccedar@mail.sos.state.mo.us (County Clerk); cawilkerson@alltel.net
http://www.morecorders.com/CountyData.asp ?COUNTY=CEDAR;
http://www.courts.mo.gov/circuits/index.nsf /County+/+Cedar/$first?OpenDocument
Peggy Kenney, County Clerk; Carole Wilkerson, Recorder of Deeds; Melinda Gumm, Circuit Clerk

Chariton County
organized 1820 from Howard County

Chariton County Circuit Clerk-Recorder
(Courthouse, 605 Jackson Street—location)
PO Box 112 (mailing address)
Keytesville, MO 65261
(660) 288-3602; (660) 288-3763 FAX
bob.widmer@courts.mo.gov
http://www.morecorders.com/CountyData.asp ?COUNTY=CHARITON;
http://www.courts.mo.gov/circuits/index.nsf /County+/+Chariton/$first?OpenDocument
Bob Widmer
(land records with Recorder of Deeds, naturalization records with Circuit Clerk, marriage licenses with Recorder's Office, probate records from 1860 to date with Circuit Court, Associate Probate Division)
no probate search service; copies of marriage licenses: $1.00 per page, $2.00 for certified copies; copies of probate records: $1.00 per page, $1.50 per certified page

Chariton County County Clerk
306 South Cherry
Keytesville, MO 65261
(660) 288-3273; (660) 288-3403 FAX
charitonclerk@centurytel.net;
ccharito@sospublicmail.state.mo.us
http://www.sos.mo.gov/elections/countyclerks. asp
Susan Littleton
(births and deaths from 1883 to 1887)

Christian County
organized 1859 from Taney, Greene and Webster counties

Christian County Courthouse
100 West Church Street
Ozark, MO 65721
(417) 485-6360 (County Clerk, Room 206); (417) 581-941 (Recorder of Deeds, PO Box 358); (417) 581-6372 (Circuit Clerk, PO Box 278); (417) 581-8331 FAX (County Clerk); (417) 581-9943 FAX (Recorder of Deeds); (417) 581-0391 FAX (Circuit Clerk)
kaybrown@christiancountymo.gov
http://www.christiancountymo.gov;
http://66.112.71.165/43solution;
http://www.morecorders.com/CountyData.a sp?COUNTY=CHRISTIAN; http://www.courts.mo.gov/circuits/index.nsf/County+/+Christian/$first?OpenDocument
Mr. Kay Brown, County Clerk; Roy Meadows, Recorder of Deeds; Richard "Rick" Lamb, Circuit Clerk

Clark County
organized 1836 from Lewis County

Clark County Courthouse
111 East Court Street
Kahoka, MO 63445
(660) 727-3283 (County Clerk, Suite 4); (660) 727-3292 (Circuit Clerk, Suite 2); (660) 727-1051 FAX (County Clerk); (660) 727-1051 FAX (Circuit Clerk)
jjclar@sospublicmail.state.mo.us;
mary.jones@courts.mo.gov
http://www.morecorders.com/CountyData.asp

?COUNTY=CLARK;
http://www.courts.mo.gov/circuits/index.nsf /County+/+Clark/$first?OpenDocument
Leih Ann Hayden, County Clerk; Mary D. Jones, Circuit Clerk and ex officio Recorder of Deeds
(deeds and mortgages from 1836, very few naturalization records, some dating from about 1850, marriages from 1836; probate records with County Probate and Associate Division, Circuit Court, 113 West Court, Kahoka, MO 63445)
probate search service: no charge ("but we can only do when time allows—we are under-staffed"); copies of land records: $1.00 each; copies of marriages: $1.00 per page; copies of probate records: $1.00 per page, no minimum

Clay County
organized 1822 from Ray County

Clay County Administration Building
1 Courthouse Square
Liberty, MO 64068
(816) 407-3570 (County Clerk); (816) 407-3550 (Recorder, PO Box 238); (816) 407-3571 FAX (County Clerk); (816) 407-3601 FAX (Recorder)
cclay01@sospublicmail.state.mo.us (County Clerk); RSevier@claycogov.com;
Robert_sevier@recorder.co.clay.mo.us
http://www.claycogov.com/county/county. php; http://recorder.claycogov.com/pages /index.asp; http://www.circuit7.net/pages /home.asp
Pamela Mason, County Clerk; Robert T. Sevier, Recorder of Deeds

Clay County Circuit Clerk
James S. Rooney Justice Center
11 South Water Street
Liberty, MO 64068
(816) 407-3900; (816) 407-3888 FAX
web@circuit7.net
http://www.circuit7.net/pages/general/contacti nfo.asp
Stephen Haymes

Clinton County
organized 1833 from Clay and Ray counties

Clinton County Courthouse
(207 North Main—location)
PO Box 275 (mailing address)
Plattsburg, MO 64477
(816) 539-3713 (County Clerk); (816) 539-3719 (Recorder); (816) 539-3731 (Circuit Clerk); (816) 539-3298 (Probate); (816) 539-3072 FAX (County Clerk); (816) 539-3893 FAX (Circuit Clerk and Recorder); (816) 539-3439 FAX (Probate)
jjclin@sospublicmail.state.mo.us (County Clerk)
http://co.clinton.mo.us; http://www.morecorderscm/CountyData.asp?COUNTY =CLINTON; http://www.courts.mo.gov/circuits/index.nsf/County+/+Clinton/$first?OpenDocument
Mary Blanton, County Clerk; Molly Livingston, Circuit Clerk-Recorder; Anna Richerson, Circuit Court, Probate Clerk
(land records from 1833 with Recorder's Office; naturalization records from 1883 to 1927 with Recorder's Office; a few births and deaths from 1833 to 1889, marriage records from 1833 with Recorder's Office; probate records with Probate Clerk)

Cole County
organized 1820 from Cooper County

Cole County Circuit Clerk
(Cole County Courthouse, 301 East High Street—location)
PO Box 1870 (mailing address)
Jefferson City, MO 65101
(573) 634-9151 (Circuit Clerk); (573) 634-9177 (Probate Division)
http://www.colecountycourts.com
Brenda Umstattd

(wills and probate estates form 1834)
no probate search service ("give full name and
date of death for search"); copies of probate
records: $1.00 per page

Cole County Clerk
Cole County Courthouse Annex
311 East High Street, Room 201
Jefferson City, MO 65101
(573) 634-9101; (573) 681-9678 FAX
mregister@colecounty.org
http://www.colecounty.org/clerk/home.htm
Marvin Register
(birth and death records)

Cole County Recorder of Deeds
(Cole County Courthouse Annex, 311 East High
Street, Room 101—location)
PO Box 353 (mailing address)
Jefferson City, MO 65101
(573-634-9115; (573) 634-4631 FAX
lrademan@colecounty.org
http://www.colecounty.org/cole1/cole/recorde
r/index.html
Larry D. Rademan
(marriages, land records)

Cooper County
organized 1818 from Howard County

Cooper County Courthouse
200 Main Street
Boonville, MO 65233-1276
(660) 882-2114; (660) 882-2232 (Circuit Clerk,
Room 26); (660) 882-2043 FAX; (660) 882-
2043 FAX (Circuit Clerk)
jjcoop@sospublicmail.state.mo.us (County
Clerk); jammey.brandes@courts.mo.gov
http://www.mo-river.net/Government/
coopercouty_gov.htm; http://www.
morecorders.com/CountyData.asp?COUNT
Y=COOPER; http://www.courts.mo.gov/
circuits/index.nsf/County+/+Cooper/$first?
OpenDocument
Darryl Kempf, County Clerk; Jammey Brandes,
Circuit Clerk-Recorder

Crawford County
organized 1829 from Gasconade County

Crawford County Circuit Clerk-Recorder
PO Box 177
Steelville, MO 65565
(573) 775-2866; (573) 775-2452 FAX
http://www.courts.mo.gov/circuits/index.nsf/
County+/+Crawford/$first?OpenDocument
Rhonda S. Jurgens
(land records, marriages, probate records [PO
Box B.C.])

Crawford County Courthouse
(203 Main Street—location)
PO Box AS (mailing address)
Steelville, MO 65565
(573) 775-2376; (573) 775-3066 FAX
ccrawfor@sospublicmail.state.mo.us
http://www.sos.mo.gov/elections/countyclerks.
asp
Connie Smith, County Clerk

Dade County
organized 1841 from Polk and Barry counties

Dade County Courthouse
300 West Water
Greenfield, MO 65661
(417) 637-2724 (County Clerk); (417) 637-5373
(Recorder); (417) 637-2271 (Circuit Clerk);
(417) 637-1006 FAX (County Clerk and
Recorder); (47) 637-5055 FAX (Circuit Clerk)
jjdade@sospublicmail.state.mo.us (County
Clerk)
http://www.ozarkspartnership.com/member_c
ontacts/?tx_tekorepmembers_pi1%5BshowU
id%4D=18&cHash=b1fd946b11;
http://www.morecorders.com/CountyData.a
sp?COUNTY=DADE;
http://www.courts.mo.gov/circuits/index.nsf
/County+/+Dade/$first?OpenDocument
Larry W. McGuire, County Clerk; Carolyn Kile,

Recorder; Brenda Adams, Circuit Clerk
$10.00 "shelving" fee for access to many
courthouse records (waived for members of
the Dade County Genealogical Society)

Dallas County
organized 1841 from Polk County

Dallas County Circuit Clerk and Recorder
PO Box 373
Bufflao, MO 65622
(417) 345-2243 (Circuit Clerk); (417) 345-2242
(Recorder); (417) 345-7641 (Probate
Division); (417) 345-5539 FAX
janice.hicks@courts.mo.gov
http://www.positech.net/~dcourt/clerks.htm;
http://www.morecorders.com/CountyData.a
sp?COUNTY=DALLAS
Janice Hicks, Judge Cody A. Hanna, Probate
Division

Dallas County Courthouse
PO Box 436
Buffalo, MO 65622-0436
(417) 345-2632 (County Clerk); (417) 345-2242
(Recorder); (417) 345-5321 FAX (County
Clerk)
cdallas@sospublicmail.state.mo.us (County
Clerk)
http://www.buffalococ.co/dallasgov.htm
Pam Louderbaugh, County Clerk; Stacy
Satterfield, Recorder of Deeds
(vital records from 1883 to 1893 with County
Clerk, land records with Recorder)
no probate search service; certified copies of
vital records: $3.00 each; copies of probate
records: 50¢ per page, no minimum

Daviess County
organized 1836 from Ray County

Daviess County Courthouse
102 North Main Street
Gallatin, MO 64640
(660) 663-2641 (County Clerk); (660) 663-3183
(Recorder, PO Box 132); (660) 663-2932
(Circuit Clerk); (660) 663-3075 FAX (County
Clerk); (660) 663-3376 FAX (Recorder); (660)
663-3876 FAX (Circuit Clerk)
jjdavi@sospublicmail.stte.mo.us (County Clerk)
http://www.morecorders.com/CountyData.asp
?COUNTY=DAVIESS;
http://www.courts.mo.gov/circuits/index.nsf
/County+/+Daviess/$first?OpenDocument
Linda Steward, County Clerk; Georgia Maxwell,
Recorder of Deeds; Linda Adkins, Circuit
Clerk
(land records from 1837, some naturalization
records in 1930s, births and deaths from 1883
to 1893, marriages from 1839, probate
records from 1890)
probate search service: no charge; copies of
probate records: 50¢ each, no minimum
("certified copies vary from office to office")

DeKalb County
organized 1845 from Clinton County

DeKalb County Courthouse
PO Box 248
Maysville, MO 64469-0248
(816) 449-5402 (County Clerk); (816) 449-2602
(Circuit Clerk); (816) 449-2440 FAX (County
Clerk); (816) 449-2440 FAX (Circuit Clerk)
dekalb@sos.mo.gov (County Clerk)
http://www.courts.mo.gov/circuits/index.nsf/
County+/+DeKalb/$first?OpenDocument
Mary Berry, County Clerk; Clifton Deshon,
Circuit Clerk-Recorder
(land records from 1845 with Recorder of
Deeds, naturalization records from 1906 to
1923 with Recorder of Deeds, some births
from 1883 to 1887 [very incomplete] with
County Clerk's Office, deaths from 1883 to
1891 and 1942 to 1943 with Recorder of
Deeds, probate records from 1878 with
Associate Circuit Court, Probate Division)
records search service: no charge; copies of land,
naturalization, vital, and probate records:

$1.00 per page, no minimum

Dent County
organized 1851 from Crawford and Shannon
counties

Dent County Courthouse
400 North Main Street
Salem, MO 65560-1436
(573) 729-4144; (573) 729-6016 FAX
dent@sos.mo.gov
http://www.salemmissouri.com/government.html
Janet Inman, County Clerk

Douglas County
organized 1857 from Ozark County

Douglas County Courthouse
(203 S.E. Second—location)
PO Box 398 (mailing adress)
Ava, MO 65608
(417) 683-4714 (County Clerk); (417) 683-4713
(Circuit Clerk); (417) 683-1017 FAX (County
Clerk); (417) 683-2794 FAX (Circuit Clerk)
cdouglas@sospublicmail.state.mo.us (County
Clerk); judith.denney@courts.mo.gov
http://www.morecorders.com/CountyData.asp
?COUNTY=DOUGLAS;
http://www.courts.mo.gov/circuits/index.nsf
/County+/+Douglas/$first?OpenDocument
Karry Davis, County Clerk; Judith Denney,
Circuit Clerk and Recorder of Deeds

Dunklin County
organized 1845 from Stoddard County

Dunklin County Courthouse
(Courthouse Square—location)
PO Box 188 (mailing address)
Kennett, MO 63857-0188
(573) 888-1374 (County Clerk); (573) 888-3468
(Recorder); (573) 888-5322 (Circuit Clerk,
Civil Division); (573) 888-2832 FAX (County
Clerk); (573) 888-8956 FAX (Recorder); (573)
888-0319 FAX (Circuit Clerk)
jjdunk@sospublicmail.state.mo.us;
slucerecorder@yahoo.com
http://www.morecorders.com/CountyData.asp
?COUNTY=DUNKLIN;
http://www.courts.mo.gov/circuits/index.nsf
/County+/+Dunklin/$first?OpenDocument
Carol Hinesly, County Clerk; Susan Luce,
Recorder of Deeds; Judith Lee Vavak, Circuit
Clerk

Franklin County
organized 1818 from St. Louis County

Franklin County Circuit Clerk
300 East Main Street, Room 301
Union, MO 63084
(636) 583-6303
bill_miller@osca.state.mo.us
http://www.franklinmo.org
Bill D. Miller
no probate search service; copies of probate
records: 35¢ each, no minimum

Franklin County Clerk
400 East Locust, Room 201
Union, MO 63084
(636) 583-6355; (636) 583-7320 FAX
frcoclerk@yhti.net
http://www.franklinmo.org
Debbie Door

Franklin County Recorder of Deeds
(300 East Main Street, Room 101, Union, MO
63084-1675—location)
PO Box 311 (mailing address)
Union, MO 63084-0311
(636) 583-6367; (636) 583-7330 FAX
fcrecordermo@yhti.net
http://www.franklincountymissouri.org/fcrd/in
dex.asp
Sharon Birkman
(land records with Assessor's Office, Union City
Auditorium, 500 East Locust, Union, MO
63084, vital records with Recorder of Deeds)

Gasconade County
organized 1820 from Franklin County

Gasconade County Courthouse
119 East First Street
Hermann, MO 65041-0295
(573) 486-5427 (County Clerk, Suite 2); (573) 486-2632 (Circuit Clerk-Recorder); (573) 486-2321 (Probate Office); (573) 486-8893 FAX (County Clerk); (573) 486-5812 FAX (Circuit Clerk-Recorder)
gasconade@sos.mo.gov (County Clerk); pam.greunke@courts.mo.gov
http://www.gscnd.com/government.html; http://www.morecorders.com/CountyData.asp?COUNTY=GASCONADE; http://www.courts.mo.gov/circuits/index.nsf/County+/+Gasconade/$first?OpenDocument
Lesa Lietzow, County Clerk; Judith Schulte, Circuit Clerk and ex Officio Recorder of Deeds
(land records from 1821 with Recorder, Suite 6, naturalization records from 1837 to 1949 with Recorder, births from 1867 to 1900, deaths from 1883 to 1900 with County Clerk, Suite 2, marriages from 1822 with Recorder, probate records with Probate Clerk, Division IV, Associate Circuit Court, PO Box 176, Hermann, MO 65041)
vital records and probate search service: no charge; copies of vital records: $1.00 per page, no minimum; copies of probate records: $10.00 per page, no minimum

Gentry County
organized 1845 from Clinton County

Gentry County Courthouse
200 West Clay Street
Albany, MO 64402-1604
(660) 726-3525 (County Clerk); (660) 726-3618 (Circuit Clerk, PO Box 27); (660) 726-4478 FAX (County Clerk); (660) 726-4102 FAX (Circuit Clerk)
gentryco@albanymo.net (County Clerk); john.whitaker@courts.mo.gov
http://www.morecorders.com/CountyData.asp?COUNTY=GENTRY; http://www.courts.mo.gov/circuits/index.nsf/County+/+Gentry/$first?OpenDocument
Carol Reidlinger, County Clerk; John Whitaker, Circuit Clerk-Recorder

Greene County
organized 1833 from Wayne and Crawford counties

Greene County Circuit Clerk
1010 Boonville
Springfield, MO 65802
(417) 868-4168; (417) 868-4186 FAX
mcarr@courts.mo.gov
http://www.greenecountymo.org/ccourt31
Michael A. Carr
(genealogy information with Green County Archives and Records Center; probate records from 1833 to 1970)

Greene County Courthouse
940 Boonville Avenue
Springfield, MO 65802
(417) 868-4055 (County Clerk, Room 113); (417) 868-4068 (Recorder of Deeds Office); (417) 868-4170 FAX (County Clerk); (417) 829-6646 FAX (Recorder); (417) 868-4807 FAX (Recorder of Deeds)
rstruckhoff@greenecountymo.org; Lmontgomery@greenecountymo.org
http://www.greenecountymo.org/web; http://www.morecorders.com/CountyData.asp?COUNTY=GREENE
Richard T. Struckhoff, County Clerk; Linda S. Montgomery, County Recorder
(genealogy information with Green County Archives and Records Center; land tax records from 1833 to 1864 [with gaps] and from 1865, land transaction records with Recorder of Deeds Office, marriage licenses with Recorder of Deeds Office)

probate search service; no charge; copies of probate records: 20¢ per page, $1.00 minimum if SASE not enclosed

Grundy County
organized 1841 from Livingston and Ray counties

Grundy County Courthouse
700 Main Street
Trenton, MO 64683-2010
(660) 359-6305 (County Clerk, Second Floor); (660) 359-5409 (Recorder); (660) 359-6605 (Circuit Clerk, Second Floor); (660) 359-6786 FAX (County Clerk); (660) 359-6604 FAX (Circuit Clerk)
recorder@grundycountymo.com
http://www.morecorders.com/CountyData.asp?COUNTY=GRUNDY; http://www.courts.mo.gov/circuits/index.nsf/County+/+Grundy/$first?OpenDocument
Kristi Urich, County Clerk; Beatrice Shaw, Circuit Clerk-Recorder

Harrison County
organized 1845 from Daviess and Ray counties

Harrison County Courthouse
(Courthouse, 1505 Main Street—location)
PO Box 525 (mailing address)
Bethany, MO 64424
(660) 425-6424 (County Clerk); (660) 425-6425 (Circuit Clerk); (660) 425-3772 FAX (County Clerk); (660) 425-6390 FAX (Circuit Clerk)
charriso@sospublicmail.state.mo.us (County Clerk); sherece.eivins@courts.mo.gov
http://www.morecorders.com/CountyData.asp?COUNTY=HARRISON; http://www.courts.mo.gov/circuits/index.nsf/County+/+Harrison/$first?OpenDocument
Sherry Seltman, County Clerk; Sherece Eivins, Circuit Clerk-Recorder
(land records with Circuit Clerk-Recorder of Deeds, naturalization records with Circuit Clerk-Recorder of Deeds, births and deaths from 1883 through 1893 only with County Clerk's Office, marriages and divorces with Circuit Clerk-Recorder of Deeds, probate records with Marjorie Butz, Clerk, Circuit Court, Probate Division II Office)
probate search service: no charge ("generally I do not answer letters as I do not have much time for doing genealogy research, but I do assist people when they come to the office; I will not copy complete files, only wills and other instruments with information relative to heirs, etc."); copies of land records: $1.00 per instrument; copies of probate records: 25¢ per page, $1.00 minimum

Henry County
organized 1834 from Lafayette County; name changed from Rives County in 1841

Henry County Courthouse
100 West Franklin Street
Clinton, MO 64735-2088
(660) 885-7204 (County Clerk); (660) 885-7211 (Recorder); (660) 885-7230 (Circuit Clerk, PO Box 487); (660) 890-2963 FAX (County Clerk); (660) 885-2264 FAX (Recorder); (660) 885-8247 FAX (Circuit Clerk)
henry@sos.mo.gov (County Clerk); henrycoclerk@hotmail.com (County Clerk); brecorder@hotmail.com
http://tacnet.missouri.org/gov/henrycou.html; http://www.morecorders.com/CountyData.asp?COUNTY=HENRY; http://www.courts.mo.gov/circuits/index.nsf/County+/+Henry/$first?OpenDocument
Gene Pogue, County Clerk; Becky Raysik, Recorder; Marsha A. Abbott, Circuit Clerk

Hickory County
organized 1845 from Benton and Polk counties

Hickory County Courthouse
(Spring and Dallas—location)
PO Box 3 (mailing address)

Hermitage, MO 65668-0003
(417) 745-6450 (County Clerk); (417) 745-6421 (Circuit Clerk, PO Box 101); (417) 745-6057 FAX (County Clerk); (417) 745-6670 FAX (Circuit Clerk)
chickory@mail.sos.mo.us (County Clerk)
http://www.hickorycountymo.com; http://www.positech.net/~dcourt/clerks.htm
Kent Parson, County Clerk; Cee Cee Smith, Circuit Clerk

Holt County
organized 1841 from Platte Purchase

Holt County Courthouse
102 West Nodaway
Oregon, MO 64473
(660) 446-3303 (County Clerk, PO Box 437); (660) 446-3301 (Circuit Clerk, PO Box 318); (660) 446-3353 FAX (County Clerk); (660) 446-3328 FAX (Circuit Clerk)
janice.radley@courts.mo.gov
http://www.morecorders.com/CountyData.asp?COUNTY=HOLT; http://www.courts.mo.gov/circuits/index.nsf/County+/+Holt/$first?OpenDocument
Kathy Kunkel, County Clerk; Janice Radley, Circuit Clerk-Recorder

Howard County
organized 1816 from St. Louis and St. Charles counties

Howard County Courthouse
1 Courthouse Square
Fayette, MO 65248
(816) 248-2284 (County Clerk); (816) 248-2194 (Circuit Clerk); (660) 248-1075 FAX (County Clerk and Circuit Clerk)
http://www.mo-river.net/Howard/Government/index.htm
Mark Hill; County Clerk; Charles J. "Charlie" Flaspohler, Circuit Clerk and Recorder; Louise Coutts, Court House Volunteer
(land records Warranty deeds, deeds of trust, surveys from 1817, naturalization records from 1850 to 1906, a few births and deaths from 1883 to 1889, marriages from 1816, estates, guardianships, intestates)
records search service: no charge, but donation appreciated; copies of records: $2.00 per page

Howell County
organized 1857 from Oregon County

Howell County Courthouse
1 Courthouse Street
West Plains, MO 65775-3400
(417) 256-2591 (County Clerk); (417) 256-3741 (Recorder, PO Box 967); (417) 256-3742 (Circuit Clerk, PO Box 967); (417) 256-2512 FAX (County Clerk); (417) 256-4650 FAX (Circuit Clerk)
chowell@sospublicmail.state.mo.us (County Clerk)
http://www.howellcounty.net; http://www.courts.mo.gov/circuits/index.nsf/County+/+Howell/$first?OpenDocument
Dennis Von Allmen, County Clerk; Cindy Weeks, Circuit Clerk-Recorder
(land records from 1867 with Recorder, births from 1883 to 1894, deaths from 1883 to 1893 with Dennis K. VonAllman, County Clerk, marriages with Recorder, probate records from 1867)
no probate search service; certified copies of vital records: $2.00 each; copies of probate records: 25¢ per page from paper originals, $1.00 per page from microfiche originals, $1.50 for certified copies

Iron County
organized 1857 from Madison, Reynolds, St. Francois, Wayne and Washington counties

Iron County Courthouse
250 Sout Main
Ironton, MO 63650-0042
(314) 546-2912 (County Clerk, PO Box 42);

(573) 546-2811 (Circuit Clerk, PO Box 24);
(473) 546-6499 FAX (County Clerk); (573)
546-2166 FAX (Circuit Clerk)
ciro01@sospublicmail.state.mo.us (County
Clerk); Brenda_Turner@osca.state.mo.us
http://www.ironcounty.homestead.com/Count
yGovernment.html
Rodney Lashley, County Clerk; Brenda Turner,
Circuit Clerk and Ex-Officio Recorder
(land records from 1857, some naturalization
records from 1887 to 1906, births and deaths
from 1883 to 1887, marriages from 1857,
probate records)
probate search service: fee determined at time of
search; certified copies of vital records: $2.00
each; copies of probate records: $1.00 to
$1.50 per page, no minimum

Jackson County
organized 1826 from Lafayette County

Jackson County Circuit Court
Jackson County Courthouse
415 East 12th Street, Third Floor
Kansas City, MO 64106
and
Independence Courthouse Annex
308 West Kansas, Second Floor
Independence, MO 64050
(816) 881-4573 (Civil Records, Third Floor);
(816) 881-3759 (Prbate Records, Ninth
Floor); (816) 881-4410 FAX (Civil Records);
(816) 881-1609 FAX (Probate Records)
mmcclure@courts.mo.gov
http://www.16thcircuit.org
Mary Ann McClure, Director, Civil Records
(marriages from 1826 with Independence)

Jackson County Clerk
Jackson County Courthouse
415 East 12th Street, Second Floor
Kansas City, MO 64106
and
Independence Office
200 South Main
Independence, MO 64050
(816) 881-3242 (Kansas City); (816) 881-1626
(Independence); (816) 881-3234 FAX (Kansas
City); (816) 881-4473 FAX (Independence)
CoClerk@jacksongov.org
http://www.jacksongov.org/content/118
9/1291/default.aspx
Mary Jo Spino
(deaths in the late 1800s)

Jackson County Recorder of Deeds
415 Est 12th Street, Room 104
Kansas City, MO 64106

Jackson County Courthouse Annex
308 West Kansas Avenue, Room 104
Independence, MO 64050
(816) 881-3193 (Kansas City); (816) 881-4483
(Independence); (816) 881-3719 FAX (Kansas
City)
bkelly@jacksongov.org
http://www.jacksongov.org/content/1167/118
9/1315/default.aspx;
http://www.morecorders.com/CountyData.a
sp?COUNTY=JACKSON
Robert Kelly
(real estate recordings from the 1800s, marriage
licenses from 1881)
vital records search service: $3.00; copies of land
records or marriage licenses: $2.00 for the
first page, $1.00 for each additional page;
copies of plates: $5.00

**16th Judicial Circuit Court of Jackson
County, Missouri**
Probate Division
415 Est 12th Street, Ninth Floor
Kansas City, MO 64106-2706
(816) 881-3755 (Info and Certified Copies,
Kansas City); (816) 881-4552 (Info and
Certified Copies, Independence)
http://www.16thcircuit.org
(early naturalization records with Circuit Court,
Kansas City, probate records)

Jasper County
organized 1841 from Barry County

Jasper County Courthouse
302 South Main Street
Carthage, MO 64836-1621
(417) 358-0416 (County Clerk, Room 102); (417)
358-0431 (Recorder of Deeds, Room 207, PO
Box 387); (417) 358-0441 (Circuit Clerk);
(417) 358-0403 (Probate Clerk, Room 108);
(417) 359-1297 FAX (County Clerk); (417)
359-1200 FAX (Recorder); (417) 358-0461
FAX (Circuit Clerk); (417) 358-0404 FAX
(Probate Clerk)
recorder@jaspercounty.org
http://www.jaspercounty.org;
http://www.courts.mo.gov/circuits/index.nsf
/County+/+Jasper/$first?OpenDocument
Ron Mosbaugh, County Clerk; Donna Grove,
Recorder; Linda Williams, Circuit Clerk;
Shelley Wiley, Probate Clerk
(land records with Recorder of Deeds, a few
births and deaths from 1883 through 1897
[none from 1898 to 1909] with County Clerk,
marriages with Recorder, probate records
with Circuit Court, Probate Division
Courthouse)

Jefferson County
organized 1818 from Sainte Genevieve and St.
Louis counties

Jefferson County Administration Center
(729 Maple Street—location)
PO Box 100 (mailing address)
Hillsboro, MO 63050-0100
(636) 797-5478 (County Clerk, Room 217); (636)
797-5486 (County Clerk); (314) 789-5414
(Recorder, Room 126); (636) 797-5443
(Circuit Clerk); (800) 748-3456 (County
Clerk); (636) 797-5360 FAX (County
Clerk); (636) 797-6310 (Recorder); (636)
797-5073 FAX (Circuit Clerk)
wwagner@jeffcomo.org; mcastle@jeffcomo.org
http://www.jeffcomo.org;
http://www.morecorders.com/CountyData.a
sp?COUNTY=JEFFERSON; http://www.
courts.mo.gov/circuits/index.nsf/County+/
+Jefferson/$first?OpenDocument
Wes Wagner, County Clerk; Marlene Castle,
Recorder of Deeds; Howard Wagner, Circuit
Clerk
(land records, marriage licenses)
copies of land records and marriages: $2.00 and up

Johnson County
organized 1834 from Lafayette County

Johnson County Circuit Court
101 West Market
Warrensburg, MO 64093
(660) 422-7413
http://www.jococourthouse.com/courts.htm
Stephanie Elkins, Circuit Clerk
probate search service: $5.00; copies of probate
records: $1.00 for the first page and 25¢ for
each additional page, no minimum ("all
payments to be made by money order only")

Johnson County Courthouse
300 North Holden Street
Warrensburg, MO 64093-1708
(660) 747-6161 (County Clerk); (660) 747-6811
(Recorder of Deeds, PO Box 32); (660) 422-
7413 (Circuit Clerk); (660) 747-9332 FAX
countyclerk@jococourthouse.com;
cjohnson@sospublicmail.state.mo.us (County
Clerk)
http://www.jococourthouse.com/CountyClerk.
htm; http://www.jococourthouse.com/
records.htm
Gilbert Powers, County Clerk; Ms. Jan Jones,
Recorder of Deeds
(land records from 1835 with Recorder of
Deeds; births and deaths from 1883 to 1893
only with County Clerk's Office; marriages
from 1835 with Recorder of Deeds)
no land records search service; copies of land
records: $1.00 for the first page and 25¢ for

each additional page of the same document

Knox County
organized 1845 from Scotland County

Knox County Circuit Clerk-Recorder
Knox County Courthouse
(100 Main Street—location)
PO Box 116 (mailing address)
Edina, MO 63537
(660) 397-2305; (660) 397-3331 FAX
ji.gibbons@courts.mo.gov
http://www.morecorders.com/CountyData.asp
?COUNTY=KNOX;
http://www.courts.mo.gov/circuits/index.nsf
/County+/+Knox/$first?OpenDocument
James R. Gibbons
(land records from 1845, naturalization records
from 1845, vital records from 1883 to 1890,
probate records from 1845)
no probate search service; copies of probate
records: 25¢ each

Knox County Clerk
107 North Fourth Street
Edina, MO 63537-1470
(660) 397-2184; (660) 397-2642 FAX
knox@sos.mo.gov
http://www.knoxcountmo.org/index.cgi?tag=o
ffices
Debbie McCurren

Laclede County
organized 1849 from Camden, Pulaski and
Wright counties

Laclede County Government Center
200 North Adams Avenue
Lebanon, MO 65536
(417) 532-5471 (County Clerk); (417) 532-4011
(Recorder); (417) 532-2471 (Circuit Clerk);
(417) 588-9288 FAX (Circuit Clerk); (417)
532-3852 FAX (Recorder)
clerk@lacledecountymissouri.org (County
Clerk); recorder@lacledecountyissouri.org;
lcc-recordfer@webound.com
http://www.lacledecountymissouri.org;
http://www.morecorders.com/CountyData.a
sp?COUNTY=LACLEDE;
http://www.courts.mo.gov/circuits/index.nsf
/County+/+Laclede/$first?OpenDocument
Glenda Mott, County Clerk; Lynn Stowe,
Recorder of Deeds; Wanda Tyree, Circuit
Clerk
(land records Warranty deeds and mortgage
records from 1849 with Recorder, platt books
from 1912 with County Clerk, births from
1884 to 1899 with County Clerk, marriages
from 1865 with Recorder, probate records
from late 1800s with Lobby of the
Courthouse)
no probate search service; copies of probate
records("cannot make copies of bound
books"): 15¢ to 50¢ each, $1.50 for certified
copies

Lafayette County
organized 1820 from Cooper County, called
Lillard County in 1821, then Lafayette County
in 1826

Lafayette County Circuit Court
(Lafayette Hall, 116 South Tenth Street—
location)
PO Box 10 (mailing address)
Lexington, MO 64067
(660) 259-6101 (Circuit and Associate
Divisions); (660) 259-2324 (Probate Division);
(660) 259-6148 FAX (Circuit and Associate
Divisions); (660) 259-4997 FAX (Probate
Division)
http://www.courts.mo.gov/circuits/index.nsf/
County+/+Lafayette/$first?OpenDocument
Deana Aversman, Circuit Clerk

Lafayette County Courthouse
1001 Main Street
Lexington, MO 64067-1344
(660) 259-4315 (County Clerk, Room 103, PO
Box 357); (660) 259-6178 (Recorder of

Deeds, Room 206, Box 416); (660) 259-6109 FAX (County Clerk); (660) 259-2918 FAX (Recorder)
clayet@sospublicmail.state.mo.us
http://www.lafayettecountyclerk.com;
http://www.morecorders.com/CountyData.asp?COUNTY=LAFAYETTE; http://www.historiclexington.com/index.html
Linda Niendick, County Clerk; Patsy Olvera, Recorder
(land records from 1821 with County Recorder, naturalization records from 1821 with Circuit Clerk, probate records from 1821 with Circuit Court—Probate Division, PO Box E, Lexington, MO 64067)
probate search service: $1.00 per legal-sized page, no minimum

Lawrence County
organized 1845 from Dade and Barry counties

Lawrence County Courthouse
1 East Courthouse Square
Mt. Vernon, MO 65712-1444
(417) 466-2638 (County Clerk, Suite 101); (417) 466-2670 (Recorder, PO Box 449); (416) 466-2471 (Circuit Clerk, Suite 201); (417) 466-4348 FAX (County Clerk); (417) 466-4995 FAX (Recorder); (417) 466-7899 FAX (Circuit Clerk)
lawrence@sos.mo.gov (County Clerk); Lawco_recorder@hotmail.com
http://www.ozarkspartnership.com/member_contacts/?tx_tekorepmembers_pi1%5BshowUid%5D=33&cHash=3a18142949; http://www.morecorders.com/CountyData.asp?COUNTY=LAWRENCE; http://www.courts.mo.gov/circuits/index.nsf/County+/+Lawrence/$first?OpenDocument
Gary Emerson, County Clerk; Pam Robertson, Recorder; Cynthia Faucett-Supiran, Circuit Clerk

Lewis County
organized 1833 from Marion County

Lewis County Courthouse
100 East Lafayette
Monticello, MO 63457
(573) 767-5205 (County Clerk, PO Box 67); (573) 767-5440 (Recorder, PO Box 97); (573) 767-5352 (Circuit Clerk, PO Box 8); (573) 767-8245 FAX (County Clerk); (573) 767-5352 FAX (Recorder); (573) 767-5342 FAX (Circuit Clerk)
clewis@sospublicmail.state.mo.us (County Clerk); william.b.smith@courts.mo.gov
http://www.morecorders.com/CountyData.asp?COUNTY=LEWIS; http://www.courts.mo.gov/circuits/index.nsf/County+/+Lewis/$first?OpenDocument
Sharon Schlager, County Clerk; Brenda Gunlock, Recorder; William Smith II, Circuit Clerk
(land records with Recorder of Deeds, naturalization records with Circuit Clerk, births and deaths from 1883 through 1887 only, probate records with Probate Office)
probate search service: no charge; copies of probate records: $1.00 each, no minimum

Lincoln County
organized 1818 from St. Charles County

Lincoln County Circuit Clerk
Lincoln County Justice Center
45 Business Park Drive
Troy, MO 63379
(636) 528-6300; (636) 528-9168 FAX
http://www.courts.mo.gov/circuits/index.nsf/County+/+Lincoln/$first?OpenDocument
Melba Houston

Lincoln County Courthouse
201 Main Street
Troy, MO 63379-1127
(636) 528-6300, ext. 1 (County Clerk); (636) 528-0325 (Recorder); (636) 528-5528 FAX (County Clerk); (636) 528-2665 FAX

(Recorder)
clincoln@sospublicmail.state.mo.us (County Clerk)
http://www.lcclerk.com; http://www.morecorders.com/CountyData.asp?COUNTY=LINCOLN
Elaine Luck, County Clerk; Dottie D. Crenshaw, Recorder

Linn County
organized 1837 from Chariton County

Linn County Courthouse
108 North High
Linneus, MO 64653
(660) 895-5417 (County Clerk, Room 102, PO Box 92); (660) 895-5216 (Recorder, Room 204); (660) 895-5212 (Circuit Clerk, PO Box 84); (660) 895-5527 FAX (County Clerk); (660) 895-5379 FAX (Recorder); (660) 895-5277 FAX (Circuit Clerk)
lincorec@grm.net
http://www.morecorders.com/CountyData.asp?COUNTY=LINN; http://www.courts.mo.gov/circuits/index.nsf/County+/+Linn/$first?OpenDocument
Peggy Ward, County Clerk; Loretta Brookshier, Recorder; E. Elaine Clough, Circuit Clerk
(land records from 1842 with Recorder's Office, naturalizations from 1850 to 1930 with Circuit Clerk's Office, naturalizations from 1889 with Circuit Clerk, a few births and deaths from 1883 to 1887 with County Clerk, marriages from 1842 with Recorder's Office, probate records from 1850 with Probate Office)
probate search service: $2.00; copies of probate records: $1.00 per page

Livingston County
organized 1837 from Carroll County

Livingston County Courthouse
(700 Webster Street—location)
PO Box 803 (mailing address)
Chillicothe, MO 64601
(660) 646-8000, ext. 3 (County Clerk, Suite 10); (660) 646-8000, ext. 6 (Recorder of Deeds; (660) 646-8000, ext. 1, then 3 (Circuit Clerk); (660) 646-8105 FAX (County Clerk); (660) 646-2734 FAX (Circuit Clerk)
countyclerk@livingstoncountymo.com; brenda.timmons@courts.mo.gov
http://www.livingstoncountymo.com; http://www.courts.mo.gov/circuits/index.nsf/County+/+Livingston/$first?OpenDocument
Ms. Kelly Christopher, County Clerk; Gordon Smith, Recorder; Brenda Timmons, Circuit Clerk

Macon County
organized 1837 from Randolph and Chariton counties

Macon County Courthouse
101 East Washington Street
Macon, MO 63552
(660) 385-2913 (County Clerk, PO Box 96); (660) 385-2732 (Recorder of Deeds, Building 2, PO Box 382); (660) 385-4631 (Circuit Clerk, Building 2, PO Box 382); (660) 385-3131 (Probate Records, PO Box 491); (660) 385-7203 FAX (County Clerk); (660) 385-4235 FAX (Circuit Clerk and Recorder)
maconcomo@yahoo.com (County Clerk); judy.roberts@courts.mo.gov
http://www.maconcountymo.com
Pat Clarke, County Clerk; Judy A. Roberts, Circuit Clerk-Recorder
(land records with Recorder of Deeds, naturalization records with Circuit Court, births and deaths from 1883 to 1893 only with County Clerk, marriages with Recorder of Deeds, probate records with Probate Records)

Madison County
organized 1818 from Sainte Genevieve and Cape Girardeau counties

Madison County Courthouse
1 Court Square
Fredericktown, MO 63645
(573) 783-2176 (County Clerk); (573) 783-3410 (Recorder); (573) 783-2102 (Circuit Clerk, PO Box 470); (573) 783-3105 (Associate and Probate Divisions); (573) 783-5351 FAX (County Clerk); (573) 783-2715 FAX (Recorder); (573) 783-2715 FAX (Circuit Clerk); (573) 783-5920 FAX (Associate and Probate Divisions)
cmadison@sospublicmail.state.mo.us (County Clerk)
http://www.morecorders.com/CountyData.asp?COUNTY=MADISON
Joan Whitener, County Clerk; Paula Francis, Recorder; Eileen Provow, Circuit Clerk
(land records from 1818 to date with Circuit Clerk and Recorder's Office, naturalization records from 1818 to date with Circuit Clerk and Recorder's Office, marriages from 1818 to date with Circuit Clerk and Recorder's Office, a few births and deaths from 1883 to 1893 with County Clerk's Office, probate records from 1822 to 1960 with Mrs. Carol King, Associate and Probate Divisions of the Madison County Circuit Court Division III, PO Box 521, Fredericktown, MO 63645)
probate search service: no charge; copies of land records, naturalization records, and marriages: $1.00 each; copies of probate records: 25¢ per page, $12.75 for fifty-one-page master list of all files from 1822 to 1960, no minimum

Maries County
organized 1855 from Gasconade, Osage and Pulaski counties

Maries County Courthouse
Fourth and Main
Vienna, MO 65582
(573) 422-3388 (County Clerk); (573) 422-3338 (Circuit Clerk and Recorder); (573) 422-3303 (Probate); (573) 422-3269 FAX (County Clerk); (573) 422-3976 FAX (Circuit Clerk and Recorder
cmaries@sospublicmail.state.mo.us (County Clerk); raymond.thompson@courts.mo.gov
http://www.morecorders.com/CountyData.asp?COUNTY=MARIES
Rhonda Brewer, County Clerk; Leo Thompson, Circuit Clerk and Recorder
(land records from 1855 with Circuit Clerk and Recorder, thirteen naturalization records; from 1874 to 1906 [Lischine, Schanning, Spielhagen, Danuser, Kleinecke, Juergens, McKenzie, Hartman, Brockman, Segrist, Spielhagan, Dette and Dette] with Historical Society of Maries County, marriages from 1881 with Circuit Clerk and Recorder, very few vital records with Record Room of Historical Society of Maries County, probate records from 1885)
no probate search service; copies of probate records: 15¢ or 25¢ each ("I don't believe there is a set charge—people usually donate")

Marion County
organized 1826 from Ralls County

Marion County Courthouse
100 South Main Street
Palmyra, MO 63461-1661
(314) 769-2549 (County Clerk, Room 107); (573) 769-2550 (Circuit Clerk, PO Box 392); (573) 769-4312 FAX (County Clerk); (573) 769-6012 FAX (Circuit Clerk)
mcco@centurytel.net (County Clerk); john.yancey@courts.mo.gov
http://www.morecorders.com/CountyData.asp?COUNTY=MARION; http://www.courts.mo.gov/circuits/index.nsf/County+/+Marion/$first?OpenDocument
Robert J. Ravenscraft, County Clerk; John E. Yancey, Circuit Clerk-Recorder, Div. 1

McDonald County
organized 1849 from Newton County

McDonald County Courthouse
602 Main Street and Highway W
Pineville, MO 64856
(417) 223-4717 (County Clerk, PO Box 665);
    (417) 223-7523 (Recorder, PO Box 157);
    (417) 223-7515 (Circuit Clerk); (417) 223-7519
    FAX (County Clerk); (417) 223-4125 FAX
    (Circuit Clerk)
jjcdo@sospublicmail.state.mo.us (County Clerk);
    kuku@olemac.net (Recorder)
http://www.courts.mo.gov/circuits/index.nsf/C
    ounty+/+McDonald/$first?OpenDocument
Barbara Williams, County Clerk; Kenny
    Underwood, Recorder of Deeds; Gene Hall,
    Circuit Clerk

Mercer County

organized 1845 from Grundy and Livingston
    counties

Mercer County Courthouse
802 Main Street
Princeton, MO 64673-1240
(660) 748-3425 (County Clerk); (660) 748-4335
    (Circuit Clerk); (660) 748-3180 FAX (County
    Clerk); (660) 748-4339 FAX (Circuit Clerk)
cmercer@sospublicmail.state.mo.us (County
    Clerk); patricia.stamper@courts.mo.gov
http://muextension.missouri.edu/mercer/cech_
    up.htm; http://www.morecorders.com/
    CountyData.asp?COUNTY=MERCER;
    http://www.courts.mo.gov/circuits/index.nsf
    /County+/+Mercer/$first?OpenDocument
Carolyn Kost, County Clerk; Patricia Stamper,
    Circuit Clerk-Recorder

Miller County

organized 1837 from Cole and Pulaski counties

Miller County Courthouse
2001 Highway 52
Tuscumbia, MO 65082-0012
(573) 369-1910 (County Clerk, PO Box 12);
    (573) 369-1935 (Recorder, PO Box 11); (573)
    369-1980 (Circuit Clerk, PO Box 11); (573)
    369-1905 FAX (County Clerk); (573) 369-
    1939 FAX (Circuit Clerk)
countyclerk@millercountymo.org;
    cmiller@sospublicmail.state.mo.us (County
    Clerk); recorder@mail.yhti.net
http://millercountymissouri.org/CountyClerk.ht
    ml; http://millercountymissouri.org/
    CircuitClerk.html
Clayton Jenkins, County Clerk; Genise L.
    Buechter, Circuit Clerk-Recorder

Mississippi County

organized 1845 from Scott County

Mississippi County Courthouse
(200 North Main Street—location)
PO Box 369 (mailing address)
Charleston, MO 63834-0369
(573) 683-2146, ext. 221 & 223 (County Clerk);
    (573) 683-2146, ext. 226 (Recorder of Deeds);
    (573) 683-2146, ext. 225 (Circuit Clerk); (573)
    683-6071 FAX (County Clerk); (573) 683-
    7696 FAX (Circuit Clerk)
mississippi@sos.mo.gov (County Clerk);
    jrolwing@misscomo.net;
    judy.rolwing@courts.mo.gov
http://www.misscomo.net/comapp.html
Hubert DeLay, Jr. County Clerk; Judy Rolwing,
    Recorder of Deeds; Leigh Ann Colson,
    Circuit Clerk
(land records and naturalization records with
    Recorder of Deeds, probate records with
    Probate Court)

Moniteau County

organized 1845 from Cole and Morgan counties,
    annexed small part of Morgan County in 1881

Moniteau County Courthouse
200 East Main
California, MO 65018
(573) 796-4661 (County Clerk, Room 106); (573)
    796-4637 (Assessor); (573) 796-2071 (Circuit
    Clerk, Room 102); (573) 796-4671 (Probate

Clerk); (573) 796-3082 FAX (County Clerk);
    (573) 796-2591 FAX (Recorder)
jjmonit@sospublicmail.state.mo.us (County
    Clerk); david.haldiman@courts.mo.gov
http://www.morecorders.com/CountyData.asp
    ?COUNTY=MONITEAU; http://www.
    courts.mo.gov/circuits/index.nsf/County+/
    +Moniteau/$first?OpenDocument
Anita Groepper, County Clerk; J. David
    Haldiman, Circuit Clerk-Recorder
(land records from 1845 with Assessor, births
    from 1883 to 1894 [incomplete], deaths from
    1883 to 1887 [incomplete], marriages from
    1845 with Circuit Clerk, probate records from
    1845 with Probate Clerk)
probate search service: ("our personnel will do
    this if time permits"); copies of probate
    records: $1.00 per page, no minimum

Monroe County

organized 1831 from Ralls County

Monroe County Courthouse
300 North Main Street
Paris, MO 65275-1399
(660) 327-5106 (County Clerk, Room 204); (660)
    327-1131 (Recorder of Deeds, Room 103, PO
    Box 246); (660) 327-5220 (Circuit Clerk and
    Probate Clerk, Room 202); (660) 327-1019
    FAX (County Clerk); (660) 327-1130 FAX
    (Recorder); (660) 327-5781 FAX (Circuit
    Clerk)
cmonroe@sospublicmail.state.mo.us
http://www2.pariso.net/county_clerk;
    http://www2.parismo.net/circuit_court.htm
Sandra "Sandy" Carter, County Clerk; Mary Sue
    Meals, Recorder; Gale Bierly, Circuit Clerk
(County Court records, plat books, road maps
    with County Clerk, land and warranty deeds
    with Circuit Clerk, marriages with Circuit
    Clerk, probate records with Probate Clerk)
probate search service: $4.00 (Lein, Circuit
    Clerk); copies of records from County Clerk:
    $15.00 plus postage for plat books, $1.00 for
    road maps; copies of probate records: $1.00
    per page, 50¢ for seal

Montgomery County

organized 1818 from St. Charles County

Montgomery County Courthouse
211 East Third
Montgomery City, MO 63361-1956
(573) 564-3357 (County Clerk); (573) 564-3157
    (Recorder); (573) 564-3341 (Circuit Clerk);
    (573) 564-8088 FAX (County Clerk); (573)
    564-3914 FAX (Recorder); (573) 564-3914
    FAX (Circuit Clerk)
montcoclerk@ktis.net
http://www.montgomerycountymo.org/Gover
    nment/government.html; http://www.
    courts.mo.gov/circuits/index.nsf/County+/
    +Montgomery/$first?OpenDocument
Pam Cartee, County Clerk; Sheila See, Recorder
    of Deeds; Patricia Bufka, Circuit Clerk

Morgan County

organized 1833 from Cooper County

Morgan County Circuit Clerk-Recorder
(Morgan County Justice Center, 211 Est
    Newton Street—location)
PO Box 687 (mailing address)
Versailles, MO 65084
(573) 378-4029 (Recorder); (573) 378-4413
    (Circuit Clerk)
http://www.morecorders.com/CountyData.asp
    ?COUNTY=MORGAN;
    http://www.courts.mo.gov/circuits/index.nsf
    /County+/+Morgan/$first?OpenDocument
Cheryl L. Morris
(land records from 1833, naturalization records
    [mixed in with court records and very hard to
    find], very few vital records [starting around
    1880], probate records from 1833)
probate search service: no charge; copies of
    probate records: 50¢ per page, no minimum

Morgan County Clerk

100 East Newton
Versailles, MO 65084
(573) 378-5436, ext. 132; (573) 378-5991 FAX
http://muextension.missouri.edu/xplor/uedivis
    /ue6070.htm
Cathy Daniels

New Madrid County

organized 1812, original county

New Madrid County Courthouse
450 Main Street
New Madrid, MO 63869
(573) 748-2524 (County Clerk, PO Box 68);
    (573) 748-5146 (Recorder, PO Box 217);
    (573) 748-2228 (Circuit Clerk); (573) 748-5556
    (Probate); (573) 748-9269 FAX (County
    Clerk); (573) 748-9271 FAX (Recorder); (573)
    748-5409 FAX (Circuit Clerk); (573) 748-9274
    FAX (Probate)
cnewmadr@sospublicmail.state.mo.us (County
    Clerk); recorder@sheltonbbs.com
http://www.morecorders.com/CountyData.asp
    ?COUNTY=NEW%20MADRID; http://
    www.courts.mo.gov/circuits/index.nsf/Coun
    ty+/+New%Madrid/$first?OpenDocument
Clement Cravens, County Clerk; Ann H.
    (Evans) Copeland, Recorder; Marsha
    Holiman, Circuit Clerk
(land records from 1805 with Recorder,
    marriages from 1805 with Recorder, probate
    records from 1806 with Paula Scobey, Clerk)
probate search service: no charge; copies of
    probate records: 25¢ each, no minimum

Newton County

organized 1838 from Barry County

Newton County Courthouse
101 South Wood Street
Neosho, MO 64850
(417) 451-8221 (County Clerk, PO Box 488);
    (417) 451-8224 (Recorder, PO Box 604);
    (417) 451-8210 (Circuit Clerk); (417) 451-7434
    FAX (County Clerk); (417) 451-8273 FAX
    (Recorder); (417) 451-8298 FAX (Circuit
    Clerk)
cnewton@sospublicmail.state.mo.us (County
    Clerk)
http://www.newtoncountymotourism.org;
    http://www.ncrecorder.org;
    http://www.courts.mo.gov/circuits/index.nsf
    /County+/+Newton/$first?OpenDocument
Kay Baum, County Clerk; Lenora Hyder,
    Recorder; Peggy L. Spicer, Circuit Clerk
(land records with Recorder of Deeds Office,
    PO Box 1307, Neosho, MO 64850, probate
    records with Division III)
probate search service: $5.00 per person; copies
    of probate records: $1.00 per page, no
    minimum

Nodaway County

organized 1845 from Andrew County

Nodaway County Circuit Clerk
303 North Market
Maryville, MO 64468
(660) 582-5431; (660) 582-4221 (Probate Clerk)
Patrick.ORiley@courts.mo.gov
http://www.nodawaycountymo.com/content/v
    iew/29/27
Kim Carmichael
(naturalization records with Circuit Clerk's
    Office, probate records with Probate Clerk)
probate search service: no charge; copies of
    probate records: $1.00 per page, no minimum

Nodaway County Courthouse
305 North Main
Maryville, MO 64468
(660) 582-2251 (County Clerk, Room 103, PO
    Box 218); (660) 582-5711 (Recorder, Room
    104); (660) 582-5282 FAX (County Clerk)
nodclerk@earthlink.net;
    nodcorecorder@earthlink.net
http://www.nodawaycountymo.com/content/v
    iew/34/27; http://www.nodawaycounty
    recorder.com

Beth (Hann) Walker, County Clerk; Sandra (Sandy) L. Smail, Recorder; Kim Carmichael, Circuit Clerk
(land records with Recorder's Office)

Oregon County
organized 1845 from Ripley County

Oregon County Courthouse
Alton, MO 65606
(417) 778-7475 (County Clerk, Room 1, Box 324); (417) 778-7460 (Recorder, PO Box 406); (417) 778-7488 FAX (County Clerk); (417) 778-7206 FAX (Recorder)
jjo33g@sospublicmail.state.mo.us (County Clerk)
http://www.morecorders.com/CountyData.asp
  ?COUNTY=OREGON;
  http://www.courts.mo.gov/circuits/index.nsf
  /County+/+Oregon/$first?OpenDocument
Gary Hensley, County Clerk; Dorothy Barton, Circuit Clerk-Recorder
(land records, naturalization records, vital records, probate records)

Osage County
organized 1841 from Gasconade County

Osage County Courthouse
Linn, MO 65051
(573) 897-2139 (County Clerk, PO Box 826); (573) 897-3114 (Circuit Clerk, PO Box 825); (573) 897-2136 (Division III); (573) 897-4741 FAX (County Clerk); (573) 897-4075 FAX (Circuit Clerk)
jjosag@sospublicmail.state.mo.us;
  charlene.eisterhold@courts.mo.gov
http://www.osagecountymo.com;
  http://www.morecorders.com/CountyData.a
  sp?COUNTY=OSAGE;
  http://www.courts.mo.gov/circuits/index.nsf
  /County+/+Osage/$first?OpenDocument
Stanley Strope, County Clerk; Charlene Eisterhold, Circuit Clerk-Recorder
(land records with Circuit Clerk and Recorder, naturalization records with Circuit Clerk and Recorder, births and deaths from 1882 to 1892 with County Clerk's Office, marriages with Circuit Clerk and Recorder, probate records with Associate Judge, Division III)
no probate search service; copies of probate records: 25¢ each

Ozark County
organized 1841 from Taney County

Ozark County Courthouse
1 Courthouse Square
Gainesville, MO 65655
(417) 679-3516 (County Clerk, PO Box 416); (417) 679-4232 (Circuit Clerk-Recorder, PO Box 36); (417) 679-3209 FAX (County Clerk); (417) 679-4554 FAX (Circuit Clerk)
cozark@sospublicmail.state.mo.us (County Clerk); becki.strong@courts.mo.gov
http://www.morecorders.com/CountyData.asp
  ?COUNTY=OZARK;
  http://www.courts.mo.gov/circuits/index.nsf
  /County+/+Ozark/$first?OpenDocument
Kelly Maddox, County Clerk; Becki Strong, Circuit Clerk-Recorder

Pemiscot County
organized 1851 from New Madrid County

Pemiscot County Courthouse
610 Ward Avenue
Caruthersville, MO 63830
(573) 333-4203 (County Clerk, Suite 2-A); (573) 333-2204 (Recorder, Suite 1A); (573) 333-0187 (Circuit Clerk, PO Box 228); (573) 333-0440 FAX (County Clerk, PO Box 34); (573) 333-0440 FAX (Recorder); (573) 333-1272 FAX (Circuit Clerk)
pemcoclerk@sbcglobal.net (County Clerk)
http://www.morecorders.com/CountyData.asp
  ?COUNTY=PEMISCOT; http://www.
  courts.mo.gov/circuits/index.nsf/County+/
  +Pemiscot/$first?OpenDocument

Larry Ray, County Clerk; Pam Strawbridge, Recorder; Kelly Maners, Circuit Clerk

Perry County
organized 1820 from Sainte Genevieve County

Perry County Circuit Clerk
15 West St. Maries Street
Perryville, MO 63775
(573) 547-6581 (Circuit Clerk, Suite 2); (573) 547-1611 (Recorder); (573) 547-9323 FAX (Circuit Clerk)
http://www.perryvillemo.com/county/county/
  circuitcourt.htm; http://www.perryvillemo.
  com/county/county/recorder.htm
Becky Paulus, Circuit Clerk; Sue Oster, County Recorder

Perry County Clerk
321 North Main, Suite 2
Perryville, MO 63775-1372
(314) 547-4242; (573) 547-7367 FAX
cperry@mail.sos.state.mo.us; rtaylor@c-b-s-i.net
http://www.perryvillemo.com/county/countycl
  erk.htm
Randy Taylor

Pettis County
organized 1833 from Saline and Cooper counties

Pettis County Courthouse
415 South Ohio
Sedalia, MO 65301-4435
(660) 826-5000, ext. 400 (County Clerk); (660) 826-5000, ext. 431 (Recorder); (660) 826-5000, ext. 453 (Circuit Clerk); (660) 829-0717 FAX (County Clerk); (660) 829-4479 FAX (Recorder)
cpettis@sospublicmail.state.mo.us (County Clerk); pettisrecorder@bcglobal.net
http://www.pettiscomo.com
Pam Doane, County Clerk; Janet Kresse, Recorder; Elaine Bryson, Circuit Clerk

Phelps County
organized 1857 from Crawford County

Phelps County Courthouse
(Third and Main Streets—location)
200 North Main Street (mailing address)
Rolla, MO 65401
(573) 458-6000; (573) 458-6115 (County Clerk, Suite 101); (573) 458-6095 (Recorder, Suite 133); (573) 458-6210 (Circuit Clerk, Suite 201); (573) 458-6119 FAX (County Clerk); (573) 458-6098 FAX (Recorder); (573) 458-6224 FAX (Circuit Clerk)
carol.bennett@phelpscounty.org;
  robin.kordes@phelpscounty.org
http://www.phelpscounty.org/coclerk/coclerk.
  htm; http://www.phelpscounty.org/recorder
  /recorder.htm; http://www.phelpscounty.
  org/circuitclerk.html
Carol A. Bennett, County Clerk; Robin Kordes, Recorder of Deeds; Sue Brown, Circuit Clerk
(land records from 1857 with Recorder's Office, naturalization records to the early or mid-50s with Recorder's Office, births and deaths from 1882 to 1892, probate records from January 1858)
probate search service: no charge; copies of probate records: $1.00 per page, no minimum

Pike County
organized 1818 from St. Charles County

Pike County Courthouse
115 West Main
Bowling Green, MO 63334-1665
(573) 324-2412 (County Clerk); (573) 324-3112; (573) 324-5154 FAX (County Clerk); (573) 324-3150
sherry.mccarty@courts.mo.gov
http://www.morecorders.com/CountyData.asp
  ?COUNTY=PIKE;
  http://www.pikecountymo.org (Pike County Development Authority)
Bob Kirkpatrick, County Clerk; Sherry McCarty, Circuit Clerk-Recorder
(land records with Recorder's Office, probate

records with Probate Office)
no probate search service ("Probate Office does not do index searches "but will refer an individual to persons that do this kind of work"); copies of probate records: 25¢ per page

Platte County
organized 1838 from Platte Purchase

Platte County Circuit Clerk
County Courthouse
328 Main Street, Suite 5-CH
Platte City, MO 64079
(816) 858-2232; (816) 858-3392 FAX
http://www.co.platte.mo.us/county_off_circ.html
Sandra Dowd
(just a few naturalization records in storage with Circuit Clerk's Office, one page of vital records in an old book, probate records from 1839 with Probate Judge)
probate search service: no charge; copies of probate records: 25¢ each, no minimum

Platte County County Clerk
County Administration Building
415 Third Street, Suite 30
Platte City, MO 64079
(816) 431-2232
skrohne@co.platte.mo.us
http://www.co.platte.mo.us/county_off_cnty_c
  lerk.html
Sandra Krohne

Platte County County Recorder
County Administration Building
415 Third Street, Suite 70
Platte City, MO 64079
(816) 858-3326 (General Information)
gboyer@co.platte.mo.us
http://www.co.platte.mo.us/county_off_rec.ht
  ml
Gloria Boyer, Chief Deputy
(land records from 1839)

Polk County
organized 1835 from Greene and Laclede counties

Polk County Courthouse
102 East Broadway
Bolivar, MO 65613
(417) 326-4031 (County Clerk, Room 11); (417) 326-4924 (Recorder, Room 8); (417) 329-4912 (Circuit Clerk); (417) 326-3525 FAX (County Clerk); (417) 326-6898 FAX (Recorder); (417) 326-4194 FAX (Circuit Clerk)
coclerk@polkcountymo.org;
  recorder@polkcountymo.org
http://www.morecorders.com/CountyData.asp
  ?COUNTY=POLK; http://www.positech.
  net/~dcourt/clerks.htm;
  http://www.ozarkspartnership.com/member
  _contacts/?tx_tekorepmembers_pi1%5Bsho
  wUid%4D=18&cHash=f9850fa9f3
Susan Entlicher, County Clerk; Carol Poindexter, Recorder; Vesta Seiner, Circuit Clerk

Pulaski County
organized 1833 from Crawford County

Pulaski County Courthouse
301 U.S. Historic 66 East
Waynesville, MO 65583-2656
(573) 774-4701 (County Clerk, Suite 101); (573) 774-4755 (Recorder, Suite 202); (573) 774-5601 FAX (County Clerk); (573) 774-6967 FAX (Recorder)
http://www.sos.mo.gov/elections/countyclerks.
  asp
Diana Linnenbringer, County Clerk; Rachelle Beasley, Circuit Clerk-Recorder
(land records from 1903 with Recorder of Deeds, some old naturalization records, probate records from 1903 with Circuit Clerk)
copies of land records: $1.00 per page; copies of probate records: 25¢ per page

Putnam County

organized 1845 from Adair, Sullivan and Linn counties, annexed Dodge County in 1853

Putnam County Courthouse
1601 Main Street
Unionville, MO 63565
(660) 947-2674 (County Clerk, Room 204); (660) 947-2071 (Circuit Clerk-Recorder, Room 202); (660) 947-2117 (Associate Ciruit Judge, Probate Court, Room 101); (660) 947-4214 FAX (County Clerk); (660) 947-2320 FAX (Circuit Clerk-Recorder); (660) 947-7348 FAX (Probate Court)
cputnam@sospublicmail.state.mo.us (County Clerk); mitzi.shipley@courts.mo.gov
http://www.morecorders.com/CountyData.asp?COUNTY=PUTNAM; http://www.courts.mo.gov/page.asp?id=1541
Sue Ann Varner, County Clerk; Mitzi Shipley, Circuit Clerk-Recorder
(land records from 1848 with Recorder of Deeds, Room 202, naturalization records from 1904 to 1905 with Circuit Clerk, Room 202, births from 1883 to 1898 with County Clerk, marriages from 1850 with Recorder of Deeds, probate records from 1845 with Probate Court, Room 101)
probate search service: no charge; copies of probate records: $1.00 per page, no minimum

Ralls County
organized 1820 from Pike County

Ralls County Courthouse
New London, MO 63459
(573) 985-7111 (County Clerk, PO Box 400); (573) 985-5631 (Recorder, PO Box 444); (573) 985-5633 (Circuit Clerk, PO Box 466); (573) 985-6100 FAX (County Clerk); (573) 985-5630 FAX (Recorder); (573) 985-3446 FAX (Circuit Clerk)
http://www.morecorders.com/CountyData.asp?COUNTY=RALLS; http://www.courts.mo.gov/page.asp?id=1585
Ernie Duckworth, County Clerk; Gina Jameson, Circuit Clerk-Recorder
(land records with Recorder of Deeds, naturalization records with Circuit Clerk, marriages with Recorder, probate records with Probate Clerk, Circuit Court)
probate search service: $3.00; copies of probate records: $1.00 per page, no minimum

Randolph County
organized 1829 from Chariton and Ralls counties

Randolph County Circuit Clerk
Justice Center, 372 Highway JJ
Huntsville, MO 65259
(660) 277-4601; (660) 277-4636 FAX
http://www.randolphcountymo.com/index.htm; http://www.courts.mo.gov/circuits/index.nsf/County+/+Randolph/$first?OpenDocument
Norma Prange

Randolph County Courthouse
110 South Main Street
Huntsville, MO 65259
(660) 277-4717 (County Clerk, Suite A); (660) 277-4718 (Recorder, Suite B); (660) 277-4834 FAX (Recorder)
rancoclerk@hotmail.com; crandolp@sospublicmail.state.mo.us (County Clerk); randolphcountyrecorder@rcao.com
http://www.randolphcountymo.com/Clerk.htm; http://www.randolphcountymo.com/recorder.htm
Jim Sears, County Clerk; Mark Price, Recorder

Ray County
organized 1820 from Howard County

Ray County Courthouse
100 West Main Street
Richmond, MO 64085-1755
(816) 776-4502 (County Clerk); (816) 776-4500 (Recorder, PO Box 167); (816) 776-3377 (Circuit Clerk); (816) 776-4512 FAX (County

Clerk and Recorder); (816) 776-6016 FAX (Circuit Clerk)
jjray0@sospublicmail.state.mo.us (County Clerk)
http://www.morecorders.com/CountyData.asp?COUNTY=RAY; http://www.courts.mo.gov/page.asp?id=1569
Paul Lynn Rogers, County Clerk; Shirley O'Dell, Recorder; Carolyn Conner, Circuit Clerk
(land records from 23 November 1820 with Recorder of Deeds, naturalization records from 1903 to 1945 with Circuit Clerk, births from 1884 to 1890, deaths from 1883 to 1886 with County Clerk, probate records from 3 April 1821 with Clerk Associate Division Circuit Court)
probate search service: $5.00 for up to three names; copies of probate records: 25¢ per page per side ("with no charge until $5.00 index search is exhausted"), $5.00 minimum

Reynolds County
organized 1845 from Shannon County

Reynolds County Courthouse
Courthouse Square
PO Box 76
Centerville, MO 63633
(573) 648-2494, ext. 12 (County Clerk, PO Box 10); (573) 648-2494, ext. 29 (Circuit Clerk-Recorder, PO Box 76); (573) 648-2296 FAX (County Clerk); (573) 648-2503 FAX (Circuit Clerk-Recorder)
jjreyn@sospublicmail.state.mo.us (County Clerk)
http://www.morecorders.com/CountyData.asp?COUNTY=REYNOLDS
Mike Harper, County Clerk; Randy Cowin, Circuit Clerk-Recorder
(land records from 1872 [courthouse burned in 1867], photocopied and hand-written naturalization records in deed books, marriage records only 1872, probate records from 1872 with Associate Judge Donald E. Lamb or Paula Gray, Clerk, Probate—Circuit Court)
probate search service ("we don't usually do this, only if time allows"); copies of probate records: $2.00 plus $1.00 per each additional page, $1.00 minimum

Ripley County
organized 1833 from Wayne County

Ripley County Courthouse
100 Courthouse Square
Doniphan, MO 63935
(573) 996-3215 (County Clerk, Suite 2); (573) 996-7941 (Recorder); (573) 996-2818 (Circuit Clerk, Suite 3) (573) 996-9774 FAX (County Clerk); (573) 996-9706 FAX (Recorder); (573) 996-5014 FAX (Circuit Clerk)
http://www.ripleycountymissouri.org/Ripley.asp; http://www.morecorders.com/CountyData.asp?COUNTY=RIPLEY; www.courts.mo.gov/page.asp?id=1651
Becky Camden York, County Clerk; Bob Featherston, Recorder; Sharon Richmond, Circuit Clerk

St. Charles County
organized 1812, original county

St. Charles County Administration Building
201 North Second Street
St. Charles, MO 63301
(636) 949-7550 (County Clerk, Room 541); (636) 949-7505 (Recorder, Room 338); (636) 949-7552 FAX (County Clerk); (636) 949-7512 FAX (Recorder)
bhall@saintcharlescounty.org; recorder@saintcharlescounty.org
http://www.saintcharlescounty.org/DesktopDefault.aspx?tabid=49
Rich Chrismer, County Clerk; Barbara Hall, Recorder; Judy Zerr, Circuit Clerk

St. Charles County Circuit Clerk
300 North Second, Suite 216
St. Charles, MO 63301
(636) 949-3080; (636) 949-7390 FAX
http://www.sccmo.org/DesktopDefault.

aspx?tabid=168
Judy Zerr

St. Clair County
organized 29 January 1841 from Rives County

St. Clair County Courthouse
655 Second Street
Osceola, MO 64776
(417) 646-2315 (County Clerk, PO Box 525); (417) 646-2950 (Recorder, PO Box 323); (417) 646-2226 (Circuit Clerk); (417) 646-8080 FAX (County Clerk); (417) 646-2951 (Recorder); (660) 646-2401 FAX (Circuit Clerk)
jjstcl@sospublicmail.state.mo.us (County Clerk); sacosageterrytory@yahoo.com
http://www.morecorders.com/CountyData.asp?COUNTY=ST.%20CLAIR; www.courts.mo.gov/page.asp?id=4776
Donna Houston, County Clerk; Pat Terry, Recorder; Barbara Taber, Circuit Clerk
(land records, naturalization records, vital records from 1883 to 1887 only, probate records)

St. Francois County
organized 1821 from Sainte Genevieve, Jefferson and Washington counties

St. Francois County Courthouse
1 North Washington Street
Farmington, MO 63640
(573) 756-5411, ext. 5 (County Clerk, Suite 206); (573) 756-2323, option 8, ext. 140 (Recorder, Room 105); (573) 756-4551 (Circuit Clerk); (573) 431-6967 FAX (County Clerk); (573) 756-3733 FAX (Circuit Clerk)
cstfranc@sospublicmail.state.mo.us; recorder@sfcgov.org
http://www.morecorders.com/CountyData.asp?COUNTY=ST.%20FRANCOIS; http://www.courts.mo.gov/page.asp?id=1626
Mark Hedrick, County Clerk; Steve Grider, Recorder; Vickie Weible, Circuit Clerk
(land records, naturalization records, vital records, probate records)

St. Louis City Circuit Clerk
10 North Tucker Boulevard, First Floor
St. Louis, MO 63101
(314) 622-4433; (314) 615-2629 (Probate, General Information); (314) 622-3462 (Archives, Second Floor, South, for pre-1980 records); (314) 622-4537 FAX; (314) 615-8293 FAX (Probate)
http://www.stlcitycircuitcourt.com
Mariano V. Favazza
(divorce and probate records; pre-1906 naturalization records)

St. Louis City Recorder of Deeds
City Hall, 1200 Market Street, Room 126
St. Louis, MO 63103
(314) 622-4610; (314) 622-3257 (Marriage License Office, Room 127); (314) 613-3016 (Birth Certificates, Room 127); (314) 613-3018 (Death Certificates, Room 124)
http://stlouis.missouri.org/citygov/recorder/index.html
Sharon Quigley Carpenter
(land records, vital records)

St. Louis County Recorder of Deeds
Lawrence K. Roos County Government Building, Fourth Floor
41 South Central Avenue
Clayton, MO 63105-1799
(314) 615-2500
recorder@stlouisco.com
http://revenue.stlouisco.com/RecorderOfDeeds
Janice M. Hammonds
(land records; marriage records)

St. Louis County
organized 1812, original county

St. Louis County Courthouse
7900 Forsyth Boulevard
Clayton, MO 63105
(314) 615-5440 (County Clerk); (314) 615-8029

(Circuit Court)
circuitcourt@stlouisco.com
http://www.stlouisco.com
Suzanne Richeda Pratl, County Clerk; Joan M.
Gilmer, Circuit Clerk
(divorce and probate records with Circuit Clerk)

Sainte Genevieve County
organized 1812, original county

Sainte Genevieve County Courthouse
55 South Third Street
Ste. Genevieve, MO 63670
(573) 883-5779 (County Clerk); (573) 883-2705
(Circuit Clerk); (573) 883-5312 FAX (County
Clerk); (573) 883-9351 FAX (Circuit Clerk)
cstegeni@sospublicmail.state.mo.us (County
Clerk)
http://www.courts.mo.gov/page.asp?id=1625
Darryle Shuh, County Clerk; David Gegg,
Recorder; Carol Steiger, Circuit Clerk

Saline County
organized 1820 from Cooper County

Saline County Courthouse
101 East Arrow Street
Marshall, MO 65340
(660) 886-3331 (County Clerk, Room 202); (660)
886-2677 (Recorder, Room 206); (660) 886-
2300 (Circuit Clerk); (660) 886-2644 FAX
(County Clerk); (660) 886-2603 FAX
(Recorder); (660) 831-5360 FAX (Circuit
Clerk)
csaline@sospublicmail.state.mo.us (County
Clerk); screcorder@mmuonline.net
http://www.courts.mo.gov/page.asp?id=1607
Kenneth Bryant, County Clerk; Jamie Nichols,
Recorder; Sharon Crawford, Circuit Clerk

Schuyler County
organized 1845 from Adair County

Schuyler County Courthouse
1 Courthouse Square
Lancaster, MO 63548
(816) 457-3842 (County Clerk, PO Box 187);
(660) 457-3784 (Circuit Clerk-Recorder, PO
Box 186); (660) 457-3016 FAX (County
Clerk); (660) 457-3016 FAX (Circuit Clerk-
Recorder)
cschuyle@sospublicmail.state.mo.us;
judy.keim@courts.mo.gov
http://www.morecorders.com/CountyData.asp
?COUNTY=SCHUYLER; http://www.
courts.mo.gov/page.asp?id=1521
Doyle Talbert, County Clerk; Judy L. Keim,
Circuit Clerk-Recorder

Scotland County
organized 1841 from Clark, Lewis and Shelby
counties

Scotland County Courthouse
117 South Market
Memphis, MO 63555
(660) 465-7027 (County Clerk, Suite 100); (660)
465-8605 (Clerk Circuit-Recorder, Suite 106);
(660) 465-7785 FAX (County Clerk); (660)
465-8673 FAX (Circuit Clerk-Recorder)
jjscol@sospublicmail.state.mo.us (County
Clerk); anita.watkins@courts.mo.gov
http://www.scotlandcounty.net/government/g
overnment.shtml;
http://www.morecorders.com/CountyData.a
sp?COUNTY=SCOTLAND; http://www.
courts.mo.gov/page.asp?id=1527
Betty Lodewegen, County Clerk; Anita Watkins,
Circuit Clerk and ex officio Recorder of
Deeds

Scott County
organized 1821 from New Madrid County

Scott County Courthouse
131 South Winchester Street
Benton, MO 63736
(573) 545-3549 (County Clerk, PO Box 188);
(573) 545-3551 (Recorder, PO Box 78); (573)

545-3596 (Circuit Clerk, PO Box 277); (573)
545-3511 (Probate Division); (573) 545-3540
FAX (County Clerk); (573) 545-3551 FAX
(Recorder); (573) 545-3597 FAX (Circuit
Clerk); (573) 545-3685 FAX (Probate
Division)
countyclerk@scottcountymo.com; ritamilan@
hotmail.com; scottcorecorder@charterin
ternet.com; circuitclerk@scottcountymo.com
http://www.scottcountymo.com/clerk.html;
http://www.courts.mo.gov/page.asp?id=1644
Rita Milam, County Clerk; Tom Dirnberger,
Recorder; Pam Glastetter, Circuit Clerk
(land records and naturalization records with
John J. Bollinger, Recorder of Deeds, PO Box
76, Benton, MO 63736, probate records with
Probate Clerk)
probate search service: no charge ("inquiries
answered on basis of clerk's time available");
copies of probate records: 50¢ each, no
minimum

Shannon County
organized 1841 from Ripley County

Shannon County Courthouse
106 Main
Eminence, MO 65466
(573) 226-3414 (County Clerk, PO Box 187);
(573) 226-3315 (Clerk-Recorder, PO Box
148); (573) 226-5321 FAX (County Clerk and
Clerk-Recorder)
shannon@sos.mo.gov (County Clerk)
http://www.courts.mo.gov/page.asp?id=1655
Shelly McAfee, County Clerk; Melany Williams,
Circuit Clerk and ex officio Recorder of
Deeds)

Shelby County
organized 1835 from Marion County

Shelby County Courthouse
100 East Main
Shelbyville, MO 63469-0186
(573) 633-2181 (County Clerk, PO Box 186);
(573) 633-2151 (Circuit Clerk-Recorder, PO
Box 176); (573) 633-1004 FAX (County Clerk
and Circuit Clerk-Recorder)
http://www.sos.mo.gov/elections/countyclerks.
asp; http://www.cityofshelbina.com/
government.htm (City of Shelbina)
Tracy Smith, County Clerk; Rosalie Shively,
Circuit Clerk-Recorder
(land records, naturalization records, and
marriages with Circuit Clerk-Recorder,
probate records with Probate Clerk, PO Box
206)
probate search service: no charge; copies of
probate records: 50¢ each, no minimum

Stoddard County
organized 1835 from Cape Girardeau County

Stoddard County Courthouse
316 South Prairie
Bloomfield, MO 63825
(573) 568-3339 (County Clerk, PO Box 110);
(573) 568-3444 (Recorder, PO Box 217);
(573) 568-2194 FAX (County Clerk); (573)
568-2545 FAX (Recorder)
jjstod@sospublicmail.state.mo.us (County
Clerk); kasbell@imsinternet.net
http://www.morecorders.com/CountyData.asp
?COUNTY=STODDARD
Don White, County Clerk; Kay Asbell, Recorder
(land records with Recorder's Office, births and
deaths from 1883 to 1886 with County
Clerk's Office)

Stoddard County Justice Center
403 South Prairie
Bloomfield, MO 63825
(573) 568-4640 (Circuit Clerk, PO Box 30); (573)
568-4640, ext. 3 (Associate Division III and
Probate, PO Box 518); (573) 568-2271 FAX
(Circuit Clerk); (573) 568-3229 FAX (Probate)
http://www.courts.mo.gov/page.asp?id=1648
Martha Ware, Circuit Clerk
(naturalization records with Circuit Clerk's

Office, probate records with Probate Office)
no probate search service ("the Stoddard County
Historical Society does some research work");
copies of probate records: 50¢ each, no
minimum

Stone County
organized 1851 from Taney County

Stone County Circuit Clerk
(Stone County Law Enforcement Center, 110 F
South Maple, Second Floor—location)
PO Box 18 (mailing address)
Galena, MO 65656
(417) 357-6114; (417) 357-3076 (Circuit Clerk);
(417) 357-3085 (Probate Division); (417) 357-
6163 FAX
Cathy_Shortt@courts.mo.gov
http://www.stoneco-mo.us/circuitcourt.htm
Cathy Shortt, Circuit Clerk; Diane Jared, Probate
Division

Stone County Courthouse
108 East Fourth Street
Galena, MO 65656
(417) 357-6127 (County Clerk, Third Floor, PO
Box 45); (417) 357-6362 (Recorder of Deeds,
108-A East Fourth Street, PO Box 186); (417)
357-6861 FAX (County Clerk); (417) 357-
8131 FAX (Recorder of Deeds)
countyclerkjudy@yahoo.com
http://www.stoneco-mo.us
Judy Berkstresser, County Clerk; Amy Larson,
Recorder of Deeds
(land records with Recorder of Deeds, marriages
only with Recorder of Deeds)
copies of land records and marriages: $2.00 each

Sullivan County
organized 1845 from Linn County

Sullivan County Courthouse
109 North Main Street
Milan, MO 63556-1369
(660) 265-3786 (County Clerk); (660) 265-3630
(Recorder); (660) 265-4717 (Circuit Clerk);
(660) 265-3724 FAX (County Clerk); (660)
265-5071 FAX (Recorder and Circuit Clerk)
jjsull@sospublicmail.state.mo.us (County Clerk)
http://www.morecorders.com/CountyData.asp
?COUNTY=SULLIVAN;
www.courts.mo.gov/page.asp?id=1576
Mike Hepler, County Clerk; John (Ike)
Morehead, Recorder; Sherry Brinkley, Circuit
Clerk

Taney County
organized 1837 from Greene County

Taney County Circuit Clerk
(110 West Elm, Second Floor—location)
PO Box 335 (mailing address)
Forsyth, MO 65653
(417) 546-7230; (417) 546-6133 FAX
BrendaNeal@courts.mo.gov
http://www.co.taney.mo.us;
http://www.courts.mo.gov/circuits/index.nsf
/County+/+Taney/$first?OpenDocument
Brenda Neal

Taney County Clerk
(226 A Main Street—location)
PO Box 156 (mailing address)
Forsyth, MO 65653
(417) 546-7200; (417) 546-2519 FAX
CountyClerk@co.taney.mo.us
http://www.co.taney.mo.us
Donna Neeley

Taney County Recorder
(240 Main Street—location)
PO Box 428 (mailing address)
Forsyth, MO 65653
(417) 546-7234; (417) 546-9021 FAX
recorder@co.taney.mo.us
http://www.co.taney.mo.us
Robert Dixon

Texas County
organized 1845 from Shannon and Wright

County Courthouse Book

counties

Texas County Courthouse
210 North Grand Avenue
Houston, MO 65483-1226
(417) 967-2112 (County Clerk); (417) 967-3742
(Circuit Clerk-Recorder); (417) 967-3837 FAX
(County Clerk); (417) 967-4220 FAX (Circuit
Clerk-Recorder)
txcomo@centurytel.net (County Clerk)
http://www.morecorders.com/CountyData.asp
?COUNTY=TEXAS; http://www.courts.
mo.gov/page.asp?id=4757
Donald R. Troutman, County Clerk; Phyllis J.
Staley, Circuit Clerk-Recorder

Vernon County
organized 1851 from Bates County

Vernon County Courthouse
100 West Cherry
Nevada, MO 64772
(417) 2500 (County Clerk); (417) 448-2520
(Recorder, Second Floor); (417) 448-2525
(Circuit Clerk); (417) 667-6035 FAX (County
Clerk); (417) 448-2524 FAX (Recorder); (417)
448-2512 FAX (Circuit Clerk)
clerk@vernoncountymo.org (County Clerk)
http://www.vernoncountymo.org;
http://www.morecorders.com/CountyData.a
sp?COUNTY=VERNON; http://www.
courts.mo.gov/page.asp?id=1637
Tammi Beach, County Clerk; Doug Shupe,
Recorder; Vickie Erwin, Circuit Clerk

Warren County
organized 1833 from Montgomery County

Warren County Courthouse
104 West Booneslick Road
Warrenton, MO 63383
(636) 456-3331 (County Clerk, Suite B); (636)
456-9800 (Recorder); (636) 456-3363 (Circuit
Clerk); (636) 456-3375 (Probate Division);
(636) 456-1801 FAX (County Clerk); (636)
456-8473 FAX (Recorder); (636) 456-2422
FAX (Circuit Clerk)
cwarren@sospublicmail.state.mo.us (County
Clerk); jerri.jordan@court.mo.gov
http://www.morecorders.com/CountyData.asp
?COUNTY=WARREN; http://www.courts.
mo.gov/page.asp?id=1595
Barbara Daly, County Clerk; Jerri Jordan, Circuit
Clerk-Recorder
(index to deeds 1833–1886, deeds 1833–1938,
marrages 1833–1915, application for marriage
licenses 1901–1920, permanent record of
births 1883–1881, register of births and
stillbirths 1883–1889, permanent record of
deaths 1884–1894, register of deaths 1883–
1889, circuit court records 1883–1886,
probate records 1883–1889, settlement
records 1868–1896, guardians/curators
records 1885–1888, will records 1833–1918)

Washington County
organized 1813 from Sainte Genevieve County

Washington County Courthouse
102 North Missouri
Potosi, MO 63664
(573) 438-6111, ext. 221 (County Clerk); (573)
438-5023 (Recorder); (573) 438-4171 (Circuit
Clerk); (573) 438-4038 FAX (County Clerk);
(573) 438-7900 FAX (Recorder and Circuit
Clerk)
jjwash@sospublicmail.stte.mo.us (County
Clerk); moyers63664@yahoo.com
http://www.morecorders.com/CountyData.asp
?COUNTY=WASHINGTON; http://www.
courts.mo.gov/page.asp?id=1627
Janet Adams, County Clerk; Judy Cresswell
Moyers, Recorder; Patti Boyer, Circuit Clerk
(land records, naturalization records, vital
records, probate records)

Wayne County
organized 1818 from Cape Girardeau and
Lawrence counties

Wayne County Courthouse
109 Walnut Street
Greenville, MO 63944
(573) 224-3012 (County Clerk, PO Box 48);
(573) 224-3014 (Recorder, PO Box 78); (573)
224-3014 (Circuit Clerk); (573) 224-3052
(Probate Division, PO Box 78); (573) 224-
5609 FAX (County Clerk); (573) 224-3015
FAX (Recorder); (573) 224-3225 FAX
(Circuit Clerk and Probate Division)
wayne@sos.mo.gov (County Clerk);
wc_recorder@semo.net
http://www.morecorders.com/CountyData.asp
?COUNTY=WAYNE; http://www.courts.
mo.gov/page.asp?id=1672
Alan R. Lutes, County Clerk; Darren Garrison,
Circuit Clerk-Recorder
(land records from December 1892 with Circuit
Clerk and Recorder's Office ["all records in
the courthouse were destroyed by fire in
December of 1892; a few of the land records
were re-recorded, but not many"], marriages
with Circuit Clerk and Recorder's Office,
probate records from December 1892 with
Associate and Probate Division of Circuit
Court)
probate search service: no charge; copies of
probate records: 25¢ per page, plus SASE, no
minimum

Webster County
organized 1855 from Greene County

Webster County Courthouse
101 South Crittenden
Marshfield, MO 65706
(417) 468-2223 (County Clerk, Room 11); (417)
859-5882 (Recorder, Room 16, PO Box 546);
(417) 859-2041 (Circuit Clerk, Criminal,
Probate, and Circuit Civil, PO Box B); (417)
859-2006 (Circuit Clerk, Civil); (417) 468-
5307 FAX (County Clerk); (417) 468-3843
FAX (Recorder); (417) 468-3786 FAX
(Circuit Clerk)
stan@fidmail.com
http://www.morecorders.com/CountyData.asp
?COUNTY=WEBSTER; http://www.
positech.net/~dcourt/clerks.htm
Stanley D. Whitehurst, County Clerk; Stacy
Atkison, Recorder of Deeds; Jill Peck, Circuit
Clerk
(land records from 1855 with Recorder of
Deeds, marriages only with Recorder's Office,
probate records with Associate Division
Probate)
probate search service: no charge; copies of
probate records: $1.00 per page, no minimum

Worth County
organized 1861 from Gentry County

Worth County Courthouse
Fourth and Front Street
Grant City, MO 64456-0530
(816) 564-2219 (County Clerk, PO Box 450);
(660) 564-2484 (Recorder, PO Box 14); (660)
564-2210 (Circuit Clerk, PO Box 340); (660)
564-2432 FAX (County Clerk); (660) 564-
2432 FAX (Recorder); (660) 564-2432 FAX
(Circuit Clerk)
worthco@ccp.com (Recorder)
http://www.morecorders.com/CountyData.asp
?COUNTY=WORTH; http://www.
courts.mo.gov/page.asp?id=1558
John Jones, County Clerk; Angela Pickering
"Angie" Steele, Recorder; Jana Smyser,
Circuit Clerk; Carmetta Jackson, Probate
(land records with Recorder, naturalization
records from 1861, vital records from 1883 to
1893 with Recorder, probate records with
Circuit Clerk)
land and probate records search service: $4.00;
copies of land and probate records: $1.00 per
document

Wright County
organized 1841 from Pulaski County

Wright County Courthouse

125 Court Square
Hartville, MO 65667
(417) 741-6661 (County Clerk, PO Box 98);
(417) 741-7322 (Recorder, PO Box 39); (417)
741-7121 (Circuit Clerk, PO Box 39); (417)
741-6142 (County Clerk); (417) 741-7504
FAX (Recorder and Circuit Clerk)
jjwrig@sospublicmail.state.mo.us (County
Clerk); joe.chadwell@courts.mo.gov
http://www.morecorders.com/CountyData.asp
?COUNTY=WRIGHT; http://www.courts.
mo.gov/page.asp?id=1680
Tony Dugger, County Clerk; Joe Chadwell,
Circuit Clerk-Recorder; Kima Harris, Deputa
Clerk, Probate
(land records from 1849 to date, probate records
from about 1900)
probate search service: no charge; copies of
probate records: 25¢ per page, no minimum

Capital: Helena. Statehood: 8 November 1889 (settled border with Canada in 1818 and 1846, was part of Washington, Nebraska, Dakota and Idaho territories before becoming a separate territory in 1864)

Montana has four courts of limited jurisdiction: the Missoula Municipal Court, City Courts in ninety-three cities, Justice of the Peace Courts in each county and the Montana Water Court.

The District Court sits in each county seat and handles all felonies, juvenile matters and probate, as well as some misdemeanors, civil actions and appeals from lower courts. The court is divided into twenty districts. First Judicial District: Broadwater and Lewis and Clark counties; Second Judicial District: Silver Bow County; Third Judicial District: Deer Lodge, Granite and Powell counties; Fourth Judicial District: Mineral, Missoula and Ravalli counties; Fifth Judicial District: Beaverhead, Jefferson and Madison counties; Sixth Judicial District: Park and Sweet Grass counties; Seventh Judicial District: Dawson, McCone, Prairie, Richland and Wibaux counties; Eighth Judicial District: Cascade County; Ninth Judicial District: Glacier, Pondera, Teton and Toole counties; Tenth Judicial District: Fergus, Judith Basin and Petroleum counties; Eleventh Judicial District: Flathead County; Twelfth Judicial District: Chouteau, Hill and Liberty counties; Thirteenth Judicial District: Big Horn, Carbon, Stillwater and Yellowstone counties; Fourteenth Judicial District: Golden Valley, Meagher, Musselshell and Wheatland counties; Fifteenth Judicial District: Daniels, Roosevelt and Sheridan counties; Sixteenth Judicial District: Carter, Custer, Fallon, Garfield, Powder River, Rosebud and Treasure counties; Seventeenth Judicial District: Blaine, Phillips and Valley counties; Eighteenth Judicial District: Gallatin County; Nineteenth Judicial District: Lincoln County; Twentieth Judicial District: Lake and Sanders counties. The Supreme Court in Helena hears appeals from all the lower courts.

Anaconda-Deer Lodge County
organized 1864, original county, city-county government consolidation 1976

Anaconda-Deer Lodge County Courthouse
800 South Main Street
Anaconda, MT 59711-2999
(406) 563-8421 (Clerk and Recorder); (406) 563-8421, ext. 223 (Clerk of District Court)
http://www.anacondamt.org;
    http://mt.gov/maco/Counties/ANACOND
    ADEERLODGE.htm
(land records from 1864 with Clerk and Recorder, naturalization records from the 1870s to the 1950s with Clerk District Court, vital records from 1898 with Clerk and Recorder, probate records from 1870 with Clerk of District Court)
land records search service: $5.00 for four or more names, $7.00 per document; vital records search service: 50¢ per year; probate search service: 50¢ per year, $5.00 maximum; copies of land records: 50¢ for the first page and 25¢ for each additional page; copies of vital records: $5.00 each for births, $3.00 each for deaths (proof of relationship required); copies of probate records: 50¢ for each of the first five pages and 25¢ for each additional page, $2.00 for certification, 50¢ minimum

Beaverhead County
organized 1864, original county

Beaverhead County Courthouse
2 South Pacific Street
Dillon, MT 59725-2713
(406) 683-3720 (County Clerk and Recorder, CL

#3); (406) 683-3725 (Clerk of District Court); (406) 683-3769 FAX (Clerk and Recorder); (406) 683-3728 FAX (Clerk of District Court)
Clerk@co.beaverhead.mt.us;
    sbrunkhorst@state.mt.us
http://www.beaverheadcounty.org/html/depart
    ments.html
Rosalee B. Richardson, Clerk and Recorder; Sheila Brunkhorst, Clerk of District Court
(land records from 1864 with County Clerk and Recorder, naturalization records from 1876 to 1929 with Clerk of District Court, births and deaths from 1900 with County Clerk and Recorder, marriages from 1867 with Clerk of District Court, probate records from 1878 with Clerk of District Court)
vital records and probate search service from Clerk of District Court: 50¢ per year; copies of land records: 50¢ each plus SASE (prefer written requests); copies of naturalizations: none; certified copies of vital records from County Clerk and Recorder: $5.00 each for births, $3.00 each for deaths; copies of vital records and probate records from Clerk of District Court: 50¢ for each of the first five pages and 25¢ for each additional page ("will accept *written* requests only; please provide prepaid return postage")

Big Horn County
organized 1913 from Rosebud and Yellowstone counties

Big Horn County Courthouse
(121 West Third Street—location)
PO Box 908 (mailing address)
Hardin, MT 59034-1905
(406) 665-3520; (406) 665-1504 (Clerk of District Court, #221, PO Box H); (406) 665-1608 FAX
cmaxwell@co.bighorn.mt.us;
    kyarlott@co.bighorn.mt.us
http://mt.gov/maco/Counties/BIGHORN.htm
Cyndy Maxwell, Clerk and Recorder; Karen Yarlott, Clerk of District Court
(land records with Clerk and Recorder, naturalization records to the mid-1950s only with Clerk of District Court, births and deaths with Clerk and Recorder, marriages with Clerk of District court, probate records with Clerk of District Court)
probate search service: 50¢ per year per name, $25.00 maximum; copies of land records: 50¢ for the first page and 25¢ for each additional page; certified copies of vital records: $5.00 each for births (some restrictions apply), $3.00 each for deaths; copies of probate records: 50¢ per page for each of the first five pages and 25¢ for each additional page, $2.00 for certification

Blaine County
organized 1895 from Chouteau and Hill counties

Blaine County Courthouse
PO Box 278
Chinook, MT 59523-0278
(406) 357-3250; (406) 357-2199 FAX
sboardman@co.blaine.mt.gov;
    kayjohnson@mt.gov
http://mt.gov/maco/Counties/BLAINE.htm
Sandra Boardman, County Clerk and Recorder/Assessor; Kay o'Brien Johnson, Clerk of District Court
(land records, naturalization records, births and deaths [closed to the public], probate records)
land, naturalization, and probate records search service: 50¢ per year per index; copies of land, naturalization, and probate records: 50¢ for the first page and 25¢ for each additional page

Broadwater County
organized 1897 from Jefferson and Meagher counties

Broadwater County Courthouse
515 Broadwater Street
Townsend, MT 59644-2325

(406) 266-9215; (406) 266-3443; (406) 266-3674 FAX
c&r@co.broadwater.mt.us;
    vmiddlemas@state.mt.us
http://townsendvalley.com
Judy Gillespie, Clerk and Recorder/Treasurer; Valerie Middlemas, Clerk of District Court
(land records with County Clerk and Recorder, naturalization records with Nellie B. Sayer, Court of District Court, vital records with Clerk and Recorder, probate records with Clerk of District Court)
probate search service: 50¢ per year, $25.00 maximum; copies of probate records: 50¢ for each of the first five pages and 25¢ for each additional page, $2.00 for certification

Butte-Silver Bow County
organized 1881 from Deer Lodge County; consolidated city-county government in 1976

Butte-Silver Bow County Courthouse
155 West Granite Street
Butte, MT 59701-9256
(406) 497-6335 (Clerk and Recorder, Room 208); (406) 497-6350 (Clerk of Court, Room 313); (406) 497-6328 FAX (Clerk and Recorder); (406) 497-6358 FAX (Clerk of Court)
clerkrec@co.silverbow.mt.us;
    lmaloney@state.mt.us
http://www.co.silverbow.mt.us
Mary M. McMahon, Clerk and Recorder; Lori Maloney, Clerk of District Court
(land records from 1881 to date with Clerk and Recorder, naturalization records with The Butte-Silver Bow Public Archives, births from about 1915 to date [sketchy before 1915, but many delayed certificates have been filed], deaths from 1907 to date [sketchy before 1907] with Clerk and Recorder, marriages with Lori Maloney, Clerk of the District Court, births from 1906 to 1921, deaths from 1901 to 1917 with Butte-Silver Bow Public Archives, probate records with Clerk of the Court)
vital records search service from Clerk of the District Court: 50¢ per name per year, payable in advance; copies of land records: 50¢ for the first page and 25¢ for each additional page (must furnish names of owners and years of ownership); certified copies of vital records from Butte-Silver Bow Public Archives: $5.00 each for births (must show proof of relationship), $3.00 each for deaths (must supply date of death within a ten-year period); copies of vital records vrom Clerk of the District Court: $1.00 each, $3.00 for certified copies; copies of probate records: 50¢ per page for each of the first five pages and 25¢ for each additional page plus postage, $2.00 for certification

Carbon County
organized 1895 from Park and Yellowstone counties

Carbon County Administration Building
17 West 11th Street
Red Lodge, MT 59068
(406) 446-1220 (Clerk and Recorder, Main Floor, PO Box 887); (406) 446-1225 (Clerk of District Court, PO Box 948); (406) 446-2640 FAX (Clerk and Recorder); (406) 446-1911 FAX (Clerk of District Court)
recorder@co.carbon.mt.us;
    sgodbey@state.mt.us; sgotte@state.mt.us
http://www.co.carbon.mt.us
Linda M. Ladvala, Clerk and Recordee; Susan L. Godbey, Clerk of District Court
(land records with Clerk and Recorder, naturalization records with Clerk of District Court, vital records with Clerk and Recorder or Clerk of District Court, probate records with Clerk of District Court)

Carter County
organized 1917 from Custer County

Carter County Courthouse
(214 Park Street—location)
PO Box 315 (mailing address)
Ekalaka, MT 59324-0315
(406) 775-8749; (406) 775-8750 FAX
Cccnrc@Midrivers.com; Ccarey@state.mt.us
http://www.cartercountymt.com
Pamela J. Castleberry, Clerk and Recorder;
    Carole Carey, Clerk of District Court
(land records with County Assessor,
    naturalization records with Clerk of District
    Court, vital records with Clerk and Recorder,
    probate records with Clerk of District Court)
search service: $7.00 per name of business or
    individual that is searched; copies of probate
    records: 50¢ for each of the first page and 25¢
    for each additional page, plus postage for
    mailings, no minimum

Cascade County
organized 1887 from Chouteau and Meagher
    counties

Cascade County Courthouse
415 Second Avenue North
Great Falls, MT 59401
(406) 454-6800 (Clerk and Recorder, Suite 1B-1);
    (406) 454-6780 (Clerk of Court, Rooms 200-
    201)
Clerkrec@co.cascade.mt.us;
    Rmoore@co.cascade.mt.us;
    mortie_46@yahoo.com
http://www.co.cascade.mt.us
Rina Fontana Moore, Clerk and
    Recorder/Auditor/Surveyor; Nancy Morton,
    Clerk of District Court
(land records with County Assessor, limited
    naturalization records with U.S. District
    Court, vital records with Clerk and Recorder,
    probate records with Clerk of District Court)
probate search service: "full search, all books,
    $25.00 per name per year"; copies of probate
    records: 50¢ for each of the first five pages
    and 25¢ for each additional page ("make
    checks payable to Clerk of District Court")

Chouteau County
organized 1865, original county

Chouteau County Courthouse
1308 Franklin Street
Fort Benton, MT 59442
(406) 622-5151 (Clerk and Recorder); (406) 622-
    5024 (Clerk of Court)
Joann59442@yahoo.com;
    Lstollfuss@state.mt.us
http://www.co.chouteau.mt.us
JoAnn L. Johnson, Clerk and Recorder; Larry
    Stollfuss Clerk of Court
(land records with Clerk and Recorder Office,
    naturalization records with Clerk of District
    Court Office, vital records with Clerk and
    Recorder Office, probate records with Clerk
    of District Court Office)
probate search service: $7.00 ("record search
    consists of Liens, Mortgages, etc."); copies of
    probate records: 50¢ each, $1.00 minimum

Custer County
organized 1865, original county

Custer County Courthouse
1010 Main Street
Miles City, MT 59301-3496
(506) 874-3343; (506) 874-3452 FAX
m.wehri@co.custer.mt.us; hparker@mt.gov
http://www.co.custer.mt.us; http://mt.gov/
    maco/Counties/CUSTER.htm
Marie Wehri, Clerk and Recorder; Hazel Parker,
    Clerk of District Court
(mortgages, deeds, patents, homesteads with
    Clerk and Recorder, naturalization records
    with Clerk of District Court, vital records
    with Clerk and Recorder, probate records
    with Clerk of District Court)
land records search service: $7.00 for the first
    five years and 50¢ for each additional year
    searched and 50¢ for each book searched for
    the additional years; vital records search

service: $6.00 for births, $4.00 for deaths
    (includes certified copy); certified copies of
    vital records: $5.00 each for births (limited to
    relatives of the registrant with proof that the
    registrant died at least thirty years ago), $3.00
    each for deaths (limited to relatives of
    registrants who died at least twenty years ago)

Daniels County
organized 1920 from Valley County

Daniels County Courthouse
(213 Main Street—location)
PO Box 247 (mailing address)
Scobey, MT 59263
(406) 487-5561; (406) 487-5583 FAX
Danclkrec@yahoo.com;
    Pmcdonnell@state.mt.us
http://mt.gov/maco/Counties/DANIELS.htm
Kristy Jones, Clerk and Recorder; Patricia
    McDonnell, Clerk of District Court
(land records from August 1920 [some
    transcribed records from July 1913] with
    Clerk and Recorder, births and deaths from
    August 1920 ["some from before"] with Clerk
    and Recorder, marriages from 1920 with
    Clerk of District Court, PO Box 67, Scobey,
    MT 59263, probate records from August
    1920 with Clerk of District Court)
probate search service: 50¢ per year per name;
    copies of land records: 50¢ for the first page
    and 25¢ for each additional page; certified
    copies of vital records: $5.00 each for births,
    $3.00 each for deaths (both confidential);
    copies of probate records: 50¢ each, $2.00 for
    certified copies, no minimum

Dawson County
organized 1865, original county

Dawson County Courthouse
207 West Bell Street
Glendive, MT 59330-1616
(406) 365-3058 (Clerk and Recorder); (406) 377-
    3967 (Clerk of Court); (406) 377-1717 FAX
    (Clerk and Recorder); (406) 377-7280 FAX
    (Clerk of Court)
Dawclerk@midrivers.com; jgalle@mt.gov
http://www.dawsoncountymontana.org
Maurine Lenhardt, Clerk and Recorder; Judy
    Galle, Clerk of District Court
(land records with Clerk and Recorder,
    naturalization records with Clerk of District
    Court, births and deaths with Clerk and
    Recorder, marriages with Clerk of District
    Court, probate records with Clerk of District
    Court)
land records search service: $10.00 per hour; no
    probate search service; copies of land records:
    25¢ each, $2.00 for certification; copies of
    vital records: $5.00 each for births (restricted
    to registrant or parents, notarized application
    required), $3.00 each for deaths (notarized
    application required); copies of probate
    records: 50¢ for each of the first five pages
    and 25¢ for each additional page, 50¢
    minimum

Deer Lodge County
(see Anaconda-Deer Lodge County)

Fallon County
organized 1913 from Custer County

Fallon County Courthouse
10 West Fallon Avenue
Baker, MT 59313
(406) 778-7106 (Clerk and Recorder, Box 846);
    (406) 778-7114 (Clerk of Court, PO Box 521);
    (406) 778-2048 FAX (Clerk and Recorder)
Falloncc@midrivers.com;
    Fcclkrc@midrivers.com; jnewell@state.mt.us
http://www.falloncounty.net
Brenda Wood, Clerk and Recorder; Jeraldine
    "Jerrie" Newell, Clerk of District Court
(land records with Clerk and Recorder,
    naturalization records with Clerk of District
    Court, vital records from about 1920 with
    Clerk and Recorder, probate records with

Clerk of District Court)
land and vital records search service: 50¢ per
    year; probate search service: no charge; copies
    of land records: 50¢ for the first page and 25¢
    for each additional page; certified copies of
    vital records: $5.00 each for births, $3.00 each
    for deaths (both confidential, but information
    can be verified); copies of probate records:
    50¢ for each of the first five pages and 25¢ for
    each additional page, no minimum

Fergus County
organized 1885 from Meagher County

Fergus County Courthouse
712 West Main Street
Lewistown, MT 59457-2562
(406) 535-5242 (Clerk and Recorder); (406) 535-
    5026 (Clerk of Court); (406) 535-9023 FAX
    (Clerk and Recorder); (406) 535-6076 FAX
    (Clerk and Recorder
clerkrecorder@tein.net; phsmith@state.mt.us
http://www.co.fergus.mt.us
Kathy A. Fleharty, Clerk and Recorder; Phyllis
    D. Smith, Clerk of District Court
(land records from about 1818 with Clerk and
    Recorder, naturalization records with Clerk of
    District Court, vital records from about 1877
    with Clerk and Recorder, probate records
    with Clerk of District Court)
probate search service: 50¢ per year, $25.00
    maximum; copies of probate records: 50¢ for
    each of the first five pages and 25¢ for each
    additional page, no minimum; "School
    Records—County Superintendent of
    Schools"

Flathead County
organized 1893 from Missoula County

Flathead County Clerk and Recorder
800 South Main Street
Kalispell, MT 59901-5435
(406) 758-5526; (406) 758-55865 FAX
robinson@co.flathead.mt.us
http://www.co.flathead.mt.us
Paula Robinson, Clerk and
    Recorder/Auditor/Surveyor
(land records, some vital records)

Flathead County Clerk of District Court
(Justice Center, 920 South Main, Third Floor—
    location)
800 South Main Street (mailing address)
Kalispell, MT 59901-5435
(406) 758-5870
pallison@co.flathead.mt.us
http://www.co.flathead.mt.us
Peggy L. "Peg" Allison

Gallatin County
organized 1864, original county

Gallatin County Courthouse
311 West Main Street, Room 203
Bozeman, MT 59715-4576
(406) 582-3050
charlotte.mills@gallatin.mt.gov
http://www.gallatin.mt.gov/Public_Documents
    /index
Charlotte Mills, Clerk and Recorder/Surveyor
(land records, births and deaths)

Gallatin County Law and Justice Center
615 South 16th, Room 302
Bozeman, MT 59715
(406) 582-2165 (Clerk of District Court)
jbrandon@state.mt.us
http://www.gallatin.mt.gov/Public_Documents
    /index
Jennifer Brandon, Clerk of Court/Public
    Administrator
(marriages and probate records)

Garfield County
organized 1919 from McCone and Valley
    counties

Garfield County Courthouse
(Leavit Street—location)

PO Box 7 (mailing address)
Jordan, MT 59337-0007
(406) 557-2760; (406) 557-2567 FAX
gccr@midrivers.com;gctreas@midrivers.com
http://mt.gov/maco/Counties/GARFIELD.htm
Janet Sherer, Clerk and Recorder; Jennifer
Crawford, Clerk of District Court/Treasurer
(land records with Clerk and Recorder;
naturalization records with Clerk of District
Court's Office, births and deaths [both
subject to restrictions] with Clerk and
Recorder, probate records with Clerk of
District Court's Office)

Glacier County
organized 1919 from Teton County

Glacier County Courthouse
512 East Main Street
Cut Bank, MT 59427-3016
(406) 873-5063; (406) 873-5063, ext. 1132, 1134,
or 1136 (Clerk of Court); (406) 873-2125
FAX; (406) 873-5627 FAX (Clerk of Court)
gmhall@co.glacier.mt.us;
dianderson@state.mt.us
http://www.glaciercountymt.org
Glenda Hall, Clerk and Recorder; Diane
Anderson, Clerk of District Court
(land records with Clerk and Recorder's Office,
naturalization records with Marty Phippen,
Clerk of District Court, vital records with
Clerk and Recorder's Office ["signing and
filling out release form for birth and death
certificates needed"], probate records with
Clerk of District Court)
probate search service: $7.00; copies of probate
records: 50¢ each, $7.00 minimum

Golden Valley County
organized 1920 from Musselshell and Sweet
Grass counties

Golden Valley County Courthouse
(107 Kemp—location)
PO Box 10 (mailing address)
Ryegate, MT 59074
(406) 568-2231; (406) 568-2598 FAX
ringlerml@yahoo.com; contact@co.golden-
valley.mt.us
http://www.co.golden-valley.mt.us;
http://mt.gov/maco/Counties/GOLDENV
ALLEY.htm
Mary Lu Ringler, Clerk and Recorder/Clerk of
District Court
(patents, births from 1909, deaths from 1911,
probate records)
probate search service: 50¢ per name per year,
$25.00 maximum; copies of probate records:
50¢ for each of the first five pages and 25¢ for
each additional page, $5.00 minimum

Granite County
organized 1893 from Deer Lodge County

Granite County Courthouse
(220 North Sansome—location)
PO Box 925 (mailing address)
Philipsburg, MT 59858-0925
(406) 859-3771; (406) 859-3817 FAX; (406) 859-
3262 FAX
graclerk@co.granite.mt.us; bkulaski@state.mt.us
http://mt.gov/maco/Counties/GRANITE.
htm; http://www.co.granite.mt.us
Blanche Mclure, Clerk and Recorder; Beverly
Kulaski, Clerk of District Court

Hill County
organized 1912 from Chouteau County

Hill County Courthouse
315 Fourth Street
Havre, MT 59501-3923
(406) 265-5481; (406) 265-5487 FAX
mellemd@co.hill.mt.us; tippetsd@co.hill.mt.us
http://www.co.hill.mt.us
Diane Mellem, Clerk and Recorder; Dena
Tippets, Clerk of District Court
(land records with Clerk and Recorder,
naturalization records with Clerk of District

Court, vital records with Clerk and Recorder,
probate records with Clerk of District Court)
no vital records search service ("long form birth
and death certificates require a questionnaire
form completed and notarized; in some
instances a court order is required"); no
probate search service; copies of land records:
50¢ for the first page and 25¢ for each
additional page; copies of probate records:
$3.00 each

Jefferson County
organized 1864, original county

Jefferson County Courthouse
(201 Centennial—location)
PO Box H (mailing address)
Boulder, MT 59632
(406) 225-4020 (Clerk and Recorder); (406) 225-
4042 (Clerk of Court); (406) 225-4149 FAX;
(406) 225-4044 FAX (Clerk of Court)
bramey@jeffco.mt.gov; mcraft@state.mt.us
http://jeffco.mt.gov/county/index.shtml
Bonnie Ramey, Clerk and Recorder; Marilyn
Craft, Clerk of District Court

Judith Basin County
organized 1920 from Fergus and Cascade
counties

Judith Basin County Courthouse
(31 First Avenue—location)
PO Box 427 (mailing address)
Stanford, MT 59479-0427
(406) 566-2301 (Clerk and Recorder); (406) 566-
2491 (Clerk of Court)
akelly@co.judith-basin.mt.us;
julanderson@state.mt.us
http://mt.gov/maco/Counties/JUDITHBASI
N.htm
Amanda Kelly, Clerk and Recorder; Julie Peevey,
Clerk of District Court
(land records with Clerk and Recorder,
Appraiser, Assessor, naturalization records to
1939, vital records with Clerk and Recorder
or Clerk of District Court, probate records
with Clerk of District Court)
probate search service: 50¢ per year; copies of
probate records: 50¢ each, no minimum

Lake County
organized 1923 from Flathead and Missoula
counties

Lake County Courthouse
106 Fourth Avenue
Polson, MT 59860-2125
(406) 883-7208 (Clerk and Recorder); (406) 883-
7254 (Clerk of Court)
clerkrecorder@lakemt.gov;
rhodges@lakemt.gov; jknutson@mt.gov
http://www.lakecounty-mt.org
Ruth E. Hodges, Clerk and Recorder/Auditor;
Julie Knutson, Clerk of District Court
(land records with Land Services, vital records
with Clerk and Recorder, probate records
with Clerk of District Court)
probate search service: $7.00; copies of probate
records: 50¢ for each of the first five pages
and 25¢ for each additional page, $1.00
minimum

Lewis and Clark County
organized 1864, original county

**Lewis and Clark County City-County
Building**
316 North Park Avenue
Helena, MT 59623
(406) 447-8334 (Clerk and Recorder); (406) 447-
8215 (Clerk of Court)
pdehart@co.lewis-clark.mt.us;
nsweeney@co.lewis-clark.mt.us
http://www.co.lewis-clark.mt.us
Paulette DeHart, Treasurer/Clerk and Recorder;
Nancy Sweeney, Clerk of District Court
(land records and vital records, naturalization
records with, vital records, probate records)
probate search service: 50¢ per year per name;

copies of probate records: 50¢ for each of the
first five pages and 25¢ for each additional
page, no minimum

Liberty County
organized 1920 from Chouteau County

Liberty County Courthouse
(111 First Street East—location)
PO Box 459 (mailing address)
Chester, MT 59522
(406) 759-5365 (Clerk and Recorder); (406) 759-
5615 (Clerk of Court)
clerk@co.liberty.mt.gov;
aseidlitzmelton@mt.gov
http://www.co.liberty.mt.gov
Rhonda Pimley, Clerk and Recorder; Anne
Seidlitz-Melton, Clerk of District Court
(land records with Clerk and Recorder,
naturalization records with Clerk of District
Court, vital records with Clerk and Recorder,
probate records with Clerk of District Court)

Lincoln County
organized 1909 from Flathead County

Lincoln County Courthouse
512 California Avenue
Libby, MT 59923-1942
(406) 293-7781, ext. 207 (Clerk and Recorder);
(406) 293-7781, ext. 224 (Clerk of Court);
(406) 293-8577 FAX (Clerk and Recorder);
(406) 293-9816 FAX (Clerk of Court)
lcclerk@libby.org; npival@stte.mt.us
http://www.lincolncountymt.us
Tammy Lauer, Clerk and Recorder; Nadine
Pival, Clerk of District Court
(land records with Clerk and Recorder,
naturalization records with Clerk of District
Court, vital records with Clerk and Recorder,
probate records with Clerk of District Court)
land, naturalization, and probate search service:
50¢ per year, $25.00 maximum; copies of land
records and naturalization records: 50¢ for the
first page and 25¢ for each additional page;
copies of vital records: $5.00 each for births,
$3.00 each for deaths

Madison County
organized 1864, original county

Madison County Courthouse
(110 West Wallace Street—location)
PO Box 185 (mailing address)
Virginia City, MT 59755
(406) 843-4270 (Clerk and Recorder, First Floor,
PO Box 366); (406) 843-4230 (Clerk of Court,
Mezzanine, PO Box 185); (406) 843-5264
FAX (Clerk and Recorder); (406) 843-5207
FAX (Clerk of Court)
pkaatz@madison.mt.gov; bubailey@mt.gov
http://madison.mt.gov
Peggy Kaatz Stemler, Clerk and Recorder;
Bundy Bailey, Clerk of District Court

McCone County
organized 1919 from Dawson and Richland
counties

McCone County Courthouse
(1004 Avenue C—location)
PO Box 199 (mailing address)
Circle, MT 59215-0199
(406) 485-3505
clerk@midrivers.com; tkirkegrd@state.mt.us
http://mt.gov/maco/Counties/McCONE.htm;
http://www.circle-montana.com
Maridel Kassner, Clerk and Recorder; Trudy
Kirkegard, Clerk of District Court
(land records with Clerk and Recorder,
naturalization records with Clerk and
Recorder, vital records with Clerk and
Recorder [proof of relationship required],
probate records with Clerk and Recorder)

Meagher County
organized 1867, original county

Meagher County Courthouse

(15 West Main—location)
PO Box 309 (mailing address)
White Sulphur Springs, MT 59645-0309
(406) 547-3612; (406) 547-3388 FAX
clowe@meaghercounty.org;
   domorris@state.mt.us
http://mt.gov/maco/Counties/MEAGHER.htm
Cameron Lowe, Clerk and Recorder; Donna
   Morris, Clerk of District Court

Mineral County
organized 1914 from Missoula County

Mineral County Courthouse
(300 River Street—location)
PO Box 550 (mailing address)
Superior, MT 59872-0550
(406) 822-3520 (Clerk and Recorder); (406) 822-
   3538 (Clerk of Court, PO Box 129)
clrkrecr@blackfoot.net
http://www.co.mineral.mt.us
Katherine Jasper, Clerk and Recorder; Kathleen
   Brown, Clerk of District Court
(land records with Clerk and Recorder, births
   and deaths with Clerk and Recorder [access
   restricted], marriages with Clerk of District
   Court, probate records with Clerk of District
   Court)
land records search service: $5.00 per name; vital
   records and probate records search service
   from Clerk of District Court: 50¢ per name
   per year; copies of land records: 50¢ for the
   first page and 25¢ for each additional page;
   copies of vital records and probate records
   from Clerk of District Court: 50¢ for each of
   the first five pages and 25¢ for each additional
   page

Missoula County
organized 14 December 1860, while part of
   Washington Territory, from Spokane County
   (all land east of longitude 115)

Missoula County Courthouse
200 West Broadway
Missoula, MT 59802-4292
(406) 523-4752 (Clerk and Recorder, Annex,
   Second Floor); (406) 258-4727 (Clerk of
   Court, Old Courthouse, Second Floor); (406)
   258-4899 FAX (Clerk of Court)
vzeier@co.missoula.mt.us;
   sfaust@co.missoula.mt.us;
   clerkofcourt@co.missoula.mt.us;
   ishelpdesk@co.missoula.mt.us
http://www.co.missoula.mt.us
Vickie Zeier, Clerk and Recorder/Treasurer;
   Shirley Faust, Clerk of District Court
(land records with County Clerk and Recorder,
   declarations of intent from 1856 with
   admissions from 1869 through the late 1940s
   ["We have a very few listed through 1979, but
   those are sporadic"] with Clerk of District
   Court, births and deaths from 1885 with
   County Clerk and Recorder, fairly complete
   marriage licenses from 1883 with Clerk of
   District Court, probate records from 1868
   [with the most complete from 1889] with
   Clerk of District Court)
vital records search service from County Clerk
   and Recorder: $10.00 per hour; probate
   search service: 50¢ per year searched, $25.00
   maximum; certified copies of vital records:
   $3.00 each ("The State of Montana
   Department of Health and Environmental
   Sciences does not permit public inspection of
   vital statistic indexes; genealogists will be
   given short-form death certificates for anyone
   who died from 1950 to present; this does not
   give family history other than birthplace for
   decedent and birth date; genealogists can
   receive a full copy if the death occurred
   before 1950; a birth certificate cannot be
   given to genealogists unless they have a
   certified copy of the person's death
   certificate"); copies of probate records: 50¢
   for each of the first five pages and 25¢ for
   each additional page, $2.00 for certified copies
   ("also must include a SASE")

Musselshell County
organized 1911 from Fergus and Yellowstone
   counties

Musselshell County Courthouse
506 Main Street
Roundup, MT 59072-2498
(406) 323-1104 (Clerk and Recorder, PO Box
   686); (406) 323-1413 (Clerk of District Court,
   PO Box 357); (406) 323-3303 FAX
mshlcocr@midrivers.com;
   cmattfield@state.mt.us
http://mt.gov/maco/Counties/MUSSELSHEL
L.htm
Jane Mang, Clerk and Recorder; Connie
   Mattfield, Clerk of District Court
(land records with Clerk and Recorder,
   naturalization records from 1911 with Clerk
   of District Court, births and deaths from
   1911 with Clerk and Recorder, marriages
   from 1911 with Clerk of District Court,
   probate records with Clerk of District Court)
probate search service: no charge; copies of
   probate records: 50¢ per page, $2.00 for
   certification

Park County
organized 1887 from Gallatin County

Park County City-County Complex
414 East Callendar
Livingston, MT 59047-2746
(406) 222-4117 (Clerk and Recorder); (406) 222-
   4125 (Clerk of Court); (406) 222-4128 FAX
   (Clerk of Court)
clerkrecorder@parkcounty.org;
   julittle@state.mt.us
http://www.parkcounty.org
Denise Nelson, Clerk and Recorder; June Little,
   Clerk of District Court
(land records with Clerk and Recorder's Office,
   naturalization records from 1887 with Clerk
   of District Court, marriage licenses from 1887
   with Clerk of District Court, probate records
   from 1887 with Clerk of District Court)
probate search service: 50¢ per year, $25.00
   maximum; copies of probate records: 50¢ for
   each of the first five pages and 25¢ for each
   additional page

Petroleum County
organized 1926 from Fergus County

Petroleum County Courthouse
(201 East Main—location)
PO Box 226 (mailing address)
Winnett, MT 59087
(406) 429-5311 (Clerk and Recorder and Clerk
   of District Court); (406) 429-6328 FAX
mbrindley@state.mt.us
http://mt.gov/maco/Counties/PETROLEUM.
htm
Mary Brindley, Clerk and Recorder
(land records from 1882 with Clerk and
   Recorder, vital records from 1890 with Clerk
   and Recorder or Clerk of District Court,
   probate records from 1890 with Clerk of
   District Court)
probate search service: 50¢ per year up to
   $25.00; copies of probate records: 50¢ for
   each of the first five pages and 25¢ for each
   additional page, no minimum

Phillips County
organized 1915 from Valley County

Phillips County Courthouse
(314 South Second Avenue, West—location)
PO Box 360 (mailing address)
Malta, MT 59538-0360
(406) 654-2429 voice & FAX
clerkrecorder@phillipscounty.mt.gov;
   clerkcourt@phillipscounty.mt.gov
http://mt.gov/maco/Counties/PHILLIPS.htm
Laurel N. Hines, Clerk and Recorder; Iris
   Robinson, Clerk of District Court
(land records with Clerk and Recorder, PO Box
   U, naturalization records with Clerk of
   District Court, PO Box I, vital records with

Clerk and Recorder, probate records with
   Clerk of District Court)
probate search service: $7.00; copies of probate
   records: $1.00 each

Pondera County
organized 1919 from Yellowstone County

Pondera County Courthouse
20 Fourth Avenue, S.W.
Conrad, MT 59425-2340
(406) 271-4001 (Clerk and Recorder, Suite 202);
   (406) 271-4026 (Clerk of Court, Top Floor);
   (406) 271-4070 FAX
clerkrec@3rivers.net; kathompson@mt.gov
http://www.ponderacountymontana.org
Janice Hoppes, Clerk and Recorder; Kara
   Thompson, Clerk of District Court
(land records with Clerk and Recorder,
   naturalization records with Clerk of District
   Court, vital records with Clerk and Recorder,
   probate records with Clerk of District Court)
probate search service: $5.00 per person; copies
   of probate records: 50¢ per page, $1.00
   minimum

Powder River County
organized 1919 from Custer County

Powder River County Courthouse
PO Box 270
Broadus, MT 59317
(406) 436-2657; (406) 436-2151 FAX
kamende@prco.mt.gov; ashannn@mt.gov
http://mt.gov/maco/Counties/POWDERRIV
ER.htm
Karen Amende, Clerk and Recorder; Aletta
   Shannon, Clerk of District Court
(land records from early 1800s with Clerk and
   Recorder ["all land records affecting present
   Powder River County were transcribed from
   the records of Custer County"], naturalization
   records from 1919 with Clerk and Recorder,
   vital records from 1919 with Clerk and
   Recorder, probate records from 1919 with
   Clerk of District Court)
probate search service: 50¢ per year per index;
   copies of probate records: 50¢ for each of the
   first five pages and 25¢ for each additional
   page, no minimum ("we also charge postage
   costs")

Powell County
organized 1907 from Deer Lodge County

Powell County Courthouse
409 Missouri Avenue
Deer Lodge, MT 59722-1084
(406) 846-3680, ext. 220 or 221; (406) 846-2991
   FAX (Commissioners and Clerk/Recorder)
dsgmt2001@yahoo.com
http://mt.gov/maco/Counties/POWELL.htm
Diane Grey, Clerk and Recorder; Mary Ann
   McKee, Clerk of District Court
(land records with Clerk and Recorder's Office
   and/or Assessor's Office, some old
   naturalization records with Clerk of District
   Court, births and deaths with Clerk and
   Recorder's Office, probate records with Clerk
   of District Court)
probate search service: 50¢ per year, $25.00
   maximum; copies of probate records: 50¢ for
   each of the first five pages and 25¢ for each
   additional page, no minimum

Prairie County
organized 1915 from Custer, Dawson and
   Fallon counties

Prairie County Courthouse
(217 West Park—location)
PO Box 125 (mailing address)
Terry, MT 59349-0125
(406) 637-5575; (406) 635-5576 FAX
clerkrecorder@prairie.t.gov
http://mt.gov/maco/Counties/PRAIRIE.htm
Lisa Kimmet, Clerk and Recorder
(land records with Clerk and Recorder,
   naturalization records with Clerk of District

Court, vital records with Clerk of District Court, probate records with Clerk of District Court)
probate search service: $7.00; copies of probate records: 25¢ per page from paper original, 50¢ per page from microfilm original, no minimum

Ravalli County
organized 1893 from Missoula County

Ravalli County Clerk and Recorder
215 South Fourth Street, Suite C
Hamilton, MT 59840
(406) 375-6555; (406) 375-6554 FAX
recorder@ravallicounty.mt.gov
http://www.co.ravalli.mt.us
Regina Plettenburg
(land records from about 1893 to date [a few earlier], births and deaths from 1893 but incomplete until about 1920)
no land records search service; copies of land records: 50¢ per page; certified copies of vital records: $5.50 each for births (restricted to the immediate family), $3.50 each for deaths (records under fifty years old restricted to the immediate family)

Ravalli County Clerk of District Court
205 Bedford Street, Suite D
Hamilton, MT 59840
(406) 375-6710; (406) 375-6721 FAX
dharmon@ravallicounty.mt.gov
http://www.co.ravalli.mt.us
Debbie Harmon

Richland County
organized 1914 from Dawson County

Richland County Courthouse
201 West Main Street
Sidney, MT 59270-4035
(406) 433-1708 (Clerk and Recorder); (406) 433-1709 (Clerk of District Court); (406) 433-3731 FAX (Clerk and Recorder)
clerkrec@richland.org;
penniclerkrec@richland.org;
ariggs@state.mt.us
http://www.richland.org
Penni D. Lewis, Clerk and Recorder; Arlene Riggs, Clerk of District Court
(land records from 1895 [transcribed from Dawson County] with Clerk and Recorder, naturalization records with Clerk of District Court, vital records from 1915 with Clerk and Recorder, probate records from 1915 with Clerk of District Court)
probate search service: no charge; copies of land records: 25¢ per page; copies of vital records: 25¢ per page (proof of relationship, registrant's date of birth and names of parents required); copies of probate records: 50¢ for each of the first five pages and 25¢ for each additional page, $2.00 for certification, $1.00 minimum

Roosevelt County
organized 1919 from Sheridan and Valley counties

Roosevelt County Courthouse
400 Second Avenue South
Wolf Point, MT 59201-1600
(406) 653-6246; (406) 653-6201 FAX
chansen@co.roosevelt.mt.us;
pstennes@state.mt.us
http://mt.gov/maco/Counties/ROOSEVELT.htm
Cheryl Hansen, Clerk and Recorder; Patricia Stennes, Clerk of Court
(land records with Clerk and Recorder, or County Assessor, naturalization records with Clerk of District Court, vital records with Clerk and Recorder, probate records with Clerk of District Court)
no vital records search service (must have name, date of birth and parents' names); copies of vital records: $1.00 each, $5.00 for certified copies of births, $3.00 for certified copies of deaths

Rosebud County
organized 1901 from Dawson County

Rosebud County Courthouse
(1200 Main Street—location)
PO Box 47 (mailing address)
Forsyth, MT 59327-0047
(406) 356-2251; (406) 346-7551 FAX
clerkandrecorder@rangeweb.net;
mhollister@state.mt.us
http://mt.gov/maco/Counties/ROSEBUD.htm
Geraldine Custer, Clerk and Recorder; Marilyn Hollister, Clerk of District Court

Sanders County
organized 1906 from Missoula County

Sanders County Courthouse
(1111 Main Street—location)
PO Box 519 (mailing address)
Thompson Falls, MT 59873-0519
(406) 827-6922 (Clerk and Recorder); (406) 827-6906 (Clerk of Court)
jrobbins@metnet.mt.gov; dirummel@mt.gov
http://www.sanderscounty.mt.gov
Jennine Robbins, Clerk and Recorder; Dianne Rummel, Clerk of District Court
(land records with Clerk and Recorder, naturalization records with Clerk of District Court, vital records with Clerk and Recorder, probate records with Clerk of District Court)
probate search service: 50¢ per year; copies of probate records: 50¢ for each of the first five pages and 25¢ for each additional page

Sheridan County
organized 1913 from Valley County

Sheridan County Courthouse
100 West Laurel Avenue
Plentywood, MT 59254-1699
(406) 765-3403 (Clerk and Recorder); (406) 765-3404 (Clerk of Court); (406) 765-2609 FAX (Clerk and Recorder)
record_supt@co.sheridan.mt.us;
jjohnson@co.sheridan.mt.us;
colson@co.sheridan.mt.us
http://www.co.sheridan.mt.us
June Johnson, Clerk and Recorder and County Superintendent of Schools; Cheryl Olson, Clerk of District Court
(land records with Clerk and Recorder's Office, naturalization records with Clerk of District Court, vital records with Clerk and Recorder's Office, probate records with Clerk of District Court)
probate search service: 50¢ per year per name; copies of probate records: 50¢ per page, no minimum

Silver Bow County
(see Butte-Silver Bow County)

Stillwater County
organized 1913 from Sweet Grass and Yellowstone counties

Stillwater County Courthouse
400 Third Avenue North
Columbus, MT 59019
(406) 322-4546
pmishler@co.stillwater.mt.us;
jcbare@state.mt.us
http://www.co.stillwater.mt.us; http://mt.gov/maco/Counties/STILLWATER.htm
Pauline Mishler, Clerk and Recorder; Jean Bare, Clerk of District Court (PO Box 367)
(land records with Clerk and Recorder, naturalization records with Clerk of District Court, Columbus, MT 59019, vital records with Clerk and Recorder, probate records with Clerk of District Court)
probate search service: $7.00; copies of probate records: 50¢ for each of the first five pages and 25¢ for each additional page, no minimum

deaths

Sweet Grass County
organized 1895 from Meagher, Park and Yellowstone counties

Sweet Grass County Courthouse
200 West First Avenue
Big Timber, MT 59011
(406) 932-5152 (Clerk and Recorder, PO Box 460); (406) 932-5154 (Clerk of Court, PO Box 698)
sgclerk1@cablemt.net; denovotny@state.mt.us
http://www.co.sweetgrass.mt.us
Sherry Bjorndal, Clerk and Recorder; Deanna Novotny, Clerk of District Court
(land records with Clerk and Recorder, naturalization records with Clerk of District Court, births and deaths with Clerk and Recorder, marriages with Clerk of District Court, probate records with Clerk of District Court)
probate search service: 50¢ per name; copies of probate records: 50¢ for each of the first five pages and 25¢ for each additional page, no minimum

Teton County
organized 1893 from Chouteau County

Teton County Courthouse
Choteau, MT 59422
(406) 466-2693 (Clerk and Recorder, PO Box 610); (406) 466-2909 (Clerk of District Court, Box 487); (406) 466-2138 FAX (Clerk and Recorder)
paula@3rivers.net; lsinton@mt.gov
http://www.tetoncomt.org
Paula Jaconetty, Clerk and Recorder; Lisa Sinton, Clerk of District Court
(land records with Clerk and Recorder, naturalization records with Clerk of District Court [must have name of person and approximate year], vital records with Clerk and Recorder, probate records with Clerk of District Court)
probate search service: 50¢ per name per year; copies of probate records: 50¢ for each of the first five pages and 25¢ for each additional page, 50¢ minimum

Toole County
organized 1914 from Teton County

Toole County Courthouse
(226 First Street, South—location)
PO Box 850 (mailing address)
Shelby, MT 59474
(406) 424-8310; (406) 434-2271; (406) 424-8301 FAX
tcclerk@3rivers.net; speers@state.mt.us
http://mt.gov/maco/Counties/TOOLE.htm
Mary Ann Harwood, Clerk and Recorder; Sandra Peers, Clerk of District Court
(land records with Clerk and Recorder, some naturalization records before the 1960s with Clerk of District Court, vital records with Clerk and Recorder, probate records with Clerk of District Court)

Treasure County
organized 1919 from Big Horn County

Treasure County Courthouse
(307 Rapelje—location)
PO Box 392 (mailing address)
Hysham, MT 59038
(406) 342-5547; (406) 342-5445 FAX
clerkrecorder@rangeweb.net
http://mt.gov/maco/Counties/TREASURE.htm
Ruth Baker, Clerk and Recorder
(land records with County Clerk and Recorder's Office, naturalization records with District Court Office, vital records with County Clerk and Recorder's Office, probate records with District Court Office)
no probate search service; copies of probate records: 50¢ for the first page and 25¢ for each additional page, $2.00 for certification, $2.00 minimum mail-out charge

Valley County

organized 1893 from Dawson County

Valley County Courthouse
(501 Court Square—location)
PO Box 1 (mailing address)
Glasgow, MT 59230-2405
(406) 228-8221, ext. 21 (Clerk and Recorder,
Suite 2); (406) 228-8221 (Clerk of District
Court, Suite 6); (406) 228-9027 FAX
lnyquist@co.valley.mt.us;
mgreenhagen@co.valley.mt.us
http://mt.gov/maco/Counties/VALLEY.htm
Lynne Nyquist, Clerk and Recorder; Melissa
Greenhagen, Clerk of District Court
(land records with Clerk and Recorder,
naturalization records to 1979 with Clerk of
District Court, vital records with Clerk and
Recorder, probate records with Clerk of
District Court)
records search service: 50¢ per page per name;
copies of records: 50¢ for each of the first five
pages and 25¢ for each additional page

Wheatland County

organized 1917 from Meagher, Fergus and
Sweet Grass counties

Wheatland County Courthouse
(201 A Avenue NW—location)
PO Box 1903 (mailing address)
Harlowton, MT 59036-1903
(406) 632-4891; (406) 632-4880 FAX
wccr@mtintouch.net; jahill@state.mt.us
http://mt.gov/maco/Counties/WHEATLAN
D.htm
Mary Miller, Clerk and Recorder; Janet Hill,
Clerk of District Court
(land records with Clerk and Recorder, Assessor,
Appraiser, naturalization records with Clerk
of District Court, births and deaths with Clerk
and Recorder [proof of relationship required],
marriages with Clerk of District Court,
probate records with Clerk of District Court)
no probate search service; copies of probate
records: 50¢ for each of the first five pages
and 25¢ for each additional page, $2.00 for
certified copies, $1.50 plus postage minimum

Wibaux County

organized 1914 from Dawson County

Wibaux County Courthouse
(200 South Wibaux—location)
PO Box 199 (mailing address)
Wibaux, MT 59353-0199
(406) 796-2481; (406) 796-2625 FAX
pazwebo@yahoo.com (Clerk and Recorder);
webodes@midrivers.com (Clerk of Court)
http://mt.gov/maco/Counties/WIBAUX.htm
Patricia Zinda, Clerk and Recorder; Michael
Schneider, Clerk of District Court

Yellowstone County

organized 1883 from Custer, Gallatin and
Meagher counties

Yellowstone County Courthouse
217 North 27th and Third North
Billings, MT 59101
(406) 256-2785 (Clerk and Recorder); (406) 256-
2862 (Clerk of Court, Rooms 702, 703 &
704); (406) 256-2736 FAX (Clerk and
Recorder)
tnave@co.yellowstone.mt.us;
lbrent@co.yellowstone.mt.us
http://www.co.yellowstone.mt.gov
Tony Nave, Clerk and Recorder; Laura A. Brent,
Clerk of District Court
(land records from 1881 with Clerk and
Recorder, births from 1800, deaths from 1895
with Clerk and Recorder, marriages with
Clerk of District Court, probate records with
Clerk of District Court)
probate search service: 50¢ per name per year;
copies of land records: 50¢ for the first page
and 25¢ for each additional page of the same
document, certified copies of births: $5.00
each; copies of deaths: $3.00 each; copies of

marriages: 50¢ each, $2.50 for certified copies,
plus 50¢ postage unless SASE included;
copies of probate records: 50¢ for each of the
first five pages and 25¢ for each additional
page per case plus 50¢ postage unless SASE
included, no minimum

<table>
<tr><td>NEBRASKA</td></tr>
</table>

*Capital: Lincoln. Statehood: 1 March 1867 (annexed
as part of the Louisiana Purchase, 1803, part of the
Territory of Orleans and later the Missouri Territory
until made a separate territory by the Kansas-Nebraska
Act of 1854)*

Nebraska has a separate Juvenile Court for
Douglas, Lancaster and Sarpy counties and a
Workers' Compensation Tribunal, but the bulk
of its civil actions, probates, guardianships,
adoptions, eminent domain matters,
misdemeanors, traffic cases, municipal
ordinance violations, felony preliminaries and
juvenile matters are heard in one of the state's
county courts, arranged in twelve judicial
districts. First District: Clay, Fillmore, Gage,
Jefferson, Johnson, Nemaha, Nuckolls, Pawnee,
Richardson, Saline, and Thayer counties; Second
District: Cass, Otoe, and Sarpy counties; Third
District: Lancaster County; Fourth District:
Douglas County; Fifth District: Boone, Butler,
Colfax, Hamilton, Merrick, Nance, Platte, Polk,
Saunders, Seward, and York counties; Sixth
District: Burt, Cedar, Dakota, Dixon, Dodge,
Thurston, and Washington counties; Seventh
District: Antelope, Cuming, Knox, Madison,
Pierce, Stanton, and Wayne counties; Eighth
District: Blaine, Boyd, Brown, Cherry, Custer,
Garfield, Greeley, Holt, Howard, Keya Paha,
Loup, Rock, Sherman, Valley, and Wheeler
counties; Ninth District: Buffalo and Hall
counties; Tenth District: Adams, Franklin,
Harlan, Kearney, Phelps, and Webster counties;
Eleventh District: Arthur, Chase, Dawson,
Dundy, Frontier, Furnas, Gosper, Hayes,
Hitchcock, Hooker, Keith, Lincoln, Logan,
McPherson, Perkins, Red Willow and Thomas
counties; Twelfth District: Banner, Box Butte,
Cheyenne, Dawes, Deuel, Garden, Grant,
Kimball, Morrill, Scotts Bluff, Sheridan, and
Sioux counties.

The state's District Courts have general
jurisdiction. A Supreme Court is the court of last
resort.

Adams County

organized 1867 from Clay County

Adams County Courthouse
500 West Fourth Street
Hastings, NE 68901
(402) 461-7107 (County Clerk); (402) 461-7143
(Clerk Magistrate of the County Court, Fifth
and Denver, PO Box 95); (402) 461-7264
(District Court, PO Box 9); (402) 461-7144
FAX (Clerk Magistrate of the County Court);
(402) 461-7269 FAX (District Court)
clewis@adamscounty.org;
tom.hawes@courts.ne.gov;
thawes@adamscounty.org;
sczaplewski@adamscounty.org
http://www.adamscounty.org
Chrisella Lewis, County Clerk; Thomas Hawes,
Clerk Magistrate of the County Court; Sue
Czaplewski, Clerk of the District Court

Adams County Register of Deeds
(500 North Denver, Hastings, NE 68901—
location)
PO Box 203 (mailing address
Hastings, NE 68902-0203
(402) 461-7148; (402) 461-7154 FAX
jjohnson@adamscounty.org
http://www.adamscounty.org/register_deeds/in
dex.htm
Janice Johnson

Antelope County

organized 1871 from Pierce County

Antelope County Courthouse
501 Main Street
Neligh, NE 68756-1466
(402) 887-4410 (County Clerk, PO Box 26);

Nebraska

183

(402) 887-4650 (Clerk Magistrate of the
County Court, Room 1, PO Box 26); (402)
887-4508 (District Court); (402) 887-4160
FAX (Clerk Magistrate of the County Court);
(402) 887-4870 FAX (District Court)
antelopeclerk@frontiernet.net; barb.finn@
courts.ne.gov; judy.cole@courts.ne.gov;
jcole@courts.state.nc.us
http://www.co.antelope.ne.us
Carolyn Pedersen, County Clerk and Register of
Deeds; Barb Finn, Clerk Magistrate of the
County Court; Judy Cole, Clerk of the District
Court
(land records from 1875 County Clerk and
Register of Deeds, naturalization records
from 1875 with Clerk of the District Court,
marriages from 1875 with County Clerk,
probate records from 1875 with Clerk
Magistrate)
no probate search service ("if we have to do the
research, we base it on the amount of time it
took us"); copies of probate records: 20¢ per
page

Arthur County
organized 1887 from unattached lands

Arthur County Courthouse
(205 First Street—location)
PO Box 126 (mailing address)
Arthur, NE 69121
(308) 764-2208; (308) 764-2201 (Clerk
Magistrate of the County Court, PO Box
146); (308) 764-2203 (District Court); (308)
764-2216 FAX (Clerk Magistrate of the
County Court and District Court)
becky.swanson@courts.ne.gov;
margaret.padgett@courts.ne.gov
http://www.nacone.org/webpages/counies/cou
ntywebs/arthur.htm
Becky Swanson, County Clerk/Register of
Deeds/Clerk of the District Court; Margaret
Padgett, Clerk Magistrate of the County Court

Banner County
organized 1888 from Cheyenne County

Banner County Courthouse
(204 State Street—location)
PO Box 67 (mailing address)
Harrisburg, NE 69345
(308) 436-5268 (Clerk Magistrate of the County
Court); (308) 436-5265 (District Court); (308)
436-4180 FAX (Clerk Magistrate of the
County Court and District Court)
angie.haun@courts.ne.gov;
sharon.sandberg@courts.ne.gov
http://www.bannercounty-gov.us
Angie Haun, Clerk Magistrate of the County
Court; Sharon Sandberg, County Clerk,
Register of Deeds, and Clerk of the District
Court
(land records, some naturalization records but
not all, vital records, probate records)
copies of records: 25¢ each

Blackbird County
(see Thurston County)

Blaine County
organized 1885 from Custer County

Blaine County Courthouse
145 Lincoln Avenue
Brewster, NE 68821
(308) 547-2222, ext. 202 (Clerk Magistrate of the
County Court, PO Box 123); (308) 547-2222,
ext. 201 (District Court, PO Box 136); (308)
547-2228 (Clerk Magistrate of the County
Court); (308) 547-2228 FAX (District Court)
soscou86@nol.org (County Clerk); sue.clark@
courts.ne.gov; april.wescott@courts.ne.gov
http://www.nol.org/blaine
Sue Clark, Clerk Magistrate of the County Court;
April Wescott, County Clerk, Register of
Deeds, and Clerk of the District Court
(land and naturalization records with County
Clerk, probate records with County Court)

Boone County
organized 1871 from Platte County

Boone County Courthouse
222 South Fourth Street
Albion, NE 68620
(402) 395-2055 voice & FAX(County Clerk);
(402) 395-6184 (Clerk Magistrate of the
County Court); (402) 395-2057 (District
Court); (402) 395-6592 FAX (Clerk
Magistrate of the County Court and District
Court)
clerk@boone.nacone.org;
lisa.langan@courts.ne.gov;
ellen.hirsch@courts.ne.gov
http://www.co.boone.ne.us
Kathy Thorberg, County Clerk and Register of
Deeds; Lisa Langan, Clerk Magistrate of the
County Court; Ellen Hirsch, Clerk of the
District Court
(land records with Register of Deeds,
naturalization records with Clerk of the
District Court, probate records with County
Court)
probate search service: $5.00 ("very helpful if we
had land descriptions or approximate year");
copies of probate records: 50¢ each, $5.00
minimum including postage

Box Butte County
organized 1886 from unorganized territory

Box Butte County Courthouse
Alliance, NE 69301-0678
(308) 762-6565 (County Clerk, PO Box 678);
(308) 762-6800 (Clerk Magistrate of the
County Court, 500 Box Butte Avenue, Suite
100, PO Box 613); (308) 762-6293 (District
Court, 515 Box Butte Avenue, Suite 300);
(308) 762-2867 FAX (County Clerk); (308)
762-2650 FAX (Clerk Magistrate of the
County Court); (308) 762-5700 FAX (District
Court)
soscou65@nol.org (County Clerk); angie.aun@
courts.ne.gov; susan.dyer@courts.ne.gov
http://www.co.box-butte.ne.us
Cheryl L. McDuffie, County Clerk and Register
of Deeds; Angie Haun, Clerk Magistrate of
the County Court; Susan Dyer, Clerk of the
District Court

Boyd County
organized 1891 from an unorganized area that
was transferred in 1882 from Dakota
Territory to Nebraska, but which, according
to the 1883 act adding it to Holt County,
required voter approval, which the courts
ruled was not done

Boyd County Courthouse
401 Thayer Street
Butte, NE 68722
(402) 775-2211 voice & FAX (Clerk Magistrate
of the County Court, PO Box 396); (402)
775-2391 (District Court, PO Box 26); (402)
775-2146 FAX (District Court)
cathy.reiman@courts.ne.gov;
tracy.reiser@courts.ne.gov
http://www.nacone.org/webpages/counies/cou
ntywebs/boyd.htm
Cathy Reiman, Clerk Magistrate of the County
Court; Tracy Reiser, County Clerk, Register of
Deeds, and Clerk of the District Court
(land records with Register of Deeds,
naturalization records with Phyllis Black,
County Clerk, probate records with County
Court)
probate search service: no charge; copies of
probate records: 25¢ each, no minimum

Brown County
organized 1883 from unorganized territory

Brown County Courthouse
148 West Fourth Street
Ainsworth, NE 69210
(402) 387-2864 (Clerk Magistrate of the County
Court); (402) 387-2705 (District Court); (402)
387-0918 FAX (Clerk Magistrate of the

County Court and District Court)
roxanne.philben@courts.ne.gov;
bcclerk@threeriver.net;
janet.huggins@courts.ne.gov
http://www.co.brown.ne.us
Roxanne Philben, Clerk Magistrate of the
County Court; Janet A. Huggins, County
Clerk, Register of Deeds, and Clerk of the
District Court
(land records with Register of Deeds,
naturalization records W.P.A. index cards
only with Clerk of District Court [copies
unavailable because of the condition of the
books], marriages with County Clerk, probate
records with County Court Clerk)
no records search service; copies of land
records: 50¢ each, $1.50 per certified page,
plus postage; certified copies of vital records:
$6.00 each plus postage; copies of probate
records: 50¢ each plus postage, $1.50 per page
for certified copies of certain records ("fees
are set by law in some matters")

Buffalo County
organized 1855, original county

Buffalo County Courthouse
1512 Central
Kearney, NE 68848
(308) 236-1226 (County Clerk's Office); (308)
236-1239 (Register of Deeds, PO Box 1270);
(308) 236-1229 (Clerk Magistrate of the
County Court, PO Box 520); (308) 236-1246
(District Court, PO Box 520); (308) 236-1291
FAX (Register of Deeds); (308) 236-1243
FAX (Clerk Magistrate of the County Court);
(308) 233-3693 FAX (District Court)
clerk@buffalogov.org; deeds@buffalogov.org;
jan.haeker@courts.ne.gov;
sharon.mauler@courts.ne.gov;
smauler@kearney.net
http://www.buffalogov.org
Janice Giffin, County Clerk; Kellie John,
Register of Deeds; Jan Haeker, Clerk
Magistrate of the County Court; Sharon K.
Mauler, Clerk of the District Court
(no county records earlier than 1870; the county
business appears to have been transacted by
the officials of Hall County before 1870, since
few people resided in Buffalo County; land
records with Register of Deeds, naturalization
records with State Archives Division,
Nebraska State Historical Society, marriage
records with County Clerk, probate records
with County Court)
probate search service (list approximate date):
no charge; copies of probate records: 25¢ per
page, 25¢ minimum

Burt County
organized 1854, original county

Burt County Courthouse
111 North 13th Street
Tekamah, NE 68061-1043
(402) 374-1955 (County Clerk, PO Box 87);
(402) 374-2950 (Clerk Magistrate of the
County Court, PO Box 87); (402) 374-2905
(District Court); (402) 374-2956 FAX (County
Clerk); (402) 374-2951 FAX (Clerk Magistrate
of the County Court); (402) 374-2909 FAX
(District Court)
burtcoclerk@huntel.net; vicki.kuhlmann@
courts.ne.gov; michele.quick@courts.ne.gov
http://www.burtcounty.ne.gov
Ila J. Davis, County Clerk and Register of
Deeds; Vicki Kuhlmann, Clerk Magistrate of
the County Court; Michele Quick, Clerk of
the District Court
(land records and marriages with County Clerk,
naturalization records with Clerk of District
Court, probate records with County Court)

Butler County
organized 1857 from unorganized territory

Butler County Courthouse
451 North Fifth Street
David City, NE 68632

(402) 367-7430 (County Clerk, PO Box 289); (402) 367-7480 (Clerk Magistrate of the County Court); (402) 367-7460 (District Court); (402) 367-3329 FAX (County Clerk); (402) 367-3249 FAX (Clerk Magistrate of the County Court and District Court)
clerk@butler.nacone.org; garlyn.beeman@courts.ne.gov; nancy.prochaska@courts.ne.gov; nprochaska@neb.rr.com
http://www.co.butler.ne.us
Christine Meysenburg, County Clerk and Register of Deeds; Garlyn Beeman, Clerk Magistrate of the County Court; Nancy L. Prochaska, Clerk of the District Court
(land records with County Clerk, naturalization records with Clerk of District Court, marriages only with County Clerk, probate records with County Court)

Cass County
organized 1854, original county

Cass County Courthouse
326 Main Street
Plattsmouth, NE 68048
(402) 296-9300 (County Clerk, Room 202); (402) 296-9330 (Register of Deeds); (402) 296-9334 (Clerk Magistrate of the County Court, Room 201); (402) 296-9339 (District Court, Room 303); (402) 296-9332 FAX (County Clerk); (402) 296-9331 FAX (Register of Deeds); (402) 296-5297 FAX (Clerk Magistrate of the County Court); (402) 296-9345 FAX (District Court)
barbw@cassne.org; clerk@cassne.org; deeds@cassne.org; davej@cassne.org; gregg.miller@courts.ne.gov; della.sullivan@courts.ne.gov; dellas@cassne.org; districtcourt@cassne.org;
http://www.cassne.org
Barbara Wohlers, County Clerk; Dave Jordan, Register of Deeds; Gregg Miller, Clerk Magistrate of the County Court; Della P. Sullivan, Clerk of the District Court

Cedar County
organized 1855, original county

Cedar County Courthouse
101 Broadway
Hartington, NE 68739
(402) 254-7411 (County Clerk, PO Box 47); (402) 254-7441 (Clerk Magistrate of the County Court, PO Box 695); (402) 254-6957 (District Court, PO Box 796); (402) 254-7410 FAX (County Clerk); (402) 254-7447 FAX (Clerk Magistrate of the County Court); (402) 254-6954 FAX (District Court)
sheryl.connolly@courts.ne.gov; janet.wiechelman@courts.ne.gov; janetw@hartel.net
http://www.co.cedar.ne.us
David Dowling, County Clerk and Register of Deeds; Sheryl Connolly, Clerk Magistrate of the County Court; Janet Wiechelman, Clerk of the District Court

Chase County
organized 1889 from unorganized territory

Chase County Courthouse
921 Broadway
Imperial, NE 69033
(308) 764-2201 (Clerk Magistrate of the County Court, PO Box 1299); (308) 882-7500 (District Court, PO Box 1299); (308) 882-7554 FAX (Clerk Magistrate of the County Court); (308) 882-7552 FAX (District Court)
alice.lindekugel@courts.ne.gov; debra.clark@courts.ne.gov
http://www.chasecounty.com
Alice Lindekugel, Clerk Magistrate of the County Court; Debra Clark, County Clerk, Register of Deeds, and Clerk of the District Court
(land records, probate records)

Cherry County
organized 1883 from unorganized territory

Cherry County Courthouse
365 North Main
Valentine, NE 69201
(402) 376-2771 (County Clerk); (402) 376-2590 (Clerk Magistrate of the County Court); (402) 376-1840 (District Court); (402) 376-3095 FAX (County Clerk); (402) 376-5942 FAX (Clerk Magistrate of the County Court); (402) 376-3830 FAX (District Court)
clerk@cherry.nacone.org; kay.morrison@courts.ne.gov; maedeane.rodgers@courts.ne.gov; rwchealth@qwest.net (District Court)
http://www.co.cherry.ne.us
Thomas E. Elliott, County Clerk and Register of Deeds; Kay Morrison, Clerk Magistrate of the County Court; Maedeane Rodgers, Clerk of the District Court
(land records, naturalization records, vital records, probate records with County Court, 365 North Main, Valentine, NE 69201)

Cheyenne County
created by proclamation in August 1870 from unorganized territory (containing the "paper" counties of Lyon and Taylor, and covering the entire south half of the Panhandle, with the north half of the Panhandle, then unorganized territory, attached for judicial purposes)

Cheyenne County Courthouse
1000 Tenth Avenue
Sidney, NE 69162
(308) 254-2141 (County Clerk, PO Box 217); (308) 254-2150 (Cheyenne County Historical Association); (308) 254-2929 (Clerk Magistrate of the County Court, PO Box 217); (308) 254-2814 (District Court, PO Box 217); (308) 254-5049 FAX (County Clerk); (308) 254-2312 FAX (Clerk Magistrate of the County Court); (308) 254-7832 FAX (District Court)
beth@hamilton.net; cindi.brown@courts.ne.gov; edith.baumbach@courts.ne.gov; ediedc@hamilton.net
http://www.co.cheyenne.ne.us
Beth Fiegenschuh, County Clerk and Register of Deeds; Cindi Brown, Clerk Magistrate of the County Court; Edie Baumbach, Clerk of the District Court
(deeds, mortgages and patent records from the 1860s, grantor/grantee index with County Clerk, naturalization records with District Court, marriages from the late 1800s with Cheyenne County Historical Association, probate records with County Court)

Clay County
organized 1855, original county (according to Thorndale and Dollarhide's Map Guide to the U.S. Federal Censuses, 1790-1920, area originally called Clay County is now part of Lancaster and Gage counties, while present-day Clay County occupies area which was unattached in 1860)

Clay County Courthouse
111 West Fairfield Street
Clay Center, NE 68933-1499
(402) 762-3463 (County Clerk, PO Box 67); (402) 762-3651 (Clerk Magistrate of the County Court); (402) 762-3595 (District Court); (402) 762-3250 FAX (County Clerk and Clerk Magistrate of the County Court); (402) 762-3604 FAX (District Court)
clerk@clay.nacone.org; julie.bergen@courts.ne.gov; joni.bitterman@courts.ne.gov; cdcbitterman@datacc.net
http://www.claycounty.ne.gov
Deborah L. Karnatz, County Clerk and Register of Deeds; Julie Bergen, Clerk Magistrate of the County Court; Joni Bitterman, Clerk of the District Court
(land records with County Clerk/Register of Deeds, naturalization records with Clerk of District Court, vital records from 1917 to 1918 with County Clerk, probate records with County Court)

Colfax County
organized 1869 from Platte County

Colfax County Courthouse
411 East 11th Street
Schuyler, NE 68661-1940
(402) 352-8504 (County Clerk); (402) 352-8511 (Clerk Magistrate of the County Court, PO Box 191); (402) 352-8506 (District Court); (402) 352-8515 FAX (County Clerk); (402) 352-8535 FAX (Clerk Magistrate of the County Court); (402) 352-8550 FAX (District Court)
clerk@colfax.nacone.org; ellen.faltys@courts.ne.gov; dori.kroeger@courts.ne.gov; colfx16@megavision.com (District Court)
http://www.colfaxcounty.ne.gov
Sharon Bohaboj, County Clerk; Ellen Faltys, Clerk Magistrate of the County Court; Dori Kroeger, Clerk of the District Court
(land records with County Clerk/Register of Deeds, naturalizations with Clerk of District Court, probate records with County Court)
probate search service: no charge; copies of land and probate probate records: 25¢ each, no minimum

Cuming County
organized 1855 from Burt County

Cuming County Courthouse
(200 South Lincoln Street—location)
PO Box 290 (mailing address)
West Point, NE 68788-0290
(402) 372-6002 (County Clerk, PO Box 290); (402) 372-6003 (Clerk Magistrate of the County Court); (402) 372-6004 (District Court); (402) 372-6030 FAX (County Clerk and Clerk Magistrate of the County Court); (402) 372-6017 FAX (District Court)
ccclerk@cableone.net; sandy.meyer@courts.ne.gov; merna.recker@courts.ne.gov; mrecker@courts.state.ne.us
http://www.co.cuming.ne.us
Bonnie Vogltance, County Clerk and Register of Deeds; Sandy Meyer, Clerk Magistrate of the County Court; Merna Recker, Clerk of the District Court
(land records with County Clerk, naturalization records with Clerk District Court, marriages with County Clerk, probate records with County Court)
no land or vital records search service; copies of vital records: 35¢ each, $4.00 or $5.00 for certified copies

Custer County
organized 1877 from unorganized territory

Custer County Courthouse
431 South Tenth Avenue
Broken Bow, NE 68822-2001
(308) 872-5701 (County Clerk); (308) 872-2221 (Register of Deeds); (308) 872-5761 (Clerk Magistrate of the County Court); (308) 872-2121 (District Court); (308) 872-6052 FAX (Clerk Magistrate of the County Court); (308) 872-5826 FAX (District Court)
clerk@custer.nacone.org; deb.hansen@courts.ne.gov; amy.oxford@courts.ne.gov
http://www.co.custer.ne.us
Constance "Conni" Gracey, County Clerk; Kyle Russell, Register of Deeds; Debra Hansen, Clerk Magistrate of the County Court; Amy Oxford, Clerk of the District Court
(land records with Register of Deeds, naturalization records with Clerk of District Court, marriage licenses with County Clerk, probate records with County Court)
no probate search service; copies of probate records: 25¢ each

Dakota County
organized 1855, original county

Dakota County Courthouse
1601 Broadway
Dakota City, NE 68731
(402) 987-2126 (County Clerk, PO Box 39); (402) 987-2166 (Register of Deeds); (402) 987-2145 (Clerk Magistrate of the County Court, PO Box 385); (402) 987-2115 (District Court, PO Box 74); (402) 471-7229 FAX (County Clerk); (402) 987-2185 (Clerk Magistrate of the County Court); (402) 987-2117 FAX (District Court)
tpiepho@dakotacountyne.org; mrahn@dakotacountyne.org (Register of Deeds); paula.jesen@courts.ne.gov; valerie.danielson@courts.ne.gov
http://www.dakotacountyne.org
Theodore "Ted" Piepho, County Clerk; Mark Dorcey, Register of Deeds; Paula Jensen, Clerk Magistrate of the County Court; Valerie Danielson, Clerk of the District Court
(land records with Register of Deeds, marriages with County Clerk, probate records with County Court)
no probate search service; certified copies of marriages: $5.00 each; copies of probate records: 25¢ each

Dawes County
organized 1885 from Sioux County

Dawes County Courthouse
451 Main Street
Chadron, NE 69337
(308) 432-0100 (County Clerk); (308) 432-0116 (Clerk Magistrate of the County Court, PO Box 806); (308) 432-0109 (District Court, PO Box 630); (308) 432-5179 FAX (County Clerk); (308) 432-0110 FAX (Clerk Magistrate of the County Court and District Court)
clerk@dawes.nacone.org; lori.miskimins@courts.ne.gov; sharon.harrison@courts.ne.gov; dawesdistrictcourt@yahoo.com
http://www.co.dawes.ne.us
Cheryl Feist, County Clerk and Register of Deeds; Lori Miskimins, Clerk Magistrate of the County Court; Sharon Harrison, Clerk of the District Court
(land records with County Clerk's Office–Register of Deeds, naturalization records with Clerk of the District Court, marriages with County Clerk's Office, probate records with County Court)
no probate search service; copies of land records: $1.00 per page, 50¢ for certification; certified copies of marriages: $5.00 each; copies of probate records: $1.00 per page

Dawson County
organized 1860 from Buffalo County

Dawson County Courthouse
700 North Washington
Lexington, NE 68850
(308) 324-2127 (County Clerk); (308) 324-4271 (Register of Deeds); (308) 324-5606 (Clerk Magistrate of the County Court); (308) 324-4261 (District Court, Third Floor); (308) 324-9837 FAX (Clerk Magistrate of the County Court); (308) 324-9876 FAX (District Court)
karlaz@cozadtel.net; lois.bliven@courts.ne.gov; sherry.warner@courts.ne.gov; swarner@cozadtel.net
http://www.dawsoncountyne.net
Karla Zlatkovsky, County Clerk; Ruth Meyer, Register of Deeds; Lois Bliven, Clerk Magistrate of the County Court; Sherry Warner, Clerk of the District Court
(land records with Register of Deeds Office, naturalization records with Clerk of District Court, marriage licenses with County Clerk's Office, probate records with County Court)
probate search service: no charge (send "name and date of death"); copies of marriage licenses: 50¢ each, $5.00 for certified copies, $2.00 for mailed copy; copies of probate records: 25¢ each, $1.00 per page for certification, no minimum

Deuel County
organized January 1889 from Cheyenne County

Deuel County Courthouse
451 Main Street
Chappell, NE 69129
(308) 874-2909 (Clerk Magistrate of the County Court, PO Box 514); (308) 874-3308 (District Court, PO Box 327); (308) 874-2994 FAX (Clerk Magistrate of the County Court); (308) 874-3472 FAX (District Court)
marian.dotson@courts.ne.gov; polly.olson@courts.ne.gov
http://www.co.deuel.ne.us
Marian Dotson, Clerk Magistrate of the County Court; Polly Olson, County Clerk, Register of Deeds, and Clerk of the District Court
(land records from 1889, naturalization records from 1889, probate records with County Court)
probate search service: no charge; copies of probate records: 10¢ per page, $1.00 per certified page, no minimum

Dixon County
organized 1856, original county

Dixon County Courthouse
302 Third Street
Ponca, NE 68770
(402) 755-5602 (County Clerk, PO Box 546); (402) 755-5607 (Clerk Magistrate of the County Court, PO Box 497); (402) 755-5604 (District Court, PO Box 395); (402) 755-5650 FAX (County Clerk); (402) 755-5651 FAX (Clerk Magistrate of the County Court and District Court)
clerk@dixon.nacone.orgsusan.smith@courts.ne.gov; jackie.kingcoughlin@courts.ne.gov
http://www.co.dixon.ne.us
Diane Mohr, County Clerk and Register of Deeds; Susan Smith, Clerk Magistrate of the County Court; Jackie King-Coughlin, Clerk of the District Court
(land records with County Clerk, naturalization records to the 1930s with Clerk of the District Court, marriages from 1872 with County Clerk, probate records with County Court)
probate search service: no charge; copies of probate records: 25¢ per page, $1.00 for certification

Dodge County
organized 1855, original county

Dodge County Courthouse
435 North Park
Fremont, NE 68025
(402) 727-2767 (County Clerk); (402) 727-2735 (Register of Deeds); (402) 727-2779 (Clerk Magistrate of the County Court, 428 North Broad Street); (402) 727-2780 (District Court, 428 North Broad Street, PO Box 1237); (402) 727-2764 FAX (County Clerk); (402) 727-2762 FAX (Clerk Magistrate of the County Court); (402) 727-2773 FAX (District Court)
clerk@dodge.nacone.org; lila.scheer@courts.ne.gov; linda.nelson@courts.ne.gov
http://www.dodgecounty.ne.gov
Fred Mytty, County Clerk; Carol Givens, Register of Deeds; Lila Scheer, Clerk Magistrate of the County Court; Linda J. Nelson, Clerk of the District Court
(land records with Register of Deeds, marriages with County Clerk, probate records with County Court)
no probate search service; copies of probate records: 50¢ each, $5.00 for certified copies, 25¢ minimum

Douglas County
organized 1854, original county, later annexed part of Washington County

Douglas County Hall of Justice
1701 Farnam Street
Omaha, NE 68183
(402) 444-7550 (Clerk Magistrate of the County Court); (402) 444-7152 (Probate Division); (402) 444-7018 (District Court, Third Floor); (402) 444-6890 FAX (Clerk Magistrate of the County Court); (402) 444-1757 FAX (District Court)
leslie.douglas@courts.ne.gov; jfriend@co.douglas.ne.us
http://www.douglas.ne.us
Leslie Douglas, Clerk Magistrate of the County Court; John Friend, Clerk of the District Court
(probate records from 1876 with County Court, Probate Division)
probate search service ("must give year of death or we will not search"): no charge; copies of probate records: 25¢ per page, no minimum

Dundy County
organized 1873 from unorganized territory

Dundy County Courthouse
102 Seventh Avenue West
Benkelman, NE 69021
(308) 423-2058 (County Clerk, PO Box 506); (308) 423-2374 (Clerk Magistrate of the County Court, PO Box 378); (308) 423-2325 FAX (County Clerk and Clerk Magistrate of the County Court)
tony.lutz@courts.ne.gov; clerk@dundy.nacone.org; deb.league@courts.ne.gov
http://www.co.dundy.ne.us
Tony Lutz, County Clerk, Register of Deeds, and Clerk of the District Court; Deborah K. League, Clerk Magistrate of the County Court

Emmett County
(see Knox County)

Fillmore County
organized 1871 from unorganized territory

Fillmore County Courthouse
900 G Street
Geneva, NE 68361
(402) 759-4931 (County Clerk, PO Box 307); (402) 759-3811 (District Court, PO Box 147); (402) 759-3514 (Clerk Magistrate of the County Court, PO Box 66); (402) 759-4307 FAX (Clerk); (402) 759-4440 FAX (District Court); (402) 759-4440 (Clerk Magistrate of the County Court)
amy.nelson@fillmore.nacone.org; districtcourt@fillmore.nacone.org;mary.saum@courts.ne.gov; cindy.carrigan@courts.ne.gov
http://www.fillmorecounty.org
Amy Nelson, County Clerk and Register of Deeds; Mary L. Saum, Clerk of the District Court; Cindy Carrigan, Clerk Magistrate of the County Court
(land records from 1 July 1871 with County Clerk/Register of Deeds, naturalization records with Clerk of District Court, marriages with County Clerk and Clerk of District Court, probate records with County Court)
no probate search service ("we refer searches to Fillmore County Genealogical Society"); copies of probate records: 35¢ each, $1.00 minimum

Franklin County
organized 1867 from Kearney County

Franklin County Courthouse
405 15th Avenue
Franklin, NE 68939-1309
(308) 425-6202 (County Clerk, PO Box 146); (308) 425-6288 (County Court, PO Box 174); (308) 425-6093 FAX (County Clerk); (308) 425-6289 FAX (County Court)
marcia.volk@courts.ne.gov; clerk@franklin.nacone.org; chris.gilpin@courts.ne.gov
http://www.co.franklin.ne.us
Marcia Volk, County Clerk, Register of Deeds, and Clerk of the District Court; Christine Gilpin, Clerk Magistrate of the County Court
(land records with Register of Deeds, naturalization records with Clerk of the District Court, probate records with County

Court)
probate search service: no charge; copies of
probate records: 25¢ per page

Frontier County
organized 1872 from unorganized territory

Frontier County Courthouse
Stockville, NE 69042
(308) 367-8641 (District Court, PO Box 40);
(308) 367-8629 (District Court, PO Box 38);
(308) 367-8730 FAX (District Court); (308)
367-8730 FAX (County Court)
darla.walther@courts.ne.gov; clerkfc@curtis-
ne.com; ron.werkmeister@courts.ne.gov
http://www.co.frontier.ne.us
Darla M. Walther, County Clerk, Register of
Deeds, and Clerk of the District Court; Ron
L. Werkmeister, Clerk Magistrate of the
County Court
(land records and naturalization records with
County Clerk and Register of Deeds, probate
records with Clerk Magistrate of the County
Court)
land records search service: $3.00 per name;
copies of land records: $1.00 per record;
copies of naturalization records: unavailable

Furnas County
organized 1873 from unorganized territory

Furnas County Courthouse
912 R Street
Beaver City, NE 68926
(308) 268-4145 (County Clerk, PO Box 387);
(308) 268-4015 (District Court, PO Box 413);
(308) 268-4025 voice and FAX (County
Court, PO Box 373); (308) 268-3205 FAX
(District Court)
clerk@furnas.nacone.org;
judy.beins@courts.ne.gov
http://www.furnascounty.ne.gov
Kennis McClelland, County Clerk and Register
of Deeds; Judy A. Beins, Clerk of the District
Court; Marjory Lambert, Clerk Magistrate of
the County Court
(land records with County Clerk, naturalization
records with Clerk of District Court, probate
records with Clerk Magistrate of the County
Court)
probate search service: $3.00 per name ("The
Furnas County Genealogical Society does
most of the searching for us and they have
their own fees"); copies of probate records:
50¢ each, 50¢ minimum

Gage County
organized 1855, original county

Gage County Courthouse
612 Grant Street
Beatrice, NE 68310-0845
(402) 223-1300 (County Clerk, PO Box 429);
(402 223-1361 (Register of Deeds, PO Box
337); (402) 223-1332 (District Court, Room
11); (402) 223-1323 (Clerk Magistrate of the
County Court, Room 17, PO Box 219); (402)
223-1371 FAX (County Clerk); (402) 223-
1313 FAX (District Court); (402) 223-1374
(Clerk Magistrate of the County Court)
clerk@gage.nacone.org; rsiems@diodecom.net;
dwells@courts.state.ne.us; diane.wells@
courts.ne.gov; Vicki.Brolhorst@courts.ne.gov
http://www.co.gage.ne.us
Dawn Hill, County Clerk; Ruth Siems, Register
of Deeds; Diane G. Wells, Clerk of the
District Court; Vicki Brolhorst, Clerk
Magistrate of the County Court
(land records with Register of Deeds,
naturalization records from 21 September
1871 to 15 February 1932 with Clerk of the
District Court, marriages only from 1860 with
County Clerk's Office, probate records from
1860 with Clerk Magistrate of the County
Court)
probate search service: no charge; copies of land
records: $1.00 per page; copies of probate
records: 25¢ per page, no minimum

Garden County
organized 1909 from unorganized territory

Garden County Courthouse
611 Main Street
Oshkosh, NE 69154
(308) 772-3924 (District Court, PO Box 486);
(308) 772-3696 (County Court, PO Box 465);
(308) 772-0124 FAX (District Court); (308)
772-4143 FAX (County Court)
teresa.mckeeman@courts.ne.gov; clerk@garden.
nacone.org; jean.kling@courts.ne.gov
http://www.co.garden.ne.us
Teresa McKeeman, County Clerk, Register of
Deeds, and Clerk of the County Court; Jean
Kling, Clerk Magistrate of the County Court
(land records with Register of Deeds, probate
records with Clerk Magistrate of the County
Court)

Garfield County
organized 1884 from Wheeler County

Garfield County Courthouse
250 South Eighth
Burwell, NE 68823
(308) 346-4161 (District Court, PO Box 218);
(308) 346-4123 (Clerk Magistrate of the
County Court, PO Box 431); (308) 346-4651
FAX (District Court); (308) 346-4069 FAX
(Clerk Magistrate of the County Court)
clerk@garfield.nacone.org; linda.heermann@
courts.ne.gov; ron.werkmeister@courts.
ne.gov
http://www.garfieldcounty.ne.gov
Linda S. Heermann, County Clerk, Register of
Deeds, and Clerk of the District Court; Judy
Simpson, Clerk Magistrate of the County
Court
(land records with County Clerk, probate
records with Clerk Magistrate of the County
Court)
no probate search service ("Garfield County has
an active Historical Society that may perform
searches if contacted"); copies of probate
records: 20¢ each

Gosper County
organized 1873 from unorganized territory

Gosper County Courthouse
Elwood, NE 68937
(308) 785-2611 (District Court, PO Box 136);
(308) 785-2531 (Clerk Magistrate of the
County Court, PO Box 55); (308) 785-2300
FAX (District Court); (308) 785-2036 FAX
(County Court)
goclerk73@atcjet.net; cynthia.evans@
courts.ne.gov; dianna.wheeler@courts.ne.gov
http://www.co.gosper.ne.us
Cynthia E. Evans, County Clerk, Register of
Deeds, and Clerk of the District Court;
Dianna Wheeler, Clerk Magistrate of the
County Court
(land records from 1873)
no land records search service ("we are
understaffed and pass any requests on to a
private individual"); copies of land records:
26¢ each, no minimum

Grant County
organized 1887 from unorganized territory (in
1870 a "paper" county called Grant covered
parts of present-day Lincoln, Frontier, Red
Willow, Furnas, Gosper, Dawson, Hayes and
Hitchcock counties, much of which area was
known as Shorter County in 1860)

Grant County Courthouse
105 East Harrison Street
Hyannis, NE 69350
(308) 458-2488 (District Court, PO Box 139);
(308) 458-2433 (County Court, PO Box 97);
(308) 458-2485 FAX (District Court); (308)
458-2262 FAX (County Court)
clerk@grant.nacone.org; tonchita.ring@
courts.ne.gov; julie.krotz@courts.ne.gov
http://www.nacone.org/webpages/counies/cou
ntywebs/grant.htm

Tonchita Ring, County Clerk, Assessor, Register
of Deeds, and Clerk of the District Court;
Julie Krotz, Clerk Magistrate of the County
Court
(land records with County Assessor, probate
records with Clerk Magistrate of the County
Court)
no probate search service; copies of probate
records: 20¢ each

Greeley County
organized 1871 from Boone County

Greeley County Courthouse
Greeley, NE 68842
(308) 428-3625 (District Court, PO Box 287);
(308) 428-2705 (County Court, PO Box 302);
(308) 428-6500 FAX (District Court)
clerk@greeley.nacone.org; mindy.grossart@
courts.ne.gov; maryjo.harrahill@courts.ne.gov
http://www.nacone.org/webpages/counies/cou
ntywebs/greeley.htm
Mindy Grossart, County Clerk and Clerk of the
District Court; Maryjo Harrahill, Clerk
Magistrate of the County Court
(land records and naturalization records with
County Clerk, probate records with Clerk
Magistrate of the County Court)
probate search service: no charge; copies of
probate records: 25¢ per page, no minimum

Hall County
organized 1858, original county

Hall County Administration Building
121 South Pine Street
Grand Island, NE 68801-6076
(308) 381-5080 (County Clerk); (308) 385-5040
(Register of Deeds, Suite 6); (308) 385-5144
(District Court, 111 West First Street, Suite 4,
Grand Island, NE 68802-1926); (308) 385-
5135 (County Court, 111 West First Street,
Suite 1); (308) 385-5107 FAX (Register of
Deeds); (308) 385-5100 FAX (District Court);
(308) 385-5138 FAX (County Court)
marlac@hallcountyne.gov; marlac@hcgi.org;
kathyb@hllcountyne.gov; kathyb@hcgi.org;
valorieb@hcgi.org;
valorie.bendixen@courts.ne.gov;
reynalda.carpenter@courts.ne.gov
http://www.hallcountyne.gov
Marla Conley, County Clerk; Kathy Baasch,
Register of Deeds; Valorie Bendixen, Clerk of
the District Court; Reynalda Carpenter, Clerk
Magistrate of the County Court

Hamilton County
organized 1867 from York County

Hamilton County Courthouse
1111 13th Street
Aurora, NE 68818
(402) 694-3443 (County Clerk, Suite 1); (402)
694-3533 (District Court, PO Box 201); (402)
694-6188 (Clerk Magistrate of the County
Court, PO Box 323); (402) 694-2297 FAX
(County Clerk); (402) 694-2396 FAX (Register
of Deeds); (402) 694-2250 (District Court);
(402) 694-2250 FAX (Clerk Magistrate of the
County Court)
clerk@hamilton.net; dcourt@hamilton.net;
rebecca.shaw@courts.ne.gov;
lynne.nylander@courts.ne.gov
http://www.co.hamilton.ne.us
Patricia L. Anderson, County Clerk and Register
of Deeds; Becky Shaw, Clerk of the District
Court; Lynne Nylander, Clerk Magistrate of
the County Court
(land records and marriages with County Clerk,
naturalization records with Clerk of District
Court, probate records from 1881 with Clerk
Magistrate of County Court)
probate search service: no charge; copies of
probate records: 25¢ per page, no minimum

Harlan County
organized 1871 from unorganized territory

Harlan County Courthouse

706 West Second Street
Alma, NE 68920
(308) 928-2179 (Clerk Magistrate of the County
Court, PO Box 379); (308) 928-2173 (District
Court, PO Box 698); (308) 928-2170 (Clerk
Magistrate of the County Court); (308) 928-
2079 FAX (District Court)
sandy.medinger@courts.ne.gov; shirley.bailey@
courts.ne.gov; clerk@harlan.nacone.org;
http://www.nacone.org/webpages/countywebs
/harlan.htm
Sandy Medinger, Clerk Magistrate of the County
Court; Shirley Bailey, County Clerk, Register
of Deeds, and Clerk of the District Court
(land records, naturalization records, probate
records with County Court)
no probate search service; copies of probate
records: 25¢ per page

Hayes County
organized 1877 from unorganized territory

Hayes County Courthouse
502 Troth Street
Hayes Center, NE 69032
(308) 286-3315 (Clerk Magistrate of the County
Court, PO Box 370); (308) 266-3413 (District
Court, PO Box 370); (308) 268-3208 FAX
(Clerk Magistrate of the County Court and
District Court)
susan.messersmith@courts.ne.gov
http://www.geocities.com/hayes_county
Kathy Jones, Clerk Magistrate of the County
Court; Joan E. Lauenroth, County Clerk,
Register of Deeds, and Clerk of the District
Court
(land records from late 1800s with Register of
Deeds, naturalization records from 1907 with
Register of Deeds, probate records from 1892
with County Court)
probate search service: no charge; copies of
probate records: 25¢ per page, no minimum

Hitchcock County
organized 1873 from unorganized territory

Hitchcock County Courthouse
229 East D Street
Trenton, NE 69044
(308) 334-5383 (Clerk Magistrate of the County
Court, PO Box 248); (308) 334-5646 (District
Court, PO Box 248); (308) 334-5351 FAX
(Clerk Magistrate of the County Court); (08)
334-5398 FAX (District Court)
peggy.rupert@courts.ne.gov;
margaret.pollmann@courts.ne.gov
http://www.co.hitchcock.ne.us
Peggy Rupert, Clerk Magistrate of the County
Court; Margaret Pollmann, County Clerk,
Register of Deeds, and Clerk of the District
Clerk
(land records with County Clerk, naturalization
records with County Clerk, vital records with
County Clerk, probate records with County
Court)
no probate search service; copies of probate
records: 50¢ per page, no minimum

Holt County
organized 1876 from Knox County

Holt County Courthouse
204 North Fourth Street
O'Neill, NE 68763
(402) 336-1762 (County Clerk, PO Box 329);
(402) 336-2250 (Register of Deeds, PO Box
329); (402) 336-1662 (Clerk Magistrate of the
County Court); (402) 336-2840 (District
Court, PO Box 755); (402) 336-1663 (Clerk
Magistrate of the County Court); (402) 336-
3601 FAX (District Court)
holtclerkcathy@morcomm.net;
midge.clark@courts.ne.gov;
junior.young@courts.ne.gov;
jyoung@courts.state.ne.us
http://www.co.holt.ne.us
Cathy Ravel, County Clerk and Register of
Deeds; Midge Clark, Clerk Magistrate of the
County Court; Junior Young, Clerk of the

District Court
(land records with Register of Deeds,
naturalization records with Clerk of District
Court, marriages with County Clerk, probate
records with County Court)
no probate search service ("Genealogical
Society, K. Manoucheri, PO Box 878,
O'Neill, NE 68763, will do probate searches
for $5.00 plus 25¢ each copy plus postage")

Hooker County
organized 1889 from unorganized territory

Hooker County Courthouse
303 NW First Street
Mullen, NE 69152
(308) 546-2244 (County Clerk, PO Box 184);
(308) 546-2855 (Register of Deeds and Clerk
of the District Court, PO Box 184); (308)
546-2249 (Clerk Magistrate of the County
Court, PO Box 184); (308) 546-2490 FAX
(Clerk Magistrate of the County Court and
District Court)
soscou93@nebnet.net (County Clerk);
cindi.walz@courts.ne.gov;
dave.sullivan@courts.ne.gov
http://www.co.hooker.ne.us
Cindi Walz, Clerk Magistrate of the County
Court; David "Dave" Sullivan, County Clerk,
Register of Deeds, and Clerk of the District
Court

Howard County
organized 1871 from Hall County

Howard County Courthouse
612 Indian Street
St. Paul, NE 68873
(308) 754-4192 (Clerk Magistrate of the County
Court, Suite #6); (308) 754-4343 (District
Court); (308) 754-4727 FAX (Clerk
Magistrate of the County Court); (308) 754-
4727 FAX (District Court)
marsha.anderson@courts.ne.gov;
marge.palmberg@courts.ne.gov;
clerk@howard.nacone.org
http://www.howardcounty.ne.gov
Marsha Anderson, Clerk Magistrate of the
County Court; Marge Palmberg, County
Clerk, Register of Deeds, and Clerk of the
District Court
(land records with RaNae Smith, County Clerk,
naturalization records with Linda M.
Scarborough, Clerk Magistrate, County Court,
probate records with Clerk Magistrate)
probate search service: no charge; copies of
probate records: 25¢ each, $1.50 for certified
copies

Jackson County
(see Lincoln County)

Jefferson County
organized 1856 from Gage County (according to
Thorndale and Dollarhide's Map Guide to the
U.S. Federal Censuses, 1790-1920, area now
called Jefferson County was called Jones
County in 1860, and in 1870 Jefferson County
covered both present-day Jefferson County
and present-day Thayer, which in 1860 was
called Nuckolls County)

Jefferson County Courthouse
411 Fourth Street
Fairbury, NE 68352-2513
(402) 729-6818 (County Clerk); (402) 729-6819
(Register of Deeds); (402) 729-6801 (Clerk
Magistrate of the County Court); (402) 729-
6807 (District Court); (402) 729-6802 FAX
(Clerk Magistrate of the County Court); (402)
729-6808 FAX (District Court)
jeffcoclerk@diodecom.net; tammie.duensing@
courts.ne.gov; boettcher@courts.ne.gov;
jeffcocdc@diodecom.net (District Court)
http://www.co.jefferson.ne.us
Sandra Stelling, County Clerk and Register of
Deeds; Tammie Duensing, Clerk Magistrate
of the County Court; Beverly Boettcher, Clerk
of the District Court

(land records from 1871 with Register of Deeds,
naturalization records from 1887 with Clerk
of District Court, marriages from 1869 only
with County Clerk, probate records from the
1870s with County Court)
probate search service: no charge; copies of land
records: $1.00 each; copies of naturalization
records: 50¢ per page; copies of marriages:
$1.00 each; copies of probate records: 25¢
each plus postage, no minimum

Johnson County
organized 1855, original county

Johnson County Courthouse
301 Broadway
Tecumseh, NE 68450-0416
(402) 335-6313 (Clerk Magistrate of the County
Court, PO Box 285); (402) 335-6300 (District
Court, PO Box 416); (402) 335-6314 FAX
(Clerk Magistrate of the County Court); (402)
335-6311 FAX (District Court)
larita.weber@courts.ne.gov;
Kathleen.nieveen@courts.ne.gov;
soscou57@nol.org (County Clerk)
http://www.co.johnson.ne.us/clerk.html
Larita Weber, Clerk Magistrate of the County
Court; Kathleen M. Nieveen, County Clerk,
Register of Deeds, and Clerk of the District
Court
(land records with Clerk, naturalization records
with Clerk of the District Court, marriages
only with Clerk, probate records with County
Court)
probate search service: no charge; copies of land
records, naturalization records, and
marriages: 25¢ each; copies of probate
records: $1.00 each, no minimum

Jones County
(see Jefferson County)

Kearney County
organized 1860, original county

Kearney County Courthouse
400 North Colorado
Minden, NE 68959
(308) 832-2723 (County Clerk); (308) 832-2719
(Clerk Magistrate of the County Court, PO
Box 377); (308) 832-1742 (District Court, PO
Box 208); (308) 832-2729 FAX (County
Clerk); (308) 832-0636 FAX (Clerk Magistrate
of the County Court and District Court)
clerk@kearney.nacone.org;
randy.eckhoff@courts.ne.gov;
jill.fritson@courts.ne.gov
http://www.kearneycounty.ne.gov
Myra Johnson, County Clerk and Register of
Deeds; Randy Eckhoff, Clerk Magistrate of
the County Court; Jill Fritson, Clerk of the
District Court
(land records with Register of Deeds,
naturalization records with Clerk of District
Court, probate records with County Court)
probate search service: no charge; copies of
probate records: $1.00 for the first copy and
10¢ for each additional copy, no minimum

Keith County
organized 1873 from Lincoln County

Keith County Courthouse
511 North Spruce Street
Ogallala, NE 69153
(308) 284-4726 (County Clerk, Room 102, PO
Box 149); (308) 284-3693 (Clerk Magistrate of
the County Court, PO Box 358); (308) 284-
3849 (District Court, Room 202); (308) 284-
6277 FAX (County Clerk); (308) 284-6825
FAX (Clerk Magistrate of the County Court);
(308) 284-3978 FAX (District Court)
clerk@keithcountyne.gov; margaret.padgett@
courts.ne.gov; susan.thomas@courts.ne.gov;
sthomas@keithcountyne.gov
http://www.co.keith.ne.us
Sandra Olson, County Clerk; Margaret Padgett,
Clerk Magistrate of the County Court; Susan
L. Thomas, Clerk of District Court

(land records from 1873 with County Clerk, probate records with County Court, marriages)

no probate search service; copies of probate records: 50¢ each, $1.50 for certified copies, no minimum; certified copies of marriages: $5.00 each

Keya Paha County

organized 1884 from Brown and Rock counties and part of the area transferred in 1882 from Dakota Territory

Keya Paha County Courthouse
310 Courthouse Drive
Springview, NE 68778
(402) 497-3021 (Clerk Magistrate of the County Court, PO Box 275); (402) 497-3791 (District Court, PO Box 349); (402) 497-3799 FAX (Clerk Magistrate of the County Court and District Court)
roxanne.philben@courts.ne.gov;
suzy.wentworth@courts.ne.gov;
clerk@keyapaha.nacone.org (County Clerk);
soscou82@nol.org (County Clerk)
http://www.co.keya-paha.ne.us
Roxanne Philben, Clerk Magistrate of the County Court; Suzy Wentworth, County Clerk, Register of Deeds and Clerk of the District Court
(land records, naturalization records from 1886, marriages from 1886, probate records from 1886)
probate search service: no charge; copies of probate records: 15¢ each (8½" x 11"), 20¢ each (8½" x 14"), no minimum

Kimball County

organized 1888 from Cheyenne County

Kimball County Courthouse
114 East Third Street
Kimball, NE 69145-1401
(308) 235-2241 (County Clerk and Register of Deeds, Suite 6); (308) 235-2831 (Clerk Magistrate of the County Court); (308) 235-3591 (District Court, Suite 7); (308) 235-3927 FAX (Clerk Magistrate of the County Court); (308) 235-3654 FAX (County Clerk, Register of Deeds, and District Court)
angie.haun@courts.ne.gov;
cathleen.sibal@courts.ne.gov;
clerk@kimball.nacone.org (County Clerk)
http://www.co.kimball.ne.us
Angie Haun, Clerk Magistrate of the County Court; Cathleen "Cathy" Sibal, County Clerk, Register of Deeds, and Clerk of the District Court
(land records from 1889 with County Clerk, naturalization records with State Historical Society, marriage licenses only with County Clerk, probate records with County Court)
certified copies of marriage licenses: $5.00 each

Knox County

county established by the Territorial Legislature in 1857, original county; name changed from L'eau Qui Court County to Emmett County; name changed from Emmett County to Knox County in 1873

Knox County Courthouse
206 Main Street
Center, NE 68724
(402) 288-5604 (County Clerk, PO Box 166); (402) 288-5613 (Register of Deeds, PO Box 166); (402) 288-5607 (Clerk Magistrate of the County Court, PO Box 125); (402) 288-5606 (District Court, PO Box 126); (402) 288-5605 FAX (County Clerk and Register of Deeds); (402) 288-5609 FAX (Clerk Magistrate of the County Court and District Court)
clerk@knox.nacone.org (County Clerk);
soscou12@nol.org (Register of Deeds);
betty.boggs@courts.ne.gov; karne.riesberg@courts.ne.gov; kriesberg@courts.state.ne.us
http://www.co.knox.ne.us
Joann M. Fischer, County Clerk and Register of Deeds; Betty Boggs, Clerk Magistrate of the

County Court; Karen K. Riesberg, Clerk of the District Court
(land records with Register of Deeds Office, naturalization records with Clerk of District Court Office, probate records with County Clerk)

Lancaster County

organized 1854, original county

Lancaster County Courthouse
555 South Tenth Street
Lincoln, NE 68508-2803
(402) 471-7481 (County Clerk, Room 108); (402) 441-7463 (Register of Deeds, Room 102); (402) 441-8728 FAX (County Clerk); (402) 441-8759 FAX (Register of Deeds)
dnolte@lancaster.ne.gov;
nagena@lancaster.ne.gov
http://www.lancaster.ne.gov
Dan Nolte, County Clerk; Norman H. Agena, Register of Deeds

Lancaster County Justice and Law Enforcement Center
575 South Tenth Street
Lincoln, NE 68508
(402) 441-7291 (Clerk Magistrate of the County Court); (402) 441-7328 (District Court); (402) 441-6056 (Clerk Magistrate of the County Court); (402) 441-6190 FAX (District Court)
Bbruckner@ci.lincoln.ne.us; sue.kirkland@courts.ne.gov; skirkland@lancaster.ne.gov; clerkdistct@lancaster.ne.gov
http://www.lancaster.ne.gov
B. Bruckner, Clerk Magistrate of the County Court; Suzanne "Sue" Kirkland, Clerk of the District Court

L'eau Qui Court County

(see Knox County)

Lincoln County

organized 1860 from unorganized territory (contained the "paper" counties of Grant and Jackson in 1870)

Lincoln County Courthouse
300 North Jeffers Street
North Platte, NE 69101
(308) 534-4350 (County Clerk, Room 101); (308) 534-4350 (Register of Deeds, Room 103); (308) 534-4350 (Clerk Magistrate of the County Court, PO Box 519); (308) 535-3504 (District Court, PO Box 1616); (308) 535-3525 FAX (Clerk Magistrate of the County Court); (308) 535-3527 FAX (District Court)http://www.co.lincoln.ne.us
clerk@co.lincoln.ne.us;
clerk@lincoln.nacone.org (County Clerk);
blockla@co.lincoln.ne.us;
randy.mccoy@courts.ne.gov;
debmccar1@yahoo.com;
debra.mccarthy@courts.ne.gov;
mccartde@co.lincoln.ne.us
http://www.co.lincoln.ne.us
Rebecca Rossell, County Clerk; Lois Block, Register of Deeds; Randy McCoy, Clerk Magistrate of the County Court; Debra McCarthy, Clerk of the District Court

Logan County

organized 1885 from Custer County

Logan County Courthouse
317 Main Street
Stapleton, NE 69163
(308) 636-2677 (Clerk Magistrate of the County Court, PO Box 8); (308) 636-2311 (District Court, PO Box 8); (308) 636-2298 FAX (Clerk Magistrate of the County Court); (308) 636-2333 FAX (District Court)
cindi.walz@courts.ne.gov;
patricia.harvey@courts.ne.gov;
soscou87@nol.org (County Clerk)
http://www.nacone.org/webpages/countywebs/logan.htm
Cindi Walz, Clerk Magistrate of the County Court; Patricia Harvey, County Clerk, Register

of Deeds, and Clerk of the District Court

Loup County

organized 1883 from unorganized territory

Loup County Courthouse
408 Fourth Street
Taylor, NE 68879
(308) 942-6035 (County Clerk, Register of Deeds, and Clerk of the District Court, PO Box 187, and Clerk Magistrate of the County Court, PO Box 146); (308) 942-3103 FAX (County Clerk, Clerk of the District Court, and Clerk Magistrate of the County Court); (308) 942-6015 FAX (Register of Deeds)
barb.strong@courts.ne.gov;
debbie.postany@courts.ne.gov;
clerk@loup.nacone.org (County Clerk)
http://www.co.loup.ne.us
Barb Strong, Clerk Magistrate of the County Court; Debbie Postany, Clerk of the District Court
(land records with County Clerk, naturalization records with County Clerk, probate records with County Court)
no land or naturalization records search service; probate search service: no charge with no copies issued; copies of land and naturlaization records: 35¢ each; copies of probate records: $1.00 for the first page (includes search) and 50¢ for each additional copy, $1.00 minimum for search with one copy

Lyon County

(see Cheyenne County)

Madison County

organized 1868 from Platte County

Madison County Courthouse
1313 North Main Street
Madison, NE 68748
(402) 454-3311, ext. 136 (County Clerk, PO Box 290); (402) 454-3311 (Register of Deeds, PO Box 229); (402) 454-3311, ext. 165 (Clerk Magistrate of the County Court, PO Box 230); (402) 454-3311 (District Court, PO Box 249); (402) 454-3438 FAX (Clerk Magistrate of the County Court); (402) 454-6528 FAX (District Court)
coclerk@co.madison.ne.us;
register@co.madison.ne.us;
lori.bohn@courts.ne.gov;
marjorie.schaffer@courts.ne.gov;
mschaffer@courts.state.ne.us
http://co.madison.ne.us
Nancy Scheer, County Clerk; Nancy Gross, Register of Deeds; Lori Bohn, Clerk Magistrate of the County Court; Marjorie Schaffer, Clerk of the District Court
(land records with Register of Deeds, vital records with County Clerk, probate records from 1868 with County Court)
probate search service: no charge; copies of land records: 50¢ per page; copies of probate records: 25¢ each, no minimum

McPherson County

organized 1887 from Lincoln and Keith counties

McPherson County Courthouse
(Fifth and Anderson—location)
PO Box 122 (mailing address)
Tryon, NE 69167
(308) 587-2363 voice & FAX
cindi.walz@courts.ne.gov;
judy.dailey@courts.ne.gov;
clerk@mcpherson.nacone.org (County Clerk)
http://www.nacone.org/webpages/counties/countywebs/mcpherson.htm
Cindi Walz, Clerk Magistrate of the County Court; Judy Dailey, County Clerk, Register of Deeds and Clerk of the District Court

Merrick County

organized 1858, original county

Merrick County Courthouse

(1502 18th Street—location)
PO Box 27 (mailing address)
Central City, NE 68826
(308) 946-2881 (County Clerk and Register of Deeds); (308) 946-2812 (Clerk Magistrate of the County Court); (308) 946-2461 (District Court); (308) 946-2332 FAX (County Clerk and Register of Deeds); (308) 946-3838 FAX (Clerk Magistrate of the County Court); (308) 946-3692 FAX (District Court)
soscou46@nol.org (County Clerk and Register of Deeds); beth.pullen@courts.ne.gov; darlene.miller@courts.ne.gov
http://www.merrickcounty.ne.gov/index_html
Gloria Broekemeier, County Clerk and Register of Deeds; Beth Pullen, Clerk Magistrate of the County Court; Darlene Miller, Clerk of the District Court
(land records from 1866 with County Clerk's Office, naturalization records with Clerk of District Court, marriages from 1869 with County Clerk's Office, probate records from 1875 with County Court)
probate search service: $5.00; copies of probate records: 25¢ per page, $1.00 for certification, no minimum

Monroe County
(see Platte County)

Morrill County
organized November 1908 from Cheyenne County

Morrill County Courthouse
600 Main Street
Bridgeport, NE 69336-0610
(308) 262-0860 (County Clerk, PO Box 610); (308) 262-0812 (Clerk Magistrate of the County Court, PO Box 418); (308) 262-1261 (District Court, PO Box 824); (308) 262-1469 FAX (County Clerk); (308) 262-1644 FAX (Clerk Magistrate of the County Court); (308) 262-1799 FAX (District Court)
souscou64@nol.org (County Clerk); clerk@morrill.nacone.org (County Clerk); linda.hayden@courts.ne.gov; marilyn.wimmer@courts.ne.gov; mccdc64@hotmail.com (District Court)
http://www.morrillcounty.ne.gov
Kathleen "Kathy" Brandt, County Clerk and Register of Deeds; Linda Hayden, Clerk Magistrate of the County Court; Marilyn Wimmer, Clerk of the District Court
(land records from 1908 with County Clerk, naturalization records from 1909 to 1945 with Clerk District Court, probate records from 1908 with Clerk Magistrate)
no probate search service; copies of probate records: 25¢ per page, no minimum

Nance County
organized 1879 from Merrick County, encompassing the entire former Pawnee Reservation

Nance County Courthouse
309 Ester Street
Fullerton, NE 68638
(308) 536-2331 (County Clerk, Register of Deeds, and Clerk of the District Court, PO Box 338); (308) 536-2675 (Clerk Magistrate of the County Court, PO Box 837); (308) 536-2742 FAX (Clerk Magistrate of the County Court); (308) 536-2742 FAX (County Clerk, Register of Deeds, and Clerk of the District Court)
angie.lewandowski@courts.ne.gov; danette.zarek@courts.ne.gov; nancecountyclerk@hamilton.net; nanceclerk@hamilton.net
http://www.co.nance.ne.us
Dianne Hollman, Register of Deeds; Angie Lewandowski, Clerk Magistrate of the County Court; Danette Zarek, County Clerk and Clerk of the District Court
(land records with County Clerk, naturalization records with Clerk of District Court, marriage licenses with County Clerk, probate records

with County Court)
probate search service: no charge; copies of probate records: 25¢ per page, no minimum ("please state approximate date of death if available")

Nemaha County
organized 1855, original county

Nemaha County Courthouse
1824 N Street
Auburn, NE 68305-2342
(402) 274-4213 (County Clerk, Suite 201); (402) 274-3008 (Clerk Magistrate of the County Court); (402) 274-3616 (Clerk of the District Court, Suite 301); (402) 274-4605 (Clerk Magistrate of the County Court); (402) 274-4478 FAX (District Court)
clerk@nemaha.nacone.org (County Clerk); nancy.hall@courts.ne.gov; amy.hector@courts.ne.gov
http://www.nemahacounty.ne.gov
Joyce Oakley, County Clerk and Register of Deeds; Nancy Hall, Clerk Magistrate of the County Court; Amy Hector, Clerk of the District Court
(land records with County Clerk, marriage certificates, probate records with County Court)
copies of land records and marriage certificates: $1.00 each

Nuckolls County
organized 1860 from unorganized territory; a county which was originally named Nuckolls is now Thayer County

Nuckolls County Courthouse
150 South Main
Nelson, NE 68961
(402) 225-4361 (County Clerk, PO Box 366); (402) 225-2371 (Clerk Magistrate of the County Court, PO Box 372); (402) 225-4341 (District Court, PO Box 362); (402) 225-4301 FAX (County Clerk); (402) 225-2373 FAX (Clerk Magistrate of the County Court and District Court)
clerk@nuckolls.nacone.org (County Clerk); linda.hayden@courts.ne.gov; danelle.whitmore@courts.ne.gov
http://www.nuckollscounty.ne.gov
Jackie L. Kassebaum, County Clerk and Register of Deeds; Linda Hayden, Clerk Magistrate of the County Court; Danelle Whitmore, Clerk of the District Court
(real estate ownership, deeds, plats, mortgages with County Clerk/Register of Deeds, naturalization records [a limited amount of information] with Clerk of the District Court, marriage licenses from 1872 with County Clerk/Register of Deeds, probate records with County Court)
no land records search service (contact Nuckolls County Genealogy Society), no vital records search service; probate search service: no charge ("we do it when we have the extra time"); copies of land records: 50¢ per standard-sized page; certified copies of vital records: $1.50 per page; copies of probate records: $1.00 per document

Otoe County
organized 1854, original county

Otoe County Courthouse
1021 Central Avenue
Nebraska City, NE 68410
(402) 873-9505 (County Clerk, PO Box 249); (402) 873-9530 (Register of Deeds, Room 203); (402) 873-9574 (Clerk Magistrate of the County Court, PO Box 487); (402) 873-9550 (District Court, PO Box 726); (402) 873-9506 FAX (County Clerk); (402) 873-9507 FAX (Register of Deeds); (402) 873-9030 (Clerk Magistrate of the County Court); (402) 873-9583 FAX (District Court)
clerk@otoe.nacone.org; deeds@otoe.nacone.org; kari.kuehn@courts.ne.gov; janis.riege@courts.ne.gov

http://www.co.otoe.ne.us
Janene Bennett, County Clerk; Janet Reed, Register of Deeds; Kari Kuehn, Clerk Magistrate of the County Court; Janis Riege, Clerk of the District Court
(land records from 4 April 1855 with Register of Deeds, naturalization records with Clerk of the District Court, marriages from 1855 with County Clerk, probate records from 1854 with Clerk Magistrate of the County Court)
probate search service: no charge; copies of land records: $1.00 each, no minimum; copies of marriage records: $3.00 each, $5.00 for certified copies; copies of probate records: 25¢ per page, $1.00 for certification, no minimum ("payment in advance of mailing copies")

Pawnee County
organized 1854, original county

Pawnee County Courthouse
625 Sixth Street
Pawnee City, NE 68420
(402) 852-2962 (County Clerk and Recorder of Deeds, PO Box 431); (402) 852-2388 voice & FAX (Clerk Magistrate of the County Court, PO Box 471); (402) 852-2963 FAX (County Clerk and Recorder of Deeds, and voice & FAX District Court)
larita.weber@courts.ne.gov; carol.young@courts.ne.gov; clerk@pawnee.nacone.org (County Clerk)
http://www.co.pawnee.ne.us
Larita Weber, Clerk Magistrate of the County Court; Carol Young, County Clerk, Register of Deeds, and Clerk of the District Court
(land records from 1854, naturalization records from 1871, probate records from 1857 with County Court)
probate search service: no charge; copies of land records: $1.00 each (if you do your own search), $2.50 for certified copies; copies of naturlaization records: $1.00 each; copies of probate records: 25¢ per page

Perkins County
organized 1887 from Keith County

Perkins County Courthouse
200 Lincoln Avenue
Grant, NE 69140
(308) 352-4415 (Clerk Magistrate of the County Court, PO Box 222); (308) 352-4643 (District Court, PO Box 156); (308) 352-4368 FAX (Clerk Magistrate of the County Court); (308) 352-2455 FAX (District Court)
karen.wilson@courts.ne.gov; rita.long@courts.ne.gov; clerk@perkins.nacone.org (County Clerk)
http://www.co.perkins.ne.us
Karen Wilson, Clerk Magistrate of the County Court; Rita A. Long, County Clerk; Clerk of the District Court
(land records with County Clerk, some naturalization records from 1890 to 1928 with County Clerk, probate records with County Court)
probate search service: no charge; copies of probate records: 25¢ per page, no minimum

Phelps County
organized 1873 from unorganized territory

Phelps County Courthouse
715 Fifth Avenue
Holdrege, NE 68949
(308) 995-4469 (County Clerk and Register of Deeds, PO Box 404); (308) 995-6561 (Clerk Magistrate of the County Court, PO Box 255); (308) 995-2281 (District Court, PO Box 462); (308) 995-4368 FAX (County Clerk and Register of Deeds); (308) 995-6562 FAX (Clerk Magistrate of the County Court); (308) 995-6562 FAX (District Court)
clerk@phelps.nacone.org (County Clerk); darrie.streeter@courts.ne.gov; jennifer.nelson@courts.ne.gov
http://www.phelpsgov.org

Sally Fox, County Clerk; Edna M. Suhr, Register of Deeds; Darrie Streeter, Clerk Magistrate of the County Court; Jennifer Nelson, Clerk of the District Court
(land records with County Clerk, naturalization records with Clerk of District Court, probate records with County Court)
probate search service: no charge; copies of probate records: 25¢ each plus postage, no minimum ("please print or type names and dates")

Pierce County
organized 1859 from Madison County

Pierce County Courthouse
111 West Court Street
Pierce, NE 68767
(402) 329-4225 (County Clerk, Room 1); (402) 329-6245 (Clerk Magistrate of the County Court, Room 11); (402) 329-4335 (District Court, Room 12); (402) 329-6439 FAX (County Clerk); (402) 329-6412 FAX (Clerk Magistrate of the County Court and District Court)
piecoclk@ptcnet.net; debra.theisen@courts. ne.gov; vickie.prince@courts.ne.gov; vprince@courts.state.ne.us
http://www.co.pierce.ne.us/court.html
Shannon Wragge, County Clerk and Register of Deeds; Deb Theisen, Clerk Magistrate of the County Court; Vickie Prince, Clerk of the District Court
(land records with County Clerk, naturalization records with Clerk of District Court, probate records with County Court)
no probate search service; copies of probate records: 25¢ each

Platte County
county created 1855 from Dodge County and was composed of the twenty-four miles square, or five hundred seventy-six square miles, included in townships 17, 18, 19 and 20 North and ranges 1, 2, 3 and 4 East of the sixth principal meridian; in 1858 it was made to include, in addition, all of Monroe County (which had been created in August 1857), on the west which was not comprised within the Pawnee Indian Reservation; in 1868 the County of Colfax was created by an act of the State Legislature, taking from Platte all of the eastern three ranges; after several changes made at different times, the southern boundary has been fixed, and it now remains at the south side of the South Channel of the Platte River, from the sixth principal meridian and at the south side of the North Channel of the river, westward from said line; Platte County now consists of townships 16, 17, 18, 19 and 20 North and ranges 1, 2, 3 and 4 West and 1 East of the sixth principal meridian

Platte County Courthouse
2610 14th Street
Columbus, NE 68601-4929
(402) 563-4904 (County Clerk, First Floor); (402) 563-4911 (Register of Deeds, First Floor); (402) 563-4905 (Clerk Magistrate of the County Court, PO Box 538); (402) 563-4906 (District Court, Second Floor, PO Box 1188); (402) 564-4164 FAX (County Clerk); (402) 562-8158 FAX (Clerk Magistrate of the County Court); (402) 562-6718 FAX (District Court)
pcclerk@megavision.com; pcroddk@ megavision.com; darla.schiefelbein@ courts.ne.gov; marlene.vetick@courts.ne.gov; distcrt@megavision.com;
http://www.plattecounty.net
Diane C. Pinger, County Clerk; Diane Kapels, Register of Deeds; Darla Schiefelbein, Clerk Magistrate of the County Court; Marlene Vetick, Clerk of the District Court
(land records with County Register of Deeds Office, marriages with County Clerk, probate records from 1869 with County Court)
no vital records search service; copies of vital

records: 50¢ each (date of marriage required)

Polk County
organized 1856, original county

Polk County Courthouse
Courthouse Square
Osceola, NE 68651
(402) 747-5431 (County Clerk, PO Box 276); (402) 747-5371 (Clerk Magistrate of the County Court, PO Box 506); (402) 747-3487 (Clerk of the District Court, PO Box 447); (402) 747-2656 FAX (County Clerk); (402) 747-5981 FAX (Clerk Magistrate of the County Court); (402) 747-8299 FAX (Clerk of the District Court)
verna.davis@courts.ne.gov; debra.girard@courts.ne.gov; clerk@polk.nacone.org (County Clerk)
http://www.polkcounty.ne.gov
Verna Davis, Clerk Magistrate of the County Court; Debra S. Girard, County Clerk, Register of Deeds, and Clerk of the District Court
(land records from 1870, naturalization records from 1876 to 1943, marriages only, probate records from 1880)
probate search service: no charge; copies of probate records: 25¢ per page, no minimum ("by written request, include date of death")

Red Willow County
organized 1873 from unorganized territory

Red Willow County Courthouse
502 Norris Avenue
McCook, NE 69001-2006
(308) 345-1552 (County Clerk); (308) 345-1904 (Clerk Magistrate of the County Court, PO Box 199); (308) 345-4583 (District Court, PO Box 847); (308) 345-4460 FAX (County Clerk); (308) 345-1904 FAX (Clerk Magistrate of the County Court); (308) 345-7907 FAX (District Court)
clerk@redwillow.nacone.org (County Clerk); clerkrod@redwillow.nacone.org; kathy. clapp@courts.ne.gov; beverly.dodge@courts. ne.gov; bdodge@courts.state.ne.us
http://www.co.red-willow.ne.us
Pauletta Gerver, County Clerk and Register of Deeds; Kathy Jones, Clerk Magistrate of the County Court; Beverly Dodge, Clerk of the District Court
(land records with Register of Deeds, naturalization records with Clerk of the District Court, probate records with County Court, marriages)
probate search service: no charge; copies of probate records: 25¢ per page, no minimum; copies of marriages: 75¢ each, $5.00 for certified copies

Richardson County
organized 1855, original county

Richardson County Courthouse
1700 Stone Street
Falls City, NE 68355
(402) 245-2911 (County Clerk); (402) 245-2812 (Clerk Magistrate of the County Court, Room 205); (402) 245-2023 (District Court); (402) 245-4192 FAX (County Clerk); (402) 245-2926 FAX (Register of Deeds); (402) 245-3352 FAX (Clerk Magistrate of the County Court); (402) 245-3725 FAX (District Court)
clerk@richardson.nacone.org (County Clerk); soscou19@nol.org (County Clerk); jeanne.mcginnis@courts.ne.gov; pam.scott@courts.ne.gov
http://www.co.richardson.ne.us
Mary Eickhoff, County Clerk and Register of Deeds; Jeanne McGinnis, Clerk Magistrate of the County Court; Pamela S. Scott, Clerk of the District Court
(land records from 1855 to date with Register of Deeds, naturalization records with State Archives Division, Nebraska State Historical Society, marriages from 1856 to date with County Clerk, probate records from 1859 to date with County Court)

copies of land records: 50¢ per page; certified copies of vital records: $5.00 each; copies of probate records: 25¢ per page, $1.00 for certification

Rock County
organized 1888 from Brown County

Rock County Courthouse
400 State Street
Bassett, NE 68714-0367
(402) 684-3601 (Clerk Magistrate of the County Court, PO Box 249); (402) 684-3933; (District Court, PO Box 367); (402) 684-2741 FAX (Clerk Magistrate of the County Court and District Court)
jenny.frick@courts.ne.gov; clerk@rock.nacone. org (County Clerk); soscou81@nol.org (County Clerk); joyce.stahl.@courts.ne.gov
http://www.co.rock.ne.us
Jenny Frick, Clerk Magistrate of the County Court; Joyce Stahl, County Clerk, Register of Deeds, and Clerk of the District Court
(land records with Register of Deeds, probate records with County Court)

Saline County
organized 18 February 1867 from Gage and Lancaster counties

Saline County Courthouse
215 South Court
Wilber, NE 68465
(402) 821-2374 (County Clerk, PO Box 865); (402) 821-2131 (Clerk Magistrate of the County Court, PO Box 865); (402) 821-2823 (District Court, PO Box 865); (402) 821-3381 FAX (County Clerk); (402) 821-2132 FAX (Clerk Magistrate of the County Court); (402) 821-3179 FAX (District Court)
clerk@saline.nacone.org; greg.baumann@ courts.ne.gov; joyce.wusk@courts.ne.gov; jwusk@courts.state.ne.us
http://www.co.saline.ne.us
Linda Kastanek, County Clerk and Register of Deeds; Greg Baumann, Clerk Magistrate of the County Court; Joyce Wusk, Clerk of the District Court
(land records with Register of Deeds, naturalization records with Clerk of District Court, marriages only with County Clerk, probate records with County Court)
probate search service: no charge; copies of probate records: 25¢ each, $5.00 minimum ("send $5.00 and we will refund money we don't need")

Sarpy County
organized 1857, original county

Sarpy County Courthouse
1210 Golden Gate Drive
Papillion, NE 68046-2845
(402) 593-2107 (County Clerk, Suite 1118); (402) 593-5773 (Register of Deeds); (402) 593-5775 (Clerk Magistrate of the County Court, Suite 3142); (402) 593-2267 (District Court); (402) 593-4360 FAX (County Clerk); (402) 593-2338 FAX (Register of Deeds); (402) 593-2193 FAX (Clerk Magistrate of the County Court); (402) 593-4403 FAX (District Court)
deb@sarpy.com; clerk@sarpy.com (County Clerk); ldowding@sarpy.com; recorder@ sarpy.com; barb.pousson@courts.ne.gov; countycourt@sarpy.com; carol.kremer@ courts.ne.gov; ckremer@sarpy.com; districtcourt@sarpy.com
http://www.sarpy.com
Debra Houghtaling, County Clerk; Lloyd J. Dowding, Register of Deeds; Barb Pousson, Clerk Magistrate of the County Court; Ms. Carol Kremer, Clerk of the District Court
(marriage licenses from 1 January 1887 with County Clerk's Office, marriage licenses before 1887 with Sarpy County Historical Society, probate records with County Court)
probate search service: no charge; copies of probate records: $1.00 per page, no minimum

Saunders County

organized 1856 from Sarpy and Douglas counties

Saunders County Courthouse
433 North Chestnut
Wahoo, NE 68066
(402) 443-8101 (County Clerk, Suite 200, PO Box 61); (402) 443-8110 (Register of Deeds, Suite 203, PO Box 184); (402) 443-8119 (Clerk Magistrate of the County Court); (402) 443-8113 (District Court, Suite 300); (402) 443-5010 FAX (County Clerk); (402) 433-8121 (Clerk Magistrate of the County Court); (402) 443-8170 FAX (District Court)
countyclerk@co.saunders.ne.us; betty.zahourek@courts.ne.gov; paul.johnson@courts.ne.gov
http://www.saunderscounty.ne.gov
Patti J. Lindgren, County Clerk; Don Clark, Register of Deeds; Betty Zahourek, Clerk Magistrate of the County Court; Paul Johnson, Clerk of the District Court
(land records with Register of Deeds Office, naturalization records with Clerk of the District Court, probate records with County Court)
no probate search service; copies of probate records: 25¢ per page

Scotts Bluff County

organized 1881 from Cheyenne County

Scotts Bluff County Administration Building
1825 Tenth Street
Gering, NE 69341-2413
(308) 456-6600 (County Clerk, First Floor); (308) 436-6775 (Clerk Magistrate of the County Court); (308) 436-6641 (District Court, PO Box 47); (308) 436-6782 FAX (Clerk Magistrate of the County Court); (308) 436-6759 FAX (District Court)
vdulaney@scottsbluffcounty.org; jbauer@scottsbluffcounty.org; dianne.lana@courts.ne.gov; ann.rosenberry@courts.ne.gov; arosenberry@scottsbluffcounty.org
http://www.scottsbluffcounty.org
Vera Dulaney, County Clerk; Jean Bauer, Register of Deeds; Dianne Lana, Clerk Magistrate of the County Court; Ann Rosenberry, Clerk of the District Court

Seward County

organized 1867 from Lancaster County

Seward County Courthouse
529 Seward Street
Seward, NE 68434
(402) 643-2883 (County Clerk, Second Floor PO Box 190); (402) 643-3241 (Clerk Magistrate of the County Court, Third Floor, PO Box 37); (402) 643-4895 (District Clerk, Third Frloor, PO Box 36); (402) 643-2950 (Clerk Magistrate of the County Court); (402) 643-2950 FAX (County Court and District Court)
sschweitzer@alltel.net; sheila.beins@courts.ne.gov; jacquelyn.stewart@courts.ne.gov
http://www.connectseward.org/cgov
Sherry Schweitzer, County Clerk and Register of Deeds; Sheila Beins, Clerk Magistrate of the County Court; Jacquelyn "Jacque" Stewart, Clerk of the District Court
(land records from 1867, vital records with State Historical Society, probate records with County Court)
no probate search service; copies of probate records: 25¢ each, $5.00 for certified copies, no minimum

Sheridan County

organized 1885 from Sioux County

Sheridan County Courthouse
301 East Second Street
Rushville, NE 69360
(308) 327-2633 (County Clerk, PO Box 39); (308) 327-5656 (Clerk Magistrate of the County Court, PO Box 430); (308) 327-5654 (District Court, PO Box 581); (308) 327-5623 FAX (Clerk Magistrate of the County Court); (308) 327-5618 FAX (District Court)
clerk@sheridan.nacone.org (County Clerk); julie.krotz@courts.ne.gov; eloise.kampbell@courts.ne.gov; kampbell@haysprings.net
http://www.nacone.org/webpages/counties/co untywcbs/sheridan.htm
Sindy Coburn, County Clerk and Register of Deeds; Julie Krotz, Clerk Magistrate of the County Court; Eloise Kampbell, Clerk of the District Court
(land records, marriages, probate records with County Court)
no records search service

Sherman County

organized 1871 from Buffalo County

Sherman County Courthouse
630 O Street
Loup City, NE 68853
(308) 745-1513, ext. 100 (County Clerk and Register of Deeds, PO Box 456); (308) 745-1513, ext. 102 (Clerk Magistrate of the County Court, PO Box 55); (308) 745-1513, ext. 103 (District Court, PO Box 456); (308) 745-0297 FAX (County Clerk); (308) 745-1510 FAX (Clerk Magistrate of the County Court); (308) 745-1820 FAX (District Court)
janelle.mostek@courts.ne.gov; marcy.sekutera@courts.ne.gov
http://www.co.sherman.ne.us
Janelle Mostek, Clerk Magistrate of the County Court; Marcy L. Sekutera, County Clerk, Register of Deeds, and Clerk of the District Court
(land records from 1870s with County Clerk, naturalization records from late 1800s with Clerk, probate records from 1870s with County Court)
probate search service: no charge; copies of land records: 50¢ per page; copies of probate records: 25¢ per page, no minimum

Shorter County

(see Grant County)

Sioux County

organized 1877 from unorganized territory

Sioux County Courthouse
325 Main Street
Harrison, NE 69346
(308) 668-2475 (Clerk Magistrate of the County Court, PO Box 477); (308) 688-2443 (District Court, PO Box 158); (308) 668-2428 FAX (Clerk Magistrate of the County Court); (308) 668-2401 FAX (District Court)
linda.roberts@courts.ne.gov; wendi.mccormick@courts.ne.gov
http://www.co.sioux.ne.us
Linda Roberts, Clerk Magistrate of the County Court; Wendi McCormick, County Clerk, Register of Deeds, and Clerk of the District Court
(land records with County Clerk, only a few naturalization records with County Clerk, probate records with County Court)
probate search service: no charge; copies of probate records: 25¢ per page, no minimum

Stanton County

organized 1865 from Dodge County

Stanton County Courthouse
(804 Ivy Street—location)
PO Box 14 (mailing address)
Stanton, NE 68779
(402) 439-2221 (Clerk Magistrate of the County Court, PO Box 536); (402) 439-2222 (District Court, PO Box 347); (402) 439-2227 FAX (Clerk Magistrate of the County Court); (402) 439-2200 FAX (District Court)
phyllis.cleveland@courts.ne.gov; martha.detlefsent@courts.ne.gov; clerk@stanton.nacone.org (County Clerk)
http://www.co.stanton.ne.us
Phyllis Cleveland, Clerk Magistrate of the County Court; Martha Detlefsen, County

Clerk and Clerk of the District Court
(land records from May 1868 with Clerk, naturalization records from 1871 with Clerk, marriage licenses from June 1869 with Clerk, probate records from late 1800s with County Court)
probate search service: no charge; copies of probate records: 25¢ per page, no minimum

Taylor County

(see Cheyenne County)

Thayer County

organized 1872 from Jefferson County

Thayer County Courthouse
225 North Fourth Street
Hebron, NE 68370
(402) 768-6126 (County Clerk, PO Box 208); (402) 768-6325 (Clerk Magistrate of the County Court, PO Box 94); (402) 768-6116 (District Court, PO Box 297); (402) 768-2129 FAX (County Clerk); (402) 768-7232 FAX (Clerk Magistrate of the County Court); (402) 768-7232 FAX (District Court)
clerk@thayer.nacone.org (County Clerk); donna.fink@courts.ne.gov; nancy.mclaughlin@courts.ne.gov
http://www.thayercounty.ne.gov
Marie E. Rauner, County Clerk and Register of Deeds; Donna Fink, Clerk Magistrate of the County Court; Nancy C. McLaughlin, Clerk of the District Court
(originally named Nuckolls County; land records with County Clerk, naturalization records with District Court, dissolution of marriages with District Court, probate records from 1871 with County Court)
probate search service: no charge; copies of probate records: 25¢ per page, $1.00 per certified page, no minimum

Thomas County

organized 1887 from Blaine County

Thomas County Courthouse
503 Main Street
Thedford, NE 69166
(308) 645-2261; (308) 645-2266 (Clerk Magistrate of the County Court, PO Box 233); (308) 645-2261 (District Court, PO Box 226); (308) 645-2623 FAX (Clerk Magistrate of the County Court and District Court)
soscou89@nol.org (Register of Deeds); cindi.walz@courts.ne.gov; wendy.rinestine@courts.ne.gov
http://www.thomascountynebraska.us
LaDonna Haake, Register of Deeds; Cindi Walz, Clerk Magistrate of the County Court; Wendy Rinestine, Clerk of the District Court
(land records with County Clerk, marriages, probate records with County Court)
probate search service: $3.00; copies of probate records: 25¢ each, $1.00 minimum

Thurston County

organized 1865 from Burt County; name changed from Blackbird County in 1889

Thurston County Courthouse
106 South Fifth
Pender, NE 68047
(402) 385-2343 (County Clerk, PO Box G); (402) 385-3136 (Clerk Magistrate of the County Court, PO Box 129); (402) 385-3318 (District Court, PO Box 216); (402) 385-3143 FAX (Clerk Magistrate of the County Court); (402) 385-2762 FAX (District Court)
clerk@thurston.nacone.org (County Clerk); vickey.nelson@courts.ne.gov; phyllis.buchholz@courts.ne.gov; pendercourts@huntel.net (District Court)
http://www.hurstoncountynebraska.us
Tammy Moore, County Clerk and Register of Deeds; Vickey Nelson, Clerk Magistrate of the County Court; Phyllis Buchholz, Clerk of the District Court
(land records with County Clerk, naturalization records with Clerk of District Court,

marriages with County Clerk, probate records with County Court)
probate search service: no charge; copies of probate records: $1.00 per page, no minimum

Valley County
organized 1871 from unorganized territory

Valley County Courthouse
125 South 15th Street
Ord, NE 68862-1409
(308) 728-3831 (Clerk Magistrate of the County Court); (308) 728-3700 (District Court); (308) 728-7725 FAX (Clerk Magistrate of the County Court); (308) 728-7725 FAX (District Court)
pauline.grooms@courts.ne.gov;
jenette.lindsey@courts.ne.gov;
clerk@valley.nacone.org (County Clerk)
http://www.co.valley.ne.us
Pauline Grooms, Clerk Magistrate of the County Court; Jenette G. Lindsey, County Cler, Register of Deeds, and Clerk of the District Court

Washington County
organized 1854, original county

Washington County Courthouse
1555 Colfax Street
Blair, NE 68008-2022
(402) 426-6822 (County Clerk, PO Box 466); (402) 426-6824 (Register of Deeds, PO Box 446); (402) 426-6833 (Clerk Magistrate of the County Court, PO Box 615); (402) 426-6899 (District Clerk, PO Box 431); (402) 426-6825 FAX (County Clerk and Register of Deeds); (402) 426-6840 FAX (Clerk Magistrate of the County Court); (402) 426-6898 FAX (District Court)
clerk@washingtoncountyne.org; soscou29@nol.org; vicki.kuhlmann@courts.ne.gov; susan.paulsen@courts.ne.gov; districtclerk@washingtoncountyne.org
http://www.co.washington.ne.us
Merry M. Truhlsen, County Clerk; Karen A. Madsen, Register of Deeds; Vicki Kuhlmann, Clerk Magistrate of the County Court; Susan Paulsen, Clerk of the District Court
(land records from 1854, naturalization records with State Historical Society, marriages only from 1867 with County Clerk's Office, probate records from latter part of 1800s with County Court)
no probate search service; copies of marriage records: 25¢ each, $5.00 for certified copies; copies of probate records: 25¢ per page, no minimum

Wayne County
organized 1867 from Thurston County

Wayne County Courthouse
510 Pearl Street
Wayne, NE 68787
(402) 375-2288 (County Clerk, PO Box 248); (402) 375-1622 (Clerk Magistrate of the County Court); (402) 375-2260 (District Court); (402) 375-4137 FAX (County Clerk); (402) 375-2342 FAX (Clerk Magistrate of the County Court); (402) 375-0103 FAX (District Court)
coclerk@bloomnet.com; sue.clark@courts.ne.gov; deb.alleman@courts.ne.gov
http://county.waynene.org
Debra Finn, County Clerk and Register of Deeds; Sue Clark, Clerk Magistrate of the County Court; Debra Alleman-Dannelly, Clerk of the District Court

Webster County
organized 1871 from unorganized territory

Webster County Courthouse
621 North Cedar Street
Red Cloud, NE 68970
(402) 746-2777 (Clerk Magistrate of the County Court); (402)746-2716 (District Court, PO Box 250); (402) 746-2771 FAX (Clerk

Magistrate of the County Court); (402) 746-2710 FAX (District Court)
jolene.duffy@courts.ne.gov;
lonnie.knehans@courts.ne.gov;
soscou45@nol.org (County Clerk);
clerk@webster.nacone.org (County Clerk)
http://www.co.webster.ne.us
Jolene Duffy, Clerk Magistrate of the County Court; Lonnie Knehans, County Clerk, Register of Deeds, and Clerk of the District Court
(land records from 1872 with County Clerk, naturalization records from 1872 with County Clerk, probate records from 1872 with County Court)
probate search service: no charge; copies of probate records: $1.00 each, no minimum ("enclose SASE"); copies of marriages: $2.00 each

Wheeler County
organized 1877 from Boone County

Wheeler County Courthouse
Third and Main
Bartlett, NE 68622
(308) 654-3376 (Clerk Magistrate of the County Court, PO Box 127); (308) 654-3235 (District Court, PO Box 127); (308) 654-3176 FAX Clerk Magistrate of the County Court); (308) 654-3470 FAX (District Court)
judy.simpson@courts.ne.gov;
lorraine.woeppel@courts.ne.gov;
clerk@wheeler.nacone.org (County Clerk)
http://www.nacone.org/webpages/counties/countywebs/wheeler.htm
Judy Simpson, Clerk Magistrate of the County Court; Lorraine Woepple, County Clerk, Register of Deeds, and Clerk of the District Court

York County
organized 1855, original county

York County Courthouse
510 Lincoln Avenue
York, NE 68467
(402) 362-7759 (County Clerk); (402) 362-4925 (Clerk Magistrate of the County Court, Room 211); (402) 362-4038 (District Court); (402) 362-2577 (Clerk Magistrate of the County Court and District Court)
dcclerk@york.nacone.org (County Clerk);
kathy.barnes@courts.ne.gov; sharon.cuda@courts.ne.gov; scuda@courts.state.ne.us;
http://www.yorkcounty.ne.gov
Cynthia D. Heine, County Clerk and Register of Deeds; Kathy Barnes, Clerk Magistrate of the County Court; Sharon Cuda, Clerk of the District Court
(land records from 1855, naturalization records with State Historical Society, probate records with County Court)
copies of land records: 25¢ each

Capital: Carson City. Statehood: 31 October 1864 (ceded by Mexico in 1848, part of the Utah Territory from 1850 to 1861, when it became a separate territory)

Nevada has several Municipal Courts of limited jurisdiction in incorporated cities and towns. The state's Judicial Courts have limited jurisdiction over civil cases, misdemeanors and small claims. The District Courts which sit at each county seat have general jurisdiction over major civil cases, equity, probate and guardianship, felonies, misdemeanors and juvenile matters. First Judicial District: Carson City (which is an independent city, not located within a county) and Storey County; Second Judicial District: Washoe County; Third Judicial District: Churchill and Lyon counties; Fourth Judicial District: Elko County; Fifth Judicial District: Esmeralda, Mineral and Nye counties; Sixth Judicial District: Humboldt, Lander and Pershing counties; Seventh Judicial District: Eureka, Lincoln and White Pine counties; Eighth Judicial District: Clark County; Ninth Judicial District: Douglas County. The Supreme Court is the court of last resort.

Churchill County
organized 1861, original county

Churchill County Courthouse
155 North Taylor Street
Fallon, NV 89406
(775) 423-6001 (Recorder, Suite 131); (775) 423-6028 (Clerk/Treasurer, Suite 110); (775) 423-8933 FAX (Recorder); (775) 423-7069 FAX (Clerk/Treasurer)
recorder@churchillcounty.org; clerktreas-gv@churchillcounty.org;
khelton@churchillcounty.org
http://www.churchillcounty.org
Vicky Tripp, Recorder; Kelly G. Helton, Clerk/Treasurer
(land records with Recorder, marriages with Clerk/Treasurer)

Third Judicial District Court
73 North Main Street
Fallon, NV 89406
(775) 423-6080; (775) 423-8578 FAX
distct-shooten@churchillcounty.org
http://www.churchillcounty.org/dcourt
Shellie Hooten, Chief Deputy Court Clerk
(probate records)

Clark County
organized September 1909 from Lincoln County

Clark County Government Center
(500 South Grand Central Parkway, Second Floor, Las Vegas, NV 89106—location)
PO Box 551510 (mailing address)
Las Vegas, NV 89155-1501
(702) 455-4336
jav@co.clark.nv.us (Recorder)
http://co.clark.nv.us/recorder/recindex.htm
Debbie Conway, Recorder
(land records)
probate search service: $1.00 per year per name; copies of probate records: $1.00 per page, no minimum

Clark County Regional Justice Center
(200 South Third Street—location)
PO Box 551601 (mailing address)
Las Vegas, NV 89101-1601
(702) 671-0500
clerkem@co.clark.nv.usparrags@co.clark.nv.us
http://www.co.clark.nv.us
Shirley B. Parraguirre, County Clerk
(marriage license applications, probate records)
certified copies of marriage license applications: $4.00 each; certified copies of marriage certificates: $7.00 each (no personal checks accepted)

Douglas County
organized 1861, original county

Douglas County Clerk's Office
(1594 Esmeralda Avenue, Room 105—location)
PO Box 218 (mailing address)
Minden, NV 89423-0218
(775) 782-9014; (775) 782-9016 FAX
breed@co.douglas.nv.us;
bjgriffin@co.douglas.nv.us
http://cltr.co.douglas.nv.us
Barbara J. Griffin, Clerk/Treasurer
(probate records)

Douglas County Recorder
Douglas County Administration Building
1616 Eighth Street
Minden, NV 89423
(775) 782-9025; (775) 783-6413 FAX
wchristen@co.douglas.nv.us
http://www.douglascountynv.gov/sites/recorde
r/index.cfm
Werner Christen
(land records from 1855, births from 1887 to
1923, deaths from 1887 to 1933)
copies of records: $1.00 per page, $3.00 for
certification

Elko County
organized 1869 from Lander County

Elko County Clerk
571 Idaho Street, Third Floor
Elko, NV 89801-3770
(775) 753-4600; (775) 753-4610 FAX
clerk@elkocountynv.net;
wsmith@elkocountynv.net
http://www.elkocountynv.net/clerk.htm
Winifred "Win" Smith, Clerk
(naturalization records, probate records from
1869)
probate search service: $1.00 per year per name;
copies of probate records: $1.00 per page, no
minimum

Elko County Recorder
571 Idaho Street, Room 103
Elko, NV 89801-3770
(775) 738-6526; (775) 738-3299 FAX
recorder@elkocountynv.net
http://www.elkocountynv.net/recorder.htm
Jerry D. Reynolds
(land records, births and deaths from 1887 to
1915, marriages from 1869)
no land records search service; vital records
search service: no charge if approximate dates
are furnished

Esmeralda County
organized 1861, original county

Esmeralda County Courthouse
Corner of Crook and Euclid
Goldfield, NV 89013
(775) 485-6337 (Auditor/Recorder, PO Box
458); (775) 485-6367 (Clerk/Treasurer, PO
Box 547); (775) 485-6338 FAX (Auditor/
Recorder); (775) 485-6309 FAX (Clerk/
Treasurer)
celgan@citlink.net
http://www.accessesmeralda.com
Karen Scott, Auditor/Recorder; LaCinda
"Cindy" Elgan, Clerk/Treasurer
(births from 1887–1911, duplicate birth
certificates 1924–1945, deaths 1887–1911,
duplicate death certificates 1924–1969,
marriage certificates from 1863, deeds from
1863, tax rolls from 1865, funeral records
1906–1969 with Recorder; naturalization
records and probate records with County
Clerk)
certified copies of probate records: $5.00

Eureka County
organized 1873 from Lander County

Eureka County Courthouse
Main Street
Eureka, NV 89316
(775) 237-5263 (Recorder/Auditor, PO Box

556); (775) 237-5262 (Clerk-Treasurer, PO
Box 677); (775) 237-5614 FAX
(Recorder/Auditor); (775) 237-6015 FAX
(Clerk-Treasurer)
mrebal@eurekanv.org;
jberg_ecct@eurekanv.org
http://www.co.eureka.nv.us
Michael N. Rebaleati, Auditor/Recorder; Jackie
Berg, Clerk/Treasurer
(land records with County Recorder,
naturalization records through the 1940s with
County Clerk, vital records with County
Recorder, probate records with County Clerk)
probate search service: $1.00 per year; copies of
probate records: $1.00 per page, $1.00
minimum

Humboldt County
organized 1861, original county

Humboldt County Courthouse
50 West Fifth Street
Winnemucca, NV 89445-0352
(775) 623-6412 (Recorder, County Annex
Building, corner of Fourth and Bridge
Streets); (775) 623-6343 (Clerk/Welfare
Director, Room 207); (775) 623-6337 FAX
(Recorder); (775) 623-6309 FAX
(Clerk/Welfare Director)
recorder@hcnv.us; coclerk@hcnv.us
http://www.hcnv.us/recorder/recorder.htm
Mary Ann Hammond, Recorder; Tami Rae
Spero, Clerk/Welfare Director
(land records with Recorder, naturalization
records, vital records with Nancy Johnson,
Registrar of Vital Statistics, City-County
Complex, Winnemucca, NV 89445, probate
records with County Clerk)
probate search service: $1.00 per year; copies of
probate records: $1.00 per page, no minimum
("must be written request")

Lake County
(see Washoe County)

Lander County
organized 1862 from Humboldt and St. Mary's
counties

Lander County Courthouse
315 South Humboldt Street
Battle Mountain, NV 89820
(775) 635-5173 (Recorder); (775) 635-5738
(Clerk); (775) 635-8272 FAX (Recorder);
(775) 635-5761 FAX (Clerk)
record@the-onramp.net; gladylind@yahoo.com;
clerk@landercounty.org
http://www.landercounty.org
Idonna Trevino, Recorder; Gladys Burris, Clerk
(land records, naturalization records, vital
records, probate records)
records search service: $1.00 per year; copies of
records: $1.00 each, $3.00 for certification

Lincoln County
organized 1866 from Nye County

Lincoln County Courthouse
1 North Main Street
Pioche, NV 89043-0090
(775) 962-5495 (Recorder, PO Box 218); (775)
962-5390 (Clerk, PO Box 90); (775) 962-5180
FAX (Recorder)
lcclerk32@hotmail.com
http://www.co.lincoln.nv.us;
http://www.lincolncountynevada.com
Leslie Boucher, Recorder/Auditor; Lisa Lloyd,
Clerk
(land records with Recorder/Auditor,
naturalization records with Clerk, vital records
with Clerk, probate records with Clerk)
probate search service: $1.00 per year; copies of
probate records: $1.00 each, no minimum

Lyon County
organized 1861, original county

Lyon County Courthouse
27 South Main Street

Yerington, NV 89447
(775) 463-6581 (Recorder); (775) 463-6501
(Clerk); (775) 463-6585 FAX (Recorder);
(775) 463-5305 FAX (Clerk)
mkassebaum@lyon-county.org;
mmilligan@lyon-county.org; nbryan@lyon-
county.org
http://www.lyon-county.org
Margie Kassebaum, Records Storage Manager;
Mary Milligan, Recorder; Nikki A. Bryan,
Clerk

Mineral County
organized 1911 from Esmeralda County

Mineral County Courthouse
105 South "A" Street
Hawthorne, NV 89415
(775) 945-3676 (Recorder, PO Box 1447); (775)
945-2446 (Clerk, Suite 1, PO Box 1450); (775)
945-1749 FAX (Recorder); (775) 945-0706
FAX (Clerk)
mincorec@gbis.com;
mineralcountyclerk@gbis.com
http://www.mineralcountygovernment.com
Christine Hoferer, Recorder; Cherrie A. George,
Clerk
(land records and marriages with Recorder; real
property tax rolls, probate records,
naturalization records to 23 August 1957 with
County Clerk and Treasurer's Office)
probate search service: $1.00 per year searched
per name; copies of probate records: $1.00
per page, no minimum

Nye County
organized 1864 from Esmeralda County

Nye County Courthouse
101 Radar Road
Tonopah, NV 89049
(775) 482-8116 (Recorder, PO Box 1111); (775)
482-8134 (Clerk, PO Box 1031); (775) 482-
8111 FAX (Recorder); (775) 482-8133 FAX
(Clerk)
bfoster@nyecounty.net; sam.merlino@
co.nye.nv.us; smerlino@nyecounty.net
http://www.nycounty.net/Recorder/recorder.html
Donna Motis, Recorder; Sandra L. "Sam"
Merlino, Clerk
(land records with County Recorder,
naturalization records through 1911 with
County Clerk, vital records with County
Recorder, probate records with County Clerk)
probate search service: $1.00 per year searched;
copies of probate records: $1.00 per page, no
minimum

Ormsby County
(see Carson City)

Pershing County
organized 1919 from Humboldt County

Pershing County Courthouse
398 Main Street
Lovelock, NV 89419
(775) 273-2408 (Recorder-Auditor, PO Box
736); (775) 273-2208 (Clerk, PO Box 820);
(775) 273-1039 FAX (Recorder-Auditor);
(775) 273-3015 FAX (Clerk)
pcrecorder@gbis.com; dmoura@pershing
county.net; dgiles@pershingcounty.net
http://www.pershingcounty.net/index.htm
Darlene Moura, Recorder; Donna Giles, Clerk
(land records with Recorder-Auditor,
naturalization records from 1919 to 1960 and
probate records with Clerk)
probate search service: $1.00 per year; copies of
probate records: $1.00 per page, no minimum

Roop County
(see Washoe County)

Storey County
organized 1861, original county

Storey County Courthouse
B Street

Virginia City, NV 89440
(775) 847-0967 (Recorder and Auditor, PO Box
1493); (775) 847-0969 (Clerk-Treasurer,
Drawer D); (775) 847-1009 FAX (Recorder
and Auditor); (775) 847-0921 FAX (Clerk-
Treasurer)
stcorecorder@775.net; recorder@
storycounty.org; ldufresne@storycounty.org;
clerk@storeycounty.org
http://www.storeycounty.org
Maggie Lowther, Recorder and Auditor;
Lorraine Dufresne, Clerk-Treasurer
(deeds from 1859 to date with County Recorder
and Auditor, births from 1887 to 1949, deaths
from 1887 to 1949, and marriages [index from
1862] with County Recorder and Auditor,
marriage licenses with Clerk-Treasurer,
probate records with Clerk-Treasurer)

Washoe County

organized 1861, original county; in 1883
annexed Roop County (called Lake County
until 1862), which was also an original county

Washoe County Clerk's Office
(75 Court Street, Room 131—location)
PO Box 30083 (mailing address)
Reno, NV 89520
(775) 328-3260; (775) 328-3110 (Court Clerk)
aharvey@mail.co.washoe.nv.us
http://www.co.washoe.nv.us
Amy Harvey, Clerk
(naturalization records and probate records)
probate search service: $1.00 per year per case;
copies of probate records: $1.00 per page, no
minimum

Washoe County Recorder
(1001 East Ninth Street, Suite 140/150—
location)
PO Box 11130 (mailing address)
Reno, NV 89520
(775) 328-3661; (775) 325-8010 FAX
kburke@mail.co.washoe.nv.us
http://www.co.washoe.nv.us
Kathryn L. "Kathy" Burke
(land records)

White Pine County

organized 1869 from Elko and Lincoln counties

White Pine County Courthouse
801 Clark Street
Ely, NV 89301
(775) 289-4567 (Recorder, Suite 1); (775) 289-
3016 (County Assessor); (775) 289-2341
(Clerk, Suite 4, PO Box 659); (775) 289-1566
FAX (Recorder); (775) 289-2544 FAX (Clerk)
wprecaud@idsely.com; wpclerk@mwpower.net
http://www.whitepinecounty.net
Martha Rivera Sindelor, Recorder; Donna Bath,
Clerk
(land records with County Assessor,
naturalization records with County Clerk,
probate records with County Clerk)
probate search service: no charge; copies of
probate records: 50¢ per page, no minimum

*Capital: Concord. Statehood: 21 June 1788 (became a
separate royal province in 1679, relinquished Vermont
in 1782)*

New Hampshire has several Municipal Courts
of limited jurisdiction whose duties, since 1964,
have been assumed by the District Courts as
vacancies occur. The District Courts handle a
variety of civil and criminal matters and have
original juvenile jurisdiction.
The Probate Court of New Hampshire has
special jurisdiction over probate matters and sits
in each county seat. The New Hampshire
Superior Court is the court of general
jurisdiction and sits at all the county seats
(except Woodsville), plus Lancaster, Manchester
and North Haverhill. The New Hampshire
Supreme Court hears appeals at Concord.
For Provincial Deeds from about 1670 to
1772, titles to state-owned property, and probate
from about 1650 to 1772, contact Division of
Records Management and Archives,
Department of State, 71 South Fruit Street,
Concord, NH 03301-2410, (603) 271-2236,
(603) 271-2272 FAX.

Heritage New Hampshire
PO Box 1776
Glen, NH 03838
(603) 383-4293
http://www.heritagenh.com

Belknap County

organized 1840 from Strafford County

Belknap County Probate Court
(64 Court Street—location)
PO Box 1343 (mailing address)
Laconia, NH 03247-1343
(603) 524-0903
http://www.courts.state.nh.us/probate/index.htm
Karen H. Brickner, Register of Probate
(probate records)
probate search service: no charge; copies of
probate records: $2.00 for the first page and
50¢ for each additional page, no minimum

Belknap County Register of Deeds
(64 Court Street—location)
PO Box 1343 (mailing address)
Laconia, NH 03247
(603) 524-5420; (603) 527-5421; (603) 527-5429
FAX
rnormandin@nhdeeds.com
http://www.belknapcounty.org
Rachel M. Normandin
(land records: index and images from 1765
available on-line at
http://www.nhdeeds.com)
copies purchased on site: $1.00 per page; copies
puchased from the Internet: $2.00 per page;
copy faxed from the Registry of Deeds office:
$3.00 per page

Belknap County Superior Court
(64 Court Street—location)
PO Box 578 (mailing address)
Laconia, NH 03247-0578
(603) 524-3570
http://www.courts.statenh.us/courtlocations.bel
ksupedir.htm
Dana Zucker, Clerk of Court
(naturalization records)

Carroll County

organized 1840 from Strafford, Coös and
Grafton counties

Carroll County Administration Building
(Route 171—location)
PO Box 152 (mailing address)
Ossipee, NH 03864
(603) 539-4872
http://publicrecords.onlinesearches.com/NH_
Carroll.htm
Lillian O. Brookes, Register of Deeds

(land records)
no land records search service; copies of land
records: $1.00 per page

Carroll County Probate Court
(County Courthouse, 96 Water Village Road—
location)
Box 1 (mailing address)
Ossipee, NH 03864
(603) 539-4123
http://www.courts.state.nh.us/probate/index.htm
Gail A. Monet, Register of Probate
(probate records from 1840 to date ["The
majority of our records prior to 1840 are at
Strafford County"])
probate search service: no charge to find out if a
named individual has a file; copies of probate
records: $2.00 for the first page and 50¢ for
each additional page (payable in advance), no
minimum; "We need a check before we send
out copies; call or write to request fee for a
copying job."

Carroll County Superior Court
(96 Water Village Road—location)
Box 3 (mailing address)
Ossipee, NH 03864
(603) 539-2201
http://www.courts.state.nh.us/courtlocations/c
arrsupedir.htm
Patricia A. Lenz, Clerk

Cheshire County

organized 1769, original county

Cheshire County Register of Deeds
(33 West Street—location)
PO Box 584 (mailing address)
Keene, NH 03431
(603) 352-0403; (603) 352-7678 FAX
ehubal@nhdeeds.com
http://www.nhdeeds.com/chsr/web/start.htm;
http://www.co.cheshire.nh.us/Deeds/index.
html
Evelyn S. Hubal
(land records: index and images from 1765
available on-line at
http://www.nhdeeds.com)
copies purchased on site: $1.00 per page; copies
puchased from the Internet: $2.00 per page;
copy faxed from the Registry of Deeds office:
$3.00 per page

Cheshire County Register of Probate
(12 Court Street—location)
PO Box 444 (mailing address)
Keene, NH 03431
(603) 357-7786
http://www.co.cheshire.nh.us/Probate/index.html
Anna Z. Tilton
(probate records)

Cheshire County Superior Court
12 Court Street
Keene, NH 03431
(603) 352-6902
http://www.co.cheshire.nh.us/SupCourt/index.
html
Barbara Hogan, Clerk of Court

Coös County

organized 1803 from Grafton County; includes
the following unincorporated areas: Atkinson
and Gilmanton Academy Grant, Bean's
Grant, Bean's Purchase, Cambridge, Cutt's
Grant, Dix's Grant, Dixville, Erving's
Location, Green's Grant, Hadley's Purchase,
Kilkenny, Lowe and Burbank's Grant,
Martin's Location, Odell, Pinkham's Grant
and Pinkham's Notch, Sargent's Purchase,
Second College Grant, Success (organized
1773), and Thompson and Meserve's
Purchase

Coös County Probate Court
55 School Street, Suite 104
Lancaster, NH 03584
(603) 788-2001 Register of Probate
http://www.courts.state.nh.us/courtlocations/c
oosprobdir.htm

Terri L. Peterson, Register of Probate

Coös County Register of Deeds
55 School Street, Suite 103
Lancaster, NH 03584
(603) 788-2392; (603) 788-4291 FAX
claimirande@ttlc.net
http://www.nhdeeds.com/coos/web/start.htm;
http://www.northnh.com (Chamber of
Commerce);
http:/extension.unh.edu/Counties/Coos/Co
os.htm (Cooperative Extension)
Carole A. Lamirande
(land records: index and images from 1765
available on-line at
http://www.nhdeeds.com)
copies purchased on site: $1.00 per page; copies
puchased from the Internet: $2.00 per page;
copy faxed from the Registry of Deeds office:
$3.00 per page

Coös County Superior Court
55 School Street, Suite 301
Lancaster, NH 03584
(603) 788-4702
http://www.courts.state.nh.us/courtlocations/c
oossupedir.htm
David P. Carlson, Clerk

Grafton County
organized 1769, original county

Grafton County Register of Probate
(Administration Building, 3855 Dartmouth
College Highway—location)
Box 3 (mailing address)
North Haverhill, NH 03774
(603) 787-6931
http://www.graftoncountynh.us; http://www.
courts.state.nh.us/courtlocations/grafprobdir.
htm
Rebecca Wyman, Register of Probate
(naturalization and probate records)

Grafton County Register of Deeds
Administration Building, 3855 Dartmouth
College Highway
North Haverhill, NH 03774
(603) 787-6921
http://www.graftoncountynh.us
Bill Sharp

Grafton County Superior Court
Administration Building, 3855 Dartmouth
College Highway
North Haverhill, NH 03774
(603) 787-6961
http://www.courts.state.nh.us/courtlocations/g
rafsupedir.htm
Robert B. Muh, Clerk

Hillsborough County
organized 1769, original county

Hillsborough County Probate Court
(30 Spring Street—location)
PO Box 387 (mailing address)
Nashua, NH 03061-0387
(603) 882-1231
http://www.courts.state.nh.us/courtlocations/h
illsprobdir.htm
Robert R. Rivard, Register of Probate
(probate records from 1771)
no probate search service; copies of probate
records: available, no minimum

Hillsborough County Register of Deeds
(Temple Street Courthouse, 19 Temple Street,
Nashua, NH 03060-3444—location)
PO Box 370 (mailing address)
Nashua, NH 03061-0370
(603) 882-6933; (603) 882-7527 FAX
jmacdon@ma.ultranet.com;
hilscopies@nhdeeds.com
http://www.hillsboroughcountynh.org; http://
www.nhdeeds.com/hils/web/start.htm
Judith A. MacDonald
(land records: index and images from 1765
available on-line at
http://www.nhdeeds.com)
copies purchased on site: $1.00 per page; copies

puchased from the Internet: $2.00 per page;
copy faxed from the Registry of Deeds office:
$3.00 per page

Hillsborough County Superior Court North
300 Chestnut Street
Manchester, NH 03101
(603) 669-7410
http://www.courts.state.nh.us/courtlocations/h
illsupedir.htm
John Safford, Clerk
(Hillsborough County naturalization records)

Hillsborough County Superior Court South
(30 Spring Street—location)
PO Box 2072 (mailing address)
Nashua, NH 03061-2072
(603) 883-6461
http://www.courts.state.nh.us/courtlocations/h
illsupedir.htm
Marshall Buttrick, Clerk
(Hillsborough County naturalization records)

Merrimack County
organized 1823 from Rockingham and
Hillsborough counties

Merrimack County Probate Court
163 North Main Street
Concord, NH 03301-5068
(603) 224-9589
http://www.courts.state.nh.us/courtlocations/
merrprobdir.htm;
http://www.ci.concord.nh.us/govmnt/
county/concordv2.asp?siteindx=Z20,09
Jane D. W. Bradstreet, Register
no probate search service; copies of probate
records: 50¢ per page, no minimum

Merrimack County Register of Deeds
(163 Nort Main Street, Concord, NH 03301—
location)
PO Box 248 (mailing address)
Concord, NH 03302-0248
(603) 228-0101; (603) 226-0868 FAX
merctydeed@aol.com
http://www.ci.concord.nh.us/govmnt/county/
concordv2.asp?siteindx=L05,22http://www.
merrimackcounty.nh.us.landata.com
Kathi L. Guay, Registrar
(land records: index and images from 1765
available on-line at
http://www.nhdeeds.com)
copies purchased on site: $1.00 per page; copies
puchased from the Internet: $2.00 per page;
copy faxed from the Registry of Deeds office:
$3.00 per page

Merrimack County Superior Court
(163 North Main Street—location)
PO Box 2880 (maiing address)
Concord, NH 03302-2880
(603) 225-5501
http://www.courts.state.nh.us/courtlocations/
merrsupedir.htm
William McGraw, Clerk

Rockingham County
organized 1769, original county

Rockingham County Probate Court
(10 Route 125, Brentwood, NH 03833—
location)
PO Box 789 (mailing address)
Kingston, NH 03848
Exeter, NH 03833
(603) 642-7117
http://co.rockingham.nh.us
Andrew Christie, Jr., Register
probate search service: $5.00; copies of probate
records: $2.00 for the first page of will and
50¢ for each additional page of will, 50¢ per
page for all other copies

Rockingham County Register of Deeds
(Courthouse, 10 Route 125, Brentwood, NH
03833—location)
PO Box 896 (mailing address)
Kingston, NH 03848
(603) 642-5526; (603) 642-8548 FAX; (603) 642-
5930 FAX

thcrock@ttlc.net
http://www.co.rockingham.nh.us; http://www.
nhdeeds.com/rock/web/start.htm
Cathy Ann Stacey
(land records: index and images from 1765
available on-line at
http://www.nhdeeds.com)
copies purchased on site: $1.00 per page; copies
puchased from the Internet: $2.00 per page;
copy faxed from the Registry of Deeds office:
$3.00 per page

Rockingham County Superior Court
(Courthouse, 10 Route 125, Brentwood, NH
03833—location)
PO Box 1258 (mailing address)
Kingston, NH 03848-1258
(603) 642-5256
http://www.courts.state.nh.us/courtlocations/r
ocksupedir.htm
Raymond Taylor, Clerk

Strafford County
organized 1769, original county

**Strafford County Justice and Administration
Building**
(259 County Farm Road—location)
PO Box 799 (mailing address)
Dover, NH 03820-0799
(603) 742-1741 (Register of Deeds); (603) 742-
3065 (Superior Court Clerk); (603) 742-2550
(Register of Probate); (603) 749-5130 FAX
(Registry of Deeds)
llessard@ttlc.net
http://co.strafford.nh.us; http://www.nhdeeds.
com/stfd/web/start.htm
Leo E. Lessard, Register of Deeds; Julie W.
Howard, Superior Court Clerk; Kimberly
Quint, Register of Probate
(land records: index and images from 1765
available on-line at
http://www.nhdeeds.com)
probate search service: no charge; copies of
probate records: "Varies by document and
size of document," 50¢ minimum; copies of
land records purchased on site: $1.00 per
page; copies of land records puchased from
the Internet: $2.00 per page; copy faxed from
the Registry of Deeds office: $3.00 per page

Sullivan County
organized 1827 from Cheshire County

Sullivan County Probate Court
(22 Main Street—location)
PO Box 417 (mailing address)
Newport, NH 03773-0417
(603) 863-3150
http://www.courts.state.nh.us/courtlocations/s
ullprobdir.htm
Diane M. Davis, Register of Probate

Sullivan County Register of Deeds
(14 Main Street, Second Floor—location)
PO Box 448 (mailing address)
Newport, NH 03773
(603) 863-2110; (603) 863-0013 FAX
sudeeds@sugar-river.net
http://www.sullivancountynh.gov;
htt://www.nhdeeds.com/slvn/web/start.htm
Sharron A. King
(land records from 1825 to date; index and
images from 1765 available on-line at
http://www.nhdeeds.com)
copies purchased on site: $1.00 per page; copies
puchased from the Internet: $2.00 per page;
copy faxed from the Registry of Deeds office:
$3.00 per page

Sullivan County Superior Court
22 Main Street
Newport, NH 03773
(603) 863-3450
http://www.courts.state.nh.us/courtlocations/s
ullsupedir.htm
James I. Peale, Clerk of Court

NEW JERSEY

Capital: Trenton. Statehood: 18 December 1787 (ceded to England in 1644, became a royal province in 1702)

New Jersey's courts of limited jurisdiction include the New Jersey Municipal Courts, the New Jersey Surrogate's Office and New Jersey Tax Court. General jurisdiction is exercised by the New Jersey Superior Court which is divided into Appellate, Law and Chancery Divisions, which sit in fifteen vicinages. Vicinage One: Atlantic and Cape May counties; Vicinage Two: Bergen County; Vicinage Three: Burlington County; Vicinage Four: Camden County; Vicinage Five: Essex County; Vicinage Six: Hudson County; Vicinage Seven: Mercer County; Vicinage Eight: Middlesex County: Vicinage Nine: Monmouth County; Vicinage Ten: Morris and Sussex counties; Vicinage Eleven: Passaic County; Vicinage Twelve: Union County; Vicinage Thirteen: Hunterdon, Somerset and Warren counties; Vicinage Fourteen: Ocean County; Vicinage Fifteen: Cumberland, Gloucester and Salem counties. The New Jersey Supreme Court is the court of last resort.

New Jersey State Archives, Division of Archives and Records Management, Department of State, 185 West State Street, CN 307, Trenton, NJ 08625-0307 has birth, death and marriage records, arranged by county, from 1 May 1848 to 30 April 1878, available for a $2.00 search/copy fee, as well as wills and inventories before 1901, deeds filed with the Secretary of State, mostly before 1790, marriage bonds or licenses filed with the Secretary before 1800. Vital records after 1 May 1878 are available from New Jersey Department of Health, State Registrar—Search Unit, Bureau of Vital Statistics, CN 370, Trenton, NJ 08625-0370.

Atlantic County
organized 1837 from Gloucester County

Atlantic County Surrogate
Altlantic County Civil Court House
1201 Bacharch Boulevard
Altantic City, NJ 08401
(609) 343-2341; (609) 343-2197 FAX
jcarney@acmail.aclink.org
http://www.aclink.org/surrogate
James A. "Jim" Carney, Surrogate
(wills, estates, probate court matters)

Atlantic County Clerk
Old Criminal Courthouse
5901 Main Street
Mays Landing, NJ 08330
(609) 641-7867; (609) 625-4011; (609) 625-4738 FAX
McGettigan_ed@aclink.org
http://www.aclink.org;
　http://www.atlanticcountyclerk.org
Edward P. McGettigan
(deeds from 1837 to date [certified copies available], declarations of intention, court hearings, petitions for naturalization and verification of naturalization records)

Bergen County
organized 1683, original county

Bergen County Clerk
1 Bergen County Plaza
Hackensack, NJ 07601
(201) 336-7000
http://co.bergen.nj.us/countyclerk
Kathleen A. Donovan

Bergen County Justice Center
Main and Essex Streets, Room 211
Hackensack, NJ 07601-7017
(201) 646-2252
http://www.co.bergen.nj.us/Surrogate/Index.htm
Michael R. Dressler, Surrogate

Burlington County
organized 1694, original county

Burlington County Courthouse
Courts Facility, 49 Rancocas Road
Mount Holly, NJ 08060-1384
(609) 265-5122 (County Clerk, First Floor, PO Box 6000); (609) 265-5005 (Surrogate, Room 102); (609) 265-0696 FAX (County Clerk)
phaines@co.burlington.nj.us;
　gkotch@co.burlington.nj.us
http://www.co.burlington.nj.us
Philip E. Haines, County Clerk; George Kotch, Surrogate

Camden County
organized 1844 from Gloucester County

Camden County Courthouse
520 Market Street, Room 102
Camden, NJ 08102-1375
(856) 225-5300; (856) 225-7100 FAX
jbeach@camdencounty.com
http://www.co.camden.nj.us/government/offic es/clerk/index.html
James Beach, County Clerk %
(land records with County Register of Deeds and Mortgages, County Clerk's Office; naturalization records from 1800 to 1933 with County Clerk)
naturalization records search service: $10.00; copies of land records: $1.00 per page, $1.00 for certification; copies of naturalizations: 75¢ for each of the first ten pages, 50¢ per page for each of the next ten pages and 25¢ for each additional page

Camden County Surrogate
415 Federal Street
Camden, NJ 08103
(856) 225-7282
patjones@camdencounty.com
http://www.co.camden.nj.us/government/offic es/surrogate/index.html
Patricia Egan Jones
(probate records)

Cape May County
organized 1692

Cape May County Courthouse
(7 North Main Street, DN 109—location)
PO Box 5000 (mailing address)
Cape May Court House, NJ 08210-5000
(609) 465-1010; (609) 465-8625 FAX
coclerk@co.cape-may.nj.us
http://www.co.cape-my.nj.us
Rita Marie Fulginiti, County Clerk %
(land records from 1692 [Liber of Deeds A, in vault, begins 1692 with deeds recorded as early as 1694], naturalization records from 1896 through 1964 [naturalization records from 1964 with Atlantic County], marriages from 1745 to 1878)

Cape May County Surrogate Court
(Court Building, 9 North Main Street—location)
4 Moore Road, Department 207 (mailing address)
Cape May Court House, NJ 08210
(609) 463-6666; (609) 463-6454 FAX
surrogate@co.cape-may.nj.us
http://www.capemaycountygov.net/Cit-e-Access/webpage.cfm?TID=5&TPID=478
W. Robert Hentges, Surrogate
(probate records from 1804 with Surrogate Court, probate records before 1804 with New Jersey Archives, Trenton)
probate search service: no charge; copies of probate records: $3.00 per page

Cumberland County
organized 1748 from Salem County

Cumberland County Courthouse
60 West Broad Street
Bridgeton, NJ 08302
(856) 451-8000, ext. 4864 (County Clerk); (856) 453-4800 (Surrogate's Office, Suite A111); (856) 455-1410 FAX (County Clerk); (856)
451-7356 FAX (Surrogate's Office)
http://www.co.cumberland.nj.us/govtserv/dep artments/county%5Fclerk;
http://www.co.cumberland.nj.us/govtserv/d epartments/surrogate
Gloria Noto, County Clerk; Arthur J. Marchand, Esq., Surrogate
(land records from late 1700s with County Clerk, naturalization records from 1800 with County Clerk, old Marriage Books A and B [first entry 1795] with County Clerk, wills from 1803 with Surrogate's Office)

Essex County
organized 1683, original county

Essex County Hall of Records
465 Martin Luther King Boulevard
Newark, NJ 07102
(973) 621-4921 (County Clerk, Room 247, PO Box 690); (973) 621-4960 (County Register of Deeds); (973) 621-4900 (Surrogate, Room 206); (973) 621-4937 (Surrogate Records); (973) 621-2654 FAX (Surrogate)
info@essexclerk.com; essexclerk@nac.net; essexreg@nac.net
http://www.essex-countynj.org
Christopher J. Durkin, County Clerk; Carole A. Graves, County Register of Deeds and Mortgages; Joseph P. Brennan, Jr., Surrogate

Gloucester County
organized 1686, original county

Gloucester County Courthouse
(1 North Broad Street—location)
PO Box 129 (mailing address)
Woodbury, NJ 08096
(856) 853-3237; (856) 853-3327 FAX
jhogan@co.gloucester.nj.us
http://www.co.gloucester.nj.us
James N. Hogan, County Clerk %

Gloucester County Surrogate's Office
(17 North Broad Street—location)
PO Box 177 (mailing address)
Woodbury, NJ 08096
(856) 853-3282; (856) 853-3311 FAX
ssalvatore@co.gloucester.nj.us
http://www.co.gloucester.nj.us
Stephen Salvatore, Surrogate

Hudson County
organized 22 February 1840 from Bergen County

Justice William J. Brennan Jr. Court House
583 Newark Avenue
Jersey City, NJ 07306-2301
(201) 795-6112 (Clerk); (201) 795-6577 (Register); (201) 795-6574 (Register's Record Room); (201) 795-2581 FAX (Clerk)
jinclan@hudsoncountynj.org (Acting County Clerk)
http://www.hudsoncountynj.org
Mary Jane Desmond, Acting County Clerk; Willie J. Flood, Register of Deeds and Mortgages
(land records with County Register, naturalization records from 1840 to 1989 with County Clerk, vital records with County Registrar)

Hudson County Surrogate's Court
Old County Administration Building
595 Newark Avenue, Room 107
Jersey City, NJ 07306
(201) 795-6377
ddeleo@hudsoncountynj.org
http://www.hudsonsurrogate.com
Donald W. DeLeo, Surrogate
probate search service: $3.00 per estate; copies of probate records: $3.00 per page, no minimum

Hunterdon County
organized 1714 from Burlington County

Hunterdon County Historic Court House
(71 Main Street, Building #3A—location)

PO Box 2900 (mailing address)
Flemington, NJ 08822-2900
(908) 788-1214; (908) 782-4068 FAX
countyclerk@co.hunterdon.nj.us
http://www.co.hunterdon.nj.us/countyclerk.htm
Mary H. Melfi, County Clerk
(land records from 1785 to date, mortgages
from 1766 to date, naturalization records
from 1808 to 1965)
copies of land and naturalization records: $1.00
per page

Hunterdon County Surrogate's Office
(65 Park Avenue—location)
PO Box 2900 (mailing address)
Flemington, NJ 08822-2900
(908) 788-1156
shoffman@co.hunterdon.nj.us
http://www.co.hunterdon.nj.us/depts/surrog/
message.htm
Susan J. Hoffman, Surrogate
(probate records)

Mercer County
organized 1838 from Hunterdon and Middlesex
counties

Mercer County Courthouse
(209 South Broad Street, Room 100—location)
PO Box 8068 (mailing address)
Trenton, NJ 08650-0068
(609) 989-6464; (609) 989-1111 FAX
cathyd@mercercounty.org
http://j.gov/counties/mercer/officials/clerk/in
dex.html
Paula Sollami-Covello, County Clerk

Mercer County Surrogate's Office
(Civil Court House, 175 South Broad Street,
Room 420, Trenton, NJ 08608—location)
PO Box 8068 (mailing address)
Trenton, NJ 08650-0068
(609) 989-6331
dgerofsky@mercercounty.org
http://nj.gov/counties/mercer/officials/surrog
ate
Diane Gerofsky, Surrogate

Middlesex County
organized 1683, original county

Middlesex County Administration Building
1 John F. Kennedy Square
New Brunswick, NJ 08901-2153
(732) 745-3005 (Clerk); (732) 745-3055
(Surrogate, First Floor)
elainef544@aol.com;
surrogate@co.middlesex.nj.us
http://www.co.middlesex.nj.us
Elaine M. Flynn, County Clerk; Kevin J.
Hoagland, Surrogate

Monmouth County
organized 1683, original county

Monmouth County Hall of Records
(1 East Main Street—location)
PO Box 1255 (mailing address)
Freehold, NJ 07728-1255
(908) 431-7324 (County Clerk); (908) 431-7330
(Surrogate)
mcfrench@co.monmouth.nj.us;
rpeters@co.monmouth.nj.us
http://www.shore.co.monmouth.nj.us
Ms. M. Claire French, County Clerk; Rosemarie
Peters, Surrogate
(deeds from 1665 to date with County Clerk,
naturalization records from 1808 to 1991 with
County Clerk, marriage returns from 1790 to
1900, probate records from the mid-1800s,
will books from 1875 to date with Surrogate)
copies of land records: 50¢ per page for each of
the first ten pages, 25¢ per page for each of
the next ten pages and 10¢ per page for each
additional page

Morris County
organized 1739 from Hunterdon County

Morris County Administration and Records

Building
Court Street
Morristown, NJ 07960
(973) 285-6059 (Clerk, PO Box 315); (973) 285-
6500 (Surrogate, Fifth Floor, PO Box 900);
(973) 829-8599 FAX (Surrogate)
jbramhall@clerk.morris.nj.us;
jpecoraro@co.morris.nj.us
http://www.co.morris.nj.us;
http://www.clerk.morris.nj.us;
http://www.morrissurrogate.com
Joan Bramhall, County Clerk; John Pecoraro,
Surrogate

Ocean County
organized 1850 from Monmouth County

Ocean County Courthouse
(118 Washington Street—location)
PO Box 2191 (mailing address)
Toms River, NJ 08754-2191
(732) 929-2018 (Clerk); (800) 722-0291 (Clerk);
(732) 929-2011 (Surrogate's Court); (732) 349-
4336 FAX (County Clerk)
cblock@co.ocean.nj.us;
occlerk@oceancountyclerk.com;
csuwak@co.ocean.nj.us
http://www.oceancountygov.com
Carl W. Block, County Clerk; Jeffrey W. Moran,
Surrogate
(land records with County Clerk, naturalization
records with Ocean County Historical
Society, probate records with Surrogate's
Court)

Passaic County
organized 1837 from Bergen and Sussex
counties

Passaic County Administration Building
401 Grand Street
Paterson, NJ 07505
(973) 225-3632; (973) 754-1920 FAX
karenb@passaiccountynj.org
http://www.passaiccountynj.org
Karen Brown, Esq., County Clerk/Register
(land records, naturalization records)

Passaic County Surrogate's Office
77 Hamilton Street
Paterson, NJ 07505-2018
(973) 881-4760; (973) 523-3449 FAX
billbate@passaiccountynj.org
http://www.passaiccountynj.org
William J. Bate, Surrogate
(probate records)

Salem County
organized 1694, original county

Salem County Courthouse
92 Market Street
Salem City, NJ 08079-1913
(856) 935-7510, ext. 8206 (County Clerk); (856)
935-7510, ext. 8323 (Surrogate); (856) 935-
8882 FAX (Clerk); (856) 339-9359 FAX
(Surrogate)
gilda.gill@salemcountynj.gov;
gwood@salemco.org
http://www.salemcountynj.gov/cmssite
Gilda Gill, County Clerk; Nicki Burke, Surrogate
(land records from 1688 to date, naturalization
records, marriage records from 1699 to 1912
with County Clerk, probate records from
1804 to date with Surrogate's Office)

Somerset County
organized 1688 from Middlesex County

Somerset County Administration Building
(20 Grove Street—location)
PO Box 3000 (mailing address)
Somerville, NJ 08876-1262
(908) 231-7006 (County Clerk); (908) 231-7003
(Surrogate); (908) 253-8853 FAX (Clerk);
(908) 429-8765 FAX (Surrogate)
CountyClerk@co.somerset.nj.us; radi@co.
somerset.nj.us; SurrogatesOffice@co.
somerset.nj.us; bruno@co.somerset.nj.us
http://www.co.somerset.nj.us

Brett I. Radi, County Clerk; Frank G. Bruno,
Surrogate
(land records with R. Peter Widin, County Clerk,
naturalization records with County Clerk,
probate records with Surrogate)

Sussex County
organized 1753 from Morris County

Sussex County Hall of Records
83 Spring Street, Suite 304
Newton, NJ 07860
(201) 579-0900 (Clerk, Suite 304); (973) 292-
4087 (Vital Statistics); (973) 383-7493 FAX
(Clerk)
scclerk@nac.net
http://www.sussex.nj.us;
http://www.sussexcountyclerk.com
Erma Gormley, County Clerk
(deeds and mortgages from 1795, naturalization
records from 1808 to 1989, marriages from
1795 through mid-1878, births and
manumissions of slaves)
no land or naturalization records search service;
copies of land and naturalization records:
$1.50 per page, no minimum

Sussex County Surrogate's Office
4 Park Place, Suite 2
Newton, NJ 07860
(973) 579-0920 (Surrogate); (973) 579-0909 FAX
scclerk@nac.net
http://www.sussex.nj.us
Nancy D. Fitzgibbons, Surrogate
(wills, trusts, probate matters, divisions, etc.)
probate search service: no charge; copies of
probate records: $3.00 per page, no minimum

Union County
organized 1857 from Essex County

Union County Courthouse
2 Broad Street
Elizabeth, NJ 07207
(908) 527-4787 (Clerk); (908) 527-4280
(Surrogate, Second Floor, Old Annex)
jrajoppi@ucnj.org; jrajoppi@unioncountynj.org;
jschwab@ucnj.org (Deputy Surrogate);
surrogate@unioncountynj.org
http://www.unioncountynj.org
Joanne Rajoppi, County Clerk; James LaCorte,
Surrogate
(deeds and mortgages from 1857 with Clerk;
probate records with Surrogate)
copies of land records: $1.50 per page; certified
copies of land records: $8.00 for the first page
and $2.00 for each additional page

Warren County
organized 1824 from Sussex County

Warren County Courthouse
413 Second Street
Belvidere, NJ 07823
(908) 475-6211 (Clerk); (908) 475-6223
(Surrogate); (908) 475-6319 FAX (Surrogate)
http://www.warrennet.org/warrencounty
Terrance "Terry" Lee, County Clerk; Susan A.
Dickey, Surrogate
(land records from 1825 with County Clerk,
naturalization records from 1825 to 1987 with
County Clerk, marriages from 1825 to 1875
with County Clerk, probate records with
Surrogate)
probate search service: no charge (for one name,
must have *first* and last names); copies of
probate records: $3.00 per page plus SASE,
no minimum ("Surrogate's records are
indexed by a letter book for first letter of *last*
name")

NEW MEXICO

Capital: Santa Fe. Statehood: 6 January 1912 (parts obtained through the annexation of Texas in 1845, the Gadsden Purchase of 1853, and the Treaty of Guadalupe-Hidalgo, 1848)

New Mexico has four courts of limited jurisdiction: Magistrate Courts (in every county except Bernalillo County), the Bernalillo County Metropolitan Court, Municipal Courts (in incorporated cities or towns with populations of 1000 or more), and Probate Courts (which sit in each county). The District Court has general jurisdiction. First Judicial District: Los Alamos, Rio Arriba, and Santa Fe counties; second Judicial District: Bernalillo County; Third Judicial District: Doña Ana County; Fourth Judicial District: Guadalupe, Mora, and San Miguel counties; Fifth Judicial District: Chaves, Eddy, and Lea counties; Sixth Judicial District: Grant, Hidalgo, and Luna counties; Seventh Judicial District: Catron, Sierra, Socorro, and Torrance counties; Eighth Judicial District: Colfax, Taos, and Union counties; Ninth Judicial District: Curry and Roosevelt counties; Tenth Judicial District: De Baca, Harding, and Quay counties; Eleventh Judicial District: McKinley and San Juan counties; Twelfth Judicial District: Lincoln and Otero counties; Thirteenth Judicial District: Cibola, Sandoval, and Valencia counties. The Court of Appeals and Supreme Court have appellate jurisdiction.

Bernalillo County
organized 1852, original county, annexed Santa Ana County 1876

Bernalillo County Courthouse
1 Civic Plaza, N.W.
Albuquerque, NM 87102
(505) 468-1290 (Clerk, Sixth Floor); (505) 468-1233 (Probate Judge, Sixth Floor)
clerk@bernco.gov; probate@bernco.gov
http://www.bernco.gov/live;
    http://www.nmsc.state.nm.us/directory/prog
    ram.php?program_id=571 (Probate Court)
Maggie Toulouse, County Clerk; Merri Rudd, Probate Judge

Second Judicial District Court
(Civil Division, 400 Lomas Boulevard N.W., Room 119—location)
PO Box 488 (mailing address)
Albuquerque, NM 07103-0488
(505) 841-8400; (505) 841-7446 FAX
albdwebmstr@nmcourts.com
http://www.nmcourts.com/seconddistrictcourt

Catron County
organized 1921 from Socorro County

Catron County Courthouse
101 Main Street
Reserve, NM 87830
(505) 533-6400 (County Clerk, PO Box 507);
    (505) 533-6400 (Probate Court, PO Box 197)
cclerk2@gilanet.com
http://www.mylocalgov.com/catroncountynm/
    Index.asp;
    http://www.nmsc.state.nm.us/directory/prog
    ram.php?program_id=575 (Probate Court)
Sharon Armijo, County Clerk; Theresa Estrada, Probate Judge
(land records from 1921, some vital records [not complete], probate records from 1921)
probate search service: no charge; copies of probate records: 10¢ per page, no minimum

Seventh Judicial District Court
(see Socorro County)

Chaves County
organized 25 February 1889 from Lincoln County

Chaves County Administrative Center
(1 St. Mary's Place—location)
PO Box 1817 (mailing address)
Roswell, NM 88203
(505) 624-6614 (Clerk and Probate, Suite 110, PO Box 580); (505) 624-6523 FAX (Clerk and Probate)
coclerk@co.chaves.nm.us
http://www.co.chaves.nm.us;
    http://www.nmsc.state.nm.us/directory/prog
    ram.php?program_id=579 (Probate Court)
Rhoda C. Coakley, County Clerk
(land records from 1890s, births and deaths from 1900s to 1961 with County Clerk, probate records with Informal Probate Court, County Clerk's Office)
probate search service ("we will try to help you as much as we can; we do not do in depth searches; my staff does not have the time for such"): no charge; copies of probate records: 25¢ per page, no minimum

Fifth Judicial District Court
(400 North Virginia, Roswell, NM 88201—location)
PO Box 1776 (mailing address)
Roswell, NM 88202-1776
(505) 622-2212 (Clerk); (505) 624-9510 FAX (Clerk)
http://www.fifthdistrictcourt.com

Cibola County
organized 19 June 1981 from Valencia County

Cibola County Courthouse
515 West High Street
Grants, NM 87020-2526
(505) 287-9431 (Clerk's Office); (505) 285-2552 (Probate); (505) 285-5434 FAX
Eileenm@cia-g.com
http://www.grants.org (Grants/Cibola County Chamber of Commerce);
    http://www.nmsc.state.nm.us/directory/prog
    ram.php?program_id=582 (Probate Court)
Eileen Martinez, County Clerk
(land records with County Clerk's Office, informal probates with County Clerk's Office, probate records with 13th Judicial District Court)
no probate search service from County Clerk's Office; copies of land records: 25¢ per page, $2.00 per document for certification; copies of probate records: 25¢ per page, $2.00 per document for certification

Thirteenth Judicial District Court
(515 West High—location)
PO Box 758 (mailing address)
Grants, NM 87020
(505) 287-8831 (Clerk); (505) 287-2104 (Judge); (505) 285-5755 FAX (Clerk); (505) 287-3658 FAX (Judge)
http://www.13districtcourt.com;
    http://www.nmsc.state.nm.us/directory/prog
    ram.php?program_id=640
Lisa Bro, Chief Clerk; Judge Camille Martinez Olguin

Colfax County
organized 1869 from Mora County

Colfax County Courthouse
PO Box 159
Raton, NM 87740
(505) 445-5551 (County Clerk); (505) 445-5585 (Eighth Judicial District Court, PO Box 160); (505) 455-9565 (Probate Court)
ccdeputyclerk@bacavalley.com
http://www.nmsc.state.nm.ujs/directory/progra
    m.php?program_id=622 (Eighth Judicial District Court);
    http://www.nmsc.state.nm.us/directory/prog
    ram.php?program_id=587 (Probate Court)
Rayetta LeDoux, County Clerk
(land records from 1864 with County Clerk, naturalization records with District Court, probate records from 1800 with County Clerk [some also filed in District Court])
probate search service: no charge; copies of

probate records: 35¢ per page, 35¢ minimum, no restrictions

Eighth Judicial District Court
(North Third Street—location)
PO Box 160 (mailing address)
Raton, NM 87740
(505) 445-5585; (505) 445-2626 FAX
http://www.nmsc.state.nm.us/directory/progra
    m.php?program_id=622

Curry County
organized 1909 from Quay and Roosevelt counties

Curry County Courthouse
(700 North Main Street, Suite 7—location)
PO Box 1168 (mailing address)
Clovis, NM 88101
(505) 763-5591, ext. 138; (505) 763-4232 FAX
mtrujillo@currycounty.org
http://www.currycounty.org; https://
    mylocalgov.com/currycountynm; http://
    www.nmsc.state.nm.us/directory/program.
    php?program_id=590 (Probate Court)
Mario Trujillo, County Clerk
(land records from 1909 with County Clerk, naturalization records with District Court Clerk, probate records from 1909 with County Clerk)
probate search service: no charge; copies of probate records: 25¢ each, no minimum

Ninth Judicial District Court
700 North Main, Suite 11
Clovis, NM 88101
(505) 762-9148; (505) 763-5160 FAX
http://www.nmcourts9thjdc.com

De Baca County
organized 1917 from Chaves, Guadalupe and Roosevelt counties

De Baca County Courthouse
PO Box 347
Fort Sumner, NM 88119
(505) 355-2601; (505) 355-7389 (Probate Court, PO Box 941)
dbclp@plateautel.net
http://www.nmsc.state.nm.us/directory/progra
    m.php?program_id=594 (Probate Court)
Laurie Pettigrew, County Manager/Clerk
(land records from 1917 with ["also have records when De Baca County was part of Chaves, Guadalupe and Roosevelt Counties"], marriage licenses, probate records from 1917)
no probate search service; copies of marriage licenses: $1.50 each; copies of probate records: 30¢ per page, $1.30 for certified copies, no minimum

Tenth Judicial District Court
514 Avenue C
Fort Sumner, NM 88119
(505) 355-2896; (505) 355-2896 FAX
http://www.nmsc.state.nm.us/directory/progra
    m.php?program_id=628

Doña Ana County
organized 1852, original county, annexed Arizona County 1861

Doña Ana County Courthouse
845 North Motel Boulevard, Room 1-200
Las Cruces, NM 88007
(505) 647-7421 (County Clerk); (505) 525-6132 (Probate Judge); (505) 6747-7419 (Probate Court, 180 West Amador, Room 106, Las Cruces, NM 88005-5691); (505) 525-6159 FAX (County Clerk); (505) 525-6159 FAX (Probate Judge); (505) 647-7224 FAX (Probate Court)
http://www.co.dona-ana.nm.us;
    http://www.nmsc.state.nm.us/directory/prog
    ram.php?program_id=599 (Probate Court);
    http://thirddistrictcourt.com/lower
Rita Torres, County Clerk; Alice M. Salcido, Probate Judge
(land records from 1853 with, probate records from 1853)

probate search service: no charge; copies of probate records: 15¢ per page, no minimum

Third Judicial District Court
201 West Picacho Avenue (corner of Alameda Boulevard and Picacho Avenue)
Las Cruces, NM 88005
(505) 523-8200; (505) 523-8296 (Probate Filings); (505) 523-8290 FAX
http://www.thirddistrictcourt.com
Nadine Sanchez, Clerk of the Court

Eddy County
organized 1887 from Lincoln County

Eddy County Courthouse
(101 West Greene Street, Carlsbad, NM 88220-6219—location)
PO Box 1139 (mailing address)
Carlsbad, NM 88221-1139
(505) 886-3383 (Clerk); (505) 886-4008 (Probate, Room 100, PO Box 850); (505) 887-1039 FAX (Probate)
eddyclerk@co.eddy.nm.us
http://www.caverns.net/ecourt;
    http://www.nmsc.state.nm.us/directory/prog ram.php?program_id=572 (Probate Court)
Darlene Rosprim, County Clerk; Charlene Wright, Probate Judge

Fifth Judicial District Court
102 North Canal, Suite 240
Carlsbad, NM 88220
(505) 885-4740 (Clerk); (505) 887-7095 FAX
http://www.fifthdistrictcourt.com

Grant County
organized 1868 from Socorro County

Grant County Courthouse
(1400 Highway 180 East, Silver City, NM 88061—location)
PO Box 898 (mailing address)
Silver City, NM 88062-0898
(505) 574-0000 (County Clerk's Office); (505) 574-0071 (Probate Judge); (505) 574-0076 FAX (Probate Judge)
howiemorales@yahoo.com
http://www.grantcountnm.com;
    http://www.nmsc.state.nm.us/directory/prog ram.php?program_id=576 (Probate Court)
Henry (Howie) Morales, County Clerk; Jo Ann F. Salcido, Probate Judge
(land records with County Clerk or Assessor, probate records with County Clerk or Probate Judge, formal probates with District Court)
probate search service: no charge; copies of probate records: 50¢ per page, no minimum

Sixth Judicial District Court
(201 North Cooper Street—location)
PO Box 2339 (mailing address)
Silver City, NM 88062
(505) 538-2975; (505) 538-3250 (Grant County); (505) 542-3411 (Hidalgo County); (505) 542-3481 FAX (Hidalgo); (505) 388-5439 FAX (Grant)
http://www.nmsc.state.nm.us/directory/progra m.php?program_id=620

Guadalupe County
organized 1891 from Lincoln and San Miguel counties

Fourth Judicial District Court
420 Parker Avenue
Santa Rosa, NM 88435
(505) 472-3888; (505) 472-4451 FAX
http://www.nmsc.state.nm.us/directory/progra m.php?program_id=615

Guadalupe County Courthouse
420 Parker Avenue
Santa Rosa, NM 88435
(505) 472-3791 (Probate); (505) 472-3735 FAX (Probate)
guadctyclerk@plateautel.net
http://www.nmsc.state.nm.us/directory/progra m.php?program_id=583 (Probate Court)
Adam Gallegos, County Clerk

(land records, probate records)
probate search service: $5.00; copies of probate records: 25¢ per page, no minimum

Harding County
organized 1921 from Mora and Union counties

Harding County Courthouse
(35 Pine Street—location)
PO Box 1002 (mailing address)
Mosquero, NM 87733-1002
(505) 673-2301; (505) 673-2922 FAX
hardingcc@plateautel.net
http://www.hardingcounty.org;
    http://www.nmsc.state.nm.us/directory/prog ram.php?program_id=585 (Probate Court)
Marie Atencio, County Clerk; Carrie Archuleta, Probate Judge
(land records, naturalization records, marriage licenses, probate records)
copies of land, naturalization, and probate records: 25¢ per page, $1.00 for certification, copies of marriage licenses: $1.50 each

Tenth Judicial District Court
Fourth and Pine Streets
Mosquero, NM 87733
(505) 673-2252 voice & FAX
http://www.nmsc.state.nm.us/directory/progra m.php?program_id=629

Hidalgo County
organized 1920 from Grant County

Hidalgo County Courthouse
300 South Shakespeare Street
Lordsburg, NM 88045-1939
(505) 542-9213 (Clerk); (505) 542-9512 (Probate)
hidclk@aznex.net
http://www.nmsc.state.nm.us/directory/progra m.php?program_id=591 (Probate Court)
Carmon Acosta, County Clerk
(land records, deeds, mortgages, etc., probate records)
probate search service: no charge; copies of probate records: 25¢ per page

Sixth Judicial District Court
(see Grant County)

Lea County
organized 1917 from Chaves and Eddy counties

Fifth Judicial District Court
(100 North Main—location)
PO Box 6C (mailing address)
Lovington, NM 88260
(505) 396-8571 (Clerk); (505) 396-2428 FAX
http://www.fifthdistrictcourt.com;
    http://www.nmsc.state.nm.us/directory/prog ram.php?program_id=616

Lea County Courthouse
(215 East Central Avenue—location)
PO Box 1507 (mailing address)
Lovington, NM 88260
(505) 396-8614 (Clerk); (505) 396-8615 (Clerk); (505) 396-8619 (Clerk); (505) 396-8648 (Probate Judge's Office); (505) 396-8877 (Probate Judge's Home); (505) 396-8521 (Probate Court)
mhughes@leacounty.net;
    mhamby@leacounty.net
http://www.leacounty.net;
    http://www.nmsc.state.nm.us/directory/prog ram.php?program_id=595 (Probate Court)
Melinda Hughes, County Clerk; Melba Hamby, Probate Judge
(land records with County Clerk, probate records with County Clerk or District Court Clerk, PO Box 6C, Lovington, NM 88260)
probate search service: no charge; copies of probate records: 50¢ per page, no minimum

Lincoln County
organized 1869 from Socorro County

Lincoln County Courthouse
(300 Central Avenue, Carrizozo, NM 88301-0711—location)

PO Box 338 (mailing address)
Carrizozo, NM 88301-0338
(505) 648-2394, ext. 131 (Clerk); (800) 687-2705 (Clerk); (505) 648-2814 (Probate Court); (505) 648-2576 FAX (Clerk)
tammiemaddox@lincolncountynm.net;
    barwrh@tularosa.net (Probate)
http://www.lincolncountynm.net;
    http://www.nmsc.state.nm.us/directory/prog ram.php?program_id=598 (Probate Court)
Tammie Maddox, County Clerk; Carrie Spencer, County Probate Judge
(deeds from 1869 with County Clerk, marriages from 1882 with County Clerk, probate records: Informal probate records from 1880s with County Clerk, other probate records with District Court)
probate search service: no charge ("This office will do a brief search; extensive searches must be done by an abstract or title company"); copies of probate records: 25¢ per page, no minimum

Twelfth Judicial District Court
(300 Central Street—location)
PO Box 725 (mailing address)
Carrizozo, NM 88310
(505) 648-2432; (505) 648-2581 FAX
http://www.12thdistrict.net
Jolene Biggs, Judicial Supervisor

Los Alamos County
organized 1949 from Sandoval and Santa Fe counties

First Judicial District Court
2300 Trinity Drive
Los Alamos, NM 87544-3051
(505) 662-9561; (505) 827-5055 FAX
http://firstdistrictcourt.com

Los Alamos County Courthouse
2300 Trinity Drive, Room 100
Los Alamos, NM 87544-3051
(505) 662-8010 (Clerk and Probate)
clerks@mail.lacnm.uskraemer@losalamos.nm.us
http://www.lac-nm.us;
    http://www.nmsc.state.nm.us/directory/prog ram.php?program_id=600 (Probate Court)
Mary Pat Kraemer, County Clerk; Janet Foster, Probate Judge

Luna County
organized 1901 from Doña Ana and Grant counties

Luna County Courthouse
(110 North Gold—location)
PO Drawer 551 (mailing address)
Deming, NM 88031
(505) 546-0491 (Clerk and Probate Judge); (505) 885-4008 (Probate Court); (505) 546-4187 FAX (Clerk and Probate Judge)
karen@lunacountynm.net
http://lunacountynm.us;
    http://www.nmsc.state.nm.us/directory/prog ram.php?program_id=573 (Probate Court)
Karen Smyer, Clerk; Delia Perez, Probate Judge
(land records from late 1800s, old birth and death index [incomplete], births from 1907 to 1932, deaths from 1907 to 1941, marriages from 1901, probate records from 1901)
no probate search service ("if you have probate number, we do make copies upon request"); certified copies of vital records: $1.50 each; copies of probate records: 50¢ per page

Sixth Judicial District Court
700 South Silver, Room 56
Deming, NM 88030
(505) 546-2344; (505) 546-2994 FAX
http://www.nmsc.state.nm.us/directory/progra m.php?program_id=619

McKinley County
organized 1899 from Bernalillo, Valencia and San Juan counties

Eleventh Judicial District Court
207 West Hill, Room 200

Gallup, NM 87301
(505) 863-6816; (505) 722-3401 FAX
webmaster@11thjdc.com
http://www.eleventhdistrictcourt.state.nm.us
Francisca P. Palochak, Judicial Manager

McKinley County Courthouse
207 West Hill Avenue
Gallup, NM 87305
(505) 722-3868; (505) 538-5240 (Probate Court,
   PO Box 1268); (505) 863-6362 FAX
boedirector@cnetco.com;
info@co.mckinley.nm.us
http://www.co.mckinley.nm.us;
   http://www.nmsc.state.nm.us/directory/prog
   ram.php?program_id=577 (Probate Court)
Jacqueline Sloan, County Clerk
(land values with Assessor, ownership transfers
   with County Clerk, naturalization records
   with Judge Joseph Rich, District Court, PO
   Box 460, Gallup, NM 87305, vital records
   with County Clerk, probate records with
   County Clerk)
probate search service: $1.00 per year; copies of
   probate records: 50¢ per page, 50¢ for
   certification

Mora County
organized 1859 from San Miguel County

Fourth Judicial District Court
(see San Miguel County)

Mora County Courthouse
PO Box 580
Mora, NM 87732
(505) 387-2448 (Clerk's Office); (505) 387-5410
   (Probate Judge); (505) 387-5702 (Probate
   Court, PO Box 36)
mora_clerk@yahoo.com
http://www.moravalley.com;
   http://www.nmsc.state.nm.us/directory/prog
   ram.php?program_id=580 (Probate Court)
Charlotte Duran, County Clerk

Otero County
organized 1899 from Doña Ana, Lincoln and
   Socorro counties

Otero County Courthouse
1000 New York Avenue, Room 108
Alamogordo, NM 88310
(505) 437-4942 (Clerk and Probate); (505) 443-
   2922 FAX (Clerk)
rsilva@co.otero.nm.us
http://www.co.otero.nm.us; http://www.
   nmsc.state.nm.us/directory/program.
   php?program_id=584 (Probate Court)
Robyn Silva, County Clerk
(land records from 1888 [not bonded for this
   search], probate records from 1888)
probate search service: no charge; copies of
   probate records: 25¢ per page, $1.00 for
   certification, no minimum

Twelfth Judicial District Court
100 New York Avenue, Room 209
Alamogordo, NM 88310
(505) 437-7310, ext. 22; (505) 434-8886 FAX
http://www.12thdistrict.net
Karen Duprey, Judicial Manager

Quay County
organized 1903

Quay County Courthouse
(300 South Third Street—location)
PO Box 1225 (mailing address)
Tucumcari, NM 88401
(505) 461-0510; (505) 461-0513
quaycountyclerk@hotmail.com
http://www.nmsc.state.nm.us/directory/progra
   m.php?program_id=588 (Probate Court)
Ellen White, County Clerk
(land records from 1892, probate records from
   1892)
probate search service: no charge; copies of
   probate records: $1.00 for the first page and
   50¢ for each additional page, no minimum

Tenth Judicial District Court
(300 South Third Street—location)
PO Box 1067 (mailing address)
Tucumcari, NM 88401
(505) 461-2764; (505) 461-4422; (505) 461-4498
   FAX
http://www.nmsc.state.nm.us/directory/progra
   m.php?program_id=627

Rio Arriba County
organized 1852, original county

First Judicial District Court
PO Drawer 40
Tierra Amarilla, NJ 87575
(505) 588-7254; (505) 588-0058; (505) 588-9898
   FAX
http://firstdistrictcourt.com

Rio Arriba County Complex
1122 Industrial Park Road
Espanola, NM 87532
or
Tierra Amarilla Court House
(7 Main Street—location)
PO Box 158 (mailing address)
Tierra Amarilla, NM 87575
(505) 753-1780 (Espanola Office); (505) 588-
   7724 (Tierra Amarilla Office); (505) 753-1258
   FAX (Clerk, Espanola Office); (505) 753-
   9397 FAX (Probate Judge); (505) 588-7418
   FAX (Tierra Amarilla Office)
jfvigil@rio-arriba.org
http://www.rio-arriba.org;
   http://www.nmsc.state.nm.us/directory/prog
   ram.php?program_id=592 (Probate Court)
J. Fred Vigil, County Clerk; Angela M. Gallegos,
   Probate Judge

Roosevelt County
organized 1903 from Chaves County

Ninth Judicial District Court
109 West First Street
Portales, NM 88130
(505) 356-4463; (505) 359-2140 FAX
http://www.nmcourts9thjdc.com
Margie F. Jones, District Court Clerk

Roosevelt County Courthouse
109 West First Street
Portales, NM 88130
(505) 356-8562 (Clerk): (505) 760-7570 (Probate
   Judge); (505) 359-1273 (Probate Court); (505)
   356-3560 FAX (Clerk); (505) 356-8218 FAX
   (Probate Court)
jcollins@rooseveltcounty.com
http://www.rooseveltcounty.com;
   http://www.nmsc.state.nm.us/directory/prog
   ram.php?program_id=596 (Probate Court)
Janet Collins, County Clerk; Nancy Gentry,
   Probate Judge
(land records, probate records with County
   Clerk)

San Juan County
organized 1887 from Rio Arriba County

Eleventh Judicial District Court
103 South Oliver
Aztec, NM 87410
and
920 Municipal Drive
Farmington, NM 87401
and
851 Andrea Drive, Suite 3
Farmington, NM 87401
(505) 334-6151 (Aztec); (505) 326-2256
   (Farmington); (505) 334-1940 FAX (Aztec);
   (505) 326-0224 FAX (Farmington)
webmaster@11thjdc.com
http://www.eleventhdistrictcourt.state.nm.us
Pat Mars, Aztec Judicial Manager; Isabel
   O'Brien, Farmington Judicial Manager

San Juan County Courthouse
100 South Oliver Drive
Aztec, NM 87410
(505) 334-9471 (Clerk and Probate Judge); (505)
   334-9471, ext. 353 (Probate Court, Suite 100,

PO Box 550); (505) 334-3635 FAX (Clerk and
   Probate Judge)
fhanhardt@sjcounty.net
http://www.sjcounty.net;
   http://www.nmsc.state.nm.us/directory/prog
   ram.php?program_id=574 (Probate Court)
Ms. Fran Hanhardt, County Clerk; Gary E.
   Risley, Probate Judge (Suite 200, PO Box 550)
(land records from 1887, marriages from 1887,
   some probate records also kept at District
   Court)
probate search service: no charge; copies of
   probate records: 50¢ per page, no minimum

San Miguel County
organized 1852, original county

Fourth Judicial District Court
(500 West National Street—location)
PO Box 1540 (mailing address)
Las Vegas, NM 87701-1540
(505) 425-7281; (505) 425-7131; (505) 425-3900;
   (505) 425-6307 FAX; (505) 454-8879 FAX
http://www.nmsc.state.nm.us/directory/progra
   m.php?program_id=614

San Miguel County Courthouse
500 West National Suite 113
Las Vegas, NM 87701
(505) 425-9331 (Clerk and Probate Judge); (505)
   454-1799 FAX (Clerk and Probate Judge)
mclerk@lasvegas-nm.com
http://www.smcounty.net; http://
   www.nmsc.state.nm.us/directory/program.
   php?program_id=578 (Probate Court)
Pecos Maez, County Clerk; Melanie Y. Rivera,
   Probate Judge
copies: $1.00 for microfiche copies, 50¢ for
   Xerox copies, $2.00 for certification

Sandoval County
organized 1903 from Rio Arriba County

Sandoval County Courthouse
(711 Camino de Pueblo—location)
PO Box 40 (mailing address)
Bernalillo, NM 87004
(505) 867-7572 (Clerk); (505) 867-7647 (Probate
   Judge); (505) 867-7500 (Probate Court); (505)
   771-8610 FAX (Clerk); (505) 720-8836
   (Probate Court)
Clerk@sandovalcounty.com;
   spadilla@sandovalcounty.com;
   kwapich@flash.net;
   marykwapich@sandovalcounty.com
http://www.sandovalcounty.com;
   http://www.nmsc.state.nm.us/directory/prog
   ram.php?program_id=601 (Probate Court)
Sally Padilla, County Clerk; Mary O. Kwapich,
   Probate Judge

Thirteenth Judicial District Court
(1500 Idalia Road, Building A—location)
PO Box 600 (mailing address)
Bernalillo, NM 87004
(505) 867-2376; (505) 867-2861 FAX
http://www.13districtcourt.com;
   http://www.nmsc.state.nm.us/directory/prog
   ram.php?program_id=639
Theresa Valencia, Chief Clerk

Santa Fe County
organized 1852, original county

First Judicial District Court
(Judge Steve Herrera Judicial Complex, 100
   Catron Street—location)
PO Box 2268 (mailing address)
Santa Fe, NJ 07504-2268
(505) 4786-0134; (505) 827-5055 FAX (Clerk)
http://firstdistrictcourt.com

Santa Fe County Courthouse
102 Grant Avenue (corner of Palace and Grant
   Avenues)
PO Box 1985 (mailing address)
Santa Fe, NM 87504-1985
(505) 984-5080 (Clerk); (505) 992-1636 (Cordilia
   Montoy, Probate Court); (505) 996-6278
   Probate Court, PO Box 276); (505) 986-6362

FAX (Probate Court)
vespinoza@co.santa-fe.nm.us
http://www.co.santa-fe.nm.us;
http://www.nmsc.state.nm.us/directory/prog
ram.php?program_id=581 (Probate Court)
Valerie Espinoza, County Clerk; Mark A.
Basham, Probate Judge; Cordilia Montoy,
Probate Court
(land records, marriages, probate records)

Sierra County
organized 1884 from Socorro County

Seventh Judicial District Court
311 North Date Street
Truth or Consequences, NM 87901
(505) 461-2764; (505) 461-4498 FAX
http://www.sapienlaw.com/Resource-
Links/New-Mexico-Courts.html

Sierra County Courthouse
100 North Date Street
Truth or Consequences, NM 87901
(505) 894-2840 (Clerk and Probate); (505) 894-
2516 FAX (Clerk and Probate)
jsanchezclerk@riolink.com
http://www.sierracounty.net;
http://www.nmsc.state.nm.us/directory/prog
ram.php?program_id=586
Janice Sanchez, County Clerk
(land records from 1884, probate records from
1913)
probate search service: $2.00; copies of probate
records: 25¢ per page

Socorro County
organized 1852, original county

Seventh Judicial District Court
(200 Church Street—location)
PO Drawer 1129 (mailing address)
Socorro, NM 87801
(505) 835-0050; (505) 838-5217 FAX
http://www.nmsc.state.nm.us/directory/progra
m.php?program_id=621

Socorro County Courthouse
PO Box I
Socorro, NM 87801
(505) 835-0423; (505) 835-3263 FAX
ajaramillo@co.socorro.nm.us
http://www.co.socorro.nm.us;
http://www.nmsc.state.nm.us/directory/prog
ram.php?program_id=589 (Probate Court)
Audrey Jaramillo, County Clerk

Taos County
organized 1852, original county

Eighth Judicial District Court
105 Albright, Suite H
Taos, NM 87571
(505) 758-3173; (505) 751-1281 FAX
http://www.nmsc.state.nm.us/directory/progra
m.php?program_id=623

Taos County Courthouse
105 Albright Street
Taos, NM 87571
(505) 737-6380 (Clerk, Suite D); (505) 737-6390
FAX (Clerk)
elaine.montano@taoscounty.org
http://www.taoscounty.org
Elaine S. Montaño, County Clerk

Torrance County
organized 1903 from Lincoln, San Miguel,
Socorro and Santa Fe counties

Seventh Judicial District Court
PO Box 78
Estancia, NM 87016
(505) 384-2974; (505) 384-2229 FAX
http://www.sapienlaw.com/Resource-
Links/New-Mexico-Courts.html

Torrance County Courthouse
(205 Ninth Street—location)
PO Box 48 (mailing address)
Estancia, NM 87016
(505) 246-4735 (Clerk, PO Box 767; Probate

Judge, PO Box 48); (505) 384-4080 FAX
(Clerk)
lkayser@torrancecountynm.org;
clerk@torrancecountyn.org
http://www.torrancecountynm.org;
http://www.nmsc.state.nm.us/directory/prog
ram.php?program_id=597 (Probate Court)
Linda Kayser, County Clerk; Mary Ann C.
Anaya, Probate Judge
(land records from 1910 with Clerk, probate
records with Judge)
no probate search service; copies of probate
records: 25¢ each, no minimum

Union County
organized 1903 from Colfax, Mora and San
Miguel counties

Eighth Judicial District Court
(200 Court Street—location)
PO Box 310 (mailing address)
Clayton, NM 88415
(505) 374-9577; (505) 374-2089 FAX
http://www.nmsc.state.nm.us/directory/progra
m.php?program_id=624

Union County Courthouse
PO Box 430
Clayton, NM 88415-0430
(505) 374-9491; (505) 374-8137 (Probate Court,
PO Box 297)
unionclerk@plateautel.net
http://www.nmsc.state.nm.us/directory/progra
m.php?program_id=602 (Probate Court)
Joyce Sowers, County Clerk
(land records, probate records)
no probate search service; copies of probate
records: 30¢ per page from paper originals,
$1.00 per page from microfilm originals, no
minimum

Valencia County
organized 1852, original county

Thirteenth Judicial District Court
(444 Luna Avenue—location)
PO Box 1089 (mailing address)
Los Lunas, NM 87301
(505) 865-4639; (505) 865-8801 FAX
http://www.13districtcourt.com;
http://www.nmsc.state.nm.us/directory/prog
ram.php?program_id=638
Geri Lynn Sanchez, Chief Clerk

Valencia County Courthouse
(444 Luna Avenue—location)
PO Box 969 (mailing address)
Los Lunas, NM 87031
(505) 866-2073; (505) 866-2023 FAX
clk@co.valencia.nm.us;
probate@co.valencia.nm.us
http://www.co.valencia.nm.us;
http://www.nmsc.state.nm.us/directory/prog
ram.php?program_id=603 (Probate Court)
Sally Perea, County Clerk and Clerk of Probate
Court; Reyna Aragon Carrejo, Probate Judge

*Capital: Albany. Statehood: 26 July 1788 (Dutch
settlement conquered by the English in 1664, became a
royal province in 1685)*

New York State has a number of courts of
limited jurisdiction. The New York Court of
Claims sits at Albany and hears claims against
the state. Town and Village Justice Courts
handle minor civil and criminal matters. New
York District Courts are established only in
Nassau and Suffolk counties and have
jurisdiction over some civil matters and
misdemeanors. The Criminal Court of the City
of New York has trial jurisdiction over
misdemeanors and violations, and the Civil
Court of the City of New York has civil
jurisdiction. New York City encompasses the
counties of Bronx, Kings (Brooklyn), New York
(Manhattan), Queens and Richmond (Staten
Island). City Courts are established in cities
outside the city of New York and have limited
jurisdiction over civil cases and criminal
jurisdiction over misdemeanors. Family Courts
established in each county and New York City
hear matters involving children and families and
have concurrent jurisdiction with the Surrogate's
Court in adoption cases. The Surrogate's Court
hears cases involving probate. In some counties
jurisdiction is handled by the County Court
Judge.
The County Courts are established in every
county except the five counties of New York
City and have general jurisdiction over criminal
offenses and some civil cases. The Supreme
Court sits in every county seat and has general
jurisdiction over cases beyond the jurisdiction of
other courts. First Judicial District: New York
County; Second Judicial District: Kings and
Richmond counties; Third Judicial District:
Albany, Columbia, Greene, Rensselaer,
Schoharie, Sullivan and Ulster counties; Fourth
Judicial District: Clinton, Essex, Franklin,
Fulton, Hamilton, Montgomery, St. Lawrence,
Saratoga, Schenectady, Warren and Washington
counties; Fifth Judicial District: Herkimer,
Jefferson, Lewis, Oneida, Onondaga and
Oswego counties; Sixth Judicial District:
Broome, Chemung, Chenango, Cortland,
Delaware, Madison, Otsego, Schuyler, Tioga and
Tompkins counties; Seventh Judicial District:
Cayuga, Livingston, Monroe, Ontario, Seneca,
Steuben, Wayne and Yates counties; Eighth
Judicial District: Allegany, Cattaraugus,
Chautauqua, Erie, Genesee, Niagara, Orleans
and Wyoming counties; Ninth Judicial District:
Dutchess, Orange, Putnam, Rockland and
Westchester counties; Tenth Judicial District:
Nassau and Suffolk counties; Eleventh Judicial
District: Queens County; Twelfth Judicial
District: Bronx County. Appeals are handled by
the Supreme Court Appellate Division and the
New York Court of Appeals.

Albany County
organized 1683, original county

Albany County Clerk
32 North Russell Road
Albany, NY 12206-1324
(518) 487-5100; (518) 487-5099 FAX
countyclerk@albanycounty.com;
TClingan@albanycounty.com
http://www.albanycouty.com/clerk
Thomas G. Clingan
(current deeds, and mortgages)

Albany County Hall of Records
95 Tivoli Street
Albany, NY 12207
(518) 436-3663; (518) 436-3678 FAX
ccarlson@albanycounty.com
http://www.albanycounty.com
Mon–Fri 8:30–4:30
(atlases from 1860 to 1941, deeds 1654–1894,

mortgages 1752–1980, declarations of intentions/naturalizations 1821–1991, Albany marriage records 1870–1954, index to wills and letters of administration 1780–1895, 1794–1895, surrogate's court records 1800–1840)

Surrogate's Court
Family Court Building, 30 Clinton Avenue
Albany, NY 12207
(518) 285-8585
http://www.nycourts.gov/courts/3jd/surrogate
s/albany/index.shtml
Stacy L. Pettit, Esq., Chief Clerk
(estate proceedings from the mid-1700s to date)
Surrogate's search service (no information given over the phone): $30.00 for under 25 years, $90.00 for over 25 years; copies: 25¢ per page or $6.00 per certified page

Allegany County
organized 1806 from Genesee County

Allegany County Clerk
County Office Building
7 Court Street, Room 18
Belmont, NY 14813-1039
(585) 268-9270; (585) 268-9659 FAX
christr@alleganyco.com;
presutje@alleganyco.com
http://www.alleganyco.com/default.asp?show=
btn_county_clerk
Robert L. Christman
(land records from 1806, naturalization records, marriages, etc.)
copies of land records: 50¢ each, $1.00 minimum, $1.00 each for certified copies, $4.00 minimum

Surrogate's Court
Courthouse, 7 Court Street
Belmont, NY 14813-1084
(585) 268-5815
cjmiller@courts.state.ny.us
http://www.nycourts.gov/courts/8jd/Allegany
/index.shtml
Carolyn Miller, Chief Clerk
(probate records)
Surrogate's search service (no information given over the phone): $30.00 for under 25 years, $90.00 for over 25 years; copies: 25¢ per page or $6.00 per certified page

Bronx County (Borough)
organized 1914 from New York County

Bronx County Clerk
851 Grand Concourse, Room 118
Bronx, NY 10451
(718) 590-3648; (718) 590-8122 FAX
webmaster@bronxcountyclerksoffice.com
http://bronxcountyclerksoffice.com/en/home
Hector L. Diaz

Surrogate's Court
851 Grand Concourse, Room 317
Bronx, NY 10451
(718) 590-4515
dcruz@courts.state.ny.us
http://www.nycourts.gov/courts/nyc/surrogate
s/index.shtml
Diana Cruz, Chief Clerk
(probate records)
Surrogate's search service (no information given over the phone): $30.00 for under 25 years, $90.00 for over 25 years; copies: 25¢ per page or $6.00 per certified page

Broome County
organized 1806 from Tioga County

Broome County Clerk
(Broome County Office Building, Department of Records, 44 Hawley Street, Third Floor—location)
PO Box 2062 (mailing address)
Binghamton, NY 13902
(607) 778-2451; (607) 763-4936 (Records Center);
clerkinfo@co.broome.ny.us

http://www.broomecounty.org/clerk/Clerk.php
Richard R. Blythe
(land records, naturalization records from 1850 [with earlier records represented to a lesser extent], marriages from 1908 to 1934)
naturalization records search service: $5.00 for every two years searched by Susan DiBencdetto, County Records Manager, provided the necessary information is supplied; requests for copies of Petition for Naturalizations should be directed to the Records Manager: 50¢ per page, $1.00 minimum

Surrogate's Court
(Broome County Courthouse, Court Street, Binghamton, NY 13904—location)
PO Box 1766 (mailing address)
Binghamton, NY 13902
(607) 778-2111; (607) 778-2308 FAX
mvescio@courts.state.ny.us
http://nycourts.gov/6jd/CountyMaps/broome
/sur/default.html
Marilyn Vescio, Chief Clerk
(probate records)
Surrogate's search service (no information given over the phone): $30.00 for under 25 years, $90.00 for over 25 years; copies: 25¢ per page or $6.00 per certified page

Cattaraugus County
organized 1808 from Genesee County

Cattaraugus County Clerk
Cattaraugus County Center
303 Court Street
Little Valley, NY 14755-1028
(716) 938-9111
ABernstein@cattco.org
http://www.co.cattaraugus.ny.us
John R. Searles

Surrogate's Court
Cattaraugus County Center
303 Court Street
Little Valley, NY 14755-1028
(716) 938-9111, ext. 2327
cwrona@courts.state.ny.us
http://www.nycourts.gov/courts/8jd/Cattaraug
us/index.shtml
Christine Wrona, Chief Clerk
(probate records)
Surrogate's search service (no information given over the phone): $30.00 for under 25 years, $90.00 for over 25 years; copies: 25¢ per page or $6.00 per certified page

Cayuga County
organized 1799 from Onondaga County

Cayuga County Clerk
(Cayuga County Office Building, 160 Genesee Street, First Floor—location)
PO Box 616 (mailing address)
Auburn, NY 13021-0616
(315) 253-1271; (315) 253-1653
sdwyer@cayugacounty.us
http://co.cayuga.ny.us/clerk/index.html
Susan M. Dwyer

Cayuga County Surrogate's Court
152 Genesee Street
Auburn, NY 13021
(315) 255-4316; (315) 255-4320; (315) 255-4322
marr@courts.state.ny.us
http://co.cayuga.ny.us/directory/judicial.htm
MaryAnne Marr
(probate records)
Surrogate's search service (no information given over the phone): $30.00 for under 25 years, $90.00 for over 25 years; copies: 25¢ per page or $6.00 per certified page

Chautauqua County
organized 1808 from Genesee County

Chautauqua County Clerk
(Gerace Office Building, Mayville, NY 14757-1007—location)
PO Box 170 (mailing address)

Mayville, NY 14757-0170
(716) 753-7111; (716) 753-4277 FAX
travis@co.chautauqua.ny.us
http://www.co.chautauqua.ny.us/clerkframe.htm
Sandra K. Sopak
(land records from 1811, naturalization records from the early 1800s through 1972, marriages from 1908 to April 1935)
land records search service: $5.00 per two-year period searched; naturalization records search service: $5.00 per name; vital records search service: $5.00 per marriage; copies of land records: $1.00 per page (copies of grantor and grantee indices not available); copies of naturalizations: $1.00 per page; copies of marriages: $5.00 each

Surrogate's Court
(Gerace Office Building, Mayville, NY 14757-1007—location)
PO Box C (mailing address)
Mayville, NY 14757
(716) 753-4339; (716) 753-4600 FAX
lromer@courts.state.ny.us
http://www.nycourts.gov/courts/8jd/Chautauq
ua/index.shtml
Lydia Romer, Chief Clerk
(probate records from 1811)
Surrogate's search service (no information given over the phone): $30.00 for under 25 years, $90.00 for over 25 years ("we do not charge this for running our records to see if we have the estates"); copies: 25¢ per page or $6.00 per certified page

Chemung County
organized 1836 from Tioga County

Chemung County Clerk
(210 Lake Street—location)
PO Box 588 (mailing address)
Elmira, NY 14902-0588
(607) 737-2920; (607) 737-2984
chughes@co.chemung.ny.us
http://www.chemungcounty.com
Catherine K. Hughes
(Tioga County deeds from 1790 to 1835, Chemung County deeds from 1836, naturalization records from 1860 to 1906)

Surrogate's Court
(Courthouse, 224 Lake Street—location)
PO Box 588 (mailing address)
Elmira, NY 14902-0588
(607) 737-2946; (607) 737-2819; (607) 737-2874 FAX
pkreitze@courts.state.ny.us
http://www.nycourts.gov/6jd/CountyMaps/ch
emung/CHMSURROG/default.html
Patricia A. Kreitzer, Chief Clerk
(probate records)
Surrogate's search service: $30.00 for under 25 years, $90.00 for over 25 years (search requests must be made in writing and appropriate fee paid prior to search); copies of probate records: 25¢ per page; certified copies: $6.00 per page

Chenango County
organized 1798 from Herkimer and Tioga counties

Chenango County Clerk
County Office Building
5 Court Street
Norwich, NY 13815-1676
(607) 337-1450
http://www.co.chenango.ny.us/CountyClerk/C
ountyClerk.htm
Mary C. Weidman
(land records, naturalization records, marriages)
naturalization records search service: $5.00 per name for a two-year search; copies of land records: $1.50 per page; copies of naturalization records: $1.50 per page; certified copies of marriages: $5.00 each

Surrogate's Court
County Office Building
5 Court Street

Norwich, NY 13815
(607) 337-1827; (607) 337-1834 FAX
lwiley@courts.state.ny.us
http://www.nycourts.gov/6jd/CountyMaps/ch
enango/CNGSURROG/default.html
Linda J. Wiley, Chief Clerk
(probate, adoptions, guardianships; genealogy
records from 1798)
Surrogate's search service (no information given
over the phone): $30.00 for under 25 years,
$90.00 for over 25 years; copies: 25¢ per page
or $6.00 per certified page

Clinton County
organized 1788 from Washington County

Clinton County Clerk
County Government Center
137 Margaret Street, First Floor, Suite 101
Plattsburgh, NY 12901
(518) 565-4700; (518) 565-4718 FAX
zurloj@co.clinton.ny.us; County
Clerk@co.clinton.ny.us
http://clintocountygov.com
John H. Zurlo
(land records from 1788, Aliens Admitted Index
and Records, naturalization records from
about 1900)

Surrogate's Court
County Government Center
137 Margaret Street
Plattsburgh, NY 12901
(518) 565-4630; (518) 565-0468 FAX
(probate records)
Surrogate's search service (no information given
over the phone): $30.00 for under 25 years,
$90.00 for over 25 years; copies: 25¢ per page
or $6.00 per certified page

Columbia County
organized 1786 from Albany County

Columbia County Clerk
560 Warren Street
Hudson, NY 12534
(518) 828-3339; (518) 828-5299 FAX
htanner@govt.co.columbia.ny.us
http://www.co.columbia.ny.us
Holly C. Tanner
(land records from mid 1800s, naturalization
records from mid 1800s to 1934)

Surrogate's Court
401 Union street
Hudson, NY 12534
(518) 828-0414
lnorton@courts.state.ny.us
http://www.nycourts.gov/courts/3jd/surrogate
s/columbia/index.shtml
Lee Norton, Chief Clerk
(probate records)
Surrogate's search service (no information given
over the phone): $30.00 for under 25 years,
$90.00 for over 25 years; copies: 25¢ per page
or $6.00 per certified page

Cortland County
organized 8 April 1808 from Onondaga County

Cortland County Clerk
(Courthouse, 46 Greenbush Street, Suite 101—
location)
PO Box 5590 (mailing address)
Cortland, NY 13045
(607) 753-5021
elarkin@cortland-co.org
http://www2.cortland-co.org/index.htm
Elizabeth P. Larkin
(deeds and mortgages from 1808, naturalization
records from 1816 through early 1960s,
marriages from 1908 to 1933 [earlier and later
records filed with city and town clerks])

Surrogate's Court
Courthouse, 46 Greenbush Street, Suite 301
Cortland, NY 13045-2725
(607) 753-5355; (607) 756-3409
mripley@courts.state.ny.us
http://www.nycourts.gov/6jd/CountyMaps/co

rtland/crtsurpg.html
Maxine B. Ripley, Chief Clerk
(probate records from 1808)
Surrogate's search service (no information given
over the phone): $30.00 for under 25 years,
$90.00 for over 25 years; copies: 25¢ per page
or $6.00 per certified page

Delaware County
organized 1797 from Ulster and Otsego counties

Delaware County Clerk
(Courthouse, Courthouse Square—location)
PO Box 426 (mailing address)
Delhi, NY 13753
(607) 746-2123
http://www.co.delaware.ny.us/depts/clerk/cler
k.htm
Sharon A. O'Dell
(land records from 1797 to date, naturalization
records from early 1800s, births, deaths and
marriages from 1847 to 1848, marriages from
1874 to 1881 and from 1909 to 1935)

Surrogate's Court
Courthouse, 3 Court Street
Delhi, NY 13753
(607) 746-2126; (607) 746-3253 FAX
http://www.nycourts.gov/6jd/CountyMaps/del
aware/DELSURROG/default.html
Nancy A. Smith, Chief Clerk
(probate records from 1797)
Surrogate's search service (no information given
over the phone): $30.00 for under 25 years,
$90.00 for over 25 years; copies: 25¢ per page
or $6.00 per certified page

Dutchess County
organized 1683, original county

Dutchess County Clerk
County Office Building
22 Market Street, Record Room, Second Floor
Poughkeepsie, NY 12601
(845) 486-2120; (845) 486-2138 FAX
clafuente@co.dutchess.ny.us
http://www.co.dutchess.ny.us/CountyGov/De
partments/CountyClerk/CCindex.htm
Colette Lafuente
(land records, naturalization records, marriage
certificates from 1908 to 1935)
no records search service; copies of records:
$5.00 per document, $6.00 per document for
certified copies

Surrogate's Court
10 Market Street
Poughkeepsie, NY 12601
(845) 486-2235; (845) 486-2234 FAX
jatherto@courts.state.ny.us
http://www.nycourts.gov/courts/9jd/Dutchess
/index.shtml
John J. Atherton, Chief Clerk
(probate records)
Surrogate's search service (no information given
over the phone): $30.00 for under 25 years,
$90.00 for over 25 years; copies: 25¢ per page
or $6.00 per certified page

Erie County
organized 1821 from Niagara County

Erie County Clerk
25 Delaware Avenue
Buffalo, NY 14202
(716) 846-8865; (716) 858-8785; (716) 858-6550
FAX
swartsd@bflo.co.erie.ny.us
http://www.erie.gov/clerk.phtml
David J. Swarts
(deeds, naturalization records from 1827 to
1929, marriages from 1878 through 29 April
1935 [very few before 1878])
records search service: $5.00 per name for each
two-year period or portion thereof, payable in
advance by money order; copies of vital
records: $5.00 each

Erie County Surrogate's Court
Erie County Hall, 92 Franklin Street

Buffalo, NY 14202
(716) 845-2560; (716) 845-2585 (Record Room);
(716) 853-3741 FAX
mmartoch@courts.state.ny.us
http://www.nycourts.gov/courts/8jd/Erie/surr
ogates/index.shtml
Mary Dee Martoche, Chief Clerk
(probate records; many records stored off-site,
and retrieval takes two to four days,
depending on staffing levels at the court at
the time of the request)
Surrogate's search service (no information given
over the phone): $30.00 for under 25 years,
$90.00 for over 25 years; copies: 25¢ per page
or $6.00 per certified page

Essex County
organized 1 March 1799 from Clinton County

Essex County Clerk
(7559 Court Street—location)
PO Box 247 (mailing address)
Elizabethtown, NY 12932
(518) 873-3601; (518) 873-3548 FAX
jprovon@co.essex.ny.us
http://www.co.essex.ny.us/cclerk.asp
Joseph Provoncha
(deeds from 1800, naturalization records,
marriage licenses and certificates from 1909
to 1912 for all towns, births, deaths and
marriages from 1847 to 1850 for the towns of
Crown Point, Keene, Moriah, Schroon,
Ticonderoga, Westport and Willsboro)
copies of vital records: 65¢ each, $5.00 for
certified copies

Surrogate's Court
Essex County Government Center, 100 Court
Street
Elizabethtown, NY 12932
(518) 873-3385; (518) 873-3731 FAX
Darlene Gough, Acting Court Clerk
(probate records)
Surrogate's search service (no information given
over the phone): $30.00 for under 25 years,
$90.00 for over 25 years; copies: 25¢ per page
or $6.00 per certified page

Franklin County
organized 1808 from Clinton County

Franklin County Clerk
(Courthouse, 355 West Main Street—location)
PO Box 70 (mailing address)
Malone, NY 12953
(518) 481-1681
wmurtagh@co.franklin.ny.us
http://www.franklincony.org/countyclerk.htm
Wanda D. Murtagh
(deeds and mortgages from 1808 to date, lis
pendens from 1820 to date, homestead
exemptions of the 1830s, land tax records
from the 1800s and early 1900s, some
naturalization records from 1825 to
September 1953, declarations of intent from
1834, marriages from 1908 to 1935)

Surrogate's Court
Courthouse, 355 West Main Street
Malone, NY 12953
(518) 481-1737
mlabarge@courts.state.ny.us
http://www.nycourts.gov/courts/4jd/franklin/
surrogates.shtml
Martha A. Labarge, Chief Clerk
(probate records)
Surrogate's search service (no information given
over the phone): $30.00 for under 25 years,
$90.00 for over 25 years; copies: 25¢ per page
or $6.00 per certified page

Fulton County
organized 1838 from Montgomery County
("oldest courthouse still in use—1776")

Fulton County Clerk
(County Building, 223 West Main Street,
Johnstown, NY 12095-2331—location)
PO Box 485 (mailing address)
Johnstown, NY 12095-0485

(518) 736-5555; (518) 736-5539
William E. Eschler
(land records, naturalization records)

Surrogate's Court
223 West Main Street
Johnstown, NY 12095
(518) 736-5685; (518) 762-6372 FAX
(probate records)
Surrogate's search service (no information given over the phone): $30.00 for under 25 years, $90.00 for over 25 years; copies: 25¢ per page or $6.00 per certified page

Genesee County
organized 1802 from Ontario County

Genesee County Clerk
(15 Main Street, Batavia, NY 14020—location)
PO Box 379 (mailing address)
Batavia, NY 14021-0379
(585) 344-2550, ext. 2242; (585) 344-8521 FAX
dread@co.genesee.ny.us
http://www.co.genesee.ny.us/dpt/countyclerk
Don M. Read
(deeds from 1802, naturalization records from 1834 to February 1962, marriages from 1908 to 1934)
land records search service: $5.00 per name; copies of land records: 50¢ per page, $1.00 minimum

Surrogate's Court
(Genesee County Courts Facility, 1 West Main Street—location)
PO Box 462 (mailing address)
Batavia, NY 14020
(585) 344-2500, ext. 2240; (585) 344-8517 FAX
http://www.nycourts.gov/courts/8jd/Genesee/index.shtml
(probate records from 1802)
Surrogate's search service (no information given over the phone): $30.00 for under 25 years, $90.00 for over 25 years; copies: 25¢ per page or $6.00 per certified page ("please read about the local history first!")

Greene County
organized 1800 from Albany and Ulster counties

Greene County Clerk
(Courthouse, 320 Main Street—location
PO Box 446 (mailing address)
Catskill, NY 12414
(518) 943-2050
mkordich@discovergreene.com
http://www.greenegovernment.com/index.htm
Mary Ann Kordich
(land records)

Surrogate's Court
(Courthouse, 320 Main Street—location)
PO Box 469 (mailing address)
Catskill, NY 12414
(518) 943-2484
emaurer@courts.state.ny.us
http://www.nycourts.gov/courts/3jd/surrogates/greene/index.shtml
Eric Maurer, Chief Clerk
(probate records)
Surrogate's search service: $30.00 for under 25 years, $90.00 for over 25 years; copies: 25¢ per page or $6.00 per certified page, no minimum, ("we ask that requests be made in writing")

Hamilton County
organized 1816 from Montgomery County

Hamilton County Clerk
County Office Building
Rt. 8, Box 204
Lake Pleasant, NY 12108
(518) 548-7111
hamcoclerk@capital.net
http://www.hamiltoncounty.com
Jane S. Zarecki

Surrogate's Court
(White Birch Lane—location)

PO Box 780 (mailing address)
Indian Lake, NY 12842-0780
(518) 648-5411; (518) 648-6286 FAX
(probate records)
Surrogate's search service (no information given over the phone): $30.00 for under 25 years, $90.00 for over 25 years; copies: 25¢ per page or $6.00 per certified page

Herkimer County
organized 1791 from Montgomery County

Herkimer County Clerk
(County Office Building, 109 Mary Street, Suite 1111, Herkimer, NY 13350-2923—location)
PO Box 471 (mailing address)
Herkimer, NY 13350-0471
(315) 867-1002; (315) 867-1129
http://herkimercounty.org/content/Departments/View/12?
Sylvia M. Rowan
(land records)

Surrogate's Court
Herkimer County Office and Court Facility
301 North Washington Street
Herkimer, NY 13350
(315) 867-1170; (315) 866-1802 FAX
cvertucc@courts.state.ny.us
http://www.nycourts.gov/courts/5jd/herkimer/index.shtml#surrogate
Constance A. Vertucci, Chief Clerk IV
(probate records)
Surrogate's search service (no information given over the phone): $30.00 for under 25 years, $90.00 for over 25 years; copies: 25¢ per page or $6.00 per certified page

Jefferson County
organized 1805 from Oneida County

Jefferson County Clerk
Jefferson County Building
175 Arsenal Street
Watertown, NY 13601-2522
(315) 785-3312
darleney@co.jefferson.ny.us
http://www.co.jefferson.ny.us/cclerk
Jo Ann M. Wilder
(deeds from 1795 [Oneida], 1805 [Jefferson], mortgages from 1805, naturalization records through 1972 [earlier and later records filed with Town Clerks], marriages from 1908 to 1933 only)

Surrogate's Court
Jefferson County Court Complex
163 Arsenal Street
Watertown, NY 13601
(315) 785-3019; (315) 785-5194 FAX
bcobb@courts.state.ny.us
http://www.nycourts.gov/courts/5jd/jefferson/index.shtml
Benjamin Cobb, Chief Clerk I
(decedent's estates from 1847)
Surrogate's search service (no information given over the phone): $30.00 for under 25 years, $90.00 for over 25 years; copies: 25¢ per page or $6.00 per certified page

Kings County
organized 1683, original county

Kings County Clerk
Supreme Court Building
360 Adams Street, Room 189, Window #6
Brooklyn, NY 11201-3712
(347) 404-9760
schepiga@courts.state.ny.us
http://www.nycourts.gov/courts/2jd/kingsclerk/index.shtml
Nancy T. Sunshine

Surrogate's Court
2 Johnson Street, Room 109
Brooklyn, NY 11201
(347) 404-9700
schepiga@courts.state.ny.us
http://www.nycourts.gov/courts/2jd/kings.shtml
Stephen Chepiga, Chief Clerk

(probate records)
Surrogate's search service (no information given over the phone): $30.00 for under 25 years, $90.00 for over 25 years; copies: 25¢ per page or $6.00 per certified page

Lewis County
organized 1805 from Oneida County

Lewis County Clerk
(Courthouse, 7660 State Street, Lowville, NY 13367-1396—location)
PO Box 332 (mailing address)
Lowville, NY 13367-1432
(315) 376-5333; (315) 376-3768 FAX
Clerk@lewiscountyny.org
http://lewiscountyny.org/content/Departments/View/24
Douglas Hanno
(land records from 1805, naturalization records from 1808 to 1906, vital records from 1848 to 1850 [incomplete])

Surrogate's Court
Courthouse, 7660 State Street
Lowville, NY 13367
(315) 376-5344; (315) 376-4145 FAX
lpfendle@courts.state.ny.us
http://www.nycourts.gov/courts/5jd/lewis/index.shtml
Lori K. Pfendler, Chief Clerk I
(estate and guardianship records; surrogate records from 1970–2000 are now available online [register at http://surrogate5th.courts.state.ny.us/public, view at http://surrogate5th.courts.state.ny.us/onbase])
Surrogate's search service (no information given over the phone): $30.00 for under 25 years, $90.00 for over 25 years; copies: 25¢ per page or $6.00 per certified page, no minimum

Livingston County
organized 1821 from Genesee and Ontario counties

Livingston County Clerk
County Government Center
6 Court Street, Room 201
Geneseo, NY 14454
(585) 243-7000; (585) 243-7928 FAX
jculbertson@co.livingston.ny.us
http://www.co.livingston.state.ny.us/home.htm
James Culbertson
(land records from 1821, naturalization records from early 1860s to 1954)

Surrogate's Court
2 Court Street
Geneseo, NY 14454
(716) 243-7095; (716) 243-7583 FAX
tmoore@courts.state.ny.us
Toni A. Moore, Chief Clerk
(probate records from 1821)
Surrogate's search service (no information given over the phone): $30.00 for under 25 years, $90.00 for over 25 years; copies: 25¢ per page or $6.00 per certified page

Madison County
organized 1806 from Chenango County

Madison County Clerk
(County Office Building #4, 138 North Court Street—location)
PO Box 668 (mailing address)
Wampsville, NY 13163-0668
(315) 366-2261
denise.roe@co.madison.ny.us
http://www.madisoncounty.org/county_clerks/CCMain.htm
Kenneth J. Kunkel, Jr.; Denise Roe, Deputy County Clerk
(land records, naturalization records, marriages to 1920)
no land or vital records search service

Surrogate's Court
(Courthouse, North Court Street—location)
PO Box 607 (mailing address)
Wampsville, NY 13163-0607

(315) 366-2392; (315) 366-2539 FAX
aslivins@courts.state.ny.us
http://www.nycourts.gov/6jd/CountyMaps/madison/Surr/default.html
Andrea L. Slivinski, Chief Clerk
(probate records)
Surrogate's search service (no information given over the phone): $30.00 for under 25 years, $90.00 for over 25 years; copies: 25¢ per page or $6.00 per certified page, no minimum

Monroe County
organized 1821 from Genesee and Ontario counties

Monroe County Clerk
County Office Building
39 West Main Street, Room 101
Rochester, NY 14614
(585) 753-1600; (585) 753-1624 FAX
mcclerk@monroecounty.gov
http://www.monroecounty.gov/clerk-index.php
Cheryl Dinolfo
(land records from 1821, naturalization records from 1821)

Surrogate's Court
99 Exchange Boulevard
Rochester, NY 14614
(585) 428-5001; (585) 428-2190 FAX
(probate records)
Surrogate's search service (no information given over the phone): $30.00 for under 25 years, $90.00 for over 25 years; copies: 25¢ per page or $6.00 per certified page

Montgomery County
organized 1772 from Albany County; name changed from Tryon County in 1784

Surrogate's Court
(New Court House, 58 Broadway, Room 50—location)
PO Box 1500 (mailing address)
Fonda, NY 12068-1500
(518) 853-8108; (518) 873-3731 FAX
(most genealogical records filed in Montgomery County Department of History and Archives)
Surrogate's search service (no information given over the phone): $30.00 for under 25 years, $90.00 for over 25 years; copies: 25¢ per page or $6.00 per certified page

Nassau County
organized 1899 from Queens County

Nassau County Clerk
240 Old Country Road, Room 106
Mineola, NY 11501
(516) 571-2663
http://www.nassaucountyny.gov/agencies/Clerk/index.html
Maureen O'Connell

Surrogate's Court
262 Old Country Road
Mineola, NY 11501
(516) 571-2847; (516) 571-2082; (516) 571-3803 FAX
http://www.nycourts.gov/courts/10jd/nassau/surrogates.shtml
(probate records)
Surrogate's search service (no information given over the phone): $30.00 for under 25 years, $90.00 for over 25 years; copies: 25¢ per page or $6.00 per certified page

New York County
organized 1683, original county

Old Merchants House Museum
29 East Fourth Street
New York, NY 10003
(212) 777-1089; (212) 777-1104 FAX
nyc1832@merchantshouse.org
http://www.merchantshouse.com
Margaret Halsey Gardiner, Executive Director
$50.00 per year membership; regular admission: $8.00

New York County Clerk
Courthouse, 60 Centre Street, Room 161
New York, NY 10007-1402
(646) 386-5955; (646) 374-4376 (Division of Old Records); (646) 374-4781 (Record Room)
http://www.ci.nyc.ny.us/html/doris/html/archives.html; http://www.tnp.com/nycgenweb/municipal.htm
Norman Goodman
(naturalization records from 1794 to 1924)
naturalization search service: $10.00 (includes copy)

Surrogate's Court
Records Search and Certifications
31 Chambers Street, Room 402
New York, NY 10007
(646) 386-5090
recordroom_general@courts.state.ny.us
http://www.courts.state.ny.us/nyc/surrogates/index.shtml
Kim Sulik, Archivist
(probate records)
Surrogate's search service (no information given over the phone): $30.00 for under 25 years, $90.00 for over 25 years; copies: 25¢ per page or $6.00 per certified page

Niagara County
organized 1808 from Genesee County

Niagara County Clerk
(Courthouse, 175 Hawley Street—location)
PO Box 461 (mailing address)
Lockport, NY 14094-0461
(716) 439-7022; (716) 439-7035 FAX
http://www.niagaracounty.com
Wayne F. Jagow
(land records, naturalization records [records from 1808 to 1821 with Erie County])

Surrogate's Court
Courthouse, 175 Hawley Street
Lockport, NY 14094
(716) 439-7130; (716) 439-7319 FAX
rsutton@courts.state.ny.us
http://www.nycourts.gov/courts/8jd/Niagara/index.shtml
Ronald Sutton, Chief Clerk
(probate records from 1821 [records from 1808 to 1821 with Erie County])
Surrogate's search service (no information given over the phone): $30.00 for under 25 years, $90.00 for over 25 years; copies: 25¢ per page or $6.00 per certified page

Oneida County
organized 1798 from Herkimer County

Oneida County Clerk
County Office Building
800 Park Avenue
Utica, NY 13501
(315) 798-5773
countyclerk@ocgov.net
http://www.oneidacounty.org/coclerkindex1.htm
Sandra DePerno
(land records)

Surrogate's Court
County Office Building
800 Park Avenue, Eighth Floor
Utica, NY 13501-2939
(315) 797-9230; (315) 797-9237 FAX
mhoffman@courts.state.ny.us
http://www.nycourts.gov/courts/5jd/oneida/index.shtml
Martha R. Hoffman, Chief Clerk V
(probate records from 1798)
Surrogate's search service (no information given over the phone): $30.00 for under 25 years, $90.00 for over 25 years; copies of probate records: 25¢ per page for short copies, 50¢ per page for long copies, $6.00 per page for certified copies

Onondaga County
organized 1794 from Herkimer County

Onondaga County Clerk

Courthouse, 401 Montgomery Street, Room 200
Syracuse, NY 13202
(315) 435-2226; (315) 435-2241; (315) 435-3455 FAX
http://www.ongov.net/Clerk
M. Ann Ciarpelli
(land records, naturalization records, vital records from 1865 to 1907, marriage certificates from 1908 to 1938)

Surrogate's Court
Courthouse, 401 Montgomery Street, Room 209
Syracuse, NY 13202
(315) 671-2100; (315) 671-1162 FAX
araphael@courts.state.ny.us
http://www.nycourts.gov/courts/5jd/onondaga/index.shtml
Ava S. Raphael, Chief Clerk VI
(probate records)
Surrogate's search service (no information given over the phone): $30.00 for under 25 years, $90.00 for over 25 years; copies: 25¢ per page or $6.00 per certified page, no minimum ("fees must be paid in advance")

Ontario County
organized 1789 from Montgomery County

Ontario County Clerk
County Municipal Building
20 Ontario Street
Canandaigua, NY 14424
(585) 396-4200; (585) 393-2951 FAX
jack.cooley@co.ontario.ny.us
http://www.co.ontario.ny.us/index.html
John H. Cooley
(land records)

Surrogate's Court
27 North Main Street, Room 130
Canandaigua, NY 14424
(585) 396-4239; (585) 396-4576 FAX
ksweeney@courts.state.ny.us
http://www.nycourts.gov/courts/7jd/Ontario/index.shtml
Kathleen D. Sweeney, Chief Clerk
(probate records)
Surrogate's search service (no information given over the phone): $30.00 for under 25 years, $90.00 for over 25 years; copies: 25¢ per page or $6.00 per certified page

Orange County
organized 1683, original county

Orange County Clerk
Orange County Government Center
255-275 Main Street
Goshen, NY 10924-1621
(845) 291-2690; (845) 291-2691 FAX
http://www.co.orange.ny.us/orgMain.asp?orgid=42&storyTypeID=&sid=&
Donna L. Benson

Surrogate's Court
30 Park Place
Goshen, NY 10924
(845) 291-2193; (845) 291-2196 FAX
jmorse@courts.state.ny.us
http://www.nycourts.gov/courts/9jd/Orange/surrogates.shtml
Joy V. Morse, Chief Clerk
(probate records, guaradianship records)
Surrogate's search service (no information given over the phone): $30.00 for under 25 years, $90.00 for over 25 years; copies: 25¢ per page or $6.00 per certified page

Orleans County
organized 1824 from Genesee County

Orleans County Clerk
Courthouse, Courthouse Square
3 South Main Street
Albion, NY 14411
(585) 589-5334; (585) 589-0181 FAX
http://www.orleansny.com/CountyClerk/coclerk.htm
Karen Lake-Maynard
(land records from 1824, naturalization records)

Surrogate's Court
Courthouse, Courthouse Square
Albion, NY 14411-1497
(585) 589-4457
dberry@courts.state.ny.us
http://www.nycourts.gov/courts/8jd/Orleans/index.shtml
Deborah Berry, Chief Clerk
(some probate records beginning in 1845)
Surrogate's search service (no information given over the phone): $30.00 for under 25 years, $90.00 for over 25 years; copies: 25¢ per page or $6.00 per certified page

Oswego County
organized 1816 from Oneida and Onondaga counties

Oswego County Clerk
46 East Bridge Street
Oswego, NY 13126-2123
(315) 349-8385; (315) 349-8383 FAX
williamsg@oswegocounty.com
http://www.co.oswego.ny.us/clerk.shtml
George J. Williams
(land records)

Surrogate's Court
Courthouse, East Oneida Street
Oswego, NY 13126
(315) 349-3295; (315) 349-8514 FAX
jcooper@courts.state.ny.us
http://www.nycourts.gov/courts/5jd/oswego/index.shtml
Judy L. Cooper, Chief Clerk I
(probate records)
Surrogate's search service (no information given over the phone): $30.00 for under 25 years, $90.00 for over 25 years; copies: 25¢ per page or $6.00 per certified page

Otsego County
organized 1791 from Montgomery County

Otsego County Clerk
(County Office Building, 197 Main Street, Cooperstown, NY 13326-1129—location)
PO Box 710 (mailing address)
Cooperstown, NY 13326
(607) 547-4276; (607) 547-7544 FAX
gardnerk@otsegocounty.com
http://www.otsegocounty.com/county%20clerk/index.htm
Kathy Sinnott Gardner
(land records from 1791, naturalization records from 1806 to 1889 and from 1895 to 1955 [incomplete], marriages from 1908 to January 1935)

Surrogate's Court
(County Office Building, 197 Main Street
Cooperstown, NY 13326-1129
(607) 547-4213; (607) 547-7566 FAX
jmcbrear@courts.state.ny.us
http://www.nycourts.gov/courts/6jd/CountyMaps/otsego/mb/otssurrogate.html
Judy M. McBrearty, Chief Clerk
(probate records)
Surrogate's search service (no information given over the phone): $30.00 for under 25 years, $90.00 for over 25 years; copies: 25¢ per page or $6.00 per certified page

Putnam County
organized 1812 from Dutchess County

Putnam County Clerk
Putnam County Office Building
40 Gleneida Avenue, Room 100
Carmel, NY 10512
(845) 225-3641, ext. 300
http://www.putnamcountyny.com/countyclerk/index.html
Dennis J. Sant
(land records, naturalization records, vital records)

Surrogate's Court
44 Gleneida Avenue
Carmel, NY 10512

(845) 225-3641, ext. 293; (845) 228-5761 FAX
http://www.nycourts.gov/courts/9jd/Putnam/index.shtml
Linda Schwark
(probate records)
Surrogate's search service (no information given over the phone): $30.00 for under 25 years, $90.00 for over 25 years; copies: 25¢ per page or $6.00 per certified page

Queens County
organized 1683, original county; includes the neighborhoods of Arverne, Astoria, Astoria Heights, Auburndale, Bayside, Bayswater, Belle Harbor, Bellerose, Breezy Point, Briarwood, Broad Channel, Cambria Heights, College Point, Corona, Douglaston, East Elmhurst, Edgemere, Elmhurst, Far Rockaway, Floral Park, Flushing, Forest Hills, Forest Hills Gardens, Fresh Meadows, Glendale, Hamilton Beach, Hammels, Hillcrest, Hollis, Hollis Hills, Howard Beach, Howard Park, Hunters Point, Jackson Heights, Jamaica, Jamaica Estates, Kew Gardens, Kew Gardens Hills, Laurelton, LeFrak City, Lindenwood, Little Neck, Locust Manor, Long Island City, Malba, Maspeth, Middle Village, Murray Hill, Neponsit, Old Howard Beach, Ozone Park, Pomonok, Queensbridge, Queens Village, Ramblersville, Rego Park, Richmond Hill, Ridgewood, Rochdale, Rockaway, Rockaway Beach, Rockaway Park, Rockwood Park, Rosedale, St. Albans, South Jamaica, South Ozone Park, Springfield Gardens, Sunnyside, Sunnyside Gardens, Utopia, Whitestone, Willets Point, Woodhaven, Woodside

Queens County Clerk
General Courthouse
88-11 Sutphin Boulevard, Room 105
Jamaica, NY 11435
(718) 520-3702
Gloria D'Amico

Surrogate's Court
General Courthouse
88-11 Sutphin Boulevard, Seventh Floor
Jamaica, NY 11435
(718) 298-0400; (718) 298-0500; (718) 298-0440 (Records); (718) 520-2204 FAX
aricc@courts.state.ny.us
http://www.nycourts.gov/courts/11jd/surrogates/index.shtml
Alicemarie E. Rice, Chief Clerk
(probate records)
Surrogate's search service (no information given over the phone): $30.00 for under 25 years, $90.00 for over 25 years; copies: 25¢ per page or $6.00 per certified page

Rensselaer County
organized 1791 from Albany County

Rensselaer County Clerk
105 Third Street
Troy, NY 12180
(518) 270-4080
http://www.rensco.com/countyclerk.htm
Frank J. Merola
(land records, naturalization records)
no land records search service; no naturalization records search or copying service

Surrogate's Court
Courthouse
Troy, NY 12180
(518) 270-3724
pmorgan@courts.state.ny.us
http://www.nycourts.gov/courts/3jd/surrogates/rensselaer/index.shtml
Paul V. Morgan, Esq., Chief Clerk
(probate records)
Surrogate's search service (no information given over the phone): $30.00 for under 25 years, $90.00 for over 25 years; copies: 25¢ per page or $6.00 per certified page

Richmond County
organized 1683, original county

Richmond County Clerk

Courthouse, 130 Stuyvesant Place
Staten Island, NY 10301
(718) 390-5386
Stephen J. Fiala
(land records from 1884 to 1929, naturalization records from 1907 to 1960 [covered by two liber indexes], card index only from 1820 to 1906, declarations of intention from about 1884 to 1929)

Surrogate's Court
18 Richmond Terrace
Staten Island, NY 10301
(718) 390-5400; (718) 390-5403; (718) 390-5404; (718) 390-8741 FAX
rcerrach@courts.state.ny.us
http://www.nycourts.gov/courts/2jd/richmond.shtml#surrogate
Ronald M. Cerrachio, Chief Clerk
(probate records)
Surrogate's search service (no information given over the phone): $30.00 for under 25 years, $90.00 for over 25 years; copies: 25¢ per page or $6.00 per certified page

Rockland County
organized 1798 from Orange County

Rockland County Clerk
Courthouse, 1 South Main Street, Suite 100
New City, NY 10956-3549
(845) 638-5070; (845) 638-5647 FAX
rocklandcountyclerk@co.rockland.ny.us
http://www.rocklandcountyclerk.com
Paul Piperato
(land records, naturalization records)

Surrogate's Court
Courthouse, 1 South Main Street
New City, NY 10956
(914) 638-5330; (845) 638-5632 FAX
vathens@courts.state.ny.us
http://www.nycourts.gov/courts/9jd/Rockland/index.shtml
Virginia Athens, Chief Clerk
(probate records)
Surrogate's search service (no information given over the phone): $30.00 for under 25 years, $90.00 for over 25 years; copies: 25¢ per page or $6.00 per certified page, no minimum

St. Lawrence County
organized 1802 from Clinton, Herkimer and Montgomery counties

St. Lawrence County Clerk
Courthouse, 48 Court Street
Canton, NY 13617-1198
(315) 379-2237; (315) 379-2302
pritchie@co.st-lawrence.ny.us
http://www.co.st-lawrence.ny.us/SLCCoClk.htm
Patricia Ritchie
(land records from 1802, naturalization records from 1802, marriages from 1908 to 1936)

Surrogate's Court
Courthouse, 48 Court Street
Canton, NY 13617-1194
(315) 379-2217; (315) 379-2372 FAX
ddow@courts.state.ny.us
http://www.nycourts.gov/courts/4jd/stlawrence/index.shtml
Debra A. Dow, Chief Clerk
(probate records)
Surrogate's search service (no information given over the phone): $30.00 for under 25 years, $90.00 for over 25 years; copies 25¢ per page ($1.00 minimum) or $6.00 per certified page

Saratoga County
organized 1791 from Albany County

Saratoga County Clerk
County Office Building
40 McMasters Street, First Floor
Ballston Spa, NY 12020-1908
(518) 885-2213; (518) 884-4726 FAX
marchiok@govt.co.saratoga.ny.us;
sarclerk@govt.co.saratoga.ny.us

http://www.co.saratoga.ny.us
Kathleen A. Marchione
(land records from 1791)

Surrogate's Court
30 McMaster Street
Balston Spa, NY 12020
(518) 885-5388, ext. 84; (518) 884-4722; (518)
884-4774 FAX
(probate records 1791)
Surrogate's search service (no information given
over the phone): $30.00 for under 25 years,
$90.00 for over 25 years; copies: 25¢ per page
or $6.00 per certified page, no minimum

Schenectady County
organized 1809 from Albany County

Schenectady County Clerk
County Office Building
620 State Street, Third Floor
Schenectady, NY 12305-2113
(518) 388-4225; (518) 388-4224 FAX
john.woodward@schenectadycounty.com
http://www.schenectadycounty.com
John J. Woodward

Surrogate's Court
Judicial Building
612 State Street
Schenectady, NY 12307
(518) 884-4722; (518) 884-4774 FAX
(probate records)
Surrogate's search service (no information given
over the phone): $30.00 for under 25 years,
$90.00 for over 25 years; copies: 25¢ per page
or $6.00 per certified page

Schoharie County
organized 1795 from Albany and Otsego
counties

**Schoharie County Clerk and Records
Management Officer**
(County Office Building, 284 Main Street, Room
130—location)
PO Box 549 (mailing address)
Schoharie, NY 12157-0549
(518) 295-8316; (518) 295-8317; (518) 295-8338
FAX
peterlopez@co.schoharie.ny.us
http://www.schohariecounty-
ny.gov/CountyClerkHome.jsp
Peter D. Lopez
(land records from 1797)

Surrogate's Court
(290 Main Street—location)
PO Box 669 (mailing address)
Schoharie, NY 12157-0669
(518) 295-8387; (518) 295-8383; (518) 295-8451
FAX
http://www.nycourts.gov/courts/3jd/surrogate
s/schoharie/index.shtml
F. Christian Spies, Chief Clerk
(probate records from 1791)
Surrogate's search service (no information given
over the phone): $30.00 for under 25 years,
$90.00 for over 25 years; copies: 25¢ per page
or $6.00 per certified page ("fees are payable
in advance; please submit SASE; many older
records are in such poor condition that we are
unable to photocopy them, and many are not
accessible to examine at this time; we do
expect at some date in the future to have our
older records placed on microfilm, at which
time copies will be available")

Schuyler County
organized 1854 from Tompkins, Steuben and
Chemung counties

Schuyler County Clerk
(105 Ninth Street—location)
Box 8 (mailing address)
Watkins Glen, NY 14891
(607) 535-8133
Lcompton@co.schuyler.ny.us
http://www.schuylercounty.us
Linda Compton

(deeds from 1855, deeds from 1796 [transcribed
from Chemung County], deeds from 1817
[transcribed from Tompkins County], deeds
from 1798 [transcribed from Steuben
County], some marriages from 1908 to 1935)

Surrogate's Court
105 Ninth Street
Watkins Glen, NY 14891
(607) 535-7144; (607) 535-4918 FAX
fpierce@courts.state.ny.us
http://www.nycourts.gov/6jd/CountyMaps/sc
huyler/SurrCt.html
Frances H. Pierce, Chief Clerk
(probate records)
Surrogate's search service (no information given
over the phone): $30.00 for under 25 years,
$90.00 for over 25 years; (whether or not the
search produces results); copies: 25¢ per page
or $6.00 per certified page, no minimum
("please include SASE with inquiry; no estate,
no charge")

Seneca County
organized 1804 from Cayuga County

Seneca County Clerk
1 Di Pronio Drive
Waterloo, NY 13165
(315) 539-5655
clotz@co.seneca.ny.us
http://www.co.seneca.ny.us
Christina Louise Lotz
(land records from 1804, naturalization records
from 1830 to 1948)

Surrogate's Court
48 West Williams Street
Waterloo, NY 13165
(315) 539-7531; (315) 539-7929 FAX
http://www.nycourts.gov/litigants/courtguides
/7thJD_seneca.pdf
Ernest C. Humbert, Chief Clerk
(probate records from 1804)
Surrogate's search service (no information given
over the phone): $30.00 for under 25 years,
$90.00 for over 25 years; (for searching and
certifying to any record for which search is
made); copies: 25¢ per page or $6.00 per
certified page, no minimum

Staten Island Borough
(see Richmond County)

Steuben County
organized 1796 from Ontario County

Steuben County County Clerk
County Office Building
3 East Pulteney Square
Bath, NY 14810
(607) 776-9631, ext. 3203
judyh@co.steuben.ny.us
http://www.steubencony.org/coclerk.html
Judith M. Hunter
(land records, naturalization records index only
from the 1820s to the 1970s, computer list
telling what clerk holds the death or marriage
record from 1885 to the 1940s [some later],
probate records [special project] 1796 to circa
1900, computer indexed)
probate search service: one name, no charge;
copies of probate records: $1.00 per page

Surrogate's Court
3 East Pulteney Square
Bath NY 14810
(607) 776-9631; (607) 776-7857 FAX
http://www.steubencony.org/ccourt.html
(probate records)
Surrogate's search service (no information given
over the phone): $30.00 for under 25 years,
$90.00 for over 25 years; copies: 25¢ per page
or $6.00 per certified page

**Middletown Historical Society of Steuben
County**
(see Town of Campbell)

Middletown Historical Society of Steuben

County
(see Town of Campbell)

**Middletown Historical Society of Steuben
County**
(see Town of Campbell)

Suffolk County
organized 1683, original county

Suffolk County Clerk
310 Center Drive
Riverhead, NY 11901-3392
(631) 852-2000; (631) 852-2004 FAX
Katherine.Satalino@suffolkcountyny.gov
http://www.co.suffolk.ny.us/webtemp3.cfm?de
pt=33&ID=2659
Judith A. Pascale
(land records)

Surrogate's Court
County Center
320 Center Drive
Riverhead, NY 11901
(631) 852-1725 (Probate Department); (631)
852-1746 (Chief Clerk)
mcipolli@courts.state.ny.us
http://www.courts.state.ny.us/courts/10jd/suff
olk/surrogates.shtml
Michael Cipollino, Chief Clerk
Surrogate's search service (no information given
over the phone): $30.00 for under 25 years,
$90.00 for over 25 years; copies: 25¢ per page
or $6.00 per certified page

Sullivan County
organized 1809 from Ulster County

Sullivan County Clerk
Sullivan County Government Center, 100 North
Street
Monticello, NY 12701-1160
(914) 794-3000, ext. 5012
http://co.sullivan.ny.us/index.asp?orgid=371&s
ID=&storyID=272
George L. Cooke, II
(land records, naturalization records, vital
records)

Surrogate's Court
Sullivan County Government Center, 100 North
Street
Monticello, NY 12701
(845) 794-3000, ext. 3450
lhering@courts.state.ny.us
http://www.nycourts.gov/courts/3jd/surrogate
s/sullivan/index.shtml
LuAnn P. Hering, Chief Clerk
(probate records)
Surrogate's search service (no information given
over the phone): $30.00 for under 25 years,
$90.00 for over 25 years; copies: 25¢ per page
or $6.00 per certified page

Tioga County
organized 1791 from Montgomery County

Surrogate's Court
(Courthouse Annex Building, 20 Court Street—
location)
PO Box 10 (mailing address)
Owego, NY 13827-0010
(607) 687-1303; (607) 687-3240 FAX
http://www.nycourts.gov/6jd/CountyMaps/tio
ga/default.html#Surr
Deborah Stone, Chief Clerk
(probate records)
Surrogate's search service (no information given
over the phone): $30.00 for under 25 years,
$90.00 for over 25 years; copies: 25¢ per page
or $6.00 per certified page

Tioga County Clerk
(16 Court Street—location)
PO Box 307 (mailing address)
Owego, NY 13827
(607) 687-8660; (607) 687-4612 FAX
http://www.tiogacountyny.com/departments/a
dministration/county_clerk.php
Robert Woodburn

Tompkins County

organized 1817 from Cayuga and Seneca
counties

Surrogate's Court
(Courthouse, 320 North Tioga Street—location)
PO Box 70 (mailing address)
Ithaca, NY 14850-0070
(607) 277-0622; (607) 256-2572 FAX
(probate records from 1817)
probate search service: no charge unless person
asks us to certify the search, then $30.00 for
under 25 years, $90.00 for over 25 years;
copies: 25¢ per page or $6.00 per certified
page, no minimum ("we prefer to receive
written requests, not telephone requests;
requests for searches do not receive high
priority unless accompanied by a check [since
we must do a receipt when payment is
received]")

Tompkins County Clerk
Courthouse, 320 North Tioga Street
Ithaca, NY 14850-4284
(607) 274-5431; (607) 274-5445 FAX
avalenti@tompkins-co.org
http://www.co.tompkins.ny.us/direct.html#Co
unty%20Clerk
Aurora Valenti
(land records from 1817, naturalization records
from 1895)
copies of land records: $1.00 per page

Ulster County

organized 1683, original county

Surrogate's Court
240 Fair Street
Kingston, NY 12401
(845) 340-3348
msulliva@courts.state.ny.us
http://www.nycourts.gov/courts/3jd/surrogate
s/ulster/index.shtml
Mary Ellen Sullivan, Chief Clerk
(probate records)
Surrogate's search service (no information given
over the phone): $30.00 for under 25 years,
$90.00 for over 25 years; copies: 25¢ per page
or $6.00 per certified page

Ulster County Clerk
(244 Fair Street, Kingston, NY 12402—location)
PO Box 1800 (mailing address)
Kingston, NY 12401-0800
(845) 340-3415 (Records Management); (845)
340-3299 FAX
http://www.co.ulster.ny.us/countyclerk
Nina Postupack
(land records from 1685 to date, naturalization
records from 1800 to 1903 [index available,
however some records are incomplete],
petitions for naturalization before March
1992, marriages from 1903 to 1935)
records search service: $5.00 for every two years
searched, payable in advance; copies: 50¢ per
page, payable in advance

Warren County

organized 1813 from Washington County

Surrogate's Court
Warren County Municipal Center
1340 State Route 9
Lake George, NY 12845
(518) 761-6512; (518) 761-6511 FAX
sfriday@courts.state.ny.us
http://www.nycourts.gov/courts/4jd/warren/s
urrogates.shtml
Shirley J. Friday, Chief Clerk
(probate records from 1813 to date)
Surrogate's search service (no information given
over the phone): $30.00 for under 25 years,
$90.00 for over 25 years; copies: 25¢ per page
or $6.00 per certified page

Warren County Clerk
Warren County Municipal Center
1340 State Route 9
Lake George, NY 12845
(518) 761-6427; (518) 761-6429; (518) 761-6455

(County Records Storage)
countyclerk@co.warren.ny.us
http://www.co.warren.ny.us
Pamela Vogel
(land records from 1813 to date, naturalization
records from 1813 to 1955, marriages from
1908 to 1935)

Washington County

organized 1772 from Albany County; name
changed from Charlotte County in 1784;
annexed towns of Cambridge and Easton
from Albany County in 1791; settled
boundary with Vermont in 1812

Surrogate's Court
383 East Broadway
Fort Edward, NY 12828
(518) 746-2545; (518) 746-2546; (518) 746-2547
FAX
mfraser@courts.state.ny.us
Mary Fraser, Chief Clerk
(probate records)
Surrogate's search service (no information given
over the phone): $30.00 for under 25 years,
$90.00 for over 25 years; copies: 25¢ per page
or $6.00 per certified page

Washington County Clerk
Municipal Center, 383 East Broadway, Building A
Fort Edward, NY 12828
(518) 746-2170; (518) 746-2136 (County
Archivist); (518) 746-2177 FAX
http://www.co.washington.ny.us/Departments
/cclerk/clk1.htm
Deborah Beahan, Clerk; Dennis Lowery,
Archivist
(deeds from 1794 to date, unrecorded
conveyances from 1742 to 1870,
naturalization records from 1794 to 1952,
from December 1977 to October 1991
[restricted], and from 1991 [index to
certificates held by INS], births, deaths and
marriages from 1848-1849, marriage licenses
from 1908 to 1935, probate records from
1786 to 1900, books of record and disposition
of real property from 1900 to date)
records search service: $10.00 plus SASE; copies
of records: $1.00 per page

Wayne County

organized 1823 from Ontario and Seneca
counties

Surrogate's Court
54 Broad Street
Lyons, NY 14489
(315) 946-5430; (315) 946-5433 FAX
Shirley Comella, Chief Clerk
(probate records)
Surrogate's search service (no information given
over the phone): $30.00 for under 25 years,
$90.00 for over 25 years; copies: 25¢ per page
or $6.00 per certified page

Wayne County Clerk
(County Office Building, Records Center, 9
Pearl Street—location)
PO Box 608 (mailing address)
Lyons, NY 14489-0608
(315) 946-7470; (315) 946-5978 FAX
mjankowski@co.wayne.ny.us
http://www.co.wayne.ny.us/ctyclerk.htm
Michael Jankowski
(land records, naturalization records)

Westchester County

organized 1683, original county

Surrogate's Court
140 Grand Street
White Plains, NY 10601
(914) 824-5656; (914) 995-3728 FAX
jkelly@courts.state.ny.us
http://www.nycourts.gov/courts/9jd/Westches
ter/surrogates.shtml
John W. Kelly, Esq., Chief Clerk
(probate records consolidated index)
Surrogate's search service (no information given
over the phone): $30.00 for under 25 years,

$90.00 for over 25 years; copies: 25¢ per page
or $6.00 per certified page

Westchester County Clerk
110 Dr. Martin Luther King, Jr., Boulevard
White Plains, NY 10601
(914) 995-3080; (914) 995-4030 FAX
cclerk@westchestergov.com
http://www.westchesterclerk.com
Timothy C. Idoni

Wyoming County

organized 1841 from Genesee County

Surrogate's Court
Courthouse, 147 North Main Street
Warsaw, NY 14569
(585) 786-3148; (585) 786-3800 FAX
wbeyer@courts.state.ny.us
http://www.nycourts.gov/courts/8jd/Wyoming
/index.shtml
William C. Beyer, Chief Clerk
(probate records)
Surrogate's search service (no information given
over the phone): $30.00 for under 25 years,
$90.00 for over 25 years; copies: 25¢ per page
or $6.00 per certified page, no minimum

Wyoming County Clerk
(143 North Main Street—location)
PO Box 70 (mailing address)
Warsaw, NY 14569-1123
(716) 786-8810; (716) 786-3703 FAX
jcoveny@wyomingco.net
http://www.wyomingco.net
Janet Coveny
(land records with, some naturalization records
for a limited period, petitions of intentions
from 1841)
copies of naturalization records: 50¢ per page

Yates County

organized 1823 from Ontario County

Surrogate's Court
Courthouse, 415 Liberty Street
Penn Yan, NY 14527
(315) 536-5130; (315) 536-5190 FAX
(probate records)
Surrogate's search service (no information given
over the phone): $30.00 for under 25 years,
$90.00 for over 25 years; copies: 25¢ per page
or $6.00 per certified page

Yates County Clerk
417 Liberty Street, Suite 1107
Penn Yan, NY 14527
(315) 536-5120
jbetts@yatescounty.org
http://www.yatescounty.org/display_page.asp?p
ID=78
Julie D. Betts

Capital: Raleigh. Statehood: 21 November 1789 (part of the Carolina Grant of 1663, gave up claims to western lands in 1790, including eastern Tennessee, the State of Franklin)

North Carolina's District Courts handle some civil actions, domestic relations, divorces, misdemeanors, felony preliminaries and juvenile cases. First Judicial District: Camden, Chowan, Currituck, Dare, Gates, Pasquotank and Perquimans counties; Second Judicial District: Beaufort, Hyde, Martin, Tyrrell and Washington counties; Third Judicial District: Carteret, Craven, Pamlico and Pitt counties; Fourth Judicial District: Duplin, Jones, Onslow and Sampson counties; Fifth Judicial District: New Hanover and Pender counties; Sixth Judicial District: Bertie, Halifax, Hertford and Northampton counties; Seventh Judicial District: Edgecombe, Nash and Wilson counties; Eighth Judicial District: Greene, Lenoir and Wayne counties; Ninth Judicial District: Franklin, Granville, Person, Vance and Warren counties; Tenth Judicial District: Wake County; Eleventh Judicial District: Harnett, Johnston and Lee counties; Twelfth Judicial District: Cumberland and Hoke counties; Thirteenth Judicial District: Bladen, Brunswick and Columbus counties; Fourteenth Judicial District: Durham County; Fifteenth Judicial District A: Alamance County; Fifteenth Judicial District B: Chatham and Orange counties; Sixteenth Judicial District: Robeson and Scotland counties; Seventeenth Judicial District A: Caswell and Rockingham counties; Seventeenth Judicial District B: Stokes and Surry counties; Eighteenth Judicial District: Guilford County; Nineteenth Judicial District A: Cabarrus and Rowan counties; Nineteenth Judicial District B: Montgomery and Randolph counties; Twentieth Judicial District: Anson, Moore, Richmond, Stanly and Union counties; Twenty-first Judicial District: Forsyth County; Twenty-second Judicial District: Alexander, Davidson, Davie and Iredell counties; Twenty-third Judicial District: Alleghany, Ashe, Wilkes and Yadkin counties; Twenty-fourth Judicial District: Avery, Madison, Mitchell, Watauga and Yancey counties; Twenty-fifth Judicial District: Burke, Caldwell and Catawba counties; Twenty-sixth Judicial District: Mecklenburg County; Twenty-seventh Judicial District A: Gaston County; Twenty-seventh Judicial District B: Cleveland and Lincoln counties; Twenty-eighth Judicial District: Buncombe County; Twenty-ninth Judicial District: Henderson, McDowell, Polk, Rutherford and Transylvania counties; Thirtieth Judicial District: Cherokee, Clay, Graham, Haywood, Jackson, Macon and Swain counties.

The Superior Courts, which sit at each county seat, are the courts of general jurisdiction. Division One: First through Eighth Judicial districts; Division Two: Ninth through Sixteenth Judicial districts; Division Three: Seventeenth through Twenty-third Judicial districts; Division Four: Twenty-fourth through Thirtieth Judicial districts. The Court of Appeals and Supreme Court have appellate jurisdiction.

The state began to record births and deaths in 1913.

Alamance County
organized 1848 from Orange County

Alamance County Clerk of Superior Court
212 West Elm Street
Graham, NC 27253-2882
(336) 438-1002 (Clerk); (336) 438-1008 (Estates)
http://www.nccourts.org/County/Alamance/Default.asp
Diane A. Pickett
no probate search service; copies of probate records: $1.00 for the first page and 25¢ for

each additional page, no minimum

Alamance County Register of Deeds
(118 West Harden Street—location)
PO Box 837 (mailing address)
Graham, NC 27253
(336) 570-6565
david.barber@alamance-nc.com
http://www.alamance-nc.com/Alamance-NC
David J. P. Barber
(land records and vital records)

Alexander County
organized 1850 from Iredell, Caldwell and Wilkes counties

Alexander County Clerk of Superior Court
(Courthouse, 100 First Street S.W.—location)
PO Box 100 (mailing address)
Taylorsville, NC 28681
(828) 632-2215; (828) 632-3550 FAX
http://www.nccourts.org/County/Alexander/Default.asp
Seth Chapman
(probate records with Clerk of Superior Court)
probate search service: no charge to individuals; copies of probate records: 25¢ per page, no minimum

Alexander County Courthouse Annex
75 First Street S.W.
Taylorsville, NC 28681-2504
(828) 632-4346 (Tax Administration, Suite 2); (828) 632-3152 (Register, Suite 1); (828) 632-3400 (Register); (828) 632-1100 FAX (Tax Administration); (828) 632-1119 FAX (Register)
bhines@co.alexander.nc.us
http://www.alexandercountync.gov/index/index.php
Benjamin Hines
(land records with County Tax Administration, vital records with Register of Deeds)

Alleghany County
organized 1859 from Ashe County

Alleghany County Clerk of Superior Court
(Courthouse, 12 North Main Street—location)
PO Box 61 (mailing address)
Sparta, NC 28675
(336) 372-8949; (336) 372-4899 FAX
http://www.nccourts.org/County/Alleghany/Default.asp
Susie J. Gambill, Clerk of Superior Court

Alleghany County Register of Deeds
(County Administration Building, 348 South Main Street—location)
PO Box 186 (mailing address)
Sparta, NC 28675
(336) 372-4342; (336) 372-2061 FAX
deeds@skybest.com
http://www.alleghanycounty-nc.gov
Lizabeth Reeves Roupe, Registrar

Anson County
organized 1749 from Bladen County

Anson County Courthouse
(114 North Greene Street—location)
PO Box 1064 (mailing address)
Wadesboro, NC 28170-1064
(704) 694-3212 (Register of Deeds, PO Box 352); (704) 694-2314 (Clerk); (704) 695-1161 FAX (Clerk)
jhuntley@co.anson.nc.us
http://www.co.anson.nc.us; http://www.nccourts.org/County/Anson/Default.asp
Joanne Huntley, Register of Deeds; M. D. Hammonds, Clerk of Superior Court
(land records from the early 1700s to date, births and deaths from 1913, and marriages from 1868 [when courthouse burned] with Register of Deeds, probate records with Clerk of Superior Court)
land and vital records search service: $2.00 per name; no probate search service; copies of land records: $1.00 for the first page and 50¢ for each additional page from handwritten

originals, 50¢ per page from typewritten originals, $3.00 for the first certified page and $1.00 for each additional certified page, plus SASE; certified copies of vital records: $3.00 each for births, deaths or marriages (available only to authorized persons), $1.50 each for marriage licenses, $1.00 each for uncertified copies of births and deaths, plus SASE

Ashe County
organized 1799 from Wilkes County

Ashe County Courthouse
(150 Government Circle—location)
PO Box 95 (mailing address)
Jefferson, NC 28640
(336) 219-2540 (Register, Suite 2300); (336) 246-5641 (Clerk); (336) 246-4276 FAX (Clerk)
registerofdeeds@ashecountygov.com
http://www.ashecountygov.com; http://www.nccourts.org/County/Ashe/Default.asp
Shirley B. Wallace, Register of Deeds; Pam W. Barlow, Clerk of Superior Court

Avery County
organized 1911 from Caldwell, Mitchell and Watauga counties

Avery County Courthouse
(200 Montezuma Street—location)
PO Box 115 (mailing address)
Newland, NC 28657
(828) 733-8260 (Register); (828) 733-2900 (Clerk); (828) 733-8261 FAX (Register); (828) 733-8410 FAX (Clerk)
averyrod@bellsouth.net
http://www.averyrod.com; http://www.nccourts.org/County/Avery/Default.asp
Tamela Baker, Register of Deeds; Lisa Daniels, Clerk of Superior Court
(land records, naturalization records, vital records, probate records)

Beaufort County
organized 1705 from Bath District, which was organized 1696 and abolished in 1739; name changed from Archdale County in 1712

Beaufort County Courthouse
(112 West Second Street—location)
PO Box 1403 (mailing address)
Washington, NC 27889-1403
(252) 946-2323 (Register, PO Box 514); (252) 946-5184 (Clerk); (252) 946-7938 FAX (Register); (252) 946-6448 FAX (Clerk)
djleggett_1999@yahoo.com
http://www.co.beaufort.nc.us; http://www.nccourts.org/County/Beaufort/Default.asp
Jennifer Whitehurst, Register of Deeds; V. Martin Paramore, Clerk of Superior Court
(land records from 1696 and vital records from 1913 with Register of Deeds; probate records with Clerk of Superior Court)

Bertie County
organized 1722 from Bath District

Bertie County Courthouse
108 Dundee Street
Windsor, NC 27983
(252) 794-5309 (Register, PO Box 340); (252) 794-3030 (Clerk–Civil, PO Box 370); (252) 794-3039 (Clerk–Criminal); (252) 794-2482 FAX (Clerk)
belinda.white@ncmail.net
http://www.co.bertie.nc.us; http://www.nccourts.org/County/Bertie/Default.asp
Belinda White, Register of Deeds; John C. P. Tyler, Clerk of Superior Court
(land records from 1722, births and deaths from 1 October 1913, and marriages from 1760 with Register of Deeds, wills from 1763 to date with Clerk of Superior Court)

Bladen County
organized 1734 from Bath District

Bladen County Courthouse

(166 Courthouse Drive—location)
PO Box 2619 (mailing address)
Elizabethtown, NC 28337
(910) 862-6710 (Register of Deeds, Main Floor);
   (910) 862-4911 (Clerk–Estates & Special
   Proceedings, Main Floor); (910) 862-6131
   FAX (Clerk)
bcrod@bladenco.org
http://www.bladninfo.org;
   http://www.nccourts.org/County/Bladen/D
   efault.asp
Charity Lewis, Register of Deeds; Nichola S.
   Dennis, Clerk of Superior Court

Brunswick County
organized 1764 from New Hanover and Bladen
   counties

Brunswick County Clerk of Superior Court
(Courthouse [Building S], 310 Government
   Center Drive, NE—location)
PO Box 127 (mailing address)
Bolivia, NC 28422
(910) 253-8502 (Civil Division); (910) 253-8509
   (Criminal Division); (910) 253-7652 FAX
http://www.nccourts.org/County/Brunswick/
   Default.asp

Brunswick County Register of Deeds
(75 Courthouse Drive—location)
PO Box 87 (mailing address)
Bolivia, NC 28422
(910)253-2690; (877) 625-9310; (910) 253-2703
   FAX
rod@brunsco.net; rod-admin@brunsco.net;
   rod-tech@brunsco.net
http://www.brunsco.net
Robert J. Robinson
(land records and vital records)

Buncombe County
organized 1792 from Burke and Rutherford
   counties (in 1812 annexed Walton County,
   which was formed in 1803 from Indian lands)

Buncombe County Courthouse
60 Court Plaza
Asheville, NC 28801
(828) 250-4300 (Register, Room 110); (828) 232-
   2600 (Clerk)
otto.debruhl@buncombecounty.org
http://www.buncombecounty.org; http://www.
   nccourts.org/County/Buncombe/Default.asp
Otto Debruhl, Register of Deeds
(land records and vital records with Register of
   Deeds, probate records with Clerk of
   Superior Court)

Burke County
organized 1777 from Rowan County

Burke County Courthouse
(201 South Green Street, Morganton, NC
   28655—location)
PO Box 796 (mailing address)
Morganton, NC 28680
(828) 438-5450 (Register of Deeds, PO Box
   219); (828) 432-2806 (Clerk, PO Box 796);
   (828) 438-5463 FAX (Register); (828) 438-
   5460 FAX (Clerk)
rod@co.burke.nc.us
http://www.
   nccourts.org/County/Burke/Default.asp
Libby Cooper, Register of Deeds; Mabel H.
   Lowman, Clerk of Superior Court
(deed transfers from 1865, births, deaths, and
   marriages with Register of Deeds, estate
   proceedings from 1865 with Clerk of Superior
   Court)
no records search service

Bute County
(see Franklin and Warren counties)

Cabarrus County
organized 1792 from Mecklenburg County

Cabarrus County Clerk of Superior Court
(Courthouse, 77 Union Street South—location)

PO Box 70 (mailing address)
Concord, NC 28026-0070
(704) 786-4137
http://www.nccourts.org/County/Cabarrus/De
   fault.asp

Cabarrus County Register of Deeds
(Governmental Center, 65 Church Street S.E.—
   location)
PO Box 707 (mailing address)
Concord, NC 28026-0707
(704) 920-2112; (704) 920-2898 FAX
lfmcabee@cabarruscounty.us
http://www.cabarruscounty.us
Linda McAbee

Caldwell County
organized 1841 from Burke and Wilkes counties

Caldwell County Clerk of Superior Court
(216 Main Street N.W.—location)
PO Box 1376 (mailing address)
Lenoir, NC 28645-1376
(828) 759-8403; (828) 757-1479 FAX
http://www.nccourts.org/County/Caldwell/De
   fault.asp
Sandie Cannon
(probate records)

Caldwell County Register of Deeds
905 West Avenue, NW
Lenoir, NC 28645
(828) 757-1310; (828) 757-1294 FAX
wrash@co.caldwell.nc.us
http://www.co.caldwell.nc.us
Wayne L. Rash
(land records with, naturalization records, and
   vital records)

Camden County
organized 1777 from Pasquotank County

Camden County Courthouse
117 North Carolina Highway 343
Camden, NC 27921
(252) 338-1919, ext. 245 (Register, PO Box 190);
   (252) 331-4871, ext. 273 (Clerk, PO Box 219);
   (252) 338-1758 FAX (Register); (252) 331-
   4827 FAX (Clerk)
pkight@ecamden.cc;
   aspivey@camdencountync.gov
http://www.camdencountync.gov
Peggy Kight, Register of Deeds; Ann D. Spivey,
   Clerk of Superior Court
(land records and vital records with Register of
   Deeds, probate records with Clerk of
   Superior Court)
no probate search service ("Any request is
   passed on to member of Historical Society");
   copies of land records: 25¢ each, $3.00 for
   certified copies; copies of probate records:
   $1.00 for the first page and 25¢ for each
   additional page

Carteret County
organized 1722 from Bath District

Carteret County Clerk of Superior Court
300 Courthouse Square Complex
Beaufort, NC 28516
(252) 728-8500; (252) 728-6502 FAX
http://www.co.carteret.nc.us
Darlene Leonard
(probate records)

Carteret County Register of Deeds
Administration Building
302 Courthouse Square Complex
Beaufort, NC 28516
(252) 728-8474
melaniea@co.carteret.nc.us
http://www.co.carteret.nc.us
Melanie Arthur
(land records and vital records)
certified copies of vital records: $3.00 each
   (must be a member of the family)

Caswell County
organized 1777 from Orange County

Caswell County Courthouse
139 East Church Street
Yanceyville, NC 27379
(336) 694-4197 (Register, PO Box 98); (336)
   694-4171 (Clerk, PO Box 790); (336) 694-
   1405 FAX (Register); (336) 694-7338 FAX
   (Clerk)
ddameron@caswellcountync.gov
http://www.caswellnc.com;
   http://www.caswellrod.net;
   http://www.nccourts.org/County/Caswell/
   Default.asp
Delores S. Dameron, Register of Deeds; John
   Satterfield, Clerk of Superior Court
(land records from 1777 and vital records from
   1913 [some delayed births from 1880] with
   Register of Deeds, probate records from 1777
   with Clerk of Superior Court)
no probate search service; copies of probate
   records: $1.00 for the first page and 25¢ for
   each additional page, no minimum ("I do not
   photocopy the probate records due to the fact
   that the records are in bound volumes and
   wear and tear on the books has nearly
   destroyed some records; all probate records
   for Caswell are available from North Carolina
   Department of Archives")

Catawba County
organized 1842 from Lincoln County

Catawba County Justice Center
(110 S.W. Boulevard, Highway 321—location)
PO Box 790 (mailing address)
Newton, NC 28658
(828) 465-1573 (Register, PO Box 65); (828)
   466-466-6104(Clerk–Civil Department, PO
   Box 728); (828) 465-1911 FAX (Register)
RDeeds@catawbacountync.gov
http://www.catawbacountync.gov
Donna Spencer, Register of Deeds; Ms. Al Jean
   Bogle, Clerk of Superior Court
(land records and vital records with Register of
   Deeds, probate records with Clerk of
   Superior Court)
no probate search service; copies not available
   of index pages

Chatham County
organized 1842 from Orange County

Chatham County Clerk of Superior Court
(12 East Street—location)
PO Box 369 (mailing address)
Pittsboro, NC 27312
(919) 542-3240; (919) 542-1402 FAX
Tammy.K.Keshler@nccourts.org
http://www.nccourts.org/County/Chatham/St
   aff/Clerk.asp
David Cooper, Clerk; Tammy K. Keshler,
   Superior Court Judicial Assistant
(probate records)
no probate search service; copies of probate
   records: $1.00 for the first page and 25¢ for
   each additional page, no minimum

Chatham County Register of Deeds
(Courthouse Annex—location)
PO Box 369 (mailing address)
Pittsboro, NC 27312-0369
(919) 542-8235
reba.thomas@ncmail.net
http://www.chathamnc.org
Reba Thomas
(land records and vital records)

Cherokee County
organized 1839 from Macon County

Cherokee County Courthouse
75 Peachtree Street
Murphy, NC 28906
(828) 837-2613 (Register); (828) 837-2522
   (Clerk); (828) 837-8178 FAX (Clerk)
daphne.dockery@cherokeecounty-nc.org;
   http://www.nccourts.org/County/Cherokee
   /Default.asp
http://www.cherokeecounty-nc.gov
Daphne Dockery, Register of Deeds; Gerald D.

Breedlove, Clerk of Superior Court

Chowan County
organized 1672 from Albemarle District

Chowan County Courthouse
(101 South Broad Street—location)
PO Box 588 (mailing address)
Edenton, NC 27932
(252) 482-2619 (Register); (252) 482-2323
(Clerk); (252) 482-3062 FAX (Register); (252)
482-2190 FAX (Clerk)
susan.rountree@ncmail.net
http://www.chowancounty-nc.gov;
http://www.nccourts.org/County/Chowan/
Default.asp
Susan Rountree, Register of Deeds; Michael J.
McArthur, Clerk of Superior Court
(land records with Register of Deeds; probate
records with Clerk of Superior Court)
copies of land records: $1.00 for the first page
and 25¢ for each additional page, no
minimum

Clay County
organized 1861 from Cherokee County

Clay County Courthouse
25 Herbert Street
Hayesville, NC 28904
(828) 389-0087 (Register, PO Box 118); (828)
389-8334 (Clerk, PO Box 506); (828) 389-
3329 FAX (Clerk)
registerofdeeds@grove.net
http://www.main.nc.us/clay;
http://www.nccourts.org/County/Clay/Defa
ult.asp
Melissa Roach, Register of Deeds; Harold
McClure, Clerk of Superior Court
(land records from 1870, births and deaths from
1913, and marriages from 1890 with Register
of Deeds, probate records from 1890 with
Clerk of Superior Court)
no probate search service; copies of land
records: 25¢ per page; copies of probate
records: $1.00 for the first page and 25¢ for
each additional page, no minimum

Cleveland County
organized 1841 from Rutherford and Lincoln
counties

Cleveland County Clerk of Superior Court
Law Enforcement Center
100 Justice Place, Third Floor
Shelby, NC 28150
(704) 484-4862
http://www.clevelandcounty.com/nav/index.htm
Mitzi McGraw Johnson, Clerk of Superior Court

Cleveland County Register of Deeds
County Administration Building
311 east Marion Street
Shelby, NC 28150
(704) 484-4834
bonnie.reece@clevelandcounty.com
http://www.clevelandcounty.com/nav/index.htm
Bonnie E. Reece

Columbus County
organized 1808 from Bladen and Brunswick
counties

Columbus County Clerk of Superior Court
(100 Courthouse Circle—location)
PO Box 1587 (mailing address)
Whiteville, NC 28472
(910) 641-3000; (910) 641-3027 FAX
http://www.nccourts.org/County/Columbus/
Default.asp
Sheila S. Pridgen, Clerk of Superior Court

Columbus County Register of Deeds
(125 Washington Street, Suite B—location)
PO Box 1086 (mailing address)
Whiteville, NC 28472
(910) 640-6625; (910) 640-2547 FAX
kwhitehead@columbusco.org;
ccdeeds@weblnk.net
http://www.columbusco.org/dotnetnuke%5F2

Kandance Whitehead

Craven County
organized 1712 from Bath District

Craven County Clerk of Superior Court
(Courthouse, 302 Broad Street—location)
PO Box 1187 (mailing address)
New Bern, NC 28563-1187
(252) 639-9004; (252) 514-4891 FAX
jan.cahoon@nccourts.org
http://www.cravencounty.com
Jan H. Cahoon
(probate records)

Craven County Courthouse
226 Pollock Street
New Bern, NC 28560
(252) 636-6617; (252) 636-1937 FAX
regdeeds@cravencounty.com
http://www.cravencounty.com
Sherri B. Richard
(land records, naturalization records, vital
records)

Cumberland County
organized 1754 from Bladen County

Cumberland County Courthouse
(117 Dick Street, Fayetteville, NC 28301-5749—
location)
PO Box 363 (mailing address)
Fayetteville, NC 28302-0363
(910) 678-7775 (Register, Room 114); (910) 678-
2902 (Clerk); (910) 323-1456 FAX (Register);
(910) 486-8556 FAX (Clerk)
getdeeds@infionline.net;
cumberlancounty@nccourts.org
http://www.co.cumberland.nc.us
J. Lee Warren, Jr., Register of Deeds; Linda
Priest, Clerk of Superior Court
(land records from 1754 and vital records from
1913 with Register of Deeds, probate records
with Clerk of Superior Court)
no probate search service; copies of land
records: 25¢ per page, $3.00 for certified
copies

Currituck County
organized 1672 from Albemarle District

Currituck County Judicial Center
2801 Caragtoke Highway
Currituck, NC 27929
(252) 232-3297 (Register, Suite 300, PO Box 71;
(252) 232-2010 (Clerk); (252) 232-2218
(Clerk); (252) 232-3906 FAX (Register); (252)
232-3722 FAX (Clerk)
cdowdy@co.currituck.nc.us;
sheila.romm@nccourts.org
http://www.co.currituck.nc.us
Charlene Y. Dowdy, Register of Deeds; Sheila R.
Romm, Clerk of Superior Court

Dare County
organized 1870 from Tyrrell, Hyde and
Currituck counties

Dare County Justice Center
(962 Marshall C. Collins Drive—location)
PO Box 1849 (mailing address)
Manteo, NC 27954-1849
(252) 475-5970 (Register); (252) 475-9100
(Clerk); (252) 473-1620 FAX (Clerk)
BarbaraG@co.dare.nc.us;
merlee.t.austin@nccourts.org
http://www.co.dare.nc.us
Barbara Gray, Register of Deeds; Merlee Austin,
Clerk of Superior Court

Davidson County
organized 1822 from Rowan County

Davidson County Courthouse
110 West Center Street, Lexington, NC 27292
Lexington, NC 27293
(336) 242-2150 (Register, PO Box 464); (336)
249-0351 (Clerk, PO Box 402); (336) 249-
6951 FAX (Clerk)
drickard@co.davidson.nc.us;

tmvm@bellsouth.net
http://www.co.davidson.nc.us/home.asp;
http://www.co.davidson.nc.us/about_the_cle
rk.html
David Rickard, Register of Deeds; Ted Michael
McKinney, Clerk of Superior Court
(land records and vital records with Register of
Deeds, naturalization records and Deeds,
probate records with Clerk of Court)
no probate search service; copies of land
records: varies; copies of probate records:
$1.00 for the first page and 25¢ for each
additional page

Davie County
organized 1836 from Rowan County

Davie County Clerk of Superior Court
Courthouse, 140 South Main Street
Mocksville, NC 27028-2425
(336) 751-3507; (336) 751-4720 FAX
http://www.co.davie.nc.us; http://www.
nccourts.org/County/Davie/Default.asp
Kenneth D. "Ken" Boger
(probate records from 1836)
probate search service: no charge; copies of
probate records: $1.00 for wills, no minimum

Davie County Register of Deeds
County Administration Building
123 South Main Street, First Floor
Mocksville, NC 27028
(336) 753-6080
brent.shoaf@co.davie.nc.us
http://www.co.davie.nc.us
Brent Shoaf
(land records from 1836, births and deaths from
1913, marriages from 1836)

Dobbs County
(see Greene, Lenoir, Wayne, and Wilson
counties)

Duplin County
organized 1749 from New Hanover County

Duplin County Clerk of Superior Court
(Courthouse, 112 Duplin Street—location)
PO Box 189 (mailing address)
Kenansville, NC 28349
(910) 296-1686 (Civil Division); (910) 296-2310
FAX
http://www.nccourts.org/County/Duplin/Defa
ult.asp
Katie Q. Harrell
(probate records)
no probate search service other than for copies
("need full name—no initials—approximate
date of death"); copies of probate records:
$1.00 for the first page and 25¢ for each
additional page, $2.00 certified copy, no
minimum

Duplin County Register of Deeds
(Courthouse Annex, 118 Duplin Street, Room
#106—location)
PO Box 970 (mailing address)
Kenansville, NC 28349-0970
(910) 296-2108; (910) 296-2344 FAX
dbrinson@duplincounty.org
http://www.duplincountync.com/government
Offices/registerOfDeeds.html;
http://rod.duplincounty.org
Davis Brinson
(land records from 1749, births and deaths from
1913, and a few marriages in the late 1800s
with Register of Deeds)
no land or vital records search service; copies of
land and vital records: $1.00 per page, $3.00
for the first certified page and $1.00 for each
additional certified page

Durham County
organized 1881 from Orange and Wake counties

Durham County Clerk of Superior Court
Judicial Building, 201 East Main Street,
Durham, NC 27701-3641
(919) 564-7030 (Criminal, Room 337); (919)
564-7050 (Civil, Room 332); (919) 560-3341

FAX
http://www.nccourts.org/County/Durham/De
fault.asp
Archie L. Smith, III
no probate search service; copies of probate
records: $1.00 for the first page and 25¢ for
each additional page, $5.00 minimum

Durham County Register of Deeds
Ground Floor, Old Courthouse
200 East Main Street
Durham, NC 27701
(919) 560-0480; (919) 560-0497 FAX
regdeeds@co.durham.nc.us
http://www.co.durham.nc.us/departments/rgds
Willie Covington
(land records and marriages)

Edgecombe County
organized 1735 from Bertie County

Edgecombe County Courthouse
301 St. Andrews Street
Tarboro, NC 27886
(252) 641-7924 (Register, PO Box 386); (252)
823-2056 (Clerk, PO Drawer 9); (252) 641-
1771 FAX (Register); (252) 823-1278 FAX
(Clerk)
rcarpenterrod@aol.com
http://www.edgecombecountync.gov;
http://www.nccourts.org/County/Edgecom
be/Default.asp
Robin W. Carpenter, Register of Deeds; Carol
A. White, Clerk of Superior Court
(real estate records from 1759, maps from 1760,
births and deaths from 1913, marriages from
1867 with Register of Deeds; old wills in book
in Clerk's handwriting back to 1760 [originals
in Department of Archives and History,
Raleigh, NC], estate records from 1945 with
Clerk of Superior Court)
no probate search service; copies of probate
records: $1.00 for the first page and 25¢ for
each additional page, no minimum ("no
copies can be made from old will books; we
refer requests for old records to the
Department of Archives and History")

Forsyth County
organized 1849 from Stokes County

Forsyth County Clerk of Superior Court
(Hall of Justice, 200 North Main Street—
location)
PO Box 20099 (mailing address)
Winston-Salem, NC 27101
(336) 761-2250; (336) 761-2470 (Estates
Division); (336) 761-2018 FAX (Clerk)
http://www.forsyth.cc/courtinfo.aspx;
http://www.nccourts.org/County/Forsyth/
Default.asp

Forsyth County Register of Deeds
102 West Third Street
Liberty Street Plaza Building
Upper Plaza
Winston-Salem, NC 27101
(9336) 703-2700; (336) 703-2701 (Recorded
information line)
wooddc@co.forsyth.nc.us
http://www.co.forsyth.nc.us
Dickie C. Wood
(land records, births and deaths from 1913 to
date, and marriage licenses from 1849 to date)
no vital records search service; copies of vital
records: 50¢ each, $3.00 for certified copies

Franklin County
organized 1779 from Bute County, which was
discontinued at that time

Franklin County Clerk of Superior Court
Courthouse, 102 South Main Street
Louisburg, NC 27549-2523
(919) 496-5104, ext. 230 (Civil Division); (919)
496-5104, ext. 234 & 237 (Estates); (919) 496-
0407 FAX
http://www.nccourts.org/County/Franklin/De
fault.asp
(wills from 1776)

no probate search service; copies of probate
records: $1.00 for the first page and 25¢ for
each additional page

Franklin County Register of Deeds
(Courthouse Annex, 113 South Main Street—
location)
PO Box 545 (mailing address)
Louisburg, NC 27549
(919) 496-3500; (919) 496-1457 FAX
lstone@co.franklin.nc.us
http://www.co.franklin.nc.us
Linda Stone

Gaston County
organized 1846 from Lincoln County

Gaston County Courthouse
325 North Marietta Street
Gastonia, NC 28052-2331
(704) 862-7684 (Register, PO Box 1578); (704)
866-3181 (Register–Recording/Real Estate);
(704) 862-7687 (Register–Vital Records);
(704) 862-7623 (Register–Marriages); (704)
852-3100 (Clerk); (704) 852-3256 (Clerk–
Estates); (704) 852-3178 (Clerk–Civil); (704)
852-3267 Fax (Clerk)
slockridge@co.gaston.nc.us
http://www.co.gaston.nc.us; http://www.
nccourts.org/County/Gaston/Default.asp
Susan Lockridge, Register of Deeds
(land records from 1847 and vital records from
1913 with Register of Deeds, probate records
with Clerk of Superior Court)
no land or vital records search service; copies of
land records: 50¢ each; certified copies: $3.00
each

Gates County
organized 1778 from Chowan, Hertford and
Perquimans counties

Gates County Courthouse
202 Court Street
Gatesville, NC 27938
(252) 357-0850 (Register, PO Box 471, 27938);
(252) 357-1365 (Clerk, PO Box 31, 27939);
(252) 357-1568 FAX (Register); (252) 357-
1047 FAX (Clerk)
gatesrod@yahoo.com
http://www.albemarle-nc.com/gates; http://
www.gatesrod.com; http://www.nccourts.
org/County/Gates/Default.asp
Sharon G. Harrell, Register of Deeds; Nell
Wiggins, Clerk of Superior Court

Glasgow County
(see Greene County)

Graham County
organized 1872 from Cherokee County; name
changed from Glasgow County in 1799

Graham County Clerk of Superior Court
(Courthouse, 12 Court Street—location)
PO Box 1179 (mailing address)
Robbinsville, NC 28771-1179
(828) 479-7986; (828) 479-6417 FAX
http://www.grahamcounty.org;
http://www.nccourts.org/County/Graham/
Default.asp
Wanda A. (Johnnie) Brooms

Graham County Register of Deeds
12 North Main Street
Robbinsville, NC 28771
(828) 479-7971
http://www.grahamcounty.org
Carolyn Stewart

Granville County
organized 1746 from Edgecombe County

Granville County Courthouse
101 Main Street
Oxford, NC 27565
(919) 693-6314 (Register, PO Box 427); (919)
693-2649 (Clerk, PO Box 219); (919) 603-
1345 FAX (Register)
rod@granvillecounty.org

http://www.granvillecounty.org; http://www.
nccourts.org/County/Granville/Default.asp
Kathryn Averett, Register of Deeds
(land records from 1746, births and deaths from
1913 to date [plus delayed births], and
marriages from 1869 to date with Register of
Deeds, probate records with Clerk of
Superior Court)
no records search service; copies of land
records: available only from 1900; copies of
probate records: 50¢ per legal-sized page, 25¢
per letter-sized page, no minimum

Greene County
organized 1791 from Dobbs County, when
Dobbs County, which was created in 1758
from the eastern half of Johnston County,
was dissolved and divided between Greene
and Lenoir counties

Greene County Courthouse
301 North Greene Street
Snow Hill, NC 28580
(252) 747-3620 (Register, PO Box 86); (252)
747-3505 (Clerk, PO Box 675); (252) 747-
2700 FAX (Clerk)
gcrod@co.greene.nc.us
http://www.co.greene.nc.us
Nancy T. Murphy, Register of Deeds; Sandra
Sutton, Clerk of Superior Court
(land records, naturalization records, vital
records, probate records)

Guilford County
organized 1770 from Rowan and Orange
counties

Guilford County Courthouse
201 South Eugene Street
Greensboro, NC 27401
(336) 373-7556 (Register, Lower Level, Room
L53; PO Box 3427); (336) 574-4302 (Clerk,
PO Box 3008, 27402); (336) 801-5252 (Clerk–
Civil/Estates); (336) 334-5020 FAX (Clerk)
jthigpe@co.guilford.nc.us
http://www.co.guilford.nc.us; http://www.
nccourts.org/County/Guilford/Default.asp
Jeff L. Thigpen, Register of Deeds; David L.
Churchill, Clerk of Superior Court
(deeds from 1771, births and deaths from 1913,
and marriages from 1865 with Register of
Deeds, probate records with Clerk of
Superior Court)
copies of marriages: 50¢ each

Halifax County
organized 1758 from Edgecombe County

Halifax County Court Services Building
357 Ferrell Lane
Halifax, NC 27839
(252) 583-2101 (Register, PO Box 67); (252)
583-5061 (Clerk, PO Box 66); (252) 583-1273
FAX (Register); (252) 583-1005 FAX (Clerk)
evans-barbeej@halifaxnc.com
http://www.halifaxnc.com; http://www.
nccourts.org/County/Halifax/Default.asp
Judy Evans-Barbee, Register of Deeds; Rebecca
(Becky) C. Spragins, Clerk of Superior Court

Harnett County
organized 1855 from Cumberland County

Harnett County Clerk of Superior Court
(301 West Cornelius Harnett Boulevard, Suite
100—location)
PO Box 849 (mailing address)
Lillington, NC 27546
(910) 814-4600; (910) 893-3683 FAX
webcoc@harnett.org
http://www.harnett.org; http://www.
nccourts.org/County/Harnett/Default.asp
Dianne L. Hatley, Clerk of Superior Court
(probate records from 1920)
no probate search service

Harnett County Register of Deeds
305 West Cornelius Harnett Boulevard, Suite
200
Lillington, NC 27546

(910) 893-7540; (910) 814-3841 FAX
webrod@harnett.org; khargrove@harnett.org
http://www.harnett.org
Kimberly Hargrove
(land records and vital records)
no probate search service

Haywood County
organized 1808 from Buncombe County

Haywood County Clerk of Superior Court
Haywood County Justice Center
285 North Main Street, Suite 1500
Waynesville, NC 28786
(828) 454-6501; (828) 456-4937 FAX
http://www.haywoodnc.net; http://www.
nccourts.org/County/Haywood/Default.asp
June L. Ray

Haywood County Register of Deeds
Courthouse, 215 North Main Street
Waynesville, NC 28786
(828) 452-6635
amurray@haywoodnc.net
http://www.haywoodnc.net
Amy Murray
(land records from 1808, births and deaths from
1913, and marriages from 1850)

Henderson County
organized 1838 from Buncombe County

Henderson County Courthouse
200 North Grove Street
Hendersonville, NC 28739
(828) 697-4901 (Register, Suite 129); (828) 697-
4851 (Clerk, Suite 163, PO Box 965); (828)
697-4879 FAX (Clerk)
http://www.hendersoncountync.org; http://
www.henderson.lib.nc.us/county/depts/
deeds.html; http://www.nccourts.org/County
/Henderson/Default.asp
Nedra Moles, Register of Deeds; Kimberly
Gasperson-Justice, Clerk of Superior Court

Hertford County
organized 1759 from Chowan, Bertie and
Northampton counties

Hertford County Courthouse
(701 King Street—location)
PO Box 86 (mailing address)
Winton, NC 27986
(252) 358-7850 (Register, PO Box 36); (252)
358-7845 (Clerk, PO Box 86); (252) 358-7914
FAX (Register); (252) 358-0793 FAX (Clerk)
kathleen.wright@ncmail.net
http://www.co.hertford.nc.us; http://www.
nccourts.org/County/Hertford/Default.asp
Mrs. Kathleen Wright, Register of Deeds;
Shirley Johnson, Clerk of Superior Court
(land records and vital records with Register of
Deeds; probate records with Clerk of
Superior Court ["the Hertford County Court
House burned down twice, about 1830 and
again in 1862; our resources are limited except
for some old wills that were recopied and put
on record many years after the death of a
person"])
probate search service: no charge; copies of
probate records: $1.00 for the first page and
25¢ for each additional page, $1.00 for
certification

Hoke County
organized 1911 from Cumberland and Robeson
counties

Hoke County Clerk of Superior Court
(304 North Main Street—location)
PO Drawer 1569 (mailing address)
Raeford, NC 28376
(910) 875-3728; (910) 904-1708 FAX
http://www.nccourts.org/County/Hoke/
Default.asp
Vera M. Hollingsworth

Hoke County Register of Deeds
113 Campus Avenue
Raeford, NC 28376

(910) 875-2035; (910) 875-9554
odudley@hokecounty.org
http://www.hokencrod.org
Onnie Dudley

Hyde County
organized 1705 from Bath District; name
changed from Wickham County in 1712

Hyde County Clerk of Superior Court
(Courthouse, 40 Oyster Creek Street—location)
PO Box 337 (mailig address)
Swan Quarter, NC 27885
(252) 926-4101; (252) 926-1002 FAX
http://www.hydecounty.org; http://www.
nccourts.org/County/Hyde/Default.asp
Sharon Sadler
(wills from late 1700s, administration records
from 1900s)
no probate search service; copies of probate
records: $1.00 for the first page and 25¢ for
each additional page, $1.00 minimum

Hyde County Register of Deeds
(23145 U.S. 264—location)
PO Box 294 (mailig address)
Swan Quarter, NC 27885
(252) 926-4182 (252) 926-3710 FAX
lbyrd@hydecountync.gov; hyderd@earthlink.net
http://www.hydecounty.org
Lora Mooney Byrd
(land records and vital records)

Iredell County
organized 1788 from Rowan County

Iredell County Clerk of Superior Court
Courthouse, 221 East Water Street
Statesville, NC 27677
(704) 878-4204; (704) 878-3261 FAX
http://www.nccourts.org/County/Iredell/Defa
ult.asp
Rena W. Turner

Iredell County Register of Deeds
(Hall of Justice Annex, 201 East Water Street—
location)
PO Box 904 (mailing address)
Statesville, NC 27677
(704) 872-7468
bbell@co.iredell.nc.us
http://www.co.iredell.nc.us/welcome.asp
Brenda D. Bell
(deeds from 1788, births and deaths from 1913,
marriages from 1850)
no copies of vital records ("Earlier records are in
poor shape and cannot be copied; originals
are in North Carolina Archives")

Jackson County
organized 1851 from Haywood and Macon
counties

**Jackson County Justice and Administration
Center**
401 Grindstaff Cove Road
Sylva, NC 28779
(828) 586-7530 (Register); (828) 586-7511
(Clerk)
jochamilton@jacksonnc.org
http://www.jacksonnc.org; http://www.
nccourts.org/County/Jackson/Default.asp
Joe Hamilton, Register of Deeds; Ann D.
Melton, Clerk of Superior Court
(land records from 1851, vital records from 1913
with Register of Deeds; probate records with
Clerk of Superior Court)
copies of land and vital records: 50¢ per page

Johnston County
organized 1746 from Craven County

Johnston County Courthouse Annex
207 East Johnston Street
Smithfield, NC 27577
(919) 989-5160 (Register, Suite 209, PO Box
118); (919) 934-3191, ext. 210 (Clerk, PO Box
297); (919) 989-5728 FAX (Clerk); (919) 934-
5857 FAX (Clerk)
craig.olive@johnstonnc.com

http://www.co.johnston.nc.us; http://www.
nccourts.org/County/Johnston/Default.asp
Craig Olive, Register of Deeds; Will R. Crocker,
Clerk of Superior Court
(land records from 1600 to 1700s, births and
deaths from 1913, and marriages from 1600s
with Register of Deeds, probate records from
late 1700s with Clerk of Superior Court)
no probate search service; copies of land records:
50¢ per page, $1.00 per map; copies of probate
records: $1.00 for the first page and 25¢ for
each additional page, no minimum

Jones County
organized 1778 from Craven County

Jones County Courthouse
(101 Market Street—location)
PO Box 280 (mailing address)
Trenton, NC 28585
(252) 448-2551 (Register, PO Box 189); (252)
448-7351 (Clerk); (252) 448-1357 FAX
(Register); (252) 448-1607 (Clerk)
gthomas@co.jones.nc.us
http://www.co.jones.nc.us; http://jonesrod.
com; http://www.nccourts.org/County/
Jones/Default.asp
Gloria Thomas, Register of Deeds; Charles C.
Henderson, Clerk of Superior Court;
(land records, naturalization records, and vital
records with Register of Deeds, probate
records with Clerk of Superior Court)

Lee County
organized 1907 from Chatham and Moore
counties

Lee County Courthouse
(1400 South Horner Boulevard, Sanford, NC
27330—location)
PO Box 4209 (mailing address)
Sanford, NC 27331
(919) 718-4585, ext. 5570 (Register); (919) 708-
4414 (Clerk)
Ann.H.Blakely@NCCourts.org
http://www.leecountync.com; http://www.
nccourts.org/County/Lee/Default.asp
Molly McInnis, Register of Deeds; Ann H.
Blakely, Clerk of Superior Court
(land records with Register of Deeds, probate
records with County Clerk of Superior Court)
no probate search service; copies of probate
records: $1.00 for the first page and 25¢ for
each additional page, no minimum

Lenoir County
organized 1791 from Dobbs and Craven
counties, when Dobbs County, which was
created in 1758 from the eastern half of
Johnston County, was dissolved and divided
between Greene and Lenoir counties

Lenoir County Clerk of Superior Court
(Copurthouse, 130 South Queen Street—
location)
PO Box 68 (mailing address)
Kinston, NC 28501
(252) 527-6231 (Clerk); (252) 527-9154 FAX
(Clerk)
http://www.nccourts.org/County/Lenoir/Defa
ult.asp
Dawn Stroud, Clerk of Superior Court
(probate records)

Lenoir County Register of Deeds
(Lenoir County Administration Building, 101
South Queen Street—location)
Po Box 3289 (mailing address)
Kinston, NC 28502
(252) 559-6420; (252) 523-6139 FAX
mseymour@co.lenoir.nc.us
http://www.co.lenoir.nc.us
Margaret Seymour
(deeds, deeds of trust, leases, etc., births and
deaths from 1914, and marriages from 1873)
copies: $1.00 per page

Lincoln County
organized 1778 from Tryon County, which was

organized in 1768 and abolished in 1779

Lincoln County Clerk of Superior Court
(1 Courthouse Square—location)
PO Box 8 (mailing address)
Lincolnton, NC 28092-0008
(704) 736-8568; (704) 736-8567 (Clerk–
Civil/Estates)
http://www.lincolncounty.org/Officials/county
officials.htm; http://www.nccourts.org/
County/Lincoln/Default.asp
Fred Hatley
(probate records)
probate search service: no charge; copies of
probate records: 50¢ per page, no minimum

Lincoln County Register of Deeds
(105-A East Court Square, Second Floor—
location)
PO Box 218 (mailing address)
Lincolnton, NC 28093
(704) 736-8530; (704) 736-8534
sdeeds@vnet.net
http://www.lincolncounty.org
Elaine Harmon
(land records and vital records)

Macon County
organized 1828 from Haywood County

Macon County Courthouse
5 West Main Street
Franklin, NC 2873-30054
(828) 349-2095 (Register); (828) 349-2041
(Clerk, PO Box 288, Franklin, NC 28744);
(828) 369-2515 FAX (Clerk)
deeds@maconnc.org
http://www.maconnc.org; http://www.
nccourts.org/County/Macon/Default.asp
Todd Raby, Register of Deeds; Victor H. Perry,
Clerk of Superior Court
(land records from 1828 and vital records from
1 October 1913; probate records with Clerk
of Superior Court)

Madison County
organized 1851 from Yancey and Buncombe
counties

Madison County Clerk of Superior Court
(Courthouse, 1 North Main Street—location)
PO Box 217 (mailing address)
Marshall, NC 28753
(828) 649-2531; (828) 649-2829 FAX
http://www.nccourts.org/County/Madison/De
fault.asp
Mark A. Cody
(probate records)

Madison County Register of Deeds
(County Administration Building, 5707 Highway
25/70—location)
PO Box 66 (mailing address)
Marshall, NC 28753
(828) 649-3131 (Register); (828) 649-3014
(Office)
susanrector@madisoncountync.org
http://www.main.nc.us/madison/index.html
Susan Rector
(land records, naturalization records, and vital
records)

Martin County
organized 1774 from Tyrrell and Halifax
counties

Martin County Governmental Center
305 East Main Street
Williamston, NC 27892
(252) 789-4320 (Register, PO Box 348); (252)
792-2515 (Clerk, PO Box 807); (252) 789-
4329 FAX; (252) 792-6668 FAX (Clerk)
tmanning@martincountyncgov.com
http://www.martincountyncgov.com; http://
www.nccourts.org/County/Martin/Default.asp
Mrs. Tina P. Manning, Register of Deeds; Tonya
C. Leggett, Clerk of Superior Court
(real estate from 1771, births and deaths from
1913 [many delayed birth certificates which
are before that time], and marriages from

1872 with Register of Deeds, probate records
with Clerk of Superior Court)
no probate search service; copies of land and
probate records: 25¢ each

McDowell County
organized 1842 from Burke and Rutherford
counties

McDowell County Courthouse
21 South Main Street
Marion, NC 28752
(704) 652-4727 (Register); (828) 652-7717
(Clerk); (828) 659-2641 FAX (Clerk)
preelmcdowel@titlesearcher.com
http://www.mcdowellgov.com; http://www.
nccourts.org/County/McDowell/Default.asp
Patricia Reel, Register of Deeds; Donald R.
Ramsey, Clerk of Superior Court
(land records and vital records with Register of
Deeds, probate records with Clerk of
Superior Court)

Mecklenburg County
organized 1762 from Anson County

**Mecklenburg County Clerk of Superior
Court**
(Courthouse, 832 East Fourth Street, Charlotte,
NC 28202—location)
PO Box 37971 (mailing address)
Charlotte, NC 28237-7971
(704) 868-0400 (Information); (704) 686-0460
(Estates Department)
martha.h.curran@nccourts.org
http://www.meckboe.org/ElectedOfficials
Report.aspx; http://www.nccourts.org/
County/Mecklenburg/Default.asp
Martha Curran
(probate records)

Mecklenburg County Register of Deeds
720 East Fourth Street
Charlotte, NC 28202
(704) 336-2443
judy.gibson@mecklenburgcountync.gov;
gibsoja@co.mecklenburg.nc.us
http://www.co.mecklenburg.nc.us/living/home
.htm
Judith Gibson
(land records and vital records)

Mitchell County
organized 1861 from Burke, Caldwell, Yancey,
McDowell and Watauga counties

Mitchell County Clerk of Superior Court
(Courthouse, 17 North Mitchell Avenue—
location)
PO Box 402 (mailing address)
Bakersville, NC 28705-0402
(828) 688-2161; (828) 688-2168 FAX
http://www.nccourts.org/County/Mitchell/Def
ault.asp
Janet L. Cook
(probate records)
no probate search service; copies of probate
records: 25¢ per page, no minimum

Mitchell County Register of Deeds
26 Crimson Laurel Circle
Bakersville, NC 28705
(828) 688-2139, ext. 320; (828) 688-3666 FAX
mcrod@mitchell.main.nc.us
http://www.mitchellcounty.org
Patty Young
(land records and vital records)

Montgomery County
organized 1778 from Anson County

Montgomery County Clerk of Superior Court
(Courthouse108 East Main Street—location)
PO Box 527 (mailing address)
Troy, NC 27371-0527
(910) 576-4211, ext. 222 (Clerk); (910) 576-4211,
ext. 241 & 242 (Clerk–Estates Department)
http://www.montgomerycountync.com; http://
www.nccourts.org/County/Montgomery/
Default.asp

Wayne Wooten, Clerk of Superior Court
(probate records)

Montgomery County Register of Deeds
(102 East Spring Street—location)
PO Box 695 (mailing address)
Troy, NC 27371-0527
(910) 576-4271; (910) 576-2209 FAX
montrod@earthlink.net
http://www.montgomerycountync.com;
http://www.montgomeryrod.net
Mrs. Kaye Norris
(land records, naturalization records, and vital
records)

Moore County
organized 1784 from Cumberland County

Moore County Clerk of Superior Court
(102 Monroe Street—loction)
PO Box 936 (mailing address)
Carthage, NC 28327
(910) 947-2396; (910) 947-1444 FAX
http://courts.co.moore.nc.us/index.htm; http://
www.nccourts.org/County/Moore/Default.asp
Catherine Phillips Graham
no probate search service; copies of probate
records: 50¢ per page

Moore County Register of Deeds
(100 Dowd Street—location)
PO Box 1210 (mailing address)
Carthage, NC 28327
(910) 947-6300 (Register); (910) 947-6370 (Vital
Records Section); (910) 947-6374 (Deed Vault
Section)
jmartin@moorecountync.gov
http://www.moorecountync.gov;
http://rod.moorecountync.gov/default.aspx
Judy D. Martin
(land records and vital records)

Nash County
organized 1777 from Edgecombe County

Nash County Courthouse
234 West Washington Street
Nashville, NC 27856-1255
(252) 459-9836 (Register, PO Box 974); (252)
459-4081 (Clerk–Civil, PO Box 759); (252)
459-9889 FAX (Register); (252) 459-6050
FAX (Clerk)
barbara.sasser@nashcountync.gov
http://co.nash.nc.us; http://www.deeds.
co.nash.nc.us; http://www.nccourts.org/
County/Nash/Default.asp
Barbara W. Sasser, Register of Deeds; Rachel
Joyner, Clerk of Superior Court
(estate records from 1777 to date, births from
October 1913 to date, deaths from 1911 to
date, marriages from 1862 to date with
Register of Deeds, wills and estates with Clerk
of Superior Court)

New Hanover County
organized 1729 from Bath and Clarendon districts

**New Hanover County Clerk of Superior
Court**
(Courthouse, 316 Princess Street, Wilmington,
NC 28401—location)
PO Box 2023 (mailing address)
Wilmington, NC 28402
(910) 341-1300; (910) 341-1111 (Court Offices);
(910) 341-1304 (Estates)
http://www.nhcgov.com; http://www.nccourts.
org/County/NewHanover/Default.asp

New Hanover County Register of Deeds
EMS Building, 216 North Second Street, Rooms
2 & 3
Wilmington, NC 28401
(910) 798-4530; (910) 798-7751 FAX
rebeccapsmith@nhcgov.com
http://www.nhcgov.com
Rebecca P. Smith

Northampton County
organized 1741 from Bertie County

Northampton County Clerk of Superior Court
(Courthouse, 104 West Jefferson Street—location)
PO Box 217 (mailing address)
Jackson, NC 27845
(252) 534-1631; (252) 534-1308 FAX
http://www.nccourts.org/County/Northampton/Default.asp
Venus M. Spruill
(probate records)

Northampton County Register of Deeds
(Jasper Ely Annex Building, Thomas Bragg Street—location)
PO Box 128 (mailing address)
Jackson, NC 27845
(252) 534-2511; (252) 534-1580 FAX
pauline.deloatch@ncmail.net
http://www.northamptonnc.com/register.asp
Pauline Deloatch, Register of Deeds; Venus M. Spruill, Clerk of Superior Court
(real estate records from 1741, naturalization records, birth and death records from 1913, and marriages from 1863)

Onslow County
organized 1734 from Bath District

Onslow County Clerk of Superior Court
Courthouse, 625 Court Street
Jacksonville, NC 28540-4797
(910) 455-4458; (910) 455-4458, ext. 223 (Estates and Special Proceedings); (910) 455-4458 FAX
http://www.nccourts.org/County/Onslow/Default.asp
Bettie Gurganus
no probate search service; copies of probate records: $1.00 for the first copy and 25¢ for each additional page

Onslow County Register of Deeds
109 Old Bridge Street
Jacksonville, NC 28540
(910) 347-3451
http://www.co.onslow.nc.us/register%5Fof%5Fdeeds
Ms. Maryland K. Washington
(land records and vital records)

Orange County
organized 1752 from the western portions of Bladen, Granville and Johnston counties

Orange County Clerk of Superior Court
New Courthouse
106 East Margaret Lane
Hillsborough, NC 27278-2546
(919) 245-2210; (919) 967-9251, ext. 2210
http://www.nccourts.org/County/Orange/Default.asp
Joan Terry
(probate records from 1754)
no probate search service (must have book and page number of a specific document); copies of probate records: $1.00 for the first page and 25¢ for each additional page, $2.00 for certification

Orange County Register of Deeds
Government Services Center
200 South Cameron Street
Hillsborough, NC 27278
(919) 245-2675
jpearson@co.orange.nc.us
http://www.co.orange.nc.us
Joyce Pearson
(land records from 1754)

Pamlico County
organized 1872 from Craven County; Lowland and Hobucken were in Beaufort County and were organized into Pamlico County in 1874

Pamlico County Courthouse
202 Main Street
Bayboro, NC 28515
(252) 745-4421 (Register, PO Box 433); (252) 745-6000 (Clerk, PO Box 38); (252) 745-7020

FAX (Register); (252) 745-6018 FAX (Clerk)
pamlico_rod@hotmail.com;
steven.e.hollowell@nccourts.org
http://www.co.pamlico.nc.us;
http://www.nccourts.org/County/Pamlico/Default.asp
Sue H. Whitford, Register of Deeds; Steven E. Hollowell, Clerk of Superior Court
(land records from 1872 with Register of Deeds, PO Box 433, Bayboro, NC 28515, births and deaths from 1913, marriages from 1872 with Register of Deeds, probate records with Clerk of Superior Court)

Pasquotank County
organized 1672 from Albemarle District

Pasquotank County Courthouse
(206 East Main Street, Elizabeth City, NC 27909—location)
PO Box 449 (mailing address)
Elizabeth City, NC 27907-0449
(252) 335-4367 (Register, Room D102, PO Box 154); (252) 331-4751 (Clerk); (252) 335-5106 FAX (Register); (252) 331-4826 FAX (Clerk)
SummerourD@co.pasquotank.nc.us
http://www.co.pasquotank.nc.us; http://www.nccourts.org/County/Pasquotank/Default.asp
Dollie Summerour, Register of Deeds; Lynne Pike, Clerk of Superior Court
(land records from 1700, births and deaths from 1913 [a few born in city back to 1903], marriage licenses from 1867, and marriage bonds from 1761 to 1866 with Register of Deeds, probate records with Clerk of Superior Court)
copies of land records: 25¢ per 11" x 14" page, 50¢ per 14" x 17" page, $1.00 minimum; copies of vital records: 25¢ each, $3.00 for certified copies, $1.00 minimum

Pender County
organized 1875 from New Hanover County

Pender County Clerk of Superior Court
(100 Wright Street—location)
PO Box 308 (mailing address)
Burgaw, NC 28425
(919) 259-1229, ext. 229 (Estates Division)
http://www.nccourts.org/County/Pender/Default.asp

Pender County Register of Deeds
(Holly Building, 300 East Fremont Street—location)
PO Box 43 (mailing address)
Burgaw, NC 28425
(910) 259-1225; (910) 259-1299 FAX
swicegoodj@pender-county.com
http://www.pender-county.com
Joyce M. Swicegood
(land records and vital records)
copies of land records: 25¢ each, $1.00 minimum; certified copies of vital records: $3.00 each (must have proper authorization)

Perquimans County
organized 1672 from Albemarle District

Perquimans County Courthouse
128 North Church Street
Hertford, NC 27944
(252) 426-5660 (Register, PO Box 74); (252) 426-1505 (Clerk, PO Box 33); (252) 426-7443 FAX (Register); (252) 426-1901 FAX (Clerk)
dreed@inteliport.com
http://www.co.perquimans.nc.us; http://www.nccourts.org/County/Perquimans/Default.asp
Mrs. Deborah S. Reed, Register of Deeds; Todd Tilley, Clerk of Superior Court

Person County
organized 1791 from Caswell County

Person County Courthouse
Courthouse Square, 105 South Main Street
Roxboro, NC 27573
(336) 597-1733 (Register); (336) 597-0554 (Clerk); (336) 597-0568 FAX (Clerk)
http://www.personcounty.net; http://www.

nccourts.org/County/Person/Default.asp
Amanda W. Garrett, Register of Deeds;
Deboarah Barker, Clerk of Superior Court

Pitt County
organized 1760 from Beaufort County

Pitt County Courthouse
100 West Third Street
Greenville, NC 27835
(252) 902-1650 (Register, PO Box 35); (252) 695-7100 (Clerk, PO Box 6067); (252) 830-3144 FAX (Clerk)
jjtart@co.pitt.nc.us
http://www.co.pitt.nc.us; http://www.nccourts.org/County/Pitt/Default.asp
Judy J. Tart, Register of Deeds; Eleanor H. Farr, Clerk of Superior Court
(land records and vital records with Register of Deeds, probate records from 1865 with Clerk Superior Court)
no probate search service; copies of probate records: $1.00 for the first page and 25¢ for each additional page

Polk County
organized 1855 from Rutherford and Henderson counties

Polk County Courthouse
1 Courthouse Square
Columbus, NC 28722
(828) 894-8450 (Register, PO Box 308); (828) 894-8231 (Clerk); (828) 894-5781 FAX (Register); (828) 894-5752 FAX (Clerk)
swhitmire@polknc.org
http://www.polknc.org; http://www.nccourts.org/County/Polk/Default.asp
Mrs. Sheila Whitmire, Register of Deeds; Charlene T. Owens, Clerk of Superior Court
(land records, naturalization records, and vital records with Register of Deeds, probate records with Clerk of Superior Court)

Randolph County
organized 1779 from Guilford County

Randolph County Clerk of Superior Court
176 East Salisbury Street
Asheboro, NC 27203
(336) 328-3001 (Clerk, Estates Division)
http://www.nccourts.org/County/Randolph/Default.asp
Lyda B. Skeen, Clerk of Superior Court
no records search service; copies of probate records: $1.00 for the first page and 25¢ for each additional page, $1.00 minimum plus SASE

Randolph County Register of Deeds
(The Shaw Building, 158 Worth Street—location)
PO Box 4588 (mailing address)
Asheboro, NC 27203
(336) 318-6960; (336) 318-6970 FAX
annshaw@randrod.com
http://www.co.randolph.nc.us
Krista M. Lowe, Department Head
(land records from 1779, births and deaths from 1913, and marriage bonds from 1779)
no records search service ("we do not have the time or personnel to do extensive genealogical research; I usually refer searchers to the Historical Society at the Asheboro Public Library; they have a very elaborate set-up with copies of all of our records and more");
copies of land records: 50¢ per page plus SASE

Richmond County
organized 1779 from Anson County

Richmond County Courthouse
(114 East Franklin Street—location)
PO Box 724 (mailing address)
Rockingham, NC 28379
(910) 997-8200; (910) 997-9100 (Clerk of Superior Court); (910) 997-8208 FAX; (910) 997-9126 FAX (Clerk)
pat.mcdonald@ncmail.net

http://www.co.richmond.nc.us; http://www.
    nccourts.org/County/Richmond/Default.asp
Pat McDonald, Register of Deeds

Robeson County
organized 1786 from Bladen County

Robeson County Clerk of Superior Court
501 North Elm Street, Room 101, Lumberton,
    NC 28358-5558—location)
PO Box 1084 (mailing address)
Lumberton, NC 28358-1084
(910) 737-5035; (910) 618-5598
vicki.locklear@co.robeson.nc.us
http://www.nccourts.org/County/Robeson/De
    fault.asp
Renae O. Hunt
(probate records)
no probate search service

Robeson County Register of Deeds
500 North Elm Street, Room 102
Lumberton, NC 28358
(910) 671-3040
vicki.locklear@co.robeson.nc.us
http://www.co.robeson.nc.us
Vicki L. Locklear
(deeds, deeds of trust, etc., and vital records)
no land records search service (contact Sam
    West, Rt. 5, Box 319, Lumberton, NC 28358);
    copies of land records: 50¢ each

Rockingham County
organized 1785 from Guilford County

Rockingham County Courthouse
1086 NC Highway 65
Wentworth, NC 27375-0127
(336) 342-8820 (Register, Basement, PO Box
    56); (336) 342-8700 (Clerk, PO Box 127);
    (336) 342-6209 FAX (Register)
rcipriani@co.rockingham.nc.us
http://www.co.rockingham.nc.us; http://www.
    nccourts.org/County/Rockingham/Default.asp
Rebecca B. Cipriani, Register of Deeds; J. Mark
    Pegram, Clerk of Superior Court
(land records from 1787, births and deaths from
    October 1913 [some delayed certificates for
    persons living in 1942 and applying for
    registration], marriage licenses from 1868,
    marriage bond index to marriages on file in
    the Department of Archives and History in
    Raleigh, marriage bonds from 1785 to 1868,
    marriage licenses from 1962 with Archives of
    the North Carolina Historical Commission in
    Raleigh with Register of Deeds; cross-index to
    wills from 1804, cross-index to administrators
    and executors from 1865, a book of old wills
    containing wills prior to 1804, a number of
    estate records with the North Carolina State
    Archives, Department of Cultural Resources,
    Division of Archives and History, with Clerk
    of Superior Court)
no land records search service (must have
    grantor, grantee, property involved and date
    of transaction); no vital records search service
    from Register of Deeds (must have
    registrant's and parents' names and date and
    place of birth or registrant's name and date
    and place of death or names of bride and
    groom and date of marriage); no probate
    search service; copies of land records: 50¢ per
    page, $3.00 for the first certified page and
    $1.00 for each additional certified page, $1.00
    minimum; copies of vital records available
    only to registrant, current spouse, sibling,
    child, parent, step-parent, grandparent or
    authorized agent

Rowan County
organized 1753 from Anson County,
    encompassing the entire northwestern
    qudrant of North Carolina and the area that
    became Tennessee

Rowan County Clerk of Superior Court
(210 North Main Street—location)
PO Box 4599 (mailing address)
Salisbury, NC 28145-4599

(704) 639-7505; (704) 639-7680 (Estates); (704)
    639-7598 FAX
http://www.nccourts.org/County/Rowan/Defa
    ult.asp
Jeffrey R. Barger

Rowan County Register of Deeds
402 North Main street
Salisbury, NC 28144
(704) 216-8626
earnhardtb@co.rowan.nc.us
http://www.co.rowan.nc.us
Bobbie Earnhardt

Rutherford County
organized 1779 from Burke and Tryon counties,
    the latter of which was organized in 1768 and
    abolished in 1779

Rutherford County Courthouse
(229 North Main Street—location)
PO Box 630 (mailing address)
Rutherfordton, NC 28139-0630
(828) 287-6155 (Register, PO Box 551); (828)
    287-6195 (Register); (828) 286-9136 (Clerk);
    (828) 286-4322 FAX (Clerk)
faye.huskey@rutherfordcountync.gov;
    rdeedrc@blueridge.net
http://www.rutherfordcountync.gov;
    http://www.nccourts.org/County/
    Rutherford/Default.asp
Faye Huskey, Register of Deeds; Keith H.
    Melton, Clerk of Superior Court
(land records from the 1700s ["but we do not
    make copies of these very old records"],
    births and deaths from 1913, marriages from
    1700s with Register of Deeds; probate
    records with Clerk of Superior Court)

Sampson County
organized 1784 from Duplin and New Hanover
    counties

Sampson County Courthouse
101 East Main Street
Clinton, NC 28328
(910) 592-8026 (Register, Room 107); (910) 592-
    5191, ext. 216 (Clerk, Estates & Special
    Proceedings); (910) 592-1803 FAX (Register);
    (910) 592-5502 FAX (Clerk)
deeds@sampsonnc.com;
    norman.w.naylor@nccourts.org
http://www.sampsonnc.com; http://www.
    nccourts.org/County/Sampson/Default.asp
Paulette W. King, Register of Deeds; Norman
    Wayne Naylor, Clerk of Superior Court
(land records from the mid-1700s, births and
    deaths from 1913, and marriages from 1865
    with Register of Deeds; wills, estates and early
    court minutes with Clerk of Superior Court)
no land records search service; copies of land
    records: $2.00 per deed, $3.00 for certified
    copies; certified copies of vital records: $3.00
    (identification needed to search vital records)

Scotland County
organized 1899 from Richmond County

Scotland County Courthouse
(212 Biggs Street, Laurinburg, NC 28352—
    location)
PO Box 769 (mailing address)
Laurinburg, NC 28353
(910) 277-2577 (Register); (910) 277-3240
    (Clerk); (910) 277-3261 FAX (Clerk)
dholcomb@scotlandcounty.org
http://www.scotlandcounty.org; http://www.
    nccourts.org/County/Scotland/Default.asp
Debra Holcomb, Register of Deeds; C.
    Whitfield Gibson, Clerk of Superior Court
(land records and vital records with Register of
    Deeds, naturalization records and probate
    records with Clerk of Superior Court)

Stanly County
organized 1841 from Montgomery County

Stanly County Courthouse
201 South Second Street
Albemarle, NC 28002

(704) 986-3640 (Register, PO Box 97); (704)
    982-2161 (Clerk, PO Box 668); (704) 98-8107
    FAX (Clerk)
calmond1@yahoo.com
http://www.co.stanley.nc.us; http://www.
    nccourts.org/County/Stanly/Default.asp
Cecil Almond, Register of Deeds; Michael
    Huneycutt, Clerk of Superior Court
(land records from 1841, births and deaths from
    October 1913, and marriages from mid-1800s
    with Register of Deeds; probate records with
    Clerk of Superior Court)
no probate search service; copies of probate
    records: $1.00 each, $1.00 minimum

Stokes County
organized 1798 from Surry County

Stokes County Clerk of Superior Court
(Gobernment Center, Highway 89, 1012 Main
    Street—location)
PO Box 50 (mailing address)
Danbury, NC 27016
(336) 593-9173; (336) 593-5459 FAX
p.jason.tuttle@aoc.state.nc.us
http://www.co.stokes.nc.us; http://www.
    nccourts.org/County/Stokes/Default.asp
Jason Tuttle
copies of probate records: 25¢ per page

Stokes County Register of Deeds
Administration Building
1014 Main Street
Danbury, NC 27016
(336) 593-2414; (336) 593-9360 FAX
kyoung@co.stokes.nc.us
http://www.co.stokes.nc.us
Kathy Young
(land records and vital records)

Surry County
organized 1770 from Rowan County

Surry County Courthouse
201 East Kapp Street
Dobson, NC 27017
(336) 386-9235 (Register, PO Box 303); (336)
    386-3700 (Clerk, PO Box 345); (336) 386-
    9879 FAX (Clerk)
http://www.co.surry.nc.us; http://www.
    nccourts.org/County/Surry/Default.asp
Carolyn Comer, Register of Deeds; Pamela M.
    Marion, Clerk of Superior Court
(land records and vital records with Register of
    Deeds, probate records with Clerk of
    Superior Court)

Swain County
organized 1871 from Jackson and Macon
    counties

Swain County Courthouse
(101 Mitchell Street—location)
PO Box 1397 (mailing address)
Bryson City, NC 28713-1397
(828) 488-9273, ext. 205 (Register, PO Box
    1183); (828) 488-2288 (Clerk); (828) 488-9360
    FAX (Clerk)
swainROD@hotmail.com
http://www.swaincounty.org; http://www.
    nccourts.org/County/Swain/Default.asp
Diane Williamson Kirkland, Register of Deeds;
    Helen C. Styles, Clerk of Superior Court

Transylvania County
organized 1861 from Jackson and Henderson
    counties

Transylvania County Clerk of Superior Court
12 East Main Street
Brevard, NC 28712
(828) 884-3120; (828) 883-2161 FAX
http://www.nccourts.org/County/Transylvania
    /Default.asp
Rita A. Ashe
no probate search service; copies of probate
    records: 25¢ each, $3.00 for certified copies

Transylvania County Register of Deeds
7 East Main Street

Brevard, NC 28712
(828) 884-3162
Cindy.Ownbey@transylvaniacounty.org;
registercmo@citcom.net
http://www.transylvaniacounty.org
Cindy M. Ownbey
(births and deaths from 1914 and deeds)

Tryon County
(see Lincoln and Rutherford counties)

Tyrrell County
organized 1729 from Albemarle District

Tyrrell County Courthouse
(403 Main Street—location)
PO Box 406 (mailing address)
Columbia, NC 27925-0406
(252) 796-2901 (Register); (252) 796-6281
(Clerk); (252) 796-0008 FAX (Clerk)
tyrrelldeeds@beachlink.com
http://www.visittyrrellcounty.com/Government;
http://albemarle-nc.com/columbia; http://
www.nccourts.org/County/Tyrrell/Default.asp
Melanie Armstrong, Register of Deeds; Nathan
T. Everett, Clerk of Superior Court
(land records and vital records with Register of
Deeds, naturalization records and probate
records with Clerk of Court)
probate search service: no charge; copies of land
records: 25¢ per page; copies of probate
records: $1.00 for the first page and 25¢ for
each additional page, no minimum

Union County
organized 1842 from Mecklenburg and Anson
counties

Union County Courthouse
400 North Main Street
Monroe, NC 28112
(704) 283-3727 (Register, Room 205, PO Box
248, 28111); (704) 296-4600 (Clerk, PO Box
5038, 28111); (704) 283-3569 FAX (Register);
(704) 289-1283 FAX (Clerk)
crystalcrump@co.union.nc.us
http://www.co.union.nc.us; http://www.
nccourts.org/County/Union/Default.asp
Crystal Crump, Register of Deeds; J. R. Rowell,
Clerk of Superior Court
(land records and vital records with Office of
the Register of Deeds, probate records with
Clerk of Superior Court)
no probate search service

Vance County
organized 1881 from Franklin, Granville and
Warren counties

Vance County Clerk of Superior Court
156 Church Street, Suite 101
Henderson, NC 27536
(252) 738-9000; (252) 492-6666 FAX
http://www.nccourts.org/County/Vance/Defa
ult.asp

Vance County Register of Deeds
County Administration Building
122 Young Street, Suite F
Henderson, NC 27536
(252) 738-2110
http://www.vancecounty.org
Cynthia Abbott

Wake County
organized 1770 from Cumberland, Johnston and
Orange counties

Wake County Clerk of Superior Court
(316 Fayetteville Street Mall, Raleigh, NC
27601—location)
PO Box 351 (mailing address)
Raleigh, NC 27602
(919) 755-4105 (Clerk); (919) 755-4116 (Estates
Division, 12th Floor)
http://web.co.wake.nc.us/courts
Lorrin Freeman, Clerk of Superior Court
(probate records)

Wake County Register of Deeds

(300 South Salisbury Street, Raleigh, NC
27601—location)
Garland Jones Building, PO Box 1897 (mailing
address)
Raleigh, NC 27602-1897
(919) 856-5460
rodtech@co.wake.nc.us; lriddick@co.wake.nc.us
http://www.wakegov.com;
http://web.co.wake.nc.us/rdeeds
Laura M. Riddick
(land records, naturalization records, vital
records)

Warren County
organized 1779 from Bute County, which was
discontinued at that time

Warren County Courthouse
109 South Main Street
Warrenton, NC 27589
(252) 257-3265 (Register, PO Box 506); (252)
257-3261 (Clerk, PO Box 709); (252) 257-
5529 FAX (Clerk)
eweldon@co.warren.nc.us
http://www.warrencountync.com; http://
www.warrencountync.org; http://www.
nccourts.org/County/Warren/Default.asp
Elsie R. Weldon, Register of Deeds
(land records from 1764, birth and death records
from 1913, and marriage records from 1867
with Register of Deeds, probate records from
1764 with Clerk of Court)
probate search service: no charge for specific
name ("send as much information as
possible"; copies of probate records: $1.00 for
the first page and 25¢ for each additional
page, $1.00 minimum

Washington County
organized 1799 from Tyrrell County

Washington County Courthouse
120 Adams Street
Plymouth, NC 27962
(919) 793-2325 (Register, PO Box 1007); (252)
793-3013 (Clerk, PO Box 901); (252) 793-
1081 FAX (Clerk)
evann@washconc.org;
denise.m.moulden@nccourts.org
http://www.washconc.org; http://www.nc
courts.org/County/Washington/Default.asp
Elaine Vann, Register of Deeds; Denise
Moulden, Clerk of Superior Court
(births and deaths from 1913, marriage index
from 1851, marriage licenses from 1881, and
land records with Register of Deeds, probate
records with Clerk of Court)
no probate search service; certified copies of
vital records: $3.00 each (restricted to
immediate family members); copies of
probate records: 25¢ per page

Watauga County
organized 1849 from Ashe, Caldwell, Wilkes,
and Yancey counties

Watauga County Courthouse
842 West King Street
Boone, NC 28607-3525
(828) 265-8000; (828) 265-8052 (Register, Room
119—location, Suite 9—mailing address);
(828) 265-5364 (Clerk, Suite 13); (828) 265-
7632 FAX (Register); (828) 262-5753 FAX
(Clerk)
joanne.townsend@ncmail.net
http://www.wataugacounty.org; http://www.
nccourts.org/County/Watauga/Default.asp
Joanne Townsend, Register of Deeds; D. Glenn
Hodges, Clerk of Superior Court
(land records and vital records with Register of
Deeds, probate records with Clerk of
Superior Court)

Wayne County
organized 1779 from Craven and Dobbs
counties

Wayne County Courthouse
224 East Walnut Street

Goldsboro, NC 27530
(919) 731-1449 (Register, PO Box 267); (919)
731-7910 (Clerk, Room 230); (919) 731-2037
FAX (Clerk)
Lois.Mooring@waynegov.com
http://www.waynegov.com; http://www.
nccourts.org/County/Wayne/Default.asp
Lois J. Mooring, Register of Deeds; Pam
Minshew, Clerk of Superior Court
(land records from 1779 and vital records from
November 1913 with Register of Deeds,
naturalization records and probate records
with Clerk of Superior Court)
probate search service: no charge; copies of
probate records: $1.00 for the first page and
25¢ for each additional page, $1.00 minimum

Wilkes County
organized 1777 from Burke and Surry counties

Wilkes County Courthouse
500 Courthouse Drive
Wilkesboro, NC 28697-2497
(336) 651-7351 (Register, Room 1000); (336)
667-1201 (Clerk); (336) 667-1985 FAX (Clerk)
http://www.wilkescounty.net; http://www.
wilkesnc.org; http://www.nccourts.org/
County/Wilkes/Default.asp
Richard L. "Rick" Woodruff, Register of Deeds;
Janet D. Handy, Clerk of Superior Court
(land records, naturalization records, vital
records, probate records)

Wilson County
organized 1855 from Edgecombe, Johnston,
Wayne and Nash counties

Wilson County Clerk of Superior Court
(115 East Nash Street—location)
PO Box 1608 (mailing address)
Wilson, NC 27894
(252) 291-7502 (Civil); (252) 291-7500
(Criminal); (252) 291-8635 FAX (Civil); (252)
291-8049 FAX (Criminal)
http://www.nccourts.org/County/Wilson/Defa
ult.asp
Andrew J. Whitley

Wilson County Register of Deeds
101 North Goldsboro Street
Wilson, NC 27893
(252) 399-2935; (252) 399-2942 FAX
aneal@wilson-co.com
http://www.wilson-co.com
Audrey Neal
(land records from 1855, births and deaths from
1913, marriages from 1855)
copies: $1.00 each for uncertified copies
(available to "anyone with a stamp stating
certain information), $3.00 each for certified
copies (restricted to parents, children, spouse,
siblings)

Yadkin County
organized 1850 from Surry County

Yadkin County Courthouse
101 South State Street
Yadkinville, NC 27055
(336) 679-4225 (Register, PO Box 211); (336)
679-8838 (Clerk, PO Box 95)
kwagoner@yadkincountync.gov
http://www.yadkincounty.gov; http://www.
nccourts.org/County/Yadkin/Default.asp
Karen Wagoner, Register of Deeds; Wayne
Dixon, Clerk of Superior Court
no probate search service; copies of probate
records: $1.00 for the first page and 25¢ for
each additional page

Yancey County
organized 1833 from Buncombe and Burke
counties

Yancey County Courthouse
110 Towne Square
Burnsville, NC 28714
(704) 682-6181 (Register, Room 4); (828) 682-
2122 (Clerk, Room 5); (828) 682-6296 FAX
(Clerk)

wjobe@yancey.main.nc.us
http://www.nccourts.org/County/Yancey/Def
ault.asp
Willoree Jobe, Register of Deeds; Warren
Hughes, Clerk of Superior Court
(land records and vital records with Register of
Deeds, probate records with Clerk of
Superior Court)
no probate search service; copies of probate
records: $1.00 for the first page and 25¢ for
each additional page, $1.00 minimum

NORTH DAKOTA

*Capital: Bismarck. Statehood: 2 November 1889 (part
of Dakota Territory in 1861, separated from South
Dakota in 1889)*

North Dakota has several Municipal Courts
of limited jurisdiction. The North Dakota
County Courts used to handle some civil
actions, misdemeanors, preliminary hearings,
mental health cases, probate, guardianship and
small claims. As of 1 January 1995 the County
Courts were consolidated with the District
Courts. The District Courts have general
jurisdiction but do not sit at each county seat.
East Central Judicial District: Cass, Steele and
Traill counties at Fargo; Northeast Judicial
District: Benson, Bottineau, Cavalier, McHenry,
Pembina, Pierce, Ramsey, Renville, Rolette,
Towner and Walsh counties at Devils Lake,
Grafton and Rugby; Northeast Central Judicial
District: Grand Forks, Griggs and Nelson
counties at Grand Forks; Northwest Judicial
District: Burke, Divide, McKenzie, Mountrail,
Ward and Williams counties at Minot and
Williston; South Central Judicial District:
Burleigh, Emmons, Grant, Kidder, Logan,
McIntosh, McLean, Mercer, Morton, Oliver,
Sheridan, Sioux and Wells counties at Bismarck,
Linton and Mandan; Southeast Judicial District:
Barnes, Dickey, Eddy, Foster, La Moure,
Ransom, Richland, Sargent and Stutsman
counties at Jamestown, Valley City and
Wahpeton; Southwest Judicial District: Adams,
Billings, Bowman, Dunn, Golden Valley,
Hettinger, Slope and Stark counties at Dickinson
and Hettinger. The state's Supreme Court is the
court of last resort.

Adams County
organized 1885 from Stark County

Adams County Courthouse
602 Adams Avenue
Hettinger, ND 58639
(701) 567-2460; (701) 456-2910 FAX
gdangeru@state.nd.us
http://www.ndaco.org/counties/county_profile
.asp?CountyID=1
Ginger Dangerud, Recorder/Clerk of Court
(land records from 1907, probate records from
1907)
probate search service: no charge; copies of
probate records: 25¢ per page, no minimum

Barnes County
organized 1875 from Cass County

Barnes County Courthouse
230 Fourth Street NW
Valley City, ND 58072
(701) 845-8506 (Recorder, Room 201); (701)
845-8512 (Clerk); (701) 845-8538 FAX
(Recorder)
kertelt@co.barnes.nd.us
http://www.co.barnes.nd.us
Kerstin Ertelt, Interim County Recorder

Benson County
organized 1883 from Ramsey County

Benson County Courthouse
311 B Avenue South
Minnewaukan, ND 58351
(701) 473-5332 (Recorder); (701) 473-5345
(Clerk); (701) 473-5571 FAX (Recorder and
Clerk)
drandle@state.nd.us; lkjohnso@state.nd.us
http://www.ndaco.org/counties/county_profile
.asp?CountyID=3
Doris E. Randle, Recorder; Lana K. Johnson,
Clerk of Court
(land records with Recorder, vital records and
probate records with Clerk of Court)
probate search service: no charge; copies of
probate records: $1.00 per document, no

minimum ("pre-payment required before
copies are mailed")

Billings County
organized 1879 from unorganized territory

Billings County Courthouse
(495 Fourth Street—location)
PO Box 138 (mailing address)
Medora, ND 58645
(701) 623-4491
dadams@state.nd.us
http://www.billingscountynd.gov
Donna Adams, Recorder/ex-officio Clerk of
Court
(land records from 1886, births from 1904,
deaths from 1909 [both very incomplete],
probate records from 1896)
probate search service: no charge; copies of
probate records: 50¢ per page, no minimum

Bottineau County
organized 1873 from unorganized territory

Bottineau County Courthouse
314 West Fifth Street
Bottineau, ND 58318
(701) 228-2786 (Recorder); (701) 228-3983
(Clerk); (701) 228-3658 FAX (Recorder);
(701) 228-2336 FAX (Clerk)
hchriste@state.nd.us
http://www.ndaco.org/counties/county_profile
.asp?CountyID=5
Helen Christenson, Recorder; Rhonda
Langehaug, Clerk of Court
(land records with Recorder, incomplete vital
records before 1944 with Clerk of Court,
probate records from 1884 with Clerk of
Courts, vital records)
probate search service: no charge; copies of land
records: $1.00 for each five pages or part
thereof, $5.00 for the first two certified pages
and $2.00 for each additional certified page;
copies of probate records: 25¢ per page, no
minimum

Bowman County
organized 1883 from Billings County

Bowman County Courthouse
104 First Street NW
Bowman, ND 58623
(701) 523-3450; (701) 523-5443 FAX
ananders@pioneer.state.nd.us;
aanderson@ndcourts.com
http://www.ndaco.org/counties/county_profile
.asp?CountyID=6
Annetta Anderson, Recorder/Clerk of Court

Buffalo County
(see Burleigh, Kidder, Logan, McHenry, Rolette,
and Sheridan counties)

Burke County
organized 1910 from Ward County

Burke County Courthouse
103 Main Street, SE
Bowbells, ND 58721
(701) 377-2818 (Recorder); (701) 377-2718
(Clerk); (701) 377-2020 FAX
solson@state.nd.us
http://www.ndaco.org/counties/county_profile
.asp?CountyID=7
Susan Olson, Recorder/Clerk of Court
(land records with Recorder, marriages from
1910 with Clerk of Court [copies: not
available], probate records from 1910 with
Clerk of Court)
probate search service: no charge; copies of
probate records: 50¢ per page, no minimum

Burleigh County
organized 1873 from Buffalo County, which was
discontinued

Burleigh County Courthouse
(221 North Fifth Street, Bismarck, ND 58501—
location)

PO Box 5518 (mailing address)
Bismarck, ND 58506-5518
(701) 222-6749 (Recorder); (701) 222-6690
(Clerk)
dkroshus@nd.gov; dsimenson@ndcourts.com
http://www.co.burleigh.nd.us
Debbie Kroshus, County Recorder; Deb
Simenson, Clerk of Court
(land records with Recorder, vital records and
probate records with Clerk of Court)
no probate search service; copies of probate
records: 20¢ per page, no minimum

Cass County
organized 1873, original county

Cass County Courthouse
(211 Ninth Street South—location)
PO Box 2806 (mailing address)
Fargo, ND 58108-2806
(701) 241-5620 (Recorder); (701) 241-5645
(Clerk); (701) 241-5621 FAX (Recorder);
(701) 241-5636 FAX (Clerk)
recorder@co.cass.nd.us;
DHoward@ndcourts.gov
http://www.casscountygov.com;
http://www.court.state.nd.us/court/counties
/dc_clerk/cass.htm
Jewel Spies, Recorder; Dorothy Howard, Clerk
of Court
(land records with Recorder; marriage licenses
from 24 March 1872 and probate and
guardianship records from January 1899 with
Clerk of Court)
probate search service: no charge; copies of
probate records: 25¢ per page, $5.00 per
certified page, no minimum

Cavalier County
organized 1873 from Pembina County

Cavalier County Courthouse
901 Third Street
Langdon, ND 58249
(701) 256-2136 (Recorder); (701) 256-2124
(Clerk); (701) 256-2546 FAX (Recorder);
(701) 256-2124 FAX (Clerk)
vkubat@state.nd.us; bgellner@ndcourts.com
http://cvaliercounty.utma.com
Vicki Kubat, Recorder; Beverly Gellner, Clerk of
Court

Dickey County
organized 1881 from La Moure County

Dickey County Courthouse
(309 North Second Street—loction)
PO Box 215 (mailing address)
Ellendale, ND 58436
(701) 349-3249, ext. 5 (Recorder); (701) 349-
3249, ext. 4 (Clerk); (701) 349-4639 FAX;
(701) 349-3560 FAX (Clerk)
tstrand@state.nd.us; aschimke@ndcourts.com
http://www.ndaco.org/counties/county_profile
.asp?CountyID=11
Tom Strand, Recorder; Andi Schimke, Clerk of
Court
(land records with Recorder, vital records and
probate records with Clerk of Court)
probate search service: no charge; copies of
probate records: $5.00 each, $5.00 minimum

Divide County
organized 1910 from Williams County

Divide County Recorder-Clerk of Court
(300 North Main—location)
PO Box 68 (mailing address)
Crosby, ND 58730-0068
(701) 965-6831; (701) 965-6943 FAX
http://www.ndaco.org/counties/county_profile
.asp?CountyID=12
Shirley Peterman
(land records, copies of vital records on file [but
certified copies must be issued by state
office], probate records)
probate search service: no charge; copies of
probate records: 25¢ per page, no minimum

Dunn County
organized 1883 from Howard County, which
was discontinued

Dunn County Courthouse
205 Owens Street
Manning, ND 58642-0105
(701) 573-4443 (Recorder); (701) 573-4447
(Clerk); (701) 573-4444 FAX
bkukla@stte.nd.us
http://www.ndaco.org/counties/county_profile
.asp?CountyID=13
Bobbi Kukla, Recorder/Clerk of Court

Eddy County
organized 1885 from Foster County

Eddy County Courthouse
524 Central Avenue
New Rockford, ND 58356-1698
(701) 947-2434; (701) 947-2067 FAX
http://www.ndaco.org/counties/county_profile
.asp?CountyID=14
Patty Hilbert, Recorder and Clerk of Court
(land records, vital records, and probate records)
probate search service: $5.00 per certificate per
person; certified copies of land records: $5.00
each; copies of probate records: $1.00 per
page out of records

Emmons County
organized 1879 from unorganized territory

Emmons County Courthouse
100 Fourth Street NW
Linton, ND 58552
(701) 254-4812; (701) 254-4012 FAX
aibach@state.nd.us
http://www.ndaco.org/counties/county_profile
.asp?CountyID=15
Anita Ibach, Recorder/Clerk of Court
(land records from August 1890, vital records
from 1903, probate records from 28 June
1884)
probate search service: 25¢ per person; copies of
probate records: $1.00 per document, $5.00
for certified copies of documents, $1.00
minimum

Foster County
organized 1883 from Dakota Territory

Foster County Courthouse
1000 Fifth Street North
Carrington, ND 58421
(701) 652-2441 (Auditor, PO Box 104); (701)
652-2491 (Recorder, PO Box 76); (701) 65-
1001 (Clerk, PO Box 257); (701) 652-2173
FAX (Auditor, Recorder, and Clerk)
rschlotm@nd.gov; llhoppe@state.nd.us;
tbeckley@nd.gov
http://mylocalgov.com/FosterCountyND/inde
x.asp
Roger Schlotman, Auditor; Lynelle Lyman-
Hoppe, Recorder; Tami Beckley, Clerk of
Court
(land records with Auditor; naturalization
records, vital records, and probate records
with Clerk of Court)

Golden Valley County
organized 1912 from Billings County

Golden Valley County Courthouse
(150 First Avenue—location)
PO Box 596 (mailing address)
Beach, ND 58621
(701) 872-3713
sdavidso@state.nd.us
http://www.beachnd.com
Susan Davidson, Recorder/Clerk of Court
(land records with Recorder, probate records
with Clerk of Court)
probate search service: $5.00; copies of probate
records: 25¢ per uncertified page, $5.00 per
certified document ("Any other problems,
contact the District Court Administrator's
Office, PO Box 1507, Dickinson, ND 58602-
1507")

Grand Forks County
organized 1873 from Pembina County

Grand Forks District Court
151 South Fourth Street
Grand Forks, ND 58206
(701) 78-8262 (Property and Records, PO Box
5066); (701) 787-2715 (Clerk, PO Box 5936);
(701) 787-270 (Clerk, Criminal, PO Box
5979); (701) 780-8212 FAX (Property and
Records)
Garlynn.helmoski@gfcounty.com
http://www.grandforkscountygov.com/homepa
ge.htm
Carolynn Helmoski, County Recorder
(land records with Property and Records
Department, probate records with Clerk of
Court)
probate search service: $5.00; copies of land
records: $1.00 per page from paper originals,
$2.00 per page from microform originals;
certified copies of probate records: $5.00 each

Grant County
organized 1916 from Morton County

Grant County Courthouse
(106 Second Avenue NE—location)
PO Box 227 (mailing address)
Carson, ND 58529
(701) 622-3615 (701) 622-3717 FAX
jstern@state.nd.us
http://www.ndaco.org/counties/county_profile
.asp?CountyID=19
Joyce Stern, Recorder/Clerk of Court
(land records with Recorder; naturalization
records, vital records, and probate records
with Clerk of Court)
no probate search service; copies of probate
records: $5.00 for the first page and $2.00 for
each additional page

Griggs County
organized 1881 from Foster County

Griggs County Courthouse
(808 Rollin Avenue SW—location)
PO Box 237 (mailing address)
Cooperstown, ND 58425-0326
(701) 797-2771 (Recorder); (701) 797-2772
(Clerk); (701) 797-3587 FAX
Janice.Steffen@griggsnd.com
http://www.ndaco.org/counties/county_profile
.asp?CountyID=20
Janice Steffen, Recorder/Clerk of Court
(land records with Recorder; vital records from
1902 to 1943 [must know the *place* of
residence at birth or death—township, city—
no alpha listings] and probate records with
Clerk of Court)
probate search service: $5.00; copies of probate
records: 25¢ per page, $5.00 for certified
copies, minimum depends on circumstances
("no phone calls")

Hettinger County
organized 1883 from Stark County

Hettinger County Courthouse
336 Pacific Avenue
Mott, ND 58646
(701) 824-2645; (701) 824-2717 FAX
sgion@state.nd.us
http://www.ndaco.org/counties/county_profile
.asp?CountyID=21
Sylvia Gion, Recorder/Clerk of Court
(land records, probate records)
probate search service: $3.00; copies of probate
records: 25¢ per page, no minimum

Howard County
(see Dunn and McKenzie counties)

Kidder County
organized 1873 from Buffalo County, which was
discontinued

Kidder County Courthouse
120 East Broadway

Steele, ND 58482-7111
(701) 475-2632, ext. 9224; (701) 475-2202 FAX
http://www.ndaco.org/counties/county_profile
.asp?CountyID=22
Barbara J. Steinke, Recorder and Clerk of Court
(land records and probate records)
land and probate records search service: $5.00

La Moure County
organized 1873 from Pembina County

La Moure County Courthouse
202 Fourth Avenue NE
La Moure, ND 58458
(701) 883-5301 and dial 6 (Recorder, PO Box
156); (701) 883-5301 and dial 4 (Clerk, PO
Box 128); (701) 883-4240 FAX (Clerk)
dmorriso@state.nd.us; lamoco@drtel.net
http://lamoco.drtel.net
Ms. Donnell Morrison Walstead, County
Recorder; Karin Boom, Clerk of Court
(land records with Recorder; vital records and
probate records with Clerk of Court)
probate search service: $5.00 (include as much
information as possible); copies of probate
records: 10¢ per page, $5.00 for certified
copies, no minimum

Logan County
organized 1873 from Buffalo County, which was
discontinued

Logan County Recorder and Clerk of Court
(301 Broadway—location)
PO Box 6 (mailing address)
Napoleon, ND 58561-0006
(701) 754-2751; (701) 754-2270 FAX
http://www.ndaco.org/counties/county_profile
.asp?CountyID=24
Dennis Schulz, Recorder and Clerk of Court
(land records with Recorder, marriages and
probate records with Clerk of Court)
probate search service: no charge; copies of
marriages: $1.00 each, $5.00 for certified
copies; copies of probate records: $1.00 per
page, $5.00 for certified copies, no minimum

McHenry County
organized 1873 from Buffalo County, which was
discontinued and whose records are in
McHenry County; organized by election on
second Tuesday in May 1885

McHenry County Courthouse
(407 Main Street, South—location)
PO Box 57 (mailing address)
Towner, ND 58788
(701) 537-5634 (Recorder); (701) 537-5729
(Clerk); (701) 537-5969 FAX (Recorder and
Clerk)
pkuk@state.nd.us; lmyers@state.nd.us
http://www.ndaco.org/counties/county_profile
.asp?CountyID=25
Pam Kuk, Recorder; Lorraine Myers, Clerk of
Court
(patents, deeds, and mortgages from 1800 to
date with Recorder, probate records with
Clerk of Court)
probate search service: no charge; copies of land
records: $1.00 per document; copies of
probate records: $1.00 each, $1.00 minimum

McIntosh County
organized 1883 from Logan County

McIntosh County Courthouse
(112 Northeast First Street—location)
PO Box 39 (mailing address)
Ashley, ND 58413
(701) 288-3589 (Recorder); (701) 288-3450
(Clerk); (701) 288-3671 FAX (Recorder and
Clerk)
http://www.ndaco.org/counties/county_profile
.asp?CountyID=26
Carol Fey, Recorder and Clerk of Court
(land records with Recorder, naturalization
records with State Archives and Historical
Research Library, State Historical Society of
North Dakota, births, deaths and marriages

with Gideon Becker, Clerk of Court, probate
records with Clerk of Court)
probate search service: $5.00 per name for a
written response; copies of probate records:
15¢ per page, $5.00 for certified copies, $2.00
minimum for mailing out a plain copy

McKenzie County
organized 1883 from Howard County, which
was discontinued

McKenzie County Courthouse
201 Fifth Street NW
Watford City, ND 58854
(701) 444-3453, ext. 289 (Recorder); (701) 444-
3452 (Clerk); (701) 444-3902 FAX (Recorder)
ajohnsrud@co.mckenzie.nd.us; lroos@nd.gov
http://www.4eyes.net
Ann Johnsrud, Recorder; Lanae Roos, Clerk of
Court

McLean County
organized 1883 from Stevens County

McLean County Courthouse
712 Fifth Avenue
Washburn, ND 58577
(701) 462-8541, ext. 226 (Recorder); (701) 462-
8541, ext. 228 (Clerk); (701) 462-3633 FAX
(Recorder); (701) 462-8212 FAX (Recorder)
mccleanco@westriv.com (Recorder); doster@
state.nd.us; maanderson@ndcourts.com;
cbailey@state.nd.us
htt://www.visitmcleancounty.com/cleanhome.
html
Dwayne J. "Dewey"Oster, Recorder; Mary Ann
Anderson, Clerk of Court; Catherine Bailey,
Deputy Clerk of Court
(land records with Recorder; naturalization
records, vital records, and probate records
with Clerk of Court)

Mercer County
organized 1875 from original territory; first
records 30 August 1884

Mercer County Courthouse
(1021 Arthur Street—location)
PO Box 39 (mailing address)
Stanton, ND 58571-0039
(701) 745-3272 (Recorder); (701) 745-3262
(Clerk)
wknutson@ndcourts.com
http://www.mercercountynd.com
Brenda Cook, County Recorder); Wanda
Knutson, Clerk of Court
(land records with Recorder, probate records
with Clerk of Court)
probate search service: $5.00; copies of probate
records: 25¢ to $1.00 depending on what it is,
$5.00 each for certified copies, 25¢ minimum
("Postage prepaid")

Morton County
organized 1873 from original territory

Morton County Courthouse
210 Second Avenue, N.W.
Mandan, ND 58554-3124
(701) 667-3305 (Recorder); (701) 667-3358
(Clerk); (701) 667-3453 FAX (Recorder)
cschaner@state.nd.us; kmarshal@ndcourts.com
http://www.co.morton.nd.us
Carrole Schaner, Recorder; Kathy Marshall,
Clerk of Court

Mountrail County
organized 25 January 1909 from Ward County

Mountrail County Courthouse
(101 North Main Street—location)
PO Box 69 (mailing address)
Stanley, ND 58784-0069
(701) 628-2945 (Recorder); (701) 628-2915
(Clerk); (701) 628-2276 FAX (Recorder and
Clerk)
dnichols@ndcourts.com
http://www.ndaco.org/counties/county_profile
.asp?CountyID=31

Marlene K. Gunderson, Recorder; Debra
Nichols, Clerk of Court
(land records with Recorder; vital records from
1909 and Court, probate records from 1909
with Clerk of Court)
probate search service: no charge; copies of land
records: $1.00 for each two-page recorded
document; copies of probate records: 25¢ per
page, $5.00 for certified copies, no minimum

Nelson County
organized 1883 from Foster and Grand Forks
counties

Nelson County Clerk of Court/Recorder
210 B Avenue West, Suite 203
Lakota, ND 58344-7410
(701) 247-2433 (Recorder); (701) 247-2462
(Clerk); (701) 247-2367 FAX (Recorder);
(701) 247-2412 FAX (Clerk)
rstevens@nd.gov; rstevens@state.nd.us
http://www.nelsonco.org
Ruth Stevens, Recorder and Clerk of Court
(land records with Recorder; vital records and
probate records with Clerk of Court)
probate search service: $1.00; copies of probate
records: 25¢ per page

Oliver County
organized 1885 from Mercer County

Oliver County Courthouse
(115 Main Street—location)
PO Box 188 (mailing address)
Center, ND 58530-0188
(701) 794-8777; (716) 794-3476 FAX
kwilkens@state.nd.us
http://www.ndaco.org/counties/county_profile
.asp?CountyID=33
Kim Wilkens, Recorder and Clerk of Court

Pembina County
organized 1867 from Indian lands

Pembina County Clerk/Recorder
301 Dakota Street West, #10
Cavalier, ND 58220
(701) 265-4373
kbraget@ndcourts.com
http://pembinacountynd.gov
Kay Newell Braget
photocopies: 10¢ each, $1.00 minimum; certified
copies: $10.00

Pierce County
organized 1887 from parts of Rolette, Bottineau
and McHenry counties and all of De Smet
County, annexed part of Church County in
1891

Pierce County Courthouse
240 S.E. Second Street
Rugby, ND 58368-1830
(701) 776-5206 (Recorder); (701) 776-6161
(Clerk); (701) 776-5707 FAX (Recorder and
Clerk)
http://www.ndaco.org/counties/county_profile
.asp?CountyID=35
Denise Pieterick, Recorder; Carla Marks, Clerk
of Court
(land records from 1889 with Recorder, vital
records from 1943 and probate records from
1889 with Clerk of Court)
probate search service: $5.00 per name; copies
of probate records: 15¢ per page

Ramsey County
organized 1873 from Pembina County

Ramsey County Courthouse
524 Fourth Avenue
Devils Lake, ND 58301
(701) 662-7018 (Recorder, #30); (701) 662-1309
(Clerk, #4); (701) 662-7093 FAX (Recorder);
(701) 662-1303 FAX (Clerk)
cabertsc@state.nd.us; FMcIntyre@ndcourts.gov
http://www.co.ramsey.nd.us; http://www.
ndcourts.gov/court/counties/ramsey.htm
Carol Bertsch, Recorder; Faye McIntyre, Clerk

of Court

Ransom County
organized 1873 from Pembina County

Ransom County Courthouse
204 Fifth Avenue West
Lisbon, ND 58054
(701) 683-5827, ext. 115 (Recorder); (701) 683-5823, ext. 120 (Clerk); (701) 683-5827 FAX (Recorder and Clerk)
sfroemke@nd.gov; vlukes@nd.gov
http://www.ransomcountynd.com
Susan Froemke, Recorder; Valorie Lukes, Clerk of Court
(land records with Recorder; marriage licenses and probate records with Clerk of Court)
probate search service: no charge; copies of probate records: 20¢ per page

Renville County
organized 1873 from Pembina County

Renville County Courthouse
(205 Main Street East—location)
PO Box 68 (mailing address)
Mohall, ND 58761-0068
(701) 756-6398
jbender@nd.gov
http://www.renvillecounty.org
Jerene Bender, County Recorder and Clerk of Court
(land records from 1910, township vital records from 1900 to about 1935, county vital records from 1935 [also at State Capitol], and probate records from 1910)
probate search service: no charge; copies of probate records: $1.00 per page, no minimum

Richland County
organized 1873, original county

Richland County Courthouse
418 Second Avenue North
Wahpeton, ND 58075
(701) 642-7800 (Recorder); (701) 671-1524 (Clerk); (701) 642-7820 FAX; (701) 671-4444 FAX (Clerk)
rquam@co.richland.nd.us; cschmitz@ndcourts.com
http://www.mylocalgov.com/richlandcountynd; http://www.ndcourts.gov/court/counties/dc _clerk/richland.htm
Ruth Quam, Recorder; Cindy Schmitz, Clerk of Court

Rolette County
organized 1873 from Buffalo County, which was discontinued (no population in 1880 census); county established 1884 or 1885

Rolette County Courthouse
(102 N.E. Second—location)
PO Box 276 (mailing address)
Rolla, ND 58367
(701) 477-3166 (Recorder); (701) 477-3816 (Clerk)
cbertsch@state.nd.us; smickelson@ndcourts.com
http://www.rolettecounty.com
Colleen Bertsch, Recorder; Susan Mickelson, Clerk of Court
(land records with Recorder; probate records with Clerk of Court)
probate search service: no charge; copies of probate records: 25¢ per page, $5.00 for the first certified copy and $2.00 for each additional certified copy

Sargent County
organized 1883 from Ransom County

Sargent County Courthouse
(355 Main Street—location)
PO Box 176 (mailing address)
Forman, ND 58032-0176
(701) 724-6241, ext. 117 (Recorder) and ext. 115 (Clerk)
joan.lee@co.sargent.nd.us

http://mylocalgov.com/SargentCountyND/index.asp
Joan A. Lee, Recorder and Clerk of Courts
(land records with Recorder, probate records with Clerk of Court)
probate search service: no charge; copies of probate records: 10¢ per page, no minimum

Sheridan County
organized 1873 from Buffalo County, which was discontinued

Sheridan County Courthouse
PO Box 668
McClusky, ND 58463-0668
(701) 363-2207
jodockte@state.nd.us
http://mylocalgov.com/SheridanCountyND/index.asp
Joyce Dockter, Recorder and Clerk of District Court
(land records from 1909 with Recorder, marriage licenses and probate records from 1909 with Clerk of Court)
no land records search service ("if asking for copies of deeds, mortgages, etc., please give complete description of land as to section, township and range"); probate search service: no charge; copies of marriage licenses: $1.00 each; copies of probate records: 25¢ per page or $1.00 per instrument if copy of a recording

Sioux County
organized 1915 from the Standing Rock Indian Reservation

Sioux County Courthouse
302 Second Avenue
Fort Yates, ND 58538
(701) 854-3853; (701) 854-3854 FAX
swaliser@state.nd.us
http://www.ndaco.org/counties/county_profile .asp?CountyID=43; http://www.ndcourts.gov/court/counties/dc _clerk/sioux.htm
Sandra L. Waliser, Recorder and Clerk of Court
(land records and probate records)
probate search service: $5.00; copies of probate records: 25¢ per page, no minimum

Slope County
organized 1915 from Billings County

Slope County Courthouse
(206 South Main Street—location)
PO Box JJ (mailing address)
Amidon, ND 58620
(701) 879-6275; (701) 879-6278 FAX
44Clerk@ndcourts.gov
http://www.ndaco.org/counties/county_profile .asp?CountyID=44; http://www.ndcourts. gov/court/counties/dc_clerk/slope.htm
Marguerite Muggsy Schatz, Recorder and Clerk of Court
(land records, not many births and deaths, some marriages, probate records)
probate search service: $5.00; copies of probate records: $1.00 per page, no minimum ("SASE is always appreciated")

Stark County
organized 1879 from unorganized territory

Stark County Courthouse
51 Third Street EastPO Box 130
Dickinson, ND 58602-0130
(701) 456-7645 (Recorder, Suite 105, PO Box 130); (701) 456-7640 FAX (Clerk, Suite 106); (701) 227-3184 (Clerk); (701) 227-3185 FAX (Clerk)
cbeckert@state.nd.us; Shartl@ndcourts.gov
http://mylocalgov.com/starkcountynd/index. asp; http://www.ndcourts.gov/court/ counties/dc_clerk/stark.htm
Carol Beckert, Recorder; Sheila J. Hartl, Clerk of Court
(land records with Recorder; naturalization records, vital records, and probate records with Clerk of Court)

no probate search service; copies of probate records: 25¢ per page, no minimum

Steele County
organized 1883 from Griggs County

Steele County Courthouse
(201 Washington Avenue West—location)
PO Box 275 (mailing address)
Finley, ND 58230
(701) 524-2152; (701) 524-1325 FAX
mharvey@state.nd.us
http://www.ndaco.org/counties/county_profile .asp?CountyID=46
Melinda Harvey, Recorder and Clerk of Court
(land records, naturalization records, vital records, probate records)

Stutsman County
organized 1873 from Pembina County

Stutsman County Courthouse
511 Second Avenue, S.E.
Jamestown, ND 58401-4210
(701) 252-9034 (Recorder); (701) 525-9042 (Vital Statistics); (701) 252-9042 (Clerk); (701) 251-1603 FAX (Recorder); (701) 251-1006 FAX (Clerk)
ksamek@nd.gov; BHill@ndcourts.gov
http://www.co.stutsman.nd.us
Karen Samek, Recorder; Barb Hill, Clerk of Court
(land records from 1883 with Recorder; births and deaths from 1882, marriages, and probate records from 1879 with Clerk of Court)
probate search service: no charge; copies of land records: $1.00 each; copies of vital records and probate records: $5.00 each

Towner County
organized 1883 from Rolette County

Towner County Courthouse
PO Box 517
Cando, ND 58324
(701) 968-4340; (701) 968-4344 FAX
jhoffert@state.nd.us
http://www.mylocalgov.com/townercountynd
Jolene D. Hoffert, Recorder and Clerk of District Court

Traill County
organized 1875 from Grand Forks County

Traill County Courthouse
114 West Caledonia
Hillsboro, ND 58045
(701) 436-4457 (Recorder); (701) 436-4454 (Clerk)
hbird@state.nd.us; pbowerso@nd.gov
http://mylocalgov.com/traillcountynd/index.asp
Hazel M. Bird, Recorder; Paulette Bowersox, Clerk of Court
(land records with Recorder; vital records from the 1900s and probate records with Clerk of Court)

Walsh County
organized 1881 from Grand Forks and Pembina counties

Walsh County Courthouse
600 Cooper Avenue
Grafton, ND 58237-1542
(701) 352-2380 (Recorder, Second Floor); (701) 352-0350 (Clerk, Third Floor); (701) 352-3340 FAX (Recorder); (701) 352-4466 FAX (Clerk)
dlink@nd.gov; bdemers@ndcourts.com
http://www.mylocalgov.com/walshcountynd
Diane Link, Recorder; Bev Demers, Clerk of Court
(deeds from 1882, mortgages from 1881, vital records from 1892, probate records from 1882)
probate search service: $5.00; copies of probate records: 25¢ per page, $5.00 for the first certified copy and $2.00 for each additional certified copy, 25¢ minimum

Ward County
organized 1885 from Renville County

Ward County Courthouse
(315 Third Street SE—location)
PO Box 5005 (mailing address)
Minot, ND 58701
(701) 857-6410 (Recorder); (701) 857-6600
   (Clerk); (701) 857-6414 FAX (Recorder);
   (701) 857-6623 FAX (Clerk)
Sheila.Dalen@co.ward.nd.us;
   51Clerk@ndcourts.gov
http://www.co.ward.nd.us;
   http://www.ndcourts.gov/court/counties/dc
   _clerk/ward.htm
Sheila Dalen, Recorder; Susan Hoffer, Clerk of
   Court
(land records with Recorder; probate records
   with Clerk of Court)
probate search service: $5.00 ("no telephone
   requests")

Wells County
organized 1873 from Sheridan County

Wells County Courthouse
700 Court Street North
Fessenden, ND 58438
(701) 547-3141 (Recorder, PO Box 125); (701)
   547-3122 (Clerk); (701) 547-3719 FAX
   (Recorder)
fschimel@nd.gov; ccolby@nd.gov
http://mylocalgov.com/wellscountynd/index.asp
Faye Schimelfenig, Recorder; Cheryl Colby,
   Clerk of Court

Williams County
organized 1890 by absorbing both Buford and
   Flannery counties

Williams County Courthouse
(205 East Broadway—location)
PO Box 2047 (mailing address)
Williston, ND 58802-2047
(701) 577-4540 (Recorder, Ground Floor); (701)
   774-4375 (Clerk, PO Box 2047); (701) 577-
   4535 FAX (Recorder); (701) 774-4379 FAX
   (Recorder)
JFixen@ndcourts.gov
http://www.williamsnd.com
Kari Evenson, Recorder; Jody Fixen, Clerk of
   Court
(land records with Recorder, vital records and
   probate records with Clerk of Court)
probate search service: no charge; copies of
   probate records: 25¢ per page, $5.00 for the
   first certified copy and $2.00 for each
   additional certified copy, no minimum

OHIO

*Capital: Columbus. Statehood: 1 March 1803 (official)
(parts claimed by Virginia, Connecticut and New York
from 1609 to 1786, part annexed by the Treaty of
Paris, 1783, included in the Northwest Territory in
1787)*

Ohio has four courts of limited jurisdiction.
Municipal Courts have jurisdiction in lesser civil
cases and in less serious criminal cases. Mayor's
Courts are created in areas without Municipal
Courts. A Court of Claims hears cases for claims
against the state. County Courts have countywide limited jurisdiction in areas not under the
Municipal Courts. These include: Adams, Ashtabula, Belmont, Brown, Butler, Carroll, Clermont, Columbiana, Darke, Erie, Fulton, Hardin,
Harrison, Highland, Holmes, Jefferson, Mahoning, Meigs, Monroe, Montgomery, Morgan,
Morrow, Muskingum, Noble, Paulding, Perry,
Pike, Putnam, Sandusky, Trumbull, Tuscarawas,
Vinton and Warren counties. The Ohio Courts
of Common Pleas sit at each county seat and
hear civil actions, domestic relations and all
probate matters as well as felonies and juvenile
cases. The Court of Appeals and Supreme Court
have appellate jurisdiction.

Adams County
organized 1797, original county

Adams County Courthouse
110 West Main Street
West Union, OH 45693-1347
(937) 544-5051 (Recorder); (937) 544-2513
   (Recorder); (937) 544-2344 (Clerk of Court,
   Room 244); (937) 544-2921 (Probate); (937)
   544-4616 FAX (Recorder); (937) 544-8911
   FAX (Clerk of Court)
http://www.adamscountyoh.com/index.html;
   http://www.occaohio.com/County/adams.htm
Mark Tolle, Recorder; Gary K. Gardner, Clerk
   of Court; Judge Brett M. Spencer, Probate
   Court
(land records with Recorder; births and deaths
   from 1888 to 1893, marriage licenses from
   1803 to 1833 and will book 1849-1860 [index
   attached] with Probate Court)
no probate search service; copies of marriage
   licenses from Probate Court: $1.00 per page
   plus SASE; copies of probate records: 50¢ per
   page, $2.00 for certified copies

Allen County
organized 1820 from Mercer County but
   remained attached to Darke County

Allen County Courthouse
301 North Main Street
Lima, OH 45801-4456
(419) 223-8517 (Recorder, Room 204, PO Box
   1243, Lima, OH 45802); (419) 223-8513
   (Clerk of Court, PO Box 1243); (419) 223-
   8501 (Research Clerk, Probate Division,
   Fourth Floor); (419) 223-8555 FAX
   (Recorder); (419) 222-8427 (Clerk of Court);
   (419) 221-3432 FAX (Probate Court)
mlosh@allencountyohio.com;
   gstaley@allencountyohio.com
http://www.co.allen.oh.us;
   http://www.allencountyohio.com/cpro.php
Mona S. Losh, Recorder; Gina C. Staley-Burley,
   Clerk of Court; Judge David R. Kinworthy,
   Probate Court
(deeds with Recorder; naturalization records
   from March 1860 through December 1925,
   births and deaths from 1867 through 1908,
   marriages from 1831 to date, estates and
   guardianships from 1835 to date with
   Research Clerk, Probate Division)
no probate search service; copies of vital
   records: $5.00 each for births and deaths, 75¢
   each for marriages, $2.00 for certified copies
   of marriages, $2.75 for certified copies of
   marriage application, plus SASE; copies of
   probate records: 75¢ per page, plus SASE

Ashland County
organized 24 February 1846 from the counties
   of Huron (Ruggles Township), Lorain
   (Sullivan and Troy townships), Richland
   (Vermillion, Montgomery, Orange, Green,
   Hanover, parts of Monroe, Mifflin and Clear
   Fork townships, also Milton and Clear Creek)
   and Wayne (Jackson, Perry, Mohican and
   Lake townships)

Ashland County Courthouse
142 West Second Street
Ashland, OH 44805
(419) 282-4238 (Recorder); (419) 282-4244
   (Recorder); (419) 282-4242 (Clerk of Court);
   (419) 282-4314 (Probate Court); (419) 281-
   5715 FAX (Recorder); (419) 282-4240 FAX
   (Clerk of Court)
clerkofcourts@ashlandcounty.org
http://www.ashlandcounty.org/recorder/index.
   htm; http://www.ashlandcounty.org/
   clerkofcourts
Barbara J. Harding, Recorder; Annette Shaw,
   Clerk of Court; Judge Damian Vercillo,
   Probate Court
(land records from 1846 with Recorder, a few
   naturalization records for 1904, 1921, 1929,
   1940, 1941, 1943, 1959 with Clerk of Court,
   naturalization records from 20 January 1860
   through 21 April 1906, births and deaths
   from 1867 to 1908, marriages from 1846, and
   probate records from 1852 with Probate
   Court)
probate search service: no charge, based on
   availability of time; copies of naturalizations:
   35¢ each, $1.00 for certified copies; copies of
   vital records: $3.00 each; copies of probate
   records: $1.00 per page by mail

Ashtabula County
organized 1807 from Trumbull County

Ashtabula County Courthouse
25 West Jefferson Street
Jefferson, OH 44047-1027
(440) 576-3767 (Recorder); (440) 576-3762
   (Recorder); (440) 576-3637 (Clerk of Court);
   (440) 576-3451 (Probate Court); (440) 576-
   3231 FAX (Recorder); (440) 576-2819 FAX
   (Clerk of Court)
jabarta@co.ashtabula.oh.us
http://www.co.ashtabula.oh.us
Judith A. Barta, Recorder; Carol A. Mead, Clerk
   of Court; Judge Charles G. Hague, Probate
   Court
(births and deaths from 1867 through 1908,
   marriages from 1811 to date with Probate
   Court)
copies of vital records: $1.00 each, $5.00 for
   certified copies, plus SASE

Athens County
organized 1805 from Washington County

Athens County Courthouse
15 South Court Street
Athens, OH 45701
(740) 592-3228 (Recorder, Room 236); (740)
   592-3242 (Clerk of Court, Fourth Floor);
   (740) 592-3251 (Probate Court, Second
   Floor); (740) 592-3229 FAX (Recorder); (740)
   592-3282 FAX (Clerk of Court)
jmscott@athenscountygovernment.com
http://athenscountygovernment.com
Julia Michael Scott, Recorder; Ann C. Trout,
   Clerk of Court; Judge Robert W. Stewart,
   Probate Court
(land records with Recorder, naturalization
   records with Clerk of Court, births, deaths,
   marriages, and probate records with Probate
   Judge)
probate search service: no charge but only
   limited searches can be performed; copies of
   probate records: $1.00 per page, $3.00 for
   certified copies, no minimum

Auglaize County
organized 14 February 1848 from Allen and

Mercer counties

Auglaize County Courthouse
Rt. 3, 201 Willipie Street
Wapakoneta, OH 45895-9803
(419) 739-6735 (Recorder, 209 South Blackhoof
Street, Suite 103); (419) 738-4219 (Clerk of
Court, Suite 211, PO Box 409); (419) 738-
7710 (Probate, Suite 103); (419) 739-6736
FAX (Recorder); (419) 739-6768 FAX (Clerk
of Court)
abillings@auglaizecounty.org;
sekohler@auglaizecounty.org
http://www.auglaizecounty.org
Ann Billings, Recorder; Sue Ellen Kohler, Clerk
of Court; Judge Mark E. Spees, Probate Court
(land records from 1848, births and deaths from
1867, marriages from 1848, probate records
from 1848)
no probate search service; copies of marriages:
$3.00 each; copies of probate records: 50¢ per
page

Belmont County
organized 1801 from Jefferson County

Belmont County Courthouse
101 West Main Street
St. Clairsville, OH 43950-1224
(740) 695-2121 (Recorder); (740) 699-2140
(Recorder); (740) 699-2169 (Clerk of Court);
(740) 699-2144 (Probate Court); (740) 699-
2140, ext. 198 FAX (Recorder)
recorder@belmontcountyohio.org
http://www.belmontcountyohio.org
Mary Catherine Nixon, Recorder; Randall L.
"Randy" Marple, Clerk of Court; Judge J.
Mark Costine, Probate Court
(births from 1867 to 20 August 1982, deaths
from 1867 to 1808 and from 1940 to 20
August 1982, marriages from 1803 to date,
and probate records with Probate Division)
no vital records or probate records search
service (must know the exact name and date
within a two-year period); certified copies of
vital records from Probate Division: $3.00
each, money order only; certified copies of
probate records: $1.00 per page (money order
only)

Brown County
organized 1817 from Adams and Clermont
counties

Brown County Courthouse
101 South Main Street
Georgetown, OH 45121
(937) 378-6478 (Recorder, Administration
Building, 800 Mt. Orab Pike, Suite 151); (937)
378-6358 (Clerk of Court, 700 Mt. Orab
Pike); (937) 378-6549 (Probate Court, PO
Box 379); (937) 378-2848 FAX (Recorder);
(937) 378-2462 FAX (Clerk of Court)
tmeranda@browncountycourt.org
http://www.county.brown.oh.us; http://www.
browncountycourt.org/srchmain.html
Gary Himes, Recorder; Tina Meranda, Clerk of
Court; Judge Margaret Ann Clark, Probate
Court
(land records, naturalization records, vital
records, probate records)

Butler County
organized 1803 from Hamilton County

Butler County Courthouse
130 High Street
Hamilton, OH 45011-2732
(513) 887-3192 (Recorder); (513) 887-3188
(Recorder); (513) 887-3278 (Clerk of Court,
315 High Street, Suite 550); (513) 887-3294
(Probate Court, Historic Butler County
Courthouse, 101 High Street, Second Floor);
(513) 887-3437 (Records Center and
Archives, 123 North Third Street); (513) 887-
3198 FAX (Recorder); (513) 887-3966 FAX
(Clerk of Court)
CrankDN@butlercountyohio.org;
bcarchives@butlercountyohio.org

http://www.butlercountyohio.org;
http://www.butlercountyclerk.org
Danny N. Crank, Recorder; Cynthia Carpenter,
Clerk of Court; Judge Randy T. Rogers,
Probate Court; Rhonda Freeze, Manager
County Archives
(land records with Recorder; naturalization
records from 1840 to 1977, births and deaths
from 1868 to 1908, marriages from 1803
[applications not on file prior to 1905], and
probate records with Records Center and
Archives [inactive case files])
probate search service: no charge if time
permits; copies of land records: $1.00 per
page; copies of naturalization records: $3.00
per page; certified copies of vital records:
$7.00 for births and deaths, $2.00 for
marriages; copies of probate records: $3.00
per page for wills, 50¢ per page for estates,
$1.00 minimum ("checks to Department")

Carroll County
organized 1832 from Columbiana, Harrison,
Jefferson and Stark counties

Carroll County Courthouse
Genealogy Department, Third Floor
119 Public Square/South Lisbon Street
Carrollton, OH 44615-1492
(330) 627-4545 (Recorder, Suite 205, PO Box
550); (330) 627-4886 (Clerk of Court); (330)
627-2323 (Probate Court, Suite 202); (330)
627-4295 FAX (Recorder)
carrollcorecorder@verizon.net
http://pages.eohio.net/carrcomm
Patricia J. Oyer, Recorder; William "Bill"
Wohlwend, Clerk of Court; Judge John H.
Weyand, Probate Court
(land records from 1833 to date, naturalization
records from 1833 to about 1900, vital
records from 1867 to 1909, probate records
from 1833 to date)

Champaign County
organized 1805 from Greene and Franklin
counties

Champaign County Courthouse
200 North Main Street
Urbana, OH 43078
(937) 484-1630 (Recorder, 1512 South U.S.
Highway 68, Suite B-200); (937) 484-1047
(Coerk of Court); (937) 484-1028 (Probate
Court); (937) 484-1628 FAX (Recorder); (937)
484-5325 FAX (Clerk of Court)
epreston@co.champaign.oh.us
http://www.co.champaign.oh.us
Carolyn J. Downing, Recorder; Edward Preston,
Clerk of Court; Judge John C. Newlin,
Probate Court
(land records from 1805 with Recorder,
naturalization records from 1805 to 1852 [in
Minute Books] with Clerk of Court,
naturalization records from 1852 to about
1906, vital records from 1867 to 1909, and
probate records from 1805 with Probate
Court)
probate search service: $2.00; copies of vital
records with Probate Court: $4.00 for births
and deaths, $2.00 for marriages; copies of
probate records: 50¢ per page, no minimum
("enclose a long SASE with every inquiry")

Clark County
organized 1817 from Champaign,.Madison and
Greene counties

Clark County Courthouse
31 North Limestone
Springfield, OH 45502
(937) 521-1705 (Recorder, PO Box 1406); (937)
328-2458 (Clerk of Court, Room 210); (937)
521-1845 (Probate Court, County
Offices/Municipal Court Building, 50
Columbia Street, Fifth Floor); (937) 328-4620
FAX (Recorder); (937) 328-2589 FAX
(Probate Court)
recorder@clarkcountyohio.gov;
clerk@clarkcountyohio.gov;

sweldy@clarkcountyohio.gov (Probate Court)
http://www.clarkcountyohio.gov;
http://www.probate.clarkcountyohio.gov
Nancy Pence, Recorder; Ronald E. Vincent,
Clerk of Court; Judge Richard P. Carey,
Probate Court

Clermont County
organized 1800, original county; changed county
seat from Williamsburg to Batavia 24
February 1824

Clermont County Courthouse
76 South Riverside Drive
Batavia, OH 45103-2602
(513) 732-7236 (Recorder, 101 East Main Street,
Batavia, OH 45103-2958); (513) 732-7964
(Clerk of Court, 270 Main Street); (513) 732-
7243 (Probate Court); (513) 732-7891 FAX
(Recorder)
recorder@co.clermont.oh.us;
cgreen@co.clermont.oh.us
http://www.co.clermont.oh.us;
http://recorder.clermontcountyohio.gov;
http://www.clermontclerk.org
Carolyn Green, Recorder; Barbara Wiedenbein,
Clerk of Court; Judge Stephanie Wyler,
Probate Court
(land records with Recorder)

Clinton County
organized 1810 from Highland County

Clinton County Courthouse
46 South South Street
Wilmington, OH 45177-2214
(937) 382-2067 (Recorder); (937) 382-2316
(Clerk of Court, Third Floor); (937) 383-3271
(Records and Archives Center); (937) 382-
2280 (Probate Court)(937) 382-8097 FAX
(Recorder); (937) 383-3455 FAX (Clerk of
Court)
skwrecorder@in-touch.net
http://co.clinton.oh.us
Sandra Wilt, Recorder; Joann M. Chamberlin,
Clerk of Court; Judge G. Allen, Gano,
Probate Court
(land records with Recorder, naturalization
records from 1880 to 1895, births and deaths
from 1867 to 1908, marriages from 1810, wills
from 1810)
no probate search service ("we have a gentleman
that comes to the court and takes our mail
and answers it"); copies of probate records:
25¢, 50¢ or $1.00 each, depending on the size
of the page, 75¢ for certification

Columbiana County
organized 1803 from Jefferson and Washington
counties

Columbiana County Courthouse
105 South Market Street
Lisbon, OH 44432-1255
(330) 424-9517, ext. 640 (Recorder); (330) 424-
7777 (Clerk of Court); (330) 424-9516
(Probate Court); (330) 424-5067 FAX
(Recorder)
cbrown@ccclerk.org
http://www.columbianacounty.org;
http://www.ccclerk.org/case_access.htm
Craig A. Brown, Recorder; Anthony Dattilio,
Clerk of Court; Judge Thomas M. Baronzzi,
Probate Court
(land records from 1803 with Recorder,
naturalization records from 1860 to 1980 and
vital records from 1803 with Clerk of Court,
births and deaths from 1867, marriages from
1803, and probate records from 1803 with
Probate Court)
no probate search service; copies of land
records: $1.00 per page; copies of
naturalization records: $1.00 per page; copies
of vital records from Clerk of Court: $1.00
per page; copies of vital records from Probate
Court: $7.00 each; copies of probate records:
50¢ per page from paper originals, $1.00 per
page from microfilm originals, 50¢ for
certification by stamp, $2.00 for certificate of

copy

Coshocton County
organized 1811 from Muskingum County

Coshocton County Courthouse Annex
(349½ Main Street—location)
PO Box 806 (mailing address)
Coshocton, OH 43812-1536
(740) 622-2817 (Recorder, PO Box 817); (740) 622-1456 (Clerk of Courts, Courthouse Square, Second Floor, 318 Main Street); (740) 622-1837 (Probate Court, 426 Main Street); (740) 295-7352 FAX (Recorder); (740) 295-0020 FAX (Clerk of Courts); (740) 623-6514 FAX (Probate Court)
davedilly@coshoctoncounty.net;
irenemiller@coshoctoncounty.net
http://www.coshoctoncounty.net
David Dilly, Recorder; Irene Miller, Clerk of Courts, Judge C. Fenning Pierce, Probate Court
(land records with Recorder; wills from 1811, births and deaths from 1867, marriages from 1811 with Probate Court)
copies of land records: $1.00 per page, 50¢ for certification; probate search service: $5.00; copies of births and deaths before 1909: $5.00; copies of marriages: $5.00; copies of probate records: $1.00 per page, $1.00 for certification

Crawford County
organized 1820 from Old Indian Territory

Crawford County Courthouse
112 East Mansfield Street
Bucyrus, OH 44820-2386
(419) 562-6961 (Recorder, Suite 206); (419) 562-2766 (Clerk of Courts, Suite 204); (419) 562-8891 (Probate Court); (419) 562-6061 FAX (Recorder); (419) 562-8011 FAX (Clerk of Courts)
clerk@crawford-co.org
http://www.crawford-co.org;
http://www.crawfordcocpcourt.org
Karen J. Scott, Recorder; Sue Seevers, Clerk of Courts, Judge Steven D. Eckstein, Probate Court
(land records with Recorder; early and later naturalization records with Clerk of Courts; other naturalization records [created between early and later records], births and deaths from 1867 to 1908, marriage licenses from 1831 to date, estates from 1834 to date, and guardianships with Probate Court)
vital records search service: no charge on as-available basis; probate search service: no charge on an as-available basis; copies of vital records: $2.00, $5.00 for certification; copies of probate records: 50¢ per page, $1.00 for certifiecation

Cuyahoga County
organized 1808 from Geauga County

Cuyahoga County Courthouse
1 Lakeside Avenue
Cleveland, OH 44113
(216) 443-7300 (Recorder, County Administration Building, 1219 Ontario Street); (216) 443-5898 (Recorder, Public Information); (216) 443-7330 (Recorder); (216) 443-8194 (Recorder); (216) 443-7952 (Clerk of Courts, Administrative Offices, Justice Center, First Floor, 1200 Ontario Street); (216) 443-8764 (Probate Court); (216) 443-8193 FAX (Recorder)
clerk_of_courts@cuyahogacounty.us
http://www.cuyahogacounty.us;
http://coc.cuyahogacounty.us;
http://probate.cuyahogacounty.us
Patrick J. O'Malley, Recorder; Gerald E. Fuerst, Clerk of Courts; Judge John J. Donnelly, Probate Court
(land records with Recorder; naturalization records ca 1818-ca 1931 generated by the Cuyahoga County Court of Common Pleas, naturalization records 1859-1901 generated by

Cuyahoga County Probate Court, and probate records with Probate Court)

Darke County
organized 1809 from Miami County

Darke County Courthouse
504 South Broadway
Greenville, OH 45331
(937) 547-7390 (Recorder); (937) 547-7335 (Clerk of Courts); (937) 547-7336 (Clerk of Courts); (937) 547-7345 (Probate Court, Garst Avenue Government Center, 300 Garst Avenue); (937) 547-7305 FAX (Clerk of Courts); (937) 547-1945 FAX (Probate Court)
sonnerj@core.com; info@co.darke.oh.us
http://www.co.darke.oh.us
Judy L. Sonner, Recorder; Cindy Pike, Clerk of Courts; Judge Michael D. McClurg, Probate Court
(land records from 1816 with Recorder; births and deaths from 1867 to December 1908, marriages from 1815 to date, and probate records with Probate Court)
land records search service: $2.00 per name; probate search service: no charge; copies of land records: $1.00 per page, no minimum; copies of marriages from Probate Court: 50¢ per page; copies of probate records: 50¢ per page, no minimum

Defiance County
organized 1845 from Williams, Henry and Paulding counties

Defiance County Courthouse
221 Clinton Street
Defiance, OH 43512
(419) 782-4741 (Recorder, Second Floor); (419) 784-4966 (Recorder); (419) 782-1936 (Clerk of Courts, 503 Jefferson Avenue, PO Box 716); (419) 782-4181 (Probate Court, Third Floor); (419) 782-3421 FAX (Recorder); (419) 784-2716 FAX (Clerk of Courts); (419) 782-2437 FAX (Probate Court)
recorder2@defiance-county.com
http://www.defiance-county.com
Jane M. Tadsen, Recorder; Jean Ziegler, Clerk of Courts; Judge Stephen W. Ruyle, Probate Court
(see Records Center for early documents)

Delaware County
organized 1808 from Franklin County

Delaware County Courthouse
91 North Sandusky Street
Delaware, OH 43015-1703
(740) 833-2460 (Recorder, 140 North Sandusky Street); (740) 833-2500 (Clerk of Courts); (740) 833-2680 (Probate Court, 88 North Sandusky Street); (740) 833-2459 FAX (Recorder); (740) 833-2499 FAX (Clerk of Courts)
abrenner@co.delaware.oh.us
http://www.co.delaware.oh.us
Andrew O. Brenner; Ms. Jan Antonoplos, Clerk of Courts; Judge Kenneth J. Spicer, Probate Court
(land records, naturalization records, vital records, probate records)

Erie County
organized 1838 from Huron and Sandusky counties

Erie County Courthouse
323 Columbus Avenue
Sandusky, OH 44870
(419) 627-7684 (Recorder, 247 Columbus Avenue, Room 225); (419) 627-7685 (Recorder); (419) 627-7705 (Clerk of Courts); (419) 627-7750 (Probate Court, Second Floor); (419) 627-6639 FAX (Recorder); (419) 624-6873 FAX (Clerk of Courts)
recorder@erie-county-ohio.net;
erieco.recorder@bright.net;
GeneralInfo@erie-county-ohio.net
http://www.erie-county-ohio.net

Barbara A. Sessler, Recorder; Barbara J. Johnson, Clerk of Courts; Judge Beverly K. McGookey, Probate Court
(land records with Recorder, naturalization records with Clerk of Courts, vital records before 1908 and probate records with Probate Court)
probate search service: no charge; copies of probate records: $1.00 each, no minimum

Fairfield County
organized 1800 from Franklin County

Fairfield County Courthouse
224 East Main
Lancaster, OH 43130-3842
(740) 687-7100 (Recorder, 210 East Main Street, PO Box 2420); (740) 687-7030 (Clerk of Courts, PO Box 370); (740) 687-7090 (Probate Court, Hall of Justice, 224 East Main Street, Room 303); (740) 687-7104 FAX (Recorder); (740) 687-0158 FAX (Clerk of Courts)
gwood@co.fairfield.oh.us
http://www.co.fairfield.oh.us;
http://www.fairfieldcountyprobate.com/index.shtml
Gene Wood, Recorder; Deborah Smalley, Clerk of Courts; Judge Steven O. Williams, Probate Court

Fayette County
organized 1810 from Ross and Highland counties

Fayette County Courthouse
110 East Court Street
Washington Court House, OH 43160-1355
(740) 335-1770 (Recorder, 133 South Main Street, Suite 305); (740) 335-6371 (Clerk of Courts, Third Floor); (740) 335-0640 (Probate Court); (740) 333-3521 FAX (Recorder); (740) 333-3522 FAX (Clerk of Courts)
cathy.templin@fayette-co-oh.com;
larry.long@fayette-co-oh.com
http://www.fayette-co-oh.com/Recorder/index.html; http://www.fayette-co-oh.com/Clerkoct/index.html; http://www.fayette-co-oh.com/Probct/index.html
Cathy Templin, Recorder; Larry Long, Clerk of Courts; Judge Nancy Drake Hammond, Probate Court
(deeds from 1810 with Recorder; naturalization records from 1828 to 1852 and from 1906 with Clerk of Courts; naturalization records from 1852 to 1906, births and deaths from 1867 to 1908, marriages from 1810, and wills and administrations from 1828 with Probate Court)
probate search service: no charge ("A courthouse fire on 19 January 1828 destroyed estate records and common pleas court records"); copies of deeds and probate records: $1.00 per page, no minimum; copies of vital records from Probate Court: $5.00 each for certified births and deaths, $1.00 per page for marriages, $2.00 per page for certified marriages

Franklin County
organized 1803 from Ross County

Franklin County Courthouse
373 South High Street
Columbus, OH 43215
(614) 462-3378 (Recorder, 18th Floor); (614) 462-3600 (Clerk of Courts, 23rd Floor); (614) 462-3621 (Clerk of Courts–Civil, Hall of Justice, 369 South High Street, Third Floor); (614) 462-3894 (Probate Court, 22nd Floor); (614) 462-4299 FAX (Recorder)
recorder@franklincountyohio.gov
http://www.co.franklin.oh.us/recorder;
http://www.franklincountyohio.gov/clerk;
http://www.franklincountyohio.gov/probate
Robert G. Montgomery, Recorder; John O'Grady, Clerk of Courts; Judge Lawrence A. Belskis, Probate Court
(land records with Recorder; births and deaths

from 1867 to 1908, marriages from 1803, and estates from 1800 with Probate Court)
probate search service: $1.00 per ten-year search; copies of vital records from Probate Court: $3.00 each; copies of probate records: 75¢ for each of the first three pages and 25¢ for each additional page, $1.00 per page for certification ("Please send cashier's check or money order and SASE")

Fulton County
organized 1850 from Lucas, Henry and Williams counties

Fulton County Courthouse
210 South Fulton
Wauseon, OH 43567-1355
(419) 337-9232 (Recorder, 152 South Fulton Street, Suite 175); (419) 337-9230 (Clerk of Courts, Room 102); (419) 337-9242 (Probate Court, Room 105); (419) 337-9282 FAX (Recorder); (419) 337-9199 FAX (Clerk of Courts); (419) 337-9284 FAX (Probate Court)
sbarber@fultoncountyoh.ocom; mgype@fultoncountyoh.com
http://www.fultoncountyoh.com
Sandra K. Barber, Recorder; Mary Gype, Clerk of Courts; Judge Michael J. Bumb, Probate Court

Gallia County
organized 1803 from Washington County

Gallia County Courthouse
18 Locust Street
Gallipolis, OH 45631
(740) 446-4612, ext. 246 (Recorder, Room 1265); (740) 446-4612 (Clerk of Courts, Room 1290); (740) 446-4612, ext. 289 (Probate Court, Room 1293); (740) 446-4804 FAX (Recorder and Clerk of Courts); (740) 446-3144 FAX (Probate Court)
recorder@gallianet.net; gcjuv@gallianet.net (Probate Court)
http://www.gallianet.net/Gallia/index.htm; http://www.occaohio.com/County/gallia.htm
Roger Walker, Recorder; Noreen M. Saunders, Clerk of Courts; Judge William S. Medley, Probate Court
(land records with Recorder; some naturalizations in probate index, births and deaths from 1864 to 1952, marriages from 1803, estates, wills, guardianships and miscellaneous records from 1803 with Probate Court)
probate search service: about $5.00 per hour; certified copies of vital records from Probate Court: $3.00 for births and deaths, $1.50 for marriages; copies of probate records: 25¢ per page, no minimum

Geauga County
organized 1805 from Trumbull County

Geauga County Courthouse
100 Short Court Street
Chardon, OH 44024
(440) 279-2020 (Recorder, Courthouse Annex, 231 Main Street, Suite 1-C, Chardon, OH 44024-1299); (440) 564-7131 (Recorder); (440) 279-1960 (Clerk of Courts); (440) 279-1830 (Probate Court, Courthouse Annex, 231 Main Street, Suite 200)
recorder@co.geauga.oh.us; dkaminski@co.geauga.oh.us
http://www.co.geauga.oh.us
Glen Eric Quigley, Recorder; Denise M. Kaminski, Clerk of Courts; Judge Charles E. Henry, Probate Court
(land records with Recorder; divorces from 1806 with Clerk of Courts; naturalization records from 1903 to 1944, births and deaths from 1867 to 1908, marriages from 1805 to 1919, marriages from 1919, and wills, estates, etc., from 1807 with Probate Court)
no probate search service ("we have very little time to do any research for people"); copies of probate records: $1.00 per page, no minimum

Greene County
organized 1803 from Hamilton and Ross counties

Greene County Courthouse
45 North Detroit Street
Xenia, OH 45385-3199
(937) 562-5270 (Recorder, 69 Greene Street, Third Floor, PO Box 100); (937) 562-5276 (Recorder); (937) 562-5290 (Clerk of Courts); (937) 376-5280 (Probate Court); (937) 562-5386 FAX (Recorder); (937) 562-5316 FAX (Probate Court)
mmorris@co.greene.oh.us; tmazur@co.greene.oh.us
http://www.co.greene.oh.us
Mary Morris, Recorder; Ms. Terri A. Mazur, Clerk of Courts, Judge Robert A. Hagler, Probate Court
(land records with Recorder; deaths, marriages, and probate records with Probate Clerk; early records with Greene County Records Center and Archives)

Guernsey County
organized 1810 from Belmont County

Guernsey County Courthouse
801 East Wheeling Avenue
Cambridge, OH 43725
(740) 432-9275 (Recorder, 627 Wheeling Avenue, Suite 305); (740) 432-9230 (Clerk of Courts, D-300); (740) 432-9262 (Probate Court, D-203); (740) 439-6258 FAX (Recorder); (740) 432-7807 FAX (Clerk of Courts)
cwheatley@guernseycounty.org; guernseycounty.clerkofcourts@verizon.net
http://www.guernseycounty.org
Colleen Doutt Wheatley, Recorder; Teresa A. "Terri" Dankovic, Clerk of Courts; Judge Robert S. Moorehead, Jr., Probate Court
(land records with Recorder, naturalization records from 1864 to 1906, births and deaths from 1867 to 1909, marriages from 1812, and probate records from 1812 with Probate Court)
probate search service: no charge; copies of naturalization records: $1.00 per page; certified copies of vital records: $2.00 for births or marriages; copies of probate records: $1.00 per page, $1.00 for certification, no minimum ("only charged for copies if we find anything; no phone requests; please direct mail to Clerk of Probate Court")

Hamilton County
organized 1790, original county

Hamilton County Administration Building
138 East Court Street
Cincinnati, OH 45202
(513) 946-4600 (Recorder–General Information); (513) 632-6014 (Recorder's computer Dial-in Access Information, need to set up an escrow account before logging on); (513) 946-4577 FAX
rebecca.groppe@hamilton-co.org; matthew.carle@hamilton-co.org
http://recordersoffice.hamilton-co.org
Rebecca Prem Groppe, Recorder; Matthew Anthony Carle, Public Relations Director
(deeds from 1794, mortgages and leases, 1939 WPA platting of cemeteries, original subdivision maps and atlases; real estate tax records, plat maps with Auditor, County Administration Building, Room 304, 138 East Court Street, Cincinnati, OH 45202, property tax records from 1883 with Treasurer's Office [off main foyer])
land records search service: no charge for index search (not permitted by law to do title search or historical searches); copies of land records: $1.00 per page

Hamilton County Courthouse
1000 Main Street
Cincinnati, OH 45202-1206
(513) 946-5656 (Clerk of Courts); (513) 946-

3600 (Probate Court, William Howard Taft Center, 230 East Ninth Street, Room 10165); (513) 946-3551 (Probate Court–Records/Genealogy); (513) 946-3565 FAX (Probate Court–Records/Genealogy)
http://www.hamilton-co.org/hc/default.asp; http://www.courtclerk.org; http://www.probatect.org
Greg Hartmann, Clerk of Courts; Judge James Cissell, Probate Court
(fire destroyed many records in 1884; naturalization records from 1850 to 1893, declarations of intent with Clerk of Courts; naturalization records from 1869 to 1884, some declarations of intention from 1846 to 1908 with Chief Deputy, Probate Court, Room 514, births from 1846 to 1908, deaths from 1882 to 1908, marriages from 1817 to date, estate cases, wills from 1791 to date, and guardianship records with Probate Court)
copies of vital records: $7.00 each; no probate search service; copies of probate records: $2.00, $2.00 minimum (no telephone requests to courthouse, enclose SASE)

Hancock County
organized 1820 from Indian lands, and attached to Wood County

Hancock County Courthouse
300 South Main Street
Findlay, OH 45840-9039
(419) 424-7091 (Recorder); (419) 424-7037 (Clerk of Courts); (419) 424-7079 (Probate Court, 308 Dorney Plaza); (419) 423-3017 FAX (Recorder); (419) 424-7801 FAX (Clerk of Courts); (419) 424-7081 FAX (Probate Court)
ammusgrave@co.hancock.oh.us; clerkofcourts@co.hancock.oh.us; probate@co.hancock.oh.us
http://www.co.hancock.oh.us
Anita M. Musgrave, Recorder; Cathy Prosser Wilcox, Clerk of Courts; Judge Allan H. Davis, Probate Court
(land records from 1830 with Recorder; some naturalization records between 1907 and 1930 with Clerk of Courts; naturalization records before 1906, births and deaths from 1867 to 1909, marriages from 1827, and estates from 1825 with Probate Court)
probate search service: no charge; copies of vital records from Probate Court: $5.00 each for births and deaths, $1.25 each for marriages; copies of probate records: 25¢ per page, no minimum

Hardin County
organized 12 February 1820 from Indian lands by an act of the Ohio legislature, but leaving it attached to Logan County; made a separate county in 1833

Hardin County Courthouse
1 Courthouse Square
Kenton, OH 43326
(419) 674-2252 (Recorder, Suite 220); (419) 674-2250 (Recorder); (419) 674-2278 (Clerk of Courts, Suite 310); (419) 674-2230 (Probate Court, Suite 210); (419) 675-2802 FAX (Recorder); (419) 674-2273 FAX (Clerk of Courts)
ssamsrecorder@hotmail.com
http://www.ohiorecorders.com/hardin.html; http://www.occaohio.com/County/hardin.htm (Clerk of Courts)
Sharon A. Sams, Recorder; Lori J. Stevenson, Clerk of Courts; Judge James S. Rapp, Probate Court
(fire destroyed records in 1853)

Harrison County
organized 1813 from Jefferson and Tuscarawas counties

Harrison County Courthouse
100 West Market Street
Cadiz, OH 43907
(740) 942-8869 (Recorder); (740) 942-8523

(Recorder); (740) 942-8863 (Clerk of Courts); (740) 942-8868 (Probate Court); (740) 942-4693 FAX (Recorder); (740) 942-4693 FAX (Clerk of Courts)
hccc@eohio.net
http://www.harrisoncountyohio.org; http://www.ohiorecorders.com/harrison.html; http://www.occaohio.com/County/harrison.htm (Clerk of Courts)
Tracy L. Boyer, Recorder; Barbara J. Yoho, Clerk of Courts; Judge Matthew P. Puskarich, Probate Court
(land records with Recorder; naturalization records with Clerk of Courts; births and deaths from 1867, marriages from 1813, and wills and estates from 1813 with Probate Court)
probate search service: depends on amount of time spent; copies of vital records: $7.00 for certified births or deaths; copies of probate records: $1.00 per page, $2.00 for certified copies, plus LSASE

Henry County
organized 1820 from Indian lands and attached to Wood County

Henry County Courthouse
(660 North Perry Street—location)
PO Box 546 (mailing address)
Napoleon, OH 43545-1702
(419) 592-1766 (Recorder, Room 202); (419) 592-8001 (Recorder); (419) 592-5886 (Clerk of Courts, Suite 302, PO Box 71); (419) 592-5926 (Probate Court, Suite 301); (419) 592-1652 FAX (Recorder); (419) 592-5888 FAX (Clerk of Courts); (419) 599-0803 FAX (Probate Court)
recorder@henrycountyohio.com; sara.myles@henrycountyohio.com; judy.sonnenberg@henrycountyohio.com; common.pleas@henrycountyohio.com (Probate Court)
http://www.henrycountyohio.com
Sara L. Myles, Recorder; Judy Sonnenberg, Clerk of Courts; Judge Keith P. Muehlfeld, Probate Court

Highland County
organized 1805 from Ross, Adams and Clermont counties

Highland County Courthouse
(105 North High Street—location)
PO Box 825 (mailing address)
Hillsboro, OH 45133
(937) 393-9954 (Recorder, 119 Gov. Foraker Place, PO Box 804); (937) 393-9957 (Clerk of Courts, PO Box 821); (937) 393-9981 (Probate Court); (937) 393-5855 FAX (Recorder); (937) 393-9878 FAX (Clerk of Courts)
recorder@co.highland.oh.us; ike.hodson@highland-co.com
http://www.highlandcounty.com/modules/mypage; http://www.ohiorecorders.com/highland.html; http://www.occaohio.com/County/highland.htm (Clerk of Courts)
Dwight "Ike" Hodson, Recorder; Paulette Donley, Clerk of Courts; Judge Kevin L. Greer, Probate Court
(some land records, vital records from 1867 to 1909, probate records)
no probate search service; copies of probate records: 25¢ per page, no minimum

Hocking County
organized 1818 from Athens and Ross counties

Hocking County Courthouse
1 East Main Street
Logan, OH 43138-1207
(740) 385-2031 (Recorder, PO Box 949); (740) 385-0147 (Recorder); (740) 385-2616 (Clerk of Courts, PO Box 108); (740) 385-3022 (Probate Court); (740) 385-0377 FAX (Recorder); (740) 385-1822 FAX (Clerk of Courts); (740) 385-6892 FAX (Probate Court)
shunt@co.hocking.oh.us

http://www.co.hocking.oh.us
Sandra K. Leach-Hunt, Recorder; Narcie Stahr, Clerk of Courts; Judge Rick Wallar, Probate Court
(land records with Recorder; very limited naturalization records from 1863 to 1900 with Probate Office, births from 1867 to 1943, deaths from 1867 to 1908, marriages from 1818, and probate records from 1837 with Probate Office)
probate search service ("no searches over phone; must put request in writing including self-addressed envelope"): $2.00; copies of probate records: 50¢ each, no minimum

Holmes County
organized 1824 from Coshocton County

Holmes County Courthouse
1 East Jackson Street
Millersburg, OH 44654
(330) 674-5916 (Recorder, 75 East Clinton Street, Suite 101, PO Box 213); (330) 674-9519 (Recorder); (330) 674-1876 (Clerk of Courts, Suite 306); (330) 674-5881 (Probate Court, Suite 201); (330) 674-0782 FAX (Recorder); (330) 674-0289 FAX (Clerk of Courts)
smiller@co.holmes.oh.us
http://www.holmescounty.com/gov; http://www.ohiorecorders.com/holmes.html; http://occaohio.com/County/holmes.htm (Clerk of Courts)
Sally Miller, Recorder; Dorcas Miller, Clerk of Courts; Judge Thomas Lee, Probate Court
(land records from 1825 with Recorder; naturalization records from 1825 to 1850 with Clerk of Courts; naturalization records from 1850, vital records from 1867 to 1908, and probate records from 1855 with Probate Court)
no probate search service (most research done by local genealogist, Dave Marshall); copies of probate records: cost "according to type and whether they are certified"

Huron County
organized 1815 from Indian lands

Huron County Courthouse
2 East Main Street
Norwalk, OH 44857
(419) 668-1916 (Recorder, 12 East Main Street); (419) 668-5113 (Clerk of Courts); (419) 668-4383 (Probate Court, First Floor); (419) 663-4052 FAX (Recorder); (419) 663-4048 FAX (Clerk of Courts)
hcrecorder@hmcltd.net; clerk@huroncountyclerk.com; susan@huroncountyclerk.com; hcjpc@accnorwalk.com
http://www.hccommissioners.com; http://www.ohiorecorders.com/huron.html; http://www.huroncountyclerk.com; http://homepages.accnorwalk.com/ncjpc/probate.htm
Karen A. Fries, Recorder; Susan S. Hazel, Clerk of Courts; Judge Tim Cardwell, Probate Court
(land records with Recorder; naturalization records before 1859 with Clerk of Courts; naturalization records from 1859, births and deaths from 1867 to 1908, marriages from 1815, and probate records from March 1852 with Probate Court)
probate search service: SASE; copies of probate records: $1.00 per page, $3.00 per record, $1.00 minimum

Jackson County
organized 1816 from Pike County

Jackson County Courthouse
226 East Main Street
Jackson, OH 45640
(740) 286-1919 (Recorder, Suite 1); (740) 286-2006 (Clerk of Courts); (740) 286-6405 (Probate Court); (740) 286-5186 FAX (Recorder); (740) 286-4061 FAX (Clerk of Courts)
http://www.ohiorecorders.com/jackson.html; http://www.occaohio.com/County/jackson.

htm (Clerk of Courts)
Rose Walters, Recorder; Robert F. Walton, Clerk of Courts; Judge Stephen D. Michael, Probate Court
(deeds from 1816 with Recorder; births and deaths from 1867 to 1908, marriages from 1817 to date, and wills from 1817 to date with Probate Court)
copies of land records: $1.00 per page

Jefferson County
organized 1797, original county

Jefferson County Courthouse
301 Market Street
Steubenville, OH 43952-2133
(740) 283-8566 (Recorder); (740) 283-8583 (Clerk of Courts, Room 200, PO Box 1326); (740) 283-8554 (Probate Court, PO Box 549); (740) 283-4007 FAX (Recorder); (740) 283-8597 FAX (Clerk of Courts)
http://www.jeffersoncountyoh.com/cgi-bin/template.pl?
Paul R. McKeegan, Recorder; John A. Corrigan, Clerk of Courts; Judge Samuel W. Kerr, Probate Court
(land records with Recorder; naturalization records, births and deaths from 1867 to 1908, marriages from 1803 to date [early records indexed by groom only, cross index begins 1976], estates and guardianships from 1838 to date, wills from 1798 to date, and trust records from 1859 to date with Probate Court)
copies of vital records: $7.00 each for certified copies of births and deaths, $3.00 for certified copies of marriages, $1.00 for uncertified copies of marriages; copies of probate records: $1.00 per page, $1.00 for certification

Knox County
organized 1808 from Fairfield County

Knox County Courthouse
111 East High Street
Mount Vernon, OH 43050
(740) 393-6755 (Recorder, 117 East High Street, Suite 114); (740) 393-6788 (Clerk of Courts, 117 East High Street, Room 201); (740) 393-6796 (Probate Court, First Floor); (740) 393-6798 (Probate Court); (740) 393-6756 FAX (Recorder); (740) 393-6832 FAX (Probate Court)
mjh@knoxcountyclerk.org
http://www.knoxcountyohio.org; http://www.recorder.co.knox.oh.us; http://www.knoxcountycpcourt.org; http://www.knoxcountyohio.org/offices/ProbateJuvenileCourt.htm
John B. Lybarger, Recorder; Mary Jo Hawkins, Clerk of Courts; Judge James M. Ronk, Probate Court

Lake County
organized 1840 from Geauga and Cuyahoga counties

Lake County Courthouse
47 North Park Place
Painesville, OH 44077
(440) 350-2510 (Recorder, 105 Main Street, PO Box 490); (440) 350-2657 (Clerk of Courts, West Annex, 25 North Park Place, PO Box 490); (440) 350-2626 (Probate Court, 25 North Park Place, PO Box 490); (440) 350-5940 FAX (Recorder); (440) 350-2628 FAX (Probate Court)
recorder@lakecountyohio.org; fsuponcic@lakecountyohio.org
http://www.lakecountyohio.org
Frank A. Suponcic, Recorder; Lynne L. Mazeika, Clerk of Courts; Judge Ted Klammer, Probate Court

Lawrence County
organized 1815 from Gallia County

Lawrence County Courthouse
1 Veterans Square
Ironton, OH 45638

(740) 533-4314 (Recorder, 111 South Fourth Street, PO Box 77); (740) 533-4312 (Recorder); (740) 533-4353 (Clerk of Courts); (740) 533-4343 (Probate Court); (740) 533-4411 FAX (Recorder)
recorder@cloh.com; lawclerk@cloh.net (Clerk of Courts)
http://www.lawrencecountyohio.org; http://www.lawrencecountyohiorecorder.org; http://www.lawrencecountyclkofcrt.org
Sharon Gossett Hager, Recorder; Less Boggs, Clerk of Courts; Judge C. David Payne, Probate Court

Licking County
organized 1808 from Fairfield County

Licking County Courthouse
Courthouse Square
Newark, OH 43055-9553
(740) 670-5300 (Recorder, County Administration Building, 20 South Second Street, Third Floor, Newark, OH 43055, PO Box 520, Newark, OH 43058-0520); (740) 670-5301 (Recorder); (740) 670-5796 (Clerk of Courts, PO Box 4370); (740) 670-5624 (Probate Court, First Floor); (740) 670-5303 FAX (Recorder); (740) 670-5886 FAX (Clerk of Courts)
blong@lcounty.com
http://www.lcounty.com
Bryan A. Long, Recorder; Gary R. Walters, Clerk of Courts; Judge Robert H. Hoover, Probate Court
(land records with Recorder; naturalization records with Clerk of Courts; births and deaths from 1875 through 1908, marriages from 1808 to 1875, and wills from 1875 with Probate Office)
no probate search service; copies of probate records: $1.00 if book and page number are known

Logan County
organized 1817 from Champaign County

Logan County Courthouse
101 South Main Street
Bellefontaine, OH 43311
(937) 599-7201 (Recorder, 100 South Madriver Street, Suite A); (937) 599-7202 (Recorder); (937) 599-7275 (Clerk of Courts, Second Floor, Room 12); (937) 599-7249 (Probate Court); (937) 599-7287 FAX (Recorder); (937) 599-7281 FAX (Clerk of Courts)
lhanson@co.logan.oh.us
http://www.co.logan.oh.us
Linda L. Hanson, Recorder; Dottie Tuttle, Clerk of Courts; Judge Michael L. Brady, Probate Court

Lorain County
organized 26 December 1822 from Huron, Cuyahoga and Medina counties

Lorain County Courthouse
308 Second Street
Elyria, OH 44035-5506
(440) 329-5148 (Recorder, Administration Building, 226 Middle Avenue); (440) 329-5536 (Clerk of Courts–Civil Division, Justice Center, 225 Court Street, Room 105, PO Box 749); (440) 244-6261 (Probate Court, Administration Building, 226 Middle Avenue); (440) 329-5477 FAX (Recorder); (440) 329-5404 FAX (Clerk of Courts)
lcrecorder@loraincounty.us
http://www.loraincounty.us/website/splash.asp
Judith Nedwick, Recorder; Ron Nabakowski, Clerk of Courts; Judge Frank J. Horvath, Probate Court
(land records with Recorder; naturalization records with Clerk of Courts; probate records from 1824 with Probate Court; early records with Lorain County Records Retention Center)
probate search service: no charge; copies of probate records: $1.00 per page, no minimum

Lucas County
organized 1835 from Wood County

Lucas County Courthouse
700 Adams Street
Toledo, OH 43624
(419) 213-4400 (Recorder, 1 Government Center, #700, Toledo, OH 43604); (419) 213-4484 (Clerk of Courts); (419) 213-4775 (Probate Court); (419) 213-4284 FAX (Recorder)
http://www.co.lucas.oh.us
Jeanine Perry, Recorder; Mr. J. Bernie Quilter, Clerk of Courts; Judge Jack R. Puffenberger, Probate Court
(births and deaths from 1865 to 1908, birth registrations from 1865 to date, marriages from 1835 to date, wills from 1865 to date, and administrations from 1891 to date with Probate Division)
copies of probate records: $1.00 per page, $2.00 per page for certified copies

Madison County
organized 1810 from Fayette County

Madison County Courthouse
1 North Main Street
London, OH 43140
(740) 852-1854 (Recorder, Room 40); (740) 852-1858 (Recorder); (740) 852-9776 (Clerk of Courts, PO Box 557); (740) 852-0756 (Probate Court, Room 205); (740) 845-1776 FAX (Recorder); (740) 845-1778 FAX (Clerk of Courts); (740) 852-7134 FAX (Probate Court)
recorder@co.madison.oh.us; juvct@co.madison.oh.us (Probate Court)
http://www.co.madison.oh.us
Charles E. Reed, Recorder; Marie Parks, Clerk of Courts; Judge Glenn S. Hamilton, Probate Court
(land records with Recorder; some scattered naturalization records with Clerk of Courts; births and deaths from 1867 to 1908, marriages from 1810, wills, estates, and guardianships from 1820 with Probate Court)
probate search service: no charge; copies of probate records: 50¢ per page, $1.00 for certification, no minimum ("we are not permitted to make change through the mail; requests for searches should be *first*; *then*, if we find the record, we will notify the individual of costs for copies; upon receiving these costs we will send the copies")

Mahoning County
organized 1846 from Columbiana and Trumbull counties

Mahoning County Courthouse
120 Market Street
Youngstown, OH 44503-1710
(330) 740-2345 (Recorder, PO Box 928); (330) 740-2104 (Clerk of Courts); (330) 740-2310 (Probate Court, First Floor); (330) 740-2105 FAX (Clerk of Courts); (330) 740-2325 FAX (Probate Court)
http://www.mahoningcountyoh.gov/Mahoning Web
Noralynn Palermo, Recorder; Tony Vivo, Clerk of Courts; Judge Timothy P. Maloney, Probate Court
(land records with Recorder ["Deeds, etc., from our parent counties were recorded here when Mahoning County was founded"]; naturalization records with Clerk of Courts; births and deaths from 1 April 1856 to 31 March 1857 and from 1 April 1864 to 20 December 1908, marriages from February 1846, and probate records on microfilm with Probate Department)
no probate search service; copies of land records: $1.00 per page; copies of probate records: 50¢ per page, no minimum ("*No checks*—cash or money order only, business size SASE a *must*; write for information about the record you are seeking before you send

money")

Marion County
organized 1820 from Indian lands by an act of the Ohio legislature but remained attached to Delaware County; separated 1824 from Delaware County

Marion County Courthouse
114 North Main Street
Marion, OH 43302-3030
(740) 223-4100 (Recorder, 222 West Center Street); (740) 223-4270 (Clerk of Courts, Courthouse Square, 100 North Main Street, Marion, OH 43302-3089); (740) 223-4109 FAX (Recorder); (740) 223-4260 (Probate Court, Courthouse Square, 100 North Main Street); (740) 223-4279 FAX (Clerk of Courts)
courtclerk@marion.net
http://www.co.marion.oh.us
Mary Jo Osmun, Recorder; Julie M. Kagel, Clerk of Courts; Judge Thomas K. Jenkins
(land records from 1822 to date with Recorder; divorce and civil court records with Clerk of the Courts; births, marriage, and probate records 1824 with Probate Court)
no probate search service; copies of probate records: $1.00 per page, no minimum

Medina County
organized 1812 from Portage County

Medina County Courthouse
93 Public Square
Medina, OH 44256-2205
(330) 725-9782 (Recorder, County Administration Building, 144 North Broadway, Room 117); (330) 725-9722 (Clerk of Courts); (330) 725-9703 (Probate Court); (330) 764-8454 FAX (Clerk of Courts)
cmswedyk@juno.com; medinaco@co.medina.oh.us
http://www.co.medina.oh.us; http://www.recorder.co.medina.oh.us; http://www.co.medina.oh.us/clerk/clrkhome.htm; http://www.medinacountyjuvenileprobatecourt.com/dynamic/default.aspx
Colleen M. Swedyk, Recorder; Kathy Fortney, Clerk of Courts; Judge John J. Lohn, Probate Court
(land records from 1795, naturalization records from 1839, births and deaths from 1867 to December 1908, marriages from 1818, estates, guardianships, trusts, etc. from 1833)
no probate search service; copies of probate records: $1.00 per page, $2.00 for certified copies ("we would prefer a money order or check and no cash for each request")

Meigs County
organized 1819 from Gallia and Athens counties

Meigs County Courthouse
100 East Second Street
Pomeroy, OH 45769
(740) 992-3806 (Recorder); (740) 992-5290 (Clerk of Courts, PO Box 151); (740) 992-3096 (Probate Court); (740) 992-2867 FAX (Recorder); (740) 992-2270 FAX (Clerk of Courts)
http://www.meigscountyohio.com; http://www.meigscountychamber.com; http://www.occaohio.com/County/meigs.htm (Clerk of Courts)
Kay Hill, Recorder; Marlene Harrison, Clerk of Courts; Judge L. Scott Powell, Probate Court
(land records, naturalization records, vital records, probate records)
no probate search service ("Due to the overwhelming amount of genealogy requests and the work load of the Meigs County Probate and Juvenile Courts, it is impossible for either office to do any more genealogy research")

Mercer County
organized 1820 from Darke County

Mercer County Courthouse

Courthouse Square, 101 North Main Street
Celina, OH 45822
(419) 586-4232 (Recorder, Room 203); (419)
586-6461 (Clerk of Courts, Room 205, PO
Box 28); (419) 586-8779 (Probate Court,
Room 306); (419) 586-3541 FAX (Recorder);
(419) 586-5826 FAX (Clerk of Courts)
recorder@mercercountyohio.org;
clerk@mercercountyohio.org
http://www.mercercountyohio.org
Tammy Barger, Recorder; James J. Highley,
Clerk of Courts; Judge Mary Pat Zitter,
Probate Court

Miami County
organized 1807 from Montgomery County

Miami County Safety Building
201 West Main Street
Troy, OH 45373-3239
(937) 440-6040 (Recorder, PO Box 653); (937)
440-6010 (Clerk of Courts, Third Floor);
(937) 332-6823 (Probate Court); (937) 440-
6041 FAX (Recorder); (937) 332-7069 FAX
(Clerk of Courts)
http://www.co.miami.oh.us
John Alexander, Recorder; Mr. Jan A. Mottinger,
Clerk of Courts; Judge Lynnita K. C. Wagner,
Probate Court

Monroe County
organized 1813 from Belmont, Washington and
Guernsey counties

Monroe County Courthouse
101 North Main Street
Woodsfield, OH 43793-1097
(740) 472-5264 (Recorder, PO Box 152); (740)
472-0761 (Clerk of Courts, Rooms 25 & 26);
(740) 472-1654 (Probate Court, Room 39);
(740) 472-2549 FAX (Clerk of Courts)
http://www.monroecountyohio.net; http://
www.ohiorecorders.com/monroe.html;
http://www.occaohio.com/County/monroe.
htm (Clerk of Courts)
Martha Louise Reid, Recorder; Beth Ann Rose,
Clerk of Courts; Judge Walter R. Starr,
Probate Court
(land records from 1837 with Recorder;
naturalization records from 1867 to 1885,
births and deaths from 1867 to 1908,
marriages from 1867, and probate records
from 1867 with Probate Court)
copies of vital records: $5.00 each; copies of
probate records: $1.00 per page, $1.00 per
document for certification

Montgomery County
organized 1803 from Hamilton and Ross
counties

Montgomery County Courts Building
41 North Perry Street
Dayton, OH 45422-2155
(937) 225-4512 (Clerk of Courts–Civil Division,
Room 104); (937) 225-4400 (Probate Court);
(937) 496-7220 FAX (Clerk of Courts–Civil
Division)
http://www.clerk.co.montgomery.oh.us;
http://www.mcohio.org/probate
Gregory A. Brush, Clerk of Courts; Judge Alice
McCollum, Probate Court

Montgomery County Recorder
(Administration Building, 451 West Third
Street—location)
PO Box 972 (mailing address)
Dayton, OH 45422-0001
(937) 225-4275; (937) 225-5405; (937) 225-5980
FAX
mcrecorder@mcohio.org
http://www.co.montgomery.oh.us; http://www.
mcohio.org/revize/montgomery/government/
recorder/index.html; http://www.mcrecorder.org
Willis E. Blackshear

Morgan County
organized 1817 from Washington County

Morgan County Courthouse

19 East Main Street
McConnelsville, OH 43756
(740) 962-4051 (Recorder, 155 East Main Street,
Room 160); (740) 962-4752 (Clerk of Courts);
(740) 962-2861 (Probate Court); (740) 962-
3364 FAX (Recorder); (740) 962-4522 FAX
(Clerk of Courts)
recorder@morgancounty-oh.gov;
clerkofcourts@morgancounty-oh.gov
http://www.morgancounty-oh.gov; http://
www.ohiorecorders.com/morgan.html;
http://www.occaohio.com/County/morgan.
htm (County Clerk)
Becky Cooley, Recorder; Mary E. Gessel, Clerk
of Courts; Judge Dan Favreau, Probate Court
(deeds with Recorder; some naturalization
records from early 1800s, births and deaths
from 1867 to 1952, marriages from 1819,
wills, and executor and administration records
from 1820 with Probate Court)
probate search service: no charge; copies of
probate records: 50¢ per page, no minimum

Morrow County
organized 1848 from Knox, Marion, Delaware
and Richland counties

Morrow County Courthouse
48 East High Street
Mount Gilead, OH 43338-1458
(419) 947-3060 (Recorder); (419) 947-2085
(Clerk of Courts); (419) 947-4515 (Probate
Court); (419) 947-5421 FAX (Clerk of Courts)
dlsmcrec@rrohio.com
http://www.morrowcounty.info
Dixie Shinaberry, Recorder; Ms. Geri Park,
Clerk of Courts; Judge Howard E. Hall,
Probate Court

Muskingum County
organized 1804 from Washington and Fairfield
counties

Muskingum County Courthouse
401 Main Street
Zanesville, OH 43701
(740) 455-7107 (Recorder, PO Box 2333,
Zanesville, OH 43702); (740) 455-7104 (Clerk
of Courts); (740) 455-7113 (Probate Court);
(740) 455-7943 FAX (Recorder); (740) 455-
7177 FAX (Clerk of Courts)
kbvincent@muskingumcounty.org
http://www.muskingumcounty.org
Karen Vincent, Recorder; Todd A. Bickle, Clerk
of Courts; Judge Joseph A. Gormley, Probate
Court

Noble County
organized 11 March 1851 from Monroe,
Morgan, Guernsey and Washington counties

Noble County Courthouse
Caldwell, OH 43724
(740) 732-4319 (Recorder, 260 Courthouse,
Room 2E); (740) 732-5604 (Clerk of Courts,
305 Courthouse); (740) 732-5047 (Probate
Court, 270 Courthouse Square); (740) 732-
5702 FAX (Recorder); (740) 732-5702 FAX
(Clerk of Courts)
http://www.noblecountyohio.com; http://
www.ohiorecorders.com/noble.html; http://
www.occaohio.com/County/noble.htm
(Clerk of Courts)
Phyllis Stritz, Recorder; Karen Starr, Clerk of
Courts; Judge John W. Nau, Probate Court
(land records with Recorder, naturalization
records with Probate Court and Clerk of
Courts; births and deaths from 1867,
marriages from 1851, and wills, estates and
guardianships from 1851 with Probate Court)
probate search service: $2.00 per category;
copies of probate records: 50¢ each, $3.00–
$7.00 for certification, $2.00 minimum (search
fee) ("always include SASE")

Ottawa County
organized 1840 from Erie, Sandusky and Lucas
counties

Ottawa County Courthouse
315 Madison Street
Port Clinton, OH 43452
(419) 734-6730 (Recorder, Room 204); (419)
734-6755 (Clerk of Courts, Room 304); (419)
734-6875 FAX(419) 734-6830 (Probate
Court); (419) 734-6919 FAX (Recorder); (419)
734-6875 FAX (Clerk of Courts)
vpark@co.ottawa.oh.us
http://www.co.ottawa.oh.us;
http://www.ottawacocpcourt.com;
http://www.ottawacountyprobatecourt.com
Virginia M. Park, Recorder; JoAn C. Monnett,
Clerk of Courts; Judge Kathleen Giesler,
Probate Court
(land records from 1840 with Recorder; vital
records before 1909 and probate records
from 1840 with Probate Court)
probate search service: no charge; copies of
probate records: $1.00 per page, $1.00 for
certification

Paulding County
organized 1820 from Indian lands and attached
to Wood County

Paulding County Courthouse
115 North Williams Street
Paulding, OH 45879
(419) 399-8275 (Recorder, Room 103); (419)
399-8276 (Recorder); (419) 399-8210 (Clerk
of Courts); (419) 399-8256 (Probate Court,
Second Floor); (419) 399-2862 FAX
(Recorder); (419) 399–8248 FAX (Clerk of
Courts)
pauldingcountyrecorder@bright.net
http://www.ohiorecorders.com/paulding.html;
http://www.occaohio.com/County/paulding.
htm
K. Sue Thrasher, Recorder; Eleanor J. Edwards,
Clerk of Courts; Judge John A. DeMuth,
Probate Court

Perry County
organized 1817 from Washington, Fairfield and
Muskingum counties

Perry County Courthouse
105 North Main Street
New Lexington, OH 43764
(740) 342-2494 (Recorder, First Floor, PO Box
147); (740) 342-1022 (Clerk of Courts, PO
Box 67); (740) 342-1493 (Probate Court, First
Floor, PO Box 167); (740) 342-5539 FAX
(Recorder); (740) 342-5527 FAX (Clerk of
Courts)
http://www.ohiorecorders.com/perry.html;
http://www.occaohio.com/County/perry.ht
m (Clerk of Courts)
Barbara J. Fox, Recorder; Timothy Wollenberg,
Clerk of Courts; Judge Luann Cooperrider,
Probate Court
(plats, liens, mortgages, oil and gas leases, armed
service discharges with Recorder;
naturalization records from 1818; births and
deaths from 1867 to 1925, marriages from
1818, and wills, estates, guardianships, trusts,
name changes, and some divorces from 1818
with Probate Court)
no probate search service; copies of land
records: 50¢ per page; copies of naturalization
records: 75¢ per page; copies of vital records
from Probate Court: 75¢ per page for births
and deaths, $5.00 for certified copies of births
and deaths, 50¢ for marriages before 1900,
75¢ for marriages after 1900, $2.00 for
certified copies of marriages; $7.00 for
certified copies; copies of probate records:
75¢ per page

Pickaway County
organized 1810 from Ross, Fairfield and
Franklin counties

Pickaway County Courthouse
207 South Court Street
Circleville, OH 43113
(740) 474-5826 (Recorder); (740) 474-5231
(Clerk of Courts); (740) 474-3117 (Probate

Court, Room 3); (740) 477-6361 FAX (Recorder); (740) 477-3976 FAX (Clerk of Courts); (740) 474-8451 FAX (Probate Court)
pickawayclerk@frognet.net
http://www.pickaway.org
Joyce R. Gifford, Recorder; James Dean, Clerk of Courts; Judge Jan Michael Long, Probate Court
(naturalization records from 1860, births and deaths from 1867, marriages from 1810, and estates from 1810 with Probate Court)
probate search service: no charge; copies of probate records: $1.00 per page, no minimum

Pike County
organized 1815 from Ross, Highland and Scioto counties

Pike County Courthouse
100 East Second Street
Waverly, OH 45690-1301
(740) 947-2622 (Recorder, 230 Waverly Plaza, Suite 500); (740) 947-2715 (Clerk of Courts, Second Floor); (740) 947-2560 (Probate Court, 230 Waverly Plaza, Suite 600, 100 East Second Street); (740) 947-7997 FAX (Recorder); (740) 947-5065 FAX (Clerk of Courts)
pcrec@bright.net
http://www.ohiorecorders.com/pike.html;
  http://www.occaohio.com/County/pike.htm
Joyce Leeth, Recorder; John E. Williams, Clerk of Courts; Judge William Wray Bevens, Probate Court
(land records, naturalization records, vital records, probate records)
probate search service: no charge; copies of probate records: $1.00

Portage County
organized 1807 from Trumbull and Jackson counties, officially formed 9 June 1808

Portage County Courthouse
203 West Main Street
Ravenna, OH 44266-2761
(330) 297-3553 (Recorder, County Administration Building, 449 South Meridian Street); (330) 297-3644 (Clerk of Courts, PO Box 1035); (330) 297-3870 (Probate Court, Room 204, PO Box 936); (330) 297-7349 FAX (Recorder); (330) 297-4554 FAX (Clerk of Courts)
bhowe@portageco.com;
  lfankhauser@portageco.com
http://www.co.portage.oh.us
Bonnie M. Howe, Recorder; Linda Fankhauser, Clerk of Courts; Judge Thomas J. Carnes, Probate Court
(land records with Recorder; birth and death records 1867–1908 and probate records with Probate Court)

Preble County
organized 1808 from Montgomery and Butler counties

Preble County Courthouse
101 East Main Street
Eaton, OH 45320
(937) 456-8173 (Recorder, PO Box 371); (937) 456-8160 (Clerk of Courts, Third Floor); (937) 456-8138 (Probate Court); (937) 456-9548 FAX (Clerk of Courts)
cwashington@preblecountyohio.net
http://www.preblecounty.com/government/county.htm; http://www.preblecountyohio.net (Clerk of Courts)
William J. Spahr, Recorder; Christopher B. Washington, Clerk of Courts; Judge Wilfred G. Dues, Probate Court

Putnam County
organized 1820 from Indian lands and attached to Wood County

Putnam County Courthouse
245 East Main Street
Ottawa, OH 45875

(419) 523-6490 (Recorder, Suite 202); (419) 523-3110 (Clerk of Courts, Suite 301); (419) 523-3012 (Probate Court, Suite 204); (419) 523-4403 FAX (Recorder); (419) 523-5284 FAX (Clerk of Courts)
http://www.putnamnet.com; http://www.putnamcountyohio.com (Putnam County Community Improvement Corporation)
Cathy Recker, Recorder; Teresa Lammers, Clerk of Courts; Judge Daniel Gerschutz, Probate Court
(land records, naturalization records, vital records, probate records)

Richland County
organized 1813 from Knox County

Richland County Administration Building
50 Park Avenue, East
Mansfield, OH 44902-1850
(419) 774-5602 (Recorder); (419) 774-5600 (Recorder); (419) 774-5549 (Clerk of Courts, PO Box 127); (419) 774-5585 (Probate Court); (419) 774-5603 FAX (Recorder); (419) 774-5547 FAX (Clerk of Courts)
adavis3288@aol.com;
  frary.l@cpcnet.richland.oh.us
http://www.richlandcountyoh.us/index.htm
Sarah M. Davis, Recorder; Linda Frary, Clerk of Courts; Judge Philip Alan B. Mayer, Probate Court
(land records, naturalization records, births and deaths from 1865 to December 1908, marriages from 1813, probate records from 1813)

Ross County
organized 1798, original county

Ross County Courthouse
2 North Paint Street
Chillicothe, OH 45601
(740) 702-3000 (Recorder, Suite E, PO Box 6162); (740) 702-3010 (Clerk of Courts, Suite B); (740) 774-1179 (Probate Court, Suite A); (740) 702-3006 FAX (Recorder); (740) 702-3018 FAX (Clerk of Courts)
rossrec@bright.net; rcclerk@bright.net
http://www.co.ross.oh.us
Kathy Dunn, Recorder; Mr. Ty D. Hinton, Clerk of Courts; Judge Richard G. Ward, Probate Court

Sandusky County
organized 1820 from Huron County

Sandusky County Courthouse
100 North Park Avenue
Fremont, OH 43420-2454
(419) 334-6226 (Recorder, Suite 217); (419) 334-6226 (Recorder); (419) 334-6161 (Clerk of Courts, Suite 320); (419) 334-6211 option 9 (Probate Court); (419) 334-6164 FAX (Clerk of Courts)
Recorder@co.sandusky.oh.us;
  Brown_Warren@co.sandusky.oh.us
http://www.sandusky-county.org
Colleen Carmack, Recorder; Warren Brown, Clerk of Courts; Judge Brad Culbert, Probate Court
(land records with Recorder, naturalization records with Clerk of Courts, probate records with Probate Court)
probate search service: no charge; copies of probate records: $1.00 plus $1.00 for certification

Scioto County
organized 1803 from Indian Territory

Scioto County Courthouse
602 Seventh Street
Portsmouth, OH 45662
(740) 355-8303 (Recorder, Room 110); (740) 355-8304 (Recorder); (740) 355-8226 (Clerk of Courts); (740) 355-8218 (Clerk of Courts); (740) 355-8360 (Probate Court); (740) 355-8355 FAX (Recorder); (740) 354-2057 FAX (Clerk of Courts)

sccourts@sciotocounty.net (Clerk of Courts)
http://www.sciotocountyohio.com
Irene Ashley, Recorder; Mildred E. Thompson, Clerk of Courts; Judge James W. Kirsch, Probate Court

Seneca County
organized 1820 from Indian land and attached to Sandusky County

Seneca County Courthouse
81 Jefferson Street
Tiffin, OH 44883-2339
(419) 447-4434 (Recorder, 109 South Washington Street, Suite 2104); (419) 447-0671 (Clerk of Courts, 117 East Market Street, Suite 4101); (419) 447-3121 (Probate Court, Probate Juvenile Court Building, 108 Jefferson Street); (419) 443-7918 FAX (Clerk of Courts)
mward@acctiffin.com
http://www.senecaco.org
Michael J. Dell, Recorder; Mary K. Ward, Clerk of Courts; Judge Paul F. Kutscher, Jr., Probate Court
(births and deaths from 1867 to 1908, marriages from 1841 with Probate Court)
vital records search service from Probate Court: $5.00; copies of vital records: $7.00 each for births and deaths, $2.00 for marriages, plus SASE

Shelby County
organized 1819 from Miami County

Shelby County Courthouse
100 East Court Street
Sidney, OH 45365
(937) 498-7270 (Recorder, Shelby County Annex, 129 East Court Street, Second Floor); (937) 498-7271 (Recorder); (937) 498-7221 (Clerk of Courts, PO Box 809); (937) 498-7265 (Probate Court, Second Floor, PO Box 4187); (937) 498-7272 FAX (Recorder); (937) 498-4840 FAX (Clerk of Courts)
jsiegel@shelbycountyrecorders.com;
  mmumford@shelbycountyclerkofcourts.com
http://www.co.shelby.oh.us;
  http://shelbycoprobate.org
Jodi L. Siegel, Recorder; Michele Mumford, Clerk of Courts; Judge Norman P. Smith, Probate Court
(birth and death records 1867–1908, marriage records from 1825, and estates, guardianships, etc. from 1825 with Probate Court)

Stark County
organized 1808 from Indian Territory

Stark County Courthouse
115 Central Plaza North (northwest corner of Market and Tuscarawas Streets)
Canton, OH 44702-1290
(330) 451-7443 (Recorder, Stark County Office Building, 110 Central Plaza South, Suite 170); (330) 451-7801 (Clerk of Courts, Suite 101); (330) 451-7752 (Probate Court, Stark County Office Building, 110 Central Plaza S, Suite 501); (330) 451-7753 (Probate Court Records Center); (330) 451-7394 FAX (Recorder); (330) 451-7066 FAX (Clerk of Courts)
recorder@co.stark.oh.us
http://www.co.stark.oh.us; http://www.recorder.co.stark.oh.us; http://www.starkclerk.org; http://www.probate.co.stark.oh.us
Rick Campbell, Recorder; Nancy Reinbold, Clerk of Courts; Judge Dixilene N. Park, Probate Court
(probate records, including estate case files from 1920 with Probate Court, Records Center)
no probate search service; copies of probate records: 50¢ per page ("always include SASE")

Summit County
organized 1840 from Portage, Medina and Stark counties

Summit County Courthouse

209 South High Street
Akron, OH 44308-1306
(330) 643-2712 (Fiscal Office, Recorder Division, Ohio Building, 175 South Main Street, Fourth Floor); (330) 643-2211 (Clerk of Courts, 205 South High Street); (330) 643-2350, Probate Court, General Office, First Floor); (330) 643-2330 (Probate Court Judge); (330) 643-2622 FAX (Fiscal Office); (330) 643-2393 FAX (Probate Court)
jdonofrio@summitoh.net; SummitCPClerk@cpcourt.summitoh.net; mdaugherty@summitoh.net; bspicer@summitohioprobate.com
http://www.co.summit.oh.us; http://www.summitohioprobate.com
John A. Donofrio, Fiscal Officer; Daniel M. Horrigan, Clerk of Courts; Mary Lou Daugherty, Chief Deputy Clerk of Courts; Judge W. F. Spicer, Probate Court
(land records with Fiscal Office, Recorder Division; naturalization records with Clerk of Courts, Naturalization Department, 53 University Avenue, Akron, OH 44308; births and deaths from 1869 through 1908, marriages from 1840, and estates, guardianships, and trusts from 1840 with Probate Court Records Room)
probate search service: no charge, but will not do extensive research (will search one or two records; "we have a list of researchers in the area to do genealogical research; we are not staffed to provide researching; fees should be in the form of a money order or certified check made out to Summit County Probate Court"); copies of vital records from Probate Court: $3.00 each for births and deaths, $1.00 each for marriages, $2.00 for certified marriages; copies of probate records: 75¢ per page, $1.00 for certification, no minimum

Trumbull County
organized 1800 from Jefferson County

Trumbull County Courthouse
161 High Street, N.W.
Warren, OH 44481-1005
(330) 675-2401 (Recorder, 160 High Street, NW); (330) 675-2557 (Clerk of Courts); (330) 675-2521 (Probate Court); (330) 675-2404 FAX (Recorder)
rsmarche@co.trumbull.oh.us
http://www.co.trumbull.oh.us; http://tcrecorder.co.trumbull.oh.us; http://www.clerk.co.trumbull.oh.us; http://www.trumbullprobate.org
Diana J. Marchese, Recorder; Karen Infante Allen, Clerk of Courts; Judge Thomas A. Swift, Probate Court
(land records with Recorder; naturalization records from 1800 to 1985, vital records, and probate records from 1805 with Probate Court)
probate search service: no charge; copies of probate records: $1.00, $2.00 per certified page, no minimum

Tuscarawas County
organized 1808 from Jefferson County

Tuscarawas County Courthouse
Public Square
New Philadelphia, OH 44663
(330) 365-3284 (Recorder, Courthouse Annex, 125 East High Street); (330) 365-3243 (Clerk of Courts, 125 East High Avenue); (330) 365-3266 (Probate Court, 101 East High Avenue, Room 103); (330) 365-3281 FAX (Recorder); (330) 343-4682 FAX (Clerk of Courts); (330) 364-3190 FAX (Probate Court)
recorder@co.tuscarawas.oh.us
http://www.co.tuscarawas.oh.us
Lori Smith, Recorder; Rockne W. Clarke, Clerk of Courts; Judge Linda A. Kate, Probate Court
(land records with Recorder, naturalization records to 1907 with Probate Court, births from 1867 to 1908, deaths from 1867 to 1924, marriages from 1808, and wills, estates, guardianships from 1808 with Probate Court)

no probate search service; copies of vital records: $7.00 each for births and deaths, $2.00 for marriages; copies of probate records: $1.00 per page, no minimum ("we do not have the staff to do extensive research for you with local genealogical society if you cannot come in yourself")

Union County
organized 1820 from Franklin, Madison and Logan counties

Union County Courthouse
215 West Fifth Street
Marysville, OH 43040
(937) 645-3032 (Recorder, County Office Building, 233 West Sixth Street); (937) 645-3006 (Clerk of Courts); (937) 645-3029 option 5 (Probate Court); (937) 642-3397 FAX (Recorder)
tmarkham@co.union.oh.us
http://www.co.union.oh.us
Teresa L. Markham, Recorder; Paula Pyers Warner, Clerk of Courts; Judge Charlotte Coleman Eufinger, Probate Court
(land records from 1820 [few deeds before] with Recorder; some naturalization records from 1860, births and deaths from 1867 to 1909, marriages from 1820 to date, and probate records from 1820 with Probate Court)
probate search service: no charge; copies of vital records: $3.00 for births and deaths; copies of probate records: 50¢ per page, $1.50 for certified copies

Van Wert County
organized 1820 from Indian Territory

Van Wert County Courthouse
121 East Main Street
Van Wert, OH 45891
(419) 238-2558 (Recorder, Suite 206); (419) 238-1022 (Clerk of Courts, Third Floor, PO Box 366); (419) 238-0027 (Probate Court, Room 104); (419) 238-5410 FAX (Recorder); (419) 238-4760 FAX (Clerk of Courts)
recorder@vanwertcounty.org; administrator@VWCommonPleas.org
http://www.vanwertcounty.org; http://www.vwcommonpleas.org/sql/calsearch.asp (Clerk of Courts)
Nancy A. Harting, Recorder; Carol Speelman, Clerk of Courts; Judge Rex D. Fortney, Probate Court
(land records from 1838 with Recorder; naturalization records 1835–1854 with Cour of Common Pleas; naturalization records 1908–1974 with Clerk of Courts; naturalization records 1855–1908, births and deaths 1867–1908, marriages from 1840, estates and wills from 1837, and guardianships from 1873 with Probate Court)
naturalization, vital and probate records search service: $3.00

Vinton County
organized 1850 from Gallia, Athens, Ross, Hocking, Meigs and Jackson counties

Vinton County Courthouse
100 East Main Street
McArthur, OH 45651
(740) 596-4314 (Recorder); (740) 596-3001 (Clerk of Courts); (740) 596-5480 (Probate Court); (740) 596-2265 FAX (Recorder)
recorder@co.vinton.oh.us; clerkofcourts@co.vinton.oh.us; court.probate@co.vinton.oh.us
http://vintoncountyoh.gov
Lori K. Graman, Recorder; Lisa A. Gilliland, Clerk of Courts; Judge N. Robert Grillo, Probate Court
(land records with Recorder, probate records with Probate Court)
no probate search service; copies of vital records: $7.00 plus SASE, exact information needed; copies of probate records: 25¢ per page plus SASE

Warren County
organized 1803 from Butler and Hamilton counties

Warren County Courthouse
320 East Silver Street
Lebanon, OH 45036-1816
(513) 695-1382 (Recorder, Administration Building, 406 Justice Drive); (513) 695-1382 (Recorder); (513) 695-1120 (Clerk of Courts, 570 Justice Drive, PO Box 238); (513) 695-1180 (Probate Court, 570 Justice Drive); (513) 695-2949 FAX (Recorder); (513) 695-2965 FAX (Clerk of Courts)
deckea@co.warren.oh.us; krista@warrenprobate.org
http://www.co.warren.oh.us/recorder; http://www.co.warren.oh.us/clerkofcourt/index.htm; http://www.co.warren.oh.us/probate_juvenile
Beth Deckard, Recorder; James L. "Jim" Spaeth, Clerk of Courts; Judge Michael E. Powell, Probate Court
(land records with Recorder, probate records with Probate Court)
no land records search service: copies of land records: $1.00 per page

Washington County
organized 1788, original county

Washington County Courthouse Annex
205 Putnam Street
Marietta, OH 45750-3085
(740) 373-6623, ext. 235 or 236 (Recorder); (740) 373-6623 (Clerk of Courts); (740) 373-6623, ext. 253 (Probate Court); (740) 373-9643 FAX (Recorder)
recorder@washingtongov.org; twright@wcgov.org; ClerkofCourts@washingtongov.org; probate-juvenile@washingtongov.org
http://www.washingtongov.org
Tracey C. Wright, Recorder; Judy R. Van Dyk, Clerk of Courts; Judge Timothy A. Williams, Probate Court
(land records with Recorder; births and deaths 1867– 20 December 1908, marriages from 1789, probate records from 1789, and naturalization records 1859–1905 with Probate Court; other naturalization records with Clerk of Courts [copies cannot be certified])
probate search service: no charge ("we must have dates and name"); certified copies of vital records from Probate Court: $5.00 each; copies of probate records: 50¢ for each of the first two pages and 25¢ for each additional page, $1.00 for certified copies, $1.00 minimum ("send to Washington County Probate Court; we do NOT take personal checks")

Wayne County
organized 15 Aug 1786, original county including parts of five states: Ohio, Indiana, Illinois, Michigan and Wisconsin; reduced in 1803 to include only a portion of Ohio; the present county was created in 1808 and organized in 1812

Wayne County Courthouse
107 West Liberty Street
Wooster, OH 44691
(330) 287-5460 (Recorder, County Administration Building, 428 West Liberty Street); (330) 287-5590 (Clerk of Courts, PO Box 507); (330) 287-5575 (Probate Court); (330) 287-5685 FAX (Recorder)
jane.carmichael@co.wayne.oh.us
http://www.waynecountyclerkofcourts.org
Jane Carmichael, Recorder; Tim Neal, Clerk of Courts; Judge Raymond E. Leisy, Probate Court
(land records with Recorder; naturalization records, births and deaths from 1867 to April 1908, marriages from 1813, probate records from 1813 with Probate Judge)
probate search service: no charge; copies of

probate records: 25¢ per page, no minimum ("should be as specific as possible")

Williams County
organized 1820 from Indian land and attached to Wood County

Williams County Courthouse
1 Courthouse Square
Bryan, OH 43506
(419) 636-3259 (Recorder); (419) 636-1551 (Clerk of Courts); (419) 636-1548 (Probate Court, Second Floor); (419) 636-7877 FAX (Clerk of Courts); (419) 636-5405 FAX (Probate Court)
recorder@wmsco.org; probate@wmsco.org
http://www.co.williams.oh.us
Patsy Mealer, Recorder; Kimberly L. Herman, Clerk of Courts; Judge Steven R. Bird, Probate Court

Wood County
organized 1820 from Indian lands, Northwest Territory

Wood County Courthouse
1 Courthouse Square
Bowling Green, OH 43402-2427
(419) 354-9140 (Recorder); (419) 354-9280 (Clerk of Courts, Second Floor); (419) 354-9230 (Probate Court); (419) 354-2039 FAX (Recorder); (419) 354-9241 FAX (Clerk of Courts); (419) 354-9357 (Probate Court)
skinder@co.wood.oh.us; bbbhaer@wcnet.org; clerkofcourts@co.wood.oh.us
http://www.co.wood.oh.us; http://www.co.wood.oh.us/recorder; http://clerkofcourt.co.wood.oh.us; http://www.probate-court.co.wood.oh.us
Sue Kinder, Recorder; Rebecca E. "Becky" Bhaer, Clerk of Courts; Judge David E. Woessner, Probate Court
(naturalization records 1859–1929 and one in 1960, and land records with Recorder; births and deaths from 1867 through 1908, marriages from 1820, estates from 1821, and guardianships from 1852 with Probate Court)
no probate search service; copies of probate records: $1.00 per page, $1.00 for certification, no minimum; certified copies: $7.00 each for births and deaths, $2.00 for abstracts of marriages

Wyandot County
organized 1845 from Marion, Crawford, Hardin, and Hancock counties

Wyandot County Courthouse
109 South Sandusky Avenue
Upper Sandusky, OH 43351-1497
(419) 294-1442 (Recorder, Room 24); (419) 294-1432 (Clerk of Courts); (419) 294-2302 (Probate Court, Room 23); (419) 294-6405 FAX (Recorder)
recorder@co.wyandot.oh.us
http://www.co.wyandot.oh.us; http://www.ohiorecorders.com/wyandot.html
Karen S. Kline, Recorder; Ann K. Dunbar, Clerk of Courts; Judge Kathleen A. Aubrey, Probate Court
(births and deaths from 1867 to 1908, marriages from 1845 to date, and estate proceedings from 1845 to date with Probate Court)
copies of vital records: $2.00 each for births and deaths, $7.00 each for certified copies of births and deaths, 50¢ each for complete marriage record (includes application, date issued, date married), $5.00 for certified copy of complete marriage record, $2.00 for marriage certificate (includes names, date married and by whom); copies of probate records: 50¢ per page, $1.00 for certification

---

OKLAHOMA

Capital: Oklahoma City. Statehood: 16 November 1907 (annexed as part of the Louisiana Territory, 1803, except for the panhandle, Indian Territory created 1820, Oklahoma Territory created 1890, merged to form state)

Oklahoma's courts of limited jurisdiction include: Court of Tax Review, Court of Bank Review, Municipal Criminal Court of Record, Workers' Compensation Court, Municipal Court Not of Record, and Court on the Judiciary. The District Courts sit in each county seat and have general jurisdiction, including civil actions, probate, domestic relations, felonies, misdemeanors, and juvenile matters. Appeals are referred to the Court of Appeals, the Court of Criminal Appeals and the Supreme Court.

Adair County
organized 1907 from Cherokee lands

Adair County Courthouse
Division Street and Highway 59
Stilwell, OK 74960
(918) 696-7198 voice & FAX (County Clerk, PO Box 169); (918) 696-97633 (Court Clerk, PO Box 426); (918) 696-5365 FAX (Court Clerk)
adaircountyclerk@alltel.net; sam.mccarter@oscn.net
http://adair.oklahomacounties.us
Carrie Philpott, County Clerk; Paula "Sam" McCarter, Court Clerk
(land records with County Clerk; probate records with Court Clerk)
land records search service: $5.00 per name; copies of land records: $1.00 per page

Alfalfa County
organized 1907 from Woods County

Alfalfa County Courthouse
300 South Grand Avenue
Cherokee, OK 73728
(580) 596-3158 (County Clerk); (580) 596-3523 (Court Clerk)
http://www.tax.ok.gov/advalcount/alfalfa.html; http://www.oscn.net/applications/oscn/start.asp?viewType=COUNTYINFO&county=Alfalfa
Bruce Martin, County Clerk; Lori Irwin, Court Clerk
(land records from 1895 with County Clerk; naturalization records, marriages, and probate records with Court Clerk)
probate search service: $5.00; copies of probate records: $1.00 per page

Atoka County
organized 1907 from Choctaw lands

Atoka County Courthouse
200 East Court Street
Atoka, OK 74525-2045
(580) 889-5157 (County Clerk); (580) 889-3565 (Court Clerk)
http://www.tax.ok.gov/advalcount/atoka.html; http://www.oscn.net/applications/oscn/start.asp?viewType=COUNTYINFO&county=ATOKA
Raylene Hammond, County Clerk; Barbara Hunt, Court Clerk
(land records with County Clerk, probate records with Court Clerk)
copies of land records: $1.00 each

Beaver County
organized 1890, original county

Beaver County Courthouse
111 West Second Street
Beaver, OK 73932
(580) 625-3141 (County Clerk, PO Box 338); (580) 625-3191 (Court Clerk, PO Box 237)
http://www.tax.ok.gov/advalcount/beaver.html; http://www.oscn.net/applications/oscn/start.asp?viewType=COUNTYINFO&county=BEAVER
Karen Schell, County Clerk; Sharon Raven, Court Clerk
(land records with County Clerk, probate records with Court Clerk)
no probate search service; copies of probate records: $1.00 per page, no minimum

Beckham County
organized 1907 from Roger Mills and Greer counties

Beckham County Courthouse
Sayre, OK 73662
(580) 928-3383 (County Clerk, PO Box 428); (580) 928-3330 (Court Clerk, PO Box 520); (580) 928-9278 FAX (Court Clerk)
http://www.tax.ok.gov/advalcount/beckham.html; http://www.oscn.net/applications/oscn/start.asp?viewType=COUNTYINFO&county=BECKHAM
Clydene Manning, County Clerk; Mary Prather, Court Clerk
(land records from 1900 with County Clerk, probate records with Court Clerk)

Blaine County
organized 1895, original county

Blaine County Courthouse
212 North Weigle
Watonga, OK 73772
(580) 623-5890 (County Clerk, PO Box 138); (405) 625-5890 (Court Clerk)
http://www.blainecountyok.com/index.htm; http://www.tax.ok.gov/advalcount/blaine.html; http://www.oscn.net/applications/oscn/start.asp?viewType=COUNTYINFO&county=BLAINE
Linda McPherson, County Clerk; Rebekah Martin, Court Clerk

Bryan County
organized 1907 from Chickasaw lands

Bryan County Courthouse
402 West Evergreen
Durant, OK 74701-4744
(580) 924-2202 (County Clerk); (580) 924-1446 (Court Clerk)
http://www.oscn.net/applications/oscn/start.asp?viewType=COUNTYINFO&county=bryan.html; http://www.oscn.net/applications/oscn/start.asp?viewType=COUNTYINFO&county=BRYAN
Patricia Brady, Court Clerk; Sandy Stroud, Court Clerk

Caddo County
organized 6 August 1901, original county

Caddo County Courthouse
201 West Oklahoma Avenue
Anadarko, OK 73005
(405) 247-6609 (County Clerk, PO Box 68); (405) 247-3393 (Court Clerk, PO Box 10)
http://www.tax.ok.gov/advalcount/caddo.html; http://www.oscn.net/applications/oscn/start.asp?viewType=COUNTYINFO&county=CADDO
Patrice Dolch, County Clerk; Opal Finch, Court Clerk
(land records through 1 July 1993 with County Clerk; probate records and some citizenship records with County Clerk)

Canadian County
organized 1890, original county

Canadian County Clerk
(201 North Choctaw Avenue—location)
PO Box 458 (mailing address)
El Reno, OK 73036
(405) 262-1070, ext. 122; (405) 422-2411 FAX
co-clerk@canadiancounty.org
http://www.canadiancounty.org
Phyllis Blair

Canadian Court Clerk

(Judicial Building, 301 North Choctaw
　Avenue—location)
PO Box 730 (mailing address)
El Reno, OK 73036
(405) 262-1070, ext. 157
dee.ray@oscn.net
http://www.canadiancounty.org
Dee Ray

Carter County
organized 1907 from Chickasaw lands

Carter County Courthouse
#20 "B Street Southwest
Ardmore, OK 73401
(580) 223-8162 (County Clerk, Suite 102, PO
　Box 1236); (580) 223-5253 (Court Clerk,
　Second Floor, PO Box 37)
cartercountyclerk@sbcglobal.net
http://www.brightok.net/cartercounty
Cynthia Harmon, County Clerk; Karen Volino,
　Court Clerk

Cherokee County
organized 1907 from Indian lands

Cherokee County Courthouse
213 West Delaware
Tahlequah, OK 74464-3639
(918) 456-3171 (County Clerk, Room 200); (918)
　456-0691 (Court Clerk, Room 302); (918)
　458-6587 FAX (Court Clerk)
http://cherokee.oklahomacounties.us;
　http://www.tax.ok.gov/advalcount/cherokee
　.htm; http://www.oscn.net/applications/
　oscn/start.asp?viewType=COUNTYINFO&
　county=CHEROKEE
Marshel Bennett, County Clerk; Shirley Glory,
　Court Clerk
(land records from 1907 with County Clerk;
　marriage licenses from 1907 and probate
　records from 1907 with County Clerk)
probate search service: $5.00 written; copies of
　marriage licenses: $5.00 each; copies of
　probate records: $1.00 for the first page and
　50¢ for each additional page, no minimum

Choctaw County
organized 1907 from Choctaw lands

Choctaw County Courthouse
300 East Duke Street
Hugo, OK 74743
(405) 326-3778 (County Clerk); (580) 326-7554
　(Court Clerk); (580) 326-0291 FAX (Court
　Clerk)
http://www.tax.ok.gov/advalcount/choctaw.ht
　ml; http://www.oscn.net/applications/oscn/
　start.asp?viewType=COUNTYINFO&count
　y=CHOCTAW
Emily VanWorth, County Clerk; Jimmy Walker,
　Court Clerk
(land records with County Clerk, naturalization
　records and probate records with Court
　Clerk)

Cimarron County
organized 1907 from Beaver County

Cimarron County Courthouse
Courthouse Square
Boise City, OK 73933
(405) 544-2251 (County Clerk, PO Box 145);
　(405) 544-2221 (Court Clerk, PO Box 788);
　(580) 544-2006 FAX (Court Clerk)
http://www.oscn.net/applications/oscn/start.as
　p?viewType=COUNTYINFO&county=cima
　rron.html
Coleen Crabtree, County Clerk; Priscilla
　Johnson, Court Clerk
(land records with County Clerk, naturalization
　records from May 1908 to February 1923 and
　probate records from February 1908 with
　Court Clerk)
probate search service: $2.00 per quarter hour;
　copies of probate records: $1.00 for the first
　page and 50¢ for each additional page, no
　minimum

Cleveland County
organized 1890 from Cherokee lands

Cleveland County Clerk
201 South Jones Avenue, Suite 210
Norman, OK 73069-6099
(405) 366-0240
http://www.oscn.net/applications/oscn/start.as
　p?viewType=COUNTYINFO&county=cleve
　land.html
Dorinda Harvey
(land records from 1889)
copies of land records: $1.00 per page

Cleveland Court Clerk
Courthouse, 200 South Peters
Norman, OK 73069
(405) 321-6402
http://www.oscn.net/applications/oscn/start.as
　p?viewType=COUNTYINFO&county=CLE
　VELAND
Rhonda Hall
(probate records)
probate search service: direct or reverse, no
　charge, if time allows; copies of probate
　records: $1.00 for the first page and 50¢ for
　each additional page, no minimum

Coal County
organized 1907 from Chickasaw lands

Coal County Courthouse
4 North Main Street
Coalgate, OK 74538-2832
(580) 927-2103 (County Clerk, Suite #1); (580)
　927-2281 (Court Clerk)
http://www.tax.ok.gov/advalcount/coal.html;
　http://www.oscn.net/applications/oscn/start
　.asp?viewType=COUNTYINFO&county=C
　OAL
Eugina Loudermilk, County Clerk; Betty Price,
　Court Clerk
(land records from 1907 with County Clerk,
　probate records from 1907 with Court Clerk)
no probate search service; copies of probate
　records: $1.00 per page, no minimum

Comanche County
organized 1901 from Cherokee lands

Comanche County Courthouse
315 S.W. Fifth Street
Lawton, OK 73501-4326
(580) 355-5214 (County Clerk, Room 304); (580)
　353-4017 (Court Clerk, Room 504)
http://www.comanchecounty.us/mainhome;
　http://comanche.oklahomacounties.us;
　http://www.tax.ok.gov/advalcount/comanch
　e.html; http://www.oscn.net/applications/
　oscn/start.asp?viewType=COUNTYINFO&
　county=COMANCHE
Earline Shriver, County Clerk; Joan Williams,
　Court Clerk
(land records with County Clerk; naturalizations
　from 28 June 1930 to 23 August 1982, mar-
　riages, and probate records with Court Clerk)
probate search service: no charge, but must have
　a date (no ten-year searches); copies of
　probate records: $1.00 for the first page and
　50¢ for each additional page

Cotton County
organized 1912 from Comanche County

Cotton County Courthouse
301 North Broadway Street
Walters, OK 73572-1271
(405) 875-3026 (County Clerk); (405) 875-3029
　(Court Clerk)
http://www.tax.ok.gov/advalcount/cotton.html;
　http://www.oscn.net/applications/oscn/
　start.asp?viewType=COUNTYINFO&count
　y=cotton
Linda Thompson, County Clerk; Debbie
　Hodnefield, Court Clerk
(land records with County Clerk, probate
　records and some births and deaths with
　Court Clerk)
no probate search service; copies of probate

records: $1.00 per page, no minimum

Craig County
organized 1907 from Cherokee lands

Craig County Courthouse
301 West Canadian
Vinita, OK 74301
(918) 256-2507 (County Clerk, PO Box 397);
　(918) 256-6451 (Court Clerk)
http://www.tax.ok.gov/advalcount/craig.html;
　http://www.oscn.net/applications/oscn/start
　.asp?viewType=COUNTYINFO&county=C
　RAIG
Tammy Malone, County Clerk; Patricia Byers,
　Court Clerk

Creek County
organized 1907 from Creek lands

Creek County Clerk
317 East Lee, Room 100
Sapulpa, OK 74066
(918) 224-4084 (County Clerk, 317 East Lee,
　Room 100)
http://www.tax.ok.gov/advalcount/creek.html
Betty Rentz
no land records search service; copies of land
　records: $1.00 each

Creek Court Clerk
Courthouse, 222 East Dewey, Suite 201
Sapulpa, OK 74066
(918) 227-2525; (918) 227-5030 FAX
http://www.oscn.net/applications/oscn/start.asp?
　viewType=COUNTYINFO&county=CREEK
Pat Creason
no probate records search service; copies of
　probate records: $1.00 each

Custer County
organized 1891, original county

Custer County Courthouse
675 B Street
Arapaho, OK 73620
(580) 323-1221 (County Clerk, PO Box 300);
　(580) 323-3233 (Court Clerk, PO Box D);
　(580) 331-1121 FAX (Court Clerk)
http://www.custercountyok.org;
　http://www.tax.ok.gov/advalcount/custer.ht
　ml; http://www.oscn.net/applications/oscn/
　start.asp?viewType=COUNTYINFO&count
　y=CUSTER
Karen Fry, County Clerk; Connie Burden, Court
　Clerk
(land records with County Clerk, marriages and
　probate records with Court Clerk)
probate search service: $5.00 per name; copies
　of probate records: $1.00 per page, no
　minimum

Day County
(see Ellis and Roger Mills counties)

Delaware County
organized 1907 from Cherokee lands

Delaware County Courthouse
327 South Fifth Street
Jay, OK 74346
(918) 253-4520 (County Clerk, PO Box 309);
　(918) 253-4420 (Court Clerk, PO Box 407);
　(918) 253-8352 FAX (County Clerk)
info@delawareclerk.org
http://www.delawareclerk.org; http://www.
　oscn.net/applications/oscn/start.asp?viewTy
　pe=COUNTYINFO&county=DELAWARE
Carol Fortner, County Clerk; Caroline Weaver,
　Court Clerk
(land records with County Clerk, probate
　records with Court Clerk)

Dewey County
organized 1892, original county

Dewey County Courthouse
Ruble and Broadway
Taloga, OK 73667-0368
(580) 328-5361 (County Clerk, PO Box 368);

(580) 328-5521 (Court Clerk, PO Box 278)
http://www.tax.ok.gov/advalcount/dewey.html;
http://www.oscn.net/applications/oscn/start
.asp?viewType=COUNTYINFO&county=D
EWEY
Sandra Clendenny, County Clerk; Nancy
Louthan, Court Clerk
(land records from 1892 with County Clerk,
probate records from 1901 with Court Clerk)
probate search service: no charge; copies of land
records: $1.00 per page; copies of probate
records: $1.00 for the first page and 50¢ for
each additional page, no minimum

Ellis County
organized 1907 from Day (which was abolished)
and Woodward counties

Ellis County Courthouse
100 South Washington
Arnett, OK 73832-0257
(580) 885-7301 (County Clerk, PO Box 179);
(580) 885-7255 (Court Clerk, PO Box 217)
http://www.tax.ok.gov/advalcount/ellis.html;
http://www.oscn.net/applications/oscn/start
.asp?viewType=COUNTYINFO&county=E
LLIS
Lynn Smith, County Clerk; Dona Folks, Court
Clerk
(land records with County Clerk, probate
records with Court Clerk)
probate search service: no charge; copies of land
records: $1.00 per page, $1.00 per instrument
for certification; copies of probate records:
$1.00 for the first page and 50¢ for each
additional page ("copies made only if money
accompanies request")

Garfield County
organized 1895, original county

Garfield County Courthouse
114 West Broadway
Enid, OK 73701
(580) 237-0225 (County Clerk, PO Box 1664);
(580) 237-0232 (Court Clerk, Second Floor);
(580) 249-5951 FAX (County Clerk and Court
Clerk)
http://www.garfieldcountyclerk.com; http://
www.oscn.net/applications/oscn/start.asp?vi
ewType=COUNTYINFO&county=GARFI
ELD
Kathy Hughes, County Clerk; Margaret Jones,
Court Clerk
(deeds and mortgages from 1893 to date with
Register of Deeds, probate records with
Court Clerk)
copies of land records: $1.00 per page, no
minimum

Garvin County
organized 1907 from Chickasaw lands

Garvin County Courthouse
201 West Grant Street
Pauls Valley, OK 73075
(405) 238-2772 (County Clerk, PO Box 926);
(405) 238-5596 (Court Clerk, PO Box 239)
http://www.tax.ok.gov/advalcount/garvin.html;
http://www.oscn.net/applications/oscn/start
.asp?viewType=COUNTYINFO&county=G
ARVIN
Gina Mann, County Clerk; Kay Brewer, Court
Clerk

Grady County
organized 1907 from Caddo and Comanche
counties

Grady County Courthouse
326 West Choctaw Avenue
Chickasha, OK 73023
(405) 224-7388 (County Clerk, PO Box 1009);
(405) 224-7446 (Court Clerk, PO Box 605);
(405) 222-4506 FAX (County Clerk)
shoe62854@aol.com
http://www.gradycountyok.com; http://www.
tax.ok.gov/advalcount/grady.html; http://
www.oscn.net/applications/oscn/start.asp?vi

ewType=COUNTYINFO&county=GRADY
Sharon Shoemake, County Clerk; Lois Foster,
Court Clerk
(land records with County Clerk, probate
records from 1907 with Court Clerk)
no probate search service; copies of probate
records: $1.00 for the first page and 50¢ for
each additional page, no minimum ("requests
for copies must be written")

Grant County
organized 1895, original county

Grant County Courthouse
112 East Guthrie
Medford, OK 73759-1243
(580) 395-2274 (County Clerk, Room 102); (580)
395-2828 (Court Clerk)
grcoclrk@sbcglobal.net
http://www.tax.ok.gov/advalcount/grant.html;
http://www.oscn.net/applications/oscn/start
.asp?viewType=COUNTYINFO&county=G
RANT
Debbie Kretchmar, County Clerk; Deana Kilian,
Court Clerk

Greer County
organized 1890, original county

Greer County Courthouse
106 East Jefferson Street
Mangum, OK 73554
(580) 782-3664 (County Clerk, PO Box 207);
(580) 782-3665 (Court Clerk, PO Box 216);
(580) 782-4026 FAX (Court Clerk)
http://www.tax.ok.gov/advalcount/greer;
http://www.oscn.net/applications/oscn/start
.asp?viewType=COUNTYINFO&county=G
REER
Sonja Wallace, County Clerk; Phyllis Denney,
Court Clerk
(land records with County Clerk, naturalization
and probate records with Court Clerk)

Harmon County
organized 1909 from Greer County

Harmon County Courthouse
114 West Hollis Street
Hollis, OK 73550
(580) 688-3658 (County Clerk); (580) 688-3617
(Court Clerk); (580) 688-2900 FAX (Court
Clerk)
http://www.tax.ok.gov/advalcount/harmon.
html; http://www.oscn.net/applications/
oscn/ start.asp?viewType=COUNTYINFO&
county=HARMON
Shirley Orr, County Clerk; Stacy Macias, Court
Clerk

Harper County
organized 1905 from Indian lands

Harper County Courthouse
311 S.E. First Street
Buffalo, OK 73834
(580) 735-2012 (County Clerk, PO Box 369);
(580) 735-2010 (Court Clerk, PO Box 347)
http://www.tax.ok.gov/advalcount/harper.html;
http://www.oscn.net/applications/oscn/
start.asp?viewType=COUNTYINFO&count
y=HARPER
Joyce Johnson, County Clerk; Linda Crouch,
Court Clerk
(land records with County Clerk, marriages and
probate records with Court Clerk)
probate search service: no charge; copies of land
records: $1.00 per page; copies of probate
records: $1.00 for the first page and 50¢ for
each additional page

Haskell County
organized 1907 from Choctaw lands

Haskell County Courthouse
202 East Main
Stigler, OK 74462-2439
(918) 967-2884 (County Clerk); (918) 967-3323
(Court Clerk); (918) 967-2819 FAX (Court

Clerk)
http://www.tax.ok.gov/advalcount/haskell;
http://www.oscn.net/applications/oscn/start
.asp?viewType=COUNTYINFO&county=H
ASKELL
Gail Brown, County Clerk; Robin Rea, Court
Clerk
(land records with County Clerk, probate
records with Court Clerk)
copies of land records: $1.00 per page, $1.00 for
certification; copies of probate records: $1.00
per page, $1.00 for certification

Hughes County
organized 1907 from Creek lands

Hughes County Courthouse
200 North Broadway Street
Holdenville, OK 74848
(405) 379-5487 (County Clerk, County Clerk,
Suite 5); (405) 379-3384 (Court Clerk, PO
Box 32)
joquita@plainsnet.net
http://www.tax.ok.gov/advalcount/hughes.html;
http://www.oscn.net/applications/oscn/
start.asp?viewType=COUNTYINFO&count
y=HUGHES
Joquita Walton, County Clerk; Sandy Moss,
Court Clerk
(land records from 1907 with County Clerk,
probate records from 1907 with Court Clerk)
probate search service: no charge; copies of
probate records: $1.00 for the first page and
50¢ for each additional page

Jackson County
organized 1907 from Greer County

Jackson County Courthouse
101 North Main Street
Altus, OK 73521
(580) 482-4070 (County Clerk, PO Box 515);
(580) 482-0448 (Court Clerk, Room 303);
(580) 482-4472 FAX (County Clerk)
jc_clerk@sbcglobal.net; sonyatutten@osen.net
http://www.jacksoncountyok.com
Louise Snodgrass, County Clerk; Sonya L.
Tutten, Court Clerk
(land records with County Clerk, naturalization
records and probate records with Court
Clerk)
records search service: $5.00; copies of records:
$1.00 per page, $1.00 for certification

Jefferson County
organized 1907 from Comanche County

Jefferson County Courthouse
220 North Main
Waurika, OK 73573-2234
(580) 228-2029 (County Clerk, Room 103); (580)
228-2961 (Court Clerk)
http://www.tax.ok.gov/advalcount/jefferson.html
Doris Pilgreen, County Clerk; Linda Graham,
Court Clerk
(deeds and mortgages from 1907 with County
Clerk, probate records with Court Clerk)
no probate search service; copies of probate
records: $1.00 per page

Johnston County
organized 1907 from Chickasaw lands

Johnston County Courthouse
403 West Main Street
Tishomingo, OK 73460
(580) 371-3184 (County Clerk, Suite 101); (580)
371-3281 (Court Clerk, Suite 201)
http://www.tax.ok.gov/advalcount/johnston.ht
ml; http://www.oscn.net/applications/oscn/
start.asp?viewType=COUNTYINFO&count
y=JOHNSTON
Kathy Ross, Court Clerk; Judy E. Beavers, Court
Clerk
(land records from 1907 with County Clerk,
marriages from 1907 and probate records
from 1907 with Court Clerk)
probate search service: no charge; copies of
probate records: $1.00 for the first page and

County Courthouse Book

50¢ for each additional page, $1.00 minimum

Kay County

opened for settlement by land run on 16 September 1893; organized 1895, original county; first named "K" County

Kay County Courthouse
Newkirk, OK 74647
(405) 362-2537 (County Clerk, PO Box 450);
(405) 362-3350 (Court Clerk, PO Box 428)
treese@courthouse.kay.ok.us;
mary.ramey@oscn.net
http://www.courthouse.kay.ok.us/home.html
Tammy Reese, County Clerk; Mary Ramey, Court Clerk
(land records from 1893 to date with County Clerk, naturalization records from 1924 to 1960, marriages, probate, and estates with Court Clerk)
land records search service: $3.00 if you have a legal description; vital records search service: $5.00 per name per type of record; probate search service: $5.00 per name per type of record; copies of land records: $1.00 per page; copies of vital records: $1.00 for the first page and 50¢ for each additional page of the same instrument; copies of probate records: $1.00 for the first page and 50¢ for each additional page of the same instrument

Kingfisher County

organized 1890, original county

Kingfisher County Courthouse
101 South Main Street
Kingfisher, OK 73750
(405) 375-3887 (County Clerk, Room 3); (405) 375-3813 (Court Clerk, PO Box 328)
kgfcoclerk@pldi.net
http://www.kingfisherco.com; http://www.tax.ok.gov/advalcount/KINGFISHER
Judy Grellner, County Clerk; Karen Mueggenborg, Court Clerk
(land records with County Clerk; naturalization records, marriages, and probate records with Court Clerk)

Kiowa County

organized 1901, original county

Kiowa County Courthouse
316 South Main Street
Hobart, OK 73651
(580) 726-5286 (County Clerk, PO Box 73);
(580) 726-5125 (Court Clerk, PO Box 854);
(580) 726-2340 FAX (Court Clerk)
http://www.tax.ok.gov/advalcount/kowa.html;
http://www.oscn.net/applications/oscn/start.asp?viewType=COUNTYINFO&county=KIOWA
Geanea Watson, County Clerk; Karen Denton, Court Clerk
(land records with County Clerk; naturalization records from 1906 to 1955, marriages from September 1901, and probate records from August 1901 with Court Clerk)
probate search service: $5.00; copies of land records: $1.00 per page; copies of probate records: $1.00 for the first page and 50¢ for each additional page, 50¢ for certification, plus SASE

Latimer County

organized 1907 from Choctaw lands

Latimer County Courthouse
109 North Central, Room 200
Wilburton, OK 74578-2440
(918) 465-3543 (County Clerk); (918) 465-2011 (Court Clerk, Room 200)
http://www.tax.ok.gov/advalcount/latimer.html;
LATIMERhttp://www.tax.ok.gov/advalcount/LATIMER
Jane Brinkley, County Clerk; Melody Littlejohn, Court Clerk
(land records with County Clerk, probate records from 1906 with Court Clerk)
probate search service: no charge; copies of probate records: $1.00 for the first page and 50¢ for each additional page

LeFlore County

organized 1907 from Choctaw lands

LeFlore County Courthouse
100 South Broadway
Poteau, OK 74953
(918) 647-5738 (County Clerk, PO Box 218);
(918) 647-3181 (Court Clerk, PO Box 688)
http://www.tax.ok.gov/advalcount/leflore.html;
http://www.tax.ok.gov/advalcount/LE%20FLORE
Alan Vickers, County Clerk; Melba Hall, Court Clerk
(land records with County Clerk, probate records with Court Clerk)

Lincoln County

organized 1891, original county

Lincoln County Courthouse
811 Manvel Avenue
Chandler, OK 74834
(405) 258-1264 (County Clerk, PO Box 126);
(405) 258-1309 (Court Clerk, PO Box 307)
http://www.tax.ok.gov/advalcount/lincoln.html;
http://www.oscn.net/applications/oscn/start.asp?viewType=COUNTYINFO&county=LINCOLN
Debbie Greenfield, County Clerk; Cindy Kirby, Court Clerk
(land records with County Clerk, naturalization records from late 1890s until 1907, marriages, and probate records with Court Clerk)
probate search service: no charge; copies of land records: $1.00 per page; copies of probate records: $1.00 for the first page and 50¢ for each additional page, no minimum

Logan County

organized 1891, original county

Logan County Courthouse
301 East Harrison
Guthrie, OK 73044
(405) 292-0266 (County Clerk, Suite 102); (405) 282-0123 (Court Clerk, Suite 201)
http://www.tax.ok.gov/advalcount/logan.html;
http://www.oscn.net/applications/oscn/start.asp?viewType=COUNTYINFO&county=LOGAN
Mary Lou Orndorff, County Clerk; ReJeania Zmek, Court Clerk
(land records with County Clerk, naturalization records and probate records with Court Clerk)
no land records search service (must have direct or indirect records by name and legal description, if known)

Love County

organized 1907 from Chickasaw lands

Love County Courthouse
405 West Main Street
Marietta, OK 73448-2848
(580) 276-3059 (County Clerk, Suite 203); (580) 276-2235 (Court Clerk, Suite 201)
http://www.tax.ok.gov/advalcount/love.html;
http://www.oscn.net/applications/oscn/start.asp?viewType=COUNTYINFO&county=LOVE
Dora Jackson, County Clerk; Kim Jackson, Court Clerk
(land records with County Clerk, marriages and probate records with Court Clerk)
copies of marriages, land records, and probate records: $1.00 per page

Major County

organized 1909 from Woods County

Major County Courthouse
500 East Broadway
Fairview, OK 73737
(580) 227-4732 (County Clerk, PO Box 379);
(580) 227-4690 (Court Clerk); (580) 227-1275 FAX (Cout Clerk)
http://major.oklahomacounties.us; http://www.tax.ok.gov/advalcount/major.html; http://www.oscn.net/applications/oscn/start.asp?viewType=COUNTYINFO&county=MAJOR
Kathy McClure, County Clerk; Shauna Hoffman, Court Clerk
(land records from 1908 with County Clerk; naturalization records from 1908 to 1928 and probate records from 1908 with Court Clerk)
probate search service: no charge; copies of probate records: $1.00 for the first page and 50¢ for each additional page, no minimum

Marshall County

organized 1907 from Chickasaw lands

Marshall County Courthouse
1 County Courthouse Street
Madill, OK 73446
(580) 795-3220 (County Clerk, Room 101); (580) 795-3278 (Court Clerk, PO Box 58)
http://www.tax.ok.gov/advalcount/marshall.html
Ann Hartin, County Clerk; Wanda Pearce, Court Clerk
(land records from about 1907 with County Clerk, marriages and probate records with Court Clerk)
no land or probate records search service: copies of land and probate records: $1.00 per page, $1.00 for certified copies

Mayes County

organized 1907 from Indian lands

Mayes County Courthouse
1 Court Place
Pryor, OK 74361
(918) 825-2426 (County Clerk, Suite 120); (918) 825-2185 (Court Clerk, Suite 200)
http://www.tax.ok.gov/advalcount/mayes.html;
http://www.oscn.net/applications/oscn/start.asp?viewType=COUNTYINFO&county=MAYES
Rita Littlefield, County Clerk; Lori Parsons, Court Clerk
(land records with County Clerk, probate records with Court Clerk)
probate search service: no charge; copies of probate records: $1.00 for the first page and 50¢ for each additional page, $1.00 minimum

McClain County

organized 1907 from Chickasaw lands

McClain County Courthouse
121 North Second
Purcell, OK 73080
(405) 527-3360 (County Clerk, PO Box 629);
(405) 527-3221 (Court Clerk, Suite 231)
http://www.tax.ok.gov/advalcount/mcclain.html; http://www.oscn.net/applications/oscn/start.asp?viewType=COUNTYINFO&county=MCCLAIN
Lois Hawkins, County Clerk; Lynda Baker, Court Clerk
(land records with County Clerk, probate records with Court Clerk)
land records search service: $3.00 per name; probate search service: $10.00 per name; copies of land records: $1.00 each; copies of probate records: $1.00 for the first page and 50¢ for each additional page

McCurtain County

organized 1907 from Choctaw lands

McCurtain County Courthouse
108 North Central Avenue
Idabel, OK 74745
(405) 286-7428; (405) 286-2370 (County Clerk, PO Box 1078); (405) 286-3693 (Court Clerk, PO Box 1378)
http://www.tax.ok.gov/advalcount/mccurtain.html; http://www.oscn.net/applications/oscn/start.asp?viewType=COUNTYINFO&county=MCCURTAIN
Karen Bryan Conaway, County Clerk; Vicki Justus, Court Clerk

(deeds and mortgages with County Clerk, probate records with Court Clerk)
probate search service: no charge; copies of probate records: $1.00 for the first page and 50¢ for each additional page, no minimum

McIntosh County
organized 1907 from Indian lands

McIntosh County Courthouse
110 North First
Eufaula, OK 74432-0108
(918) 689-2741 (County Clerk, PO Box 110); (918) 689-2282 (Court Clerk, PO Box 426)
http://mcintosh.oklahomacounties.us
Shirley Irvin, County Clerk; Carrie Pittman, Court Clerk

Murray County
organized 1907 from Chickasaw lands

Murray County Courthouse
Tenth and Wyandotte Street
Sulphur, OK 73086
(580) 622-3920 (County Clerk, PO Box 442); (580) 622-3223 (Court Clerk, PO Box 578); (580) 622-2979 FAX (Court Clerk)
http://murray.oklahomacounties.us; http://www.tax.ok.gov/advalcount/murray.h tml; http://www.oscn.net/applications/ oscn/start.asp?viewType=COUNTYINFO& county=MURRAY
David Thompson, County Clerk; Jo Freeman, Court Clerk
(land records with County Clerk, probate records with Court Clerk)

Muskogee County
organized 1907 from Cherokee lands

Muskogee County Courthouse
3000 North Street
Muskogee, OK 74402
(918) 682-7781 (County Clerk, PO Box 1008); (918) 682-7873 (Court Clerk, PO Box 1350)
muskogeecounty@sbcglobal.net (County Clerk)
http://www.tax.ok.gov/advalcount/muskogee.h tml; http://www.oscn.net/applications/ oscn/start.asp?viewType=COUNTYINFO& county=MUSKOGEE
Karen Anderson, County Clerk; Paula Sexton, Court Clerk
(land records with County Clerk, probate records with Court Clerk)
probate search service: no charge; copies of probate records: $1.50 for the first page and 50¢ for each additional page, 50¢ for certification, no minimum

Noble County
organized 1897 from Indian lands

Noble County Courthouse
300 Courthouse Drive
Perry, OK 73077
(580) 336-2141 (County Clerk, Room 11); (580) 336-5187 (Court Clerk, Room 14)
http://www.tax.ok.gov/advalcount/noble.html; http://www.oscn.net/applications/oscn/start .asp?viewType=COUNTYINFO&county= NOBLE
Ronita Coldiron, County Clerk; Hillary Vondran, Court Clerk
(final certificates from the U.S., U.S. patents, deeds, mineral deeds, etc. from 1892 with County Clerk; some naturalization records from 1893, marriages from 1893, and probate records from 1893 with Court Clerk)
land, naturalization, vital, and probate records search service: $5.00 per name; copies of land records: $1.00 per page, $1.00 per page for certification; copies of naturalization, vital, and probate records: $1.00 for the first page and 50¢ for each additional page per instrument

Nowata County
organized 1907 from Cherokee lands

Nowata County Courthouse
229 North Maple Street
Nowata, OK 74048-2654
(918) 273-2480 (County Clerk); (918) 273-0127 (Court Clerk)
http://www.tax.ok.gov/advalcount/nowata.html; http://www.oscn.net/applications/oscn/ start.asp?viewType=COUNTYINFO&count y=NOWATA
Teresa Jackson, County Clerk; Beverly McKee, Court Clerk
(land records with County Clerk, probate records with Court Clerk)
copies of land records: $1.00 per page, $1.00 for certification

Okfuskee County
organized 1907 from Creek lands

Okfuskee County Courthouse
209 North Third
Okemah, OK 74859
(918) 623-1724 (County Clerk, PO Box 108); (918) 623-0525 (Court Clerk, PO Box 30)
http://www.tax.ok.gov/advalcount/okfuskee. html; http://www.oscn.net/applications/ oscn/start.asp?viewType=COUNTYINFO county=OKFUSKEE
Diane Flanders, County Clerk; Kay Adams, Court Clerk

Oklahoma County
organized 1891, original county

Oklahoma County Courthouse
320 N.W. Robert S. Kerr Avenue
Oklahoma City, OK 73102-3441
(405) 713-7184 (County Clerk, Room 108); (405) 713-1864 (County Clerk, Room 141); (405) 713-1705 (Recorded Information, Court Clerk, County Office Building/Courthouse Annex, Room 409); (405) 278-1539 (Registrar of Deeds); (405) 713-1722 (Court Clerk); (405) 713-1728 (Probate Department)
ccchaphi@oklahomacounty.org
http://www.oklahomacounty.org
Carolynn Caudill, County Clerk; Patricia Presley, Court Clerk
(land records with Registrar of Deeds, probate records with Court Clerk)
probate search service: no charge; copies of probate records: $1.00 for the first page and 50¢ for each additional page, no minimum

Okmulgee County
organized 1907 from Creek lands

Okmulgee County Courthouse
314 West Seventh Street
Okmulgee, OK 74447
(918) 756-0788 (County Clerk, PO Box 904); (918) 756-3042 (Court Clerk)
http://www.tax.ok.gov/advalcount/okmulgee.h tml; http://www.oscn.net/applications/ oscn/ start.asp?viewType=COUNTYINFO& county=OKMULGEE
Becky Thomas, County Clerk; Linda Beaver, Court Clerk
(land records with County Clerk, probate records with Court Clerk)
no probate search service; copies of land records: $1.00 per page, $1.00 for certification; copies of probate records: $1.00 for the first page and 50¢ for each additional page, no minimum

Osage County
organized 1907 from Osage Indian lands

Osage County Courthouse
600 Grandview Street
Pawhuska, OK 74056-0087
(918) 287-3136 (County Clerk, PO Box 87); (918) 287-4104 (Court Clerk, Room 304)
http://osage.oklahomacounties.us
Denny Hutson, County Clerk; Angie Bruce, Court Clerk
(land records from 1907 with County Clerk, marriage licenses and probate records with

Court Clerk)
no probate search service; copies of land and probate records: $1.00 per page, no minimum

Ottawa County
organized 1907 from Indian lands

Ottawa County Courthouse
102 East Central Avenue
Miami, OK 74354
(918) 542-3332 (County Clerk, Suite 203); (918) 542-2801 (Court Clerk); (918) 540-3278 FAX (Court Clerk)
http://www.tax.ok.gov/advalcount/ottawa.html; http://www.oscn.net/applications/oscn/ start.asp?viewType=COUNTYINFO&count y=OTTAWA
Reba G. Sill, County Clerk; Cathy Williams, Court Clerk

Pawnee County
organized 1897 from Indian lands

Pawnee County Courthouse
500 Harrison Street
Pawnee, OK 74058
(918) 762-2732 (County Clerk, Room 202); (918) 762-2547 (Court Clerk, Room 300)
http://www.tax.ok.gov/advalcount/pawnee.ht ml; http://www.oscn.net/applications/oscn/ start.asp?viewType=COUNTYINFO&count y=PAWNEE
Marcelee Welch, County Clerk; Janet Dallas, Court Clerk

Payne County
organized 1890, original county

Payne County Clerk
County Administration Building, 315 West Sixth, #202
Stillwater, OK 74074-4020
(405) 747-8310; (405) 747-8304 FAX
sschieffer@paynecounty.org
http://www.paynecounty.org
Sherri Schieffer
(land records)

Payne Court Clerk
Courthouse, 606 South Husband, Room 206
Stillwater, OK 74074
(405) 372-4774
Lisa.Lambert@oscn.net
http://www.paynecounty.org
Lisa S. Lambert
no probate search service; copies of probate records: $1.00 for the first page and 50¢ for each additional page, plus certification, $1.00 minimum

Pittsburg County
organized 1907 from Choctaw lands

Pittsburg County Courthouse
115 East Carl Albert Parkway
McAlester, OK 74501-5020
(918) 423-6865 (County Clerk, Suite 1A); (918) 423-4859 (Court Clerk, PO Box 460)
http://www.tax.ok.gov/advalcount/pittsburg. html; http://www.oscn.net/applications/ oscn/ start.asp?viewType=COUNTYINFO& county=PITTSBURG
Debbie Lenox-Burch, County Clerk; Cindy Eller, Court Clerk
(land records with County Clerk, probate records with Court Clerk)
no land records search service ("we do not do genealogy searches"); copies of land records: $1.00 per page

Pontotoc County
organized 1907 from Choctaw lands

Pontotoc County Courthouse
120 West 13th Street
Ada, OK 74820
(580) 332-1425 (County Clerk, PO Box 1425); (580) 332-5763 (Court Clerk, PO Box 427); (580) 332-5766 FAX (Court Clerk)
http://www.tax.ok.gov/advalcount/pontotoc.ht

ml; http://www.oscn.net/applications/oscn/
start.asp?viewType=COUNTYINFO&count
y=PONTOTOC
Lynn Lofton, County Clerk; Ernestine Eubank,
Court Clerk
(land records with County Clerk, probate
records with Court Clerk)

Pottawatomie County
organized 1891 as Pottawatomie-Shawnee
County, original county; later named
Pottawatomie County

Pottawatomie County Courthouse
325 North Broadway
Shawnee, OK 74801
(405) 273-8222 (County Clerk, PO Box 576);
(405) 273-3624 (Court Clerk)
clerkpc@swbell.net (County Clerk)
http://www.tax.ok.gov/advalcount/pottawatom
ie.html;
http://www.oscn.net/applications/oscn/
start.asp?viewType=COUNTYINFO&count
y=POTTAWATOMIE
Nancy Bryce, County Clerk; Reta Head, Court
Clerk
(land records with County Clerk; naturalization
records, marriage licenses, and probate
records with Court Clerk)
land records search service: no charge for index
search; no probate search service; copies of
land records: $1.00 per page; copies of
probate records: $1.00 per page

Pushmataha County
organized 1907 from Indian lands

Pushmataha County Clerk and Court Clerk
302 Southwest "B"
Antlers, OK 74523
(580) 298-3626 (County Clerk); (580) 298-2274
(Court Clerk)
http://www.tax.ok.gov/advalcount/pushmatah
a.html; http://www.oscn.net/applications/
oscn/start.asp?viewType=COUNTYINFO&
county=PUSHMATAHA
Jane Dunlap, County Clerk; Kathy D. Milam,
Court Clerk

Roger Mills County
organized 1895, original county; annexed part of
Day County when it was abolished in 1907

Roger Mills County Courthouse
480 Mays and Broadway
Cheyenne, OK 73628
(580) 497-3395 (County Clerk, PO Box 708);
(580) 497-3361 (Court Clerk); (580) 497-2167
FAX (Court Clerk)
http://www.tax.ok.gov/advalcount/rogermills.h
tml; http://www.oscn.net/applications/
oscn/start.asp?viewType=COUNTYINFO&
county=ROGER%20MILLS
Jimmy Beavin, County Clerk; Geneece Cook,
Court Clerk
(tract records, indirect/direct, grantor/grantee
records with County Clerk and Recorder,
probate records with Court Clerk)
probate search service; copies of land records:
$1.00 per page; copies of probate records:
$1.00 for the first page and 50¢ for each
additional page, no minimum

Rogers County
organized 1907 from Cherokee lands

Rogers County Courthouse
219 South Missouri
Claremore, OK 74017-7832
(918) 341-2518 (County Clerk, Room #1-104);
(918) 341-5711 (Court Clerk, PO Box 839);
(918) 341-4529 FAX (County Clerk)
peggy@rogerscounty.org
http://www.rogerscounty.org; http://www.
oscn.net/applications/oscn/start.asp?viewTy
pe=COUNTYINFO&county=ROGERS
Peggy Armstrong, County Clerk; Candi
Czpansky, Court Clerk

Seminole County
organized 1907 from Seminole lands

Seminole County Courthouse
120 South Wewoka Avenue
Wewoka, OK 74884
(405) 257-2501 (Court Clerk, PO Box 1180);
(405) 257-6236 (Court Clerk, PO Box 130);
(405) 257-2631 FAX (Court Clerk)
http://www.tax.ok.gov/advalcount/seminole.ht
ml; http://www.oscn.net/applications/oscn/
start.asp?viewType=COUNTYINFO&count
y=SEMINOLE
Tim Anderson, County Clerk; Sharon Post,
Court Clerk

Sequoyah County
organized 1907 from Cherokee lands

Sequoyah County Courthouse
120 East Chickasaw Street
Sallisaw, OK 74955-4655
(918) 775-4516 (County Clerk); (918) 775-4411
(Court Clerk)
http://www.tax.ok.gov/advalcount/sequoyah.ht
ml; http://www.oscn.net/applications/oscn/
start.asp?viewType=COUNTYINFO&count
y=SEQUOYAH
Donna Jamison, County Clerk; Maudeen Vann,
Court Clerk

Stephens County
organized 1907 from Comanche County

Stephens County Courthouse
101 South 11th Street
Duncan, OK 73533
(580) 255-0977 (County Clerk, Room 203); (580)
470-2000 (Court Clerk)
http://www.tax.ok.gov/advalcount/stephens.ht
ml; http://www.oscn.net/applications/oscn/
start.asp?viewType=COUNTYINFO&count
y=STEPHENS
Jo Johnson, County Clerk; Connie Elam, Court
Clerk
(land records with County Clerk, probate
records with Court Clerk)
land records search service: no charge; probate
search service: $5.00 per search; copies of
land records: $1.00 each; copies of probate
records: $1.00 for the first page and 50¢ for
each additional page, no minimum

Texas County
organized 1907 from Beaver County

Texas County Courthouse
319 North Main Street
Guymon, OK 73942
(580) 338-3141 (County Clerk, PO Box 197);
(580) 338-3003 (Court Clerk, PO Box 1081)
http://www.guymonok.org/CountyGovernmen
t.html (under construction); http://www.tax.
ok.gov/advalcount/texas.html; http://www.
oscn.net/applications/oscn/start.asp?viewTy
pe=COUNTYINFO&county=TEXAS
Marcia Hollingshead, County Clerk; Karen
Parrish, Court Clerk
(land records with County Clerk, probate
records with Court Clerk)
no land records search service (must have book
and page number); copies of land records:
$1.00 per page

Tillman County
organized 1907 from Comanche lands

Tillman County Courthouse
101 North Main
Frederick, OK 73542
(580) 335-3421 (County Clerk, PO Box 992);
(580) 335-3023 (Court Clerk, PO Box 116)
http://www.tax.ok.gov/advalcount/tillman.html;
http://www.oscn.net/applications/oscn/
start.asp?viewType=COUNTYINFO&
county=TILLMAN
Jerri Boyd, County Clerk; Daralene Kidwell,
Court Clerk
(land records with County Clerk; ten or twelve

naturalization records from during World War
II [other naturalization records with Court
Clerks in Lawton or Altus, OK], vital records,
and probate records with Court Clerk)
no probate search service; copies of land
records: $1.00 per page, $1.00 per instrument
for certification; copies of probate records:
$1.00 for the first page and 50¢ for each
additional page of same instrument, $1.00
minimum

Tulsa County
organized 1907 from Creek lands

Tulsa County Courthouse
500 South Denver Avenue
Tulsa, OK 74103-3826
(918) 596-5801 (County Clerk); (918) 596-5000
(Court Clerk, Room 200); (918) 596-5819
FAX (County Clerk)
cwilson@tulsacounty.org; sallysmith@oscn.net
http://www.tulsacounty.org
Earlene Wilson, County Clerk; Sally Howe-
Smith, Court Clerk
(land records with County Clerk; probate
records from 1907 with Court Clerk)
probate search service: $5.00 per name; copies
of probate records: $1.00 for the first page
and 50¢ for each additional page, 50¢ for
certification, no minimum

Wagoner County
organized 1907 from Creek lands

Wagoner County Courthouse
307 East Cherokee
Wagoner, OK 74467-4729
(918) 485-2216 (County Clerk, PO Box 156);
(918) 485-4508 (Court Clerk, PO Box 249)
http://wagoner.oklahomacounties.us; http://
www.oscn.net/applications/oscn/start.asp?vi
ewType=COUNTYINFO&county=WAGO
NER
Jerry Fields, County Clerk; Sue Wells, Court
Clerk

Washington County
organized 1907 from Cherokee lands

Washington County Courthouse
420 South Johnstone Avenue
Bartlesville, OK 74003-6605
(918) 337-2840 (County Clerk, Room 100); (918)
337-2870 (Court Clerk); (918) 337-2897 FAX
(Court Clerk)
clerk@countycourthouse.org;
martha.mersch@oscn.net
http://www.countycourthouse.org
Marjorie Parrish, County Clerk; Martha Mersch,
Court Clerk
(land records with County Clerk; naturalization
records, vital records, and probate records
with Court Clerk)

Washita County
organized 1897 from Indian lands

Washita County Courthouse
111 East Main Street
Cordell, OK 73632
(580) 832-3548 (County Clerk, PO Box 380);
(580) 832-3836 (Court Clerk, PO Box 397)
http://www.tax.ok.gov/advalcount/washita.ht
ml; http://www.oscn.net/applications/oscn/
start.asp?viewType=COUNTYINFO&count
y=WASHITA
Marita McKee, County Clerk; Tena Arganbright,
Court Clerk
(land records with County Clerk; some
naturalization records to about 1907
[indexed], marriage applications/certificates
from 1892 to date [indexed], and probate
records from 1903 to date with Court Clerk)
land records search service (must have complete
name, year, and legal description [section,
township, range] of the land, if known;
naturalization, vital, and probate records
search service: no charge for a single record in
a known year, $5.00 for more extensive

searches; copies of naturalization, vital, and probate records: $1.00 for the first page and 50¢ for each additional page

Woods County
organized 1893, original county

Woods County Courthouse
407 Government Street
Alva, OK 73717
(580) 327-0942 (County Clerk, PO Box 386); (580) 327-3119 (Court Clerk, PO Box 924)
small@pldi.net
http://www.tax.ok.gov/advalcount/woods.html; http://www.oscn.net/applications/oscn/start.asp?viewType=COUNTYINFO&county=WOODS
Pam Inman, County Clerk; Della Dunnigan, Court Clerk
(land records with County Clerk, naturalization records and probate records with Court Clerk)
probate search service: no charge; copies of land records: $1.00 per page; copies of probate records: $1.00 for the first page and 50¢ for each additional page

Woodward County
organized 1907 from Indian lands

Woodward County Courthouse
1600 Main Street
Woodward, OK 73801-3046
(580) 256-3625 (County Clerk, Suite 8); (580) 256-3413 (Court Clerk); (580) 254-6840 FAX (County Clerk)
http://woodwardcounty.org
Ron Hohweiler, County Clerk; Jenny Hopkins, Court Clerk
(land records from 1893 to date with County Clerk; naturalization records, marriages, and probate records with Court Clerk)

OREGON

Capital: Salem. Statehood: 14 February 1859 (annexed when Great Britain relinquished claim in 1846, became a separate territory 14 August 1848, including all lands north of the 42nd parallel and west of the Rockies)

Oregon has some 145 Municipal Courts of limited jurisdiction. Nine County Courts have probate jurisdiction in Gilliam, Grant, Harney, Malheur, Sherman and Wheeler counties, and have juvenile jurisdiction in Crook, Gilliam, Harney, Jefferson, Morrow, Sherman and Wheeler counties. Justice Courts in Baker, Columbia, Curry, Douglas, Gilliam, Grant, Harney, Hood River, Jackson, Klamath, Lake, Lane, Lincoln, Linn, Malheur, Marion, Morrow, Sherman, Tillamook, Washington and Wheeler counties handle most civil actions, misdemeanors and traffic matters. District Courts in twenty-eight counties (all except Baker, Gilliam, Grant, Harney, Lake, Malheur, Sherman and Wheeler counties) have jurisdiction over some criminal cases, some civil cases, traffic violations and small claims. The District Courts in Curry, Hood River and Wasco counties hear probate cases. The state's Tax Court has statewide jurisdiction over tax cases.

The Circuit Courts have general jurisdiction and sit at each county seat. First Judicial District: Jackson County; Second Judicial District: Lane County; Third Judicial District: Marion County; Fourth Judicial District: Multnomah County; Fifth Judicial District: Clackamas County; Sixth Judicial District: Morrow and Umatilla counties; Seventh Judicial District: Gilliam, Hood River, Sherman, Wasco and Wheeler counties; Eighth Judicial District: Baker and Grant counties; Ninth Judicial District: Harney and Malheur counties; Tenth Judicial District: Union and Wallowa counties; Eleventh Judicial District: Crook, Deschutes and Jefferson counties; Twelfth Judicial District: Polk and Yamhill counties; Thirteenth Judicial District: Klamath and Lake counties; Fourteenth Judicial District: Josephine County; Fifteenth Judicial District: Coos and Curry counties; Sixteenth Judicial District: Douglas County; Seventeenth Judicial District: Lincoln County; Nineteenth Judicial District: Clatsop, Columbia and Tillamook counties; Twentieth Judicial District: Washington County; Twenty-first Judicial District: Benton and Linn counties. The Court of Appeals and Supreme Court hear appeals.

Baker County
organized 1862 from unorganized territory

Baker County Courthouse
1995 Third Street
Baker, OR 97814-3363
(541) 523-6414; (541) 523-6305 (Circuit Court, Suite #220); (541) 523-9738 FAX (Circuit Court)
tgreen@bakercounty.org
http://www.bakercounty.org; http://www.ojd.state.or.us/bak/index.shtml (Circuit Court)
Tamara "Tami" Green, County Clerk
(land records with County Clerk's Office, probate records with Circuit Court)
probate search service: no charge; copies of probate records: 25¢ per page, $1.00 minimum

Benton County
organized 1847, original county

Benton County Circuit Court
(Courthouse, 120 NW Fourth Street, Corvallis, OR 97330—location)
PO Box 1870 (mailing address)
Corvallis, OR 97339-1870
(541) 766-6825 (Probate)
http://www.ojd.state.or.us/ben/index.htm

Benton County Records and Licenses Office
120 NW Fourth Street

Corvallis, OR 97330
(541) 776-6831; (541) 766-6675 FAX
http://www.co.benton.or.us/admin/records/index.php
(assessment and tax rolls, circuit court case files, county court case files, deeds and indexes, federal land grant recordsland title registers, marriage records, military records, mortgage records, naturalization certificates, naturalization declarations of intention, naturalization petitions and orders, pension and relief records, prisoner register, probate case files probate estate records school district records, births and deaths from 1907 to 1944)
land and vital records search service from Department of Records and Elections: $3.75 per name; no probate search service; copies of land, vital, and probate records: 25¢ per page, $3.75 for certification, no minimum

Clackamas County
organized 1843, original county

Clackamas County Circuit Court
County Courthouse, 807 Main Street, Room 104
Oregon City, OR 97045
(503) 655-8447; (503) 650-3962 FAX
http://www.ojd.state.or.us/courts/circuit/clackamas.htm

Clackamas County Courthouse
2051 Kaen Road, Second Floor
Oregon City, OR 97045
(503) 655-5686; (503) 650-5687 FAX
sherryhal@co.clackamas.or.us
http://www.clackamas.us/clerk
Sherry Hall, County Clerk
(land records from 1856, marriages from 1847)
no land or vital records search service; copies of land and vital records: $4.00 for the first page and 25¢ for each additional page of the same document, $3.75 per document for certification

Clatsop County
organized 1844, original county

Clatsop County Circuit Court
(749 Commercial Street—location)
PO Box 835 (mailing address)
Astoria, OR 97103
(503) 325-8555; (503) 325-9300 FAX (Civil)
Bryant.Baehr@ojd.state.or.us
http://www.ojd.state.or.us/clt/index.htm
Bryant Baehr, Trial Court Administrator

Clatsop County Public Services Building
820 Exchange Street, Suite 220
Astoria, OR 97103
(503) 325-8511; (503) 325-9307 FAX
clerk@co.clatsop.or.us
http://www.co.clatsop.or.us/index.asp
Nicole Williams, County Clerk

Columbia County
organized 1854 from Washington County

Columbia County Courthouse
230 Strand Street
St. Helens, OR 97051
(503) 397-3796 (County Clerk); (503) 397-2327 (Circuit Court)
huserb@co.columbia.or.us; susan.j.hill@ojd.state.or.us
http://www.co.columbia.or.us/home.asp; http://www.ojd.state.or.us/col (Circuit Court)
Elizabeth "Betty" Huser, County Clerk; Susan Hill, Trial Court Administrator
(deeds and mortgages from the 1800s, some naturalization records [no copies], marriages from 1800s, probate records from 1880)
probate search service: $3.75; copies of probate records: 25¢ per page, no minimum

Coos County
organized 1853 from Umpqua and Jackson counties

Coos County Courthouse

County Courthouse Book

250 North Baxter Street
Coquille, OR 97423-1899
(503) 396-3121, ext. 228 (County Clerk); (503) 396-3121, ext. 556 (Probate)
coosclerk@co.coos.or.us
http://www.co.coos.or.us;
http://cooscurrycourts.org
Terri Turi, County Clerk
(land records with County Clerk, some naturalization indexes on file with County Clerk, marriages with Circuit Court Clerk, probate records before 1 January 1983 with County Clerk, probate records after 1 January 1983 with Circuit Court Clerk)
no probate search service; copies of probate records: $3.75 plus 25¢ per page, no minimum

County Circuit Court
316 Main Street
Klamath Falls, OR 97601
(541) 883-5503, ext. 221 (Civil Division)
Klamath.Webmaster@ojd.state.or.us
http://www.ojd.state.or.us/kla

Crook County
organized 1882 from Wasco and Grant counties

Crook County Courthouse
300 NE Third Street
Prineville, OR 97754-1949
(541) 447-6553 (County Clerk, Room 23); (541) 447-6541 (Circuit Court, ext. 107 for Probate); (541) 416-2145 FAX (County Clerk)
dee.berman@co.crook.or.us
http://www.co.crook.or.us; http://www.ojd.state.or.us/cro (Circuit Court)
Deanna Berman, County Clerk
(land records with Clerk, naturalization records with Clerk, old births and deaths to about 1950 with Clerk's Office, probate records with Circuit Court)
no probate search service ("any records search prior to August 1986 we refer to private research person"); copies of probate records: 25¢ per page, $3.75 for certification, no minimum

Curry County
organized 1855 from Coos County

Curry County Courthouse
29821 North Ellensburg
Gold Beach, OR 97444
(541) 247-3295 (County Clerk-Recording, PO Box 746); (541) 247-4511 (Circuit Court, PO Box 810); (800) 243-7620 (County Clerk); (541) 247-6440 FAX (County Clerk)
denneys@co.curry.or.us
http://www.co.curry.or.us;
http://cooscurrycourts.org
Reneé Kolen, County Clerk; Shelley Denney, Product Admin/Records Manager, Recording Division
(land records, naturalization records from 1856 to 1907, marriages)
copies: 25¢ per page

Deschutes County
organized 1916 from Crook County

Deschutes County Circuit Court
(Courthouse, 1164 NW Bond Street [Gray Building], File Room, Second Floor—location)
1100 NW Bond Street, (mailing address)
Bend, OR 97701
(541) 388-5300, ext. 2090 (Civil), ext. 2160 (Court Records Supervisor); ext. 2080 (Probate/Name Changes)
http://www.ojd.state.or.us//index.htm

Deschutes County Clerk
Deschutes Services Center
1300 NW Wall Street, Suite 200
Bend, OR 97701
(541) 388-6549
nancyb@co.deschutes.or.us;
recording@co.deschutes.or.us
http://www.co.deschutes.or.us/go/living-here
Nancy Blankenship

(deeds from 1882 to date, mortgages from 1897 to date, plats, mine claims, petitions for naturalization from 1917 to 1970, marriage applications from 1947 to date, some death certificates [in deeds])
land, naturalization, and vital records search service: $3.75; copies of land, naturalization, and vital records: 25¢ per page

Douglas County
organized 1852 from Umpqua County, which was organized in 1851 and whose remnant, after Coos County was broken off in 1855, was annexed to Douglas County in 1862

Douglas County Justice Building
1036 S.E. Douglas
Roseburg, OR 97470-3317
(541) 440-4325 (County Clerk, Room 221, PO Box 10); (541) 957-2471 (Circuit Court); (541) 440-4408 FAX (County Clerk)
benielse@co.douglas.or.us
http://www.co.douglas.or.us
Barbara Nielson, County Clerk

Gilliam County
organized 1885 from Wasco County

Gilliam County Courthouse
(221 South Oregon Street—location)
PO Box 427 (mailing address)
Condon, OR 97823
(503) 384-2311; (541) 384-3572 (Circuit Court, PO Box 622); (541) 384-2166 FAX (Circuit Court)
http://www.oregoncities.us/gilliamcounty; http://seventhdistrict.ojd.state.or.us/html/gilliam.html
Rena Kennedy, County Clerk
(land records, limited incomplete naturalization records, and probate records)
probate search service: $3.75; copies of probate records: 25¢ per page, $3.75 per document minimum ("if we have to find it")

Grant County
organized 1864 from Harney County

Grant County Circuit Court
(205 South Humbolt Street—location)
PO Box 159 (mailing address)
Canyon City, OR 97820
(541) 575-1438; (541) 575-2165 FAX
http://www.ojd.state.or.us/grant

Grant County Courthouse
(201 South Humbolt—location)
PO Box 220 (mailing address)
Canyon City, OR 97820-0220
(503) 575-0059
grantco@oregontrail.net
http://bluebook.state.or.us/local/counties/counties12.htm; http://www.grancounty.cc (Chamber of Commerce)
Kathy McKinnon, County Clerk
(deeds, mortgages, land patents from 1864, naturalization records [cannot be photocopied], births and deaths from 1915 to 1948, marriages from 1872, probate records from 1864)
probate search service: $3.75; copies of probate records: 25¢ each, no minimum

Harney County
organized 1889 from Grant County

Harney County Courthouse
450 North Buena Vista Avenue
Burns, OR 97720
(541) 573-6641 (County Clerk); (541) 573-5207 (Circuit Court); (541) 573-8370 FAX (County Clerk); (541) 573-5715 FAX (Circuit Court)
clerk@co.harney.or.us
http://www.co.harney.or.us;
http://www.ojd.state.or.us/har/index.shtml
Maria Iturriaga, County Clerk
(land records, marriage licenses, probate records)
probate search service: $12.50; certified copies of land records: $3.75 per instrument; copies of probate records: $1.00 per page, no

minimum

Hood River County Courthouse
309 State Street
Hood River, OR 97031-2093
(541) 386-1442 (Records); (541) 386-3535 (Circuit Court); (541) 386-4=6864 FAX (Records and Assessment); (541) 386-3465 FAX (Circuit Court)
http://www.co.hood-river.or.us; http://seventhdistrict.ojd.state.or.us/html/hood_river.html
Sandra Berry, Director of Records and Assessment
(deeds, mortgages, etc., very few naturalization records, marriages from July 1908 with Department of Records and Assessment, probate records with Trial Court Clerk)
land records search service: $3.75; probate search service: no charge; copies of land records: 25¢ each, $3.75 for certification; copies of probate records: 25¢ per page

Hood River County
organized 1908 from Wasco County

Jackson County
organized 1852 from Wasco County

Jackson County Circuit Court
100 South Oakdale
Medford, OR 97501
(541) 776-7171, ext. 584 (Probate), ext. 582 (Circuit Court Civil); (541) 776-7057 FAX
http://www.ojd.state.or.us/jac/index.htm
Jim Adams, Trial Court Administrator

Jackson County Clerk
10 South Oakdale, Room 216
Medford, OR 97501-2952
(541) 774-6147; (541) 774-6714 FAX
becketks@jacksoncounty.org
http://www.co.jackson.or.us
Kathleen S. "Kathy" Beckett
(deeds from 1908)

Jefferson County
organized 1914 from Crook County

Jefferson County Courthouse
75 S.E. C Street
Madras, OR 97741-1707
(541) 475-4451 (County Clerk); (541) 475-3317 (Circuit Clerk, General Information, Suite C); (541) 325-5018 FAX (County Clerk)
kathy.marston@co.jefferson.or.us
http://www.co.jefferson.or.us; http://www.ojd.state.or.us/cro (Circuit Court)
Kathleen Marston, County Clerk
(land records with County Clerk, naturalization records with County Clerk, probate records with Trial Court Clerk, Circuit Court)
land and naturalization records search service: $3.75; copies of probate records: 50¢ per page from microfilm originals

Josephine County
organized 1856 from Jackson County

Josephine County Courthouse
500 NW Sixth Street
Grants Pass, OR 97526
(541) 474-5240 (County Clerk); (541) 476-2309 (Circuit Court); (541) 474-5246 FAX (County Clerk); (541) 471-2079 FAX (Circuit Court)
clerk@co.josephine
http://www.co.josephine.or.us;
http://www.ojd.state.or.us/jos/index.shtml
Georgette Brown, County Clerk

Klamath County
organized 1882 from Lake County

Klamath County Clerk
Government Center, 305 Main Street
Klamath Falls, OR 97601
(541) 883-5134; (541) 885-6757 FAX
lsmith@co.klamath.or.us
http://www.co.klamath.or.us
Linda Smith

Lake County
organized 1874 from unorganized territory

Lake County Courthouse
513 Center Street, corner of Highway 395
Lakeview, OR 97630-1539
(541) 947-6006 (County Clerk, Room 219); (541)
947-6051 (Circuit Court); (541) 947-6015
FAX (County Clerk); (541) 947-3724 FAX
(Circuit Court)
info@co.lake.or.us; sgeaney@co.lake.or.us
http://www.lakecountyor.org
Stacie Geaney, County Clerk; Val Paulson, Trial
Court Administrator

Lane County
organized 1851 from Linn and Benton counties

Lane County Courthouse
125 East Eighth Avenue
Eugene, OR 97401-2922
(541) 682-4274 (County Clerk, Records); (541)
682-4020 (Circuit Court); (541) 682-4255
(Probate Center)
annette.newingham@co.lane.or.us
http://www.co.lane.or.us;
http://www.ojd.state.or.us/lan
Annette Newingham, County Clerk

Lincoln County
organized 1893 from Benton County

Lincoln County Courthouse
225 West Olive Street
Newport, OR 97365
(541) 265-4131 (County Clerk, Room 201); (541)
265-4236 (Circuit Court, PO Box 100); (541)
265-4950 FAX (County Clerk)
djenkins@co.lincoln.or.us;
countyclerk@co.lincoln.or.us
http://www.co.lincoln.or.us
Mr. Dana W. Jenkins, County Clerk
(land records with County Clerk's Office,
marriages only with County Clerk's Office,
probate records with State Court
Administration Office, Room 202)
copies of land records: 25¢ per page

Linn County
organized 1847, original county

Linn County Courthouse
300 SW Fourth Avenue
Albany, OR 97321
(503) 967-3829 (County Clerk-Recording, PO
Box 100); (541) 967-3802 (Circuit Court,
Room 107, PO Box 1749); (541) 926-5109
FAX (County Clerk)
SDruckenmiller@co.linn.or.us
http://www.co.linn.or.us;
http://www.ojd.state.or.us/linn (Circuit
Court)
Steve Druckenmiller, County Clerk
(land records from 1850 with County Clerk,
naturalization records from July 1855 to
November 1956 via Clerk's accession number
with Archives Division, Salem, births and
deaths from 1903 to 1915 and 1921 to 1945
with Archives, marriages from 1847 with
County Clerk, probate records with Circuit
Court Records)

Malheur County
organized 1887 from Baker County

Malheur County Courthouse
251 B Street, South
Vale, OR 97918
(541) 473-5151 (County Clerk, Suite 4); (541)
473-5171 (Circuit Court, PO Box 670); (541)
473-5523 FAX (County Clerk or Circuit
Court)
ddelong@malheurco.org
http://www.malheurco.org;
http://www.ojd.state.or.us/mal/index.shtml
Deborah R. DeLong, County Clerk and
Recorder
(land records from 1887, probate records from
1887)

probate search service: $3.75; copies of probate
records: 25¢ per page, no minimum

Marion County
organized 1843, original county

Marion County Courthouse
100 High Street NE
Salem, OR 97301
(503) 588-5225 (County Clerk, Room 1331, PO
Box 14500, Salem, OR 97309); (503) 588-
5105 (Circuit Court); (503) 373-4360 FAX
(Circuit Court)
bburgess@co.marion.or.us;
clerk@co.marion.or.us
http://www.co.marion.or.us
Bill Burgess, County Clerk
(land records with County Clerk's Office,
probate records with State of Oregon, County
Courthouse)

Morrow County
organized 1885 from Umatilla County

Morrow County Courthouse
100 Court Street
Heppner, OR 97836
(541) 676-5601 (County Clerk, Suite 102, PO
Box 338); (541) 676-5264 (Circuit Court, PO
Box 609); (541) 676-9902 FAX (Circuit
Court)
bchilders@co.morrow.or.us
http://www.morrowcountyoregon.com; http://
www.ojd.state.or.us/uma/morrow.htm
Bobbi Childers, County Clerk
(land records with Office of the County Clerk,
naturalization records with Office of the
County Clerk, vital records with Office of the
County Clerk, probate records with Circuit
Court Trial Court Clerk)
probate search service: no charge; copies of
probate records: 25¢ each, no minimum

Multnomah County
organized 1854 from Clackamas and
Washington counties

Multnomah County Courthouse
1021 S.W. Fourth
Portland, OR 97204-1110
(503) 248-3277; (503) 988-3957 (District Court)
http://www.co.multnomah.or.us;
http://www.ojd.state.or.us/mul/index.html
probate search service: no charge ("need
complete name and approximate date of
death and/or case number"); copies of
probate records: 25¢ per page, no minimum

Polk County
organized 1845, original county

Polk County Courthouse
850 Main Street
Dallas, OR 97338-3116
(503) 623-9217 (County Clerk, Room 201); (503)
623-3154 (Circuit Court, Room 301)
unger.valerie@co.polk.or.us
http://www.co.polk.or.us/Clerk/default.asp;
http://www.ojd.state.or.us/plk/index.htm
Valerie Unger, County Clerk
(land records with County Surveyor, 751 S.W.
Clay Street, Dallas, OR 97338, deeds from
1856, mortgages, leases with Clerk's Office,
deaths [indexed under direct deeds], marriages
from 1849 with Clerk's Office, probate
records from 1926 with Circuit Court;
probate records before 1926 with Archives
Division, Secretary of State, 800 Summer
Street, N.E., Salem, OR 97310)
probate search service: $12.50; copies of probate
records: 25¢ per page, no minimum

Sherman County
organized 1889 from Wasco County

Sherman County Courthouse
500 Court Street
Moro, OR 97039
(503) 565-3606 (County Clerk, PO Box 365);

(541) 565-3650 (Circuit Court, PO Box 402);
(541) 565-3249 FAX (Circuit Court)
dhayden@sherman-county.com
http://www.sherman-county.com; http://seventh
district.ojd.state.or.us/html/sherman.html
Linda Cornie, County Clerk; Debbie Hayden,
Chief Deputy Clerk

Tillamook County
organized 1853 from Clatsop, Polk and Yamhill
counties

Tillamook County Courthouse
201 Laurel Avenue
Tillamook, OR 97141
(503) 842-3402 (County Clerk, First Floor);
(800) 488-8280, ext. 4000 (County Clerk);
(503) 842-2596 (Circuit Court, Main Floor);
(503) 842-1599 FAX (County Clerk); (503)
842-2597 FAX (Circuit Court)
toncil@co.tillamook.or.us
http://www.co.tillamook.or.us; http://www.
ojd.state.or.us/til/index.html (Circuit Court)
Tassi O'Neil, County Clerk; Beverly E. Lutz,
Trial Court Administrator
(land records with County Clerk, marriages with
County Clerk, probate records with Circuit
Court)
no probate search service; copies of probate
records: 25¢ per page, $3.75 for certified
copies

Umatilla County
organized 1862 from Wasco County

Umatilla County Courthouse
216 S.E. Fourth Avenue
Pendleton, OR 97801-2500
(541) 278-6236 (Office of County Records, PO
Box 1227); (541) 278-0341 (Circuit Court, PO
Box 1307); (541) 278-6345 FAX (Office of
County Records)
http://www.co.umatilla.or.us;
http://www.ojd.state.or.us/uma/index.htm
Records: Mon–Fri 9:00–5:00; Circuit Court:
Mon–Fri 8:00–noon & 1:00–5:00
(land records from 1862 to date and scattered
naturalization records from various years with
the Department of Administrative Services,
Office of County Records, probate records
with State Courts Office)
copies of naturalization records: 25¢ per page

Union County
organized 1864 from Umatilla County

Union County Circuit Court
1007 Fourth Street
La Grande, OR 97850
(541) 962-9500
union.county@ojd.state.or.us
http://www.ojd.state.or.us/courts/circuit/
union.htm
Michelle Leonard, Trial Court Administrator
probate search service: $12.00 minimum

Union County County Clerk
1001 Fourth Street, Suite D
La Grande, OR 97850
(541) 963-1006; (541) 963-1013 FAX
clerk31@union-county.org
http://www.union-county.org
Robin Church, Interim County Clerk
(land records, naturalization records, births from
1922 to 1944, deaths from 1921 to 1944,
marriages from 1864 to date)

Wallowa County
organized 1887 from Union County

Wallowa County Courthouse
101 South River Street
Enterprise, OR 97828
(541) 426-4543, ext. 15 (Room 100); (541) 426-
4991 (Circuit Court, Room 204)
wcclerk@co.wallowa.or.us
http://www.co.wallowa.or.us/cc; http://www.
ojd.state.or.us/courts/circuit/wallowa.htm
Dana Roberts, County Clerk; Michelle Leonard,
Trial Court Administrator

(land records, naturalization records, vital records, probate records)
copies of land, naturalization, vital, and probate records: $3.75 per book pulled plus 25¢ per page copied

Wasco County

organized 1854, created from the original Champoeg District by the Territorial Legislature; it embraced all of Oregon east of the Cascade Range, most of Idaho, and parts of Montana and Wyoming

Wasco County Courthouse
511 Washington Street
The Dalles, OR 97058
(541) 506-2530 (County Clerk, Room 201); (541) 506-2700 (Circuit Court, PO Box 1400); (541) 506-2711 FAX (Circuit Court)
karenl@co.wasco.or.us
http://www.co.wasco.or.us; http://seventh district.ojd.state.or.us/html/wasco.html
Karen LeBreton Coats, County Clerk; Charles B. Wall, Trial Court Administrator
(land records from 1854 with County Clerk, marriages from 1854 with County Clerk, probate records from 1854 with Trial Court)
land, vital, and probate records search service: no charge; copies of land and vital records: $4.00 for the first page of each document and 25¢ for each additional page; copies of probate records: 25¢ per page

Washington County

organized 1843, original county

Washington County Public Services Building
155 North First Avenue
Hillsboro, OR 97124
(503) 846-8752 (Department of Assessment and Taxation, Suite 130, MS 9); (503) 648-8879 (Probate); (503) 648-8767 (Trial Court Administrator); (503) 846-3909 FAX (Department of Assessment and Taxation)
at@co.wshington.or.us
http://www.co.washington.or.us/cgi/home/wa shco.pl; http://www.ojd.stte.or.us/wsh/ default.htm
Diana Bradrick, Supervisor, Assessment and Taxtion Department, Recording Division; Richard Moellmer, Trial Court Administrator, District Court
(land records from 1850 with Recording Section, Department of Assessment and Taxation—County Clerk, Mapping and Records Division, naturalization records with State of Oregon Court Services, Circuit and District Courts of Oregon, probate records with State of Oregon Court Services)
land records search service: $3.75 per document plus 25¢ per page; no probate search service; copies of land records: 50¢ each for self-made copies, which cannot be certified, $3.75 for certified copies; copies of probate records: 25¢ per page, $3.75 for certification ("All fees payable in advance")

Wheeler County

organized 1899 from Crook, Gilliam and Grant counties

Wheeler County Courthouse
701 Adams Street
Fossil, OR 97830-0327
(503) 763-2400 (General, PO Box 327); (541) 763-2541 (Circuit Court, PO Box 308); (541) 763-2026 FAX (Circuit Court)
bsitton@ncesd.k12.or.us
http://www.wheelercounty-oregon.com; http://bluebook.state.or.us/local/counties/ counties35.htm http://seventhdistrict.ojd. state.or.us/html/wheeler.html
Barbara Sitton, County Clerk; Charles B. Wall, Trial Court Administrator
(land records from 1899, naturalization records from 1899, abstracts only of vital records with, probate records from 1899)
probate search service: $3.75 per file; copies of

probate records: 25¢ per page up to legal size, no minimum ("for extensive searches the charge is $15.00 per hour")

Yamhill County

organized 1843, original county

Yamhill County Circuit Court
Court Records, Room 202
535 NE Fifth Street
McMinnville, OR 97128
(503) 434-7530, ext. 4260 (Probate)
http://www.ojd.state.or.us/yam/Pages/Home.htm
Phil McCollister, Trial Court Administrator
(probate records from 1852 with Trial Court Office)
probate search service: no charge; copies of probate records: 1–5 pages $1.00, 6–25 pages $2.00, 26–100 pages $3.00, 101-200 pages $5.00

Yamhill County Clerk
414 NE Evans Street
McMinnville, OR 97128-4607
(503) 434-7518; (503) 434-7520 FAX
colemanj@co.yamhill.or.us
http://www.co.yamhill.or.us/clerk/index.asp
Jan Coleman
(deeds from 1853, mortgages and plats, marriages from 1854)
land and vital records search service: $15.00 per hour; copies of land records: 25¢ per page; certified copies of vital records: $10.00 each

PENNSYLVANIA

Capital: Harrisburg. Statehood: 12 December 1787 (obtained royal charter in 1681, Mason-Dixon Line settled 1763-1767)

Philadelphia has a Municipal Court and a Traffic Court, and Pittsburgh has a Magistrates Court. These three courts, along with the District Justice Courts, which exist in magisterial districts throughout the state except in Philadelphia County, have limited jurisdiction over lesser civil and minor criminal offenses. The Court of Common Pleas, which sits at each county seat, has general jurisdiction over all civil and criminal matters. The Orphans Court Division handles probate. Each of the state's sixty Judicial Districts has one county except the following: Seventeenth Judicial District: Snyder and Union counties; Twenty-sixth Judicial District: Columbia and Montour counties; Thirty-seventh Judicial District: Forest and Warren counties; Thirty-ninth Judicial District: Franklin and Fulton counties; Forty-first Judicial District: Juniata and Perry counties; Forty-fourth Judicial District: Sullivan and Wyoming counties; Fifty-ninth Judicial District: Cameron and Elk counties. The Commonwealth Court hears cases involving the government and its agencies. Superior Court hears some intermediate appeals, and the Supreme Court is the court of last resort.

Adams County

organized 1800 from York County

Adams County Courthouse
111-117 Baltimore Street
Gettysburg, PA 17325-2312
(717) 337-9826 (Register and Recorder, Room 102); (717) 337-9834 (Prothonotary, Room 104); (717) 337-9806 (Clerk of Courts); (717) 334-1758 FAX (Register and Recorder); (717) 334-2091 FAX (Prothonotary); (717) 334-9333 FAX (Clerk of Courts)
registerrecorder@adamscounty.us; pfunt@ adamscounty.us; klawver@adamscounty.us
http://www.adamscounty.us/adams/site/ default.asp
Patsy Gochenauer, Register of Wills and Recorder of Deeds; Patricia A. Funt, Prothonotary; Kelly A. Lawver, Clerk of Courts
(land records from 1800 with Register and Recorder, naturalization records with Prothonotary's Office, vital records [index to births 1852–1855 and 1893–1905, index to deaths 1852–1855 and 1893–1905, index to marriages 1852–1855] with Clerk of Courts, probate records with Register and Recorder)
probate search service: $5.00 per hour, $3.00 minimum; copies of probate records: 25¢ per page, $9.00 for the first page of certified documents and $4.00 for each additional certified page, plus LSASE

Allegheny County

organized 1788 from Washington and Westmoreland counties

Allegheny County Courthouse
436 Grant Street
Pittsburgh, PA 15219-2495
(412) 350-5322 (Clerk of Courts, Room 114)
george.matta@court.allegheny.pa.us
http://www.county.allegheny.pa.us/cofc
George F. Matta, Clerk of Courts

Allegheny County Office Building
542 Forbes Avenue
Pittsburgh, PA 15219
(412) 350-4266 (Room 101); (412) 350-6877 FAX
webmaster.deeds@county.allegheny.pa.us
http://www.county.allegheny.pa.us/deeds
Valerie McDonald Roberts, Recorder of Deeds

City County Building
414 Grant Street, First Floor
Pittsburgh, PA 15219-2469
(412) 350-4200 (Prothonotary); (412) 350-4180
(Register of Wills); (412) 350-5260 FAX
(Prothonotary)
webmaster.regwills@county.allegheny.pa.us
http://www.county.allegheny.pa.us/protho;
http://www.county.allegheny.pa.us/regwills
Michael E. Lamb, Prothonotary; Eileen Wagner,
Register of Wills
(naturalization records with Prothonotary;
births, deaths, marriage licenses, and wills
with Register of Wills)

Armstrong County
organized 1800 from Allegheny, Lycoming and
Westmoreland counties

Armstrong County Courthouse
500 Market Street
Kittanning, PA 16201
(724) 548-3256 (Recorder); (724) 548-3251
(Prothonotary); (724) 548-3236 FAX
(Recorder); (724) 548-3351 FAX
(Prothonotary)
prothonotary@co.armstrong.pa.us
http://www.co.armstrong.pa.us
Beverly A. Casella, Register of Wills/Recorder
of Deeds/Clerk of Orphans' Court; Brenda
George, Prothonotary/Clerk of Courts
(land records with Recorder, naturalization
records with Prothonotary, vital records with
Clerk of Orphans Court, probate records with
Register of Wills)
no probate search service; copies of probate
records: $1.00 per page by mail, plus SASE,
no minimum ("very helpful to have names
spelled correctly and approximate dates")

Beaver County
organized 1800 from Allegheny and Washington
counties

Beaver County Courthouse
810 Third Street
Beaver, PA 15009
(724) 728-5700 (Recorder); (724) 728-3934, ext.
11279 (Prothonotary); (724) 728-3934, ext.
11322 (Clerk of Courts, Room 207); (724)
728-3934, ext. 11273 (Register of Wills); (724)
728-8479 FAX (Recorder); (724) 728-3360
FAX (Prothonotary); (724) 728-8853 FAX
(Clerk of Courts); (724) 728-9810 FAX
(Register of Wills)
jbeal@co.beaver.pa.us;
nwerme@co.beaver.pa.us;
jenslen@co.beaver.pa.us;
cfiorucci@co.beaver.pa.us
http://www.co.beaver.pa.us
Janice Jeschke-Beal, Recorder of Deeds; Nancy
Werme,, Prothonotary; Judy R. Enslen, Court
Clerk; Carol Fiorucci, Register of Wills
(land records with Recorder of Deeds/Tax
Assessment, naturalization records with
Prothonotary, vital records with Register of
Wills, probate records with Register of Wills)
probate search service: cost varies; copies of
probate records: $1.00 per page

Bedford County
organized 9 March 1771 from Cumberland
County

Bedford County Courthouse
(Public Square, 203 South Julieanna Street,
Bedford, PA 15522-1714—location)
PO Box 166 (mailing address)
Bedford, PA 15522-0166
(814) 623-4836 (Register); (814) 623-4833
(Prothonotary); (814) 623-0488 FAX
(Register); (814) 623-4831 FAX
(Prothonotary)
regrec@bedford.net; bcproth@pennswoods.net
http://bedford.pacounties.org/bedford/site/def
ault.asp
Faith A. Zembower, Register of Wills/Recorder
of Deeds; Cathy Fetter, Prothonotary/Clerk
of Courts

(deeds from 1771 with Register and Recorder,
naturalization records with Prothonotary,
births and deaths from 1852 to 1854 and
from 1893 to 1905, marriage licenses from
1852 to 1854 and from 1885 with
Prothonotary's Office, wills from 1771 with
Recorder's Office and Register of Wills)
no land records search service (search requires
first and last names); probate search service:
no charge (require first and last names);
copies of probate records: 50¢ per page plus
postage, no minimum

Berks County
organized 1751 from Bucks, Lancaster and
Philadelphia counties

Berks County Courthouse
633 Court Street, 13th Floor
Reading, PA 19601
(215) 378-8000; (215) 378-8015 (Recorder of
Deeds, Third Floor); (215) 378-8039
(Prothonotary, Second Floor); (215) 378-8048
(Register of Wills Second Floor)
http://www.co.berks.pa.us
Ellie Antoine, Recorder of Deeds; Marianne
Sutton, Prothonotary; Lawrence Madaglia,
Register of Wills
(land records from 1752 with Recorder of
Deeds, naturalization records from 1798 with
Prothonotary [Chief Clerk—Civil Division
Courts], probate records from 1752 with
Register of Wills)
probate search service: $5.00; copies of probate
records: $1.00 per page, no minimum

Blair County
organized 1846 from Bedford and Huntingdon
counties

Blair County Courthouse
423 Allegheny Street
Holidaysburg, PA 16648-2022
(814) 693-3095 (Recorder of Deeds, Suite 145);
(814) 693-3092 (Register of Wills, Suite 145);
(814) 693-3093 FAX
http://blair.pacounties.org/blair/site;
http://www.blaircountyrecorder.com
Mary Ann Bennis, Register of Wills and
Recorder of Deeds; Carol Newman,
Prothonotary ad Clerk of Courts

Bradford County
organized 1810 from Luzerne and Lycoming
counties

Bradford County Courthouse
301 Main Street
Towanda, PA 18848-1824
(570) 265-1702 (Register/Recorder); (570) 265-
1705 (Prothonotary); (570) 265-1721 FAX
(Register/Recorder)
http://www.bradfordcountypa.org;
http://bradford-pa.com/gov
Shirley Rockefeller, Register/Recorder, Clerk of
Orphans Court; Sally F. Vaughn,
Prothonotary and Clerk of Courts
(deeds and mortgages from 1812, oil leases from
September 1930 with Register and Recorder's
Office; naturalization records from 1840 with
Prothonotary's Office, births from 1893
through 1905, deaths from 1895 through
1905, marriages from 1885 with Register and
Recorder's Office, wills from 1812 [indexed
by decedent's name or by
executor/administrator] with Register and
Recorder's Office)
probate search service: $10.00; copies of land,
naturalization, vital and probate records: 50¢
per page, no minimum ("please send a
SASE")

Bucks County
organized 1682, original county

Bucks County Courthouse
55 East Court Street
Doylestown, PA 18901
(215) 348-6209 (Recorder of Deeds, Second

Floor); (215) 348-6191 (Prothonotary); (215)
348-6389 (Clerk of Courts); (215) 348-6265
(Register of Wills, Third Floor); (215) 348-
6271 (Orphan's Court); (215) 348-6184 FAX
(Prothonotary); (215) 348-6740 FAX (Clerk
of Courts); (215) 348-6156 FAX (Register of
Wills)
cocassociates@co.bucks.pa.us;
registerofwills@co.bucks.pa.us;
orphanscourt@co.bucks.pa.us
http://www.bucksounty.org
Edward Gudknecht, Recorder of Deeds; Patricia
L. Bachtel, Prothonotary; Mary K. Smithson,
Clerk of Courts; Barbara G. Reilly, Register of
Wills and Orphan's Court
(land records with Recorder of Deeds,
naturalization records with Prothonotary, vital
records with Register of Wills, probate
records with Register of Wills)
probate search service: $25.00 estate charge;
copies of probate records: $1.00 per page,
$10.00 minimum

Butler County
organized 1800 from Allegheny County

Butler County Government Center
(124 West Diamond Street, Butler, PA 16001—
location)
PO Box 1208 (mailing address)
Butler, PA 16003
(724) 284-5340 (Recorder of Deeds, Floor L);
(724) 284-5214 (Prothonotary, First Floor);
(724) 284-5233 (Clerk of Courts); (724) 284-
1409 (Register); (724) 285-9099 FAX
(Recorder); (724) 284-5278 FAX (Recorder)
mmustell@co.butler.pa.us;
llotz@co.butler.pa.us; jmoser@co.butler.pa.us
http://www.co.butler.pa.us
Michelle Mostello, Recorder of Deeds; Glenna
Walters, Prothonotary; Lisa Lotz, Clerk of
Courts; Judy Moser, Register of Wills and
Clerk of Orphans Court
(deeds and other instruments for the transfer of
interest in land with Recorder of Deeds
Office, naturalization records with
Prothonotary's Office, probate records and
estate administration with Register of Wills
and Clerk of Courts Office)
no probate search service

Cambria County
organized 1804 from Bedford, Huntingdon and
Somerset counties

Cambria County Courthouse
200 South Center Street
Ebensburg, PA 15931
(814) 472-1473 (Recorder); (814) 472-1636
(Prothonotary); (814) 472-1540 (Clerk of
Courts); (814) 472-1440 (Register); (814) 472-
1412 FAX (Recorder); (814) 472-5632 FAX
(Prothonotary); (814) 472-0761 FAX (Clerk
of Courts)
pberkebile@co.cambria.pa.us;
skuhar@co.cambria.pa.us
http://www.co.cambria.pa.us/cambria/site/def
ault.asp
Andrea Fedore Sims, Recorder of Deeds; Patty
Berkebile, Prothonotary; Susan M. Kuhar,
Clerk of Courts; Patty J. Sharbaugh, Register
of Wills and Clerk of Orphans' Court

Cameron County
organized 1860 from Clinton, Elk, McKean and
Potter counties

Cameron County Courthouse
20 East Fifth Street
Emporium, PA 15834
(814) 486-2315; (814) 486-3176 FAX
http://www.cameroncountypa.com
David J. Reed, Prothonotary, Recorder of
Deeds, Clerk of Courts, and Register of Wills
(land records from 1860 with Recorder of
Deeds, naturalization records from 1860 to
1907 with Prothonotary, vital records from
1860 to 1907, probate records from 1860 with
Register of Wills)

no probate search service; copies of probate records: 50¢ per page, $2.00 minimum

Carbon County

organized 13 March 1843 from Monroe and Northampton counties

Carbon County Courthouse
(4 Broadway—location)
PO Box 129 (mailing address)
Jim Thorpe, PA 18229-0129
(570) 325-2651 (Recorder of Deeds, PO Box 87); (570) 325-3637 (Clerk of Courts); (717) 325-2261 (Register of Wills/Clerk of Orphans Court, PO Box 286); (570) 325-5705 FAX (Clerk of Courts)
http://www.carboncounty.com;
http://www.carboncourts.com/CLERK
Emmett McCall, Recorder of Deeds; William McGinley, Clerk of Court; Judith Moon, Register of Wills
(deeds, mortgages, assignments, leases, etc. with Recorder of Deeds, births from 1892 through 1905, marriages from 1 October 1885 and wills from December 1843 with Register of Wills/Clerk of Orphans Court)
vital records and probate records search service: $12.00 per hour, $7.00 for ½ hour or less; copies of land records: 50¢ per page, $1.50 for certification; copies of vital records and probate records from Register of Wills: 25¢ per page from paper originals, 50¢ per page from microfilm originals

Centre County

organized 1800 from Huntingdon, Lycoming, Mifflin and Northumberland counties

Centre County Courthouse
Bellefonte, PA 16823
(814) 355-6796
http://www.co.centre.pa.us/default.asp
Debra C. Immel, Prothonotary and Clerk of Courts
(naturalization records)

Centre County Office Building
414 Holmes Street
Bellefonte, PA 16823
(814) 355-6801 (Recorder); (814) 355-6724 (Register); (814) 355-8685 FAX (Register)
rodinfo@co.centre.pa.us;
rabierly@co.centre.pa.us
http://www.co.centre.pa.us/default.asp
Joseph L. Davidson, Recorder of Deeds; Roger A. Bierly, Register of Wills
(land records with Recorder of Deeds, births from 1893 to 1905 and probate records with Register of Wills)
probate search service: no charge; copies of probate records: costs vary

Chester County

organized 1682, original county

Chester County Courthouse
(2 North High Street—location)
PO Box 2748 (mailing address)
West Chester, PA 19380-0991
(610) 344-6300 (Prothonotary, Suite 130); (610) 344-6135 (Clerk of Courts); (610) 344-6335 (Register, Suite 109); (610) 344-6218 FAX (Register)
http://dsf.chesco.org
Bryan D. Walters, Prothonotary; Teena Peters, Clerk of Courts; Paula Gowen, Register of Wills and Clerk of the Orphans' Court
(naturalization records after 1900 with Prothonotary; marriages after 1930 with Clerk of Orphans Court; probate records after 1923 with Register of Wills)
vital records search service: $5.00 for three years (includes copy of the record if found)

Chester County Recorder of Deeds
(121 North Walnut Street—location)
PO Box 2748 (mailing address)
West Chester, PA 19380-0991
(610) 344-6330; (610) 344-6408
rodinfo@chesco.org

http://dsf.chesco.org/recorder/cwp/view.asp?A=1519&Q=606686
Terence Farrell
(deeds after 1805; online database from 1960 only)

Clarion County

organized 1839 from Armstrong and Venango counties

Clarion County Courthouse
401 Main Street
Clarion, PA 16214
(814) 226–4000, ext. 2500 (Register and Recorder, First Floor); (814) 226-1119, ext. 2402 (Prothonotary)
mjmccall@co.clarion.pa.us
http://www.co.clarion.pa.us/offices.html
Greg Mortimer, Register and Recorder; Mary Jane McCall, Prothonotary
(land records from 1840 with Recorder's Office, naturalization records to late 1800s with Prothonotary's Office, births and deaths from 1893 to 1906, marriages from 1885 with Recorder's Office, probate records from 1840 with Recorder's Office)
probate search service: $5.00; copies of probate records: $1.00 per page, plus SASE, no minimum

Clearfield County

organized 1804 from Lycoming and Northumberland counties

Clearfield County Courthouse
(230 East Market Street—location)
PO Box 361 (mailing address)
Clearfield, PA 16830-0316
(814) 765-2641 (Register and Recorder); (814) 765-2641, ext. 1331 (Prothonotary, PO Box 549)
http://www.clearfieldco.org
Karen L. Starck, Recorder and Register; William A. Shaw, Prothonotary/Clerk of Courts
(land records from 1804 with Register and Recorder, naturalization records from 1850 with Prothonotary, births and deaths from 1893 to 1905, marriages from 1885 with Register and Recorder, probate records from 1820 with Register and Recorder)
no probate search service; copies of probate records: 50¢ per page

Clinton County

organized 21 June 1839 from Centre and Lycoming counties

Clinton County Courthouse
232 East Main Street
Lock Haven, PA 17745
(717) 893-4010 (Register and Recorder, First Floor); (717) 893-4007 (Prothonotary, First Floor)
regrec@clintoncountypa.com;
syarrison@clintoncountypa.com
http://www.clintoncountypa.com
Gail Gephart, Register and Recorder; Sherry L. Yarrison, Prothonotary and Clerk of Courts
(land records from 1839 with Registrar and Recorder, naturalization records with Prothonotary, births and deaths from 1893 through 1905, marriages from 1885 to date [no general index] with Register and Recorder, probate records from 1839 with Registrar and Recorder)
probate search service: no charge; copies of land and naturalization records: $1.00 for the first page and 50¢ for each additional page; copies of probate records: $1.00 for the first page and 50¢ for each additional page

Columbia County

organized 1813 from Northumberland County

Columbia County Courthouse
35 West Main Street
Bloomsburg, PA 17815
(570) 389-5632 (Register and Recorder); (570) 389-5614 (Prothonotary)

bmichael@columbiapa.org;
tkline@columbiapa.org
http://www.columbiapa.org/offices
Beverly J. Michael, Register and Recorder; Tami B. Kline, Prothonotary, Clerk of Courts, and Clerk of Orphans Court
(land records with Tax Records, naturalization records with Prothonotary/Clerk of Courts, vital records from 1893 to 1905 with Prothonotary/Clerk of Courts, probate records from 1813 with Register of Wills)
no probate search service; copies of probate records: 25¢ each, no minimum

Crawford County

organized 1800 from Allegheny County

Crawford County Courthouse
903 Diamond Park
Meadville, PA 16335-2677
(814) 373-2537 (Register and Recorder); (814) 336-1151
cstainbrook@co.crawford.pa.us
http://www.co.crawford.pa.us
Carol A. Stainbrook, Register of Wills and Recorder of Deeds; Mary Courtney, Clerk of Courts
(land records from 1800 with Register and Recorder, naturalization records with Prothonotary, vital records from 1893 through 1905 with Clerk of Courts, probate records from 1800 with Register and Recorder)
probate search service: $10.00; copies of naturalization records: 50¢ per page; copies of probate records: $1.00 per page, no minimum

Cumberland County

organized 1750 from Lancaster County

Cumberland County Courthouse
1 Courthouse Square
Carlisle, PA 17013
(717) 240-6370 (Recorder); (717) 240-6195 (Prothonotary); (717) 240-6345 (Register of Wills, First Floor); (717) 240-7797 FAX (Register)
recorderofdeeds@ccpa.net; clong@ccpa.net; gfarner@ccpa.net; regofwills@ccpa.net
http://www.ccpa.net/cumberland/site/default.asp
Robert Ziegler, Recorder of Deeds; Curtis R. Long, Prothonotary; Glenda Farner Strasbaugh, Register of Wills/Clerk of Orphans' Court

Dauphin County

organized 1785 from Lancaster County

Dauphin County Courthouse
Front and Market Streets
Harrisburg, PA 17108
(717) 780-6560 (Recorder, Room 102); (717) 780-6520 (Prothonotary, First Floor, PO Box 945); (717) 780-6530 (Clerk of Courts, Third Floor); (717) 780-6500 (Register of Wills, Room 103)
jzugay@dauphinc.org
http://www.dauphincounty.org/publicly-elected-officials
James M. Zugay, Esq., Recorder of Deeds; Stephen E. Farina, Prothonotary; Lowell A. Witmer, Clerk of Courts; Sandy Snyder, Register of Wills and Clerk of the Orphans' Court
(land records from 1785 with Recorder of Deeds, naturalization records from 1845 [except 1900 to 1917 inclusive filed with Clerk of Court, Federal Courthouse, Scranton, PA] with Prothonotary, births and deaths from 1893 to 1906, marriages from 1885 with Register of Wills and Clerk of the Orphans' Court Division, probate records from 1785 with Register of Wills and Clerk of the Orphans' Court Division)
probate search service: $10.00 per individual; copies of probate records: $1.00 per page ("we duplicate from original documents")

Delaware County
organized 1789 from Chester County

Delaware County Government Center Building
201 West Front Street
Media, PA 19063
(610) 891-4152 (Recorder of Deeds, Room 107);
(610) 891-4400 (Register, Room 102)
archives@co.delaware.pa.us;
http://www.co.delaware.pa.us/depts/recorder.
html; http://www.co.delaware.pa.us/
registerofwills/index.html
Thomas J. Judge, Sr., Recorder of Deeds; Hugh
Donaghue, Register of Wills and Clerk of
Orphans' Court

Elk County
organized 1843 from Clearfield, Jefferson and
McKean counties

Elk County Courthouse
240 Main Street
Ridgway, PA 15853
(814) 776-5349 (Register, PO Box 314); (814)
776-5344 (Prothonotary, PO Box 237); (814)
776-5382 FAX (Register); (814) 776-5303
FAX (Prothonotary)
webmaster@elkoes.ncentral.com
http://www.co.elk.pa.us
Peter W. Weidenboerner, Register of Wills,
Recorder of Deeds, and Clerk of Orphans'
Court; David A. Frey, Prothonotary and Clerk
of Courts
(land records from 1843 to date with Recorder
of Deeds, naturalization records from 1944 to
date with Prothonotary, births and deaths
from 1893 to 1905 with Register of Wills,
births and deaths from 1906 to date with Vital
Records, PO Box 1528, New Castle, PA
16103, probate records from 1843 to date
with Register of Wills)

Erie County
organized 1800 from Allegheny County

Erie County Courthouse
140 West Sixth Street
Erie, PA 16501-1011
(814) 451-6246 (Recorder); (814) 451-6250
(Prothonotary, Room 120); (814) 451-6221
(Clerk of Courts, Room 103); (814) 451-6260
(Register of Wills, Room 122); (814) 451-6213
FAX (Recorder)
recorder@eriecountygov.org
http://www.eriecountygov.org
Patrick Fetzner, Clerk of Records
(Clerk of Records Offices includes Recorder of
Deeds, Register of Wills, Prothonotary, and
Clerk of Courts; land records with Recorder
of Deeds, naturalization records with
Prothonotary, vital records with
Prothonotary, probate records with Register
of Wills)
probate search service: $5.00; copies of probate
records: $1.00 each, no minimum

Fayette County
organized 1783 from Westmoreland County

Fayette County Courthouse
61 East Main Street
Uniontown, PA 15401-3514
(724) 430-1479 (Records Department); (724)
430-1238 (Recorder of Deeds); (724) 430-
1272 (Prothonotary); (724) 430-1253 (Clerk of
Courts); (724) 430-1206 (Register of Wills);
(724) 430-4857 FAX (Records Department);
(724) 430-1458 FAX (Recorder of Deeds);
(724) 430-4555 FAX (Prothonotary); (724)
430-8410 FAX (Clerk of Courts); (724) 430-
1275 FAX (Register of Wills)
csutherland@fayettepa.org;
jsnyder_fayette@atlanticbb.net
http://www.co.fayette.pa.us/fayette/site/
default.asp
Colleen Sutherland, Records Department; David
G. Malosky, Recorder of Deeds; Lance
Winterhalter, Prothonotary; Janice Snyder,

Clerk of Courts; Donald Redman, Register of
Wills
(land records, naturalization records, vital
records, probate records)
probate search service: no charge (must have
given name and surname and approximate
dates); copies of probate records: 50¢ per
page, no minimum

Forest County
organized 1848 from Jefferson and Venango
counties

Forest County Courthouse
526 Elm Street
Tionesta, PA 16353
(814) 755-3526 (Prothonotary, Box 2)
http://www.forestcounty.com
Tammy McKee Schwab, Prothonotary,
Recorder, and Register
(land records from 1857 with Recorder,
naturalization records [dates are questionable]
with Prothonotary, births from 1893 to 1905,
deaths from 1893 to 1907, marriages from
1885 with Clerk of Orphans Court, probate
records from 1855 with Register of Wills)
probate search service: $5.00; copies of probate
records: 25¢ per page, $1.00 minimum

Franklin County
organized 1784 from Cumberland County

Franklin County Courthouse
157 Lincoln Way, East
Chambersburg, PA 17201-2211
(717) 261-3872 (Register and Recorder, First
Floor); (717) 261-3861 (Prothonotary); (717)
261-3805 (Clerk of Courts); (717) 263-5717
FAX (Register and Recorder); (717) 264-6772
FAX (Prothonotary); (717) 261-3896 FAX
(Clerk of Courts)
http://www.co.franklin.pa.us/franklin/site/defa
ult.asp
Linda Miller, Register of Wills and Recorder of
Deeds; Linda Beard, Prothonotary; Bill
Vandrew, Clerk of Court
(land records with Register and Recorder,
naturalization records with Prothonotary, vital
records with Clerk of Courts, probate records
with Register and Recorder)
no probate search service; copies of probate
records: 25¢ per page, $1.00 minimum

Fulton County
organized 1850 from Bedford County

Fulton County Courthouse
201 North Second Street
McConnellsburg, PA 17233
(717) 485-4212
http://www.fultoncntypa.org/CountyGovernm
ent/Prothonotary/tabid/106/Default.aspx
Patty Fix, Prothonotary/Clerk of
Courts/Recorder of Deeds/Register of
Wills/Orphans' Court Clerk
(land records from 1850 with Prothonotary's
Office, naturalization records from 1843 to
1915 with Prothonotary's Office, births and
deaths from 1895 to 1905 with
Prothonotary's Office, probate records from
1850 with Prothonotary's Office)
probate search service: no charge; copies of
probate records: 25¢ each for regular-sized
copies, 50¢ for large copies, $1.00 minimum

Greene County
organized 1796 from Washington County

Greene County Courthouse
10 East High Street
Waynesburg, PA 15370
(724) 852-5283 (Recorder, Room 103); (724)
852-5288 (Prothonotary, Room 103); (724)
852-5284 (Register); (724) 852-5281 (Clerk of
Courts, Room 103); (724) 627-4716 FAX
(Recorder and Register); (&24) 852-5353
FAX (Prothonotary)
theadlee@co.greene.pa.us;
swhite@co.greene.pa.us

http://www.co.greene.pa.us/secured/gc/depts/
lo/rr/index.htm
Thomas (Tom) Headlee, Register of Wills and
Recorder of Deeds; Susan White,
Prothonotary; Shirley Stockdale, Clerk of
Courts
(deeds, mortgages, leases, agreements, right of
ways, etc. from 1796 to date with Recorder's
Office, naturalization records from 1796 to
early 1900s with Prothonotary's Office, births
and deaths from 1893 to 1915, marriages
from 1885 with Clerk of Courts, probate
records from 1796 to date with Recorder's
Office)
probate search service: no charge (need first and
last names); copies of probate records: $4.00
for births, $3.00 for deaths, $5.00 for
marriages; copies of probate records: $5.00
for the first page and 50¢ for each additional
page

Huntingdon County
organized 1787 from Bedford County

Huntingdon County Courthouse
223 Penn Street
Huntingdon, PA 16652
(814) 643-2740 (Register and Recorder); (814)
643-1610 (Prothonotary); (814) 643-8152
FAX (Register and Recorder); (814) 643-4271
FAX
register_recorder@huntingdoncounty.net;
kcoons@huntingdoncounty.net
http://huntingdoncounty.net/hunt%5Fco/site/
default.asp
Janet Hanks, Register of Wills, Recorder of
Deeds, Clerk of the Orphans' Court; Kay
Coons, Prothonotary and Clerk of Courts
(land records from 1787 to date with Recorder
of Deeds, naturalization records from 1787
with Prothonotary, births and deaths from
1894 to 1905, marriages from October 1885
to date with Clerk of Orphans Court, probate
records from 1787 to date with Register of
Wills)

Indiana County
organized 1803 from Lycoming and
Westmoreland counties

Indiana County Courthouse
825 Philadelphia Street
Indiana, PA 15701-3934
(412) 465-3860 (Register and Recorder, Second
Floor); (412) 465-3855 (Prothonotary and
Clerk of Courts); (412) 465-3863 FAX
(Register and Recorder)
http://www.countyofindiana.org/prothon.htm
Patricia Streams-Warman, Recorder of Deeds;
Linda Moore-Mack, Prothonotary and Clerk
of Courts
(land records from 1803 with Register and
Recorder, naturalization records from 1806 to
1958 with Prothonotary and Clerk of Courts,
births and deaths from 1893 to 1905 with
Register and Recorder, probate records from
1803 with Register and Recorder)
no probate search service; copies of probate
records: 25¢ per page, $3.00 minimum

Jefferson County
organized 1804 from Lycoming County

Jefferson County Courthouse
200 Main Street
Brookville, PA 15825-1236
(814) 849-8031 (Recorder); (814) 849-1606
(Prothonotary)
Diane Maihle Kiehl, Register of Deeds,
Recorder of Wills, and Clerk of the Orphans'
Court; Virginia Ishman, Clerk of Courts and
Prothonotary
(land records from 1828 to date with Recorder
of Deeds, naturalization records with
Prothonotary, vital records from 1893 to 1906
with Clerk of the Orphans' Court, probate
records from 1828 to date with Register of
Wills)
land, vital, and probate records search service:

$5.00 per name; copies of land, vital, and probate: 50¢ per page plus $2.50 for mailing

Juniata County
organized 1831 from Mifflin County

Juniata County Courthouse
(Bridge and Main Streets—location)
PO Box 68 (mailing address)
Miffintown, PA 17059-0068
(717) 436-7709 (Register and Recorder); (717) 436-7715 (Prothonotary); (717) 436-7756 FAX (Register and Recorder); (717) 436-7734 FAX (Prothonotary)
http://www.co.juniata.pa.us
Nancy Lebkicher, Register and Recorder; Joan E. Clark, Prothonotary and Clerk of Courts

Lackawanna County
organized 1878 from Luzerne County

Lackawanna County Clerk of Judicial Records
Brooks Building
436 Spruce Street
Scranton, PA 18503
(570) 963-6723 (Civil); (570) 963-6759 (Criminal); (570) 963-6387 FAX (Civil); (570) 963-6459 FAX (Criminal)
Rinaldim@lackawannacounty.org
http://www.lackawannacounty.org/viewDepartment.aspx?DeptID=20
Mary F. Rinaldi
research: see Genealogical Research Society of Northeastern Pennsylvania, Inc. (GRSNP)

Lackawanna County Recorder and Register
Scranton Electric Building
507 Linden Street
Scranton, PA 18503
(570) 963-6775 (Recorder, Suite 800); (570) 963-6702; (Register, Suite 400); (570) 963-6390 FAX (Recorder); (570) 963-6377 FAX (Register)
mcNultye@lackawannacounty.org;
registerofwills@lackawannacounty.org
http://www.lackawannacounty.org/viewDepartment.aspx?DeptID=9 (Recorder);
http://www.lackawannacounty.org/viewDepartment.aspx?DeptID=35 (Register)
Evie Rafalko-McNulty, Recorder of Deeds; Linda Munley, Register of Wills
research: see Genealogical Research Society of Northeastern Pennsylvania, Inc. (GRSNP)

Lancaster County
organized 1729 from Chester County

Lancaster County Courthouse
(50 North Duke Street, Lancaster, PA 17602-2805—location)
PO Box 83480 (mailing address)
Lancaster, PA 17608-3480
(717) 299-8238 (Recorder, Second Floor); (717) 299-8282 (Prothonotary, Second Floor); (717) 299-8275 (Clerk of Courts); (717) 299-8243 (Register of Wills, Second Floor); (717) 299-8318 (Records and Archives)
mcdonald@co.lancaster.pa.us; wengerr@co.lancaster.pa.us; DenlingD@co.lancaster.pa.us; Reinaker@co.lacaster.pa.us; craterd@co.lancaster.pa.us
http://www.co.lancaster.pa.us
Steve McDonald, Recorder of Deeds; Randall O. Wenger, Prothonotary; Dale R. Denlinger, Clerk of Courts; Donna S. Reinaker, Register of Wills; Dory Crater, Director, Office of Records and Archives
(noncurrent records with Records and Archives: land records from 1729, births from 1893 to 1907 for Lancaster County, from 1881 to 1906 for Lancaster City, marriages from 1885, probate records)

Lawrence County
organized 1849 from Beaver and Mercer counties

Lawrence County Government Center
430 Court Street

New Castle, PA 16101
(724) 656-2127 (Recorder of Deeds); (724) 656-2126 (Prothonotary); (724) 656-2159 (Register)
recorder@co.lawrence.pa.us;
prothonotary@co.lawrence.pa.us
http://www.co.lawrence.pa.us
Janet Kalajainen, Register and Recorder; Helen Morgan, Prothonotary and Clerk of Courts
(land records with Recorder of Deeds' Office, naturalization records with Prothonotary's Office, births and deaths from 1893 to 1905, marriages with Prothonotary's Office, probate records with Register of Wills)
copies of probate records: $1.00 for the first page (includes mail search) and 50¢ for each additional page

Lebanon County
organized 1815 from Dauphin and Lancaster counties

Lebanon County Municipal Building
400 South Eighth Street
Lebanon, PA 17042-6794
(717) 274-2801, ext. 2223 (Recorder); (717) 274-2801, ext. 2120 (Prothonotary, Room 104); (717) 274-2801, ext. 2118 (Clerk of Courts, Room 102); (717) 274-2801, ext. 2217 (Register, Room 105); (717) 228-4456 FAX (Recorder); (717) 228-4467 FAX (Prothonotary); (717) 228-4467 FAX (Clerk of Courts); (717) 274-8094 FAX (Register and Commissioners)
dlutz@lebcnty.org;
ClerkofCourts102@lebcnty.org
http://dsf.pacounties.org/lebanon/site/default.asp
Donna J. Lutz, Recorder of Deeds; Lisa Arnold, Prothonotary and Clerk of Court; Dawn L. Resanovich, Register of Wills and Clerk of the Orphans' Court
(land records with Recorder of Deeds, naturalization records from about 1861 to date with Prothonotary's Office, births from 1893 through 1906, marriages from 1885 to date with Register of Wills, Orphans Court
probate records with Register of Wills Office

Lehigh County
organized 1812 from Northampton County

Lehigh County Courthouse
455 West Hamilton Street
Allentown, PA 18101
(610) 782-3077 (Clerk of Courts, Criminal, Room 132); (610) 782-3148 (Clerk of Courts, Civil, Room 132); (610) 782-3170 (Register); (610) 770-6797 FAX (Clerk of Courts, Criminal); (610) 770-3840 FAX (Clerk of Courts, Civil); (610) 782-3932 FAX (Register)
andreanaugle@lehighcounty.org
http://www.lehighcounty.org
Andrea E. Naugle, Clerk of Courts; Sandra L. Schantz, Register of Wills

Lehigh County Government Center
17 South Seventh Street
Allentown, PA 18101
(610) 782-3162 (Recorder, Room 350); (610) 782-3116 FAX
http://www.lehighcounty.org
Marie Dean, Recorder of Deeds
(land records, naturalization records, vital records, probate records)

Luzerne County
organized 1786 from Northumberland County

Luzerne County Courthouse
200 North River Street
Wilkes-Barre, PA 18711
(570) 825-1641 (Recorder); (570) 825-1743 (Prothonotary); (570) 825-1585 (Clerk of Courts); (570) 970-4580 FAX (Recorder)
http://www.luzernecounty.org
Jannell L. Decker, Esq., Recorder of Deeds; Jill A. Moran, Esq., Prothonotary; Robert F. Reilly, Clerk of Court

(land records with Recorder of Deeds, naturalization records with Prothonotary, births and probate records with Register of Wills)
probate search service: $5.00 per search; copies of probate records: $1.00 per page

Luzerne County Register of Wills
Penn Place Annex
20 North Pennsylvania Avenue
Wilkes-Barre, PA 18702
(570) 825-1668
http://www.luzernecounty.org/county/row_offices/register_of_wills
Dorothy Stankovic

Lycoming County
organized 1795 from Northumberland County

Lycoming County Courthouse
48 West Third Street
Williamsport, PA 17701-6519
(717) 327-2263 (Register and Recorder, First Floor); (717) 327-2251 (Prothonotary, First Floor)
http://www.lyco.org/lyco/site/default.asp
Annabel R. Miller, Register and Recorder
(land records from 1795 with Register and Recorder, naturalization records from 1804 to 1956 with Prothonotary, births from 1893 to 1905, deaths from 1893 to 1898, marriages from 1885 with Register and Recorder, probate records from 1850 with Register and Recorder)
probate search service: $5.00; copies of probate records: 25¢ per page, $1.00 minimum

McKean County
organized 1804 from Lycoming County

McKean County Courthouse
500 West Main Street
Smethport, PA 16749
(814) 887-3250 (Recorder); (814) 887-3260 (Register); (814) 887-3255 FAX (Recorder); (814) 887-3255 FAX (Register)
http://www.mckeancountypa.org
Anne Bosworth, Recorder of Deeds; Bonnie Moore-Howard, Prothonotary and Clerk of Courts; Harrijane Hannon, Register of Wills and Clerk of Orphans' Court
(land records with Betty Comes, Recorder of Deeds, naturalization records with Bonnie Moore, Prothonotary, marriage licenses with Carol P. Christensen, Register of Wills, probate records with Register of Wills)
probate search service: no charge; certified copies of marriage records: $10.00 each for licenses, $15.00 each for applications; copies of probate records: $1.00 per page, $10.00 for the first certified page and $5.00 for each additional certified page, no minimum

Mercer County
organized 1800 from Allegheny County

Mercer County Courthouse
5 Diamond Street
Mercer, PA 16137-0066
(724) 662-7573 (Recorder); (724) 662-7561 (Prothonotary); (724) 662-7548 (Clerk of Courts and Register of Wills); (724) 662-2021 FAX (Prothonotary)
webmaster@mcc.co.mercer.pa.us (Prothonotary)
http://www.mcc.co.mercer.pa.us
Rhonda McClelland, Recorder; Elizabeth F. Fair, Prothonotary; Kathleen Kloos, Clerk of Courts and Register of Wills
(land records with Recorder of Deeds, naturalization records with Prothonotary, vital records with Clerk of Courts and Clerk of Orphans Court, probate records with Register of Wills)

Mifflin County
organized 1789 from Cumberland and Northumberland counties

Mifflin County Courthouse

20 North Wayne Street
Lewistown, PA 17044-1770
(717) 242-1449 (Register and Recorder); (717)
248-8146 (Prothonotary); (717) 248-2503
FAX (Register and Recorder); (717) 248-5275
FAX (Prothonotary)
bstringer@co.mifflin.pa.us;
prothonotary@co.mifflin.a.us
http://www.co.mifflin.pa.us/mifflin/site/defaul
t.asp
Barb Stringer, Register of Wills and Recorder of
Deeds; Patti Burke, Prothontary and Clerk of
Courts

Monroe County
organized 1836 from Northampton and Pike
counties

Monroe County Courthouse
Seventh and Monroe Streets
Stroudsburg, PA 18360
(570) 517-3969 (Register and Recorder); (570)
517-3370 (Prothonotary); (570) 517-3385
(Clerk of Courts); (570) 517-3873 FAX
(Register and Recorder)
http://www.co.monroe.pa.us/monroe/site/def
ault.asp
Helen Diecidue, Register of Wills and Recorder
of Deeds; George Warden, Prothonotary and
Clerk of Courts
(land records with Recorder of Deeds,
naturalization records with Prothonotary, vital
records with Prothonotary, probate records
with Register of Wills)
probate search service: no charge for one name
if time warrants; copies of probate records:
25¢ per page ("old records all on microfiche
up to end of 1981; reader-printers are
available; 1981 to present files may be used
from file folders")

Montgomery County
organized 1784 from Philadelphia County

Montgomery County Courthouse
(1 Montgomery Plaza, Swede and Airy Streets—
location)
PO Box 311 (mailing address)
Norristown, PA 19404
(610) 278-3289 (Recorder, Suite 303, PO Box
311); (610) 278-3360 (Prothonotary, First
Floor); (610) 278-3346 (Clerk of Courts,
Second Floor); (610) 278-3400 (Register,
Second Floor, PO Box 311); (610) 278-3869
FAX (Recorder); (610) 278-5994 FAX
(Prothonotary); (610) 278-5188 FAX (Clerk
of Courts)
mcrod@mail.montcopa.org; mccoc@
mail.montcopa.org; registerofwillsorphans
court@mail.montcopa.org
http://www2.montcopa.org/montco/site/
default.asp
Nancy J. Becker, Recorder of Deeds; William E.
Donnelly, Prothonotary; Jane B. Markley,
Clerk of Courts; Frances V. Pierce, Register
of Wills

Montour County
organized 1850 from Columbia County

Montour County Courthouse
29 Mill Street
Danville, PA 17821-1945
(570) 271-3012 (Register and Recorder); (570)
271-3010 (Prothonotary); (570) 271-3071
FAX (Register and Recorder); (570) 271-3089
FAX (Prothonotary)
Montourregrec@yahoo.com
http://www.montourco.org/montour/site/defa
ult.asp
Linda L. Weaver, Register and Recorder; Susan
M. Kauwell, Prothonotary/Clerk of
Courts/Clerk of Orphans' Court
(land records from 1850 with Register and
Recorder's Office, naturalization records from
1850 to 1940 with Prothonotary, births and
deaths from 1893 to 1905, marriage licenses
from 1885 with Clerk of Courts, probate
records from 1850 with Register and

Recorder's Office)
probate search service: $5.00; copies of probate
records: 50¢ each, no minimum

Northampton County
organized 1752 from Bucks County

Northampton County Courthouse
669 Washington Street
Easton, PA 18042-7475
(610) 559-3077 (Recorder); (610) 559-3094
(Register)
NCInfo@northamptoncounty.org
http://www.northamptoncounty.org/northamp
ton/site/default.asp
Ann Achatz, Recorder of Deeds; Holly
Ruggiero, Clerk of Court of Civil Division
(Prothonotary); Dorothy Cole, Register of
Wills

Northumberland County
organized 1772 from Bedford, Berks,
Cumberland, Lancaster and Northampton
counties

Northumberland County Courthouse
201 Market Street
Sunbury, PA 17801-3408
(570) 988-4143 (Register and Recorder); (570)
988-4151 (Prothonotary); (570) 988-4151
(Clerk of Courts); (570) 988-4141 FAX
(Register and Recorder)
regrecmz@norrycopa.net
http://www.northumberlandco.org
Mary Zimmerman, Register of Wills and
Recorder of Deeds
(land records from 1772 with Recorder,
naturalization records with Prothonotary, vital
records with Recorder, probate records from
1772 with Register of Wills)
no probate search service; copies of probate
records: 25¢ each, $2.00 minimum

Perry County
organized 1820 from Cumberland County

Perry County Courthouse
1 Courthouse Square
New Bloomfield, PA 17068
(717) 582-2131; (717) 582-5167 FAX
(Register/Recorder and Prothonotary)
http://www.perryco.org/perry/site/default.asp
Wendy Welfley, Register and Recorder; Brenda
Albright, Prothonotary
(land records from 1820, naturalization records
from 1904 to 1973 with Prothonotary, births
from 1893 to 1918, probate records from
1820)
probate search service: $2.00; copies of probate
records: 50¢ per page plus 25¢ per ounce
postage and handling, no minimum

Philadelphia County
organized 1682, original county; coterminous
with the City of Philadelphia

Register of Wills
City Hall
Philadelphia, PA 19107
(215) 686-6250 (Register of Wills, Room 180);
(215) 686-6268 FAX (Register of Wills)
rowonline@phila.gov
http://secureprod.phila.gov/wills
Honorable Ronald R. Donatucci, Esq.

Pike County
organized 1814 from Wayne County

Pike County Administration Building
506 Broad Street
Milford, PA 18337
(570) 296-3508; (570) 296-3514 FAX
lmurcko@pikepa.org
http://www.pikepa.org/Recorder.htm;
http://www.pikepa.org/Regofwills.htm
Lynn A. Murcko, Recorder of Deeds and
Register of Wills
(land records from 1814, births and deaths from
1895 to 1905 only, probate records from

1820)
no probate search service; copies of probate
records: 25¢ (in person only)

**Pike County Prothonotary and Clerk of
Courts**
412 Broad Street
Milford, PA 18337
(570) 296-7231
http://www.pikepa.org/clerkofcourt.htm
Denise Fitzpatrick

Potter County
organized 1804 from Lycoming County

Potter County Courthouse
1 East Second Street, Room 22
Coudersport, PA 16915
(814) 274-8290 (Recorder of Deeds); (814) 274-
8370 (Register of Wills)
http://www.pottercountypa.net
Amy Moshier, Prothonotary and Clerk of Courts
(land records, naturalization records, vital
records, probate records)

Schuylkill County
organized 1811 from Berks and Northampton
counties

Schuylkill County Courthouse
401 North Second Street
Pottsville, PA 17901-2528
(570) 628-1481 (Recorder, First Floor); (570)
628-1270 (Prothonotary, First Floor); (570)
628-1382 (Register, First Floor); (570) 628-
1384 FAX (Register)
http://www.co.schuylkill.pa.us
A. Matthew Dudish, Recorder of Deeds; Peter J.
Symons, Jr., Prothonotary; George A. Uritis,
Register of Wills and Clerk of the Orphans'
Court
(births and deaths from 1893 to 1905, marriages
from 1885 to date, wills from 1811 to date,
estates [minors' and decedents', indexed from
1888 to date], Orphans' Court proceedings
[indexed from 1888 to date])
copies of land records: $8.00; certified copies of
vital records: $4.00 each for births, $3.00 each
for deaths and marriages, plus SASE; copies
of probate records: 50¢ per page

Snyder County
organized 1855 from Union County

Snyder County Courthouse
(9 West Market Street—location)
PO Box 217 (mailing address)
Middleburg, PA 17842
(570) 837-4224 (Register and Recorder); (570)
837-4202 (Prothonotary); (570) 837-4299
FAX (Register and Recorder)
hkreamer@snydercounty.org;
prothonotary@snydercounty.org
http://www.snydercounty.org
Harvey J. Kreamer, Jr., Register and Recorder;
Teresa J. Berger, Prothonotary and Clerk of
Courts
(land records from 1855 with Recorder of
Deeds, births and deaths from 1893 to 1905
inclusive, marriages from 1885 with
Prothonotary, probate records from 1855
with Register of Wills)
no probate search service; copies of probate
records: 50¢ each for regular-sized copies,
$1.00 each for oversized copies, no minimum

Somerset County
organized 1795 from Bedford County

Somerset County Courthouse
111 East Union Street
Somerset, PA 15501
(814) 445-1547 (Recorder, Suite 400); (814) 445-
1428 (Prothonotary, Suite 190); (814) 445-
1435 (Clerk of Courts, Suite 180); (814) 445-
1548 (Register, Suite 170); (814) 445-1563
FAX (Recorder); (814) 444-9270 FAX
(Prothonotary); (814) 445-1542 FAX
(Register)
brantp@co.somerset.pa.us;

prothonotary@co.somerset.pa.us;
ackermans@co.somerset.pa.us
http://www.co.somerset.pa.us
Patricia Brant, Recorder of Deeds; Angie
Svonavec, Prothonotary; Mary Dinning, Clerk
of Courts; Sharon Ackerman, Register of
Wills and Clerk of Orphans' Court
(land records with Recorder of Deeds,
naturalization records with Prothonotary,
births and deaths from 1893 to 1906 [a few
for 1907 and 1908], marriages from 10
October 1885 to date with Register of Wills,
probate records from 1795 to date with
Register of Wills)
probate search service: no charge; copies of
probate records: 50¢ each, $5.00 for certified
copies, plus SASE

Sullivan County
organized 1847 from Lycoming County

Sullivan County Courthouse
Main and Muncy Streets
Laporte, PA 18626
(570) 946-7351
register_recorder@sullivancounty-pa.us;
fdoyle@sullivancounty-pa.us
http://www.sullivancounty-
pa.us/courthouse.html
Francine Doyle, Recorder of Deeds,
Prothonotary/Clerk of Courts, and Register
of Wills

Susquehanna County
organized 1810 from Luzerne County

Susquehanna County Courthouse
(11 Maple Street—location)
PO Box 218 (mailing address)
Montrose, PA 18801
(717) 278-4600, ext. 110 (Recorder and
Register); (570) 278-4600 ext. 198 (Historical
Records); (570) 278-2963 FAX (Recorder and
Register)
http://www.susqco.com
Mary F. Evans, Recorder of Deeds and Register
of Wills; Marilyn Holly, Prothonotary and
Clerk of Courts; Shari Whitney, Historical
Records
(deeds from 1810, mortgages from 1813 with
Recorder's Office, naturalization records with
Prothonotary, births and deaths from 1893 to
1906, marriages from 1885 with Recorder's
Office, probate records from 1810 with
Recorder's Office)
no land records search service ("need a first
name when looking up deeds and mortgages,
also an approximate year"); probate search
service: $5.00; copies of probate records:
$2.00 per page

Tioga County
organized 26 March 1804 from Lycoming
County [townships and dates of organization:
Tioga from Lycoming 1808; Delmar from
Lycoming 1808; Deerfield from Delmar 1814;
Elkland from Delmar 1814; Covington from
Tioga, February 1815; Jackson from Tioga,
September 1815; Sullivan from Covington,
February 1816; Lawrence from Tioga and
Elkland, December 1816; Charleston from
Delmar, December 1820; Westfield from
Deerfield, December 1821; Middlebury from
Delmar and Elkland, September 1822; Liberty
from Delmar and Covington, February 1823;
Shippen from Delmar, February 1823;
Richmond from Covington, February 1824;
Morris from Delmar, September 1824;
Rutland from Jackson and Sullivan, February
1828; Chatham from Deerfield, February
1828; Farmington from Elkland, February
1830; Union from Sullivan, February 1830;
Gaines from Shippen, March 1838; Bloss
from Covington, June 1841; Clymer (formerly
Middlebury) from Westfield and Gaines,
December 1850; Ward from Sullivan and
Union, February 1852; Elk from Delmar and
Morris, February 1856; Osceola from Elkland,

December 1854; Nelson from Elkland,
December 1857; Hamilton from Bloss,
December 1872; Duncan from Delmar,
Charleston and Morris, December 1873;
Brookfield from Westfield 1827; Putnam
from Covington Township and Borough 1
October 1918; boroughs and dates: Wellsboro
from Delmar, May 1830; Lawrenceville from
Lawrence, May 1831; Covington from
Covington Township, May 1831; Elkland
from Elkland Township, May 1831; Knoxville
from Deerfield, May 1850; Mansfield from
Richmond, February 1857; Mainesburg from
Sullivan, February 1859; Tioga from Tioga
Township, February 1860; Fall Brook from
Ward, August 1864; Westfield from Westfield
Township, January 1867; Blossburg from
Bloss, August 1871; Roseville from Rutland,
August 1876; Nelson from Nelson Township;
Osceola from Osceola Township, November
1882; Liberty from Liberty Township, July
1893]

Tioga County Courthouse
116-118 Main Street
Wellsboro, PA 16901-1410
(570) 724-9260 (Register and Recorder, First
Floor); (570) 724-9281 (Prothonotary, First
Floor); (570) 724-9286 FAX (Prothonotary)
http://www.tiogacountypa.us
Jane Wetherbee, Recorder of Deeds
(deeds from 1807, mortgages from 1812
Register of Deeds, Recorder of Wills, and
Clerk of Orphans Court, naturalization
records with Prothonotary, births and deaths
from 1893 to 1905, marriage licenses from
1885 with Register and Recorder, wills and
administrations from 1806 with Register and
Recorder)
land and vital records search service: $5.00 per
surname; probate search service from Tioga
County Historical Society: $40.00 per
surname (includes grantee and grantor deeds
index 1807-1874, wills and administrations
1807-1880, orphans court 1807-1880, alien
records 1813-1903, marriage licenses 1885-
1905, and births and deaths 1893-1905);
probate search servide from Register and
Recorder: $5.00 per name; copies of land
records: $2.00 per page, $1.50 for
certification; copies of vital records: $7.00
each; copies of probate records: $7.00 for the
first certified page and $3.00 for each
additional certified page

Union County
organized 1813 from Northumberland County

Union County Courthouse
103 South Second Street
Lewisburg, PA 17837-1903
(570) 524-8761 (Register); (570) 524-8753
(Prothonotary/Clerk of Courts)
tschrawder@unionco.org;
lrichards@unionco.org
http://www.seda-
cog.org/union/site/default.asp
Teresa S. Schrawder, Acting Register of Deeds;
Linda Richards, Prothonotary/Clerk of
Courts
(grantor/grantee records with Register,
naturalization records from 1813 to 1956 with
Prothonotary, births and deaths from 1893 to
1905, marriage licenses from 1885 with Clerk
of the Orphans Court, wills and letters of
administration with Register)
probate search service: $5.00; copies of probate
records: $1.00 per page, $5.00 minimum
(includes search), plus LSASE

Venango County
organized 1800 from Allegheny and Lycoming
counties

Venango County Courthouse
(1174 Elk Street—location)
PO Box 831 (mailing address)
Franklin, PA 16323
(814) 432-9539 (Register and Recorder, First

Floor); (814) 432-9577 (Prothonotary, First
Floor); (814) 432-9569 FAX (Register and
Recorder)
sbuchanan@co.venango.pa.us;
pmiller@co.venango.pa.us
http://www.co.venango.pa.us/home/index.htm
Sue A. Buchanan, Register and Recorder; Peggy
L. Miller, Prothonotary and Clerk of Courts
(land records from 1805 with Register of Wills,
Recorder of Deeds, Clerk of Orphans Court
Division, naturalization records from 1806 to
1929 with Prothonotary and Clerk of Courts,
births and deaths from 1893 through 1905
inclusive, marriages from 1 October 1885
with Register of Wills, Recorder of Deeds,
Clerk of Orphans Court Division, probate
records from 1805 with Register of Wills,
Recorder of Deeds, Clerk of Orphans Court
Division)
probate search service (cost determined by
amount and kind of work to be done); copies
of probate records: 50¢ per page plus postage,
no minimum

Warren County
organized 1800 from Allegheny and Lycoming
counties

Warren County Courthouse
204 Fourth Street
Warren, PA 16365-2318
(814) 728-3430 (Register-Recorder); (814) 728-
3440 (Prothonotary)
lbimber@warren-county.net; skosinski@warren-
county.net
http://www.warren-county.net
Lori Bimber, Register of Wills and Recorder of
Deeds; Susan Kosinski, Prothonotary and
Clerk of the Courts
(land records from 1819 with Recorder of
Deeds, naturalization records from 1847 to
1969 with Prothonotary, vital records from
1893 through 1905 with Clerk of Orphans
Court, probate records from 1819 with
Register of Wills)
probate search service: $5.00; copies of probate
records: $1.00 per page ("must be paid in
advance with SASE for return of papers")

Washington County
organized 28 March 1781 from Westmoreland
County

Washington County Courthouse
1 South Main Street
Washington, PA 15301
(724) 228-6770 (Prothonotary, Suite 1001); (724)
228-6787 (Clerk of Courts, Suite 1005); (724)
228-6775 (Register, Suite 1002)
http://www.co.washington.pa.us
Phyllis Ranko-Matheny, Prothonotary; Barbara
Gibbs, Clerk of Courts; Kathleen Flynn Reda,
Register of Wills
births and deaths 1893–1906, marriage records
from 1885, estate records from 1785 from
Register of Wills)
Register of Wills search service: $10.00 plus
SASE

Washington County Recorder of Deeds
100 West Beau Street, Room 204
Washington, PA 15301
(724) 228-6806; (724) 228-6737 FAX
recorder@sgi.net
http://www.co.washington.pa.us
Deborah "Debbie" Bardella
copies of land records (by mail/phone): $10.00
per document

Wayne County
organized 1798 from Northampton County

Wayne County Courthouse
925 Court Street
Honesdale, PA 18431-1996
(717) 253-5970, ext. 4040 (Recorder of Deeds,
Annex); (570) 253-5970, ext. 4030
(Prothonotary, Second Floor Annex)
http://www.co.wayne.pa.us

Ginger Golden, Recorder of Deeds and Register of Wills; Edward "Ned" Sandercock, Prothonotary and Clerk of Courts
(land records from 1798 with Register and Recorder, naturalization records from 1798 through 1956 with Prothonotary and Clerk of Courts, vital records from 1893 to 1906 with Prothonotary and Clerk of Courts, probate records from 1798 with Register and Recorder)
no probate search service; copies of probate records: 50¢ per page, no minimum; "Some records are missing due to a flood"

Westmoreland County
organized 1773 from Bedford County

Westmoreland County Courthouse
2 North Main Street
Greensburg, PA 15601
(724) 830-3518 (Recorder, Suite 503); (724) 830-3502 (Prothonotary, Suite 501); 0-3734 (Clerk of Courts, Suite 203); (724) 830-3177 (Register, Suite 301); (724) 850-3979 FAX (Clerk of Courts); (724) 850-3976 FAX (Register)
wcclkcrt@co.westmoreland.pa.us; ekeim@co.westmoreland.pa.us
http://www.co.westmoreland.pa.us
Thomas "Tom" Murphy, Recorder of Deeds; Ronald "Ron" Diehl, Prothonotary; David L. "Dave" Patterson, Clerk of Courts; Earl S. Keim, II, Register of Wills
(land records from 1773 with Recorder of Deeds; copies and dockets for naturalization cases from 20 September 1902 to 20 January 1907, petitions from 1874 to date, and a group of volumes listing immigrants and their naturalizations in alphabetical order with Prothonotary; births and deaths from 1893 to 1905, marriages from 1885 to date, probate records from 1773 to date with Register of Wills Office)
probate search service: $3.00 minimum per will (must have both first and last names, and approximate date); copies of naturalization records: $2.00 per page; certified copies of vital records: $5.00 each; copies of probate records: 50¢ per page plus postage

Wyoming County
organized 1842 from Luzerne County (consists of the eighteen townships of Braintrim, Clinton, Eaton, Exeter, Falls, Forkston, Lemon, Mehoopany, Meshoppen, Monroe, Nicholson, North Branch, Northmoreland, Noxen, Overfield, Tunkhannock, Washington, and Windham)

Wyoming County Courthouse
1 Courthouse Square
Tunkhannock, PA 18657-1216
(717) 836-3200, exts. 232, 233, 234, 299 (Prothonotary)
http://www.pacounties.org/wyoming/site/default.asp
Paulette A. Burnside, Prothonotary, Clerk of Courts, and Clerk of Orphans' Court

York County
organized 1749 from Lancaster County

York County Administrative Center
28 East Market Street
York, PA 17401-1590
(717) 771-9644 (Recorder of Deeds); (717) 771-9582 FAX (Recorder of Deeds); (717) 771-9675; (717) 771-9727 (County Archives); (717) 771-9607 (Register of Wills)
http://www.york-county.org
Randi L. Reisinger, Recorder of Deeds
(land records with Recorder of Deeds)
no probate search service; copies of probate records: $1.00 per page, no minimum

York County Judicial Center
45 North George Street
York, PA 17401
(717) 771-9611 (Prothonotary); (717) 771-9612

(Clerk of Courts); (717) 771-9607 (Register, Second Floor); (717) 771-9096 FAX (Clerk of Courts); (717) 771-4678 FAX (Register)
http://www.york-county.org/prothonotary.html; http://www.york-county.org/clerkofcourts.html
Pamela S. Lee, Prothonotary; Don O'Shell, Clerk of Courts; Bradley C. Jacobs, Register of Wills
(vital records with Orphans Court and Register of Wills, probate records with Register of Wills)

Rhode Island 247

RHODE ISLAND

Capital: Providence. Statehood: 29 May 1790 (officially called Rhode Island and Providence Plantations, chartered 1663)

Rhode Island has Municipal Courts of limited jurisdiction.

District Courts sit in places designated by the chief judge and hear some civil actions, small claims, mental health matters, housing code violations, misdemeanors, felony arraignments and administrative agency appeals.

Note that town records, vital records, probate records, and land records are not held at the county level. The Supreme Court Judicial Records Center has some early court and naturalization records.

Supreme Court Judicial Records Center
5 Hill Street
Pawtucket, RI 02860
(401) 721-2640
archives@courts.state.ri.us
http://www.courts.state.ri.us/records/defaultrecords.htm
(civil cases 1671–1900, criminal cases 1671–1900, divorces 1749-1900, naturalization papers 1793–1974)

Bristol County
organized 1747 from Newport County; includes the towns of Barrington (formed 1717 from Massachusetts as part of Warren in 1747, reestablished as Barrington 1770), Bristol (formed 1681 from Massachusetts), and Warren (formed 1747 from the Massachusetts towns of Barrington, Swansea, and Rehoboth, added part from Bristol in 1873), plus the locations of Annawomscutt, Bay Spring, Beach Terrace, Bristol Highlands, Coggeshall, East Warren, Laurel Park, Nayatt, Peck Corner, Touisset, Touisset Highlands, and West Barrington

District Court
Sixth Division
(see Providence County)

Kent County
organized 1750 from Washington County; includes the city of Warwick (founded 1642, an original town, called Shawomet until 1648, city incorporated 1931), the towns of Coventry (incorporated 1741 from Warwick), East Greenwich, formed 1677, called Dedford from 1686 to 1689), West Greenwich (incorporated 1741 from East Greenwich), and West Warwick (incorporated November 1913 from Warwick), plus the locations of Anthony, Apponaug, Arctic, Arkwright, Bartons Corner, Bayside, Birch Hill (historical), Buttonwoods, Centerville, Chepiwanoxet, Clyde, Coles, Colvintown, Conimicut, Cooks Corner, Cowesett, Crompton, East Natick, Escoheag, Fairbanks Corner, Folly Landing, Frenchtown, Frys Corner, Gortons Corner, Greene, Greenwood, Harris, Highland Beach, Hillsgrove, Hopkins Hollow, Hoxsie, Kettle Corner, Kitts Corner, Lakewood, Lincoln Park, Lippitt, Longmeadow, Meadow View, Mishnock, Moosehorn Corner, Natick, Nausauket, Nichols Corner, Nooseneck, Norwood, Oakland Beach, Palace Garden, Phenix, Places Corner, Pontiac, Potowomut, Potterville, Quidnick, Rice City, River Point, River View, Rocky Point, Shawomet, Shippee Corner, Silver Hook, Spencers Corner, Spring Green, Spring Lake, Tarbox Corner, Vaughn Hollow, Washington, Westcott, and Wildes Corner

District Court
Third Division
Kent County Court House, 222 Quaker Lane

Warwick, RI 02886-0107
(401) 822-1771
http://www.courts.state.ri.us/district/divisions.
htm
(serves Coventry, East Greenwich, Warwick, West Greenwich, and West Warwick)

Newport County

organized 1703, original county; includes the cities of Newport (town initially incorporated 1639) and Portsmouth (town initially incorporated 1638) and the towns of Jamestown (incorporated 1678, Indian name Conanicut), Little Compton (incorporated 1682, from Massachusettes in 1747), Middletown (incorporated 1743 from Newport), and Tiverton (founded 1694, incorporated from Massachusetts 1747), plus the locations of Adamsville, Bliss Corners, Brenton Village, Bridgeport (historical), Bristol Ferry, Clarks Village, Conanicut Park, Eagleville, Grayville, Hamiltons Corner, Homestead, Island Park, Jamestown, Jamestown Shores, Lawtons, Melville, North Tiverton, Pottersville, Purgatory, Rockville, Sachuest, Sakonnet, South Portsmouth, Whitehall, Wightmans Corner, Woods Corner

District Court
Second Division
Murray Judicial Complex
45 Washington Square
Newport, RI 02840
(401) 841-8350
http://www.courts.state.ri.us/district/divisions.
htm
(serves Jamestown, Little Compton, Middletown, Newport, Portsmouth, and Tiverton)

Providence County

organized 1703, original county; includes the cities of Central Falls (incorporated 1895 from Lincoln), Cranston (incorporated 1754 from Providence), East Providence (founded 1862, incorporated 1863 from Massachusetts, originally Rehoboth, then Seekonk), Pawtucket (formed 1828, incorporated 1862 from Massachusetts 1862, part from North Providence 1874), Providence (incorporated 1636, an original town), and Woonsocket (incorporated 1867 from part of Cumberland, part from Smithfield in 1871), and the towns of Burrillville (incorporated 1806 from Glocester), Cumberland (incorporated 1747 from Massachusetts, formerly Attleborough), Foster (incorporated 1781 from Scituate), Glocester (incorporated 1731 from Providence), Johnston (incorporated 1759 from Providence), Lincoln (incorporated 1871 from Smithfield), North Providence (incorporated 1765 from Providence), North Smithfield (incorporated 1871 from Smithfield), Scituate (incorporated 1731 from Providence), and Smithfield (incorporated 1731 from Providence), plus the locations of Abbott Run, Albion, Allendale, Arlington, Armington Corner, Arnold Mills, Ashland (historical), Ashton, Auburn, Bellefonte, Berkeley, Bishop Heights, Branch Village, Bridgeton, Carpenters Corner, Centerdale, Chepachet, Cherry Valley, Chopmist, Clarkville, Clayville, Comstock Gardens, Cumberland, Cumberland Hill, Darlington, Diamond Hill, Dryden Heights, Dyerville, East Providence Center, Edgewood, Elmdale (historical), Elmwood, Esmond, Fairlawn, Federal Hill, Fiskeville, Foresdale, Fountain Spring, Fruit Hill, Garden City, Gazzaville, Geneva, Georgiaville, Glendale, Globe, Graniteville, Grants Mills, Greenville, Greystone, Hamlet, Harmony, Harrisdale, Harrisville, Hope, Hopkins Mills, Hughesdale, Huntsville, Jackson, Kent (historical), Kent Corner, KKnightsville, Leonard Corner, Lime Rock, Lippitt Estate, Lonsdale, Luther Corner, Lymansville, Manton, Manville, Mapleville, Marieville, Merino, Meshanticut,

Mohegan, Mooseup Valley, Narragansett Terrace, Nasonville, North Foster, North Scituate, Oak Valley, Oakland, Oaklawn, Olneyville, Pascoag, Pawtuxet, Phillipsdale, Pocasset, Ponaganset (historical), Primrose, Quinnville, Richmond (historical), Riverside, Rockland (historical), Round Top, Rumford, Saundersville, Sayles Bleachery, Saylesville, Saylesville Highlands, Silver Spring, Simmons Corner, Simmonsville, Slatersville, Social, Sockanosset, South Foster, South Scituate (historical), Spragueville, Spring Grove, Stillwater, Tarkiln, Union Village, Valley Falls, Vernon, Vue de l'eau, Waldron Corners, Wanskuck, Waterford, Wayland, West Gloucester, West Greenville, Whipple, Woodlawn, and Woodville

District Court
Sixth Division
Joseph Garrahy Judicial Complex, 1 Dorrance Plaza
Providence, RI 02903-2719
(401) 458-5400
http://www.courts.state.ri.us/district/divisions.
htm
(serves Barrington, Bristol, and Warren, Bristol County, and Burrillville, Central Falls, Cranston, Cumberland, East Providence, Foster, Gloucester, Johnston, Lincoln, North Providence, North Smithfield, Pawtucket, Providence, Scituate, Smithfield, and Woonsocket, Providence County)

Providence Probate Court
City Hall, 25 Dorrance Street, Fifth Floor
Providence, RI 02903
(401) 421-7740, ext. 307; (401) 861-6208 FAX
http://www.providenceri.com/probate
Paul V. Jabour, Esq., Clerk

Washington County

organized 1729 from Newport County; includes Block Island
(incorporated 1661 as the Town of New Shoreham, established 1664 as Block Island and admitted to the colony, originally part of Newport County) and the towns of Charlestown (incorporated 1738 from Westerly), Exeter (incorporated 1742/3 from North Kingstown), Hopkinton (incorporated 1757 from Westerly), Narragansett (town incorporated 22 March 1888, formed 1901 from South Kingstown), North Kingstown (formed 1641, incorporated as Kingstown 1674, called Rochester 1686–1689, known as North Kingstown after 1723), Richmond (incorporated 1747 from Charlestown), South Kingstown (incorporated 1723 from Kingstown when divided North and South), and Westerly (incorporated 1669, called Haversham 1686–1689), plus the locations of Allenton, Alton, Annaquatucket, Arcadia, Ashaway, Avondale, Barberville, Belleville, Bethel, Black Plain, Bonnet Shores, Bradford, Bridgetown, Brudickville, Canonchet, Carolina, Centerville, Charlestown Beach, Cold Spring Beach, Columbia Heights, Curtis Corner, Davisville, Dunn Corner, Dunn Landing, Ellis Flats, Elmhurst, Fisherville, Fort Ninigret, Galilee, Glen Rock, Gould, Green Hill, Hamilton, Haversham, Hillsdale, Hope Valley, Indian Lake Shores, Isaacs Corner, Jerusalem, Kenyon, Kiefer Park, Kingston, Kingston Station, Lafayette, Langworthy Corner, Liberty, Locustville, Matunuck, McGowan Corners, Millville, Misquamicut, Mooresfield, Moscow, Mount View, Narragansett Beach, Narragansett Pier, New Shoreham Center, North Quidnessett, Old Harbor Landing, Peace Dale, Perryville, Pettaquamscutt Lake Shores, Pine Hill, Plum Beach, Point Judith, Potter Hill, Quidnessett, Quonochontaug, Quonochontaug Beach, Rocky Brook, Rodman Crossing (historical), Saunderstown, Scarborough Hills, Seaweed Beach, Shady Harbor, Shannock, Shelter Harbor, Shore Acres, Slocum, Snug Harbor, South Hopkinton, Stillmanville, Tripps

Corner, Tuckertown, Tuckertown Four Corners, Tug Hollow, Usquepaug, Wakefield, Weekapaug, Weekapaug Beach, West Kingston, White Rock, Wickford, Wood River Junction, Woodville, and Wyoming

District Court
Fourth Division
McGrath Judicial Complex
4800 Tower Hill Road
Wakefield, RI 02879
(401) 783-5441
http://www.courts.state.ri.us/district/divisions.
htm
(naturalization records; serves Charlestown, Exeter, Hopkinton, Narragansett, New Shoreham, North Kingstown, Richmond, South Kingstown, and Westerly)

SOUTH CAROLINA

Capital: Columbia. Statehood: 23 May 1788 (included in the Carolina Grant of 1663, ceded western lands in 1787)

South Carolina's Municipal Courts have limited jurisdiction to try offenses for which the penalty is under $200 or thirty days imprisonment. Over three hundred Magistrate Courts have jurisdiction over civil matters under $1,000 and criminal matters similar to the Municipal Courts. Probate Courts in each county handle estates, guardianships, and mental health issues. Family Court sits at each county seat and has jurisdiction over marriage, divorce, custody, support, etc. South Carolina's Circuit Court has general jurisdiction and sits in each county seat. First Judicial Circuit: Calhoun, Dorchester and Orangeburg counties; Second: Aiken, Bamberg and Barnwell counties; Third: Clarendon, Lee, Sumter and Williamsburg counties; Fourth: Chesterfield, Darlington, Dillon and Marlboro counties; Fifth: Kershaw and Richland counties; Sixth: Chester, Fairfield and Lancaster counties; Seventh: Cherokee and Spartanburg counties; Eighth: Abbeville, Greenwood, Laurens and Newberry counties; Ninth: Berkeley and Charleston counties; Tenth: Anderson and Oconee counties; Eleventh: Edgefield, Lexington, McCormick and Saluda counties; Twelfth: Florence and Marion counties; Thirteenth: Greenville and Pickens counties; Fourteenth: Allendale, Beaufort, Colleton, Hampton and Jasper counties; Fifteenth: Georgetown and Horry counties; Sixteenth: Union and York counties. Its judicial circuits are the same as those for the Family Courts. A Court of Appeals and Supreme Court hear appeals.

In 1683 three "counties" were laid out in South Carolina: Berkeley, Colleton and Craven counties. Carteret (later changed to Granville) was added somewhat later. However, no records were kept in the counties. In 1706 "parishes" took the place of the former counties. In 1768 the area was divided into seven "judicial districts": Beaufort, Camden, Charles Town, Cheraws, George Town, Ninety Six and Orangeburg. Pickney and Washington districts were added in 1793. In 1798 the nine districts were divided into twenty-four. Beaufort District: no change; Camden District: Chester, Fairfield, Kershaw, Lancaster, Sumter and York; Charles Town District: Charlestown and Colleton; Cheraws District: Chesterfield, Darlington and Marlborough; Georgetown District: George Town and Marion; Ninety Six District: Abbeville, Edgefield, Greenville, Laurens, Newberry, Pendleton, Spartanburg and Union; Orangeburg District: Barnwell and Orangeburg. Between 1800 and 1858 Richland was taken from Kershaw, Williamsburg from Georgetown, Horry from Georgetown, Lexington from Orangeburg, Anderson and Pickens from Pendleton, and Clarendon from Sumter. Some of these districts had been organized as "counties" within their parent districts prior to being formally designated as districts in their own right. In 1868 all districts were renamed counties.

Abbeville County Courthouse
102 Court Square
Abbeville, SC 29620
(864) 366-5312, ext. 55 (Clerk, Room 103, PO Box 99); (864) 366-5312, ext. 62 (Probate, Room 102, PO Box 70); (864) 366-9188 FAX (Clerk); (864) 366-4023 FAX (Probate)
emily.McMahan@abbevillecounty.sc.gov
http://www.abbevillecountysc.com; http://www.sccounties.org/counties/abbeville.htm
Emily Y. McMahan, Clerk of Court; Charles M. Sumner, Probate Judge
(land records from 1873 to date [older records burned while in storage] with Clerk of Court,

plats from 1780 to 1788 from the Old Ninety-Six District collection with Probate Court, 29620, marriages from 1911 to date with Probate Court, wills from 1776 to date; inventories and accounts from 1783)
no vital records search service (must have name of groom, maiden name of bride and year of marriage); probate search service: $5.00 for out-of-state requests (send LSASE for price quote); copies of land records from Clerk of Court: send LSASE for price quote; copies of plats: $2.00 each on 11" x 17" sheets; copies of vital records: $5.00 each; copies of probate records: 50¢ per side plus $1.50 handling for each file, pack or volume

Aiken County
organized 1871 from Edgefield County

Aiken County Probate Court
(Judicial Center, Room E126, 109 Park Avenue SW, Aiken, SC 29801—location)
PO Box 1576 (mailing address)
Aiken, SC 29802-1576
(803) 642-2001
probatecourt@aikencountysc.gov
http://www.aikencountysc.gov
(marriage licenses from 1904 and probate records from 1904, estates with Probate Judge)
no probate search service; copies of probate records: 25¢ per page, $1.00 for certification

Aiken County Register Mesne Conveyance
828 Richland Avenue West, Room 100
Aiken, SC 29802
(803) 642-2072
http://www.aikencountysc.gov
(land records online from 1990)

Allendale County
organized 1919 from Barnwell and Hampton counties

Allendale County Courthouse
292 Barnwell Highway
Allendale, SC 29810
(803) 584-2737 (Clerk of Court, PO Box 126); (803) 584-5157 (Probate Judge PO Box 603); (803) 584-7046 FAX (Clerk of Court)
esabb@bellsouth.net;
bbennett@allendalecounty.com
http://www.allendalecounty.com
Elaine Sabb, Clerk of Court; Brenda Bennett, Probate Judge

Anderson County
organized 1826 from Pendleton District, which was abolished at that time

Anderson County Courthouse
(100 South Main Street, Anderson, SC 29621—location)
PO Box 8002 (mailing address)
Anderson, SC 29622
(864) 260-4054 (Register); (864) 260-4049 (Probate); (864) 260-4443 FAX (Register); (864) 260-4811 FAX (Probate)
mnewton@andersoncountysc.org
http://www.andersoncountysc.org
Shirley McElhannon, Register of Deeds; Martha Newton, Probate Judge

Bamberg County
organized 1897 from Barnwell County

Bamberg County Courthouse
Bamberg, SC 29003
(803) 245-3025 (Clerk, PO Box 150); (803) 245-3008 (Probate, PO Box 180); (803) 245-3027 FAX
http://www.sccounties.org/counties/Bamberg.htm
James B. Hiers, Clerk of Court; Nancy H. Green, Probate Judge
(land records from 1897; probate records)
copies of land records: 50¢ per page, $2.00 for certification

Barnwell County
organized 1798 from Orangeburg District

Barnwell County Courthouse
(57 Wall Street—location)
PO Box 723 (mailing address)
Barnwell, SC 29812-0723
(803) 541-1020 (Clerk); (803) 541-1031 (Probate, Room 112)
GFK@barnewellsc.com;
bcedc@barnwellsc.com
http://www.barnwellcountysc.com
George Fickling, Jr., Clerk of Court; Dale M. Gable, Probate Judge
(land records with Courthouse, probate records with Probate Court)
probate search service: no charge; copies of probate records: 50¢ per page

Beaufort County
organized 1764, original district

Beaufort County Probate Court
(102 Ribaut Road—location)
PO Box 1083 (mailing address)
Beaufort, SC 29901
(843) 470-5319; (843) 470-5324 FAX
judgefms@bcgov.net
http://www.sccourts.org/probate/index.cfm?fuseaction=countyno=7
Francis M. "Frank" Simon, Probate Judge

Beaufort County Register of Deeds
(100 Ribaut Road, Room 205—location)
PO Drawer 1197 (mailing address)
Beaufort, SC 29902
(843) 470-2705 (Research Clerk); (843) 470-2709 FAX
maryl@bcgov.net
http://www.bcgov.net/Reg_Deed/ROD.php
Mary Lamie, Research Clerk
land records search service: $7.00 per half hour plus 50¢ per page for copies and postage; certified copies $1.00 plus 50¢ per page and search fee

Berkeley County
organized 1882 from Charleston County, which was formerly Charlestown District

Berkeley County Probate Court
300 California Avenue
Moncks Corner, SC 29461
(843) 719-4519
http://www.co.berkeley.sc.us
Keith W. Kornahrens, Probate Judge
(marriages, wills and estates, guardianships and conservatorships)

Berkeley County Register of Deeds
(1003 Highway 52—location)
PO Box 6122 (mailing address)
Moncks Corner, SC 29461-6120
(843) 719-4084; (843) 719-4851 FAX
http://www.co.berkeley.sc.us
Cynthia B. Forte, Register
(deeds, mortgages and liens from 1882)

Calhoun County
organized 1908 from Lexington County

Calhoun County Courthouse
302 FR Huff Drive
St. Matthews, SC 29135
(803) 874-3524 (Clerk of Court, PO Box 709); (803) 874-3514 (Probate Judge,); (803) 874-1242 FAX
http://www.calhouncountychamber.org; http://www.sccounties.org/counties/calhoun.htm
Ken Hasty, Clerk of Court; Frederick Robinson, Probate Judge
(land records and marriage licenses with Clerk of Court, probate records with Probate Court)
no probate search service; certified copies of marriage licenses: $2.00 each; copies of probate records: 25¢ per page

Charleston County

organized 1769, as Charles Town and later Charlestown, an original district

Charleston County Probate Court
Judicial Center
100 Broad Street
Charleston, SC 29401
(843) 958-5180 (Commitment Division, Suite 469); (843) 958-5183 (Marriage License Division, Suite 469); (843) 958-5191 FAX
http://www.charlestoncounty.org

Charleston County Probate Court
Estate Division
Historic Courthouse
84 Broad Street, Third Floor
Charleston, SC 29401
(843) 958-5030; (843) 958-5044 FAX
irvcondon@charlestoncounty.org
http://www.charlestoncounty.org
Irvin Condon, Probate Judge

Charleston County Register of Mesne Conveyance
O. T. Wallace County Office Building
101 Meeting Street, Room 201
Charleston, SC 29402
(843) 958-4800; (843) 958-4803 FAX
publicinfo@charlestoncounty.org
http://www.charlestoncounty.org
Charlie Lybrand, Register

Cherokee County

organized 1897 from Union and York counties

Cherokee County Courthouse
Administration Building
210 North Limestone Street
Gaffney, SC 29342
(864) 487-2574 (Clerk of Court); (864) 487-2584 (Probate Clerk); (864) 902-8426 FAX (Probate Court)
lynne.price@cherokeecountysc.com
http://delisac.web.aplus.net/cherokeecounty southcarolina
Brandy McBee, Clerk of Court; Lynne Price, Probate Clerk
(land records from the 1700s, births and deaths from 1853, marriages from the 1700s, probate records from the 1700s)
copies of land records, vital records and probate records: $1.50 for the first two pages and $1.00 for each additional page

Chester County

organized 1785 from Camden District

Chester County Courthouse
(140 Main Street—location)
PO Box 580 (mailing address)
Chester, SC 29706-0580
(803) 385-2605 (Clerk of Court); (803) 385-2604 (Probate); (803) 581-5180 FAX (Probate)
scarpenter@chestercounty.org; lroddey@chestercounty.org
http://www.chestercounty.org
Sue K. Carpenter, Clerk of Court; Lois H. Roddey, Probate Judge
(land records and naturalization records with Clerk of Court, marriage records from 1911 and probate records from the late 1780s)
no probate search service; copies of probate records: 50¢ per page

Chesterfield County

organized 1798 from Cheraws District

Chesterfield County Courthouse
200 West Main Street
Chesterfield, SC 29709
(843) 623-2574 (Clerk, PO Box 529); (843) 623-2376 (Probate)
clerkofcc@shtc.net; pcourt@shtc.net
http://www.sccounties.org/counties/ Chesterfield.htm
Faye Sellers, Clerk of Court; Edwin Davis, Probate Judge
(deeds and mortgages with Clerk's Office, probate records with Probate Judge's Office)

Clarendon County

organized 1855 from Sumter District

Clarendon County Courthouse
3 West Keitt Street
Manning, SC 29102
(803) 435-4443 (Clerk, PO Box 136); (803) 435-4444 (Register Mesne Conveyance); (803) 435-8774 (Probate, PO Box 307); (803) 435-4844 FAX (Clerk)
clerkofcourt@sc.rr.com; clarendonrmc@ sc.rr.com; clarendonprobate@sc.rr.com
http://www.clarendoncounty.sc.gov
Beulah G. Roberts, Clerk of Court; Linda Ard, Register Mesne Conveyance); Barney Lee Morris, Probate Judge
(land records, naturalization records, vital records, probate records)

Colleton County

organized 1798 from Charleston District

Colleton County Clerk of Court
(Courthouse, 101 Hampton Street—location)
PO Box 620 (mailing address)
Walterboro, SC 29488-0620
(843) 549-5791 (Clerk); (843) 542-2745 (Register); (843) 549-2875 FAX (Clerk); (843) 549-2749 FAX (Register)
pgrant@colletoncounty.org
http://www.colletoncounty.org/legal/clerk.aspx
Patricia C. Grant, Clerk of Court; Regina M. Brown, Office Manager/Register of Deeds
(land records from about 1865 to date with Clerk of Court Office, Register of Deeds Office)
land records search service: no charge; copies of land records: 25¢ each

Colleton County Probate Court
(200 East Washington Street—location)
PO Box 1036 (mailing address)
Walterboro, SC 29488
(843) 549-7216; (843) 549-5571 FAX
ccpj@lowcountry.com
http://www.colletoncounty.org/probate_court/ default.aspx
I. A. Smoak III, Probate Judge

Darlington County

organized 1785 from Cheraws District

Darlington County Courthouse
1 Public Square
Darlington, SC 29532-3213
(843) 398-4330 (Clerk, Room B-4); (843) 398-4310 (Probate, Room 208)
clerk@darcosc.com; jcarter@darcosc.com; mlawson@darcosc.com
http://www.darcosc.com
Scott B. Suggs, Clerk of Court; Marvin I. Lawson, Probate Judge
(land records from 1806 with Clerk of Court, naturalization records from about 1845 to about 1890 with Darlington County Historical Commission, marriages only from 1911 with Probate Judge, probate records from about 1789 with Historical Commission)
probate search service: no charge; copies of probate records: $1.00 for the first page and 50¢ for each additional page, plus $2.50 for mailing first fifty pages, no minimum

Dillon County

organized 1910 from Marion County

Dillon County Courthouse
Dillon, SC 29536
(843) 774-1425 (Clerk of Court, PO Drawer 1220); (843) 774-1423 (Probate, PO Box 189); (843) 774-1443 FAX
dilloncac@bellsouth.net (Clerk)
http://www.sccounties.org/counties/Dillon.htm
Gwen Hyatt, Clerk of Court; S. Kay Turner, Probate Judge
(land records with Clerk of Court, probate records with Probate Court)
probate search service: $1.00 per year; copies of probate records: $5.00, no minimum

Dorchester County

organized 1868 from Ninety Six District

Dorchester County Probate Court
101 Ridge Street
St. George, SC 29477-2443
(843) 832-0105 (Administrative Division); (843) 563-0136 (Estate Division); (843) 563-0105 (Marriage License Division)
dcprobate@msn.com
http://www.dorchestercounty.net/Probate.htm
Tiffany Provence, Probate Judge
probate search service: no charge; copies of probate records: 25¢ per page

Dorchester County Register of Deeds
201 Johnston Street
St. George, SC 29477
(843) 832-0181 voice & FAX
mbailey@dorchestercounty.net
http://www.dorchestercounty.net/RMC/RMC Main.aspx
Margaret Bailey

Edgefield County

organized 1785 from Ninety Six District

Edgefield County Courthouse
129 Courthouse Square
Edgefield, SC 29824
(803) 637-4080 (Clerk, PO Box 34); (803) 637-4076 (Probate, PO Box 45)
admininfo@edgefieldcounty.sc.gov
http://www.edgefieldcounty.sc.gov
Shirley F. Newby, Clerk of Court; Robert E. Peeler, Probate Judge
(land records from 1839 to date; probate records)

Fairfield County

organized 1785 from Camden District

Fairfield County Courthouse
Winnsboro, SC 29180
(803) 712-6526 (Clerk, PO Drawer 299); (803) 712-6519 (Probate, PO Box 385)
prenwick@fairfieldsc.com
http://www.sccounties.org/counties/Fairfield.htm
Betty Jo Beckham, Clerk of Court; Pamela W. Renwick, Probate Judge
(land records, naturalization records, vital records, probate records)
no records search service

Florence County

organized 1888 from Clarendon, Darlington, Marion, and Williamsburg counties

Florence County City-County Complex
180 North Irby Street
Florence, SC 29501-3456
(843) 665-3031 (Clerk); (843) 665-3035 (Probate, MSC-L); (843) 665-3068 FAX
creel-shearin@florenceco.org; keaton@florenceco.org
http://www.florenceco.org
Connie Reel-Shearin, Clerk of Court; Kenneth Eaton, Probate Judge

Georgetown County

organized 1769, original district

Georgetown County Courthouse
129 Screven Street, Room 109
PO Box 421270 (mailing address)
Georgetown, SC 29442-1270
(843) 545-3088 (Registrar, Room 109); (843) 545-3274 (Probate, Room 226)
wmaring@georgetowncountysc.org
http://www.georgetowncountysc.org
Wanda Prevatte, Registrar of Deeds; Waldo Maring, Probate Judge

Greenville County

organized 1798 from Ninety Six District

Greenville County Courthouse
Greenville County Square
301 University Ridge
Greenville, SC 29601

(864) 467-7240 (Register, Suite 1300); (864) 467-7170 (Probate, Suite 1200); (864) 467-7107 FAX (Register)
Dfaulkner@greenvillecounty.org
http://www.greenvillecounty.org
Timothy Nanney, Register of Deeds; Debora Faulkner, Probate Judge
(land records from the 1700s to date; marriage licenses from 1911 to date and probate records from 1800 to date with Probate Court)
copies of land records: 50¢ each

Greenwood County
organized 3 June 1897 from Abbeville and Edgefield counties

Greenwood County Courthouse
528 Monument Street
Greenwood, SC 29646-2643
(864) 942-8546 (Clerk of Court, Room 114); (864) 942-8613 (Register); (864) 942-8625 (Probate, Room 205); (864) 942-8620 FAX (Probate)
franka@co.greenwood.sc.us
http://www.co.greenwood.sc.us
Ingram B. Moon, Clerk of Court; Freda Sartin, Register Mesne Conveyance; Frank Addy, Jr., Probate Judge
(marriage licenses from 1895 and probate records from 1895 with Probate Court)
no vital or probate records search service; certified copies of probate records: $5.00 for the first page and 25¢ for each additional page of the same document, plus at least $1.00 for mailing, no minimum ("fee for copies to precede copies' being mailed")

Hampton County
organized 1878 from Beaufort County

Hampton County Clerk of Court
1 Courthouse Square
Hampton, SC 29924
(803) 943-7510; (803) 943-7596 FAX
mnettles@hamptoncountysc.org; hcclerk@yahoo.com
http://www.hamptoncountysc.org
Mylinda Nettles, Clerk of Court
(land records with Register of Deeds in Clerk of Court office)

Hampton County Probate Court
(B. T. DeLoach Building, 201 Jackson Avenue West—location)
PO Box 601 (mailing address)
Hampton, SC 29924
(803) 914) 2172; (803) 914-2174 FAX
sodom@hamptoncountysc.org; sheilabelle70@yahoo.com
http://www.hamptoncountysc.org
Shelia B. Odom, Probate Judge
(naturalization records and probate records)

Horry County
organized 1802 from Georgetown District

Horry County Government and Justice Center
Justice Wing
1301 Second Avenue
Conway, SC 29526
(843) 915-5080 (Clerk); (843) 915-5370 (Probate, Second Floor, PO Box 288, Conwy, SC 29528); (843) 915-6081 FAX (Clerk); (843) 915-6370 FAX (Probate)
hugginsm@horrycounty.org; edmondsd@horrycounty.org
http://www.horrycounty.org/hcgPortal.asp
Melanie Huggins, Clerk of Court; Deirdre W. Edmonds, Probate Judge
(land records with Register Mesne Conveyance, PO Box 470, Conway, SC 29526, naturalization records with Billie G. Richardson, Clerk of Court, probate records)

Horry County Register of Deeds
(Horry County Government and Justice Center, Government Wing, 1301 Second Avenue—location)

PO Box 470 (mailing address)
Conway, SC 29526
(843) 915-5430; (843) 915-6430 FAX
bskipper@horrycounty.org
http://www.horrycounty.org/depts/finance/register.asp
Ms. Ballery V. Skipper, Director

Jasper County
organized 1912 from Beaufort and Hampton counties

Jasper County Registrar of Deeds
305 Russell Avenue
Ridgeland, SC 29936
(843) 726-7718; (843) 726-5173 FAX
jasperprobatecourt@earthlink.net
http://www.jaspercountysc.org
Joseph N. Malphrus, Jr., Probate Judge

Jasper County Registrar of Deeds
(224 Second Avenue—location)
PO Box 836 (mailing address)
Ridgeland, SC 29936
(843) 726-7755
http://www.jaspercountysc.org
Patsye M. Greene, Registrar

Kershaw County
organized 1798 from Camden District

Kershaw County Probate Court
1121 Broad Street
Camden, SC 29020
(803) 425-1500
http://www.sccounties.org/counties/kershaw.htm
Harriett Pierce, Probate Judge

Kershaw County Register of Deeds
515 Walnut Street, Room 180
Camden, SC 29020
(803) 425-1500
http://www.sccounties.org/counties/kershaw.htm
Billie O. McLeod, Register of Deeds

Lancaster County
organized 1798 from Camden District

Lancaster County Offices
PO Box 1809
Lancaster, SC 29720
(803) 416-9440 (Register, 101 North Main Street); (803) 285-1581 (Clerk, 116 West Dunlap Street); (803) 283-3379 (Probate, Lancaster County Administration Building 101, North Main Street); (803) 283-3370 FAX
fourlane@infoave.net (Register); jhammond@lancastercountysc.net; sandyestridge@lancastercountysc.net
http://www.lancastercountysc.net
John Lane, Register of Deeds; Jeffrey Hammond, Clerk of Court; Sandra Estridge, Probate Judge
(naturalization records with Clerk of Court, probate records from 1860 with Probate Judge)
probate search service: $10.00; copies of probate records: $1.00 per page, $10.00 minimum

Laurens County
organized 1785 from Ninety Six District

Laurens County Courthouse
100 Hillcrest Square
Laurens, SC 29360-0287
(864) 984-3538 (Clerk, Suite B, PO Box 287); (864) 984-7315 (Probate, Suite A, PO Box 194); (864) 984-7023 FAX (Clerk); (864) 984-3779 FAX (Probate)
http://www.laurenscounty.org
Lynn W. Lancaster, Clerk of Court; Ms. Kaye W. Fridy, Probate Judge

Lee County
organized 1902 from Darlington and Kershaw counties

Lee County Courthouse
Courthouse Square
Bishopville, SC 29010

(803) 484-5341 (Clerk, PO Box 387, and Probate, PO Box 24); (803) 484-6512 FAX
charris@leecountysc.org
http://www.sccounties.org/counties/Lee.htm
James I. Davis, Clerk of Court; Catherine Harris, Probate Judge
(land records with Clerk of Court, probate records with Probate Judge)

Lexington County
organized from 1804 Orangeburg District

Lexington County Probate Court
205 East Main Street, Suite 134
Lexington, SC 29072
(803) 785-8324
deckstrom@lex-co.com
http://www.lex-co.com
Daniel Eckstrom, Probate Judge

Lexington County Register of Deeds
(Administration Building, Third Floor—location)
212 South Lake Drive (mailing address)
Lexington, SC 29072
(803) 785-8168 (803) 785-8189 FAX
dgunter@lex-co.com
http://www.lex-co.com
Debra Gunter
copies: 35¢ per page, pluse SASE

Marion County
organized 1800 with boundaries identical with those of Liberty County, created 1798 within Georgetown District

Marion County Courthouse
Marion, SC 29571-0295
(843) 423-8240 (Clerk, PO Box 295); (843) 423-8244 (Probate, PO Box 583); (843) 423-8306 FAX
http://www.co.marion.sc.us; http://www.sccounties.org/counties/marion.htm
Sherry R. Rhodes, Clerk of Court; T. Carroll Atkinson III, Probate Judge

Marlboro County
organized 1798 from Cheraws District

William P. Wallace, Sr. Administration Building
Main Street
Bennettsville, SC 29512
(843) 479-5613 (Clerk, PO Drawer 996); (843) 479-5610 (Probate, PO Box 455); (843) 479-5639 FAX
jstubbsfc@bellsouth.net; mcprobate@bellsouth.net
http://www.marlborocounty.sc.gov
William Funderburk, Clerk of Court; Paul Mark Heath, Probate Judge
(deeds with Clerk of Court's Office, estates and wills with Probate Judges' Office)
no probate search service; copies of probate records: 25¢ per page ("subject to change")

McCormick County
organized 1914 from Edgefield County

McCormick County Courthouse
133 South Mine Street
McCormick, SC 29835
(864) 465-2195 (Clerk, Room 102); (864) 465-2630 (Probate)
clerkcourt@wctel.net; mccormickpro@wctel.net
http://www.sccounties.org/counties/mccormick.htm; http://www.sciway.net/cnty/mccormick.html
Kathryne P. Butler, Clerk of Court; Ronnie D. Kidd, Probate Judge

Newberry County
organized 1785 from Ninety Six District

Newberry County Courthouse
1226 College Street
Newberry, SC 29108
(803) 321-2110 (Clerk, Room 5); (803) 321-2118 (Probate, PO Box 442); (803) 321-2111 FAX (Clerk); (803) 321-2119 FAX (Probate)

jbowers@newberrycounty.net;
knobles@newberrycounty.net
http://www.newberrycounty.net
Jackie Bowers, Clerk of Court; Kelly Baker
Nobles, Probate Judge

Oconee County
organized 1868 from Pickens County

Oconee County Courthouse
415 South Pine Street
Walhalla, SC 29691
(864) 638-4285 (Register); (864) 638-4280
(Clerk, PO Box 678); (864) 638-4275
(Probate, PO Box 471); (864) 638-4287 FAX
(Register); (864) 638-4282 FAX (Clerk); (864)
638-4278 FAX (Probate)
dbutts@oconeesc.com; ssmith@oconeesc.com;
sorr@oconeesc.com
http://www.oconeesc.com
Dale L. Butts, Register of Deeds; Sallie C. Smith,
Clerk of Court; Sandra Burgess Orr, Probate
Judge
(land records and vital records with Clerk of
Court, probate records with Probate Judge)
no probate search service; copies of probate
records: 50¢ per page, 50¢ minimum

Orangeburg County
organized 1769, original district

Orangeburg County Courthouse
(190 Gibson Street—location)
PO Box 9000 (mailing address)
Orangeburg, SC 29116-9000
(803) 533-6260 (Clerk); (803) 533-6280
(Probate); (803) 533-6279 FAX (Probate
mbrandhorst@orangeburgcounty.org;
Lrael@orangeburgcounty.org
http://www.orangeburgcounty.org
Lisa Mizell, Clerk of Court; Marcia Brandhorst,
Deputy Clerk of Court/Court Administrator;
Pandora LaShawn Jones-Glover, Probate
Judge; Loxie Rael, Clerk of Probate Court
(land records from 1865 with Register Mesne
Conveyance, probate records from 1865 with
Judge of Probate)
no land records search service; probate search
service: no charge; copies of land records: 50¢
per page, $1.00 per document minimum;
copies of probate records: 50¢ per page, $1.00
minimum ("all records in courthouse were
destroyed by fire in 1865; fees may be
increased in the near future—amounts yet to
be determined")

Pickens County
organized 1826 from Pendleton District, which
was abolished at that time

Pickens County Administration Facility
222 McDaniel Avenue
Pickens, SC 29671
(864) 898-898-5868 (Register, B-5); (864) 898-
5903 (Probate, B-16); (864) 898-5924 FAX
(Register)
http://www.co.pickens.sc.us; http://www.
sccounties.org/counties/pickens.htm
Paul McGuffin, Register of Deeds; Kathy Zorn,
Probate Judge

Pickens County Clerk of Court
(214 East Main Street, A100—location)
PO Box 215 (mailing address)
Pickens, SC 29671
(864) 898-5657; (864) 898-5863 FAX
lejetteg@co.pickens.sc.us
http://www.co.pickens.sc.us
Lejette H. Gatlin, Clerk of Court

Richland County
organized 1799 from Kershaw District

Richland County Judicial Center
(1701 Main Street—location)
PO Box 1781 (mailing address)
Columbia, SC 29202
(803) 576-1910 (Register of Deeds, PO Box
192); (803) 576-1950 (Clerk, PO Box 2766);
(803) 576-1961 (Probate Court, Estate

Division, Suite 207, PO Box 192); (803) 576-
1785 FAX (Clerk); (803) 576-1993 FAX
(Probate, Estate Division)
barbarascott@richlandonline.com;
amymcculloch@richlandonline.com
http://www.richlandonline.com
Barbara A. Scott, Clerk of Court; Amy
McCulloch, Probate Judge
(land records with Register of Deeds, probate
records with Judge of Probate)

Saluda County
organized 1896 from Edgefield County

Saluda County Courthouse
100 East Church Street
Saluda, SC 29138
(864) 445-4500, ext. 2214 (Clerk, Suite 6); (864)
445-3303 (Register); (864) 445-4500, ext. 2220
(Probate, Suite 4); (864) 445-3772 FAX
(Clerk)
db.holmes@saludacounty.sc.gov;
m.upchurch@saludacounty.sc.gov
http://www.saludacounty.sc.gov
Doris B. Holmes, Clerk of Court/Register of
Deeds; Margaret N. Upchurch, Probate Judge

Spartanburg County
organized 1785 from Ninety Six District

Spartanburg County Judicial Center
180 Magnolia Street
Spartanburg, SC 29306
(864) 596-2591 (Clerk, Second Floor, Suite 500);
(803) 596-3337 (Spartanburg Health
Department); (803) 596-2556 (Probate, First
Floor, Suite 302); (864) 596-2011 FAX
(Probate)
clerksoffice@spartanburgcounty.org
http://www.spartanburgcounty.org
Marcus W. Kitchens, Clerk of Court; Ponda
Caldwell, Probate Department Head
(births and marriages with probate records with
Probate Judge)
probate search service: $5.00 per search; copies
of vital records: $5.00 each; copies of probate
records: 50¢ per page

Spartanburg County Register of Deeds
Administration Building
Main Leve, Suite 100
366 North Church Street
Spartanburg, SC 29303
(864) 596-2514; (864) 596-2477 FAX
sford@spartanburgcounty.org
http://www.spartanburgcounty.org
Steve Ford, Department Head

Sumter County
organized 1798 from Camden District

Sumter County Courthouse
141 North Main Street
Sumter, SC 29150
(803) 436-2177 (Register, Room 202); (803) 436-
2227 (Clerk, Room 311, General Sessions
Department); (803) 436-2228, Clerk, Room
309, Civil Court); (803) 436-2232 (Clerk,
Criminal Court); (803) 436-2266 (Clerk,
Family Court); (803) 436-2166 (Probate,
Room 111); (803) 436-2223 FAX (Clerk);
(803) 436-2407 FAX (Probate
jacampbell@sumtercountysc.org
http://www.sumtercountysc.org
Vicki McCarthy, Register of Deeds; James C.
Campbell, Clerk of Court; Dale Atkinson,
Probate Judge
probate search service: no charge; copies of
probate records: $1.00 for the first page and
50¢ for each additional page, no minimum
("records prior to 1900s are on microfiche")

Union County
organized 1798 from Ninety Six District

Union County Courthouse
210 West Main Street
Union, SC 29379
(864) 429-1630 (Clerk); (864) 429-1625 (Probate)
clerkofcourt@countyofunion.com;

pjudge@countyofunion.com
http://www.countyofunion.com
Brad Morris, Clerk of Court and Registrar of
Mesne Conveyance; Donna Cudd, Probate
Judge
(land records from 1785 with Clerk of Court,
marriage records from 1911 and probate
records from late 1700s with Probate Court)
no probate search service; copies of probate
records: 20¢ per page plus postage and
handling

Williamsburg County
organized 1802 from Georgetown District

Williamsburg County Courthouse
125 West Main Street
Kingstree, SC 29556
(843) 355-9321, ext. 153 (Clerk); (843) 355-9321,
ext. 558 (Probate, PO Box 1005); (843) 355-
7821 FAX (Clerk)
wmsbcofc@ftc-i.net (Clerk);
williamsburgprobatecourt@yahoo.com
http://www.williamsburgsc.com
Carolyn Wiliams, Clerk of Court and Register of
Deeds; Rudell Gamble, Probate Judge
(land records with Clerk of Court, probate
records with Probate Judge)

York County
organized 1798 from Camden District

York County Courthouse
(1675-1G York Highway—location)
PO Box 649 (mailing address)
York, SC 29745
(803) 684-8510 (Property Deeds and Records);
(803) 684-8507 (Civil Records); (803) 628-
3036 (Criminal Court); (803) 909-7100
(Family Court); (803) 684-8505; (803) 628-
3133 FAX
clerk.court@yorkcountygov.com;
david.hamilton@yorkcountygov.com
http://www.yorkcountygov.com
David Hamilton, Clerk of Court

York County Probate Court
(Belk Building, 1 North Congress Street—
location)
PO Box 219 (mailing address)
York, SC 29745
(803) 684-8513; (803) 684-8536 FAX
probate@yorkcountygov.com
http://www.yorkcountygov.com
John Gettys, Probate Judge

SOUTH DAKOTA

Capital: Pierre. Statehood: 2 November 1889 (part of Dakota Territory in 1861)

South Dakota Magistrate Courts have limited jurisdiction over civil suits, small claims, mental health matters, misdemeanors, ordinance violations, etc. They are divided into circuits which are identical to those of the Circuit Courts, which sit at each county seat and have concurrent jurisdiction with the Magistrate Courts, plus exclusive jurisdiction over felony cases and civil cases involving land title or boundary disputes, domestic relations, probate and juvenile hearings. First Judicial Circuit: Bon Homme, Charles Mix, Clay, Douglas, Hutchinson, Lincoln, Turner, Union and Yankton counties; Second Judicial Circuit: Minnehaha County; Third Judicial Circuit: Beadle, Brookings, Clark, Codington, Deuel, Grant, Hamlin, Hand and Kingsbury counties; Fourth Judicial Circuit: Aurora, Brule, Buffalo, Davison, Hanson, Jerauld, Lake, McCook, Miner, Moody and Sanborn counties; Fifth Judicial Circuit: Brown, Campbell, Day, Edmunds, Faulk, Marshall, McPherson, Roberts, Spink and Walworth counties; Sixth Judicial Circuit: Bennett, Gregory, Haakon, Hughes, Hyde, Jackson, Jones, Lyman, Mellette, Potter, Stanley, Sully, Todd (attached to Tripp) and Tripp counties; Seventh Judicial Circuit: Custer, Fall River, Pennington and Shannon (attached to Fall River) counties; Eighth Judicial Circuit: Butte, Corson, Dewey, Harding, Lawrence, Meade, Perkins and Ziebach counties.

Lay magistrates, some of whom are clerks of Circuit Courts, can hear some uncontested civil actions and guilty pleas. The Supreme Court is the court of last resort.

Aurora County
county created by an act of legislature 22 February 1879 and organized 8 August 1881 from land that had been part of Hanson County (what was later Davison, Jerauld and Cragin counties); organization ratified November 1882; in 1881 annexed the western tier of townships from Davison County (township 109 is now part of Jerauld County; Cragin County was organized in 1873 and abolished in 1879)

Aurora County Courthouse
(Main Street—location)
PO Box 397 (mailing address)
Plankinton, SD 57368-0397
(605) 942-7161 (Register of Deeds, PO Box 334); (605) 942-7165 (Clerk of Courts, PO Box 366)
Arlene.Koch@state.sd.us
http://www.state.sd.us/doh/Genealogy/aurora.htm
Arlene Koch, Register of Deeds
(land records with Register of Deeds, naturalization records with Clerk of Courts, vital records with Register of Deeds, probate records with Clerk of Courts)
probate search service: $2.00 per name; copies of probate records: 10¢ per page plus postage charge if there are a lot of pages, no minimum

Beadle County
organized 1879 from Spink and Clark counties

Beadle County Courthouse
Huron, SD 57350
(605) 353-8412 (Register of Deeds, PO Box 55); (605) 353-7165 (Clerk of Courts, PO Box 1358); (605) 353-8402 FAX (Register of Deeds)
bcregdeeds@midco.net
http://www.beadlecounty.org/registerdeeds.html
Barbara O'Riley, Register of Deeds

Bennett County
organized 1909 from Indian lands

Bennett County Courthouse
(Main Street—location)
PO Box 460 (mailing address)
Martin, SD 57551-0460
(605) 685-6054 (Register of Deeds, PO Box 433); (605) 685-6969 (Clerk of Courts, PO Box 281)
Nancy.Sterkel@state.sd.us
http://www.state.sd.us/doh/Genealogy/bennett.htm
Nancy Sterkel, Register of Deeds

Bon Homme County
organized 1862 from Charles Mix County

Bon Homme County Courthouse
300 West 18th Avenue
Tyndall, SD 57066
(605) 589-3302 (Register of Deeds, PO Box 3); (605) 589-4215 (Clerk of Courts, PO Box 6)
elton.rokusek@state.sd.us
http://www.state.sd.us/doh/Genealogy/bonhomme.htm
Elton Rokusek, Register of Deeds

Brookings County
organized 1862 from unorganized territory

Brookings County Courthouse
314 Sixth Avenue
Brookings, SD 57006-2041
(605) 696-8240 (Register of Deeds); (605) 688-4200 (Clerk of Courts); (605) 696-8245 FAX (Register of Deeds)
bchapman@brookingscountysd.gov
http://www.brookingscountysd.gov
Beverly Chapman, Register of Deeds
(land records from the 1870s, vital records from 1905, probate records with Clerk of Courts)

Brown County
organized 1879 from Beadle County

Brown County Courthouse
25 Market Street
Aberdeen, SD 57401
(605) 626-7140 (Register of Deeds, PO Box 1307); (605) 626-2451 (Clerk of Courts, PO Box 1087); (605) 626-4010 FAX (Register of Deeds)
bcrdeeds@midco.net
http://www.brown.sd.us
Carol Sherman, Register of Deeds
(land records with Register of Deeds, vital records with Register of Deeds, probate records with Register of Deeds and Clerk of Courts)
probate search service: $4.00; copies of probate records: $1.00 per page, no minimum

Brule County
organized 1875 from Buffalo County

Brule County Courthouse
300 South Courtland
Chamberlain, SD 57325-1508
(605) 234-4434 voice & FAX (Register of Deeds, Suite 110); (605) 734-4580 (Clerk of Courts, Suite 111)
brulrod@midstatesd.net judy.busack@statee.sd.us
http://brulecounty.org
Judith Busack, Register of Deeds
(land records with Register of Deeds, naturalization records with Clerk of Courts, vital records with Register of Deeds, probate records with Clerk of Courts)

Buffalo County
organized 1873 from territorial county; first county officials appointed 5 January 1885 at Gann Valley

Buffalo County Courthouse
PO Box 174
Gann Valley, SD 57341-0174
(605) 293-3239 (Register of Deeds); (605) 734-4580 (Clerk of Courts, Brule County Courthouse, 300 South Courtland, Suite 111, Chamberlain, SD 57325)
buffco@midstatesd.net
http://www.state.sd.us/doh/Genealogy/buffalo.htm
Elaine Wulff, Register of Deeds
(land records with Register of Deeds, naturalization records with Clerk of Courts, births and deaths from 1905 to date, burials from 1941 to date with Register of Deeds, probate records with Clerk of Courts)
copies of land records: $1.00 plus 20¢ per page for each page after five, $2.00 for certified copies, $10.00 for the first page of plats and $5.00 for the second page; copies of vital records: $7.00 for certified copies of births and deaths, $5.00 for certified copies of marriages, $3.00 for the first page of coroner's records and $2.00 for each additional page

Butte County
organized 1883 from Harding County

Butte County Courthouse
839 Fifth Avenue
Belle Fourche, SD 57717-1729
(605) 892-2912; (605) 892-2516 (Clerk of Courts, PO Box 237)
Bc-Rod@Blackhills.com
http://www.state.sd.us/doh/Genealogy/butte.htm
Paula Walker, Register of Deeds
(land records with Register of Deeds, vital records with Register of Deeds, probate records with Clerk of Courts)
copies of land records: $1.00 per document (up to five pages) and 20¢ for each additional page; copies of vital records: $7.00 each for births and deaths, $5.00 each for marriages

Campbell County
organized 1873 from Buffalo County, when the legislature of Dakota Territory divided the territory into counties; surveyed 1883 and 1884, when settlers began to arrive; first board of county commissioners appointed 1883 and met 17 April 1884

Campbell County Courthouse
(Second and Main—location)
PO Box 37 (mailing address)
Mound City, SD 57646
(605) 955-3505 (Register of Deeds, PO Box 148); (605) 955-3536 (Clerk of Courts, PO Box 146); (605) 955-3308 FAX (Register of Deeds)
http://www.state.sd.us/doh/Genealogy/campbell.htm
Joyce Krokel, Register of Deeds; Kathleen E. Fuehrer, Clerk of Courts
(land records with Register of Deeds, naturalization records from 1884 to 1942 with Clerk of Courts, births from 1905 [earliest delayed birth from 1883], deaths from 1905, marriage licenses from 10 May 1890 with Register of Deeds, probate records from 1891 to date with Clerk of Courts)
probate search service: $2.00 per name; copies of land records: $1.00 per instrument, $2.00 per instrument for certified copies; certified copies of vital records: $7.00 for births and deaths, $5.00 for marriages; copies of probate records: 25¢ per page

Charles Mix County
organized 1862, original county

Charles Mix County Courthouse
(Main Street—location)
PO Box 490 (mailing address)
Lake Andes, SD 57356
(605) 487-7141 (Register of Deeds, PO Box 206); (605) 487-7511 (Clerk of Courts, PO Box 640)
cmixrod@hcinet.net
http://www.state.sd.us/doh/Genealogy/charlesmix.htm
Monica Waldner, Register of Deeds

Clark County
formed 1873, organized 1881

Clark County Courthouse
(200 North Commercial—location)
PO Box 294 (mailing address)
Clark, SD 57225-0294
(605) 532-5363 (Register of Deeds); (605) 532-5851 (Clerk of Courts)
janet.hurlbut@state.sd.us
http://www.state.sd.us/doh/Genealogy/clark.htm; http://www.clarksd.com
Janet Hurlbut, Register of Deeds; Roberta Heim, Clerk of Courts
(land records with Register of Deeds, births and deaths from 1905, marriages from the 1890s with Register of Deeds, probate records from 1882 with Clerk of Courts)
probate search service: $2.00; copies of land records: $1.00 per instrument; certified copies of vital records: $7.00 for births and deaths, $5.00 for marriages; copies of probate records: 20¢ each

Clay County
organized 1862 from unorganized territory

Clay County Courthouse
(211 West Main Street—location)
PO Box 403 (mailing adress)
Vermillion, SD 57069-0403
(605) 677-7130 (Register of Deeds, Suite 202); (605) 677-6756 (Clerk of Courts, PO Box 377); (605) 677-7104 FAX (Register of Deeds)
Betty.McCambridge@state.sd.us
http://www.claycountysd.org
Betty McCambridge, Register of Deeds
(land records from 1870 with Register of Deeds, naturalization records from 1867 with Clerk of Courts, vital records from 1905 with Register of Deeds, probate records from 1875 with Clerk of Courts)
probate search service: $2.00; copies of probate records: 10¢ per page, $2.00 for certification, $2.00 minimum

Codington County
organized 1877 from Indian lands

Codington County Courthouse
14 First Avenue, SE
Watertown, SD 57201
(605) 882-6278 (Register of Deeds); (605) 882-6274 (Ezualization); (605) 882-5095 (Clerk of Courts, PO Box 1054); (605) 882-5230 FAX (Register of Deeds); (605) 882-5387 FAX (Equalization)
coddoc@codington.org
http://www.codington.org
Ann Siefel, Register of Deeds
(land records with Register of Deeds/Director of Equalization, vital records with Register of Deeds, probate records with Clerk of Courts)
probate search service: no charge; copies of probate records: 20¢ each, no minimum

Corson County
organized 1909 from Dewey County

Corson County Courthouse
20-0 First Street, East
McIntosh, SD 57641
(607) 273-4395 (Register of Deeds, PO Box 256); (605) 273-4201 (Clerk of Courts, PO Box 175)
regdeeds@dakota-web.com; corsonrod@sdplains.com
http://www.state.sd.us/doh/Genealogy/corson.htm
Virginia Sauer, Register of Deeds
(land records, naturalization records, vital records, probate records)
no probate search service; copies of land records and vital records: $1.00 each, $2.00 for certified copies; certified copies of naturalization records: $2.00 each; copies of vital records: $1.00 each, $2.00 for certified copies; copies of probate records: 25¢ per page, $2.00 for certified copies

Custer County
organized 1875 from Indian lands

Custer County Courthouse
420 S.W. Mt. Rushmore Road
Custer, SD 57730-1934
(605) 673-8171 (Register of Deeds); (605) 673-4816 (Clerk of Courts); (605) 673-8148 FAX (Register of Deeds)
flarsen@custercountysd.com
http://www.custercountysd.com
Frances M. Larsen, Register of Deeds; Debbie Salzsieder, Clerk of Courts

Davison County
organized 1873 from Hanson County

Davison County Courthouse
200 East Fourth Street
Mitchell, SD 57301-2631
(605) 995-8616 (Register of Deeds); (605) 995-8105 (Clerk of Courts, PO Box 927); (605) 995-8648 FAX (Register of Deeds)
registerofdeeds@davisoncounty.org
http://www.davisoncounty.org/RegisterofDeeds/rodindex.htm
Debra Young, Register of Deeds
(land records with Register of Deeds, vital records with Register of Deeds, probate records with Clerk of Courts)
probate search service: $2.00; copies of probate records: two for 25¢ plus postage, no minimum

Day County
organized 1879 from Clark County

Day County Courthouse
711 West First Street
Webster, SD 57274-1396
(605) 345-9506 (Register of Deeds); (605) 345-3771 (Clerk of Courts, 711 West First Street, Webster, SD 57274-1359); (605) 345-3375 (Clerk of Courts); (605) 345-9507 FAX (Register of Deeds)
http://www.state.sd.us/doh/Genealogy/day.htm
Janet Knapp, Register of Deeds
(land records with Register of Deeds, naturalization records with Clerk of Courts, vital records with Register of Deeds, probate records with Clerk of Courts)
no probate search service; copies of probate records: 10¢ per page, no minimum

Deuel County
organized 1862 from Brookings County

Deuel County Courthouse
(408 Fifth Street West—location)
PO Box 616 (mailing address)
Clear Lake, SD 57226
(605) 874-2268 (Register of Deeds, Second Floor, PO Box 125); (605) 874-2120 (Clerk of Courts, Second Floor, PO Box 308)
mary.ingalls@state.sd.us
http://www.deuelcountysd.com
Mary Jane Ingalls, Register of Deeds; Karna Lindner, Clerk of Courts

Dewey County
organized 1873 from Indian lands

Dewey County Courthouse
PO Box 277
Timber Lake, SD 57656-0277
(605) 865-3661 (Register of Deeds, PO Box 117); (605) 865-3566 (Clerk of Courts, PO Box 96); (605) 865-3672 (Auditor)
deborah.goldade@state.sd.us
http://www.state.sd.us/doh/Genealogy/dewey.htm
Deborah Goldade, Register of Deeds
(land records with Register of Deeds, naturalization records with Clerk of Courts, vital records with Register of Deeds and/or Clerk of Courts, probate records with Clerk of Courts)
probate search service: $2.00; copies of land records: 25¢ per page, $2.00 for the first five

pages and 25¢ for each additional page of the same instrument for certified copies; certified copies of vital records: $7.00 each; copies of probate records: 25¢ per page, $2.00 for certified copies

Douglas County
organized 1873 from Charles Mix County

Douglas County Courthouse
PO Box 159
Armour, SD 57313
(605) 724-2204 (Register of Deeds); (605) 724-2585 (Clerk of Courts, PO Box 36)
http://www.state.sd.us/doh/Genealogy/douglas.htm
Randall Larson, Register of Deeds

Edmunds County
organized 1873 from Buffalo County

Edmunds County Courthouse
PO Box 97
Ipswich, SD 57451-0097
(605) 426-6431 (Register of Deeds, PO Box 386); (605) 426-6671 (Clerk of Courts, PO Box 384)
ed.dosch@state.sd.us
http://www.state.sd.us/doh/Genealogy/edmunds.htm
Edward Dosch, Register of Deeds
(land records with Director of Equalization, PO Box 247, Ipswich, SD 57451, naturalization records with Clerk of Courts, vital records with Register of Deeds, probate records with Clerk of Courts)
probate search service: $2.00 and up; copies of probate records: 10¢ or 15¢ per page, no minimum

Fall River County
organized 1883 from Custer County

Fall River County Courthouse
906 North River Street
Hot Springs, SD 57747-1399
(605) 745-5139 (Register of Deeds); (605) 745-5131 (Clerk of Courts)
frshrod@gwtc.net (Register of Deeds)
http://www.state.sd.us/doh/Genealogy/fallriver.htm
Anita Gilkey, Register of Deeds
(land records with Register of Deeds, vital records with Register of Deeds, probate records with Clerk of Courts)
probate search service: $2.00 per name; copies of probate records: $2.00 per certified copy of each document, $2.00 minimum

Faulk County
organized 1873 from Buffalo County and unorganized territory

Faulk County Courthouse
PO Box 309
Faulkton, SD 57438-0309
(605) 598-6228 (Register of Deeds); (605) 598-6223 (Clerk of Courts, PO Box 357)
http://www.state.sd.us/doh/Genealogy/faulk.htm
Sally Snow, Register of Deeds

Grant County
organized 1873 from Codington and Deuel counties

Grant County Courthouse
210 East Fifth Avenue
Milbank, SD 57252-2433
(605) 432-4752 (Register of Deeds); (605) 432-5482 (Clerk of Courts, PO Box 509)
Karen.Hooth-Quade@state.sd.us
http://www.state.sd.us/doh/Genealogy/grant.htm
Karen Hooth-Quade, Register of Deeds
(land records with Register of Deeds Office, naturalization records from about 1895 with Clerk of Courts, vital records with Register of Deeds Office, probate records from about 1895 with Clerk of Courts)
probate search service: no charge; copies of

probate records: 20¢ per page, no minimum

Gregory County
organized 1862 from Yankton County

Gregory County Courthouse
PO Box 437
Burke, SD 57523-0437
(605) 775-2624 (Recorder of Deeds); (605) 775-2665 (Clerk of Courts, PO Box 430)
Sodakpete@hotmail.com
http://www.state.sd.us/doh/Genealogy/gregory.htm
Jerry Peterson, Register of Deeds

Haakon County
organized 1914 from Stanley County

Haakon County Courthouse
(140 South Howard—location)
PO Box 698 (mailing address)
Philip, SD 57567
(605) 859-2785 (Register of Deeds, PO Box 100); (605) 859-2627 (Clerk of Courts, PO Box 70)
haakonrod@gwtc.net
http://www.state.sd.us/doh/Genealogy/Haakon.htm
Karyl Sandal, Register of Deeds
(land records with Register of Deeds, naturalization records with Clerk of Courts, vital records with Register of Deeds, probate records with Clerk of Courts)
probate search service: $2.00; copies of probate records: 20¢ per page, no minimum

Hamlin County
organized 1873 from Deuel County

Hamlin County Courthouse
PO Box 237
Hayti, SD 57241
(605) 783-3206 (Register of Deeds, PO Box 56); (605) 783-3751 (Clerk of Courts, PO Box 256)
Marlene.Schaefer@state.sd.us
http://www.state.sd.us/doh/Genealogy/hamlin.htm
Marlene Schaefer, Register of Deeds
(land records with Register of Deeds, naturalization records with Clerk of Courts, vital records with Register of Deeds, probate records with Clerk of Courts)
probate search service: $2.00; copies of probate records: 15¢ per letter-sized page, 20¢ per legal-sized page, $2.00 minimum plus SASE

Hand County
county created 1873; organized 1882

Hand County Courthouse
415 West First Avenue
Miller, SD 57362-1346
(605) 853-3512 (Register of Deeds); (605) 853-3337 (Clerk of Courts, PO Box 122)
Registrar.Hand.com@Midconetwork.com
http://www.state.sd.us/doh/Genealogy/hand.htm
Sheila Cross, Register of Deeds
(land records from 1881 with Register of Deeds, naturalizations with State Archives, births and deaths from July 1905 ([some delayed births registered], marriages from 1883 with Register of Deeds, probate records with Clerk of Courts)
probate search service: $2.00 per name; copies of land records: 50¢ per page, $2.00 per instrument for certification; certified copies: $7.00 each for births and deaths, $5.00 each for marriages; copies of probate records: 20¢ per page

Hanson County
organized 1873 from Buffalo and Deuel counties

Hanson County Courthouse
PO Box 500
Alexandria, SD 57311-0500
(605) 239-4512 (Register of Deeds, PO Box 8);

(605) 239-4446 (Clerk of Courts, PO Box 127)
debra.zens@state.sd.us
http://www.state.sd.us/doh/Genealogy/hanson.htm
Debra Zens, Register of Deeds

Harding County
organized 1909 from Butte County

Harding County Courthouse
PO Box 26
Buffalo, SD 57720-0026
(605) 375-3321 (Register of Deeds, PO Box 101); (605) 375-3351 (Clerk of Courts, PO Box 534)
hcrod@sdplains.com
http://www.state.sd.us/doh/Genealogy/harding.htm
Sue Litzel, Register of Deeds
(land records from 1909 [numerical and alphabetical] with Register of Deeds, vital records with Register of Deeds, probate records with Clerk of Courts)
probate search service: $2.00; copies of probate records: $1.00 per page, $2.00 for certified copies

Hughes County
organized 26 November 1880 from Buffalo County

Hughes County Courthouse
104 East Capital
Pierre, SD 57501-2589
(605) 224-7895 (Register of Deeds); (605) 773-3713 (Clerk of Courts, PO Box 1238)
http://www.state.sd.us/doh/Genealogy/hughes.htm
Norine Riis, Register of Deeds
(land records, vital records, probate records)

Hutchinson County
organized 1862 from unorganized territory, in 1879 annexed Armstrong County, which was created in 1871

Hutchinson County Courthouse
140 Euclid
Olivet, SD 57052
(605) 387-4217 (Register of Deeds, Room 37); (605) 387-4215 (Clerk of Courts, Room 36, PO Box 7)
regod@gwtc.net
http://www.state.sd.us/doh/Genealogy/hutchinson.htm
Julie Herrboldt, Register of Deeds
(land records with Register of Deeds, vital records with Register of Deeds, probate records with Clerk of Courts)
probate search service: $2.00 per name; copies of land records: $1.00 per document; certified copies of vital records: $7.00 each for births and deaths, $5.00 each for marriages; copies of probate records: 10¢ per page, no minimum

Hyde County
organized 1873 from Buffalo County

Hyde County Courthouse
(112 Commercial, S.E.—location)
PO Box 379 (mailing address)
Highmore, SD 57345-0379
(605) 852-2517 (Register of Deeds, PO Box 342); (605) 852-2512 (Clerk of Courts, PO Box 306)
Hyderod@Venturecomm.net
http://www.state.sd.us/doh/Genealogy/hyde.htm
Duane Johnson, Register of Deeds; Alfred F. Jetty, Clerk of Courts
(land records with Register of Deeds Office, naturalization records with Clerk of Courts, vital records with Register of Deeds Office, probate records with Clerk of Courts)
land records search service: $2.00 in advance

Jackson County
organized 1914 from Stanley County; in 1976

annexed Washabaugh County, which was organized 1883 from Indian lands and continued as an Indian reservation

Jackson County Courthouse
PO Box 280
Kadoka, SD 57543-0280
(605) 837-2420 (Register of Deeds, PO Box 248); (605) 837-2122 (Clerk of Courts, PO Box 128)
http://www.state.sd.us/doh/Genealogy/jackson.htm
Harvey T. Byrd, Register of Deeds
(land records with Register of Deeds, naturalization records with Clerk of Courts, vital records with Register of Deeds, probate records with Clerk of Courts)
probate search service: no charge; certified copies of land records: $1.00 each; certified copies of naturalization records: $2.00 each; certified copies of vital records: $5.00 each; copies of probate records: 15¢ each, $2.00 for certified copies, no minimum

Jayne County
(see Turner County)

Jerauld County
organized 1883 from Aurora County

Jerauld County Courthouse
(205 South Wallace—location)
PO Box 422 (mailing address)
Wessington Springs, SD 57382-0422
(605) 539-1221 (Register of Deeds, PO Box 452); (605) 539-1202 (Clerk of Courts, PO Box 435)
http://www.state.sd.us/doh/Genealogy/jerauld.htm
Lila Teeslink, Register of Deeds
(deeds from 1884 with Register of Deeds, naturalization records from 1884 with Clerk of Courts, vital records from 1905 with Register of Deeds [proof of relationship required], probate records from 1905 with Clerk of Courts)
probate search service: $2.00 per name; copies of deeds: $1.00 each, $2.00 for certified copies; copies of probate records: 20¢ per page, no minimum; no telephone requests

Jones County
organized 1916 from Lyman County

Jones County Courthouse
PO Box 307
Murdo, SD 57559-0307
(605) 669-7104 (Register of Deeds, PO Box 446); (605) 669-2361 (Clerk of Courts, PO Box 448)
http://www.state.sd.us/doh/Genealogy/jones.htm
Terri Volmer, Register of Deeds

Kingsbury County
organized 1873 from Hanson County

Kingsbury County Courthouse
PO Box 196
De Smet, SD 57231
(605) 854-3591 (Register of Deeds, PO Box 146); (605) 854-3811 (Clerk of Courts, PO Box 176)
caryn.hojer@state.sd.us
http://www.state.sd.us/doh/Genealogy/kingsbury.htm
Caryn Hojer, Register of Deeds
(land records with Register of Deeds, vital records from 1905 with Register of Deeds, probate records with Clerk of Courts)
probate search service: $2.00; copies of probate records: 20¢ per page, no minimum

Lake County
organized 1873 from Brookings and Hanson counties

Lake County Courthouse
(200 East Center—location)
PO Box 447 (mailing address)

Madison, SD 57042-0447
(605) 256-7614 voice & FAX (Register of
   Deeds, PO Box 266); (605) 256-5644 (Clerk
   of Courts)
penny.boatright@state.sd.us
http://www.lakecountysd.com
Penny Boatwright, Register of Deeds
(land records with Register of Deeds,
   naturalization records with Clerk of Courts,
   vital records from 1 July 1905 with Register of
   Deeds, probate records with Clerk of Courts)
probate search service: no charge; copies of
   probate records: 25¢ per page, no minimum

Lawrence County
organized 1875 from unorganized territory

Lawrence County Administrative Building
90 Sherman Street
Deadwood, SD 57732
(605) 578-3930 (Register of Deeds, PO Box
   565); (605) 578-2040 (Clerk of Courts, PO
   Box 626); (605) 722-6212 FAX (Register of
   Deeds)
jmeverde@lawrence.sd.us;
   deedsoff@lawrence.sd.us
http://www.lawrence.sd.us
Judy Meverden, Register of Deeds

Lincoln County
organized 1867 from Minnehaha County

Lincoln County Courthouse
100 East Fifth Street
Canton, SD 57013-1732
(605) 987-5661 (Register of Deeds); (605) 987-
   5891 (Clerk of Courts, 425 North Dakota
   Avenue, Sioux Falls, SD 57104-2470)
Lincolnrod@IW.net
http://www.state.sd.us/doh/Genealogy/
   lincoln.htm
Kathleen Hill, Register of Deeds
(land records with Register of Deeds,
   naturalization records First papers from 1870,
   second papers to 1941 with Clerk of Courts,
   births and deaths from 1905 [delayed births
   from 1870], marriages from 1873 with
   Register of Deeds, probate records from June
   1880 with Clerk of Courts)
probate search service: $2.00 per name; copies
   of land records: $1.00 each, $2.00 for certified
   copies; certified copies of vital records: $5.00
   each; copies of probate records: 15¢ each for
   short pages, 20¢ for long pages, $2.00 for
   certified copies, no minimum

Lyman County
organized 1873 from unorganized territory

Lyman County Courthouse
Kennebec, SD 57544
(605) 869-2297 (Register of Deeds, PO Box 98);
   (605) 869-2277 (Clerk of Courts, PO Box
   235); (605) 869-2177 FAX (Clerk of Courts);
   (605) 869-2203 FAX (Register of Deeds)
Tracy.Brakke@state.sd.us
http://s92375618.onlinehome.us/content.
   php?content.1
Tracy Brakke, Register of Deeds; Denise
   Anderson, Clerk of Courts
(land records with Register of Deeds, births and
   deaths with Register of Deeds, probate
   records with Clerk of Courts)
probate search service: $2.00; copies of land
   records: $1.00 per document plus 20¢ per
   page for each page after five, $2.00 for
   certified copies; certified copies of vital
   records: $7.00 each; copies of probate
   records: 25¢ each, $2.00 minimum

Marshall County
organized 1885 from Day County

Marshall County Courthouse
(Vanderhorck Avenue—location)
PO Box 130 (mailing address)
Britton, SD 57430-0130
(605) 448-2352 (Register of Deeds); (605) 448-
   5213 (Clerk of Courts)

mcregister@sbtc.net
http://www.state.sd.us/doh/Genealogy/
   marshall.htm
Marlene Sime, Register of Deeds
(land records with Register of Deeds; probate
   records with Clerk of Courts)
land records search service: $2.00; copies of land
   records: 10¢ each, $2.00 for certified copies

McCook County
organized 1873 from Hanson County

McCook County Courthouse
PO Box 190
Salem, SD 57058-0190
(605) 425-2701 (Register of Deeds, PO Box
   338); (605) 425-2781 (Clerk of Courts, PO
   Box 504)
Laurie.Schwans@state.sd.us
http://www.state.sd.us/doh/Genealogy/
   mccook.htm
Laurie Schwans, Register of Deeds
(land records with Director of Equalization,
   naturalization records with Clerk of Courts,
   vital records with Register of Deeds, probate
   records with Clerk of Courts)
probate search service: $2.00; copies of probate
   records: 20¢ per page, no minimum

McPherson County
organized 1873 from Buffalo County

McPherson County Courthouse
PO Box L
Leola, SD 57456-0448
(605) 439-3151 (Register of Deeds, PO Box
   129); (605) 439-3361 (Clerk of Courts, PO
   Box 248)
Mcphersonrod@Valleytel.net
http://www.state.sd.us/doh/Genealogy/
   mcpherson.htm
John Hilgeman, Register of Deeds
(land records from 1884 with Register of Deeds,
   naturalization records from 1884 to 1943 with
   Clerk of Courts, vital records from 1905 with
   Register of Deeds, probate records from 1887
   with Clerk of Courts)
probate search service: $2.00; copies of land
   records: $1.00 each; certified copies of vital
   records: $7.00 each; copies of probate
   records: 30¢ per page, $2.25 certified, no
   minimum

Meade County
organized 1889 from Lawrence County

Meade County Courthouse
1425 Sherman Street
Sturgis, SD 57785-1452
(605) 347-2356 (Register of Deeds); (605) 347-
   4411 (Clerk of Courts, PO Box 939); (605)
   347-5925 FAX (Register of Deeds)
mcrod@dtgnet.com; meade@meadecounty.org
http://www.meadecounty.org
Angela Ross, Register of Deeds

Mellette County
organized 1909 from Tripp County

Mellette County Courthouse
PO Box C
White River, SD 57579-0403
(605) 259-3371 (Register of Deeds, PO Box
   183); (605) 259-3230 (Clerk of Courts, PO
   Box 257)
karen.obrien@state.sd.us
http://www.state.sd.us/doh/Genealogy/
   mellette.htm
Karen O'Brien, Register of Deeds
(land records with Register of Deeds,
   naturalization records with Clerk of Courts,
   vital records with Register of Deeds, probate
   records with Clerk of Courts)
no probate search service; copies of vital
   records: $7.00 for births and deaths; copies of
   probate records: 25¢ each

Miner County
organized 1873 from Hanson County

Miner County Courthouse
401 North Main
Howard, SD 57349
(605) 772-5621 (Register of Deeds, PO Box
   546); (605) 772-4612 (Clerk of Courts, PO
   Box 265)
minerdeeds@alliancecom.net;
   minerdeeds@splitrocktel.net
http://www.howardsd.com; http://www.state.
   sd.us/doh/Genealogy/miner.htm
Karla Neises, Register of Deeds
(land records with Register of Deeds,
   naturalization records with Clerk of Courts,
   vital records with Register of Deeds, probate
   records with Clerk of Courts)

Minnehaha County
organized 1862 from territorial county

Minnehaha County Administration Building
415 North Dakota Avenue, First Floor
Sioux Falls, SD 57102-0136
(605) 335-4223
jristy@minnehahacounty.org
http://www.minnehahacounty.org
Julie Risty, Register of Deeds
(land records from 1870, some vital records
   from late 1800s but not complete)

Minnehaha County Clerk of Courts
425 North Dakota Avenue
Sioux Falls, SD 57102-0136
(605) 367-5900
http://www.sdjudicial.com/circuit_courts/inde
   x.asp?circuit=mc_county&nav=3
(probate records)
probate search service: $2.00; certified copies of
   vital records: $7.00 each; copies of probate
   records: 20¢ per page, no minimum but must
   enclose SASE

Moody County
organized 1873 from Brookings and Minnehaha
counties

Moody County Courthouse
(101 East Pipestone Avenue—location)
PO Box 152 (mailing address)
Flandreau, SD 57028
(605) 997-3151 (Register of Deeds, Suite C);
   (605) 997-3181 (Clerk of Courts, PO Box
   226)
mcrod@mcisweb.com
http://www.state.sd.us/doh/Genealogy/
   moody.htm
Gail Meyer, Register of Deeds

Pennington County
organized 1875 from unorganized territory

Pennington County Courthouse
315 St. Joseph Street
Rapid City, SD 57709
(605) 394-2177 (Register of Deeds, Suite 104);
   (605) 394-2575 (Clerk of Courts, PO Box
   230)
donnam@co.pennington.sd.us
http://www.co.pennington.sd.us
Donna Mayer, Register of Deeds
(land records with Register of Deeds, vital
   records with Register of Deeds, probate
   records with Clerk of Courts)
probate search service: no charge; copies of
   probate records: 25¢ each, no minimum

Perkins County
organized 1909 from Harding and Butte
counties

Perkins County Courthouse
PO Box 126
Bison, SD 57620
(605) 244-5620 (Register of Deeds, PO Box
   127); (605) 244-5626 (Clerk of Courts, PO
   Box 426)
pkrod@sdplains.com
http://www.state.sd.us/doh/Genealogy/
   perkins.htm
Darlene Lockert, Register of Deeds

(land records with Register of Deeds, naturalization records, vital records with Register of Deeds, probate records from 1908)

land records search service: $4.00; vital records search service: $5.00; probate search service: $2.00; copies of land records: 25¢ each for 8½" x 11", 50¢ each for 11" x 14"; certified copies of vital records: $7.00 each; copies of probate records: 25¢ each for letter-sized copies, 50¢ for legal-sized copies, $2.00 minimum ("written requests only")

Potter County
organized 1875 from Buffalo County

Potter County Courthouse
201 South Exene
Gettysburg, SD 57442-1521
(605) 765-9467 (Register of Deeds); (605) 765-9472 (Clerk of Courts, PO Box 67)
pcrod@venturecomm.net
http://www.state.sd.us/doh/Genealogy/potter.htm
Elaine Storkson, Register of Deeds

Roberts County
organized 1883 from Grant County

Roberts County Courthouse
411 Second Avenue East
Sisseton, SD 57262-1495
(605) 698-7152 (Register of Deeds); (605) 698-3395 (Clerk of Courts)
http://www.state.sd.us/doh/Genealogy/roberts.htm
Carol Martenson, Register of Deeds
(land records with Register of Deeds, births, deaths and marriages with Register of Deeds; probate records with Clerk of Courts)
probate search service: $2.00 by mail (no random searches; will search only specific names); certified copies of vital records: $7.00 each for births and deaths, $5.00 each for marriages; copies of probate records: 15¢ per page, $2.00 per document for certification, no minimum

Sanborn County
organized 1883 from Miner County

Sanborn County Courthouse
(604 West Sixth Street—location)
PO Box 7 (mailing address)
Woonsocket, SD 57385
(605) 796-4516 (Register of Deeds, PO Box 295); (605) 796-4515 (Clerk of Courts, PO Box 56)
sancorod@santel.net
http://www.state.sd.us/doh/Genealogy/sanborn.htm
Lynelle Brueske, Register of Deeds
(land records with Register of Deeds, PO Box 295, Woonsocket, SD 57385, naturalization records [cannot be photocopied], vital records with Register of Deeds, probate records with Clerk of Courts, PO Box 56, Woonsocket, SD 57385)
probate search service: $2.00; copies of probate records: 25¢ per page, no minimum

Shannon County
organized 1875 from territorial county, in 1943 reannexed Washington County, which was organized in 1883 from Shannon County

Shannon County Courthouse
c/o Fall River County Courthouse
906 North River Street
Hot Springs, SD 57747-1399
(605) 745-3996; (605) 745-5139 (Register of Deeds); (605) 745-5131 (Clerk of Courts)
acaglm@gwtc.net
http://www.state.sd.us/doh/Genealogy/shannon.htm
Anita Gilkey, Register of Deeds
(land records with Register of Deeds, vital records with Register of Deeds, probate records with Clerk of Courts)

probate search service: $2.00 per name; copies of probate records: $2.00 per certified copy of each document, $2.00 minimum

Spink County
organized 1873 from Hanson and Walworth counties

Spink County Courthouse
210 East Seventh Avenue
Redfield, SD 57469-1266
(605) 472-0150 (Recorder of Deeds, PO Box 266); (605) 472-4535 (Clerk of Courts); (605) 472-4352 FAX (Clerk of Courts)
Spinkrod@nrctv.com; 5thcircuit@ujs.state.sd.us
http://www.state.sd.us/doh/Genealogy/spink.htm; http://ujs.sd.gov/5thCircuit/scounty.htm; http://growspink.com
Sharon Jungwirth, Register of Deeds; Donna Fredrickson, Clerk of Courts
(land records with Register of Deeds, naturalization records from 1884 with Clerk of Courts Office, vital records with Register of Deeds, probate records from 1928 with Clerk of Courts)
probate search service: $2.00; copies of land records: $1.00 for each of the first five pages and 20¢ for each additional page; certified copies of vital records: $7.00 each for births and deaths, $5.00 each for marriages; copies of probate records: 15¢ per page plus postage, no minimum ("our records are alphabetized, so most of the time dates are not necessary")

Stanley County
organized 1873 from unorganized territory

Stanley County Courthouse
Ft. Pierre, SD 57532
(605) 223-2610 (Register of Deeds, PO Box 595); (605) 223-7735 (Clerk of Courts, PO Box 758)
Bstoes@hotmail.com
http://www.state.sd.us/doh/Genealogy/stanley.htm
Bev Stoeser, Register of Deeds

Sully County
organized 1873 from Potter County

Sully County Courthouse
Onida, SD 57564
(605) 258-2331 (Register of Deeds, PO Box 265); (605) 258-2535 (Clerk of Courts, PO Box 188)
sullydeeds@sbtc.net; hollymcknight@state.sd.us
http://www.state.sd.us/doh/Genealogy/sully.htm
Holly McKnight, Register of Deeds
(land records and vital records with Register of Deeds, naturalization records and probate records with Clerk of Courts)

Todd County
organized 1909 from Indian lands

Todd County Courthouse
c/o Tripp County Courthouse
200 East Third Street
Winner, SD 57580-1806
(605) 842-2208 (Register of Deeds); (605) 842-2266 (Clerk of Courts, PO Box 311)
http://www.state.sd.us/doh/Genealogy/todd.htm
Louise Flisram, Register of Deeds
(land records and vital records from 1909 with Register of Deeds Office, naturalization records from 1909 and probate records from 1907 with Clerk of Courts)
probate search service: $2.00; copies of land records: $1.00 per instrument (up to five pages) and 20¢ for each additional page; certified copies of vital records: $7.00 per document; copies of probate records: 10¢ per page, no minimum

Tripp County
organized 1873 from unorganized territory

Tripp County Courthouse
200 East Third Street

Winner, SD 57580-1806
(605) 842-2208 (Register of Deeds); (605) 842-2266 (Clerk of Courts, PO Box 311)
http://www.state.sd.us/doh/Genealogy/tripp.htm
Louise Filsram, Register of Deeds
(land records from 1909 with Register of Deeds Office, naturalization records from 1909 with Clerk of Courts, vital records from 1909 with Register of Deeds, probate records from 1907 with Clerk of Courts)
probate search service: $2.00; copies of land records: $1.00 per instrument (up to five pages) and 20¢ for each additional page; certified copies of vital records: $7.00 per document; copies of probate records: 10¢ per page, no minimum

Turner County
organized 1871 from Lincoln County and part of the now-defunct Jayne County

Turner County Courthouse
(Main Street—location)
PO Box 368 (mailing address)
Parker, SD 57053
(605) 297-3443 (Register of Deeds, PO Box 485); (605) 297-3115 (Clerk of Courts, PO Box 446)
turegod@dtgnet.com
http://www.state.sd.us/doh/Genealogy/turner.htm
Carol J. Viet, Register of Deeds
(land records from 1871 with Register of Deeds, naturalization records from 1887 with South Dakota Historical Society, vital records from July 1905 with Register of Deeds, probate records from 1884 with Clerk of Courts, probate records from May 1927 through March 1949 with Record Storage, East Hiway Bypass, Pierre, SD 57501)
land records search service: no charge (but must have legal description of the land); vital records search service: no charge (but must have first, middle, and last name of child, father's name, mother's maiden name, place of birth for birth certificate; decedent's full name, date and place of death for death certificate; full names of bride and groom, date and place of marriage for marriage certificate); probate search service: $2.00 per name; copies of land records: $1.00 per document; certified copies of vital records: $7.00 each for births and deaths, $5.00 for marriages, payable in advance; copies of probate records: 25¢ each, no minimum

Union County
organized 1862 from unorganized territory

Union County Courthouse
(209 East Main Street—location)
PO Box 757 (mailing address)
Elk Point, SD 57025-0757
(605) 356-2191 (Recorder of Deeds, Suite 210, PO Box 490); (605) 356-2132 (Clerk of Courts, Suite 230); (605) 356-3047 FAX (Recorder of Deeds)
Ucrod@iw.net; ucrod2@iw.net
http://www.state.sd.us/doh/Genealogy/union.htm
Jana Foltz, Register of Deeds

Walworth County
organized 1873 from territorial county

Walworth County Courthouse
PO Box 199
Selby, SD 57472-0199
(605) 649-7057 (Register of Deeds, PO Box 159); (605) 649-7311 (Clerk of Courts, PO Box 328)
Walrod@midco.net; rod.walworthco@midconetwork.com
http://www.state.sd.us/doh/Genealogy/walworth.htm
Susan Eisemann, Register of Deeds
(land records with Register of Deeds, vital records with Register of Deeds, probate records with Clerk of Courts)

no probate search service; copies of probate
   records: $1.00 per page

Yankton County
organized 1862 from territorial county

Yankton County Courthouse
(321 West Third Street—location)
PO Box 137 (mailing address)
Yankton, SD 57078
(605) 260-4400, ext. 5 (Register of Deeds, PO
   Box 694); (605) 668-3080 (Clerk of Courts,
   PO Box 155)
brian@co.yankton.sd.us
http://www.co.yankton.sd.us/departments.html
Brian Hunhoff, Register of Deeds
(probate records from 1905)
probate search service: $2.00 per name; copies
   of probate records: 20¢ per page, no
   minimum ("correct name on probate and year
   it was filed would be helpful in locating the
   file")

Ziebach County
organized 1911 from Pennington County

Ziebach County Courthouse
Main Street
Dupree, SD 57623
(605) 365-5157; (605) 365-5165 (Register of
   Deeds, PO Box 68); (605) 365-5159 (Clerk of
   Courts, PO Box 306)
Lila.Lafferty@state.sd.us
http://www.state.sd.us/doh/Genealogy/
   ziebach.htm
Lila Lafferty, Register of Deeds
(land records with Register of Deeds,
   naturalization records with Clerk of Courts,
   vital records with Register of Deeds, probate
   records with Clerk of Courts)
probate search service: $2.00; copies of land
   records: $1.00 per page, $2.00 per certified
   page; certified copies of vital records: $7.00
   each for births and deaths, $5.00 each for
   marriages; copies of probate records: 25¢ per
   page, no minimum

Capital: Nashville. Statehood: 1 June 1796
(acknowledged as part of the U.S. by Great Britain in
1783, eastern part constituted the State of Franklin,
1784 to 1788; North Carolina relinquished its claims
in 1790)

Tennessee has more than 300 Municipal
Courts in home-rule municipalities that hear city
ordinance violations and various other matters.
Special Juvenile Courts have been set up in
some fourteen counties, exercising authority
otherwise given to the General Sessions Courts.
Davidson and Shelby counties have Probate
Courts, whose duties are elsewhere handled by
the General Sessions Courts. The General
Sessions Courts sit at each county seat and have
limited jurisdiction over civil controversies and
some misdemeanors, as well as conducting
preliminary felony hearings and, in some
counties, presiding over probate and juvenile
matters.
   In 1984 the State Trial Courts were divided
into thirty-one judicial districts, consisting of the
Criminal Courts, the Chancery Courts and the
Circuit Courts, sitting at each county seat.
Thereby the Law and Equity Courts of Gibson,
Montgomery and Sullivan counties became
Chancery Courts, and the Law and Equity Court
of Dyer County became a Circuit Court.
Criminal Courts, having original jurisdiction
over criminal matters, are established in thirteen
of the thirty-one judicial districts in the state
(marked below[1]). Chancery Courts, having
jurisdiction over all equity matters (over $50),
most civil cases (except torts), divorce and
adoption, as well as some probate matters, exist
in twenty-five judicial districts (marked below[2]).
Circuit Courts have general jurisdiction in each
of the thirty-one judicial districts.
   First Judicial District[1,2]: Carter, Johnson,
Unicoi and Washington counties; Second[1,2]:
Sullivan County; Third[1,2]: Greene, Hamblen,
Hancock and Hawkins; Fourth[2]: Cocke,
Grainger, Jefferson and Sevier; Fifth: Blount
County; Sixth[1,2]: Knox County; Seventh[2]:
Anderson County; Eighth[1,2]: Campbell,
Claiborne, Fentress, Scott and Union; Ninth[1,2]:
Loudon, Meigs, Morgan and Roane; Tenth[1,2]:
Bradley, McMinn, Monroe and Polk;
Eleventh[1,2]: Hamilton County; Twelfth[2]:
Bledsoe, Franklin, Grundy, Marion, Rhea and
Sequatchie; Thirteenth[1,2]: Clay, Cumberland,
DeKalb, Overton, Pickett, Putnam and White;
Fourteenth: Coffee County; Fifteenth[1,2]:
Jackson, Macon, Smith, Trousdale and Wilson;
Sixteenth[2]: Cannon and Rutherford;
Seventeenth[2]: Bedford, Lincoln, Marshall and
Moore; Eighteenth[1,2]: Sumner County;
Nineteenth[2]: Montgomery and Robertson;
Twentieth[1,2]: Davidson County; Twenty-first:
Hickman, Lewis, Perry and Williamson; Twenty-
second: Giles, Lawrence, Maury and Wayne;
Twenty-third: Cheatham, Dickson, Houston,
Humphreys and Stewart; Twenty-fourth[2]:
Benton, Carroll, Decatur, Hardin and Henry;
Twenty-fifth[2]: Fayette, Hardeman, Lauderdale,
McNairy and Tipton; Twenty-sixth[2]: Chester,
Henderson and Madison; Twenty-seventh[2]:
Obion and Weakley; Twenty-eighth[2] Crockett,
Gibson and Haywood; Twenty-ninth[2]: Dyer and
Lake; Thirtieth[1,2]: Shelby County; Thirty-first:
Van Buren and Warren. Appeals are heard by
the Court of Appeals, Court of Criminal
Appeals and Supreme Court.

Anderson County
organized 1801 from Grainger and Knox
counties

Anderson County Courthouse
100 North Main Street
Clinton, TN 37716
(865) 457-6235 (Register of Deeds, Room 205);
   (865) 463-6842 (Circuit Court Clerk); (865)
457-6228 (County Clerk, Room 111); (865)
   457-6248 (Chancery Court Clerk and Master,
   Room 308); (865) 463-6892 FX (County
   Clerk)
tshelton@titlescarcher.com;
   jcole@andersontn.org
http://www.andersontn.org
Tim Shelton, Register of Deeds; Barry Pelizzari,
   Circuit Court Clerk; Jeff Cole, County Clerk;
   Steve Queener, Chancery Court Clerk and
   Master

Bedford County
organized 1807 from Rutherford County and
Indian lands

Bedford County Courthouse
1 Public Square
Shelbyville, TN 37160
(931) 684-5719 (Register of Deeds, 108
   Northside Square); (931) 684-3223 (Circuit
   Court Clerk, Suite 200); (931) 684-1921
   (County Clerk, 104 Northside Square); (931)
   684-1672 (Chancery Court Clerk and Master,
   Room 302); (931) 685-2086 FAX (Register of
   Deeds); (931) 685-9590 FAX (County Clerk)
Kathy.Prater@state.tn.us;
   TN02CH001@smtpaoc.tsc.state.tn.us
   (Chancery Court Clerk and Master)
http://www.bedfordcountytn.org
John H. Reed, Jr., Register of Deeds; Thomas A.
   Smith, Circuit Court Clerk; Kathy K. Prater,
   County Clerk; Patricia Finney, Chancery
   Court Clerk and Master
(land records from the early or mid-1800s with
   Register of Deeds; births from 1909 to 1911,
   and from 1925 to 1939, deaths from 1925 to
   1939, marriages from 1 January 1861 to date
   and probate records from 1861 to 31 August
   1982 with County Clerk, probate records after
   1 September 1982 with Howard Barton,
   Chancery Court Clerk and Master)
copies of vital records: $2.00 each, $4.00 for
   certified copies; copies of probate records:
   $1.00 per page, $2.00 each for certified copies

Benton County
organized 1835 from Henry and Humphreys
counties

Benton County Courthouse
(1 East Court Square—location)
PO Box 8 (mailing address)
Camden, TN 38320-0008
(731) 584-6661 (Register of Deeds, Room
   105);(731) 584-6711 (Circuit Court Clerk);
   (731) 584-6053 (County Clerk); (731) 584-
   4435 (Chancery Court Clerk and Master);
   (731) 584-4640 FAX (Register of Deeds)
debbiehargis10@hotmail.com;
   Wanda.Malin@state.tn.us;
   timothy.burrus@tscmail.state.tn.us
http://www.bentoncountynet.com/countymeeti
   ngs.html
Debra Hargis, Register of Deeds; Terry Hudson,
   Circuit Court Clerk; Wanda Malin, County
   Clerk; Timothy Burrus, Chancery Court Clerk
   and Master
(marriage licenses from 1852 to date and
   probate records to 1984 with County Clerk,
   probate records from 1984 with Chancery
   Court Clerk and Master)
vital records search service: $5.00

Bledsoe County
organized 1807 from Roane County and Indian
lands

Bledsoe County Courthouse
116 Main Street
Pikeville, TN 37367
(423) 447-2020 (Register of Deeds, PO Box
   385); (423) 447-6488 (Circuit Court Clerk);
   (423) 447-2137 (County Clerk, PO Box 212);
   (423) 447-2484 (Chancery Court Clerk and
   Master); (423) 447-6856 FAX (Register of
   Deeds); (423) 447-6856 FAX (County Clerk)
TN04CC003@smtpaoc.tsc.state.tn.us (Circuit
   Court Clerk); Carolyn.Terry@state.tn.us;

TN04CH001@smtpaoc.tsc.state.tn.us
(Chancery Court Clerk and Master)
http://www.pikeville-bledsoe.com
Emma S. Boynton, Register of Deeds; Carolyn
M. Terry, County Clerk; Jamey Roberson,
Circuit Court Clerk; Greg Forgey, Chancery
Court Clerk and Master
(land records from 1908 to date (most earlier
records destroyed by fire], one will book and
some old court minutes have been restored
[but cannot be copied] with Register of
Deeds)
no land records search service

Blount County
organized 1795 from Knox County

Blount County Courthouse
349 Court Street
Maryville, TN 37803-5906
(865) 273-5880 (Register of Deeds); (865) 273-
5400 (Circuit Court Clerk, 926 East Lamar
Alexander Parkway, 37804-6201); (865) 273-
5800 (County Clerk, 345 Court Street, 37804-
5906); (865) 273-5500 (Chancery Court Clerk
and Master, Blount County Justice Center,
930 East Lamar Alexander Prkway, 37804-
5002); (865) 273-5890 FAX (Register of
Deeds); (865) 273-5815 FAX (County Clerk);
(865) 273-5519 FAX (Chancery Court Clerk
and Master)
pwhaley@mail.blount.state.tn.us; thatcher@
blounttn.org; rcrawford@mail.blount.
state.tn.us; jcarroll@blounttn.org
http://www.blounttn.org
Penny H. Whaley, Register of Deeds; Thomas
Hatcher, Circuit Court Clerk; Roy Crawford,
Jr., County Clerk; Brenda Flowers, Chancery
Court Clerk and Master

Bradley County
organized 1836 from Indian lands

Bradley County Courthouse
355 Ocoee Street
Cleveland, TN 37311
(423) 728-7201 (Archives); (423) 728-7240
(Register of Deeds); (423) 728-7214 (Circuit
Court Clerk); (423) 728-7048 (Circuit Court
Clerk); (423) 728-7226 (County Clerk); (423)
728-7206 (Chancery Court Clerk and Master);
(423) 476-0488 FAX (Circuit Court Clerk);
(423) 478-8845 FAX (County Clerk); (423)
339-0723 FAX (Chancery Court Clerk and
Master)
ahindman@bradleyco.net;
ntrimble@bradleyco.net (Register of Deeds);
asimpson@bradleyco.et;
Donna.Simpson@state.tn.us;
TN06CH001@smtpaoc.tsc.state.tn.us
(Chancery Court Clerk and Master)
http://www.bradleyco.net
Amy Hindman, Archives Director; Raymond
Swafford, Register of Deeds; Gayla Miller,
Circuit Court Clerk; Donna Simpson, County
Clerk; Carl Shrewsbury, Chancery Court Clerk
and Master
(deeds, wills, old marriage bonds, and family
files with all the original court records with
Archives)

Campbell County
organized 1806 from Anderson and Claiborne
counties

Campbell County Courthouse
195 Kentucky Street
Jacksboro, TN 37757
(423) 562-3864 (Register of Deeds, PO Box 85);
(423) 562-2624 (Circuit Court Clerk); (423)
562-4985 (County Clerk, Suite 2, PO Box
450); (423) 562-3496 (Chancery Court Clerk
and Master); (423) 562-9833 FAX (Register of
Deeds); (423) 566-3852 FAX (County Clerk)
Don.Nance@state.tn.us;
TN07CH001@smtpaoc.tsc.state.tn.us
(Chancery Court Clerk and Master)
http://co.campbell.tn.us
Dormas Miller, Register of Deeds; Brenda

Boshears, Circuit Court Clerk; Don Nance,
County Clerk; Bill Archer, Chancery Court
Clerk and Master

Cannon County
organized 1836 from Rutherford, Warren and
Smith counties

Cannon County Courthouse
Woodbury Public Square
Woodbury, TN 37190
(615) 563-2041 (Register of Deeds); (615) 563-
4461 (Circuit Court Clerk); (615) 563-8142
(County Clerk); (615) 563-5936 (Chancery
Court Clerk and Master); (615) 563-5696
FAX (Register of Deeds); (615) 563-1289
FAX (County Clerk)
debbie.morris@vcourthouse.com;
Bobby.P.Smith@state.tn.us
http://www.cannoncounty.info
Deborah Morris, Register of Deeds; Bobby
Smith, County Clerk; Robert H. "Hoppy"
Davenport, Circuit Court Clerk; Harold
Patrick, Chancery Court Clerk and Master

Carroll County
organized 1821 from Western District (Indian
lands)

Carroll County Courthouse
625 High Street
Huntingdon, TN 38344
(731) 986-1952 (Register of Deeds, PO Box
432); (731) 986-1990 (Health Department);
(731) 986-1926 (Circuit Court Clerk, 99 Court
Square, Suite 103); (731) 986-1960 (County
Clerk, Suite 103); (731) 986-1920 (Chancery
Court Clerk and Master); (731) 986-1955
FAX (Register of Deeds); (731) 986-1978
FAX (County Clerk)
natalie.mccullough@vcourthouse.com
(Register); Crolyn.Lutz@state.tn.us;
kenneth.todd@tscmail.state.tn.us
http://www.tennesseeanytime.org/local/carroll.
html
Natalie Porter, Register of Deeds; Bertha Taylor,
Circuit Court Clerk; Carolyn Lutz, County
Clerk; Kenneth Todd, Chancery Court Clerk
and Master
(land records with Register of Deeds, vital records
with Health Department, marriages from 1838
with County Clerk, probate records with
Chancery Court Clerk and Master)

Carter County
organized 1796 from Washington County; name
changed from Carteret County

Carter County Courthouse
801 East Elk Avenue
Elizabethton, TN 37643
(423) 542-1830 (Register of Deeds); (423) 542-
1835 (Circuit Court Clerk, Carter County
Justice Center, 924 East Elk Avenue); (423)
542-1814 (County Clerk); (423) 542-1812
(Chancery Court Clerk and Master)
Mary.Gouge@state.tn.us
http://www.cartercountyt.com
Jody Bristol, Register of Deeds; John Paul
Mathes, Circuit Court Clerk; Mary Gouge,
County Clerk; Melissa Moreland, Chancery
Court Clerk and Master

Cheatham County
organized 1856 from Dickson, Montgomery,
Davidson and Robertson counties

Cheatham County Criminal Justice Center
100 Public Square
Ashland City, TN 37015-1711
(615) 792-4317 (Register of Deeds, 210 South
Main, Suite 109); (615) 792-3272 (Circuit
Court Clerk, Suite 106); (615) 792-5179
(County Clerk, 264 South Main Street, Suite
108); (615) 792-4620 (Chancery Court Clerk
and Master, Suite 106); (615) 792-2039 FAX
(Register of Deeds); (615) 792-2094 FAX
(County Clerk)
dolores.moulton2@courthouse.com;

dolores.moulton@vcourthouse.com;
WJHall@state.tn.us
http://www.cheathamcounty.net
Dolores Moulton, Register of Deeds; Julie
Womack, Circuit Court Clerk; W. J. Hall,
County Clerk; Pamela Jenkins, Chancery
Court Clerk and Master
(land records with Register of Deeds; marriages
from 1956 to date, wills and testaments from
1856 to 1982 with County Clerk; wills and
testaments from 1982 with Chancery Court
Clerk and Master)
probate search service from Chancery Court: no
charge; copies of marriages: 25¢ each (from
old records only), $1.00 for certified copies;
copies of wills and testaments from County
Clerk: $1.00 per page; copies of probate
records from Chancery Court: $2.00 per page,
$2.00 for certification, no minimum

Chester County
organized 1879 from Hardeman, Henderson,
Madison and McNairy counties

Chester County Courthouse
159 East Main Street
Henderson, TN 38340
(731) 989-4991 (Register of Deeds, PO Box
292); (731) 989-2233 (County Clerk, 133 East
Main, PO Box 205); (731) 989-2454 (Circuit
Court Clerk, PO Box 133); (731) 989-7171
(Chancery Court Clerk and Master, 126 Crook
Street, PO Box 262); (731) 989-7282 FAX
(Register of Deeds)
judy.cranford@vcourthouse.com;
johnny.garner@state.tn.us
http://www.tennesseeanytime.org/local/chester
.html
Judy H. Cranford, Register of Deeds; Keith
Frye, Circuit Court Clerk; Johnny Garner,
County Clerk; Cornelia Hall, Chancery Court
Clerk and Master

Claiborne County
organized 1801 from Grainger and Hawkins
counties

Claiborne County Courthouse
1740 Main Street
Tazewell, TN 37879
(423) 626-3325 (Register of Deeds, PO Box
117); (423) 626-8181 (Circuit Court Clerk,
Criminal Justice Center, 415 Straight Creek
Road, 37825); (423) 626-3283 (County Clerk,
PO Box 173); (423) 626-3284 (Chancery
Court Clerk and Master, PO Box 180); (423)
626-1661 FAX (Register of Deeds); (423)
626-1661 FAX (County Clerk)
TN13CC001@smtpaoc.tsc.state.tn.us (Circuit
Court Clerk); evelyn.hill@state.tn.us
http://www.claibornecounty.com
Kimberly H. Reece, Register of Deeds; Billy Ray
Cheek, Circuit Court Clerk; Evelyn Hill,
County Clerk; Frances Cardwell, Chancery
Court Clerk and Master

Clay County
organized 1870 from Jackson and Overton
counties

Clay County Courthouse
Celina, TN 38551
(931) 243-3298 (Register of Deeds, PO Box
430); (931) 243-2557 (Circuit Court Clerk, PO
Box 156); (931) 243-2249 (County Clerk, PO
Box 218); (931) 243-3145 (Chancery Court
Clerk and Master, PO Box 332)
Patricia.Hix@state.tn.us;
tn14ch003@tscmail.state.tn.us (Chancery
Court Clerk and Master)
http://www.dalehollowlake.org/county.htm
Brenda Browning, Register of Deeds; Peggy
Ballard, Circuit Court Clerk; Patricia Hix,
County Clerk; Corrinne McLerran, Chancery
Court Clerk and Master
(land records with Register of Deeds, probate
records with Chancery Court Clerk and
Master)

Cocke County

organized 1797 from Jefferson County

Cocke County Courthouse Annex
360 East Main Street
Newport, TN 37821
(423) 623-7540 (Register of Deeds, 111 Court Avenue, Room 102); (423) 623-6124 (Circuit Court Clerk); (423) 623-6176 (County Clerk, County Records Commission, 111 Court Avenue, Room 101); (423) 623-3321 (Chancery Court Clerk and Master); (423) 623-6178 FAX (County Clerk)
janice.a.butler@state.tn.us;
tn15ch001@smtpaoc.tsc.state.tn.us (Chancery Court Clerk and Master)
http://www.cockecounty.net/county_officials.htm
Linda H. Benson, Register of Deeds; Peggy Lane, Circuit Court Clerk; Janice Butler, County Clerk; Craig Wild, Chancery Court Clerk and Master
(land records with Register of Deeds, marriages from 1877 to date with County Clerk, probate records with Chancery Court Clerk and Master)
copies of open records: $1.00 each, $2.00 for certified copies

Coffee County

organized 1836 from Bedford, Franklin and Warren counties

Coffee County Courthouse
101 West Fort Street
Manchester, TN 37355
(931) 723-5130 (Register of Deeds, PO Box 178); (931) 723-5110 (Circuit Court Clerk, 300 Hillsboro Boulevard, PO Box 629, Manchester, TN 37349); (931) 723-5106 (County Clerk, 1327 McArthur Street); (931) 723-5132 (Chancery Court Clerk and Master, 300 Hillsboro Boulevard, Box 8, Manchester, TN 37355); (931) 723-8248 FAX (County Clerk)
evaughn@coffeecountytn.org; teresa.mcfadden @state.tn.us; cvbroyles@cafes.net
http://www.coffeecountytn.org
Ellen P. Vaughn, Register of Deeds; Heather H. Duncan, Circuit Court Clerk; Teresa McFadden, County Clerk; Charlotte V. Broyles, Chancery Court Clerk and Master
(deeds from 1835 with Register of Deeds)

Crockett County

organized 1871 from Dyer, Gibson, Haywood and Madison counties

Crockett County Courthouse
1 South Bells Street
Alamo, TN 38001
(731) 696-5455 (Register of Deeds, Suite 2); (731) 696-5462 (Circuit Court Clerk, Suite 6); (731) 696-5452 (County Clerk, Suite 1); (731) 696-5458 (Chancery Court Clerk and Master, Suite 5); (731) 696-4101 FAX (Register of Deeds); (731) 696-3261 FAX (County Clerk)
alan.castellaw@vcourthouse.com;
Ernest.Bushart@state.tn.us;
kim.kail@tscmail.state.tn.us
http://www.tennesseeanytime.org/local/crockett.html
Alan K. Castellaw, Register of Deeds; Kim Kail, Circuit Court Clerk; Ernest Bushart, County Clerk; Betty Johnson, Chancery Court Clerk and Master

Cumberland County

organized November 1855 from Bledsoe, Fentress, Morgan, Putnam, Rhea, Roane, Van Buren and White counties; boundary lines established by 1856

Cumberland County Courthouse
2 North Main Street
Crossville, TN 38555-9428
(931) 484-5559 (Register of Deeds, Suite 204); (931) 484-6647 (Circuit Court Clerk, Suite 302); (931) 484-6442 (County Clerk, Suite 206); (931) 484-4731 (Chancery Court Clerk and Master, Suite 101); (931) 484-6440 FAX (County Clerk)
Jule.Bryson@state.tn.us;
tn18ch001@smtpaoc.tsc.state.tn.us (Chancery Court Clerk and Master)
http://www.brockhill.org; http://www.tennesseeanytime.org/local/cumberland.html
Judy Graham Swallows, Register of Deeds, Larry Sherrill, Circuit Court Clerk; Jule Bryson, County Clerk; Sue Tollett, Chancery Court Clerk and Master
(land records from 1856 [sketchy before 1905 courthouse fire] with Registrar of Deeds and Tax Assessor, vital records with County Court Clerk; probate records with Chancery Court Clerk and Master)

Davidson County

organized 1783 (Middle Tennessee) by act of North Carolina; consolidated with the City of Nashville in 1962

Davidson County Courthouse
1 Public Square
Nashville, TN 37201-5007
(615) 862-6790 (Register of Deeds, Gaylord Entertainment Center, 501 Broadway PO Box 196398, 372-19-6398); (615) 862-5181 (Circuit Court Clerk, Suite 302, PO Box 196303, 37219-6303); (615) 862-6256 (County Clerk, Marriage and Notary Department, 523 Mainstrem Drive, 37228); (615) 862-5710 (Chancery Court Clerk and Master, Suite 308); (615) 862-5191 FAX (Circuit Court Clerk);
rod.infodesk@nashville.gov; bill.garrett@nashville.gov; circuit@nashville.gov; CountyClerk@nashville.gov; RickyRooker@jis.Nashville.org
http://www.nashville.org; http://www.tennesseeanytime.org/local/davidson.html
Bill Garrett, Register of Deeds; Richard Rooker, Circuit Court Clerk; John Arriola, County Clerk; Claudia Bonnyman, Chancery Court Clerk and Master
(land records from 1784 to date with Register of Deeds; births from 1881 to 1908, deaths from 1874-1908 for Nashville with Tennessee State Library and Archives)

Decatur County

organized 1845 from Perry County

Decatur County Courthouse
(22 West Main Street—location)
PO Box 488 (mailing address)
Decaturville, TN 38329-0488
(731) 852-3712 (Register of Deeds); (731) 852-3125 (Circuit Court Clerk); (731) 852-3417 (County Clerk); (731) 852-3422 (Chancery Court Clerk and Master)
davisd@decaturcountytn.org;
tannerd@decaturcountytn.org;
poper@decaturcountytn.org;
Randy.Pope@state.tn.us;
tn20ch001@smtpaoc.tsc.state.tn.us (Chancery Court Clerk and Master)
http://www.decaturcountytn.org
Donald Davis, Register of Deeds; Danny Tanner, Circuit Court Clerk; Randy Pope, County Clerk; Elizabeth Carpenter, Chancery Court Clerk and Master

DeKalb County

organized 1837 from Cannon, Warren, White, Wilson and Jackson counties

DeKalb County Courthouse
1 Public Square
Smithville, TN 37166
(615) 597-4153 (Register of Deeds, Room 201); (615) 597-5711 (Circuit Court Clerk, Room 303); (615) 597-5177 (County Clerk, Room 205); (615) 597-4360 (Chancery Court Clerk and Master, Room 302)
tn21cc001@smtpaoc.tsc.state.tn.us (Circuit Court Clerk); Mike.Clayborn@state.tn.us; tn21ch001@smtpaoc.tsc.state.tn.us (Chancery Court Clerk and Master)
http://www.smithvilletn.com/government/indexhtm
Jeffrey McMillen, Register of Deeds; Mrs. Katherine Pack, Circuit Court Clerk; Michael Clayborn, County Clerk; Mrs. Debra "Debbie" Malone, Chancery Court Clerk and Master

Dickson County

organized 1803 from Montgomery and Robertson counties

Dickson County Courthouse
1 Court Square
Charlotte, TN 37036
(615) 789-4171, ext. 242 (Register of Deeds, PO Box 200); (615) 789-4171 (Circuit Court Clerk, Courthouse Annex, PO Box 70); (615) 789-7010 (Circuit Court Clerk); (615) 789-5093 (County Clerk, Room 126, PO Box 220); (615) 789-4171 (Chancery Court Clerk and Master, Courthouse Annex, PO Box 547); (615) 789-7011 (Chancery Court Clerk and Master); (615) 789-0128 FAX (County Clerk)
Jackdeeds@aol.com; jackie.farthing@vcourthouse.com; tn22cc001@smtpaoc.tsc.state.tn.us (Circuit Court Clerk); phil.simons@state.tn.us; tn22ch001@smtpaoc.tsc.state.tn.us (Chancery Court Clerk and Master)
http://www.dicksoncounty.net
Jackie Wall Farthing, Register of Deeds; Pam Myatt, Circuit Court Clerk; Phil Simons, County Clerk; Nancy Miller, Chancery Court Clerk and Master
(land records with Register of Deeds, probate records with County Clerk)
no probate search service ("I most times turn it over to someone and set the charges by them")

Dyer County

organized 1823 from Western District (Indian lands)

Dyer County Courthouse
PO Box 1360
Dyersburg, TN 38025-1360
(731) 286-7806 (Register of Deeds, 1 Veteran's Square); (731) 288-7898 (Register of Deeds); (731) 286-7808 (Circuit Court Clerk); (731) 286-7814 (County Clerk, 115 Market Street); (731) 286-7818 (Chancery Court Clerk and Master, Room 201); (731) 288-7724 FAX (Register of Deeds); (731) 288-7719 FAX (County Clerk)
danny.fowlkes@vcourthouse.com;
dfowlkes@co.dyer.th.us;
diane.moore@state.tn.us;
jhoff_38024@yahoo.com
http://www.co.dyer.tn.us (coming soon)
John Fowlkes, Register of Deeds; Tom T. J. Jones, Circuit Court Clerk; Diane Moore, County Clerk; John H. Hoff, Chancery Court Clerk and Master

Fayette County

organized 1824 from Shelby and Hardeman counties

Fayette County Courthouse
1 Court Square
Somerville, TN 38068
(901) 465-5251 (Register of Deeds, PO Box 99); (901) 465-5205 (Circuit Court Clerk, Room 201, PO Box 670); (901) 465-5213 (County Clerk, Room 101, PO Box 218); (901) 465-5219 (Chancery Court Clerk and Master, Room 104, PO Box 220); (901) 465-5293 FAX (County Clerk)
Sue.Culver@state.tn.us
http://www.fayettetn.us
Edward Pattat, Register of Deeds; Connie Doyle, Circuit Court Clerk; Sue Culver, County Clerk; Vip Lewis, Chancery Court Clerk and Master
(land records with Register of Deeds; early naturalization records with Circuit Court Clerk; marriages with County Clerk; probate records with Chancery Court Clerk and

Master)
probate search service: no charge; copies of
probate records: 30¢ each

Fentress County
organized 1823 from Overton, White and
Morgan counties

Fentress County Courthouse
101 Main Street South
Jamestown, TN 38556
(931) 8779-7818 (Register of Deeds, PO Box
341); (931) 879-7919 (Circuit Court Clerk, PO
Box 699); (931) 879-8014 (County Clerk, PO
Box 823); (931) 879-8615 (Chancery Court
Clerk and Master, PO Box 66); (931) 879-
4502 FAX (Register of Deeds); (931) 879-
8438 FAX (County Clerk)
fentress@titlesearcher.com; countyclerk@
twlakes.net; Marilyn.L.Stephens@state.tn.us
http://www.tennesseeanytime.org/local/
fentress.html
Loyce Stephens, Register of Deeds; Tammy
Smith, Circuit Court Clerk; Marilyn Stephens,
County Clerk; Kathryn Robbins, Chancery
Court Clerk and Master

Franklin County
organized 1807 from Rutherford County and
Indian lands

Franklin County Courthouse
1 South Jefferson Street
Winchester, TN 37398
(931) 967-2840 (Register of Deeds); (931) 967-
2923 (Circuit Court Clerk); (931) 967-2541
(County Clerk); (931) 967-2843 (Chancery
Court Clerk and Master); (931) 962-1463
FAX (Register of Deeds); (931) 962-3394
FAX (County Clerk)
lydiadarlene61@hotmail.com; nancysilver
tooth@bellsouth.net; Nina.Tucker@state.tn.us
http://www.franklncotn.us
Lydia Johnson, Register of Deeds; Nancy
Silvertooth, Circuit Court Clerk; Nina Tucker,
County Clerk; Brenda Clark, Chancery Court
Clerk and Master

Gibson County
organized 1823 from Western District (Indian
lands)

Gibson County Courthouse
1 Court Square
Trenton, TN 38382
(731) 855-7627 (Register of Deeds, Suite 201);
(731) 855-7615 (Circuit Court Clerk, 295
North College, PO Box 147); (731) 855-7628
(Register of Deeds); (731) 855-7615 (Circuit
Court Clerk); (731) 855-7642 (County Clerk,
Suite 100, PO Box 228); (731) 855-7639
(Chancery Court Clerk and Master, 204
Nourth Court Square, PO Box 290); (731)
855-7643 FAX (County Clerk)
hilda.patterson@vcourthouse.com;
Diane.P.Taylor@state.tn.us;
loislockhart701@hotmail.com
http://www.gibsoncountytn.com
Hilda T. Patterson, Register of Deeds; Janice
Jones, Circuit Court Clerk; Diane Taylor,
County Clerk; Lois Lockhart, Chancery Court
Clerk and Master
(land records with Tax Assessor, vital records
with County Clerk, Chancery Court Clerk and
Master at Humboldt and Trenton, and Circuit
Clerk, probate records with Chancery Court
Clerk and Master, Trenton)
no probate search service; copies of probate
records: 50¢ per page, no minimum

Giles County
organized 1809 from Maury County

Giles County Courthouse
(1 Public Square—location)
PO Box 678 (mailing address)
Pulaski, TN 38478-0678
(931) 363-8434 (Old Records Department);
(931) 363-5137 (Recorder of Deeds); (931)

363-5311 (Circuit Court Clerk); (931) 424-
7000 (County Clerk); (931) 363-2620
(Chancery Court Clerk and Master); (931)
424-4795 FAX (County Clerk)
gilesrod@titlesearcher.com;
Carol.Wade@state.tn.us
http://www.rackleyhost.com/GilesCounty
Clara M. Parker, Director of Old Records
Department; Kay Gibbons, Register of
Deeds; Crystal Greene, Circuit Court Clerk;
Carol H. Wade, County Clerk; Merry Sigmon,
Chancery Court Clerk and Master
(deeds from 1810 to 1900, Survey-Entry from
1828 to 1848, tax books from 1875, tax lists
1812 and 1836, marriages from 1865 to 1900
[a few early marriages before 1865], will
books from 1860 to 1900, some early loose
wills, Chancery Court Original Court Cases
from the 1830s, some County Court loose
records and cases with Old Records
Department)
probate search service: $10.00; vital records
search service: $10.00; land records search
service: $10.00; copies of land records: 25¢
per page (back and front); copies of vital
records: 25¢ per page (back and front); copies
of probate records: 25¢ per page (back and
front)

Grainger County
organized 1796 from Hawkins County

Grainger County Courthouse
Rutledge, TN 37861
(865) 850-8549 (Archives, PO Box 408); (865)
828-3523 (Register of Deeds); (865) 828-3605
(Circuit Court Clerk, PO Box 157); (865) 828-
3511 (County Clerk, PO Box 116); (865) 828-
4436 (Chancery Court Clerk and Master);
(865) 828-4284 FAX (Register of Deeds);
(865) 828-3203 FAX (County Clerk)
graingerarchives@msn.com;
Angie.Lamb@state.tn.us
http://www.graingertn.com
Stevvi Cook, Archives Manager; Dorothy
Reagan, Register of Deeds; Rhonda Reagan,
Circuit Court Clerk; Angie Jackson Lamb,
County Clerk; Vickie L. Greenlee, Chancery
Court Clerk and Master

Greene County
organized 1783 from Washington County

Greene County Courthouse
101 South Main Street
Greeneville, TN 37743
(423) 798-1726 (Register of Deeds, 204 North
Cutler Street, 37745); (423) 638-4332 (Circuit
Court Clerk); (423) 798-1760 (Circuit Court
Clerk); (423) 798-1708 (County Clerk,
Courthouse Annex, 204 North Cutler Street,
Suite 200, 37745); (423) 638-6501 (Chancery
Court Clerk and Master); (423) 798-1742
(Chancery Court Clerk and Master); (423)
798-1822 FAX (County Clerk)
jump4joyr@yahoo.com; David.Thompson@
state.tn.us; greenecm@earthlink.net
http://www.tennesseeanytime.org/local/greene.
html
Joy Rader, Register of Deeds; Gail Davis Jeffers,
Circuit Court Clerk; David Thompson,
County Clerk; Kay Armstrong, Chancery
Court Clerk and Master

Grundy County
organized 1844 from Franklin and Warren
counties

Grundy County Courthouse
Cumberland Street
Altamont, TN 37301
(931) 692-3621 (Register of Deeds, PO Box 35);
(931) 692-3368 (Circuit Court Clerk, PO Box
161); (931) 692-3622 (County Clerk,
Courthouse Circle, Grundy Street, PO Box
215); (931) 692-3455 (Chancery Court Clerk
and Master, PO Box 174); (931) 692-3627
FAX (Register of Deeds); (931) 692-3659
FAX (County Clerk)

gayle.vanhooser@vcourthouse.com;
Jimmy.Rogers@state.tn.us
http://www.tennesseeanytime.org/local/grundy
.html
Gayle VanHooser, Register of Deeds; Marcia
Bess, Circuit Court Clerk; Jimmy Rogers,
County Clerk; Phyllis Dent, Chancery Court
Clerk and Master

Hamblen County
organized 1870 from Grainger, Hawkins and
Jefferson counties

Hamblen County Courthouse
511 West Second North Street
Morristown, TN 37814-3964
(423) 586-6551 (Register of Deeds); (423) 586-
5640 (Circuit Court Clerk, 510 Allison Street);
(423) 586-1993 (County Clerk); (423) 586-
9112 (Chancery Court Clerk and Master,
Room 303); (423) 318-2505 FAX (Register of
Deeds); (423) 585-2015 FAX (County Clerk)
Linda.Wilder@state.tn.us; kjt59@hotmail.com
http://www.hamblencountygovernment.us
Jim R. Clawson, Register of Deeds; Kathy
Mullins, Circuit Court Clerk; Linda Wilder,
County Clerk; Kathy Jones-Terry, Chancery
Court Clerk and Master
(land records with Register of Deeds, vital
records and probate records with County
Clerk)
probate search service: per time charge; copies
of probate records: 10¢ per page, $2.00 for
certified copies, no minimum

Hamilton County
organized 1819 from Rhea County and Indian
lands, and in January 1920 annexed James
County, which was organized 1871 from
Hamilton and Bradley counties

Hamilton County Courthouse
625 Georgia Avenue
Chattanooga, TN 37402
(423) 209-6560 (Register of Deeds, 400
Courthouse, PO Box 1639); (423) 209-6700
(Circuit Court Clerk, 500 Courthouse); (423)
209-6500 (County Clerk, 201 Courthouse);
(423) 209-6600 (Chancery Court Clerk and
Master, 300 Courthouse); (423) 209-6561
FAX (Register of Deeds); (423) 209-6701
(Circuit Court Clerk); (423) 209-6501 FAX
(County Clerk); (423) 209-6601 FAX
(Chancery Court Clerk and Master)
PHurst@exch.HamiltonTN.gov;
CountyClerk@mail.hamiltontn.gov;
LeeAkers@exch.hamiltontn.gov
http://www.hamiltontn.gov
Pamela Hurst, Register of Deeds; Paula
Tompson, Circuit Court Clerk; William F.
"Bill" Knowles, County Clerk; Mr. S. Lee
Akers, Chancery Court Clerk and Master
(births from 1879 to 1908, deaths from 1872 to
1908 for Chattanooga with Tennessee State
Library and Archives)

Hancock County
organized 1844 from Claiborne and Hawkins
counties

Hancock County Courthouse
1237 Main Street
Sneedville, TN 37869
(423) 733-4545 (Register of Deeds, PO Box
347); (423) 733-2954 (Circuit Court Clerk, PO
Box 347); (423) 733-2519 (County Clerk (PO
Box 575); (423) 733-4524 (Chancery Court
Clerk and Master, Suite 104, PO Box 347);
(423) 733-4509 FAX (County Clerk)
janie.lamb@vcourthouse.com;
Wayne.Dean@state.tn.us
http://www.hancockcountytn.com
Janie Lamb, Register of Deeds; Bill McMurry,
Circuit Court Clerk; Wayne Dean, County
Clerk; Scott Collins, Chancery Court Clerk
and Master

Hardeman County
organized 1823 from Hardin County and

Western District (Indian lands)

Hardeman County Courthouse
100 North Main Street
Bolivar, TN 38008-2322
(731) 658-3476 (Register of Deeds); (731) 658-6524 (Circuit Court Clerk); (731) 658-3541 (County Clerk); (731) 658-3142 (Chancery Court Clerk and Master, PO Box 45)
lily.barnes@vcourthouse.net;
   Jerry.Armstrong@state.tn.us;
   Janice.Bodiford@tscmail.state.tn.us
http://www.hardemancotn.org
Lily D. Barnes, Register of Deeds; Linda K. Fulghum, Circuit Court Clerk; Mr. Jerry W. Armstrong, County Clerk; Mrs. Janice M. Bodiford, Chancery Court Clerk and Master

Hardin County
organized 1819 from Western District (Indian lands), to run to the Mississippi, but eleven days later Shelby County was organized from Hardin County

Hardin County Courthouse
601 Main Street
Savannah, TN 38372
(731) 925-4936 (Register of Deeds); (731) 925-3583 (Circuit Court Clerk, 465 Main Street); (731) 925-3921 (County Clerk, Courthouse Annex Building, 65 Court Street, Suite 1); (731) 925-8166 (Chancery Court Clerk and Master, 465 Main Street); (731) 926-4313 FAX (County Clerk)
juliegail@vcourthouse.com;
   Connie.S.Stephens@state.tn.us;
   tn36ch001@smtpaoc.tsc.state.tn.us (Chancery Court Clerk and Master)
http://www.tennesseeanytime.org/local/hardin.html
Julie Gail Adkisson, Register of Deeds; Diane B. Polk, Circuit Court Clerk; Connie Stephens, County Clerk; Martha Smith, Chancery Court Clerk and Master

Hawkins County
organized 1786 from Sullivan County

Hawkins County Courthouse
150 Washington Street
Rogersville, TN 37857-3346
(423) 272-8304 (Register of Deeds, PO Box 235); (423) 272-3397 (Circuit Court Clerk, 100 East Main Street, Room 203); (423) 272-7002 (County Clerk, 100 East Main Street, Room 204, PO Box 790); (423) 272-8150 (Chancery Court Clerk and Master, 100 East Main Street, Room 103, PO Box 908); (423) 921-3170 FAX (Register of Deeds); (423) 272-5801 FAX (County Clerk)
jckirkpatrick@chartertn.net;
   tn37cc001@smtpaoc.tsc.state.tn.us (Circuit Court Clerk); Carroll.Jenkins@state.tn.us;
   Shirley.Graham@tscmail.state.tn.us
http://www.hawkinscountytn.gov
Judy Kirkpatrick, Register of Deeds; Holly H. Jaynes, Circuit Court Clerk; A. Carroll Jenkins, County Clerk; Shirley Graham, Chancery Court Clerk and Master
(land records with Register of Deeds, naturalization records with Circuit Court Clerk, probate records from 1787 through 1982 with County Clerk, probate records from 1982 with Chancery Court Clerk and Master)
no probate search service from the County Clerk's Office; copies of probate records: 25¢ per page, $2.00 for certified copies

Haywood County
organized 1823 from Western District (Indian lands)

Haywood County Courthouse
1 North Washington Street
Brownsville, TN 38012-2557
(731) 772-0332 (Register of Deeds); (731) 772-1112 (Circuit Court Clerk); (731) 772-2362 (County Clerk); (731) 772-0122 (Chancery

Court Clerk and Master, PO Box 356); (731) 772-1213 FAX (County Clerk)
ann.d.medford@state.tn.us;
   judy.hardister@tscmail.state.tn.us
http://www.tennesseeanytime.org/local/haywood.html
Steven Smith, Register of Deeds; Elma Pirtle, Circuit Court Clerk; Ann D. Medford, County Clerk; Judy Hardister, Chancery Court Clerk and Master
(land records with Register of Deeds, naturalization records with County Clerk, vital records with County Clerk, probate records with Chancery Court Clerk and Master)
probate search service: depends on amount of research; copies of probate records: 25¢ each, no minimum

Henderson County
organized 1821 from Western District (Indian lands)

Henderson County Courthouse
17 Monroe Avenue
Lexington, TN 38351
(731) 968-2941 (Register of Deeds, Main Street); (731) 968-2031 (Circuit Court Clerk, Suite 9); (731) 968-2856 (County Clerk, Suite 2); (731) 968-2801 (Chancery Court Clerk and Master, Suite 2); (731) 968-6644 FAX (County Clerk)
denny.phillips@vcourthouse.com;
   Carolyn.Holmes@state.tn.us;
   tn39ch001@smtpaoc.tsc.state.tn.us (Chancery Court Clerk and Master)
http://www.tennesseeanytime.org/local/henderson.html
Denny H. Phillips, Register of Deeds; Kenny Cavness, Circuit Court Clerk; Carolyn Holmes, County Clerk; Leigh Milam, Chancery Court Clerk and Master

Henry County
organized 1821 from Western District (Indian lands)

Henry County Courthouse
101 West Washington
Paris, TN 38242
(731) 642-4081 (Register of Deeds, PO Box 44); (731) 642-0162 (Assessor of Property, PO Box 564); (731) 642-0461 (Circuit Court Clerk, PO Box 429); (731) 642-2412 (County Clerk, Suite 102, PO Box 24); (731) 642-4234 (Chancery Court Clerk and Master, PO Box 313); (731) 642-2123 FAX (Register of Deeds); (731) 644-0947 FAX (County Clerk)
alice.d.webb@vcourthouse.com;
   tn40cc001@smtpaoc.tsc.state.tn.us (Circuit Court Clerk); Jerry.Bomar@state.tn.us;
   tn40ch001@smtpaoc.tsc.state.tn.us (Chancery Court Clerk and Master)
http://www.henryco.com
Alice D. Webb, Register of Deeds; Charles Van Dyke, Assessor of Property; Rondall Myers, Circuit Court Clerk; Jerry D. Bomar, County Clerk; Mary Burns Chancery Court Clerk and Master
(land records with Register of Deeds or Assessor of Property, PO Box 564, Paris, TN 38242, marriages and probate records with County Clerk)

Hickman County
organized 1807 from Dickson County

Hickman County Courthouse
South Public Square
Centerville, TN 37033
(931) 729-4882 (Register of Deeds, #1 Courthouse); (931) 729-2211 (Circuit Court Clerk, 104 College Street, Suite 204); (931) 729-2621 (County Clerk, 114 North Central Avenue, Suite 202); (931) 729-2522 (Chancery Court Clerk and Master, 104 College Street, Suite 202); (931) 729-6113 FAX (Register of Deeds); (931) 729-6141 FAX (Circuit Court Clerk); (931) 729-6131 FAX (County Clerk); (931) 729-3726 FAX (Chancery Court Clerk and Master)

hickman@titlesearcher.com; circuitcourt@hickmanco.com; tn41cc006@tscmail.state.tn.us (Circuit Court Clerk); rtotty@state.tn.us; Randell.Totty@state.tn.us; chancerycourt@hickmanco.com; tn41ch001@smtpaoc.tsc.state.tn.us (Chancery Court Clerk and Master)
http://www.hickmanco.com
Patty Sisk, Register of Deeds; Dana Nicholson, Circuit Court Clerk; Randel Totty, County Clerk; Sue Smith, Chancery Court Clerk and Master

Houston County
organized 1871 from Dickson, Montgomery, Stewart and Humphreys counties

Houston County Courthouse
Erin, TN 37061
(931) 289-3510 (Register of Deeds, PO Box 412); (931) 289-4673 (Circuit Court Clerk, PO Box 402); (931) 289-3141 (County Clerk, 4725 East Main Street, Room 100); (931) 289-3870 (Chancery Court Clerk and Master, PO Box 332); (931) 289-2603 FAX (County Clerk)
sherrill.moore@vcourthouse.com;
   register103@hotmail.com;
   robert.reed.brown@state.tn.us
http://www.tennesseeanytime.org/local/houston.html
Sherrill P. Moore, Register of Deeds; Sharon Tomlinson, Circuit Court Clerk; Robert Brown, County Clerk; Patsy Brooks, Chancery Court Clerk and Master

Humphreys County
organized 1809 from Stewart County

Humphreys County Courthouse
Court Square
Waverly, TN 37185
(931) 296-7681 (Register of Deeds, Courthouse Annex, 102 Thompson Street); (931) 296-2461 (Circuit Court Clerk, Courthouse, 106 Court Square); (931) 296-7671 (County Clerk, Courthouse Annex, 102 Thompson Street, Room 2); (931) 296-2558 (Chancery Court Clerk and Master, Courthouse, 202 Court Squaare); (931) 296-0823 FAX (County Clerk)
shirleyf@titlesearcher.com (Register of Deeds); Betty.Etheridge@state.tn.us;
   mikebullion@yahoo.com
http://www.tennesseeanytime.org/local/humphreys.html
Janet "Jan" Crowell, Register of Deeds; Elaine Choate, Circuit Court Clerk; Betty Etheridge, County Clerk; Mike Bullion, Chancery Court Clerk and Master

Jackson County
organized 1801 from Smith County and Indian lands

Jackson County Courthouse
Gainesboro, TN 38562
(913) 268-9012 (Register of Deeds, PO Box 301); (931) 268-9314 (Circuit Court Clerk, PO Box 205); (931) 268-9212 (County Clerk, PO Box 346); (931) 268-9516 (Chancery Court Clerk and Master, PO Box 342); (931) 268-4555 FAX (Circuit Court Clerk); (931) 268-4149 FAX (County Clerk); (931) 268-9512 FAX (Chancery Court Clerk and Master)
jackson@titlesearcher.com;
   belinda.ward@state.tn.us
http://www.jacksonco.com
Kimberly "Kim" Barham, Register of Deeds; Aaron Thomas, Circuit Court Clerk; Belinda Ward, County Clerk; Garry Jones, Chancery Court Clerk and Master
(land records with Register of Deeds, probate records with County Clerk)
probate search service: $1.00; copies of probate records: 15¢ each

Jefferson County
organized 1792 from Greene and Hawkins counties

Jefferson County Courthouse

202 West Main Street
Dandridge, TN 37725
(865) 397-4904 (Museum and Archives, PO Box
1193); (865) 397-2918 (Register of Deeds, PO
Box 58); (865) 397-2786 (Circuit Court Clerk);
(865) 397-2935 (County Clerk, 214 West Main
Street, PO Box 710); (865) 397-2404
(Chancery Court Clerk and Master, 202 West
Main Street, Second Floor, PO Box 5); (865)
397-5689 FAX (Circuit Court Clerk); (865)
397-3839 FAX (County Clerk); (865) 397-
5645 FAX (Chancery Court Clerk and
Master)
archives@jeffersoncountytn.gov;
PMurphy@jeffersoncountytn.gov;
Rick.Farrar@state.tn.us;
countyclerk@jeffersoncountytn.gov;
chancerycourt@jeffersoncountytn.gov;
tn45ch001@smtpaoc.tsc.state.tn.us (Chancery
Court Clerk and Master)
http://www.jeffersoncountytn.gov
Lura B. "Lu" Hinchey, Director of Museum and
Archives; Sarah Webb, Register of Deeds;
Penny Murphy, Circuit Court Clerk; R. E.
Farrar III, County Clerk; Nancy C. Humbard,
Chancery Court Clerk and Master
(land records with Register of Deeds, marriages
and probate records with County Clerk)
probate search service: $2.00; copies of probate
records: $1.00 each; "SASE helpful"

Johnson County
organized 1836 from Carter County

Johnson County Courthouse
222 West Main Street
Mountain City, TN 37683-1612
(423) 727-7841 (Register of Deeds); (423) 727-
9012 (Circuit Court Clerk, PO Box 73); (423)
727-9633 (County Clerk); (423) 727-7853
(Chancery Court Clerk and Master, PO Box
196); (423) 727-7047 FAX (Register of
Deeds); (423) 727-7047 FAX (County Clerk)
trish@titlesearcher.com; ltmorefield@juno.com
http://www.johnsoncountytn.org;
http://www.johnsoncountychamber.org
Patricia W. "Trish" Hartley, Register of Deeds;
Carolyn Wilson Hawkins, Circuit Court Clerk;
Tammie Fenner, County Clerk; Linda
Morefield, Chancery Court Clerk and Master)
(land records from 1836 with Register of Deeds,
marriages from 1836 and wills from 1836 with
County Clerk)
land, vital, and probate records search service:
no charge

Knox County
organized 1792 from Greene and Hawkins
counties

Knox County City County Building
400 Main Avenue
Knoxville, TN 37902-2406
(865) 215-2330 (Register of Deeds, Suite 225;
(865) 215-2400 (Circuit Court Clerk, Suite M-
30); (865) 215-2385 (County Clerk, Old
Courthouse, 300 Main Street, PO Box 1566);
(865) 215-2555 (Chancery Court Clerk and
Master, Suite 125); (865) 215-2332 FAX
(Register of Deeds); (865) 215-4251 FAX
(Circuit Court Clerk); (865) 215-2620 FAX
(County Clerk); (865) 215-2920 (Chancery
Court Clerk and Master)
threebt@aol.com (Register of Deeds);
county.clerk@knoxcounty.org;
chancery.court@knoxcounty.org
http://www.knoxcounty.org
Sherry Witt, Register of Deeds; Catherine F.
Quist, Circuit Court Clerk; Billy G. Tindell,
County Clerk; Howard G. Hogan, Chancery
Court Clerk and Master
(warranty deeds after 1929 with Register of
Deeds; marriages from 1992 to date with
County Clerk, Marriage Records)

Lake County
organized 1870 from Obion County

Lake County Courthouse

229 Church Street
Tiptonville, TN 38079
(731) 253-7462 (Register of Deeds, PO Box 5);
(731) 253-7137 (Circuit Court Clerk, PO Box
11); (731) 253-7582 (County Clerk, 116 South
Court Street); (731) 253-8926 (Chancery
Court Clerk and Master, PO Box 12); (731)
253-9815 FAX (Register of Deeds); (731)
253-6815 FAX (County Clerk)
Claudia.Adcock@vcourthouse.net;
Joann.Mills@state.tn.us;
tn48ch001@smtpaoc.tsc.state.tn.us
http://rach.reelfootareachamber.com
Claudia Adcock, Register of Deeds; Debbie
Beasley, Circuit Court Clerk; Jo Ann Mills,
County Clerk; Nanette Cook, Chancery Court
Clerk and Master

Lauderdale County
organized 1835 from Dyer, Tipton, and
Haywood counties

Lauderdale County Courthouse
100 Court Square
Ripley, TN 38063
(731) 635-2171 (Register of Deeds); (731) 635-
0101 (Circuit Court Clerk, PO Box 509);
(731) 635-2561 (County Clerk); (731) 635-
1941 (Chancery Court Clerk and Master, PO
Box 265); (731) 635-9682 FAX (Register of
Deeds); (731) 635-9682 FAX (County Clerk)
anniejennings@msn.com;
Linda.Summar@state.tn.us;
tn49ch002@smtpaoc.tsc.state.tn.us (Chancery
Court Clerk and Master)
http://www.tennesseeanytime.org/local/lauder
dale.html
Annie Laura Jennings, Register of Deeds;
Richard Jennings, Circuit Court Clerk; Linda
Summer, County Clerk; Sandra Burnham,
Chancery Court Clerk and Master

Lawrence County
organized 1817 from Hickman and Maury
counties

Lawrence County Courthouse
240 West Gaines Street
Lawrenceburg, TN 38464
(615) 762-2407 (Mrs. Coffey); (931) 766-4180
(Register of Deeds, NBU #18); (931) 766-
4177 (Circuit Court Clerk, NBU #12); (931)
762-7700 (County Clerk, NBU #2); (931)
766-4182 (Chancery Court Clerk and Master,
NBU #13)
ttdunkin@yahoo.com;
countyclerk@co.lawrence.tn.us;
Kristy.Gang@tscmail.state.tn.us
http://www.co.lawrence.tn.us
Teresa Dunkin, Register of Deeds; Debbie
Riddle, Circuit Court Clerk; Chuck Kizer,
County Clerk; Kristy Gang, Chancery Court
Clerk and Master
(historical land and probate records with Mrs. F.
L. Coffey, Jr., 200 Parkes Avenue,
Lawrenceburg, TN 38464)

Lewis County
organized 1843 from Hickman, Maury, Wayne
and Lawrence counties

Lewis County Courthouse
110 Park Avenue North
Hohenwald, TN 38462
(931) 796-3255 (Register of Deeds); (931) 796-
3724 (Circuit Court Clerk, Room 201); (931)
796-2200 (County Clerk, Room 105); (931)
796-3734 (Chancery Court Clerk and Master,
Room 208); (931) 796-6010 FAX (County
Clerk)
ophelia.green@vcourthouse.com;
Sandra.Clayton@state.tn.us;
janet.williams@tscmail.state.tn.us
http://www.tennesseeanytime.org/local/lewis.
html
Ophelia Green, Register of Deeds; Robert G.
"Bob" Johnston, Assessor of Property;
Donna Couch, Circuit Court Clerk; Sandra
Clayton, County Clerk; Janet Williams,

Chancery Court Clerk and Master
(land records with Assessor of Property, vital
records with County Clerk, probate records
with Chancery Court Clerk and Master)
probate search service: $2.00 ("Please send as
much information as possible"); copies of
probate records: $1.00 per page, no minimum

Lincoln County
organized 1809 from Bedford County

Lincoln County Courthouse
112 Main Avenue South
Fayetteville, TN 37334
(931) 433-5366 (Register of Deeds, Room 104);
(931) 433-2334 (Circuit Court Clerk, Room
203); (931) 433-2454 (County Clerk, Room
102); (931) 433-1482 (Chancery Court Clerk
and Master, Room B-109); (931) 433-9312
FAX (Register of Deeds); (931) 438-1577
(Circuit Court Clerk); (931) 433-9304 FAX
(County Clerk)
rdelap@titlesearcher.com;
Anne.Underwood@state.tn.us
http://www.vallnet.com/lincolncounty
Randy Delap, Register of Deeds; Gail Corder,
Circuit Court Clerk; Anne J. Underwood,
County Clerk; Becky Bartlett, Chancery Court
Clerk and Master

Loudon County
organized 1870 from Blount, Monroe, McMinn
and Roane counties

Loudon County Courthouse
100 River Road
Loudon, TN 37774
(865) 458-2605 (Register of Deeds, PO Box
395); (865) 458-2042 (Circuit Court Clerk, PO
Box 280); (865) 458-3314 (County Clerk, 101
Mulberry Street, Suite 200); (865) 458-2630
(Chancery Court Clerk and Master, PO Box
509); (865) 458-9028 FAX (Register of
Deeds); (865) 458-2043 FAX (Circuit Court
Clerk); (865) 458-0829 FAX (Chancery Court
Clerk and Master)
tracie@titlesearcher.com; Lisa.Niles@tscmail.
state.tn.us; tn53cc001@smtpaoc.tsc.state.tn.us
(Circuit Court Clerk); Riley.Wampler@state.
tn.us; tn53cc001@smtpaoc.tsc.state.tn.us
(Chancery Court Clerk and Master)
http://www.loudoncounty-tn.gov
Tracie Littleton, Register of Deeds; Lisa Niles,
Circuit Court Clerk; Riley D. Wampler,
County Clerk; Fred Chaney, Chancery Court
Clerk and Master

Macon County
organized 1842 from Smith and Sumner
counties

Macon County Courthouse
Public Square
Lafayette, TN 37083
(615) 666-2353 (Register of Deeds, 102 County
Courthouse); (615) 666-2354 (Circuit Court
Clerk, 904 Highway 52 East); (615) 666-2333
(County Clerk, 104 County Courthouse);
(615) 666-2000 voice & FAX (Chancery
Court Clerk and Master, 906 Highway 52
East); (615) 666-2691 FAX (Register of
Deeds); (615) 666-3001 FAX (Circuit Court
Clerk); (615) 666-2202 FAX (County Clerk)
James. Howser@state.tn.us;
gwenhlinville@yahoo.com
http://www.maconcountytn.com
Melinda Ferguson, Register of Deeds; Rick
Gann, Circuit Court Clerk; James Ralph
Howser, County Clerk; Gwen Linville,
Chancery Court Clerk and Master
(deeds with Register of Deeds; marriage records
from April 1901, probate records from 1901)
probate search service: $5.00; copies of probate
records: 50¢ each, no minimum

Madison County
organized 1821 from Western District (Indian
lands)

Madison County Courthouse
100 East Main Street
Jackson, TN 38301-6299
(731) 423-6028 (Register of Deeds, Suite 109);
(731) 423-6065 (Assessor of Property, 118
East Baltimore, Suite 4, Jackson, TN 38301-
6346); (731) 423-6035 (Circuit Court Clerk,
515 South Liberty Street, Suite 200); (731)
423-6022 (County Clerk, Suite 105); (731)
423-6032 (Chancery Court Clerk and Master)
Linda@TitleSercher.com; Judy.Barnhill@
tscmail.state.tn.us; freddie.pruitt@state.tn.us
http://www.co.madison.tn.us
Linda Walden, Register of Deeds; Frances
Hunley, Assessor of Property; Judy Barnhill,
Circuit Court Clerk; Freddie Pruitt, County
Clerk; Pam Carter, Chancery Court Clerk and
Master
(land records with Assessor of Property, vital
records with Register of Deeds, old marriage
licenses and probate records with County
Clerk)
probate search service: $10.00 for five years
search; certified copies of old marriage
licenses available (or photocopies of original
documents but not of "old books"); copies of
probate records: $1.00 per page, $2.00 for
certification, $10.00 minimum

Marion County
organized 1817 from Western District (Indian
lands)

Marion County Courthouse
Jasper, TN 37347
(423) 942-2573 (Register of Deeds, 24
Courthouse Square, PO Box 789); (423) 942-
8020 (Circuit Court Clerk, Marion County
Justice Center, PO Box 789); (423) 942-2515
(County Clerk, Room 101, PO Box 789);
(423) 942-2601 (Chancery Court Clerk and
Master, Courthouse, 5 Oak Street, PO Box
789); (423) 942-1327 FAX (Register of
Deeds); (423) 942-0815 FAX (County Clerk)
Dwight.Minter@state.tn.us;
tn56ch001@smtpaoc.tsc.state.tn.us (Chancery
Court Clerk and Master)
http://www.tennesseeanytime.org/local/
marion.html
Winfred Haggard, Register of Deeds; Evelyn
Griffith, Circuit Court Clerk; Dwight Minter,
County Clerk; Levoy Gudger, Chancery Court
Clerk and Master

Marshall County
organized 1836 from Giles, Bedford, Lincoln
and Maury counties

Marshall County Courthouse
Public Square
Lewisburg, TN 37091
(931) 359-4933 (Register of Deeds); (931) 359-
0536 (Circuit Court Clerk); (931) 359-1072
(County Clerk); (931) 359-2181 (Chancery
Court Clerk and Master)
dwweaver@vcourthouse.com;
tn57cc001@smtpaoc.tsc.state.tn.usDaphne.Fa
gan@state.tn.us;
thomashigdon@hotmail.com
http://www.marshallcountytn.com
Dorris Weaver, Register of Deeds; Elinor
Foster, Circuit Court Clerk; Daphne Fagan,
County Clerk; Tommy Higdon, Chancery
Court Clerk and Master
(land records from 1836 with Register of Deeds,
probate records from 1836 with County
Clerk)
probate search service: $5.00; copies of probate
records: 30¢ per page, no minimum

Maury County
organized 1807 from Williamson County and
Indian lands

Maury County Courthouse
Public Square
Columbia, TN 38401
(931) 381-3690, ext. 358 (Register of Deeds, 1
Public Square, Room #108); (931) 375-1100

(Circuit Court Clerk, 41 Public Square, Room
202); (931) 381-3690, option 4 (County Clerk,
10 Public Square); (931) 375-1300 (Chancery
Court Clerk and Master, 41 Public Square);
(931) 375-5219 FAX (County Clerk)
nancy.w.thompson@state.tn.us;
jbailey@maurycounty-tn.gov;
Cheryl.Church@tscmail.state.tn.us
http://www.maurycounty-tn.gov
John Fleming, Register of Deeds; James Bailey,
County Executive; Kathy Kelley, Circuit
Court Clerk; Nancy Thompson, County
Clerk; Cheryl P. Church, Chancery Court
Clerk and Master
(land records with Register of Deeds, vital
records from 1807 with County Executive,
probate records with Chancery Court Clerk
and Master)
no probate search service; copies of land
records: 50¢ per page; copies of probate
records: 25¢ each, no minimum

McMinn County
organized 1819 from Cherokee Indian lands

McMinn County Courthouse
6 East Madison Avenue
Athens, TN 37303
(423) 745-1232 (Register of Deeds, Main Floor,
PO Box 1074); (423) 745-1923 (Circuit Court
Clerk); (615) 745-4440 (County Clerk,
Courthouse Annex, Madison Park Shopping
Center, 5 South Hill Street, Suite A, Athens,
TN 37303); (423) 745-1281 (Chancery Court
Clerk and Master); (423) 744-1642 FAX
(Circuit Court Clerk); (423) 744-1657 FAX
(County Clerk); (423) 744-1652 FAX
(Chancery Court Clerk and Master)
Evonne.Jones@state.tn.us; circuitcourtclerk@
mcminncounty.org; pgaines@yahoo.com
http://www.mcminncounty.org
Nadean Cunningham, Register of Deeds;
Rhonda Cooley, Circuit Court Clerk; Evonne
Hoback, County Clerk; Patty Gaines,
Chancery Court Clerk and Master
(land records with Register of Deeds, marriages
from 1820 with County Clerk, probate
records with Circuit Court Clerk)

McNairy County
organized 1823 from Hardin County

McNairy County Courthouse
Court Avenue
Selmer, TN 38375
(731) 645-3656 voice & FAX (Register of
Deeds, PO Box 158); (731) 645-1015 (Circuit
Court Clerk, Criminal Justice Center, 300
Industrial Park Drive); (731) 645-3511
(County Clerk, Room 102); (731) 645-5446
(Chancery Court Clerk and Master, Room
205); (731) 646-1414 FAX (County Clerk)
Brian.Dickey@vcourthouse.com;
ronnie.price@state.tn.us
http://www.tennesseeanytime.org/local/
mcnairy.html
Brian Neal Dickey, Register of Deeds; Ronnie
Brooks, Circuit Court Clerk; Ronnie Price,
County Clerk; Kim Harrison, Chancery Court
Clerk and Master

Meigs County
organized 1836 from Hamilton, McMinn, Rhea
and Roane counties

Meigs County Courthouse
Main Street, 17214 State Highway 58
Decatur, TN 37322-0218
(423) 334-5228 voice & FAX (Register of
Deeds, PO Box 245); (423) 334-5821 (Circuit
Court Clerk, Second Floor, PO Box 205);
(423) 334-5747 voice & FAX (County Clerk,
PO Box 218); (423) 334-5243 (Chancery
Court Clerk and Master, Second Floor, PO
Box 5)
janie.rowland@state.tn.us
http://www.tennesseeanytime.org/local/meigs.
html
Janie Stiner, Register of Deeds; Darrell Davis,

Circuit Court Clerk; Janie Rowland, County
Clerk; Jim Mercer, Chancery Court Clerk and
Master

Monroe County
organized 1819 from Hiwassee Purchase (Indian
lands)

Monroe County Courthouse
105 College Street
Madisonville, TN 37354-2400
(423) 442-2440 (Register of Deeds, 103 College
Street, Suite 4); (423) 442-2396 (Circuit Court
Clerk, Suite 103); (423) 442-2220 (County
Clerk, 103 College Street); (423) 442-2644
(Chancery Court Clerk and Master, Suite 2);
(423) 442-2405 FAX (Register of Deeds);
(423) 442-9542 FAX (County Clerk)
ccclerkmon@tellico.net; larry.sloan@state.tn.us;
monroeclerk@bellsouth.net
http://www.monroegovernment.org
Mildred "Millie" Estes, Register of Deeds;
Martha Cook, Circuit Court Clerk; Larry
Sloan, County Clerk; Robert J. Pennington,
Chancery Court Clerk and Master

Montgomery County
organized 1796 by the division between
Montgomery and Robertson counties of
Tennessee County, which had been organized
in 1788 from Davidson County and was then
abolished, and whose records were deposited
with Montgomery County

Montgomery County Courthouse
350 Pageant Lane
Clarksville, TN 37042
(931) 648-5713 (Register of Deeds, Suite 101-A,
PO Box 1124); (931) 648-5700 (Circuit Court
Clerk, 2 Millennium Plaza, Suite 115); (931)
648-5711 (County Clerk); (931) 648-5703
(Chancery Court Clerk and Master, Courts
Center, 2 Millennium Plaza, Suite 101,
Clarksville, TN 37041); (931) 553-5157 FAX
(Register of Deeds); (931) 648-5729 FAX
(Circuit Court Clerk); (931) 648-5759 FAX
Chancery Court Clerk and Master)
cccmont@montgomerycountytn.orgcjcastle@m
ontgomerycountytn.org;
kajackson@montgomerycountytn.org
http://www.montgomerycountytn.org/county/i
ndex.htm
Connie W. Bell, Register of Deeds; Cheryl
Castle, Circuit Court Clerk; Kellie Jackson,
County Clerk; Ted A. Crozier, Jr., Chancery
Court Clerk and Master

Moore County
organized 1871 from Bedford, Franklin, Lincoln
and Coffee counties; consolidated with the
City of Lynchburg in 1987

Moore County Courthouse
196 Main Street
Lynchburg, TN 37352
(931) 759-7913 (Register of Deeds, PO Box
206); (931) 759-5673 (Circuit Court Clerk,
Suite 404, PO Box 206); (931) 759-7346
(County Clerk, PO Box 206); (931) 759-7028
(Chancery Court Clerk and Master, Suite 312,
PO Box 206); (931) 759-6394 FAX (Register
of Deeds); (931) 759-6394 FAX (County
Clerk)
cwbell@montgomerycountytn.com;
nancy.hatfield@state.tn.us;
tn64ch001@smtpaoc.tsc.state.tn.us
http://www.tennesseeanytime.org/local/moore.
html
Barbara Durm, Register of Deeds; Trixie H.
Harrison, Circuit Court Clerk; Nancy
Hatfield, County Clerk; Tammy Roberts,
Chancery Court Clerk and Master

Morgan County
organized 1817 from Roane County, and in 1903
annexed part of Anderson County

Morgan County Courthouse
Main Street

Wartburg, TN 37887
(423) 346-3105 (Register of Deeds, PO Box 311); (423) 346-3503 (Circuit Court Clerk, PO Box 163); (423) 346-3480 (County Clerk, 415 South Kingston Street, PO Box 301); (423) 346-3881 (Chancery Court Clerk and Master, PO Box 789); (423) 346-3609 FAX (Register of Deeds); (423) 346-4161 FAX (County Clerk)
sandy.dalton@vcourthouse.com;
Carol.Hamby@state.tn.us;
angandcm@yahoo.comhttp://www.tennessee anytime.org/local/morgan.html
Sandy Leach-Dalton Register of Deeds; Pam Lively, Circuit Court Clerk; Carol Hamby, County Clerk; Angela Anderson, Chancery Court Clerk and Master

Obion County
organized 1823 from Western District (Indian lands)

Obion County Courthouse
Court Square
Union City, TN 38261
(731) 885-9351 (Register of Deeds, PO Box 514); (731) 885-1372 (Circuit Court Clerk, 7 Bill Burnett Circle); (901) 885-3831 (County Clerk, 2 Bill Burnett Circle); (731) 885-2562 (Chancery Court Clerk and Master, 6 Bill Burnett Circle, PO Box 187); (731) 885-0287 FAX (County Clerk)
Vollie.Boehms@state.tn.us;
tn66ch001@smtpaoc.tsc.state.tn.us (Chancery Court Clerk and Master)
http://www.obioncountytennessee.com
Vickie O. Long, Register of Deeds; Harry Johnson, Circuit Court Clerk; Vollie Jean Boehms, County Clerk; Paula Rice, Chancery Court Clerk and Master
(land records from Register of Deeds, marriages and some births and deaths from County Clerk, probate records from Chancery Court Clerk and Master)

Overton County
organized 1806 from Jackson County and Indian lands

Overton County Courthouse
Livingston, TN 38570
(931) 823-4011 (Courthouse Annex, 317 East University Street); (931) 823-2312 (Circuit Court Clerk, 1000 John Tom Poindexter Drive); (931) 823-2631 (County Clerk, Courthouse Annex, 317 East University Street, Room 22); (931) 823-2536 (Chancery Court Clerk and Master, 1000 East Court Square, Suite A, PO Box 127); (931) 823-7036 FAX (County Clerk)
hugh.ogletree@state.tn.us;
tn67ch001@smtpaoc.tsc.state.tn.us
http://www.overtoncountytn.com
Franklin D. "Peck" Smith, Register of Deeds; Johnny Brown, Circuit Court Clerk; Hugh Ogletree, County Clerk; Dorothy Stanton, Chancery Court Clerk and Master

Perry County
organized 1821 from Hickman and Humphreys counties (petitioned for formation 1819, legislation passed 1820, first court held the first Monday of January 1821)

Perry County Courthouse
PO Box 16
Linden, TN 37096-0016
(931) 589-2210 (Register of Deeds, PO Box 354); (931) 589-2218 (Circuit Court Clerk, PO Box 91); (931) 589-2219 (County Clerk, Main Street, PO Box 58); (931) 589-2217 (Chancery Court Clerk and Master, PO Box 251); (931) 589-2215 FAX (County Clerk)
Jane.Lewis@state.tn.us; jlewis@netease.net;
tn68ch001@smtpaoc.tsc.state.tn.us (Chancery Court Clerk and Master)
http://www.perrycountytennessee.com
Patricia W. Bell, Register of Deeds; Peggy Smotherman, Circuit Court Clerk; Jane Lewis,

County Clerk; Joyce Marshall, Chancery Court Clerk and Master
(land records from 1841 [only reconstructed records available from before courthouse fire of 1865, but most records saved from fire of 1928] with Perry County Public Library, Rt. 10, Box 3A, Linden, TN 37096, births and deaths from 1912, probate records)
land, vital, and probate records search service: donation; copies: 15¢ per page

Pickett County
organized 1879 from Fentress and Overton counties

Pickett County Courthouse
1 Courthouse Square
Byrdstown, TN 38549
(931) 864-3316 (Register of Deeds, Suite 204); (931) 864-3114 (Assessor of Property, Suite 202); (931) 864-3958 (Circuit Court Clerk, Suite 100); (931) 864-3879 (County Clerk, Suite 201, PO Box 5); (931) 864-3359 (Chancery Court Clerk and Master, Suite 203); (931) 864-7087 FAX (County Clerk)
Robert.E.Lee@state.tn.us
http://www.dalehollow.com/government.htm
Phyllis Ford, Register of Deeds; Larry Anderson, Assessor of Property; Larry Brown, Circuit Court Clerk; Charlie Lee, County Clerk; Sue Whited, Chancery Court Clerk and Master
(land records with Assessor of Property, naturalization records with County Agent, Community Center, Byrdstown, TN 38549, vital records and probate records with County Clerk)
probate search service: no set rate; copies of probate records: 25¢ per page, no minimum

Polk County
organized 1839 from Bradley and McMinn counties

Polk County Courthouse
6239 Highway 411 North
Benton, TN 37307
(423) 338-4537 (Register of Deeds, PO Box 293); (423) 338-4524 (Circuit Court Clerk, PO Box 256); (423) 338-4526 (County Clerk, Room 102, PO Box 158); (423) 338-4522 (Chancery Court Clerk and Master, Suite 307, PO Drawer L); (423) 338-4551 FAX (County Clerk)
tn70ch001@tscmail.state.tn.us (Chancery Court Clerk and Master)
http://www.tennesseeanytime.org/local/polk.html
Donna (Kandi) Bramlett, Register of Deeds; Connie H. Clark, Circuit Court Clerk; Angie Sanford, County Clerk; Kimberly Ingram, Chancery Court Clerk and Master
(land records with Register of Deeds, marriages with County Clerk, probate records with Chancery Court Clerk and Master)

Putnam County
organized 1842 from Smith, White, DeKalb, Overton and Jackson counties

Putnam County Courthouse
29 North Washington Avenue
Cookeville, TN 38501
(931) 526-7101 (Register of Deeds, PO Box 487); (931) 528-1508 (Circuit Court Clerk, 421 East Spring Street, Room 1C, Suite 49A); (931) 526-7106 (County Clerk, PO Box 220); (931) 526-6321 (Chancery Court Clerk and Master, 421 East Spring Street, Suite 1C38); (931) 526-7106 (Probate Court Clerk); (931) 372-8201 FAX (County Clerk)
harold.burrus@vcourthouse.com;
Wayne.Nabors@state.tn.us
http://www.putnamcountytn.gov
Harold Burris, Register of Deeds; Marcia Borys, Circuit Court Clerk; Wayne Nabors, County Clerk; Linda F. Reeder, Chancery Court Clerk and Master

Rhea County
organized 1807 from Roane County

Rhea County Courthouse
1475 North Market Street
Dayton, TN 37321
(423) 775-7841 (Register of Deeds); (423) 775-7805 (Circuit Court Clerk, Suite 102); (423) 775-7808 (County Clerk, 375 Church Street, Suite 101); (423) 775-7895 FAX (Register of Deeds); (423) 775-7806 (Chancery Court Clerk and Master, Suite 301); (423) 775-7898 FAX (County Clerk)
Linda.Shaver@state.tn.us;
tn72cc001@smtpaoc.tsc.state.tn.us (Chancery Court Clerk and Master)
http://www.rheacountyetc.com; http://www.tennesseeanytime.org/local/rhea.html
Gladys Best, Register of Deeds; Regina Metts, Circuit Court Clerk; Linda Shaver, County Clerk; John Fine, Chancery Court Clerk and Master

Roane County
organized 1801 from Knox County and Indian lands

Roane County Courthouse
200 East Race Street
Kingston, TN 37763
(865) 376-5578 (Records Department, PO Box 643); (865) 376-4563 (Register of Deeds); (865) 376-2390 (Circuit Court Clerk, Suite 11); (865) 376-5556 (County Clerk, PO Box 546); (865) 376-2487 (Chancery Court Clerk and Master, PO Box 402); (865) 717-4121 FAX (County Clerk)
Barbara.Anthony@state.tn.us;
tn73ch001@smtpaoc.tsc.state.tn.us (Chancery Court Clerk and Master)
http://www.tennesseeanytime.org/local/roane.html
Sharon Brackett, Register of Deeds; Angela Randolph, Circuit Court Clerk; Barbara Anthony, County Clerk; Shannon Conley, Chancery Court Clerk and Master
(deeds from 1801, marriages from 1801, wills and estates from 1803 with Records Department)
probate search service: $3.00; certified copies of land and probate records: $5.00 each ("need approximate dates and SASE included with letter")

Robertson County
organized 1796 by the division between Montgomery and Robertson counties of Tennessee County, which had been organized in 1788 from Davidson County and was then abolished, and whose records were deposited with Montgomery County

Robertson County Courthouse
501 Main Street
Springfield, TN 37172
(615) 898-7870 (Register of Deeds, Courthouse Annex, 525 South Brown Street); (615) 384-7864 (Circuit Court Clerk, Room 206); (615) 384-5895 (County Clerk, 511 South Brown Street); (615) 384-5650 (Chancery Court Clerk and Master, Room 207); (615) 384-2218 FAX (County Clerk)
frankie.fletcher@vcourthouse.net;
Susan.Atchley@state.tn.us;
tn74ch001@smtpaoc.tsc.state.tn.us (Chancery Court Clerk and Master)
http://www.tennesseeanytime.org/local/robertson.html
Frankie Fletcher, Register of Deeds; Lisa M. Cavender, Circuit Court Clerk; Susan Atchley, County Clerk; Kenneth Hudgens, Chancery Court Clerk and Master
(land records with Register of Deeds)

Rutherford County
organized 1803 from Davidson, Williamson, and Wilson counties

Rutherford County Judicial Building
20 Public Square North
Murfreesboro, TN 37130
(615) 898-7820 (Circuit Court Clerk–Civil

Division, Room 202); (615) 898-7812 Circuit
Court Clerk–Criminal Division); (615) 898-
7860 (Chancery Court Clerk and Master, Suite
302); (615) 217-7119 FAX (Circuit Court
Clerk); (615) 849-9553 FAX (Chancery Court
Clerk and Master)
egaither@rutherfordcounty.org;
    jbratcher@rutherfordcounty.org
http://www.rutherfordcounty.org/departments.
htm
Eloise Gaither, Circuit Court Clerk; John
    Bratcher, Chancery Court Clerk and Master
(probate records with Judge of Probate)
no probate search service

**Rutherford County Register of Deeds and
    County Clerk**
319 North Maple Street
Murfreesboro, TN 37130
(615) 898-7870 (Register of Deeds, Suite 133);
    (615) 898-7800 (County Clerk, Suite 121);
    (615) 898-7987 FAX (Register of Deeds);
    (615) 898-7830 FAX (County Clerk)
jennifer.gerhart@vcourthouse.com;
    register@rutherfordcounty.org;
    Georgia.Lynch@state.tn.us;
    glynch@rutherfordcounty.org
http://www.rutherfordcounty.org/departments.
htm
Jennifer M. Gerhart, Register of Deeds; Georgia
    Ann Lynch, County Clerk

Scott County
organized 1849 from Fentress, Morgan,
    Anderson and Campbell counties

Scott County Courthouse
283 Court Street
Huntsville, TN 37756
(423) 663-2417 (Register of Deeds, PO Box 61);
    (423) 663-2420 (Assessor of Property, PO
    Box 74); (423) 663-2440 (Circuit Court Clerk,
    PO Box 330); (423) 663-2588 (County Clerk,
    PO Box 87); (423) 663-2627 (Chancery Court
    Clerk and Master, PO Box 195); (423) 663-
    3969 FAX (County Clerk)
patricia.phillips@state.tn.us
http://www.scottcounty.com
Porter B. Rector, Jr., Register of Deeds; Steve
    Thompson, Assessor of Property; Verda B.
    Cope, Jr., Circuit Court Clerk; Patricia
    Phillips, County Clerk; Jane Lloyd, Chancery
    Court Clerk and Master
(land records with Assessor of Property, probate
    records with Clerk)

Sequatchie County
organized 1857 from Hamilton County (and
    previously from Bledsoe, Marion and Grundy
    counties)

Sequatchie County Courthouse
PO Box 595
Dunlap, TN 37327-0595
(423) 949-2512 (Register of Deeds, 307 Cherry
    Street East); (423) 949-2618 (Circuit Court
    Clerk, Justice Center, 351 Fredonia Road,
    Suite B); (423) 949-2522 (County Clerk, 22
    Cherry Street, PO Box 248); (423) 949-3670
    (Chancery Court Clerk and Master, PO Box
    1651); (423) 949-6554 FAX (Register of
    Deeds); (423) 949-6316 FAX (County Clerk)
connie1949@bwonline.com;
    Charlotte.Cagle@state.tn.us;
    tn77ch001@smtpaoc.tsc.state.tn.us (Chancery
    Court Clerk and Master)
http://www.tennesseeanytime.org/local/sequat
chie.html
Connie E. Green, Register of Deeds; Karen
    Millsaps, Circuit Court Clerk; Charlotte Cagle,
    County Clerk; Thomas Goins, Chancery
    Court Clerk and Master
(deed books from 1858, a few births in 1881 and
    from 1908 to early 1940; a few deaths in 1881
    and from 1908 to 1938; marriages from 1858,
    some probate records in old court minutes
    and fairly complete to present with Chancery
    Court Clerk and Master)
probate search service: no charge; copies of

probate records: 25¢ per page plus postage,
    no minimum ("clerks are busy; a delay in
    answering is sometimes necessary")

Sevier County
organized 1794 from Jefferson County (territory
    south of River Ohio), effective 4 July 1796

Sevier County Courthouse
125 Court Avenue
Sevierville, TN 37862
(865) 453-2758 (Register of Deeds, Suite 209W);
    (865) 453-5536 (Circuit Court Clerk, Room
    204E); (865) 453-5502 (County Clerk, Suite
    202); (865) 453-4654 (Chancery Court Clerk
    and Master, Suite 108W, PO Box 4426); (865)
    453-0290 FAX (Register of Deeds); (865)
    774-9792 FAX (Circuit Court Clerk); (865)
    453-6830 FAX (County Clerk)
joe.keener@state.tn.us;
    tn78ch001@smtpaoc.tsc.state.tn.us (Chancery
    Court Clerk and Master)
http://www.seviercountytn.org
Sharon Robertson Huskey, Register of Deeds;
    Rita Ellison, Circuit Court Clerk; Joe T.
    Keener II, County Clerk; Carolyn P.
    McMahan, Chancery Court Clerk and Master
(deeds from January 1846 to date, survey books
    from April 1824 to March 1903 [indexed],
    probate records from April 1856 [after
    courthouse burned 26 March 1856] to date)
no land records search service (must have
    specific name and date); no probate search
    service (must have specific name and date)

Shelby County
organized 1819 from Hardin County, eleven
    days after its parent county was organized

Shelby County Courthouse
140 Adams
Memphis, TN 38103-2018
(901) 454-4366 (Register of Deeds, 160 North
    Main, Room 519); (901) 544-7608 (Health
    Department, Office of Vital Records, 814
    Jefferson Avenue, Room 101-103, Memphis,
    TN 38105); (901) 379-7051 (Circuit Court
    Clerk, Shelby County Complex, 1075 Mullins
    Station, Room W115, Memphis, TN 38134);
    (901) 545-4244 (County Clerk, 150
    Washington Avenue); (901) 545-4002
    (Chancery Court Clerk and Master, Suite 308);
    (901) 545-4040 (Probate Court Clerk); (901)
    545-3837 FAX (Register of Deeds); (901)
    544-7610 (Health Department); (901) 545-
    3779 FAX (County Clerk)
tom.leatherwood@shelbycountytn.gov;
    tleatherwood@co.shelby.tn.us; moore-
    j@co.shelby.tn.us;
    jimmy.moore@shelbycountynh.gov;
    debbie.stamson@shelbycountytn.gov
http://www.shelbycountytn.gov;
    http://co4.shelbycountytn.gov/court_clerks/
    circuit_court/index.htm;
    http://co4.shelbycountytn.gov/court_clerks/
    chancery_court/index.htm
Tom Leatherwood, Register of Deeds;
    Cassandra L. Brown, Local Registrar, Health
    Department; James "Jimmy" Moore, Circuit
    Court Clerk; Debbie Stamson, County Clerk;
    Dewun R. Settle, Chancery Court Clerk and
    Master
(land records with Register of Deeds, vital
    records with Health Department, probate
    records with Clerk)
probate search service: $1.00 per name; copies
    of probate records: $2.00 for wills, $2.00 for
    certification, $3.00 for letters, no minimum

Smith County
organized 1799 from Sumner County and Indian
    lands

Smith County Courthouse
211 North Main Street
Carthage, TN 37030
(615) 735-1760 (Register of Deeds, 122 Turner
    Circle, Suite 113); (615) 735-0500 (Circuit
    Court Clerk); (615) 735-9833 (County Clerk,

122 Turner High Circle, Suite 101); (615) 735-
    2092 (Chancery Court Clerk and Master);
    (615) 735-8263 FAX (Register of Deeds);
    (615) 735-8252 FAX (County Clerk)
Jimmy.Norris@state.tn.us;
    tn80ch001@smtpaoc.tsc.state.tn.us (Chancery
    Court Clerk and Master)
http://www.tennesseeanytime.org/local/smith.
html
Jerri Lynn Vaden, Register of Deeds; Myra
    Hardcastle, Circuit Court Clerk; James Norris,
    County Clerk; Dianna Dillehay, Chancery
    Court Clerk and Master

Stewart County
organized 1803 from Montgomery County

Stewart County Courthouse
225 Donelson Parkway
Dover, TN 37058
(931) 232-5990 (Register of Deeds, PO Box 57);
    (931) 232-7042 (Circuit Court Clerk, PO Box
    193); (931) 232-7616 (County Clerk, PO Box
    67); (931) 232-5665 (Chancery Court Clerk
    and Master, PO Box 102); (931) 232-3111
    FAX (Register of Deeds); (931) 232-4934
    FAX (County Clerk)
ruth.mathis@vcourthouse.com;
    jimmy.fitzhugh@state.tn.us;
    tn81ch001@smtpaoc.tsc.state.tn.us (Chancery
    Court Clerk and Master)
http://www.stewartcountygovernment.com
Ruth Mathis, Register of Deeds; Jason Wallace,
    Circuit Court Clerk; Jimmy Fitzhugh, County
    Clerk; Jane C. Link, Chancery Court Clerk
    and Master

Sullivan County
organized 1779 from Washington County

Sullivan County Courthouse
Blountville, TN 37617
(423) 323-6420 (Register of Deeds, 3411
    Highway 126, Suite 101); (423) 279-2780
    (Health Department); (423) 279-2752 (Circuit
    Court Clerk, Justice Center, 140 Blountville
    Bypass, PO Box 585); (423) 323-6428
    (County Clerk, 3258 Highway 126, Suite 101);
    (423) 323-6483 (Chancery Court Clerk and
    Master, Justice Center, 140 Blountville
    Bypass); (423) 279-2771 FAX (Register of
    Deeds); (423) 279-2725 FAX (County Clerk);
    (423) 279-2780 (Health Department)
circuit@sullivancounty.org;
    coclerk@sullivancounty.org;
    jeanie.gammon@state.tn.us;
    slhousewright@yahoo.com;
    chancery@sullivancounty.org
http://www.sullivancounty.org;
    http://www.sullivanhealth.org/content/defau
    lt.asp?General_ID=54
Mary Lou Duncan, Register of Deeds; Tommy
    Kerns, Circuit Court Clerk; Jeanie Gammon,
    County Clerk; Sarah Housewright, Chancery
    Court Clerk and Master
(land records with Register of Deeds, marriages
    with County Clerk or County Health
    Department, probate records with Chancery
    Court Clerk and Master and Probate Clerk)

Sumner County
organized 1786 from Davidson County (North
    Carolina), becoming part of the Territory
    South of the River Ohio (popularly called the
    Southwest Territory) from its creation in May
    1790 until Tennessee became a state in 1796

Sumner County Courthouse
Public Square
Gallatin, TN 37066
(615) 452-3892 (Register of Deeds, County
    Administration Building, 355 North
    Belvedere Drive, Room 201, PO Box 299);
    (615) 452-4367 (Circuit Court Clerk, 101
    Public Square, PO Box 549); (615) 452-4063
    (County Clerk, 355 North Belvedere Drive,
    Room 111); (615) 452-4282 (Chancery Court
    Clerk and Master); (615) 451-6027 FAX
    (Circuit Court Clerk); (615) 452-9371 FAX

(County Clerk); (615) 451-6031 FAX (Chancery Court Clerk and Master) pwhitaker@sumnertn.org; mahailiah.hughes@tscmail.state.tn.us; BKemp@SumnerTN.org; Bill.Kemp@state.tn.us; tnch0011@tsc.state.tn.us (Chancery Court Clerk and Master)
http://www.sumnertn.org
Pamela L.Whitaker, Register of Deeds; Mahailiah Hughes, Circuit Court Clerk; William Kemp, County Clerk; Brenda M. Page, Chancery Court Clerk and Master

Tipton County
organized 1823 from Western District (Indian lands)

Tipton County Courthouse
100 Court Square
Covington, TN 38019
(901) 476-0204 (Register of Deeds, Room 105, PO Box 626); (901) 475-3310 (Circuit Court Clerk, 1801 South College Street, Suite 102); (901) 476-0207 (County Clerk, 220 Highway 51, North, Suite 2, PO Box 528); (901) 476-0209 (Chancery Court Clerk and Master, 1801 South College Street, Suite 110); (901) 476-0228 FAX (Register of Deeds); (901) 476-0297 FAX (Chancery Court Clerk and Master)
registerofdeeds@tiptonco.com; claudia.peeler@vcourthouse.com; Pam.Deen@state.tn.us; tn84cc001@smtpaoc.tsc.state.tn.us (Circuit Court Clerk); tcounty@netten.net (County Clerk); tn84ch001@smtpaoc.tsc.state.tn.us (Chancery Court Clerk and Master)
http://www.tiptonco.com
Claudia Peeler, Register of Deeds; Mike Forbess, Circuit Court Clerk; Pam Deen, County Clerk; Judy Billings, Chancery Court Clerk and Master
(land records, naturalization records, vital records, probate records)

Trousdale County
organized 1870 from Macon, Smith, Wilson and Sumner counties; consolidated with the City of Hartsville in 2000

Trousdale County Courthouse
200 East Main Street
Hartsville, TN 37074
(615) 374-2921 (Register of Deeds, Room 8); (615) 374-3411 (Circuit Court Clerk, Room 5); (615) 374-2906 (County Clerk, Room 2); (615) 374-2996 (Chancery Court Clerk and Master, Room 1); (615) 374-1100 FAX (County Clerk)
mary.holder@vcourthouse.com; Rita.Crowder@state.tn.us
http://www.hartsvilletrousdale.com; http://www.tennesseeanytime.org/local/trousdale.html
Mary G. Holder, Register of Deeds; Kim Taylor, Circuit Court Clerk; Rita Crowder, County Clerk; Shelly Brown, Chancery Court Clerk and Master
(land records with Register of Deeds, naturalization records with Clerk, vital records and probate records with Chancery Court Clerk and Master)
no probate search service; copies of probate records: $1.00 per page, $3.00 minimum

Unicoi County
organized 1875 from Washington and Carter counties

Unicoi County Courthouse
100 Main Street
Erwin, TN 37650
(423) 743-6104 (Register of Deeds, PO Box 305); (423) 743-3541 (Circuit Court Clerk, PO Box 2000); (423) 743-3381 (County Clerk, Suite 100, PO Box 340); (423) 743-9541 (Chancery Court Clerk and Master, PO Box 46); (423) 743-8007 FAX (Register of Deeds); (423) 743-5430 FAX (County Clerk)
debbiet@titlesearcher.com;

registerdeeds@earthlink.net; Ruby.McLaughlin@state.tn.us; tsimerly@preferred.com
http://www.unicoicounty.org
Debbie Tittle, Register of Deeds; Tracie Pate, Circuit Court Clerk; Ruby H. McLaughlin, County Clerk; Teresa W. Simerly, Chancery Court Clerk and Master
(births from 1909 to 1912 and from 1925 to 1939, deaths from 1909 to 1911, marriages, probate records)
probate search service: $2.00; copies of probate records: $1.00 per page

Union County
organized 1850 from Anderson, Campbell, Grainger, Claiborne and Knox counties

Union County Courthouse
901 Main Street
Maynardville, TN 37807
(865) 992-8024 (Register of Deeds, PO Box 57); (865) 992-5493 (Circuit Court Clerk, Suite 220); (865) 992-8043 (County Clerk, Suite 119); (865) 992-5942 (Chancery Court Clerk and Master, Suite 215); (865) 992-8025 FAX (Register of Deeds)(865) 992-4992 FAX (County Clerk)
Pam.Ailor@state.tn.us
http://www.unioncountytn.org
Mary Beth Kitts, Register of Deeds; Barbara J. Williams, Circuit Court Clerk; Pam Ailor, County Clerk; Doris Seymour, Chancery Court Clerk and Master

Van Buren County
organized 1840 from Bledsoe, Warren and White counties

Van Buren County Courthouse
PO Box 126
Spencer, TN 38585-0126
(931) 946-2263 (Register of Deeds, PO Box 9); (931) 946-2121 (County Clerk, Smith Street, Administrative Building, PO Box 827); (931) 946-2153 (Circuit Court Clerk, PO Box 126); (931) 946-7175 (Chancery Court Clerk and Master, PO Box 153); (931) 946-7363 FAX (Register of Deeds); (931) 946-2876 FAX (County Clerk)
LSimmons@titlesearcher.com; Linda.Pettit@state.tn.us
http://www.tennesseeanytime.org/local/vanburen.html
Linda L. Davis Simmons, Register of Deeds; Teresa S. Delong, Circuit Court Clerk; Linda Pettit, County Clerk; Tina Shockley, Chancery Court Clerk and Master
(land records from 1840, some births and deaths, marriages, probate records from 1840)
probate search service: no charge ("we have no personnel for such except County Historian, Mr. Earl J. Madewell, Rt. 1, Spencer, TN 38585"); copies of probate records: 50¢ per page, no minimum

Warren County
organized 1807 from White, Jackson and Smith counties, and Indian lands

Warren County Courthouse
111 South Court Square
McMinnville, TN 37110
(931) 473-2926 (Register of Deeds); (931) 473-2373 (Circuit Court Clerk, PO Box 639); (931) 473-2623 (County Clerk, 201 Locust Street, Suite 2P); (931) 473-2364 (Chancery Court Clerk and Master, Suite 101, PO Box 639); (931) 474-2114 FAX (Register of Deeds); (931) 473-8622 FAX (County Clerk)
terry.smith@vcourthouse.com; wcregdeeds@blomand.net; Lesa.Scott@state.tn.us; trenena.wilcher@tscmail.state.tn.us
http://www.tennesseeanytime.org/local/warren.html
Terry Smith, Register of Deeds; Bernie Morris, Circuit Court Clerk; Lesa Scott, County Clerk; Trenena Wilcher, Chancery Court Clerk and

Master
(deed books from 1808 [excluding Books "X" and "T", destroyed during Civil War] with Register of Deeds, marriages from 1852 [prior records destroyed during Civil War] with County Clerk, wills from 1827 with Chancery Court Clerk and Master)
no probate search service; copies of probate records: 25¢ each plus postage

Washington County
organized 1777, original county by act of North Carolina

Washington County Courthouse
101 East Market Street
Jonesboro, TN 37659
(423) 753-1644 (Register of Deeds, PO Box 69); (423) 753-1611 (Circuit Court Clerk, PO Box 356); (423) 753-1622 (County Clerk, PO Box 218); (423) 753-1631 (Chancery Court Clerk and Master)
washingtoncountyclerk@yahoo.com; Doyle.Cloyd@state.tn.us
http://www.washingtoncountytn.com
Ginger Jilton, Register of Deeds; Karen Guinn, Circuit Court Clerk; Doyle Cloyd, County Clerk; Brenda Sneyd, Chancery Court Clerk and Master

Wayne County
organized 1817 from Hickman and Humphreys counties

Wayne County Courthouse
200 Court Square
Waynesboro, TN 38485
(931) 722-5518 (Register of Deeds, PO Box 465); (931) 722-5519 (Circuit Court Clerk, PO Box 869); (931) 722-5544 (County Clerk, PO Box 367); (931) 722-5517 (Chancery Court Clerk and Master, 100 Court Circle, PO Box 101); (931) 722-6410 FAX (County Clerk)
rbutler@titlesearcher.com; ruth.butler@vcourthouse.com; Stan.Horton@state.tn.us; tn91ch001@smtpaoc.tsc.state.tn.us (Chancery Court Clerk and Master)
http://www.waynecountytn.org; http://www.tennesseeanytime.org/local/wayne.html
Ruth Butler, Register of Deeds; Billy G. Crews, Circuit Court Clerk; Stan Horton, County Clerk; Carolyn Mathis, Chancery Court Clerk and Master

Weakley County
organized 1823 from Western District (Indian lands)

Weakley County Courthouse
Court Square
Dresden, TN 38225
(731) 363-3646 (Recorder of Deeds, PO Box 45); (731) 364-3455 (Circuit Court Clerk,Second Floor, PO Box 28); (731) 364-2285 (County Clerk, Room 104, PO Box 587); (731) 364-3454 (Chancery Court Clerk and Master, 116 Main, Suite 301, PO Box 197); (731) 364-5284 (Recorder of Deeds); (731) 364-5236 FAX (County Clerk)
weakley@titlesearcher.com; pat.scarbrough@state.tn.us
http://globegte.utm.edu/french/globegate_mirror/weakley.html
Donna Winstead, Register of Deeds; Pam Belew, Circuit Court Clerk; Pat Scarbrough, County Clerk; Susan Collins, Chancery Court Clerk and Master
(land records with Register of Deeds, probate records with Chancery Court Clerk and Master)
probate search service; copies of probate records: 50¢ per page

White County
organized 1806 from Jackson and Smith counties

White County Courthouse
1 East Bockman Way
Sparta, TN 38583
(931) 836-2817 (Register of Deeds, Room 118, PO Box 86); (931) 836-3205 (Circuit Court Clerk, Justice Center, 111 Depot Street, Suite 1); (931) 836-3712 (County Clerk, Room 115); (931) 836-3787 (Chancery Court Clerk and Master, Room 303); (931) 836-8418 FAX (Register of Deeds); (931) 836-2601 FAX (County Clerk)
Pinoak62@blomand.net (Register of Deeds); Connie.Jolley@state.tn.us; Liberty62@blomand.net (County Clerk); tn93ch001@smtpaoc.tsc.state.tn.us (Chancery Court Clerk and Master)
http://www.sparta-chamber.net/main.htm
Gary Brogden, Register of Deeds; Beverly Templeton, Circuit Court Clerk; Connie Jolley, County Clerk; Lynda K. McCoy, Chancery Court Clerk and Master

Williamson County
organized 1799 from Davidson County

Williamson County Administrative Complex
1320 West Main Street
Franklin, TN 37064
(615) 790-5706 (Register of Deeds, PO Box 808, Franklin, TN 37065-0808); (615) 790-5454 (Circuit Court Clerk, Judicial Center, 135 Fourth Avenue South, Room 203, Franklin, TN 37064); (615) 790-5712 (County Clerk, Suite 135); (615) 790-5428 (Chancery Court Clerk and Master, Judicial Center, 135 Fourth Avenue South, Room 236, Franklin, TN 37064, PO Box 1661, Franklin, TN 37065); (615) 790-5459 FAX (Register of Deeds); (615) 790-5610 FAX (County Clerk); (615) 790-5626 FAX (Chancery Court Clerk and Master)
tn94cc001@smtpaoc.tsc.state.tn.us (Circuit Court Clerk); Elaine.Anderson@state.tn.us; elainea@williamson-tn.org
http://www.wililiamsoncounty-tn.gov/williamson/live/default.asp
Sadie Wade, Register of Deeds; Debbie McMillan Barrett, Circuit Court Clerk; Elaine Anderson, County Clerk; Elaine B. Beeler, Chancery Court Clerk and Master

Wilson County
organized 1799 from Sumner County

Wilson County Courthouse
228 East Main Street
Lebanon, TN 37087
(615) 443-2611 (Register of Deeds, Room 108); (615) 444-2042 (Circuit Court Clerk, 134 South College Street, First Floor); (615) 444-0314 (County Clerk, Room 101, PO Box 950); (615) 444-2835 (Chancery Court Clerk and Master, 134 South College Street, Second Floor); (615) 443-2615 FAX (County Clerk)
beth@wilsondeeds.com (Beth Howard, Office Administrator, Register of Deeds); tn95cc018@smtpaoc.tsc.state.tn.us (Circuit Court Clerk); Jim.Goodall@state.tn.us; jgoodall@state.tn.us; tn95ch001@smtpaoc.tsc.state.tn.us (Chancery Court Clerk and Master)
http://www.wilsoncountytn.com
John "Bev" Spickard, Register of Deeds; Linda Neal, Circuit Court Clerk; Jim Goodall, County Clerk; Barbara Webb, Chancery Court Clerk and Master
(land records from 1793 to date with Register of Deeds)

TEXAS

Capital: Austin. Statehood: 29 December 1845 (declared independence from Mexico as the Republic of Texas on 2 March 1836, boundaries fixed by the Treaty of Guadalupe-Hidalgo, 1848)

Texas has some 839 Municipal Courts and 948 Justice of the Peace Courts which have limited jurisdiction over minor matters. Probate matters are dealt with either in the District Courts or Constitutional County Courts except in the special Probate Courts organized in Bexar, Dallas, Galveston, Harris and Tarrant counties. County Courts at Law, organized primarily in metropolitan counties, relieve the Constitutional County Courts of some of their responsibilities: Anderson, Angelina, Austin, Bastrop, Bell, Bexar, Brazoria, Brazos, Caldwell, Calhoun, Cameron, Cherokee, Collin, Comal, Dallas, Denton, Ector, Ellis, El Paso, Fort Bend, Galveston, Grayson, Gregg, Guadalupe, Harris, Harrison, Hays, Henderson, Hidalgo, Houston, Hunt, Jefferson, Johnson, Kerr, Kleberg, Liberty, Lubbock, McLennan, Medina, Midland, Montgomery, Moore, Nacogdoches, Nolan, Nueces, Orange, Panola, Parker, Polk, Potter, Randall, Reeves, Rusk, Smith, Starr, Tarrant, Taylor, Tom Green, Travis, Val Verde, Victoria, Walker, Waller, Webb, Wichita, Williamson and Wise counties.
The Constitutional County Courts in each county have probate jurisdiction (except in counties with Probate Courts), jurisdiction over misdemeanors involving fines over $200 or sentences under two years, criminal jurisdiction (except where a Criminal District Court exists), and appellate jurisdiction over the Municipal and Justice of the Peace Courts. The District Courts have general jurisdiction, which varies somewhat from district to district. Most exercise both criminal and civil jurisdiction, but in Dallas, Jefferson and Tarrant counties Criminal District Courts exist. Special Family District Courts exist in Districts 300 to 330 and 360.
There are 364 Judicial Districts, some of which cover more than one county, or a single county may contain as many as fifty-eight districts. Appeals are heard by the Court of Appeals, the Court of Criminal Appeals and Supreme Court.

Anderson County
organized 1846 from Houston County

Anderson County Courthouse
500 North Church Street
Palestine, TX 75801
(903) 723-7402 (County Clerk, Room 10); (903) 723-7412 (District Clerk, Second Floor); (903) 723-7494 FAX
jstaples@co.anderson.tx.us
http://www.co.anderson.tx.us
Wanda Burke, County Clerk; Janice Staples, District Clerk
(land records from 1846, births and deaths from 1903, marriages from 1846, probate records from 1846)
probate search service: $5.00; copies of probate records: $1.00 per page, no minimum

Andrews County
organized 1876 from Bexar County

Andrews County Courthouse
(201 North Main Street—location)
PO Box 727 (mailing address)
Andrews, TX 79714
(915) 524-1426 (County Clerk, PO Box 727); (432) 524-1417 (District Clerk, Room 102)
bhoermann@co.andrews.tx.us; cjones@co.andrews.tx.usccollingsworth@co.andrews.tx.us (District Clerk)
http://www.co.andrews.tx.us
F. Wm. Hoermann, County Clerk; Cynthia Jones, District Clerk

(land records, vital records, probate records)
probate search service: no charge; copies of probate records: $1.00 per page, $5.00 for certification, no minimum

Angelina County
organized 1846 from Nacogdoches County

Angelina County Clerk
(Courthouse, 215 East Lufkin Avenue—location)
PO Box 908 (mailing address)
Lufkin, TX 75902-0908
(936) 634-8339 (County Clerk, First Floor); (936) 4312 (District Clerk, First Floor); (936) 5915 FAX (District Clerk)
jch50@angelinacounty.net; rsquyres@angelinacounty.net
http://www.angelinacounty.net
Jo Ann Chastain, County Clerk; Rega Squyres, District Clerk
(land records from 1846, births from 1928, and deaths from 1904 [some delayed further back] with County Clerk, probate records from 1838 with District Clerk)
no probate search service; land records search service: $10.00; copies of land records: $1.00 per page, plus $1.00 for certification on Real Property; certified copies of vital records: $9.00 each (births within the last fifty years and deaths within the last twenty-five years, subject to restrictions, no genealogists unless they have a certified letter from parent or qualified legal representative)

Aransas County
organized 1871 from Refugio County

Aransas County Courthouse
301 North Live Oak
Rockport, TX 78382-2744
(361) 790-0122 (County Clerk, Room 101); (361) 790-0128 (District Clerk); (361) 790-0119 FAX (County Clerk); (361) 790-5211 FAX (District Clerk)
acclerk@sbcglobal.net
http://www.co.aransas.tx.us
Peggy L. Friebele, County Clerk; Pam Heard, District Clerk

Archer County
organized 1858 from Fannin County

Archer County Courthouse
PO Box 458
Archer City, TX 76351
(940) 574-4302 (County Clerk); (940) 574-4615 (District Clerk)
http://www.co.archer.tx.us
Karren Winter, County Clerk; Jane Ham, District Clerk

Armstrong County
organized 1876 from Bexar County

Armstrong County Courthouse
PO Box 309
Claude, TX 79019-0309
(806) 226-2081
http://www.co.armstrong.tx.us
Joe Reck, County/District Clerk

Atascosa County
organized 1856 from Bexar County

Atascosa County Courthouse
1 Courthouse Circle Drive
Jourdanton, TX 78026
(830) 767-2511 (County Clerk, #102); (830) 769-3011 (District Clerk, #52); (830) 769-1021 FAX (County Clerk); (830) 769-2841 FAX (District Clerk)
laquita.hayden@co.atascosa.tx.us
http://www.co.atascosa.tx.us
Laquita Hayden, County Clerk; Jerome Brite, District Clerk
(land records from 1856, vital records from 1856 [births within the last fifty years and deaths within the last twenty-five years, subject to

restrictions] with County Clerk , probate records from 1856 with District Clerk)
probate search service: no charge; copies of probate records: $1.00 per page

Austin County
organized 1836 from Old Mexican Municipality

Austin County Courthouse
1 East Main
Bellville, TX 77418-1521
(979) 865-5911 (County Clerk and District Clerk); (979) 865-0336 FAX (County Clerk)
countyc@industryinet.com;
smurphy@industryinet.com
http://www.austincounty.com
Carrie Gregor, County Clerk; Sue Murphy, District Clerk
(land records from 1833 with County Clerk, naturalization records from 1854 with County Clerk and District Clerk, vital records from 1903 with County Clerk, probate records from 1837 with County Clerk)
copies of land, vital, or probate records: $1.00 per page, $5.00 for certification

Bailey County
formed without officials 1876 from Bexar County, organized 1917

Bailey County Courthouse
300 South First Street
Muleshoe, TX 79347
(806) 272-3044 (County Clerk); (806) 272-3165 (District Clerk)
elaine.parker@co.bailey.tx.us
http://www.co.bailey.tx.us
Paula Benton, County Clerk; Elaine Parker, District Clerk
(land records from 1882, vital records from 1919, probate records from 1919)
probate search service: $5.00; copies of probate records: $1.00 per page, no minimum

Bandera County
organized 1856 from Uvalde County

Bandera County Courthouse
500 Main Street
Bandera, TX 78003
(830) 796-3332 (County Clerk, PO Box 823); (830) 796-4606 (District Clerk, PO Box 2688); (830) 796-8323 FAX (County Clerk); (830) 796-8499 FAX (District Clerk)
cancyw@indian-creek.net; tammykdc@indian-creek.net
http://www.banderacounty.org
Candy Wheeler, County Clerk; Tamera S. "Tammy" Kneuper, District Clerk
(land records from 1856, very few naturalization records; some vital records from 1856, but most are after 1903, some probate records from 1856)
probate search service: $5.00; copies of probate records: $1.00 each ("we prefer to look them up for the person in our older records because of the condition of the books—very old")

Bastrop County
organized 1836 from Old Mexican Municipality

Bastrop County Courthouse
804 Pecan Street
Bastrop, TX 78602
(512) 332-7234 (County Clerk, 803 Pine, Room 112, PO Box 577); (512) 332-7244 (District Clerk, PO Box 770); (512) 332-7241 FAX (County Clerk); (512) 332-7249 FAX (District Clerk)
rpietsch@bastropcounty.com
http://www.co.bastrop.tx.us
Rose Pietsch, County Clerk; Cathy Oliver Smith, District Clerk
(land records from 1837 with County Clerk, naturalization records from about 1837 with County Clerk [some records with District Clerk], vital records from 1903 with County Clerk [not open to the public, but clerks will

check for names], probate records from 1837 with County Clerk)
probate search service: no charge; copies of probate records: $1.00 per page ("we do not do searches over the phone; a request must be in writing and include a SASE for an answer")

Baylor County
organized 1858 from Fannin County

Baylor County Courthouse
101 South Washington
Seymour, TX 76380
(940) 889-3322; (940) 889-4300 FAX
http://www.tshonline.org/handbook/online/articles/BB/hcb4.html;
http://www.cityofseymour.org (city government)
Clara Coker, District/County Clerk

Bee County
organized 1857 from Goliad and Refugio counties

Bee County Courthouse
105 West Corpus Christi
Beeville, TX 78102-5627
(361) 362-3245 (County Clerk, Room 103); (361) 362-3242 (District Clerk, Room 304, PO Box 666); (361) 362-3247 FAX (County Clerk); (361) 362-3282 FAX (District Clerk)
mirella.davis@co.bee.tx.us
http://www.co.bee.tx.us
Mirella Escamilla Davis, County Clerk; Anna Marie Silvas, District Clerk
(land records from 1858, vital records from 1903, probate records from 1859)
probate search service: $5.00 per estate name; copies of probate records: $1.00 and $2.00 (small and large books), no minimum ("fees due before copies are issued")

Bell County
organized 1850 from Milam County

Bell County Courthouse
Belton, TX 76513
(254) 933-5165 (County Clerk, Courthouse Annex, 550 East Second Street, PO Box 480); (254) 933-5197 (District Clerk, District Courts Center, 1201 Huey Road, PO Box 909); (254) 933-5176 FAX (County Clerk); (254) 933-5199 FAX (District Clerk)
shelley.coston@co.bell.tx.us;
shelia.norman@co.bell.tx.us;
snorman@vvm.com
http://www.bellcountytx.com
Shelley Coston, County Clerk; Sheila F. Norman, District Clerk
(land records from 1850 to date with County Clerk, naturalization records with District Clerk, vital records from 1903 to date with County Clerk, probate records from 1850 to date with County Clerk)
land, vital and probate records search service: $5.00 per name; copies of land, vital, and probate records: $1.00 per page

Bexar County
organized 1835 from Old Mexican Municipality

Bexar County Courthouse
100 Dolorosa Street
San Antonio, TX 78285-5100
(210) 553-6982 (Archives); (201) 335-2216 (County Clerk, #108, 78205); (210) 335-2113 (District Clerk, First Floor, 78205); (210) 335-2197 FAX (County Clerk); (210) 335-3424 FAX (District Clerk)
mmontemayor@co.bexar.tx.us
http://www.co.bexar.tx.us
Gary Gauntt, Supervisor-Archives; Gerard C. "Gerry" Rickhoff, County Clerk; Margaret G. Montemayor, District Clerk
(land records from 1736 [Spanish, Mexican, Republic, and up-to-date], naturalization records from 1837 to 1890, church records of San Fernando Cathedral, others, probate records from Spanish, Mexican period, up-to-

date also)
probate search service: $5.00 for the first five years and $1.00 for each additional year; copies of probate records: $1.00 per page, no minimum

Blanco County
created on 11 February 1858 from Burnet, Comal, Gillespie and Hays counties

Blanco County Courthouse
Johnson City, TX 78636
(830) 868-7357 (County Clerk, PO Box 65); (830) 868-0973 (District Clerk, PO Box 382); (830) 868-4158 FAX (County Clerk); (830) 868-2084 FAX (District Clerk)
http://www.co.blanco.tx.us
Karen Newman, County Clerk; Deborah Elsbury, District Clerk
("Our courthouse burned in 1876; we have nothing before then"; land records with Clerk, naturalization records with Clerk, births and deaths from 1903, marriages from 1876 with Clerk, probate records from 1876)
probate search service: $5.00 per search; copies of probate records: $1.00 per page

Borden County
organized 1876 from Bexar County

Borden County Courthouse
PO Box 124
Gail, TX 79738
(806) 756-4312; (806) 756-4405 FAX
bordenco@poka.com
http://www.co.borden.tx.us
Norma Herridge, District/County Clerk

Bosque County
organized 1854 from McLennan and Milam counties

Bosque County Courthouse
Meridian, TX 76665
(254) 435-2201 (County Clerk, PO Box 617); (254) 435-2234 (District Clerk, PO Box 674); (254) 435-2152 FAX (County Clerk); (254) 435-2152 FAX (District Clerk)
room106@htcomp.net (County Clerk)
http://users.htcomp.net/bosque
Betty Outlaw, County Clerk; Sandra Woosley, District Clerk

Bowie County
organized 1840 from Red River County

Bowie County Courthouse
710 James Bowie Drive—location)
PO Box 248 (mailing address)
New Boston, TX 75570
(903) 628-6740 (County Clerk); (903) 628-6775 (District Clerk, PO Box 248); (903) 628-6729 FAX (County Clerk); (903) 628-2217 FAX (District Clerk)
http://www.co.bowie.tx.us/ips/cms
Velma Moore, County Clerk; Ms. Billy Fox, District Clerk
(births, delayed births, deaths, marriage licenses)
copies of vital records: $9.00 each for births, deaths and marriages, $25.00 for delayed births ("must have name and dates in order to do searches")

Brazoria County
organized 1836 from Old Mexican Municipality

Brazoria County Courthouse
111 East Locust, Suite 200
Angleton, TX 77515
(979) 864-1355 (County Clerk, Suite 200); (979) 864-1385 (County Clerk–Civil Division); (979) 864-1830 (County Clerk–Criminal Division); (979) 864-1374 (County Clerk—Deed Records); (979) 864-1366 (County Clerk—Probate); (979) 864-1357 (County Clerk–Vital Statistics); (979) 864-1316 (District Clerk, Suite 500); (979) 864-1314 (District Clerk–Records)
joyceh@brazoria-county.com;

jerrydeere@brazornia-county.com
http://www.brazoria-county.com
Joyce Hudman, County Clerk; Jerry Deere,
District Clerk
(land records, vital records, probate records)
probate search service: $5.00; copies of probate
records: $1.00 per page, no minimum

Brazos County
organized 1841 from Washington County

Brazos County Courthouse
300 East 26th Street
Bryan, TX 77803
(979) 361-4528 (County Clerk, Suite 120); (979)
361-4230 (District Clerk, Suite 216)
kmcqueen@co.brazos.tx.us;
mhamlin@co.brazos.tx.us
http://www.co.brazos.tx.us
Karen McQueen, County Clerk; Marc Hamlin,
District Clerk

Brewster County
organized 1887 from Presidio County

Brewster County Courthouse
PO Drawer 119
Alpine, TX 79831
(432) 837-3355 (County Clerk); (432) 837-6216
(District Clerk); (432) 837-6217 FAX (County
Clerk); (432) 837-6217 FAX (District Clerk)
bertam@overland.net; joanns@overland.net
http://www.co.brewster.tx.us/ips/cms
Berta R. Martinez, County Clerk; JoAnn
Salgado, District Clerk
(land records from 1877, births and deaths from
1903, marriages from 1887, probate records
from 1887)
probate search service: $9.00 each; copies of
probate records: $1.00 per page, no minimum

Briscoe County
organized 1876 from Bexar County

Briscoe County Courthouse
PO Box 555
Silverton, TX 79257
(806) 823-2134; (806) 823-2359 FAX
http://www.co.briscoe.tx.us
Bena Hester, District/County Clerk
(land records, naturalization records, vital
records, probate records)
probate search service: $5.00; copies of probate:
$1.00 per page, no minimum

Brooks County
organized 1911 from Starr and Zapata counties

Brooks County Courthouse
Falfurrias, TX 78355
(361) 325-5604, ext. 248 (County Clerk, PO Box
427); (361) 325-5604, ext. 238 (District Clerk,
Po Box 534); (361) 325-4944 FAX (District
Clerk)
http://www.co.brooks.tx.us/ips/cms
Frutoso "Pepe" Garza, County Clerk; Noe
Guerra, Jr., District Clerk

Brown County
organized from Caldwell County by an act of the
legislature, passed 27 August 1856; after the
election of 21 March 1857, the county lines
were found not to be exact; boundaries
corrected and a second election held 2 August
1858

Brown County Courthouse
200 South Broadway
Brownwood, TX 76801-3136
(325) 643-2594 (County Clerk); (325) 646-5514
(District Clerk); (325) 643-1685 FAX (County
Clerk)
brncntyclk@hotmail.com
http://www.ci.brownwood.tx.us (City of
Brownwood)
Margaret Wood, County Clerk; Janice "Jan"
Brown, District Clerk
(land records from 1880, births and deaths from
1903, marriages from 1880, probate records

from 1880)
records search service: no charge (births within
the last fifty years and deaths within the last
twenty-five years, subject to restrictions);
copies of land and probate records: $1.00 per
page, no minimum

Burleson County
organized 1846 from Milam and Washington
counties

Burleson County Courthouse
100 West Buck
Caldwell, TX 77836
(979) 567-2329 (County Clerk, Suite 203); (979)
567-2336 District Clerk, Suite 303); (979) 567-
2376 FAX (County Clerk)
http://www.co.burleson.tx.us
Anna L. Schielack, County Clerk; Joy Brymer,
District Clerk
(land records, delayed births, marriages from 21
September 1846, probate records with County
Clerk; naturalization records with District
Clerk)
probate search service: no charge at this time
("however our searching time is *limited*");
copies of probate records: $1.00 per page, no
minimum

Burnet County
organized 1852 from Travis County

Burnet County Courthouse
220 South Pierce Street
Burnet, TX 78611-3136
(512) 756-5406 (County Clerk, First Floor);
(512) 756-5450 (District Clerk (Courthouse
Annex North, 1701 East Polk Street, Suite 90,
Burnet, TX 78611-2757); (512) 756-5410
FAX (County Clerk)
countyclerk@burnetcountytexas.org;
districtclerk@burnetcountytexas.org
http://www.burnetcountytexas.org
Janet Parker, County Clerk; Dana Deberry,
District Clerk

Caldwell County
organized 1848 from Gonzales County

Caldwell County Courthouse
110 South Main Street
Lockhart, TX 78644
(512) 398-1804 (County Clerk, First Floor, PO
Box 906); (512) 398-1806 (District Clerk, 201
East San Antonio, PO Box 749, Lockhart, TX
78644; (512) 398-1805 FAX (District Clerk)
http://www.co.caldwell.tx.us
Nina Sells, County Clerk; Tina Morgan, District
Clerk
(land records, vital records, and probate records
with County Clerk; naturalization records
with District Clerk)
no probate search service; copies of probate
records: $1.00 each, no minimum

Calhoun County
organized 1846 from Victoria County

Calhoun County Courthouse
211 South Ann Street
Port Lavaca, TX 77979-4249
(361) 553-4411 (County Clerk); (361) 553-4630
(District Clerk, PO Box 658); (361) 553-4420
FAX (County Clerk)
calhoun@tisd.net
http://www.tisd.net/~calhoun
Anita Fricke, County Clerk; Pamela Martin-
Hartgrove, District Clerk

Callahan County
organized 1877 from Milam and Travis counties

Callahan County Courthouse
100 West Fourth Street
Baird, TX 79504
(2325) 854-5815 (County Clerk, Suite 104); (325)
854-5825 (District Clerk, Suite 300); (325)
854-5816 FAX (County Clerk); (325) 854-
5826 FAX (District Clerk)

callahandc@hotmail.com
http://www.callahancounty.org
Jeanie Bohannon, County Clerk; Sharon Owens,
District Clerk
(land records from 1877, births and deaths from
1903 [early years are sketchy], marriages from
1877, probate records from 1877)
probate search service: $6.00 ("we need full
names and an approximate date for any
record we search"); copies of probate records:
$1.00 per page, $5.00 for certification, no
minimum

Cameron County
organized 1848 from Nueces County

Cameron County Courthouse
1100 East Monroe Street
Brownsville, TX 78520
(956) 544-0815 (County Clerk, Administration
Building, 964 East Harrison Street, Second
Floor); (956) 544-0817 (County Clerk–Vital
Statistics); (956) 548-9586 (County Clerk–
Probate Department); (956) 544-0838
(District Clerk–Civil, Judicial Building, 974
East Harrison Street, Third Floor); (956) 548-
0894 FAX (County Clerk); (956) 544-0841
FAX (District Clerk)
jgrivera@co.cameron.tx.us;
mayra.medrano@co.cameron.tx.usadelagarza
@co.cameron.tx.us
http://www.co.cameron.tx.us
Joe Rivera, County Clerk; Ms. Mayra Medrano,
Supervisor, Probate Department; Aurora De
La Garza, District Clerk
(land records with County Clerk–Recording
Department, vital records with County Clerk–
Vital Statistics, probate records with County
Clerk–Probate Department)
probate search service: $5.00; copies of probate
records: $1.00 per page, no minimum

Camp County
organized 1874 from Upshur County

Camp County Courthouse
126 Church Street, Room #102
Pittsburg, TX 75686-1346
(903) 856-2731 (County Clerk, Room 102); (903)
856-3221 (District Clerk, Room 204); (903)
856-2309 FAX (County Clerk); (903) 856-
0560 FAX (District Clerk)
http://www.co.camp.tx.us/ips/cms
Elaine Young, County Clerk; Ms. Mignon Cook,
District Clerk
(land records from 1874, births, deaths and
marriages from 1903, probate records from
1894)
probate search service: no charge; copies of vital
records: $9.00 each for births and deaths,
$7.00 each for marriages; copies of probate
records: 50¢ per page, no minimum

Carson County
organized 1876 from Bexar County

Carson County Courthouse
PO Box 487
Panhandle, TX 79068-0487
(806) 537-3873; (806) 537-3623 FAX
celeste5204@msn.com
http://www.co.carson.tx.us/ips/cms
Celeste Bichsel, District/County Clerk

Cass County
organized 1846 from Bowie County; name
changed from Davis County in 1871

Cass County Courthouse
Linden, TX 75563
(903) 756-5071 (County Clerk, PO Box 449);
(903) 756-7514 (District Clerk, PO Box 510);
(903) 756-8057 FAX (County Clerk); (903)
756-5253 FAX (District Clerk)
jmitchell.countyclerk@casscountytx.org;
bwilbanks.districtclerk@casscountytx.org
http://www.co.cass.tx.us/ips/cms
Jannis Mitchell, County Clerk; Becky Wilbanks,
District Clerk

(land records from 1846, vital records from early 1900s, probate records from 1846)
probate search service: $5.00 per search; copies of probate records: $1.00 per page, no minimum

Castro County
organized 1876 from Wheeler County

Castro County Courthouse
100 East Bedford Street, Room 101
Dimmitt, TX 79027-2643
(806) 647-3338; (806) 647-5438 FAX
jmtclerk@castrocounty.org
http://ww.co.castro.tx.us
Joyce Thomas, District/County Clerk

Chambers County
organized 1858 from Jefferson and Liberty counties

Chambers County Courthouse
404 Washington
Anahuac, TX 77514
(409) 267-8309 (County Clerk, PO Box 728); (409) 267-8276 (District Clerk–Civil, PO Box NN); (409) 267-8315 FAX (County Clerk)
hhawthorne@co.chambers.tx.us
http://www.co.chambers.tx.us
Heather Hawthorne, County Clerk; Robert B. Scherer, Jr., District Clerk
(land records from 1 January 1875, vital records from 1903, probate records from 1 January 1875)
probate search service: no charge; copies of probate records: $1.00 each, no minimum

Cherokee County
organized 1846 from Nacogdoches County

Cherokee County Courthouse
520 North Main Street
Rusk, TX 75785
(903) 683-2447 (County Clerk, PO Drawer 420); (903) 683-6908 (District Clerk, PO Drawer C); (903) 683-5931 FAX (County Clerk); (903) 683-2971 FAX (District Clerk)
http://www.co.cherokee.tx.us/ips/cms
Laverne Lusk, County Clerk; Janet Gates, District Clerk
(land records from 1846, births and deaths from 1903, marriages from 1846, probate records from 1839)
probate search service: $5.00; copies of land records: $1.00 per page; copies of vital records: $9.00 each for births, $2.00 each for non-certified deaths before 1950, $9.00 each for certified deaths before 1950 or any deaths after 1950, $2.00 each for non-certified marriage licenses before 1950, $5.00 each for certified marriage licenses before 1950 or any marriages after 1950; copies of probate records: $1.00 per page

Childress County
organized 1887 from Bexar and Fannin counties

Childress County Courthouse
100 Avenue E, NW
Courthouse Box 4
Childress, TX 79201-3755
(940) 937-6143; (940) 937-3708 FAX
clerks@srcaccess.net
http://www.co.childress.tx.us
Zona Prince, District/County Clerk
(land records, vital records, probate records)
records search service: $10.00; copies of records: $1.00 per page, $5.00 for certification

Clay County
organized 1857 from Cooke County

Clay County Courthouse
100 North Bridge Street (On the Square)
Henrietta, TX 76365
(940) 538-4631 (County Clerk, PO Box 548); (940) 538-4561 (District Clerk, PO Drawer 568); (940) 538-4008 FAX (County Clerk)
ccjudge@claycountytx.com (Kenneth Liggett, County Judge)
http://www.co.clay.tx.us/ips/cms
Kay Hutchison, County Clerk; Dan Slagle, District Clerk
(land records from 1870s, vital records from 1903, probate records from 1873 with County Clerk; naturalization records [proceedings discontinued 1917] with District Clerk)
probate search service: no charge; copies of probate records: $1.00 per page

Cochran County
organized 1876 from Bexar County

Cochran County Courthouse
100 North Main Street, Room 102
Morton, TX 79346
(806) 266-5450; (806) 266-9027 FAX
cclerk@door.net
http://www.co.cochran.tx.us/ips/cms
Rita Tyson, District/County Clerk

Coke County
organized 1889 from Tom Green County

Coke County Courthouse
PO Box 150
Robert Lee, TX 76945-0150
(325) 453-2631; (325) 453-2650 FAX
marylgclerk@juno.com; mary.grim@co.coke.tx.us
http://www.co.coke.tx.us/ips/cms
Mary Grim, District/County Clerk
(land records, vital records, probate records)
probate search service: no charge; copies of probate records: $1.00 per page, $5.00 for certification, no minimum

Coleman County
organized 1858 from Travis County

Coleman County Courthouse
Coleman, TX 76834
(325) 625-2889 (County Clerk, 100 West Live Oak Street, Suite 105, PO Box 591); (325) 625-2568 (District Clerk, PO Box 512)
cclerk@web-access.net
http://www.co.coleman.tx.us/ips/cms
Jo Ann Hale, County Clerk; Jo Chapman, District Clerk

Collin County
organized 1846 from Fannin County

Collin County Government Center
210 South McDonald Street
McKinney, TX 7506
(972) 548-4185 (County Clerk, Annex A, First Floor, 200 South McDonald, Suite 120); (972) 548-4320 (District Clerk, Suite 130); (972) 547-5731 FAX (County Clerk)
ctyclerks@collincountytx.gov; distclk@co.collin.tx.us
http://www.co.collin.tx.us
Stacey Kemp, County Clerk; Hannah Kunkle, District Clerk
(land records from 1846, vital records from 1903, probate records from about 1858)
no probate search service; copies of probate records: $1.00 per page, no minimum

Collingsworth County
organized 1876 from Bexar and Fannin counties

Collingsworth County Courthouse
(800 West Avenue—location)
PO Box 10 (mailing address)
Wellington, TX 79095
(806) 447-2408; (806) 447-2409 FAX
http://www.co.collingsworth.tx.us/ips/cms
Jackie Johnson, District/County Clerk
(probate records from 1890s, deeds and vital records from 1890s)
records search service: $5.00 each; copies of records: $1.00 per page, no minimum

Colorado County
organized 1836 from Old Mexican Municipality

Colorado County Courthouse
400 Spring Street
Columbus, TX 78934
(979) 732-2155 (County Clerk, Room 103); (979) 732-2536 (Room 210E); (979) 732-8852 FAX (County Clerk); (979) 732-2591 FAX (District Clerk)
harvey.vornsand@co.colorado.tx.us
http://www.co.colorado.tx.us/ips/cms
Darlene Hayek, County Clerk; Harvey Vornsand, District Clerk

Comal County
organized 1846 from Bexar and Gonzales counties

Comal County Courthouse
150 North Seguin
New Braunfels, TX 78130
(830) 620-5513 (County Clerk, Suite 101); (830) 620-5574 (District Clerk); (830) 620-3410 FAX (County Clerk); (830) 608-2006 FAX (District Clerk)
cckajs@co.comal.tx.us; dckkhf@co.comal.tx.us
http://www.co.comal.tx.us
Joy Streater, County Clerk; Kathy Faulkner, District Clerk
(naturalization records from 1847 with District Clerk; index to the naturalization records, land records from 1846, births and deaths from 1903, marriages from 1846, and probate records from 1846 with County Clerk)
probate search service: $5.00 per name; copies of probate records: $1.00 per page, no minimum

Comanche County
organized 1856 from Bosque and Coryell counties

Comanche County Courthouse
101 West Central Avenue
Comanche, TX 76442-3264
(325) 356-2655 (County Clerk); (325) 356-2342 (District Clerk, PO Box 206)
ccclerk@htcomp.net
Ruby Lesley, County Clerk; La Nell Williams, District Clerk
(land records from 1856, births and deaths from 1903, marriages from 1856, probate records from 1856)
no probate search service; copies of vital records: $7.50 each for births and deaths, $3.00 each for marriages; copies of probate records: $1.00 per page

Concho County
organized 1858 from Bexar County

Concho County Courthouse
(Highway 83—location)
PO Box 98 (mailing address)
Paint Rock, TX 76866-0098
(325) 732-4322; (325) 732-2040 FAX
barbara.hoffman@co.concho.tx.us
http://www.co.tx.us/ips/cms
Barbara K. Hoffman, District/County Clerk
(land records, births, deaths, and marriage licenses)
copies: $1.00 per page, $5.00 for certification; copies of vital records: $9.00 each for births and deaths

Cooke County
organized 1848 from Fannin County

Cooke County Courthouse
100 South Dixon Street
Gainesville, TX 76240
(940) 668-5420 (County Clerk); (940) 668-5450 (District Clerk); (940) 668-5486 FAX (County Clerk)
districtclerk@nortexinfo.net
http://www.co.cooke.tx.us/ips/cms
Rebecca Lawson, County Clerk; Patricia Payne, District Clerk
(land records from 1850, vital records from 1903, probate records from 1850s with County Clerk; naturalization records from late 1890s with District Clerk)

probate search service: no charge ("be as specific on dates as possible"); copies of probate records: $1.00 each (uncertified), no minimum

Coryell County

organized 1854 from Bell and McLennan counties

Coryell County Courthouse
620 East Main Street—location
Gatesville, TX 76528
(254) 865-5911, ext. 235 (County Clerk, PO Box 237); (254) 865-5911, ext. 241 (District Clerk, PO Box 4); (254) 865-8631 FAX (County Clerk); (254) 865-5064 FAX (District Clerk)
coryellcountyclerk@htcomp.net;
barbara.simpson@co.coryell.tx.us;
jmay52dc@aol.com
http://www.coryellcounty.org
Barbara Simpson, County Clerk; Janice Gray, District Clerk
(land records, births and deaths, probate records)
land and probate records search service: $10.00 per index; copies of land and probate records: $1.00 per page, certified copies: $5.00 for the first page and $1.00 for each additional page (money order only); copies of vital records: $9.00 (money order only, births within the last fifty years and deaths within the last twenty-five years, subject to restrictions)

Cottle County

organized 1892 from Childress County

Cottle County Courthouse
PO Box 717
Paducah, TX 79248
(806) 492-3823; (806) 492-2625 FAX
http://www.co.cottle.tx.us/ips/cms
Beckey Tucker, District/County Clerk
(land records from 1892, vital records: All births that were reported [but many were born at home and not reported; lots of delayed births were recorded in the 1940s], death records not complete before 1929, probate records [all are indexed and complete])
probate search service: $5.00; copies of probate records: $1.00 per page

Crane County

organized 1927 from Ector County

Crane County Courthouse
PO Box 578
Crane, TX 79731-0578
(432) 558-3581; (432) 558-1148 FAX
judy.crawford@co.crane.tx.us
http://www.co.crane.tx.us/ips/cms
Judy Crawford, District/County Clerk
(births and deaths [births within the last fifty years and deaths within the last twenty-five years, subject to restrictions], and probate records)
probate search service: $5.00; copies of probate records: $1.00 per page, $5.00 per certificate

Crockett County

organized 1875 from Bexar County

Crockett County Courthouse
PO Drawer C
Osona, TX 76943-2502
(325) 392-2022; (325) 392-3742 FAX
dpmoore54@hotmail.com
http://www.co.crockett.tx.us/ips/cms
Debbi Puckett-Moore, District/County Clerk
(vital records, probate records)
probate search service: $10.00; copies of probate records: $1.00 each, no minimum

Crosby County

organized 1876 from Baylor County

Crosby County Courthouse
(201 West Aspen—location)
PO Box 218
Crosbyton, TX 79322

(806) 675-2334 (County Clerk, Suite 102); (806) 675-2071 (District Clerk, Suite 207); (806) 675-2804 FAX (District Clerk)
ccdc72nd@flash.net
http://www.co.crosby.tx.us/ips/cms
Betty J. Pierce, County Clerk; Karla Isbell, District Clerk
(land records, vital records from 1886, probate records from 1886)
probate search service: no charge; copies of land records: $1.00 per page; copies of probate records: $1.00 per page, no minimum

Culberson County

organized 1911 from El Paso County

Culberson County Courthouse
PO Box 158
Van Horn, TX 79855-0158
(432) 283-2058; (432) 283-9234 FAX
http://www.co.culberson.tx.us
Linda McDonald, District/County Clerk
(land records, vital records, probate records)
land, vital, and probate records search service: $5.00 per name; copies of land, vital, and probate records: $1.00 per page

Dallam County

organized 1876 from Bexar County

Dallam County Courthouse
PO Box 1352
Dalhart, TX 79002-1352
(806) 249-4751
clerk@dallam.org
http://www.dallam.org/county
Ms. Terri Banks, District/County Clerk
(deeds, deed of trust, etc. [all indexed by name], some vital records [Dalhart is in two counties—Dallam and Hartley; the hospital is located in Hartley County, where most births and deaths occur], probate records)
probate search service ("give as much information as possible—names, dates, etc."): no charge; copies of probate records: $1.00 per page, no minimum

Dallas County

organized 1846 from Nacogdoches County

Dallas County Courthouse
Dallas, TX 75202
(214) 653-7099 (County Clerk, Records Building, 500 Main Street, Second Floor); (214) 653-7149 (District Clerk, 600 Commerce Street, Suite 103); (214) 653-7176 FAX (County Clerk)
http://www.dallascounty.org
John F. Warren, County Clerk; Gary Fitzsimmons, District Clerk
birth certificate: $23.00, death certificate: $20.00, land records: $1.00 per page

Dawson County

organized 1858 from Bexar County

Dawson County Courthouse
PO Box 1268
Lamesa, TX 79331-1268
(806) 872-3778 (County Clerk); (806) 872-7373 (District Clerk); (806) 872-2473 FAX (County Clerk); (806) 872-9513 FAX (District Clerk)
dawsonclerk@pics.net; districtclerk@pics.net
http://www.co.dawson.tx.us
Gloria Vera, County Clerk; Carolyn Turner, District Clerk
(land records, vital records, probate records)
probate search service: no charge; copies of probate records: $1.00 per page, no minimum

Deaf Smith County

organized 1876 from Bexar County

Deaf Smith County Courthouse
235 East Third
Hereford, TX 79045
(806) 363-7077 (County Clerk, Room 203); (806) 364-3901 (District Clerk, Room 304); (806) 363-7023 FAX (County Clerk); (806) 363-

7007 FAX (District Clerk)
david.ruland@co.deaf-smith.tx.us
http://www.co.deaf-smith.tx.us/ips/cms
David Ruland, County Clerk; Jean Schumacher Coody, District Clerk
(land records from 1876, vital records from 1876, probate records from 1876)
probate search service: $2.00; copies of probate records: $1.00 per page, no minimum

Delta County

organized 1870 from Lamar County

Delta County Courthouse
200 West Dallas Avenue
Cooper, TX 75432-1726
(903) 395-4400, ext. 222; (903) 395-4260 FAX
http://www.co.delta.tx.us/ips/cms
Jane Jones, District/County Clerk

Denton County

organized 1846 from Fannin County

Denton County Courts Building
1450 East McKinney Street
Denton, TX 76209-4524
(940) 349-2012 (County Clerk, PO Box 2187, Denton, TX 76202-2187); (940) 349-2200 (District Clerk, PO Box 2146, Denton, TX 76202-2146); (940) 349-2013 FAX (County Clerk); (940) 349-2231 FAX (District Clerk)
cynthia.mitchell@dentoncounty.com;
sherri.adelstein@dentoncounty.com
http://www.co.denton.tx.us
Cynthia Mitchell, County Clerk; Sherri Adelstein, District Clerk
(land records from 1876, vital records from 1903, some delayed births from 1870s, probate records from 1876 with County Clerk; early naturalization records with Historical Museum)
probate search service: $5.00 for the first five years and $1.00 for each additional year; copies of probate records: $1.00 per page ("no personal checks; all money orders or cashier's check")

De Witt County

organized 1846 from Goliad, Gonzales and Victoria counties

De Witt County Courthouse
307 North Gonzales Street
Cuero, TX 77954-2970
(361) 275-3724 (County Clerk); (361) 275-2221 (District Clerk, PO Box 845); (361) 275-8994 FAX (County Clerk); (361) 275-5910 FAX (District Clerk)
dewittcc@gvec.net; dewittcc@dewittec.net;
dewittdistclk@sbcglobal.net;
dewittdistclk@dewittec.net
http://www.co.dewitt.tx.us
Elva Petersen, County Clerk; Tabeth Gardner, District Clerk
(land records from 1846, naturalization records from 1846, vital records from 1903, some births registered during 1873 to 1876 and probate births [cities of Cuero and Yoakum have births and deaths from 1951], probate records from 1846 with County Clerk)
probate search service: no charge; copies of probate records: $1.00 per page, no minimum

Dickens County

organized 1876 from Bexar County

Dickens County Courthouse
PO Box 120
Dickens, TX 79229
(806) 623-5531
coclerk@caprock-spur.com
Winona Humphreys, District/County Clerk
(deeds from 1891, naturalization records from 1891, births and deaths from 1901, marriages from 1891 [births within the last fifty years and deaths within the last twenty-five years, subject to restrictions], probate records from about 1900)
probate search service: $5.00; copies of probate

records: $1.00 per page, no minimum

Dimmit County
organized 1858 from Bexar and Maverick counties

Dimmit County Courthouse
103 North Fifth Street
Carrizo Springs, TX 78834-3101
(830) 876-4838 (County Clerk); (830) 876-4244 (District Clerk); (830) 876-4202 FAX (County Clerk)
Mario_Garcia@faxmail.com
Mario Z. Garcia, County Clerk; Maricela Lopez Gonzalez, District Clerk

Donley County
organized 1876 from Jack County

Donley County Courthouse
PO Drawer U
Clarendon, TX 79226-2020
(806) 847-3436; (806) 874-3351 FAX
districtclerk@donleytx.com
http://www.donleytx.com
Alice Fay Vargas, District/County Clerk
(land records from 1882, births from 1878, deaths from 1903, marriages from 1882, probate records from 1886)
records search service: $5.00 per name; copies of land and probate records: $1.00 per page up to thirty pages, then 85¢ for the next page and 15¢ for each additional page, no minimum; certified copies of vital records: $9.00 each

Duval County
organized 1858 from Live Oak, Starr and Nueces counties

Duval County Courthouse
San Diego, TX 78384
(361) 279-3322, ext. 272 (County Clerk, PO Box 248); (361) 279-3322, ext. 239 (District Clerk, PO Drawer 428); (361) 279-3159 FAX (County Clerk)
Oscar_Garcia@faxmail.com
Oscar Garcia, Jr., County Clerk; Richard M. Barton, District Clerk
(land records, vital records from 1800, probate records from 1800 with County Clerk)
probate search service: no charge; copies of land records: $1.00 each, $1.00 for certification; copies of vital records: $8.00 each for long form of birth certificate and death certificate, $5.00 each for birth cards or marriage certificates (request for birth certificate must include name, date of birth and parents; for death certificate: name and date of death; for marriage certificate: names of husband and wife and date of marriage); copies of probate records: $1.00 per page, no minimum

Eastland County
organized 1858 from Bosque, Coryell and Travis counties

Eastland County Clerk
100 West Main
Eastland, TX 76448
(254) 629-1583 (County Clerk, Suite 102, PO Box 110); (254) 629-2664 (District Court, Suite 206); (254) 629-8125 FAX (County Clerk); (254) 629-2070 (District Clerk)
ecco@eastlandcountytexas.com (County Clerk); ecdc@eastlandcountytexas.com (District Clerk)
http://county.eastlandcountytexas.com
Cathy Jentho, County Clerk; Karen Moore, District Clerk
(land records from 1873, births and deaths from 1903 [other than delayed records], marriages from 1873, probate records from 1873)
no probate search service; certified copies of vital records: $9.00 each for births and deaths, $5.00 each for marriages (births within the last fifty years and deaths within the last twenty-five years, subject to restrictions); copies of probate records: $1.00 per page plus $5.00 for certification, no minimum

Ector County
organized 1887 from Tom Green County

Ector County Courthouse
1010 East Eighth Street
Odessa, TX 79763
(432) 498-4130 (County Clerk, 300 North Grant, Room 111, Odessa, TX 79761, PO Box 707, Odessa, TX 79760); (432) 498-4290 (District Clerk, 300 North Grant, Room 301); (432) 498-4177 FAX (County Clerk); (432) 498-4292 FAX (District Clerk)
http://www.co.ector.tx.us
Linda Haney, County Clerk; Janis Morgan, District Clerk
(land records, births, deaths, marriages, and probate records with County Clerk)
probate search service: no charge; copies of probate records: $1.00 per page, no minimum

Edwards County
organized 1858 from Bexar County

Edwards County Courthouse
PO Box 184
Rocksprings, TX 78880-0184
(830) 683-2235; (830) 683-5376 FAX
Joanna Baker, District/County Clerk
(land records, vital records [certified copies only], probate records)
probate search service: $5.00 per name; copies of probate records: $1.00 each ("send cash or check")

Ellis County
organized 1849 from Navarro County

Ellis County Courthouse
101 West Main
Waxahachie, TX 75165-3759
(972) 923-5070 (County Clerk, Records Building, 117 West Franklin Street, Waxahachie, TX 75168); (972) 825-5000 (District Clerk, 1201 North Highway 77, Suite 103); (972) 923-5075 FAX (County Clerk)
cindy.polley@co.ellis.tx.us
http://www.co.ellis.tx.us
Cindy Polley, County Clerk; Melanie Price-Reed, District Clerk
(deeds from 1845, births from 1903 [unless delayed birth], deaths from 1903, marriages from 1850, and estates and wills from 1845 with County Clerk; naturalization records with District Clerk)
land and probate records search service: $5.00 for five-year search per name; vital records search fee: $9.00 per birth, death or marriage, includes certified copy if found; copies of land or probate records: 50¢ per page if made by individual in person, $1.00 per page if made by office staff, no minimum, $5.00 for certification ("must have dates and names in order to check any of the above")

El Paso County
organized 1850 from Bexar County

El Paso County Courthouse
500 East San Antonio
El Paso, TX 79901-2421
(915) 546-2071 (County Clerk, Suite 105); (915) 546-2021 (District Clerk, Suite 103); (915) 546-2012 FAX (County Clerk); (915) 546-8139 FAX (District Clerk
countyclerk@epcounty.com; districtclerk@epcounty.com
http://www.co.el-paso.tx.us
Delia Briones, County Clerk; Gilbert Sanchez, District Clerk

Erath County
organized 1856 from Bosque and Coryell counties

Erath County Courthouse
100 Graham Street
Stephenville, TX 76401-4219
(254) 965-1482 (County Clerk, 100 West Washington); (254) 965-1486 (District Clerk,

112 West College Street); (254) 965-5732 FAX (County Clerk); (254) 965-7156 FAX (District Clerk)
http://www.co.erath.tx.us/ips/cms
Gwinda Jones, County Clerk; Wanda Pringle, District Clerk
(deeds from 1867, births [also delayed records before 1903] and deaths from 1903, marriages [recorded in the county where the license was purchased] from 1869, probate records from 1876)
probate search service: $2.00 ("we cannot make extensive searches but will search for any record if names and dates are supplied; enclosing a SASE with any request for information will get you a reply"); certified copies of vital records: $9.00 each (includes search; births within the last fifty years and deaths within the last twenty-five years, subject to restrictions; restricted records may be made available to a properly qualified applicant, with positive identification, upon submission of a written, signed application that fully identifies the record); copies of probate records: $1.00 per page plus $5.00 for certification

Falls County
organized 1850 from Limestone and Milam counties

Falls County Courthouse
Marlin, TX 76661
(254) 883-1408 (County Clerk, PO Box 458); (254) 883-1419 (District Clerk, PO Box 229); (254) 883-1406 FAX (County Clerk)
Frances Braswell, County Clerk; Larry Hoelscher, District Clerk
(land records from 1835, births and deaths from 1903, marriages from 1854, probate records from 1880)
copies of land, probate, and vital records for genealogy: $1.00 per page, no minimum

Fannin County
organized 1837 from Red River County

Fannin County Courthouse
101 East Sam Rayburn Drive
Bonham, TX 75418
(903) 583-7486 (County Clerk, Suite 102); (903) 583-7459 (District Clerk, Suite 201); (903) 583-9598 FAX (County Clerk); (903) 640-1826 FAX (District Clerk)
tjrich@fanninco.net; njyoung@fanninco.net
http://www.co.fannin.tx.us/ips/cms
Tammy Rich, County Clerk; Nancy Young, District Clerk
(land records from 1838, some naturalization records, vital records from 1903, probate records from 1838)
no probate search service; copies of probate records: $1.00 per page

Fayette County
organized 1837 from Bastrop and Colorado counties

Fayette County Courthouse
151 North Washington Street
La Grange, TX 78945-2657
(979) 968-3251 (County Clerk, PO Box 59); (979) 968-3548 (District Clerk, Room 102); (979) 968-8531 FAX (County Clerk); (979) 968-2618 FAX (District Clerk)
fcclerk@cvtv.net; virginia.wied@co.fayette.tx.us
http://www.co.fayette.tx.us
Carolyn Kubos Roberts, County Clerk; Virginia Wied, District Clerk
(land records from 1838, vital records from 1903, and probate records from 1838 with County Clerk; naturalization records from 1850, indexed with District Clerk)
probate search service: $5.00; copies of probate records: $1.00 per page, no minimum

Fisher County
organized 1876 from Bexar County

Fisher County Courthouse
Roby, TX 79543
(325) 776-2401 (County Clerk, PO Box 368);
(325) 776-2279 (District Clerk, PO Box 88);
(325) 776-3274 FAX (County Clerk); (325)
776-3253 FAX (District Clerk)
fcclerk180@yahoo.com
http://www.co.fisher.tx.us/ips/cms
Pat Thomson, County Clerk; Tammy Haley,
District Clerk

Floyd County
organized 1876 from Bexar County

Floyd County Courthouse
100 Main Street
Floydada, TX 79235
(806) 983-4900 (County Clerk, Room 101, PO
Box 476); (806) 983-4923 (District Clerk, PO
Box 67); (806) 983-3236 (County Clerk)
http://members.tripod.com/proagency/floydco
unty.html
Marilyn Holcomb, County Clerk; Patty
Davenport, District Clerk
(land records, vital records, probate records)
probate search service: no charge; copies of
probate records: $1.00 per page, $1.00
minimum

Foard County
organized 1891 from Cottle, Hardeman, King
and Knox counties

Foard County Courthouse
PO Box 539
Crowell, TX 79227
(940) 684-1365; (940) 684-1918 FAX
Patricia Aydelott, District/County Clerk
(land records, naturalization records, vital
records from 1903, probate records from
1893)
land, vital, and probate records search service:
$10.00; copies of land, vital, and probate
records: $1.00 per page, no minimum

Fort Bend County
organized 1837 from Austin County

Fort Bend County Courthouse
301 Jackson Street
Richmond, TX 77469
(281) 341-8685 (County Clerk); (281) 344-3953
(401 Jackson Street, Room 106); (281) 341-
8697 FAX (County Clerk); (281) 341-4519
FAX (District Court)
cclerk@co.fort-bend.tx.us; wilsondh@co.fort-
bend.tx.us; distclerk@co.fort-bend.tx.us
http://www.co.fort-bend.tx.us
Dianne Wilson, Ph.D.County Clerk; Annie
Elliot, District Clerk
(births from 1900, delayed births from late
1800s, deaths from 1903, marriages from
1837, probate records from 1838)
probate search service ("please give the years to
be searched; we do not do searches for last
name only; we need a first name, also"): $2.00
per name; copies of probate records: $1.00
per page, $2.00 for certified copies, no
minimum

Franklin County
organized 1875 from Titus County

Franklin County Clerk
Mount Vernon, TX 75457
(903) 537-4252, ext. 6 (County Clerk, 200 North
Kaufman Street); (903) 537-8337 (District
Clerk, 208 South Highway 37); (903) 537-
4252 FAX (County Clerk); (903) 537-8338
FAX (District Clerk)
fcclerk@mt-vernon.com
http://www.co.franklin.tx.us/ips/cms
Betty Crane, County Clerk; Ellen Jaggers,
District Clerk
(land records from 1849, births and deaths from
1903, marriages from 1875, probate records
from 1875)
probate search service: $5.00 per name; copies
of probate records: $1.00 per page, $1.00 for

certification, no minimum

Freestone County
organized 1850 from Limestone County

Freestone County Clerk
Fairfield, TX 75840
(903) 389-2635 (County Clerk, PO Box 1010);
(903) 389-2534 (District Clerk, PO Box 722);
(903) 389-3839 FAX; (903) 389-5289 FAX
(District Clerk)
http://www.co.freestone.tx.us/ips/cms
Mary Lynn White, County Clerk; Janet Haydon
Chappell, District Clerk
(land records from 1851, births and deaths from
1903, and probate records from 1851 with
County Clerk; naturalization records before
1910 with District Clerk)
no probate search service; certified copies of
vital records: $9.00 each (births within the last
fifty years and deaths within the last twenty-
five years, subject to restrictions); copies of
probate records: $1.00 per page

Frio County
organized 1858 from Bexar and Uvalde counties

Frio County Courthouse
500 East San Antonio
Pearsall, TX 78061
(830) 334-2214 (County Clerk, Box 6); (830)
334-8073 (District Clerk, Box 8); (830) 334-
0021 FAX (County Clerk); (830) 334-0047
FAX (District Clerk)
http://www.co.frio.tx.us/ips/cms
Angelina "Angie" Tullis, County Clerk; Ramona
Rodriguez, District Clerk

Gaines County
organized 1876 from Bexar County

Gaines County Courthouse
101 South Main
Seminole, TX 79360-4341
(432) 758-4003 (County Clerk, Room 107, PO
Box 847); (432) 758-4014 (District Clerk,
Room 213, PO Box 847); (432) 758-1442
FAX (County Clerk); (432) 758-4036 FAX
(District Clerk
vicki.phillips@co.gaines.tx.us;
virginia.stewart@co.gaines.tx.us
http://www.gainescountyonline.us
Vicki Phillips, County Clerk; Virginia Stewart,
District Clerk
(land records from 1906, births, deaths and
marriage licenses from 1906, probate records
from 1906)
records search service: no charge; copies: $1.00
per page, $9.00 per certified page (births
within the last fifty years and deaths within
the last twenty-five years, subject to
restrictions)

Galveston County
organized 1838 from Brazoria County

Galveston County Courthouse
Galveston, TX 77553
(409) 766-2200 (County Clerk, 600 59th Street,
Suite 2001, Galveston, TX 77551-4180, PO
Box 17253, Galveston, TX 77552-7253); (409)
765-2690 (District Clerk, Room 4001, 77551-
2388); (409) 765-3160 FAX (County Clerk);
(409) 766-2292 FAX (District Clerk)
http://www.co.galveston.tx.us
Mary Ann Daigle, County Clerk; Latonia D.
Wilson, District Clerk
(land records from 1838 [index under the
grantors' and grantees' names, not by
property description], some naturalization
records in 1879, and applications, births and
deaths from June 1903 to February 1909 for
city and county, births and deaths from 1941
to 1951 for City of Galveston or Texas City,
and probate records from 1838 with County
Clerk; later naturalization records with
District Court; births and deaths from 1910 to
1941 for City of Galveston and births and
deaths for Bolivar with City Hall, Galveston,

TX 77553, births and deaths from November
1954 from Memorial Hospital with City Hall,
City Registrar, PO Box 2608, Texas City, TX
77590)
probate search service: $5.00; copies of probate
records: $1.00 per page, $1.00 for certification
per instrument ("we do not bill")

Garza County
organized 1876 from Bexar County

Garza County Courthouse
(300 West Main Street, First Floor—location)
PO Box 366 (mailing address)Post, TX 79356-
3242
(806) 495-4430; (806) 495-4431 FAX
james.plummer@co.garza.tx.us
http://www.garzacounty.net
James "Jim" Plummer, District/County Clerk

Gillespie County
organized 1846 from Bexar County

Gillespie County Courthouse
101 West Main
Fredericksburg, TX 78624
(830) 997-6515 (County Clerk); (830) 997-6517
(District Clerk); (830) 997-9958 FX (County
Clerk)
mlrusche@gillespiecounty.org;
bmeyer@gillespiecounty.org
http://www.gillespiecounty.org
Mary Lynn Rusche, County Clerk; Barbara
Meyer, District Clerk
(land records, births from 1846, deaths from
1903, marriages and marriage index from
1850, and probate records with County Clerk;
naturalization records with Barbara Meyer,
District Clerk)
no probate search service; copies of land
records: $1.00 per page; copies of vital
records: $9.00 each for births and deaths,
$6.00 each for marriages (births within the last
fifty years and deaths within the last twenty-
five years, subject to restrictions); copies of
probate records: $1.00 per page

Glasscock County
organized 1887 from Tom Green County

Glasscock County Courthouse
PO Box 190
Garden City, TX 79739-0190
(432) 354-2371; (432) 354-2348 FAX
rebecca.batla@co.glasscock.tx.us
http://www.co.glasscock.tx.us
Rebecca Batla, District/County Clerk

Goliad County
organized 1836 from Old Mexican Municipality

Goliad County Courthouse
PO Box 50
Goliad, TX 77963
(361) 645-3294
gturley@goliadcogovt.org
http://www.co.goliad.tx.us/ips/cms
Gail M. Turley, District/County Clerk
(land records from the late 1800s [after
courthouse fire of June 1870], naturalization
records to 1915, births and deaths from 1903,
with some from the late 1800s, marriages
from 1876, probate records)
records search service: $5.00 per name and index
searched; copies of land, naturalization, and
probate records: $1.00 per page, $5.00 for
certification; certified copies of vital records:
$9.00 each for births and deaths (births within
the last fifty years and deaths within the last
twenty-five years, subject to restrictions)

Gonzales County
organized 1836 from Old Mexican Municipality

Gonzales County Courthouse
Gonzales, TX 78629
(830) 672-2801 (County Clerk, Courthouse
Annex, 1709 Sarah DeWitt Drive, PO Box
77); (830) 672-2326 (District Clerk, 414 St.

Joseph Street, Suite 300); (830) 672-2636 FAX (County Clerk); (830) 672-9313 FAX (District Clerk)
http://www.co.gonzales.tx.us/ips/cms
Ms. Lee Riedel, County Clerk; Sandra J. Baker, District Clerk

Gray County
organized 1876 from Bexar County

Gray County Courthouse
200 North Russell Street
Pampa, TX 79065-6442
(806) 669-8004 (County Clerk, PO Box 1902); (806) 669-8010 (District Clerk, PO Box 1139)
graycoclerk@centramedia.net;
dcghonderich@graycch.com
http://www.co.gray.tx.us/ips/cms
Susan Winborne, County Clerk; Gaye Honderich, District Clerk
(land records from 1880s [some prior], vital records, probate records with County Clerk)
no probate search service; copies of probate records: $1.00 per page

Grayson County
organized 1846 from Fannin County

Grayson County Courthouse
100 West Houston
Sherman, TX 75090
(903) 813-4238 (County Clerk–Real Property); (903) 813-4243 (County Clerk–Vital Statistics, Suite 17); (903) 813-4241 (County Clerk–Probate Clerk, Suite 17); (903) 813-4352 (District Clerk, Justice Center, 200 South Crockett, Suite 120A); (903) 870-0609 FAX (District Clerk)
realproperty@co.grayson.tx.us (Real Property); frontdesk@co.grayson.tx.us (Vital Statistics); garciar@co.grayson.tx.us; powerst@co.grayson.tx.us
http://www.co.grayson.tx.us
Wilma Blackshear-Bush, County Clerk; Dottie Carlson, Vital Statistics Clerk; Reina Garcia, Probate Clerk; Ms. Tracy Powers, District Clerk
(land records from 1846, vital records from 1900, probate records from 1900)
vital records search service: $5.00 for five-year search per name; no probate search service; certified copies of land records: $5.00 per document plus $1.00 per page, plus $1.00 if staff makes the copy; copies of vital records: $9.00 each for births and deaths, $5.00 each for marriage licenses; copies of probate records: $1.00 per page, certification $5.00 per document or $2.00 per page

Gregg County
organized 1873 from Rusk and Upshur counties

Gregg County Courthouse
101 East Methvin Street
Longview, TX 75601
(903) 236-8430 (County Clerk–Main, Suite 200); (903) 237-2637 (County Clerk–Birth/Records); (903) 237-2663 (District Clerk, Suite 334, PO Box 711, Longview, TX 75606); (903) 237-2574 FAX (County Clerk)
Gladyce.Carver@co.gregg.tx.us (County Clerk); Barbara.Duncan@co.gregg.tx.us
http://www.co.gregg.tx.us
Connie Wade, County Clerk; Barbara Duncan, District Clerk

Grimes County
organized 1846 from Montgomery County

Grimes County Courthouse
Anderson, TX 77830
(936) 873-2111 (County Clerk, PO Box 209); (936) 873-2111, ext. 240 (District Clerk, PO Box 234); (936) 873-3308 FAX (County Clerk); (936) 873-2514 FAX (District Clerk)
http://www.co.grimes.tx.us/ips/cms
David Pasket, County Clerk; Gay Wells, District Clerk
(land records from 1837, vital records from 1903, and probate records from 1847 with

County Clerk; naturalization records from 1892 with District Clerk)
no probate search service; copies of probate records: 75¢ each, $1.00 per certified page plus $1.00 for certification

Guadalupe County
organized 1846 from Bexar and Gonzales counties

Guadalupe County Courthouse
101 East Court Street
Seguin, TX 78155
(830) 303-8859 (County Clerk–Deeds, Suite 208); (830) 303-8863 (County Clerk–Vital Statistics); (830) 303-8867 (County Clerk–Probate); (830) 303-8873 (District Clerk–Court Collections, Suite 308); (830) 401-0300 FAX (County Clerk); (830) 379-1943 FAX (District Clerk)
tkiel@co.guadalupe.tx.us
http://www.co.guadalupe.tx.us
Teresa Kiel, County Clerk; Debi Crow, District Clerk
(land records from 1854, vital records from 1933 [births within the last fifty years and deaths within the last twenty-five years, subject to restrictions], and probate records from 1854 with County Clerk; naturalization records from 1887 to 1906 with District Clerk)
no probate search service; copies of probate records: $1.00 each, $5.00 for certification, no minimum

Hale County
organized 1876 from Bexar County

Hale County Clerk
500 Broadway
Plainview, TX 79073
(806) 291-5205 (County Clerk, Room 140); (806) 291-5261 (County Clerk); (806) 291-5226 (District Clerk, Room 200); (806) 291-9810 FAX (County Clerk)
hccleerk@Plainview.com
http://www.co.hale.tx.us
Latrice Kemp, County Clerk; Carla Cannon, District Clerk
(land records from 1884, vital records, and probate records from 1908 with County Clerk)
land and probate records search service: $5.00; vital records search service: $10.00 for three names; copies of land and probate recordsrecords: $1.00 each, $5.00 per document for certification; certified copies of vital records: $9.00 each for births and deaths (births within the last fifty years and deaths within the last twenty-five years, subject to restrictions)

Hall County
organized 1876 from Bexar County

Hall County Courthouse
512 Main Street, Suite 8
Memphis, TX 79245
(806) 259-2627
cclerk@count.net
http://www.co.hall.tx.us/ips/cms
Raye Bailey, District/Courty Clerk

Hamilton County
county created 22 January 1858 and organized 2 June 1858, being part of the Milam Land District of Texas and developed from parts of Bosque, Lampasas and Comanche counties

Hamilton County Courthouse
104 East Main
Hamilton, TX 76531
(254) 386-3518 (County Clerk, 101 East Main); (254) 386-3417 (District Clerk, 100 North Rice); (254) 386-8727 FAX (County Clerk); (254) 386-8610 FAX (District Clerk)
hamcoclerk@htcomp.net;
districtclerk@htcomp.net
http://www.co.hamilton.tx.us
Debbie Rudolph, County Clerk; Leoma Larance

District Clerk
(land records from 1852, vital records from 1903 [incomplete until 1939], and probate records from 1878 with County Clerk; naturalization records with District Clerk)
probate search service: $5.00; copies of probate records: $1.00 each, no minimum

Hansford County
organized 1876 from Bexar County

Hansford District/County Clerk
15 Northwest Court
Spearman, TX 79081
(806) 659-4110; (806) 659-4168 FAX
kvcdc@hotmail.com
http://www.co.hansford.tx.us/ips/cms
Kim V. Vera
(land records, vital records, probate records)
copies of land and probate records: $1.00 per page

Hardeman County
organized 1858 from Fannin County

Hardeman County Courthouse
PO Box 30
Quanah, TX 79252
(940) 663-2901; (940) 663-2961; (940) 663-5161 FAX
Linda Walker, District/County Clerk
(land records from 1871, vital records from 1903, and probate records from 1886)
probate search service: no charge; copies of probate records: 25¢ per page, $1.00 for certified copies

Hardin County
organized 1858 from Jefferson and Liberty counties

Hardin County Courthouse
300 Monroe
Kountze, TX 77625
(409) 246-5185 (County Clerk, PO Box 38); (409) 246-5150 (District Clerk, PO Box 2997); (409) 246-3208 FAX (County Clerk); (409) 246-3208 FAX (District Clerk)
glenda.alston@co.hardin.tx.us;
vicki.johnson@co.hardin.tx.us, District Clerk
http://www.co.hardin.tx.us/ips/cms
Glenda Alston, County Clerk; Vicki Johnson, District Clerk
(land records, vital records, probate records)
probate search service: $5.00; copies of probate records: $1.00 per page, no minimum, $5.00 per certification ("need to know date of death")

Harris County
organized 1836 from Austin and Liberty counties (Old Mexican Municipality); name changed from Harrisburg County

Harris County Civil Courts Building
201 Caroline
Houston, TX 77251
(713) 755-6405 (County Clerk, Fourth Floor, PO Box 1525); (713) 755-6425 (County Clerk—Probate Courts Department, Eighth Floor); (713) 755-9463 (District Clerk, Historical Documents Room, Room 200, PO Box 4651); (713) 755-5700 FAX (District Clerk)
bkaufman@cco.hctx.net; ccinfo@cco.hctx.net; charles_bacarisse@dco.co.harris.tx.us; historicalreadingroom@hcdistrictclerk.com
http://www.co.harris.tx.us
Beverly B. Kaufman, County Clerk; Charles Bacarisse, District Clerk
(land records from 1836 to date, naturalization records from 1892 through 1905, county births from 1903 to date, city births from October 1941 through April 1951, probate records from 1836 to date)

Harrison County
organized 1839 from Shelby County

Harrison County Courthouse
200 West Houston Street
Marshall, TX 75671
(903) 935-8403 (County Clerk, Suite 143); (903) 935-8409 (District Clerk, Suite 234, PO Box 1119)
patsyc@co.harrison.tx.us;
   sherryg@co.harrison.tx.us
http://www.co.harrison.tx.us
Patsy Cox, County Clerk; Sherry Haynes-Griffis, District Clerk
(land records from 1839, most vital records from 1903, probate records from about 1840)
no probate search service; copies of probate records: $1.00 per page, no minimum

Hartley County
organized 1876 from Bexar County

Hartley County Courthouse
PO Box Q
Channing, TX 79018
(806) 235-3582; (806) 235-2316 FAX
diane.thompson@co.hartley.tx.us
http://www.co.hartley.tx.us/ips/cms
Diane Thompson, District/County Clerk

Haskell County
organized 1858 from Fannin and Milam counties

Haskell County Courthouse
PO Box 905
Haskell, TX 79521
(940) 864-2451 (County Clerk); (940) 864-2030 (District Clerk); (940) 864-6164 FAX (County Clerk)
Rhonda.Moeller@co.haskell.tx.us;
   haskellcc@yahoo.com; dclerk@westex.net
http://www.co.haskell.tx.us/ips/cms
Rhonda Hewitt Moeller, County Clerk; Penny Young Anderson, District Clerk

Hays County
organized 1848 from Travis County

Hays County Courthouse
111 East San Antonio Street
San Marcos, TX 78666
(512, 393-7330 (County Clerk, Records Building, 137 North Guadalupe Street); (512) 939-7660 (District Clerk, 110 MLK Drive); (512) 393-7337 FAX (County Clerk)
fritsche@co.hays.tx.us;
   distclerk@co.hays.tx.usdcca@co.hays.tx.us
http://www.co.hays.tx.us
Linda C. Fritsche, County Clerk; Cecelia Adair, District Clerk
(land records from 1848, a few naturalization records in deed records, births and deaths from 1903, and probate records with County Clerk; births in City of San Marcos from 1950 with City Registrar)
probate search service: no charge ("need to know approximate date of death"); copies of probate records: $1.00 per page, no minimum

Hemphill County
organized 1876 from Bexar County

Hemphill County Courthouse
400 Main Street
PO Box 867
Canadian, TX 79014-0867
(806) 323-6212; (806) 323-5271 FAX
Brenda Perrin, District/County Clerk
(real estate records from 1887, a few naturalization records in early 1900s, a few vital records from 1896, probate records from 1887)
probate search service: $1.00 and up, depending on length; copies of probate records: 50¢ per page, no minimum

Henderson County
organized 1846 from Houston County

Henderson County Courthouse
100 East Tyler

Athens, TX 75751
(903) 675-6140 (County Clerk, Suite 107, PO Box 632); (903) 675-6115 (District Clerk, Suite 203); (903) 675-6105 FAX (County Clerk); (903) 677-7274 FAX (District Clerk)
gwendolyn.moffeit@co.henderson.tx.us;
   bhanks@co.henderson.tx.us
http://www.co.henderson.tx.us/ips/cms
Gwen Moffeit, County Clerk; Becky Hanks, District Clerk
(deeds, births, deaths, and marriage licenses)
copies of land records: $1.00 per page; copies of vital records: $9.00 each for births and deaths, $3.00 each for marriage licenses

Hidalgo County
organized 1852 from Cameron County

Hidalgo County Courthouse
100 North Closner
Edinburg, TX 78539
(956) 318-2100 (County Clerk, PO Box 58, Edinburg, TX 78540-0058); (956) 318-2200 (District Clerk, First Floor, PO Box 87); (956) 318-2105 FAX (County Clerk); (956) 318-2251 FAX (District Clerk)
acmuniz@hidalgocountyclerk.us
http://www.co.hidalgo.tx.us
Arturo Guajardo, Jr., County Clerk; Annette C. Muñiz, Chief Deputy County Clerk; Laura Hinojosa, District Clerk

Hill County
organized 1853 from Navarro County

Hill County Courthouse
Corner Elm and Waco Streets
Hillsboro, TX 76645
(254) 582-4030 (County Clerk, PO Box 398); (254) 582-4042 (District Clerk, PO Box 634); (254) 582-4035 FAX (County Clerk); (254) 582-4035 FAX (District Clerk)
countyclerk@co.hill.tx.us;
   districtclerk@co.hill.tx.us;
   cbdistrictclerk@hillsboro.net
http://www.co.hill.tx.us/ips/cms
Nicole Tanner, County Clerk; Charlotte Barr, District Clerk
(land records from 1860, births from 1875, deaths from 1903, marriages from 1878, probate records from late 1800s [about the 1890s])
probate search service: no charge; copies of probate records: $1.00 per page, $1.00 minimum

Hockley County
organized 1921 (other sources say organized 1876); first federal census: 1880 with no population

Hockley County Courthouse
802 Houston Avenue
Levelland, TX 79336
(806) 894-3185 (County Clerk, Suite 213); (806) 894-4404 (County Clerk); (806) 894-8527 (District Clerk, Suite 316)
hcdc286@hotmail.com
http://www.co.hockley.tx.us
Irene Gonzalez, County Clerk; Dennis Price, District Clerk
(land records, vital records, or probate records with County Clerk; naturalization records with District Clerk)
probate search service: no charge; copies of probate records: $1.00 per page, no minimum

Hood County
organized 1865 from Johnson County

Hood County Courthouse
100 East Pearl Street
Granbury, TX 76048
(817) 579-3222 (County Clerk, PO Box 339); (817) 408-2600 (District Clerk, Justice Center, 1200 West Pearl Street, Room 21); (817) 579-3239 FAX (District Clerk)
hooddistclrk@itexas.net
http://www.co.hood.tx.us

Sally Oubre, County Clerk; Tonna Trumble, District Clerk
(land records from 1865, naturalization records, vital records from 1903, probate records)
records search service: $5.00 ("no phone search"); copies of land, vital and probate records: $1.00 each, no minimum; certification fee: $5.00 plus $1.00 per page

Hopkins County
organized 1846 from Lamar and Nacogdoches counties

Hopkins County Courthouse
118 Church Street
Sulphur Springs, TX 75482
(903) 438-4074 (County Clerk, 306 North Davis, PO Box 288); (903) 438-4081 (District Clerk, PO Box 391)
hopcoclk@yahoo.com
http://www.hopkinscountytx.org
Debbie Shirley, County Clerk; Patricia Dorner, District Clerk
(land records from 1846, vital records from 1903, probate records from 1846)
probate search service: $10.00 per hour; copies of probate records: $1.00 per page, no minimum

Houston County
organized 1837 from Nacogdoches County

Houston County Courthouse
401 East Houston Avenue, Town Square
Crockett, TX 75835
(936) 544-3255, ext. 240 (County Clerk, First Floor, PO Box 370); (936) 544-3255, ext. 222 (District Clerk, PO Box 1186)
bridget.lamb@co.houston.tx.us
http://www.co.houston.tx.us/ips/cms
Bridget Lamb, County Clerk; Carolyn Rains, District Clerk
(land records from 1881, vital records from 1903, and probate records from 1859)
no probate search service; copies of probate records: $1.00 per page, no minimum

Howard County
organized 1876 from Bexar County

Howard County Courthouse
300 Main Street
Big Spring, TX 79721
(432) 264-2213 (County Clerk, PO Box 1468); (432) 264-2223 (District Clerk, PO Box 2138); (432) 264-2206 FAX (County Clerk); (432) 264-2256 FAX (District Clerk)
dwright@howard-county.lib.tx.us
http://www.co.howard.tx.us/ips/cms
Donna Wright, County Clerk; Colleen Barton, District Clerk

Hudspeth County
organized 1917 from El Paso County

Hudspeth County Courthouse
PO Drawer 58
Sierra Blanca, TX 79851
(915) 369-2301; (915) 369-2361 FAX
http://www.co.hudspeth.tx.us
Paula Hoover, District/County Clerk
(official land records from 1917 [however they do have transcribed records from El Paso County], births, deaths and marriages from 1917, and probate records from 1917)
probate search service: no charge; copies of probate records: $1.00 per page, no minimum

Hunt County
organized 1846 from Fannin and Nacogdoches counties

Hunt County Courthouse
2500 Lee Street
Greenville, TX 75403
(903) 408-4130 (County Clerk, Second Floor); (903) 408-4172 (District Clerk, Second Floor)
http://www.huntcounty.net
Linda Brooks, County Clerk; Stacey Landrum,

District Clerk
(land records from 1846 with, births and deaths
from 1903 [delayed births from the 1800s],
marriages from 1846, probate records from
1847)
probate search service: $5.00 for five-year
search; copies of vital records: $9.00 each for
births, deaths and marriages (births within the
last fifty years and deaths within the last
twenty-five years, subject to restrictions);
copies of probate records: $1.00 per page,
$5.00 for certification, no minimum

Hutchinson County
organized 1876 from Bexar County

Hutchinson County Courthouse
500 Main
Stinnett, TX 79083
(806) 878-4048 (County Clerk, PO Box 1186);
(806) 878-4017 (District Clerk, PO Box 580);
(806) 878-4003 (County Clerk); (806) 878-
4042 FAX (District Clerk)
co.clerk@hutchinsoncnty.com
http://www.co.hutchinson.tx.us/ips/cms
Beverly A. Turner, County Clerk; Joan Carder,
District Clerk
(deeds from 1875, births and deaths from 1927
[proof of relationship required with
application for copies of births and deaths],
probate records from 1927)
probate search service: $5.00 for each name
searched; copies of probate records: $1.00 per
page, no minimum

Irion County
organized 1889 from Tom Green County

Irion County Courthouse
(209 Park View—location)
PO Box 736 (mailing address)
Mertzon, TX 76941
(915) 835-2421
reba.criner@co.irion.tx.us
http://www.co.irion.tx.us
Reba Criner, District/County Clerk

Jack County
organized 4 July 1857 from Cooke County

Jack County Courthouse
100 North Main Street
Jacksboro, TX 76458
(940) 567-2111 (County Clerk, Suite 208); (940)
567-2141 (District Clerk); (940) 567-6441
FAX (County Clerk)
http://www.jackcounty.org
Shelly Clayton, County Clerk; Tracie Pippin,
District Clerk
(deeds from 1858, births and deaths from 1903,
marriage licenses from 1858, probate records
from 1858 with County Clerk; naturalization
records from 1900 with District Clerk)
probate search service: $5.00; copies of probate
records: depends on the copy, no minimum

Jackson County
organized 1836 from Old Mexican Municipality

Jackson County Courthouse
115 West Main Street
Edna, TX 77957-2733
(361) 782-3563 (County Clerk, Room 101); (361)
782-3812 (District Clerk); (361) 782-3132
FAX (County Clerk); (361) 782-3056 FAX
(District Clerk)
jcclerk@co.jackson.tx.usjcclerk@ykc.com;
smathis@co.jackson.tx.us
http://www.co.jackson.tx.us/ips/cms
Kenneth McElveen, County Clerk; Sharon
Mathis, District Clerk

Jasper County
organized 1836 from Old Mexican Municipality

Jasper County Courthouse
121 North Austin
Jasper, TX 75951
(409) 384-2632 (County Clerk, PO Box 2070);

(409) 384-2721 (District Clerk, PO Box 2088);
(409) 384-7198 FAX (County Clerk); (409)
383-7501 FAX (District Clerk)
debbie.newman@co.jasper.tx.us;
linda.ryall@co.jasper.tx.us
http://www.co.jasper.tx.us/ips/cms
Debbie Newman, County Clerk; Linda Ryall,
District Clerk

Jeff Davis County
organized 1887 from Presidio County

Jeff Davis County Courthouse
(101 State Street—location)
PO Box 398 (mailing address)
Fort Davis, TX 79734-0398
(432) 426-3251; (432) 426-3760 FAX
http://www.co.jeff-davis.tx.us/ips/cms
Sue Blackley, District/County Clerk
(land records, naturalization records, vital
records, probate records)

Jefferson County
organized 1836 from Old Mexican Municipality

Jefferson County Courthouse
1149 Pearl Avenue
Beaumont, TX 77701-3619
(409) 835-8475 (County Clerk, PO Box 1151);
(409) 835-8580 (District Clerk); (409) 835-
8527 FAX (District Clerk)
countyck@co.jefferson.tx.us
http://www.co.jefferson.tx.us
Carolyn L. Guidry, County Clerk; Lolita Ramos,
District Clerk

Jim Hogg County
organized 1913 from Brooks and Duval counties

Jim Hogg County Courthouse
(102 East Tilley Street—location)
PO Box 729 (mailing address)
Hebbronville, TX 78361
(512) 527-4031; (361) 527-5843 FAX
http://www.co.jim-hogg.tx.us/ips/cms
Noemi G. Salina, District/County Clerk

Jim Wells County
organized 1911 from Nueces County

Jim Wells County Courthouse
200 North Almond
Alice, TX 78332-4845
(361) 668-5702 (County Clerk, PO Box 1459);
(361) 668-5717 (District Clerk, PO Box 2219);
(361) 668-8671 FAX (County Clerk)
http://www.co.jim-wells.tx.us/ips/cms
Ruben Sandoval, County Clerk; R. David
Guerrero, District Clerk
(land records from 1911, a few vital records in
delayed records from early 1900s, probate
records from 1911)
probate search service: no charge; copies of
probate records: $1.00 per page, no minimum

Johnson County
organized 1854 from McLennan and Navarro
counties

Johnson County Guinn Justice Facility
204 South Buffalo Avenue
Cleburne, TX 76033
(817) 556-6310 (County Clerk, Recording
Section, Third Floor, PO Box 1986); (817)
556-6839 (District Clerk, Suite 206, PO Box
495)
curtisd@johnsoncountytx.org; courtney@
johnsoncountytx.org (District Clerk)
http://www.johnsoncountytx.org
Curtis H. Douglas, County Clerk; David R.
Lloyd, District Clerk

Jones County
organized 1881 from Bexar and Bosque counties

Jones County Courthouse
Anson, TX 79501
(325) 823-3762 (County Clerk, PO Box 552);
(325) 823-3731 (District Clerk, PO Box 308);
(325) 823-4223 FAX (County Clerk); (325)

823-4223 FAX (District Clerk)
http://www.co.jones.tx.us/ips/cms
Julia McCray, County Clerk; Nona Carter,
District Clerk
(land records from 1881, births and deaths from
1903, probate records)
no land record search service ("we do not do
this regularly, but if only a few requests, will
look when we have time"); no probate search
service: ("if only one or two names to search
will do at our time when can, and let you
know the number of pages"); copies of
probate records: $1.00 per page, $2.00
minimum

Karnes County
organized 1854 from Goliad County

Karnes County Courthouse
101 North Panna Maria Avenue
Karnes City, TX 78118-2959
(830) 780-3938 (County Clerk, Suite 9); (830)
780-2562 (District Clerk, Suite 2); (830) 780-
4576 FAX (County Clerk); (830) 780-3227
FAX (District Clerk)
http://www.co.karnes.tx.us
Alva Jonas, County Clerk; Robbie Shortner,
District Clerk
(land records from 1854, births, deaths and
marriages from 1903, and probate records
from 1854 with County Clerk; naturalization
records from 1880 with District Clerk)

Kaufman County
organized 1848 from Van Zandt County

Kaufman County Courthouse
100 West Mulberry Street
Kaufman, TX 75142
(972) 932-4331, ext. 1200 (County Clerk, First
Floor, Suite 5); (972) 932-4331, ext. 1274
(District Clerk); (972) 962-8018 FAX (County
Clerk)
countyclerk@kaufmancounty.net
http://www.kaufmancounty.net
Laura Hughes, County Clerk; Sandra
Featherston, District Clerk
(land records from 1840s, one book of
naturalization records, births from 1870s [if
put on by affidavit], deaths from 1903,
probate records from middle 1800s)
land records search service (for search, need year
in which deed transaction was done); vital
records search service (for search, need years);
probate search service: $5.00 for a ten-year
span; copies of probate records: $1.00 per
page, $5.00 for certification, $5.00 minimum
(search fee)

Kendall County
organized 1862 from portions of Blanco and
Kerr counties

Kendall County Courthouse
201 East San Antonio Street
Boerne, TX 78006
(830) 249-9343, ext. 230 (County Clerk); (830)
249-9343, ext. 260 (District Clerk)
darlene.herrin@co.kendall.tx.us;
shirley.stehling@co.kendall.tx.us
http://www.co.kendall.tx.us
Darlene Herrin, County Clerk; Shirley Stehling,
District Clerk

Kenedy County
organized 1911 from Hidalgo and Cameron
counties; name changed from Willacy County
in 1921, at which time a new Willacy County
was created from Cameron and Hidalgo
counties and a 1.4-mile strip of old Willacy

Kenedy County Courthouse
PO Box 227
Sarita, TX 78385
(361) 294-5220; (361) 294-5218 FAX
http://www.co.kenedy.tx.us/ips/cms
Veronica Vela, County/District Clerk
(land records from 1849, vital records from
1912, probate records from 1860)

probate search service: $5.00; copies of probate records: $1.00 per page, no minimum

Kent County
organized 1876 from Bexar County

Kent County Courthouse
PO Box 9
Jayton, TX 79528-0009
(806) 237-3881; (806) 237-2632 FAX
kcdclerk@caprock-spur.com
http://www.co.kent.tx.us/ips/cms
Richard Craig Harrison, District/County Clerk
(land records from 1892, vital records from 1903 [a few delayed births earlier than that], probate records from 1893)
probate search service: $5.00; copies of probate records: $1.00 per page; certification: $5.00 plus $1.00 per page

Kerr County
organized 1856 from Bexar County

Kerr County Courthouse
700 Main Street
Kerrville, TX 78028-5389
(830) 792-2255 (County Clerk, Suite 122); (830) 792-2281 (District Clerk); (830) 792-2274 FAX (County Clerk)
clerk@ktc.com (County Clerk); kerrdc9@ktc.com (District Clerk)
http://www.co.kerr.tx.us
Jannett Pieper, County Clerk; Linda Uecker, District Clerk
(land records from 1856, very few naturalization records from 1858 to 1862, declarations of intent to become U.S. Citizen from 1876 to 1906, births from 1875, deaths from 1903, marriages from 1856, probate records from 1856)
probate search service: no charge; copies of probate records: 50¢ per page, $1.00 per page certified plus $1.00 for certification, no minimum

Kimble County
organized 1858 from Bexar County

Kimble County Courthouse
501 Main Street
Junction, TX 76849-4763
(325) 446-3353; (325) 446-2986 FAX
haydee.torres@co.kimble.tx.us
http://www.co.kimble.tx.us
Haydee Torres, District/County Clerk
(land records from 1884, births, deaths and marriages from 1900, and probate records from 1884)
records search service: $5.00; copies of vital records: $9.00 each for births and deaths, $5.00 each for marriages; copies of probate records: $1.00 per page

King County
organized 1850 from Fannin County

King County Courthouse
PO Box 135
Guthrie, TX 79236
(806) 596-4412; (806) 596-4664 FAX
Jammye D. Timmons, District/County Clerk

Kinney County
organized 1873 from Bexar County

Kinney County Courthouse
PO Drawer 9
Brackettville, TX 78832-0009
(830) 563-2521; (830) 563-2644 FAX
http://www.co.kinney.tx.us/ips/cms
Dora Elia Sandoval, District/County Clerk
(land records from 1841, probate records from about 1841, births, deaths and marriages)
records search service: $10.00 per name per record group; copies of land and probate records: $1.00 per page; certified copies of vital records: $9.00 each for births and deaths, $5.00 each for marriages (births within the last fifty years and deaths within the last twenty-

five years, subject to restrictions)

Kleberg County
organized 1913 from Nueces County

Kleberg County Courthouse
Kingsville, TX 78364
(361) 595-8548 (County Clerk, PO Box 1327); (361) 595-8561 (District Clerk, PO Box 312); (361) 593-1355 FAX (County Clerk)
misolizdc@yahoo.com
http://www.co.kleberg.tx.us
Leo Alacon, County Clerk; Martha Soliz, District Clerk
(land records from 1913, vital records from 1913 [photo I.D. required for birth certificates], probate records from 1913)
probate search service: $5.00 per name; copies of probate records: $1.00 per page

Knox County
organized 1858 from Fannin County

Knox County Courthouse
PO Box 196
Benjamin, TX 79505
(940) 454-2441; (940) 459-2005 FAX
Annette Offutt, District/County Clerk
(land records, births from 1905, deaths from 1910, marriages from 1886, probate records)
probate search service: no charge; copies of probate records: $1.00 per page, no minimum

Lamar County
organized 1840 from Red River County

Lamar County Courthouse
119 North Main Street
Paris, TX 75460-4265
(903) 737-2420 (County Clerk); (903) 737-2427 (District Clerk); (903) 737-2451 FAX (County Clerk); (903) 785-4905 FAX (District Clerk)
kmarlow@co.lamar.tx.us; map@co.lamar.tx.us
http://www.co.lamar.tx.us
Kathy Marlowe, County Clerk; Marvin Patterson, District Clerk
(land records from 1836, births from 1903, delayed births from the 1800s, deaths from 1903 but were not required by the state until 1940, probate records from 1836)
no vital records search service (must provide full names, dates and places, and proof of relationship); no probate search service; copies of land records: $1.00 per page, $5.00 per document for certification; certified copies of vital records: $9.00 each for births and deaths, $8.00 each for marriages, $1.00 each for uncertified copies of marriages; copies of probate records: $1.00 per page, $1.00 for certification, $20.00 deposit

Lamb County
organized 1876 from Bexar County

Lamb County Courthouse
100 Sixth Street
Littlefield, TX 79339
(806) 385-4222 (County Clerk, Room 103, Box 3); (806) 385-4222, ext. 240 (District Clerk, Room 212); (806) 385-6485 FAX (County Clerk)
lambdc@hotmail.com
http://www.co.lamb.tx.us/ips/cms
Bill Johnson, County Clerk; Stephanie Chester, District Clerk
(land records, vital records, and probate records)
probate search service: no charge; copies of probate records: $1.00 per page plus $1.00 for certification, no minimum

Lampasas County
organized 1856 from Bell and Travis counties

Lampasas County Courthouse
400 South Live Oak
Lampasas, TX 76550
(512) 556-8271 (County Clerk, PO Box 347); (512) 556-8271 (District Clerk, PO ox 327); (512) 556-8270 FAX (County Clerk); (512)

556-9463 FAX (District Clerk)
http://www.co.lampasas.tx.us/ips/cms
Connie Hartmann, County Clerk; Terri Cox, District Clerk
(deeds, births and deaths, and probate records from 1856 with County Clerk; ad valorem tax records with County Appraisal District Office)
probate search service: no charge, unless very time consuming; copies of probate records: $1.00 per page, $5.00 for certification, if needed, no minimum

La Salle County
organized 1880 from Bexar and Webb counties

La Salle County Courthouse
101 Courthouse Square, Suite 107
Cotulla, TX 78014
(830) 879-4432; (830) 879-2933 FAX
http://www.lasallecountytx.org
Margarita Esqueda, District/County Clerk
(land, vital, and probate records from 1881, naturalization records)
probate search service: no charge unless extensive search; copies of probate records: $1.00 per page, no minimum ("fee must be paid in advance")

Lavaca County
organized 1846 from Colorado, Victoria and Jackson counties

Lavaca County Courthouse
Hallettsville, TX 77964
(361) 798-3612 (County Clerk, PO Box 326); (361) 798-2351 (District Clerk, 109 North La Grange Street, PO Box 306); (361) 798-1610 FAX (County Clerk)
elizabeth.kouba@co.lavaca.tx.us; lavacadc@sbcglobal.net
http://www.co.lavaca.tx.us/ips/cms
Elizabeth A. Kouba County Clerk; Calvin Albrecht, District Clerk
(direct and reverse land records from 1846, just one volume of naturalization records [from about the 1880s], births from 1859, deaths from 1903, marriages from 1847, probate records from 1847)
no land records search service (must have record volume and page reference or a specific name and date for transaction, no copies of indexes); naturalization search service: $5.00 per for up to five names per record; no birth or death records search service (must have specific names and dates), $5.00 for search of marriage records; probate search service: no charge for a single name and date; certified copies of vital records: $9.00 each for births and deaths, $5.00 each for marriages, $1.00 each for uncertified copies of marriages (births within the last fifty years and deaths within the last twenty-five years, subject to restrictions); copies of probate records: $1.00 each, no minimum

Lee County
organized 1874 from Bastrop, Burleson, Washington and Fayette counties

Lee County Courthouse
Giddings, TX 78942
(979) 542-3684 (County Clerk, 898 East Richmond, PO Box 419); (979) 542-2947 (District Clerk, 289 South Main, PO Box 176); (979) 542-2623 FAX (County Clerk); (979) 542-2444 FAX (District Clerk)
leecoclk@bluebon.net; leedistclk@bluebon.net
http://www.co.lee.tx.us/ips/cms
Sharon Blasig, County Clerk; Lisa Teinert, District Clerk
(land records from 1874, vital records from 1903, and probate records from 1874 with County Clerk; naturalization records from 1874 with County Clerk and District Clerk)
probate search service: $5.00; copies of probate records: $1.00 per page, no minimum

Leon County

organized 1846 from Robertson County

Leon County Courthouse
Centerville, TX 75833
(903) 536-2352 (County Clerk, 204 East St.
    Mary, PO Box 98); (903) 536-2227 (District
    Clerk, 139 East Main, PO Box 39); (903) 536-
    2431 FAX (County Clerk); (903) 536-5058
    FAX (District Clerk)
http://www.co.leon.tx.us/ips/cms
Carla Neyland McEachern, County Clerk; Diane
    Davis, District Clerk
(land records from 1848, births and deaths from
    1903, marriages from 1885, probate records
    from 1846)
probate search service: no charge; copies of
    probate records: $1.00 per page, no minimum

Liberty County

organized 1836 from Bexar County

Liberty County Courthouse
1923 Sam Houston Street
Liberty, TX 77575-4815
(936) 336-4670 (County Clerk, PO Box 369);
    (936) 336-4686 (District Clerk, Room 303);
    (936) 336-8174 FAX (County Clerk)
delia.sellers@co.liberty.tx.us; distclerk@co.
    liberty.tx.us; melody.gilmore@co.liberty.tx.us
http://www.co.liberty.tx.us
Delia Sellers, County Clerk; Melody Gilmore,
    District Clerk

Limestone County

organized 1846 from Robertson County

Limestone County Courthouse
200 West State Street
Groesbeck, TX 76642-1702
(254) 729-5504 (County Clerk, PO Box 350);
    (254) 729-3206 (District Clerk, PO Box 230);
    (254) 729-2951 FAX (County Clerk); (254)
    729-2960 FAX (District Clerk)
coclerk@co.limestone.tx.us
http://www.co.limestone.tx.us/ips/cms
Peggy Beck, County Clerk; Carol Sue Jenkins,
    District Clerk
(land records from about 1900, births from
    1900, deaths from 1903, marriages from 1873,
    probate records from 1900)
no probate search service (must have dates and
    names); copies of land records: $1.00 per
    page; copies of vital records: $9.00 each for
    births and deaths, $6.00 each for marriages;
    copies of probate records: $1.00 per page, no
    minimum

Lipscomb County

organized 1876 from Bexar County

Lipscomb County Courthouse
PO Box 70
Lipscomb, TX 79056
(806) 862-3004 voice & FAX
http://www.co.lipscomb.tx.us/ips/cms
Kim Blau, County/District Clerk
(land records, naturalization records from 1925
    to 1926, vital records, probate records)
probate search service: $5.00; copies of probate
    records: $1.00 per page, no minimum;
    "SASE"

Live Oak County

organized 1856 from Nueces County

Live Oak County Courthouse
George West, TX 78022
(361) 449-2733 (County Clerk, PO Box 280);
    (361) 449-2733 (District Clerk, PO Drawer
    O); (361) 449-3155 FAX (County Clerk);
    (361) 449-3155 FAX (District Clerk)
http://www.co.live-oak.tx.us/ips/cms
Karen Irving, County Clerk; Lois Shannon,
    District Clerk

Llano County

organized 1856 from Bexar County

Llano County Clerk

107 West Sandstone
Llano, TX 78643
(325) 247-4455 (County Clerk, PO Box 40);
    (325) 247-5036 (District Clerk, PO Box 877);
    (325) 247-2406 FAX (County Clerk); (325)
    248-0492 FAX (District Clerk)
coclerk@co.llano.tx.us; dcllano@moment.net;
    joyce.gillow@co.llano.tx.us
http://www.co.llano.tx.us/ips/cms
Betty Sue Hoy, County Clerk; Joyce Gillow,
    District Clerk
(land records from 1880)

Loving County

organized 1887 from Tom Green County

Loving County Courthouse
PO Box 194
Mentone, TX 79754
(432) 377-2441; (432) 377-2701 FAX
lovingco@nwol.net
http://www.co.loving.tx.us
Beverly Hanson, District/County Clerk

Lubbock County

organized 1891 from Baylor County (other
    sources say organized 1876; first federal
    census: 1880)

Lubbock County Courthouse
(904 Broadway—location)
PO Box 10536 (mailing address)
Lubbock, TX 79408
(806) 775-1630 (County Clerk, Room 207); (806)
    775-1623 (District Clerk, Room 105)
http://www.co.lubbock.tx.us
Kelly Pinion, County Clerk; Barbara Sucsy,
    District Clerk
(land records, vital records, and probate records
    with County Clerk)
no land records search service; probate search
    service: $5.00 per name; copies of probate
    records: $1.00 per page, no minimum

Lynn County

organized 1876 from Bexar County

Lynn County Courthouse
PO Box 1256
Tahoka, TX 79373-1256
(806) 561-4750 (County Clerk, PO Box 937);
    (806) 561-4274 (District Clerk, PO Box 939);
    (806) 561-4988 FAX (County Clerk); (806)
    561-4151 FAX (District Clerk)
susan.tipton@co.lynn.tx.us;
    sandra.laws@co.lynn.tx.us
http://www.co.lynn.tx.us/ips/cms
Susan Tipton, County Clerk; Sandra Laws,
    District Clerk

Madison County

organized 1854 from Montgomery, Walker,
    Grimes and Leon counties

Madison County Courthouse
101 West Main Street
Madisonville, TX 77864
(936) 348-2638 (County Clerk, Room 102); (936)
    348-9203 (District Clerk, Room 226); (936)
    348-5858 FAX (County Clerk); (936) 348-
    9204 FAX (District Clerk)
charlotte.barrett@madisoncountytx.org;
    distclk@txucom.net
http://www.co.madison.tx.us/ips/cms
Charlotte Barrett, County Clerk; Joyce Batson,
    District Clerk
(land records from 1873, vital records from
    1903, probate records from 1873)
probate search service: $5.00; copies of land
    records: $1.00 per page, $5.00 per instrument
    for certified copies; copies of vital records:
    $9.00 each ("records are closed to public,
    need as much information as possible for us
    to search"); copies of probate records: $1.00
    per page, $5.00 per instrument for certified
    copies, no minimum

Marion County

organized 1860 from Cass County

Marion County Courthouse
102 West Austin Street
Jefferson, TX 75657
(903) 665-3971 (County Clerk, Room 301, PO
    Box 763); (903) 665-2441 (District Clerk,
    Room 303); (903) 665-8732 FAX
mcclerk@sydcom.net; mcdistclerk@sydcom.net
http://www.co.marion.tx.us/ips/cms
Betty Smith, County Clerk; Janie McCay,
    District Clerk
(land records from 1860, vital records from 1903
    [very few in earlier years, births within the last
    fifty years and deaths within the last twenty-
    five years, subject to restrictions], and probate
    records from 1860 with County Clerk; very
    few old naturalization records with District
    Clerk)
probate search service: $5.00 for index search;
    copies of probate records: $1.00 per page, no
    minimum

Martin County

organized 1876 from Bexar County

Martin County Courthouse
PO Box 906
Stanton, TX 79782
(432) 756-3412; (432) 607-2212 FAX
susiehull@crcom.net
Susie Hull, District/County Clerk
(land records from 1883, births from 1885,
    deaths from 1910 and marriages from 1885,
    probate records from 1888)
records search service: no charge; copies of
    records: $1.00 each for births over fifty years
    old, deaths over twenty-five years old or
    marriages, $9.00 each for certified copies of
    births and deaths, $5.00 each for certified
    copies of marriages; copies of probate
    records: $1.00 per page, no minimum

Mason County

organized 1858 from Bexar County

Mason County Courthouse
PO Box 702
Mason, TX 76856-0702
(325) 347-5253; (325) 347-6868 FAX
http://www.co.mason.tx.us/ips/cms
Pam Beam, District/County Clerk

Matagorda County

organized 1836 from Old Mexican Municipality

Matagorda County Courthouse
1700 Seventh Street
Bay City, TX 77414-5034
(979) 244-7680 (County Clerk, Room 202); (979)
    244-7621 (District Clerk, Room 307); (979)
    244-7688 FAX (County Clerk)
gail.denn@co.matagorda.tx.us;
    beckydenn@hotmail.com
http://www.co.matagorda.tx.us/ips/cms
Gail Denn, County Clerk; Becky Denn, District
    Clerk
(land records from early 1800s, vital records
    from 1903, probate records from early 1800s)
no probate search service; copies of probate
    records: $1.00 per page, no minimum

Maverick County

organized 1856 from Kenedy County

Maverick County Courthouse
500 Quarry Street
Eagle Pass, TX 78853
(512) 773-2829 (County Clerk, Suite 2); (830)
    773-2629 (District Clerk, Suite 5); (830) 773-
    0129 FAX (County Clerk); (830) 773-6450
    FAX (District Clerk)
countyclerk@maverickcounty.org;
    districtclerk@maverickcounty.org
http://www.maverickcounty.org
Sara Montemayor, County Clerk; Irene
    Rodriguez, District Clerk

McCulloch County
organized 1856 from Bexar County

McCulloch County Courthouse
199 Courthouse Square
Brady, TX 76825
(325) 597-0733, ext. 103 (County Clerk, Room 101); (325) 597-0733, ext. 6 (District Clerk, Room 205); (325) 597-1731 FAX (County Clerk); (915) 597-0606 FAX (District Clerk)
http://www.co.mcculloch.tx.us
Tina A. Smith, County Clerk; Mackye Johnson, District Clerk
(land records from 1875; vital records from 1903 [earlier for delayed], probate records from 1876)
no probate search service ("names and dates are required"); copies of probate records: $1.00 per page plus certification if required, no minimum

McLennan County
organized 1850 from Milam, Robertson and Navarro counties

McLennan County Courthouse
501 Washington Street
Waco, TX 76701-1364
(254) 757-5078 (County Clerk, Records Building, 215 North Fifth Street, Room 223-A, Waco, TX 76701, PO Box 1727, Waco, TX 76703); (254) 757-5057 (District Clerk–Civil, 300 Courthouse Annex, 501 Washington Aven, Waco, TX 76701, PO Box 2451, Waco, TX 76703); (254) 757-5054 (District Clerk–Criminal); (254) 757-5146 FAX (County Clerk)
http://www.co.mcclennan.tx.us
J. A. "Andy" Harwell, County Clerk; Karen Matkin, District Clerk
(land records, vital records, and probate records with County Clerk; naturalization records with District Clerk)
no probate search service; copies of probate records: $7.50, no minimum

McMullen County
organized 1858 from Bexar and Live Oak counties

McMullen County Courthouse
PO Box 235
Tilden, TX 78072-0235
(361) 274-3858 FAX; (361) 274-3618 FAX
Dorairene Garza, District/County Clerk
(land records from 29 November 1871, naturalization records from 1877, vital records from 1903, probate records from 1877)
probate search service: $5.00; copies of probate records: $1.00 each, no minimum

Medina County
organized 1848 from Bexar County

Medina County Courthouse
1100 16th Street
Hondo, TX 78861
(830) 741-6040 (County Clerk, Room 109); (830) 741-6070 (District Clerk, Room 209); (830) 741-6015 FAX (County Clerk)
countyclerk@medinacountytexas.org;
districtclerk@medinacountytexas.org
http://www.medinacountytexas.org
Lisa J. Wernette, County Clerk; Maria Eva Soto, District Clerk

Menard County
organized 1858 from Bexar County

Menard County Courthouse
PO Box 1028
Menard, TX 76659
(325) 396-4682; (325) 396-2047 FAX
menardck@mairmail.net
http://www.menardtexas.com
Polly Reeves, District/County Clerk

Midland County
organized 1885 from Tom Green County

Midland County Courthouse
200 West Wall Street
Midland, TX 79701-4620
(432) 688-4401 (County Clerk, Suite 105); (432) 688-4500 (District Clerk, Suite 301); (432) 688-4902 FAX (County Clerk); (432) 688-4934 FAX (District Clerk)
shauna_brown@co.midland.tx.us;
wilda_smith@co.midland.tx.us (District Clerk)
http://www.co.midland.tx.us
Shauna Brown, County Clerk; Vivian Wood, District Clerk
(land records, vital records, probate records)
no land records search service (need date of transaction and name of buyer and seller, do not index under property description); vital records search service: births and deaths closed to public, will assist in finding same if have name of person and date of birth or death), marriages (need name of male and female and date of marriage); probate search service: no charge (open to the public except for mentally ill cases or alcoholic cases); copies of land records: $1.00 per page, $1.00 for certification; copies of vital records: $7.50 each for births and deaths, $2.00 each for marriage licenses; copies of probate records: $1.00 per page, $1.00 for certification ("please send cash, cashier's check or money order; we cannot accept personal checks or out of town checks")

Milam County
organized 1836 from Old Mexican Municipality

Milam County Courthouse
107 West Main
Cameron, TX 76520
(254) 697-7049 (County Clerk); (254) 697-7052 (District Clerk, PO Box 999); (254) 697-7055 FAX (County Clerk)
http://www.co.milam.tx.us
Barbara Vansa, County Clerk; Cindy Fechner, District Clerk
(land records from 1874, some vital records from 1878, and probate records from 1874 with County Clerk; naturalization records with District Clerk)
probate search service: no charge if not too many; copies of probate records: $1.00 per page

Mills County
organized 1887 from Brown, Comanche, Lampasas and Hamilton counties

Mills County Courthouse
PO Box 646
Goldthwaite, TX 76844-0646
(325) 648-2711; (325) 648-3251 FAX
http://www.co.mills.tx.us/ips/cms
Carolyn Foster, District/County Clerk
(land records from 1836, naturalization records until 1925, vital records from 1903, probate records from 1887)
no probate search service ("do not do genealogy research"); copies of probate records: $1.00 per page

Mitchell County
organized 1881 from Bexar County

Mitchell County Courthouse
349 Oak Street
Colorado City, TX 79512
(325) 728-3481 (County Clerk, Room 103); (325) 728-5918 (District Clerk, Room 302); (325) 728-5322 FAX (County Clerk)
dscarlock@co.mitchell.tx.us;
sharon@co.mitchell.tx.us
Debby Carlock, County Clerk; Sharon Hammond, District Clerk
(land records, births and deaths, probate records)
probate search service: $5.00 if over five names per request; copies of land records: $1.00 per page; certified copies of vital records: $9.00 for the first copy and $3.00 for each additional copy of the same record (births within the last fifty years and deaths within the last twenty-five years, subject to restrictions); copies of probate records: $1.00 per page plus $5.00 to certify

Montague County
organized 1857 from Cooke County

Montague County Clerk
Montague, TX 76251
(940) 894-2461 (County Clerk, PO Box 77); (940) 894-2571 (District Clerk, PO Box 155); (940) 894-6601 FAX (County Clerk); (940) 894-2077 FAX (District Clerk)
countyclerk@wavelinx.net
http://www.co.montague.tx.us/ips/cms
Glenda Henson, County Clerk; Lesia Darden, District Clerk
(grantor and grantee indexes from 1873, births and deaths from 1903, marriages from 1873, probate records from 1873)
probate search service: no charge; copies of vital records: $9.00 each for births and deaths, $6.00 each for certified copies of marriages, $1.00 each for plain copies of marriages ("when requesting birth and death records we require name of person, birth date, place of birth, parents' names and the reason for needing this record"; births within the last fifty years and deaths within the last twenty-five years, subject to restrictions; copies of probate records: $1.00 each, $1.00 for certification

Montgomery County
organized 1837 from Washington County

Montgomery County Courthouse
301 North Thompson
Conroe, TX 77301
(409) 539-7885 (County Clerk, 210 West Davis [Highway 105], Conroe, TX 77301, PO Box 959, Conroe, TX 77305); (936) 539-7855 (District Clerk, 301 North Main Street, Conroe, TX 77301; PO Box 2985, Conroe, TX 77305); (936) 760-6990 FAX (County Clerk)
turnbull@co.montgomery.tx.us;
badamick@co.montgomery.tx.us
http://www.co.montgomery.tx.us
Mark Turnbull, County Clerk; Barbara Adamick, District Clerk
(land records, births and deaths from 1903, probate records from 1838)
probate search service: $5.00; copies of probate records: $1.00 per page for plain copies, $2.00 per page for certified copies, no minimum

Moore County
organized 1876 from Bexar County

Moore County Courthouse
715 Dumas Avenue
Dumas, TX 79029
(806) 935-2009 (County Clerk, Room 105); (806) 935-4218 (District Clerk, Room 109); (806) 935-9004 FAX (County Clerk); (806) 935-6325 FAX (District Clerk)
bmckanna@moorecountytexas.com;
distclerk@moorecountytexas.com
http://www.co.moore.tx.us/ips/cms
Brenda McKanna, County Clerk; Diane Hoefling, District Clerk
(land records, vital records, probate records)

Morris County
organized 1875 from Titus County

Morris County Courthouse
500 Broadnax Street
Daingerfield, TX 75638-1304
(903) 645-3911 (County Clerk); (903) 645-2321 (District Clerk); (903) 645-4026 FAX (County Clerk); (903) 645-3433 FAX (District Clerk)
mccountyclerk@bluebonnet.net
http://www.co.morris.tx.us/ips/cms
Vicki Camp, County Clerk; Gwen Oney, District Clerk

(transcribed land records from Titus County from 1849, births and deaths from 1904 [closed to the public, we will check], marriages from about 1875, and probate records from 1875 with County Clerk; divorces with District Clerk)
no probate search service ("we do it as a courtesy unless it takes more time than we can afford, then we advise"); copies of vital records: $9.00 each for births, deaths and marriage licenses; copies of probate records: $1.00 per plain copy, no minimum

Motley County
organized 1876 from Bexar County

Motley County Courthouse
(701 Dundee Street—location)
PO Box 600 (mailing address)
Matador, TX 79224
(806) 347-2621; (806) 347-2220 FAX
http://www.co.motley.tx.us/ips/cms
Kate Hurt, District/County Clerk
(deeds, deeds of trust, releases, births, deaths and marriage licenses, probate records)
probate search service: $10.00 per estate; copies of probate records: $1.00 per page plus $1.00 for certification

Nacogdoches County
organized 1836 from Old Mexican Municipality

Nacogdoches County Courthouse
101 West Main Street
Nacogdoches, TX 75961-5119
(936) 560-7733 (County Clerk); (936) 560-7740 (District Clerk, Suite 120); (936) 559-5926 FAX (County Clerk); (936) 560-7839 FAX (District Clerk)
county.clerk@co.nacogdoches.tx.us; carol.wilson@co.nacogdoches.tx.us; donna.phillips@co.nacogdoches.tx.us
http://www.co.nacogdoches.tx.us/ips/cms
Ms. Carol Wilson, County Clerk; Donna Phillips, District Clerk
(land records from 1833, vital records from 1903, some delayed birth records back into the 1800s, probate records from 1838)
no probate search service; copies of probate records: $1.00 per page, $1.00 minimum

Navarro County
organized 1846 from Robertson County

Navarro County Courthouse
300 West Third Avenue
Corsicana, TX 75110
(903) 654-3035 (County Clerk, Suite 101, PO Box 423, Corsicana, TX 75151-0423); (903) 654-3040 (District Clerk, Suite 201, PO Box 1439, Corsicana, TX 75151); (903) 654-3097 FAX (County Clerk)
mgreer@airmail.net
http://www.co.navarro.tx.us/ips/cms
Sherry Dowd, County Clerk; Marilyn Greer, District Clerk
(land records, naturalization records, vital records, and probate records)
probate search service: $5.00 per hour; copies of probate records: $1.00 per page, no minimum

Newton County
organized 1846 from Jasper County

Newton County Courthouse
Newton, TX 75966
(409) 379-5341 (County Clerk, 115 Court Street, PO Box 484); (409) 379-3951 (District Clerk, 117 Court Street, PO Box 535); (409) 379-9049 FAX (County Clerk); (409) 379-9087 FAX (District Clerk)
mary.cobb@co.newton.tx.us; newtoncc@mail.com; bree.allen@co.newton.tx.us
http://www.co.newton.tx.us/ips/cms
Mary Cobb, County Clerk; Bree Allen, District Clerk
(land records from 1846, vital records from 1903, and probate records from 1846 with County Clerk; naturalization records with

District Clerk)
probate search service: no charge; copies of probate records: $1.00 per page, no minimum

Nolan County
organized 1876 from Bexar County

Nolan County Clerk
100 East Third
Sweetwater, TX 79556
(325) 235-2462 (County Clerk, Suite 108); (325) 235-2111 (District Clerk, Suite 200); (325) 236-9416 FAX (County Clerk)
cclerk@sweetwaternet.com
http://www.co.nolan.tx.us/ips/cms
Patricia McGowan, County Clerk; Patti Neill, District Clerk
(land records from 1880, vital records from 1880, probate records from 1881)
land, vital, and probate records search service: $5.00 per name ("we do not do extensive searches; to search our index, names and dates are required; persons may do own searches"); copies: $1.00 per page, no minimum

Nueces County
organized 1846 from San Patricio County

Nueces County Courthouse
901 Leopard Street
Corpus Christi, TX 78401-3606
(361) 888-0580 (County Clerk, Room 201); (361) 888-0450 (District Clerk, Room 313); (361) 888-0329 FAX (County Clerk)
http://www.co.nueces.tx.us
Diana Barrera, County Clerk; Patsy Perez, District Clerk

Ochiltree County
organized 1876 from Bexar County

Ochiltree County Courthouse
511 South Main Street
Perryton, TX 79070-3154
(806) 435-8039 (County Clerk); (806) 435-8054 (District Clerk); (806) 435-2081 FAX (County Clerk); (806) 435-8058 FAX (District Clerk)
http://www.co.ochiltree.tx.us/ips/cms
Jane Hammerbeck, County Clerk; Shawn Bogard, District Clerk
(deeds, vital records, probate records with County Clerk)
no land records search service; probate search service: no charge; copies of probate records: $1.00 per page, no minimum

Oldham County
organized 1876 from Jack County

Oldham County Clerk
PO Box 360
Vega, TX 79092-0360
(806) 267-2667; (806) 267-2671 FAX
ocdc@amaonline.com
http://www.co.oldham.tx.us/ips/cms
Becky Groneman, District/County Clerk
(land records, naturalization records, births and deaths, probate records)
records search service: $5.00; copies of vital records: birth certificates available to the public on or after the fiftieth anniversary of the date on which the record was filed, $11.00 each; death certificates available on or after the twenty-fifth anniversary of the date on which the record was filed, $9.00 each; copies of probate records: $1.00 per page, $5.00 for certified copies

Orange County
organized 1852 from Jefferson County

Orange County Courthouse
801 Division Street
Orange, TX 77630
(409) 882-7055 (County Clerk, 123 South Sixth Street); (409) 882-7825 (District Clerk); (409) 882-7012 FAX; (409) 882-7083 FAX (District Clerk)

mgilbert@co.orange.tx.us
http://www.co.orange.tx.us
Karen Jo Vance, County Clerk; Michael Gilbert, Chief Deputy County Clerk; Vickie Edgerly, District Clerk
(land records from 1852, births and deaths from 1903 for those who were born or died outside of city limits, probate records from 1852)
no probate search service; copies of vital records: $7.50 each for births and deaths; copies of probate records: $1.00 per page

Palo Pinto County
organized 1856 from Navarro County

Palo Pinto County Clerk
Palo Pinto, TX 76084
(940) 659-1219 (County Clerk, PO Box 219); (940) 659-1279 (District Clerk, PO Box 189); (940) 659-2289 FAX (County Clerk); (940) 659-2590 FAX (District Clerk)
bobbie.smith@co.palo-pinto.tx.us; janie.glover@co.palo-pinto.tx.us
http://www.co.palo-pinto.tx.us/ips/cms
Bobbie Smith, County Clerk; Janie Glover, District Clerk
(land records from 1857, births and deaths from 1903, marriages from 1857, probate records from 1857)
probate search service: no charge; copies of probate records: $1.00 per page plus $5.00 for certification, payable in advance, no minimum

Panola County
organized 1846 from Harrison and Shelby counties

Panola County Courthouse Building
1010 South Sycamore
Carthage, TX 75633
(903) 693-0302 (County Clerk, Room 201); (903) 693-0306 (District Clerk, Room 227); (903) 693-2726 FAX (County Clerk); (903) 693-6914 FAX (District Clerk)
Mickey.Dorman@co.panola.tx.us; Sandra.King@co.panola.tx.us
http://www.carthagetexas.com/panolacounty/index.htm
Mickey Dorman, County Clerk; Debra Johnson, District Clerk
(land records from 1846, vital records from 1903, some delayed births before 1903 [births within the last fifty years or deaths within the last twenty-five years, subject to restrictions], and probate records from 1846 with County Clerk)
probate search service ("have to have approximate date for all searches"): $10.00; copies of probate records: $1.00 per page, no minimum

Parker County
organized 1855 from Bosque and Navarro counties

Parker County Courthouse
1 Courthouse Square
Weatherford, TX 76086
(817) 594-7461 (County Clerk, 1112 Santa Fe Drive); (817) 598-6114 District Clerk–Civil, 117 Ft. Worth Highway); (817) 598-6194 (District Clerk–Felony); (817) 594-9540 FAX (County Clerk); (817) 598-6131 FAX (District Clerk)
jeane.brunson@parkercountytx.com; elvera.johnson@parkercountytx.com
http://www.co.parker.tx.us/ips/cms
Jeane Brunson, County Clerk; Elvera Johnson, District Clerk

Parmer County
organized 1876 from Bexar County

Parmer County Courthouse
401 Third Street
Farwell, TX 79325
(806) 481-3691 (County Clerk, PO Box 356); (806) 481-3419 (District Clerk); (806) 481-9154 FAX (County Clerk); (806) 481-9416

FAX (District Clerk)
http://www.co.parmer.tx.us/ips/cms
Colleen Stover, County Clerk; Sandra Warren,
District Clerk

Pecos County
organized 1871 from Presidio County

Pecos County Courthouse
103 West Callaghan Street
Fort Stockton, TX 79735-7101
(432) 336-7555 (County Clerk); (432) 336-3503
(District Clerk, 400 South Nelson); (432) 336-
6437 FAX (District Clerk)
pcclerk@co.pecos.tx.us;
districtclerk@co.pecos.tx.us
http://www.co.pecos.tx.us
Judy Deerfield, County Clerk; Gayle Henderson,
District Clerk

Polk County
organized 1846 from Liberty County

Polk County Clerk
100 West Church Street
Livingston, TX 77351
(936) 327-6804 (County Clerk, PO Drawer 2119);
(936) 327-6805 (County Clerk); (936) 327-6814
(District Clerk, 101 West Church Street, Suite
205); (936) 327-6874 FAX (County Clerk);
(936) 327-6857 FAX (District Clerk)
bhmiddleton_2000@yahoo.com;
keclifton@yahoo.com
http://www.co.polk.tx.us/ips/cms
Barbara Middleton, County Clerk; Kathy
Clifton, District Clerk
(land records from 1846, vital records from
1903, probate records from 1846)
land and probate records search service: $10.00
per name; copies of probate records: $1.00
per page

Potter County
organized 1876 from Bexar County

Potter County Courthouse
500 South Fillmore Street
Amarillo, TX 79101
(806) 379-2275 (County Clerk, Room 205, PO
Box 9638, Amarillo, TX 79105-9638); (806)
379-2300 (District Clerk, 501 South Fillmore,
Suite 1B, Amarillom, TX 79101, PO Box
9570, Amarillo, TX 79105)
districtclerk@co.potter.tx.us;
carolinewoodburn@co.potter.tx.us
http://www.co.potter.tx.us/home.html
Julie Smith, County Clerk; Caroline Woodburn,
District Clerk

Presidio County
organized 1850 from Bexar County

Presidio County Courthouse
PO Box 789
Marfa, TX 79843-0789
(432) 729-4812; (432) 729-4313 FAX
http://www.co.presidio.tx.us/ips/cms
Brenda Silva, District/County Clerk
(a few land records from 1832 [most from late
1880s], a few births from 1868 [most from
1903; some birth records of the 1950s with
The City of Marfa], deaths from 1903, and
probate records from 1878)
land and probate records search service: $5.00;
copies of vital records: $7.50 each for births
and deaths, $5.00 each for marriage licenses
("No telephone requests honored; need
written request of person for self or relative
to include parents' names, date of birth or
death, place of birth or death, purpose for
which birth certificate is to be used, and form
of birth certificate needed—I.D. Card or long
form"); copies of land records: $1.00 per page
plus $1.00 for certification

Rains County
organized 1870 from Hopkins and Hunt
counties

Rains County Courthouse Annex
(220 West Quitman Street—location)
PO Box 187 (mailing address)
Emory, TX 75440-0187
(903) 474-9999, ext. 4 (County Clerk); (903) 474-
9999, ext. 10 (District Clerk); (903) 474-9390
FAX (County Clerk); (903) 473-0163 FAX
(District Clerk)
rcclerk@globeco.net
http://www.co.rains.tx.us/ips/cms
Linda Wallace, County Clerk; Deborah Traylor,
District Clerk

Randall County
organized 1876 from Bexar County

Randall County Courthouse
2309 Russell Long Boulevard
Canyon, TX 79015
(806) 468-5505 (County Clerk, 2309 Russell
Long Boulevard, Suite 101, PO Box 660);
(806) 468-5600 (District Clerk, Suite 110);
(806) 468-5509 FAX (County Clerk)
countyclerk@randallcounty.org;
sbarto@randallcounty.org;
districtclerk@randallcounty.org;
jcarter@randallcounty.org
http://www.randallcounty.org
Sue Wicker Bartolino, County Clerk; Jo Carter,
District Clerk

Reagan County
organized 1903 from Tom Green County

Reagan County Courthouse
PO Box 100
Big Lake, TX 76932-0100
(325) 884-2442; (325) 884-1503 FAX
rcclerk@wcc.net
Terri Pullig, District/County Clerk

Real County
organized 1913 from Bandera, Edwards and
Kerr counties

Real County Courthouse
PO Box 750
Leakey, TX 78873
(830) 232-5202; (830) 232-6888 FAX
realcl@hctc.net
http://www.co.real.tx.us/ips/cms
Bella A. Rubio, District/County Clerk
(land records, births and deaths, and probate
records)
copies of land records and probate records:
$1.00 per page, $5.00 per document for
certification; copies of vital records: $9.00
each for births and deaths (births within the
last fifty years and deaths within the last
twenty-five years, subject to restrictions)

Red River County
organized 1836 from Old Mexican Municipality

Red River County Courthouse
400 North Walnut Street
Clarksville, TX 75426
(903) 427-2401 (County Clerk, 200 North
Walnut); (903) 427-3761 (District Clerk, 1007
East Main Street); (903) 427-5510 FAX
(County Clerk); (903) 427-9004 FAX (District
Clerk)
redriver@neto.com
http://www.co.red-river.tx.us/ips/cms
Lorie Moose, County Clerk; Janice Gentry,
District Clerk
(land records from 1835, not very many
naturalization records from 1839, vital records
from 1903, probate records from 1835)
probate search service: $5.00 per name with
approximate date that you want searched
("when making a request for a search of the
records be specific as to name and date of
search"); copies of probate records: $1.00 per
page; $6.00 minimum (search and copy)

Reeves County
organized 1885 from Pecos County

Reeves County Courthouse
100 East Fourth Street
Pecos, TX 79772
(915) 445-5467 (County Clerk, PO Box 867);
(915) 445-2414 (District Clerk, PO Box 848)
Dianne O. Florez, County Clerk; Patricia Tarin,
District Clerk
(land records from 1885, vital records from
1885, probate records from 1885)
no land records search service; probate search
service: $10.00; copies of probate records:
$1.00 each, no minimum

Refugio County
organized 1856 from Old Mexican Municipality

Refugio County Courthouse
(808 Commerce Street—location)
PO Box 704 (mailing address)
Refugio, TX 78377-0704
(361) 526-2233; (361) 526-2727; (361) 526-1325
FAX
rjvg211@aol.com
http://www.co.refugio.tx.us/ips/cms
Ruby Garcia, District/County Clerk
(land records from 1835 with, naturalization
records from 1854, births, deaths, and
marriage licenses from 1903 to 1974, probate
records from 1840)
probate search service: $10.00; vital records
search service: $10.00; copies of vital records:
$9.00 each for births and deaths, $5.00 each
for marriage licenses; copies of probate
records: $1.00 per page, no minimum

Roberts County
organized 1876 from Bexar County

Roberts County Courthouse
PO Box 477
Miami, TX 79059-0477
(806) 868-2341; (806) 868-3381 FAX
robertstx@centramedia.net
http://www.co.roberts.tx.us/ips/cms
Donna Goodman, District/County Clerk

Robertson County
organized 1837 from Bexar County

Robertson County Courthouse
PO Box 1029
Franklin, TX 77856-1029
(979) 828-4130 (County Clerk, PO Box 1029);
(979) 828-3636 (District Clerk, PO Box 250);
(979) 828-1260 FAX (County Clerk); (979)
828-5523 FAX (District Clerk)
c-clerk@txcyber.com
http://www.co.robertson.tx.us/ips/cms
Kathryn Brimhall, County Clerk; Barbara W.
Axtell, District Clerk
(land records from 1838, vital records from
1903, and probate records from 1836 with
County Clerk; naturalization records with
District Clerk)
probate search service: no charge; copies of
probate records: $1.00 per page, $5.00 for
certification, no minimum

Rockwall County
organized 1873 from Kaufman County

Rockwall County Historic Courthouse
101 East Rusk Road
Rockwall, TX 75087
(972) 882-0220 (County Clerk, Rockwall
Government Building, 1101 Ridge Road,
Suite 209); (972) 882-0260 (District Clerk,
Rockwall Government Building, 1101 Ridge
Road, Suite 209); (972) 882-0229 FAX
(County Clerk); (972) 882-0268 FAX (District
Clerk)
kmcdaniel@rockwallcountytexas.com
http://www.rockwallcountytexas.com
Lisa Constant, County Clerk; Kay McDaniel,
District Clerk
(land records from 1873, vital records from
1873, probate records from 1873)
probate search service: $5.00; copies of probate
records: $1.00 each, no minimum

Runnels County
organized 1858 from Coleman County

Runnels County Courthouse
600 Courthouse Square
613 Hutchings Avenue and Broadway
Ballinger, TX 76821
(915) 365-2720 (County Clerk, Room 106, Box 189); (325) 365-2638 (District Clerk, PO Box 166); (325) 365-3408 FAX (County Clerk); (325) 365-9229 FAX (District Clerk)
elesa.ocker@co.runnels.tx.us
http://www.co.runnels.tx.us/ips/cms
Elesa Ocker, County Clerk; Tammy Burleson, District Clerk
(land records from 1880, vital records from 1880, probate records from 1880)
no land records search service (must have grantor or grantee and year of transaction; probate search service: no charge; copies of land records: $1.00 per page plus $5.00 for certification; copies of vital records: $9.00 each for births and deaths (births within the last fifty years and deaths within the last twenty-five years, subject to restrictions); copies of probate records: $1.00 per page plus $5.00 for certification

Rusk County
organized 1843 from Nacogdoches County

Rusk County Courthouse
115 North Main Street
Henderson, TX 75653
(903) 657-0330 (County Clerk, PO Box 758); (903) 657-0353 (District Clerk); (903) 657-0062 FAX (County Clerk); (903) 657-1914 FAX (District Clerk)
joyce.lewis@co.rusk.tx.us
http://www.co.rusk.tx.us/ips/cms
Joyce Lewis, County Clerk; Jean Hodges, District Clerk
(land records from 1844, births and deaths from 1904, marriages from 1844, probate records from 1844)
probate search service: no charge; copies of probate records: $1.00 per page, no minimum

Sabine County
organized 1836 from Old Mexican Municipality

Sabine County Courthouse
Hemphill, TX 75948
(409) 787-3786 (County Clerk, PO Drawer 580); (409) 787-2912 (District Clerk, PO Box 850); (409) 797-2044 FAX (County Clerk)
Janice McDaniel, County Clerk; Tanya Walker, District Clerk

San Augustine County
organized 1836 from Old Mexican Municipality

San Augustine County Courthouse
100 West Columbia
San Augustine, TX 75972
(936) 275-2452 (County Clerk, Room 106); (936) 275-2231 (District Clerk, Room 202)
diana.kovar@co.san-augustine.tx.us; jean.steptoe@co.san-augustine.tx.us
http://www.co.san-augustine.tx.us/ips/cms
Diana Kovar, County Clerk; Jeannie Steptoe, District Clerk
(land records from 1834, births from late 1800s, deaths from 1903, probate records from 1838)
probate search service: $5.00; copies of probate records: $1.00 per page plus $5.00 if certified

San Jacinto County
organized 1870 from Liberty County

San Jacinto County Courthouse
1 State Highway 150
Coldspring, TX 77331
(936) 653-2324 (County Clerk, Room 2); (936) 653-2909 (District Clerk, Room 4); (936) 653-4659 FAX (District Clerk)
http://www.co.san-jacinto.tx.us/ips/cms
Angelia Steele, County Clerk; Rebecca "Becky"

Capers, District Clerk
(deeds from 1800, births, deaths and marriages from 1870, wills from 1800)
no probate search service; copies of vital records: $9.00 each for births and deaths; copies of probate records: $1.00 per page, no minimum

San Patricio County
organized 1836 from Old Mexican Municipality

San Patricio County Courthouse
400 West Sinton Street
Sinton, TX 78387
(361) 364-2490 (County Clerk, Room 124, PO Box 578); (361) 364-6225 (District Clerk, Room 210, PO Box 1084); (361) 364-6137 FAX (District Clerk)
graciella.alaniz.gonzales@co.san-patricio.tx.us
http://www.co.san-patricio.tx.us/ips/cms
Gracie Alaniz-Gonzales, County Clerk; Laura Miller, District Clerk
(land records from 1846, births and deaths from 1903, probate records from 1847)
probate search service: no charge; copies of probate records: $1.00 each, $1.00 for certification, no minimum

San Saba County
organized 1856 from Bexar County

San Saba County Courthouse
500 East Wallace Street, Room 202
San Saba, TX 76877
(325) 372-3614; (325) 372-5425 FAX
clerk@sansabacounty.org; ssco.dc@centex.net
http://www.sansabacounty.org
Kim Wells, District/County Clerk

Schleicher County
organized 1887 from Crockett County

Schleicher County Courthouse
PO Drawer 580
Eldorado, TX 76936
(325) 853-2833; (325) 853-2768 FAX
http://www.co.schleicher.tx.us/ips/cms
Peggy Williams, District/County Clerk

Scurry County
organized 1876 from Bexar County

Scurry County Clerk
1806 25th Street
Snyder, TX 79549
(325) 573-5332 (County Clerk, Suite 300); (325) 573-5641 (District Clerk, Suite 402); (325) 573-7396 FAX (County Clerk); (325) 573-1081 FAX (District Clerk)
http://www.co.scurry.tx.us/ips/cms
Joan Bunch, County Clerk; Candace Jones, District Clerk
(land records, births and deaths, probate records)
no land records search service (contact local abstract companies); probate search service: no charge; certified copies of vital records: $9.00 each, with documentary evidence; copies of probate records: $1.00 per page, no minimum

Shackelford County
organized 1858 from Bosque County

Shackelford County Courthouse
PO Box 247
Albany, TX 76430-0247
(325) 762-2232, ext. 3; (325) 762-3966 FAX
cdclerk@sbcgobal.net
http://www.co.shackelford.tx.us/ips/cms
Cheri Hawkins, District/County Clerk
(land records, vital records, probate records)

Shelby County
organized 1836 from Old Mexican Municipality

Shelby County Courthouse
200 San Augustine
Center, TX 75935
(936) 598-6361 (County Clerk, PO Box 1987);

(936) 598-4164 (District Clerk, PO Box 1953); (936) 598-3701 FAX (County Clerk); (936) 598-3323 FAX (District Clerk)
cogovoff@ktsnet.com
http://www.co.shelby.tx.us/ips/cms
Allison Harbison, County Clerk; Lori Oliver, District Clerk
(land records from 1882 [after courthouse fire], births, deaths after the late 1920s and marriages from 1882 to date, probate records)
land and probate records search service: $9.00, applied to cost of copies, if record is found; copies of land and probate records: $2.00 per page, $5.00 per instrument for certification; certified copies of vital records: $9.00 each

Sherman County
organized 1876 from Bexar County

Sherman County Courthouse
PO Box 270
Stratford, TX 79084-0270
(806) 396-2371; (806) 366-5670 FAX
gina.jones@co.sherman.tx.us
http://www.co.sherman.tx.us/ips/cms
Gina Jones, District/County Clerk

Smith County
organized 1846 from Nacogdoches County

Smith County Courthouse
100 North Broadway
Tyler, TX 75702
(903) 590-4670 (County Clerk, 200 East Ferguson, Suite 300, Tyler, TX 75702, PO Box 1018, Tyler, TX 75710); (903) 590-1672 (District Clerk, PO Box 1077); (903) 590-4689 FAX (County Clerk); (903) 590-1661 FAX (District Clerk)
http://www.smith-county.com
Judy Carnes, County Clerk; Lois Rogers, District Clerk
(land records from 1846, probate records from 1846, rural births from 1903, deaths from 1875, and marriage licenses with County Clerk)
probate search service: $5.00; copies of probate records: $1.00 per page, $1.00 minimum

Somervell County
organized 1875 from Hood County

Somervell County Courthouse
PO Box 1098
Glen Rose, TX 76043-1098
(254) 897-4427; (254) 897-3233 FAX
clerk@glenrose.org
http://www.glenrose.org
Candace Garrett, District/County Clerk
(land records from 1875, births and deaths from 1903, probate records from 1800)
probate search service: no charge; copies of probate records: $1.00 per page, no minimum

Starr County
organized 1848 from Nueces County

Starr County Courthouse
401 North Britton Avenue
Rio Grande City, TX 78582
(956) 487-8032 (County Clerk, Room 201); (956) 487-8482 (District Clerk, Room 304); (956) 487-8674 FAX (County Clerk); (956) 487-8493 FAX (District Clerk)
dennis.gonzalez@co.starr.tx.us
http://www.co.starr.tx.us/ips/cms
Dennis D. Gonzales, County Clerk; Eloy R. Garcia, District Clerk
(filing of deeds, deeds of trust, liens, release of liens, oil & gas mineral leases, cemetery deeds, etc., births, deaths and marriage licenses, and probate records with County Clerk; naturalization records with District Clerk)
probate search service: no charge; copies of land records: $1.00 per page, $5.00 for certification; copies of vital records: $9.00 each for each birth or death certificate or certified copy of marriage license; copies of probate records: $1.00 per page, no minimum

Stephens County

organized 1858 from Bosque County, formerly Buchanan County

Stephens County Courthouse
200 West Walker Street
Breckenridge, TX 76024
(254) 559-3700 (County Clerk); (254) 559-3151 (District Clerk); (254) 559-9645 FAX (County Clerk); (254) 559-8127 FAX (District Clerk)
90thdc@texasisp.com
http://www.co.stephens.tx.us/ips/cms
Helen Haddock, County Clerk; Christie Coapland, District Clerk

Sterling County

organized 1891 from Tom Green County

Sterling County Courthouse
PO Box 55
Sterling City, TX 76951-0055
(915) 378-5191; (325) 378-3111 FAX
http://www.co.sterling.tx.us/ips/cms
Susan Wyatt, District/County Clerk
(land records, vital records from 1902, probate records)
no probate search service; copies of probate records: $1.00 per page, no minimum

Stonewall County

organized 1876 from Fannin County

Stonewall County Courthouse
PO Box P
Aspermont, TX 79502-0914
(940) 989-2272; (940) 989-2032 FAX
Belinda Page, District/County Clerk

Sutton County

organized 1887 from Wood County

Sutton County Courthouse
300 East Oak, Suite 3
Sonora, TX 76950
(325) 387-3815; (325) 387-6028 FAX
sutton@sonoratx.net
http://www.co.sutton.tx.us/ips/cs
Veronica Hernandez, District/County Clerk

Swisher County

organized 1876 from Bexar County

Swisher County Courthouse
119 South Maxwell Avenue
Tulia, TX 79088-2245
(806) 995-3294; (806) 995-4121 FAX
brenda.hudson@swisher-tx.net
http://www.co.swisher.tx.us/ips/cms
Brenda Hudson, District/County Clerk

Tarrant County

was once part of the Peters Colony, organized 1849 from Navarro County, with Birdville as the first county seat, moved to Fort Worth in 1856

Tarrant County Courthouse
100 West Weatherford Street
Fort Worth, TX 76196
(817) 334-1195 (County Clerk–Records Library, Rooms B20 and B30, Civil Division: Probate Court Clerks, Room 233, Real Property, Room 130A, Vital Statistics, Room 180A); (817) 884-1870 (District Clerk–Records Division, 200 East Weatherford); (817) 884-1075 FAX (County Clerk)
shenderson@tarrantcounty.com; dclerk@tarrantcounty.com
http://www.co.tarrant.tx.us
Suzanne Henderson, County Clerk; Thomas A. Wilder, District Clerk
(deeds from 1876 [date of courthouse fire], plats from 1876, births from 1876, deaths from 1903, marriages from 1876, and probate records from 1876 [pre-1876 probate records, contact Records Management Center for originals or Fort Worth Public Library for microfilm copies] with County Clerk; divorce and civil court records with District Clerk)

probate search service: no charge; copies of probate records: $1.00 per page plus $1.00 for certification, no minimum ("money in advance and cause number if available")

Taylor County

organized 1858 from Bexar County

Taylor County Courthouse
300 Oak Street
Abilene, TX 79608
(325) 674-1202 (County Clerk); (325) 674-1316 (District Clerk); (325) 674-1365 FAX
bevill@taylorcountytexas.org; hendersp@taylorcountytexas.org
http://www.taylorcountytexas.org
Larry G. Bevill, County Clerk; Patricia Henderson, District Clerk

Terrell County

organized 1905 from Pecos County

Terrell County Courthouse
(105 East Hackberry—location)
PO Box 410 (mailing address)
Sanderson, TX 79848-0410
(432) 345-2391; (432) 345-2740 FAX
martha.allen@co.terrell.tx.us
http://www.co.terrell.tx.us/ips/cms
Martha Allen, District/County Clerk

Terry County

organized 1876 from Bexar County

Terry County Courthouse
500 West Main
Brownfield, TX 79316-4328
(806) 637-8552 (County Clerk, Room 105); (806) 637-8551 (County Clerk; (806) 637-4202 (District Clerk, Room 209E); (806) 647-4874 FAX (County Clerk); (806) 637-1333 FAX (District Clerk)
terrycoclerk@door.net
http://www.co.terry.tx.us/ips/cms
Ann Willis, County Clerk; Paige Lindsey, District Clerk

Throckmorton County

organized 1858 from Bosque County

Throckmorton County Courthouse
PO Box 309
Throckmorton, TX 76083-0309
(940) 849-2501; (940) 849-3032 FAX
http://www.co.throckmorton.tx.us/ips/cms
Mary "Susie" Walraven, District/County Clerk

Titus County

organized 1846 from Red River County

Titus County Courthouse
100 West First Street
Mount Pleasant, TX 75455
(903) 577-6796 (County Clerk, Suite 204); (903) 577-6721 (District Clerk, PO Box 492); (903) 572-5078 FAX (County Clerk); (903) 577-6719 (District Clerk)
http://www.co.titus.tx.us
Teresa Price, County Clerk; Debra Absten, District Clerk

Tom Green County

organized 1874 from Bexar County

Tom Green County Courthouse
112 West Beauregard Avenue
San Angelo, TX 76903
(325) 659-6553 (County Clerk, 124 West Beauregard Avenue); (325) 659-6579 (District Clerk–Family/Civil); (325) 659-3251 FAX (County Clerk); (325) 659-3241 FAX (District Clerk)
elizabeth.mcgill@co.tom-green.tx.us; sheri.woodfin@co.tom-green.tx.us
http://www.co.tom-green.tx.us/ips/cms
Elizabeth McGill, County Clerk; Sherilyn Woodfin, District Clerk
(land records, vital records, and probate records with County Clerk; naturalization records with District Clerk)

probate search service: $5.00 per name; copies of probate records: $1.00 per page, $5.00 per instrument for certification

Travis County

organized 1840 from Bastrop County

Travis County Courthouse
1000 Guadalupe
Austin, TX 78701-2336
(512) 473-9188 (County Clerk–Recording Division, PO Box 1748); (512) 473-9595 (County Clerk–Probate Division); (512) 854-9457 (District Clerk, Third Floor, PO Box 67903); (512) 854-4526 FAX (County Clerk); (512) 854-9549 FAX (District Clerk)
dana.debeauvoir@co.travis.tx.us; amalia.rodriguez-mendoza@co.travis.tx.us
http://www.co.travis.tx.us
Dana DeBeauvoir, County Clerk; Amalia Rodriguez-Mendoza, District Clerk
(land records from 1840 to date with County Clerk, Recording Division, naturalization records from 1903 with County Clerk, births and deaths for all of Travis County and the city of Austin from 1903 to 1917 and from 1941 to 1956, births and deaths for Travis County outside the city limits of Austin from 1917 to 1941 and from 1956 to date [births and deaths within the city of Austin from 1917 to 1941 and from 1956 to date with City of Austin Health Department], marriage licenses from 1840 to date with County Clerk, probate records from 1845 to date with County Clerk, Probate Division)
land records and naturalization records search service: $10.00 per name per ten-year period per index (grantor or grantee index); vital records search service from County Clerk: $11.00 each for birth records, $9.00 each for death records, $10.00 per name per ten-year period per index (male or female index) for marriage records; copies of land records, naturalization records, and probate records: $1.00 per page plus $5.00 per document for certification, no minimum ("payment must be received before service can be performed; checks and correspondence addressed to Travis County Clerk"); copies of vital records: $1.00 per page plus $5.00 per document for certification of marriage records (births within the last fifty years and deaths within the last twenty-five years, subject to restrictions)

Trinity County

organized 1850 from Houston County

Trinity County Courthouse
Groveton, TX 75845
(936) 642-1208 (County Clerk, PO Box 456); (936) 642-1118 (District Clerk, PO Box 549); (936) 642-3004 FAX
http://www.co.trinity.tx.us/ips/cms
Diane McCrory, County Clerk; Cheryl Cartwright, District Clerk
(land records from 1800s, index from 1900, naturalization records, vital records from 1903, probate records from 1900s)
no probate search service; copies of probate records: $1.00 each, no minimum

Tyler County

organized 1846 from Liberty County

Tyler County Courthouse
100 West Bluff, Courthouse Square
Woodville, TX 75979
(409) 283-2281 (County Clerk, Room 110); (409) 283-2162 (District Clerk, Room 110); (409) 283-6305 FAX (County Clerk); (409) 283-6305 FAX (District Clerk)
coclerk@inu.net
http://www.co.tyler.tx.us/ips/cms
Donece R. Gregory, County Clerk; Melissie Evans, District Clerk
(land records from 1840s, vital records from 1850s, probate records from 1840s)
land, vital, and probate records search service: $5.00; copies of land and probate records:

$1.00 per page, no minimum

Upshur County
organized 1846 from Harrison and Nacogdoches counties

Upshur County Courthouse
Gilmer, TX 75644
(903) 680-8123 (County Clerk—Deed Office, PO Box 730); (903) 680-8127 (County Clerk–Courts Office); (903) 843-5031 (District Clerk, PO Box 950); (903) 843-5492 FAX (County Clerk); (903) 843-5492 FAX (County Clerk)
http://www.countyofupsher.com
Peggy LaGrone, County Clerk; Carolyn Bullock, District Clerk

Upton County
organized 1887 from Tom Green County

Upton County Courthouse
(205 East Tenth Street—location)
PO Box 465 (mailing adress)
Rankin, TX 79778-0465
(915) 693-2861; (432) 693-2129 FAX
monetta.sides@co.upton.tx.us
http://www.co.upton.tx.us/ips/cms
Monetta Sides, District/County Clerk
(land records, vital records, probate records)
no probate search service; copies of vital records: $9.00 each for births, deaths and marriages; copies of probate records: $1.00 per page plus $1.00 for certification, no minimum ("copies are not provided until payment is made")

Uvalde County
organized 1850 from Bexar County

Uvalde County Courthouse
Uvalde, TX 78802
(830) 278-6614 (County Clerk, PO Box 284, Uvalde, TX 78802-0284); (830) 278-3918 (District Clerk, Courthouse Plaza, Box 15, Uvalde, TX 78801); (830) 278-8692 FAX (County Clerk)
uvcoclk@uvaldecounty.com
http://www.uvaldecounty.com
Lucille C. Hutcherson, County Clerk; Lydia Steele, District Clerk
(land records from 1856, vital records from 1856, probate records from 1856)
land records search service: $10.00 per name per ten-year period; vital records search service: $9.00 per name for births and deaths, $8.00 per name for marriages (includes one certified copy); probate search service: $10.00 per name; copies of land and probate records: $1.00 per page, $5.00 per document for certification

Val Verde County
organized 1885 Kinney and Pecos counties

Val Verde County Courthouse
Del Rio, TX 78841
(830) 774-7564 (County Clerk, PO Box 1267); (830) 774-7538 (District Clerk, PO Box 1544); (830) 774-7608 FAX (County Clerk)
distclk@delrio.com
http://www.cityofdelrio.com (City of Del Rio)
Generosa G. Ramon, County Clerk; Luz Balderas, District Clerk
(land records from 1885, probate records from June 1885)
probate search service: $5.00 per name; copies of probate records: $1.00 each, no minimum ("fee on any service must be paid before delivery of service")

Van Zandt County
organized 1848 from Henderson County

Van Zandt County Courthouse
121 East Dallas Street
Canton, TX 75103
(903) 567-6503 (County Clerk, Room 202, PO Box 515); (903) 567-6576 (District Clerk, Suite 302); (903) 567-6722 FAX (County Clerk); (903) 567-1283 FAX (District Clerk)
countyclerk@vanzandtcounty.org; districtclerk@vanzandtcounty.org
http://www.vanzandtcounty.org
Charlotte Bledsoe, County Clerk; Karen Wilson, District Clerk
(land records, vital records, probate records)
probate search service: $5.00; copies of probate records: $1.00

Victoria County
organized 1836 from Old Mexican Municipality

Victoria County Courts Building
(115 North Bridge—location)
PO Box 2410 (mailing address)
Victoria, TX 77901-6513
(361) 575-1478 (County Clerk, Room 103, PO Box 1968); (361) 575-0581 (District Clerk, Third Floor); (361) 575-6276 FAX (County Clerk); (361) 572-5682 FAX (District Clerk–Civil Department); (361) 575-9549 FAX (District Clerk–Criminal Division)
stuart@ccorridor.com
http://www.victoriacountytx.org
Val D. Huvar, County Clerk; Cathy Stuart, District Clerk
(land records from 1838, naturalization records from 1870, which is very limited [Federal and District Clerk's Office have some naturalization records, also], vital records from 1903, and probate records from 1838 from County Clerk)
probate search service: $5.00 prepaid; no vital records search service (births and deaths closed to the public, but will "check on one or more" for researchers); copies of probate records: $1.00 per page plus $5.00 for the certificate, no minimum

Walker County
organized 1846 from Montgomery County

Walker County Courthouse
1100 University Avenue
Huntsville, TX 77340
(936) 436-4922 (County Clerk, Suite 201, PO Box 210, Huntsville, TX 77342-0210); (936) 436-4972 (District Clerk, Suite 209); (936) 936-4973 FAX (District Clerk)
jpatton@co.walker.tx.us; rflowers@co.walker.tx.us
http://www.co.walker.tx.us
James D. Patton, County Clerk; Ms. Robyn Flowers, District Clerk
(land records from 1846, births and deaths from 1903, marriages from 1846, and probate records from 1846 with County Clerk; naturalization records with District Clerk)
probate search service: $5.00; copies of probate records: $1.00 per page plus $1.00 for certification, no minimum

Waller County
organized 1873 from Austin County

Waller County Courthouse
836 Austin Street
Hempstead, TX 77445-4667
(979) 826-7711 (County Clerk, Suite 211); (979) 826-7735 (District Clerk, Suite 318); (979) 826-8317 FAX (County Clerk); (979) 826-7738 FAX (District Clerk)
pj.spadachene@wallercotx.com
http://www.co.waller.tx.us/ips/cms
Cheryl Peters, County Clerk; Patricia J. Spadachene, District Clerk

Ward County
organized 1892 from Tom Green County (other sources say organized 1887; first federal census: 1890)

Ward County Courthouse
400 South Allen Street
Monahans, TX 79756
(432) 943-3294 (County Clerk, Suite 101); (432) 943-2751 (District Clerk, Suite 202); (432) 943-6054 FAX (County Clerk); (432) 943-3810 FAX (District Clerk)
natrell.cain@co.ward.tx.us
http://www.co.ward.tx.us/ips/cms
Natrell Cain, County Clerk; Patricia Oyerbides, District Clerk
(land records with, vital records, probate records)
probate search service: $5.00 per search per name; copies of probate records: $1.00 per page plus $1.00 per certificate, no minimum ("fee must accompany written request; NO personal checks, NO food store money orders; bank or U.S. Post Office Checks or money orders only")

Washington County
organized 1836 from Texas Municipality

Washington County Courthouse
100 East Main Street
Brenham, TX 77833
(979) 277-6200, ext. 115 (County Clerk, Suite 102); (979) 277-6200, ext. 152 (District Clerk, Suite 304); (979) 277-6278 FAX (County Clerk)
brothermel@wacounty.com; districtclerk@wacounty.com
http://www.co.washington.tx.us/ips/cms
Beth A. Rothermel, County Clerk; Vicki Lehmann, District Clerk
(land records from 1837 to date, births and deaths from 1903 to date, marriages from 1837 to date, and probate records from 1837 to date with County Clerk; naturalization records with District Clerk)
land, vital, and probate records search service: $5.00 per name; copies: $1.00 per page (picture I.D. or two other forms of I.D. required for vital records)

Webb County
organized 1848 from Bexar County

Webb County Justic Center
1110 Victoria Street
Laredo, TX 78040
(956) 523-4265 (County Clerk, Second Floor); (956) 523-4268 (District Clerk, Suite 203, Laredo, TX 78040); (956) 523-5035 FAX (County Clerk)
mgutierrez@webbcounty.com
http://www.webbcountytx.gov
Margie Ramirez Ibarra, County Clerk; Manuel "Meme" Gutierrez, District Clerk

Wharton County
organized 1846 from Colorado and Jackson counties

Wharton County Courthouse
Wharton, TX 77488
(979) 532-2381 (County Clerk, 309 East Milam, Suite 700, PO Box 69); (979) 532-5542 (District Clerk, PO Drawer 391); (979) 532-8426 FAX (County Clerk); (979) 532-1299 FAX (District Clerk)
http://www.co.wharton.tx.us/ips/cms
Sandra K. Sanders, County Clerk; Denice Malota, District Clerk
(land records, vital records, and probate records with County Clerk; naturalization records with District Clerk)
no probate search service; copies of probate records: $1.00 per page

Wheeler County
organized 1876 from Bexar County

Wheeler County Courthouse
401 Main Street
Wheeler, TX 79096
(806) 826-5544 (County Clerk, PO Box 465); (806) 826-5931 (District Clerk, PO Box 528); (806) 826-3282 FAX (County Clerk); (806) 826-5503 FAX (District Clerk)
whecoclk@nts-online.net
http://www.co.wheeler.tx.us/ips/cms
Margaret Dorman, County Clerk; Sherri Jones,

District Clerk
(land records from early 1900s, vital records from early 1900s, probate records from early 1900s)
no probate search service ("we do not search for you unless you request a specific name; you are welcome to use our records for your own search"); copies of probate records: $1.00 per page

Wichita County
organized 1858 from Fannin County

Wichita County Courthouse
900 Seventh Street
Wichita Falls, TX 76301
(940) 766-8195 (County Clerk, Room 250); (940) 766-8190 (District Clerk–Civil Records, Room 303); (940) 716-8554 FAX (County Clerk)
Lori.Bohannon@co.wichita.tx.us; Dorsey.Trapp@co.wichita.tx.us
http://www.co.wichita.tx.us
Lori Bohannon, County Clerk; Mr. Dorsey Ray Trapp, District Clerk

Wilbarger County
organized 1858 from Bexar County

Wilbarger County Courthouse
1700 Wilbarger Street
Vernon, TX 76384-4742
(940) 552-5486 (County Clerk, Room 15); (940) 553-3411 (District Clerk, Room 33); (940) 553-2320 FAX (County Clerk); (940) 553-2316 FAX (District Clerk)
http://www.co.wilbarger.tx.us
Bettie Thompson, County Clerk; Brenda Peterson, District Clerk
(land records from 1881, vital records from 1890, probate records from 1900)
probate search service: $5.00; copies of probate records: $1.00 per page, $5.00 minimum

Willacy County
organized 1921 from Cameron and Hidalgo counties and a 1.4-mile strip of a former Willacy County, which was renamed Kenedy County at the same time that the new county was created

Willacy County Courthouse
190 North Third Street
Raymondville, TX 78580-3533
(512) 689-2710 (County Clerk, 540 West Hidalgo Street); (956) 689-2532 (District Clerk, 546 West Hidalgo Street); (956) 689-6127 FAX (County Clerk); (956) 689-5713 FAX (District Clerk)
http://www.co.willacy.tx.us/ips/cms
Terry Flores, County Clerk; Gilbert Lozano, District Clerk

Williamson County
organized 1848 from Milam County

Williamson County Justice Center
405 Martin Luther King Street
Georgetown, TX 78626
(512) 943-1515 (County Clerk, Justice Center, PO Box 18); (512) 943-1212 (District Clerk, PO Box 24); (512) 943-1616 FAX (County Clerk)
nrister@wilco.org
http://www.wilco.org
Nancy E. Rister, County Clerk; Lisa David, District Clerk
(land records from 1848, vital records from 1903, probate records from 1848)
no land or vital records search service; no probate search service; copies of probate records: $1.00 per page

Wilson County
organized 1860 from Bexar County

Wilson County Courthouse
1420 Third Street
Floresville, TX 78114
(830) 393-7308 (County Clerk, Suite 105, PO Box 27); (830) 393-7322 (District Clerk, Suite 202, PO Box 812); (830) 393-7334 FAX (County Clerk); (830) 393-7319 FAX (District Clerk)
http://www.co.wilson.tx.us/ips/cms
Eva S. Martinez, County Clerk; Deborah Bryan, District Clerk
(land records, vital records [proof of relationship required], probate records)
no probate search service (must have names and dates); copies of probate records: $1.00 each, no minimum

Winkler County
organized 1887 from Tom Green County

Winkler County Courthouse
Kermit, TX 79745
(915) 586-3401 (County Clerk, PO Box 1007); (915) 586-3359 (District Clerk, PO Box 1065)
http://www.co.winkler.tx.us
Shethelia Reed, County Clerk; Sherry Terry, District Clerk
(land records from 1883 [no title searches made on real estate without volume and page numbers], vital records from 1912, probate records from 1912)
probate search service: $5.00 per single name; copies of probate records: $1.00 per page, $1.00 for certification

Wise County
organized 1856 from Cooke County

Wise County Courthouse
Decatur, TX 76234
(940) 627-3351 (County Clerk, PO Box 359); (940) 627-5535 (District Clerk, PO Box 308); (940) 627-6404 FAX (County Clerk); (940) 627-0705 FAX (District Clerk)
countyclerk@co.wise.tx.us; districtclerk@co.wise.tx.us
http://www.co.wise.tx.us
Sherry Parker, County Clerk; Cristy Fuqua, District ClerkClerk
(land records from 1852, vital records from 1903, probate records from 1882)
vital records search service: $9.00 (includes one copy; requires a properly completed application for certified copies); probate search service: no charge; copies of land records: $1.00 each; copies of probate records: $1.00 each

Wood County
organized 1850 from Van Zandt County

Wood County Clerk
1 Main Street
Quitman, TX 75783
(903) 763-2711 (County Clerk, PO Box 1796); (903) 763-2361 (District Clerk, Room 302); (903) 763-5641 FAX (County Clerk); (903) 763-1511 FAX (District Clerk)
btaylor@co.wood.tx.us; jdturner@co.wood.tx.us
http://www.co.wood.tx.us/ips/cms
Brenda Taylor, County Clerk; Jenica Turner, District Clerk
(land records from 1879 to date, vital records from 1903 or 1904 to date, probate records from 1879 to date)

Yoakum County
created 1876 from Bexar County; organized 1907

Yoakum County Courthouse
Plains, TX 79355
(806) 456-7491, ext. 294 (County Clerk, PO Box 309); (806) 456-7491, ext. 297 (District Clerk, PO Box 899); (806) 456-2258 FAX (County Clerk); (806) 456-8767 FAX (District Clerk)
dlynrushing@hotmail.com; vicki.blundell@co.yoakum.tx.us
http://www.co.yoakum.tx.us/ips/cms
Deborah L. Rushing, County Clerk; Vicki Blundell, District Clerk
(land records, births, deaths and marriage licenses, probate records)
no vital records search service (must furnish name of child or decedent, year of birth or death); probate search service: $5.00 by Clerk's Office; certified copies of vital records: $9.00 each for births or deaths, $3.00 each for marriage licenses; copies of probate records: $1.00 per page, no minimum

Young County
organized 1856 from Bosque County

Young County Courthouse
516 Fourth Street
Graham, TX 76050
(940) 549-8432 (County Clerk, Room 104); (940) 549-0086 (District Clerk, Room 201); (940) 521-0305 FAX (County Clerk)
s.choate@youngcounty.org; c.collins@youngcounty.org
http://www.co.young.tx.us
Shirley Choate, County Clerk; Carolyn Collins, District Clerk
(land records from March 1854, births and deaths from 1903, probate records from 1876)
probate search service: $5.00 per name; copies of probate records: $1.00 per page

Zapata County
organized 1858 from Starr and Webb counties

Zapata County Courthouse
PO Box 789
Zapata, TX 78076
(956) 765-9915; (956) 765-9933 FAX
Mary Jayne Villarreal-Bonoan, District/County Clerk

Zavala County
organized 1884 from Uvalde and Maverick counties

Zavala County Courthouse
200 East Uvalde Street
Crystal City, TX 78839-3547
(830) 374-2331 (County Clerk, Suite 7, PO Box 5008); (830) 374-3456 (District Clerk, PO Box 704); (830) 374-5955 FAX (County Clerk); (830) 374-2632 FAX (District Clerk)
oralia.trevino@co.zavala.tx.us
http://www.co.zavala.tx.us/ips/cms
Oralia G. Trevino, County Clerk; Rachel P. Ramirez, District Clerk
(land records from 1886 to date with, vital records from 1900 to date [births within the last fifty years and deaths within the last twenty-five years, subject to restrictions], probate records from 1900 to date)

UTAH

Capital: Salt Lake City. Statehood: 4 January 1896 (annexed by the Treaty of Guadalupe-Hidalgo, 1848, became a territory in 1850 from the provisional State of Deseret, south of the 42nd parallel and west of the Rockies)

Utah has about 180 Justice of the Peace Courts which hear lesser civil cases, small claims, some misdemeanors and felony preliminaries. Juvenile Court sits at each county seat and has special jurisdiction; its six districts are different from either the Judicial Districts of the District Court or the Circuits of the Circuit Court. Circuit Court handles some civil cases, some criminal cases and some small claims, and sits in each county seat (some of them as secondary locations), except Farmington in Davis County and Parowan in Iron County. First Circuit: Box Elder County; Second Circuit: Cache and Rich counties; Third Circuit: Morgan and Weber counties; Fourth Circuit: Davis County; Fifth Circuit: Salt Lake and Summit counties; Sixth Circuit: Tooele County; Seventh Circuit: Daggett, Duchesne and Uintah counties; Eighth Circuit: Juab, Utah and Wasatch counties; Ninth Circuit: Beaver, Iron, Millard and Washington counties; Tenth Circuit: Garfield, Kane, Piute, Sanpete, Sevier and Wayne counties; Eleventh Circuit: Carbon and Emery counties; Twelfth Circuit: Grand and San Juan counties.

District Court sits at each county seat and hears criminal felonies, review of administrative agencies, and all civil matters not heard by the lower courts. First Judicial District: Box Elder, Cache and Rich counties; Second Judicial District: Davis, Morgan and Weber counties; Third Judicial District: Salt Lake, Summit and Tooele counties; Fourth Judicial District: Juab, Millard, Utah and Wasatch counties; Fifth Judicial District: Beaver, Iron and Washington counties; Sixth Judicial District: Garfield, Kane, Piute, Sanpete, Sevier and Wayne counties; Seventh Judicial District: Carbon, Daggett, Duchesne, Emery, Grand, San Juan and Uintah counties. The Court of Appeals and Supreme Court hear appeals.

Beaver County
organized 1856 from Iron and Millard counties

Beaver County Clerk of the Fifth District Court
Cedar City Hall of Justice
40 North 100 East
Cedar City, UT 84720
(435) 867-3201; (435) 867-3212 FAX
carolybb@email.utcourts.gov
http://www.utcourts.gov/directory/courthouse.
   cgi?county=1
Carolyn Bulloch
(probate records)

Beaver County Recorder
(105 East Center—location)
PO Box 431 (mailing address)
Beaver, UT 84713-0431
(435) 438-6480; (435) 438-6481 FAX
rbbrown@beaver.state.ut.us
http://www.beaver.state.ut.us/recorder.htm
R. Bruce Brown
(land records)

Box Elder County
organized 1856 from unorganized territory

Box Elder County Clerk of the First District Court
 (43 North Main—location)
PO Box 873 (mailing address)
Brigham City, UT 84302-0873
(435) 734-4600; (435) 734-4610 FAX
joed@email.utcourts.gov
http://www.utcourts.gov/directory/courthouse.
   cgi?county=2
Joe Derring

(probate records)
probate search service: $4.00 per hour; copies of probate records: 25¢ per page, $2.00 per page certification

Box Elder County Recorder/Clerk/Surveyor
Box Elder County Courthouse
1 South Main Street
Brigham City, UT 84302
(435) 734-3351; (435) 723-7562 FAX
ladams@boxeldercounty.org
http://www.boxeldercounty.org/recclerk/
   clerk-top.html; http://www.boxeldercounty.
   org/recclerk/rec-top.html
LuAnn Adams, Recorder/Clerk/Surveyor
(land records and naturalization records)

Cache County
organized 4 April 1857 from unorganized territory

Cache County Clerk
Cache County Courthouse
179 North Main Street, Suite 102
   Logan, UT 84321-5081
(435) 716-7150
jillzoll@cacheco.state.ut.us
http://www.cachecounty.org/clerk
Jill N. Zollinger
(marriages)

Cache County Clerk of the First District Court
135 North 100 West
Logan, UT 84321
(435) 750-1310; (435) 750-1355 FAX
sherylm@email.utcourts.gov
http://www.utcourts.gov/directory/courthouse.
   cgi?county=3
Sheryl Morris
(probate records)

Cache County Recorder
Cache County Courthouse
179 North Main Street, Suite 101
Logan, UT 84321
(435) 755-1530
mike@yoda.state.ut.us
http://www.cachecounty.org/recorder
Michael Gleed
(land records)

Carbon County
organized 1894 from Emery County

Carbon County Clerk
120 East Main Street
Price, UT 84501-3050
(435) 636-3227
smerrell@co.carbon.ut.us
http://www.carboncountyutah.com/clerks/inde
   x.htm
Sulika Merrell, Deputy Clerk
(naturalization and marriages)

Carbon County Clerk of the Seventh District Court
Carbon County Court Complex
149 East 100 South
Price, UT 84501
(435) 636-3409; (435) 637-7349 FAX
pollya@email.utcourts.gov
http://www.utcourts.gov/directory/courthouse.
   cgi?county=4
Polly Atwood
(probate records)

Carbon County Recorder
120 East Main Street
Price, UT 84501-3050
(435) 636-3244
smurdock@co.carbon.ut.us
http://www.carboncountyutah.com
Sharon Murdock
(land records)

Daggett County
organized 1918 from Uintah County

Daggett County Auditor/Recorder
PO Box 219

Manila, UT 84046-029
(435) 784-3210; (435) 784-3335 FAX
rwilde@daggett.state.ut.us
http://www.daggettcounty.org
RaNae Wilde
(land records)

Daggett County Clerk
PO Box 219
Manila, UT 84046-0219
(435) 784-3154
vmckee@daggett.state.ut.us
http://www.daggettcounty.org
Vickie McKee
(naturalization records, marriages)

Daggett County Clerk of the Eighth District Court
(920 East Highway 40, Vernal, UT 84078—location)
PO Box 219 (mailing address)
Manila, UT 84046
(435) 784-3154; (435) 784-3335 FAX
http://www.utcourts.gov/directory/courthouse.
   cgi?county=5
Joanne McKee
(probate records)

Davis County
organized 1850 from Salt Lake County

Davis County Clerk
(28 East State Street, Room 136—location)
PO Box 618 (mailing address)
Farmington, UT 84025-0618
(801) 451-3324; (801) 451-3421 FAX
rawlings@co.davis.ut.us
http://www.co.davis.ut.us/clerkauditor
Steve Rawlings
(naturalization records from 1905 to 1925, marriages from June 1888)

Davis County Clerk of the Second District Court
(800 West State Street—location)
PO Box 769 (mailing address)
Farmington, UT 84025
(801) 447-3820; (801) 447-3881 FAX
alysonb@email.utcourts.gov
http://www.utcourts.gov/directory/courthouse.
   cgi?county=6
Alyson Brown
(probate records)
probate search service: $10.00 per hour; copies of probate records: 25¢ per page

Davis County Recorder
(28 East State Street, Room 119—location)
PO Box 618 (mailing address)
Farmington, UT 84025-0618
(801) 451-3225; (801) 451-3141 FAX
http://www.co.davis.ut.us/recorder
(land records from 1886)

Duchesne County
organized 5 January 1915 from Wasatch County

Duchesne County Clerk/Auditor
(734 North Center—location)
PO Box 910 (mailing address)
Duchesne, UT 84021-0910
(435) 738-1123; (435) 738-5522 FAX
dfreston@co.duchesne.ut.us
http://www.duchesnegov.net/clerkauditor/
   clerk.html
Diane Freston
(marriage licenses from 1915)

Duchesne County Clerk of the Eighth District Court
(920 East Highway 40, Vernal, UT 84078—location)
PO Box 219 (mailing address)
Manila, UT 84046
(435) 784-3154; (435) 784-3335 FAX
http://www.utcourts.gov/directory/courthouse.
   cgi?county=7
Joanne McKee
(probate records from 1915)
probate search service: no charge; copies of probate records: 25¢ per page plus postage,

no minimum

Duchesne County Recorder
(734 North Center—location)
PO Box 916 (mailing address)
Duchesne, UT 84021-0916
(435) 738-1160
http://www.duchesnegov.net/recorder/
    recorder.html
Carolyne Madsen
(land records from 1875, only what
    naturalization records may have been
    recorded by certain individuals)
no land records search service (can be accessed
    with a legal description or a name)

Emery County
organized 1880 from Sanpete and Sevier
    counties

Emery County Clerk/Auditor
(75 East Main—location)
PO Box 907 (mailing address)
Castle Dale, UT 84513-0907
(435) 381-5106; (435) 381-5183 FAX
brenda@co.emery.ut.us
http://www.emerycounty.com/auditor
Brenda Dugmore

**Emery County Clerk of the Seventh District
    Court**
Carbon County Court Complex
149 East 100 South
Price, UT 84501
(435) 636-3409; (435) 637-7349 FAX
pollya@email.utcourts.gov
http://www.utcourts.gov/directory/courthouse.
    cgi?county=8
Polly Atwood
(probate records)
probate search service: available; copies of
    probate records: available; 7/06
    www.utcourts.gov/directory lists

Emery County Recorder
(75 East Main, Room 104—location)
PO Box 698 (mailing address)
Castle Dale, UT 84513-0698
(435) 381-2414; (435) 381-2614 FAX
swasey@co.emery.ut.us
http://www.emerycounty.com/recorder
Dixie Swasey
(land records)

Garfield County
organized 9 March 1882 from Iron, Kane and
    Sevier counties

Garfield County Clerk
PO Box 77
Panguitch, UT 84759-0077
(435) 676-1100; (435) 676-8239 FAX
gcclerk@mountainwest.net
http://utahreach.org/garfield/clerk.htm
Camille Moore

**Garfield County Clerk of the Sixth District
    Court**
(Garfield County Courthouse, 55 South Main
    Street—location)
PO Box 77 (mailing address)
Panguitch, UT 84759-0077
(435) 676-1100; (435) 676-8239 FAX
http://www.utcourts.gov/directory/courthouse.
    cgi?county=9; http://www.utcourts.gov/
    courts/dist/distsites/6th/#map
Camille Moore
(marriage licenses probate records)
probate search service: $8.00 per hour; copies of
    marriage licenses: $6.00 each; copies of
    probate records: 50¢ per page, no minimum

Garfield County Recorder
PO Box 77
Panguitch, UT 84759-0077
(435) 676-1112; (435) 676-8239 FAX
gcrec@color-country.net
http://utahreach.org/garfield/govt/recorder.htm
A. Les Barker
(land records)

Grand County
organized 1890 from Emery and Uintah
    counties

Grand County Clerk
125 East Center Street
Moab, UT 84532-2429
(435) 259-1321; (435) 259-2959 FAX
frannyt@grand.state.ut.us
http://www.grandcountyutah.net/clerk
Fran Townsend

**Grand County Clerk of the Seventh District
    Court**
Grand County Courthouse
125 East Center Street
Moab, UT 84532
(435) 259-1350; (435) 259-4081 FAX
claudiap@email.utcourts.gov
http://www.utcourts.gov/directory/courthouse.
    cgi?county=10
Claudia Page
(probate records)
probate search service: no charge; copies of
    probate records: 25¢ per page, no minimum

Grand County Recorder
125 East Center
Moab, UT 84532-2449
(801) 259-1331
mmosher@grand.state.ut.us
http://www.grandcountyutah.net/recorder
Merlene Mosher
(land records)

Iron County
organized 1850 from unorganized territory;
    name changed from Little Salt Lake County in
    1850

Iron County Clerk
PO Box 429
Parowan, UT 84761-0429
(435) 477–8341; (435) 477-8847 FAX
david@ironcounty.net
http://www.ironcounty.net/departments/Clerk
David I. Yardley
(naturalization records; marriage licenses from
    1896 to date)

Iron County Clerk of the Fifth District Court
Cedar City Hall of Justice
40 North 100 East
Cedar City, UT 84720
(435) 867-3201; (435) 867-3212 FAX
carolybb@emailutcourts.gov
http://www.utcourts.gov/directory/courthouse.
    cgi?county=11
Carolyn Bulloch
(probate records)
probate search service: $7.65 per hour; copies of
    probate records: 25¢ each, no minimum

Iron County Recorder
68 South 100 East
Parowan, UT 84761
(435) 477-8350; (435) 477-8847 FAX
recorder@ironcounty.net
http://www.ironcounty.net/departments/
    Recorder
Dixie B. Matheson
(land records)

Juab County
organized 1852, original county

Juab County Clerk
160 North Main Street
Nephi, UT 84648-1412
(435) 623-3410; (435) 623-5936 FAX
pati@co.juab.ut.us
http://www.co.juab.ut.us/County/Clerk/Index.
    htm
Patricia Ingram

**Juab County Clerk of the Fourth District
    Court**
(160 North Main—location)
PO Box 249 (mailing address)
Nephi, UT 84648

(435) 623-0901; (435) 623-0922 FAX
cindyj@email.utcourts.gov
http://www.utcourts.gov/directory/courthouse.
    cgi?county=12
Cindy Jacquart, Assistant Clerk of Court
(probate records from 1890)
probate search service: $7.50 per hour; copies of
    probate records: 25¢ per page, no minimum

Juab County Recorder
160 North Main
Nephi, UT 84648-1412
(435) 623-3430; (435) 623-5936 FAX
craigs@co.juab.ut.us
http://www.co.juab.ut.us/County/Recorder/In
    dex.html
Craig Sperry
(land records from 1890, naturalization records
    from 1900 to 1905, vital records from 1898 to
    1905)

Kane County
organized 1864 from Washington County

Kane County Clerk
Courthouse, 76 North Main Street
Kanab, UT 84741-3209
(435) 644-2458; (435) 644-2052 FAX
clerk@xpressweb.com
http://www.kaneutah.com
Karla Johnson

**Kane County Clerk of the Sixth District
    Court**
Kane County Courthouse
76 North Main
Kanab, UT 84741
(435) 644-2458; (435) 644-2052 FAX
karlaj@email.utcourts.gov
http://www.utcourts.gov/directory/courthouse.
    cgi?county=13; http://www.utcourts.gov/
    courts/dist/distsites/6th/#map
Karla Johnson, Clerk
(probate records)
copies of probate records: 25¢ per page plus
    postage

Kane County Recorder
Courthouse, 76 North Main Street
Kanab, UT 84741-3209
(435) 644-2360; (435) 644-2052 FAX
recorder@kane.state.ut.us
http://www.kaneutah.com
VerJean Caruso
(land records)

Millard County
organized 1851 from Juab County

Millard County Clerk
765 South Highway 99, Suite 6
Fillmore, UT 84631-5032
(435) 743-6223; (435) 743-6923 FAX
normab@email.utcourts.gov
http://www.millardcounty.com
Norma Brunson

**Millard County Clerk of the Fourth District
    Court**
765 South Highway 99, Suite 6
Fillmore, UT 84631
(435) 743-6223; (435) 743-6923 FAX
normab@email.utcourts.gov
http://www.utcourts.gov/directory/courthouse.
    cgi?county=14
Norma Brunson
(probate records)
probate search service: no charge for one name,
    one time, otherwise $5.00 per hour; copies of
    probate records: 25¢ per page plus postage
    costs ("call for instructions")

Millard County Recorder
50 South Main Street
Fillmore, UT 84631-5504
(435) 743-6210; (435) 743-4221 FAX
chansen@co.millard.ut.us
http://www.millardcounty.com
Connie Hansen
(land records)

Morgan County

organized 1862 from Davis and Summit
counties

Morgan County Clerk
PO Box 886
Morgan, UT 84050-0886
(801) 845-4011; (801) 829-6176 FAX
slafitte@morgan-county.net
http://www.morgan-county.net/Clerk.htm
Stacy Lafite

**Morgan County Clerk of the Second District
Court**
2525 Grant Avenue
Ogden, UT 84401
(801) 395-1060; (801) 395-1182 FAX
maureem@email.utcourts.gov
http://www.utcourts.gov/directory/courthouse.
cgi?county=15
Maureen Magagna
(probate records)
probate search service: no charge; copies of
probate records: 25¢ per page, $2.00 per
document plus 50¢ per page for certified
copies, plus postage, no minimum

Morgan County Recorder
PO Box 886
Morgan, UT 84050-0886
(801) 829-3277; (801) 829-6176 FAX
http://www.morgan-county.net/recorder.htm
Debbie Weaver
(land records, marriage licenses)

Piute County

organized 1865 from Sevier County

Piute County Clerk
(550 North Main—location)
PO Box 99 (mailing address)
Junction, UT 84740-0099
(435) 577-2840; (435) 577-2433
valeenb@hotmail.com
http://www.piute.org
Valeen H. Brown

**Piute County Clerk of the Sixth District
Court**
(Piute County Courthouse, 550 North Main—
location)
PO Box 99 (mailing address)
Junction, UT 84740
(435) 577-2840; (435) 577-2433 FAX
valeenb@hotmail.com
http://www.utcourts.gov/directory/courthouse.
cgi?county=16; http://www.utcourts.gov/
courts/dist/distsites/6th/#map
Valeen Brown, Clerk
(probate records)

Piute County Recorder
(500 North Main—location)
PO Box 116 (mailing address)
Junction, UT 84740-0116
(435) 577-2505; (435) 577-2433 FAX
http://www.piute.org
(land records)

Rich County

organized 1864, original county; name changed
from Richland County

Rich County Clerk
(20 South Main—location)
PO Box 218 (mailing address)
Randolph, UT 84064-0218
(435) 793-2415; (435) 793-2410 FAX
rcclerk@allwest.net
http://www.richcountyut.org
Pamela Shaul

Rich County Clerk of the First District Court
Rich County Courthouse
20 South Main
Randolph, UT 84064
(435) 793-2415; (435) 793-2410 FAX
pamelas@email.utcourts.gov
http://www.utcourts.gov/directory/courthouse.
cgi?county=17

Pamela Shaul
(probate records)

Rich County Recorder
(20 South Main—location)
PO Box 322 (mailing address)
Randolph, UT 84064-0322
(435) 793-2005; (435) 793-2410 FAX
rcrecord@allwest.net
http://www.richcountyut.org
Debra Lee Ames

Salt Lake County

organized 1849, original county; name changed
from Great Salt Lake County in 1868

Salt Lake County Clerk
Salt Lake County Complex
2001 South State Street, Suite 2200
Salt Lake City, UT 84190-1050
(801) 468-3519; (801) 468-3440 FAX
sswensen@co.slc.ut.us
http://www.clerk.slco.org
Sherrie Swensen

**Salt Lake County Clerk of the Third District
Court**
(450 South State Street—location)
PO Box 1860 (mailing address)
Salt Lake City, UT 84114-1860
(801) 238-7455; (801) 238-7430 FAX
scotth@email.utcourts.gov
http://www.utcourts.gov/directory/courthouse.
cgi?county=18
Scott Hennessy
(probate records)

Salt Lake County Recorder
Salt Lake County Complex
2001 South State Street, Suite N1600
Salt Lake City, UT 84190-0002
(801) 468-3391; (801) 468-3335 FAX
gott@slco.org
http://slcorecorder.siredocs.com/rechome/
main.aspx
Gary Ott
(land records)

San Juan County

organized 1880 from Kane County

San Juan County Clerk
(117 South Main—location)
PO Box 338 (mailing address)
Monticello, UT 84535-0338
(435) 587-3223, ext. 4113; (435) 587-2425 FAX
njohnson@sanjuancounty.org
http://www.sanjuancounty.org
Norm Johnson

**San Juan County Clerk of the Seventh
District Court**
Grand County Courthouse
125 East Center Street
Moab, UT 84532
(435) 259-1350; (435) 259-4081 FAX
claudiap@email.utcourts.gov
http://www.utcourts.gov/directory/courthouse.
cgi?county=19
Claudia Page
(probate records)
probate search service: $2.00 per name/$7.00
per hour; copies of probate records: 50¢ each,
$2.00 minimum

San Juan County Recorder
(117 South Main, Room 103—location)
PO Box 789 (mailing address)
Monticello, UT 84535-0789
(435) 587-3228; (435) 587-2447 FAX
lcjones@sanjuancounty.org
http://www.sanjuancounty.org
Louise Jones
(land records)

Sanpete County

organized 1849, original county

Sanpete County Clerk
(160 North Main—location)
PO Box 100 (mailing address)

Manti, UT 84642-0100
(435) 835-2131; (435) 835-2135 FAX
krisf@email.utcourts.gov
http://utahreach.org/sanpete/govt/clerk.htm
Kristine Frischknecht
(births and deaths from 1898 to 1905, marriages)

**Sanpete County Clerk of the Sixth District
Court–Manti**
(Sanpete County Courthouse, 160 North
Main—location)
PO Box 100 (mailing address)
Manti, UT 84642
(435) 835-2131; (435) 835-2135 FAX
sandycn@email.utcourts.gov
http://www.utcourts.gov/directory/courthouse.
cgi?county=20;
http://www.utcourts.gov/courts/dist/distsite
s/6th/#map
Sandy Neill
(probate records)
probate search service: $10.00 per hour (longer
than ten minutes); copies of probate records:
15¢ to 25¢ per page, $2.00 per document plus
25¢ per page for certified copies, no minimum

Sanpete County Recorder
Sanpete County Courthouse
160 North Main
Manti, UT 84642-1266
(435) 835-2181; (435) 835-2182 FAX
rdh@sanpetecounty-ut.gov
http://www.sanpetecounty.org/page/recorder
Reed Hatch
(land records)

Sevier County

organized 1865 from Sanpete County

Sevier County Clerk
Sevier County Courthouse
250 North Main Street, Suite 101
Richfield, UT 84701-2165
(435) 893-0401; (435) 896-8888 FAX
steve@sevierutah.net
http://www.sevierutah.net/clerk_auditor/clerk_
auditor.html
Steven C. Wall

**Sevier County Clerk of the Sixth District
Court–Richfield**
895 East 300 North
Richfield, UT 84701
(435) 896-2720; (435) 896-8047 FAX
peggyj@email.utcourts.gov
http://www.utcourts.gov/directory/courthouse.
cgi?county=21; http://www.utcourts.gov/
courts/dist/distsites/6th/#map
Peggy K. Johnson
(probate records)

Sevier County Recorder
Sevier County Courthouse
250 North Main Street
Richfield, UT 84701-2156
(435) 896-9262, ext. 210–214; (435) 896-8888
FAX
jayrene@sevierutah.net
http://www.sevierutah.net/recorder/recorder.
html
Jayrene Nielsen
(land records)

Summit County

organized 1854 from Salt Lake County

Summit County Clerk
PO Box 128
Coalville, UT 84017-0128
(435) 336-3203; (435) 336-3030 FAX
sfollett@co.summit.ut.us
http://www.summitcounty.org/clerk
Susan Follett
(naturalization records, vital records)

**Summit County Clerk of the Third District
Court**
(450 South State Street—location)
PO Box 1860 (mailing address)
Salt Lake City, UT 84114-1860
(801) 238-7455; (801) 238-7430 FAX

scotth@email.utcourts.gov
http://www.utcourts.gov/directory/courthouse.
cgi?county=22
Scott Hennessy
(probate records)
probate search service: $7.65 per hour after ten
minutes; copies of probate records: 25¢ per
page, no minimum ("fees paid in advance")

Summit County Recorder
PO Box 128
Coalville, UT 84017-0128
(435) 336-3238; (435) 336-3055 FAX
aspriggs@co.summit.ut.us
http://www.summitcounty.org/recorder
Alan Spriggs
(land records from 1856 to date)
no land records search service; copies of land
records: 50¢ per page, $2.00 each for plats up
to 18" x 18", $4.00 each for larger plats

Tooele County
organized 1849, original county; includes
Shambip County, which was abolished in
1862

Tooele County Clerk
47 South Main Street, Room 130
Tooele, UT 84074-2131
(435) 843-3140; (866) 704-3443, ext. 3140; (435)
882-7317 FAX
dewing@co.tooele.ut.us
http://www.co.tooele.ut.us/clerk.htm
Dennis D. Ewing
(early naturalization records, births and deaths
from 1897 to 1905)

**Tooele County Clerk of the Third District
Court**
(450 South State Street—location)
PO Box 1860 (mailing address)
Salt Lake City, UT 84114-1860
(801) 238-7455; (801) 238-7430 FAX
scotth@email.utcourts.gov
http://www.utcourts.gov/directory/courthouse.
cgi?county=23
Scott Hennessy
(probate records)
probate search service: $6.00 per hour; copies of
probate records: 25¢ each, no minimum

Tooele County Recorder
47 South Main Street, Room 213
Tooele, UT 84074-2131
(435) 843-3180; (866) 704-3443, ext. 31
cpeshell@co.tooele.ut.us
http://www.co.tooele.ut.us/recorder.htm
Calleen Peshell
(land records)

Uintah County
organized 1880 from Wasatch County

Uinta County Clerk
147 East Main Street
Vernal, UT 84078-2603
(435) 781-5361; (435) 781-6701 FAX
mwilkins@co.uintah.ut.us
http://www.co.uintah.ut.us/clerk_auditor/
clrkaud.php
Mike Wilkins

**Uintah County Clerk of the Eighth District
Court**
(920 East Highway 40, Vernal, UT 84078—
location)
PO Box 219 (mailing address)
Manila, UT 84046
(435) 784-3154; (435) 784-3335 FAX
http://www.utcourts.gov/directory/courthouse.
cgi?county=24
Joanne McKee
(probate records)

Uintah County Recorder
147 East Main Street
Vernal, UT 84078-2603
(435) 781-5398
randyjsimmons@co.uintah.ut.us
http://www.co.uintah.ut.us/recorder/rec.php
Randy Simmons

(land records)

Utah County
organized 1849, original county; includes Cedar
County, which was abolished in 1862

Utah County Clerk
100 East Center Street, Room 3600
Provo, UT 84606-3106
(801) 851-8109; (801) 851-8232 FAX
kristens.ucadm@state.ut.us
http://www.co.utah.ut.us/Dept/ClerkAud/
index.asp
Kim T. Jackson

**Utah County Clerk of the Fourth District
Court**
125 North 100 West
Provo, UT 84603
(801) 429-1176; (801) 429-1020 FAX
http://www.utcourts.gov/directory/courthouse.
cgi?county=25
Lori Woffinden
(probate records)
probate search service: $8.00 per hour plus
SASE; copies of probate records: 25¢ each,
no minimum

Utah County Recorder
100 East Center Street, Suite 1300
Provo, UT 84606-3106
(801) 851-8179; (801) 851-8181 FAX
ucadm.randyc@state.ut.us
http://www.co.utah.ut.us/Dept/Record/index.
asp
Randall Covington, III
(land records and vital records)

Wasatch County
organized 1870 from Salt Lake and Utah
counties

Wasatch County Clerk
25 North Main Street
Heber City, UT 84032-1827
(435) 657-3190; (435) 654-9924 FAX
btitcomb@co.wasatch.ut.us
http://www.co.wasatch.ut.us/d/auditor.html
Brent R. Titcomb
(marriage licenses and some births)

**Wasatch County Clerk of the Fourth District
Court**
(1361 South Highway 40—location)
PO Box 730 (mailing address)
Heber City, UT 84032
(435) 654-4676; (435) 654-3281 FAX
roseb@email.utcourts.gov
http://www.utcourts.gov/directory/courthouse.
cgi?county=26
Diann Burgener
(probate records)

Wasatch County Recorder
25 North Main Street
Heber City, UT 84032-1827
(435) 657-3210; (435) 654-9924 FAX
lpalmier@co.wasatch.ut.us
http://www.co.wasatch.ut.us/d/recorder.html
Liz Palmier
(land records, naturalization records)

Washington County
organized 1856 from unorganized territory

Washington County Clerk
Washington County Administration Building
197 East Tabernacle Street
St. George, UT 84770-3443
(435) 634-5712; (435) 634-5753 FAX
clerk@washco.state.ut.us;
calvinr@washco.state.ut.us
http://www.washco.state.ut.us
Calvin R. Robison

**Washington County Clerk of the Fifth
District Court**
Washington County Hall of Justice
220 North 200 East
St. George, UT 84770
(435) 986-5706; (435) 986-5723 FAX

carolyns@email.utcourts.gov
http://www.utcourts.gov/directory/courthouse.
cgi?county=27
Carolyn Smitherman
(probate records)
probate search service: $2.00 per hour; copies of
probate records: 15¢ each

Washington County Recorder
87 North 200 East, Suite 101
St. George, UT 84770-5019
(435) 634-5709
russells@washco.state.ut.us
http://www.washco.state.ut.us
Russell Shirts
(land records with County Recorder,
naturalization records with County Clerk,
marriage licenses only with County Clerk)

Wayne County
organized 1892 from Piute County

Wayne County Clerk
18 South Main Street
Loa, UT 84747
(435) 836-1300
ryan@wco.state.ut.us
http://www.waynecnty.com/clerk.htm
Ryan Torgerson
(vital records from 1898 to 1947)

**Wayne County Clerk of the Sixth District
Court**
Wayne County Courthouse
18 South Main
Loa, UT 84747-0189
(435) 836-1300; (435) 836-2479 FAX
ryat@email.utcourts.gov
http://www.utcourts.gov/directory/courthouse.
cgi?county=28; http://www.utcourts.gov/
courts/dist/distsites/6th/#map
Ryan Torgerson
(probate records from 1898)
probate search service available; copies of
probate records: 50¢ per page, $6.00 for
certified copies, no minimum

Wayne County Recorder
Wayne County Courthouse
18 South Main Street
Loa, UT 84747
(435) 836-1303
http://www.waynecnty.com/treasurer.htm
(land records)

Weber County
organized 1849, original county

Weber County Clerk
2380 Washington Boulevard, Suite 320
Ogden, UT 84401-1456
(801) 399-8400; (801) 399-8300 FAX
lluncefo@co.weber.ut.us
http://www1.co.weber.ut.us/Clerk_Auditor
Linda Lunceford

**Weber County Clerk of the Second District
Court**
2525 Grant Avenue
Ogden, UT 84401
(801) 395-1060; (801) 395-1182 FAX
maureem@email.utcourts.gov
http://www.utcourts.gov/directory/courthouse.
cgi?county=29
Maureen Magagna
(probate records)

Weber County Recorder
Municipal Building
2380 Washington Boulevard, Suite 370
Ogden, UT 84401-1465
(801) 399-8441; (801) 399-8320 FAX
dcrofts@co.weber.ut.us
http://www1.co.weber.ut.us/recorder
Doug Crofts

<table>
</table>

VERMONT

Capital: Montpelier. Statehood: 4 March 1791 (claims relinquished by Massachusetts in 1781, by New Hampshire in 1782, and by New York in 1790, although Vermont asserts that it was an "independent republic" from 1777 until it joined the U.S. in 1791)

Vermont's Probate Court is divided into eighteen districts. It sits at the county seats in Addison, Caledonia, Chittenden, Franklin, Grand Isle, Lamoille, Orange, Orleans and Washington Districts. The Probate Court in Bennington District sits at Bennington and includes the towns of Bennington, Glastenbury, Pownal, Readsboro, Searsburg, Shaftsbury, Stamford and Woodford; Essex District sits at Island Pond; Fair Haven District sits at Fair Haven and includes the towns of Benson, Castleton, Fair Haven, Hubbardton, Pawlet, Poultney, Sudbury, Wells and West Haven; Hartford District sits at Woodstock and includes the towns of Barnard, Bethel, Bridgewater, Hartford, Hartland, Norwich, Pomfret, Rochester, Royalton, Sharon, Stockbridge and Woodstock; Manchester District sits at Manchester and includes the towns of Arlington, Dorset, Landgrove, Manchester, Peru, Rupert, Sandgate, Sunderland and Winhall; Marlboro District sits at Brattleboro and includes the towns of Brattleboro, Dover, Dummerston, Guilford, Halifax, Marlboro, Newfane, Stratton, Somerset, Vernon, Wardsboro, Whitingham and Wilmington; Rutland District sits at Rutland City and includes the towns of Brandon, Chittenden, Clarendon, Danby, Ira, Mendon, Middletown Springs, Mount Holly, Mount Tabor, Pittsfield, Pittsford, Proctor, Rutland Town, Rutland City, Sherburne, Shrewsbury, Tinmouth, Wallingford and West Rutland; Westminster District sits at Bellows Falls and includes the towns of Athens, Brookline, Grafton, Jamaica, Londonderry, Putney, Rockingham, Townshend, Westminster and Windham; Windsor District sits at North Springfield and includes the towns of Andover, Baltimore, Cavendish, Chester, Ludlow, North Springfield, Plymouth, Reading, Springfield, Weathersfield, West Windsor, Weston and Windsor.

The District Courts have limited jurisdiction over civil, criminal and juvenile matters and are organized into three multi-county units, with each county constituting a district within the unit, and two special units: Brandon (at the town of Brandon, having jurisdiction over the Brandon Training School, a mental health facility) and Waterbury (at Barre, exercising mental health jurisdiction only). Unit One: Bennington, Rutland, Windham and Windsor Circuits (at Bennington, Rutland, Brattleboro and White River Junction); Unit Two: Addison, Chittenden, Orange and Washington Circuits (at Middlebury, Burlington, Chelsea and Barre); Unit Three: Caledonia, Essex, Franklin, Grand Isle, Lamoille and Orleans Circuits (at St. Johnsbury, St. Albans, Hyde Park and Newport). Superior Court sits at each county seat and has general jurisdiction over criminal and civil actions, real estate and domestic relations. The Supreme Court is the court of last resort.

The town offices house land records and vital records. Vital records from 1760–1954 are also at Vermont Public Records Division.

Addison County
organized 1785 from Rutland and Chittenden counties

Addison County Clerk
7 Judge Frank Mahady Court
Middlebury, VT 05753
(802) 388-7741
http://www.addisoncounty.com (Chamber of Commerce)
Kylie Dixon

Addison Probate District
Marbleworks Building
7 Mahady Court
Middlebury, VT 05753-1405
(802) 388-2612
http://www.vermontjudiciary.org/courts/probate/index.htm
Maureen Mulligan, Register
(probate records for all of Addison County, including City of Vergennes and the towns of Addison, Bridport, Bristol, Cornwall, Ferrisburg, Goshen, Granville, Hancock, Leicester, Lincoln, Middlebury, Monkton, New Haven, Orwell, Panton, Ripton, Salisbury, Shoreham, Starksboro, Waltham, Weybridge, and Whiting)

Bennington County
organized 1779, original county

Bennington County Clerk
(207 South Street—location)
PO Box 4157 (mailing address)
Bennington, VT 05201
(802) 447-2700
Betty Loftus
(Glastenbury [unorganized town] land and vital records from 1833)

Bennington Probate District
(207 South Street—location)
PO Box 65 (mailing address)
Bennington, VT 05201-0065
(802) 447-2705
http://www.vermontjudiciary.org/courts/probate/index.htm
Debbie J. Briggs, Register
(probate records from the 1770s for the towns of Bennington, Glastenbury, Pownal, Readsboro, Searsburg, Shaftsbury, Stamford and Woodford [remainder of Bennington County covered by Manchester District Probate Court])
no probate search service; copies of probate records: 25¢ per page, $1.00 minimum

Manchester District Probate Court
PO Box 446
Manchester, VT 05254
(802) 362-1410
http://www.vermontjudiciary.org/courts/probate/index.htm
Michele M. Pacheco, Register
(district organized 1771; probate records from 1771 for the towns of Arlington, Dorset, Landgrove, Manchester, Peru, Rupert, Sandgate, Sunderland and Winhall [remainder of Bennington County covered by Bennington Probate District])
probate search service: no charge; copies of probate records: 25¢ per page, $1.00 minimum

Caledonia County
organized 1792 from unorganized territory

Caledonia County Clerk
1126 Main Street, Suite 1
St. Johnsbury, VT 05819-2637
(802) 748-6600
Kathleen Pearl

Caledonia Probate District
(27 Main Street—location)
PO Box 511 (mailing address)
St. Johnsbury, VT 05819
(802) 748-6605
http://www.vermontjudiciary.org/courts/probate/index.htm
Pam Comeau, Register
(probate records for all of Caledonia County, including the towns of Barnet, Burke, Danville, Groton, Hardwick, Kirby, Lyndon, Newark, Peacham, Ryegate, St. Johnsbury, Sheffield, Stannard, Sutton, Walden, Waterford, and Wheelock)

Chittenden County
organized 1787, original county

Chittenden County Clerk
(175 Main Street—location)
PO Box 187 (mailing address)
Burlington, VT 05402
(802) 863-3467
Diane Lavallee

Chittenden Probate District
(175 Main Street—location)
PO Box 511 (mailing address)
Burlington, VT 05402
(802) 864-7481
http://www.vermontjudiciary.org/courts/probate/index.htm
Debra Brunell and Judith Joly, Registers
(probate records for all of Chittenden County, including Buel's Gore, Essex Junction, City of Burlington, City of Winooski and the towns of Bolton, Charlotte, Colchester, Essex, Hinesburg, Huntington, Jericho, Milton, Richmond, St. George, Shelburne, South Burlington, Underhill, Westford, and Williston)
probate search service: no charge; copies of probate records: 25¢ per page, $1.00 minimum ("prepaid—we cannot bill")

Essex County
organized 1792 from unorganized territory

Essex County Clerk
(Courthouse, 75 Courthouse Drive—location)
PO Box 75 (mailig address)
Guildhall, VT 05905
(802) 676-3910
Angelina Desiletes
(vital records only for unorganized towns and government of Essex County)

Essex District Probate Court
(Main Street—location)
PO Box 426 (mailing address)
Island Pond, VT 05846
(802) 723-4770
http://www.vermontjudiciary.org/courts/probate/index.htm
Fay Moore, Register
(estates, trusts and guardian estates from about 1869 ([index cards for the prior years] for all of Essex County, including Avery's Gore, Warner's Grant, Warren's Gore and the towns of Averill, Bloomfield, Brighton, Brunswick, Canaan, Concord, East Haven, Ferdinand, Granby, Guildhall, Lemington, Lewis, Lunenburg, Maidstone, Norton, and Victory)
probate search service: no charge; copies of probate records: 25¢ per page, $1.00 minimum

Franklin County
organized 1792 from Chittenden County

Franklin County Clerk
(Church Street—location)
PO Box 808 (mailing address)
St. Albans, VT 05478-0808
(802) 524-3863
James A. Pelkey

Franklin Probate District
17 Church Street
St. Albans, VT 05478
(802) 524-7948
http://www.vermontjudiciary.org/courts/probate/index.htm
Mary Wright, Register
(probate records: For all of Franklin County, including St. Albans City and the towns of Bakersfield, Berkshire, Enosburg, Fairfax, Fairfield, Fletcher, Franklin, Georgia, Highgate, Montgomery, Richford, St. Albans, Sheldon, and Swanton)

Grand Isle County
organized 1802 from Franklin County

Grand Isle County Clerk
(Route 2—location)
PO Box 7 (mailing address)

North Hero, VT 05474-0007
(802) 372-8350
sbritton@mail.crt.state.vt.us
Sherry Britton, County Clerk and Court Clerk

Grand Isle Probate District
PO Box 7
North Hero, VT 05474-0007
(802) 372-8350
sbritton@mail.crt.state.vt.us
http://www.vermontjudiciary.org/courts/
    probate/index.htm
Sherry Britton, Register
(probate records from 1820 for all of Grand Isle
    County, including the towns of Alburg, Isle
    La Motte, Grand Isle, North Hero and South
    Hero)
no probate search service; copies of probate
    records: 10¢ each

Lamoille County
organized 1835 from Orleans and Chittenden
    counties

Lamoille County Clerk
(Main Street—location)
PO Box 303 (mailing address)
Hyde Park, VT 05655-0303
(802) 888-2207
Kathleen B. Hobart
(limited and badly indexed land records,
    naturalization records to the year transferred
    to Burlington and St. Albans)

Lamoille Probate District
PO Box 102
Hyde Park, VT 05655
(802) 888-3306
http://www.vermontjudiciary.org/courts/
    probate/index.htm
Doreen Blake, Register
(vital records [corrections only], probate records
    for all of Lamoille County, including the
    towns of Belvidere, Cambridge, Eden,
    Elmore, Hyde Park, Johnson, Morristown,
    Stowe, Waterville and Wolcott from 1837)
probate search service: no charge; copies of
    probate records: 25¢ per page, $1.00
    minimum

Orange County
organized 1781 from Windsor and Caledonia
    counties

Bradford Probate District
(consolidated into Orange District Probate
    Court)

Orange County Clerk
5 Court Street
Chelsea, VT 05038-9746
(802) 685-4610; (802) 685-3173 FAX
Emily Newman
(land records from 1771 to 1850 [most land
    records in Town Clerks' Offices])

Orange District Probate Court
5 Court Street
Chelsea, VT 05038
(802) 685-4610
http://www.vermontjudiciary.org/courts/
    probate/index.htm
Marilyn Newman, Register
(consolidated Randolph [organized 1781] and
    Bradford districts 1 June 1994; probate
    records for all of Orange County, including
    the towns of Bradford, Braintree, Brookfield,
    Chelsea, Corinth, Fairlee, Newbury, Orange,
    Randolph, Strafford, Thetford, Topsham,
    Tunbridge, Vershire, Washington, West
    Fairlee and Williamstown)

Randolph District Courthouse
(consolidated into Orange District Probate
    Court)

Orleans County
organized 1792, original county

Orleans County Clerk
247 Main Street

Newport, VT 05855
(802) 334-3344; (802) 334-4429 FAX
Laura Dolgin
(naturalization records to 1990)

Orleans Probate District
247 Main Street
Newport, VT 05855
(802) 334-3366
http://www.vermontjudiciary.org/courts/
    probate/index.htm
Lorraine Gray, Register
(probate records for all of Orleans County,
    including Newport City and the towns of
    Albany, Barton, Brownington, Charleston,
    Coventry, Craftsbury, Derby, Glover,
    Greensboro, Holland, Irasburg, Jay, Lowell,
    Morgan, Newport, Troy, Westfield and
    Westmore)
probate search service: varies; copies of probate
    records: 25¢ per page, $1.00 minimum for
    document of less than four pages

Rutland County
organized 1781, original county

Fair Haven Probate Court
3 North Park Place
Fair Haven, VT 05743
(802) 265-3380
http://www.vermontjudiciary.org/courts/
    probate/index.htm
Sheri C. Brown, Register
(probate records from 1797 for the towns of
    Benson, Castleton, Fair Haven, Hubbardton,
    Pawlet, Poultney, Sudbury, Wells and West
    Haven [remainder of Rutland County covered
    by Rutland Probate Court])
no probate search service; copies of probate
    records: 25¢ per page, $1.00 minimum

Rutland County Clerk
83 Center Street
Rutland, VT 05701-4017
(802) 775-4394
Gay S. Johnson

Rutland Probate Court
(83 Center Street—location)
PO Box 339 (mailing address)
Rutland, VT 05701-4017
(802) 775-0114; (802) 775-0115
http://www.vermontjudiciary.org/courts/
    probate/index.htm
Susan Burnett and Nanette Weir, Registers
(probate records for Rutland City and the towns
    of Brandon, Chittenden, Clarendon, Danby,
    Ira, Mendon, Middletown Springs, Mount
    Holly, Mount Tabor, Pittsfield, Pittsford,
    Proctor, Rutland, Sherburne, Shrewsbury,
    Tinmouth, Wallingford and West Rutland
    [remainder of Rutland County covered by
    Fair Haven Probate Court])
probate search service: no charge for check of
    index; copies of probate records: 25¢ per
    page, $1.00 minimum

Washington County
organized 1810 from Addison and Orange
    counties

Washington County Clerk
(65 State Street—location)
PO Box 426 (mailing address)
Montpelier, VT 05602-0426
(802) 223-2091
Claire Mee

Washington Probate District
(10 Elm Street #2—location)
PO Box 15 (mailing address)
Montpelier, VT 05601-0015
(802) 828-3405
http://www.vermontjudiciary.org/courts/
    probate/index.htm
Donna Murray, Register
(probate records for all of Washington County,
    including Barre City, City of Montpelier and
    the towns of Barre, Berlin, Cabot, Calais,
    Duxbury, East Montpelier, Fayston,

Marshfield, Middlesex, Moretown, Northfield,
    Plainfield, Roxbury, Waitsfield, Warren,
    Waterbury, Woodbury, and Worcester)
probate search service: no charge; copies of
    probate records: 25¢ per page

Windham County
organized 1779, original county

Marlboro Probate District
80 Flat Street, Suite 104
Brattleboro, VT 05302
(802) 257-2898
http://www.vermontjudiciary.org/courts/
    probate/index.htm
Susan Dunham, Register
(probate records for the towns of Brattleboro,
    Dover, Dummerston, Guilford, Halifax,
    Marlboro, Newfane, Stratton, Somerset,
    Vernon, Wardsboro, Whitingham and
    Wilmington [remainder of Windham County
    covered by Westminster District Probate
    Court])

Westminster District Probate Court
PO Box 47
Bellows Falls, VT 05101-0047
(802) 463-3019
http://www.vermontjudiciary.org/courts/
    probate/index.htm
Judith Lidie, Register
(district organized 1700s; probate records from
    the 1700s for the towns of Athens, Brookline,
    Grafton, Jamaica, Londonderry, Putney,
    Rockingham, Townshend, Westminster and
    Windham [remainder of Windham County
    covered by Marlboro Probate District])
probate search service: no charge; copies of
    probate records: 25¢ per page, $1.00
    minimum; "Fees must be paid in advance."

Windham County Clerk
(Route 30—location)
PO Box 207 (mailing address)
Newfane, VT 05345
(802) 365-7979
Larry C. Robinson

Windsor County
organized 1781, original county

The Hartford District Probate Court
(62 Pleasant Street—location)
PO Box 275 (mailing address)
Woodstock, VT 05091
(802) 457-1503
http://www.vermontjudiciary.org/courts/
    probate/index.htm
Donna G. Pearsons, Register
(estates, adoptions [confidential], trust,
    guardianships and change of names for the
    towns of Barnard, Bethel, Bridgewater,
    Hartford, Hartland, Norwich, Pomfret,
    Rochester, Royalton, Sharon, Stockbridge and
    Woodstock [remainder of Windsor County
    covered by Windsor District Probate Court])
probate search service: 25¢ per page, $1.00
    minimum

Windsor County Clerk
(12 The Green—location)
PO Box 458 (mailing address)
Woodstock, VT 05091-1212
(802) 457-2121
Jane E. Ammel

Windsor District Probate Court
(Route 106, Cota Fuel Building—location)
PO Box 402 (mailing address)
North Springfield, VT 05150-0402
(802) 886-2284
http://www.vermontjudiciary.org/courts/
    probate/index.htm
Brenda S. Neronsky, Register
(district organized 1763; corrections of birth,
    marriage or death certificates from Middlesex
    and Burlington; estates, guardianships,
    adoptions for the towns of Andover,
    Baltimore, Cavendish, Chester, Ludlow,
    Plymouth, Reading, Springfield,

Weathersfield, West Windsor, Weston and Windsor [remainder of Windsor County covered by The Hartford District Probate Court])

probate search service: no charge; copies of probate records: 25¢ per page, $1.00 minimum

VIRGINIA

Capital: Richmond. Statehood: 25 June 1788

Virginia has had independent cities since Williamsburg was chartered in 1722. As of 1980 they are now officially outside county boundaries. Three previously incorporated cities are now absorbed into counties: Manchester, formed 1874, merged into Richmond County in 1910; South Norfolk, formed 1921, merged with all of Norfolk County in 1962 to form the city of Chesapeake; Warwick, formed 1952 from all of Warwick County, merged into the city of Newport News in 1957. Also, Elizabeth City County merged with the city of Hampton in 1952, and Princess Anne County merged with the city of Virginia Beach in 1962.

Virginia's Juvenile and Domestic Relations Courts sit in all county seats and independent cities but are not courts of record. The District Courts hear some civil actions, plus misdemeanors, ordinance violations, traffic and felony preliminaries. First Judicial District: Chesapeake City; 2nd: Virginia Beach City; 2nd A: Accomack and Northampton cos.; 3rd: Portsmouth City; 4th: Norfolk City; 5th: Franklin and Suffolk cities & Isle of Wight and Southampton cos.; 6th: Emporia and Hopewell cities & Brunswick, Greensville, Prince George, Surry and Sussex cos.; 7th: Newport News City; 8th: Hampton City; 9th: Poquoson and Williamsburg cities & Charles City, Gloucester, James City, King and Queen, King William, Mathews, Middlesex, New Kent and York cos.; 10th: South Boston City & Appomattox, Buckingham, Charlotte, Cumberland, Halifax, Lunenburg, Mecklenburg and Prince Edward cos.; 11th: Petersburg and Amelia cities & Dinwiddie, Nottoway and Powhatan cos.; 12th: Colonial Heights City & Chesterfield County; 13th: Richmond City; 14th: Henrico County; 15th: Fredericksburg City & Caroline, Essex, Hanover, King George, Lancaster, Northumberland, Richmond, Spotsylvania, Stafford and Westmoreland cos.; 16th: Charlottesville and Albemarle City & Culpeper, Fluvanna, Goochland, Greene, Louisa, Madison and Orange cos.; 17th: Arlington County; 18th: Alexandria City; 19th: Falls Church and Fairfax cities & Fairfax County; 20th: Fauquier, Loudoun, and Rappahannock cos.; 21st: Martinsville City & Henry and Patrick cos.; 22nd: Danville City & Franklin and Pittsylvania cos.; 23rd: Roanoke and Salem cities & Roanoke County; 24th: Bedford and Lynchburg cities & Amherst, Bedford, Campbell and Nelson cos.; 25th: Buena Vista, Clifton Forge, Covington, Lexington, Staunton and Waynesboro cities & Alleghany, Augusta, Bath, Botetourt, Craig, Highland and Rockbridge cos.; 26th: Harrisonburg and Winchester cities & Clarke, Frederick, Page, Rockingham, Shenandoah and Warren cos.; 27th: Galax and Radford cities & Carroll, Floyd, Grayson, Montgomery, Pulaski and Wythe cos.; 28th: Bristol City & Smyth and Washington cos.; 29th: Bland, Buchanan, Dickenson, Giles, Russell and Tazewell cos.; 30th: Norton City & Lee, Scott and Wise cos.; 31st: Manassas and Manassas Park cities & Prince William County. The Circuit Court has general civil and criminal jurisdiction and sits in Judicial Circuits which are the same as the District Courts' Judicial Districts, except that the Second Circuit includes both the Second and Second A districts. The Court of Appeals and the Supreme Court hear appeals.

Accawmack County
(see Northampton County)

Accomack County
organized 1663 from Northampton County

Accomack County Clerk of the Circuit Court
(23316 Courthouse Avenue—location)
PO Box 126 (mailing address)
Accomac, VA 23301
(757) 787-3776; (757) 787-1849 FAX
SHCooper@courts.state.va.us
http://www.co.accomack.va.us/index2.html;
    http://www.courts.state.va.us/courts/circuit/
    Accomack/home.html
Samuel Cooper, Jr.
(land records, naturalization records, vital records, probate records)
no probate search service (contact Mrs. Mary Francis Carey, C.G., New Church, VA 23415, (804) 824-4615)

Albemarle County
organized 1744 from Goochland County

Albemarle County Clerk of the Circuit Court
501 East Jefferson Street, Court Square
Charlottesville, VA 22901
(434) 972-4083; (434) 293-0298 FAX
SMarshal@albemarle.org
http://www.albemarle.org;
    http://www.courts.state.va.us/courts/circuit/
    Albemarle/home.html
Shelby J. Marshall
(land records from 1744 to date, vital records from 1780 to date, probate records from 1744 to date)

Alexandria Clerk of the Circuit Court
Courthouse, 520 King Street
Alexandria, VA 22314
(703) 838-4044
ed.semonian@alexandriava.gov
http://www.courts.state.va.us/courts/circuit/Al
    exandria/home.html
Edward Semonian, Jr.
(land records from 1782, marriage licenses only from 1870, probate records from 1797)
no probate search service; copies of probate records: $1.00 for each of the first two pages and 50¢ for each additional page per document; "Some of the older books cannot be photocopied due to age; they must either be copied by hand or by using a camera."

Alleghany County
organized 1822 from Bath and Botetourt counties, Virginia, and Monroe County (now West Virginia)

Alleghany County Clerk of the Circuit Court
(266 West Main Street—location)
PO Box 670 (mailing address)
Covington, VA 24426-0670
(540) 965-1730; (540) 965-1732 FAX
dbyer@courts.state.va.us
http://www.co.alleghany.va.us;
    http://www.courts.state.va.us/courts/circuit/
    Alleghany/home.html
Debra N. Byer
(land records from 1822 [records include independent city of Covington], vital records from 1822 [records include independent city of Covington], probate records from 1822 [records include independent city of Covington])
no land or probate search service; copies of land and probate records: 50¢ per page; certified copies of vital records: $2.50 per page

Amelia County
organized 1734 from Brunswick and Prince George counties

Amelia County Clerk of the Circuit Court
PO Box 237
Amelia, VA 23002-0237
(804) 561-2128; (804) 561-6364 FAX
info@ameliava.com
http://www.ameliava.com;
    http://www.courts.state.va.us/courts/circuit/
    Amelia/home.html
Marilyn Wilson
(land records, vital records, probate records)

Amherst County Clerk of the Circuit Court
(113 Taylor Street—location)
PO Box 462 (mailing address)

Amherst, VA 24521
(434) 929-9321; (434) 946-9323 FAX
http://www.countyofamherst.com; http://www.
courts.state.va.us/courts/circuit/Amherst/
home.html
Roy C. Mayo III
(land records, marriages, probate records)
probate search service: no charge; copies of
probate records: $1.00 per page

Amherst County
organized 1761 from Albemarle County

Appomattox County
organized 1845 from Buckingham, Campbell,
Charlotte and Prince Edward counties

**Appomattox County Clerk of the Circuit
Court**
(Court Street—location)
PO Box 672 (mailing address)
Appomattox, VA 24522-0672
(434) 352-5275; (434) 352-2781 FAX
brwilliams@courts.state.va.us
http://www.appomattox.com; http://www.
courts.state.va.us/courts/circuit/
Appomattox/home.html
Barbara K. Williams
(land and probate records from 1892, marriages
from 1892)
no probate search service; copies of probate
records: 50¢ per page, no minimum; copies of
marriages: $5.00

Arlington County
Alexandria County organized 1801 from part of
the District of Columbia which had been
ceded by Virginia to the federal government
in 1791, being then part of Fairfax County; in
1846 the county was retroceded back to
Virginia, and the area was renamed Arlington
County in March 1920

Arlington County Clerk of the Circuit Court
1425 North Courthouse Road, Suite 6700
Arlington, VA 22201
(703) 228-4370
Circuit Court@arlingtonva.us
http://www.co.arlington.va.us;
http://www.courts.state.va.us/courts/circuit/
Arlington/home.html
David A. Bell

Augusta County
organized 1745 from Orange County

Augusta County Clerk of the Circuit Court
(1 East Johnson Street, Staunton, VA 24401—
location)
PO Box 689 (mailing address)
Staunton, VA 24402-0689
(540) 245-5321; (540) 245-5318 FAX
jbdavis@courts.state.va.us;
coadmin@co.augusta.va.us
http://www.co.augusta.va.us;
http://www.courts.state.va.us/courts/circuit/
Augusta/home.html
John B. Davis
(deeds from November 1745, land tax records
from 1786, survey books from 1745 to about
1840, naturalization records from 1790 to
1900 ([must be searched for], births and
deaths from 1853 to 1896, marriages from
1785, probate records from 1745)
probate search service: "Do not do extensive
searches—charge only for copies in brief
searches"; certified copies of marriages: an
additional $2.00 per record for certification;
copies of probate records: 50¢ per page, no
minimum

Bath County
organized 1790 from Augusta and Botetourt
counties, Virginia, and Greenbrier County
(now West Virginia)

Bath County Clerk of the Circuit Court
PO Box 180
Warm Springs, VA 24484-0180

(540) 839-7226; (540) 839-7248 FAX
DCarpenter@courts.state.va.us
http://www.bathcountyva.org;
http://www.courts.state.va.us/courts/circuit/
Bath/home.html
Darlene W. Carpenter
(land records from 1791, births from 1853 to
1950, deaths from 1853 to 1912, wills from
1791)
probate search service: depends on amount of
time involved; copies of probate records:
$1.00 for each of the first two pages and 50¢
for each additional page per instrument, no
minimum

City of Bedford Clerk of the Circuit Court
(see Bedford County Clerk of the Circuit Court)

Bedford County
organized 1753 from Albemarle and Lunenburg
counties

Bedford County Clerk of the Circuit Court
(County Administration Building, 122 East Main
Street, Suite 201—location)
PO Box 235 (mailing address)
Bedford, VA 24523
(540) 586-7632; (540) 586-6197
chogan@courts.state.va.us
http://www.co.bedford.va.us/index.asp;
http://www.courts.state.va.us/courts/circuit/
Bedford/home.html
Cathy C. Hogan
(deeds and probate records from 1754, births
from 1853, deaths from 1853, marriages from
1754)
probate search service: yes, but "We do not do
family history"; copies of land and probate
records: 50¢ per page, no minimum; copies of
vital records: $3.00 each

Bland County
organized 1861 from Giles, Tazewell and Wythe
counties

Bland County Clerk of the Circuit Court
PO Box 295
Bland, VA 24315-0295
(276) 688-4562; (276) 688-2438 FAX
dijohnson@courts.state.va.us
http://www.bland.org; http://www.courts.state.
va.us/courts/circuit/Bland/home.html
Rebecca I. "Becky" Johnson

Botetourt County
organized 1769 from Augusta and Rockbridge
counties

Botetourt County Clerk of the Circuit Court
(Courthouse, 1 West Main Street—location)
PO Box 219 (mailing address)
Fincastle, VA 24090-0219
(540) 473-8274; (540) 473-8209 FAX
tmoore@co.botetourt.va.us
http://www.co.botetourt.va.us;
http://www.courts.state.va.us/courts/circuit/
Botetourt/home.html
Tommy L. Moore, Clerk of Circuit Court
(land records from 1770, a few naturalization
records recorded in the Court Order Books,
births and deaths from 1853 to 1870,
marriages from 1770, Court Order and
Minute Books from 1770, Surveyor's Records
from 1799, probate records from 1770)
probate search service: no charge for cursory
search; copies of land and probate records:
50¢ per page, no minimum; copies of vital
records: $2.00 each

Bristol Clerk of the Circuit Court
Courthouse, 497 Cumberland
Bristol, VA 24201-4394
(276) 645-7321; (276) 821-6097 FAX
TRohr@courts.state.va.us
http://www.courts.state.va.us/courts/circuit/Br
istol/home.html
Terry G. Rohr

Brunswick County
organized 1732 from Prince George, Isle of

Wight and Surry counties

Brunswick County Clerk of the Circuit Court
Circuit Court of Brunswick County
216 North Main Street
Lawrenceville, VA 23868-0160
(434) 848-2215; (434) 848-4307 FAX
http://www.brunswickco.com;
http://www.courts.state.va.us/courts/circuit/
Brunswick/home.html
V. Earl Stanley, Jr., Clerk
(maps, survey plats from 1902, deed books from
1732, and deed of trust books, marriages from
1732, probate records from 1732)
no probate search service (must have at least
name(s), type of transaction and general time
period); copies of probate records: 50¢ each,
$1.00 minimum, plus SASE

Buchanan County
organized 1858 from Tazewell and Russell
counties

Buchanan County Clerk of the Circuit Court
(Courthouse—location)
PO Box 929 (mailing address)
Grundy, VA 24614
(276) 935-6567
http://www.buchanancounty.org;
http://www.courts.state.va.us/courts/circuit/
Buchanan/home.html
Beverly S. Tiller
(land records, naturalization records, vital
records, probate records)

Buckingham County
organized 1758 from Albemarle and
Appomattox counties

**Buckingham County Clerk of the Circuit
Court**
(Highway 60—location)
PO Box 107 (mailing address)
Buckingham, VA 23921
(434) 969-4734; (434) 969-2043 FAX
http://www.courts.state.va.us/courts/circuit/B
uckingham/home.html
Malcolm Booker, Jr.
(land and probate records from 1869, vital
records from 1869 to 1918)

Buena Vista Clerk of the Circuit Court
Municipal Building, 2039 Sycamore Avenue
Buena Vista, VA 24416-3123
(540) 261-8627; (540) 261-8625 FAX
ccoleman@courts.state.va.us
http://www.courts.state.va.us/courts/circuit/
Buena_Vista/home.html
Christopher W. Coleman

Campbell County
organized 1782 from Bedford County

Campbell County Clerk of the Circuit Court
(732 Village Highway—location)
PO Box 7 (mailing address)
Rustburg, VA 24588-0007
(434) 592-9517
http://www.co.campbell.va.us;
http://www.courts.state.va.us/courts/circuit/
Campbell/home.html
Deborah Hughes
(land records, vital records, probate records)
probate search service: no charge; copies of
probate records: $1.00 per page, no minimum

Caroline County
organized 1728 from Essex, King and Queen
and King William counties

Caroline County Clerk of the Circuit Court
(112 Courthouse Lane and Main Street, Suite
A—location)
PO Box 309 (mailing address)
Bowling Green, VA 22427-0309
(804) 633-5800
rcampbell@co.caroline.va.us
http://www.co.caroline.va.us;
http://www.courts.state.va.us/courts/circuit/
Caroline/home.html

Ray S. Campbell, Jr.

Carroll County
organized 1842 from Grayson and Patrick counties

Carroll County Clerk of the Circuit Court
(Governmental Center, 605 Pine Street, Suite A-230—location)
PO Box 218 (mailing address)
Hillsville, VA 24343-0218
(276) 730-3070; (276) 236-8008, ext. 3070; (276) 730-3071 FAX
choneycutt@courts.state.va.us
http://www.carrollcountyva.org;
    http://www.courts.state.va.us/courts/circuit/ Carroll/home.html
Carolyn H. Honeycutt

Charles City County
organized 1634, original county

Charles City County Clerk of the Circuit Court
(10780 Courthouse Road—location)
PO Box 86 (mailing address)
Charles City, VA 23030-0086
(804) 652-2105; (804) 652-2107; (804) 829-5647 FAX
http://co.charles-city.va.us;
    http://www.courts.state.va.us/courts/circuit/ Charles_City/home.html
Edith K. Holmes
(land records from 1789, vital records from 1850, probate records from 1790)
probate search service: no charge; copies of probate records: $1.00 per page, no minimum

Charlotte County
organized 1765 from Lunenburg County

Charlotte County Clerk of the Circuit Court
(115 LeGrande Avenue—location)
PO Box 38 (mailing address)
Charlotte Court House, VA 23923
(434) 542-5147; (434) 542-4336 FAX
http://www.co.charlotte.va.us/community_res. htm#courts; http://www.courts.state.va.us/ courts/circuit/Charlotte/home.html
Stuart B. Fallen
(deeds, marriages, and wills from 1765)
no probate search service ("we check will, deed, marriages for specific name and date"); copies of probate records: $1.00 per page, no minimum

Charlottesville Clerk of the Circuit Court
315 East High Street
Charlottesville, VA 22902
(434) 970-3766
http://www.charlottesville.org;
    http://www.courts.state.va.us/courts/circuit/ Charlottesville/home.html
Paul C. Garrett

City of Chesapeake Clerk of the Circuit Court
General District and Circuit Court Building
307 Albemarle Drive, Suite 300A
Chesapeake, VA 23322-5579
(757) 382-3000; (757) 382-3034 FAX
ccclerk@cityofchesapeake.net
http://www.chesapeake.va.us/services/depart/c ircourt/index.shtml
Faye W. Mitchell
(deeds from 1637, births from 1853 to 1917 [not complete], deaths from 1853 to 1917 and from 1870 to 1917 [not complete], marriage bonds from 1706 to 1850 [not complete], marriages from 1850 [not complete], wills from 1637 to 1755 and from 1756 [not complete])
probate search service: no charge; copies of probate records: 50¢ per page, $1.00 minimum; "Must send check or money order with request"

Chesterfield County
organized 1749 from Henrico County

Chesterfield County Circuit Court
(9500 Courthouse Road—location)
PO Box 125 (mailing address)
Chesterfield, VA 23832-0125
(804) 748-1209 (Record Room); (804) 748-1241 (Clerk); (804) 796-5625 FAX
circuitcourtclerk@chesterfield.gov;
    worthingtonj@chesterfield.gov
http://www.co.chesterfield.va.us;
    http://www.courts.state.va.us/courts/circuit/ Chesterfield/home.html
Judy L. Worthington
(land and probate records from 1749, marriages from 1771)
probate search service: no charge for a five-year span; copies of probate records: 50¢ per page, no minimum

Clarke County
organized 1836 from Frederick County

Clarke County Clerk of the Circuit Court
(102 North Church Street—location)
PO Box 189 (mailing address)
Berryville, VA 22611-0189
(540) 955-5116; (540) 955-0284 FAX
hbutts@courts.state.va.us
http://www.co.clarke.va.us;
    http://www.courts.state.va.us/courts/circuit/ Clarke/home.html
Helen Butts
(land records, marriages, probate records)

Town of Clifton Forge Clerk of the Circuit Court
PO Box 27
Clifton Forge, VA 24422-0027
(540) 863-5091
questions@cliftonforge.org
http://www.cliftonforge.org
(land records, marriages, and probate records from 1906)
no probate search service; copies of probate records: 50¢ per page, no minimum

Colonial Heights Clerk of the Circuit Court
(401 Temple Avenue—location)
PO Box 3401 (mailing address)
Colonial Heights, VA 23834
(804) 520-9364
Sstafford@courts.state.va.us
http://www.courts.state.va.us/courts/circuit/C olonial_Heights/home.html
Stacy L. Stafford
(land and probate records from 1 February 1961)
no probate search service; copies of probate records: 50¢ per page

Covington Clerk of the Circuit Court
(see Alleghany County Clerk of the Circuit Court)

Craig County
organized 1851 from Botetourt, Giles and Roanoke counties, Virginia, and Monroe County (now West Virginia)

Craig County Clerk of the Circuit Court
(Courthouse, 303 Main Street—location)
PO Box 185 (mailing address)
New Castle, VA 24127-0185
(540) 864-6141; (540) 864-7471 FAX
http://www.courts.state.va.us/courts/circuit/ Craig/home.html
Peggy A. Bostic
(land records from 1864, births and deaths from 1864 to 1896, probate records from 1851)
probate search service: no charge ("due to our small staff we can only do these as time allows"); copies of probate records: 50¢ per page

Culpeper County
organized 1748 from Orange County

Culpeper County Clerk of the Circuit Court
Courthouse Building
135 West Cameron Street, Suite 103
Culpeper, VA 22701-3097
(540) 727-3438
jcorbin@courts.state.va.us
http://www.culpepercounty.gov;
    http://www.courts.state.va.us/courts/circuit/ Culpeper/home.html
Janice J. Corbin
(land and probate records)

Cumberland County
organized 1749 from Goochland County

Cumberland County Clerk of the Circuit Court
PO Box 8
Cumberland, VA 23040
(804) 492-4442; (804) 492-4876 FAX
COwnby@courts.state.va.us
http://www.cumberlandva.com;
    http://www.courts.state.va.us/courts/circuit/ Cumberland/home.html
Carol Ownby
(land records from 1749, naturalization records from 1917 to 1925, births and deaths from 1853 to the 1880s [varies], marriages from 1749, probate records from 1749)
probate search service: no charge unless research is extensive; copies of probate records: 50¢ per page, no minimum

Danville Clerk of the Circuit Court
(401 Patton Street—location)
PO Box 3300 (mailing address)
Danville, VA 24543
(434) 799-5168; (434) 799-6502 FAX
ggibson@courts.state.va.us
http://www.danville-va.gov/officials.asp? menuid=2816&sub1menuid=2842
Gerald A. Gibson
(land records from 15 May 1841, marriage licenses only from 13 July 1841, probate records from 16 July 1857)
no land records search service; no vital records search service; no probate search service; copies of probate records: 50¢ per page, no minimum ("all records are open to the public")

Dickenson County
organized 1880 from Buchanan, Russell and Wise counties

Dickenson County Clerk of the Circuit Court
(Courthouse, Main Street, First Floor—location)
PO Box 190 (mailing address)
Clintwood, VA 24228-0190
(276) 926-1616; (276) 926-1617; (276) 926-6465 FAX
joe.tate@clerk.dcwin.org;
    jhtate@courts.state.va.us; clerkt@yahoo.com
http://www.dickensonctyva.com;
    http://www.courts.state.va.us/courts/circuit/ Dickenson/home.html
Joseph H. "Joe" Tate
(land records, marriage licenses and one book of old births and deaths, probate records)
no land, probate or vital records search service, but will look up records; copies: 50¢ per page, $2.00 for certification

Dinwiddie County
organized 1752 from Prince George County

Dinwiddie County Clerk of the Circuit Court
(Courthouse, 14008 Boydton Plank Road, Third Floor—location)
PO Box 63
Dinwiddie, VA 23841
(804) 469-4540; (804) 469-5383 FAX
http://www.dinwiddieva.us;
    http://www.courts.state.va.us/courts/circuit/ Dinwiddie/home.html
Annie Lee Williams
(land and probate records from 1833, naturalization records from 1903 to 1916, marriages, and a few births and deaths from 1865 to 1896)
no probate search service; copies of probate records: 25¢ per page, $2.00 for certified copies; copies of marriages: $3.00

Emporia Clerk of the Circuit Court
(see Greensville County Clerk of the Circuit
Court)

Essex County
organized 1692 from Old Rappahannock
County, which was organized 1656 from
Lancaster County and abolished 1692

Essex County Clerk of the Circuit Court
(305 Prince Street—location)
PO Box 445 (mailing address)
Tappahannock, VA 22560-0445
(804) 443-3541; (804) 443-4381; (804) 445-1216
FAX
gashworth@courts.state.va.us
http://www.essex-virginia.org;
http://www.courts.state.va.us/courts/circuit/
Essex/home.html
Gayle Ashworth
(deeds from 1656, births and deaths from 1853
to about 1912, marriages from 1804 to date,
wills from 1656)

City of Fairfax Clerk of the Circuit Court
(see Fairfax County Clerk of the Circuit Court)

Fairfax County
organized 1742 from Prince William and
Loudoun counties

Fairfax County Circuit Court Archives
Judicial Center, 4110 Chain Bridge Road, Level C
Fairfax, VA 22030-4009
(703) 246-4168 (Archives Section); (703) 246-
2770 (General
Information)john.frey@co.fairfax.va.us
arch@fairfaxcounty.gov
http://www.fairfaxcounty.gov/courts/circuit/ar
chives.htm
John Frey, Clerk of the Circuit Court
(land records from 1742 [some early years
missing], very spotty naturalization records
from 1785 to 1900, births, deaths and
marriages from 1853 [incomplete except for
marriages], probate records from 1742)
probate search service: no charge; copies of
probate records: 50¢ each, 25¢ each for
seniors and students, no minimum

Falls Church Clerk of the Circuit Court
(see Arlington County Clerk of the Circuit
Court)

Fauquier County
organized 1759 from Prince William County

Fauquier County Clerk of the Circuit Court
(29 Ashby Street—location)
PO Box 985 (mailing address)
Warrenton, VA 22186-0985
(703) 347-8610
clerk@fauquiercounty.gov
http://www.fauquiercounty.gov/government/d
epartments/circuitcourt
Gail Barb
(grantor/grantee indices from 1759, births and
deaths from 1853 to 1896 and 1913 to 1916,
marriages from 1759 ["Early official records
of births and deaths in Virginia are almost
nonexistent, as the recording was not required
by law; by an act passed in 1853, the state
required the recording of vital statistics; birth
records were not routinely filed during the
period 1896 to 1912"], probate records from
1759)
probate search service: no charge; copies of
probate records: $1.00 for each of the first
two pages and 50¢ for each additional page

Floyd County
organized 1831 from Montgomery and Franklin
counties

Floyd County Clerk of the Circuit Court
Courthouse, 100 East Main Street, Room 200
Floyd, VA 24091
(540) 745-9330; (540) 745-9303 FAX (Court
Work Only)
info@floydcova.org

http://www.floydcova.org/departments/circuit
_court.shtml
Wendell G. Peters
(land and probate records from 1831, births and
deaths from 1853 to 1873, marriages from
1831)
no probate search service (name provided for
private search); copies of land and probate
records: 50¢ per page; copies of vital statistics:
$2.50 each for marriages

Fluvanna County
organized 1777 from Albemarle County

Fluvanna County Clerk of the Circuit Court
(132 Main Street—location)
PO Box 550 (mailing address)
Palmyra, VA 22963
(434) 591-1970; (434) 591-1971 FAX
BPeterson@courts.state.va.us
http://www.co.fluvanna.va.us;
http://www.courts.state.va.us/courts/circuit/
Fluvanna/home.html
Bouson E. Peterson, Jr.
(land and probate records from 1777, births and
deaths from 1853 to 1896, marriages from
1777)
no probate search service; copies of probate
records: about $1.00 per page

Franklin Clerk of the Circuit Court
(see Southampton County Clerk of the Circuit
Court)

Franklin County
organized 1786 from Bedford, Henry and
Patrick counties

Franklin County Clerk of the Circuit Court
(275 South Main Street, Suite 280—location)
PO Box 567 (mailing address)
Rocky Mount, VA 24151
(540) 483-3065; (540) 483-3042 FAX
ahall@courts.state.va.us
http://www.franklincountyva.org;
http://www.courts.state.va.us/courts/circuit/
Franklin/home.html
Alice Hall
(land and probate records)
no land or probate search service (must give
book and page); copies of land and probate
records: $1.00 per page, $2.00 for certification

Frederick County
organized 1743 from Orange County

Frederick County Clerk of the Circuit Court
The Judicial Center
5 North Kent Street
Winchester, VA 22601
(540) 667-5770; (540) 545-8711
rhogan@courts.state.va.us
http://www.co.frederick.va.us;
http://www.winfredclerk.com
Rebecca P. Hogan
(land records from 1743, births from 1853 to
1912, deaths from 1853 to 1896, marriages
from 1782, wills from 1743)
no probate search service; copies of probate
records: 50¢ per page, no minimum; "We do
not do extensive research work or copying; if
they have Book and Page Numbers for one or
two instruments we will copy at a reasonable
rate; otherwise we refer to a local genealogist,
Rebecca H. Good, 30 West 13th Street, Front
Royal, VA 22630"

Fredericksburg Clerk of the Circuit Court
(815 Princess Anne Street—location)
PO Box 359 (mailing address)
Fredericksburg, VA 22404-0359
(540) 372-1066; (540) 310-0637
smitchell@courts.state.va.us
http://www.courts.state.va.us/courts/circuit/Fr
edericksburg/home.html
Sharron S. Mitchell, Clerk
(land records from 1782 [all loose papers are
sealed during reformatting and indexing
project], marriages from 1782, probate
records from 1782)

no probate search service (referred to local
researchers who charge for their services);
copies of probate records: 50¢ per page, no
minimum

Galax Clerk of the Circuit Court
(see Carroll or Grayson counties)

Giles County
organized 1806 from Montgomery, Tazewell and
Wythe counties, Virginia, and Monroe County
(now West Virginia)

Giles County Clerk of the Circuit Court
501 Wenonah Avenue
Pearisburg, VA 24134
(540) 921-1722; (540) 921-3825 FAX
http://www.gilescounty.org;
http://www.courts.state.va.us/courts/circuit/
Giles/home.html
Scarlet B. Ratcliffe
(deeds, etc., from 1806, births and deaths from
1855 to 1896, marriages from 1806, probate
records from 1806)
probate search service ("we do not have a
particular fee; research service limited due to
small size of staff"); copies of probate
records: 50¢ per page, no minimum

Gloucester County
organized 1651 from York County

Gloucester County Clerk of Circuit Court
7400 Justice Drive, Room 327
Gloucester, VA 23061
(804) 693-2502; (804) 693-0552 (Records
Room); (804) 693-2186 FAX
agentry@courts.state.va.us;
agentry@gloucesterva.info
http://www.co.gloucester.va.us;
http://www.courts.state.va.us/courts/circuit/
Gloucester/home.html
C. Ann Gentry
(land and probate records)
no probate search service; copies of probate
records: $1.00 per page

Goochland County
organized 1727 from Henrico County

**Goochland County Clerk of the Circuit
Court**
(2938 River Road West—location)
PO Box 196 (mailing address)
Goochland, VA 23063-0196
(804) 556-5353; (804) 556-4962 FAX
webmaster@co.goochland.va.us
http://www.co.goochland.va.us;
http://www.courts.state.va.us/courts/circuit/
Goochland/home.html
Lee G. Turner
(land records from 1728, probate records from
1728)
probate search service: $5.00; copies of probate
records: $1.00 per page, no minimum

Grayson County
organized 1793 from Wythe and Patrick
counties

Grayson County Clerk of the Circuit Court
(129 Davis Street, Independence, VA 24348-
9602—location)
PO Box 130 (mailing address)
Independence, VA 24348
(276) 773-2231; (276) 773-3338 FAX
http://www.graysoncountyva.com;
http://www.courts.state.va.us/courts/circuit/
Grayson/home.html
Charles T. Sturgill
(land and probate records and marriages from
1793)
no probate search service; copies of probate
records: 50¢ per page, $2.00 for certification

Greene County
organized 1838 from Orange County

Greene County Clerk of the Circuit Court
(22 Court Street, to the right of the courthouse

on Court Square—location)
PO Box 386 (mailing address)
Stanardsville, VA 22973-0386
(434) 985-5208; (434) 985-6723 FAX
webmaster@gcva.us
http://www.gcva.us;
 http://www.courts.state.va.us/courts/circuit/
 Greene/home.html
Marie C. Durrer
(land records from 1838 with Marie C. Durrer,
 Clerk, Circuit Court, PO Box 386,
 Stanardsville, VA 22973, births and deaths
 from 1838 to the late 1800s [not complete],
 marriage licenses from 1838 with Clerk,
 probate records from 1838 to the late 1800s,
 probate of wills from 1838 to date)
no records search service (must have complete
 names); copies of probate records: 50¢ per
 page

Greensville County
organized 1780 from Brunswick and Sussex
 counties

**Greensville County Clerk of the Circuit
Court**
(337 South Main Street, Emporia, VA 23847-
 2027—location)
PO Box 631 (mailing address)
Emporia, VA 23847-0631
(434) 348-4215; (434) 348-4020 FAX
http://www.greensvillecountyva.gov;
 http://www.courts.state.va.us/courts/circuit/
 Greensville/home.html
Robert C. Wrenn
(land and probate records, marriages)
probate search service: no charge; copies of
 probate records: $1.00 per page, no minimum

Halifax County
organized 1752 from Lunenburg County

Halifax County Clerk of the Circuit Court
(Main Street—location)
PO Box 729 (mailing address)
Halifax, VA 24558-0729
(434) 476-2141; (434) 476-6211; (434) 476-2890
 FAX
rconner@courts.state.va.us
http://www.oldhalifax.com;
 http://www.courts.state.va.us/courts/circuit/
 Halifax/home.html
Robert W. Conner, Jr.

City of Hampton Clerk of the Circuit Court
(101 King's Way Mall—location)
PO Box 40 (mailing address)
Hampton, VA 23669-0040
(757) 727-6105; (757) 728-3505 FAX
LSmith@courts.state.va.us
http://www.hampton.va.us;
 http://www.courts.state.va.us/courts/circuit/
 Hampton/home.html
Linda Batchelor Smith
(deeds from 1689 to 1699 [incomplete and not
 indexed] and from 1865 [complete],
 marriages, wills from 1689 to 1699
 [incomplete and not indexed], from 1701 to
 1859 [restored and indexed in 1968], and
 from 1865 [complet])
probate search service: no charge ("we do not
 research unindexed records prior to 1865");
 copies of probate records: $1.00 for each of
 the first two pages and 50¢ for each additional
 page, no minimum

Hanover County
organized 1720 from New Kent

Hanover County Clerk of the Circuit Court
Government Complex, 7497 County Complex
 Road
Hanover, VA 23069
(804) 365-6120
fhargrove@courts.state.va.us
http://www.co.hanover.va.us/circuitct/default.
 htm
Frank D. Hargrove, Jr.
(grantor and grantee inexes from 1865, deed

books from 1865 [deed books 1720–1865
 were burned in April 1865, except for 1733–
 1735 & 1783–1792], marriage records form
 1865, wills from 1865, chancery suit papers
 from 1832)

Harrisonburg Clerk of the Circuit Court
(see Rockingham County Clerk of the Circuit
 Court)

Henrico County
organized 1634, original county

Henrico County Clerk of the Circuit Court
(Government Center, 4301 East Parham and
 Hungary Spring Roads—location)
PO Box 27032 (mailing address)
Richmond, VA 23273-0001
(804) 501-5334 (Clerk); (804) 501-4202 (General
 Information)
smi22@co.henrico.va.us
http://www.co.henrico.va.us/clerk
Yvonne G. Smith
(deeds from 1781, marriages from 1900 to date,
 wills from 1781 to date)

Henry County
organized 1777 from Pittsylvania and Patrick
 counties

Henry County Clerk of the Circuit Court
3160 Kings Mountain Road, Suite B
Martinsville, VA 24112-3966
(276) 634-4880
vhelmstutler@courts.state.va.us
http://www.co.henry.va.us;
 http://www.courts.state.va.us/courts/circuit/
 Henry/home.html
Vickie Stone Helmstutler

Highland County
organized 1847 from Bath County, Virginia, and
 Pendleton County (now West Virginia)

Highland County Clerk of the Circuit Court
PO Box 190
Monterey, VA 24465
(540) 468-2447; (540) 468-3447 FAX
http://www.highlandcounty.org;
 http://www.courts.state.va.us/courts/circuit/
 Highland/home.html
Sue K. Dudley
(land and probate records, births from 1853 to
 1896 and from 1912 to 1917, deaths from
 1853 to 1870 and from 1912 to 1917,
 marriages from 1847)
probate search service: no charge; copies of
 probate records: $1.00 per page, no minimum

City of Hopewell Clerk of the Circuit Court
(100 East Broadway, Room 251—location)
PO Box 310 (mailing address)
Hopewell, VA 23860
(804) 541-2239; (804) 541-2438 FAX
krackley@courts.state.va.us
http://www.courts.state.va.us/courts/circuit/H
 opewell/home.html
Kay H. Rackley
(land and probate records from 1 July 1916)
probate search service: no charge; copies of
 probate records: $1.00 for the first page and
 50¢ for each additional page, plus SASE

Isle of Wight County
organized 1634 from Upper Norfolk (which was
 organized 1636 from New Norfolk County
 and renamed Nansemond County 1642/3);
 name changed from Warrossauosacke County
 in 1637

**Isle of Wight County Clerk of the Circuit
Court**
(17122 Monument Circle—location)
PO Box 110 (mailing address)
Isle of Wight, VA 23397
(757) 365-6233
http://www.co.isle-of-wight.va.us;
 http://www.courts.state.va.us/courts/circuit/
 Isle_of_Wight/home.html
William E. Laine, Jr.

(dees from the early 1700s, births 1853–1885,
 deaths 1853–1876, marriages vrom 1772, wills
 from the 1600s) and probate records,
 marriages)
no probate search service ("The Court Clerk
 does not have a research staff, however, if the
 person can provide the book and page
 number they will copy and send; the Court
 Clerk staff can assist in the location of a local
 genealogist"); copies of probate records: 50¢
 per page, no minimum

James City County
organized 1634, original county

**James City County/Williamsburg Clerk of
the Circuit Court**
5201 Monticello Avenue, Suite 6
Williamsburg, VA 23188-8218
(757) 564-2242; (757) 564-2329 FAX
bwoolridge@courts.state.va.us
http://www.jccegov.com/courts/index.html;
 http://www.courts.state.va.us/courts/circuit/
 James_City_County~Williamsburg/home.html
Betsy B. Woolridge

King and Queen County
organized 1691 from New Kent County

**King and Queen County Clerk of the Circuit
Court**
(234 Allen's Circle—location)
PO Box 67 (mailing address)
King and Queen Courthouse, VA 23085-0067
(804) 785-5984; (804) 769-5010; (804) 785-5698
 FAX; (804) 769-5081 FAX
DLongest@courts.state.va.us
http://www.kingandqueenco.net;
 http://www.courts.state.va.us/courts/circuit/
 King_and_Queen/home.html
Deborah F. Longest
(land and probate records from 1864 ["all
 records prior to 1865 destroyed by fire"])
no probate search service; copies of probate
 records: $1.00 per page, $1.00 minimum

King George County
organized 1721 from Richmond and
 Westmoreland counties

**King George County Clerk of the Circuit
Court**
9483 Kings Highway, Suite 3
King George, VA 22485-3444
(703) 775-3322
CMason@courts.state.va.us
http://www.king-george.va.us;
 http://www.courts.state.va.us/courts/circuit/
 King_George/home.html
Charles V. Mason
(land and probate records from 1721, very few,
 scattered vital records
probate search service: no charge; copies of
 probate records: 50¢ per page, $2.00
 minimum

King William County
organized 1702 from King and Queen County

**King William County Clerk of the Circuit
Court**
PO Box 216
King William, VA 23086-0216
(804) 769-4936; (804) 769-4937; (804) 769-4938;
 (804) 769-4991 FAX
pnorman@courts.state.va.us
http://www.co.king-william.va.us; http://www.
 kingwilliamva.com; http://www.courts.state.
 va.us/courts/circuit/King_William/home.html
Patricia M. Norman
(land and probate records from 1885 [date of
 courthouse fire])
no land or probate search service

Lancaster County
organized 1651 from York and Northumberland
 counties

Lancaster County Clerk of the Circuit Court

PO Box 99
Lancaster, VA 22503
(804) 462-5611; (804) 462-9978 FAX
ckennedy@lancova.com
http://www.lancova.com;
   http://www.courts.state.va.us/courts/circuit/
   Lancaster/home.html
Constance Kennedy

Lee County
organized 1793 from Russell and Scott counties

Lee County Clerk of the Circuit Court
PO Box 326
Jonesville, VA 24263-0326
(276) 346-7763; (276) 346-3440 FAX
banderson@courts.state.va.us
http://www.leecountyvirginia.com;
   http://www.courts.state.va.us/courts/circuit/
   Lee/home.html
Beverly R. Anderson
(land records from 1793, vital records from 1857
   to 1875, probate records from 1793)
probate search service: $10.00; copies of probate
   records: 25¢ per page, no minimum

Lexington Clerk of the Circuit Court
(see Rockbridge County Clerk of the Circuit
   Court)

Loudoun County
organized 1757 from Fairfax County

Loudoun County Clerk of the Circuit Court
(18 East Market Street—location)
PO Box 550 (mailing address)
Leesburg, VA 22075-0550
(703) 777-0270; (703) 777-0376 FAX
circuitclerk@loudoun.gov
http://www.co.loudoun.va.us;
   http://www.courts.state.va.us/courts/circuit/
   Loudoun/home.html
Gary M. Clemens
(land records, very few naturalization records
   from the early to mid-1800s [unindexed],
   probate records)
no records search service (must have full name
   and time period; "I know of one individual
   who is a member of the Historical Society,
   who may be willing to do some research: Mrs.
   Mary Fishback, 20 North Street, N.E.,
   Leesburg, VA 22075"); copies of probate
   records: 50¢ per page, no minimum

Louisa County
organized 1742 from Hanover County

Louisa County Clerk of the Circuit Court
(100 West Main Street—location)
PO Box 37 (mailing address)
Louisa, VA 23093-0037
(540) 967-5312; (540) 967-2705 FAX
SHopkins@courts.state.va.us
http://www.courts.state.va.us/courts/circuit/L
   ouisa/home.html
Susan R. Hopkins

Lunenburg County
organized 1746 from Brunswick County

**Lunenburg County Clerk of the Circuit
Court**
11435 Courthouse Road
Lunenburg, VA 23952
(434) 696-2132; (434) 696-3931 FAX
info@lunenburgva.org
http://lunenburgva.org;
   http://www.courts.state.va.us/courts/circuit/
   Lunenburg/home.html
Gordon F. Erby
(land records, only one or two Orders of
   Naturalization on record in the Order Books,
   vital records, probate records)

Lynchburg Clerk of the Circuit Court
(900 Court Street—location)
PO Box 4 (mailing address)
Lynchburg, VA 24505-0004
(434) 455-2620; (434) 847-1864 FAX
LPalmer@courts.state.va.us

http://www.courts.state.va.us/courts/circuit/
   Lynchburg/home.html
Larry B. Palmer
(land and probate records, marriages and
   divorces only [no births and deaths])
no probate search service; copies of probate
   records: 50¢ per page, $2.00 for certification,
   no minimum

Madison County
organized 1793 from Culpeper County

Madison County Clerk of the Circuit Court
(1 Main Street—location)
PO Box 220 (mailing address)
Madison, VA 22727
(540) 948-6888; (540) 948-3759 FAX
cwatts@courts.state.va.us
http://www.madisonco.virginia.gov;
   http://www.courts.state.va.us/courts/circuit/
   Madison/home.html
Caroline Watts
(land and probate records and marriages from
   1793)
no probate search service ("We refer all requests
   to local genealogist")

Manassas Clerk of the Circuit Court
(see Prince William County Clerk of the Circuit
   Court)

Manassas Park Clerk of the Circuit Court
(see Prince William County Clerk of the Circuit
   Court)

Martinsville Clerk of the Circuit Court
(55 West Church Street—location)
PO Box 1206 (mailing address)
Martinsville, VA 24114-1206
(276) 403-5106; (276) 403-5232 FAX
APritchett@courts.state.va.us
http://www.courts.state.va.us/courts/circuit/M
   artinsville/home.html
Ashby R. Pritchett

Mathews County
organized 1791 from Gloucester County

Mathews County Clerk of the Circuit Court
(10622 Buckley Hall Road—location)
PO Box 463 (mailing address)
Mathews, VA 23109
(804) 725-2550
ecallis@co.mathews.va.us
http://www.co.mathews.va.us;
   http://www.courts.state.va.us/courts/circuit/
   Mathews/home.html
E. Eugene Callis III

Mecklenburg County
organized 1765 from Lunenburg County

**Mecklenburg County Clerk of the Circuit
Court**
PO Box 530
Boydton, VA 23917-0530
(434) 738-6191, ext. 4222; (434) 738-6861 FAX
ecoleman@courts.state.va.us
http://www.mecklenburgva.com;
   http://www.courts.state.va.us/courts/circuit/
   Mecklenburg/home.html
E. E. Coleman, Jr.

Middlesex County
organized 1673 from Lancaster County

Middlesex County Clerk of the Circuit Court
(Courthouse, Routes 17 & 33—location)
PO Box 158 (mailing address)
Saluda, VA 23149
(804) 758-5317; (804) 758-8637 FAX
pwalton@courts.state.va.us
http://www.co.middlesex.va.us/middlesex_cou
   nty_constitutional_.htm;
   http://www.courts.state.va.us/courts/circuit/
   Middlesex/home.html
Peggy W. Walton
(land records from 1675, marriages from 1742,
   probate records from 1674 with County
   Research Department)

probate search service: $1.00 per name; copies
   of probate records: $1.00 for each of the first
   two pages and 50¢ for each additional page;
   $1.00 minimum

Montgomery County
organized 1777 from Fincastle (organized 1772
   from Botetourt County and abolished 1777),
   Botetourt and Pulaski counties

Montgomery County Circuit Court
(1 East Main Street, Suite B-5—location)
PO Box 6309 (mailing address)
Christiansburg, VA 24068-6309
(540) 382-5760; (540) 382-6937 FAX
Aburke@courts.state.va.us; aburke@naxs.com
http://www.montva.com;
   http://www.courts.state.va.us/courts/circuit/
   Montgomery/home.html
Allan C. Burke
(land records from 1773 to date, vital records
   from 1853 to 1868 only, probate records from
   1773 to date)
no detailed land or vital records searches or a lot
   of requests at one time; no probate search
   service (contact Dorothy S. Kessler, PO Box
   67, Fincastle, VA 24090); copies of probate
   records: 50¢ per page

Nelson County
organized 1808 from Amherst County

Nelson County Clerk of the Circuit Court
(84 Courthouse Square, First Floor—location)
PO Box 10 (mailing address)
Lovingston, VA 22949-0010
(434) 263-7020; (434) 263-7027 FAX
http://www.nelsoncounty.com;
   http://www.courts.state.va.us/courts/circuit/
   Nelson/home.html
Judy Stevens Smythers

New Kent County
organized 1654 from York and James City
   counties

New Kent County Clerk of the Circuit Court
(Courthouse, 12001 Courthouse Circle—
   location)
PO Box 98 (mailing address)
New Kent, VA 23124-0098
(804) 966-9520; (804) 966-9528 FAX
http://www.courts.state.va.us/courts/circuit/N
   ew_Kent/home.html
Karen A. Butler
(land and probate records and deaths and
   marriages from 1865)
no probate search service; copies of probate
   records: 50¢ per page, no minimum
   ("Payment must be received before copies are
   mailed")

Newport News Clerk of the Circuit Court
(Courthouse Building, 2500 Washington Avenue
Newport News, VA 23607-4307
(757) 926-8561; (757) 926-8531 FAX
city@nngov.com
http://www.newport-news.va.us;
   http://www.courts.state.va.us/courts/circuit/
   Newport_News/home.html
Rex A. Davis
(land and probate records from 1863 [date of
   fire], marriages from 1863)

Norfolk Clerk of the Circuit Court
100 St. Paul's Boulevard
Norfolk, VA 23510
(757) 664-4580
GSchaefer@courts.state.va.us
http://www.courts.state.va.us/courts/circuit/N
   orfolk/home.html
George E. Schaefer

Northampton County
organized 1634, original county; name changed
   from Accawmack County 1642/3

**Northampton County Clerk of the Circuit
Court**
(5229 The Hornes—location)

PO Box 36 (mailing address)
Eastville, VA 23347-0036
(757) 678-0465; (757) 678-5410 FAX
tljohnson@courts.state.va.us
http://www.co.northampton.va.us;
    http://www.courts.state.va.us/courts/circuit/
    Northampton/home.html
Ms. Traci L. Johnson
(land records and records)
probate search service: no charge, time
    permitting; copies of probate records: 50¢ per
    page

Northumberland County
organized 1648 from Chickacoun Indian District

**Northumberland County Clerk of the Circuit
Court**
(39 Judicial Place—location)
PO Box 217 (mailing address)
Heathsville, VA 22473-0217
(804) 580-3700; (804) 580-2261 FAX
http://www.co.northumberland.va.us;
    http://www.courts.state.va.us/courts/circuit/
    Northumberland/home.html
Linda L. Booth
(deeds from 1650 [from 1672 to 1706 missing
    unless re-recorded and from 1729 to 1738
    missing], land tax from 1850, some early
    births [and a few deaths] of the St. Stephens
    parish from 1661 to 1810, no births of the
    Wicomico parish for this period, births from
    1853 to 1896, deaths from 1861 to 1895,
    some marriages from 1735 to 1795, marriage
    bonds from 1783 to 1850, unindexed register
    of minister's returns from 1850 to 1853,
    marriages from 1854, probate records from
    1650 [with some missing years as land
    records]), naturalization records: denizations
    [in Colonial era] in order books)
copies: $1.00 per page if envelope and postage
    are sent, no minimum; "Please send an
    envelope, self-addressed, large enough to
    include all records requested; include
    sufficient postage; since the General Index for
    both wills and deeds does not commence
    until 1750, one must know the Record Book
    and page in requesting documents before
    1750; in requesting documents after 1750,
    give full name and approximate dates; for
    those requesting genealogical research, they
    will be given names of genealogists to
    contact."

City of Norton Clerk of the Circuit Court
(see Wise County/Norton City Clerk of the
    Circuit Court)

Nottoway County
organized 1789 from Amelia County

Nottoway County Clerk of the Circuit Court
(328 West Courthouse Road—location)
PO Box 25 (mailing address)
Nottoway, VA 23955-0025
(434) 645-9043; (434) 645-2201 FAX
clerking@meckcom.net
http://www.nottoway.org/home.shtml;
    http://www.courts.state.va.us/courts/circuit/
    Nottoway/home.html
Jane L. Brown
(land and probate records from 1789 to 1842
    and from 1865)
probate search service: $5.00; copies of probate
    records: $1.00 per page, no minimum

Orange County
organized 1734 from Spotsylvania County

Orange County Clerk of the Circuit Court
110 North Madison Road, Suite 3
PO Box 230
Orange, VA 22960
(540) 672-4030; (540) 672-2939 FAX
http://www.orangecova.com;
    http://www.courts.state.va.us/courts/circuit/
    Orange/home.html
Linda S. Timmons
(land and probate records from 1734, marriages

from 1857)
no probate search service; copies of probate
    records: 50¢ per page, no minimum

Page County
organized 1831 from Rockingham and
    Shenandoah counties

Page County Circuit Court
116 South Court Street, Suite A
Luray, VA 22835-1224
(540) 743-4064; (540) 743-6902; (540) 743-2338
    FAX
clerkwilson@hotmail.com
http://www.co.page.va.us;
    http://www.courts.state.va.us/courts/circuit/
    Page/home.html
C. R. Wilson
(land records, probate records)
no land or probate records search service: copies
    of land and probate records: 50¢ per page

Patrick County
organized 1791 from Henry County

Patrick County Clerk of the Circuit Court
(101 West Blue Ridge Street—location)
PO Box 148 (mailing address)
Stuart, VA 24171-0148
(276) 694-7213; (276) 694-6943 FAX
sgasperini@courts.state.va.us
http://www.co.patrick.va.us;
    http://www.courts.state.va.us/courts/circuit/
    Patrick/home.html
Susan C. Gasperini
(land and probate records from 1791, births
    from 1853 to 1896, deaths from 1853 to 1870,
    marriages from 1791)
no probate search service; copies of probate
    records: 50¢ per page, additional fee for
    certified copies

Petersburg Clerk of the Circuit Court
7 Courthouse Avenue
Petersburg, VA 23803
(804) 733-2367; (804) 732-5548 FAX
BScott@courts.state.va.us
http://www.courts.state.va.us/courts/circuit/Pe
    tersburg/home.html
Benjamin O. Scott

Pittsylvania County
organized 1767 from Halifax County

**Pittsylvania County Clerk of the Circuit
Court**
(3 North Main Street—location)
PO Drawer 31 (mailing address)
Chatham, VA 24531-0031
(434) 432-7887; (434) 432-7913 FAX
HfHaymore@courts.state.va.us
http://www.pittgov.org/home.htm;
    http://www.courts.state.va.us/courts/circuit/
    Pittsylvania/home.html
H. F. Haymore, Jr.

Poquoson Clerk of the Circuit Court
(see York County-Poquoson Clerk of the Circuit
    Court)

Portsmouth Clerk of the Circuit Court
(601 Crawford Street, Portsmouth, VA 23704—
    location)
PO Box 1217 (mailing address)
Portsmouth, VA 23705-1217
(757) 393-8671
CMorrison@courts.state.va.us
http://www.courts.state.va.us/courts/circuit/P
    ortsmouth/home.html
Cynthia P. Morrison
(land records, vital records, probate records)
copies: 50¢ per page, no restrictions

Powhatan County
organized 1777 from Cumberland and
    Chesterfield counties

Powhatan County Clerk of the Circuit Court
(Courthouse Complex, 3834 Old Buckingham
    Road, Suite C, Powhatan, VA 23139-7019—

location)
PO Box 37 (mailing address)
Powhatan, VA 23139-0037
(804) 598-5660; (804) 598-5608 FAX
wmaxey@courts.state.va.us
http://www.powhatanva.gov;
    http://www.courts.state.va.us/courts/circuit/
    Powhatan/home.html
William E. Maxey, Jr.

Prince Edward County
organized 1754 from Amelia County

**Prince Edward County Clerk of the Circuit
Court**
(111 South Street, Second Floor—location)
PO Box 304 (mailing address)
Farmville, VA 23901-0304
(434) 392-5145; (434) 392-3913 FAX
meppes@courts.state.va.us
http://www.co.prince-edward.va.us;
    http://www.courts.state.va.us/courts/circuit/
    Prince_Edward/home.html
Machelle J. Eppes

Prince George County
organized 1703 from Charles City County

**Prince George County Clerk of the Circuit
Court**
(6601 Courts Drive—location)
PO Box 98 (mailing address)
Prince George, VA 23875-0098
(804) 733-2640; (804) 861-5721 FAX
bknott@courts.state.va.us
http://www.princegeorgeva.org;
    http://www.courts.state.va.us/courts/circuit/
    Prince_George/home.html
Bishop Knott, Jr.
(land records from 1710 to 1728, from 1787 to
    1792, and from 1842 to date, naturalization
    records, vital records, probate records)

Prince William County
organized 1731 from King George and Stafford
    counties

**Prince William County Clerk of the Circuit
Court**
(Judicial Center, 9311 Lee Avenue, Third Floor,
    Suite 302, Manassas, VA 20110—location)
PO Box 191 (mailing address)
Prince William, VA 22110
(703) 335-6015
http://www.pwcgov.org/default.aspx?topic=04
    0017
Wendy Jones, Acting Clerk of the Circuit Court
(deeds from 1731, marriages from 1859, and
    probate records from 1731)
probate search service: $10.00; copies of probate
    records: 50¢ per page, no minimum

Pulaski County
organized 1839 from Montgomery and Wythe
    counties

Pulaski County Clerk of the Circuit Court
45 Third Street, NW, Suite 101
Pulaski, VA 24301
(540) 980-7825; (540) 980-7835 FAX
http://www.pulaskicounty.org;
    http://www.courts.state.va.us/courts/circuit/
    Pulaski/home.html
Maetta H. Crewe
(land and probate records from 1839, births and
    deaths from 1853 to 1933, marriages from
    1854 to 1933)
no probate search service; copies of marriages:
    $2.00; copies of probate records: $1.00 per
    page, no minimum

Radford Clerk of the Circuit Court
619 Second Street, West
Radford, VA 24141-1431
(540) 731-3610; (540) 731-3612 FAX
zclerk@yahoo.com
http://www.courts.state.va.us/courts/circuit/R
    dford/home.html
Zelda S. Vaughn
(land records from 1892, marriage licenses [if

obtained licenses in Radford, if living in Radford at the time], probate records)
no probate search service; copies of probate records: 50¢ per page

Rappahannock County

organized 1833 from Culpeper County (not to be confused with Old Rappahannock County, with county seat at Lancaster, which was organized 1656 from Lancaster County and abolished 1692)

Rappahannock County Clerk of the Circuit Court
(238 Gay Street—location)
PO Box 517 (mailing address)
Washington, VA 22747-0517
(540) 675-5350; (540) 675-5351 FAX
ldbruce@courts.state.va.us; dbruce@summit.net
http://www.rappahannockcountyva.gov;
    http://www.courts.state.va.us/courts/circuit/
    Rappahannock/home.html
Diane Bruce
(land records, a few births and deaths [1850s and 1890s], marriage licenses from 1833, probate records from 1833)
no probate search service

Richmond Clerk of the Circuit Court
John Marshall Courts Building
400 East Marshall Street
Richmond, VA 23219
(804) 646-6505; (804) 646-6562 FAX
Bevill.Dean@Richmondgov.com
http://www.ci.richmond.va.us;
    http://www.courts.state.va.us/courts/circuit/
    Richmond/home.html
Bevill M. Dean
(land and probate records)

Richmond County

organized 1692 from Old Rappahannock County, which was organized 1656 from Lancaster County and abolished 1692

Richmond County Clerk of the Circuit Court
(101 Court Street—location)
PO Box 1000 (mailing address)
Warsaw, VA 22572
(804) 333-3781; (804) 333-5396 FAX
rforrester@courts.state.va.us
http://www.co.richmond.va.us;
    http://www.courts.state.va.us/courts/circuit/
    Richmond/home.html
Rosa S. Forrester
(land records from 1692, vital records: Church registers from 1672 to 1800 includes births, deaths and marriages, probate records from 1699)
probate search service: refer to State Library; copies of probate records: 50¢ to 75¢ per page, $1.00 minimum plus SASE

Roanoke Clerk of the Circuit Court
315 Church Avenue, S.W.
Roanoke, VA 24016
(540) 853-6702 (Civil Division); (540) 853-6723 (Criminal Division); (540) 853-6711 (Estates); (540) 853-1024 FAX
brenda.hamilton@roanokeva.gov
http://www.roanokeva.gov/WebMgmt/
    ywbase61b.nsf/DocName/$circlerk
Brenda S. Hamilton

Roanoke County

organized 1838 from Botetourt and Montgomery counties

Roanoke County Clerk of the Circuit Court
(Courthouse, 305 East Main Street, Room 200—location)
PO Box 1126 (mailing address)
Salem, VA 24153-1126
(540) 387-6205; (540) 387-6145 FAX
smcgraw@roanokecountyva.gov;
    smcgraw@co.roanoke.va.us
http://www.roanokecountyva.gov/Departments/
    CircuitCourtClerksOffice/Default.htm
Steven A. McGraw, Sr.
(land records, marriages but no deaths, probate

records)
probate search service: $5.00; copies of probate records: 50¢ per page, no minimum ("all record searches must be in writing; with a limited staff there may be delays in responding to the search requests")

Rockbridge County

organized 1778 from Augusta and Botetourt counties

Rockbridge County Clerk of the Circuit Court
Courthouse Square
2 South Main Street
Lexington, VA 24450
(540) 463-2644; (540) 463-2232; (540) 463-3850 FAX
dbpatterson@courts.state.va.us
http://www.co.rockbridge.va.us;
    http://www.courts.state.va.us/courts/circuit/
    Rockbridge/home.html
D. Bruce Patterson
(land records from 1778 to date, some naturalizations recorded in an old order book [unsure of the number], births from 1853 to 1896 [very limited], deaths from 1853 to 1870 [very limited], marriages from 1778 to date, probate records from 1778 to date)
no land or probate search service ("we do not have manpower to do general index searches for land records, etc. Our office is not staffed to do genealogical research; we will assist persons who come to our office but can answer mailed requests only when time allows [usually during summer months]; requests for copywork received through the mail must be accompanied by SASE and should request specific documents"); copies: $1.00 for each of the first two pages and 50¢ for each additional page, no minimum

Rockingham County

organized 1778 from Augusta County

Rockingham County Clerk of the Circuit Court
Court Square
Harrisonburg, VA 22801
(540) 564-3111; (540) 564-3126 (Land Records); (540) 564-3118 (Criminal Division); (540) 564-3124 (Probate, Genealogy); (540) 564-3114 (Civil Division)
wharper@rockinghamcountyva.gov
http://www.rockinghamcountyva.gov/showpag
    e.aspx?PageID=137
L. Wayne Harper
(land and probate records from 1778)
no probate search service; copies of probate records: 50¢ each, no minimum

Russell County

organized 1786 from Washington County

Russell County Clerk of the Circuit Court
(Main Street—location)
PO Box 435 (mailing address)
Lebanon, VA 24266-0435
(276) 889-8023; (276) 889-8003 FAX
dollie_compton@yahoo.com
http://www.courts.state.va.us/courts/circuit/R
    ussell/home.html
Dollie M. Compton

Salem Clerk of the Circuit Court
PO Box 891
Salem, VA 24153-0891
(540) 375-3067; (540) 375-4039 FAX
CCrawford@courts.state.va.us
http://www.courts.state.va.us/courts/circuit/
    Salem/home.html
Chance Crawford
(land, probate, and vital records from 1968)

Scott County

organized 1814 from Lee, Russell and Washington counties

Scott County Clerk of the Circuit Court
104 East Jackson Street, Suite 2

Gate City, VA 24251
(276) 386-3801; (276) 386-2430 FAX
http://www.scottcircuitclerk.com
Mark A. "Bo" Taylor

Shenandoah County

organized 1772 from Frederick County; name changed from Dunmore County in 1778

Shenandoah County Clerk of the Circuit Court
(112 South Main Street—location)
PO Box 406 (mailing address)
Woodstock, VA 22664-0406
(540) 459-6150; (540) 459-6155 FAX
info@shenandoahcountyva.us
http://www.shenandoahcountyva.us;
    http://www.courts.state.va.us/courts/circuit/
    Shenandoah/home.html
Denise F. Barb
(land records from 1772 to date, births and deaths from 1853 to 1869 [some years missing], marriages from 1772 to date ["We can do certification of marriages on record in indexes"; originals filed at Virginia State Library and Archives; copies from microfilm available from Shenandoah County Historical Society]; probate records from 1772 to date from Research Team)
probate search service: $5.00 per search (includes up to five copies from Will Book A-F only); copies of probate records: $1.00 each

Smyth County

organized 1832 from Washington and Wythe counties

Smyth County Clerk of the Circuit Court
109 West Main Street, Room 144
Marion, VA 24354
(276) 782-4044; (276) 782-4045 FAX
http://www.smythcounty.org;
    http://www.courts.state.va.us/courts/circuit/
    Smyth/home.html
Jimmy L. Warren
(land and probate records)
probate search service: $15.00 per hour; copies of probate records: $1.00 per page, $2.00 minimum

South Boston Clerk of the Circuit Court
(see Halifax County Clerk of the Circuit Court)

Southampton County

organized 1749 from Isle of Wight and Nansemond counties

Southampton County Clerk of the Circuit Court
(22350 Main Street—location)
PO Box 190 (mailing address)
Courtland, VA 23837
(757) 653-2200
WCosby@courts.state.va.us
http://www.southamptoncounty.org;
    http://www.courts.state.va.us/courts/circuit/
    Southampton/home.html
Wayne M. Cosby

Spotsylvania County

organized 1721 from Essex, King and Queen and King William counties

Spotsylvania County Clerk of the Circuit Court
(9115 Courthouse Road—location)
PO Box 96 (mailing address)
Spotsylvania, VA 22553-0096
(540) 507-7600; (540) 582-2169 FAX
spotsyclerk@aol.com
http://www.spotsylvania.va.us;
    http://www.courts.state.va.us/courts/circuit/
    Spotsylvania/home.html
Paul M. Metzger
(land records, naturalization records, vital records, probate records)

Stafford County

organized 1664 from Westmoreland County

Stafford County Circuit Court Clerk
(Judicial Center, 1300 Courthouse Road, Second Floor—location)
PO Box 69 (mailing address)
Stafford, VA 22555
(540) 659-8750; (540) 658-8752 (Lnd Records); (540) 658-4640 FAX
bdecatur@co.stafford.va.us
http://www.co.stafford.va.us/Departments/Courts_&_Legal_Services/Index.shtml
Barbara Decatur
(land and probate records [mostly post-war; for pre-war records, contact Virginia State Library and Archives])

Staunton Clerk of the Circuit Court
(113 East Beverley Street, Third Floor—location)
PO Box 1286 (mailing address)
Staunton, VA 24402-1286
(540) 332-3874; (540) 332-3970 FAX; (540) 851-4029 FAX
customer_relations@ci.staunton.va.us
http://www.staunton.va.us;
http://www.courts.state.va.us/courts/circuit/Staunton/home.html
Thomas E. Roberts
(land and probate records from 1802, some old births and deaths from 1853 to 1898)

Suffolk Clerk of the Circuit Court
441 Market Street
Suffolk, VA 23434-5237
(757) 923-2251; (757) 538-3204 FAX
WRCarter@courts.state.va.us
http://www.courts.state.va.us/courts/circuit/Suffolk/home.html
W. R. Carter, Jr.

Surry County
organized 1652 from James City County

Surry County Clerk of the Circuit Court
(203 Church Street, Routes 10 and 31—location)
PO Box 203 (mailing address)
Surry, VA 23883-0203
(757) 294-3161; (757) 294-0471 FAX
GClayton@courts.state.va.us
http://www.surrycounty.govoffice2.com;
http://www.courts.state.va.us/courts/circuit/Surry/home.html
Gail P. Clayton

Sussex County
organized 1754 from Surry County

Sussex County Clerk of the Circuit Court
(15088 Courthouse Road, Route 735—location)
PO Box 1337 (mailing address)
Sussex, VA 23884-0337
(434) 246-1012; (434) 246-5511, ext. 1012; (434) 246-2203 FAX
http://www.courts.state.va.us/courts/circuit/Sussex/home.html
Gary M. Williams
(deeds from 1754, naturalization records interspersed in court minutes [not readily available], births and deaths from 1853 to 1869 and 1892 to 1896, marriages from 1754, probate records from 1754)
probate search service: generally no charge; copies of vital records: $3.00 for marriages; copies of probate records: $1.00 for each of the first two pages and 50¢ for each additional page, no minimum; "A limit of five archival records per customer copied at one time"

Tazewell County
organized 1800 from Logan, Russell, Washington and Wythe counties

Tazewell County Clerk of the Circuit Court
(Courthouse, 101 West Main Street—location)
PO Box 968 (mailing address)
Tazewell, VA 24651-0968
(276) 988-1222; (276) 988-7501 FAX
bblevins@courts.state.va.us
http://www.tazewellcounty.org;
http://www.courts.state.va.us/courts/circuit/Tazewell/home.html

James E. "Buddy" Blevins
(deeds and wills from 1800, births and deaths from 1853 to 1870, marriages from 1800)
no probate search service; copies of probate records: $1.00 for each of the first two pages and 50¢ for each additional page per document; "Office employees are forbidden to do index searches"

Upper Norfolk County
(see City of Suffolk and Isle of Wight County)

Virginia Beach Circuit Court Clerk's Office
Virginia Beach Judicial Center, Building 10B
2425 Nimmo Parkway, Third Floor
Virginia Beach, VA 23456
(757) 427-4181
pio@vbgov.com (Public Information)
http://www.vbgov.com/vgn.aspx?dept_list=d47c7e192ca49010VgnVCM100000870b640aRCRD&x=11&y=9
Tina E. Sinnen
(land and probate records from 1691 to date, marriage licenses from 1821 to date)

Warren County
organized 1836 from Frederick and Shenandoah counties

Warren County Circuit Court
1 East Main Street
Front Royal, VA 22630-3382
(540) 635-2435; (540) 636-3274 FAX
jsims@courts.state.va.us
http://www.warrencountyva.net;
http://www.courts.state.va.us/courts/circuit/Warren/home.html
Jennifer R. Sims
(land records from 1836, vital records from 1836 to 1895, probate records from 1836)
no probate search service; copies of probate records: 50¢ per page, $1.00 minimum

Washington County
organized 1777 from Fincastle (organized 1772 from Botetourt County and abolished 1777) and Montgomery counties

Washington County Circuit Court
(Courthouse, 191 East Main Street—location)
PO Box 289 (mailing address)
Abingdon, VA 24212-0289
(276) 676-6224; (276) 676-6226; (276) 676-6218 FAX
washcocirct@naxs.com;
tphipps@courts.state.va.us
http://www.washcova.com/wps/portal;
http://www.courts.state.va.us/courts/circuit/Washington/home.html
Patricia S. Phipps
(land records from about 1778, marriages, probate records from 1778)
no probate search service ("we prefer you get a genealogist to do the research"); copies of probate records: 50¢ per page, $1.00 for certified copies, 50¢ minimum

Westmoreland County
organized 1653 from Northumberland County

Westmoreland County Clerk of the Circuit Court
(Courthouse—location)
PO Box 307 (mailing address)
Montross, VA 22520-0307
(804) 493-0108; (804) 493-0393 FAX
http://www.courts.state.va.us/courts/circuit/Westmoreland/home.html
Gwynne J. Chatham
(land records from 1653, naturalization records ["We may have some but do not know dates"], births and deaths from 1855 to 1895, wills from 1653)
probate search service ("we usually don't charge to look, but for copies"); copies of probate records: $2.00 for each of the first four pages and 50¢ for each additional page, $2.00 minimum; "We do research when we have

time, so there may be a delay in getting an answer because we haven't had the time to look it up"

Williamsburg Clerk of the Circuit Court
(see James City County/Williamsburg Clerk of the Circuit Court)

Winchester Clerk of the Circuit Court
The Judicial Center
5 North Kent Street
Winchester, VA 22601-5037
(540) 667-5770; (540) 667-6638 FAX
dlpayne@courts.state.va.us
http://www.winfredclerk.com
Terry H. Whittle
(land records from 1790, marriages from 1790 [very incomplete until 1853, complete from 1866], probate records from 1790)
no probate search service; copies of probate records: 50¢ per page, no minimum ("we will copy pages of specific requests when name, book and page number given; to have individual research done, contact Historical Society")

Wise County
organized 1856 from Lee, Russell and Scott counties

Wise County/Norton City Clerk of the Circuit Court
(206 East Main Street, Room 245—location)
PO Box 1248 (mailing address)
Wise, VA 24293-1248
(276) 328-6111
clerk@courtbar.org
http://www.wisecounty.org;
http://www.courtbar.org
Jack Kennedy
(deeds, marriages, and probate records)
no probate search service; copies of probate records: 50¢ per page

Wythe County
organized 1790 from Montgomery and Grayson counties

Wythe County Clerk of the Circuit Court
Circuit Court Building, 225 South Fourth Street, Room 105
Wytheville, VA 24382
(276) 223-6050; (276) 223-6057 FAX
HHorney@courts.state.va.us
http://www.wytheco.org;
http://www.courts.state.va.us/courts/circuit/Wythe/home.html
Hayden H. Horney
(land records from 1790, only one Birth and Death Record Book ["starts 1853 for a span of about 10 to 12 years"], probate records from 1790)
no land, naturalization, or probate records search service (contact Mary B. Kegley, PO Box 134, Wytheville, VA 24382 or Mrs. W. T. Trevillian, 665 West Washington Street, Wytheville, VA 24382); copies of probate records: $1.00 per page from large-format, early books, 50¢ per page from small books

York County
organized 1634, original county; name changed from Charles River County in 1642

York County- Poquoson Clerk of the Circuit Court
(300 Ballard Street—location)
PO Box 371
Yorktown, VA 23690
(757) 890-3350
http://www.yorkcounty.gov/circuitcourt
Ms. Lynn S. Jenkins

Capital: Olympia. Statehood: 11 November 1889 (territory organized 2 March 1853 out of Oregon Territory, including the present-day states of Washington, Idaho and Montana, west of the Rockies)

Washington has some 136 Municipal and Police Courts with limited jurisdiction over municipal ordinance violations. Seventy-one District Courts, having jurisdiction over some civil actions, small claims, misdemeanors, traffic and felony preliminaries, serve Washington's thirty-nine counties, sitting in each county seat and elsewhere. Those District Courts which are the only one in their county sit at the county seat and are named after the county; for example, Asotin District Court in Asotin County. The following counties have more than one District Court within their boundaries: Adams County: Othello and Ritzville District Courts; Clallam County: Clallam District Courts No. 1 (at Port Angeles) and No. 2 (at Forks); Douglas County: Douglas (at East Wenatchee) and Bridgeport Branch District Courts; Grays Harbor County: Grays Harbor District Courts No. 1 (at Montesano) and No. 2 (at Aberdeen); King County: Airport (at Seattle), Aukeen (at Auburn), Bellevue, Federal Way, Issaquah, Mercer Island, Northeast King (at Redmond), Renton, Roxbury (at Seattle), Seattle, Shoreline (at Seattle) and Vashon Island District Courts; Kittitas County: Lower Kittitas (at Ellensburg) and Upper Kittitas (at Cle Elum) District Courts; Klickitat County: East Klickitat (at Goldendale) and West Klickitat (at White Salmon); Pacific County: North Pacific (at South Bend) and South Pacific (at Long Beach) District Courts; Pierce County: Pierce District Courts No. 1 (at Tacoma), No. 2 (at Gig Harbor), No. 3 (at Eatonville) and No. 4 (at Buckley); Snohomish County: Cascade (at Arlington), Everett, Evergreen (at Monroe) and South Snohomish (at Lynwood) District Courts; Spokane County: Cheney, Deer Park, Millwood (at Spokane) and Spokane District Courts; Walla Walla County: College Place and Walla Walla District Courts; Whitman County: Whitman (at Colfax) and Pullman Branch District Courts; Yakima County: Sunnyside, Toppenish and Yakima District Courts.

Superior Court sits at each county seat and has general jurisdiction over all civil matters except small claims, probate, divorce, criminal and juvenile matters. Seven of the thirty judicial districts include more than one county: Asotin-Columbia-Garfield, Benton-Franklin, Chelan-Douglas, Ferry-Pend Oreille-Stevens, Island-San Juan, Klickitat-Skamania and Pacific-Wahkiakum. The Court of Appeals and Supreme Court hear appeals.

Adams County
organized 1883 from Whitman County

Adams County Courthouse
210 West Broadway
Ritzville, WA 99169-1860
(509) 659-3247 (Auditor); (509) 659-3257 (Clerk, PO Box 187); (509) 659-3254 FAX (Auditor); (509) 659-0118 FAX (Clerk)
NancyM@co.adams.wa.us
http://www.co.adams.wa.us
Nancy McBroom, County Auditor; Susan K. Kirkendall, County Clerk and Superior Court Clerk
(land records from 1879 to date with County Auditor, births and deaths from 1891 to 1907 with County Auditor, probate records and naturalization records with County Clerk)
land and probate search service: $8.00 per hour; copies of land and probate records: $1.00 each, $3.00 for certified copies

Asotin County
organized 1883 from Garfield County

Asotin County Courthouse
135 Second Street
Asotin, WA 99402-0159
(509) 243-2016 (Assessor, PO Box 69); (509) 243-4978 (Clerk, PO Box 159); (509) 243-2099 FAX (Assessor); (509) 243-2081 FAX (Clerk)
arogers@co.asotin.wa.us; l_hough_acriver@yahoo.com
http://www.co.asotin.wa.us
Anthony Rogers, County Assessor; Linda Hough, County Clerk-Superior Court
(land records with Assessor, probate records with Clerk)
probate search service: $8.00 per hour; copies of probate records: statutory fee

Benton County
organized 1855, original county

Benton County Courthouse
620 Market Street
Prosser, WA 99350-0190
(509) 786-2046 (Assessor); (509) 786-5624 (Clerk)
barb.wagner@co.benton.wa.us; kay.staples@co.benton.wa.us
http://www.co.benton.wa.us
Barbara Wagner, County Assessor; Ms. Josie Delvin, County Clerk

Chehalis County
(see Grays Harabor County)

Chelan County
organized 1899 from Kittitas and Okanogan counties

Chelan County Law and Justice Building
350 Orondo Street
Wenatchee, WA 98801
(509) 667-6365 (Assessor); (509) 667-6380 (Clerk, Fifth Level, PO Box 3025); (509) 667-6664 FAX
assessor@co.chelan.wa.us; russ.griffith@co.chelan.wa.us; SuperiorCourt.Clerk@co.chelan.wa.us; siri.a.woods@co.chelan.wa.us
http://www.co.chelan.wa.us
Russell Griffith, County Assessor; Siri Woods, County Clerk and Superior Court Clerk
(land records only as awarded through litigation, adoptions [confidential], probate records from 1900)
probate search service: $20.00 minimum; copies of probate records: $2.00 for the first page and $1.00 for each additional page, $2.00 minimum

Clallam County
organized 1854 from Jefferson County

Clallam County Courthouse
223 East Fourth Street
Port Angeles, WA 98362-3098
(360) 417-2222 (Auditor, Suite 1); (360) 417-2231 (Clerk); (360) 417-2517 FAX (Auditor)
auditor@co.clallam.wa.us; mlingvall@co.clallam.wa.us; web_clerk@co.clallam.wa.us
http://www.clallam.net
Patty Rosand, Auditor; Mollie Lingvall, County Clerk and Superior Court Clerk
(deeds with Auditor, naturalization records with County Clerk, births, deaths and marriages to 1907 [not complete] with Auditor, probate records with County Clerk)
probate search service: $8.00 per hour; copies of probate records: $2.00 for the first page and $1.00 for each additional page

Clark County
organized 1845, original county

Clark County Clerk
(1200 Franklin Street—location)
PO Box 5000 (mailing address)
Vancouver, WA 98666-5000
(206) 699-2292
countyclerk@clark.wa.gov

http://www.clark.wa.gov/courts/clerk/access-records.html
Sherry W. Parker, County Clerk; Teri A. Nielsen, Chief Deputy Clerk
(naturalization records and probate records)
probate search service: $8.00; copies of probate records: $2.00 for the first page and $1.00 for each additional page; "If papers leave Clerk's office they need to be certified"

Columbia County
organized 1875 from Walla Walla County

Columbia County Courthouse
341 East Main Street
Dayton, WA 99328-1361
(509) 382-4541 (Auditor, Suite 2); (509) 382-4321 (Clerks); (509) 382-4830 FAX (Auditor)
sharon_richter@co.columbia.wa.us
http://wei.secstate.wa.gov/WEI/Colubmia (Auditor)
Sharon Richter, Auditor and County Clerk
(land records from 1864 with Auditor, naturalization records from 1875 to 1942 [index only], births and deaths from July 1891 to July 1906 with Auditor, probate records from 1875 with Clerks)
probate search service: $20.00 per hour, $8.00 minimum; copies of probate records: $1.00 per page

Cowlitz County
organized 1854, original county

Cowlitz County Clerk
Hall of Justice
312 S.W. First Street, Room 233
Kelso, WA 98626-1798
(360) 577-3016
http://www.co.cowlitz.wa.us/clerk
Roni A. Booth, County Clerk and Clerk of Superior Court
(index to wills from 6 December 1878, probate fee book from 13 February 1894)
probate search service: $20.00 per hour, $10.00 per name minimum (especially for pre-1925 records); copies of probate records: $1.00 per page, $1.00 for certification of pleadings

Douglas County
organized 1883 from Lincoln County

Douglas County Courthouse
213 South Rainier
PO Box 516
Waterville, WA 98858-0516
(509) 745-8527 (Auditor, PO Box 456); (509) 745-8529 (Clerk); (509) 745-8812 FAX (Auditor)
tduvall@co.douglas.wa.us; jkoch@co.douglas.wa.us
http://www.douglascountywa.net
Thad Duvall, County Auditor; Juanita Koch, County Clerk and Clerk of Superior Court
(land records, probate records)
probate search service: $8.00 per hour; copies of probate records: $2.00 for the first page and $1.00 for each additional page

Ferry County
organized 1899 from Stevens County

Ferry County Courthouse
(350 East Delaware Avenue—location)
PO Box 498 (mailing address)
Republic, WA 99166-0498
(509) 775-5200 (Auditor); (509) 775-5245 (Clerk); (509) 775-5208 FAX (Auditor)
auditor@co.ferry.wa.us; ferryclerks@hotmail.com
http://www.ferry-county.com
Clydene V. Bolinger, County Auditor; Jean Bremner-Booher, County Clerk
(land records from 1898 with Auditor's Office, naturalization records from 1920 to 1930 only with Clerk, marriages from 1898 with Auditor's Office, probate records with Clerk's Office)
land, vital, and probate records search service:

$8.00 per hour; copies of land and vital records: $1.00 per page, $2.00 for certification; copies of probate records: 50¢ per page, no minimum

Franklin County
organized 1883 from Whitman County

Franklin County Courthouse
1016 North Fourth Avenue
Pasco, WA 99301-3706
(509) 545-3536 (Auditor, Main Floor, PO Box 1451); (509) 545-3525 (Clerk, Room 306); (509) 545-2243 FAX (Clerk)
zlenhart@co.franklin.wa.us;
mkkillian@co.franklin.wa.us
http://www.co.franklin.wa.us
Zona Lenhart, County Auditor; Michael J. "Mike" Killian, County Clerk

Garfield County
organized 1881 from Columbia County

Garfield County Courthouse
Pomeroy, WA 99347
(509) 843-1411 (Auditor, PO Box 278); (509) 843-3731 (Clerk, PO Box 915); (509) 843-3941 FAX (Auditor); (509) 843-1224 FAX (Clerk)
ddeal@co.garfield.wa.us;
superiorcourt@co.garfield.wa.us
http://www.wacounties.org/waco/county/garvield.html;
http://www.palouse.org/garfield.htm
Donna J. Deal, County Auditor; Linda Bartels, County Clerk and Clerk of Superior Court
(land records with Auditor, naturalization records with Clerk, births from 1891 to 1952, deaths from 1891 to 1955 with Auditor, probate records from 1882 with Clerk)
probate search service: no charge; copies of probate records: 25¢ per page

Grays Harbor County
organized 1855, original county; name changed from Chehalis County in 1915

Grays Harbor County Clerk
102 West Broadway
Montesano, WA 98563
(360) 249-3842; (306) 249-6381 FAX
cherylb@co.grays-harbor.wa.us
http://www.co.grays-harbor.wa.us/info/clerk/index.htm
Cheryl Brown, County Clerk and Clerk of Superior Court
(probate records from 1856 [microfilm used])
no probate search service; copies of probate records: $2.00 for the first page and $1.00 for each additional page, $8.00 minimum for written report

Grays Harbor County Courthouse
(100 West Broadway—location)
PO Box 590 (mailing address)
Montesano, WA 98563-0590
(360) 249-4121 (Assessor, Suite 21); (360) 249-4232 (County Auditor, Suite 2); (306) 249-3330 FAX (Auditor)
eprkut@co.grays-harbor.wa.us;
vspatz@co.grays-harbor.wa.us
http://www.co.grays-harbor.wa.us
Cherri Rose-Konschu, County Assessor; Vern Spatz, County Auditor
(current land ownership records, but no history of ownership with Assessor, chain of title with County Auditor)
no land records search service (contact Coast Title and Escrow, Inc., 211 East Market Street, Aberdeen 98520)

Grant County
organized 24 February 1909 from Douglas County

Grant County Law and Justice Center
(35 C Street NW—location)
PO Box 37 (mailing address)
Ephrata, WA 98823-0037
(509) 754-2011 (Main number); (509) 754-2011, ext. 430 or 630 (Clerk, Room 218); (509) 754-6098 FAX
bvarney@grantcounty-wa.com;
lgrammer@co.grant.wa.us;
kallen@grantcounty-wa.com
http://www.co.grant.wa.us
Bill Varney, County Auditor; Laure Grammer, County Assessor; Kimberly A. Allen, County Clerk and Clerk of Superior Court
(deeds, etc. with Auditor's Office, land records with County Assessor, naturalization records with Clerk, vital records with County Health District, marriage licenses with Auditor, probate records with Clerk)
probate search service: $8.00 per hour per name; copies of probate records: $2.00 for the first page and $1.00 for each additional page, no minimum

Island County
organized 1854, original county

Island County Courthouse
(1 NE Seventh Street—location)
PO Box 5000 (mailing address)
Coupeville, WA 98239
(360) 679-7366 (Auditor); (360) 679-7303 (Assessor); (360) 679-7359 (Clerk); (360) 240-5553 FAX (Auditor); (360) 240-5565 FAX (Assessor)
suzannes@co.island.wa.us;
sharonf@co.island.wa.us
http://www.islandcounty.net
Suzanne Sinclair, County Auditor; Tom Baenen, County Assessor; Sharon Franzen, County Clerk
(land records with Auditor/Assessor/Treasurer, probate records with Clerk)
probate search service: $20.00 per hour; copies of probate records: $2.00 for the first page and $1.00 for each additional page per document ("no personal checks")

Jefferson County
organized 1854, original county

Jefferson County Courthouse
1820 Jefferson Street
Port Townsend, WA 98368
(360) 385-9105 (Assessor, PO Box 1220); (360) 385-9116 (Auditor, PO Box 563); (360) 385-9125 (Superior Court, PO Box 1220); (360) 385-9197 FAX (Assessor); (360) 385-9228 FAX (Auditor); (360) 385-5672 FAX (Superior Court)
jwesterman@co.jefferson.wa.us;
deldridge@co.jefferson.wa.us
http://www.co.jefferson.wa.us
Jack Westerman III, County Assessor; Donna M. Eldridge, County Auditor; Ruth Gordon, County Clerk and Clerk of Superior Court
(land records with Assessor, naturalization records from 1854 to September 1906 with County Clerk, births and deaths to 1907 with Auditor, probate records with Superior Court)
probate search service: $8.00 per hour; copies of probate records: $1.00 for the first page and 50¢ for each additional page, $2.00 for the first certified page and $1.00 for each additional certified page, $8.00 minimum

King County
organized 1852, original county

King County Superior Court Clerk's Office
Seattle Courthouse
516 Third Avenue
Seattle, WA 98104
(206) 296-9300
clerksofficecustomerservice@metrokc.gov
http://www.metrokc.gov/kcscc
Barbara Miner, Director and Superior Court Clerk
(probate records)
no probate search service; copies of probate records: $2.00 for the first page and $1.00 for each additional page ("correspondence requests: $8.00")

Kitsap County
organized 1857 from Jefferson County

Kitsap County Courthouse
614 Division Street
Port Orchard, WA 98366-4614
(360) 337-7160 (Assessor, MS-22); (360) 876-7164 (Clerk, MS-34)
personal-roperty@co.kitsap.wa.us;
javery@co.kitsap.wa.us;
dpeterso@co.kitsap.wa.us
http://www.kitsapgov.com/assr/pp/p_prop.htm; http://www.kitsapgov.com/clerk/default.htm
Jim Avery, County Assessor; Dave Peterson, County Clerk
(land records with Assessor, probate records with County Clerk)
probate search service: $8.00; copies of probate records: $1.00 per page, $2.00 per document for certification, no minimum

Kittitas County
organized 1883 from Yakima County

Kittitas County Courthouse
205 West Fifth Avenue
Ellensburg, WA 98926-2887
(509) 962-7501 (Assessor, Suite 101); (509) 962-7504 (Auditor, Suite 105); (509) 962-7531 (Clerk, Suite 210); (509) 962-7666 FAX (Assessor); (509) 962-7687 FAX (Auditor); (509) 962-7667 FAX (Clerk)
assessors@co.kittitas.wa.us; auditor@co.kittitas.wa.us; clerk@co.kittitas.wa.us; joyce@co.kittitas.wa.us
http://www.co.kittitas.wa.us
Marsha Weyand, County Assessor; Jerry V. Pettit, County Auditor; Joyce Julsrud, County Clerk and Clerk of Superior Court
(land records Appraisals of land with Assessor, land ownership, deeds, plats, surveys with Auditor, naturalization records from 1889 with Clerk, vital records with Auditor, probate records from 1889 with Clerk)
probate search service: $8.00 per hour; copies of probate records: $1.00 per page

Klickitat County
organized 1859, original county (or from Clark County)

Klickitat County Courthouse
205 South Columbus Avenue
Goldendale, WA 98620-9286
(509) 773-4001 (Auditor, Room 203, MS-CH-2); (509) 773-5744 (County Clerk, Room 204, MS-CH-3); (509) 773-4244 FAX (Auditor)
brendas@co.klickitat.wa.us;
saundraol@co.klickitat.wa.us
http://www.klickitatcounty.org
Brenda Sorensen, County Auditor; Saundra Olson, County Clerk
(land records from 1866 with Nancy J. Evans, Auditor, Room 203, naturalization records from March 1889 to 1906 with County Clerk's Office, Room 204, births from 1882 to July 1907, deaths from 1891 to 12 March 1907, marriages with Auditor, probate records from January 1880 with Clerk's Office)
land, vital, and probate records search service: $8.00 per hour; copies of land records: $1.00 per page, $3.00 for certified copies; copies of vital records: $3.00 each; copies of probate records: $2.00 for the first page and $1.00 for each additional page, $3.00 for the first certified page and $1.00 for each additional certified page, no minimum

Lewis County
organized 1845, original county

Lewis County Courthouse
344 West Main
Chehalis, WA 98532-1922
(360) 740-1156 (Auditor); (800) 562-6130 (Auditor); (360) 740-1163 (Recording Department)
https://fortress.2a.gov/lewisco/home/LC/

Default.aspx
Gary E. Zandell, County Auditor; Kathy Brack, County Clerk
(land records Plats, surveys with Gary E. Zandell, Auditor, 351 N.W. North Street, PO Box 29, Chehalis, WA 98532-0029, births and deaths before 1 June 1907 with Auditor, marriage licenses with Recording Department, Auditor's Office, births and deaths from 1954 to date with County Health Department, 360 N.W. North Street, Chehalis, WA 98532, probate records with Donna Karvia, County Clerk, 360 N.W. North Street, Chehalis, WA 98532)
land records search service: $8.00 per name; copies of land records: $1.00 per page, $2.00 per document for certification; copies of vital records: $11.00 each

Lincoln County
organized 1883 from Spokane County

Lincoln County Courthouse
450 Logan Street
Davenport, WA 99122-9501
(509) 725-4971 (Auditor, PO Box 28); (509) 725-7011 (Assessor, PO Box 400); (509) 725-1401 (Clerk, PO Box 68); (509) 725-0820 FAX (Auditor); (509) 725-1150 FAX (Clerk)
sjohnston@co.lincoln.wa.us;
ffreeze@co.lincoln.wa.us;
psemprimoznik@co.lincoln.wa.us
http://www.co.lincoln.wa.us
Shelly Johnston, County Auditor; Jon F. "Frosty" Freeze, County Assessor; Peggy Semprimoznik, County Clerk
(naturalization records and probate records with County Clerk's Office)
probate search service: $8.00 per hour, $4.00 minimum; copies of probate records: 25¢ per page, $2.00 for certified documents plus $1.00 per page

Mason County
organized 1854 from Thurston County; name changed from Sawanish County in 1864

Mason County Clerk
(419 North Fourth Street—location)
PO Box 340 (mailing address)
Shelton, WA 98584
(360) 427-9670, ext. 422
pms@co.mason.wa.us
http://www.co.mason.wa.us
Pat Swartos
(probate records from 1890)
probate search service: $8.00 per hour, $4.00 minimum; copies of probate records: $2.00 for the first page and $1.00 for each additional page plus SASE, no minimum

Okanogan County
organized 2 February 1888 from the west part of Stevens County

Okanogan County Courthouse
149 Third North
Okanogan, WA 98840
(509) 422-7190 (Assessor, Room 202, PO Box 152); (509) 422-7240 (Auditor, Room 104, PO Box 1010); (509) 422-7275 (Clerk); (509) 422-7163 FAX (Auditor)
assessor@co.okanogan.wa.us;
sfurman@co.okanogan.wa.us;
jbradley@co.okanogan.wa.us
http://www.okanogancounty.org
Scott D. Furman, County Assessor; Laurie K. Thomas, County Auditor; Jackie Bradley, County Clerk
(land records in County Assessor's Office, some naturalization records [none after 1976] with the County Clerk, probate records from 1895 with the County Clerk)
probate search service: $8.00 per hour; copies of probate records: 50¢ per page, no minimum

Pacific County
organized 1854, original county

Pacific County Courthouse
300 Memorial Drive
South Bend, WA 98586
(360) 875-9315 (Auditor, PO Box 97); (360) 875-9301 (Assessor, PO Box 86); (360) 875-9320 (Clerk, PO Box 67); (360) 875-9333 FAX (Auditor); (360) 875-9321 FAX (Clerk)
pgardner@co.pacific.wa.us;
assessor@co.pacific.wa.usbwalker@co.pacific.wa.us; vleach@co.pacific.wa.us
http://www.co.pacific.wa.us
Pat Gardner, County Auditor; Bruce Walker, County Assessor; Virginia Leach, County Clerk

Pend Oreille County
organized 1911 from Stevens County

Pend Oreille County Clerk
(229 South Garden—location)
PO Box 5020 (mailing address)
Newport, WA 99156-5020
(509) 447-2435; (509) 447-2734 FAX
townbey@pendoreille.org
http://w.co.pend-oreille.wa.us/District%20Court/superior%20court%20index.htm
Tammie A. Ownbey, County Clerk and Clerk of Superior Court
(probate records)
copies of probate records: $2.00 for the first page and $1.00 for each additional page, no minimum

Pend Oreille County Courthouse
625 West Fourth Street
Newport, WA 99156-5015
(509) 447-3185 (Auditor, PO Box 5075); (509) 447-4312 (Assessor, PO Box 5010); (509) 447-2475 FAX (Auditor); (509) 447-0318 FAX (Assessor)
mnichols@pendoreille.org;
jwalker@pendoreille.org
http://www.co.pend-oreille.wa.us
Marianne Nichols, County Auditor; Janet Walker, County Assessor
(information concerning land with Assessor's Office, statutory warranty deeds, quit claim deeds, easements, agreements, plats, liens, mortgages, UCCs, patent records, quartz locations, mining locations, lis pendens and water right locations with Auditor, marriages with Auditor)
records search service from Auditor: $8.00 per hour; copies of land records: $1.00 per page, $2.00 per document for certification, $5.00 for the first page of surveys or plats and $3.00 for each additional page; copies of vital records: $8.00 each

Pierce County
organized 1853, original county

Pierce County Assessor-Treasurer
2401 South 35th Street, Room 142
Tacoma, WA 98409
(206) 798-2775
pcatr@co.pierce.wa.us
http://www.co.pierce.wa.us/PC
Ken Madsen, County Assessor/Treasurer
(land records)
records search service: $10.00; copies: $1.00 for the first page and $1.00 for each additional page, no minimum

Pierce County Clerk
City-County Building, Room 110
930 Tacoma Avenue South
Tacoma, WA 98402-2102
(206) 591-7455 (Clerk's Office—Divorces); (206) 591-7461 (Clerk's Office—Probate)
pcclerk@co.pierce.wa.us;
kstock@co.pierce.wa.us
http://www.co.pierce.wa.us/PC
Kevin Stock, County Clerk and Clerk of Superior Court
records search service: $10.00; copies: $1.00 for the first page and $1.00 for each additional page, no minimum

San Juan County
organized 1873 from Whatcom County

San Juan County Courthouse
350 Court Street
Friday Harbor, WA 98250
(360) 378-2172 (Assessor, PO Box 1519); (360) 378-2161 (Auditor, PO Box 638); (360) 378-2163 (Clerk, Second Floor, No. 7); (360) 378-6256 FAX (Auditor); (360) 378-3967 FAX (Clerk)
assessor@co.san-juan.wa.us;auditor@co.san-juan.wa.us
http://www.co.san-juan.wa.us
Charles Zalmanek, County Assessor; Milene Henley, County Auditor; Joan P. White, County Clerk and Clerk of Superior Court
(land records with County Assessor, surveys and plat maps with County Auditor, marriages to July 1907 with County Auditor, probate records from 1800s and early 1900s with Washington State Archives, Northwest Region, recent probate records with County Clerk's Office)
probate search service: $8.00 per hour; copies of land records: $1.00 per page, $2.00 per document for certification, $1.50 per page for reduced size surveys and plats; copies of marriages: $1.00 each, $11.00 for certified copies; copies of probate records: $2.00 for the first page and $1.00 for each additional page, $8.00 minimum

Skagit County
organized 1883 from Whatcom County

Skagit County Clerk
205 West Kincaid, Room 103
Mount Vernon, WA 98273
(360) 336-9440
supcrtclerk@co.skagit.wa.us
http://www.skagitcounty.net
Nancy Scott, County Clerk and Clerk of Superior Court
probate search service: $20.00 per hour per name (prepaid); copies of probate records: $2.00 for the first page and $1.00 for each additional page, $2.00 per document for certification

Skamania County
organized 1854 from Clark County

Skamania County Courthouse
(240 NW Vancouver Avenue—location)
PO Box 790 (mailing address)
Stevenson, WA 98648-0790
(509) 427-3720 (Assessor); (509) 427-3730 (Auditor, Second Floor); (509) 427-3770 (Clerk, Room 33); (509) 427-3728 FAX (Assessor); (509) 427-3777 FAX (Clerk)
spencer@co.skamania.wa.us;
garvison@co.skamania.wa.us;
vance@co.skamania.wa.us
http://www.skamaniacounty.org
Gabe Spencer, County Assessor; J. Michael Garvison, County Auditor; Sharon Vance, County Clerk and Clerk of Superior Court
(land records with Assessor, naturalization records with Clerk, marriages with Auditor, dissolutions with Clerk, probate records with Clerk)
probate search service: $8.00 per hour; copies of probate records: $2.00 for the first page and $1.00 for each additional page, no minimum

Snohomish County
organized 1861 from Island County

Snohomish County Courthouse
3000 Rockefeller Avenue
Everett, WA 98201
(425) 388-3483 (Auditor, Public Information, M/S 505); (206) 388-3466 (Clerk, Room M-206, Second Floor Mission Building, M/S 605)
county.auditor@co.snohomish.wa.us;
contact.clerk@co.snohomish.wa.us;
daniels@co.sohomish.wa.us

http://www1.co.snohomish.wa.us
Carolyn Diepenbrock, County Auditor; Pam L.
Daniels, County Clerk and Ex-officio Clerk of
Superior Court
(land records with County Auditor, Recording
and Filing, First Floor Administration
Building, 3000 Rockefeller, M/S 204, probate
records with County Clerk, Room 246
Mission Building, 3000 Rockefeller)
probate search service: $12.00 for 1 to 10 names,
$16.00 for 11 to 15 names, $20.00 for 16 to
20 names; copies of probate records: $2.00
for the first page and $1.00 for each additional
page of document, no minimum ("the Clerk's
Office cannot accept personal checks;
cashier's check or money order acceptable;
SASE requested")

Spokane County
created 29 January 1858 in the legislature's
1858–59 session, from Walla Walla County;
Missoula County (now Montana) created 7
May 1860, from all land east of longitude 115
(eastern third of Spokane County); Stevens
County created 20 January 1863, with Stevens
County attached to Spokane County for
judicial purposes; Washington Territory
divided by Congress 3 March 1863, with all
east of longitude 117 and the Snake River in
Idaho Territory, thus shrinking Stevens
County so that Spokane County was
eliminated 19 January 1864 and annexed to
Stevens County; Spokane County recreated 30
October 1879

Spokane County Courthouse
1116 West Broadway Avenue
Spokane, WA 99201
(509) 477-1721; (509) 477-1725 FAX
PublicRecordsOfficer@spokanecounty.org
http://www.spokanecounty.org
Public Disclosure Officer
(all requests for public records should be sent to
the county's Public Records Officer)

Stevens County
Spokane County created 29 January 1858 in the
legislature's 1858–59 session, from Walla
Walla County; Missoula County (now
Montana) created 7 May 1860, from all land
east of longitude 115 (eastern third of
Spokane County); Stevens County created 20
January 1863, with Stevens County attached
to Spokane County for judicial purposes;
Washington Territory divided by Congress 3
March 1863, with all east of longitude 117 and
the Snake River in Idaho Territory, thus
shrinking Stevens County so that Spokane
County was eliminated 19 January 1864 and
annexed to Stevens County; Spokane County
recreated 30 October 1879

Stevens County Courthouse
215 South Oak Street
Colville, WA 99114
(509) 684-7510 (Auditor); (509) 684-7575
(Clerk); (509) 684-8310 FAX (Auditor and
Clerk)
tgray@co.stevens.wa.us;
pchester@co.stevens.wa.us
http://www.co.stevens.wa.us
Tim Gray, County Auditor; Patricia Chester,
County Clerk
(land records with Tim Gray, County Auditor)
land records search service: $8.00 per hour,
$4.00 minimum; copies of land records: $1.00
per page, $2.00 for certification

Thurston County
organized 1852 from Lewis County

Thurston County Courthouse
2000 Lakeridge Drive, S.W.
Olympia, WA 98502-6045
(360) 786-5224 (Auditor); (360) 786-5430 (Clerk,
Building 2)
wymank@co.thurston.wa.us;
GouldB@co.thurston.wa.us
http://www.co.thurston.wa.us/index.asp

Ms. Kim Wyman, County Auditor; Betty J.
Gould, County Clerk
(land records, births and deaths from 1890 to
1907, marriages from 1852 with Auditor,
probate records with Clerk)

Wahkiakum County
organized 1854 from Lewis County

Wahkiakum County Courthouse
64 Main Street
Cathlamet, WA 98612
(360) 795-3219 (Auditor, Second Floor, PO Box
534); (360) 795-3791 (Assessor, PO Box 145);
(360) 795-3558 (Clerk, PO Box 116); (360)
795-0824 FAX (Auditor); (360) 795-0540
FAX (Assessor); (360) 795-8813 FAX (Clerk)
tischerd@co.wahkiakum.wa.us; zerrs@co.
wahkiaium.wa.us; blixb@co.wahkiakum.wa.us
http://www.co.wahkiakum.wa.us
Diane L. Tischer, County Auditor; Sulema Zerr,
County Assessor; Barbara A. Blix, County
Clerk and Ex-officio Clerk of Superior Court

Walla Walla County
organized 1854 at the first session of the
Washington Territorial Legislature, original
county

Walla Walla County Courthouse
315 West Main Street
Walla Walla, WA 99362-2838
(509) 524-2549 (Auditor, Room 201, PO Box
1856); (509) 524-2780 (Clerk, PO Box 836);
(509) 524-2779 FAX (Clerk)
kmmartin@co.walla-walla.wa.us (Auditor);
wwcoauditor@co.walla-walla.wa.us; ;
kmartin@co.walla-walla.wa.us (Clerk)
http://www.co.walla-walla.wa.us
Karen Martin, County Auditor, Kathy Martin,
County Clerk and Clerk of Superior Court
(land records from 1860 with County Auditor;
naturalization records from 1800s to
September 1906 with Washington State
Archives, Eastern Regional Branch,
naturalization records from September 1906
to September 1950 moved to Yakima, WA
[must request certificates from Spokane, WA],
marriages from 1862 to date, probate records
from 1800s with County Clerk)
land records search service: $8.00 per hour per
name; probate search service: $20.00 per
hour; copies of land records: $1.00 per page;
copies of probate records: $2.00 for the first
page and $1.00 for each additional page

Whatcom County
organized 1854 from Island County

Whatcom County Courthouse
311 Grand Avenue
Bellingham, WA 98225-4038
(360) 676-6740 (Auditor, Suite 103); (360) 676-
6790 (Assessor, Suite 106); (360) 676-6777
(Superior Court, Suite 301); (360) 738-4556
FAX (Auditor)
auditor@co.whatcom.wa.us; sforslof@
co.whatcom.wa.us; assessor@co.whatcom.
wa.us; kwillnau@co.whatcom.wa.us;
sccustomer_service@whatcomcounty.us;
nfjackson@whatcomcounty.us
http://www.co.whatcom.wa.us
Shirley Forslof, County Auditor; Keith
Willnauer, County Assessor; N. F. Jackson,
Jr., County Clerk and Clerk of Superior Court

Whitman County
created 29 November 1871 from Stevens
County, organized 1 January 1872 by an 1871
act of the legislature

Whitman County Courthouse
400 North Main Street
Colfax, WA 99111-0390
(509) 397-6270 (Auditor); (509) 397-6220
(Assessor); (509) 397-6240 (Clerk); (509) 397-
6351 FAX (Auditor); (509) 397-6223 FAX
(Assessor); (509) 397-3546 FAX (Clerk)
Auditor@co.whitman.wa.us; Assessor@

co.whitman.wa.us; Clerk@co.whitman.wa.us
http://www.whitmancounty.org
Eunice Coker, County Auditor; Joe Reynolds,
County Assessor; Shirley Bafus, County Clerk
(land records, naturalization records, vital
records, probate records)
copies of land, naturalization, vital, and probate
records: 25¢ per page

Yakima County
organized 1865 from Indian Territory

Yakima County Courthouse
128 North Second Street
Yakima, WA 98901
(509) 574-1400 (Auditor, Room 117); (509) 574-
1430 (Clerk, Room 323); (509) 574-1341 FAX
(Auditor)
corky.mattingly@co.yakima.wa.us
http://www.co.yakima.wa.us
Corky Mattingly, Auditor; Kim M. Eaton,
County Clerk and Ex-officio Clerk of
Supreme Court
(land records from the late 1800s to date by
name, date only—no legal description with
Auditor, limited naturalization records
records retained with County Clerk, births
and deaths before 1907, marriages from the
late 1800s to date, probate records with
County Clerk)
land records search service: $8.00 per hour; vital
records search service: $8.00 per hour (please
submit correct spelling of names and
approximate dates); probate search service:
$20.00 per hour (please submit correct
spelling of names and approximate dates);
copies of land records: $1.00 per page, $2.00
per document for certification; copies of vital
records: $1.00 per page, $2.00 per document
for certification; copies of probate records:
10¢ per page, minimum, $2.00 for the first
certified page and $1.00 for each additional
certified page

WEST VIRGINIA

Capital: Charleston. Statehood: 20 June 1863 (part of Virginia until the Civil War)

West Virginia has about fifty-five Magistrate Courts and fifty-four Municipal Courts of limited jurisdiction. The Court of Claims hears damage claims against the government and claims made under the Crime Victims Compensation Act. The County Commissions, formerly the County Courts, are established in every county to administer probate, mental commitments, guardianships, etc.

Thirty-one Circuit Courts have general jurisdiction in civil and criminal matters. The following Judicial Circuits include more than one county: First Judicial Circuit: Brooke, Hancock and Ohio counties; Second Judicial Circuit: Marshall, Tyler and Wetzel counties; Third Judicial Circuit: Doddridge, Pleasants and Ritchie counties; Fourth Judicial Circuit: Wirt and Wood counties; Fifth Judicial Circuit: Calhoun, Jackson and Roane counties; Eleventh Judicial Circuit: Greenbrier, Monroe, Pocahontas and Summers counties; Fourteenth Judicial Circuit: Braxton, Clay, Gilmer and Webster counties; Nineteenth Judicial Circuit: Barbour and Taylor counties; Twenty-first Judicial Circuit: Grant, Mineral and Tucker counties; Twenty-second Judicial Circuit: Hampshire, Hardy and Pendleton counties; Twenty-third Judicial Circuit: Berkeley, Jefferson and Morgan counties; Twenty-fifth Judicial Circuit: Boone and Lincoln counties; Twenty-sixth Judicial Circuit: Lewis and Upshur counties; Twenty-ninth Judicial Circuit: Mason and Putnam counties; Thirty-first Judicial Circuit: Berkeley, Jefferson and Morgan counties. Note that the Twenty-third and Thirty-first Judicial Circuits are the same. The following counties comprise single-county judicial circuits: Cabell, Fayette, Harrison, Kanawha, Logan, Marion, McDowell, Mercer, Mingo, Monongalia, Nicholas, Preston, Raleigh, Randolph, Wayne, and Wyoming counties. The Supreme Court of Appeals is the court of last resort.

Barbour County

organized 1843 from Harrison, Lewis and Randolph counties

Barbour County Courthouse
(8 North Main Street—location)
PO Box 310 (mailing address)
Philippi, WV 26416-0310
(304) 457-2232; (304) 457-4572 FAX
http://www.wv.gov/county.aspx?regID=5&cID=33
Debra Harris Talbott, County Clerk; Jerry A. Lantz, Circuit Clerk

Berkeley County

organized 1772 from Frederick County (now Virginia)

Berkeley County Courthouse
126 West King Street
Martinsburg, WV 25401
(304) 264-1927 (County Clerk, Room 1); (304) 264-1918 (Circuit Clerk); ; (304) 267-9723 FAX
http://www.berkeleycountycomm.org
John W. Small, Jr., County Clerk; Virginia M. Sine, Circuit Clerk
(deeds from 1772 [books 14, 22, 28, 37, 42, 56 and the last half of 59 and 62 lost)], land grants from 1772, surveyor's records from 1771, land books from 1782 to 1900 [last not open to the public], births and deaths from 1865 to date, marriage bonds from 1781 to 1870 [originals not open to the public, but available in printed form], probate records from 1772 [will books 11, 17, 18, 19 and 20 lost, some lost wills re-recorded], inventories and settlements of accounts [listed separately

from will books after the Civil War], guardian bonds from 1776 to 1847 and from 1865 to 1873 [not open to the public])
no land, vital records or probate search service

Boone County

organized 1847 from Cabell, Kanawha and Logan counties

Boone County Courthouse
206 Court Street
Madison, WV 25130
(304) 369-7330; (304) 369-7329 FAX
suezickefoose@courtswv.org
http://www.wv.gov/county.aspx?regID=6&cID=37
Gary W. Williams, County Clerk; Sue Ann Zickefoose, Circuit Clerk

Braxton County

organized 1836 from Kanawha, Lewis, Nicholas and Randolph counties

Braxton County Courthouse
300 Main Street
Sutton, WV 26601
(304) 765-2833 (County Clerk); (304) 765-2837 (Circuit Clerk); (304) 765-2093 FAX
jdjordanwv@netscape.net
http://www.braxtonwv.org/CourtHouse.htm
John D. Jordan, County Clerk; J. W. Morris, Circuit Clerk
(land records from 1836, births and deaths from 1853, marriages from 1856, probate records from 1836)
land, vital records and probate search service: no charge ("We do not search the indexes without specific periods of time within the request"); copies of vital records: $2.00 each; copies of probate records: $1.50 for the first two pages and $1.00 for each additional page, no minimum

Brooke County

organized 1796 from Ohio County

Brooke County Courthouse
632 Main Street
Wellsburg, WV 26070
(304) 737-3661; (304) 737-4023 FAX
madamclerk@aol.com
http://www.wv.gov/county.aspx?regID=8&cID=53
Sylvia J. Benzo, County Clerk; Glenda Brooks, Circuit Clerk
(deeds, births and deaths from 1853, marriages from 1797, wills from 1797, letters of administration with County Clerk; naturalization records with Circuit Clerk)
no probate search service; copies of probate records: $3.00 for the first two pages of deeds and 50¢ for each additional page, plus stamps, $2.00 each for plats up to 120 square inches and 1¢ for each additional square inch; copies of vital records: copies: $2.00 each; copies of probate records: $1.00 each, $1.50 to certify long form

Cabell County

organized 1809 from Kanawha County

Cabell County Courthouse
750 Fifth Avenue
Huntington, WV 25701
(304) 526-8625 (County Clerk, Suite 108); (304) 526-8622 (Circuit Clerk, Room 114); (304) 526-8632 FAX (County Clerk); (304) 526-8699 FAX (Circuit Clerk)
kcol@cabellcountyclerk.org; adellc@cabellct.com
http://www.cabellcounty.org
Karen S. Cole, County Clerk; Adell Chandler Meadows, Circuit Clerk

Calhoun County

organized 1856 from Gilmer County

Calhoun County Courthouse
PO Box 230

Grantsville, WV 26147-0230
(304) 354-6725; (304) 354-6725 FAX
circuitcl@hotmail.com
http://www.wv.gov/county.aspx?regID=7&cID=49
Richard D. Kirby, County Clerk; Shelia Garettson, Circuit Clerk
(grantor and grantee land records, births, deaths, marriages, wills)
probate search service: no charge (supply names and dates); copies of probate records: $1.50 for the first two pages and $1.00 for each additional page of the same document, $1.50 minimum

Clay County

organized 1858 from Braxton and Nicholas counties

Clay County Courthouse
PO Box 196
Clay, WV 25043-0196
(304) 587-4259; (304) 587-7329 FAX
claycoclerk@hotmail.com
http://www.wv.gov/county.aspx?regID=4&cID=20
Judy R. Moore, County Clerk; Mike Asbury, Circuit Clerk
(land records from 1858, vital records from 1858, probate records from 1858)
no probate search service; copies of probate records: $1.50 for the first two pages and $1.00 for each additional page, $1.50 minimum

Doddridge County

organized 1845 from Harrison, Tyler, Ritchie and Lewis counties

Doddridge County Courthouse
118 East Court Street
West Union, WV 26456
(304) 873-2631; (304) 873-1840 FAX
doddcoclerk3@yhoo.com
http://www.wv.gov/county.aspx?regID=5&cID=27
Janice Ellifritt Cox, County Clerk; Dwight E. Moore, Circuit Clerk
(land records from 1845, births, deaths and marriages from 1845, probate records from 1845)
no probate search service; copies of vital records: $1.50 each; copies of probate records: $1.50 for the first two pages and $1.00 for each additional page

Fayette County

organized 1831 from Kanawha, Greenbrier, Nicholas and Logan counties

Fayette County Courthouse
(100 Court Street—location)
PO Box 307 (mailing address)
Fayetteville, WV 25840-0307
(304) 574-4225; (304) 574-4314 FAX
kelvin@cwv.net
http://www.fayettecounty.com; http://www.wv.gov/county.aspx?regID=3&cID=13
Kelvin Holliday, County Clerk; Danny Wright, Circuit Clerk
(land records from 1830s, births and deaths from 1866, marriages from 1831, probate records)
no probate search service ("need date of death, name of decedent"); copies of probate records: $1.50 for the first two pages and $1.00 for each additional page, $1.50 minimum

Gilmer County

organized 1845 from Lewis and Kanawha counties

Gilmer County Courthouse
10 Howard Street
Glenville, WV 26351
(304) 462-7641; (304) 462-5134 FAX
bjmclerk@yahoo.com; gccc@rtol.net

http://www.wv.gov/county.aspx?regID=4&cID=21
Beverly Marks, County Clerk; David Lane Smith, Circuit Clerk
(land records from 1845, vital records from 1853, probate records from 1845)
probate search service: no charge (no genealogy searches, but will look up specific items when pertinent information is provided); copies of probate records: $1.50 for the first two pages and $1.00 for each additional page, no minimum

Grant County
organized 1866 from Hardy County

Grant County Courthouse
5 Highland Avenue
Petersburg, WV 26847-1705
(304) 257-4550; (304) 257-4207 FAX
gccomm@access.mountain.net (County Clerk); gccc@mountain.net (Circuit Clerk)
http://www.wv.gov/county.aspx?regID=1&cID=3
Harold G. Hiser, County Clerk; Betty C. Moomau, Circuit Clerk
(land records from 1866, vital records from 1866, probate records from 1866)
no probate search service; copies of probate records: 25¢ for each of the first ten pages and 15¢ for each additional page, 25¢ minimum

Greenbrier County
organized 1778 from Montgomery and Botetourt counties (now Virginia)

Greenbrier County Courthouse
PO Box 506
Lewisburg, WV 24901-0506
(304) 647-6602; (304) 647-6694 FAX
gbrctyclerk@hotmail.com
http://www.wv.gov/county.aspx?regID=3&cID=12
William B. J. Livesay, County Clerk; Louvonne Arbuckle, Circuit Clerk
(land records from late 1700s, vital records from 1853, probate records from late 1700s)
probate search service: $5.00; copies of probate records: $1.00 per standard page or $1.00 per reduced page, no minimum

Hampshire County
organized 1754 from Frederick and Augusta counties (now Virginia)

Hampshire County Courthouse
PO Box 806
Romney, WV 26757-0806
(304) 822-5112; (304) 822-4039 FAX
http://www.wv.gov/county.aspx?regID=1&cID=2
Sharon H. Link, County Clerk; Sonji Embrey, Circuit Clerk
(deeds from 1754, births, deaths and marriage records from 1865, probate records from 1754 [although some of these are missing])
probate search service: no charge ("we need names and dates before we will research any record"); copies of probate records: $1.50 for the first two pages and $1.00 for each additional page, no minimum

Hancock County
organized 1848 from Brooke County

Hancock County Courthouse
102 North Court Street
New Cumberland, WV 26047
(304) 564-3311, ext. 266 (County Clerk, PO Box 367); (304) 564-3311, ext. 287 (Circuit Clerk, PO Box 428); (304) 564-5941 FAX (County Clerk); (304) 564-5014 FAX (Circuit Clerk)
estraight@hancockcountywv.org; bjackson@hancockcountywv.org
http://www.hancockcountywv.org; http://www.wv.gov/county.aspx?regID=8&cID=52
Eleanor Straight, County Clerk and Assessor;

Brenda Jackson, Circuit Clerk
(land records, vital records, probate records)
no probate search service; copies of probate records: $1.50 for the first two pages and $1.00 for each additional page, $1.50 minimum

Hardy County
organized 1786 from Hampshire County

Hardy County Courthouse
204 Washington Street
Moorefield, WV 26836
(304) 530-0252; (304) 530-0251 FAX
hcsheriff@hardynet.com (Robert Ferrell, Sheriff)
http://www.wv.gov/county.aspx?regID=1&cID=4
Greg Lee Ely, County Clerk; Janet Ferrell, Circuit Clerk
(land records, vital records, probate records)
probate search service: $5.00 ("we do very little genealogy research; we refer requests to a local genealogist"); copies of probate records: $1.50 for the first two pages and $1.00 for each additional page, $1.50 minimum

Harrison County
organized 1784 from Monongalia, Randolph and Ohio counties

Harrison County Courthouse
301 West Main Street
Clarksburg, WV 26301-2909
(304) 624-8672 (County Clerk); (304) 624-8640 (Circuit Clerk); (304) 624-8675 FAX (County Clerk)
sthomas@harrisoncountywv.com; dkopp@harrisoncountywv.com
http://www.harrisoncountywv.com
Susan Thomas, County Clerk; Donald L. Kopp II, Circuit Clerk
(land records from 1800s, births and deaths from 1853, marriages from 1700s, probate records from 1881)
no probate search service; copies of vital records: $2.00 per page; copies of probate records: $1.50 for the first two pages and $1.00 for each additional page

Jackson County
organized 1831 from Kanawha, Mason and Wood counties

Jackson County Courthouse
(116 Court Street—location)
PO Box 800 (mailing address)
Ripley, WV 25271
(304) 373-2250; (304) 372-1107 FAX
countyclerk@jacksoncountywv.com
http://www.wv.gov/county.aspx?regID=7&cID=47
Jeff Waybright, County Clerk; Keith Brotherton, Circuit Clerk
(land records from 1831, births and deaths from 1853, marriages from 1831 [no restrictions], probate records from 1831)
no probate search service: copies: $1.50 for the first two pages and $1.00 for each additional page

Jefferson County
created from Berkeley County in an act passed by the General Assembly of Virginia 8 January 1801 (area contained in Virginia's Northumberland County, 1648-1652, Lancaster County 1652-1656, Old Rappahannock County 1656-1691, Essex County 1691-1720, Spotsylvania County 1720-1734, Orange County 1734-1738, Frederick County 1738-1772, and Berkeley County 1772-1801)

Jefferson County Circuit Clerk
(110 North George Street—location)
PO Box 1234 (mailing address)
Charles Town, WV 25414
(304) 728-3213; (304) 728-3398 FAX
circuitclerk@hotmail.com

http://www.jeffersoncountywv.org/circlk.html
Patricia A. Noland
(naturalization records)

Jefferson County Clerk
(Courthouse, 100 East Washington Street—location)
PO Box 208 (mailing address)
Charles Town, WV 25414-0250
(304) 728-3215 (Recording); (304) 728-3230 (Probate); (304) 728-1957 FAX
clerkjeff@yahoo.com
http://www.jeffersoncountywv.org/coclk.html
Jennifer Maghan
(land records from 1801, births and deaths from 1853, marriages from 1801, wills from 1801)
copies: $1.00 per page

Kanawha County
organized 1789 from Greenbrier County (now West Virginia) and Montgomery County (now Virginia)

Kanawha County Courthouse
111 Court Street
Charleston, WV 25332
(304) 357-0440; (304) 357-0473 FAX
cathygatson@courtswv.org
http://www.kanawha.us/default.aspx
Cathy Gatson

Kanawha County Clerk
(409 Virginia Street, East—location)
PO Box 3226 (mailing address)
Charleston, WV 25332
(304) 357-0130; (304) 357-0585 FAX
veramccormick@kanawha.us
http://www.kanawha.us/default.aspx
Vera J. McCormick
(land records from 1790, births and deaths from 1853, marriages from 1854, wills from 1790)

Lewis County
organized 1816 from Harrison and Randolph counties

Lewis County Courthouse
PO Box 466
Weston, WV 26452
(304) 269-8200; (304) 269-8202 FAX
coclk21000@yahoo.com
http://www.wv.gov/county.aspx?regID=4&cID=25
Mary Lou Myers, County Clerk; John B. Hinzman, Circuit Clerk
(land records from early 1800s, births and deaths from 1853, marriages from early 1800s, probate records from early 1800s)
probate search service: $5.00; copies of land records: $2.00 each; copies of probate records: $1.50 for the first two pages and $1.00 for each additional page, no minimum

Lincoln County
organized 1867 from Boone, Cabell and Kanawha counties

Lincoln County Courthouse
(8000 Court Street—location)
PO Box 497 (mailing address)
Hamlin, WV 25523
(304) 824-3336; (304) 824-2012 FAX
http://www.wv.gov/county.aspx?regID=6&cID=41
Donald C. Whitten, County Clerk; Greg Stowers, Circuit Clerk
(land records, naturalization records, vital records, probate records)

Logan County
organized 1824 from Cabell and Kanawha counties, and Giles and Tazewell counties (now Virginia)

Logan County Courthouse
300 Stratton Street
Logan, WV 25601
(304) 792-8600; (304) 792-8621 FAX
http://www.wv.gov/county.aspx?regID=6&cID=38

Glenn Adkins, County Clerk; Alvis Porter, Circuit Clerk
(land records, vital records, probate records)
probate search service: no charge; copies of probate records: $1.50 for the first two pages and $1.00 for each additional page, $1.50 minimum

Marion County
organized 1842 from Harrison and Monongalia counties

Marion County Courthouse
217 Adams Street
Fairmont, WV 26554
(304) 367-5440 (County Clerk, First Floor, PO Box 1267); (304) 367-5361; (Circuit Clerk, Second Floor, PO Box 1269); (304) 367-5448 FAX (County Clerk); 304) 367-5374 FAX (Circuit Clerk
janicecosco@marioncountyclerk.com; bcore@marioncountywv.com
http://www.marioncountywv.com
Janice Cosco, County Clerk; Barbara A. Core, Circuit Clerk

Marshall County
organized 1835 from Ohio County

Marshall County Courthouse
(600 Seventh Street—location)
PO Drawer B (mailing address)
Moundsville, WV 26041
(304) 845-1220; (304) 845-5891 FAX
janpest@aol.com; Marshallwv@aol.com (Circuit Clerk)
http://www.wv.gov/county.aspx?regID=8&cID=55
Jan Pest, County Clerk; David R. Ealy, Circuit Clerk

Mason County
organized 1804 from Kanawha County

Mason County Courthouse
200 Sixth Street
Point Pleasant, WV 25550
(304) 675-1997; (304) 675-2521 FAX
masoncoclerk@eurekanet.com; masoncircuitclk@citynet.net
http://www.wv.gov/county.aspx?regID=6&cID=34
Diana N. Pearson Cromley, County Clerk; Bill Withers, Circuit Clerk

McDowell County
organized 1858 from Tazewell County (now Virginia)

McDowell County Courthouse
90 Wyoming Street
Welch, WV 24801
(304) 436-8544; (304) 436-8576 FAX
http://www.wv.gov/county.aspx?regID=3&cID=16
Donald L. Hicks, County Clerk; Michael D. Brooks, Circuit Clerk

Mercer County
organized 1837 from Giles and Tazewell counties (now Virginia)

Mercer County Courthouse
1501 West Main Street
Princeton, WV 24740
(304) 487-8311; (304) 487-8351 FAX
am970wwyo@hotmail.com (County Clerk)
http://www.wv.gov/county.aspx?regID=3&cID=17
Rudolph Jennings, County Clerk; Brenda Davis, Circuit Clerk
(land records from 1837, vital records from 1853, probate records from 1853)
no probate search service; copies of probate records: $1.50 for the first two pages and $1.00 for each additional page

Mineral County
organized 1866 from Hampshire County

Mineral County Commission
150 Armstrong Street
Keyser, WV 26726-3505
(304) 788-3924 (County Clerk); (304) 788-1562 (Circuit Clerk, Second Floor); (304) 788-4109 FAX (County Clerk); (304) 788-4109 FAX (Circuit Clerk)
countyclerk@mineralcountywv.org; circuitclerk@mineralcountywv.com
http://www.mineralcountywv.com/index.asp
Lauren Ellifritz, County Clerk; Mary Margaret Rinehart, Circuit Clerk
(land records from 1865; births, deaths and marriages from 1865)
no vital records search service (must have date of event within two or three years); copies of land and probate records: $1.50 for the first two pages and $1.00 for each additional page; copies of vital records: $1.50 each

Mingo County
organized 1895 from Logan County

Mingo County Courthouse
PO Box 1197
Williamson, WV 25661-1197
(304) 235-0330; (304) 235-0328 FAX
http://www.wv.gov/county.aspx?regID=6&cID=39
Jim Hatfield, County Clerk; Grant Preece, Circuit Clerk
(land records with Assessor, Tax Department, County Clerk, naturalization records, vital records, and probate records with County Clerk)
no probate search service ("records are public, you may search"); copies of probate records: $1.50 for the first two pages and $1.00 for each additional page, no minimum

Monongalia County
organized 1776 from District of West Augusta

Monongalia County Courthouse
243 High Street
Morgantown, WV 26505-5491
(304) 291-7230 (County Clerk); (304) 291-7234 (Vital Statistics); (304) 291-7236 (Estates); (304) 291-7237 (Records Room); (304) 291-7240 (Circuit Clerk); (304) 291-7233 FAX
moncoclerk@yahoo.com; tennant95@hotmail.com; circuitclerk@sbccom.com
http://www.co.monongalia.wv.us
Michael A. Oliverio, County Clerk; Betty Tennant, Administrative Assistant; Jean Friend, Circuit Clerk
(some land and probate records in 1700s, births and deaths from 1853, marriages from 1796)
no search service ("we do not have anyone employed to do genealogy research"; contact Monongalia County Historical Society); copies: $1.50 for the first two pages and $1.00 for each additional page

Monroe County
organized 1779 from Greenbrier County (now West Virginia) and Botetourt County (now Virginia)

Monroe County Courthouse
(Main Street—location)
PO Box 350 (mailing address)
Union, WV 24983-0350
(304) 772-3096; (304) 772-4191 FAX
dje@inetone.net; jlight@monroecountywv.net
http://www.wv.gov/county.aspx?regID=3&cID=19
Donald J. Evans, County Clerk; Julia L. Light, Circuit Clerk
(land records, naturalization records, vital records probate records)
no records search service; copies of land, naturalization, vital and probate records: $1.00 each

Morgan County
organized 1820 from Berkeley and Hampshire counties

Morgan County Courthouse
(83 Fairfax Street—location)
Box 28 (mailing address)
Berkeley Springs, WV 25411
(304) 258-8547; (304) 258-8545 FAX
morgancountyclerk@hotmail.com; mccircuitclerk@hotmail.com
http://www.wv.gov/county.aspx?regID=2&cID=9
Debra Kesecker, County Clerk; Betsy R. Moss Miller, Circuit Clerk

Nicholas County
organized 1818 from Greenbrier, Kanawha and Randolph counties

Nicholas County Courthouse
700 Main Street
Summersville, WV 26651
(304) 872-7820; (304) 872-9600 FAX
countyclerk@geoweb.net
http://www.wv.gov/county.aspx?regID=4&cID=23
Wanda Henderson, County Clerk; June Foster Gower, Circuit Clerk

Ohio County
organized 1776 from Augusta County

Ohio County Courthouse
City County Building
1500 Chapline Street
Wheeling, WV 26003-3553
(304) 234-3656; (304) 234-3829 FAX
brendamiller@courtswv.org
http://www.wv.gov/county.aspx?regID=8&cID=54
Patty Fahey, County Clerk; Brenda Miller, Circuit Clerk
(deed books from 1778, no naturalizations, just index ["All records kept in Library in Morgantown, WV"], births and deaths from 1853 ["Births were not required to be recorded until 1923, some we have, others we don't"], marriages from 1790, settlements from 1777, wills from late 1700s)
vital records search service: $1.00 per name; no probate search service (contact Wheeling Area Genealogical Society, 2237 Marshall Avenue, Wheeling, WV 26003); copies of land and probate records: 50¢ per page (no copies of index records), no minimum; certified copies of vital records: $2.00 each

Pendleton County
organized 1788 from Hardy County (now West Virginia) and Augusta and Rockingham counties (now Virginia)

Pendleton County Courthouse
(100 South Main Street—location)
Box 187 (mailing address)
Franklin, WV 26807
(304) 358-2505; (304) 358-2473 FAX
http://www.wv.gov/county.aspx?regID=1&cID=6
Nancy K. Gonshor, County Clerk; Shalee Wilburn, Circuit Clerk
(land records from 1788, births and deaths from 1853, marriages from 1800, probate records from 1789)
no probate search service; copies of probate records: $1.00 per page, $1.50 minimum

Pleasants County
organized 1851 from Ritchie, Tyler and Wood counties

Pleasants County Courthouse
301 Court Lane
St. Marys, WV 26170
(304) 684-7637; (304) 684-7569 FAX
smorgan_clerk@yahoo.com
http://www.wv.gov/county.aspx?regID=7&cID=43
Sue Morgan, County Clerk; Millie Farnsworth, Circuit Clerk
(land records, vital records, and probate records with County Clerk; naturalization records

with Circuit Clerk)
probate search service: no charge, but accurate years must be provided; copies of probate records: $1.50 for the first two pages and $1.00 for each additional page, $1.50 each for certified copies

Pocahontas County

organized 1821 from Pendleton, Randolph and Greenbrier counties (now West Virginia) and Bath County (now Virginia)

Pocahontas County Courthouse
900-C Tenth Avenue
Marlinton, WV 24954-1333
(304) 799-4549; (304) 799-6947 FAX
http://www.wv.gov/county.aspx?regID=1&cID=8
Patricia D. Dunbrack, County Clerk; Sandra Friel, Circuit Clerk
(land and probate records from 1822, births from 1854, deaths from 1853, naturalization records from 1904 to 1929 with Circuit Clerk's Office)
probate search service: 50¢ per name; copies of probate records: $1.50 for the first two pages and $1.00 for each additional page per document, no minimum

Preston County

organized 1818 from Monongalia and Randolph counties

Preston County Courthouse
101 West Main Street
Kingwood, WV 26537-1121
(304) 329-0700; (304) 329-0198 FAX
nireckart@hotmail.com;
betclerk2ork@hotmail.com
http://www.wv.gov/county.aspx?regID=5&cID=31
Nancy L. Reckart, County Clerk; Betsy Castle, Circuit Clerk

Putnam County

organized 1848 from Kanawha, Mason and Cabell counties

Putnam County Courthouse
3389 Winfield Road
Winfield, WV 25213
(304) 586-0202; (304) 586-0200 FAX
bwood@wvnet.edu; dsmith@wvnet.edu (Circuit Clerk)
http://countycommission.putnamcounty.org
Brian Wood, County Clerk; Donald A. Wright, Circuit Clerk
(land and probate records from 1848, vital records from 1848)
probate search service: $2.00 per name; copies of probate records: $1.50 for the first two pages and $1.00 for each additional page

Raleigh County

organized 1850 from Fayette County

Raleigh County Courthouse
(215 Main Street—location)
PO Drawer AN (mailing address)
Beckley, WV 25801
(304) 255-9123 (County Clerk); (304) 255-9135 (Circuit Clerk); (304) 255-9352 FAX
betty@raleighcounty.com
http://www.raleighcounty.com;
http://www.wv.gov/county.aspx?regID=3&cID=14
Betty Riffe, County Clerk; Janice Davis, Circuit Clerk
(land records with Assessor, naturalization records with Circuit Clerk, vital records from 1853 with County Clerk, probate records from 1853 with County Clerk)
probate search service: no charge; copies of probate records: $1.50 for the first two pages and $1.00 for each additional page, $2.00 each for certified copies ("we only check years that the incident occurred, we don't do genealogical searches")

Randolph County

organized 1787 from Harrison County

Randolph County Courthouse
PO Box 368
Elkins, WV 26241-0368
(304) 636-0543; (304) 636-5989 FAX
pdr@citynet.met (Circuit Clerk)
http://www.randolphcountywv.com (Convention and Visitors Bureau); http://www.wv.gov/county.aspx?regID=1&cID=7
Sandra Pawelczyk; Phil Riggleman, Circuit Clerk

Ritchie County

organized 1843 from Harrison, Lewis, and Wood counties

Ritchie County Courthouse
115 East Main Street
Harrisville, WV 26362
(304) 643-2164; (304) 643-2906 FAX
sjscott@clerk.state.wv.us; ;
recox@circuit.state.wv.us
http://www.wv.gov/county.aspx?regID=7&cID=44
Susan J. Scott, County Clerk; Rose E. Cox, Circuit Clerk
(land and probate records from 1853, vital records from 1853)
no probate search service; copies of probate records: $1.50 for the first two pages and $1.00 for each additional page

Roane County

organized 1856 from Gilmer, Jackson, and Kanawha counties

Roane County Courthouse
(200 Main Street—location)
PO Box 69 (mailing address)
Spencer, WV 25276
(304) 927-2860; (304) 927-2489 FAX
cwhite2@clerk.state.wv.us;
bbreat@circuit.state.wv.us
http://www.wv.gov/county.aspx?regID=7&cID=48
Charles B. White, Jr., County Clerk; Beverly Greathouse, Circuit Clerk
(land records, vital records, probate records)
probate search service: $1.00 per name per book; copies of land records: $1.50 for the first two pages and $1.00 for each additional page; copies of vital records: $2.00 each; copies of probate records: $1.50 for the first two pages and $1.00 for each additional page, no minimum

Summers County

organized 1871 from Greenbrier, Monroe, and Mercer counties

Summers County Courthouse
PO Box 97
Hinton, WV 25951-0097
(304) 466-7104; (304) 466-7146 FAX
summersclerk@hotmail.com
http://www.wv.gov/county.aspx?regID=3&cID=18
Mary Beth Merritt, County Clerk; Linda Barumit, Circuit Clerk
(land, probate and vital records from 1871)
probate search service: no charge; copies of probate records: $1.50 for the first two pages and $1.00 for each additional page, no minimum

Taylor County

organized 1844 from Harrison, Barbour, and Marion counties

Taylor County Courthouse
214 West Main Street
Grafton, WV 26354
(304) 265-1401; (304) 265-5450 FAX
http://www.wv.gov/county.aspx?regID=5&cID=32
Nancy V. Fowler, County Clerk; Elaine Bennett, Circuit Clerk

Tucker County

organized 1856 from Randolph County

Tucker County Courthouse
215 First Street
Parsons, WV 26287
(304) 478-2866; (304) 478-4464 FAX
ttucsing@access.mountain.net (County Clerk); bava@ncumedia.net
http://www.wv.gov/county.aspx?regID=1&cID=5
Linda Cale, County Clerk; Donna Jean Bava, Circuit Clerk
(land, probate, and vital records from 1856, naturalization records)
probate search service: $5.00; copies of probate records: $1.50 for the first two pages and $1.00 for each additional page, $1.50 minimum

Tyler County

organized 1814 from Ohio County

Tyler County Courthouse
(121 Main Street—location)
PO Box 66 (mailing address)
Middlebourne, WV 26149-0066
(304) 758-2102; (304) 758-2126 FAX
tylerco@clerk.state.wv.us
http://www.wv.gov/county.aspx?regID=8&cID=57
Lora G. Thomas, County Clerk; Kay L. Keller, Circuit Clerk
(land records with Clerk and Assessor's Office, vital records from 1853 with Clerk's Office, probate records with Clerk's Office)
probate search service (fees depending on the research); copies of probate records: $1.50 for the first two pages and 50¢ for each additional page, $2.00 each for certified copies, $1.50 minimum

Upshur County

organized 1851 from Randolph, Barbour, and Lewis counties

Upshur County Courthouse
38 West Main Street
Buckhannon, WV 26201
(304) 472-1068; (304) 472-1029 FAX
dtwilfong@upshurcounty.org; sirclk@aol.com
http://www.wv.gov/county.aspx?regID=4&cID=26
Debbie Wilfong, County Clerk; Teresa Beer, Circuit Clerk

Wayne County

organized 1842 from Cabell County

Wayne County Courthouse
700 Hendricks Street
Wayne, WV 25570
(304) 272-6369; (304) 272-5318 FAX
wayneco@citynet.net (County Clerk)
http://www.wv.gov/county.aspx?regID=6&cID=40
Robert Pasley, County Clerk; James "Jamie" Ferguson, Circuit Clerk
(deeds from 1842, births, deaths and marriages from 1853, supplemental fiduciary [list of heirs] from 1909, appraisements from 1878, settlements from 1886, wills from 1843)
probate search service: no charge; copies of probate records: $1.50 for the first two pages and $1.00 for each additional page, $1.50 minimum

Webster County

organized 1860 from Braxton, Nicholas and Randolph counties

Webster County Commission
2 Court Square
Webster Springs, WV 26288
(304) 847-2508; (304) 847-5780 FAX
webstercoclerk@frontiernet.net;
beamer1@citlink.net (Circuit Clerk)
http://www.websterwv.com (Webster County Economic Development Authority);

http://www.wv.gov/county.aspx?regID=4&cID=24

Terry J. Payne, County Clerk; Jeanine Moore, Circuit Clerk

(land records, naturalization records, births, deaths and marriages

copies: $1.50 each

Wetzel County
organized 1846 from Tyler County

Wetzel County Courthouse
PO Box 156
New Martinsville, WV 26155-0156
(304) 455-8224; (304) 455-5256 FAX
http://www.wv.gov/county.aspx?regID=8&cID=56
Carol Marshall Haught, County Clerk; Sharon M. Dulaney, Circuit Clerk
(land and probate records from 1846, births, deaths and marriage licenses from 1846; naturalization records from 1846 with Circuit Clerk's Office)
no probate search service (will look up a name but will not do index searches; contact Wetzel County Genealogical Society, which charges $10.00 per half day); copies of land and probate records: $1.50 for the first two pages and $1.00 for each additional page; copies of vital records: $2.00 each

Wirt County
organized 1848 from Jackson and Wood counties

Wirt County Courthouse
PO Box 53
Elizabeth, WV 26143-0053
(304) 275-4271; (304) 275-3418 FAX
http://www.wv.gov/county.aspx?regID=7&cID=46
Suellen Calebaugh, County Clerk; Theresa Rollins, Circuit Clerk
(land, probate and vital records)
no probate search service; copies of probate records: $1.50 for the first two pages and $1.00 for each additional page, no minimum

Wood County
organized 1798 from Harrison and Kanawha counties

Wood County Circuit Clerk
Wood County Judicial Building, Room 133
Parkersburg, WV 26101-5353
(304) 424-1700; (304) 424-1804 FAX
circuitclerk@woodcountywv.com
http://www.woodcountywv.com
Carole Jones

Wood County Clerk
(Courthouse, 1 Court Square—location)
PO Box 1474 (mailing address)
Parkersburg, WV 26101
(304) 424-1850 (County Clerk); (304) 424-1870 (Record Room, First Floor); (304) 424-1845 (Vital Statistics, Second Floor); (304) 424-1860 (Marriages, Fourth Floor); (304) 424-1898 (Probate, Second Floor); (304) 424-1982 FAX
jamiesix@woodcountywv.com
http://www.woodcountywv.com
James R. Six
(land records from 1798, vital records from 1801, probate records from 1880)
probate search service: no charge; copies of probate records: $1.50 for the first two pages and $1.00 for each additional page, no minimum

Wyoming County
organized 1850 from Logan County

Wyoming County Courthouse
100 Main Street
Pineville, WV 24874
(304) 732-8000; (304) 732-7262 FAX
http://www.wv.gov/county.aspx?regID=3&cID=15
D. Michael "Mike" Goode, County Clerk; David

Stover, Circuit Clerk
(land records from 1850, vital records from 1850, probate records from 24 January 1931 with County Clerk; naturalization records with Circuit Clerk)
no probate search service; copies of probate records: $1.50 for the first two pages and $1.00 for each additional page; copies of naturalization records: 25¢ per page

---

WISCONSIN

Capital: Madison. Statehood: 29 May 1848 (recognized as part of the U.S. by great Britain in 1783, claims relinquished by Virginia, Massachusetts and Connecticut, in the Northwest Territory 1787, Indiana Territory 7 May 1800, Illinois Territory 3 February 1809, Michigan Territory 18 April 1818, and organized as a separate territory in 20 April 1836)

Wisconsin has over 200 Municipal Courts with limited jurisdiction over local ordinances. There are sixty-nine Circuit Courts with general jurisdiction which sit at each county seat except in the following combined districts: Buffalo-Pepin at Alma, Forest-Florence at Crandon, and Shawano-Menominee at Shawano. The Court of Appeals and Supreme Court hear appeals.

Adams County
organized 1848 from Portage County

Adams County Courthouse
400 Main Street
Friendship, WI 53934
(608) 339-4206 (Register of Deeds, PO Box 219); (608) 339-4208 (Clerk of Circuit Court, PO Box 220); (608) 399-4200 (County Clerk, PO Box 278); (608) 339-4213 (Register in Probate, 402 Main Street, PO Box 200); (608) 339-4514 FAX (County Clerk)
adamsrod@co.adams.wi.us; dianna.helmrick@wicourts.gov; cphillippi@co.adams.wi.us; terry.warner@wicourts.gov
http://209.200.70.10; http://www.co.adams.wi.gov/default.asp?id=5&mnu=5
Jodi Helgeson Register of Deeds; Dianna D. Helmrick, Clerk of Circuit Court; Cindy Phillippi, County Clerk; Terry Reynolds Warner, Register in Probate
(deeds from 1853, births from 1860, deaths from 1876, marriages from 1859)
copies of deeds: $2.00 each; copies of vital records: $10.00 each for births, $7.00 each for deaths and marriages

Ashland County
organized 1860 from unorganized territory

Ashland County Courthouse
201 West Main Street
Ashland, WI 54806
(715) 682-7008 (Register of Deeds); (715) 682-7016 (Clerk of Circuit Court); (715) 682-7000 (County Clerk); (715) 682-7009 (Register in Probate); (715) 682-7035 FAX (Register of Deeds); (715) 682-7919 FAX (Clerk of Circuit Court); (715) 682-7032 FAX (County Clerk)
karen.miller@co.ashland.wi.us; kathleen.colgrove@wicourts.gov; pat.somppi@co.ashland.wi.us; rosalind.wilhelm@wicourts.gov
http://www.co.ashland.wi.us
Karen Miller, Register of Deeds, Kathleen Colgrove, Clerk of Circuit Court; Patricia Somppi, County Clerk; Rosalind Wilhelm, Register in Probate
(land records with Register of Deeds, naturalization records from 1890 with Clerk of Circuit Court, vital records from 1890 with Register of Deeds, probate records from 1890 with Register in Probate)
probate search service: $4.00 per name; copies of probate records: $1.00 per page, no minimum

Bad Ax County
(see Vernon County)

Barron County
organized 1859; name changed from Dallas County in 1869

Barron County Courthouse
330 East LaSalle Avenue
Barron, WI 54812-9801

(715) 537-6210 (Register of Deeds, Room 2500);
(715) 537-6200 (County Clerk, Room 210);
(715) 537-6817 FAX (Register of Deeds)
joyce.kaseno@co.barron.wi.us;
deeann.cook@co.barron.wi.us
http://www.co.barron.wi.us
Joyce K. Kaseno, Register of Deeds; DeeAnn
Cook, County Clerk
(land records and vital records with Register of
Deeds)

Barron County Justice Center
1420 State Highway 25 North
Barron, WI 54812
(715) 537-6260 (Clerk of Circuit Court, Room
2601); (715) 537-6265 (Clerk of Circuit Court,
Room 2201); (715) 537-6261 (Register in
Probate, Room 2700); (715) 537-6269 FAX
(Clerk of Circuit Court); (715) 537-6769 FAX
(Register in Probate)
judith.espeseth@wicourts.gov;
deanne.alsbury@wicourts.gov
http://www.co.barron.wi.us;
http://www.co.barron.wi.us/courts.htm
Judith W. Espeseth, Clerk of Circuit Court;
Deanne E. Alsbury, Register in Probate

Bayfield County
organized 1845 from Ashland County; name
changed from LaPointe County in 1866

Bayfield County Courthouse
117 East Fifth Street
Washburn, WI 54891
(715) 373-6119 (Register of Deeds, PO Box
813); (715) 373-6108 (Clerk of Circuit Court);
(715) 373-6100 (County Clerk)
polson@bayfieldcounty.org; Kay.Cederberg@
wicourts.gov; sfibert@bayfieldcounty.org
http://www.bayfieldcounty.org
Patricia Olson, Register of Deeds; Kay
Cederberg, Clerk of Circuit Court and
Register in Probate; Scott Fibert, County
Clerk
(land records with Tax Lister's Office;
naturalization records, births from the late
1870s, deaths from the late 1800s, and
marriages from the mid-1800s with Register
of Deeds; probate records with Clerk of
Courts)
probate search service: $5.00; copies of birgh
certificates: $12.00; copies of death certificates
and marriage records: $7.00; copies of probate
records: $1.25 per page

Brown County
organized 1818 from territorial county, annexed
part of Shawano and Oconto counties in 1919

Brown County Office Building
305 East Walnut Street
Green Bay, WI 54301
(920) 448-4470 (Register of Deeds, Northern
Building, Room 260, PO Box 23600); (414)
448-4471 (Tract Index); (920) 448-4016
(County Clerk, Room 120); (920) 448-4449
FAX (Register of Deeds); (920) 448-4498
FAX (County Clerk)
bc_register_of_deeds@co.brown.wi.us;
bc_county_clerk@co.brown.wi.us
http://www.co.brown.wi.us
Cathy Williquette, Register of Deeds; Darlene
Marcelle, County Clerk
(land records, births from 1746, deaths from
1834, marriages from 1821 with Register of
Deeds)
copies of vital records: $8.00 each for births,
$5.00 each for deaths and marriages (cashier's
check or money order)

Brown County Courthouse
100 South Jefferson Street
Green Bay, WI 54301
(920) 448-4155 (Clerk of Courts, Lower Level);
(920) 448-4275 (Register in Probate, Room
160, PO Box 23600)
bc_clerk_of_courts@co.brown.wi.us;
james.queoff@wicourts.gov
http://www.co.brown.wi.us

Lisa Wilson, Clerk of Courts; James Queoff,
Register in Probate
(naturalization records from 1940 with Clerk of
Courts; probate records with Register in
Probate)
probate search service: $4.00; copies of probate
records: $1.00 per page ("all county offices
require the fee before we search or issue
copies of documents")

Buffalo County
organized 6 July 1853 from Jackson County to
include all of what is now Trempealeau
County, west of the line between ranges 7 and
8, south of the Buffalo River and north of the
line between townships 18 and 19, enlarged in
1854 north to the line between townships 24
and 25, west to the Chippewa River, south to
the Mississippi and the line between
townships 18 and 19

Buffalo County Courthouse
407 South Second Street
Alma, WI 54610
(608) 685-6230 (Register of Deeds, PO Box 28);
(608) 685-6212 (Clerk of Court, PO Box 68);
(608) 685-6206 (County Clerk, PO Box 58);
(608) 685-6202 (Register in Probate, PO Box
68); (608) 685-6213 FAX (Register of Deeds
and County Clerk); (608) 685-6211 FAX
(Clerk of Court and Register in Probate)
donna.carothers@buffalocounty.com;
roselle.urness@wicourts.gov;
roxann.halverson@buffalocounty.com;
renee.pronschinske@wicourts.gov
http://www.buffalocounty.com
Donna J. Carothers, Register of Deeds; Roselle
Urness, Clerk of Circuit Court; Roxann
Halverson, County Clerk; Renee
Pronschinske, Register in Probate
(land records with Register of Deeds,
naturalization records with Clerk of Court,
vital records with Register of Deeds, probate
records with Circuit Court's Register in
Probate)
copies of land records: $2.00 for the first page
and $1.00 for each additional page, 25¢ per
document for certification; certified or
uncertified copies of vital records: $10.00
each for births, $7.00 each for deaths and
marriages (certified copies restricted to
persons with a "direct and tangible interest"
in the records)

Burnett County
organized 1856 from Polk County

Burnett County Government Center
7410 County Road K
Siren, WI 54872
(715) 349-2183 (Register of Deeds, #103); (715)
349-2147 (Clerk of Court, #115); (715) 349-
2173 (County Clerk, #105); (715) 349-2177
(Register in Probate, #110); (715) 349-2037
FAX (Register of Deeds); (715) 349-7659
FAX (Clerk of Court); (715) 349-2169 FAX
(County Clerk)
jechell@burnettcounty.org;
Trudy.Schmidt@wicourts.gov;
Wanda.Hinrichs@dss.co.burnett.wi.us;
dorothy.richard@wicourts.gov
http://www.burnettcounty.com
Jeanine Chell, Register of Deeds; Trudy
Schmidt, Clerk of Circuit Court; Wanda
Hinrichs, County Clerk; Dorothy Richard,
Register in Probate
(land records with Register of Deeds, vital
records with Register of Deeds, probate
records with Register in Probate, #110)
probate search service: $4.00; copies of land
records: $2.00 for the first page and $1.00 for
each additional page; certified copies of vital
records: $1.00 each for births, $7.00 each for
deaths and marriages; copies of probate
records: $1.00 per page, $1.00 minimum

Calumet County
organized 1836 from territorial county

Calumet County Courthouse
206 Court Street
Chilton, WI 53014-1127
(920) 849-1441 (Register of Deeds); (920) 849-
1414 (Clerk of Courts); (920) 849-1458
(County Clerk); (920) 849-1455 (Register in
Probate); (920) 849-1469 FAX; (414) 849-
2361
Gregory.Shirley@co.calumet.wi.us;
Barb.VanAkkeren@wicourts.gov;
Hauser.Beth@co.calumet.wi.us;
Janice.Marose@wicourts.gov
http://www.co.calumet.wi.us
Shirley Gregory, Register of Deeds; Barbara
VanAkkeren, Clerk of Courts; Beth Hauser,
County Clerk; Janice Marose, Register in
Probate
(land records and vital records with Register of
Deeds, probate records with Register in
Probate)

Chippewa County
organized 1845 from Crawford County (not to
be confused with a former Chippewa County
which existed at the time of the 1830 census,
covering much of what is now Ashland,
Bayfield, Douglas, Iron and Vilas counties)

Chippewa County Courthouse
711 North Bridge Street
Chippewa Falls, WI 54729-1876
(715) 726-7994 (Register of Deeds); (715) 726-
7758 (Clerk of Circuit Court, Room 220);
(715) 726-7980 (County Clerk); (715) 726-
7737 (Register in Probate, Room 218); (715)
726-4582 FAX (Register of Deeds); (715)
726-7987 FAX (County Clerk)
mgeissler@co.chippewa.wi.us; khepfler@
co.chippewa.wi.us; kbernier@co.chippewa.
wi.us; kstelzner@co.chippewa.wi.us;
kay.stelzner@wicourts.gov
http://www.co.chipewa.wi.us
Marge L. Geissler, Register of Deeds; Karen
Hepfler, Clerk of Circuit Court; Kathleen
Bernier, County Clerk; Katherine Stelzner
(land records with Register of Deeds,
naturalization records with Clerk of Circuit
Court, vital records with Register of Deeds,
probate records with Register in Probate)

Clark County
organized 1853 from Marathon County

Clark County Courthouse
517 Court Street
Neillsville, WI 54456-1971
(715) 743-5162 (Register of Deeds, Room 303,
PO Box 384); (715) 743-5181 (Clerk of
Circuit Court, Room 405); (715) 743-5148
(County Clerk, Room 301); (715) 743-5172
(Register in Probate, Room 403); (715) 743-
5154 FAX (Register of Deeds and County
Clerk)
http://www.co.clark.wi.us/ClarkCounty
lois.hagedorn@co.clark.wi.us;
gail.walker@wicourts.gov;
christina.jensen@co.clark.wi.us;
stephen.walter@wicourts.gov
Lois Hagedorn, Register of Deeds; Gail Walker,
Clerk of Circuit Court; Christina M. Jensen,
County Clerk; Stephen J. Walter, Registrar
(land records, naturalization records [incomplete
before 1895], and vital records [incomplete
before 1905] with Register of Deeds, probate
records from 1874 with Register in Probate
["files prior to 1901 are on microfilm at State
Historical Society"])
probate search service: $4.00; copies of land
records: $2.00 for the first page and $1.00 for
each additional page of the same document;
certified or uncertified copies of vital records:
$10.00 each for births, $7.00 each for deaths
and marriages; copies of probate records: 15¢
each, no minimum

Columbia County
organized 1846 from Portage, Brown and
Crawford counties

Columbia County Carl Frederick Administration Building
400 DeWitt Street
Portage, WI 53901
(608) 742-9677 (Register of Deeds, PO Box 133); (608) 742-9640 (Clerk of Circuit Court, PO Box 587); (608) 742-9654 (County Clerk); (608) 742-9636 (Register in Probate, PO Box 587); (608) 742-9875 FAX (Register of Deeds); (608) 742-9601 FAX (Clerk of Circuit Court); (608) 742-9602 FAX (County Clerk); (608) 742-9601 FAX (Register in Probate)(
Lisa.Walker@co.columbia.wi.us;
Susan.Raimer@wicourts.gov;
Sue.Moll@co.columbia.wi.us;
Joan.Maxwell@wicourts.gov
http://www.co.columbia.wi.us/ColumbiaCounty
Lisa Walker, Register of Deeds; Susan Raimer, Clerk of Circuit Court; Sue Moll, County Clerk; Joan Maxwell, Register in Probate
(land records from 1828 to date with Register of Deeds, naturalization records with Clerk of Circuit Court, vital records from the 1850s with Register of Deeds, probate records with Register in Probate)
probate search service: $4.00 (cost of search applied to copies); copies of land records: $2.00 for the first page and $1.00 for each additional page of the same document; vital records search service: $10.00 for births, $7.00 for deaths and marriages (includes one copy, if the record is found); copies of probate records: $1.00 per page, no minimum

Crawford County
organized 26 October 1818 from territorial county

Crawford County Courthouse
220 North Beaumont Road
Prairie du Chien, WI 53821
(608) 326-0219 (Register of Deeds); (608) 326-0200 (County Clerk)
donna.steiner@wicourts.gov;
jgeisler@centurytel.net;
nancy.dowling@wicourts.gov
http://www.wisconline.com/counties/crawford
Melissa Mezera, Register of Deeds; Donna Steiner, Clerk of Cicruit Court; Janet Geisler, County Clerk; Nancy Dowling, Register in Probate
(land records with Register of Deeds, naturalization records with Clerk of Courts, vital records with Register of Deeds, probate records with Joan Hurda, Register in Probate)
no probate search service; copies of probate records: $2.00 per page, no minimum

Dallas County
(see Barron County)

Dane County
organized 1839 from Iowa County

Dane County City-County Building
210 Martin Luther King, Jr. Boulevard
Madison, WI 53709
(608) 266-4141 (Register of Deeds, Room 110, PO Box 1438); (608)266-4121 (County Clerk); (608) 267-3110 FAX (Register of Deeds); (608) 266-2611 FAX (County Clerk)
chlebowski@co.dane.wi.us;
ohlsen@co.dane.wi.us
http://www.co.dane.wi.us
Kristi Chlebowski, Register of Deeds; Bob Ohlsen, County Clerk;
(deeds, mortgages, land contracts, satisfactions, etc., from 1835 to date with Register of Deeds, land records with Planning and Development, Room 116, naturalization records with The State Historical Society of Wisconsin, vital records from the 1850s to date [early records incomplete] with Register of Deeds)
copies of land records with Register of Deeds: $2.00 for the first page and $1.00 for each additional page, 25¢ for certification; certified or uncertified copies of vital records: $1.00

for births and $7.00 for deaths and marriages (certified copies restricted to persons with a "direct and tangible interest" in the records)

Dane County Clerk of Circuit Court and Register in Probate
Courthouse, Room 1000
215 South Hamilton Street
Madison, WI 53703
(608) 266-4311; (608) 266-4679; (608) 266-4625 FAX; (608) 267-8859 FAX
carlo.esqueda@wicourts.gov
http://www.countyofdane.com/clrkcort/clrkhome.htm
Carlo Esqueda

Dodge County
organized 1836 from territorial county

Dodge County Administration Building
127 East Oak Street
Juneau, WI 53039
(920) 386-3720 (Register of Deeds, Third Floor); (920) 386-3602 (County Clerk); (920) 386-3902 FAX (Register of Deeds); (920) 386-3928 FAX (County Clerk)
rod@co.dodge.wi.us;
cplanasch@co.dodge.wi.us;
kgibson@co.dodge.wi.us
http://www.co.dodge.wi.us
Chris Planasch, Register of Deeds; Karen J. Gibson, County Clerk
(land records from 1877 [date of fire], index cards to naturalization records [original naturalization records with University of Wisconsin—Oshkosh, Area Research Center, Citizenship Records], births, deaths and marriages)
no land records search service (contact Jeanne Dornfeld, W4402 Raasch's Hill Road, Horicon, WI 53032); copies of land records: $2.00 for the first page and $1.00 for each additional page; copies of vital records: $10.00 each for births, $7.00 each for deaths and marriages (certified copies restricted to persons with a "direct and tangible interest" in the records)

Dodge County Justice Facility
210 West Center Street
Juneau, WI 53039
(920) 386-3820 (Clerk of Circuit Court); (920) 386-3550 (Register in Probate)
Lynn.Hron@wicourts.gov;
kathy.munro@wicourts.gov
http://www.co.dodge.wi.us
Lynn Hron, Clerk of Circuit Court; Kathleen Munro, Register in Probate
(probate records from 1840s)
probate search service: $4.00 each; copies of probate records: $1.00 each, no minimum

Door County
organized 1851 from Brown County

Door County Courthouse
(421 Nebraska Street—location)
PO Box 670 (mailing address)
Sturgeon Bay, WI 54235-0670
(920) 746-2270 (Register of Deeds); (920) 746-2447 FAX; (414) 743-5511
cpetersilka@co.door.wi.us;
nancy.robillard@wicourts.gov;
nbemmann@co.door.wi.us
http://www.co.door.wi.gov
Carey Petersilka, Register of Deeds; Nancy Bemmann, County Clerk
(land records from 1857, vital records from 1857 [not a lot of records in the late 1800s] with Register of Deeds)
copies of vital records: $10.00 each for births, $7.00 each for deaths and marriages (certified copies restricted to persons with a "direct and tangible interest" in the records)

Door County Justice Center
1205 South Duluth Avenue
Sturgeon Bay, WI 54235
(920) 746-2205 (Clerk of Circuit Court); (920) 746-2482 (Register in Probate); (920) 746-

2520 FAX (Clerk of Circuit Court and Register in Probate)
nancy.robillard@wicourts.gov;
judith.schneider@wicourts.gov
http://www.co.door.wi.gov
Nancy Robillard, Clerk of Circuit Court; Judith Schneider, Register in Probate
(probate records from 1863)
probate search service: $4.00; copies of probate records: $1.00 each, no minimum

Douglas County
county created by an act of legislature on 8 February 1854 from unorganized territory

Douglas County Courthouse
1313 Belknap Street
Superior, WI 54880-2730
(715) 395-1350 (Register of Deeds, Room 108); (715) 395-1203 (Clerk of Circuit Court, Room 309); (715) 395-1341 (County Clerk, Room 101); (715) 395-1229 (Register in Probate); (715) 395-1553 FAX (Register of Deeds); (715) 395-1421 FAX (County Clerk); (715) 395-1633 FAX (Register in Probate)
gayle.wahner@douglascountywi.org;
joan.osty@wicourts.gov;
sue.sandvick@douglascountywi.org;
kathy.reed@wicourts.gov
http://www.douglascountywi.org
Gayle I. Wahner, Register of Deeds; Joan Osty, Clerk of Circuit Court; Susan Sandvick, County Clerk; Kathy Reed, Register in Probate
(land records with Register of Deeds or County Clerk, vital records with Register of Deeds)
certified copies of vital records (restricted to persons with a "direct and tangible interest" in the records): $10.00 each for births, $7.00 each for deaths and marriages, $1.00 each for uncertified copies

Dunn County
organized 1854 from Chippewa County

Dunn County Government Center
800 Wilson Avenue
Menomonie, WI 54751-2717
(715) 232-1228 (Register of Deeds, Room 135); (715) 232-1677 (County Clerk, Room 147); (715) 232-1229 FAX (Register of Deeds); (715) 232-2534 FAX (County Clerk)
rod@co.dunn.wi.us; jmrdutt@co.dunn.wi.us; cco@co.dunn.wi.us
http://www.co.dunn.wi.us
James Mrdutt, Register of Deeds; Marilyn Hoyt, County Clerk
(land records and vital records with Register of Deeds)
no land or vital records search service ("Register of Deeds Office will not do land or vital record searches over the telephone; the office does not have the staff to handle verbal requests; please send SASE with requests; the fee should be sent, and if a record is found a copy will be sent"); copies of vital records: $8.00 each for births, $5.00 each for deaths and marriages; copies of probate records: $1.00 per page, no minimum

Dunn County Justice Center
615 Stokke Parkway
Menomonie, WI 54751
(715) 232-2611 (Clerk of Circuit Court); (715) 232-6782 (Register in Probate, Suite 1300); (715) 232-6888 FAX (Clerk of Circuit Court); (715) 232-6787 (Register in Probate)
clara.minor@wicourts.gov;
nancy.greene@wicourts.gov
http://www.co.dunn.wi.us
Clara D. Minor, Clerk of Circuit Court; Nancy Greene, Register in Probate
probate search service: $4.00; copies of probate records: $1.00 per page, no minimum

Eau Claire County
organized 1856 from Clark County

Eau Claire County Courthouse

721 Oxford Avenue
Eau Claire, WI 54703-5481
(715) 839-4745 (Register of Deeds); (715) 839-4816 (Clerk of District Court); (715) 839-4803 (County Clerk); (715) 839-4823 (Register in Probate, Room 2201)
mary.kaiser@co.eau-claire.wi.us; EauClaire.Info@wicourts.gov; diana.miller@wicourts.gov; Janet.Loomis@co.eau-claire.wi.us; jean.gay@wicourts.gov
http://www.co.eau-claire.wi.us
Mary L. Kaiser, Register of Deeds; Diana J. Miller, Clerk of Circuit Court; Janet Loomis, County Clerk; Jean Gay, Register in Probate
(land records from 1856 with Register of Deeds, naturalization records with Clerk of Court, vital records from 1907 with Register of Deeds, probate records with Register in Probate)
probate search service: $4.00; copies of vital records: $10.00 each for births, $7.00 each for deaths and marriages; copies of probate records: $1.00 per page, $3.00 for certification, no minimum

Florence County
organized 1882 from Marinette and Oconto counties

Florence County Courthouse
(501 Lake Avenue—location)
PO Box 410 (mailing address)
Florence, WI 54121-0410
(715) 528-4252 (Register of Deeds); (715) 528-3205 (Clerk of Circuit Court); (715) 528-3201 (County Clerk); (715) 528-4272 FAX (Register of Deeds); (715) 528-5470 FAX (Clerk of Circuit Court); (715) 589-4762 FAX (County Clerk)
flocorod@florencewi.net; paula.coraggio@wicourts.gov; jmeyer@co.florence.wi.us
http://www.florencewisconsin.com
Pattie Gehlhoff, Register of Deeds; Paula Coraggio, Clerk of Circuit Court and Register in Probate; Geraldine "Jerri" Meyer, County Clerk
(land records and vital records with Register of Deeds, naturalization records and probate records with Clerk of Circuit Court)
copies of land records: $2.00 for the first page and $1.00 for each additional page

Fond du Lac County
organized 1836 from territorial county

Fond du Lac County Courthouse
160 South Macy Street
Fond du Lac, WI 54935-4241
(920) 929-3034 (Clerk of Circuit Court, Civil/Family); (920) 929-3084 (Register in Probate); (920) 929-3293 FAX (Register of Deeds); (920) 929-3933 FAX (Clerk of District Court); (920) 929-3293 FAX (County Clerk); (920) 906-5540 FAX (Register in Probate)
register.deeds@co.fond-du-lac.wi.us; mary.karst@co.fond-du-lac.wi.us; county.clerk@co.fond-du-lac.wi.us; joyce.buechel@co.fond-du-lac.wi.us; ardell.klaske@wicourts.gov
http://www.co.fond-du-lac.wi.us
Patricia Kraus, Register of Deeds; Mary Karst, Clerk of Circuit Court; Joyce Buechel, County Clerk; Ardell Klaske, Register in Probate
(land records and vital records with Register of Deeds, probate records with Register in Probate)
vital records search service: $10.00 (applied to cost of copy if found); probate search service: $4.00 ("send searching fee and summary of what information you want; we will advise as to what we have and cost of copies"); copies of land records: $2.00 for the first page and $1.00 for each additional page; copies of vital records: $10.00 each for births, $7.00 for deaths and marriages; copies of probate records: $1.00 per page, no minimum

Forest County
organized 1885 from Langlade and Oconto counties

Forest County Courthouse
200 East Madison Street
Crandon, WI 54520-1414
(715) 478-3823 (Recorder of Deeds); (715) 478-3323 (Clerk of Circuit Court); (715) 478-2422 (County Clerk); (715) 478-2418 (Register in Probate); (715) 478-3837 FAX (Register of Deeds Office); (715) 478-3211 FAX (Clerk of Circuit Court); (715) 478-5175 FAX (County Clerk)
forestrd@co.forest.wi.us; fcclerk@co.forest.wi.us; kathy.flannery@wicourts.gov
http://www.co.forest.wi.gov; http://www.forestcountywi.com
Paul Aschenbrenner, Recorder of Deeds; Penny Carter, Clerk of Circuit Court; Ann Mihalko, County Clerk; Kathy Flannery, Register in Probate

Grant County
organized 1836 from Iowa County

Grant County Courthouse
130 West Maple
Lancaster, WI 53813-1625
(608) 723-2675 (County Clerk); (608) 723-2697 (Register in Probate); (608) 623-4048 FAX (County Clerk)
diane.perkins@wicourts.gov; gcoclerk@pcii.net; jody.bartels@wicourts.gov
http://www.grantcounty.org
Diane Perkins, Clerk of Circuit Court; Chris Carl, County Clerk; Jody Bartels, Register in Probate

Grant County Register of Deeds
(111 South Jefferson Street—location)
PO Box 391 (mailing address)
Lancaster, WI 53813-0391
(608) 723-2727; (608) 723-4048 FAX
http://www.wrdaonline.org/Biography/Grant.htm
Marilyn Pierce

Green County
organized 1836 from Iowa County

Green County Courthouse
1016 16th Avenue
Monroe, WI 53566
(608) 328-9430; (608) 328-9439 (Register of Deeds); (608) 328-9433 (Clerk of Circuit Court); (608) 328-9430 (County Clerk); (608) 328-9567 (Register in Probate); (608) 328-2835 FAX (Register of Deeds); (608) 328-2835 FAX (Clerk of Circuit Court); (608) 328-2835 FAX (County Clerk)
cmeudt@greencountywi.org; carol.thompson@wicourts.gov; mdoyle@greencountywi.org; jean.goepfert@wicourts.gov
http://www.co.green.wi.gov
Cynthia Meudt, Register of Deeds; Carol Thompson, Clerk of Circuit Court; Michael Doyle, County Clerk; Jean Goepfert, Register in Probate
(real estate records from 1837, legitimate births from 1852, deaths from 1874, and marriages from 1843 [incomplete before 1 June 1907] with Register of Deeds, probate records with Register in Probate)
probate search service: $4.00 per name; copies of land records: $2.00 for the first page and $1.00 for each additional page, 25¢ for certification; certified copies of naturalization records: $3.50 each; certified or uncertified copies of vital records: $10.00 each for births, $7.00 each for deaths and marriages (certified copies restricted to persons with a "direct and tangible interest" in the records); copies of probate records: $1.00 per page, no minimum

Green Lake County
organized 1858 from Marquette District

Green Lake County Courthouse
(492 Hill Street—location)

PO Box 3188 (mailing address)
Green Lake, WI 54941
(920) 294-4021 (Register of Deeds, Room 290); (920) 294-4142 (Clerk of Circuit Court, Room 390); (920) 294-4005 (County Clerk, Room 230); (920) 294-4044 (Register in Probate); (920) 294-4165 FAX (Register of Deeds); (920) 294-4009 FAX (County Clerk)
rod@co.green-lake.wi.us; susan.krueger@wicourts.gov; clerk@co.green-lake.wi.us; lee.huenerberg@wicourts.gov
http://www.co.green-lake.wi.us
Leone Seaman, Register of Deeds; Susan Krueger, Clerk of Circuit Court; Margaret Bostelmann, County Clerk; Lee Huenerberg, Register in Probate
(land records from 1845, births and deaths from 1876, and marriages from 1852 with Register of Deeds, probate records with Register in Probate Office)

Iowa County
organized 1829 from territorial county

Iowa County Courthouse
222 North Iowa Street
Dodgeville, WI 53533-1557
(608) 935-0396 (Register of Deeds); (608) 935-0395 (Clerk of Circuit Court); (608) 935-0399 (County Clerk); (608) 935-0347 (Register in Probate)
dixie.edge@iowacounty.org; greg.klusendorf@iowacounty.org; Carolyn.Olson@wicourts.gov; tari.engels@wicourts.gov
http://www.iowacounty.org
Dixie L. Edge, Register of Deeds; Carolyn Olson, Clerk of Circuit Court; Greg Klusendorf, County Clerk; Tari Engels, Register in Probate
(land records from 1835 [grantee/grantor index only] with Register of Deeds, naturalization index from 1835 to 1906 with Clerk of Courts Office, births and deaths from 1877 [a few earlier], marriages from 1849 [most are indexed by groom only] with Register of Deeds, probate records from 1830s with Register in Probate, some wills and final judgments for estates recorded in land records with Register of Deeds)
land records search service: no charge, as time permits; no probate search service; copies of land records: $2.00 for the first page and $1.00 for each additional page, copies of probate records: $1.00 per page

Iron County
organized 1893 from Ashland and Oneida counties

Iron County Courthouse
300 Taconite Street
Hurley, WI 54534
(715) 561-3375; (715) 561-2945 (Register of Deeds, Suite 102); (715) 561-3434 (Register in Probate, Room 209)
register@ironcountywi.org; irod1@cheqnet.net; Karen.Ransanici@wicourts.gov; clerk@ironcountywi.org; diane.erickson@wicourts.gov
http://www.wrdaonline.org/Biography/Iron.htm (Register of Deeds); http://www.ironcountywi.com (Iron County Development Zone Council)
Robert Traczyk, Register of Deeds; Karen Ransanici, Clerk of Circuit Court; Michael Saari, County Clerk; Diane Erickson, Register in Probate

Jackson County
organized 11 May 1853 from Crawford and La Crosse counties

Jackson County Courthouse
307 Main Street
Black River Falls, WI 54615
(715) 284-0205 (Register of Deeds); (715) 284-0208 (Clerk of Circuit Court); (715) 284-0201 (County Clerk); (715) 284-0213 (Register in Probate); (715) 284-0270 FAX (Clerk of

Circuit Court); (715) 284-0278 FAX (County Clerk)

shari.marg@co.jackson.wi.us; claudia.singleton @wicourts.gov; kyle.deno@co.jackson.wi.us; kathy.powell@wicourts.gov

http://www.co.jackson.wi.us

Shari Marg, Register of Deeds; Claudia Singleton, Clerk of Circuit Court; Kyle Deno, County Clerk; Kathy Powell, Register in Probate

(land records with Treasurer or Tax Lister, naturalization records with Clerk of Circuit Court, vital records with Register of Deeds, probate records with Register in Probate)

probate search service: $4.00; copies of probate records: $1.00 each, no minimum

Jefferson County
organized 1836 from Dodge and Waukesha counties

Jefferson County Courthouse
320 South Main Street
Jefferson, WI 53549-1718
(920) 674-7235 (Register of Deeds, PO Box 356); (920) 674-7150 (Clerk of Circuit Court); (920) 674-7140 (County Clerk, Room 109); (920) 674-7245 (Register in Probate); (920) 674-7238 FAX (Register of Deeds); (920) 674-7368 FAX (County Clerk)

stacih@co.jefferson.wi.us; Carla.Robinson@ wicourts.gov; barbf@co.jefferson.wi.us; thomas.lafleur@wicourts.gov

http://www.co.jefferson.wi.us

Staci Hoffman, Register of Deeds; Carla Robinson, Clerk of Circuit Court; Barbara Frank, County Clerk; Thomas Lafleur, Register in Probate

Juneau County
organized 1856 from Adams County

Juneau County Courthouse
220 East State Street
Mauston, WI 53948
(608) 847-9325 (Register of Deeds, Room 212); (608) 847-9300 (County Clerk, Room 112); (608) 847-9402 FAX (Register of Deeds); (608) 847-9402 FAX (County Clerk)

juneaurd@co.juneau.wi.us; jcclerk@co.juneau.wi.us

http://www.co.juneau.wi.gov

Christie Bender, Register of Deeds; Kathleen Kobylski, County Clerk

(land records with Real Property Description Office, vital records with Register of Deeds Office)

Juneau County Courthouse
(200 Oak Street—location)
PO Box 246 (mailing address)
Mauston, WI 53948
(608) 847-9356 (Clerk of Courts); (608) 847-9346 (Register in Probate Office, Room 2300); (608) 847-9360 FAX (Clerk of Court)

louise.schulz@wicourts.gov; diane.mortensen@wicourts.gov

http://www.co.juneau.wi.gov

Louise Schulz, Clerk of Circuit Court; Diane Mortensen, Register in Probate

(naturalization records with Clerk of Courts Office, probate records with Register in Probate)

probate search service: $4.00; copies of probate records: $1.00 per page, $3.00 certified

Kenosha County
organized 1850 from Racine County

Kenosha County Administration Building
1010 56th Street
Kenosha, WI 53140
(414) 653-2414 (Register of Deeds—Real Estate); (414) 653-2444 (Register of Deeds—Vitals); (262) 653-2477 (County Clerk); (262) 653-2564 FAX (County Clerk)

lprincipe@co.kenosha.wi.us; chighland@co.kenosha.wi.us

http://www.co.kenosha.wi.us

Louise I. Principe, Register of Deeds; Edna

Highland, County Clerk

(land records and vital records with Register of Deeds)

copies of land records: $2.00 for the first page and $1.00 for each additional page, $3.00 each for plats, 25¢ for certification; copies of vital records: $10.00 each for births, $7.00 each for deaths and marriages

Kenosha County Courthouse
912 56th Street
Kenosha, WI 53140
(262) 653-2664 (Clerk of Circuit Court); (262) 653-2678 (Register in Probate); (262) 653-2435 FAX (Clerk of Circuit Court—Records); (262) 653-2753 FAX (Clerk of Circuit Court—Family); (262) 653-2673 FAX (Clerk of Circuit Court—Probate)

Rebecca.Matoska-Mentink@wicourts.gov; marilyn.lemke@wicourts.gov

http://www.co.kenosha.wi.us

Rebecca Matoska-Mentink, Clerk of Circuit Court; Marilyn Lemke (Register in Probate)

(naturalization records with Clerk of Courts, probate records with Register in Probate)

no probate search service

Kewaunee County
organized 1852 from Manitowoc County

Kewaunee County Courthouse
613 Dodge Street
Kewaunee, WI 54216
(920) 388-7144 (Clerk of Circuit Court); (920) 388-7123 (County Clerk); (920) 388-7143 (Register in Probate); (920) 388-7049 FAX (Clerk of Circuit Court); (920) 388-7195 FAX (County Clerk)

rebecca.deterville@wicourts.gov; teskel@ kewauneeco.org; juliet.schleis@wicourts.gov; julie.gallenberger@wicourts.gov

http://www.kewauneeco.org

Rebecca "Becky" Deterville, Clerk of Circuit Court; Linda Teske, County Clerk; Juliet Schleis, Register in Probate

Kewaunee County Register of Deeds
810 Lincoln Street
Kewaunee, WI 54216
(920) 388-7126 (Register of Deeds); (920) 388-7129 FAX (Register of Deeds)

wolfj@kewauneeco.org; rebecca.deterville@wicourts.gov

http://www.kewauneeco.org

Janet Wolf, Register of Deeds; Rebecca Deterville, Clerk of Circuit Court

La Crosse County
organized 1851 Crawford County

La Crosse County Administration Center
400 North Fourth Street
La Crosse, WI 54601-3227
(608) 785-9644 (Register of Deeds, Room 1220); (608) 785-9645 (Register of Deeds); (608) 785-9581 (County Clerk, Room 1210)

mcbride.cheryl@co.la-crosse.wi.us; naegle.marion@co.la-crosse.wi.us

http://www.co.la-crosse.wi.us

Cheryl McBride, Register of Deeds; Marion I. Naegle, County Clerk

(land records from 1851 with Real Property Lister, Land, Title, Mapping Department, vital records from late 1800s with Register of Deeds)

La Crosse County Law Enforcement Center
333 Vine Street
La Crosse, WI 54601
(608) 785-9590 (Clerk of Circuit Court); (608) 785-9882 (Register in Probate, Room 312)

Pam.radtke@wicourts.gov; lois.groeschel@wicourts.gov

http://www.co.la-crosse.wi.us

Pamela Radtke, Clerk of Circuit Court; Lois Groeschel, Register in Probate

(probate records from the late 1890s)

probate search service: $4.00; copies of probate records: $1.00 per page, no minimum

Lafayette County
organized 1846 from Iowa County

Lafayette County Courthouse
(626 Main Street—location)
PO Box 40 (mailing address)
Darlington, WI 53530-0040
(608) 776-4838 (Register of Deeds); (608) 776-4832 (Clerk of Circuit Court); (608) 776-4850 (County Clerk); (608) 776-4811 (Register in Probate); (608) 776-4991 FAX (Register of Deeds); (608) 776-8893 FAX (County Clerk)

joe.boll@lafayettecountywi.org; catherine. mcgowan@wicourts.gov; linda.bawden@la fayettecountywi.org; lauretta.lade@wicourts.gov

http://www.wicip.uwplatt.edu/lafayette

Joseph Boll, Register of Deeds; Catherine McGowan, Clerk of Circuit Court; Linda Bawden, County Clerk; Lauretta Lade, Register in Probate

(government entry book from 1835, births from 1855 ["very sparse, not good until 1900"], deaths from 1876, and marriages from 1847 with Register of Deeds Office)

probate search service: $4.00; copies of probate records: $1.00 per page, no minimum; "If mailed out, payment is required before"

Langlade County
organized 1879 from Oconto County

Langlade County Courthouse
800 Clermont Street
Antigo, WI 54409-1985
(715) 627-6209 (Register of Deeds); (715) 627-6215 (Clerk of Circuit Court); (715) 627-6200 (County Clerk); (715) 627-6213 (Register in Probate); (715) 627-6270 FAX (Register of Deeds); (715) 627-6316 FAX (Clerk of Circuit Court); (715) 627-6329 FAX (Register in Probate)

sfischer@co.langlade.wi.us; langrod@newnorth. net; victoria.adamski@wicourts.gov; kjacob@ co.langlade.wi.us; joy.pecha@wicourts.gov

http://www.co.langlade.wi.us

Sandra Fischer, Register of Deeds; Victoria A. "Vicky" Adamski, Clerk of Circuit Court; Kathryn Jacob, County Clerk; Joy S. Pecha, Register in Probate

(land records from 1883 and vital records with Register of Deeds, probate records with Register in Probate)

probate search service: $4.00 per file; copies of land records: $2.00 for the first page and $1.00 for each additional page; copies of vital records: $1.00 each for births, $7.00 each for deaths and marriages; copies of probate records: $1.00 per page

LaPointe County
(see Bayfield County)

Lincoln County
organized 1874 from Marathon County

Lincoln County Courthouse
1110 East Main Street
Merrill, WI 54452-2577
(715) 536-0475 (Register of Deeds, Suite 201); (715) 536-0319 (Clerk of Circuit Court, Suite 200); (715) 536-0312 (County Clerk, Suite 202); (715) 536-0342 (Register in Probate); (715) 536-0360 FAX (Register of Deeds); (715) 536-0361 FAX (Clerk of Circuit Court); (715) 536-6528 FAX (County Clerk)

jcallahan@co.lincoln.wi.us; ckimmons@ co.lincoln.wi.us; cindy.kimmons@wicourts. gov; becky.byer@wicourts.gov

http://www.co.lincoln.wi.us

Sarah Koss, Register of Deeds; Cindy Kimmons, Clerk of Circuit Court; Becky Byer, Register in Probate

(land records and vital records with Register of Deeds, probate records with Register in Probate)

probate search service: $4.00; copies of vital records: $10.00 each for births, $7.00 each for deaths and marriages; copies of probate records: 25¢ per page, no minimum, "enclose SASE")

Manitowoc County
organized 1836 from territorial county

Manitowoc County Courthouse
1010 South Eighth Street
Manitowoc, WI 54220-5392
(920) 683-4010 (Register of Deeds, Room 104, PO Box 421); (920) 6783-4030 (Clerk of Circuit Court, Room 105, PO Box 2000); (920) 683-4003 (County Clerk, Room 115); (414) 683-4015 (Register in Probate, Room 116)(920) 683-2702 FAX (Register of Deeds); (920) 683-2733 FAX (Clerk of Circuit Court); (920) 683-4007 FAX (County Clerk)
prestonjones@co.manitowoc.wi.us; lynn.zigmunt@wi.courts.gov; jamieaulik@co.manitowoc.wi.us; patricia.koppa@wicourts.gov
http://www.manitowoc-county.com
Preston F. Jones, Register of Deeds; Lynn Zigmunt, Clerk of Circuit Court; Jamie Aulik, County Clerk; Patricia Koppa, Register in Probate
(land records from the early 1800s and births, deaths and marriages from the 1850s with Register of Deeds, probate files from 1850 with Register in Probate)
probate search service: $4.00; copies of probate records: $1.00 per page, $1.00 minimum ("we will review file and advise requester of documents we feel will be of genealogical value")

Marathon County
organized 1850 from Portage County

Marathon County Courthouse
500 Forest Street
Wausau, WI 54403-5568
(715) 261-1470 (Register of Deeds); (715) 261-1300 (Clerk of Circuit Court); (715) 261-1500 (County Clerk); (715) 261-1261 (Register in Probate); (715) 261-1488 FAX (Register of Deeds); (715) 261-1319 FAX (Clerk of Circuit Court); (715) 261-1515 FAX (County Clerk)
ucc@mailco.marathon.wi.us (Register of Deeds); clerkofcourts@mail.co.marathon.wi.us; nrkottke@mail.co.marathon.wi.us; countyclerk@mail.co.marathon.wi.us; jenni.lemmer@wicourts.gov
http://www.co.marathon.wi.us
Michael J. Sydow, Register of Deeds; Diane Sennholz, Clerk of Circuit Court; Nan Kottke, County Clerk; Jenni Lemmer, Register in Probate
(land records and vital records with Register of Deeds, naturalization records with Clerk of Court, probate records with Register in Probate)
probate search service: $4.00 per name; copies of vital records: $10.00 each for births, $7.00 each for deaths and marriages; copies of probate records: $1.00 per page, no minimum ("return postage appreciated; old probate files stored in basement, not available for immediate review")

Marinette County
organized 1879 from Oconto County

Marinette County Courthouse
1926 Hall Avenue
Marinette, WI 54143-1728
(715) 732-7550 (Register of Deeds, Room C105); (715) 732-7450 (Clerk of Circuit Court); (715) 732-7406 (County Clerk); (715) 732-7475 (Register in Probate, Room C-210); (715) 732-7556 FAX (Register of Deeds); (715) 732-7461 FAX (Clerk of Circuit Court); (715) 732-7532 FAX (County Clerk); (715) 732-7461 FAX (Register in Probate)
MCROD@marinettecounty.com; mhuempfner@marinettecounty.com; linda.dumke@wicourts.gov; mcclerk@marinettecounty.com; linda.keller@wicourts.gov
http://www.marinettecounty.com
Melanie I. Huempfner, Register of Deeds; Linda L. Dumke-Marquardt, Clerk of Circuit Court; Katherine "Kathy" Brandt, County Clerk, Linda Keller, Register in Probate
(land records and vital records with Register of Deeds, naturalization records with Clerk of Court, probate records with Register in Probate)
probate search service: $4.00; fee for copies, no minimum

Marquette County
organized 1836 from Marquette District

Marquette County Courthouse
77 West Park Street
Montello, WI 53949-0186
(608) 297-9136, ext. 232 (Register of Deeds, PO Box 236); (608) 297-9136, ext. 202 (Clerk of Circuit Court); (608) 297-9136, ext. 214 (County Clerk); (608) 297-9105 (Register in Probate, PO Box 142)
bwegner@co.marquette.wi.us; shari.rudolph@wicourt.gov; jthalacker@co.marquette.wi.us; carol.polk@wicourts.gov
http://www.co.marquette.wi.us
Bernice Wegner, Register of Deeds; Shari Rudolph, Clerk of Circuit Court; James "Jim" Thalacker, County Clerk/Auditor; Carol Polk, Register in Probate
(land records from 1836 and vital records from 1870 [better records after 1911] with Register of Deeds, probate records with Register in Probate)
probate search service: $4.00, but depends on extent of search; copies of probate records: $1.25 each

Menominee County
organized 1961 from the Menominee Indian Reservation (Shawano and Oconto counties)

Menominee County Courthouse
(Courthouse Lane—location)
PO Box 279 (mailing address)
Keshena, WI 54135-0279
(715) 799-3312 (Register of Deeds); (715) 799-3313 (Clerk of Circuit Court); (715) 799-3311 (County Clerk)
ruthwa@co.menominee.wi.us
http://www.wisconline.com/counties/menominee
Pamela Waukau, Register of Deeds and Clerk of Circuit Court; Ruth Waupoose, County Clerk

Menominee County Register in Probate
311 North Main Street
Shawano, WI 54166
(715) 526-8631; (715) 526-8622 FAX
cheryl.strauss@wicourts.gov
Cheryl Strauss

Milwaukee County
organized from the Northwest Territory; by an act of the Michigan Territorial Legislature, Milwaukee County became a distinct political division in August 1835, some eight months before the Territory of Wisconsin was created

Milwaukee County Courthouse
901 North Ninth Street
Milwaukee, WI 53233
(414) 278-4021 (Register of Deeds, Room 103); (414) 278-4000 (Register of Deeds—land); (414) 278-4003 (Register of Deeds—vital records); (414) 278-5362 (Clerk of Circuit Court, Room 104); (414) 278-4067 (County Clerk, Room 105); (414) 278-4516 (Register in Probate, Room 207); (414) 223-1257 FAX (Register of Deeds); (414) 223-1260 FAX (Clerk of Circuit Court)
regdeeds@milwcnty.com; RODVitalRecords@milwcnty.com; john.barrett@wicourts.gov; ctimail@wicourts.gov; mryan@milwcnty.com; countyclerk@milwcnty.com; robert.knoll@wicourts.gov
http://www.milwaukeecounty.org
John La Fave, Register of Deeds; John Barrett, Clerk of Circuit Court; Mark Ryan, County Clerk; Robert Knoll, Register in Probate
(land records with Register of Deeds; naturalization records with Milwaukee County Historical Society, vital records with Register of Deeds, probate records with Register in Probate)
probate search service: $4.00; copies of probate records: $1.00 per page, no minimum

Monroe County
organized 1854 from unorganized territory

Monroe County Clerk of Circuit Court and Register in Probate
112 South Court Street
Sparta, WI 54656-0165
(608) 269-8745 (Clerk of Circuit Court); (608) 269-8701 (Register in Probate, Room 301)
carol.thorsen@wicourts.gov; diane.berendes@wicourts.gov
http://www.co.monroe.wi.us/pub/home.php
Carol Thorsen, Clerk of Circuit Court; Diane Berendes, Register in Probate
(probate records from the early 1870s with Register in Probate)
copies of probate records: 50¢ per page, no minimum ("please include a SASE for use in returning information")

Monroe County Register of Deeds and County Clerk
202 South K Street
Sparta, WI 54656
(608) 269-8716 (Register of Deeds, Room 2); ; (608) 269-8705 (County Clerk, Room 1); (608) 269-8747 FAX (County Clerk)
smatson@co.monroe.wi.us
http://www.co.monroe.wi.us/pub/home.php
John D. Burke, Register of Deeds; Susan Matson, County Clerk
http://www.co.monroe.wi.us/pub/home.php
(land records, births from 1850, deaths from 1867, and marriages from 1854 with Register of Deeds)
land records search service: $5.00 plus SASE; copies of land records: $2.00 for the first page and $1.00 for each additional page of the same document; copies of vital records: $10.00 each for births, $5.00 each for deaths and marriages (send for application form first, certified copies restricted to persons with a "direct and tangible interest" in the records)

Oconto County
organized 1851 from Brown County

Oconto County Courthouse
301 Washington Street
Oconto, WI 54153-1675
(920) 834-7113 (Register of Deeds); (920) 834-6857 (Clerk of Circuit Court); (920) 834-6800 (County Clerk); (414) 834-6839 (Register in Probate); (920) 834-6805 FAX (Register of Deeds); (920) 834-6867 FAX (Clerk of Circuit Court); (920) 834-6805 FAX (County Clerk); (920) 834-6867 FAX (Register in Probate)
coc@co.oconto.wi.us; judy.ferries@co.oconto.wi.us; Pat.Pawlak@wicourts.gov
http://www.co.oconto.wi.us
Loralee Lasley, Register of Deeds; Michael C. Hodkiewicz, Clerk of Circuit Court; Judy Ferris, County Clerk; Patricia L. Pawlak, Register in Probate
(land records, births and deaths from 1872, marriages from 1855 with Register of Deeds, probate records with Register in Probate)
probate search service: $4.00; copies of probate records: $1.00 per page, no minimum ("payment in advance; mentals, adoptions and juvenile files are sealed and not for public view")

Oneida County
organized 1885 from Lincoln County

Oneida County Courthouse
(1 Courthouse Square—location)

PO Box 400 (mailing address)
Rhinelander, WI 54501-0400
(715) 369-6150 (Register of Deeds); (715) 369-6120 (Clerk of Circuit Court); (715) 369-6144 (County Clerk); (715) 369-6159 (Register in Probate); (715) 369-6222 FAX (Register of Deeds); (715) 369-6160 FAX (Clerk of Circuit Court); (715) 369-6230 FAX (County Clerk)
ocrod1@newnorth.net; tleighton@co.oneida.wi.us; ken.gardner@wicourts.gov; kenneth.gardner@wicourts.gov; bbruso@co.oneida.wi.us; susanne.ohman@wicourts.gov
http://www.co.oneida.wi.gov
Thomas H. Leighton, Register of Deeds; Kenneth J. Gardner, Clerk of Circuit Court; Robert Brusco, County Clerk; Susanne Ohman, Register in Probate
(land records and vital records with Register of Deeds, probate records with Register in Probate)
probate search service: $4.00; copies of land records: $1.00 per page; copies of vital records: $10.00 each for births, $7.00 each for deaths and marriages (proof of relationship required; copies of probate records: $1.00 per page, no minimum

Outagamie County
organized 1851 from Brown County

Outagamie County Administrative Building
410 South Walnut Street
Appleton, WI 54911-5936
(920) 832-5095 (Register of Deeds); (920) 832-5077 (County Clerk, Room 213); (920) 832-2177 FAX (Register of Deeds);
flenzjm@co.outagamie.wi.us; lonnie.wolf@wicourts.gov; sue.lutz@wicourts.gov
http://www.co.outagamie.wi.us
Janice Flenz, Register of Deeds
(land records from 1851 and vital records [not required by law until 1907] with Register of Deeds)
copies of vital records: $10.00 each for births, $7.00 each for deaths and marriages (certified copies restricted to persons with a "direct and tangible interest" in the records)

Outagamie County Justice Center
320 Walnut Street
Appleton, WI 54911
(920) 832-5131 (Clerk of Circuit Court); (920) 832-5601 (Register in Probate); (920) 832-5115 FAX (Clerk of Circuit Court)
lonnie.wolf@wicourts.govsue.lutz@wicourts.gov
http://www.co.outagamie.wi.us
Lonnie Wolf, Clerk of Circuit Court; Sue Lutz, Register in Probate
(probate records from 1855 with Register in Probate)
probate search service: $4.00; copies of probate records: $1.00 per page, no minimum ("not all of our records are kept at the courthouse so we may not be able to supply file the day of the search")

Ozaukee County
organized 1853 from Washington County

Ozaukee County Administration Building
(121 West Main Street—location)
PO Box 994 (mailing address)
Port Washington, WI 53074-0994
(262) 284-8260 (Register of Deeds, Room 120); (262) 284-8110 (County Clerk); (414) 284-8100 FAX (Register of Deeds)
rvoigt@co.ozaukee.wi.us; jwinkelhorst@co.ozaukee.wi.us
http://www.co.ozaukee.wi.us
Ronald A. Voigt, Register of Deeds; Julianne B. "Julie" Winkelhorst, County Clerk
(land records, naturalization records and vital records with Register of Deeds)
no land, naturalization, or vital records search service; copies of vital records: $10.00 each for births, $7.00 each for deaths and marriages

Ozaukee County Administration Building
1201 South Spring Street
Port Washington, WI 53074
(262) 284-8409 (Clerk of Courts); (262) 284-8370 (Register in Probate, PO Box 994); (262) 284-8491 FAX (Clerk of Courts and Register in Probate)
courtservices@co.ozaukee.wi.us; jschmidt@co.ozaukee.wi.us; marylou.mueller@wicourts.gov
http://www.co.ozaukee.wi.us
Jeffrey S. Schmidt, Clerk of Circuit Court; Mary Lou Mueller, Register in Probate

Pepin County
organized 1858 from Chippewa County

Pepin County Government Center
(740 Seventh Avenue West—location)
PO Box 39 (mailing address)
Durand, WI 54736
(715) 672-8856 (Register of Deeds); (715) 672-8861 (Clerk of Circuit Court); (715) 672-8857 (County Clerk); (715) 672-8859 (Register in Probate); (715) 672-8677 FAX (Register of Deeds)
rconlin@co.pepin.wi.us; audrey.lieffering@wicourts.gov; countyclerk@co.pepin.wi.us; corine.bien@wicourts.gov
http://www.co.pepin.wi.us
Rita Conlin, Register of Deeds; Audrey Lieffering, Clerk of Circuit Court; Marcia R. Bauer, County Clerk; Corine Bien, Register in Probate
(deeds, mortgages, land contracts, etc., and vital records with Register of Deeds; naturalization records with Clerk of Court; probate records with Register in Probate)
naturalization records search service: $5.00; probate search service: $4.00; copies of probate records: $1.00 each, $4.00 certified, no minimum other than search fee

Pierce County
organized 1853 from St. Croix County

Pierce County Courthouse
(414 West Main Street—location)
PO Box 119 (mailing address)
Ellsworth, WI 54011-0119
(715) 273-6748, ext. 6416 (Register of Deeds, PO Box 267); (715) 273-6741, ext. 6405 (Clerk of Circuit Court, PO Box 129); (715) 273-6744, ext. 6688 (County Clerk, PO Box 119); (715) 273-6752 (Register in Probate, PO Box 97); (715) 273-6861 FAX (Register of Deeds and County Clerk); (715) 273-6855 FAX (Clerk of Circuit Court); (715) 273-6794 FAX (Register in Probate)
vnelson@co.pierce.wi.us; peg.feuerhelm@wicourts.gov; jamie.feuerhelm@co.pierce.wi.us; dee.novak@wicourts.gov
http://www.co.pierce.wi.us
Vicki Nelson, Register of Deeds; Peg Feuerhelm, Clerk of Circuit Court; Jamie Feuerhelm, County Clerk; Dee Novak, Register in Probate

Polk County
organized March 1853 from St. Croix County

Polk County Government Center
100 Polk County Plaza
Balsam Lake, WI 54810
(715) 485-9240 (Register of Deeds, PO Box 576); (715) 485-9226 (County Clerk, Suite 110); (715) 485-9202 FAX (Register of Deeds); (715) 485-9104 FAX (County Clerk)
regdeeds@co.polk.wi.us; cathya@co.polk.wi.us
http://www.co.polk.wi.us
Laurie Anderson, Register of Deeds; Catherine L. Albrecht, County Clerk
(land records from about 1854 to date and births, deaths and marriages from about 1865 to date with Register of Deeds)
copies of land records: $2.00 for the first page and $1.00 for each additional page; certified or uncertified copies of vital records: $10.00 each for births, $7.00 each for deaths and marriages (certified copies restricted to

persons with a "direct and tangible interest" in the records)

Polk County Justice Center
1005 West Main Street
Balsam Lake, WI 54810
(715) 485-9299 (Clerk of Circuit Court, PO Box 549, Suite 300); (715) 485-9238 (Register in Probate, Suite 500); (715) 485-9262 FAX (Clerk of Circuit Court)
lois.hoff@wicourts.gov; jenell.anderson@wicourts.gov
http://www.co.polk.wi.us
Lois Hoff, Clerk of Circuit Court; Jenell Anderson, Register in Probate
(naturalization records with Clerk of Courts Office, probate records with Register in Probate's Office)

Portage County
organized 1836 from territorial county in the area now occupied by much of Columbia County, expanded northward in 1841 (into territory from Crawford County), and Columbia County detached in 1846

Portage County City-County Building
1516 Church Street
Stevens Point, WI 54481
(715) 346-1351; (715) 346-1428 (Register of Deeds); (715) 346-1364 (Clerk of Circuit Court); (715) 346-1351 (County Clerk); (715) 346-1362 (Register in Probate); (715) 346-1236 FAX (Clerk of Circuit Court); (715) 346-1486 FAX (County Clerk)
wisinskc@co.portage.wi.us; bernadete.flatoff@wicourts.gov; simoniss@co.portage.wi.us; info@co.portage.wi.us (County Clerk); theresa.gagas@wicourts.gov
http://www.co.portage.wi.us
Cynthia A. Wisinski, Register of Deeds; Bernadette Flatoff, Clerk of Circuit Court; Shirley Simonis, County Clerk; Theresa Gagas, Register in Probate
(land records with Register of Deeds, Land Description Office, naturalization records with Clerk of Courts Office, vital records with Register of Deeds Office, probate records with Circuit Court Branch II)

Price County
organized 1879 from Chippewa and Lincoln counties

Price County Courthouse
126 Cherry Street
Phillips, WI 54555
(715) 339-2515 (Register of Deeds, Room 108); (715) 339-2353 (Clerk of Circuit Court, Room 206); (715) 339-3325 (County Clerk, Room 106); (715) 339-3078 (Register in Probate); (715) 339-5114 FAX (Clerk of Circuit Court)
rgdeeds@co.price.wi.us; chris.cress@wicourts.gov; jean.gottwald@co.price.wi.us; jeanne.larson@wicourts.gov
http://www.co.price.wi.us
Judith Chizek, Register of Deeds; Chris Cress, Clerk of Circuit Court; Jean Gottwald, County Clerk; Jeanne Larson, Register in Probate
(land records and vital records with Register of Deeds, naturalization records with Clerk of Courts, probate records with Register in Probate)

Racine County
organized 1836 from territorial county

Racine County Courthouse
730 Wisconsin Avenue
Racine, WI 53403-1238
(262) 636-3862; (262) 636-3208 (Register of Deeds, 1st Floor); (262) 636-3333 (Clerk of Circuit Court, 6th & 8th Floors); (262) 636-3121 (County Clerk, 1st Floor); (262) 636-3868 (Register in Probate); (262) 636-3851 FAX (Register of Deeds); (262) 636-3491 FAX (County Clerk)
james.ladwig@goracine.org; RCRegisterofDeeds@goracine.org; taraesa.wheary@

goracine.org; RCClerkofCourts@goracine. org; joan.rennert@goracine.org; RCClerk@ goracine.org; carol.mills@wicourts.gov
http://www.racineco.com
James Ladwig, Register of Deeds; Taraesa Wheary, Clerk of Circuit Court; Joan Rennert, County Clerk; Carol Mills, Register in Probate
(land records with Register of Deeds, probate records from 1836 with Register in Probate)
probate search service: $4.00; copies of probate records: $1.00 per page

Richland County
organized 1842 from Crawford, Sauk and Iowa counties

Richland County Courthouse
181 Seminary Street
Richland Center, WI 53581
(608) 647-2197; (608) 647-3011 (Register of Deeds, PO Box 337); (608) 647-3956 (Clerk of Circuit Court, PO Box 6655, PO Box 655); (608) 647-2197 (County Clerk, PO Box 310); (608) 647-2626 (Register in Probate, PO Box 427); (608) 647-6134 FAX (Register of Deeds and County Clerk)
regofdeeds@co.richland.wi.us; ann.robinson@ wicourts.gov; vlasakv@co.richland.wi.us; sandra.mcnamer@wicourts.gov
http://www.co.richland.wi.us
Susan Triggs, Register of Deeds; Ann Robinson, Clerk of Circuit Court; Victor Vlasak, County Clery; Sandra McNamer, Register in Probate

Rock County
organized 1836 from territorial county

Rock County Courthouse
51 South Main Street
Janesville, WI 53545-3951
(608) 757-5650 (Register of Deeds); (608) 743-2200 (Clerk of Circuit Court, Second Floor); (608) 757-5660 (County Clerk); (608) 757-5633 (Register in Probate, Third Floor); (608) 757-5563 FAX (Register of Deeds); (608) 743-2223 FAX (Clerk of Circuit Court); (608) 757-5662 FAX (County Clerk); (608) 757-5769 FAX (Register in Probate)
leyes@co.rock.wi.us; eldred.wielke@ wicourts.gov; kayo@co.rock.wi.us; louis.mineau@wicourts.gov
http://www.co.rock.wi.us
Randal Leyes, Register of Deeds; Eldred Mielke, Clerk of Circuit Court; Kay O'Connell, County Clerk; Louis X. Mineau, Register in Probate
(land records from 1830, births from 1860, deaths from 1873, and marriages from 1849 with Register of Deeds; naturalizations from 1839 with Clerk of Courts; index of probate records from 1850 with Register in Probate, probate records from Files #1 through 20394 with Rock County Historical Society)
vital records search service: $10.00 for births, $7.00 for deaths and marriages (includes one copy, if found); probate search service: $4.00; copies of probate records: 25¢ per page plus SASE

Rusk County
organized 1901 from Chippewa County

Rusk County Courthouse
311 East Miner Avenue
Ladysmith, WI 54848-1829
(715) 532-2139 (Register of Deeds, Suite 132N); (715) 532-2108 (Clerk of Circuit Court); (715) 532-2100 (County Clerk); (715) 532-2147 (Register in Probate); (715) 532-2194 FAX (Register of Deeds)
linda@ruskcountywi.us; renae.baxter@ wicourts.gov; dnelson@ruskcountywi.us; genevieve.mikula@wicourts.gov
http://www.ruskcounty.org
Linda Ann Effertz, Register of Deeds; Renae R. Baxter, Clerk of Circuit Court; Denise Nelson, County Clerk; Genevieve Mikula, Register in Probate
(land records and vital records with Register of

Deeds; probate records with Register in Probate)

St. Croix County
organized 1840 from territorial county

St. Croix County Government Center
1101 Carmichael Road
Hudson, WI 54016
(715) 386-4652 (Register of Deeds); (715) 386-4630 (Clerk of Circuit Court); (715) 386-4609 (County Clerk); (715) 386-4618 (Register in Probate); (715) 386-4687 FAX; (715) 381-4396 FAX (Clerk of Circuit Court); (715) 381-4400 FAX (County Clerk); (715) 381-4318 FAX (Register in Probate)
kayw@co.saint-croix.wi.us; lori.meyer@wicourts.gov; cindyc@co.saint-croix.wi.us; ericka.nelson@wicourts.gov
http://www.co.saint-croix.wi.us
Kathleen H. "Kay" Walsh, Register of Deeds; Lori Meyer, Clerk of Circuit Court; Cindy Campbell, County Clerk; Ericka S. Nelson, Register in Probate
(vital records with Register of Deeds, probate records with Register in Probate)
probate search service: $4.00; copies of probate records: $1.00 per page, $3.00 certification fee, no minimum

Sauk County
organized 1840 from territorial county

Sauk County Courthouse
515 Oak Street
Baraboo, WI 53913-2416
(608) 355-3287 (Clerk of Circuit Court); (608) 355-3226 (Register in Probate); (608) 355-3480 (Clerk of Circuit Court); (608) 355-3514 (Register in Probate)
vicki.meister@wicourts.gov; james.daniels@wicourts.gov
http://www.co.sauk.wi.us
Vicki Meister, Clerk of Circuit Court; James Daniels, Register in Probate

Sauk County West Square Building
505 Broadway
Baraboo, WI 53913
(608) 355-3288 (Register of Deeds, Room 122); (608) 355-3286 (County Clerk, Room 144); (608) 355-4439 FAX (Register of Deeds); (608) 355-3292 FAX (County Clerk)
bbailey@co.sauk.wi.us; bmielke@co.sauk.wi.us
http://www.co.sauk.wi.us
Brent Bailey, Register of Deeds; Beverly Mielke, County Clerk
(land records and vital records with Register of Deeds)

Sawyer County
organized 1883 from Ashland and Chippewa counties

Sawyer County Courthouse
10610 Main Street
Hayward, WI 54843
(715) 634-4867 (Register of Deeds, PO Box 686); (715) 634-3564 (Mapping Department, PO Box 441); (715) 634-4887 (Clerk of Circuit Court, PO Box 508); (715) 634-4866 (County Cler, PO Box 836); (715) 634-7519 (Register in Probate, PO Box 447); (715) 634-6839 FAX (Register of Deeds); (715) 634-3666 FAX (County Clerk)
reg.of.deeds@sawyercountygov.org; ricki.briggs@wicourts.gov; county.clerk@sawyer countygov.org; bonnie.struska@wicourts.gov
http://www.sawyercountygov.org
Paula Chisser, Register of Deeds; Ricki Briggs, Clerk of Circuit Court; Kris Mayberry, County Clerk; Bonnie Struska, Register in Probate
(land records with Register of Deeds and Mapping Department, naturalization records and vital records with Register of Deeds, probate records with Register in Probate)

Shawano County
organized 1853 from Oconto County

Shawano County Courthouse
311 North Main Street
Shawano, WI 54166-2145
(715) 526-9150; (715) 524-2129 (Register of Deeds, First Floor); (715) 526-9347 (Clerk of Circuit Court, Second Floor); (715) 526-9150 (County Clerk, First Floor); (715) 526-8631 (Register in Probate); (715) 524-2130 FAX (Register of Deeds); (715) 526-4915 FAX (Clerk of Circuit Court); (715) 524-5157 (County Clerk); (715) 526-8622 FAX (Register in Probate)
rgdamy@co.shawano.wi.us; sue.krueger@ wicourts.gov; cheryl.strauss@wicourts.gov
http://www.co.shawano.wi.us
Amy Dillenburg, Register of Deeds; Susan Krueger, Clerk of Circuit Court; Rosemary Bohm, County Clerk; Cheryl Strauss, Register in Probate

Sheboygan County
organized 1836 from territorial county

Sheboygan County Administration Building
508 New York Avenue
Sheboygan, WI 53081
(920) 459-3023 (Register of Deeds, Room 218, PO Box 416); (920) 459-3872 (Vital Records); (920) 459-3003 (County Clerk, Foom 129); (920) 459-1338 FAX (Register of Deeds); ;(920) 459-0304 FAX (County Clerk)
glancjmg@co.sheboygan.wi.us
http://www.co.sheboygan.wi.us
Ellen R. Schleicher, Register of Deeds; Julie Glancey, County Clerk
(land records from 1836, vital records from the 1840s, and probate records from the 1800s to the 1950s with Register of Deeds)
vital records search service: $7.00; no probate search service; copies of vital records: $7.00 each, $10.00 each for certified copies of births, $7.00 each for certified copies of deaths and marriages (satisfactory proof of identity required); copies of probate records: $2.00 per page from Register of Deeds

Sheboygan County Courthouse
615 North Sixth Street
Sheboygan, WI 53081-4612
(920) 459-3068 (Clerk of Circuit Court, First Floor–South); (920) 459-3050 (Register in Probate, Fourth Floor); (920) 459-3921 FAX (Clerk of Circuit Court)
nan.todd@wicourts.gov; glancjmg@co.sheboygan.wi.us; sandy.graumann@wicourts.gov
http://www.co.sheboygan.wi.us
Nan Todd, Clerk of Circuit Court; Sandy L. Graumann, Register in Probate
(probate records after 1950s with Register in Probate)
no probate search service

Taylor County
organized 1875 from Clark and Lincoln counties

Taylor County Courthouse
224 South Second Street
Medford, WI 54451
(715) 748-1483 (Register of Deeds); (715) 748-1465 (Real Property Lister); (715) 748-1428 (Clerk of Circuit Court, Second Floor); (715) 748-1460 (County Clerk, First Floor); (715) 748-1435 (Register in Probate); (715) 748-1446 FAX (Register of Deeds)
marvel.lemke@co.taylor.wi.us; maggie.gebauer@wicourts.gov; bruce.strama@ co.taylor.wi.us; toni.matthias@wicourts.gov
http://www.co.taylor.wi.us
Marvel A. Lemke, Register of Deeds; Margaret Gebauer, Clerk of Circuit Court; Bruce P. Strama, County Clerk; Toni Matthias, Register in Probate
(land records with Register of Deeds or Real Property Lister, naturalization records with Clerk of Court, vital records with Register of Deeds, probate records with Register in Probate)
naturalization and probate records search

service: $5.00; copies of naturlization records: $1.25 per page; copies of probate records: $1.00 per page

Trempealeau County

created as Trempe a l'eau by an act approved 24 January 1854 from Chippewa County [north of the Buffalo River], Jackson County [south of the Buffalo River, east of the line between ranges 7 and 8, and north of the line between townships 18 and 19], Buffalo County [south of the Buffalo River, west of the line between ranges 7 and 8, and north of the line between townships 18 and 19], and La Crosse County [south of the line between townships 18 and 19]; boundaries adjusted with La Crosse County along the Black River and with Buffalo County along the Trempealeau and Mississippi rivers in 1857

Trempealeau County Courthouse
36245 Main Street
Whitehall, WI 54773-0067
(715) 538-2311, ext. 244 (Register of Deeds, Room 106, PO Box 67); (715) 538-2311, ext. 240 (Clerk of Circuit Court, PO Box 67); (715) (715) 538-2311, ext. 238 (Register in Probate); (715) 538-4400 FAX (Circuit Court)
rose0@tremplocounty.com; angela.sylla@icourts.gov; tcclerk@tremplocounty.com; kay.vold@wicourts.gov
http://www.tremplocounty.com
Rose Ottum, Register of Deeds; Angeline Sylla, Clerk of Circuit Court; Paul L. Syverson, County Clerk; Kay Vold, Register in Probate
(land records and vital records with Register of Deeds, probate records with Register in Probate)
no land or vital records search service by mail; probate search service: $4.00 ("as work load permits"); certified copies of vital records: $10.00 for births, $7.00 for deaths and marriages (application must be completed and fee paid in advance, restricted to immediate family); copies of probate records: $1.00 per page

Vernon County

organized 1851 from Richland and Crawford counties; name changed from Bad Ax County in 1862

Vernon County Courthouse
400 Courthouse Square
Viroqua, WI 54665
(608) 637-5371 (Register of Deeds, PO Box 46); (608) 637-5340 (Clerk of Circuit Court, PO Box 426); (608) 637-5380 (County Clerk, Courthouse Annex, Room 108); (608) 637-5347 (Register in Probate, PO Box 448)
kspaeth@vernoncounty.org; kathleen.buros@icourts.gov; sue.thompson@wicourts.gov
http://www.wisconline.com/counties/vernon
Konna Spaeth, Register of Deeds; Kathleen Buros, Clerk of Circuit Court; Ron Hoff, County Clerk; Sue Thompson, Register in Probate
(land records from the late 1850s to date and vital records from the late 1860s to date [scattered early records] with Register of Deeds, naturalization records with Clerk of Court, probate records with Register in Probate)

Vilas County

organized 1893 fron Oneida County

Vilas County Courthouse
(330 Court Street—location)
PO Box 369 (mailing address)
Eagle River, WI 54521-0369
(715) 479-3660 (Register of Deeds); (715) 479-3632 (Clerk of Circuit Court); (715) 479-3600 (County Clerk); (715) 479-3642 (Register in Probate); (715) 479-3695 FAX (Register of Deeds); (715) 479-3605 FAX (County Clerk)
johans@co.vilas.wi.us; jean.numrich@icourts.gov; daalle@co.vilas.wi.us; amy.franzen@wicourts.gov
http://www.co.vilas.wi.us
Joan Hansen, Register of Deeds; Jean Numrich, Clerk of Circuit Court; David R. Alleman, County Clerk; Amy Franzen, Register in Probate

Walworth County

organized 1836 from territorial county

Walworth County Courthouse
100 West Walworth Street
Elkhorn, WI 53121
(262) 741-4233 (Register of Deeds, Room 102, PO Box 995); (262) 741-4241 (County Clerk, PO Box 1001); (262) 741-4947 FAX (Register of Deeds); (262) 741-4287 FAX (County Clerk)
walcord@co.walworth.wi.us; kbushey@co.walworth.wi.us
http://www.co.walworth.wi.us
Connie J. Woolever, Register of Deeds; Kimberly S. Bushey, County Clerk
(grantor/grantee index from 1839, births from 1856, deaths from 1873, marriages from 1839 with Register of Deeds)

Walworth County Courthouse
(1800 County Trunk NN—location)
PO Box 1001 (mailing address)
Elkhorn, WI 53121
(262) 741-7012 (Clerk of Circuit Court, Room 2080); (262) 741-7015 (Register in Probate, Room 2085, PO Box 1001); (262) 741-7002 FAX (Register in Probate)
reiff@co.walworth.wi.us; gloria.niemetscheck@wicourts.gov
http://www.co.walworth.wi.us
Sheila Reiff, Clerk of Circuit Court; Gloria Niemetscheck, Register in Probate
probate search service: $4.00 per name; copies of probate records: $1.00 per page, no minimum

Washburn County

organized 1883 from Burnett County

Washburn County Courthouse
10 Fourth Avenue
Shell Lake, WI 54871
(715) 468-7808; (715) 468-4616 (Register of Deeds, PO Box 607); (715) 468-4677 (Clerk of Circuit Court, PO Box 339); (715) 468-4600 (County Clerk, PO Box 639); (715) 468-4688 (Register in Probate, PO Box 316); (715) 468-4658 FAX (Register of Deeds); (715) 468-4678 FAX (Clerk of Circuit Court); (715) 468-4725 FAX (County Clerk)
regdeeds@co.washburn.wi.us; deeann.mclellan@wicourts.gov; coclerk@co.washburn.wi.us; lhoeppne@co.washburn.wi.us; karen.nord@wicourts.gov
http://www.co.washburn.wi.us
Diane M. Poach, Register of Deeds; DeeAnn McLellan, Clerk of Circuit Court; Lynn K. Hoeppner, County Clerk; Karen Nord, Register in Probate
(land records and vital records with Register of Deeds, probate records with Register in Probate)
probate search service: $4.00; copies of probate records: $1.00 per page, no minimum

Washington County

organized 1836 from territorial county

Washington County Courthouse
(432 East Washington Street—location)
PO Box 1986 (mailing address)
West Bend, WI 53095-7986
(262) 335-4318 (Register of Deeds); (262) 335-4341 (Clerk of Circuit Court); (262) 335-4400 (County Clerk); (262) 335-4333 (Register in Probate, PO Box 82)
sharon.martin@co.washington.wi.us; washington.coc@wicourts.gov; kristine.deiss@wicourts.gov; clkbrenda@co.washington.wi.us; kay.morlen@wicourts.gov
http://www.co.washington.wi.us/washington/home.jsp

Sharon Martin, Register of Deeds; Kristine Deiss, Clerk of Circuit Court; Brenda Jaszewski, County Clerk; Kay Morlen, Register in Probate
(land records and vital records with Register of Deeds, probate records with Register in Probate, Room 3008)
certified copies of vital records: $10.00 each for births, $7.00 each for deaths and marriages

Waukesha County

organized 1846 from Milwaukee County

Waukesha County Administration Building
1320 Pewaukee Road
Waukesha, WI 53188-2485
(414) 548-7583 (Register of Deeds, Room 110); (262) 548-7010 (County Clerk, Room 120); (262) 548-7722 FAX (County Clerk)
registerofdeeds@waukeshacounty.gov; mhasslinger@waukeshacounty.gov
http://www.waukeshacounty.gov/cm
Michael J. Hasslinger, Register of Deeds; Kathy Nickolaus, County Clerk
(land records from 1840 to date, deaths from 1872, marriages from 1846, with Register of Deeds)
copies of vital records from Register of Deeds: $10.00 each for births and deaths, $7.00 each for deaths and marriages (certified copies restricted to persons with a "direct and tangible interest" in the records)

Waukesha County Courthouse
515 West Moreland Boulevard
Waukesha, WI 53188-2428
(262) 896-8525 (Clerk of Circuit Court, Room C108); (262) 548-7472 (Register in Probate, Room C380)
Carolyn.Evenson@wicourts.gov; sally.lunde@wicourts.gov
http://www.waukeshacounty.gov/cm
Carolyn Evenson, Clerk of Circuit Court; Sally Lunde, Register in Probate

Waupaca County

organized 1851 from Winnebago and Brown counties

Waupaca County Courthouse
(811 Harding Street—location)
PO Box 307 (mailing address)
Waupaca, WI 54981
(715) 258-6250 (Register of Deeds); (715) 258-6460 (Clerk of Circuit Court); (715) 258-6200 (County Clerk); (715) 258-6429 (Register in Probate); (715) 258-4990 FAX (Register of Deeds)
mmazem@co.waupaca.wi.us; terrie.tews@wicourts.gov; mrobbi@co.waupaca.wi.us; angela.dahle@wicourts.gov
http://www.co.waupaca.wi.us
Michael Mazemke, Register of Deeds; Terrie Tews, Clerk of Circuit Court; Mary A. Robbins, County Clerk; Angela Dahle, Register in Probate
(land records from 1852 and vital records from 1852 with Register of Deeds [proof of relationship required], probate records from 1860 with Register in Probate)

Waushara County

organized 1851 from Marquette County

Waushara County Courthouse
209 South St. Marie Street
Wautoma, WI 54982
(920) 787-0444 (Register of Deeds, First Floor, PO Box 338); (920) 787-0441 (Clerk of Circuit Court, Second Floor, PO Box 507); (920) 787-0442 (County Clerk, First Floor, PO Box 488); (920) 787-0448 (Register in Probate, PO Box 508)
rod.courthouse@co.waushara.wi.us; courts.courthouse@co.waushara.wi.us; jane.putskey@wicourts.gov; countyclerk.courthouse@co.waushara.wi.us; john.courthouse@co.waushara.wi.us; rebecca.gramse@wicourts.gov

http://www.1waushara.com

Barbara Struzynski, Register of Deeds; Jane Putskey, Clerk of Circuit Court; John Benz, County Clerk; Rebecca Gramse, Register in Probate

(land records from 1852, births and deaths from 1876, and marriages from 1852 with Register of Deeds; probate records with Register in Probate)

Winnebago County
organized 1840 from Brown County

Winnebago County Courthouse
415 Jackson Street
Oshkosh, WI 54901-4751
(920) 236-4881 (Register of Deeds–Real Estate, Room 170, PO Box 2808, 54903-2808); (920) 236-4882 (Register of Deeds–Vital Records, Room 30); (920) 236-4848 (Clerk of Circuit Court, Fourth Floor, PO Box 2808); (920) 236-4888 (County Clerk, Room 110); (920) 236-4831 (Register in Probate)
jpagel@co.winnebago.wi.us; diane.fremgen@ wicourts.gov; sertmer@co.winnebago.wi.us; sara.henke@wicourts.gov
http://www.co.winnebago.wi.us;
Julie Pagel, Register of Deeds; Diane Fremgen, Clerk of Circuit Court; Sue Ertmer, County Clerk; Sara Henke, Register in Probate
(land records from 1864, births from 1838, deaths from 1876, and marriages from 1867 [all records sparse before July 1907] with Register of Deeds, probate records with Register in Probate)
no land records search service ("we do not do genealogy research in person or by mail; local genealogists will do research for a fee"); vital records search service: $10.00 for births and $7.00 for deaths or marriages (includes one copy, must have approximate date of the event, within a five-year span); probate search service: $4.00 per name; copies of probate records: $1.00 per page, no minimum

Wood County
organized 1856 from Portage County

Wood County Courthouse
400 Market Street
Wisconsin Rapids, WI 54494
(715) 421-8450 (Register of Deeds, PO Box 8095); (715) 421-8490 (Clerk of Circuit Court); (715) 421-8460 (County Clerk, Room 203 A-B, PO Box 8095); (715) 421-8523 (Register in Probate, PO Box 8095); (715) 421-8446 FAX (Register of Deeds); (715) 421-8691 (Clerk of Circuit Court)
register@co.wood.wi.us; rkrause@co.wood. wi.us; cindy.joosten@wicourts.gov; ctyclerk@ co.wood.wi.us; cmeyers@co.wood.wi.us; sherry.masephol@wicourts.gov;
http://www.co.wood.wi.us/courts/index.htm
http://www.co.wood.wi.us
René L. Krause, Register of Deeds; Cindy Joosten, Clerk of Circuit Court; Cynthia Meyers, County Clerk; Sherry Masephol, Register in Probate
(land records with Register of Deeds, naturalization records from 1856 with Clerk of Circuit Court, births and deaths with Register of Deeds, probate records with Register in Probate)
probate search service: $4.00 per file ("search fee must be sent in before the records will be looked up, and copies will not be mailed until the copying fee is received"); copies of probate records: $1.00 per page

---

WYOMING

Capital: Cheyenne. Statehood: 10 July 1890 (annexed as part of the Louisiana Purchase, 1803, territory gained from Great Britain in 1846 and from Texas in 1850, became a separate territory in 1868)

Wyoming has Municipal Courts in incorporated cities and towns with local jurisdiction. Justice Courts have limited jurisdiction in counties where there are no County Courts: Big Horn, Crook, Hot Springs, Johnson, Niobrara, Park, Platte, Sublette, Teton, Washakie and Weston counties. County Courts are required in counties with populations over 30,000, but may be established in smaller counties with the consent of the state legislature.

The District Court has general jurisdiction in civil, criminal and juvenile matters and sits at each county seat. The Supreme Court is the court of last resort.

Albany County
organized 1868, original county

Albany County Clerk
525 Grand Avenue
Laramie, WY 82070-3836
(307) 721-2543; (307) 721-2547 (Real Estate); (307) 721-2544 FAX
acclerkgonzales@yahoo.com
http://www.co.albany.wy.us
Jackie R. Gonzales
(land records from January 1869)

Second Judicial District
(525 Grand Avenue, Suite 305—location)
PO Box 1106 (mailing address)
Laramie, WY 82070
(307) 721-2508; (307) 721-2520 FAX
http://www.co.albany.wy.us
Janice Sexton, Clerk of the District Court
(naturalization records from early 1900, probate records from 1889)
probate search service: no charge; copies of probate records: $1.00 for the first page and 50¢ for each additional page

Big Horn County
organized 1896 from Fremont, Johnson and Sheridan counties

Big Horn County Clerk
(420 West C Street—location)
PO Box 31 (mailing address)
Basin, WY 82410
(307) 568-2357; (307) 568-9375 FAX
cclerk@tctwest.net
http://www.bighorncountywy.gov
Dori Noyes
(land records and marriages)

Fifth Judicial District
(420 West C Street—location)
PO Box 670 (mailing address)
Basin, WY 82410-0670
(307) 568-2381; (307) 568-2791 FAX
vickie_larchick@yahoo.com
http://www.bighorncountywy.gov
Vicki Larchick, Clerk of the District Court
(probate records)
probate search service: no charge; copies of probate records: $1.00 for the first page and 50¢ for each additional attached page, 50¢ for certification of each document, no minimum; "All fees must be prepaid before we will mail out any requested documents."

Campbell County
organized 1911 from Crook and Weston counties

Campbell County Clerk
(500 South Gillette Avenue, Suite 1600, Gillette, WY 82716-4239—location)
PO Box 3010 (mailing address)
Gillette, WY 82717-3010

---

(307) 682-7285; (307) 687-6455 FAX
http://ccg.co.campbell.wy.us
Susan Saunders
(land records from late 1800s, marriages from 1913)
land records: copies: $1.00 per page, $2.00 per instrument for certification

Sixth Judicial District
(500 South Gillette Avenue, Suite 2400, Gillette, WY 82716-4239—location)
PO Box 817 (mailing address)
Gillette, WY 82717
(307) 682-3424; (307) 687-6209 FAX
http://ccg.co.campbell.wy.us
Nancy Ratcliff, Clerk of the District Court
(probate records from 1913)
probate search service: no charge; copies of probate records: $1.00 for the first page and 50¢ for each additional page, no minimum

Carbon County
organized 1868, original county

Carbon County Clerk and Recorder
(Fifth and Spruce—location)
PO Box 6 (mailing address)
Rawlins, WY 82301
(307) 328-2668
cclerk@trib.com
http://carboncountyclerk.wyo.gov
Gwynn G. Rothenberger
(land records from 1868)

Second Judicial District
PO Box 67
Rawlins, WY 82301
(307) 328-2628
lindy@vcn.com
http://carboncountyclerk.wyo.gov/distclerk.htm
Lindy Glode, Clerk of the District Court
(naturalizataion records and probate records)
probate search service: no charge (written requests only, none by phone); copies of probate records: $1.00 for the first page and 25¢ for each additional page, 50¢ per page for certification, no minimum

Converse County
organized 1888 from Albany County

Converse County Clerk
(107 North Fifth Street, Suite 114—location)
PO Box 990 (mailing address)
Douglas, WY 82633-0990
(307) 358-2244; (307) 358-5998 FAX
ccclerk@communicomm.com
http://www.conversecounty.org
Lucile Taylor
(land records from 1888; naturalization records from late 1890s and early 1900s to 2 April 1941 [all files not complete], marriages from 1888)

Eighth Judicial District
(107 North Fifth Street, Suite 228—location)
PO Box 189 (mailing address)
Douglas, WY 82633-0189
(307) 358-3165
jwinte@state.wy.us
http://www.conversecounty.org/gov_admin/ clerk_of_court.htm
Jo Winters, Clerk of the District Court
(probate records from 1892)
probate search service: no charge; copies of probate records: 25¢ per page, 50¢ for certification plus $1.00 for the first certified page and 50¢ for each additional certified page, no minimum

Crook County
organized 1875

Crook County Clerk
PO Box 37
Sundance, WY 82729-0037
(307) 283-1323
http://www.newedc.net/crook/index.htm
(Northeast Wyoming Economic Development Coalition)

Connie Tschetter
(land records from 1875)

Sixth Judicial District
PO Box 904
Sundance, WY 82729
(307) 283-2523
http://courts.state.wy.us/CircuitCourtDirectory.
aspx
Christina Wood, Clerk of the District Court
(naturalization records from 1885, probate
records)
probate search service: no charge; copies of
probate records: $1.00 for the first page and
50¢ for each additional page, no minimum;
"SASE"

Fremont County
organized 1884 from Sweetwater County

Fremont County Clerk
450 North Second Street, Room 220
Lander, WY 82520
(307) 332-2405; (307) 332-1132 FAX
fcclerkfreese@yahoo.com
http://fremontcountywy.org
Julie Freese
(land records)

Ninth Judicial District
PO Box 370
Lander, WY 82520
(307) 332-1134
cclan@courts.state.wy.us
http://courts.state.wy.us/CircuitCourtDirectory.
aspx
Lorelie Calvert, Clerk of the District Court

Goshen County
organized 1911 from Laramie and Platte
counties

Eight Judicial District
(2125 East A Street—location)
PO Box 818 (mailing address)
Torrington, WY 82240-0818
(307) 532-2155; (307) 532-8608 FAX
http://goshencounty.org/CDC
Bonnie Petsch, Clerk of the District Court

Goshen County Clerk
(2125 East A Street—location)
PO Box 160 (mailing address)
Torrington, WY 82240
(307) 532-4051; (307) 532-7375 FAX
http://goshencounty.org/clerk
Connie Addy
(land records)

Hot Springs County
organized 1911 from Fremont County

Fifth Judicial District
415 Arapahoe Street
Thermopolis, WY 82443
(307) 864-3323; (307) 864-3210 FAX
lharris@hscounty.com
http://www.hscounty.com/cofcourt.html
Linda R. Harris, Clerk of the District Court

Hot Springs County Clerk
415 Arapahoe Street
Thermopolis, WY 82443
(307) 864-3515; (307) 864-3333 FAX
hanso@hscounty.com/clerk.html
http://www.hscounty.com
Hans Odde
(land records)

Johnson County
organized 1875 from Pease County

Fourth Judicial District
76 North Main Street
Buffalo, WY 82834
(307) 684-7271
taxber@state.wy.us
http://www.johnsoncountywyoming.org/distric
tcourt.html
Thelma Axberg, Clerk of the District Court

Johnson County Clerk
76 North Main Street
Buffalo, WY 82834-1847
(307) 684-7272
http://www.johnsoncountywyoming.org
Linda Barnhart
(land records)

Laramie County
organized 1867, original county

First Judicial District
(309 West 20th Street, Suite 3205—location)
PO Box 787 (mailing address)
Cheyenne, WY 82001-0787
(307) 638-4270; (307) 633-4277 FAX
districtcourtlc@laramiecounty.com
http://www.laramiecounty.com/departments/di
strict_court/index.asp
Gerrie E. Bishop, Clerk of the District Court
(naturalization records, probate records)
no probate search service; copies of probate
records: $1.00 for the first page and 50¢ for
each additional page

Laramie County Clerk
(309 West 20th Street—location)
PO Box 608 (mailing address)
Cheyenne, WY 82001
(307) 633-4268 (Clerk); (307) 633-4374 (Records
Center)
office@laramiecountyclerk.com;
dlathrop@laramiecountyclerk.com;
dan@laramiecountyclerk.com
http://webgate.co.laramie.wy.us
Debbye Balcaen Lathrop, County Clerk; Dan
Siglin, Records Center Manager
(land records)

Lincoln County
organized 1911 from Uinta County

Lincoln County Clerk
925 Sage Avenue, Suite 101
Kemmerer, WY 83101
(307) 877-9056; (307) 877-3101 FAX
jwagner@lcwy.org
http://www.lcwy.org
Jeanne Wagner
(land records)

Third Judicial District
(925 Sage Avenue, Second Floor—location)
PO Drawer 510 (mailing address)
Kemmerer, WY 83101
(307) 877-3320; (307) 877-9056
http://www.lcwy.org/clerkdistrict.asp
Kenneth Roberts, Clerk of the District Court
(naturalization records, probate records from
1960)
probate search service: no charge; copies of
probate records: $1.00 for the first page and
50¢ for each additional page, no minimum;
for probate records prior to 1960, see
Wyoming State Archives, Cheyene

Natrona County
organized 1888 from Carbon County

Natrona County Clerk
(200 North Center
Casper, WY 82601-1949
(307) 235-9206
rvitto@natronacounty-wy.gov
http://www.natrona.net
Renea Vitto
(Natrona County land records from 1890 and
Carbon County transcripts from 1887,
marriages from 1890)

Seventh Judicial District
(200 North Center, Suite 205, Casper, WY
82601—location)
PO Box 2510 (mailing address)
Casper, WY 82602
(307) 235-9243
cdc@natronacounty-wy.gov
http://www.natrona.net
Gen Tuma, Clerk of the District Court
(naturalization records from 1907 and probate

records from 1892)
probate search service: no charge; copies of
probate records: $1.00 for the first page and
50¢ for each additional page, no minimum;
"payment in advance"

Niobrara County
organized 1911 from Converse County

Eighth Judicial District
(424 South Elm—location)
PO Box 420 (mailing address)
Lusk, WY 82225
(307) 334-2211 (Commissioners Office); (307)
334-3013 FAX (Commissioners)
http://courts.state.wy.us/CircuitCourtDirectory.
aspx
Linda Fosher, Clerk of the District Court
(land records from patent, marriages, probate
records)
copies of land records: $1.00 per page; copies of
marriages: $1.00 each, $8.00 for certified
copies

Niobrara County Clerk
(424 South Elm Street—location)
PO Box 1238 (mailing address)
Lusk, WY 82225
(307) 334-2211 (Commissioners Office); (307)
334-3013 FAX (Commissioners)
http://www.newedc.net/niobrara (Northeast
Wyoming Economic Development Coalition);
http://www.luskwyoming.co/chamber.html
(Chamber of Commerce)
Becky Freeman
(land records)

Park County
organized 1909 from Big Horn County

Fifth Judicial District
(Courthouse, 1002, Sheridan Avenue, Addition
Section, First Floor—location)
PO Box 1960 (mailing address)
Cody, WY 82414-1960
(307) 527-8690; (800) 786-2844, ext. 8690; (307)
527-8687 FAX
jboyer@parkcounty.us
http://www.parkcounty.us/distcourtclerk.htm
Joyce Boyer, Clerk of the District Court
(old naturalization records, probate records)

Park County Clerk
1002 Sheridan Avenue, Addition Section, First
Floor
Cody, WY 82414
(307) 527-8600; (800) 786-28744, ext. 8600
kjensen@parkcounty.us
http://www.parkcounty.us
Kelly Jensen
(land records)

Platte County
organized 1911 from Laramie County

Eighth Judicial District
PO Box 158
Wheatland, WY 82201
(307) 322-3857
pccdc@communicomm.com
http://courts.state.wy.us/CircuitCourtDirectory.
aspx
Susan Artery, Clerk of the District Court

Platte County Clerk
PO Box 728
Wheatland, WY 82201-0728
(307) 322-3555
pcclerk@wyomingwireless.com
http://www.plattechamber.com (Chamber of
Commerce)
Jean Dixon
(land records)

Sheridan County
organized 1888 from Johnson County

Fourth Judicial District
224 South Main, Suite B-11
Sheridan, WY 82801

(307) 674-2960
http://www.sheridancounty.com/court_clerk/index.html
Doree Kobold, Clerk of the District Court
(naturalization and probate records)
probate search service: $5.00 per name; copies of probate records: 50¢ for the first page and 25¢ for each additional page

Sheridan County Clerk
224 South Main, Suite B-2
Sheridan, WY 82801
(307) 674-2500
clerk@sheridancounty.com
http://www.sheridancounty.com
Audrey Koltiska
(land records)
land records search service: $5.00 per name; naturalization records search service: $5.00 per name (records over fifty years old are open to the public); copies of probate records: 50¢ for the first page and 25¢ for each additional page

Sublette County
organized 1921 from Fremont and Lincoln counties

Ninth Judicial District
PO Box 764
Pinedale, WY 82941
(307) 367-4376
http://courts.state.wy.us/CircuitCourtDirectory.aspx
Marilyn Jensen, Clerk of the District Court
(probate records)
probate search service: no charge; copies of probate records: $1.00 for the first page and 50¢ for each additional page, no minimum

Sublette County Clerk
(21 South Tyler Street—location)
PO Box 250 (mailing address)
Pinedale, WY 82941
(307) 367-4372
ccsublet@quest.state.wy.us
http://www.sublette.com
Mary Lankford, Clerk
(land records and marriages)

Sweetwater County
organized 1869, original county

Sweetwater County Clerk
(80 West Flaming Gorge Way—location)
PO Box 730 (mailing address)
Green River, WY 82935-0730
(307) 872-6400; (307) 872-6337 FAX
davisd@sweet.wy.us
http://www.co.sweet.wy.us/clerk/index.html
Dale Davis
(land records, marriages)
copies of land records: $1.00 per page, $2.00 for certification; certified copies of marriages: $5.00 each

Third Judicial District
PO Box 430
Green River, WY 82935
(307) 872-6448
http://www.co.sweet.wy.us
Ellen Smith, Clerk of the District Court
(naturalization and probate records)

Teton County
organized 1921 from Lincoln County

Ninth Judicial District
(Courthouse, 180 South King Street, Second Floor—location)
PO Box 4460 (mailing address)
Jackson, WY 83001
(307) 733-2533; (307) 734-1562 FAX
dmahoney@tetonwyo.org
http://www.tetonwyo.org/codc
Dee Mahoney, Clerk of the District Court

Uinta County
organized 1869, original county

Third Judicial District
(Courthouse, 225 Ninth Street—location)
PO Box 1906 (mailing address)
Evanston, WY 82930
(307) 783-0456; (307) 783-0400 FAX (call first)
annlavery@uintacounty.com
http://www.uintacounty.com
Ann Lavery, Clerk of the District Court
(naturalization and probate records)

Uinta County Clerk and Recorder
(225 Ninth Street, Evanston, WY 82930-3415—location)
PO Box 810 (mailing address)
Evanston, WY 82931
(307) 783-0306; (307) 783-0376 FAX
lyfox@uintacounty.com
http://www.uintacounty.com
Lynne Fox
(land records)

Washakie County
organized 1911 from Big Horn County

Fifth Judicial District
PO Box 862
Worland, WY 82401
(307) 347-4821; (307) 347-4325 FAX
http://www.washakiecounty.net
SuZann Whitlock, Clerk of the District Court
(naturalization and probate records)
no probate search service; copies of probate records: $1.00 for the first page and 50¢ for each additional page, $1.00 minimum

Washakie County Clerk
(Courthouse, 1001 Big Horn Avenue—location)
PO Box 260 (mailing address)
Worland, WY 82401-0260
(307) 347-3131; (307) 347-9366 FAX
strauc5@rtconnect.net
http://www.washakiecounty.net
Mary Grace Strauch
(land records with County Clerk or County Assessor)

Weston County
organized 1890 from Crook County

Sixth Judicial District
1 West Main
Newcastle, WY 82701
(307) 746-4778
http://courts.state.wy.us/CircuitCourtDirectory.aspx
Sandra Walford, Clerk of the District Court

Weston County Clerk
1 West Main Street
Newcastle, WY 82701-2106
(307) 746-4744
http://www.newedc.net/weston (The Northeast Wyoming Economic evelopment Coalition)
Paulette Thompson
(land records)

American Samoa

Capital: Pago Pago.

Includes Tutuila, Aunu'u, Manu'a Group (Ta'u, Olosega, Ofu), Rose, and Swains Island. U.S received sovereignty over the eastern islands from Great Britain and Germany in 1899. Local chiefs ceded Tutuila and Aunu'u in 1900, and the Manu'a Group and Rose in 1904. Swains Island was annexed in 1925.

Guam

Capital: Agana. Ceded December 1898

Superior Court of Guam
Guam Judiciary Building
120 West O'Brien Drive
Agana, GU 96910
(671) 475-3420
(organized 1945; land records with Department of Land Management, naturalization records with District Court of Guam, vital records with Department of Public Health and Social Services, limited probate jurisdiction from 1945 to 1974, general jurisdiction from 1974 to date with Alfredo M. Borlas, Clerk of Court)
probate search service: $1.00 per year plus $10.00 retrieval fee; copies of probate records: 50¢ per page, $1.00 for certification per document

Commonwealth of the Northern Mariana Islands

Capital: Garapan

Six inhabited islands, including Saipan, Rota, and Tinian.

Commonwealth of Puerto Rico
(Estadu Libre Asociado de Puerto Rico)

Capital: San Juan. Ceded 10 December 1898

Puerto Rico's Justice of the Peace Courts and Municipal Courts handle civil investigations, probable cause hearings, warrants and summonses, but hold no trials. The District Courts have general jurisdiction over certain misdemeanors and violations and over lesser civil actions, including torts, contracts, real property rights and domestic relations. The Superior Courts (in twelve districts) hear major civil actions, juvenile and criminal matters and have exclusive jurisdiction over estates. The Supreme Court hears appeals.

Aguadilla Superior Court
Centro Judicial
Progreso Street, Box 1010
Aguadilla, PR 00605
(809) 891-0115
http://welcome.topuertorico.org/government.shtml
Fernando Castillo-Velez, Chief Clerk
land records, naturalization records, vital records probate records)

Aibonito Superior Court
18th Street—Bo. Robles
Urb. El Roble
Aibonito, PR 00609
(809) 735-7201
http://welcome.topuertorico.org/government.shtml
Lucia Santiago Rivera, Chief Clerk

Arecibo Superior Court
Rotario Avenue
Box 1238
Arecibo, PR 00613
(809) 878-0060
http://welcome.topuertorico.org/government.shtml

María del Carmen Cruz, Chief Clerk
(land records, naturalization records, vital
   records, probate records)
copies: $1.00 each (money order payable to
   Secretario de Hacienda)

Bayamon Superior Court
State Highway #2
Corner Estaban Padilla, Box 60-619
Bayamon, PR 00619
(809) 780-8402
http://welcome.topuertorico.org/government.s
   html
Rosa M. Carrillo Batista, Chief Clerk

Caguas Superior Court
Highway 9
Corner Rafael Cordero
Caguas, PR 00625
(809) 744-0953
http://welcome.topuertorico.org/government.s
   html
Nelly Gonzalez Cabrera, Chief Clerk

Carolina Superior Court
Chief Clerk
Carolina, PR 00630
(809) 752-6810
http://welcome.topuertorico.org/government.s
   html
Chief Clerk

Guayama Superior Court
McArthur Street
Guayama, PR 00654
(809) 864-1202
http://welcome.topuertorico.org/government.s
   html
Edna Ramos de Alicea, Chief Clerk

Humacao Superior Court
Atanacio Cuadra Street
Humacao, PR 00661
(809) 852-5370
DomingaG@tribunales.gobierno.pr
http://welcome.topuertorico.org/government.s
   html
Dominga Gómez Foster, Chief Clerk

Mayaguez Superior Court
Leon Street, Corner Nenadich
Box 97
Mayaguez, PR 00708
(809) 832-6340
http://welcome.topuertorico.org/government.s
   html
Gladys Falu Olivencia, Chief Clerk

Ponce Superior Court
State Highway #1, Box 1791
Ponce, PR 00733
(809) 840-7380
http://welcome.topuertorico.org/government.s
   html
Paulita Colon Rivera, Clerk

San Juan Superior Court
Munoz Rivera Avenue
Corner Coll y Toste, Stop 35½
PO Box 887
Hato Rey, PR 00919
(809) 763-0590
RebeccaR@tribunales.gobierno.pr
http://welcome.topuertorico.org/government.s
   html
Rebecca Rivera Torres, Chief Clerk

Utuado Superior Court
Box 950
New Avenue
Utuado, PR 00761
(809) 894-2476
http://welcome.topuertorico.org/government.s
   html
Edwin Barreiro Figueroa, Chief Clerk

Trust Territories

Virgin Islands

Capital: Charlotte Amalie. Acquired 1917

The Virgin Islands' Territorial Courts are
courts of general jurisdiction. The U.S. District
Court for the District of the Virgin Islands
handles all appeals.

Consists of three larger islands (St. John, St.
Croix, and St. Thomas), plus fifty smaller islands
and cays.

Territorial Court of the Virgin Islands,
   Division of St. Croix
(R. H. Amphlett Leader Justice Complex, First
   Floor, Room 101—location)
PO Box 9000 (mailing address)
Kingshill
St. Croix, VI 00850
(340) 778-9750; (340) 778-4044 FAX
Chiefdeputyclerk.Stx@visuperiorcourt.org
http://www.visuperiorcourt.org
Venetia H. Velazquez, Clerk of the Court

Territorial Court of the Virgin Islands,
   Division of St. Thomas-St. John
(Alexander A. Farrelly Justice Center, 5400
   Veteran's Drive, First Floor, East Wing,
   Room E111—location)
PO Box 70 (mailing address)
Charlotte Amalie
St. Thomas, VI 00801
(809) 774-6680; (340) 776-8690
Chiefdeputyclerk.Stx@visuperiorcourt.org
http://www.visuperiorcourt.org/clerk/contactI
   nfoClerk.aspx
Venetia H. Velazquez, Clerk of the Court

DISCARD

LaVergne, TN USA
20 August 2009
155358LV00001B/4/P